Human
Resource
Management

Nicky Wolfe

Human Resource Management

Fourth Edition

Derek Torrington and Laura Hall

PRENTICE HALL EUROPE
LONDON · NEW YORK · TORONTO · SYDNEY · TOKYO ·
SINGAPORE · MADRID · MEXICO CITY · MUNICH · PARIS

First edition published 1987
Second edition published 1991
Third edition published 1995

This fourth edition first published 1998 by
Prentice Hall Europe
Campus 400, Maylands Avenue
Hemel Hempstead
Hertfordshire, HP2 7EZ
A division of
Simon & Schuster International Group

Typeset in 10/12pt Meridien
by Meridian Colour Repro Ltd, Pangbourne-on-Thames, Berkshire

Printed and bound by Rotolito Lombarda, Italy

Library of Congress Cataloging-in-Publication Data

Torrington, Derek, 1931–
    Human resource management / Derek Torrington and Laura Hall. —
4th ed.
      p.   cm.
    Rev. ed. of: Personnel management. 1995.
    Includes bibliographical references and index.
    ISBN 0-13-626532-4
    1. Personnel management.   I. Hall, Laura, 1952–   .
II. Torrington, Derek, 1931–   Personnel management.   III. Title.
HF5549.T675   1998
658.3—dc21   97-46376
                                                 CIP

British Library Cataloguing in Publication Data

A catalogue record for this book is available from
the British Library

ISBN 0-13-626532-4

1 2 3 4 5 02 01 00 97 98

Brief contents

Main contents

8 Interactive skill: presentation *151*

Part III **Resourcing**

9 Strategic aspects of resourcing *170*

Preface

Those of you who are familiar with previous editions of this text will notice that the title has now changed to *Human Resource Management*. We have done this to reflect both the fact that this is the term employed virtually throughout the academic world, and because of the increasing influence of the HRM concept on personnel practice. This change of title should not be taken as a fundamental change in the underlying content and approach of the material of this new edition since the objective of this text remains to provide a comprehensive and practical introduction to the personnel functions and processes in and around a business, and to support this through extensive illustrative material and evidence from company practices.

There was a considerable amount of restructuring for the third edition of this text. In response to market research and in order to assist continuity and familiarity with the organisation of the text for those recommending this text for courses, the structural changes we have made for this edition have been limited to the following:

- Shortening Part I (Introduction) by removing Chapter 2 of the third edition.
- Removing the 'International HRM' chapter of the third edition, and integrating comparative international material and illustrations at relevant points in the text.
- Including a new final chapter on 'Ethics' to reflect renewed interest in and popular debate on professional standards.

The text has therefore retained its logical flow and overall eight-part structure, with the core of the text covered in the 33 chapters which comprise Parts II–VII. Each of these parts begins with an opening chapter reviewing the strategic aspects of the personnel function that is the subject of the part, thereby reflecting the current interest in strategy and making the necessary link to the concept of HRM, but without becoming involved in its sometimes incoherent lack of agenda. This is followed by several chapters each describing and discussing the core operational aspects. The final chapter in each part addresses the practical interactive skills required by personnel employees in relation to the heart of the function that has been explored in the part. The logic of including these chapters is that personnel management incorporates more of these face-to-face skills than any other aspect of business management. Parts II–VII, therefore, have the following framework of chapters which, our market research concludes, remains a popular approach for effective teaching and learning:

Strategy

Operation

Interaction

We have comprehensively updated and revised the material in the third edition to encompass legislative changes (including disability, pensions and data protection), emerging issues of professional and academic debate, previously unpublished findings and commentary from our own recent research into contemporary business practices, and other recent data and survey findings. In addition, we have expanded and developed many topics which were new to the third edition, but have since gained more prominence, including the management of diversity, the learning organisation and performance management.

This new edition has introduced a range of assessment material and new illustrations, as well as several new design features to assist further both full- and part-time students in using and learning from the text; these include:

▶ Integrated Window on Practice boxes – provide a range of illustrative material throughout the text, including examples of real company practice, survey results, anecdotes and quotes, and court cases. The number of these illustrations has been increased for this edition.

▶ Integrated Activity Boxes – encourage students to review and critically apply their understanding at regular intervals throughout the text, either by responding to a question or by undertaking a small practical assignment, individually or as part of a group. In recognition that this text is used on both professional and academic courses, we have amended many of the exercises from the third edition to reflect better the fact that many undergraduate students will have little or no business experience. Of those we have retained in their original format, some may appear to exclude students who are not in employment by asking readers to consider an aspect in their own organisation; however, the organisation could be a college or university, the students' union, a political body or sports team.

▶ New Discussion Topics – at the end of each of the strategy and operations chapters, as well as the introductory and final chapters, there are two or three short questions intended for general discussion in a tutorial or study group.

▶ New Exercises – at the end of each of the interaction chapters, there are two or three role-play style exercises intended for students to practise the skills which have been covered. These were previously provided in the Lecturer's Manual only.

▶ New Case Study Problems – at the end of each part we have included one short case study and several questions to enable students to review, link and apply their understanding of the previous chapters to a business scenario.

▶ New Examination Questions – at the end of each part of the text (except Part VIII) we have included eight sample questions from past examinations, each of which has been graded to indicate its level of difficulty: introductory undergraduate, intermediate/advanced undergraduate, masters and professional. These questions have been drawn from a number of universities, including Bradford, Cranfield, Manchester Metropolitan, Warwick and UMIST, and the IPD.

Each part of the text now includes a brief introduction to its scope and purpose. The extensive end-of-chapter references and bullet-point summary propositions from previous editions have been retained and updated.

Lecturer support material

This edition has an improved content and range of supplementary materials to assist lecturers in the preparation and delivery of courses using the text. All of the following items are available on application to the publisher:

- Resource Manual – includes comprehensive lecture and seminar outlines for both one- and two-semester courses; and indicative answers and debriefs for all the text exercises and case study problems.
- OHP Masters Pack – includes over 100 black/white A4 sheets containing a variety of specially prepared bullet-point material, and selected enlarged illustrations, figures and tables from the text.
- PowerPoint Slides – includes the above material on CD-ROM in full-colour presentation format.

Acknowledgements

As usual we are grateful for the assistance of a number of people and wish to acknowledge the help of those anonymous reviewers, who were kind enough to make comments at various stages of the writing, to Andy Goss and Jill Birch at Prentice Hall, and Stephen Taylor and Margaret Lees at UMIST. We acknowledge the following permissions from: the Academy of Management for Figure 2.1; Braybrook Press for Figure 2.2 and Table 9.1; John Wiley and Sons Inc. for Figure 2.3, Figure 2.4, Figure 2.6, Figure 9.4, Figure 19.1 and 'High Performance Teams at Digital, Ayr' (Window on Practice in Chapter 2); The Free Press (a division of Simon and Schuster) for Figure 2.5; David Guest for Figure 2.7; The Institute of Personnel and Development for Figure 6.1, Figure 7.2, Figure 7.3, and Figure 34.2; Findlay Publications for Figure 6.3; Burn and Thompson for Table 7.2; the Institute for Employment Research for Figure 9.1; John Atkinson for Figure 9.2 and Figure 9.3; *Human Resource Management Journal* for Table 12.3 and Table 16.1; McGraw-Hill Book Company for Figure 16.1 and Figure 16.2; Stanley Thornes Publishers for Figure 17.2; Idea Group Publishing for Figure 18.2; Vikki Ford for Table 19.2; Paul Miller for Table 21.1; the American Academy of Management for Figure 23.3 and Table 23.1; and Harcourt Brace and Company for Figure 24.2.

Derek Torrington and Laura Hall
Manchester, December 1997

PART I
Introduction

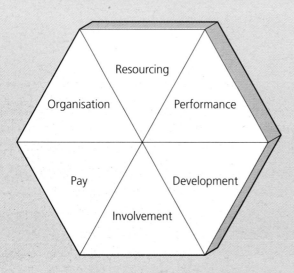

The first part of the book has only two chapters and forms the basis for all that is to follow. Chapter 1 sets the scene by describing the way in which personnel works today and then explains how it has evolved to its present form over the hundred years of its existence as a separate function of management. It shows that present-day practice is not only a response to contemporary business demands and social expectations, but also an amalgam of different features which have built up throughout the twentieth century. At the close of the chapter there is a model of the remainder and a philosophy for personnel management.

Chapter 2 concentrates on strategy in personnel and human resource management, drawing on research carried out by the authors over a ten-year period. We see the way in which personnel specialists make their strategic contribution, drawing a distinction between a human resource strategy and strategic human resource initiatives.

CHAPTER 1

The nature of personnel and human resource management

Jobs, careers and our whole experience of employment have changed more in the last decade than in the previous two centuries. The social impact of this change is scarcely recognised and frequently attributed to the temporary hiatus of 'the recession'. The fundamental change is a steady reversal of the trend of the last 200 years, during which the organisation has been not only the central feature of economic activity but also the boundary within which most people work, in which they find their personal security, their career prospects and the means to meet their work-related needs.

There is no longer this certainty. Organisations are getting smaller and less reliable. Entrepreneurs are less likely to found a dynasty for their children to inherit, and more likely to launch a project to be developed, exploited and then closed down or sold on within two or three years. The movement and availability of investment capital is less at the disposal of the tycoon following a dream with remorseless determination and more disposed of by 9–5 manipulators of yield ratios yawning in front of computer terminals. Organisations are becoming leaner and smaller. We have delayering and downsizing; rightsizing and outplacement: core/periphery workforces; subcontracting and temporary contracts; a growth in self-employment and part-time working. The organisation as an entity is going out of fashion and the above terms have arrived in the management vocabulary to describe the process of keeping the business as small as possible and the jobs within the business as flexible (and as insecure) as possible.

The American analyst Rifkin states:

> Transnational corporations are blazing a path across national boundaries, transforming and disrupting the lives of billions of people in their search for global markets. The casualties . . . are beginning to mount as millions of workers are riffed to make room for more efficient and profitable machine surrogates. Unemployment is rising and tempers are flaring in country after country caught up in the corporate crossfire to improve production performance at all costs.
>
> (Rifkin 1995, p. 287)

Rifkin describes an experience of employment, dominated not by individual entrepreneurs or lantern-jawed chief executives, but by anonymous corporations; our destinies determined not by the goodwill or illwill of powerful individuals, but by the remorseless, grim logic of market forces and discounted cash flow

– all this against a background not of security and confidence, but of acute anxiety and uncertainty. Charles Handy spells out the employment implications:

> The employee society is on the wane. New models are needed, new role players who will make the new ways less frightening. Political society will also have to make changes: resolving once and for all that children grow up with something to sell to the world . . . and that the helpless and the failures of this new order do not suffer too much, or bring too much suffering.
>
> (Handy 1995, p. 31)

Handy's reference to 'the employee society' reminds us of the irony that we now regret the passing of a form of life which our early nineteenth-century predecessors resisted: the factory system. Regular employment was virtually unknown and the idea of spending all one's working day in a specific place outside the home was unpalatable to most people, even though the alternative of a very hard, indigent life in agriculture was so gruelling. The early factory owners resorted to harsh discipline and long hours as a crude method of converting men, women and children to this radically new way of working:

> The new virtues that the workers were persuaded to adopt were those requisite for a material civilisation: regularity, punctuality, obedience, thrift, providence, sobriety and industry.   (Chapman and Chambers 1970)

The practice of personnel management has followed changing patterns of employment and, as a new millennium is about to dawn, contemporary personnel and HR specialists – perhaps – stand ready to be Handy's 'new role players to make the new ways less frightening'.

Personnel management is going through the biggest change in its history. Many commentators believed that the arrival of human resource management was to be the great change in emphasis, but that was no more than rethinking the processes inside the organisation; we now have to think beyond the organisation as entity. Personnel management has grown and developed with the increasing size and variety of organisations. It is in the throes of fundamental change because that process has gone into reverse and organisation *as entity* is in decline. We are rediscovering organisation *as a process*.

ACTIVITY BOX 1.1

We use the word organisation to describe an entity, when we are describing the place where we work ('my organisation'), a particular business enterprise ('Shell is an international organisation') or as a general term to describe undertakings ('over 200 organisations were represented at the conference').

Organisation as a process describes how something is done ('the organisation of the conference was very efficient'; 'The project failed due to poor organisation').

Think of examples of personnel work which are organisation as a process.

Consider the following imaginary scenario. There are six people to watch among the crowds thronging the railway station. First is Charles, Personnel Director, who is on his way to London for yet another strategy meeting. There is the possible closure of the plant in South Korea in order to take advantage of the lower labour costs in Sri Lanka. Then there is the meeting with the executive search consultants to review the candidates for the Chief Executive post in the new subsidiary at Luton before flying out to L.A. to propose that the design function should be relocated to Rome – they won't like that!

Also walking briskly along to the first class section of the London train is Sam (who may be Samantha or Samuel) a freelance consultant specialising in management development, setting off to run a three-day event for a large company that is rapidly developing its overseas activities and needs Sam's expertise to bring some of the senior executives up to date on European issues. During the journey Sam hopes to do some more work on the distance learning package which the business school has requested.

On a different platform Sharon has got off her commuter train and is hurrying towards the office, hoping that the computer system is working properly, so that she can pull off those reports that are needed for the management meeting later in the day. She is Personnel Administration Manager for her company and is regularly required to produce personnel projections and analyses for meetings. She has just spotted Adrian and has decided to dodge round the other side of the platform to avoid him. Adrian has been hired on a temporary six-month contract to develop the computer system, but he seems more interested in developing his own career and making sure that his work cannot possibly be finished in the time allotted.

John and Mary are some way ahead and exchanging views on what it is like to be a line manager. There used to be quite a lot of expertise in the personnel department to help with things like absence, discipline, performance management and all the range of matters relating to people at work, but now everything is left to 'the line'. The Chief Executive called it 'empowerment'. John and Mary feel that it is having responsibility dumped on you without really knowing what you are doing, and without much reward either.

ACTIVITY BOX 1.2

In the above scenario some roles were assigned explicitly to women or to men, others were gender-neutral. What was the significance of this? Were they realistic? Is there any connection between the way those roles were assigned and the decline of organisation as entity?

Charles, Sam, Sharon, Adrian, John and Mary could well be going to work that day for the same company, but specialisation, rationalisation and the emphasis on market mechanisms mean that there is less emphasis on the company being an organisation of which they are a part, although their individual activities still have to be co-ordinated.

There is a major shift in emphasis for personnel managers. Less and less do they administer the contract of **employment**: more and more do they administer the contract for **performance**, and the performance may come from employees, but it is just as likely to come from non-employees. Personnel specialists lead the way from within their own ranks with the training function being dismantled and the specialist work of developing skills, competences and capacities being contracted out to consultants and specialist suppliers. Other aspects of the

Macclesfield, in the north of England was the centre of silk manufacture from the beginning of the eighteenth century through to the middle of the twentieth. The town's heritage museum portrays vividly how people were engaged in making silk buttons, working individually or as small family units in garrets producing buttons to the order of merchandisers and being paid by the piece, as and when there was an order. They were all home workers.

Ten miles away the village of Styal developed around a mill which represented a different mode of working. Instead of work being put out to people, people were brought in to the work. There is an apprentice house, where foundlings were housed and both cared for and exploited during their teen years. Begun in 1783, the firm employed 2,000 people by 1834 (Rose 1986, p. 13). This was the beginning of a trend that

was to continue uninterrupted until very recently. The entity of the organisation was the focus for economic activity and it was also the vehicle for our working lives. We became employees, the organisation took over responsibility for our jobs and our livelihood, our training and our security in old age. Welfare officers were invented and later turned into personnel officers. Trade unions developed. We acquired elaborate structures of authority and lines of responsibility.

Today Styal Mill is a textile museum still surrounded by the village of houses built by the mill owner for his employees. It is owned by the National Trust and visited by thousands of people every year. It is a flourishing, successful business, but it employs only a handful of people on a full-time, permanent basis. Many more are temporary, part-time employees or volunteers.

personnel function that are increasingly contracted out are recruitment, selection and many aspects of payment. The new activity of outplacement is typically handed to consultants and the even newer concept of employee assistance programmes are usually regarded as necessarily being contracted out if they are to be credible.

The make-up of contemporary personnel management

Despite the enormous discussion about the significance of human resource management, personnel specialists remain largely committed to the term 'personnel' as the appropriate label for themselves, their departments and their professional body. In our research we found an extraordinarily wide range of titles, but the departmental title incorporating 'personnel' outnumbered those with 'human resources' by just over 4:1. For individual jobs 'personnel' had a majority of just over 3:1.

As the function has evolved it has added new dimensions without shedding those developed in earlier periods. For years personnel managers tried to disown their welfare officer origins, yet employee welfare remains a central feature of the role. In the 1980s many people claimed that human resource management had replaced personnel management but, except as a label, this was rarely true. If we are to understand personnel management today, we need to trace its development, to see how new dimensions have been added progressively to make personnel management the most varied, fascinating and demanding of all management roles.

Although we cannot attribute any particular ideology to a complete group of people at any one time, it is possible roughly to show the development of the personnel function by suggesting a general self-image, which obtained at different periods.

The social reformer

Before personnel emerged as a specialist management activity, there were those in the nineteenth century who tried to intervene in industrial affairs to support the position of the severely underprivileged factory worker at the hands of a rapacious employer. The Industrial Revolution had initially helped people to move away from the poverty and harshness of rural life, or from the hopelessness of the orphanage, and into the factories and the cities, but the organisation of the work soon degraded human life and dehumanised working people. In the words of William Wordsworth:

Men, maidens, youths,
Mothers and little children, boys and girls,
Enter, and each the wonted task resumes
Within this temple, where is offered up
To Gain, the master idol of the realm,
perpetual sacrifice.

Free enterprise, the survival of the fittest and the ruthless exploitation of the masses were seen as laws of nature, and it was social reformers like Lord Shaftesbury and Robert Owen who went some way to mitigating this hardship, mainly by standing outside the organisation and the workplace, offering criticism of employer behaviour within, and inducing some changes. This was aided by the more general social commentary of Dickens' novels and the observations of Friedrich Engels.

We need to trace the evolution of personnel management to this type of person, as it was their influence and example that enabled personnel managers to be appointed, and provided the first frame of reference for the appointees to work within. It would also be incorrect to say that this type of concern is obsolete. There are regular reports of employees being exploited by employers flouting the law, and the problem of organisational distance between decision-makers and those putting decisions into practice remains a source of alienation from work. In one large company an inscription was printed on a report stating that it should not be bent, twisted or defaced. A group of employees in the same company made a muted complaint about their lack of identity by producing lapel badges with the caption: 'I am a human being, do not bend, twist or deface'.

The acolyte of benevolence

The first people to be appointed with specific responsibility for improving the lot of employees were usually known as welfare officers; they saw their role as dispensing benefits to the deserving and unfortunate employees. The motivation was the Christian charity of the noble employer, who was prepared to provide these comforts, partly because the employees deserved them, but mainly because the employer was disposed to provide them.

The leading examples of this development were the Quaker families of Cadbury and Rowntree, and the Lever Brothers' soap business. All set up progressive schemes of unemployment benefit, sick pay and subsidised housing for their employees during the latter part of the nineteenth century. Although later accused of paternalism, these initiatives marked a fundamental shift of employer philosophy. Seebohm Rowntree became a renowned sociologist as well as being chairman of his company for sixteen years and putting into practice the reforms he advocated in his writings. Cadbury Schweppes and Unilever remain among the most efficient and profitable businesses in the United Kingdom a hundred years after the foundation of the Bournville village and Port Sunlight.

In other instances the philosophy was perverted by relatively cheap welfare provisions being offered as a substitute for higher wages, and was used extensively to keep trade unions at bay.

The Institute of Welfare Officers was established in 1913 at a meeting in the Rowntree factory in York and the welfare tradition remains strong in personnel management, although it keeps re-emerging in different forms. There is constant comment on the provision of facilities like childcare and health screening, as well as the occasional discussion about business ethics (for example, Pocock 1989). The extent to which contemporary working practices for professional and executive employees make unreasonable demands of time and inconvenience is receiving increasing attention, as is the need for employees of all types to balance work and domestic responsibilities:

> Care-friendly employment practices will be the phenomenon of the future. Only by addressing the needs of employees caring for children, dependants with disabilities and the elderly, will employers be able to attract and retain the non-traditional sectors of the workforce which are forecast to form the workforce of the 1990s.
> (Worman 1990)

The humane bureaucrat

The first two phases were concerned predominantly with the physical environment of work and the amelioration of hardship among 'the workers'. We now come to the stage where employing organisations were taking a further step in increasing their size, and specialisation was emerging in the management levels as well as on the shopfloor. This led to the growth of personnel work on what is loosely called staffing, with great concern about role specification, careful selection, training and placement. The personnel manager was learning to operate within a bureaucracy, serving organisational rather than paternalist-employer objectives, but still committed to a basically humanitarian role.

For the first time there was a willingness to look to social science for support. Much of the scientific management philosophy of F. W. Taylor informed personnel thinking:

> First. Develop a science for each element of a man's work, which replaces the old rule-of-thumb method.
> Second. Scientifically select and then train, teach, and develop the workman, whereas in the past he chose his own work and trained himself as best he could.
> Third. Heartily cooperate with the men so as to insure all of the work being done in accordance with the principles which have been developed.

> Fourth. There is an almost equal division of the work and the responsibility between the management and the workmen. The management take over all work for which they are better fitted than workmen, while in the past almost all of the work and the greater part of the responsibility was thrown upon the men.   (Taylor 1911, pp. 36–7)

Work was to be made more efficient by analysis of what was required and the careful selection and training of the workman, who would then be supported by the management in a spirit of positive co-operation.

The Frenchman Henri Fayol (1949) considered not the worker but the management process, and his analytical framework for management is sometimes known as scientific administration, as his approach had much in common with Taylor's.

The humane bureaucracy stage in the development of personnel thinking was also influenced by the Human Relations school of thought, which was in many ways a reaction against scientific management, or a reaction against the way in which scientific management was being applied. Just as the high ideals of the Cadburys and Rowntrees had been debased by some of their imitators, so Taylor found his managerial philosophy was seldom fully appreciated, and scientific management became identified with hyper-specialisation of work and very tight systems of payment.

The human relations approach appealed immediately to those who were concerned about industrial conflict and the apparent dehumanising potential of scientific management. The main advocate was Elton Mayo (1933), and the central idea was to emphasise informal social relationships and employee morale as contributors to organisational efficiency.

It was during this stage of development that personnel managers began to develop a technology as well as an approach, and many of the methods developed at this time remain at the heart of what personnel managers do; the idea of fitting together two sets of requirements is a theme to which we shall return.

The consensus negotiator

Personnel managers next added expertise in bargaining to their repertoire of skills. The acolytes of benevolence had not been numerous or strong enough to satisfy employee aspirations as a result of employer voluntary provision. In the period after the Second World War there was relatively full employment, and labour became a scarce resource. Trade unions extended their membership and employers had to change firm, traditional unitarism as the reality of what Allan Flanders, the leading industrial relations analyst of the 1960s, was to call 'the challenge from below' was grudgingly recognised. Where the personnel manager could at best be described as a 'remembrancer' of the employees, the trade union official could be their accredited representative.

Trade union assertiveness brought a shift towards bargaining by the employer on at least some matters. There was a growth of joint consultation and the establishment of joint production committees and suggestion schemes. Nationalised industries were set up, with a statutory duty placed on employers to negotiate with unions representing employees. The government encouraged the appointment of personnel officers and set up courses for them to be trained at universities. A personnel management advisory service was set up at the Ministry of Labour, and this still survives as the first A in ACAS (Advisory, Conciliation and Arbitration Service).

The trend began during the early 1940s but received a major boost when the sellers' market of the immediate postwar period began to harden and international competition made more urgent the development of greater productive efficiency and the elimination of restrictive (or protective) practices. The personnel manager acquired bargaining expertise to deploy in search of a lost consensus.

Organisation man

Next came a development of the humane bureaucracy phase into a preoccupation with the effectiveness of the organisation as a whole, with clear objectives and a widespread commitment among organisation members to those objectives. The approach was also characterised by candour between members and a form of operation that supported the integrity of the individual and provided opportunities for personal growth. There was an attempt to understand the interaction of organisational structures between, on the one hand, the people who make up the organisation and, on the other, the surrounding society in which it is set.

This development was most clearly seen in the late 1960s and is most significant because it marks a change of focus among personnel specialists, away from dealing with the rank-and-file employee on behalf of the management towards dealing with the management and integration of managerial activity. Its most recent manifestation has been in programmes of organisation and management development, as companies have subcontracted much of their routine work to peripheral employees, and concentrated on developing and retaining an élite core of people with specialist expertise on whom the business depends for its future.

Manpower analyst

The last of our historical stereotypes is that of manpower analyst, associated with the term 'management of human resources'. A development of the general management anxiety to quantify decisions has been a move towards regarding people as manpower or human resources. A relatively extreme form of this is human asset accounting, which assigns a value to individual employees in accounting terms and estimates the extent to which that asset will appreciate or depreciate in the future, so eventually everyone is written off in more ways than one.

More widespread was the use of manpower planning, which was:

> a strategy for the organization, utilization and improvement of an
> organization's human resources. It comprises three main activities:
> (a) assessing what manpower of what different grades, categories and
> skills will be needed in the short term and long term (i.e. manpower
> demand); (b) deciding what manpower an organization is likely to have in
> the future, based on current trends and anticipated external circumstances
> (i.e. manpower supply); and (c) taking action to ensure that supply meets
> demand (e.g. training, retraining, recruitment).   (Message 1974)

Although originally based on an assumption of organisational expansion, manpower planning was reshaped during the onset of organisational contraction to ensure the closest possible fit between the number of people and skills required and what was available. The activity was boosted by the advent of the computer, which made possible a range of calculations and measurements that were unrealistic earlier.

Human resource management

The concept of human resource management (HRM) took the management world by storm during the 1980s and has represented a significant change of direction. The difference needs to be explored, even though the nature and degree of the difference remain largely matters of opinion rather than fact, and the similarities are much greater than the differences.

Personnel management is *workforce-centred*, directed mainly at the organisation's employees; finding and training them, arranging for them to be paid, explaining management's expectations, justifying management's actions, satisfying employees' work-related needs, dealing with their problems and seeking to modify management action that could produce an unwelcome employee response. The people who work in the organisation are the starting point, and they are a resource that is relatively inflexible in comparison with other resources, like cash and materials.

Although indisputably a management function, personnel is never totally identified with management interests, as it becomes ineffective when not able to understand and articulate the aspirations and views of the workforce, just as sales representatives have to understand and articulate the aspirations of the customers. There is always some degree of being in between the management and the employees, mediating the needs of each to the other. Thomason quotes from both Miller and Spates to express this idea:

> Miller argues that the personnel management role is 'different from other staff jobs in that it has to serve not only the employer, but also act in the interests of employees as individual human beings, and by extension, the interests of society' (Miller 1975). Similarly, Spates finds a conception of the personnel management role which provides a place for the goals and aspirations of workers. . . . For him, the function of personnel administration is concerned with 'organizing and treating individuals at work so that they will get the greatest possible realisation of their intrinsic abilities, thus attaining maximum efficiency for themselves and their group and thereby giving to the concern of which they are a part its determining competitive advantage and its optimum results'.   (Thomason 1981, p. 38)

HRM is *resource-centred*, directed mainly at management needs for human resources (not necessarily employees) to be provided and deployed. Demand rather than supply is the focus of the activity. There is greater emphasis on planning, monitoring and control, rather than mediation. Problem-solving is undertaken with other members of management on human resource issues rather than directly with employees or their representatives. It is totally identified with management interests, being a general management activity, and is relatively distant from the workforce as a whole, as employee interests can be enhanced only through effective overall management.

Underpinning personnel management are the twin ideas that people have a right to be treated as dignified human beings while at work, that they are only effective as employees when their job-related personal needs are met, and that this will not happen without personnel management intervention in the everyday manager/subordinate relationships. Personnel managers are involved in a more direct way in the relationship between other managers and their

WINDOW ON PRACTICE

The rock-hard, steely-eyed film star Clint Eastwood has appeared in several films as tough cop Harry Callaghan, whose approach to law and order is to shoot first and not bother asking too many questions afterwards. On one occasion he had killed rather a lot of people even by his own high standards, so that he was becoming politically embarrassing to the authorities. Something had to be done. The Chief of Police nerved himself and called Harry into his office, taking care that there was a large table between them, and gave him the news that he was being transferred to personnel. There was a moment of electric silence. A nervous tic flickered briefly on Harry Callaghan's right cheek. His jaw locked and those famous cold-blue eyes gave the Chief a look that could have penetrated armour plate as he hissed his reply through clenched teeth: 'Personnel is for assholes.' Whereupon he left the room, slamming the door with sufficient vigour to splinter the woodwork in several places.

Being a man of few words, Harry Callaghan did not explain further, but we can interpret his view as being the common one that personnel work is typically undertaken by deviant innovators, who have their own 'soft' agenda of being nice to people and who shirk the hard, competitive world of marketing, the precision of finance, or the long hours and hard knocks of manufacturing. It is soft, ineffectual and unimportant.

subordinates, because the personnel aspects of management are often perceived by line managers as not central to their role.

Underpinning human resource management is the idea that management of human resources is much the same as any other aspect of management and an integral part of it that cannot be separated out for specialists to handle. People have a right to considerate treatment while at work, and they will be effective when their personal career and competence needs are met within a context of efficient management and a mutually respectful working relationship. The specialist role is directed towards getting the deployment of right numbers and skills at the right price, supporting other managers in their people management and contributing to major strategic change.

This is how we interpret the distinction between personnel management and human resource management, but the distinction is one over which there is much debate and uncertainty (see, for example, Guest 1989; Legge 1989; Sisson 1989; Hart 1993; Torrington 1994). Legge provides the most scrupulous analysis and concludes that there is very little difference in fact between the two, but there are some differences that are important; first, that human resource management concentrates more on what is done to managers rather than on what is done by managers to other employees; second, that there is a more proactive role for line managers; and third, that there is a top management responsibility for managing culture. We return to all these matters later in the book.

It would be inaccurate to suggest that one approach has taken over from the other, just as it would be wrong to suggest that one is modern and the other old-fashioned, or that one is right and the other wrong. Both are usually present in one organisation; sometimes in one person. This can cause tension and ambiguity. As an emphasis for the work of personnel specialists there is a tendency for human resource management to increase at the expense of personnel management, and we suggest the following reasons for this change:

1. The devolution of personnel duties to line managers means that more of the mediation and reconciliation of needs associated with personnel management is being undertaken by line managers, like John and Mary at the opening of this chapter. Managers of all sorts are increasingly their own personnel managers as part of a tendency for all managers to become more general ('all-singing, all-dancing') than specialised in their responsibilities.

2. With widespread unemployment, much temporary and part-time working, a gradual reduction in normal working hours and a shortening of the working lifetime as a proportion of the total lifetime, the workplace is not quite as significant as a source of personal self-esteem and as an arena for achieving personal objectives, as it was 10–15 years ago. When full-time employment is an experience shared by all for most of their adult lives, then it is the source of most opportunities and the means of self-actualisation. Now it is an experience which a significant minority do not share at all and a further significant minority only experience in the 'peripheral workforce'. Even those employed full-time in 'proper jobs' probably spend no more than 20 per cent of their time for half their lifetime at work. In this situation the meeting of personal goals at work is a prospect denied to many and an instrumental orientation to work becomes more common.

ACTIVITY BOX 1.3

Although men are tending to retire well before the state retirement age of 65, the retirement age for women is being raised from 60 to 65. How will this alter the relative experience of employment between men and women?

3. Personnel specialists have long sought organisational power. Karen Legge (1978, pp. 67–94) described contrasted approaches used by them in this quest. First was *conformist innovation*, whereby personnel specialists identify their activities with the objective of organisational success, emphasising cost-benefit and conforming to the criteria of organisational success adopted by managerial colleagues, who usually have greater power. In contrast are the *deviant innovators*, who identify their activities with a set of norms or values that are distinct from, but not necessarily in conflict with, the norms of organisational success. They will emphasise social values rather than cost-benefit. HRM is a form of conformist innovation: close identification with central management interests. Human resources management theoretically provides a repositioning of the personnel function to make it more influential.

4. There is an ever-increasing range of mini-expertise needed within the personnel area. The range of activities covered by the function has tended to expand and that range of activities requires a wide variety of specialist knowledge. The law is the most obvious of these additions, including the areas of concern that have a dimension based on law, such as equal opportunity, but there has also been growing involvement with organisational change, pensions, statutory and occupational sick pay, more sophisticated approaches to payment, government initiatives on training

and employment, and the application of the computer. This leads to an increasing use of external resources, reinforcing the tendency for personnel managers to become deployers of resources and knowledgeable about sources, rather than just deployers of skills and knowledgeable about people.

5. The reduced assertiveness of most trade unions has made industrial action less likely and has reduced managerial apprehensiveness about unfavourable employee response.

6. The prolonged economic recession of the late 1980s stimulated management concern with immediate survival at the expense of longer-term development. Some new companies grew very quickly but then declined quickly, emphasising the benefits of working at the here-and-now rather than contemplating the future. This has usually been accompanied by a narrow human resource management approach with a greater emphasis on the present and avoidance of long-term commitments other than to key personnel.

7. The emphasis of employment legislation has shifted away from employee rights towards union containment, so lessening the degree of management anxiety about this 'frightener'.

8. There is an increasing need for personnel activities to be justified in cost terms, as, for instance, in the direct charging for internal training events, so that the training function operates in the same way as an external supplier, with the same need constantly to justify its activities. The gradual advance in the application of computerisation makes it easier for costs, or notional costs, to be attached to an increasing range of activities that were previously part of general overheads.

The seven stereotypes we have identified have all blended together to make the complex of contemporary personnel management. Although they have emerged roughly in sequence, all are still present to a varying degree in different types of personnel post and the nature of personnel work today can only be understood by an appreciation of its varied components.

ACTIVITY BOX 1.4

Which of these seven stereotypes do you personally find most attractive as describing the sort of job you would like to do? Which one, or combination, of the seven most accurately describes the job you have?

Ways of organising the personnel function

Personnel departments vary considerably in size from one person only up to several hundreds. We examined forty-two organisation charts of the personnel function in different establishments and found that in every case jobs were defined on a functional basis (employee relations manager, recruitment officer, management development adviser, and so forth) or as general responsibilities, such as personnel manager, factory personnel officer, group personnel manager, or manager, human resources. The most significant influence on the organisation of the personnel function seems to be either the degree of centralisation or the degree of attenuation.

The degree of centralisation is an issue affecting only larger organisations. Sisson and Scullion (1985) reported on research in the largest 100 companies in the United Kingdom to show that some companies have very large corporate personnel departments, others have a small head office team, others have a single executive, and others have no corporate personnel activity at all. They explain this in terms of whether or not the management at the centre have retained responsibility for a number of aspects of operating management that are critical as well as discharging responsibility for strategic management. If personnel is a critical function in which a common approach is needed because of the organisation being in a single business, like Marks & Spencer or Ford, then there is likely to be a strong corporate personnel function, although the moves away from national-level bargaining have reduced the imperatives behind this sort of centralisation. In the multidivisional corporation, there is not the same logic behind centralisation.

The degree of attenuation is a more localised issue stemming from making the business leaner and fitter. The organisation retains a senior personnel manager with significant rank and responsibility but little specialist support at middle to senior management levels and a personnel administration manager keeping excellent records and dealing with a host of routine matters, rather like Charles and Sharon at the opening of this chapter. The degree of attenuation varies, but the greater it is the fewer specialist roles there will be. Though there are no standard forms of organisation, three samples are shown in Figures 1.1, 1.2 and 1.3.

Figure 1.1 shows the situation of a personnel department in a subsidiary of an organisation with a strong corporate personnel function determining most policy questions and maintaining consistency of practice across a number of different establishments. Figure 1.2 is an establishment of similar size, but Figure 1.3 is a well-developed, independent function in a large, integrated organisation. Notice the dotted lines in Figure 1.1, indicating split accountability between the local manager and head office.

Most job-holders within the personnel function carry several responsibilities. The following are some of the most common job titles and the duties attaching to them.

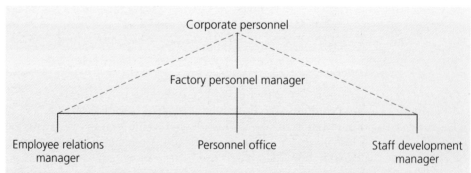

Figure 1.1 Sample structure of the personnel function in an establishment that is part of an organisation with a strong corporate personnel department

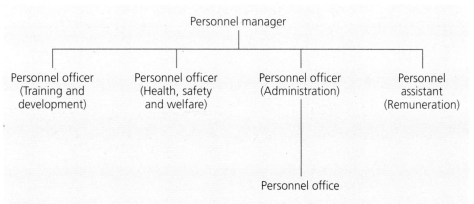

Figure 1.2 Sample structure of the personnel function in an autonomous establishment

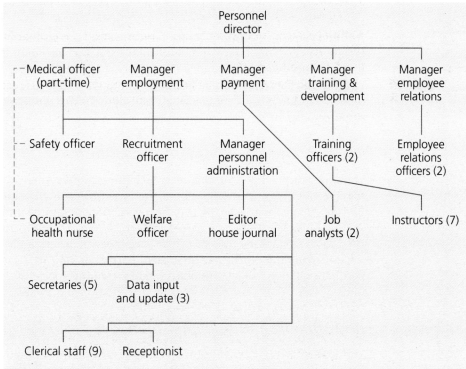

Figure 1.3 Sample structure of the personnel function in a large integrated organisation

Personnel or HR manager/director

This is the general manager in charge of the personnel function, who acts as its figurehead and main spokesperson, representing personnel issues in all senior management discussions and policy-making. There are usually one or more specialist responsibilities attaching to the post. In Figure 1.2, for instance, the personnel manager is responsible for employee relations and all pay matters. This is the role, together with most of those that follow, for which the Institute of Personnel Management's membership examinations provide the most appropriate and widely regarded qualification.

Personnel officer

In most establishments this is the title of the person who deals with all personnel issues, being a second type of generalist role. In larger establishments it is a general title with a specific explanatory responsibility following in brackets. Figure 1.2 again provides an example.

Employee relations manager

The most common specialist role is that dealing with the collective relationship between management and employees, especially where this is formalised through union recognition and procedure agreements. It often includes responsibility for pay issues, employee involvement and communication.

Management development manager

Another strong tradition is to concentrate responsibility for training and employee development in the hands of a specialist, although there is an increasing tendency to deal with development matters by heavy reliance on outside facilities, such as consultants, like Sam. There is also a focus on *management* development rather than on *employee* development to emphasise the managers' responsibility for developing their staff.

Training and development consultants

Training officers have similar responsibilities to personnel officers in that they may be single trainers with general training duties in an establishment, or they may be charged with specific training tasks, like operator training. The term 'consultant' is increasingly being used instead of 'officer' to ensure that the work is used as a consultancy by managers to arrange the training *they* want rather than what the training officer has organised. Formal qualifications in organisational or occupational psychology are often held by training specialists, and IPD qualifications devote a large proportion of their standards and total syllabus to this area.

Recruitment and selection manager

These posts are not as widespread as they were and usually these duties are the regular part-time responsibility of several people in a personnel department, yet the work remains highly skilled and many large organisations still retain specialist personnel, usually with an occupational psychology background expertise.

Human resource planner

This is a much less clear job title with many variations, used to describe someone whose expertise is basically in human resource planning and statistics, and who will do much of the preliminary work on personnel planning and strategy.

Organisation development consultant

This role specialises in enabling the organisation to adapt to its changing environment and its members to develop their roles to meet the new challenges and opportunities that are emerging. It is a job with few administrative features and is usually held by someone with an independent, roving commission.

Safety officer/welfare officer

The area of health, safety and welfare is one where there are strong legal constraints on employer action and the Safety Officer is not always a part of the personnel function at all. Large organisations often have one or more welfare officers to deal with general issues of employee support and there has recently been an increase in employee assistance programmes, which perform part of the welfare function through the use of an outside agency.

Personnel administration manager

The final role in this sample list is a longstanding one, which is changing direction. There is some tendency for personnel administration to increase, and a part of the expanding numbers in personnel departments is in the clerical/administrative/keyboard area, with the demands of such tasks as statutory sick pay and the need to maintain a personnel database on the computer. This part of the operation is run by someone who used to be called 'office manager', but who is now more likely to be described as 'personnel administration manager'.

So far this chapter has been devoted to considering the personnel specialism, but the personnel function of management as a whole is equally important. Each manager has inescapable responsibilities and duties of a personnel type, so that personnel management is not only of interest to specialists but to all managers. The degree and nature of the involvement differs, but the need for a philosophy or set of beliefs to underpin one's actions remains the same.

Many organisations do not have personnel specialists at all. The existence of a specialised personnel function is clearly related to size, and the increasing number of small businesses do not need, or cannot afford, this type of specialism. They may use consultants, they may use the advisory resources of university departments, they may use their bank's computer to process the payroll, but there is still a personnel dimension to their management activities.

A philosophy of personnel management

The philosophy of personnel management that is the basis of this book has been only slightly modified since it was first put forward in 1979 (Torrington and Chapman 1979, p. 4). Despite all the changes in the labour market and in the government approach to the economy, this seems to be the most realistic and constructive approach, based on the earlier ideas of Enid Mumford (1972) and McCarthy and Ellis (1973). As it has a further slight development for this edition, it is worth showing how it has changed from 1979 to today. The original was:

> Personnel management is most realistically seen as a series of activities enabling working man and his employing organisation to reach agreement about the nature and objectives of the employment relationship between them, and then to fulfil those agreements.
>
> (Torrington and Chapman 1979, p. 4)

Our definition for 1995 was, and remains:

> Personnel management is a series of activities which: first enables working people and the business which uses their skills to agree about the objectives and nature of their working relationship and, secondly, ensures that the agreement is fulfilled.   (Torrington and Hall 1995, p. 21)

Only by satisfying the needs of the individual contributor will the business obtain the commitment to organisational objectives that is needed for organisational success, and only by contributing to organisational success will individuals be able to satisfy their personal employment needs. It is when employer and employee – or business and supplier of skills – accept that mutuality and reciprocal depen-

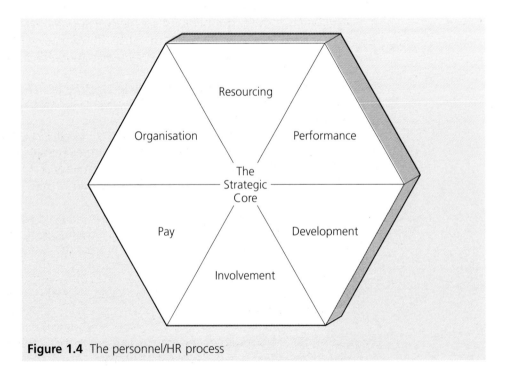

Figure 1.4 The personnel/HR process

dence that personnel management is exciting, centre-stage and productive of business success. Where the employer is concerned with employees only as factors of production, personnel management is boring and a cost that will always be trimmed. Where employees have no trust in their employer and adopt an entirely instrumental orientation to their work, they will be fed up and will make ineffectual the work of any personnel function.

Personnel managers are great grumblers, and some will react to the last paragraph by saying that they do not get the support they deserve. Personnel decisions are always taken last, never get proper resources, and so forth. Sometimes this is correct, but all too often it is a self-fulfilling prophecy, because the personnel people are pursuing the wrong objectives, or carefully keeping out of the way when things get really tough; which was exactly Harry Callaghan's point.

Figure 1.4 represents the contents of this book in the six main parts. After the two chapter introduction in Part I come the six parts, which each have the same format: strategic aspects, operational features, and a keynote chapter on an interaction that is central to that set of operations. This is the personnel/HRM process, a strategic core with operational specialist expertise and a strong focus on dealing with people face to face.

Personnel managers are like managers in every other part of the business. They have to make things happen rather than wait for things to happen, and to make things happen they not only have to have the right approach; they also have to know their stuff. Read on!

Summary propositions

1.1   Personnel management is undergoing its biggest-ever change as *organisation-as-entity* declines and we rediscover organisation-as-process.
1.2   Contemporary personnel management work is made up of seven facets, which have been dominant at various times during the evolution of personnel management ideas.
1.3   Personnel management is the work of personnel specialists; human resource management is a feature of the work of all managers, including personnel specialists.
1.4   The philosophy of personnel management in this book is that it is a series of activities which: first enables working people and the business which uses their skills to agree about the nature and objectives of their working relationship; and, secondly, ensures that the agreement is fulfilled.

References

Chapman, S. D. and Chambers, J. D. (1970) *The Beginnings of Industrial Britain*, quoted in Quarry Bank Mill Trust (1986) *Mill Life at Styal*, Willow Publishing: Altrincham, Cheshire.

Fayol, H. (1949) *General and Industrial Management*, London: Pitman.

Guest, D. E. (1989) 'Personnel and HRM – can you tell the difference?', *Personnel Management*, Vol. 21, No. 1, January.

Handy, C. B. (1995) *Beyond Certainty*, London: Random House.

Hart, T. J. (1993) 'Human resource management: time to exorcise the militant tendency', *Employee Relations*, Vol. 15, No. 3, pp. 29–36.

Legge, K. (1978) *Power, Innovation and Problem-solving in Personnel Management*, London: McGraw-Hill.

Legge, K. (1989) 'Human resource management: a critical analysis', in J. Storey (ed.), *New Perspectives on Human Resource Management*, London: Routledge.

Mackay, L. E. and Torrington, D. P. (1986) *The Changing Nature of Personnel Management*, London: Institute of Personnel Management.

Mayo, E. (1933) *The Human Problems of an Industrial Civilisation*, New York: Macmillan.

McCarthy, W. E. J. and Ellis, N. D. (1973) *Management by Agreement*, London: Hutchinson.

Message, M. C. (1974) 'Manpower planning', in D. P. Torrington (ed.), *Encyclopaedia of Personnel Management*, Aldershot: Gower.

Mumford, E. (1972) 'Job satisfaction: a method of analysis', *Personnel Review*, Vol. 1, No. 3.

Pocock, P. (1989) 'Is business ethics a contradiction in terms?' *Personnel Management*, Vol. 21, No. 11, December.

Rifkin, J. R. (1995) *The End of Work*, New York: Archer/Putnam.

Rose, M. B. (1986) *The Gregs of Quarry Bank Mill*, Cambridge: Cambridge University Press.

Sisson, K. (1989) 'Personnel management in perspective', and 'Personnel management in transition', in K. Sisson (ed.), *Personnel Management in Transition*, Oxford: Blackwell.

Sisson, K. and Scullion, H. (1985) 'Putting the corporate personnel department in its place', *Personnel Management*, December.

Taylor, F. W. (1911) *Scientific Management*, New York: Harper & Row.

Thomason, G. F. (1981) *A Textbook of Personnel Management*, London: IPM.

Torrington, D. P. (1994) 'How dangerous is human resource management? A reply to Tim Hart', *Employee Relations*, Vol. 15, No. 5, pp. 40–53.

Torrington, D. P. and Chapman, J. B. (1979) *Personnel Management*, Hemel Hempstead: Prentice Hall.

Worman, D. (1990) 'The forgotten carers', *Personnel Management*, Vol. 22, No. 1.

General discussion topics

1. In what ways does the decline of the organisation as an entity make working more attractive to members of the group, and in what ways does it become less attractive?

2. How do you understand the suggestion that the contract of employment is gradually changing to a contract for performance?

3. The philosophy of personnel management set out at the end of this chapter makes no reference to the customer. David Ulrich, a professor at Michigan Business School, believes that it is important to refocus personnel/HR activities away from the firm towards the customer so that suppliers, employees and customers are woven together into a value-chain team. What difference do you think that would make?

CHAPTER 2

Human resource strategy

We have seen how interest in strategy has taken personnel management by storm. The rhetoric of strategic involvement is now embedded in 'personnel speak' and the strategy for human resources is seen to be a central component of business strategy. The key question for personnel managers is whether or not they are involved in the decision-making. Storey has described how this presents a dilemma for personnel directors:

> If, in order to win business credibility on the board, they suppressed traditional personnel perspectives, the whole question of their distinctive contribution would be open to question. . . . If, on the other hand, the personnel director seeks to give a higher profile to the distinctive attributes of a 'personnel view', this may be seen to renege on the 'business primacy' axiom . . .
>
> (Storey 1992, p. 275)

In this chapter we set out the nature of human resource strategy, its development and integration with organisational strategy.

What is human resource strategy?

Human resource strategy involves a central philosophy of the way that people in the organisation are managed, and the translation of this into personnel policies and practices. It requires personnel policies and practices to be integrated so that they make a coherent whole, and also that this whole is integrated with the business or organisational strategy. These themes of integration and a central philosophy of people management have been drawn out by a number of writers (e.g. Handy *et al.* 1989; Hendry and Pettigrew 1986). Baird *et al.*, as early as 1983, went one step beyond this and argued that there can be no organisational strategy without the inclusion of human resources. A third theme identified by Handy *et al.* is that the above demands a strategic view of the role of personnel management in the organisation. We shall come back to these themes later on.

So far we have a definition of what is involved in human resource strategy, but what does one look like? Human resource strategy is generally behaviour-based. In the traditional ideal model there would be analysis of the types of employee behaviour required to fulfil business objectives, and then an identification of personnel policies and practices which would bring about and reinforce this behaviour. A very good example of this is found in Schuler and Jackson

(1987). They used the three generic business strategies defined by Porter (1974) and for each identified employee role behaviour and HRM policies required. Their conclusions are shown below in Table 2.1.

Table 2.1 Business strategies, and associated employee role behaviour and HRM policies

Strategy	Employee role behaviour	HRM policies
1. Innovation	A high degree of creative behaviour	Jobs that require close interaction and co-ordination among groups of individuals
	Longer-term focus	Performance appraisals that are more likely to reflect longer-term and group-based achievements
	A relatively high level of co-operative, interdependent behaviour	Jobs that allow employees to develop skills that can be used in other positions in the firm
		Compensation systems that emphasise internal equity rather than external or market-based equity
	A moderate degree of concern for quality	Pay rates that tend to be low, but that allow employees to be stockholders and have more freedom to choose the mix of components that make up their pay package
	A moderate concern for quantity; an equal degree of concern for process and results	Broad career paths to reinforce the development of a broad range of skills
	A greater degree of risk-taking; a higher tolerance of ambiguity and unpredictability	
2. Quality enhancement	Relatively repetitive and predictable behaviours	Relatively fixed and explicit job descriptions
	A more long-term or intermediate focus	High levels of employee participation in decisions relevant to immediate work conditions and the job itself
	A moderate amount of co-operative, interdependent behaviour	A mix of individual and group criteria for performance appraisal that is mostly short term and results orientated
	A high concern for quality	A relatively egalitarian treatment of employees and some guarantees of employment security
	A modest concern for quantity of output	Extensive and continuous training and development of employees
	High concern for process: low risk-taking activity; commitment to the goals of the organisation	
3. Cost reduction	Relatively repetitive and predictable behaviour	Relatively fixed and explicit job descriptions that allow little room for ambiguity
	A rather short-term focus	Narrowly designed jobs and narrowly defined career paths that encourage specialisation expertise and efficiency
	Primarily autonomous or individual activity	Short-term results-orientated performance appraisals
	Moderate concern for quality	Close monitoring of market pay levels for use in making compensation decisions
	High concern for quantity of output	Minimal levels of employee training and development
	Primary concern for results; low risk-taking activity; relatively high degree of comfort with stability	

Source: Schuler and Jackson (1987). Reproduced with permission of the Academy of Management.

Similar analyses can be found for other approaches to business strategy, for example in relation to the Boston matrix (Purcell 1992) and the developmental stage of the organisation (Kochan and Barocci 1985). Some human resource strategies describe the behaviour of all employees, but others have concentrated on the behaviour of Chief Executives and senior managers; Miles and Snow (1978), for example, align appropriate managerial characteristics to three generic strategies of prospector, defender and analyser. The rationale behind this matching process is that if managerial attributes and skills are aligned to the organisational strategy, then a higher level of organisational performance will result. There is little empirical evidence to validate this link, but some recent work by Thomas and Ramaswamy (1996) does provide some support. They used statistical analysis to investigate if there was a match between manager attributes and skills in organisations with either a defender or a prospector strategy in 269 of the *Fortune 500* companies in the United States. They found an overall statistical relationship between manager attributes and strategy. Taking the analysis a step further they then compared thirty organisations which were misaligned with thirty which were aligned and found that performance in the aligned companies (whether prospector or defender) was statistically superior. Whilst this work can be criticised, it does provide an indication of further research which can be developed to aid our understanding of the issues. The type of strategies described above are at a fairly general level, and there is much more concentration now on tailoring the approach to the particular needs of the specific organisation.

Many human resource strategies aim to target not just behaviour, but through behaviour change to effect a change in the culture of the organisation. The target is, therefore, to change the common view of 'the way we do things around here' and to attempt to change the beliefs and values of employees. There is much debate as to whether this is achievable.

Before we move on to look at the different degrees to which human resource strategy is and can be integrated with organisational strategy, it is important to consider how human resource strategy relates to human resource planning. Our starting point is Bramham who in 1989 identified, along with other authors at the time, the difference between manpower planning and human resource planning. His view was that:

> There are particularly important differences in terms of process and purpose. In human resource planning the manager is concerned with motivating people – a process in which costs, numbers, control and systems interact to play a part. In manpower planning the manager is concerned with the numerical elements of forecasting, supply-demand matching and control, in which people are a part. There are therefore important areas of overlap and interconnection but there is a fundamental difference in underlying approach.
>
> (Bramham 1989, p. 147)

The emphasis in Bramham's book is on motivating employees to achieve organisational objectives by defining plans and targets that enable the personnel function to manage the culture of the organisation. This appears very little different from our definition of human resource strategy, above.

What is the difference, then, between strategy and planning? A common view has been that they are virtually one and the same – hence the term 'strategic planning'. In an article in the *Harvard Business Review* (February 1994, p. 108),

Henry Mintzberg gives us his view. He distinguishes between strategic thinking which is about creating a vision of how things could be, and strategic planning which is about collecting the relevant data and also programming the vision into what needs to be done to get there:

> Strategic thinking, in contrast, is about synthesis. It involves intuition and creativity. The outcome of strategic thinking is an integrated perspective of the enterprise, a not-too-precisely articulated vision of direction . . .

In this chapter we shall concentrate on the strategic vision, and in Chapter 4 we shall concentrate on the planning process.

The degree of integration with organisational strategy

The degree of integration between organisational strategy and human resource strategy varies considerably between different organisations. Figure 2.1 shows a range of possible relationships.

In the *separation model* (A) there is no relationship at all, if indeed organisational and human resource strategy *did* exist in an explicit form in the organisation. This is a typical picture of twenty years ago, but it still exists today, particularly in smaller organisations.

The *fit model* (B) represents a growing recognition of the importance of people in the achievement of organisational strategy. Employees are seen as key in the implementation of the declared organisational strategy, and human resource strategy is designed to fit the requirements of the organisation's strategy. Some of the early formal models of human resource strategy, particularly that proposed by Fombrun *et al.* (1984), concentrate on how the human resource strategy can be designed to ensure a close fit, and the same approach is used in the Schuler and Jackson example in Table 2.1.

This whole approach depends on a view of strategy formulation as a logical rational process, which remains the view in many organisations. The relationship in the fit model is exemplified by organisations which cascade their business objectives down from the senior management team through functions, through departments, through teams, and so on. Functions, for example, have to propose a functional strategy which enables the organisational strategy to be achieved. Departments have to propose a strategy which enables the functional strategy to be achieved, and so on. In this way the personnel function (as with any other) is required to respond to organisational strategy by defining a strategy which meets organisational demands.

The *dialogue model* (C) takes the relationship one step further, as it recognises the need for two-way communication and some debate. What is demanded in the organisation's strategy may not be viewed as feasible and alternative possibilities need to be reviewed. The debate, however, is often limited, as shown in the example in the Window on Practice on page 28.

The holistic model and the HR driven model (D and E) show a much closer involvement between organisational and human resource strategy.

The *holistic model* (D) represents the people of the organisation being recognised as the key to competitive advantage rather than just the way of implementing organisational strategy. In other words HR strategy is not just the means

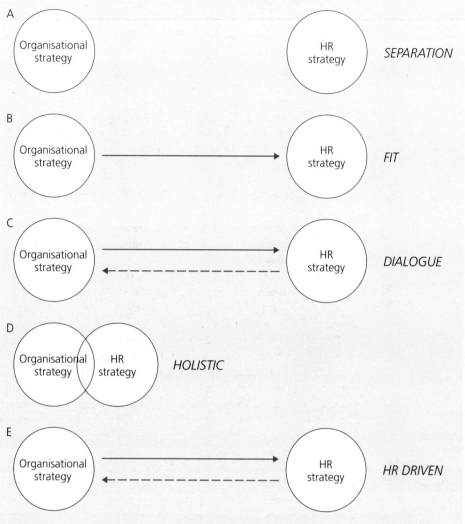

Figure 2.1 Potential relationships between organisational strategy and HR strategy

for achieving business strategy (the ends), but an end in itself. Human resource strategy therefore becomes critical and, as Baird argued, there can be no strategy without human resource strategy. Boxall (1996) develops this idea in relation to the resource-based firm, and argues convincingly that business strategy can usefully be interpreted as more broad than a competitive strategy (or positioning in the marketplace). In which case business strategy can encompass a variety of other strategies including HRM, and he describes these strategies as the pieces of a jigsaw. This suggests mutual development and some form of integration. It appears that the personnel function has finally made it. The bad news is that the empirical evidence suggests that in most organisations this is not the case. People issues may count for a lot, but the personnel function still has some way to go. Storey (1989), reporting on a large-scale research project, found a clear emphasis on people strategies, for example total quality, but also found that the

WINDOW ON PRACTICE

In one large, multinational organisation an objectives-setting cascade was put in place. This cascade did allow for a dialogue between the planned organisation strategy and the response of each function. In the organisation strategy there was some emphasis on people growth and development and job fulfilment. The Personnel Department's response included amongst other things an emphasis on line management involvement in these areas, which would be supported by consultancy help from the Personnel Department.

The top management team replied to this by asking the Personnel Department to add a strategic objective about employee welfare and support. The Personnel Department strongly argued that this was a line management responsibility, along with coaching, development, and so on. The Function saw its customers as the managers of the organisation, not the employees. The result of the debate was that the Personnel Function added the strategic objective about employee welfare.

Although the approach in this case appeared two-way, the stronger of the parties was the management team, and they were determined that their vision was the one that would be implemented!

personnel function has rarely been involved in developing them. However more recent research (for example, Kelly and Gennard 1996) suggests that some progress has been made.

The *HR driven model* (E) offers a more extreme form, which places human resource strategy in prime position. The argument here is that if people are the key to competitive advantage, then we need to build on our people strengths. Logically, then, as the potential of our employees will undoubtedly affect the achievement of any planned strategy, it would be sensible to take account of this in developing our strategic direction. Butler (1988) identifies this model as a shift from human resources as the implementors of strategy to human resources as a driving force in the formulation of the strategy. He sees this within the context of a model of emergent strategy as shown in Figure 2.2.

ACTIVITY BOX 2.1

▶ Which of these approaches to human resource strategy most closely fits your organisation? (If you are a full-time student read one or two relevant cases

in *People Management* and interpret these as 'your organisation'.)
▶ Why did you come to this decision?
▶ What are the advantages and disadvantages of the approach used?

So far we have considered human resource strategy and its relationship to organisational strategy and have only mentioned in passing the role of the personnel or human resource function in this. We shall now explore that role.

The role of the personnel function in strategy

The extent to which the personnel function is involved in both organisational and human resource strategy development is dependent on a range of factors.

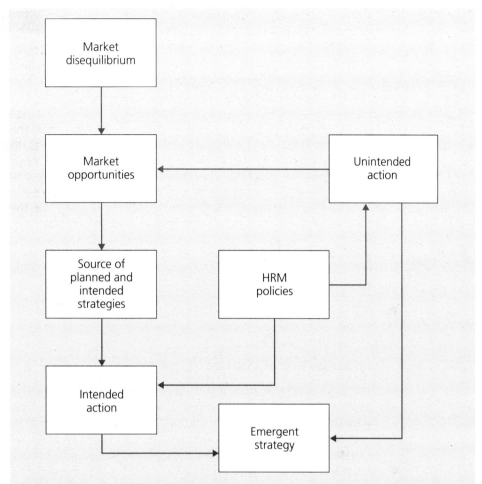

Figure 2.2 Butler's unified model of HRM, strategy formulation and market dynamics (Butler 1988). Reproduced with permission of Brayrooke Press Ltd

Factors influencing the role

The personnel role in the organisation

Involvement in strategy is clearly dependent on the level of regard for the personnel function. There is a variety of ways to describe the way that the personnel function is seen in the organisation, as shown in Chapter 1. One specific way that this can be viewed is through the role of the most senior personnel person.

There is a greater likelihood of involvement in strategy when the most senior personnel person is at Director level on the Main Board. John Purcell (1994), found that only 30 per cent of companies in the private sector with 1,000 or more employees had such a Director. He found that many more had an executive with the title of Director, but without Main Board membership and the influencing potential that is allied with this. The IPM (1992) found two-thirds of personnel functions represented on the top management team, and Brewster and Smith (1990) found the same proportions in large organisations. They also found, however, that a smaller percentage (around half) were involved in strategic planning. Even looking at the most favourable evidence from the research, a picture emerges of limited involvement in strategic matters. The good news is that the IPM's survey found that representation on the top management team was predicted to increase, although there is contradictory evidence (Tyson 1995). Our research suggests an increase in Board membership over the period 1984–94. In our survey in 1983 (Mackay and Torrington 1986) 21 per cent of respondents indicated that the most senior personnel person was a member of the Board, and using a sample contacted in a similar way in 1994 we found that this percentage had risen to 63 per cent – a threefold increase (Hall *et al.* 1996). Not all of these personnel managers had a decision-making role, but 53 per cent did, compared with only 10 per cent who did not. However, our interviews revealed that Board representation is not 'simply' increasing. Two businesses had previously had an HR Director on the Board but had one no longer, and in one organisation the title of HR Director was held by someone outside the function.

Organisational culture

The organisation's view of the importance of people and how they should be treated is inevitably an important factor in personnel involvement. For example, does the organisation see people as a cost or an investment? Buller (1988) found that the degree of integration between organisational and human resource strategy was influenced by the philosophy towards people. Our research supports this finding.

Organisational environment

Buller also found that in organisations placed in a more turbulent environment, the personnel function were more likely to be involved in strategy. If an organisation operates in a stable and comfortable environment there is no pressure to change, whereas a turbulent environment demands that the organisation looks for new approaches and ways of doing things. A major crisis often operates in this way, and brings with it a new Chief Executive for the organisation. The influence of a Chief Executive is critical regarding personnel involvement. The Chief Executive is the one person who can begin to shake up the traditional culture in the organisation where the personnel function may not have been valued or involved in the past. In our recent research the mindset of the Chief Executive was identified as a critical influence on the extent and integration of HR strategy, as was the competitive environment in which the organisation in which the organisation existed. Five of the interviewees explicitly expressed a view that the current role and importance of the function (and this included specifically their involvement in strategy) was affected by the business environment. In all cases the impact of this was that they had become more central, more important and more involved. Consequently the argument was also made that if the circumstances changed, then the role and importance of the function would also change, especially their strategic role. These interviewees represented a range of sectors – manufacturing (2), local government, communications and the health sector. When asked why the change in role had taken place, interviewees commented on how changes and the increasing pace of change currently being experienced were bringing HR issues to the fore at a strategic level and hence the Personnel function was seen as key within the organisation. Some could see circumstances changing yet again to those where HR would no longer be such a key focus.

In general the function's position in the organisation seems to be constantly on the move which is well exemplified by the following:

> But it's at a real crisis point [the personnel function]. Either it goes forward and actually takes on a much more strategic role than it has been able to do up until now or it gets pushed down again.
>
> (Personnel Manager, Education)

These three influences are not particularly easy to manipulate, but what the personnel function *can* do is look for windows of opportunity in these areas, and *use* them. In order to do this the function needs to use business and financial language; describe the rationale for personnel activities in terms of business benefits; act as a business manager first and a personnel manager second; appoint line managers into the personnel function; concentrate on priorities as defined by the business; and offer well-developed change management skills that can be immediately used. In addition, the function needs to prepare itself by thinking strategically; identifying a functional mission and strategy and involving line management in the development of human resource strategy. Indeed, we found, as did Kelly and Gennard (1996), that Board membership does not guarantee the involvement of personnel specialists in strategy. Whilst a place on the Board was generally identified as desirable, it was not necessarily seen as essential to strategic involvement:

> The Head of Finance has just been taken onto the Board, so I'm beginning to see the opportunity. Having said that I feel we're well enough represented at the moment . . . the way our Board operates is that you join in when there is something relevant and appropriate and I find myself going along to Board meetings often – so there's ready access.
>
> (Head of Personnel, Central Government)

We found clear evidence of HR strategy and a commitment to people issues in organisations without an Board Director representing the Personnel function. One of our interviewees explained this well when he talked of the impact of the mindset of the Chief Executive:

> I'm not entirely convinced of the argument which says that there's got to be an HR Director on the Board. I think it's very much down to the mindset of the Chief Executive and to what extent he's basically got an HRM mindset.   (Head of Retail HR, Building Society)

A further important factor in HR strategic involvement was the relationship of the most senior personnel person with the Chief Executive. In some cases a direct formal reporting relationship was found to be helpful, and in others the building up of a good working relationship:

    . . . time spent with her [the Chief Executive], discussing issues gets HR onto her agenda, gets her agenda onto the HR side as well, so we know what's in her mind, and given the way this organisation revolves around the Chief Executive . . .'
(Personnel Manager)

Another key dimension was the skills and personality of the most senior HR person – they were often involved, not because of their formal role but because of their individual skills and their potential contribution to the organisation. However, two Personnel Managers had the confidence and skills to 'gatecrash' Board meetings, and others talked of constantly influencing other managers and campaigning in respect of personnel issues.

WINDOW ON PRACTICE

Frank Sharp, Head of Human Resources, explains the functional vision at Ilford Mobberly as: 'Develop innovative HR strategies to improve the profit of the business . . .'

    The functional goals which the HR team needed to commit to are:

> By 1998 the HR team will be acknowledged by our internal customers and external peers as a professional customer-oriented, innovative, progressive, influence in the Imaging Products Division. This will be achieved by establishing a long-term successful partnership with line managers to ensure the achievement of the empowerment of all employees on the Mobberley site, thereby contributing to the expectations of customers both internal and external.

Specific personnel roles in strategy

Specific roles that the personnel function is in a good position to fulfil are those of co-ordinating people issues across the organisation; providing organisational people information; asking questions about the people implications of business strategy; acting as a consultant or facilitator to line managers and the top team on strategy matters; selling the strategy; and acting as a role model for strategic changes.

    In our recent research we asked personnel managers about their broad role in HR strategy across a range of HR areas, shown in Table 2.2. We found that the most common experience was that of Personnel Managers acting in partnership with line managers in developing strategy (Torrington and Hall 1996), rather than developing HR strategy alone or being excluded from strategy (as, for example Storey (1989) found in his research).

    Putting aside the differences between the content areas, there are two clear messages in Table 2.2. The first is that – with the exception of quality initiatives and work design – only a small percentage of senior personnel practitioners felt they lacked any strategic involvement. Secondly, if we follow Mintzberg's (1994) division of strategy and planning and compare the two options which clearly focus on strategy development (columns 1 and 2) with those that focus on implementation of strategy and on information input (columns 3 and 4), then the emphasis is on strategy development as opposed to implementation. In all content areas, except for work design, the combined percentage from columns 1 and 2 exceeds the combined percentage from columns 3 and 4.

Table 2.2 Personnel roles in HR strategy

Answers to the question 'Which of the following most closely describes the nature of the personnel function's involvement at a strategic level in each of the areas listed below?

	Develops strategy alone %	Develops strategy with the line %	Provides information to inform strategic decisions %	Implements strategic decisions %	None %
HR planning	9 (n=18)	49 (n=93)	26 (n=49)	6 (n=11)	10 (n=19)
Recruitment and selection	15 (n=29)	49 (n=92)	14 (n=27)	16 (n=31)	5 (n=10)
Work design	2 (n=4)	25 (n=46)	24 (n=44)	13 (n=23)	35 (n=64)
Performance management	7 (n=13)	44 (n=82)	23 (n=43)	10 (n=18)	16 (n=29)
Quality initiatives	4 (n=8)	38 (n=70)	17 (n=32)	11 (n=20)	29 (n=54)
Training	10 (n=19)	60 (n=113)	12 (n=23)	7 (n=14)	11 (n=20)
Management development	10 (n=18)	57 (n=105)	10 (n=19)	7 (n=13)	16 (n=30)
Career planning	7 (n=12)	50 (n=93)	16 (n=30)	6 (n=11)	22 (n=40)
Communications	10 (n=19)	53 (n=101)	17 (n=32)	10 (n=18)	10 (n=19)
Employee relations/ involvement	16 (n=30)	56 (n=105)	15 (n=29)	7 (n=14)	5 (n=10)
Health & safety	13 (n=23)	38 (n=69)	15 (n=28)	14 (n=25)	21 (n=39)
Reward	8 (n=14)	45 (n=84)	17 (n=31)	14 (n=25)	17 (n=31)
Redundancy & dismissal	11 (n=21)	46 (n=86)	23 (n=43)	14 (n=26)	6 (n=12)

Respondents were asked to select just *one* choice for each content area.
Row totals = 100% (plus or minus, due to rounding).

We also found in our interviews evidence that personnel involvement in HR strategy was increasing, although it is important to remember that this increase may well be from a low base. Gunnigle and Moore (1994), for example, when analysing the Irish respondents from the Price Waterhouse Cranfield Project, found that only 29 per cent of organisations had a written HR strategy. We found that although strategic involvement was increasing, strategy was developed in an opportunistic manner on an issue-by-issue basis. This meant that although HR strategy was vertically integrated with business strategy on an issue-by-issue basis, there was virtually no evidence of a fully formed horizontally integrated HR strategy. Whilst there was some strong evidence of strategic decision-making and strategic thinking as a response or reaction to business demands, there did not exist a proactive HR strategy as a discrete entity.

WINDOW ON PRACTICE

Frank Sharp from Ilford Mobberley has a clear view on the personnel role in strategy which is to:

Diagnose and analyse the blocks to the organisation achieving its business mission.

Interpret and prioritise what human resource activities can be used to get over or around those blocks.

Develop a concept and vision of what the organisation could look like with the blocks removed, and then sell this.

Lead change through action, and doing what it's selling.

More specifically he identifies ongoing skills to use working with managers in the achievement of the strategy as:

Remove barriers – for example, payment systems that get in the way of a new approach, even though our first

perspective may be that these things can't be changed.

Slay dragons/myths – for example, talk to opinion leaders and ask them what it would be like in an ideal organisation and what would get in the way of achieving it. Having elicited responses like 'you'll never get the unions to agree to that' go out and demonstrate that it can be done.

Facilitate – meetings and encourage managers to do that.

Coach – managers as we work with them. Identify their inherent strengths and help to develop them.

Train – managers in organisational development and give them a tool-kit to use.

Recognise – when they have done something significant.

ACTIVITY BOX 2.2

Which personnel skills are most valued in your organisation, and why?
In what specific ways could you use the ones that Frank Sharp describes?

OR

Read three relevant case examples from *People Management* and identify the personnel skills which are most valued

Formal models of human resource strategy

We now turn to review some of the formal models of human resource strategy from the academic literature before reviewing some examples of strategies in use. These models have appeared increasingly since 1984 and provide us with analytical tools to understand how human resource strategy is developed and some prescriptions of a recommended way to develop strategy and of appropriate strategy content. We shall review some of the most influential models, but for a more detailed evaluation, see Boxall (1992).

Fombrun, Tichy and Devanna's matching model

In their book *Strategic Human Resource Management* (1984) Fombrun *et al.*, based in Michigan, proposed the basic framework shown in Figures 2.3 and 2.4. Figure 2.3 represents the location of human resource management in relation to organisational strategy, and you should be able to note how the Fit Model (B) (page 26)

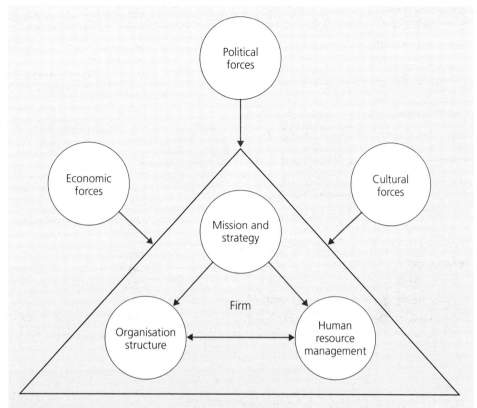

Figure 2.3 Strategic management and environmental pressures (Fombrun, Tichy and Devanna 1984, p. 35), in *Strategic Human Resource Management* © John Wiley and Sons Inc. 1984. Reprinted by permission of John Wiley and Sons, Inc.

is used. Figure 2.4 shows how activities within human resource management can be unified and designed in order to support the organisation's strategy.

The strength of this model is that it provides a simple framework to show how selection, appraisal, development and reward can be mutually geared to produce the required type of employee performance. For example, if an organisation required co-operative team behaviour with mutual sharing of information and support, the broad implications would be:

Selection: successful experience of team work and sociable, co-operative personality; rather than an independent thinker who likes working alone.
Appraisal: based on contribution to the team, and support of others; rather than individual outstanding performance.
Reward: based on team performance and contribution; rather than individual performance and individual effort.

There is little doubt that this type of internal fit is valuable. However, question-marks have been raised over the model owing to its simplistic response to organisation strategy. The question 'what if it is not possible to produce a human resource response that enables the required employee behaviour and

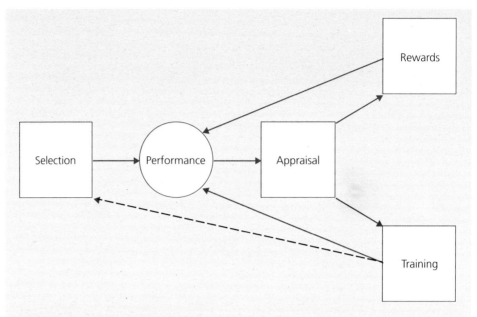

Figure 2.4 The human resource cycle (Fombrun, Tichy and Devanna 1984, p. 41), in *Strategic Human Resource Management* © John Wiley and Sons Inc. 1984. Reprinted by permission of John Wiley and Sons, Inc.

performance?' is never addressed. So, for example, the distance between now and future performance requirements, the strengths, weaknesses and potential of the workforce, the motivation of the workforce, and employee relations issues are not considered.

This model has been criticised because of its dependence on a rational strategy formulation rather than on an emergent strategy formation approach; and because of the nature of the one-way relationship with organisational strategy. It has also been criticised owing to its unitarist assumptions, as no recognition is made for employee interests and their choice of whether or not to change their behaviour.

The Harvard model

This model, produced by Beer, Spector, Lawrence, Quinn Mills and Walton, also in 1984, is an analytical model rather than a prescriptive one and has been adopted more readily in the UK. The model, shown in Figure 2.5, recognises the different stakeholder interests which impact on employee behaviour and performance, and also gives greater emphasis to factors in the environment which will help to shape human resource strategic choices – identified in the **Situation factors** box. Poole (1990) also notes that the model has potential for international or other comparative analysis, as it takes into account different sets of philosophies and assumptions which may be operating.

Although Beer *et al.*'s model is primarily analytical, there are prescriptive elements leading to some potential confusion. These prescriptive elements are rather

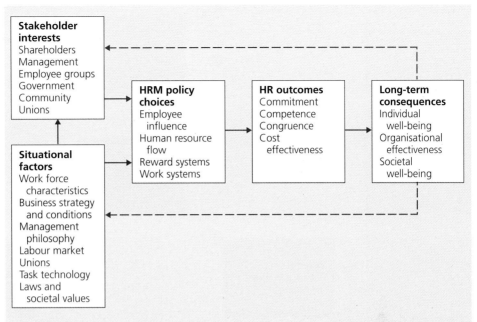

Figure 2.5 The Harvard framework for human resource management. Reprinted with permission of The Free Press, a Division of Simon and Schuster, from *Managing Human Assets* by Michael Beer, Bert Spector, Paul R. Lawrence, D. Quinn Mills, Richard E. Walton. Copyright © 1984 by The Free Press

different from those in Fombrun *et al.*'s model, which prescribe matching fit with organisational strategy and a process for engaging what are identified as the key human resource activities. The prescription in Beer *et al.*'s model is found in the **HR outcomes** box, where specific outcomes are identified as desirable.

The Warwick model

This model, based on the Harvard model, emanates from the Centre for Strategy and Change at Warwick University. As Figure 2.6 shows (from Hendry and Pettigrew 1992), the prescriptive elements of the Harvard model are absent and there is a greater emphasis on an analytical approach to human resource strategy. The model gives full recognition to the external context of human resource strategy; and also identifies a two-way rather than a one-way relationship with organisational strategy as explained in the dialogue and HR driven models on pages 26 and 28. There is also the important recognition of the impact of the role of the personnel function on the human resource strategy content.

In a key statement Hendry and Pettigrew warn against 'treating the design of HRM systems in an overly rational way' and note the importance of learning to the formation of strategy. The authors of this model recognise Mintzberg's perspective of emergent strategy rather than a purely rational, top-down planned approach.

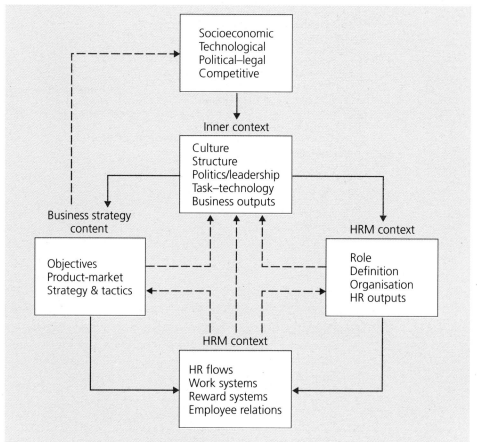

Figure 2.6 Model of strategic change and human resource management (Hendry and Pettigrew 1992, p. 139) in 'Patterns of strategic change in the development of Human Resource Management', in *British Journal of Management*, copyright © 1992 John Wiley and Sons Ltd. Reprinted by permission of John Wiley and Sons Ltd

Guest's model

Guest (1989a) has adapted the Harvard model in a very different way. His model is a prescriptive one based on the four HR outcomes. He has developed these into four policy goals: strategic integration, commitment, flexibility and quality. These policy goals are related to HRM policies and expected organisational outcomes as shown in Figure 2.7.

Guest describes the four policy goals as follows:

Strategic integration – ensuring that HRM is fully integrated into strategic planning, that HRM policies are coherent, that line managers use HRM practices as part of their everyday work.

Commitment – ensuring that employees feel bound to the organisation and are committed to high performance via their behaviour.

Flexibility – ensuring an adaptable organisation structure, and functional flexibility based on multi-skilling.

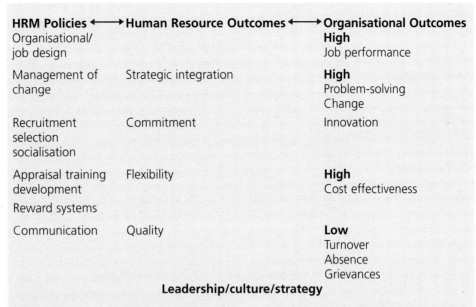

HRM Policies ←——→	Human Resource Outcomes ←——→	Organisational Outcomes
Organisational/ job design		**High** Job performance
Management of change	Strategic integration	**High** Problem-solving Change
Recruitment selection socialisation	Commitment	Innovation
Appraisal training development	Flexibility	**High** Cost effectiveness
Reward systems		
Communication	Quality	**Low** Turnover Absence Grievances

Leadership/culture/strategy

Figure 2.7 A theory of HRM (Guest 1989a, p. 49). Reproduced with permission of the author.

> **Quality** – ensuring a high quality of goods and services through high quality, flexible employees.

Guest sees these goals as a package – all need to be achieved to create the desired organisational outcomes

Clarity of goals gives a certain attractiveness to this model – but this is where the problems also lie. Whipp (1992) questions the extent to which such a shift is possible, and Purcell (1991) sees the goals as unattainable. The goals are also an expression of human resource management, as opposed to personnel management, and as such bring us back to the debate about what human resource management really is and the inherent contradictions in the approach (see, for example, Legge 1991, 1995). Because of the prescriptive approach bringing with it a set of values, it suggests that there is only one best way and this is it. Although Guest (1987) has argued that there is no best practice, he also encourages the use of the above approach as the route to survival of UK businesses.

Human resource management strategic themes

The range of current human resource strategic themes includes flexibility, quality, customer orientation, empowerment, commitment, team working, leadership and continuous learning. Many of these themes are interlinked and typically each organisation will combine a range of themes appropriate to its needs. We shall look first in some more detail at some of the themes and then see how one organisation has used them in practice.

Flexibility is commonly identified as an organisational goal, although Blyton and Morris (1992) argue that there is only limited evidence of its being used strategically as opposed to a short-term 'fix'. Flexibility can be defined in a wide variety of different ways: Bramham (1989), for example, identifies eight definitions. Blyton and Morris (1992) concentrate on four key types of flexibility:

1. **Task or functional flexibility**: where employees may be multi-skilled and involved in a wide range of tasks, with fewer boundaries between jobs. This type of flexibility encourages team working practices, and in its ultimate form destroys the distinction between craft and operator jobs and tasks.
2. **Numerical flexibility**: where the labour supply is made flexible by the use of different types of employment contracts and subcontracting. For example, Hakim (1990) found some core/periphery strategies.
3. **Temporal flexibility**: where the number and timing of hours worked can be varied to meet organisational needs, as for example in annual hours contracts.
4. **Wage flexibility**: where wages offered are individualised rather than standardised, by the use, for example, of performance related pay or pay for skills offered rather than tasks allocated.

Although flexibility is high on the agenda, there are some potential contradictions with other strategic themes. The use of functional flexibility which decreases the use of specialist skills and the use of subcontractors to provide numerical flexibility, may have undesirable consequences for the achievement of a quality strategy.

Quality is another key theme. The achievement of a quality service or a quality product demands a culture of quality where everyone in the organisation feels responsible for seeking out and solving problems in the production process, and where everyone desires and takes part in continuous improvement. In this way quality is built into the process rather than being checked at the end. To achieve this, responsibility needs to be delegated to the lowest possible level in the organisation, and full participation and involvement of all employees is expected. Individuals are 'empowered' by being given the resources and support to take on this responsibility. Team-based environments are usually operated where the team is given a target and it is up to them how they control themselves and achieve the task. One of the platforms of a quality culture is often the requirement to 'get it right first time'.

Very closely tied up with quality is the notion of customer orientation. Quality is often defined in terms of the product being fit for the purpose intended, understanding customer needs and meeting customer expectations (see, for example, Dale and Cooper 1992). This brings with it an emphasis on getting to know the customer and their needs and responding appropriately. In human resource terms this requires a culture which always puts the customer first in everything that is done. This customer orientation does not only apply to external customers of the organisation, but internal ones too. In this way one department or team will be the 'customer' for the work that is produced by another department or team. For example, all line departments will be customers of the training courses and consultancy offered by the training department.

Also closely tied up with the achievement of quality is a strategic emphasis on employee commitment. Given this commitment employees can be trusted to take responsibility and make the right decisions. This commitment removes the need for a high level of control. Commitment is seen to flow from involvement and empowerment and also from appropriate leadership. This increased emphasis on leadership underlines the value of vision and the ability to inspire employees rather than traditional management skills.

Continuous learning is a strategic theme which is increasingly apparent, and which we would argue is perhaps the most critical. A learning culture is based on the idea that it's OK to say, 'I don't know the answer . . . but I'm going to find out'; and where it's OK to get things wrong – as long as we learn something from that. We shall look at continuous learning in the next section, but it is worth noting at this point that there are some inherent contradictions between a quality strategy based on 'right first time' and a learning strategy based on 'it's OK to get it wrong'.

The following example shows how one organisation has used and adapted some of the strategic themes we have just discussed.

WINDOW ON PRACTICE

High performance teams at Digital, Ayr

In an extremely competitive market the Ayr plant had to demonstrate that they could manufacture specified computer systems at a 'landed cost' competitive with other Digital plants, especially those in the Far East. To do this management had to rapidly introduce a package of changes. They had a strategic focus and a clear vision of the changes (both technical and organisational) required to promote success and they 'sold' this to the employees and corporate management. The high performance team concept they sold had two great advantages – inbuilt quality and flexibility. Supportive policies were put in place – such as a new skills-based pay system. Employment policies in terms of career planning, training and development and other reward policies were also designed to be consistent with and reinforce the initiative. Management introduced unsupervised autonomous groups called 'high performance teams' with around a dozen members with full 'back to front' responsibility for product assembly, test, fault finding, and problem-solving, as well as some equipment maintenance. They used flextime without timeclocks and organised their own team discipline. Individuals were encouraged to develop a range of skills and help others in developing their capability. The ten key characteristics of the teams were as follows:

- self-managing, self-organising, self-regulating
- front-to-back responsibility for core process
- negotiated production targets
- multi-skilling – no job titles
- share skills, knowledge, experience and problems
- skills-based payment system
- peer selection, peer review
- open layout, open communications
- support staff on the spot
- commitment to high standards and performance

Management had to learn to stand back and let the groups reach their own decisions – an approach that eventually released considerable management time. A great deal of attention was given to how the transition was managed and this was seen as critical to the success of the approach. Time was taken to ensure maximum formal and informal communication and consultation, and there was a critical mass of key individuals prepared to devote themselves to ensure success. Employees were involved to the fullest extent so they eventually felt they owned the concepts and techniques which they used. Training covered job skills, problem solving techniques and 'attitude training' in the concepts of high performance organisational design.

(Adapted from Buchanan 1992.)

Strategy, learning and change

Learning needs to be a key theme in human resource strategy. We argue this on three counts:

1. We have noted elsewhere that we live in turbulent times with constant change, and that much of the emphasis in strategy is providing a coherent view on how to deal with changing demands in the environment. Bob Garratt (1990) argues that for an organisation to survive learning in the organisation has got to be greater or at least equal to the degree of change.
2. We accept Mintzberg's proposition of emergent strategy, as outlined on page 37, and that strategy formation results from:
   ready—fire—aim—fire—aim—fire—aim
   rather than:
   ready—aim—fire
   We therefore need to act in order to think as well as think in order to act. This being the case we learn from experimentation (both successful and unsuccessful), with successful experiments gradually converging and becoming the strategy. To benefit from our actions we need an organisation which is open to the potential for learning available.
3. A resource-based view of the firm is a useful perspective in relation to HR strategy. This view emphasises the building of strategic capability (rather than implementing predetermined strategies) and the long-term resilience of the firm. This encompasses not only historical strengths, but continued development and growth of employees and the organisation in building the core competencies on which competitive advantage depends. See Boxall (1996) for a further exploration of this perspective.

In order to form successful strategy in response to a changing environment it appears critical that the organisation becomes a learning organisation, which as defined by Pedler *et al.* (1989) is:

An organisation which facilitates the learning of all its members and continuously transforms itself.

We have already noted some of the behavioural characteristics of this, which include the acceptability of making mistakes, as long as we learn from them; and being able to admit lack of knowledge or skill and ask for help when needed. Also included would be a free flow of accurate information, decisions being taken at the lowest possible level and continuous self-development for all. We look at the characteristics of learning organisations in much more detail in Chapter 16 on Organisational Performance.

For an in-depth discussion of strategic approaches and issues Mabey and Salaman (1995) is an excellent source of reference.

Summary propositions

2.1 Human resource strategy is a central philosophy of the way that people in the organisation should be managed. It requires consistent and mutually reinforcing policies in all areas of personnel management.

2.2   It usually involves descriptions of required employee behaviour, and sometimes of the culture of the organisation.

2.3   In an ideal world the development of human resource strategy would be fully integrated with the development of organisational strategy, in reality this relationship is often of a different nature.

2.4   The extent to which personnel specialists are involved in HR strategy is influenced by the environment of the business, its culture, the perspective of the Chief Executive, Personnel Board membership, and the qualities, characteristics and working relationships of the most senior personnel specialist.

2.4   There are many different academic models of human resource strategy. Some are analytical, some are prescriptive and some combine elements of both.

2.5   Human resource strategy themes currently centre on quality, customer orientation, flexibility, commitment, involvement, leadership, team working and continuous learning.

2.6   We propose that the most critical human resource strategy centres around organisational learning.

References

Baird, L., Meshoulam, I. and DeGive, G. (1983) 'Meshing human resources planning with strategic business planning: a model approach', *Personnel*, Vol. 60, Part 5 (Sept./Oct.), pp. 14–25.

Beer, M., Spector, B., Lawrence P. R., Quinn, Mills D. and Walton R. E. (1984) *Managing Human Assets*, New York: Free Press.

Blyton, P. and Morris, J. (1992) 'HRM and the limits of flexibility', in Blyton, P. and Turnbull, P. (eds.), *Reassessing Human Resource Management*, California: Sage Publications.

Boxall, P. F. (1992) 'Strategic human resource management: beginnings of a new theoretical sophistication?, *Human Resource Management Journal*, Vol. 2, No. 3.

Boxall, P. F. (1996) 'The strategic HRM debate and the resource-based view of the firm', *Human Resource Management Journal*, Vol. 6, No. 3, pp. 59–75.

Bramham, J. (1989) *Human Resource Planning*, London: IPM.

Buchanan, D. A. (1992) 'High performance: new boundaries of acceptability in worker control', in G. Salaman *et al.* (eds.) *Human Resource Strategies*, California: Sage Publications.

Buller, P. F. (1988) 'Successful partnerships: HR and strategic planning at eight top firms', *Organisational Dynamics*, Vol. 36, No. 1.

Butler, J. (1988/89) 'Human resource management as a driving force in business strategy', *Journal of General Management*, Vol. 13, No. 4.

Dale, B. and Cooper, C. (1992) *Total Quality and Human Resources: An executive guide*, Oxford: Blackwell.

Fombrun, C., Tichy, N. M. and Devanna, M. A. (1984) *Strategic Human Resource Management*, New York: John Wiley and Sons.

Garratt, B. (1990) *Creating a Learning Organisation*, Hemel Hempstead: Director Books.

Guest, D. (1987) 'Human resource management and industrial relations', *Journal of Management Studies*, Vol. 24, No. 5.

Guest, D. (1989a) 'Human resource management: its implications for industrial relations and Trade Unions', in J. Storey (ed.) *New Perspectives on Human Resource Management*, London: Routledge.

Guest, D. (1989b) 'Personnel and HRM: Can you tell the difference?' *Personnel Management* (January).

Gunningle, P. and Moore, S. (1994) 'Liking business strategy and human resource management: issues and implications', *Personnel Review*, Vol. 23, No. 1, pp. 63–84.

Hakim, C. (1990) 'Core and periphery in employees' workforce welfare strategies: evidence from the 1987 ELKS survey', *Work, Employment and Society*, Vol. 4, No. 2, pp. 157–88.

Hall, L., Allen, C. and Torrington, D. (1996) 'Human resource strategy and the personnel function', *Contemporary developments in Human Resource Management*, Paris: Editions ESKA.

Handy, L., Barnham, K., Panter, S. and Winhard, A. (1989) 'Beyond the personnel function – the strategic management of human resources', *Journal of European Industrial Training*, Vol. 13, No. 1.

Hendry, C. and Pettigrew, A. (1986) 'The practice of strategic human resource management', *Personnel Review*, Vol. 13, No. 3.

Hendry, C. and Pettigrew, A. (1992) 'Patterns of strategic change in the development of Human Resource Management', *British Journal of Management*.

IPM (1992) *Issues in People Management, No. 4, The Emerging Role of the Personnel/HR Manager: A United Kingdom and Irish Perspective*, London: IPM.

Kelly, J. and Gennard, J. (1996) 'The role of personnel directors in the Board of Directors', *Personnel Review*, Vol. 25, No. 1, pp. 7–24.

Legge, K. (1991) 'Human resource management: a critical analysis', in J. Storey (ed.) *New Perspectives on Human Resource Management*, London: Routledge.

Legge, K. (1995) *Human Resource Management: Rhetorics and realities*, Basingstoke: Macmillan.

Kochan, T. A. and Barocci, T. A. (1985) *Human Resource Management and Industrial Relations: Text, Readings and Cases*, Boston: Little Brown.

Mabey, C. and Salaman, G. (1995) *Strategic Human Resource Management*, Oxford: Blackwell.

Mackay, L. E. and Torrington, D. P. (1986) *The Changing Nature of Personnel Management*, London: IPD.

Miles, R. E. and Snow, C. C. (1978) 'Organisation strategy, structure and process', *Academy of Management Review*, Vol. 2, pp. 546–62.

Mintzberg, H. (1994) 'The fall and rise of strategic planning', *Harvard Business Review* (February).

Pedler, M., Boydell, T. and Burgoyne, J. (1989) 'Towards the learning company', *Management Education and Development*, Vol. 20, Pt 1.

Poole, M. (1990) 'Editorial: HRM in an international perspective', *International Journal of Human Resource Management*, Vol. 1, No. 1.

Porter, M. (1974) *Competitive Advantage*, New York: Free Press.

Purcell, J. (1991) 'The impact of corporate strategy on human resource management', in J. Storey (ed.) *New Perspectives on Personnel Management*, London: Routledge.

Purcell, J. (1992) 'The impact of corporate strategy on human resource management', in G. Salaman *et al.* (eds.) *Human Resource Strategies*, London: Sage Publications.

Purcell, J. (1994) 'Personnel earns a place on the Board', *Personnel Management* (February).

Schuler, R. S. and Jackson, S. E. (1987) 'Linking competitive strategies with human resource management practices', *Academy of Management Executive*, No. 3 (August).

Storey, J. (ed.) (1989) *New Perspectives on Human Resource Management*, London: Routledge.

Storey, J. (1992) *Developments in the Management of Human Resources*, Oxford: Blackwell.

Thomas, A. and Ramaswamy, K. (1996) 'Matching managers to strategy: further tests of the Miles and Snow typology', *British Journal of Management*, Vol. 7, pp. 247–61.

Torrington, D. and Hall, L. (1996) 'Chasing the rainbow: Why seeking status through strategy misses the point for the personnel function', *Employee Relations*, Vol. 18, No. 6, pp. 70–6.

Tyson, S. (1995) *Human Resource Strategy*, London: Pitman.

Whipp, R. (1992) 'Human resource management, competition and strategy: some productive tensions', in P. Blyton and P. Turnbull (eds.) *Reassessing Human Resource Management*, California: Sage Publications.

General discussion topics

1. Is it feasible to link business strategy with the management of people in organisations?
2. Does it really matter whether the most senior personnel person is on the Board of Directors, or are personal work relationships, political alliances and personal track-records more important?
3. Human resource strategies can be stimulating to produce and satisfying to display, but how can we make sure that they are implemented?

Case study problem

You have just been appointed to replace the personnel manager in an organisation where members of the Board felt that personnel practice had become over-preoccupied with 'fads and gimmicks' rather than with the needs of the business and the people who worked there. They have asked you to:

1. Review the ways in which human resource management is being conducted across the entire business, within the line as well as by the personnel specialists.
2. Identify aspects of best practice currently being employed by leading-edge personnel practitioners.
3. Draft proposals for a programme of strategic initiatives to enhance human resource management throughout the business.

On investigation you find:

1. Moves towards a single union agreement have foundered because of implacable resistance from two unions with members in the organisation whose representatives were excluded from discussions about the proposals.
2. The concept of performance management has been introduced at the same time as moves to empower line managers. Many line managers feel that empowerment means no more than taking the blame for things that go wrong, and many of their subordinates feel that they are now cut off from the centralised, expert services of the personnel function.
3. A case for the Investors in People award was turned down because practice failed to match the policy.
4. Members of the personnel function say that they have lost credibility and job satisfaction by a series of grandiose schemes that were not fully developed and which could not be fully implemented in a short time.

Required

Produce outline, costed proposals, with a timetable, for the Board to consider on what you would do in the first six months and in the next twelve months to deal with this situation.

Locate the organisation in whatever industry you prefer.

Part I

Examination questions

Undergraduate introductory

1. Summarise the stages in development of personnel management and human resource management.
2. How has the concept of human resource management changed management approaches to the employment of people?

Undergraduate finals

3. Explain the problems of integrating HR strategy with corporate strategy. How can these problems be addressed?
4. What were the shortcomings in the traditional personnel management approach that caused the HRM approach to become so popular?

Masters

5. Analyse the links between business strategy and HRM, using examples to support your answer.
6. Tom Keenoy (1990) claims:

   > Far from indicating a new era of humane people-oriented employment management, the primary purpose of the rhetoric of HRM might be to provide a legitimatory managerial ideology to facilitate the intensification of work. (*Personnel Review*, Vol. 19, No. 2)

   Discuss this proposition in the light of *both* your studies and your working experience.

Professional

7. In May 1993 *Fortune* magazine set out 'six trends that will re-shape the workplace':
   (a) The average organisation will become smaller, employing fewer people.
   (b) The traditional hierarchical organisation will give way to a variety of forms, foremost being the network of specialists.
   (c) Technicians will replace manufacturing operatives as the worker élite.

(d) The vertical division of labour will be replaced by a horizontal division.

(e) The paradigm of doing business will shift from making a product to providing a service.

(f) Work will be redefined towards constant learning, more higher-order thinking, less nine-to-five.

How far do you see these trends exemplified in (a) the economy generally and (b) your own organisation?

8. 'In my business my colleagues and I undertake a number of strategic initiatives, but it is unrealistic to claim that we have a human resource strategy, as that would bring us into futile conflict with our managerial colleagues.'

Discuss that comment, by an HR Director, in the light of your own experience.

Organisation

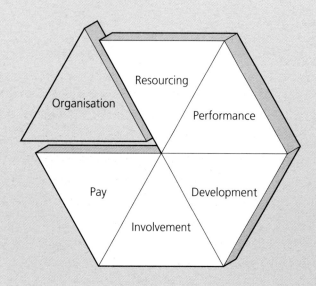

Resourcing

Organisation

Performance

Pay

Development

Involvement

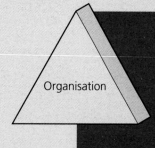

Organisation

The management of people takes place in, or in relation to, some organisation and co-ordination of their activities. This produces synergy: working together to produce a result that is greater than the sum of the individual parts. That co-ordination spreads beyond the employees of the business along the supply chain, or value chain, to include suppliers and customers.

The processes of organisation are concerned with communication and information. We all need to know who does what, where we can find the information we need and who needs information from us so that they can do their jobs. One of the main instruments in organisation is planning requirements before then working out how those requirements can be met, and one of the main methods of co-ordination is organisation structure and culture. The structure describes the bare bones of the various working relationships between the people in the business, while the culture is a collection of values and attitudes that the people of the business have in common to energise them and get them working effectively together.

CHAPTER 3

Strategic aspects of organisation

Personnel managers have always been involved in the organisation of the business in their operational role. This is why there was the development phase, described in Chapter 1, of the humane bureaucrat, as businesses grew bigger and became more specialised. The interest in organisation development provided a further twist to the tale. In this part of the book we examine several aspects of personnel activities which are linked in to the organisation-as-entity and organisation-as-process. Structure and culture are largely concerned with the entity; planning, information, communication and presentation are all to do with organisaton as a process.

Strategic aspects of organisation are grounded in the simple proposition of Alfred Chandler (1962) that 'structure follows strategy'. Whatever strategy for growth a business pursued, the structure of the business followed and reflected the demands of that strategy. He was, of course, writing at a time when the idea of growth was universally accepted as an automatic objective for any business, but his analysis remains a central feature of understanding business organisations.

Chandler's three stages of business development

After examining the growth of seventy large American businesses, Chandler concluded that they all pass through three stages of development: unit, functional and multi-divisional.

Any business begins by being on a single location, with a single product and a single decision-maker. It may be Rolls and Royce or Hewlett and Packard, rather than Eddie Land or Clive Sinclair but it is still a single decision-making function with two or three people working very closely together and doing almost everything. The first stage of development into the *unit firm* involves the process of vertical integration, with specialist functions being set up and other people employed as there is increasing turnover, the beginning of hierarchy and attempts to achieve some economies of scale. One further feature of this is to expand forwards or backwards in the operating chain, by acquiring other business, such as a supplier or raw materials or a retail outlet.

Evolving into a *functional organisation* introduces specialisation as departments are established to deal with different functions, such as marketing, personnel and finance. If the business expands still further and diversifies into different industries and products, there is then the final stage of turning into *a multi-divisional form*. Chandler observed that the process of transition was usually delayed and often very dissatisfying to the original entrepreneur. His explanation for this was that the entrepreneur/founder was typically brilliant at strategy (otherwise there would not be a continuing business) but rarely interested in, or skilful at, structuring a business, especially as the structuring process put power and decision into other hands.

Chandler's thesis has been examined by a number of researchers in the period since it was first propounded. Three slight modifications are worth mentioning here, particularly in relation to the evolution of the multi-divisional form. First, Rumelt (1982) showed that the likelihood of a firm having a multi-divisional structure increased as it diversified. Miles and Snow (1984) carried out extensive studies to examine what they called 'strategic fit': the match between strategy, structure and internal management processes. They demonstrate that businesses need organisation structures and management processes that are appropriate to their strategy, or there is a likelihood that their strategy will fail. Both of these may seem unsurprising, even obvious, conclusions: their value is to confirm the enduring potency of Chandler's ideas. A more significant modification comes from Waterman and Peters (1980), who suggested that businesses could make temporary structural changes to cope with the more rapidly changing contemporary environment without abandoning its overall structure.

Having a structure that matches the strategy is thus crucial to the success of strategy, and structure (organisation-as-entity) interrelates closely with the management processes (organisation-as-process).

WINDOW ON PRACTICE

One of the most remarkable entrepreneurs and technological innovators of the 1970s was Clive Sinclair. The dramatic success of the first pocket calculator was quickly followed by the digital watch and the first home computers, ZX81 and Spectrum. An admiring prime minister gave him a knighthood and it seemed that he could do no wrong, but there was no appropriate structure to sustain the strategy. There was a shortage of management skills, especially in marketing and distribution, so there was a retreat. Sir Clive re-established his company to undertake only research and invention. Everything else was sub-contracted, while the handful of people who made up Sinclair Research concentrated on the next technological breakthrough: the electric car. Technically ingenious, the product was a flop. There had been no authoritative marketing guidance to demonstrate that the product would never sell. The strategy could not succeed without the appropriate structure and management processes.

Centralisation and decentralisation

One of the popular ideas of the 1980s was the strategic business unit, which was a method of empowerment, except that it was not an individual manager being empowered, but a complete operating unit of the business. The management of a particular unit was given an agreed budget and an agreed set of targets for the forthcoming period. Thereafter they had freedom to manage themselves in whatever way they thought fit, providing that they first submitted regular reports and secondly that they met the targets and complied with the budget expectations.

This was a form of decentralisation, and many managers in strategic business units made the wry comment that the one thing that was not decentralised was the strategy!

What is to be decentralised and what is to remain central or drawn into the centre? Chris Hendry (1990, p. 93) makes the interesting observation that in the process of a business decentralising its operations, personnel often remains one of the last centralising forces. He attributes this to the belief of personnel people and Chief Executives about issues such as equity, order, consistency and control. The personnel function will relinquish these only reluctantly as they see great risks in, for instance, methods of payment being set up on different principles in separate parts of the business. What about coercive comparisons? What about equal value claims if we do not monitor closely from the centre?

The focus of this concern is changing. Control of collective bargaining and pay structures – the traditional strongholds of the Personnel Director – are being gradually abandoned and decentralised in favour of new power bases, such as group contracts, succession planning, management development and graduate recruitment (*ibid.*, p. 99).

There is, however, a different dimension to the centralisation/decentralisation question. In writing about international companies Kobrin (1988) has demonstrated that managers have to centralise and decentralise at the same time. It does not need the international dimension to make this comment valid. Each component of the business has to have its strengths and knowledge developed and exploited to the full if it is to be effective, and this requires a greater degree of empowerment than most advocates of budget-driven strategic business units acknowledge. At the same time the individual operating unit has to maximise its contribution to group objectives, and that will inevitably lead to occasional profound conflict between unit and group objectives. The strategic role for the personnel people here is not simply to cope with the conflict when it breaks out, but somehow to develop a culture that succeeds in delivering the apparently irreconcilable requirements: enough autonomy for people to really deploy their skills, enthusiasm and commitment, but enough control for group-wide considerations ultimately to prevail, when they have been tested in the furnace of unit aggressive interrogation. The last part is vital.

Personnel people increasingly have as a part of their role those aspects of co-ordination that go beyond budgetary and planning controls. There are two particular suggestions.

The first is *evangelisation*, the process of winning the acceptance throughout the business of a common mission and a shared purpose. This idea of needing to win hearts and minds has been a common thread in management thinking for most of the twentieth century, and a specialised example is provided later in this chapter from the work of Hopfl (1993). It takes on particular significance in the decentralised business and it is indeed a remarkable management team that will be able to commit themselves with enthusiasm to closing down their local operation on the grounds that the business as a whole will benefit if an operation elsewhere is developed.

Co-ordination through evangelisation works through **shared belief**. The beliefs may be interpreted in different ways and may produce varied behaviours, but there is the attempt to promulgate relatively simple doctrines to which members of the organisation subscribe and through which they are energised. Some readers of this book will have learned their catechism as children, or will have

WINDOW ON PRACTICE

Henry was the Managing Director of a growing business with six operating subsidiaries. Fiona was the Financial Director, who had just joined from a rather larger company. One of the six operating subsidiaries was in difficulties and it appeared to Henry, Fiona and their Board colleagues that it would need to be closed. Fiona said she would work out the numbers over the week-end.

On Monday Fiona showed her proposals to Henry, including the cost of severance for all employed at the subsidiary, including Barry, the General Manager. She sighed and said she supposed he would like her to go down and get it done with. Henry asked if she had consulted with the Personnel Director, George. She had not, so George was asked in and a different strategy was agreed: Barry would be called up to Head Office.

Barry came, clearly having a shrewd idea of what was afoot. Henry explained the situation and said there really seemed no alternative but to close the plant, but Barry was not to worry; he would be looked after. Barry replied that the plant would only close over his dead body and that they did not know what they were talking

about. Fiona produced her analysis and was closely questioned by Barry and strongly challenged on certain of her assumptions. After three hours of vigorous argument Henry called a halt by asking Barry to come back within a week with counter-proposals. Henry still felt that Fiona's analysis was correct and that the plant should close, but if Barry could produce watertight, convincing alternatives, they would be listened to. Fiona complained that her professional judgement was being doubted, but George shepherded Barry out of the room.

Five days later Barry was back with a plan that he had discussed with the General Managers of two other subsidiaries and which they said they could make work by slight variations in the way they worked together. The plan involved a drastic reduction in the workforce, but Barry's plant would remain open, targets would be met and they would be back within budget in six months' time. Now it was the turn of Henry and Fiona to question Barry closely, but eventually they agreed that his proposal was a better strategy for the group as a whole.

studied the thirty-nine articles defining the doctrinal position of the Church of England. Although this may seem inappropriate to the business world, in the 1970s a British company, Vitafoam, was established by a man who required his senior executives to copy out his annual policy statement by hand, three times, before handing it back to him. It is now commonplace for companies to have mission statements, which come close to being unifying articles of faith.

> At the top is the mission statement, a broad goal based on the organization's planning premises, basic assumptions about the organization's purpose, its values, its distinctive competencies, and its place in the world. A mission statement is a relatively permanent part of an organization's identity and can do much to unify and motivate its members.
>
> (Stoner and Freeman 1992, p. 188)

Evangelisation also works through **parables**. Ed Schein (1985, p. 239) identified 'stories and legends' as one of the key mechanisms for articulating and reinforcing the organisation's culture.

The company house magazine helps in circulating the good news about heroic deeds in all parts of the company network. Better are the word-of-mouth exchanges and accounts of personal experience. Evangelisation can use **apostles** – ambassadors sent out to preach the faith. These are the people – usually in senior positions – who move round the company a great deal. They know the business well and can describe one component to another, explaining company policy, justifying particular decisions and countering parochial thinking. They can also move ideas around ('In Seoul they are wondering about . . . what do think?') and help in the development of individual networks ('Try getting in touch with Oscar Jennings in Pittsburgh . . . he had similar problems a few weeks ago'). At times of crisis, apostles are likely to be especially busy, countering rumour and strengthening resolve. It may be important that most of the apostles come from headquarters and have personally met, and can tell stories about, the founder. Anita Roddick's Body Shop is an organisation that grew rapidly on the basis of working in a way that was markedly different from the conventions of the cosmetics industry that it was challenging. Its growth seemed to need people in all parts to identify closely with the vision and personality of the founder:

> The inductresses' eyes seem to light up whenever Anita's name is mentioned. We are told, in semi-joyous terms, the great tale concerning that first humble little shop in Brighton. And . . . one of our inductressses uses the phrase, 'And Anita saw what she had done, and it was good.'
>
> (Keily 1991, p. 3)

Co-ordination can be improved by the development and promulgation of *standards and norms*. Many companies have sought the accreditation of BS 5750, the British Standard for quality; others claim to be equal opportunity employers. Thinking companies will wish to set standards for many aspects of their operation, especially in personnel matters. The Human Resources Section at Shell Centre are charged with developing and maintaining standards relating to alcohol and drug abuse. If standards are adopted throughout a company, they become a form of co-ordination. Furthermore, it is not necessary for all of them to be developed at the Centre. Decentralised standard formulation can enable different parts of the business to take a lead as a preliminary to universal adoption of the standard they have formulated: an excellent method of integration.

Planning

Just as the concept of strategy has somewhat overwhelmed the use of policy as a management instrument, it has also shaded out the use of planning. Planning had its heyday in management thinking during the 1960s, when the clever ideas of operations research were seen as a means whereby future activities could be forecast with confidence so that plans could then be made to deliver that future, 'the past is history . . . the future is planning'. The attraction of planning was that you could make the future happen instead of waiting for it to happen to you. To be a reactive manager was almost as bad as having a communicable disease.

The trouble was that the future rarely turned out as expected; some completely unforeseen event scuppered the plans. The great example was the use of Programme Evaluation Review Technique (PERT) in planning the development and production of the Polaris missile system. Sapolsky (1972, p. 246) studied its application and decided that as a planning technique it was as effective as rain dancing, and that its obvious success was due not to its technical efficiency but to the mystique of infallibility that its managers were able to promote.

As enthusiasm for change took over from a commitment to planning among managers, there was a tendency to think that all action needed to be spontaneous. Particularly in Britain, the predilection for short-term thinking received an unfortunate boost, with the concomitant difficulties of a reluctance to invest and an unwillingness to make provision – through training, for instance – to a future that might not happen. Tom Peters appeared to dismiss planning altogether, producing less than two pages devoted to the topic in a 560-page tome:

> The long-range strategic plan, of voluminous length, is less useful than before. But a strategic 'mind-set', which focuses on skill/capability building (e.g. adding value to the work force via training to prepare it to respond more flexibly and be more quality-conscious) is more important than ever.
>
> (Peters 1989, p. 394)

There we have another clue to the future orientation of personnel management, as we think of organisation as process rather than entity. Peters sees little scope for the strategic plan of the type beloved by the marketing specialists and the MBA graduate, but calls instead for some forward-looking, creative personnel work. This echoes the Japanese concern with the longer term. Holden (1994, p. 125) gives the example of a Japanese computer company with a development plan for all employees that takes 42 years to complete!

As will be seen in the next few chapters, personnel work requires an approach to planning that is rather more flexible and imaginative – soft as well as hard – than that of the manpower planning textbooks of the 1970s.

Information and communication

Information is a prerequisite for all decision-making, and the handling of information is crucial to all personnel work: aggregated data on numbers, ages, skills, hours, rates of pay and so on, and information relating to invididuals.

Communication is a varied process whereby information of the above, specific type is merged with other types of data, understanding, feeling and image to create the process whereby the organisation functions. This requires care with organisational structure, for what is an organisation chart except a statement about responsibilities, status, channels of communication and job titles? It requires an appreciation of organisational culture, an effective set of systems, procedures and drills, and it requires personal competence in members of the organisation, especially managers.

One of the main strategic aspects of communication is communicating across national and cultural boundaries, where feedback is especially important both to monitor what is happening and to develop understanding between the operations. Those in country A will inevitably have limited understanding about the situation of those in country B, to say nothing of the cultural and linguistic uncertainties that feedback can help clear up.

Recently, business expansion has been frequently by acquisition rather than simple growth of what Alfred Chandler described as the unit firm. This produces a particularly intense communications problem. Employees in the acquired company will feel a greater sense of community with each other than with those who have acquired them. They will see corporate affairs from their own standpoint and will tend to be cautious in their behaviour and suspicious in their interpretation of what they hear from their new owners. Personnel people can have a crucial part to play in managing the requisite communications and information flow.

When the expansion is by acquisition of businesses in a different country, with a different set of cultural norms, the problems are intensified. Even when initial suspicion begins to unwind, there are still difficulties. For example:

Rivalry

Whatever is done to develop a shared sense of purpose and a common identity, companies in different countries tend to take pride in their own accomplishments and to disparage the accomplishments of other nationality groups. As long as this stimulates healthy competition, rivalry can benefit the company, but it quickly becomes destructive, like the situation of the car assembly plant in Britain which constantly rejected and returned gear boxes made by a plant of the same company in a different country.

Distorted perceptions

National boundaries produce distorted ideas about the 'other' people, whose achievements are underestimated and undervalued in comparison with the achievements of your own group, which may be overestimated.

Resource allocation

Allocation of resources between competing interests is always problematical, but becomes even more difficult in international comparisons. A company in a vulnerable situation may go as far as to provide disinformation about a rival in order to win additional resources.

WINDOW ON PRACTICE

Rover Group was the largest car manufacturer in Britain and the last of the major manufacturers that could claim to be British. In view of the tradition of car manufacture, this was a point of symbolic significance. When the company developed a technical collaboration with the Japanese Honda company, there was considerable discussion and uncertainty, but the collaboration proved fruitful. At the beginning of 1994 a controlling interest in Rover Group was sold to the German company BMW. This produced a very strong reaction and anxiety that the future of the British operation would be blighted. The Honda association was also regarded as being vitiated by this move. Despite many assurances, the management had to engage in unrelenting communication and consultation for months in order to reassure company employees and to avoid uncertainties in the product and financial markets.

Brandt and Hulbert (1976) studied organisational feedback in a number of multinational companies which had their headquarters in Europe, Japan and the United States. They found that the American organisations had many more feedback reports and meetings between headquarters and subsidiaries than their European or Japanese counterparts. In contrast, Pascale (1978) found that Japanese managers in Japan used face-to-face contacts more than American managers as well as more upwards and lateral communication. Japanese managers in America used communication in the same way as Americans.

One of the few values of management jargon is that the jargon quickly becomes universally understood by the experts, no matter what their nationality. JIT, QWL, TQM are understood by managers everywhere, although NVQ and IIP are understood only by a more select audience.

Disseminating information and other messages within the organisation helps develop corporate culture and a sense of collaboration across national boundaries to integrate the business. Members of the different units in the business have to understand why a company has been acquired in Korea or Chile, even though it seems to threaten the livelihood of some parts of the parent organisation. Comprehensive communication can raise awareness of the wider market and the opportunities that are waiting to be grasped. Foulds and Mallet (1989, p. 78) suggest the following as purposes of international communication, most of which are just as relevant if one is operating within a single national boundary:

to reinforce group culture so as to improve the speed and effectiveness of decision taking;

to encourage information exchange in internationally related activities and prevent the 'reinvention of the wheel';

to form the background to the succession planning activity – certain cultures demand certain types of people;

to establish in people's minds what is expected of them by the parent company;

to facilitate change in a way acceptable to the parent company;

to undermine the 'not invented here' attitudes and thereby encourage changes;

to improve the attractiveness of the company in the recruitment field – particularly where the subsidiary is small and far from base;

to encourage small activities, which may be to-morrow's 'cream', and give such activities a perspective within the international activities.

WINDOW ON PRACTICE

The problem of communicating across linguistic boundaries is illustrated by this official translation from a government announcement in Prague:

Because Christmas Eve falls on a Thursday, the day has been designated a Saturday for work purposes. Factories will close all day, with stores open a half day only. Friday, December 25 has been designated a Sunday, with both factories and stores open all day. Monday, December 28, will be a Wednesday for work purposes. Wednesday, December 30, will be a business Friday. Saturday, January 2, will be a Sunday, and Sunday, January 3, will be a Monday.

The organisation must operate holistically. It is not the sum of its parts: the whole exists in every part, like the human body. If you are ill, a sample of your blood or the taking of your temperature is just as good an indicator to a doctor whatever part of your body it comes from. Customers have a holistic view of the organisation because they are interested in what it delivers as a product or service, not in whether the design section is more efficient than the warehouse. Managers cannot work effectively in their part of the business without understanding its simultaneous relationship to the whole. Businesses function holistically and holism is a function of constant, efficient communication, like the bloodstream and the central nervous system.

A major development in information and communication has, of course, been the arrival of personnel management information systems, discussed in Chapters 7 and 8. These enable information to be stored, located, summarised and analysed instantaneously, although one the leading European experts on the subject feels that progress has been painfully slow:

> the development of imaginative CPISs is pathetically slow. Todays CPISs still look very much like those of 10 to 15 years ago. [They] may use a mouse to point arrows at icons, store endless amounts of data, be in technicolour and they may be networked, but the differences in value they offer . . . do not represent 15 years of development.   (Richards-Carpenter 1994, p. 63)

A strategic issue for personnel specialists is to consider how the potential of this facility can be realised more effectively.

A quite different aspect of communication for the personnel specialist is the need for propaganda or public relations.

Delegation of responsibility for aspects of personnel management by empowering the line manager is a theme to which there is frequent reference in this book. This empowerment goes both ways, as managers from other backgrounds bring their perspective more intrusively into what personnel specialists have liked to regard as their own preserve. The public relations approach is a clear example, with many businesses running communications with employees along similar lines to communications with customers. Often privately derided as 'hard-sell gimmicks' these methods are not always popular in the personnel community. Perhaps the best-known of these activities was a series of commitment-raising projects in British Airways. Heather Hopfl describes the opening of a three-day workshop, 'Visioning the Future':

> This event requires a level of stage management that would not be unfamiliar to a touring rock band. . . . One of the trainers stands at the door to ensure that no-one gets in early to 'spoil' the experience. Nine o'clock. The doors to the conference room are opened . . . the opening music from 'Also Sprach Zarathustra' . . . blasts out a triumphal welcome. . . . The lights dim and the corporate logo appears before them. Three days of management development have begun.   (Hopfl 1993, p. 120)

Although this is alien to many personnel people, they soon realised that people are so used to slick presentation in all departments of their lives, that presentation of information at work needs to use contemporary techniques if it is to have impact.

Summary propositions

3.1   Organisational strategy is inextricably linked with the structure of the business; one cannot be changed without changing, or requiring change, in the other.

3.2   One common strategic initiative is to decentralise, using the strategic business unit as the locus of business activity. This requires specific measures to co-ordinate the decentralised fragments.

3.3   The international, or global, business can have considerable problems in co-ordination. Ways of dealing with them include evangelisation, the development of standards and norms and planning.

3.4   Communication in any business confirms the holistic nature of the enterprise.

References

Brandt, W. K. and Hulbert, J. M. (1976) 'Patterns of communication in the multinational company', *Journal of International Business Studies* (Spring), pp. 57–64.

Chandler, A. D. (1962) *Strategy and Structure*, Cambridge, Mass: MIT Press.

Foulds, J. and Mallet, L. (1989) 'The European and international dimension', in T. Wilkinson (ed.) *The Communications Challenge*, London: IPM.

Hendry, C. (1990) 'Corporate management of human resources under conditions of decentralisation', *British Journal of Management*, Vol. 1, No. 2, pp. 91–103.

Holden, N. J. (1994) 'International HRM with vision', in D. P. Torrington, *International Human Resource Management*, Hemel Hempstead: Prentice Hall International.

Hopfl, H. (1993) 'Culture and commitment: British Airways', in D. Gowler, K. Legge and C. Clegg (eds.) *Case Studies in Organizational Behaviour*, 2nd edn, London: Paul Chapman Publishing.

Keily, D. (1991) 'Body Shop blues', in *The Sunday Times*, 8 December, p. 3.

Kobrin, S. J. (1988) 'Expatriate reduction and strategic control in American multi-national corporations', *Human Resource Management*, Vol. 27, No. 1, pp. 63–75.

Miles, R. E. and Snow, C. E. (1984) 'Fit, failure and the hall of fame', *California Management Review*, Vol. 26, No. 3, pp. 10–28.

Pascale, R. T. (1978) 'Communication and decision making across cultures: Japanese and American comparisons', *Administrative Science Quarterly*, March, pp. 91–110.

Peters, T. J. (1989) *Thriving on Chaos*, London: Pan Books.

Richards-Carpenter, C. (1994) 'Why the CPIS is a Disappointment', *Personnel Management*, Vol. 26, No. 5, pp. 63–4.

Rumelt, R. P. (1982) 'Diversification strategy and profitability', *Strategic Management Journal*, Vol. 3, pp. 359–69.

Sapolsky, H. (1972) *The Polaris System Development*, Cambridge, Mass: Harvard University Press.

Schein, E. H. (1985) *Organizational Culture and Leadership*, San Francisco: Jossey-Bass.

Stoner, J. A. F. and Freeman, R. E. (1992) *Management*, 5th edn., Englewood Cliffs, NJ: Prentice Hall Inc.

Waterman, R. H. and Peters, T. J. (1980) 'Structure is not organisation', *Business Horizons*, June.

General discussion topics

1. How do you understand the ideas of evangelisation, parables, apostles and standards and norms? What are the advantages and drawbacks of using religious imagery in this context?
2. What lessons should Henry, Fiona and Barry learn from their discussions?
3. What is the difference between information and communication?

CHAPTER 4

Planning: jobs and people

In 1994 Henry Mintzberg asserted that 'the most successful strategies are visions, not plans'. The usefulness of the human resource planning process has always been questioned on the basis of feasibility and implementation problems. In this chapter we will show that human resource planning is a valuable process, which, as Walker (1992a) maintains, is necessary to support strategy.

The role of planning

Mintzberg identifies the role of planning in terms of programming the strategic vision, and also in terms of providing information which stimulates the visioning process. It is helpful to look at human resource planning in the same way, which is demonstrated in Figure 4.1. In more detail Mintzberg identifies:

Planning as strategic programming – planning cannot generate strategies, but it can make them operational by clarifying them; working out the consequences of them; and identifying what must be done to achieve each strategy.

Planning as tools to communicate and control – planning can ensure co-ordination and encourage everyone to pull in the same direction; planners can assist in finding successful experimental strategies which may be operating in just a small part of the organisation.

Figure 4.1 Human resource strategic visioning and strategic planning

> **Planners as analysts** – planners need to analyse hard data – both external and internal which managers can then make use of the strategy development process.
>
> **Planners as catalysts** – raising difficult questions and challenging the conventional wisdom which may stimulate managers into thinking in more creative ways.

Planners, therefore, whether organisational planners or human resource planners, have an essential contribution to make to the strategic visioning carried out by senior managers.

Feasibility and use of human resource planning

Concerns raised about the feasibility of human resource plans focus on the nature of the human resource, the nature of the planning in an uncertain environment, and the difficulty of implementing plans.

Hussey (1982), in a book about corporate planning, argues that the human resource is far more complex to plan for than the financial resource. He comments on the critical differences between people, the difficulty of moving them around, the costs of overstaffing, and on the importance of treating people as people and not an inanimate resource. In addition, individuals have their personal set of values and motivations, and these need to be accounted for in the potential achievement of identified plans.

The balance between visioning and planning will be different depending on the environment. In a highly uncertain environment the emphasis needs to be more on the visioning process. Where things are slightly less chaotic planning has a greater contribution to make. Even so, plans need to be viewed as flexible and reviewed regularly, rather than seeing them as an end point in the process. Planning need not be seen as an isolated event, but rather something that has to be continuously monitored, refined and updated. Bell (1989) argues that while there may be an annual cycle of planning, this should represent a review activity that goes on throughout the year; and that each cycle should feed into the next.

In spite of the difficulties with planning, Manzini (1984) comments that 'a plan, imperfect though it may be, will generally get us closer to the target than if we had not planned'.

Implementation issues are tied up with the weight that line managers attach to human resource plans. They are more likely to be supportive if they have been involved in the human resource planning process, if the analyses used are simple rather than complex. Walker (1992b) comments that human resource plans are becoming more flexible and shorter-term, with a clearer focus on human resource issues, simpler data analysis, and an emphasis on action planning and implementation. All these suggest that the output of the planning process needs to be user-friendly, and owned by line management rather than the personnel function (see for example Greer *et al.* 1989). Ulrich (1989) points to the need for human resource plans to be seen as the means to an end (achieving the vision), rather than an end in themselves.

WINDOW ON PRACTICE

Tony, the Personnel Manager shouted at Ian the Chief Executive: 'What do you mean, it wasn't agreed?'

'I mean it's the first I've heard that you need £22k for a new apprentice scheme.'

'Well, it was in the plan.'

'What plan?'

'The manpower plan, what other f*****g plan would I mean!'

'You didn't ask me for the money.'

'I asked you in the plan, and you didn't come back and say we couldn't have it.'

'I didn't come back and say you could – now let's start at the beginning – tell me why we need to spend it and what will happen if we don't.'

The conversation continued and finally Tony and Ian began to talk about the real issues. Ian never told Tony that he had filed the manpower plan unread, but he did tell him that he wanted next year's plan to be five pages of interpretation and recommendations and not eighty-five pages of figures.

A model of human resource planning

Increasingly there is a need for organisations to integrate the process of planning for numbers and skills or employees; employee behaviour and organisational culture; organisation design and the makeup of individual jobs; and formal and informal systems. These aspects are all critical in terms of programming and achieving the vision. Each of these aspects interrelates with the others. However in the area of human resource planning reality has always been recognised as a long way from identified best practice (see, for example, Ulrich 1989).

Undoubtedly different organisations will place different emphases on each of these factors, and may well plan each separately or plan some and not others. Traditionally human resource planning, generally termed manpower planning, was concerned with the numbers of employees and skill levels and types in the organisation. A typical model of traditional manpower planning is shown in Figure 4.2. In this model the emphasis is on balancing the projected demand for and supply of labour, in order to have the right number of the right employees in the right place at the right time. The demand for manpower is influenced by corporate strategies and objectives, the environment and the way that staff are utilised within the business. The supply of manpower is projected from current employees (via calculations about expected leavers, retirements, promotions, etc.) and from the availability of the required skills in the labour market. Anticipated demand and supply are then reconciled by considering a range of options, and plans to achieve a feasible balance are designed.

The model we shall use in this chapter attempts to bring all aspects of planning together, incorporating the more traditional model of 'manpower planning', but going beyond this to include behaviour, culture, systems, and so on. Our model identifies 'where we want to be' translated from response to the strategic vision; 'where we are now'; and 'what we need to do to make the transition' – all operating within the organisation's environment. The model is shown in diagrammatic form in Figure 4.3.

We shall now look in more depth at each of these four areas. It is important to remember that although the steps may logically follow on in the way that they are presented, in reality they may be carried out in parallel, and/or in an informal fashion, and each area may well be revisited a number of times.

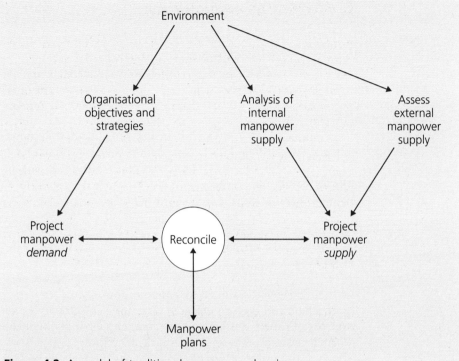

Figure 4.2 A model of traditional manpower planning

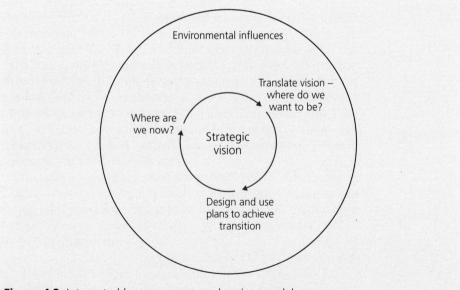

Figure 4.3 Integrated human resource planning model

Analysing the environment

In this chapter we refer to the environment broadly as the context of the organisation, and this is clearly critical in the impact that it has on both organisational and human resource strategy. Much strategy is based on a response to the environment – for example, what our customers now want or what competitors are now offering – or a proactive effort to guess what customers will want or to persuade them what they will need. In human resource terms we need to identify, for example, how difficult or easy it will be to find employees with scarce skills and what these employees will expect of an employer so that we can attract them. (See Appendix, note 1.) We shall be concerned with legislation which will limit or widen the conditions of employment that we offer, with what competitors are offering, and what training schemes are available locally or nationally.

Data on relevant trends can be collected from current literature, company annual reports, conferences/courses and from contacts and networking. Table 4.1 gives examples of the many possible sources against each major area.

Table 4.1 Sources of information on environment trends

Trend area	Possible sources
Social	Census information
	IPM journals
	News media
	Social Trends
	General Household Survey
	Employment Gazette
	Local papers
Demographics	*Labour Market Quarterly*
	Census information
	Employment Gazette
	Local Council, TEC
Political and legislative	News media
	Proceedings of European Parliament
	Proceedings of British Parliament
	Hansard
	Industrial Relations Review and Report
	Industrial Low Journal
	IDS Brief
Industrial and technological	*Employment Digest*
	Journals specifically for the industry
	Financial Times
	Employers' association
	Trade association
Competitors	Annual reports
	Talk to them!

Having acquired and constantly updated data on the environment, one of the most common ways of analysing this is to produce a map of the environment, represented as a wheel. The map represents a time in the future, say three years out. In the centre of the wheel can be written the core purpose of the organisation as it relates to people, or potential future strategies or goals. Each spoke of the wheel can then be filled in to represent a factor of the external environment, for example, potential employees, a specific local competitor, competitors generally, regulatory bodies, customers, government. From all the spokes the six or seven regarded as most important need to be selected.

These can then be worked further by asking what demands each will make of the organisation, and how the organisation will need to respond in order to achieve its goals. From these responses can be derived the implications for human

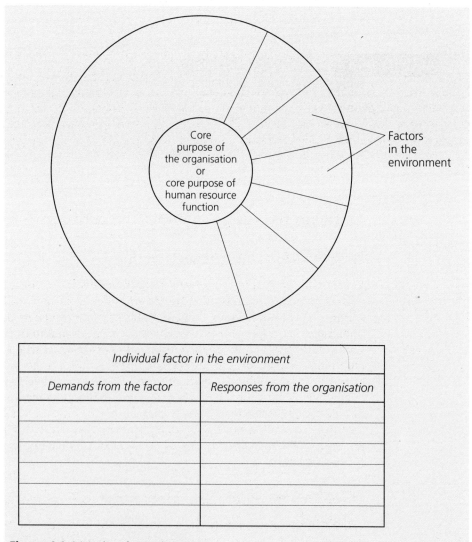

Figure 4.4 Mapping the environment

resource activities. For example, the demands of potential employees may be predicted as:

> ❯ We need a career not just a job.
> ❯ We need flexibility to help with childrearing.
> ❯ We want to be treated as people and not machines.
> ❯ We need a picture of what the organisation has in store for us.
> ❯ We want to be better trained.

And so on.

Managers then consider what the organisation would need to offer to meet these needs – in order to meet a declared organisational goal or strategy. It is a good way of identifying human resource issues which need to be addressed. The analysis can also be fed back into identifying and clarifying the future vision or goals in human resource terms. Figure 4.4 gives an outline for the whole process. (For a worked example see Appendix, note 2.)

ACTIVITY BOX 4.1

Draw a map of the external environment for any organisation in which you are involved for three to five years ahead. Individually or as a group, brainstorm all the spokes in the wheel and select the six most important ones. Draw up a demands and responses list for each. Write a one-side of A4 summary of what you think your organisation's priorities should be in the people area over the next 3–5 years.

Defining the future in human resource terms

Organisation, behaviour and culture

There is little specific literature on the methods used to translate the strategic objectives of the organisation and environmental influences into qualitative or soft human resource goals. In general terms, they can be summed up as the use of managerial judgement. If the activity is seen as vital to the organisation, then senior managers will be involved in the processes and it will be more likely to be identified as part of the strategic visioning rather than a planning activity. Brainstorming, combined with the use of structured checklists or matrices, can encourage a more thorough analysis. Organisation change literature and corporate planning literature are helpful as a source of ideas in this area. Three simple techniques are a human resource implications checklist (see Figure 4.5), a strategic brainstorming exercise (Figure 4.6) and a behavioural expectation chart (Appendix, note 3).

Employee numbers and skills (demand forecasting)

There is far more literature in the more traditional area of forecasting employee number demand based on the organisation's strategic objectives. Both objective and subjective approaches can be employed:

Corporate goal	Human resource implications in respect of:	Methods of achieving this
	New tasks?	
	For whom?	
	What competencies needed?	
	Relative importance of team/individual behaviour	
	Deleted tasks?	
	How will managers need to manage?	

Figure 4.5 The beginnings of a human resource implications checklist

Objective methods

Statistical methods

Some statistical methods depend on the assumption that the future situation will display some continuity from the past. Past trends are projected into the future to simulate or 'model' what would happen if they continued – for example, historical trends of employee numbers could be projected into the future. These methods are rarely used in the present climate as they are inappropriate in a context of rapid and often discontinuous change.

Other statistical models relate employee number demand to more specific organisational and environmental circumstances. These models are used to calculate people demand as a result of, usually, organisational activities. Models can take account of determining factors, such as production, sales, passenger-miles, level of service. These factors can be used separately or in combination with other determining factors. A simple model might relate people demand to production, using a constant relationship, without making any assumptions about economies of scale. In this model if output is to be doubled, then employees would also need to be doubled. (See Appendix, note 4.)

Managers write a corporate goal in the centre and brainstorm changes that need to take place in each of the four areas, one area at a time

Figure 4.6 Strategic brainstorming exercise

More complicated equations can be formulated, which describe the way that a combination of independent factors have affected the dependent employee demand. By inserting new values of the independent factors, such as new projected sales figures, the demand for employees can be worked out from the equation. The equations can also be represented as graphs making the relationships clear to see. These models can be adapted to take account of projected changes in utilisation, owing to factors such as the introduction of new technology, or alternative organisational forms, such as high performance teams.

Work study

This method is based on time-study and a thorough analysis of the work done to arrive at the person-hours needed per unit of output. Standards are developed for the numbers and levels of employees that are needed to do the work tasks. These standards may be developed within the organisation or elsewhere and are most useful when studying production work. It is important that the standards are checked regularly to make sure they are still appropriate. Work study is usually classified as an objective measure, but Verhoeven (1982) argues that since the development of standards and the grouping of tasks is partly dependent on human judgement, it should be considered as a subjective method.

Subjective methods

Managerial judgement

Sometimes called executive judgement, managerial opinion or inductive method, it can also include the judgements of other operational and technical staff, as well as all levels of managers. This method is based on managers' estimates of manpower demand based on past experience and on corporate plans. Managerial judgements can be collected from the 'bottom up' with lower-level managers providing estimates to go up the hierarchy for discussion and redrafting. Alternatively, a 'top-down' approach can be used with estimates made by the highest level of management to go down the hierarchy for discussion and redrafting. Using this method it is difficult to cope with changes that are very different from past experiences. It is also less precise than statistical methods, but it is more comprehensive. Managerial judgement is a simple method, which can be applied fairly quickly and is not restricted by lack of data, particularly historical data, as are statistical techniques. Stainer makes the point that managerial judgement is important even when statistical techniques are used when he says:

> The aim in employing statistical techniques is to simplify the problem to the extent that the human mind can cope with it efficiently, rather than to eliminate subjective judgement altogether. (Stainer 1971)

(See Appendix, note 5.)

Delphi technique

This is a specialised procedure for the collection of managerial opinions based on the idea of the oracle at Delphi. A group of managers anonymously and independently answer questions about anticipated manpower demand. A compilation of the answers is fed back to each individual, and the process is repeated until all the answers converge. Empirical data suggest that this technique is little used at present, although it is often referred to as a common method.

Taking account of changing employee utilisation

The emphasis on employee utilisation varies considerably between different authors – some see it as the most critical issue, whereas others give it only passing attention. There is a vast range of ways to change the way that employees are used:

1. Introducing new materials or equipment, particularly new technology.
2. Introducing changes in work organisation, such as:
   (a) quality circles,
   (b) job rotation,
   (c) job enlargement,
   (d) job enrichment,
   (e) autonomous work-groups,
   (f) high-performance teams
   (g) participation.
3. Organisation development.
4. Introducing changes in organisation structure, such as:
   (a) centralisation/decentralisation,
   (b) new departmental boundaries,
   (c) relocation of parts of the organisation,
   (d) flexible project structures.
5. Introducing productivity schemes, bonus schemes or other incentive schemes.
6. Encouraging greater staff flexibility and work interchangeability.
7. Altering times and periods of work.
8. Training and appraisal of staff.
9. Developing managers and use of performance management

Some of these methods are interrelated or overlap and would therefore be used in combination. (See Appendix, note 6.) Interconnections between most of these areas and soft human resources planning are also apparent.

Analysing the current situation

Organisation, behaviour and culture

It is in this area that more choice of techniques is available, and the possibilities include the use of questionnaires to staff (Appendix, note 7), interviews with staff and managerial judgement. Focus groups are an increasingly popular technique where, preferably, the Chief Executive meets with, say, twenty representative staff from each department to discuss their views of the strengths and weaknesses of the organisation, and what can be done to improve. These approaches can be used to provide information on, for example:

- Motivation of employees.
- Job satisfaction.
- Organisational culture.
- The way that people are managed.
- Attitude to minority groups and equality of opportunity.
- Commitment to the organisation and reasons for this.

▶ Clarity of business objectives.
▶ Goal-focused and other behaviour.
▶ Organisational issues and problems.
▶ What can be done to improve.
▶ Organisational strengths to build on.

WINDOW ON PRACTICE

Jennifer Hadley is the Chief Executive of Dynamo Castings, a long-established organisation which had experienced rapid growth and healthy profits until the past three years. Around 800 staff were employed mostly in production, but significant numbers were also employed in marketing/sales and research/development. Poor performance over the last three years was largely the result of the competition who were able to deliver a quality product at a competitive price more quickly. Dynamo retained the edge in developing new designs, but this consumed a high level of resources and was a lengthy process from research to eventual production. Most employees had been with the company for a large part of their working lives and the culture was still appropriate to the times of high profit where life had been fairly easy and laid back. Messages about difficult times, belt tightening and higher productivity with less people had been filtered down to employees who did not change their behaviour but did feel threatened.

It was with some trepidation that Jennifer decided to personally meet with a cross-section of each department to talk through company and departmental issues. The first was with research/development. As expected, the meeting began with a flood of concerns about job security. No promises could be given. However the mid-point of the meeting was quite fruitful, and the following, among other, points became clear:

▶ that development time could be reduced to one year from two if some production staff were involved in the development process from the very beginning;
▶ that many development staff felt their career prospects were very limited and a number expressed the wish to be able to move into marketing – they felt this would have an advantage also when it came to marketing new products;
▶ that staff felt fairly paid and would be prepared to forgo salary rises for a year or two if this would mean job security, they liked working for Dynamo and didn't want to move;
▶ that staff were aware of the difficult position the company was in but they really didn't know what to do to make it any better;
▶ development staff wanted to know why Dynamo didn't collaborate with Castem Ltd on areas of mutual interest (Jennifer didn't know the answer to this one).

The meeting not only gave Jennifer a better understanding of what employees felt, but also some good ideas to explore. Departmental staff knew their problems had not been wiped away, but did feel that Jennifer had at least taken the trouble to listen to them.

Turnover figures, performance data, recruitment and promotion trends and characteristics of employees, may also shed some light on these issues.

Data relating to current formal and informal systems, together with data on the structure of the organisation, also need to be collected, and the effectiveness, efficiency and other implications of these need to be carefully considered. Most data will be collected from within the organisation, but data may also be collected from significant others, such as customers, who may be part of the environment.

Current and projected employee numbers and skills (employee supply)

Current employee supply can be analysed in both individual and overall statistical terms.

Statistical analysis

Analysis may be made for any of the following factors, either singly or in combination: number of employees classified by function, department, occupation job title, skills, qualifications, training, age, length of service, performance appraisal results. (See Appendix, note 8.)

Forecasting of employee supply is concerned with predicting how the current supply of manpower will change over time, primarily in respect of how many will leave, but also how many will be internally promoted or transferred. These changes are forecast by analysing what has happened in the past, in terms of staff retention and/or movement, and projecting this into the future to see what would happen if the same trends continued. Bell (1989) provides an extremely thorough coverage of possible analyses, on which this section is based. However, although statistical analyses are most well developed for the forecasting of employee supply, behavioural aspects are also important (see Timperley 1980). These include investigating the reasons why staff leave and criteria that affect promotions and transfers. Changes in working conditions and in personnel policy would be relevant here. Statistical techniques fall broadly into two categories: analyses of staff leaving the organisation, and analyses of internal movements.

Analyses of staff leaving the organisation

Annual labour turnover index

This is sometimes called the percentage wastage rate, or the conventional turnover index. This is the simplest formula for wastage and looks at the number of staff leaving during the year as a percentage of the total number employed who could have left.

$$\frac{\text{Leavers in year}}{\substack{\text{Average number of staff} \\ \text{in post during year}}} \times 100 = \text{per cent wastage rate}$$

(See Appendix, note 9.)

This measure has been criticised because it gives only a limited amount of information. If, for example, there were twenty-five leavers over the year, it would not be possible to determine whether twenty-five different jobs had been left by twenty-five different people, or whether twenty-five different people had tried and left the same job. Length of service is not taken into account with this measure, yet length of service has been shown to have a considerable influence on leaving patterns – such as the high number of leavers at the time of induction.

Stability index

This index is based on the number of staff who could have stayed throughout the period. Usually, staff with a full year's service are expressed as a percentage of staff in post one year ago.

$$\frac{\text{Number of staff with one year's service at date}}{\text{Number of staff employed exactly one year before}} \times 100 = \text{per cent stability}$$

(See Appendix, note 10.)

This index however ignores joiners throughout the year and takes little account of length of service.

Bowey's Stability Index (Bowey 1974) attempts to take account of the length of service of employees.

Cohort analysis

A cohort is defined as a homogeneous group of people. Cohort analysis involves the tracking of what happens, in terms of leavers, to a group of people with very similar characteristics who join the organisation at the same time. Graduates are an appropriate group for this type of analysis. A graph can be produced to show what happens to the group. The graph can be in the form of a survival curve or a log-normal wastage curve, which can be plotted as a straight line and can be used to make predictions. The disadvantage of this method of analysis is that it cannot be used for groups other than the specific type of group for which it was originally prepared. The information has also to be collected over a long time-period, which gives rise to problems of availability of data and their validity.

Half-life

This is a figure which expresses the time taken for half the cohort to leave the organisation. The figure does not give as much information as a survival curve, but it is useful as a summary and as a method of comparing different groups.

Census method

The census method is an analysis of leavers over a reasonably short period of time – often over a year. The length of completed service of leavers is summarised by using a histogram, as shown in Figure 4.7. (See Appendix, note 11.)

Retention profile

Staff retained, that is those who remain with the organisation, are allocated to groups depending on the year they joined. The number in each year group is translated into a percentage of the total number of individuals who joined during that year.

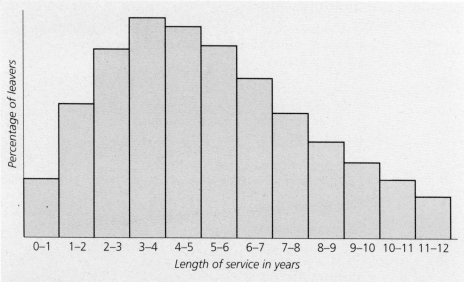

Figure 4.7 Census analysis: percentage of leavers with differing length of service

Analyses of internal movements

These techniques tend to be more sophisticated than those dealing with the analysis of wastage.

Age and length of service distributions can be helpful to indicate problems that may arise in the future, such as promotion blocks. They need to be used in conjunction with an analysis of previous promotion patterns in the organisation. (See Appendix, note 12.) More sophisticated tools such as the Markov chain and renewal models are rarely used.

A simpler and more popular technique is a stocks and flows analysis of the whole organisation or a part of it, such as a department. The model is constructed to show the hierarchy of positions and the numbers employed in each. Numbers moving between positions, and in and out of the organisation over any time-period, can be displayed. An example of a stocks and flows analysis is given in Figure 4.8. The model is a visual way of displaying promotion and lateral move channels in operation, and shows what happens in reality to compare with the espoused approach.

Individual analysis

Similar information to the above can be collected on an individual basis to facilitate succession, career, redundancy and relocation planning. Replacement and succession planning are increasingly used and often represented in the form of charts, as shown in Figure 4.9.

Succession planning is usually only carried out for a select group in the organisation – those who are identified as having high potential – and generally

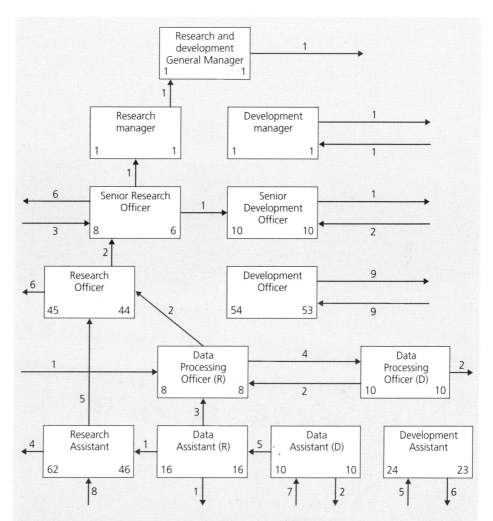

Figure 4.8 Stocks and flows: current establishment and staff in post with movements over the last year. Left side: number inside box = number of posts. Right side: number inside box = actual number in post. Arrow into box = recruitment or promotion or sideways move. Arrow from box = leavers or movers. No line between boxes = no movement between those positions in last year

centres on the most senior jobs. The emphasis is on organisation needs – identifying who will be equipped to fill the most senior positions and over what timescale. It is usually a closed process, so that an individual is not likely to know whether they are on a succession list or chart. In these ways succession is very different from career planning, which we look at in detail in Chapter 24. Walker (1992a) examines the difference between succession planning and replacement planning. He identifies the characteristics of replacement planning as:

▶ an informal approach, often based on personal knowledge of possible candidates;

Post	Current post holder	Ready now	Ready soon	Ready future
Marketing Manager	D. Peters	F. Davis	F. Heald	B. Baker
Development Manager	R. Trice	D. Peters	M. Marks	B. Baker L. Brice
Research Manager	J. Moore		J. Old	C. Chane F. Davis
Data Manager	T. Totter	D. Peters	K. James J. Old	C. Churcher

Candidate	Present	Probable	Possible	Future	Development/ experience needed for each role
D. Peters	Marketing manager	Development manager	Data manager	Marketing manager	
F. Davis	Unit leader	Marketing manager		Research manager	
M. Marks	Development team leader		Development manager		

Figure 4.9 Two formats for succession planning

- often lacking in a thorough analysis of the challenges within the jobs, usually short-term;
- concentrates on vertical moves with little consideration of lateral or diagonal moves.

Walker describes succession planning as overcoming these weaknesses, being more systematic and longer term, with a thorough analysis of the demands of future jobs and of the strengths, weaknesses and experiences of key employees. The emphasis is on developing individuals for the potential challenges ahead of them.

ACTIVITY BOX 4.2

1. Why do employees leave organisations?
2. What are the determinants of promotion in your organisation? Are they made explicit? Do staff understand what the determinants are?
3. What would be your criteria for promotion in your organisation?

Reconciliation, decisions and plans

We have already said that, in reality, there is a process of continuous feedback between the different stages of human resource planning activities, as they are all interdependent. On the soft side (organisation, behaviour and culture) there is a dynamic relationship between the future vision, environmental trends and the current position. Key factors to take into account during reconciliation and deciding on action plans are the acceptability of the plans to both senior managers and other employees, the priority of each plan, key players who will need to be influenced, and the factors that will encourage or be a barrier to successful implementation. Piercy (1989), in relation to strategic planning generally, offers a series of tools to help managers work through these issues.

On the hard side feasibility may centre on the situation where the supply forecast is less than the demand forecast. Here, the possibilities are to:

1. Alter the demand forecast by considering the effect of changes in the utilisation of employees, such as training and productivity deals, or high-performance teams.
2. Alter the demand forecast by considering using different types of employees to meet the corporate objectives, such as employing a smaller number of staff with higher level skills, or employing staff with insufficient skills and training them immediately.
3. Change the company objectives, as lack of manpower will prevent them from being achieved in any case. Realistic objectives may need to be based on the manpower that is, and is forecast to be, available.

When the demand forecast is less than the internal supply forecast in some areas, the possibilities are to:

1. Consider and calculate the costs of overemployment over various timespans.
2. Consider the methods and cost of losing staff.
3. Consider changes in utilisation: work out the feasibility and costs of retraining, redeployment, and so on.
4. Consider whether it is possible for the company objectives to be changed. Could the company diversify, move into new markets, etc.?

We have also noted the interrelationship between the soft and the hard aspects of planning. For example, the creation of high-performance teams may have implications for different staffing numbers, a different distribution of skills, alternative approaches to reward and a different management style. The relocation of supplier's staff on customer premises, in order to get really close to the customer, could have implications for relocation, recruitment, skills required and culture encouraged. The development of a learning organisation may have implications for turnover and absence levels, training and development provision, culture encouraged, and approach to reward.

Once all alternatives have been considered and feasible solutions decided upon, specific action plans can be designed covering all appropriate areas of human resource management activity. For example:

1. **Human resource supply plans**: Plans may need to be made concerning the timing and approach to recruitment or downsizing. For example, it may have been decided that in order to recruit sufficient staff, a public

relations campaign is needed to promote a particular company image. Promotion, transfer and redeployment and redundancy plans would also be relevant here.

2. **Organisation and structure plans**: These plans may concern departmental existence, remit and structure and the relationships between departments. They may also be concerned with the layers of hierarchy within departments and the level at which tasks are done, and the organisational groups within which they are done. Changes to organisation and structure will usually result in changes in employee utilisation.

3. **Employee utilisation plans**: Any changes in utilisation that affect human resource demand will need to be planned. Some changes will result in a sudden difference in the tasks that employees do and the numbers needed; others will result in a gradual movement over time. Managers need to work out new tasks to be done, old ones to be dropped and the timescale by which they need the right number of people fully operational. Other plans may involve the distribution of hours worked, for example the use of annual hours contracts; or the use of functional flexibility where employees develop and use a wider range of skills. There are implications for communications plans as the employees involved will need to be consulted about the changes and be prepared and trained for what will happen. There will be interconnections with supply plans here, for example, if fewer employees will be needed, what criteria will be used to determine who should be made redundant and who should be redeployed and retrained, and in which areas.

4. **Training and management development plans**: There will be training implications from both the manpower supply and manpower utilisation plans. The timing of the training can be a critical aspect. For example, training for specific new technology skills loses most of its impact if it is done six months before the equipment arrives. If the organisation wishes to increase recruitment by promoting the excellent development and training that it provides for employees, then clear programmes of what will be offered need to be finalised and resourced so that these can then be used to entice candidates into the organisation. If the organisation is stressing customer service or total quality, then appropriate training will need to be developed to enable employees to achieve this.

5. **Performance plans**: Performance plans directly address performance issues, for example, the introduction of an objective-setting and performance-management system; setting performance and quality standards; or culture change programmes aimed at encouraging specified behaviour and performance

6. **Appraisal plans**: The organisation needs to make sure that it is assessing the things that are important to it. If customer service is paramount, then employees need to be assessed on aspects of customer service relevant to their job, in addition to other factors. This serves the purpose of reinforcing the importance of customer service, and also provides a mechanism for improving performance in this area, and rewarding this where appraisal is to be linked to pay.

7. **Reward plans**: It is often said that what gets rewarded gets done, and it is key that rewards reflect what the organisation sees as important. For

example, if quantity of output is most important for production workers, bonuses may relate to number of items produced. If quality is most important, then bonuses may reflect reject rate, or customer complaint rate. If managers are only rewarded for meeting their individual objectives there may be problems if the organisation is heavily dependent on team work.

8. **Employee relations plans**: These plans may involve unions, employee representatives or all employees. They would include any matters which need to be negotiated or areas where there is the opportunity for employee involvement and participation.

9. **Communications plans**: The way that planned changes are communicated to employees is critical. Plans need to include methods for not only informing employees what managers expect of them, but also methods to enable employees to express their concerns and needs for successful implementation. Communications plans will also be important if, for example, managers wish to generate greater employee commitment by keeping employees better informed about the progress of the organisation.

Once the plans have been made and put into action, the planning process still continues. It is important that the plans be monitored to see if they are being achieved and if they are producing the expected results. Plans will also need to be reconsidered on a continuing basis in order to cope with changing circumstances.

Summary propositions

4.1   Human resource planning activities are all interdependent.
4.2   Human resource planning methods range from sophisticated statistical techniques to simple diagnostic tools to analyse judgemental data.
4.3   As human resource planning deals with people, planners need to plan for what is acceptable as well as what is feasible.
4.4   Human resource planning is a continuous process rather than a one-off activity.
4.5   Human resource plans cover areas such as people supply, communications, training/development, appraisal, organisation and pay.

References

Bell, D. J. (1989) *Planning Corporate Manpower*, London: Longman.
Bowey, A. (1974) *A Guide to Manpower Planning*, London: Macmillan.
Greer, C. R., Jackson, D. L. and Fiorito, J. (1989) 'Adapting human resources planning in a changing business environment', *Human Resource Management*, Vol. 28, No. 1 (Spring).
Hussey, D. (1982) *Corporate Planning: Theory and practice*, 2nd edn, Oxford: Pergamon.
Manzini, A. O. (1984) 'Human resource planning: observations on the state of the art and the state of practice', *Human Resource Planning*, Vol. 7, Pt 2, pp 105 10.

Mintzberg, H. (1994) 'The fall and rise of strategic planning', *Harvard Business Review* (January/February).

Piercy, N. (1989) 'Diagnosing and solving implementation problems in strategic planning', *Journal of General Management*, Vol. 15, No. 1, pp. 19–38.

Schuler, R. S. and Walker, J. W. (1990) 'Human resources strategy: focusing on issues and actions', *Organisational Dynamics* (Summer).

Smith, A. R. (ed.) (1980) 'Corporate manpower planning: a personnel review', *Review Monograph*, Aldershot: Gower.

Stainer, G. (1971) *Manpower Planning*, London: Heinemann.

Timperley, S. R. (1980) 'Towards a behavioural view of manpower planning', in A. R. Smith (ed.), *Corporate Manpower Planning*, Aldershot: Gower.

Ulrich, D. (1989) 'Strategic human resource planning: why and how?', *Human Resource Planning*, Vol. 10, No. 1.

Verhoeven, C. T. (1982) *Techniques in Corporate Manpower Planning*, Boston/The Hague/London: Kluwer Nijhoff.

Walker, J. W. (1992a) *Human Resource Strategy*, Maidenhead: McGraw-Hill.

Walker, J. W. (1992b) 'Human resource planning, 1990s-style', *Human Resource Planning*, Vol. 13, No. 4.

Appendix

The City Hotel is located in the middle of a medium-sized city. It caters mainly for business trade during the week and for holiday trade during the weekends and in the summer. In the summer and at weekends there is, therefore, a greater demand for catering and waiting staff as there is a greater demand for lunches. During the same periods there is a lesser demand for housekeeping staff as the customers are mostly longer-stay. The hotel has been gradually improved and refurbished over the past five years, and trade, although reasonably good to begin with, has also gradually improved over the period. There are plans to open an extension with a further twenty bedrooms next year.

Note 1

There has been a particular problem in recruiting kitchen assistants, waiting and bar staff. This is partly due to local competition, but also to the fact that early starting and late finishing times make travel very difficult. Often there are no buses at these times and taxis are the only available transport. One or two hotels in the area have begun a hotel transport system, and the City Hotel management have decided to investigate this idea in order to attract a higher number of better quality applicants. A second problem has been identified as the lack of availability of chefs and receptionists of the required level of skill. It is felt that the local colleges are not producing potential staff with sufficient skills, and therefore the management of the City Hotel have decided to consider:

1. A training scheme, either run internally or in conjunction with other hotels.
2. Better wages to attract the better trained staff from other employers.
3. Investigation of other localities and the possibility of providing more staff.

Table A4.1 Demands and responses for the 'customer' factor

Customer demands	Responses
Polite staff	Our staff pride themselves on being courteous
Staff understand that we are busy	We will make procedures quick and simple, people and staff will respond to needs immediately
Sometimes we need facilities we have not arranged in advance	We will be flexible and enthusiastic in our response
And so on.	

Note 2

Having mapped the environment, the hotel management looked at the demands and responses for each priority area. For 'customers' the beginnings of the list are shown in Table A4.1.

Note 3

The management of the City Hotel decided that one of their key objectives over the next three years was to become known for excellence in customer service. This was seen as a key tool to compete with adjacent hotels. Managers used brainstorming to identify the staff behaviours that they wanted to see in place, and summarised their ideas in the format in Table A4.2.

Table A4.2 Behavioural expectations chart: organisation goal – excellence in customer service

Behaviours needed	How to create or reinforce
Address customers by name	A customer service training course to be developed
Smile at customer	A group incentive bonus to be paid on basis of customer feedback. Customer service meetings to be held in company time once per week
Respond to requests, e.g. room change in positive manner	
Ask customers if everything is to their satisfaction	
Answer calls from rooms within four rings	
And so on.	

In addition to this a suggestion scheme was instigated to collect ideas for improvement in customer service. A payment of £50 to be made for each successful suggestion.

Note 4

The City Hotel management has plans to open a further twenty bedrooms in a new extension during the coming year. On the basis of this simple model the additional staff required could be worked out as follows:

- Fifty-five bedrooms requires 60 staff.
- The ratio of staff to bedrooms is therefore 1.09 staff per bedroom.
- If the same relationship were maintained (i.e. without any economies of scale) the additional number of staff needed would be: 20 bedrooms × 1.09 staff = 21.8 extra staff needed. Thus total staff needed would = 81.2 full-time equivalent staff.

Note 5

The managerial staff at the City Hotel exercised judgements on the following human resource planning matters:

1. Management considered the probable reasons for the relationship between people demand and time. It was felt that this was most probably due to the gradual improvement in the hotel over the last five years. Since this improvement had virtually reached its potential it was felt that the relationship between employee demand and time would change.
2. Judgements had to be made on whether the occupancy of the new wing would immediately justify all the additional staff to be appointed.
3. The management considered that since the weather had been very poor in the preceding summer, the bookings for the following summer period might be slightly down on the last year and this shortfall might not be made up by increasing business trade.
4. Judgements were made as to whether staff could be better utilised, with the effect that the additional numbers of staff projected might not be so great.

Note 6

The managers of the City Hotel decided to encourage greater staff flexibility and interchangeability. This interchangeability would be particularly useful between waiting duties and chamber duties. At the present time waiting duties are great-est at the weekend and least during weekdays, whereas chamber duties are the other way around. The effect of this is that waiting staff and chamber staff both have a number of hours of enforced idle time, and the feeling was that there was some overstaffing. By securing flexibility from staff (by paying a flexibility bonus) it was felt that the smooth running and efficiency of the hotel would be consid-erably increased. It was calculated that the nine chamber posts and eight waiting posts could be covered by sixteen combined posts (all FTEs).

Note 7

Managers of the City Hotel assessed the levels of customer service at present by collecting questionnaire data from both staff and customers and conducting a series of interviews with staff. They also asked in what areas service could be improved and asked staff how this might be achieved. As well as specific targets for improvement, they found many examples of systems and organisation that did not help staff give the best customer service. Staff understood that getting the paperwork right was more important than service to the customer in checking out and in. The paperwork systems were over-complex and could be simplified. Also, shift-change times were found to correspond with busy checkout times. Plans were developed to improve systems, organisation and communication.

Note 8

The statistical analysis of staff (Table A4.3) was aimed at occupation, age and full-time equivalent posts. This analysis was used primarily for three main purposes:

1. Full-time equivalents needed to be worked out so that this figure could be used in other manpower planning calculations.
2. To consider the occupational balance of staff and to give information which would be useful from the point of view of staff interchangeability.
3. To plan for future retirements and, in consequence, look at recruitment plans and promotion plans.

Note 9

At the City Hotel eighteen staff had left during the preceding year. The annual labour turnover index was therefore worked out to be:

$$\frac{18}{70*} \times 100 = 25.7 \text{ per cent}$$

(*The average number of staff employed over the year is different from the maximum number of staff that have been employed and were desired to be employed.)

Table A4.3 Staff by occupation, number and age

Broad occupational group	FTE	Actual number of staff	Ages
General managers and department heads	4 + 5	4 + 5	(45, 43, 30, 21) (51, 47, 45, 35, 32)
Reception/accounts/clerical	7	8	(55, 24, 24, 23, 21, 21, 21, 18)
Chamber staff	9	12	(52, 51, 35, 35, 34, 33, 31, 31, 30, 29, 20, 19)
Porters	3	3	(64, 51, 20)
Chefs	8	8	(49, 47, 41, 40, 39, 24, 23, 21)
Other kitchen staff	12	16	(59, 59, 57, 52, 51, 31, 29, 28, 27, 27, 24, 24, 24, 23, 19, 18)
Bar/waiting staff	10	14	(51, 45, 35, 35, 33, 32, 30, 29, 26, 26, 25, 25, 20, 21)
Handyperson/gardener	2	2	(64, 63)
Total	**60**	**72**	

Note 10

At the City Hotel, of the eighteen staff that had been recruited over the year, three had been replacements for the same kitchen assistant's job, and two had been replacements for another kitchen assistant's job. The stability index was therefore worked out as:

$$\frac{54}{69*} \times 100 = 78.26 \text{ per cent stability}$$

(*At exactly one year before there were only 69 of the desired 72 staff in post.)

Note 11

A histogram (Figure A4.1) was plotted of leavers over the past year from the City Hotel. It shows how the majority of leavers had shorter lengths of service, with periods of employment of less than six months being most common.

Note 12

Analysis of the age distribution (Table A4.3) indicates that there may be some difficulties with promotions. In particular, a problem was identified for management promotions. There are four general managers, the youngest being 21. In the past such a junior manager would have been promoted after two years' service, which they had just completed. The ages of the other managers indicate that there will be no retirements in the immediate future and management staff turnover has, in the past few years, been low. In view of this it was thought likely that the

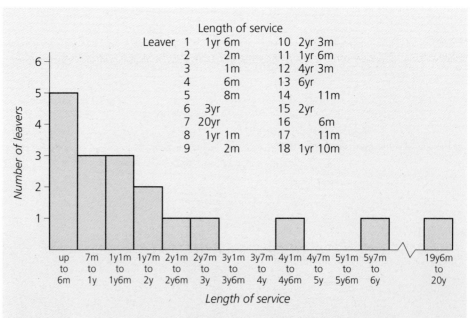

Figure A4.1 A histogram of the lengths of service of eighteen employees leaving the City Hotel in the previous year

junior manager would leave shortly. This was not desired since they were particularly able, so ways of dealing with this promotion block were considered, such as creating a new post, which might retain the junior manager's services until a promotion became available.

General discussion topics

1. Discuss the proposition that traditional (numbers) human resource planning is only of interest to organisations in periods of growth when unemployment levels are low.
2. 'It is worthwhile planning even if you have no strategy'. For what reasons might you agree or disagree with this statement.

CHAPTER 5

Structure and culture

Organisations have both a structure and a culture. The structure is a framework that can be described and altered at will. The culture is much more difficult to grasp and understand; it is also much more difficult to change. There are theories of organisational design that are directed towards the structure; no one has yet claimed to design a culture. Yet structure and culture are as interdependent as lungs and oxygen in providing the business with life and purpose.

Gradually attitudes towards structure are altering. Few people now see the design of an organisation as a single act of creation, deploying power and wisdom to put people in a constructive working relationship with each other: the moment comes and the organisation is created in an instantaneous big bang. However attractive this idea may be, it is the minority of managers who find themselves in that situation. For most people the organisation is in a steady state of being not right: a pattern of working relationships bedevilled by inefficiency, frustration and obsolescence. For them, organisation design is a process of tinkering, pushing and shoving, getting bits and pieces of improvement where possible and occasionally coping with a cataclysm – like a need to shed half the workforce – that seems to leave the worst possible combination of human resources in its wake.

This used to be the experience of personnel officers especially. In the 1980s our research showed personnel specialists to be involved usually only at the margin of significant changes in work organisation. Our 1990s study showed that this was changing with the increased emphasis on strategic involvement, but the specious attraction of structural change remains. Changing the structure is easy – it can be done almost literally by the stroke of a pen – but ensuring appropriate culture change as well is much harder. Pursuing the lungs and oxygen analogy, there is no point in repairing a damaged lung if there is no oxygen to inflate it. Too often involvement is in sorting out a mess rather than in finding ways of avoiding the mess.

Whether one is creating the single grand design, coping with the steady state or trying to change the structure, it is necessary first to understand the process of organising, and the alternative main forms of organisation, before proceeding to consider methods of intervention and the significance of culture.

The fundamentals of the organising process

Organising requires both **differentiation** and **integration**. The process of differentiation is setting up the arrangements for an individual job or task to be undertaken effectively, while integration is co-ordinating the work of individuals so that the whole task is completed satisfactorily. There is no one best way of doing either. The organising of the individual job will vary according to the degree of predictability in what has to be done, so that the organising of manufacturing jobs tends to emphasise sticking to a routine of clearly defined tasks and much specialisation. Jobs that have constantly fresh problems and unpredictable requirements, like marketing and social work, produce frequent redefinitions of job boundaries, a tendency to flexible networks of working relationships rather than a clear hierarchy and a greater degree of individual autonomy.

The greater the differentiation, the harder will be the task of co-ordination. Lawrence and Lorsch (1967), in probably the most influential work on organisation ever written, demonstrated that the nature of the integration problem varies with the rate at which new products are introduced. Galbraith (1977) further showed the importance of the capacity of the organisation to process information about events that cannot be predicted in advance. As the level of uncertainty increases, more information has to be processed with organisation being needed to provide the processing capacity.

We can now see how differentiation and integration are put into action in the face of uncertainty to produce a working organisation. There are three fundamentals: task identity and job definition, structure and decision-making complexes.

Task identity and job definition

A job holder has a label or title which provides the basic identity, content and boundaries of what the job holder does. Some titles are explicit and understood well enough to meet most organisational requirements. Hearing that someone's job is marketing director, office cleaner, commissionaire, plumber, photographic model or train driver provides you with a good initial understanding of that person's role in the business. Other titles are imprecise or confusing. A single issue of a national newspaper includes the following among the advertised vacancies: clerical assistant, jazz assistant administrator, plastics executive, administrator, information specialist, third party products manager, sub titler and editorial services controller. Some of these are general titles, which are widely used to cover jobs without highly specific content; others probably are precisely understood by those with experience in a particular industry or business, even though they puzzle those of us without that insider knowledge.

There are still many questions to be answered so that other members of the business can understand the job holder's status, power, expertise, scope of responsibility and reliability. These questions are especially important where jobs adjoin each other. Where does A's responsibility finish and B's begin? Do areas of responsibility overlap? Are there matters for which no one appears to be responsible? Precise definition can be a nightmare, as there is as much definition of what **not** to do as on what to do. Some analysts believe that task definition stifles potential and frustrates people's contribution, so they advocate terms like 'key result areas' or 'responsibilities'.

> Job duties tell you what you have to do. Responsibilities tell you what you have to **accomplish**. Objectives are **targets**, Key result areas are areas in which **results** are expected. These differences are part and parcel of the whole move away from jobs. The twin brother of TIM-J ('That isn't my job')

is IDM-J, or 'I've done my job (So don't expect anything else out of me)!'
You can do your job and still fail to achieve the results your job was
originally meant to serve. It's like the operation that was a success –
although the patient died.   (Bridges 1995, p. 155)

ACTIVITY BOX 5.1

Write down job titles in your organisation that
you do not understand, or which you regard as
confusing. How would you change them so
that they become more effective labels? How
many job titles include words like 'senior', 'principal' or 'manager' which have no significance
other than to confer status on the job holder?

Although the standard device for clarifying task identity and job definition is
the job description, it is frequently seen as the epitome of stifling, irrelevant
bureaucracy, as well as being lost in a filing cabinet. There is always the risk that
it becomes a straitjacket rather than a framework.

In stable organisations the job description is probably an acceptable mechanism for clarifying the boundaries and content of jobs. In businesses where
uncertainty is the only thing that is certain, job descriptions will be less acceptable and appropriate, but identifying the task and defining the job remain fundamentals of the organising process.

Structure

People work together, even though the extent to which jobs interlock will vary,
so the organisation designer has to decide how identified tasks should be grouped
together. There are four common bases for such groupings. First is grouping
according to **function**, so that the sales personnel are put together in one group,
public relations in another group, research in another, and so on. The logic here
is that the group members share an expertise and can therefore understand each
other, offering valid criticism, leadership and mutual support.

A second principle is to group people on the basis of **territory**, with employees of different and complementary skills being co-ordinated in a particular local-
ity. This is usually where there is a satellite separated geographically from the
main body of the organisation, like the Glasgow office of a nationwide business
having a handful of people based in Glasgow covering duties such as sales,
service and maintenance, warehousing, invoicing and stock control. The best-
known example is the department store or the high street branch of a national
bank.

A third alternative is to group on the basis of **product**, so that varied skills and
expertise are again brought together with a common objective; not this time a
group of customers in a particular territory, but a product that depends on the
interplay of skill variety. John Child gives the example of the hospital, where personnel with medical, nursing, clerical and technical skills are deployed in groups
specialising with such 'products' or activities as maternity, paediatrics and accidents. He then explains the difference between the functional and product logics:

The product-based logic of tasks recognizes how the contributions of different specialists need to be integrated within one complete cycle of work. . . . The product logic is primarily technological, envisaging a flow of work laterally across functional areas. The functional logic is primarily hierarchical, drawing attention to the vertical grouping of people in depth within the boundaries of separate, specialized sections of the company.

(Child 1984, p. 87)

WINDOW ON PRACTICE

The location of kettles

In a school the number and location of kettles is a main determinant of the informal structure. Usually there is at least a kettle – and sometimes more elaborate water-boiling equipment – in the staffroom. There is also a kettle in the general office which supplies the Headteacher and some or all of the Deputies and senior teachers. This is a valuable clue to status in the informal structure:

who within the senior staff is part of the inner coffee cabinet? Some staff have kettles in their classroom or office and **may** invite a colleague or two to join them in the early morning or at break times. These are usually Heads of Department or Heads of Year marking out a clear status divide. Departmental offices and prep. rooms often have kettles used to make coffee during non-contact periods for members of staff in that particular grouping.

The fourth alternative grouping logic is by **time-period**, a form which is dictated by operating circumstances. Where a limited number of people work together at unusual times, like a night shift, then that time-period will be the group boundary for organisational purposes, and group members would probably identify first with the group and may feel estranged from the rest of the organisation.

Decision-making complexes

Organisational affairs are pushed along by decisions being made, some by individuals and some made collectively. The scope of decisions to be made by individuals is usually determined by their labelling or by their position in the hierarchy. Some matters, however, are reserved for collective decision. The strategies that emerge from the boardroom have to have majority support among those taking part in the discussion, even if one person may dominate due to ownership influence or personal status. Decisions about the corporate plan, overall marketing strategy and policy on acquisitions are other decisions that are usually made collectively. The organisation designer is interested in determining the nature of the groups that make these decisions and in resolving which matters should be decided in this way.

We use the term decision-making **complexes** rather than decision-making groups as the decision is made on the basis of more consultation than just the face-to-face discussion in the meeting which produces the decision. In large undertakings a decision-making group is surrounded by working parties, aides, personal assistants, special advisers and secretaries, who provide position papers, draft reports, mediate between factions and prepare the ground. All these preliminaries partly shape the decision that is eventually made.

Alternative forms of organisation structure

Charles Handy (1985/1993) drew on earlier work by Roger Harrison (1972) to produce a four-fold classification of organisations, which has caught the imagination of most managers who have read it. Here we present a slightly different explanation, but acknowledge the source of the main ideas. There is no single ideal organisational form:

> organizations are as different and varied as the nations and societies of the world. They have differing cultures – sets of values and norms and beliefs – reflected in different structures and systems. And the cultures are affected by the events of the past and by the climate of the present, by the technology of the type of work, by their aims and the kind of people that work in them.
>
> (Handy 1993, p. 180)

Despite this variety, three broad types of structure are found most often and a fourth type is becoming more common.

The entrepreneurial form

The entrepreneurial form emphasises central power. It is like the spider's web, with one person or group so dominant that all power stems from the centre, all decisions are made and all behaviour reflects expectations of the centre (Figure 5.1). There are few collective decisions, much reliance on individuals, and actions stem from obtaining the approval of key figures. It is frequently found in busi-

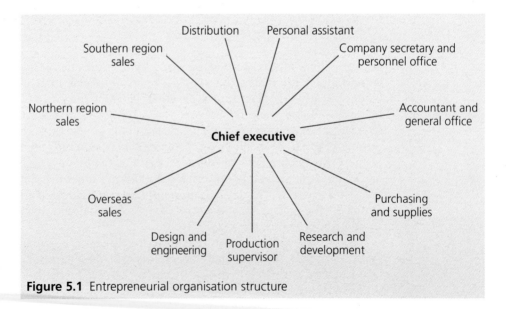

Figure 5.1 Entrepreneurial organisation structure

nesses where decisions must be made quickly and with flair and judgement rather than careful deliberation. Newspaper editing has an entrepreneurial form of organisation and most of the performing arts have strong centralised direction.

This is the form of most small and growing organisations as they owe their existence to the expertise or initiative of one or two people, and it is only by reflecting accurately that originality that the business can survive. As the business expands this type of structure can become unwieldy because too many peripheral decisions cannot be made without approval from the centre, which then becomes overloaded. It is also difficult to maintain if the spider leaves the centre. A successor may not have the same degree of dominance. In some instances the problem of increasing size has been dealt with by maintaining entrepreneurial structure at the core of the enterprise and giving considerable independence to satellite organisations, providing that overall performance targets are met.

The bureaucratic form

The bureaucratic form emphasises the distribution rather than centralisation of power and responsibility. It has been the conventional means of enabling an organisation to grow beyond the entrepreneurial form to establish an existence that is not dependent on a single person or group of founders (Figure 5.2). Through emphasising role rather than flair, operational processes become more predictable and consistent, with procedure and committee replacing individual judgement. Responsibility is devolved through the structure and it is a method of organisation well suited to stable situations, making possible economies of scale and the benefits of specialisation. There is seldom the flexibility to deal with a volatile environment and a tendency to be self-sufficient:

> The bureaucratic approach is intended to provide organizational control through ensuring a high degree of predictability in people's behaviour. It is also a means of trying to ensure that different clients or employees are treated fairly through the application of general rules and procedures. The problem is that rules are inflexible instruments of administration which

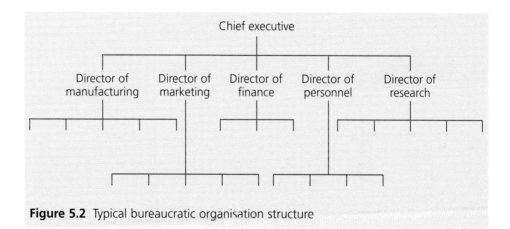

Figure 5.2 Typical bureaucratic organisation structure

enshrine experience of past rather than present conditions, which cannot be readily adapted to suit individual needs, and which can become barriers behind which it is tempting for the administrator to hide.   (Child 1984, p. 8)

Bureaucracy has been the standard form of structure for large organisations for thousands of years and remains the dominant form today. It has, however, come under criticism recently because of its inappropriateness in times of change and a tendency to frustrate personal initiative. 'Bureaucracy' is definitely a dirty word, so companies work hard at overcoming its drawbacks.

The matrix form

The matrix form emphasises the co-ordination of expertise into project-oriented groups of people with individual responsibility. It has been developed to counter some of the difficulties of the entrepreneurial and bureaucratic forms (Figure 5.3). It was first developed in the United States during the 1960s as a means of satisfying the government on the progress of orders placed with contractors for the supply of defence material. Checking on progress proved very difficult with a bureaucracy, so it was made a condition of contracts that the contractor should appoint a project manager with responsibility for meeting the delivery commitments and keeping the project within budget. In this way the government was able to deal with a single representative rather than with a number of people with only partial responsibility. The contractors then had to realign their organisation so that the project manager could exercise the degree of control necessary to make the responsibility effective. This is done either by appointing a product manager with considerable status and power, or by creating product teams with specialists seconded from each functional area. The first method leaves the weight

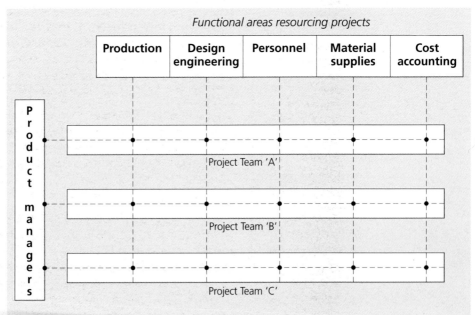

Figure 5.3 Typical matrix organisation structure

of authority with the functional hierarchy, while the product managers have a mainly co-ordinating, progress-chasing role as lone specialists. The second method shifts power towards the product managers, who then have their own teams of experts, with the functional areas being seen as a resource rather than the centre of action and decision. A third, but less common, situation is a permanent overlay of one set of hierarchical connections laid horizontally over a pre-existing conventional, vertical hierarchy. This brings the relative power distribution into approximate balance, but can also make decision-making very slow as a result of that equilibrium.

Matrix is the form that appeals to many managers because it is theoretically based on expertise and provides scope for people at relatively humble levels of the organisation to deploy their skills and carry responsibility. It has, however, recently lost favour because it can generate expensive support systems for product managers needing additional secretaries, assistants and all the panoply of office, as well as the unwieldy administration referred to above.

One way in which matrix has found a new lease of life is in the increasing internationalisation of business, where the impracticability of bureaucracy is most obvious. International business tends to run on matrix lines with complex patterns of working relationship and a greater emphasis on developing agreement than on telling people what to do.

The independence form

The independence form emphasises the individual and is almost a form of non-organisation. The other three are all methods of putting together the contributions of a number of people so that the sum is greater than the parts, results being achieved by the co-ordination of effort. The independence form is a method of providing a support system so that individuals can perform, with the co-ordination of individual effort being either subsidiary or absent (Figure 5.4).

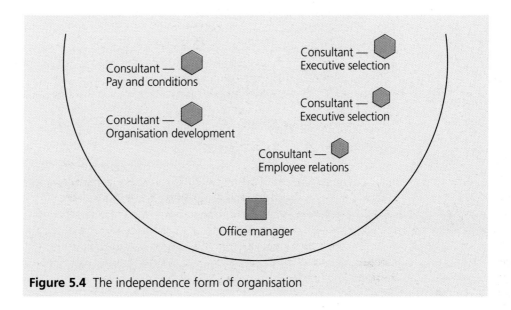

Figure 5.4 The independence form of organisation

Barristers' chambers and doctors' clinics work in this way and it is a form of organisation attractive to those of independent mind who are confident of their ability to be individually successful. Some firms of consultants and craft work-shops operate similarly, with a background organisation to enable the specialists to operate independently. It has been regarded as unsuitable for most types of undertaking because of the lack of co-ordination and control, but there is grow-ing interest in it with the increasing emphasis on individual responsibility and professional skill in business. The vague shape can be discerned in many busi-nesses for the reasons outlined in Chapter 1: the decline of organisation as entity.

ACTIVITY BOX 5.2

Which of the four forms of organisation would you regard as most important for the following:

(a) The operating theatre of a hospital
(b) A kibbutz
(c) A library
(d) A university department
(e) A department store
(f) A primary school
(g) A psychiatric ward
(h) A hotel
(i) A fashion house
(j) A trade union

Differentiated structures

This four-fold classification is a means of analysis rather than a description of four distinct types of organisation with any undertaking being clearly one of the four (Table 5.1). Bureaucracies will typically have matrix features at some points and few entrepreneurial structures are quite as 'pure' as described here. Probably any

Table 5.1 Conditions favouring different organisational forms

Form	Conditions
Entrepreneurial	▶ Dominance of single person or group at centre, due to ownership, expertise or the need of the operation for a strong controlling figure ▶ Modest size, simple technology and single, dominant technical expertise ▶ Uncertain or rapidly changing environment
Bureaucratic	▶ Complex organisation with devolved power and expertise ▶ Large size, complex technology and varied technical expertise ▶ Stable environment
Matrix	▶ Complex organisation with bureaucratic features and need to devolve responsibility and enhance responsiveness to clients
Independence	▶ Simple organisation form to support independent activities of specialists, with little co-ordination ▶ Professional rather than management orientation among specialists

organisation you could name could be classified as having one of these four features dominant and in some there is one form dominant in one section of the business and another form dominant elsewhere. Large banks, for example, are bureaucratic in their retailing operations as consistency is of paramount importance and any changes need to be put into operation simultaneously by a large number of people while being comprehensible to a large number of customers. The same banks will, however, tend to an entrepreneurial emphasis in their merchant banking activities and to independence in currency dealings.

New forms of structure?

There is much discussion about new forms of organisation that will be needed in the future, based on an assessment of current and evolving activities that could make a new form of organisation viable. The following are some of the reasons for this view:

Big is no longer always beautiful

Most organisational structures evolved on an implicit assumption that the business would expand, but this is no longer seen as the sole form of growth: diversification and change are equally interesting, and sometimes wiser, alternatives.

Business is not necessarily directed towards permanence

Until quite recently enterprises were established with the objective of continuing indefinitely, often with a semi-dynastic objective: 'All this will be yours one day, my lad.' There is now greater emphasis on terms like project and venture, setting up an enterprise that will run for a time and then be closed or sold on.

The customer is king

There is increased emphasis on the importance of the customer and meeting the customer's needs, so that gradually preoccupation with internal affairs and organisational politics declines and the people of the organisation become less inward-looking, with issues of hierarchical status having less importance.

The proliferation of expertise

Running a business requires an increasing variety of skills and diverse expertise, so that management relies on people knowing what to do and being required to get on with it. Seldom is a single business big enough to employ all the experts it requires, so many skills have to be bought in on a temporary basis from consultants or contractors.

Information technology

Gradually computerised management information systems are able to produce the quality of control data that can depersonalise the management process to a greater extent. Objectives for individuals and sections have a greater degree of quantification and performance is measurable.

The boundaryless organisation

In our discussion above about job descriptions, one of the reasons for them was to define the boundaries between jobs. The idea that a job has boundaries is very unpopular with some managers, as they believe it limits and constrains, but some commentators (for example, Devanna and Tichy 1990) describe the boundaryless organisation. This is taking the concept of the core and periphery workforce rather further, particularly in reference to the supply chain, and loosens many familiar constraints:

> A boundaryless organization eliminates barriers that separate functions (e.g., marketing versus manufacturing), domestic and foreign operations, different levels of work (managerial versus hourly), and between the organization and its customers and suppliers. Boundaryless organizations ensure that the specifications and requirements of the suppliers, producers, and consumers are all well integrated to achieve objectives.
>
> (Milkovich and Boudreau 1994, p. 123)

Delayering

A popular managerial pastime has become the process of taking out layers of management in the hierarchy in order to speed response times and make the operation more efficient. Drucker (1988) suggests the need for a considerable reduction in the number of layers in the management hierarchy, with the idea that the organisation of the future will be like a symphony orchestra, with a range of highly skilled experts, who know exactly what to do, provided that a conductor provides co-ordination and *brio*. That superb metaphor is slightly weakened, as he concedes, by the fact that a business does not have the main co-ordinating mechanism of the symphony orchestra: the score to read from.

We believe that the key to finding a new organisational form lies in reviewing the notion of both hierarchy and boundary. The analyses of some economists (notably Marglin 1974; and Williamson 1975) give us a different angle on working relationships within organisations, as they look for a rational basis. The entrepreneurial, bureaucratic and matrix forms all take hierarchy as a given and the guiding principle is 'to whom are you accountable', just as the law sees employees as servants of a master – the employer – and the legal basis on which most of us work is a contract of **employment**. If you start without the hierarchical assumption, it is just as feasible to construe working relationships as transactions. This produces a choice, as the working relationship can either be set in a market, where one buys services from another, or it can be set in a hierarchy, where one obtains work from another.

Charles Handy has used the apt concept of the mercenary to describe the situation:

> we are on hire to the best bidder for as long as we are useful to that bidder and then we hope we will be useful to another bidder. We are mercenaries, all of us, and organisations too. You can see why that might make sense in terms of short-term efficiency but . . . it does not build continuity, any sense of pride or any sense of commitment.
>
> (Handy 1997, p. 35)

Turning, then, to the organisational boundary, we have two complementary aspects. Supply-chain development is the process of expanding the activity of the business along the supply-chain, by moving some activities to suppliers and moving some on towards the customer. The best-known example is probably Marks & Spencer underwear. Although marketed by Marks & Spencer, it is not made by them, but by their suppliers. In this instance the retailer has long controlled supply by maintaining a strict quality and price regime, but this approach has become a much more common feature of flexibility of shifting an activity and all its attendant responsibilities to a supplier. The same sort of shift can be seen in the way manufacturers increase their control over agents and retailers. Most motor manufacturers control the price of servicing their vehicles as well as specifying the standards to which servicing should be carried out. Supply-chain development reduces the risk for the core business and integrates more closely the activities of several separate businesses.

In some cases, of course, the customer is also involved in doing a part of the work. The concept of the supermarket started the trend of eliminating the need for sales staff to pick, weigh and wrap prior to cash. Various other elements of self-service extend this practice. A useful example is IKEA, who not only expect customers to serve themselves, by providing a catalogue delivered to the home for prior selection, but also expect the customer to assemble the piece of furniture that is collected.

De-emphasising the hierarchy and blurring the boundary are both aspects of looking at organisation as process rather than as entity. This requires a new approach to organisation structure, which we tentatively describe as **professional**. It has many features of the independence form and some of the matrix. Fundamental to its operation is the core/periphery-type split in the business and in the workforce. The core contains all those activities which will be carried out by employees, while the periphery contains activities that will be put out to tender by contractors or moved elsewhere in the supply-chain, including the customer. The crucial decisions relate to which activities should be in which area. The core should contain those skills which are specialised to the business, rare or secret. Logically, all the other activities are put in the periphery, but suppose there is an unexpected shortage of people to provide peripheral skills. In approaching privatisation several British water authorities reduced their employment of civil engineers, because they were expensive and the work could be done on an *ad hoc* basis by consultants. Gradually, however, there developed a shortage of civil engineers in the consultancy firms, so that the simple rules of the marketplace ceased to operate. The consultants were normally too small to carry trainees in the same way that the water authorities had done. Should water authorities now employ more core civil engineers?

ACTIVITY BOX 5.3

If you were running an airport, which of the following activities would you locate in the core and which on the periphery of your business:
1. Baggage handling
2. The fire service
3. Catering
4. Newsagency
5. Airport information
6. Car park attendance
7. Maintenance of premises and services
8. Cleaning

The approach to the core employees is to give them a strong sense of identification with the business and its success, usually through developing a corporate culture, with shared values and reinforced, consistent behaviours. Those on the periphery have a close specification of what is required from them and their continued engagement depends on meeting the terms of the contract.

The obvious way in which this form of organisation is unattractive to most people is the lack of secure employment. Kanter (1989, p. 358) believes there is no escape from this and that security in the future will come from **continued employability** rather than continuity of employment. There will be no safe havens for those who can no longer keep up. This seemingly harsh message may nevertheless be the way of overcoming the greatest weaknesses of bureaucracy, as the safe havens are usually in senior posts!

The lessons of the last twenty years for the organisation designer are that tinkering with structure will be fruitless without thinking through the purpose of the organisation, the nature of the demands being placed on it from outside, the types of operation which are to be organised, and the people available. Efficient bureaucrats may not make good entrepreneurs, independence is clearly inappropriate if the operation is one with closely interlocking tasks, and moving to a matrix may not be the best way of dealing with a dramatic change in the product market.

Organisational culture

Organisational culture is an alternative way of describing the same thing as structure, but as the concept and the language are different, our approach and resultant methods are different as well. Here are some of the ways in which the approach differs:

- Structure is firm; culture is soft.
- Structure is clear; culture is intangible.
- Structure is about systems to which people have to adapt; culture is about people who have norms and values in common.
- Structure is about the distribution of authority; culture is about how people work together.

Organisational culture is the characteristic spirit and belief of an organisation, demonstrated, for example, in the norms and values that are generally held about how people should behave and treat each other, the nature of working relationships that should be developed and attitudes to change. These norms are deep, taken-for-granted assumptions which are not always expressed, and are often known without being understood.

Through the 1980s in particular there was great interest in organisational culture as the key to improved organisational effectiveness (for example, Deal and Kennedy, 1982; Handy 1985) and this has complemented the earlier preoccupation with organisational structure. Organisation charts may be useful in clarifying reporting relations and subtleties of seniority, but the culture or ethos of the business is believed to be an equally important determinant of effectiveness. Just as most of the developments described earlier in this chapter have been attempts to reduce the rigidity of structure – particularly in bureaucracies – the interest in culture is an attempt to achieve the same objective, but by redefining the problem.

The history and traditions of an organisation reveal something of its culture because the cultural norms develop over a relatively long period, with layers and layers of practice both modifying and consolidating the norms and providing the framework of ritual and convention in which people feel secure, once they have internalised its elements.

Although it sounds strange to attribute human qualities to organisations, they do have distinctive identities. Wally Olins (1989) cites the example of the world's great chemical companies, which superficially seem similar and produce virtually identical products selling at the same price. Yet they each have strong identities and in culture are as different as individual human beings.

Corporate culture

Corporate culture is a more self-conscious expression of specific types of objective in relation to behaviour and values. This entices customers to buy, it entices prospective employees to seek jobs and causes them to feel committed to the organisation:

> research demonstrates that a good organisation which is well known is admired more and liked better than an equally good company which is not so well known. It will attract more and better people to work for it, can more readily make acquisitions and more effectively launch new products: it will perform better.   (Olins 1989, p. 53)

This identity can be expressed and reinforced in various ways, such as a formal statement from the Chief Executive, or in such comments as 'we don't do things that way here'. There is the logo, the stationery, the uniform. In one way or another it is an attempt to ensure commitment. Through all employing organisations there is inevitably some withholding of co-operation by staff, even where they accept the authority of managers and their right to manage (Anthony 1986, p. 41). This is, in part, because managers have an unrealistic expectation about co-operation and in part because of the limited extent to which the authority of position can be exercised. Corporate culture can get round this problem.

It is important that those employed in an organisation should try to understand the culture they share. Managers in general, and personnel managers in particular, have to understand the extent to which culture can be changed and how the changes can be made, even if the changes may be much harder and slower to make than most managers believe and most circumstances allow.

As we have said, culture is often not expressed and may be known without being understood. It is none the less real and powerful, so that the enthusiasts who unwittingly work counter-culturally will find that there is a metaphorical but solid brick wall against which they are beating their heads. Enthusiasts who pause to work out the nature of the culture in which they are operating can at least begin the process of change and influence the direction of the cultural evolution, because culture can never be like a brick wall. It is living and growing, able to strengthen and support the efforts of those who use it, as surely as it will frustrate the efforts of those who ignore it.

A further important aspect of organisational cultures is the extent to which they are typically dominated by traditional male values of rationality, logic, competition and independence, rather than the traditional female values of emotional expression, intuition, caring and interdependence (Marshall 1985). Is it necessary that organisational cultures should be so biased? Is that the only way to prosper? Perhaps not, but it seems that an organisation has to be set up from scratch by women if it is to develop a different culture:

> Women . . . may not be properly represented at important levels of big corporations, but they are now doing remarkably well in the firms they have set up themselves. Here, they don't have to play the male game according to male rules. They are free to make up their own rules, make relationships rather than play games, run their businesses more on a basis of trust than of fear, co-operation rather than rivalry . . .   (Moir and Jessell 1989, p. 167)

Goffee and Scase (1985) studied women executives and found abundant evidence of women being very successful when able to operate outside a male-dominated culture. Indeed, the cause of equality for women at work may well be jeopardised rather than helped by the argument that the only non-genital differences between men and women are socially determined (Tiger 1970).

ACTIVITY BOX 5.4

Is your organisation dominated by male characteristics? Where are there signs of female values? How could the female values spread further in the organisation? What would be the effect on the success of the organisation?

Culture in national context

No organisation is an island, so attempts to foster or alter corporate culture must take account not only of the intentions of those in charge and the expectations of those employed, but also of developments in the surrounding society, both nationally and internationally.

In Britain the idea of an enterprise culture in the 1980s was more than the platform of a political party, it was the articulation of an idea whose time had come. There was a sudden upsurge of new businesses, mostly small and specialised, but there was also an associated change in values and expectations among many working people, especially the young, which was to increase interest in careers, mentoring, customised pay arrangements, networking and others. Whatever business you were in, you had to internalise this change of cultural emphasis. Through the 1990s, the enterprise emphasis has lost some of its momentum, although people remain more willing to take risks in order to get what they want out of life.

Concern for the environment has developed rapidly in the 1990s, so that the expression of environmental responsibility is becoming necessary in the product market, but it is also necessary as a feature of the corporate culture to which employees will respond. It is becoming more difficult to get people to commit themselves to projects that they regard as unworthy. They may do it for the money, but will not offer commitment. Increasingly people look to their workplace for their personal opportunities to do what is worthwhile. The extraordinary success of such television spectaculars as Bandaid and Children in Need have been mainly built on money raised by groups of people operating in, or from, their place of work. Marketing specialist Elizabeth Nelson reports the result of consumer surveys:

Throughout the political spectrum there is a growing awareness that the State should be made more efficient, via competition. Individual responsibility plus collective efficiency is a model for the next twenty years. Our surveys show that there is a strong majority even among the very rich prepared to pay more in tax to alleviate poverty. (Nelson 1989, p. 296)

Concern for the environment is growing apace at the national political level. At the local level there is not only concern about the ozone layer and the greenhouse effect, but noise, dirt, smells and inconvenience to fellow citizens. Corporate culture has to assimilate these concerns.

ACTIVITY BOX 5.5

▶ How could your organisation be more protective of the environment ?

▶ What would be the costs of the changes you describe?
▶ What would be the benefits of the changes you describe?

Culture in international context

As business becomes increasingly international, personnel managers have to become international as well, although not at quite the same speed as their marketing colleagues. International cultural issues are a puzzle. The history of the European Union in attempting to establish a supranational institution is one of constant, but reluctant recognition of the stubbornness of national differences and the accentuation of regional differences among, for instance, the Basques and the Flemish. Nationality is important to personnel management because of its effect on human behaviour and the consequent constraints on management action.

Identity

Nationality is a root source of our individual identity, with all its affiliations and allegiances. Arabs have a tradition of hospitality to guests which can cause them to be deeply offended when invitations are declined; the Japanese have great difficulty about losing face; and the Germans have made efficiency and attention to detail a national characteristic. There is also the difficulty that we tend to associate certain characteristics unthinkingly with certain nationalities, yet not all Spaniards are hot-tempered and not all Scots are mean.

Conditioning

Family conventions, religious traditions and forms of education differ markedly between countries, and every adult is partly a product of these features of conditioning, with the attendant values, imperatives and beliefs that shape behaviour and expectation. American children are taught very early the values of individuality and doing your own thing; Japanese children are taught to conform, to work within a group and to develop team spirit.

Political and legal system

Different nations are distinct political units, so that the political institutions and the ways in which they are used are different. This is not just the formal but also the informal political realities that are resistant to change. The laws and the systems of law differ, so that some countries, like Australia and the United States, have legally binding arbitration as a way of resolving industrial disputes. Not only is this a practice that we do not have in Britain, it also means that the status of the contract of employment is different.

Geert Hofstede (1980) analysed no fewer than 116,000 questionnaires administered to employees in forty different countries and concluded that national cultures could be explained by four key factors.

Individualism

This is the extent to which people expect to look after themselves and their family only. The opposite is collectivism, which has a tight social framework and in which people expect to have a wider social responsibilty to discharge because others in the group will support them. Those of a collectivist persuasion believe they owe absolute loyalty to their group.

Power distance

This factor measures the extent to which the less powerful members of the society accept the unequal distribution of power. In organisations this is the degree of centralisation of authority and the exercise of autocratic leadership.

Uncertainty avoidance

The future is always unknown, but some societies socialise their members to accept this and take risks, while members of other societies have been socialised to be made anxious about this and seek after the security of law, religion or technology.

Masculinity

The division of roles between the sexes varies from one society to another. Where men are assertive and have dominant roles these values permeate the whole of society and the organisations that make them up, so there is an emphasis on showing off, performing, making money and achieving something visible. Where there is a larger role for women, who are more service-oriented with caring roles, the values move towards concern for the environment and the quality of life, putting the quality of relationships before the making of money and not showing off.

Hofstede found some clear national cultural differences between nationalities. The findings were then compared with the large-scale British study of organisations carried out in the 1970s (Pugh and Hickson, 1976) and an unpublished analysis of MBA students' work at INSEAD, which suggested that there were clusters of national cultures that coincided with different organisational principles. Hofstede argues (1991, pp. 140–6) that countries emphasising large power distance and strong uncertainty avoidance tended to have forms of organisation that relied heavily on hierarchy and clear orders from superiors: **a pyramid of people**.

In countries with small power distance and strong uncertainty avoidance the implicit form of organisation relies on rules, procedures and clear structure: **a well-oiled machine**.

The implicit model of organisation in countries with small power distance and weak uncertainty avoidance was a reliance on *ad hoc* solutions to problems as they arose, as many of the problems could be boiled down to human relations difficulties: **a village market**.

The picture is completed by the fourth group of countries where there is large power distance and weak uncertainty avoidance. Here problems are resolved by constantly referring to the boss who is like a father to an extended family, so there is concentration of authority without structuring of activities: **the family**. Table 5.2 shows which countries are in the different segments.

This classification of cultural diversity helps us to make sense of how people in different countries operate. The implicit form of organisation for Britain is a village market, for France it is a pyramid of people, for Germany it is a well-oiled machine and for Hong Kong it is a family. If we can understand the organisational

Table 5.2 Types of organisation implicit in various countries

Pyramid of people	Well-oiled machine	Village market	Family
Arab speaking	Austria	Australia	East Africa
Argentina	Costa Rica	Britain	Hong Kong
Belgium	Finland	Canada	India
Brazil	Germany	Denmark	Indonesia
Chile	Israel	Ireland	Jamaica
Colombia	Switzerland	Netherlands	Malaysia
Ecuador		New Zealand	Philippines
France		Norway	Singapore
Greece		South Africa	West Africa
Guatemala		Sweden	
Iran		United States	
Italy			
Japan			
Korea			
Mexico			
Pakistan			
Panama			
Peru			
Portugal			
Salvador			
Spain			
Taiwan			
Thailand			
Turkey			
Uruguay			
Venezuela			
Yugoslavia			

realities and detail in those four countries, we then have clues about how to cope in Denmark, Ecuador, Austria or Indonesia because they each share the implicit organisational form of one of the original four.

WINDOW ON PRACTICE

In this chapter there is not space to consider some of the problems in the world-wide use of English as the language of business, and therefore the language of luxury hotels. Here are two examples.
From the Petaling Jaya Hilton in Malaysia:

'Do not use the lift in case of fire.'

From the Chicago Grosvenor in USA:

'Walk up one floor and down two floors for improved elevator service.'

In Hofstede's second book he produces a refinement of the uncertainty avoidance dimension: 'Confucian dynamism', or long-term versus short-term orientation. Management researchers are typically from Western Europe or the United States, with that type of cultural bias. Working with the Canadian Michael Bond, Hofstede used a Chinese value survey technique in a fresh study and uncovered a cultural variable – long-term orientation – that none of the original, western questions had reached. The highest scoring countries on this dimension were China, Hong Kong, Taiwan, Japan and South Korea. Singapore was placed ninth. Leaving out the special case of China, we see that the other five countries are those known as the 'Five Dragons' because of their dramatic rate of economic growth. As Hofstede says:

> The correlation between certain Confucian values and economic growth is a surprising, even a sensational, finding.   (Hofstede 1991, p. 167)

The 'Confucian' values attached to this long-term orientation included perseverance, clearly maintained status differentials, thrift and having a sense of shame. In many ways these values are valuable for business growth, as they put social value on entrepreneurial initiative, support the entrepreneur by the willing compliance of others seeking a place in the system, encourage saving and investment, and put pressure on those who do not meet objectives.

Developing corporate culture

It is harder to change attitudes than to change behaviour: having a test drive in the car you think you *might* buy is much more likely to make you decide than a lengthy explanation of its virtues. In developing corporate culture we therefore have to start with trying to change norms of behaviour; over time those changed behaviours may lead to a change in the more deeply held beliefs of shared norms. When the behaviour pays off, then the attitudes and beliefs gradually shift.

The most penetrating analysis of organisational culture is by Schein (1985), who distinguishes between the ways in which an organisation needs to develop a culture which enables it to adapt to its changing environment (pp. 52–65) and, at the same time, build and maintain itself through processes of internal integration (pp. 65–83).

How do cultures change? How do they become consolidated? The general comment of Schein is that there are primary and secondary mechanisms. The primary mechanisms being:

1. what leaders pay most attention to;
2. how leaders react to crises and critical incidents;
3. role modelling, teaching and coaching by leaders;
4. criteria for allocating rewards and determining status;
5. criteria for selection, promotion and termination. (pp. 224–37)

These place great emphasis on example-setting by those in leadership roles. If the manager walks round a construction site without a hard hat, then it is unlikely that other people will regard such headgear as important. The comment about how leaders react to crises and critical incidents is interesting. At one level this is to do with reactions like calmness or urgency, but it is also a question of what is identified by leaders as crises and critical incidents. If there is great attention paid by managers to punctuality and less to quality, then punctuality receives greater emphasis in the eyes of everyone.

The comment about coaching and teaching by leaders indicates the degree of social integration there needs to be between the opinion formers and those holding the opinions and producing the behaviour that those opinions shape. Research on how people learn demonstrates quite clearly that attitude formation is developed effectively by social interaction and scarcely at all by other methods. Exhortation and written instructions or assurances are likely to do little to change the culture of an organisation: working closely with people can.

The most significant reinforcement of attitudes and beliefs comes from that which is tangible and visible. What do people need to do to get a pay rise? What do you have to do to get promoted? What can lead to people being fired? Those working in and around organisations usually want the first two and try to avoid the third. If loyalty is rewarded you will get loyalty, but may not get performance. If performance is rewarded, people will at least try to deliver performance.

This line of argument by Schein presents two difficulties. First, such emphasis on 'leadership' can imply dependence on one Great Leader to whom everyone else responds. Second, it is too easy to confuse cultural leadership with position leadership; those who are most effective in setting the tone may not be those in the most senior posts, even though they are well placed for this.

Focusing on the Great Leader also emphasises hierarchical principles of organisation, with all the drawbacks we have already seen. Organisational culture is the concern of all members and change in a culture is effective and swift only when there is wide agreement, and ownership concerning the change to be sought. Wide agreement about important aspects of culture seem to be best obtained, paradoxically, through a recognition and toleration of a legitimate plurality of views and styles on less central matters. Differences will not be resolved by the Great Leader exercising 'the right to manage', but through discussion amongst all parties concerned.

Elevated position in a hierarchy, though possibly helpful, is not a guarantee of effectiveness in the pursuit of, or opposition to, cultural change.

A third difficulty is an assumption, in much of the theory, that the stamp of its culture leaves an identical mark across all of an organisation. We referred above to a 'legitimate plurality of views and styles' as a counterweight to the Great Leader. In fact, we have to go further because all organisations, especially

ACTIVITY BOX 5.6

Think of an organisation of which you are or have been a member that had a strong leader. This may not necessarily have been an employing organisation, but a school, youth club, operatic society, political association etc.

▶ Did the leader shape the culture?
▶ Did the culture resist the leader?
▶ How did the shaping or resistance manifest itself?

professional organisations, contain groupings each with a distinctive culture, depending on its members' views, the nature of its expertise or tasks, its history, and so on. A visitor walking round the premises of any organisation notices different cultures in different areas; when this variety is respected, the culture of the organisation as a whole will be quite different from that in an organisation where such variety is suppressed.

Schein's secondary mechanisms for the articulation and reinforcement of culture are:

1. the organisational structure;
2. systems and procedures;
3. space, buildings and façades;
4. stories and legends about important events and people;
5. formal statements of philosophy and policy. (pp. 237–42)

These introduce a wider range of possible actions, but notice what comes last! So often we find in practice that attempts to develop aspects of culture actually begin with formal statements of policy, or that cultural inertia is attributed to the lack of such statements. The connection with structure cannot be emphasised enough, as a bureaucratic structure will, for instance, be the biggest single impediment to introducing a corporate culture emphasising risk-taking and personal initiative. The use of space, façades and stories appeals to the romance that is in all of us. The company logo now assumes extraordinary significance in providing a symbol of corporate identity, which everyone can see, understand and share. The stories that go round the grapevine may be those of management incompetence or greed. On the other hand, they may be stories of initiative or dedication to duty. There may be stories only about managers in key positions or there may be stories about how X saved the day by extraordinary initiative and Y got a letter from the overseas visitor who had appreciated a small act of kindness. These are the things which shape culture and managers can influence all of them, for it is the cultural leaders who will make all of these things happen.

Without a central sense of unity, organisations are no more than a collection of people who would rather be somewhere else because they lack effectiveness and conviction in what they are doing. The effective organisation has a few central ideals about which there is a high degree of consensus and those ideals are supported and put into operation by simple rules and clear procedures. The organisation that depends principally on rules for its cohesion is in the process of decay.

Rosabeth Moss Kanter (1989, pp. 361–5) believes that the demands of the future will require seven particular qualities from managers. First, the ability **to operate without relying on the might of hierarchy** behind them. Managers will have to rely on their personal capacities to achieve results rather than depending on the authority of their position.

Second will be a need **to compete in a way that enhances rather than undercuts co-operation**. This is a tall order, but the argument is that the nature of competitive striving must be to stimulate those with whom one has a working relationship, instead of trying to win the fight.

Her third quality is a **high standard of ethics**. Her reasoning follows closely from the previous point and is very similar to the old-fashioned British idea of 'a gentleman's word is his bond'. Collaborations, joint ventures and similar alliances make it necessary for people to be candid and to reveal information, but also being able to rely on partners not to violate that trust. This sounds optimistic, but the logic is clear enough.

The fourth requirement is **humility**, as there will always be new things to learn.

Fifth is **the need to develop a process focus**. How things are done will be just as important as what is to be done. There may be problems to solve that present intriguing intellectual challenges, but success lies not in being able to decide what should be done, but in being able to implement the decision: to make it happen.

The sixth suggestion is **the need to be multifaceted and ambidextrous**:

> able to work across functions and business units to find synergies that multiply value, able to form alliances when opportune but to cut ties when necessary, able to swim effectively in the mainstream and in newstreams.
>
> (Kanter 1989, p. 364)

Her final suggestion is that it is necessary **to gain satisfaction from results**. A shift of emphasis from status to contribution and from attainment of position to attainment of results.

ACTIVITY BOX 5.7

▶ How many of Kanter's seven qualities have you got?
▶ How appropriate are these qualities for where you are in your organisation now?
▶ How necessary do you think each of these qualities will be in your future career?

Summary propositions

5.1 Organisation design is occasionally a process of creating an entire organisation from scratch, but for most people it is modifying bits of an existing organisation.

5.2 Personnel officers play an increasingly significant role in organisation design.

5.3 The fundamentals of organisation design are task identity and job definition, structure and decision-making complexes.

5.4 Alternative forms of structure are entrepreneurial, bureaucratic, matrix and independence. A new form of professional organisation can also be seen.

5.5 The culture of an organisation is the characteristic spirit and belief of its members, demonstrated by the behavioural norms and values held by them in common.

5.6 Corporate culture is a culture that those directing the organisation seek to create and foster in the interests of the organisation achieving its objectives.

5.7 No organisation is an island, so attempts to foster or alter corporate culture must take account not only of the intentions and expectations of those within the organisation, but also of developments in the surrounding society, both nationally and internationally.

References

Anthony, P. D. (1986) *The Foundation of Management*, London: Tavistock.

Bridges, W. (1995) *Jobshift: How to prosper in a workplace without jobs*, London: Nicholas Brearley.

Child, J. (1984) *Organization: A guide to problems and practice*, 2nd edn, London: Harper & Row.

Deal, T. E. and Kennedy, A. A. (1982) *Corporate Cultures: The rites and rituals of corporate life*, Reading, Mass: Addison-Wesley

Devanna, M. A. and Tichy, N. (1990) 'Creating the competitive organization of the 21st century: the boundaryless corporation', *Human Resource Management*, Vol. 29, No. 4, Winter, pp. 455–71.

Drucker, P. F. (1988) 'The coming of the new organization', *Harvard Business Review*, Vol. 66, No. 1, January–February.

Galbraith, J. R. (1977) *Organization Design*, Wokingham: Addison-Wesley.

Goffee, R. and Scase, R. (1985) *Women in Charge*, London: Allen & Unwin.

Handy, C. B. (1985/1993) *Understanding Organizations*, 3rd and 4th edns, Harmondsworth: Penguin Books.

Handy, C. B. (1997) 'What's it all for?: re-inventing capitalism for the next decade', *Royal Society of Arts Journal*, Vol. CXLIV, No. 5475, pp. 33–40.

Harrison, R. (1972) 'How to describe your organization', *Harvard Business Review*, September/October.

Hofstede, G. (1980) *Culture's Consequences*, Beverly Hills, Calif.: Sage.

Hofstede, G. (1991) *Cultures and Organizations: Software of the mind*, London: McGraw-Hill.

Kanter, R. M. (1989) *When Giants Learn to Dance*, New York: Simon & Schuster.

Lawrence, P. R. and Lorsch, J. W. (1967) *Organization and Environment*, Cambridge, Mass: Harvard University Press.

Marglin, S. (1974) 'What do bosses do?', in A. Gorz (ed.), *Division of Labour*, Brighton: Harvester Press.

Marshall, J. (1985) 'Paths of personal and professional development for women managers', *Management Education and Development*, Vol. 16, pp. 169–79.

Milkovich, G. T. and Boudreau, J. W. (1994), *Human Resource Management*, 7th edn, Burr Ridge, Ill.: Richard D. Irwin Inc.

Moir, A. and Jessel, D. (1989) *Brain Sex*, London: Michael Joseph.

Nelson, E. (1989) 'Marketing in 1992 and beyond', *Royal Society of Arts Journal*, Vol. CXXXVI, No. 5393, April, pp. 292–304.

Olins, W. (1989) *Corporate Identity*, London: Thames & Hudson.

Pugh, D. S. and Hickson, D. J. (1976) *Organisational Structure in its Context*, Farnborough: Saxon House.

Schein, E. H. (1985) *Organizational Culture and Leadership*, San Francisco: Jossey-Bass.

Tiger, L. (1970) 'The biological origins of sexual discrimination', *The Impact of Science on Society*, Vol. 20, No. 1.

Williamson, O. E. (1975) *Markets and Hierarchies: Analysis and antitrust implications*, New York: Free Press.

General discussion topics

1. What are the strengths and weaknesses of the bureaucratic form of organisation? Have downsizing and customer care made it obsolete?
2. To what extent do you think it is realistic to talk of organisations having predominantly male or female characteristics? Could there be a neutral form?
3. What do you think of the analysis by Geert Hofstede about how norms vary across cultures? Does it help management action in an international context, or simply make it confusing?

CHAPTER 6

Organisational communication and systems

Without communication a business would not exist, let alone survive. Communication is the essence of organisation both as entity and as process that we have considered in earlier chapters. The mission statement, strategies, policies, procedures and drills, the organisation chart, the balance sheet, budget, the training manual, job descriptions, appraisal forms, plans, forecasts, memoranda, briefings, contracts, statements of objectives, electronic mail, computer conferencing, presentations, conversations, meetings and interviews are all different manifestations of this one activity which holds everything together and makes things happen. In this chapter we look first at the scope of communicating in organisations, then consider in more detail the processes and the barriers to their effectiveness, before reviewing different techniques and systems.

Meaning and scope of communication

Communication involves both the giving out of messages from one person and the receiving and understanding of those messages by another or others. If a message has been given out by one person but has not been received or understood by another, then communication has not taken place. The methods of communicating in organisations include speech, non-verbal communication, writing, audiovisual and electronic means. These methods are considered in greater detail later in this chapter. The method used will depend on the precise message that needs to be passed on. In general, messages may contain factual information, opinion or emotion.

In organisations a wide variety of messages will need to be communicated. Some messages are individually specific – for example, a supervisor giving feedback on a completed task or expressing concern at continued lateness; or an individual explaining his or her future career plans. Others are team- or group-oriented – for example, current group objectives; a change in team structure or office accommodation; or sharing action plans for the week. A third group of messages is concerned with all employees – for example, quarterly business results, new company image, revised payment system; or expressions of employee confusion over a new organisational programme or change being introduced. In this chapter we shall concentrate on communication relevant to all or groups of employees. Individually specific communication is dealt with elsewhere in this book, in the chapters on performance management, appraisal, discipline and grievance.

From the above examples it is clear that organisational communication is not only top-down, but also bottom-up and lateral. All aspects are important and all are included in this chapter. The key to success of many organisational communications systems is the extent to which they provide for two- or three-way communication, rather than just one-way traffic.

Within any organisation there are both formal and informal channels of communication. The formal channels are those that are officially acknowledged and approved, such as circulars, meetings, posters, and so on. Informal channels of communication can either facilitate or inhibit communication through official channels (Glen 1975). Foy (1983) argues that in order to improve corporate communication the grapevine should not be eliminated, but an effort should be made to ensure that official communication channels match the informal ones. The informal channels of communication are not officially acknowledged, but are, however, often privately acknowledged and approved, and sometimes deliberately used: government 'leaks' are a good example. In other organisations the same type of leak may be used from time to time to see what the reaction would be to a proposed management initiative, so that the initiative can be modified before being made official. It is a form of consultation that can save face by avoiding a formal espousal of a strategy that is shown to be unsatisfactory.

Within organisations the existence of such informal channels of communication often encourages managers to communicate officially, as the information will in any case be passed on. On these grounds it may be assumed that an increase in official communication would result in a decrease in the unofficial informal communication. Interestingly, this has been shown not to be the case and that increasing official communication results in increasing informal communication. Effectiveness in communication usually requires a careful blend of both formal and informal channels, with formal statements of fact and reasons, supported by informal explanations and interpretations.

In this chapter we shall concentrate on information which was deliberately intended to be communicated, and which is backed up by an explicit system of communication.

Purposes of communication in organisation

Greenbaum (1974) described four major purposes of organisation communication. He identified **regulation** purposes where communication is intended to ensure that employee behaviour is consistent and congruent with the goals of the organisation. Second, **innovation** purposes whereby the organisation seeks to change the way that things are done. Third, **integration** purposes where the aim is to encourage employees to identify with the organisation and raise morale. And fourth, **information** purposes, which involve the passing on of factual information which employees will need in order to do their jobs.

Clutterbuck and Dearlove (1993) offer a slightly different classification. They identify **task** communication which is specific information needed to do the job; **educational** or **context** communication, which is the background information, and **motivational** communications. In order to achieve some of these purposes communications may well be designed to be persuasive – for example, safety campaigns. There is, however, an increasing emphasis on upwards communications and in particular a focus on involving employees, as in, for example, suggestion schemes, focus groups and quality circles (although revitalised circles as part of a TQM approach may have a different emphasis). We look in more detail at focus groups towards the end of this chapter and return to the other approaches in Part VI on Involvement.

Upwards communication is important for the following reasons:

1. It helps managers to understand employees' concerns.
2. It helps managers to keep more in touch with employees' attitudes and values.
3. It can alert managers to potential problems.
4. It can provide managers with workable solutions to problems.
5. It can provide managers with the information that they need for decision-making.
6. It helps employees to feel that they are participating and contributing, and can encourage motivation and commitment to future courses of action.
7. It provides some feedback on the effectiveness of downwards communication, and ideas on how it may be improved.

McClelland (1988) suggests that the following factors, among others, are important for successful upwards communication: access to senior managers, sufficient business understanding, an atmosphere of trust with no fear of reprisals, and sufficient feedback.

Lateral communication is important, among other reasons, for ensuring co-ordination of activities and goals.

ACTIVITY BOX 6.1

In your organisation, or any organisation with which you are familiar:

1. What formal channels of lateral communication are there?
2. How effective are these and why?
3. Suggest ways in which lateral communication could be improved.

Organisational communication is directed at the outside world as well as at employees. Company newspapers, for example, are aimed at informing employees of what's going on in the company, but are also seen as a way to project an image to the outside world. Carlisle (1982) notes this function as a key part of organisational communication.

The process of communicating: the telecommunications analogy

A convenient and well-established method of approaching and understanding communication is to draw an analogy with telecommunications. Here one examines the human process by comparing it with the electronic process. Figure 6.1 shows how the communication process begins with some abstract idea or thought

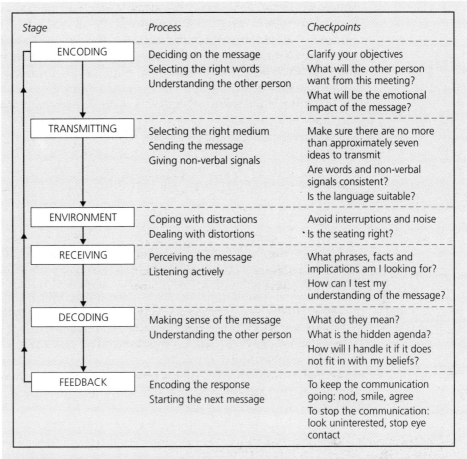

Stage	Process	Checkpoints
ENCODING	Deciding on the message Selecting the right words Understanding the other person	Clarify your objectives What will the other person want from this meeting? What will be the emotional impact of the message?
TRANSMITTING	Selecting the right medium Sending the message Giving non-verbal signals	Make sure there are no more than approximately seven ideas to transmit Are words and non-verbal signals consistent? Is the language suitable?
ENVIRONMENT	Coping with distractions Dealing with distortions	Avoid interruptions and noise Is the seating right?
RECEIVING	Perceiving the message Listening actively	What phrases, facts and implications am I looking for? How can I test my understanding of the message?
DECODING	Making sense of the message Understanding the other person	What do they mean? What is the hidden agenda? How will I handle it if it does not fit in with my beliefs?
FEEDBACK	Encoding the response Starting the next message	To keep the communication going: nod, smile, agree To stop the communication: look uninterested, stop eye contact

Figure 6.1 The process of communication (Torrington *et al.* 1985). Used with the permission of the Institute of Personnel Management

in the mind of the person seeking to convey information. The first step in the communication process is for the central nervous system of that person to translate the abstractions through the vocal organs into speech patterns or into some form of written or other visual message. If the channel of communication is speech, then the patterns of speech travel through the air as sound waves to be received by the ears and conveyed as nerve impulses to the brain. If the channel of communication is visual, as in written communications, the message is either manually, mechanically or electronically transferred and is received by the eyes and conveyed again by nerve impulses to the brain.

The message is unscrambled in the central nervous system of the receiver, which then instructs the listener to understand; the final stage comes when there is registration and the receiver understands.

Through these various stages of translation from the mind of one to the mind of the other there is a number of points at which error is possible, and even likely. It is almost impossible to know whether the abstract idea in the mind of one person has been transferred accurately to the mind of the other. One essential element in the whole process is feedback. This completes the circuit so that there is some indication from the listener that the message has been received and understood. It is probable that the feedback response will give some indication to the transmitter of the quality of the message that has been received. If the transmitter expects a reaction of pleasure and the feedback received is a frown, then it is immediately known that there is an inaccuracy in the picture that has been planted in the mind of the receiver, and the opportunity arises to identify the inaccuracy and correct it.

A further element in the communication process is that of 'noise'. This is used as a generic term to describe anything that interferes in the transmission process: inaudibility, inattention, physical noise, and so forth. The degree to which some noise element is present will impair the quality of both transmission and feedback.

More recent analysis of the communication process has led to a greater understanding of the setting in which communication takes place, so that now perhaps we focus more on understanding the process and the activity of receiving and interpreting information than we do on the activities involved in transmitting information. Shoveller (1987) lists no fewer than twenty-four reasons why communications in organisations may fail. These range from people failing to accept the responsibility to communicate to lack of interest on behalf of the recipient.

Peter Drucker (1970) has described the four fundamentals of communication as: (1) perception, (2) expectation, (3) involvement, and (4) not information. Here Drucker is emphasising that it is the recipient who communicates. The traditional communicator only 'utters'. Unless somebody hears, there is no communication, only noise. The utterer does not communicate, but only makes it possible or difficult for the recipient to perceive.

Barriers to communication

It is the listener or reader who will determine the extent to which the message is understood. What we hear, see or understand is shaped very largely by our own experience and background, so for example, instead of hearing what people tell us, we hear what our minds tell us they have said – the two may be different. There are various ways in which expectation determines communication content and a number of these ways of determination can impair the accuracy of message transmission. They act as 'noise', interfering with both transmission and feedback. We shall look at some of the principal difficulties.

The frame of reference

Few of us change our opinions alone. We are likely to be influenced by the opinions developed within the group with which we identify ourselves: the reference group. If a particular group of people hold certain values in common, individual members of that group will not easily modify their values unless and until there is a value shift in the group as a whole. This is perhaps most apparent in the relative intractability of opinions relating to political party allegiance. There are certain clearly identifiable social class groupings who tend to affiliate to particular political parties; and a change in that affiliation by an individual is rare and difficult. Managers frequently direct to an individual a message, request, instruction or rebuke which would find a more likely response if it were mediated through a representative of the group of employees rather than being directed at an individual. An interesting example of this is the way in which safety campaigns (Strauss and Sayles 1972) are mounted, where the attempt is usually by the use of slogans and posters in order to persuade individual employees about the importance of safe working practices and similar aspects of behaviour rather than negotiating a change of behaviour through group representatives.

Whenever a matter is being discussed, the people among whom it is being considered will view it from their particular personal frame of reference. Where the frames of reference of transmitter and receiver differ widely, there may be substantial difficulties in accurate transmission of messages and even greater difficulties in ensuring that the response of the receiver is that which the transmitter intended.

Cultural differences provide a frame of reference through which an individual interprets meaning. Hofstede (1990) has done considerable work on describing

WINDOW ON PRACTICE

Tixier (1994) has researched management and communication styles in Europe, and whilst she argues that the diversity of styles is so complex that it is difficult to draw conclusions, she does identify six dimensions of communications styles. These are:

1. Preference for either oral or written communication – she found that the Germans, Dutch and Portuguese favoured written communication, and could not, for example understand the high telephone bills of French subsidiaries who rely much more heavily on oral communication. She also found that verbal agreements have a different value in different countries.

2. Length of written communication – she argues that, partly as a result of the nature of the language and partly a result of early conditioning, there are differences in the length of written communication considered to be appropriate in different countries. She suggests that it is difficult to be concise in French, and that for Greeks a longer communication is considered to create a more favourable impression.

3. Implicit and explicit communication – Tixier suggests that while some countries prefer simple and tight communications with no room for ambiguity (for example,

Germany), others prefer a more subtle and suggestive approach which needs reading between the lines (France, for example).

4. Clarity – this is linked to the dimension above, and relates to the degree of preciseness required. For example, the British and Swedes allow more room for individual initiative in responding to a communication.

5. Formality – Tixier suggests that such countries as Italy, Portugal Germany and Austria prefer a more formal style of address (as in the formal version of 'you', and the use of titles), whereas in Ireland, Luxembourg, Switzerland and the Scandinavian countries a less formal approach is preferred. She associates these differences partly with the importance of symbols of power and recognition in different countries and the extent to which the culture is 'egalitarian'.

6. More or less direct modes of communication – related to the above, Tixier suggests that preferences in directness are expressed in both written and oral communication. For example, the acceptability of criticism and overt conflict. She suggests the Nordics are very careful about how criticism is expressed, where in Spain and Italy it is acceptable to have a more 'noisy and scathing' approach.

cultural differences (see pages 104–6 for a fuller explanation) and has written widely about how this affects the interactions between employees from different countries.

The stereotype

An extreme form of letting expectation determine communication content is stereotyping, where we expect a particular type of statement or particular type of attitude from a stereotype of a person. It is, for instance, quite common for the English to expect certain types of behaviour and intention from the Irish ('Never stop talking and always ready for a fight'). Equally, there is a stereotype expectation about the Scots, that they will be mean or at least extremely careful with their money. People also have stereotypes of certain office holders. There is a widespread stereotype of shop stewards which shows them as being militant, politically extreme in one, and only one, direction, unreasonable, unintelligent and obstructive. Equally, there are widespread stereotypes of different types of manager and for some people there is a stereotype of managers as a whole. One of the greatest difficulties in achieving equal opportunities at work is the challenging of deeply held stereotypes about men and women. Stereotypes about women include the view that they are unwilling to be away from home due to family commitments, that they do not want to rise too high in the hierarchy and that they will invariably leave to have children. Men, on the other hand, are often seen as career-driven and intent on promotion. There are also stereotypes relating to age, such as an older person being seen as unable to stand the pace, no longer able to think quickly and unwilling to change.

The effect of these stereotypes in communication matters is that the person who encounters someone for whom they have a stereotype will begin hearing what the person says in the light of the stereotype held.

Cognitive dissonance

Another area of difficulty, which has been explored extensively by Festinger (1957) and others, is the extent to which people will cope successfully with information inputs that they find irreconcilable in some particular way. If someone receives information that is consistent with what they already believe, they are likely to understand it, believe it, remember it and take action upon it. If, however, they receive information that is inconsistent with their established beliefs, then they will have genuine difficulty in understanding, remembering and taking action. This is because one of the ways of dealing with the discomfort of dissonance is to distort the message so that what they hear is what they want to hear, what they expect to hear and can easily understand rather than the difficult, challenging information that is being put to them.

The halo or horns effect

A slightly different aspect of expectation determining communication content is the halo or horns effect, which causes the reaction of receivers of information to move to extremes of either acceptance or rejection. When we are listening to somebody in whom we have confidence and who has earned our trust we may be predisposed to agree with what they say because we have placed an imaginary halo around their head. Because of our experience of their trustworthiness and reliability we have an expectation that what they say will be trustworthy and reliable. On the other hand, if we have learned to distrust someone, then what we hear them say will be either ignored or treated with considerable caution. Perhaps the most common example of this is the reaction that people have to the leaders of political parties when they appear on television.

Semantics and jargon

One difficulty about transferring ideas from one person to another is that ideas cannot be transferred because meaning cannot be transferred – all the communicators can use as their vehicle is words or symbols, but unfortunately the same symbols may suggest different meanings to different people. The meanings are in the hearers rather than the speakers and certainly not in the words themselves. A simple example of this is 'quite ill' which could have a variety of weightings according to how it was heard and the circumstances in which the comment was made.

The problem of jargon is where a word or a phrase has a specialised meaning that is immediately understandable by the *cognoscenti*, but meaningless or misleading to those who do not share the specialised knowledge. The Maslovian hierarchy of human needs is by now well known in management circles. On one occasion a lecturer was describing the ideas that were implicit in this notion and was rather surprised some months later in an examination paper to see that one of the students had heard not 'hierarchy' but 'high Iraqi'. The unfamiliarity of the word 'hierarchy' had been completely misinterpreted by that particular receiver, who had imposed her own meaning on what she heard because of the need to make sense of what it was that she received.

Another interesting example was in a school of motoring, where for many years trainee drivers were given the instruction 'clutch out' or 'clutch in', which nearly always confused the trainee. Later the standard instruction was altered to 'clutch down' or 'clutch up'.

Not paying attention and forgetting

The final combination of problems to consider here is first the extent to which people do not pay attention to what is being said or to what they see. There is a human predilection to be selective in attention. There are many examples of this, perhaps the most common being the way in which a listener can focus attention on a comment being made by one person in a general babble of sound by a group of people. This is complicated by the problem of noise, which we have already considered, but it has the effect of the listener trying very hard to suppress all signals other than the particular one that they are trying to pick up.

The rate at which we forget what we hear is considerable. We have probably forgotten half the substance of what we hear within a few hours of hearing it, and no more than 10 per cent will remain after two or three days. Figure 6.2 provides a summary of the main phases in communication and the barriers to effectiveness.

	Sender	Recipient	Social/environmental
Barriers in sending message	Unaware message needed Inadequate information in message Pre-judgements about message Pre-judgements about recipient		
Barriers to reception		Needs and anxieties Beliefs and values Attitudes and opinions Expectations Pre-judgements Attention to stimuli	Effects of other environmental stimuli
Barriers to understanding	Semantics and jargon Communication skills Length of communication Communication channel	Semantics problems Concentration Listening abilities Knowledge Pre-judgements Receptivity to new ideas	
Barriers to acceptance	Personal characteristics Dissonant behaviour Attitudes and opinions Beliefs and values	Attitudes, opinions and prejudices Beliefs and values Receptivity to new ideas Frame of reference Personal characteristics	Interpersonal conflict Emotional clashes Status differences Group frame of reference Previous experience of similar interactions
Barriers to action	Memory and retention Level of acceptance	Memory and attention Level of acceptance Flexibility for change of attitudes, behaviour, etc. Personal characteristics	Conflicting messages Actions of others Support/resources

Figure 6.2 The main barriers to effective communication

ACTIVITY BOX 6.2

When a computer system is designed in-house, analysts from the computer services department will liaise with members of the user department. Why is the computer system that results from this rarely what the user department wanted?

WINDOW ON·PRACTICE

Gill (1996) analysed a communications exercise within a medium-sized private sector company. The company were introducing gainsharing and implemented a communications and involvement programme to support the design and implementation of the scheme. Gill used group and individual interviews together with a questionnaire to find out to what extent employees understood the objectives of the new scheme, whether they considered the involvement and communications processes to have been effective and their desire to participate in the scheme.

She found that employees had a different understanding of the objectives of the scheme compared to senior management. To senior management the objectives were behavioural and in particular were to motivate employees, increase commitment, improve/develop teamworking and improve communications, with the anticipation that this would result in improved profitability. Employees, on the other hand, considered that the two key objectives were to increase output and improve profits. Other objectives they identified were to get people to work harder, improve the product, improve motivation, commitment and teamworking and increase employees' earnings. In terms of the effectiveness of the communications process 93 per cent of employees thought this to be ineffective and felt that their views had not been taken into account. Senior management felt that communications were better than they ever had been. They felt that they had sought employees' views and taken them on board, and could provide examples of this, although some also acknowledged that could have done even better. However 90 per cent of employees did want to participate in the scheme.

In her analysis Gill identified recent company history and levels of trust between different levels of management and employees as critical factors in the effectiveness of the communications, in addition to the actual methods used.

Ways of communicating in organisations

As discussed at the beginning of this chapter, there are many communication media: speech, non-verbal communication, writing, audio-visual and electronic means. Using each medium there is a variety of methods of communication which can be employed in organisations. A summary of communication media and the main methods of organisational communication are found in Table 6.1. Some methods are appropriate only for downwards communication, such as films and posters, other methods are suitable for upwards communication only, such as suggestion schemes. Many methods, however, are suitable for both downwards and upwards communication as well as for lateral communication. The choice of communication method will depend not only on the direction of the communication, but also on the specific nature of the message to be communicated. Notifying employees about a reorganisation which directly affects them would not be best communicated solely via an official memo. Many messages, however, are best transmitted by the use of more than one communication medium. Company rules, for example, might most effectively be communicated verbally; communication on an induction course supported by a written summary for employees to take away as a reminder. Company performance may well be written about in the company newspaper, but may also be displayed diagrammatically via a poster or on the noticeboard. As a general rule, messages are more successfully communicated if more than one communication medium is used.

Table 6.1 Different methods of communicating within organisations

Used mainly for communication	Downwards	Upwards	Laterally
Medium			
Written	X	X	X
Official paperwork	X		X
Information bulletins	X		
Newsletters/house journals	X		X
Company newspapers	X		X
Company reports	X		
Objective-setting cascade	X		
Employee reports	X		
Notice boards	X		
Manuals	X		X
Training handouts	X		X
Suggestion scheme		X	
Attitude survey		X	
Customer surveys			X
Speech			
Mass meetings	X		
Meetings of reps.	X		X
Departmental meetings	X	X	X
Interdepartmental meetings	X		X
Briefing groups	X	X	
Focus groups		X	
Formal presentations	X		
Conferences/seminars	X		X
'Open door' policy		X	
Audiovisual			
Slides	X		
Tape-slides	X		
Film strips	X		
Film	X		
Television/video	X		
Audio tape	X		
Company radio	X		X
Posters/flip-chart/blackboard	X		
Video conferencing	X		X
Electronic			
Electronic mail	X	X	X
CBT	X		
Non-verbal			
Present during any communication via speech and some audiovisual communications			

If more than one medium is used it is imperative that each message reinforces the other, and that conflicting messages are avoided. Variety is another important factor when choosing a communication method. If any particular channel of communication is overloaded, this may result in escape, queuing, loss of quality,

Communicating change at Grants of St James

Grants of St James were embarking on a radical reorganisation, and recognised that communication was a critical factor in its success. They introduced a business briefing system and developed the capacity of managers to communicate and manage change. In supporting briefers Grants were open about why changes were required, allowed managers to question the strategy and also involved them in planning the communications needed and the implementation of change.

They produced a briefing pack for supervisors and managers which included a script and visual aids outlining the changes; answers to anticipated questions; an information pack for each employee; copies of all press releases and guidance on how to handle questions from the press; guidance on follow-up communications and how to handle disputes; a process for follow-up meetings.

As well as direct communications to employees, there were communications via union representatives, and also via the Communications Co-ordination Group. This group was set up to co-ordinate communications over thirteen locations, and it liaised with line managers on each site, the Board and the Press Office. They provided a hot-line service to managers for the week immediately following the announcement of changes.

For a fuller explanation, see Withers and Hurley (1990).

delegation or prioritising. If, for example, a company tries to communicate too many messages by means of posters, then employees may escape by ceasing to read any posters, or not read them properly, and so on. If a communication channel is overused, it becomes less effective, and some authors have noted the danger of a general communications overload.

For a full description of all the different methods of communication, see Bland (1980). We do not have the space here to review all the different methods of communication within the work organisation, but we shall discuss team briefing in some depth and then briefly cover objective setting cascades, focus groups, staff surveys and customer surveys.

Team briefing

Team briefing is a method of face-to-face communication in groups of about 10–20 employees. The leader of the group provides up-to-date organisational information, with explanation and rationale, and group members are given an opportunity to ask questions. Townley (1989) suggests team briefing is probably the most systematic method of providing top-down information to employees. It is a method of communication pioneered by the Industrial Society, particularly John Garnett, and has been encouraged in some form since the mid-1960s.

In 1975 a BIM survey established that 51 per cent of firms regularly used team briefing; a decade later Millward and Stevens (1986) reported that 62 per cent of organisations contacted in the Second Workplace Industrial Relations Survey used team briefing. Marchington *et al.* (1993), in smaller-scale research, reported team briefing in 19 out of 25 organisations that were contacted. Team briefing is adopted to improve communications with the workforce and to gain the advantages of upwards and downwards communication (p. 135). The *Industrial Relations Review and Report* comments that organisations introduce team briefing 'as a means of communicating with their employees, improving employee attitudes and increasing their involvement at work' (*Industrial Relations Review and Report*, 4 February 1986, p. 2).

Team briefing is often seen as a way of encouraging employee commitment to the organisation, particularly to major organisational change, by providing the reasons behind intended changes and an opportunity for employees to ask questions. Marchington (1987) also suggests other reasons behind the growth of team briefing: employers' desire to avoid industrial action by trade unions by diverting conflict; increasing expectations of employees to have more influence over their lives at work; and legislation requiring employers to develop employee involvement, such as the 1982 Employment Act, are all mentioned.

Team briefing also provides other potential advantages, which include the strengthening of the supervisor's role and the discouragement of reliance on shop stewards and informal networks. This is because in the team briefing system the shopfloor workers will be briefed as a group by their supervisor. In particular, Marchington suggests, it enhances the supervisor's reputation as the provider of information and reinforces the role as being accountable for team performance.

The type of information that is transmitted in briefing groups includes management information, sales figures, progress made, policies, and the implications of all these for the workers involved. It is critical that the information passed on is made relevant to those who will hear it.

The team briefing system works from the top downwards in gradual stages: it is suggested that these stages do not exceed four. The system starts with a board meeting, or meeting of executives, and this is followed by briefing groups being held at the next level down, using as their base briefing notes issued by the first meeting, but adding any other information that may be relevant at this level. The last level of briefing group is the level of the supervisor or first line manager briefing the shopfloor workers. Briefing notes from the next level of briefing group are used here, together with local information. It is usually suggested that those who are 'briefers' and lead the briefing group should, between meetings, make notes of any items of importance that should be included in the next meeting. Meetings are held at intervals varying from fortnightly to quarterly, depending on the circumstances, but it is important that meetings are arranged well in advance so that they are clearly seen as part of the structure. Many organisations have a regular interval between meetings.

Training is important for all those who take part in briefing groups, and particularly for those who will act as briefers, as they may be unused to dealing with groups as opposed to individuals. The success of team briefing depends critically on the skills of the briefer.

Briefing groups are not intended to replace other channels of communication but to supplement them, and urgent matters should be dealt with immediately and not saved for the next team briefing session (*Industrial Relations Review and Report* 1986). However, the potential importance of briefing groups in the whole communications structure is exemplified by a comment from Mike Judge of Talbot Motors (in Romano 1984): 'Team briefing is the cornerstone of our communications policy.' Some guidelines on team briefing are found in Figure 6.3.

There can be difficulties, however, in establishing a team briefing system. Marchington (1987) notes that team briefing is 'managerial in tone' and is concerned with reinforcing 'managerial prerogative', and can therefore be seen by the trade unions as a way of weakening their power. He goes on to comment that team briefing stands most chance of success either where there is little or no

Team briefing should be:
Held at regular intervals and not just at times of crisis.
Brief, ideally lasting no longer than 30 minutes.
Led by the immediate foreman or supervisor of the work group.
Face-to-face and not reduced to a series of circulars and memos.
Structured to cover –

- progress: how we are doing
- people: who is coming and going
- policy: any changes affecting the team
- points: for further action.

Monitored to assess their success or failure.

How team briefing works:

1. The briefer collects information relating to progress, people, policy and points for action in preparation for the meeting.
2. A few days before the meeting he or she prepares a local brief, which is checked by the manager.
3. Following a board meeting, for example, three or four relevant items are typed and sent to briefers at the next level.
4. Directors meet their teams and any questions which cannot be answered immediately are noted and answered within 48 hours. In addition to local information, the brief will have explained the items passed down from the board.
5. This process continues down the line, ensuring there is a local brief and that management points have been included.
6. The majority of people should be briefed at the same time and the number of levels through which information passes should be no more than four.
7. After meetings, briefers should find and feedback answers to unanswered questions Absentees should be briefed on their return.

Figure 6.3 Guidelines for team briefing (Romano 1984, p. 40). Reproduced with permission of Findlay Publications Ltd

union organisation, or where the union is well established and supported by the company with good channels of communication. The prognosis is not good where there has been previous union conflict or mistrust. In 1993 he found that customised systems were more effective that those bought 'off the peg', and that briefing was more effective where it was consistent with other management practices. He also reported that less than 20 per cent of employees said that it improved their commitment to the organisation, 66 per cent felt that it had not changed their understanding of management decisions, and 40 per cent said that it did not lead to an increase in information received.

Beaumont (1993) reports on a team briefing pilot study in the public sector and discovered that there was little employee participation at the sessions. On surveying employees he found that they felt there was overlap between team briefing and the in-house newspaper, that they felt the decisions had already been made and that some items were held back rather than disclosed.

In spite of potential problems with team briefing, we found, in our recent research, that 63 per cent of the organisations surveyed were currently operating a team briefing system, and that around half of these had been operating for over ten years. A small number, amounting to 5 per cent of organisations, however, had discontinued team briefing over the last ten years.

Objective-setting cascades

Objective-setting cascades are frequently used to communicate the mission and strategic objectives of the organisation to the whole organisation. The purpose is to ensure that all employees can then pull in the same direction and have something to guide their priorities. To make the organisational mission and strategic objectives more usable they are normally translated into strategic objectives for each level in the organisation, as shown in Figure 6.4.

So the organisation's strategic objectives determine objectives at the functional level, which in turn determine objectives at the department level, which in turn determine objectives at the group level, which in turn determine objectives at the individual level. In theory, if all parts of the organisation achieve their strategic objectives, then the strategic objectives at the organisational level will have been achieved.

The effectiveness of the cascade is partly determined by the way in which the objectives are communicated. If this is done in a one-way top-down manner, with objectives being imposed, the results may well be different from using a two-way approach where each level 'offers up' its own objectives in response to higher level objectives.

A further option is for the team leader, for example, to set objectives jointly with their team rather than carrying out this task independently. This allows the opportunity to gain commitment to the objectives via employee involvement.

Focus groups

Focus groups are an increasingly popular way for Chief Executives and the senior team to gather grounded information from all levels in the organisation, rather than from the senior managers with whom they normally communicate. They are usually organised on a departmental basis with the Chief Executive meeting

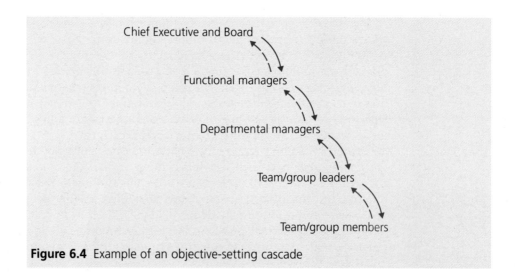

Figure 6.4 Example of an objective-setting cascade

around twenty employees from all levels in the department. The focus is on how this group sees the organisation. What from their perspective are the strengths and weaknesses? What are the difficulties and opportunities? And how can difficulties be overcome and opportunities seized?

Customer feedback systems

Customer feedback systems are a particularly good way of encouraging lateral communication in the organisation. They apply especially to departments that service a wide range of other departments – for example, computer services, site services, personnel – although all departments can identify some internal customers. The focus is on what do we do well, what could be improved and how could we improve. Most feedback systems are paper-based, although some will be face-to-face.

Staff surveys

Staff surveys are mainly carried out anonymously via questionnaires, although sometimes interviews are held between staff members and an external agency so anonymity can still be maintained. They are a systematic means of collecting the views of employees. Farnham (1993) suggests that they can be used to diagnose organisational problems; assess the effects of change; compare attitudes pre- and post-changes; gather feedback on management action, plans and policies; and identify collective concerns.

ACTIVITY BOX 6.3

What do you think would be the most effective way(s) of communicating the following in a non-unionised organisation with 3,000 employees:

1. Instructions from the computer services department on how to use the new computer system.
2. Sales targets for the forthcoming year.
3. Plans to relocate to a new plant 5 miles away.
4. New absence and holiday reporting procedures.

Summary propositions

6.1 Communication is the flow of information through the organisation structure that can produce understanding and action, but may produce mistrust and inefficiency.

6.2 Formal communication is supported by informal communication, and managerial use of both systems has to be kept in balance.

6.3 Effective communication is multilateral and 'bottom-up' not simply 'top-down'.

6.4 Barriers to communication include the frame of reference, stereotyping, cognitive dissonance, the halo or horns effect, semantics, jargon and not paying attention or forgetting.

6.5 Team briefing, objective setting cascades, focus groups, customer feedback systems and staff surveys are all popular approaches to communication in organisations.

References

Beaumont, P. B. (1993) *Human Resource Management: Key concepts and skills*, London: Sage Publications.

Bland, M. (1980) *Employee Communication in the 1980's: A personnel manager's guide*, London: Kogan Page.

Carlisle, H. M. (1982) *Management: Concepts, methods and applications*, 2nd edn, Chicago: Science Research Associates Ltd.

Clutterbuck, D. and Dearlove, D. (1993) *Raising the Profile: Marketing the HR function*, London: IPM.

Drucker, P. (1970) 'What communication means', *Management Today*, March.

Farnham, D. (1993) *Employee Relations*, London: IPM.

Festinger, L. (1957) *A Theory of Cognitive Dissonance*, Stanford, Calif: Stanford University Press.

Foy, N. (1983) 'Networkers of the world unite', *Personnel Management*, March.

Gill, J. (1996) 'Communication – is it really that simple?' *Personnel Review*, Vol. 25, No. 5, pp. 23–36.

Glen, F. (1975) *The Social Psychology of Organizations*, Essential Psychology Series, London: Methuen.

Greenbaum, H. W. (1974) 'The audit of organisational communication', *Academy of Management Journal*, pp. 739–54.

Hofstede, G. (1990) *Culture's Consequences*, Beverly Hills, Calif.: Sage.

Industrial Relations Review and Report (1986) *Team Briefing: Practical steps in employee communications*, IRRR, 4 February.

Marchington, M. (1987) 'Employee participation', in B. Towers (ed.), *A Handbook of Industrial Relations Practice*, London: Kogan Page.

Marchington, M., Wilkinson, A. and Askers, P. (1993) 'Waving or drowning in participation', *Personnel Management*, March.

McClelland, V. A. (1988) 'Communication: upward communication: is anyone listening?' *Personnel Journal*, June.

Millward, N. and Stevens, M. (1986) *The Second Workplace Industrial Relations Survey, 1980–1984*, Aldershot: Gower.

Parsloe, E. (1980) 'Why bother? Overcoming the attitudes barrier' in M. Bland, *Employee Communications in the 1980's*, London: Kogan Page.

Romano, S. (1984) 'Shopfloor briefing: Talbot proves its value', *Works Management*, April.

Shoveller, S. E. (1987) 'A problem of communications', *Work Study*, June.

Strauss, G. and Sayles, L. R. (1972) *Personnel: The human problems of management*, Englewood Cliffs, NJ: Prentice Hall.

Tixier, M. (1994) 'Management and communication styles in Europe: can they be compared and matched?', *Employee Relations*, Vol. 16, No. 1, pp. 8–26.

Torrington, D. P., Weightman, J. and Johns, K. (1985) *Management Methods*, London: IPM.

Townley, B. (1989) 'Employee communication programmes', in K. Sisson, *Personnel Management in Britain*, Oxford: Blackwell.

Withers, M. and Hurley, B. (1990) 'Grants grows its own grapevine', *Personnel Management*, November.

General discussion topics

1. We have used a rational approach to communication in this chapter, but in practice communication in organisations is affected by politics and individual agendas. What types of impact do politics and individual agendas have on organisational communications?
   ▶ Should organisations seek to address these issues?
   ▶ How might they do this, and is it feasible?
2. How does the culture of an organisation affect its communications systems?

CHAPTER 7

Information

'I was making decisions by the seat of my pants on the basis of information on one side of A4', a personnel manager told one of the authors when describing what life was like before installing a personnel computer system. In this chapter we will look briefly at just how the computer has changed the nature of personnel information.

The opposite problem is the personnel manager who is suffocating under a surfeit of information which has been collected with no real purpose in mind. This means that we need to concentrate on the reasons for collecting information and how it can be used to improve the organisation, as well as what to collect and how to collect it. Four main types of personnel information are explored: individual operating information; strategic aggregate information; information on the effectiveness and efficiency of personnel systems; and information on the personnel function. We conclude by reviewing the implications of the Data Protection Act and the Data Protection Directive.

A computer revolution?

Since the early 1980s there has been a gradual increase in the number of personnel departments using a computer system, and early expectations centred not only on increased efficiency, but also on a change in personnel processes and the personnel role in the organisation (see, for example, Kinnie and Arthurs 1993). Such changes have only been evident in a very small number of organisations which use the computer in a sophisticated way (Hall and Torrington 1989). There is much evidence to show that personnel functions do not develop the potential of the computer (Kinnie and Arthurs 1993; Broderick and Boudreau 1992). Further research by Kinnie and Arthurs (1996) indicates that little has changed in personnel specialists' approach to computers since the 1980s. Richards-Carpenter (1996), reporting on the 1996 survey of Computers in Personnel and Training, found personnel generalists to be more closely involved than any other group with routine and operational matters in computer terms – such as updating data, answering routine queries and producing standard reports.

In our recent research (Table 7.1), we found that there was still a tendency to retain paper as well as computer records (rather than relying solely on the computer), and a tendency to keep only paper records for sensitive areas (such as test results, appraisal reviews and career development plans).

Table 7.1 Computer- and paper-based records in our research sample of 1994

	Stored on paper only %	Stored on computer only %	Stored on both %	Not available %
Personal information records	17	2	81	nil
Test results	50	4	19	31
Training records	39	6	52	3
Appraisal and development reviews	67	1	19	12
Personal growth profiles	30	2	8	61
Career development plans	46	1	10	43
Strategic HR plan	43	2	22	32
Job grades/ categories	25	11	57	5
Person specifications	60	3	23	15
Career structures	27	2	22	50

Barriers to extensive and sophisticated computer use have variously been found to be: the use of a centrally imposed system which does not meet local needs; problems of inadequate access; a system which does not operate in real time; a system which does not provide for on-line enquiries; a system which does not provide for flexible enquiries; lack of integration between systems holding different pieces of personnel information; and lack of training.

As these traditional practical barriers are gradually eroded, how do we explain the continued lack of sophisticated use at a strategic level? Kinnie and Arthurs (1996) explain the emphasis on routine transactional systems as opposed to expert and decision support systems in relation to three broad influences on IT development in HR. First, that although the presence of a personnel specialist was significantly associated with the use of HR information systems, these specialists were most concerned with the use of a system *within* their own department which encouraged transactional applications. Second, the IT skills and abilities of HR specialists helped to explain low expectations and limited use of advanced applications. Third, 'personnel specialists were also anxious to preserve, and if possible extend, their political power within the organisation by the use of an HRIS. They sought to place themselves at the centre of an employee information system through which the use of transactional applications, rather than [the] use of expert systems which potentially weakened their power.'

Acquiring a system which meets the department's needs and to which staff are committed is clearly a critical first step. Robertson (1992) describes a helpful approach to designing and installing a new computer system which was used in the Prudental Insurance Company. Yet implementing a new HR information system represents a major form of organisation change, and there has been little research from this perspective (Kossek *et al.* 1994).

WINDOW ON PRACTICE

Kossek *et al.* (1994), in North America, report on a longitudinal case study of the implementation of a new corporate HRIS specifically designed to enhance strategic and business decision-making at 'Opco', a worldwide business. They were particularly concerned with the reactions of members of the HR department to the new corporate system. Four major themes emerged: that the new HRIS symbolised the wish of the HR department to become more of a strategic business partner; second, that the new HRIS will enable HR to perform new or enhanced roles of information brokers and decision enabler; and third, that the new HRIS is a catalyst for altering power dynamics and communications patterns between HR and other management functions. In comparison with these positive perspectives the fourth theme revealed that 'real' HR managers don't directly use the HRIS or don't view HRIS use as a critical competency. Alongside this it is interesting to note that as the implementation of the system progresses their expectations of the system remained high, but their intention to use the system significantly decreased. Kossek *et al.* concluded that 'implementing a new HRIS requires new frames or socially constructed views and ways of thinking'. They argue that a sophisticated HRIS cannot just be bolted on, but requires organisational development. For effective organisational change to occur they also argue that there must be congruence between the capabilities of the innovation and employees' ideals and beliefs regarding the change. If HR specialists do not value HRIS skills or comprehend the significance of the new system then little change will happen and the use of the system will remain geared to administrative support rather than decision support.

ACTIVITY BOX 7.1

▶ If you do *not* use a computer in the personnel department, how could a computer be used to meet the department's and the organisation's needs? What specific objectives would you set for a computer system?

▶ If you do use a computer in the personnel department, how is the computer used to meet the department's and the organisation's needs? What needs are not being met? Why not? What specific objectives would you set for a new or improved system?

▶ **If you are not employed in an organisation.** For an organisation of 300 employes with a personnel department of three staff: what questions would you ask, of whom, in order to come to a recommendation about whether a computerised HRIS would be useful and the ways in which it could be best used.

In spite of the barriers identified above, personnel people are certainly becoming more familiar with the computer's potential contribution to personnel information and in writing the bulk of this chapter we have assumed such facilities as:

▶ producing employee listings according to specified criteria,
▶ producing a wide range of aggregate statistics in a variety of forms, including matrices, graphs and charts,

◗ administrative/operational systems which produce required letters and provide residue data of transactions and timings.

It is the ability to produce such information within minutes or hours rather than days or months that has been the real benefit of the computer so far. We do not discuss the use of different types of systems. For further information on employee database systems – the foundation of most personnel information – see Callagher (1986) or Norman and Edwards (1984). For further details on administrative systems see, for example, Ive (1982), and for the use of expert systems, for example, Glover (1988). The conference papers resulting from the annual Computers in Personnel Conferences are an excellent source of information and ideas.

Personnel information: a model

The framework in Figure 7.1 shows different types of personnel information that are helpful to the organisation. **Individual information** is an employee's individual record which would include personal information and job and employment history. This information is helpful as a factual record of past events which can assist operational decisions in respect of the employee, such as a promotion decision based on employee performance and potential ratings, job experiences, qualifications, skills and abilities.

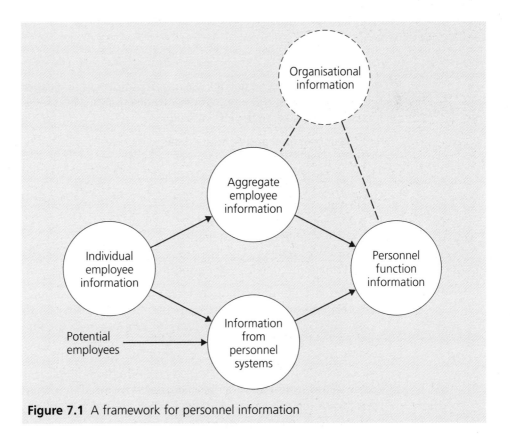

Figure 7.1 A framework for personnel information

Individual information about each employee is the foundation of **aggregate employee information** and this provides a basis for strategy and policy decisions which would apply across departments, functions, or the whole organisation. Aggregate information can also be analysed against organisational information to identify the effectiveness of the workforce as a whole.

Information from **personnel systems and activities** can also provide aggregate information about employees or potential employees, for example, an ethnic breakdown of all applicants to the organisation. It can also provide information about the workload which has been undertaken and the speed and timing of different activities. An example would be volume and pace of recruitment activity over a specified period. This information is helpful for staffing levels, and personnel standards and service agreements with different departments or the whole organisation. It can be helpful in identifying targets or benchmarks towards which the function can strive.

The **information on personnel function** is derived from data about personnel systems, aggregate employee data and other organisational data. Together these will provide information about the function's efficiency, particularly in financial terms. An example here would be personnel staffing ratios and cost-benefit analyses of training activity.

In addition there exists **external information** which can be used for comparative purposes.

We shall now take each one of these information areas and explore them in some more detail.

Individual employee information

Individual employee data chiefly comprise information gleaned from the application form together will employment history that has built up since the employee joined. Areas covered usually include:

- Basic personal and contract details.
- Training/development/education details.
- Appraisal details/career progression.
- Payment and pension details.
- Fringe benefits.
- Discipline/grievance details.
- Health/safety/welfare details.
- Absence details.
- Termination details, e.g. reason for leaving.

Information relating to these areas may be stored in varying amounts of depth depending on the needs of the particular department, as illustrated in Table 7.2.

One of the chief users of this type of information is the individual's line manager, for example to check previous training courses attended before agreeing to a training course request, or checking absence history when an employee has had a recent spate of absences. In many cases the line manager does not have easy access to this information, either because it is stored in a folder in the personnel department, or it is on a computer system to which the line manager does not have access.

Table 7.2 Individual information stored in a computerised personnel information system: an example showing various levels of information that may be stored

⟶ *Increasing depth of information*

Definition of level of depth	Level 1	Level 2	Level 3	Level 4
Example of how definition relates to an area of personnel information; educational qualifications	Highest educational qualification	Highest educational qualification, date and subject	All educational qualifications since leaving school with dates and subjects	All educational qualifications, with dates and subject for those after leaving school
Individual example	HND	HND Business Studies 1974	ONC Business Studies 1972 HND Business Studies 1974	5 'O' Levels 1 'A' Level ONC Business Studies 1972 HND Business Studies 1974

In terms of collecting information to update the file or folder it is the line manager who has current information on absence, training courses attended, appraisal results and so on, yet it is usually the personnel department who input the new data into the system.

WINDOW ON PRACTICE

In a multinational business unit of around 3,500 employees the personnel function used a computer system which had been specified and designed for the Organisational Head Office Personnel Function. The system was helpful but not user-friendly, and information was input by personnel staff daily and updated into the records on-screen on a monthly basis. There was a large volume to input and only critical areas were updated, for example absence data at the expense of training details. Many departments found that they were unable to get complete and accurate information from the system that could help them in managing their staff. One department dealt with this by buying their own PC and inputting and updating all the personnel data that they required.

ACTIVITY BOX 7.2

What are the respective roles of the personnel function and line managers in your organisation in relation to individual employee data?

What are the reasons for this?

What are the advantages and disadvantages of the way that the roles are divided?

How would you recommend that this situation be changed, and why?

If you are not employed in an organisation. How should individual data be managed in an organisation of 150 staff with no personnel department and two payroll staff?

The organisation as a whole also has an interest in individual employee data, which can be used to select individuals for promotion or lateral moves, for relocation or a secondment. If the data are on a computer system it is relatively easy to produce a list of employees who have, for example, electronic engineering skills, French as a second language, a specified performance rating and have worked for the organisation for two years or more. Individual data of a similar nature can also be transferred into a succession planning system (described in more detail in Chapter 4). Lastly individual information can be used in redundancy situations to identify a list of individuals who meet the agreed redundancy criteria.

Aggregate employee information

Aggregated employee information describes the characteristics of the current workforce. It is used at a strategic level in the planning process as described in Chapter 4, and it is also used to inform policy and design changes to improve the current position. Typical areas of information that are analysed include:

Skills profile
Length of service profile
Absence levels and costing
Turnover levels and costing
Age profile
Gender profile
Ethnic profile
Disability profile
Internal organisational movement
Salary and benefits costs

In addition aggregate employee information can be used in conjunction with organisational data to gain measures of workforce effectiveness.

We shall look in more detail at some of the above analyses.

Absence analysis and costing

Huczynski and Fitzpatrick (1989) suggest three main approaches to analysing absence, which can be applied on an individual or a aggregate workforce basis. For aggregate analysis **absence rate** is the number of days absence, that is when attendance would have been expected, of all employees. **Absence percentage rate** is this figure divided by the total number of actual working days for all employees over the year, multiplied by 100. This simple percentage figure is the one most often used and enables the organisation's absence level to be compared with national figures, or other organisations in the same sector.

Absence frequency rate is the number of spells of absence over the period, usually a year. Comparing this and the absence percentage rate gives critical information about the type of absence problem that the organisation is experiencing.

As well as external comparisons, absence data can be analysed by department, work group, occupation, grade, and so on. In this way the analysis will throw up problem areas, and additional analysis can be used to try to identify the causes of differing levels of absence in different parts of the organisation. The data may be supplemented by information from questionnaires or interviews with employees or line managers.

The purpose of producing this information is to understand the causes and extent of absence in order to manage it effectively. So, for example, such analysis may result in a new absence policy, employee communications about the impact of absence, appropriate training for line managers, changes to specific groups of jobs, and the introduction of a new type of attendance system such as flextime. The information provides a base for future monitoring.

Further analysis of the data can be used to provide guidelines to line managers in managing individual absence issues. Behrend (1978) provides a method of analysing overall absence so that it shows the absence levels of the highest 25 per cent of the workforce, and of the other three quartiles. This gives line managers an indication of how the absence level of a particular employee compares with the rest of the workforce, and can be used to provide realistic guidelines about what action managers should take when an individual's absence has reached a specified level. Figure 7.2 shows the analysis.

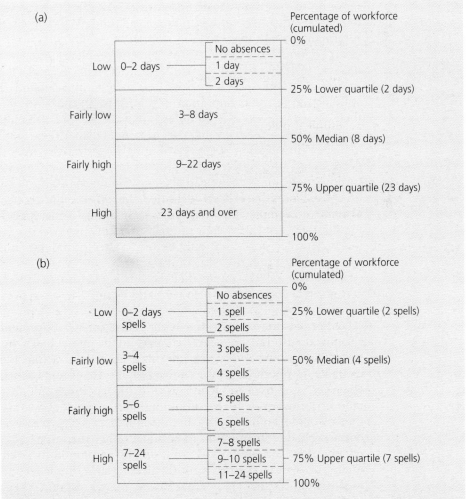

Figure 7.2 An example of the analysis of absence: (a) classification of employees by number of days lost; (b) classification of employees by number of absence spells (Behrend 1978, p. 13). Used with permission of IPD Publications.

The costing of absence needs to have a wider focus that just the pay of the absent individual. Other costs include:

▶ line manager costs in finding a temporary replacement or rescheduling work,
▶ the actual costs of the temporary employee,
▶ costs of showing a temporary employee what to do,
▶ costs associated with a slower work rate or more errors from a temporary employee,
▶ costs of contracts not be completed on time.

These costs can be calculated and provide the potential for productivity improvement.

Turnover analysis and costing

In Chapter 4 we looked at the ways of measuring employee turnover, so now we move on to look at its causes and costs. There is little that an organisation can do to manage turnover unless there is an understanding of the reasons for it. Information about these reasons is notoriously difficult to collect. Most commentators recommend exit interviews, but the problem here is whether the individual will feel able to tell the truth, and this will depend on the culture of the organisation, the specific reasons for leaving, and support that the individual will need from the organisation in the future in the form of references. Despite their disadvantages, exit interviews may be helpful if handled sensitively and confidentially – perhaps by the personnel department rather than the line manager. In addition analyses of differing turnover rates between different departments and different job groups may well shed some light on causes of turnover. Attitude surveys can also provide relevant information.

Once causes have been identified the organisation is in a position to take action. For example, if the reason for staff leaving is that higher wages are offered for similar jobs nearby then the organisation could decide to improve its wage levels. This decision could only be made after consideration of the costs of this compared with the true costs of turnover.

Hugo Fair (1992) argues that there is a wide range of costs to be taken into account when calculating turnover, and Figure 7.3 shows the process of analysis which he suggests.

Other reasons for turnover might centre on lack of promotion; difficulties in relating to the line manager; change in the individual's work preferences or needs. Some of these can be improved by actions within the organisation, for example, by developing career progression systems and facilitating lateral moves. However, in spite of the high cost of turnover it may not always be desirable to reduce turnover rates to the minimum level possible. Low turnover reduces promotion opportunities, limits the introduction of new blood and new ideas, and encourages the organisation to be static rather than dynamic. Turnover in some organisations can be too low, with employees bound by golden handcuffs from finding a better opportunity elsewhere. These employees may stay with the organisation to maintain their living standards, but their enthusiasm and commitment to the job itself may be low.

On the basis of all the turnover information produced the organisation needs to decide on, and target, the **optimum** turnover rate for the time being.

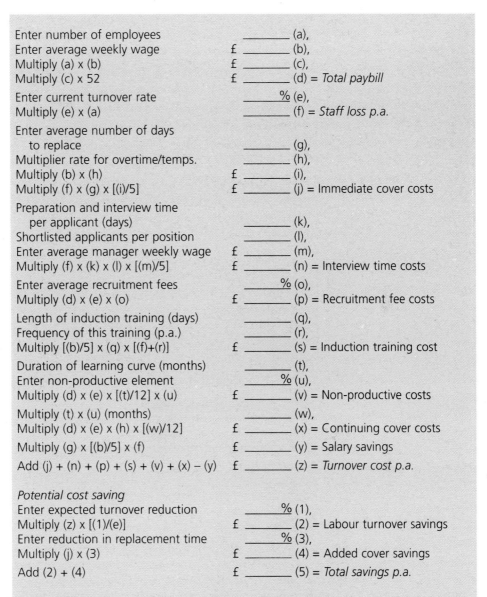

```
Enter number of employees                        _____ (a),
Enter average weekly wage              £ _____ (b),
Multiply (a) x (b)                     £ _____ (c),
Multiply (c) x 52                      £ _____ (d) = Total paybill

Enter current turnover rate                      ____%  (e),
Multiply (e) x (a)                               _____ (f) = Staff loss p.a.

Enter average number of days
   to replace                                    _____ (g),
Multiplier rate for overtime/temps.              _____ (h),
Multiply (b) x (h)                     £ _____ (i),
Multiply (f) x (g) x [(i)/5]           £ _____ (j) = Immediate cover costs

Preparation and interview time
   per applicant (days)                          _____ (k),
Shortlisted applicants per position              _____ (l),
Enter average manager weekly wage      £ _____ (m),
Multiply (f) x (k) x (l) x [(m)/5]     £ _____ (n) = Interview time costs

Enter average recruitment fees                   ____%  (o),
Multiply (d) x (e) x (o)               £ _____ (p) = Recruitment fee costs

Length of induction training (days)              _____ (q),
Frequency of this training (p.a.)                _____ (r),
Multiply [(b)/5] x (q) x [(f)+(r)]     £ _____ (s) = Induction training cost

Duration of learning curve (months)             _____ (t),
Enter non-productive element                     ____%  (u),
Multiply (d) x (e) x [(t)/12] x (u)    £ _____ (v) = Non-productive costs

Multiply (t) x (u) (months)                      _____ (w),
Multiply (d) x (e) x (h) x [(w)/12]    £ _____ (x) = Continuing cover costs

Multiply (g) x [(b)/5] x (f)           £ _____ (y) = Salary savings
Add (j) + (n) + (p) + (s) + (v) + (x) - (y)  £ _____ (z) = Turnover cost p.a.


Potential cost saving
Enter expected turnover reduction                ____%  (1),
Multiply (z) x [(1)/(e)]               £ _____ (2) = Labour turnover savings
Enter reduction in replacement time              ____%  (3),
Multiply (j) x (3)                     £ _____ (4) = Added cover savings
Add (2) + (4)                          £ _____ (5) = Total savings p.a.
```

Figure 7.3 A sample form for costing labour turnover (Fair 1992, p. 41). Used with permission of IPD Publications.

Equal opportunities analysis

This analysis aims to provide an organisational profile of ethnic origin, gender, age and disability. The resulting percentages from this can be compared with national and local community figures to give an initial idea of how representative the organisation is. Further analyses break these figures down to compare them by department, job category and grade. It is in this type of analysis that startling differences are likely to be found, for example as shown in Figure 7.4.

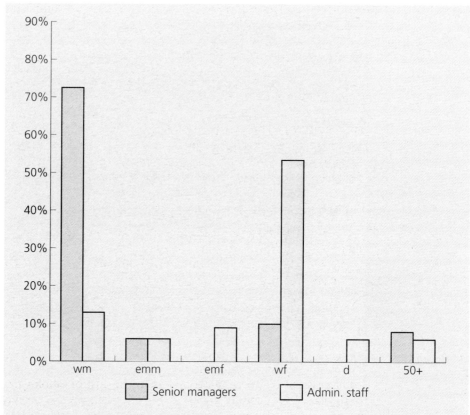

Figure 7.4 Breakdown of senior manager staff group and administrative staff group. wm, white males; emm, ethnic minority males; emf, ethnic minority females; wf, white females; d, disabled; 50+, more than fifty. Percentages of senior manager category and administrative category; each add to over 100 per cent as there is some overlap between groups into which they are subdivided.

The information gleaned can be used to:

▶ question the extent and spread of disadvantaged groups in the organisation,
▶ identify specific barriers to a more representative spread,
▶ formulate appropriate policy and action plans,
▶ set targets to be achieved and monitor year on year compared with these base figures.

Other analyses can be carried out to show promotion, internal moves and secondment figures for disadvantaged groups compared with advantages groups, for example, white males. Further mention is made of these and the recruitment system in the following section.

The workforce and organisational performance

There is a range of analyses which can relate the contribution of the workforce to organisational performance. These relationships can be used to control headcount, measure organisational effectiveness and compare this with similar organisations. The information can also be used to communicate to employees what their contribution is to the business.

Profit per employee

One of the ratios used most often is produced by dividing annual profit by the number of employees. This is useful for monitoring improvement, but especially helpful in demonstrating to each employee the importance of cost consciousness. If an employee of an organisation employing 3,000 employees realises that profit per employee is only £900 this means far more to that individual than expressing profit as £2.7 million. Cost-consciousness suddenly becomes important as the fragile and marginal nature of profits is demonstrated.

Turnover per employee

This is a similar ratio, but using gross turnover instead of profit. This gives a much clearer idea of the volume of business and the workload of employees. Comparing this ratio to the previous ratio gives pointers to organisational efficiency and again can be used to give employees a better understanding of organisation performance, particularly when turnover is increasing and profit is decreasing. This ratio can also be used to monitor headcount to ensure that it does not rise more rapidly than the workload as expressed by turnover.

People costs

Another piece of information relates to the cost of employees in relation to the total costs of production. To work this out turnover less profit (that is the cost of production) is compared with employee costs (salary plus on-costs). The percentage of production costs accounted for by employees will vary markedly according to the nature of the business. For example, in some pharmaceutical businesses people costs will account for 70 per cent of all production costs (due to a heavy emphasis on research and development) whereas in a less people-intensive business, as found in other parts of the manufacturing sector, people costs may only account for around 15 per cent. Changes in the percentage of people costs over time would need to be investigated. People costs are a good way of communicating to employees just how important they are to the success of the business.

For a more detailed description of people and organisational costs, see Fair (1992).

Information from personnel systems and activities

Information, including costs can be collected from a range of personnel systems and activities, the most common areas being:

- recruitment systems,
- training activities,
- health and safety systems,
- promotions, relocations and secondments,
- succession planning systems,
- employee support and health programmes,

▶ assessment centres and other selection procedures,
▶ administrative systems.

In this section we briefly review a sample of systems and activities. Further details are found in the chapter relevant to the activity itself.

Recruitment systems

Information collected from a computerised, or otherwise well-documented, recruitment system may involve the following over a specified period:

▶ number of vacancies advertised,
▶ number of vacancies filled,
▶ number of applications,
▶ number of candidates selected for first interviews,
▶ number of candidates attended first interviews,
▶ number of candidates selected for tests/second interviews,
▶ number of candidates tested/second interviews,
▶ number of offers made.

This analysis will give information on the workload of the recruitment section. Further analysis by vacancy will give information about hard to find skills; accuracy of person specification; appropriateness of advertisement wording and so on. For example, *if* an advertisement for one job:

▶ brought in 400 applications,
▶ fifteen candidates attended first interview,
▶ three (out of eight) attended tests and second interview,
▶ two were offered the post and none accepted,

then something in the recruitment process is going wrong!

Further analysis by advertising media can indicate the effectiveness of media and the cost of recruitment as shown in Chapter 11.

Organisations seriously interested in equal opportunities can develop the analysis by breaking down the numbers at each stage by ethnic origin, gender, age and disability. This form of monitoring can identify stages in the procedure where discrimination is most likely to be taking place. The information gleaned can be useful in indicating the use of different advertising media, different selection methods and training for recruiting managers. Continued monitoring and target setting can be used to improve the situation.

WINDOW ON PRACTICE

One of the authors of this book marked 150 answers to an examination question on improving equal opportunities. There were many excellent answers describing how organisations carefully monitored all job applications at various stages – particularly in the public sector. The use to which this information was put was less impressive. Most candidates explained that nothing was done with the information. Sometimes monitoring was done using separate sheets sent along with application forms – these sheets were carefully collected, sorted and stored – but not analysed! In other organisations statistical summaries were produced but never discussed, used to inform strategy or policy, or acted upon.

Recruitment data can also be broken down by speed and timings of stages which can be helpful in quantifying workload and its peaks and troughs. It can also be used to monitor service contracts with departments where time based recruitment targets have been agreed.

Training activities

Training course information can cover:

▶ demand for courses,
▶ applications for courses,
▶ places booked,
▶ cancellations,
▶ actual attendance,
▶ effectiveness/benefit from courses.

Effectiveness and benefit from courses are clearly the most difficult of these to define. End of course 'happy sheets' can provide some information about specific sessions and how they might be improved, but they say little about the eventual effectiveness of the training once the participants are back on the job.

In manual jobs it may be possible to measure resulting performance by speed or error rate. In other jobs – for example, management roles – resulting performance may best be measured by structured interviews with the participant and their immediate manager or through questionnaires. It is important that pre-course performance is compared with post-course performance. However, any changes will not only be due to the course itself as there may be many other intervening factors.

Cost of training can be compared against performance improvement to give a cost-benefit analysis. Costs amount to far more than the money equivalent of the participant's time off the job.

ACTIVITY BOX 7.3

Identify a training course at work which runs over around one week, or any training/educa- tion course which you have attended List and quantify all the costs involved and work out the cost per participant.

Employee health programmes

Often referred to as wellness programmes in the United States, these programmes include such activities as healthy eating and drinking promotions, no smoking campaigns, health screening, stress counselling and physical fitness facilities. The rationale behind some programmes is that the cost of the programmes is less than the cost of ill and absent employees, employee rehabilitation, employee turnover and employee replacement. Some organisations will also have more altruistic motives.

The cost of these programmes includes cost of materials, facilities, support staff and employee time off the job where appropriate. These programmes are mostly provided free of charge, although there may be some small charges in relation to the use of fitness centres.

Cascio (1991) lists a range of potential outcomes of the use of such programmes which may be costed, which include absence costs, accident costs, turnover costs, productive costs and costs of hospital visits. These outcomes look attractive to the organisation, but clearly identifying the impact of wellness programmes on these, as opposed to other factors, is no easy matter.

Information on the personnel function

A range of figures are often calculated in relation to the size and effectiveness of the personnel function. Probably the most common is the ratio between headcount in the personnel function and total organisational headcount. One use of this is to control the number of personnel staff linked to the size of the organisation, once a workable ratio has been identified. Typical ratios lie between 1:50 and 1:100. Other figures concentrate on the expenditure for which the personnel function is responsible. So, for example, the operating budget of the personnel function is added to personnel staff salaries and on-costs. This figure will be monitored annually. Further analyses take this cost and divide it by the number of employees in the organisation, which gives personnel costs per employee.

Another way of reviewing personnel costs is to compare them with all other costs of the organisation. This ratio can then be monitored for changes, and as a way of assessing the productivity of the function.

Berkshire County Council have taken a serious approach to auditing the personnel function, and their approach has three stages (see Burn and Thompson 1993). The first stage is collecting data about the operation of the department compared with others including corporate statistics and cost effectiveness. This information is then used to identify benchmarks for the future. Some of their key statistics with averages are shown in Table 7.3. The second stage of the process assesses the satisfaction of the customers with the personnel function, using such criteria as professionalism, delivery and commitment. The third step is a check that the department operates good practice in relation to legal and professional codes of practice.

Table 7.3 Some key statistics (with their averages) for Berkshire County Council (Burn and Thompson 1993, p. 29). Reproduced with permission of the authors.

Personnel staff to full-time employees	1:95
Managerial/professional personnel staff to full-time employees	1:166
Salary and bonus costs of personnel department staff per organisation employee	£208
Personnel salary and bonus costs as a percentage of the total	1.5%
Overall cost of the personnel function as a percentage of overall organisation costs	1.7%
Recruitment costs per new recruit	£650
Training costs per employee year (internal and external) – private sector	£172 pa

Confidentiality, privacy and security

Concerns about confidentiality, privacy and security of personal information have always been present but have been highlighted by the growing use of computers.

Confidentiality

Confidentiality relates to information sought, obtained or held by an organisation, the disclosure of which might be detrimental to that organisation or to the third party that supplied it.

   The guarantee given to the reference writer that everything they say will be treated in the strictest confidence is to protect the reference writer, the third party, rather than the person about whom the reference is written.

Privacy

This relates to information sought, obtained or held by an organisation about a past, present or prospective employee, the use of which might be detrimental to that employee. A Home Office document on computers and privacy suggests that there are three areas of potential danger to privacy:

1. Inaccurate, incomplete or irrelevant information.
2. The possibility of access to information by people who should not need to have it.
3. The use of information in a context or for a purpose other than that for which it was obtained.

The Data Protection Act 1984

The Data Protection Act attempts to regulate the above dangers.

When does the Data Protection Act apply?

The Act applies to organisations holding personal data. Personal data have been defined as:

> data which relates to a living individual who can be identified from the information including an expression of opinion about an individual but not any indication of the intentions of the data user in respect of that individual.
>
> (Data Protection Act, s. 1(3))

All organisations using a computerised personnel information system have to be registered, giving the sources and purposes of the information that is held.

Each purpose must be registered. Information that is held manually is not covered by the Act, only data that can be processed by automatic equipment. Users of personal data have an obligation to follow the data protection principles outlined in the Act.

Data protection principles

There are eight data protection principles. These are:

1. Personal data shall be obtained and processed fairly and lawfully.
2. Personal data shall be held only for specified purposes.
3. Personal data shall not be used or disclosed in a manner incompatible with the specified purposes.
4. Personal data shall be adequate, relevant and not excessive in relation to purpose.
5. Personal data shall be accurate and where relevant kept up to date.
6. Personal data shall not be kept for longer than necessary.
7. An individual is entitled to be informed where data are held about him or her and is entitled to access to the data and where appropriate to have the data corrected or erased.
8. Appropriate security measures should be taken against unauthorised access, alteration, disclosure or destruction, and against accidental loss or destruction.

Implications for personnel managers

In our research in 1986 we found one organisation that had used a HRIS, but had ceased to do so, partly due to worries about the Data Protection Act. Most organisations, however, felt that the Data Protection Act was going to have little effect on the way that they handled personal data. Bell comments that:

> The most significant part of the legislation for personnel managers concerns the seventh principle – the right of access to personal data by the 'data subject', in this case the employee or the applicant for a job, if details are kept on a computer or word processor.
> (Bell 1984)

It is in this area that personnel managers expressed most concern. Most, though, were happy for individuals to see data about themselves, and in many cases these data had been directly supplied by the individual. There was, however, a distinct tendency not to keep sensitive information on the computer. A few employers expressed concern about occupational health data, as there were occasions, for example, where an employee had a terminal illness, but for good reasons was not told of their condition. If such data were kept on computer, there would be no way to shield the employee from this information. A number commented that appraisal data were deliberately not kept on the system, partly due to the Data Protection Act, but also because it was already their policy to send an individual's computerised details to them each year for verification. Personnel managers often pointed to a locked drawer in their desk as the place where assessment of performance and potential data and succession planning data were kept. The Data Protection Act gives individuals the right to see any expression of opinion about themselves, but not any indication of the intentions of the data user regarding themselves. Although in many organisations appraisal records are 'open', employers are usually less keen to reveal succession planning and employee potential information. There is concern that some information regarding employee potential may be classified as an expression of opinion, and therefore, if kept on the computer, may be viewed by the individual employee. Top executives were omitted from the system in most cases.

Security

Appropriate security is necessary in order to protect both the individual, as outlined in the Act, and to protect the employer. The most common methods are the use of passwords to gain access to the data, careful positioning of VDUs and printers, regular back-up copies and the use of audit trails to log the day's transactions.

The EU Directive relating to paper records

In addition to the Data Protection Act, there was a further Act, the Access to Health Records Act 1992, which allowed employees to view their medical records in *both* computer and paper form. The 1995 Data Protection Directive extends this right to all employee records. The Directive comes into force on 24 October 1998 Aikin (1996) suggests that before that date, wise employers will conduct a thorough audit of existing records and decide which ones need to be kept; draft instructions for staff who will list the purposes for which information is kept; and clarify access and security arrangements for this data. However as the Directive refers to 'structured' personal data only, there is the question of handwritten notes which exist outside a structured filing system. If these are unstructured, handwritten notes or those written on a date basis, in a diary for example, then they are not covered by the Act.

The Act requires that an Information Controller must be appointed within the organisation, who will be responsible for any breaches of the Act, unless they can show otherwise. The Act has a broader coverage than the Data Protection Act in that it covers not only the 'use' of personal data, but also the 'processing' of this, and as such can include collection, recording, alteration, disclosure and erasure, amongst other activities.

Article Six of the Act requires that data be:

▶ processed fairly and lawfully, and ensuring that employees are notified in advance of how the data will be processed,
▶ collected for specified, explicit and legitimate purposes, and processed only in relation to these,
▶ adequate, relevant and not excessive for the purpose,
▶ kept for no longer than necessary.

There are some transitional arrangements, over the following twelve years, for data that were collected prior to 1998.

Individuals will have access to, and the opportunity to correct, all personal data at reasonable intervals, and can claim damages if they have suffered a loss as the result of the Act being breached. For some employers this may encourage further use of, or the introduction of, an HRIS where the reason for recording information on paper only may have been motivated by a desire to withhold sensitive data (such as career potential information) from employees.

WINDOW ON PRACTICE

E-mail is a rapidly growing form of communication, and research in this area, although relatively thin until recently, is steadily growing. Initial work concentrated on e-mail use in relation to the technology, and work concentrated on the barriers to individual e-mail use, such as lack of user involvement, avoidance of change and difficulties in relation to user cognitive style. More recently collective level explanations have been explored (see for example Markus 1994) considering cultural and situational factors and pressure from others. In addition early work concentrated on the characteristics which affected the adoption, use and successful implementation of e-mail. There is a growing trend to consider the **impact** of e-mail use on employee and organisational behaviour.

Sproull and Kiesler (1991) argue that it has social features which distinguish it from other technologies and which can result in a democratising effect. For example, it has the potential to facilitate communication between those at the bottom of the organisation and those at the top, and to enable people at the periphery of the organisation to become more visible. Pliskin *et al.* (1997) studied a 2½-year long strike of academics in Israel where e-mail was used as the medium of communication between the strikers. They found that it enabled unity to develop within the striker group as they were in constant communication, sharing information, jokes and boosting morale. It was also used to distribute offers of practical help, debate issues and as a vehicle through which they consolidated their support of their leadership. In particular it also provided contact between the strike leaders and the strikers (where there is often a communication gap) so that the leaders did not become separate from the strikers. It also facilitated the negotiation process by involving everyone in the debate about what should be done next and what solutions to the strike were acceptable.

Brigham and Corbett (1997) in their study of e-mail in a large UK organisation found that it had an impact on power relations in the organisation. Although some managers stated that it made their job easier, they also felt that it was a mechanism for monitoring their work. An example was given of opening e-mail post – where the sender received not only confirmation of delivery, but of the post being opened and the time it was opened. Some felt inundated by information which they could not use.

Summary propositions

7.1　Too much information can be as bad as too little – the organisation needs to be clear of the purpose for collecting it.

7.2　Personnel information can be seen in four parts – individual employee information; aggregate employee information; information on personnel systems and activities and information on the contribution of the personnel function.

7.3　Personnel information can be used for operational and strategic purposes.

7.4　It is increasingly important to identify the costs and benefits of personnel activities.

7.5 The data protection legislation and the EU Directive relating to paper records provide legal enforcement for good personnel practice in the areas of confidentiality, privacy and security.

References

Aikin, O. (1996) 'Be prepared for a data remember', *People Management*, 30 May.

Behrend, H. (1978) *How to Monitor Absence from Work: From headcount to computer*, London: IPD.

Bell, D. (1984) 'Practical implications of the Data Protection Act', *Personnel Management*, June.

Brigham, M. and Corbett, J. M. (1997) 'E-mail, power and the constitution of organisational reality', *New Technology, Work and Employment*, Vol. 12, No. 1, pp. 25–35.

Broderick, R. and Boudreau, J. W. (1992) 'HRM, IT and competitive advantage', *Academy of Management Executive*, Vol. 6, No. 2, pp. 7–17.

Burn, D. and Thompson, L. (1993) 'When Personnel calls in the Auditors', *Personnel Management*, January.

Callagher, M. (1986) *Computers and Personnel Management*, London: Heinemann.

Cascio, W. F. (1991) *Costing Human Resources*, Boston: PWS Kent Publishing Company.

Fair, H. (1992) *Personnel and Profit*, London: IPM.

Glover, D. (1998) 'Expert systems', in T. Page (ed.), *Computers in Personnel: A generation on*. The CIP 88 Conference Book, London: IPM and IMS.

Hall, L. A. and Torrington, D. P. (1986) 'Why not use the computer? The use and lack of computers in personnel', *Personnel Review*, Vol. 15, No. 8.

Hall, L. A. and Torrington, D. P. (1989) 'How personnel managers come to terms with the computer', *Personnel Review*, Vol. 18, No. 6.

Huczynski, A. A. and Fitzpatrick, M. J. (1989) *Managing Employee Absence for a Competitive Edge*, London: Pitman.

Ive, T. (1982) 'Ready made package or sharing the mainframe?', *Personnel Management*, July.

Kinnie, N. and Arthurs, A. (1993) 'Will personnel people ever learn to love the computer?', *Personnel Management*, June.

Kinnie, N. and Arthurs, A. (1996) 'Personnel specialists' advanced use of information technology – evidence and explanations', *Personnel Review*, Vol. 25, No. 3, pp. 3–19.

Kossek, E. E., Young, W., Gash, D. C. and Nichol, V. (1994) 'Waiting for innovation in the Human Resources Department: Godot implements a human resource information system', *Human Resource Management Journal*, Spring, Vol. 33, No. 1, pp. 135–59.

Markus, M. L. (1994) 'Electronic mail as a medium of choice', *Organisation Science*, Vol. 5, No. 4, pp. 502–27.

Norman, M. and Edwards, T. (1984) *Microcomputers in Personnel*, London: IPM.

Pliskin, N., Romm, C. T. and Markey, R. (1997) 'E-mail as a weapon in an industrial dispute', *New Technology, Work and Employment*, Vol. 12, No. 1, pp. 3–12.

Richards-Carpenter, C. (1996) 'Make a difference by doing IT better', *People Management*, 13 June.

Robertson, D. (1992) 'A Prudent review of data systems', *Personnel Management*, June.

Sproull, L. and Kiesler, S. (1991) *Connections: New ways of working in networked organisations*, Bambridge, Mass: MIT Press.

General discussion topics

1. 'Getting too involved in HRI systems is a dangerous step for the HR professional because it pulls them away from their area of core expertise (people and people systems) which they need to continuously develop and exploit.' Do you agree?
2. Discuss the notion that information is power, and apply this to the specialist personnel function.

CHAPTER 8

Interactive skill: presentation

Every manager makes presentations. It has become an integral part of organisational life, as it may be that some people read the executive summary sheets at the beginning of reports, and some may even read the report itself, but the main mechanism for conveying ideas is the oral presentation. There are two main reasons for this.

First is the change of emphasis in organisation, which we have already considered at some length: the decline of organisation-as-entity with the associated rise of organisation-as-process, and the move away from structure towards culture. Socialisation is valued as a means of creating commitment, and the oral presentation to stimulate discussion is the central method of explanation in order to get everyone on the same wavelength.

Second is the decision-making process. Some managers used to cherish the notion that there was always a correct decision lying hidden somewhere like buried treasure which could be reached either by rigorous analysis or by individual wisdom. Although the elaborate decision-making complexes described in Chapter 5 may eventually come up with the best decision they can, and although individual flair can occasionally reach a decision that is breathtaking in its originality, the critical feature of any decision is not only whether it is 'right', but how effectively it can be implemented. Effective implementation means getting people involved, so that they shape the decision and then own it and make it happen. Presentation is a part of the process of setting a framework within which people can gradually work out the details and commit themselves to action.

Furthermore, having to make a presentation means that at least one person at a meeting is well prepared. Also, all of us in contemporary, television-dominated society are conditioned to respond to the impact of the soundbite and its accompanying projected image.

Personnel managers make presentations in all sorts of situations: induction courses, trade union negotiations, employee consultation, training programmes, explanations of company policy, representation at industrial tribunal, and so forth. We have placed this chapter at this point in the book in order to emphasise the value to the personnel specialist of presentation on aspects of organisation, strategy and planning. Whatever plans you have, someone has got to accept and endorse them, and the personnel dimension to anything can be the hardest on which to win support through the difficulty of backing up a case with hard evidence.

I wish we could get more impact from our personnel people when it comes to meetings of the Board. It is crucial that we get that type of input to the total decision-making process, but time after time they cock it up. The marketing people come in all flash and well-polished. They give you clear and simple messages with state-of-the-art visual aids and lots of impact. The finance people come in and are as miserable as sin, but they explain it with numbers that you can't get away from. The personnel people are woolly, wordy and don't know what they want. What's more, they bang on as if they, and they alone, have some direct line to the Almighty on what is right and wrong, implying that we're just a collection of money-grubbing bastards. (Director of Manfuacturing)

Excellence in presentation is rare, even with the most elaborate of technical and professional assistance. It comes from qualities that by now you either do or do not have, like mastery of language, fluency, disciplined thinking and social poise. Everyone, however, can become effective in presentation, through appreciating some of the basics, through practice and through feedback.

There is little scope for oratory in organisational life, though there are frequent attempts by individual managers to incorporate aspects of propaganda into addresses they make to groups of employees in an attempt to change their attitudes and behaviour.

More common are addresses intended to increase the knowledge and understanding of audience members, such as on a training course or at a sales presentation. This is where few are effective and many are frightened. It is the widespread fear of speaking in public that gives such power to those who seem to have conquered the fear. Considerable self-confidence comes to those who can cope with something that daunts most people they know. Too many managers regard speaking in public as something beyond them:

> Many managers, both male and female, suffer from the delusion that
> speaking in public is the same as a theatrical performance, or something
> suitable only for extroverts. This delusion often serves as a defence. The
> plain truth is that they fear exposure of their limitations as speakers . . . .
> If a man has something worth saying, he should not only say it but also
> learn to say it with full effect. (Bell 1989, p. 46)

There is an old saying that beauty lies in the eye of the beholder: beauty only exists when it is seen and appreciated, so that creating a thing of beauty is creating something that will be seen as beautiful. Everything depends on the reaction of the beholder. Presentation is somewhat similar. Success lies not just in saying the right thing, but in saying it right: what matters is the reaction.

Reverting to the telecommunications analogy in Chapter 6, there may be many different receivers, all of whom have to be kept switched on and tuned in by the speaker. In selection, counselling, appraisal and discipline there is only one receiver; in training there will seldom be more than five or six, and negotiations involve only small groups. Presentation will often involve dozens or hundreds of receivers.

Another important difference between this interaction and others is the length of transmission. There is less scope for two-way traffic than there is in the other situations, yet the multitude of receivers will all be operating at varying levels of efficiency. Some will be working efficiently while others are switched off. Some will be producing a decoding of the transmitted message that is quite different from what is intended. It would be unduly optimistic to say that the speaker should get all the receivers working on the same wavelength in the same way, but that should always be the objective.

This can be illustrated by examples from entertainment. As the performance at a pop concert becomes more frenzied and libidinous nearly all members of the audience will combine in a united response, with postural echoes, hands high above heads, glazed expressions and general ecstasy. Some, however, will react quite differently, sitting silent or inattentive. Even the comedian, getting a steadily rising level of laughter from the audience with every succeeding joke, will never make all the audience laugh.

The speaker in the lecture room, at the shareholders' meeting or at the sales conference will never get everyone's attention, but still needs to win over as many members of the audience as possible. As with other performances there is scope for preparation, rehearsal and careful manipulation of the physical environment to achieve the maximum effect. This is why we place great emphasis on preparation.

Preparing the presentation

Objectives

As with almost every aspect of management, the starting point is the objective. What are you aiming to achieve? What do you want the listeners to do, to think or to feel? Note that the question is not 'What do you want to say?'; the objective is in the response of the listeners. That starting point begins the whole process with a focus on results and pay-off, turning attention away from ego. It also determines tone. If your objective is to inform, you will emphasise facts. If you aim to persuade, you will try to appeal to emotion as well to reason.

The status of the speaker

Are you the right person to deliver this message to this audience? The audience will turn up their receivers if the speaker has authority that fits the message; if not, they will turn off or not even tune in. The main determinant of appropriateness to deliver a message is the credence the audience gives to the speaker's standing and expertise. If they see the speaker as a person with information that will be of use to them, then they will accord the necessary status and listen. If the ensuing presentation disappoints them they will not only become inattentive, they are likely to signal their disillusion with demoralising clarity. Audiences show little compunction about humiliating speakers, who assume authority with all its ritual trappings, such as standing while the audience sits, occupying special, distant space and anticipating their attention.

Another aspect of status is hierarchy. Senior members of organisations are expected to speak on important matters ('We want it from the horse's mouth'). When the level of the message does not match the level of the speaker, there will be mistrust.

At a British Gypsum factory in northwest England the general manager called all the shop stewards together simply to announce that the toilet doors were to be painted white. The reason for this was to cope with a long-running problem with graffiti, but the members of the audience dispersed asking each other what he really meant, as it seemed inconceivable that a person in that position should call them together solely for that reason. A few days later a lowly placed charge-hand announced that the factory was to be closed; the audience would not believe him and demanded corroboration.

Who you are and the position you occupy influences what your audience hear you say. The small exception to this is the way in which those with power can invest it in their close aides, like the Buckingham Palace spokesperson. In informal situations, at least, private secretaries and personal assistants to managing directors speak with considerable authority.

The room

Presentations frequently suffer because the arrangements of the room are designed to facilitate some activity other than the presentation. Speaking after a meal is usually worst, because the arrangements are geared to the serving and consumption of food, rather than paying attention to a presentation. Many of the people will be facing the wrong way and pondering the turmoil in their digestive system rather than listening to the presenter, who will have the additional problem that there is nowhere to put notes and the overhead projector is in the wrong place. The contrast to the carefully staged event is striking:

> In the conference room the trainers are busy adjusting their equipment, making sure their speakers are properly positioned, checking the large screen and playing with the lights. This event requires a level of preparation that would not be unfamiliar to a touring rock band.   (Hopfl 1993, p. 120)

The arrangements of the room affect the quality of the presentation. Eye contact with the audience is essential as a means of control and is made difficult if anyone is too close. The seating is best arranged so that there are approximately the right number of seats. Too many will tend to scatter the members of the audience, making it harder for the speaker to get them to behave like an audience rather than a collection of individuals. Too few seats can have slight advantages, if the presentation is to be quite brief, if the entrance is at the back of the room and there will be few latecomers. To have all seats full and a small number standing can create a lively atmosphere. However, the drawbacks of having too few seats will usually outweigh the advantages. If the audience is quiet, a single latecomer entering on tip-toe with bated breath will attract the attention of everyone, and half of them will exchange knowing smiles with their neighbours. But latecomers seldom enter on tip-toe with bated breath. They usually say 'Sorry I'm late' with a sheepish grin and then mutter something inaudible about the traffic before tripping over somebody's briefcase, while all members of the audience look round to assure themselves that there really isn't any room and commenting on how hot it is.

The position from which to speak is dictated by the arrangements for the audience, but problems that typically curse unprepared speakers are a lack of anywhere to put notes, a distracting background behind the speaker, problems with microphones or some problem with visual aids. Visual aids are referred to shortly, but the problem of the distracting background is not always appreciated. The audience need to look at the speaker so as to concentrate on what they are hearing. Visual aids should embellish the presentation; other visual images will be a distraction. Examples are murals, stained glass windows, blackboards that are not being used or charts on the wall. Speakers who scorn the blackboard because they have a sheaf of acetate sheets to show on the overhead projector often overlook the fact that members of the audience will tend to read what is on the blackboard, even though it was written by someone else the day before.

WINDOW ON PRACTICE

One large company has a lecture room in its training centre that is used for management training sessions. On the wall to one side of the speaker's position is a wall chart of the periodic table of chemical elements. During any session all members of an audience spend some time examining the chart, whether they be chemists making sure they can remember the sequence or non-chemists trying to understand it.

Often there is someone introducing the speaker, and this can be the biggest distraction of all if the person deliberately or accidentally impersonates Eric Morecambe listening to Ernie Wise. If you are in the position of introducing someone else, remember not to yawn, pick your nose or register amused disbelief.

ACTIVITY BOX 8.1

The next time you attend a presentation or listen to a speech given by someone else, study the arrangement of the room and note the changes that you would (and could) make if you were the speaker.

The material

What is to be said or, more accurately, what should members of the audience go away having understood and remembered?

> Organise your material with an introduction that previews, a body that develops, and a conclusion that reviews. When you organize the body of your presentation, start by sorting out the theme. The theme is a planning device that holds together the various ideas you want to discuss. If the theme of your presentation is informative, then the body should provide facts. If the theme is persuasive, the body should develop persuasive arguments.
>
> (Fandt 1994, p. 159)

In the introduction the speaker establishes rapport with the audience. Apart from their attention, the speaker will include here an answer to the unspoken question – is it going to be worth our while listening? A useful introduction is to explain what the members of the audience will know or be able to do at the end. It is also helpful to sketch out the framework of what is to come, so that people can follow it more readily. But stick to what you promise. If you say there are going to be five points, the audience will listen for five to make sure that they have not missed one. In the main body is the message that is to be conveyed, the development of the argument and the build-up of what it is that the audience should go away having understood and remembered. The conclusion is where the main points are reiterated and confirmed in a brief, integrated summary.

The main body will need to be effectively organised. This will not only help members of the audience to maintain attention, it will also discipline the speaker to avoid rambling, distracting irrelevance or forgetting. The most common methods are:

> ▶ Chronological sequence, dealing with issues by taking the audience through a series of events. A presentation to an industrial tribunal often follows this pattern.
> ▶ Known to unknown, or simple to complex. You start either with a brief review of what the audience already knows or can easily understand and then develop to what they do not yet know or cannot yet understand. The logic of this method is to ground the audience in something they can handle so that they can make sense of the unfamiliar. This is the standard method of organising teaching sessions.
> ▶ Problem to solution is almost the exact opposite of simple to complex. A problem is presented and a solution follows. The understanding of the audience is again grounded, but this time grounded in anxiety that the speaker is about to relieve.
> ▶ Comparison is a method of organisation which compares one account with another. Selling usually follows this path, as the new is compared with the old.

Whatever the method of organisation for the material, the main body will always contain a number of key thoughts or ideas. This is what the speaker is trying to plant in the minds of the audience: not just facts, which are inert, but the ideas which facts may well illustrate and clarify. The idea that inflation is dangerously high is only illustrated by the fact that it is at a particular figure in a particular month.

The ideas in a presentation can be helpfully linked together by a device that will help audience members to remember them and to grasp their interdependence. One method is to enshrine the ideas in a story. If the story is recalled, the thoughts are recalled with it, as they are integral to the structure. The classic examples of this are the New Testament parables, but every play, novel or film uses the same method. Another method is to use key words to identify the points that are being made, especially if they have an alliterative or mnemonic feature, like 'People Produce Prosperity'. In a lecture it is common to provide a framework for ideas by using a drawing or system model to show the interconnection of points.

Facts, by giving impact, keep together the framework of ideas that the speaker has assembled. They clarify and give dimension to what is being said. The danger is to use too many, so that the audience are overwhelmed by facts and figures which begin to bemuse them. If the presentation is to be accompanied by a hand-out, facts may be usefully contained in that, so that they can be referred to later, without the audience having to remember them.

Humour is the most dangerous of all aids to the speaker. If the audience laughs at a funny story, the speaker will be encouraged and may feel under less tension, but how tempting to try again and end up 'playing for laughs'. Laughter is a most seductive human reaction, but too many laughs are even more dangerous than too many facts. What will the audience remember – the joke, or what the joke was intended to illustrate? Attempted humour is also dangerous for the ineffective comedian. If you tell what you think is a funny story and no one laughs, you have made a fool of yourself (at least in your own eyes) and risk floundering.

Very few people speak effectively without notes. And although there is a tendency to marvel at those who can, relying solely on memory risks missing something out, getting a fact wrong or drying up completely. Notes follow the pattern of organisation you have established, providing discipline and limiting the tendency to ramble. It is both irritating and unhelpful for members of an audience to cope with a speaker who wanders off down a blind alley, yet this is very common. When an amusing anecdote pops up in your brain, it can be almost irresistible to share it.

There are two basic kinds of notes: headlines or a script. Headlines are probably the most common, with main points underlined and facts listed beneath. Sometimes there will also be a marginal note about an anecdote or other type of illustration. The alternative, the script, enables the speaker to try out the exact wording, phrases and pauses to achieve the greatest effect. The script will benefit from some marking or arrangement that will help you to find your place again as your eyes constantly flick from the page to the audience and back again. This can be underlining or using a highlighter.

There are many variations of these basic methods, so that one approach is to use varying line length, while another is to use rows of dots to indicate pause or emphasis.

Some people like to have their notes on small cards, so that they are unobtrusive, but this is difficult if the notes are more than headlines. Standard A4 paper should present no problem, if the notes are not stapled, are well laid out and can be handled discreetly. Never forget to number the pages or cards, as the next time you speak they may slip off your lap moments before you are due to begin.

The speaker

The final aspect of preparation is to prepare the speaker, who has to bring the notes to life. Rehearsal can help eliminate potential difficulties, but you need to have someone else in to listen and to comment: the mirror is a poor substitute. Only in this way will there be guidance on what is heard and understood, as well as on what is being said. So the first rehearsal check is on the clarity of expression: does it hang together and make sense? The second rehearsal check is on audibility. Occasional speakers often find it difficult to speak loud enough to be heard at the same time as speaking naturally. Also there is a strange tendency to drop the voice at the end of sentences, losing the last few words. Can you be heard, and can you be heard all the time, or do the last few words in every sentence fade away?

Few people avoid stagefright. This is useful up to a point as it keys up the speaker to produce as vivid a performance as possible. Too much stage fright, however, can destroy it. Confidence is essential in getting the audience to listen. Diffidence and nervousness may be engaging qualities in athletes who have just broken a world record or in bridegrooms at wedding receptions, but not for business speakers. It can be reduced by deliberate relaxation, moving consciously a little more slowly than usual and concentrating on the deliberate relaxation of different muscles. There are various ways of relaxing, but some of them require a degree of privacy that may not be feasible. Here are some suggestions, ranging from the simple and discreet to the more elaborate:

▶ Take several long, deep breaths, filling the base of the lungs from the bottom up.

▶ Breathe in to a steady count of three and out to an equally steady count of nine; in to four and out to twelve; in to five and out to fifteen, and so on.

▶ Smile as much as possible before starting, as this will remove traces of an anxious frown and relax facial muscles before confronting the audience. It takes 64 muscles to frown and only 14 to smile.

Making the presentation

Now begins the experience that some people find more frightening than any other: facing the audience. Sometimes the result can be exhilarating; all too frequently it is humiliating. The ritual is of one person asserting authority over others and the speaker cannot avoid that role. Disclaimers, apologies and appeals to the better nature of the audience are of no use as the only reason for the event is that the speaker has some authority that members of the audience respect, and that is the expectation to which you have to rise. The audience that is satisfied will 'applaud' and flatter you in a dozen ways; the dissatisfied audience is merciless.

Rapport

Rapport is a French word (although familiar to most English-speaking personnel specialists) for which there is no English equivalent, meaning to set up some sort of bond or mutual sympathy between people. In presentation it involves presenting yourself before the audience in a way that gets them to perk up and take notice, wanting to hear what you have to say. It does not just happen; you have to **make** it happen.

Appearance is particularly important, not in the sense of best suits or polished shoes, but what the appearance of the speaker says to the audience. The way we present ourselves to others says something of our attitude towards them – we have taken trouble to get ready, or we have not. This may be regarded as the trivia of manners, but virtually everyone works on their appearance in order to feel confident and to create an effect. An audience will scrutinise your appearance closely as they are trapped, with very little else to look at. Do you look prepared and organised? Do you look as if you care what they think? Appearance can also distract. I wonder where she got those earrings? I'm sure he's got odd socks on. That bracelet must have cost a fortune! Is that lapel badge for Round Table or blood donors?

Stance is an expression of authority: you stand, they have to sit. It is not always essential to stand as the organisation of the room will probably give you enough special space to maintain your authority while sitting, but you deny yourself the chance for building up initial confidence slightly if you do not take this opportunity. The speaker's confident manner can make the audience believe that it is all going to be worthwhile. It is not enough, but it helps.

The speaker will also demonstrate and foster contact with the audience and involvement with them. One way is to explain the structure of the presentation, the reasons for it, why the exponent is the person doing it and what the outcome could be for the audience. You need to avoid the risk of creating false hopes, as it is pointless to generate a positive response at the beginning which is let down by what follows, so that the audience leaves disgruntled.

The best method of contact is to look at the audience. This is difficult for inexperienced speakers, who regard the audience as a Hydra-headed monster and dare not look it in the eye, preferring to gaze intently either at their notes, a spot on the floor six inches in front of their feet or the top right-hand corner of the ceiling. Such faint hearts should remember a figure from Greek mythology – the Gorgon, one glance from whom turned the observer to stone. The roles of speaker and listener are so clearly dominant and submissive that people in the audience who see the speaker looking at them will appear interested, stop yawning, sit up straight, stop talking, defer the crossword till later, or whatever other behaviour is consistent with being observed by an authority figure.

The American Evelyn Mayerson, writing at a time when the male gender was still used almost universally in management texts, suggests that there are three significant non-verbal cues that the speaker gives to affect audience response. The first is energy level:

> If he looks as if he needs a lectern to prop him up, he conveys a low energy level. If he seems bursting with vigor, he conveys a high energy level. The freedom with which he turns his head, smiles and moves his hands, the control of the breath as he sends forth his words, his speech volume, his articulation, and his spacing and using all contribute to an image of energy level.
> (Mayerson 1979, p. 183)

Secondly is flexibility of movement and thirdly comes the speaker's warmth and enthusiasm:

> Enthusiasm is contagious. If a speaker wants to convince, he has to believe in the issue himself. His belief helps to get the message across. There is a difference between 'We have to do something about wasted materials' said as the speaker picks lint off his trousers, scans the horizon, stifles a yawn, or scratches his head, and 'We have to do something about wasted materials' said with inflection, pausing, direct eye contact and an erect posture.
> (*ibid.*, p. 184)

Do not start by telling a joke unless you are absolutely sure you can get the audience to laugh and that the joke will contribute to, rather than distract from, your message. If you are planning to start by saying, 'My wife (husband, brother, mother, sister) said I should stop boring if I did not strike oil in the first fifteen minutes,' think again.

Preview

After you have won over the audience, so that they are eating out of the palm of your hand, you give them a preview. Think of this as an agenda, or as the trailer of a film. You are summarising what is to come, so that the listeners have a framework into which they can fit what they are about to hear.

Development

The form of development is predetermined by the preparation that has been made: the number of ideas, the relevant facts, the illustrations, and so on. It is now that the value of that preparation is felt. Do not, however, fall into the trap of thinking that your opening funny story, with eye contact and a list of points to be covered is all the 'performance' that is required. Audience attention and involvement has to be sustained through the manner of the exposition:

> interest and motivation should be sustained throughout by the use of material or examples which are intrinsically interesting to the audience, dramatic, or simply funny. Concrete examples and stories make the material easier to assimilate, and should be subordinated to the main argument.
>
> (Argyle 1972, p. 209)

It is important not to attempt too much, as listeners cannot process as much information as readers can. Reverting to the comments at the opening of this chapter, the predisposition towards listening to a presentation instead of reading a report appears to show a preference for the quick and easy rather than for the thorough.

> Most people cannot easily comprehend more than three to five main points in a speech. This doesn't mean that you say three things and sit down. It means that you should group your complex ideas into three to five major areas and select supporting visuals that will reinforce your main points.
>
> (Fandt 1994, p. 164)

Voice

The voice is the means by which the material is transmitted and the quality of the voice usage will govern what is heard and understood. Try to speak with expression and enthusiasm, remembering inflection and pace.

Inflection refers to the variations in volume and in pitch which give your words expressiveness. Volume is easy to understand, but pitch is less obvious. It describes the range between a squeak and a growl. A low-pitched voice can well express solemnity, while a high-pitched voice is more expressive of excitement.

Pace describes the speed at which you speak. Most inexperienced presenters speak too fast, mainly because of nervousness, so that what they say comes out as a gabble. Those who speak too slowly are likely to bore their audience, who feel that they could cope with things coming at them rather more briskly. Also, the speaking goes on for a much longer period without interruption than in normal conversation, so that the speaker needs a slower pace to permit breathing and thinking. There is still the need to vary pace to provide selective emphasis. As ever the key is to get the right pace, and to vary that pace. A good example is to listen to a commentary on a race, where both pace and pitch rise as the race proceeds. Among the ways of getting pace right are:

- Immediately before starting take a few deep breaths.
- Don't start too quickly, and look across the audience for a moment or two first.
- Use pauses and sometimes additional emphasis to mark a change in direction, to separate stages in the presentation and when using key terms.

Pauses help by enabling breathing and emphasis and aiding audience comprehension. They also help to eliminate the nonsense words or 'verbal pauses' that frequently occur as someone is speaking: 'you know', 'as it were', 'at the end of the day', 'um', 'by and large', 'right' and 'OK' being some of the most common. The reason for this type of distracting interjection is that the flow of ideas and the operation of the tongue are not correctly synchronised, so that contentless words and sounds are produced occasionally to fill the void that the brain has momentarily left. Practice can replace nonsense words with pauses, which are better for the audience and for the speaker.

At all times keep the presentation slow enough to be understood, but fast enough to keep the audience on their toes.

All speakers seem to have a natural tendency for volume to drop at the end of sentences, partly because they are running out of breath. In trying to overcome this difficulty there is the risk of becoming monotonous, as everything is on the same level, without any appropriate reference to the meaning of the words being spoken.

Visual aids

We remember what we see for longer than we remember what we are told, and we can sometimes understand what we see better than we can understand what we hear. This is the rationale for the use of whiteboards, flip charts, overhead projectors, powerpoint slides, films, television, working models and experiments. They are, however, aids to, and not substitutes for, the presentation. Too much displayed material can obscure rather than illuminate what is being said. Television news provides a good example of how much can be used. The dominant theme is always the talking head with frequently intercut pieces of film. Very seldom do words appear on the screen and then usually as extracts from a speech or report, where a short sentence or passage is regarded as being especially meaningful. The other way in which words and numbers appear is when facts are needed to illustrate an idea, so that ideas like football scores or a change in the value of the pound sterling almost always have the figures shown on the screen to clarify and illustrate. Seldom, however, will more than two or three numbers be displayed at the same time.

Recently presentation has been made much smarter by the development of computer packages like POWERPOINT. This is basically a way of organising material to project, either through a computerised system, or as masters for the overhead projector. It is, however, much more comprehensive, as it suggests how to make the presentation and helps with such things as speaker's notes and hand-outs.

Speakers need to remember the size of what they are displaying as well as its complexity. Material has to be big enough for people to read and simple enough for them to follow. Material also has to be timed to coincide with what is being said. Where a speaker is using a display with quite a lot of information, it may be sensible to mask it and reveal one section at a time as the exposition proceeds, so that some members of the audience do not move on to a part of the diagram or table that has not yet been explained and that they do not yet understand. Equally, do not leave on an overhead projector an illustration of something from which you have moved on. The audience will be drawn to the powerful, projected image rather than to what you are saying.

Make sure you are familiar with the equipment before you start. If using a flip-chart or whiteboard, ensure that there are pens of the right sort, which have not dried up. If there is a blackboard, clean it. If there is an overhead projector, make sure it is plugged in, that you know how to switch it on and that the bulb has not blown. Then check that the glass is clean (toilet tissue is good for this) so that the image is sharp and that the size and focus of the display is correct.

Hand-outs

It is a common and helpful practice to prepare a hand-out to accompany the presentation. A typed synopsis of what has been said, or a copy of a diagram that has been displayed, can be helpful in reinforcement, but may reduce the level of concentration during the presentation itself. The hand-out should not duplicate the presentation or make it irrelevant. Issued beforehand, like a long report, it can form the basis of a presentation that is pointing up or adding to the main points. Issued afterwards, it can reiterate factual details and summarise the main points of the presentation.

Language

Language needs to be what the audience will understand. The larger and more heterogeneous the audience, the more difficult for the speaker to cover that wide range of capacities. Marks (1980, pp. 54–60) has some helpful advice on this and points out how easy it is for professionals to slip into jargon that can puzzle many people, like the marketing manager to whom everything is a mix and the personnel manager to whom everything is a package. Few things can antagonise an audience more than the feeling that the speaker is trying to impress them with cleverness rather than putting the message over.

Closing

At the end, the speaker summarises the points that have been made, reinforces them and leads the audience to some sort of follow-up action. That action may often be no more than to remember something of what has been heard, or to feel reassured, but it is the closing that will lead to the action. The speaker has to avoid an anti-climax, which can be caused by signalling the end too clearly: 'Let me sum up what I have been trying to say. . .'. That both indicates that there is nothing new and confirms the view of the audience that it has not been well done. Instead the exponent aims for a climax – a positive close. Among the ways to do this are telling a story, which brings together and illustrates the points that have been made; raising rhetorical questions to which members of the audience can now see answers where they could not at the beginning; and a straightforward statement which shows the interrelationship of points made earlier.

Pitfalls

The inexperienced speaker should guard against some of the more common pitfalls, one of which is apology. If members of the audience are disciplining themselves to sit still and listen, it will not make them more responsive if you start by telling them of your incompetence. Your best hope is to try to conceal it, rather than emphasise it. Shortly after a serious airport disaster, a fire officer addressed a press conference with the opening, 'I cannot promise you that I have expert knowledge on this subject, so perhaps I may share with you some of my own confusion.'

All of us can recall situations in which a speaker's mannerisms distracted us from what was being said. They are a form of displacement activity and should not be restrained to the point of making the presentation wooden or stilted, but can be modified to avoid too much distraction. A common mannerism is walking about. In moderation this provides a mild variation in scene, but some of the more distracting variations are the walks that follow a precise, oft-repeated path to and fro, or those that include little flourishes like a slow motion, modified goosestep. Standing still can be little better if it is accompanied by the act of balancing on the outside edges of one's shoes or using a toe to sketch, with great care and precision, a cross or triangle in the imaginary dust on the floor.

Some people reserve for their public speeches a minute examination of their fingernails or a series of isometric exercises to relieve muscular aches in their shoulders. Rings and bracelets are frequently played with incessantly, but the greatest distractor of all is probably the pair of spectacles that goes on, comes off, gets folded and put away, only to be taken out, unfolded, put on. . . .

Some speakers lose their audience by not stopping when they have finished, rambling from one anti-climactic afterthought to another as the audience chafes because the coffee will be getting cold. When you have said, 'And finally . . .' you have no more than two minutes left. If you follow this with 'To conclude . . .' and later, 'As a last word . . .' and later still, 'And this really is my last word . . .' you may excite sufficient wrath in the audience for them to start throwing things.

Summary propositions

8.1   Oral presentation is a central skill for all managers; personnel managers have to make presentations in a wider variety of situations than most of their managerial colleagues.

8.2   The key aspects of preparation are: objectives, the status of the speaker, preparation of the room, organising the material, preparing oneself.

8.3   The key features of the presentation itself are: rapport, preview, development, the use of the voice, visual aids, hand-outs, language, closing and avoiding pitfalls.

References

Argyle, M. (1972) *The Psychology of Interpersonal Behaviour*, London: Pelican.
Bell, G. (1989) *Speaking and Business Presentations*, London: Heinemann.
Fandt, P. M. (1994) *Management Skills: Practice and experience*, St Paul, Minn.: West Publishing.
Hopfl, H. (1993) 'Culture and commitment: British Airways', in D. Gowler, K. Legge and C. Clegg (eds.), *Case Studies in Organizational Behaviour and Human Resource Management*, London: Paul Chapman Publishing.

Marks, W. (1980) *How to Give a Speech*, London: IPM.
Mayerson, E. W. (1979) *Shoptalk*, Philadelphia: W. B. Saunders.

Practical exercises in presentation

1. When attending a presentation or listening to a speech given by someone else, study the arrangement of the room and note the changes that you would (and could) make if you were the speaker. Why have you done that?
2. Obtain from your library a book or audio cassette of speeches made by an effective orator, such as Winston Churchill, Billy Graham, John Kennedy or Martin Luther King, and make notes of the plan of their material.
3. Prepare a five-minute speech on one of these topics:
   (a) Music
   (b) Health and fitness
   (c) Your favourite sport
   (d) Your hobby
   (e) Your first boyfriend/girlfriend.
   After preparation, deliver the speech in an empty room (the garage would do) and record (audio) it. Play it back several times, making critical notes of energy level, voice, pace, pauses, etc., following the points in the chapter, then deliver the speech again whilst making a recording.

▶ In what ways is it better?
▶ In what ways not as good?
▶ What have you learned about the way you speak?
▶ What can you still improve?

If you can move on to video-recording, the benefits of the exercise is greater, but it is wise to start with audio recording and probably better not to video-record for a wider audience than yourself. Group discussion of video-recorded presentations can be very inhibiting.

Case study problem

Setting up a call centre

Recently there has been a dramatic growth in the number of call centres. These are large groups of staff gathered together at a centre to deal with much, if not all, of the dealings between the business and its customers. This development is made possible by advances in telecommunications and is made necessary to overcome many of the inefficiencies and delays that come from having to rely mainly on communication by post. Typically the call centre is geographically remote from the rest of the business. Often this is to avoid the high labour costs of southeast England, but there is also a view that regional accents are more acceptable to customers than those from the southeast.

One of the earliest call centres was Direct Line Insurance, which sold policies by telephone, reducing the need for personal, face-to-face discussion with customers. This produced economies of scale and reduced charges, which generated very successful business. Another example was Littlewoods Mail Order, where the well-established routine was for agents to have a catalogue and sell to their friends from the catalogue and then send in a postal order form. The practice developed of the order being 'phoned in, instead of posted. Both these developments, and the many others that have followed, required well-trained staff, who can deal with a wide range of enquiries and issues in a manner that will induce the uncertain customer to buy and persuade the dissatisfied customer that something will be done.

The majority of staff are female and it is increasingly an area of graduate employment as a preliminary to seeking greater responsibility.

You have to set up the staffing and organisation of a new call centre that is to operate on a seven-day week, open to telephone callers from 08.00 to 22.00 daily. The centre is to handle a new range of financial services products and the business plan calls for a minimum of 120 operators to be available at all times. From 10.00 to 17.00, 200 need to be available, and 350 are needed from 17.00 to 21.00.

The majority of the work will be selling in direct response to customer calls, where the operator will sell the product, but then arrange for the necessary follow-up: information and/or communication through the post, the raising of an invoice, a return call by someone with specialist expertise, checking of customer references prior to confirmation, a follow-up call in one week by the operator, and so on.

There will also be some cold calling by other staff, as well as the management and supervision of the administrative system and financial control.

Required

You now have to set up the centre, starting with the following questions:

1. What number of operative staff will you require to meet the staffing levels needed?
2. How will you organise the shift rotas for maximum effectiveness?
3. What mix will you aim for of full-time and part-time staff?
4. What type of organisational structure will you need to produce effective co-ordination of, and communication between, the numbers of staff you have identified in answer to questions 2 and 3?
5. How do you overcome the problems of communication that are likely to arise when people spend their working day in the 'blinkered' workplace of headset and computer terminal?
6. How will you develop an organisational culture to overcome the potential for this sort of work to become alienating in the same way as many mass-production operations in manufacturing?

Part II Examination questions

Undergraduate introductory

1. Explain the thinking behind the statement by Alfred Chandler that structure follows strategy.
2. Explain the telecommunications analogy and how it helps you to understand what happens in organisations.

Undergraduate finals

3. Of the four organisational forms identified (Entrepreneurial, Bureaucratic, Matrix and Independence) what would be the problems facing a firm moving from one form to one of the other forms? Explain which change you are discussing.
4. Evaluate the typical problems facing personnel managers in trying to organise effective communication in businesses. How can these problems be overcome?

Masters

5. 'Consumption is more important than work for modern identity.' Discuss.
6. Critically appraise the current role of the personnel specialist in the area of HR planning and information systems.

Professional

7. 'Giving feedback lies at the heart of coaching and mentoring, and it should also feature in all managers' informal day-to-day working contacts with their staff,' writes Alan Fowler (*People Management*). Why is giving feedback so difficult? What do's and don'ts advice would you give to a manager who seeks your help on two matters: (a) the effective use of feedback as a motivational tool for the encouragement of good performers; (b) how feedback may be constructively deployed in remedial scenarios where poor performance is linked to abrasive and uncooperative behaviour?
8. What are the key criteria for assessing the effectiveness of a personnel information system?

PART III
Resourcing

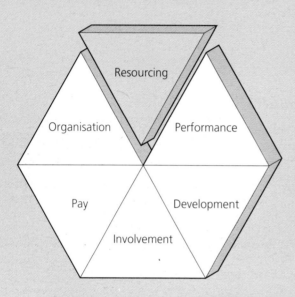

The first major activity of the personnel specialist is to find and bring in the people that the business needs for its success. The people may not be employees – they may be consultants or subcontractors. They may be temporary, full-time, part-time or occasional, and the working relationship between the business and its people is the contract, which sums up the features of that relationship so that both parties know where they stand. Nearly always there is a face-to-face meeting between the parties to agree terms before the relationship begins. The process of 'coming to terms' is one of mutual appraisal. Many prospective employees reject a prospective employer by deciding not to apply for a post, or by discontinuing their application. Employers always choose between many – and often feel there are too few applicants. Contracts end as well as begin, and we have to be sure that the arrangements to end the contract are as sound as those for it to start.

Strategic aspects of resourcing

'Angela's leaving – quick we must make sure to get the ad in this month's journal.' 'It's hopeless – they all leave just as soon as we've trained them. What's the point?' 'It's not my fault – we just can't get the staff. No wonder quality is so poor.' 'That's it. The results are so bad we'll have to let some of them go. Tony, draw up a shortlist of possibles and we'll try and get it sorted this week.'

All too often employee resourcing is a reactive activity, with the absence of any link to organisational strategy and a lack of internal coherence. In order to bridge this gap we suggest the consideration of a range of aspects which together can form the framework for a resourcing strategy that can facilitate the future direction of the organisation. Each of these aspects offers choices for the organisation. We first consider the organisation's response to the resourcing environment, and then look at some different approaches to flexible resourcing. We review the choice to recruit experienced staff or home-grow them, the choice to target specific skills or groups, and the choice of appropriate levels of turnover for the organistion. Finally, we take a strategic view of resourcing roles in the organisation.

Responding to external labour markets and demographics

There are four major issues facing employers in the 1990s in relation to the external labour market.

Labour shortages

In 1971 there were around 900,000 live births in the United Kingdom. By 1977, it was below 700,000 and has since failed to reach 800,000 per annum. Thus, although the workforce is still growing, the extra numbers are in the middle and older age groups rather than among the young. The late 1990s are likely to be characterised by labour shortages, an underlying problem which has been so far been masked by the recession. The joker in the pack on this question may well be the effect of the single European market. If some forecasts are proved correct (for example, Rajan 1990), the United Kingdom could suffer substantial job losses in the early years of the single market.

Age composition

By the year 2000 there will be about 2.3 million more people aged between 25 and 64 in the labour force than there are now, and about 1.3 million fewer aged under 25. The result is a growing workforce of which a higher proportion is older than now. Employers who rely on young people in certain jobs, or as trainees for specific career plans, will experience particular problems. However, it is likely that the majority of employers will be forced to review policy as regards the preferred age of new recruits.

Sex composition

As a result of the decline in population growth, employers will have to rely more on increasing the readiness of individuals to work. Current civilian activity rates (the proportion of the population in or seeking work) are expected to continue their trend of recent years, which means that while male activity rates decline, female rates will continue to increase. So marked are these effects that almost all (90 per cent) of the expected increase in labour supply to 2000 is among women. By 2000, women will comprise 44 per cent of the labour force. The ability of employers to attract female recruits may well depend on provision of facilities such as crèches, training for returners and career-breaks.

Skill shortage

Demand for labour in manual and unskilled jobs is expected to continue to contract during the 1990s. The growth in demand for labour will therefore be concentrated among the higher skilled occupations, and in particular among professional, scientific and technical occupations (Figure 9.1).

University graduates are the main source of supply for these higher skilled occupations, but higher education is also influenced by demographic factors and

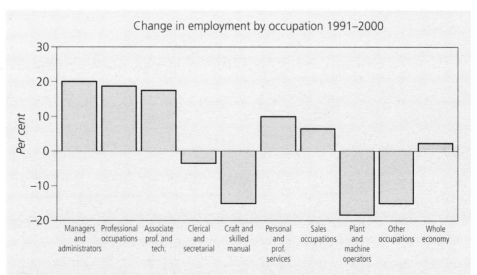

Figure 9.1 Predictions of labour market demands (Institute for Employment Research 1993). Used with permission of the Institute for Employment Research.

the need to compete with employers anxious to recruit 'A' level school-leavers. While demand for graduates generally is up, there is a particular need for two specific types: the technologist, required by the electronic, electrical engineering and computing sectors; and the high-flyer, increasingly sought to meet the long-term needs of senior management. Many employers are attempting to solve their problems by broadening the entry requirements, so that now nearly half the vacancies currently advertised are open to all graduates.

There is some evidence to suggest that so far as these highly qualified staff and new graduates are concerned, eventually the implementation of the single European market will produce a net worsening of supply in the United Kingdom as more potential recruits seek employment overseas (Pearson and Pike 1989). This anticipated trend has so far been held back by practical difficulties in arranging European employment such as the differences required in vocational qualifications, difficulties in transfer of pension rights and more general factors such as housing and children's education issues. This potential worsening of our supply of well-qualified staff may not be offset by the predicted UK job losses, as jobs lost are more likely to be those at a lower level in the organisation.

A planned response to demographic change

Overall, these demographic and labour supply factors are certain to cause a tightening of labour markets in all parts of the country. However, what may well exacerbate the situation is the failure of employers to devise and implement suitable responses. John Atkinson has suggested a sequential response by firms to the predicted demographic downturn (Figure 9.2) and notes that:

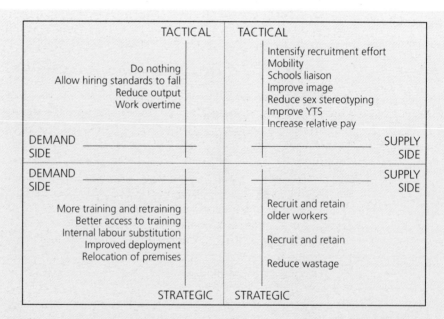

Figure 9.2 Employer's response to shortages (Atkinson 1989, p. 23). Used with permission of the author.

This shows the most likely types of response and the sequence in which they will be introduced. It suggests that we will see a progression from the tactical towards more strategic responses, and towards an external labour market (supply side) perspective, back to an internal one (demand side). It suggests that firms will progress from doing little or nothing, through competing for available labour, to identifying substitutes for it, ending with the improved deployment and performance of the existing workforce.

(Atkinson 1989, p. 22)

Awareness of labour market changes, although masked at present, can have an impact on current as well as future resourcing strategies. For example, when Ilford were seeking to reduce the size of their current workforce they considered lowering the company retirement age. Although this option had many immediate benefits it was dismissed as it would cause severe problems in the longer term.

Flexible resourcing choices

In Chapter 2 we noted that flexibility was identified as one of the main planks of human resource strategy (see for example, Guest 1989). We now consider how this may influence resourcing strategy. Organisations have choices in achieving numerical flexibility, temporal flexibility and in how they balance these two aspects. (Other aspects of flexibility – functional and pay – are discussed in Chapters 2 and 31, respectively.)

Numerical flexibility

Numerical flexibility allows the organisation to respond quickly to the environment in terms of the numbers of people employed. This is achieved by using alternatives to traditional full-time, permanent employees. The use, for example, of short-term contract staff, staff with rolling contracts, staff on short-term, government-supported training schemes, outworkers, and so on, enable the organisation to reduce or expand the workforce quickly and cheaply.

Atkinson is one of a number of commentators who has described the way in which firms may develop flexibility in their approach to employment, as shown in Figure 9.3. The flexible firm in this analysis has a variety of ways of meeting the need for human resources. First are core employees, who form the primary labour market. They are highly regarded by the employer, well-paid and involved in those activities that are unique to the firm or give it a distinctive character. These employees have improved career prospects and offer the type of flexibility to the employer that is so prized in the skilled craftsworker who does not adhere rigidly to customary protective working practices.

There are then two peripheral groups: First, those who have skills that are needed but not specific to the particular firm, like typing and word processing. The strategy for these posts is to rely on the external labour market to a much greater extent, to specify a narrow range of tasks without career prospects, so that the employee has a job but not a career. This is a further development of the labour process described by Braverman (1974). Some employees may be able to transfer to core posts, but generally limited scope is likely to maintain a fairly high turnover, so that adjustments to the vagaries of the product market are eased.

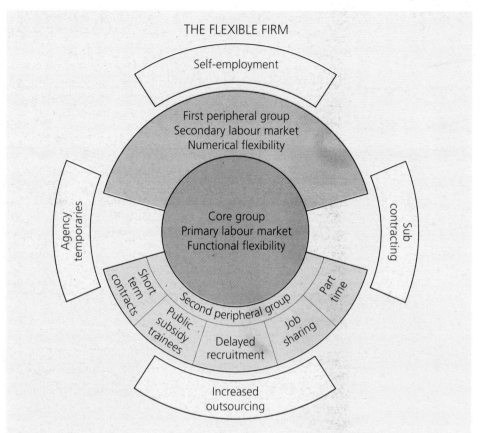

Figure 9.3 Atkinson's model of the flexible firm (from Atkinson 1984). Used with permission of the authors.

The second peripheral group is made up of those enjoying even less security, as they have contracts of employment that are limited, either to a short-term or to a part-time attachment. There may also be a few job sharers and many participants on government training schemes find themselves in this category. An alternative or additional means towards this flexibility is to contract out the work that has to be done, either by employing temporary personnel from agencies or by the entire operation, as subcontracting.

As we saw in the chapter on organisation structure, a slightly different version of the peripheral workforce is the way in which the organisation boundary may be adjusted by redefining what is to be done in-house and what is to be contracted out to various suppliers.

Temporal flexibility

This type of flexibility concerns varying the pattern of hours worked in order to respond to business demands and employee needs. Moves away from the 9–5, 38-hour week include the use of annual hours contracts, increased use of part-time work, job-sharing and flexible working hours. For example, an organisation subject to peaks and troughs of demand (such as an icecream manufacturer) could use annual hours contracts so that more employee hours are available at peak periods and less are used when business is slow. Flextime systems can benefit the employer by providing employee cover outside the 9–5 day and over lunchtimes, and can also provide employee benefits by allowing personal demands to be fitted more easily around work demands. Blyton and Morris (1992) also note the opportunity that temporal flexibility offers to improve the utilisation of staff. Evidence suggests that the use of annual hours contracts is increasing, and an IPM survey in 1993 found that 60 per cent of employers using this type of contract had introduced the scheme since 1989 (Hutchinson 1993a).

WINDOW ON PRACTICE

Welsh Water introduced a pilot scheme for annual hours contracts in 1991 (Hutchinson 1993b) and found they produced a range of benefits which included a firmer control over overtime, less need for temporary contract labour, increased output, improved management control, reduced absence and a more flexible, co-operative and committed workforce. Since the pilot scheme was introduced they have found that other employees are pressing to be included in the system.

Gall (1996) found in his research in forty-nine organisations that annual hours contracts were used most often to 'promote work practice changes', and were often introduced as part of a larger package of measures. Other reasons for introduction were to reduce overtime or special payments; due to variable/ seasonal demand and to reduce the working week. He found that organisations had experienced problems due to the complexity of designing the system; working out the pay due and sometimes in paying for hours that were not worked. Some organisations had experimented with annual hours but had reverted to traditional systems.

Flexibility: rhetoric and reality

Flexibility has been identified as a key characteristic of an HRM approach, as distinct from a personnel approach to the management of people in the organisation (see, for example, Guest 1987; Legge 1989; and Storey 1989). It has also been identified as a competitive response to the rapidly changing business environment. There has been a continuing debate as to whether Atkinson's model of core and periphery was a description of trends or a prescription for the future. Pollert (1991) and Atkinson and Meager (1986) found the use of such approaches to be *ad hoc* rather than strategic. Legge (1995) concludes that the empirical evidence suggests that flexibility is used in a pragmatic and opportunistic way rather than as a strategic HRM initiative. Hakim (1990) found few firms explicitly pursuing a core/periphery strategy, and Blyton and Turnbull (1992) suggest that empirical studies demonstrate a gap between the rhetoric and the reality of flexibility. In characterising the difference between the approach to flexibility which has generally been found and the potential for a long-term strategic approach, Boyer (1988) categorises flexibility as either defensive, when pursued on an *ad hoc* basis, and offensive when part of an explicit strategy. In a similar vein Rojot (1989) distinguishes between a short-term approach to flexibility which was likely to emphasise numerical flexibility and long-term approaches which were more likely to involve functional flexibility. In our recent research we found much evidence of numerical flexibility which was generally adopted in a reactive and opportunistic way. Of the twenty interview respondents with whom we discussed flexibility, seventeen were able to give examples of flexible resourcing, and the emphasis was on the use of short-term contract and temporary staff. There was no strategic view of the future intended shape of the organisation, and flexible practices were adopted due to operational demands such as cost-cutting, the introduction of computerisation, seasonal business demands, no-redundancy policies and the inability to recruit the desired full-time permanent staff. Only a small amount of functional flexibility was reported and only two organisations had a strategic approach to this.

WINDOW ON PRACTICE

Tuselmann (1996) argues that a high degree of interdependence exists between the different forms of flexibility, that there are costs and benefits of each, and that organisations choose an optimal mix dependent on their market conditions and the country in which they operate. He suggests that a high degree of functional flexibility may be generally inconsistent with a high degree of numerical or financial flexibility. It has been argued that whilst Britain pursues numerical flexibility, in an unregulated and decentralised labour market, there is a greater emphasis in other parts of Europe on functional flexibilty. In particular Germany has successfully followed this route within a high regulatory framework and high degree of centralisation and industrial relations consensus. Tuselmann notes that this framework also constrains their pursuit of numerical, temporal

and financial flexibility, and that as Germany experiences increasing competitive pressures, their model of labour flexibility is at a crossroads.

There are other balances in resourcing strategy that can be addressed, for example the balance between numbers of permanent staff employed and the hours that each employee works. In November 1993 Volkswagen in Germany announced that in their current poor financial situation they were employing too many people. In order to avoid redundancies they agreed with the workforce that hours would be reduced by 20 per cent so that they worked a four day week, and that wages would be reduced by 10 per cent. There is a good deal of emphasis in Europe on reducing the working week to help reduce redundancies, unemployment and absence levels, and to improve family life.

ACTIVITY BOX 9.1

What evidence can you find in your organisation to support a more flexible approach to resourcing?

What were the driving forces behind these changes ?

How have employees responded and why?

Ready-made or home-grown

Organisations have a choice whether to depend extensively on the talent available in the external labour market or to invest heavily in training and development and career systems to exploit the potential in the internal labour market.

Some organisations thrive on high levels of turnover, while others thrive on the development of employees which remain with the organisation in the long term. The emphasis on either approach, or a balance between the two, can be chosen to support organisational strategy.

Sonnenfield *et al.* (1992) propose a model which relates entry and exit of staff with promotion and development of staff in the organisation. One axis of the model is supply flow. They argue that, strategically, organisations that focus on internal supply tend to see people as assets with a long-term development value rather than costs in terms of annual expenditure. The other axis is labelled the assignment flow, which describes the basis on which individuals are assigned new tasks in the organisation. The criteria for allocation may be in terms of individual contribution to organisational performance, or on group contribution which Sonnenfield *et al.* identify as factors such as loyalty, length of service and support of others. They argue that, strategically, organisations that emphasise individual contribution expect individuals to provide value on a continuous basis, whereas those that emphasise group contribution see employees as having intrinsic value.

The model proposed describes the combination of these two aspects of resourcing and results in four typical 'career systems' as shown in Figure 9.4. In

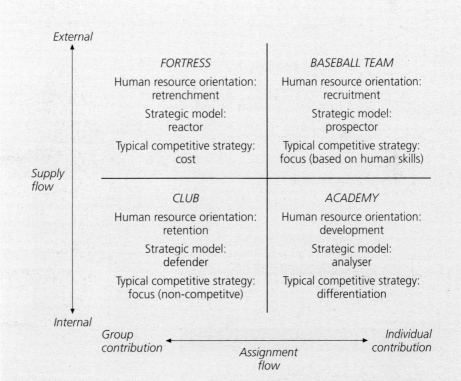

Figure 9.4 A typology of career systems (Sonnenfield *et al.* 1992), in 'Strategic determinants of managerial labour markets', *Human Resource Management* 27 (4). Copyright © John Wiley and Sons, Inc. Used with permission of John Wiley and Sons, Inc.

each box alongside the career system label (academy, club, baseball team and fortress) Sonnenfield *et al.* identify the strategic organisation model and the competitive strategy which are most likely to drive each career system. They also identify the likely orientation of the personnel function.

In this chapter we are concerned with the characteristics of the career systems which are as follows:

Academies

In academies there is a heavy emphasis on individual contribution, in terms of reward and promotion. They are characterised by stability and low turnover of staff with many employees remaining until retirement. There is an emphasis on development and often competitions for promotion and barriers to leaving the organisation. Examples of typical industries where academies operate are pharmaceuticals and automobiles.

Clubs

Again there is a heavy emphasis on the internal labour market, but promotion is more likely to be based on loyalty, length of service, seniority and equality rather than individual contribution. There is an emphasis on staff retention. Sectors where this is likely to operate include public bodies, although the introduction of competitive forces will mean that a different career system may be appropriate.

Baseball teams

These organisations use external labour sources at all levels to seek the highest contributors. There is an emphasis on recruitment to maintain staffing levels. Employees will tend to identify with their profession rather than the organisation, and examples given are advertising, accountancy and legal firms.

Fortresses

These organisations are concerned with survival and cannot afford to be concerned with individuals, either in terms of reward or promotion. They are more likely to depend on external recruitment, often for generalists who meet the needs of a retrenchment or turnaround situation. Examples given are publishing, retailing and the hotel sector.

ACTIVITY BOX 9.2

▶ Which of the four career systems in the Sonnenfield *et al.* model typifies your organisation?
▶ What characteristics lead you to this conclusion?
▶ How does this career systems strategy fit with your organisational strategy and organisational mission (either explicitly stated or implicit)?

From this discussion it is clear that the balance between retention and turnover is not just a cost factor but also a critical factor in relating human resource strategy to organisational strategy. Some writers, for example Cann (1993), argue that high turnover levels need not be associated with low training and development levels, and that reasonable levels of turnover are helpful for some industries in terms of distributing skills.

We shall return to the career system model in Chapter 21 on strategic aspects of development.

Targeting specific competencies

The use of tight job descriptions prepared for recruitment purposes has been questioned in a climate of rapid and constant change (see, for example, Evenden 1993). Although job descriptions remain of value, the way that they are defined is changing to allow more flexibility within a given job and to describe outputs rather than inputs. The emphasis is moving to the person specification, not necessarily restricted to the initial job, but with a focus on qualities and attributes that fit with the strategic direction and culture of the organisation.

WINDOW ON PRACTICE

A large and previously successful manufacturing organisation needed to change from its bureaucratic approach in order to remain competitive in a tougher marketplace. The organisation decided that it wanted employees to have a 'can do' attitude; be prepared to try something new and difficult; focus on ends, not means; have a flexible approach to their job; admit their mistakes and learn from them.

This vision of the future clearly had implications for the culture of the organisation and also for the characteristics that would be sought in individuals who were recruited and promoted.

Purcell (1992) suggests how employee characteristics and resourcing emphasis can be matched to the strategic position of the organisation in terms of the Boston matrix. For **wildcat** organisations he suggests that employees need to be willing and able to work in a variety of areas with broad skills. For **star** organisations he suggests a high degree of individualism is required with careful recruitment and selection to employ the best. **Cash cow** organisations, he suggests, need order and stability, and this may result in overmanning in a comfortable organisation. In this type of organisation there may be more encouragement to recruit employees who will not 'rock the boat'. Finally in **dog** organisations he suggests the emphasis will be on reducing surplus labour rather than recruitment in order to enable cost reductions.

Writing from the perspective of differentiated reward structures for chief executives, Miller and Norburn (1981) identify the characteristics of a Chief Executive which would match the prevailing business strategy, as shown in Table 9.1. This gives a clear indication of the competencies required for the external recruitment or promotion to the position of Chief Executive in each strategic situation.

Table 9.1 Matching managers to strategy (Miller and Norburn 1981, p. 24). Reproduced with permission of Braybrooke Press Ltd.

The objective of the business	The main business activities	The chief executive should be
Growth	1. Pursuit of increased *market share* 2. Earnings generation *subordinate* to building dominant position 3. Focus on *longer-term* results 4. Emphasis on *technical innovation* and market development	A. *Young*, ambitious, aggressive B. Strong development and growth potential C. High tolerance for *risk-taking* D. Highly *competitive* by nature
Earnings	1. Pursuit of *maximum earnings* 2. Balanced focus on *short-range/long-range* 3. Emphasis on complex analysis and clearly articulated *plans* 4. Emphasis on increased *productivity*, cost improvements, strategic pricing	A. *Tolerates* risk, but doesn't seek it B. Comfortable with variety and flexibility C. *Careful* but not conservative D. *Trade-off* artist; short/long, risk/reward
Cash flow	1. Pursuit of maximum positive *cash flow* 2. Sell off market share to *maximise* profitability 3. Intensive *pruning* of less profitable product/market segments 4. Intensive *short-range* emphasis/minimise 'futures' activities	A. *Seasoned* and experienced B. Places high premium on *efficiency* C. High tolerance for stability, no change for sake of it D. *Not* a dreamer, turned on by results *now*

Strategic resourcing roles

Increasingly, a strategic view is being taken of how resourcing roles are allocated. The traditional view of a heavy involvement of the personnel function in order to provide consistency and expertise is being challenged. There is a shift to greater line manager involvement in resourcing activities with personnel role being devolved. This is not necessarily happening, in an uncontrolled way however. Personnel Officers at Heinz, for example, have produced training for line managers and support material to enable line managers to carry out recruitment activities without direct personnel support.

Summary propositions

9.1 A strategic approach to resourcing requires that account is taken of the changes taking place in the labour market.

9.2 There is an increase in resourcing activities which encourage temporal and numerical flexibility.

9.3 Organisations have strategic choices concerning the use they make of their internal and the external labour market.

9.4 The characteristics sought in recruiting and promoting individuals can be matched to the organisation's strategic direction.

9.5 Organisations have strategic choices about which members of the organisation carry out resourcing activities.

References

Atkinson, J. (1984) 'Manpower strategies for flexible organisations', *Personnel Management*, August.

Atkinson, J. (1989) 'Four stages of adjustment to the democratic downturn', *Personnel Management*, August.

Atkinson, J. and Meager, N. (1986) *New Forms of Work Organisation*, IMS Report 121, IMS: Brighton.

Benson, J. (1996) 'Management strategy and labour flexibility in Japanese manufacturing enterprises', *Human Resource Management Journal*, Vol. 6, No. 2, pp. 44–57.

Blyton, P. and Morris, J. (1992) 'HRM and the limits of flexibility' in P. Blyton and P. Turnbull, *Reassessing Human Resource Management*, London: Sage.

Blyton, P. and Turnbull, P. (1992) *Reassessing Human Resource Management*, London: Sage.

Boyer, R. (ed.) (1988) *The Search for Labour Market Flexibility*, Oxford: Clarendon Press.

Braverman, H. (1974) *Labor and Monopoly Capital*, New York: Monthly Review Press.

Cann, T. (1993) 'Why poaching is good practice', *Personnel Management*, October.

Employment Department Group (1993) *Labour Market and Skill Trends 94/5*, Crown Copyright, London: HMSO.

Evenden, R. (1993) 'The strategic management of recruitment and selection', in R. Harrison (ed.), *Human Resource Management – Issues and Strategies*, Wokingham: Addison-Wesley.

Gall, G. (1996) 'All year round: the growth of annual hours in Britain', *Personnel Review*, Vol. 25, No. 3, pp. 35–52.

Guest, D. (1987) 'Human resource management and industrial relations', *Journal of Management Studies*, Vol. 24, No. 5, pp. 503–21.

Guest, D. (1989) 'Personnel and HRM, can you tell the difference?', *Personnel Management*, January, pp. 48–51.

Hakim, C. (1990) 'Core and periphery in employers' workforce strategies: evidence from 1987 ELUS survey', *Work Employment and Society*, Vol. 4, No. 2, pp. 157–88.

Hutchinson, S. (1993a) *Issues in People Management No 5. Annual hours working in the UK*, London: IPM.

Hutchinson, S. (1993b) 'The changing face of annual labour', *Personnel Management*, April.

Institute for Employment Research (1993) 'Change in employment by occupation 1991–2000', in *Review of Economy and Employment*, Institute for Employment Research.

Legge, K. (1989) 'Human resource management – a critical analysis, in J. Storey (ed.), *New Perspectives in Human Resource Management*, London: Routledge.

Legge, K. (1995) *Human Resource Management: Rhetorics and realities*, Basingstoke: Macmillan.

Miller, P. and Norburn, D. (1981) 'Strategy and executive reward: the mismatch in the strategic process', *Journal of General Management*, Vol. 6, No. 4, pp. 17–27.

Pearson, R. and Pike, G. (1989) *The Graduate Labour Market in the 1990s*, Falmer: Institute of Manpower Studies.

Pollert, A. (1991) 'The Orthodoxy of Flexibility', in A. Pollert (ed.), *Farewell to Flexibility*, Oxford: Blackwell.

Purcell, J. (1992) 'The impact of corporate strategies on human resource management', in G. Salaman *et al.* (eds.), *Human Resource Strategies*, London: Sage.

Rajan, A. (1990) *A Zero Sum Game*, Birmingham: The Industrial Society.

Rojot, J. (1989) 'National experience in labour market flexibility', in Organisation for Economic Cooperation and Development (ed.), *Labour Market Flexibility: Trends in enterprises*, Paris: OECD, pp. 37–60.

Sonnenfield, J. A. *et al.* (1992) 'Strategic determinants of managerial labour markets', in G. Salaman *et al.* (eds.), *Human Resource Strategies*, London: Sage.

Storey, J. (ed.) (1989) *New Perspectives on Human Resource Management*, London: Routledge.

Tuselmann H.-J. (1996) 'The path towards greater labour flexibility in Germany: hampered by past success?' *Employee Relations*, Vol. 18, No. 6, pp. 26–47.

General discussion topics

1. In spite of continued high levels of unemployment, many employers still continue to experience skills shortages. What steps can *employers* take to alleviate this situation. What steps might the *Government* take?
2. Discuss the claim that flexible resourcing strategies should be welcomed by the individual as they provide new areas of opportunity rather than a threat.

CHAPTER 10

Contracts of employment, contractors and consultants

Although the emphasis of the contract under which we are employed has changed towards that of a contract for performance, the overall, formal title is still the contract of employment.

It has been conventional to think of employment as full-time employment, but gradually a range of alternative forms is emerging. Full-time employment has been in steady decline for some time and the fall in the numbers of people registered as unemployed in the 1990s has been attributable mainly to the increasing number of part-time jobs available. Employers increasingly use a number of different forms of contract: not only different contracts of employment, but also contracts for the provision of services from subcontractors and consultants.

The proportion of the labour force that works part-time varies across the European Union. Table 10.1 shows the figures for 1991.

Since the development of the factory system employees have always been required to attend work at rigidly predetermined blocks of time, with some

Table 10.1 Proportion of the labour force working part-time in the European Union in 1991

Spain	3%
Greece	4%
Italy	5.5%
Luxembourg	7%
Portugal	7%
Ireland	8%
Belgium	12%
France	12%
Germany	15%
United Kingdom	22%
Denmark	23%
Netherlands	33%

Source: *Labour Force Survey* (1993), p.119.

variation through the use of overtime. The logic of this was not seriously questioned until 1968 when the concept of flexible working hours developed in West Germany. Although the majority of people still work some version of 9 to 5, there is a growing range of different practices, which have been evolving since the idea of flexible working hours broke the mould.

By the 1980s there was considerable interest in finding variations in order to introduce greater flexibility in the staffing of business and to provide individual employees with the scope to match working requirements with personal and domestic preferences. This interest was reflected in a number of reports and publications, such as BIM (1985) and Clutterbuck (1985).

The development of working patterns

By 1850 the **normal working week** in Britain had been established as 60 hours spread over 6 days of 10 hours each. Bienefeld (1972) analyses how normal weekly hours fell at four distinct periods (Table 10.2).

Since then there has been a further drop to approximately 38 hours a week, although the pattern of a normal week is now harder to distinguish. Furthermore, there is a wide variation according to type of employment. Taking all hours worked, including paid and unpaid overtime, the level in the Spring of 1996 was an average of 45.8 hours for men and 40.6 for women (Central Statistical Office 1997, p. 79).

Bienefeld argues that these reductions all came at a time when economic conditions were favourable, unemployment was low and union bargaining power high, and that the reason for unions seeking the reductions was in anticipation of future unemployment when the trade cycle moved from relative prosperity to relative recession:

> The four periods during which there were reductions in hours were marked by a configuration of economic factors that distinguished rises in money wages; they were periods of great prosperity, hence low unemployment, and hence great union bargaining power; finally, they were periods when unemployment was not felt to be a serious threat.   (Bienefeld 1972, p. 224)

While that analysis may be an accurate explanation of the decline in working hours in the past, it must be a poor predictor for the future, as it is difficult to envisage all the factors ever again being present at the same time. There has always been an obvious tension between unions seeking a reduction in the working week without a loss of earnings while employers have needed to be

Table 10.2 Percentage reduction in British working hours between 1850 and early 1960s

Period	Weekly hours' reduction	Percentage fall
1850–75	60–50	10%
1896–1920	54–48	11%
Late 1940s	48–44	8%
Early 1960s	44–40	9%

convinced that reductions in hours will not reduce productivity. When hours were very long there was a convincing argument based on fatigue. More recently, moves have been based on a bargain: a reduction in hours in exchange for some major union concession, such as a change in working practices, that gives management greater control of operations. The whole concept of a normal working week has been eroded as work becomes less rigidly constrained in predetermined blocks of time.

It is interesting that during industrial action by electricity power workers in the early 1970s, the Government introduced a three-day week to save fuel. In most instances production remained as high, or nearly as high, as it had been during the previous five-day week.

Shift working can be traced back to the dawn of human history, with many examples for soldiers and sailors, for instance. In industry split-shifts were operated as early as 1694 in glassmaking, and there was a 1785 experiment in the largest ironworks in South Wales of three eight-hour shifts as an alternative to the norm of two twelve-hour shifts. Recently, there has been an extension of shift working patterns and an increase in the number of people working shifts. Atkinson (1982, p. 2) calculated that by 1980 25 per cent of manual workers worked on shifts in the manufacturing sector and that 22 per cent of all industrial workers were employed in this way. An official analysis for 1993 (Table 10.3) shows a remarkably large proportion of the workforce employed in non-traditional ways.

It would be misleading to add all the percentages and conclude that two-thirds of the working population work 'unsocial' hours, as some work on more than one of the periods. It is still striking that a quarter of all those in employment worked on Saturdays, although many of these will be part-timers.

The need to stagger working hours grows greater rather than less. The bank that is open only from 10.00 a.m. to 3.00 p.m. is a now a rarity; the airport channelling people onto aircraft will be operating from very early morning to late evening; public houses remain open all day and a high street store will typically be open for at least 70 hours a week. Initially, most attempts to stagger working hours were in order to ease public transport problems: now they are to find ways of staffing the business.

At one time **part-time working** was relatively unusual and was scarcely economic for the employer as the national insurance costs of the part-time employee were disproportionate to those of the full-timer. The part-time contract was

Table 10.3 People usually engaged in weekend working, shift work and night work, Spring 1993

	Total number	Percentage of all in employment
Saturdays only	6,054,000	23.9%
Both Saturdays and Sundays	2,543,000	10.0%
Sundays only	2,990,000	11.8%
Shifts, including both weekend and night shifts	3,954,000	15.6%
Nights	1,544,000	6.1%

Source: Central Statistical Office 1994, p. 60

regarded as an indulgence for the employee and only a second-best alternative to the employment of someone full-time. This view was endorsed by lower rates of pay, little or no security of employment and exclusion from such benefits as sick pay, holiday pay and pension entitlement. How things have changed!

In the last twenty-five years the proportion of the workforce on part-time contracts has increased so dramatically that it had reached 22 per cent of total employees by 1991. By 1996 the proportion of jobs in Britain that were part-time had increased to 25 per cent, having almost doubled to 28 per cent in 1994 since reaching 15 per cent in 1971. Table 10.1 showed that this proportion seems to be greater than that in most other EU countries, although there is some difficulty of definition. What is part-time? At the moment the British method of calculation classifies anything less than the normal weekly hours at the place of work to be part-time, so a part-timer could be working 6 hours a week or 35.

Ninety per cent of the recent rise in part-time working has been female. This has coincided with campaigns to enhance the employment opportunities of women, with the Equal Opportunities Commission advocating the development of job-sharing. Part-time still, however, lacks the status of full-time employment and it is now more often described as a problem to be overcome rather than an opportunity for flexibility. A leavening of part-time posts provides flexibility to the management in staffing the operation and employment opportunity for those who do not seek full-time work. Too many part-time posts destabilises the staffing of the operation through increasing the training costs, requiring close supervision and costly administration while deploying people who have little understanding of the business. At the same time people who are seeking full-time work are denied the opportunity. In 1996 8 per cent of all male employees and 45 per cent of all female employees were working part-time (Central Statistical Office 1997, p. 76).

WINDOW ON PRACTICE

The Times (14 June 1994, p. 29) reports that Marks & Spencer is the blue-chip operator of part-time working, with forty years' experience and frequently sought out by other businesses to find out how it is done. They now feel that some stores are using too many part-timers and are aiming to reduce the part-time workforce from 80 per cent to 70 per cent.

Flexible working hours were initially seen as a way of overcoming travel-to-work problems and as an inducement to prospective employees to join a company that offered this type of flexibility. By the 1980s interest in this type of scheme was falling, but it remains in wide use, both to provide flexibility and as a means of achieving better management control of employee working hours (IDS 1983). In 1996 10 per cent of all full-time employees was working flexible hours (Central Statistical Office 1997, p. 80). Union resistance has reduced, but there is still fear that overtime opportunities may be reduced and attention distracted from the need to reduce working hours (Lee 1983).

Compressed hours are a method of reducing the working week by extending the working day, so that people work the same number of hours but on fewer days. An alternative method is to make the working day more concentrated by reducing the length of the midday meal-break. The now commonplace four-night week on the night shift in engineering was introduced in Coventry as a result of absenteeism on the fifth night being so high that it was uneconomic to operate.

Other more unusual variations include the idea of **annual hours contracts**, whereby the employee contracts to provide the employer with a specified number of hours' work per year and then enjoys considerable latitude in deciding when to work those hours, subject to employer needs and priorities. A **zero hours contract** is the least attractive form of part-time working, as the employee is not guaranteed any hours' work at all, but may be called in if there is a need.

There are already considerable changes in working patterns and further extension of variations seems likely. The advantage to the employer is flexibility, not only to cope with the commercial ebb and flow, but also to maintain a level of manning for a period of organisational operation that is now almost always longer than a standard working week for an individual employee. The appeal to the employee is more diverse. For some there is the attraction of working only part-time, for others there is a more comfortable interface between work and non-work, and for yet others there is the opportunity of combining more than one form of employment.

Flexibility is, however, not valued in organisations if it leads to instability, and it is not welcome to those doing the work of the organisation if it denies them the satisfaction of their reasonable, work-related personal needs.

ACTIVITY BOX 10.1

What types of job would you regard as most appropriate for the following variations of the conventional 9-to-5 working pattern?

1. shift working,
2. part-time working,
3. job sharing,
4. flexible hours,
5. compressed hours,
6. annual hours.

What types of job would not be suitable for each of these?

Shift working

There are situations where there is no alternative to working shifts or at least abnormal hours. In the continuous process industries like steel-making and glass manufacture, the need for employees to be in attendance at all hours is dictated by the impracticality of interrupting the manufacturing cycle. In other circumstances there is the overwhelming imperative of customer demand, so that commuter trains are used more out of normal working hours than within them, and morning newspapers have to be prepared in the middle of the night.

The operation of shifts carries an implicit assumption that it is unattractive to the individual employee: it carries a premium payment all of its own and the drafters of incomes policies in the 1970s brought a new phrase into common usage by introducing the notion of special treatment for those who work 'unsocial hours'. Such a generalisation may make sound industrial relations sense, but is no more accurate a statement about individuals than the statement that gentlemen prefer blondes. Wedderburn gives examples of the range of reactions he discovered in interviewing 500 shiftworkers:

One young couple work the same shift so that they can use their spare time together working on their old house; another couple work opposing shifts, so that they can manage a handicapped child between them. One young father loves shiftwork because he sees more of his infant children; another feels he is losing contact with his time-locked school children. One can fish all day in uncrowded waters; another gave up fishing because weekend shiftwork meant that he missed crucial competitions. One foreman enjoys the total responsibility that shiftwork gives him; another fears that he has missed his chances of promotion, isolated on shiftwork.

(Wedderburn 1975, p. 181)

For most people the prospect of working shifts may well be appalling, but for a substantial minority it provides a welcome element of flexibility in the employment contract at a time in their lives when it is perhaps very convenient for them to spend a period working unusual hours, and for a higher rate of pay.

There are various patterns of working shifts, each of which brings with it a slightly different set of problems and opportunities.

The part-timer shift

Here a group of people are employed for a few hours daily at the beginning or end of normal working hours. The most common group are office cleaners, who may work from 6 a.m. to 9 a.m. or for a similar period in the evening. Also there are some shifts for four or five hours in the evening. Common here are supermarket shelvers, who stock shelves in readiness for the store opening the following morning.

The advantage to employers is in using relatively small units of time that would be insufficient for a full-time employee, and it is a very convenient working arrangement for a fairly large number of people. Where the employer is seeking a short spell of additional work from people who require little training (either because the work is straightforward or because the skills are generally available) the part-timer shift may be an ideal arrangement. It may be less satisfactory as a permanent type of employment.

The permanent night shift

The permanent night shift is another arrangement which creates a special category of employee who is set apart (or cut off) from everyone else. They are working full-time, but have no contact with the rest of the organisation's members, who leave before they arrive and return after they have left. Apart from the specialised applications like national newspapers, this form is usually used either to undertake cleaning and maintenance of plant while it is idle, or to increase output on a rather more permanent basis than can be achieved through part-timer shifts.

The attraction of this arrangement is that it makes use of plant at times when it would otherwise be idle and, if it is used for maintenance, it avoids maintenance interrupting production. It also avoids the upheaval of the existing workforce that would be involved by introducing double-day shifts.

The drawbacks can be considerable. Employees are operating permanently outside normal working hours, and as they are full-time employees that may be even more critical than it is with part-timers. There is an inevitable 'apartheid' for the regular night worker, who is out of touch with the mainstream of union and company activities. A further problem is the provision of services, like catering, medical and routine personnel services. For the evening worker these are either unnecessary or can be provided relatively cheaply by a few daily employees working occasional overtime. For night workers the services are both more difficult to provide and more costly. Night working is the form that is likely to be most difficult for employees to sustain as most people are diurnal rather than nocturnal creatures. A small minority seem genuinely to prefer working regular nights and maintain this rhythm for their working lives over many years, but for most it will be undertaken either reluctantly or for relatively short periods.

Alternating day and night shifts

If night working is being used to increase output rather than for cleaning and maintenance, then alternation is a possibility. It mitigates many of the difficulties of regular night working, but does present employees with the problem of regular, drastic changes in their daily rhythms.

Double-day shifts

The double-day shift variation is surprisingly unpopular. Instead of working a normal day shift, employees work either 6 till 2 or 2 till 10. This means that plant is in use for sixteen hours, all employees are present for a large part of the 'normal' day, there is no night working and the rotation between the early and late shift enables a variety of leisure activities to be followed.

One problem is the fact that it may be the first experience of shifts for the bulk of employees, if it is introduced in place of a system of regular days or regular days and nights. There may be difficulties about transport in the early morning and there is all the inconvenience of eating at unfamiliar times.

Three-shift working

Three-shift working represents a further development and is the most widespread pattern: 6 till 2, 2 till 10 and 10 till 6. The 24-hour cycle is covered so that there is continuous operation. There is a further subdivision: *discontinuous* three-shift working is where the plant stops for the weekend, and *continuous* shift-working, whereby the plant never stops. Here we have the inescapable night shift and, with continuous working, the final loss of the sacrosanct weekend. If shifts are run on the traditional pattern of changing every week the shift workers have the unattractive feature of the 'dead fortnight' of two weeks when normal evening social activities are not possible because of late return home after a 2 till 10 shift or early departure for a 10 till 6 shift. The most common solution to this is to accelerate the rotation with a 'continental' shift pattern, whereby a shift team spend no more than three consecutive days on the same shift.

Reductions in the number of hours in the basic working week have induced a range of variations in shiftworking pattern that were not necessary until the 40-hour barrier was broken. Useful examples of such variations have been described by IDS (1985).

Part-time working

Although there has been some increase in part-time working for men, it has grown rapidly among women, because so many women wish to work only part-time or because their share of domestic responsibilities allows them to work in this way only. Many of them will be working short shifts and sometimes two will share a full working day. Others will be in positions for which only a few hours within the normal day are required or a few hours at particular times of the week. As described, retailing is an occupation that has considerable scope for the part-timer, as there is obviously a greater need for counter personnel on Saturday mornings than on Monday mornings. Also many shops are now open for longer periods than would be normal hours for a full-time employee, so that the part-timer helps to fill the gaps and provide the extra manning at peak periods. Catering is another example, as are market research interviewing, office cleaning, typing and some posts in education. Another aspect of the increasing number of women returning to part-time employment is the provision of funded crèche facilities for children (Falconer 1990). As labour shortages become more acute, this issue is likely to become of greater importance to both employers and potential employees.

A specialised form of part-time work is that which is a kind of overtime in which a person works extra time for a second employer in order to increase earnings. Known as *moonlighting*, this includes such jobs as taxi-driving and bartending, as well as the more specialised tasks like dealing with other people's income tax claims. The second employer gains considerable benefit, obtaining the services of perhaps a skilled and experienced employee without having to invest in that person's training or future career.

Flexible working hours

A typical arrangement for flexible working hours is where the organisation abandons a fixed starting and finishing time for the working day. Instead, employees start work at a predetermined time in the period between 8.00 a.m. and 10.00 a.m. and finish between 4.00 p.m. and 6.00 p.m. They are obliged to be present during the core time of 10 till 4, but can use the flexible time at the beginning and end of the working day to produce a pattern of working hours that suits their personal needs and preferences. The main advantage of this scheme is that it enables people to avoid peak travel times and the awkward rigidity of the inflexible starting time. From the organisation's point of view it can eliminate the tendency towards a frozen period at the beginning and end of the day when nothing happens – for the first 20 minutes everyone is looking at the paper or making coffee, and for the last 20 minutes everyone is preparing to go home. If the process of individual start-up and slow-down is spread over a longer period, the organisation is operational for longer.

The scheme described above assumes that the necessary number of hours will be worked each day. The variations on the theme increase flexibility by allowing a longer settlement period, so that employees can work varying lengths of time on different days, provided that they complete the quota appropriate for the week or month or whatever other settlement period is agreed. This means that someone can take a half-day for shopping or a full day for a long weekend, as long as the quota is made up within a prescribed period.

As most organisations depend on a high degree of interaction between staff members for their operations to be viable, all are required to be in attendance for the core time period of the day, although this is waived in schemes where people are allowed to take half or whole days off. A further control is on the bandwidth, which is the time between the earliest feasible starting time and the latest possible finishing time. If this becomes too great the working day attenuates in a rather costly way.

One feature of flexible hours which is often resented by employees is the way in which their attendance is registered, as there has been a tendency to reintroduce time clocks or the more sophisticated elapsed time recorders as a way of controlling the attendance of the individual person. While it is conventional for employees to 'fight' mechanical time recording because of its rigidity, there is also the feeling that it is at least fair. There can be no suspicion that some people are not putting in their full complement of hours, nor that some have bluer eyes than others. On the other hand, it is less likely to generate an atmosphere where people develop the type of open-ended approach to working hours that some managers regard as commitment.

In many areas of white-collar employment time-keeping is a matter of mutual trust rather than of control. In this type of situation there might be strong resistance to mechanical time recording, largely because the motives for its introduction would be suspect. Management will also have reservations about installing expensive time-recording equipment that has not previously been necessary.

Annual hours

New working patterns offer the opportunity to reduce costs and improve performance. Organisations need a better match between employee working hours and the operating profile of the business in order to improve customer response time and increase productivity.

The 'annual hours' approach has proved to be an effective method of tackling the problem. Central to each annual hours agreement is that the period of time within which full-time employees must work their contractual hours is defined over a whole year. All normal working hours contracts can be converted to annual hours; for example, an average 38-hour week becomes 1,732 annual hours, assuming five weeks' holiday entitlement. The principal advantage of annual hours in manufacturing sectors which need to maximise the utilisation of expensive assets, comes from the ability to separate employee working time from the operating hours of the plant and equipment. Thus we have seen the growth of five-crew systems, in particular in the continuous process industries. Such systems are capable of delivering 168 hours of production a week by rotating five crews. In 365 days there are 8,760 hours to be covered, requiring 1,752 annual hours from each shift crew, averaging just over 38 hours for 46 weeks. All holidays can be rostered into 'off' weeks, and 50 or more weeks of production can be planned in any one year without resorting to overtime. Further variations can be incorporated to deal with fluctuating levels of seasonal demand.

In our research we found just over one respondent in ten reporting some form of annualised hours arrangement working in their business. Official statistics show 3.9 per cent of full-time employees and 3.1 per cent of part-time employees working on annualised hours (Central Statistical Office 1997, p. 80).

The move to annual hours is an important step for a company to take and should not be undertaken without careful consideration and planning. Managers need to be aware of all the consequences. The tangible savings include all those things that are not only measurable but are capable of being measured before the scheme is put in. Some savings, such as reduced absenteeism, are quantifiable only after the scheme has been running and therefore cannot be counted as part of the cost justification. A less tangible issue for both parties is the distance that is introduced between employer and employee, who becomes less a part of the business and more like a subcontractor. Another problem can be the carrying forward of assumptions from the previous working regime to the new. One agreement is being superseded by another and, as every industrial relations practitioner knows, anything that happened before which is not specifically excluded from a new agreement then becomes a precedent. In October 1996 such a situation had to be resolved by the Court of Appeal:

> In the Court of Appeal's view it was in the nature of such an agreement that it had to be clear and concise in order to be readily understood by all who were concerned with its operation. . . . If any topic were left uncovered by the agreement, the natural inference, in the Court's opinion, was. . . that the topic had been purposefully left out of the agreement on the basis that it was considered too controversial or too complicated to justify any variation of the main terms of the agreement to take account of it.   (IDS 1996b, p. 3)

Zero hours

For most people a very unattractive form of part-time working is where the employee is not guaranteed any hours of work at all, but may be called in if there is a need. This has long been the practice in some areas of employment, such as agency nurses and members of the acting profession, but it has recently been used to some extent in other areas, such as retailing, to deal with emergencies or unforeseen circumstances.

Temporary contracts

Although no contract is permanent, most continue indefinitely and will only be terminated if something goes wrong. It is widely believed that more people are currently on temporary contracts, either with an explicit termination date or with an understanding that the job is for a limited time without a termination date being predetermined. Our research gave some interesting indications about the prevalence of this practice. First we asked about the proportion of all those employed by the respondent organisations who had temporary contracts. Table 10.4 shows a modest proportion. The implication seems clearly that the numbers of individual people with temporary contracts is small.

Table 10.4 Employees with temporary contracts

	Manual	Non-manual	Managers
Percentage of employees in this category who have temporary contracts	10%	6%	2%

Table 10.5 Establishments having employees with temporary contracts

	Manual	Non-manual	Managers
Percentage of establishments having at least one employee on a temporary contract	71%	64%	26%

Another approach is to see the number of establishments having at least one person on a temporary contract (Table 10.5).

If one asks the question taking a longer retrospective view, and including the possibility of subcontracting, a different picture emerges (Table 10.6).

This suggests that the practice of temporary contracts is more widespread than the number of individual people affected, and the majority of businesses are likely to use temporary appointments at some time. Official statistics, however, show a different picture, with job tenure being long. Since 1986 average job tenure has fallen slightly for men from 9.4 years to 8.9 and has risen for women from 6.5 to 7.1. Furthermore:

> Overall 1.5 million people, 7 per cent of employees, in the United Kingdom had a temporary job in 1995. This proportion is low compared with most other countries in the European Union . . . only in Austria and Belgium was it lower.   (Central Statistical Office 1997, pp. 77–8)

Why do employers choose this method? Some of the reasons are obvious. Retail stores need more staff immediately before Christmas than in February and icecream manufacturers need more people in July than November, so both types of business have seasonal fluctuations. Nowadays, however, there is the additional factor of flexibility in the face of uncertainty. Will the new line sell? Will there be sustained business after we have completed this particular contract?

There are a number of ways in which managers find the temporary employee to be an asset. In the early days of the Government-funded Youth Training Scheme (YTS), it was referred to as the 'free trial offer'. A manager was able to try out a prospective new employee without any commitment, and could decide after a few weeks or months whether the person was worth appointing or not. This remains a common view, so that the early months are almost a form of probation. Increasingly graduate recruitment by smaller employers operates on this basis.

Table 10.6 Establishments using temporary staff in previous year

	Manual	Non-manual	Managers
Establishments which have used temporary staff as an alternative to appointing a permanent employee in the previous year	76%	79%	22%
Establishments which have used subcontracting as an alternative to appointing a permanent employee in the previous year	45%	26%	12%

Research by Geary (1992) in the Republic of Ireland found that the use of temporary contracts gave management a greater degree of control over labour. The temporary employee worked under the constant, unspoken threat of dismissal and felt the need to behave with total compliance to avoid this. Managers were uncomfortable about the working relationship, feeling that it was divisive and unfair, but maintained that the main reason for employing temporary staff was their motivation. They put a lot of effort into their work in the hope of being made permanent and were seldom absent. Their presence also improved control over permanent staff:

> Very often when temporary workers felt obliged to do overtime, for instance, so did their permanent counterparts. A shop steward who had worked in the plant for eight years told me of the frustration by many permanent employees, 'People complain to me about the level of overtime. But what can you do when you have 20 temps and 5 permanent people on a line? Temps feel obliged to come in at the week-end and so do permanent people as a result.'
>
> (Geary 1992, p. 56)

Unpublished research by Curtis (1996) in the West Midlands largely supports Geary's conclusions, but adds the fear by managers of having to go through the trauma of redundancies. Having had to make large proportions of the workforce redundant in previous years, they were anxious to avoid a repetition of that at all costs.

There was also a strong tendency for managers to regard temporary workers quite differently from permanent workers, often not regarding them as employees at all: 'people who are not here'. This is reflected in the relatively low level of benefits available to temporary staff, such as sick pay, holiday pay and the general raft of workers' rights to which they have no statutory entitlement.

Distance working and subcontracting

In the quest for greater flexibility many employers are beginning to explore new ways of getting work done which do not involve individuals working full-time on their premises.

Working overseas, selling in the field and home-working are the most obvious types of distance working. Other types of distance employment include teleworking, working on far-flung sites, or off-site as subcontractors and consultants. Contractually, 'distant' or 'peripheral' working can include anything that is different from the traditional full-time contract even though employees may be geographically present for part or all of the time; for example, part-time and job-sharing, temporary and short-term working, on-site subcontracting and consultancy.

There is increasing interest in the concepts of teleworking and tele-cottaging. *Tele* is from the Greek for distant, and is familiar to us in terms like telegram and television. A more specific definition is provided by Incomes Data Services from a survey by Huws (1996) which puts it in two categories:

> The first is the individualised form of teleworking which involves work completed away from the employer's premises, such as home-based teleworking or multi-locational working. The second category is a collective

form of teleworking which covers work completed on non-domestic premises and managed by the employer or third party. This includes call centres and tele-cottages.
(IDS 1996a, p. 22)

The number of people engaged in distance working or teleworking is difficult to estimate, as there are so many people who have always worked in this way, such as sales representatives, and by no means all fall into the stereotype category of someone sitting at a remote computer terminal. The total number is small, but it is certainly growing, despite some of the drawbacks mentioned in the last chapter. The main advantage, for both the employer and the employee, is the flexibility it provides, but the employer also benefits from reduced office accommodation costs and an increase in productivity.

The scale of tele-cottaging is easier to assess, as there is a Tele-Cottage and Tele-centre Association which reported 90 telecottages in 1994 and 154 in 1996. A typical centre provides computer and telecommunications equipment for use by its members. The staple activity is usually training in IT skills, but commercial usage by members is also an important feature.

Between 1986 and 1993 the number of self-employed people in Britain increased from 2,566,000 to 2,902,000, moving from 11 per cent to just over 12 per cent of the working population, although the proportion was slightly higher in 1991 (Central Statistical Office 1994, p. 58). The number has scarcely altered since then.

Rothwell (1987) has identified several issues relating to the employment of distance workers. These are considered next.

Finding the right people

One source may be existing staff who would prefer more flexible working arrangements, or those who have left employment for family reasons, travel, redundancy or early retirement. Subcontractors whose businesses have been set up as a result of company hive-offs or buy-outs are another potential source. Information regarding the relevant public and private agencies, subcontractors and consultants may well be something which more managers need to acquire. More effective relationships can be established by taking time to classify needs and developing longer-term arrangements with public/private agencies and with subcontractors.

Job specification and selection

Job specification is important in all selection processes but is critical in most forms of geographically and contractually distant working, particularly in subcontracted work. It is important to set out clearly defined parameters of action, criteria for decision and issues which need reference back. Person specifications are also crucial since in much distance working there is less scope for employees to be trained or socialised on the job. In addition, 'small business' skills are likely to be needed by teleworkers, networkers, consultants and subcontractors.

Communication and control

Attention needs to be given to the initial stages of settling in these distance workers. Those off-site need to know the pattern of regular links and contacts to be followed. Those newly recruited to the company need the same induction information as regular employees. In fact, those working independently with less supervision may need additional material, particularly on health and safety. Heightened team building skills will also be needed to encompass staff who are working on a variety of different contracts and at different locations.

Pay and performance

A key aspect of the employment of distance workers is the close link between pay and performance. Managers must be able to specify job targets and requirements accurately and to clarify and agree these with the employees or contractors concerned. Where a fee rather than a salary is paid, the onus is on the manager to ensure the work has been completed satisfactorily. Others (consultants, tele-workers, networkers) may be paid on the basis of time, and it is for the supervisor to ensure the right level and quality of output for that payment.

It is doubtful whether pay levels of peripheral staff can be related to existing job-evaluated systems or salary structures. Indeed, one advantage of extending the variety of peripheral workers is the ability to move outside those constraints, which may no longer be appropriate. Concepts of the total compensation package may need to be examined more closely in relation to distance workers – will financial services (e.g. low interest loans) and provision of home computers become more important?

ACTIVITY BOX 10.2

Consider either the organisation where you work or an organisation where you have a fair idea of what is involved in a number of different jobs, like a hospital or a television company. Which jobs would it be most suitable, from a management point of view, to staff on the following bases?
- ▶ Compressed hours
- ▶ Annual hours
- ▶ Short-term contracts
- ▶ Consultancy

The contract of employment

The contract of employment governs the relationship between an employer and an employee. Other types of contract will be made between an employing organisation and those who do the work of the business without being its employees. The contract will be one of the following:

Permanent: This is open-ended and without a date of expiry.

Fixed-term: This has a fixed start and finish date, although it may have provision for notice before the agreed finish date.

Temporary: Temporary contracts are for people employed explicitly for a limited period, but with the expiry date not precisely specified. A specialised form of temporary contract is where someone is employed to carry out a specified task, so that the expiry date is when the task is complete.

Employees who work 16 hours a week or more have the same legal rights as full-timers, but those who work between 8 and 16 hours acquire these rights only when they have been in continuous service with the employer for five years. Employers are not legally obliged to pay the same rates to those working part-time as to those working full-time, but they are bound by the Equal Pay Act, so that part-timers could have a claim for equal pay if they can identify a full-time worker of the opposite sex carrying out similar work.

Expiry or performance of contract may be the most normal form of termination for most contracts, consultants or short-term workers. Termination of part-timers will be likely to follow the same legal and contractual procedures as for full-time staff, depending on their length of service, notice of period of terms and conditions agreed with unions and incorporated into their contracts. Where dismissal is for reasons of redundancy, selection of part-timers or other peripheral groups only could constitute unlawful 'indirect' discrimination if these were mainly of one sex; proportionate percentage selection of part-time and full-time employees might be more appropriate unless the work was performed by only one group and no suitable alternative offers at all could be made.

A special type of contract is that for apprenticeship. Although this is to be seen as a contract of employment for the purpose of accumulating employment rights, it is a form of legally-binding working relationship that pre-dates all current legislative rights in employment, and the apprentice therefore has additional rights at common law relating to training. An employer cannot lawfully terminate an apprentice's contract before the agreed period of training is complete, unless there is closure or a fundamental change of activity in the business to justify redundancy.

Termination of peripheral workers' contracts or disciplinary dismissal may call for legal advice, given the complexity of the position of many categories of flexi-workers.

Checklist for preparing a contract of employment

1. Name of employer; name of employee.
2. Date on which employment began.
3. Job title.
4. Rate of pay, period and method of payment.
5. Normal hours of work and related conditions, such as meal-breaks.
6. Arrangements for holidays and holiday pay, including means whereby both can be calculated precisely.
7. Terms and conditions relating to sickness, injury and sick pay.
8. Terms and conditions of pension arrangements, including a note about whether or not the employment is contracted out under the provisions of the Social Security Pensions Act 1975.
9. Length of notice due to and from employee.
10. Disciplinary rules and procedure.
11. Arrangements for handling employee grievances.
12. (Where applicable) Conditions of employment relating to trade union membership.

Employing consultants

The Bertie Ramsbottom Ballad on page 198 incorporates nearly all the nightmares about consultants. Although the ballad is directed at external consultants, whose services are bought in, many of the reservations also apply to much personnel work, which is advisory and seeking to bring about change in the attitudes and practices of managerial colleagues.

WINDOW ON PRACTICE

The Preying Mantis

Of all the businesses, by far,
Consultancy's the most bizarre.
For, to the penetrating eye,
There's no apparent reason why,
With no more assets than a pen,
This group of personable men
Can sell to clients more than twice
The same ridiculous advice,
Or find, in such a rich profusion,
Problems to fit their own solution.

The strategy that they pursue –
To give advice instead of do –
Keeps their fingers on the pulses
Without recourse to stomach ulcers,
And brings them monetary gain,
Without a modicum of pain.
The wretched object of their quest,
Reduced to cardiac arrest,
Is left alone to implement
The asinine report they've sent.

Meanwhile the analysts have gone
Back to client number one,
Who desperately needs their aid
To tidy up the mess they made.
And on and on – ad infinitum –
The masochistic clients invite 'em.
Until the merciful reliever
Invokes the company receiver.

No one really seems to know
The rate at which consultants grow,
By some amoeba-like division?
Or chemobiologic fission?
They clone themselves without an end
Along their exponential trend.
The paradox is each adviser,
If he makes his client wiser,
Inadvertently destroys
The basis of his future joys.
So does anybody know
Where latter-day consultants go?

(Ralph Windle 1985)

One is entitled to some scepticism about the value of using external consultants:

> The naive might have imagined that as management disciplines matured and executives increasingly mastered them, the need for outside advisers would fade. Think again . . . the global consultancy market is now worth around $40 billion . . . and employs upwards of 100,000 of the most highly-qualified people in the world.   (Caulkin 1997, p. 33).

Daily fees frequently are £3,000 per person-day, with some of the superstars asking five times that amount. The odd thing is the rare occasion when anyone says it was worth every penny. The typical comment is exactly the opposite. Simon Caulkin quotes Lord Weinstock and Anita Roddick:

> [Lord Weinstock] Consultants are invariably a waste of money. There has been the occasional instance where a useful idea has come up, but the input we have received has usually been banal and unoriginal, wrapped up in impressive sounding but irrelevant rhetoric.

> Anita Roddick says that having consultants tramping through the Body Shop was the most uncomfortable period in its history.   (Caulkin 1997, p. 34)

Some personnel activities are undoubtedly best undertaken by consultants. An example is the use of personnel tests in selection. These have been available for many years as a means of making selection more systematic and objective, yet their use remains limited and is sometimes misguided. Few employing organisations are big enough to have a scale of recruitment *for similar posts* which produces a large enough set of results for analysis and comparison to be fruitful. The Royal Air Force selects trainee pilots using a battery of tests developed over many years. There is also a wealth of evidence from tests and subsequent performance, for the ability to fly an aircraft to be predicted with reasonable accuracy from test results alone.

Few other employers can accumulate enough evidence to make comparable predictions, but specialist firms of consultants can, at least theoretically, produce occupational norms to provide useful performance indicators from test results.

Duncan Wood (1985, p. 41) asked senior representatives of fourteen well-established consultancies to rank seven reasons for their use in personnel work. The result was:

> First: To provide specialist expertise and wider knowledge not available within the client organisation.
> Second: To provide an independent view.
> Third: To act as a catalyst.
> Fourth: To provide extra resources to meet temporary requirements.
> Fifth: To help develop a consensus when there are divided views about proposed changes.
> Sixth: To demonstrate to employees the impartiality/objectivity of personnel changes or decisions.
> Seventh: To justify potentially unpleasant decisions.

In earlier research it was found that confident and competent personnel managers can call on the services of outside experts without fear of jeopardising their own position and being able to specify closely what they require (Torrington and Mackay, 1986).

Where the personnel function is under-resourced, or where the personnel manager lacks professional expertise, then consultants will be used reluctantly, with a poor specification of requirements and the likelihood of an unsatisfactory outcome for both client and consultant.

ACTIVITY BOX 10.3

What personnel problems currently facing your organisation do you think might best be approached by using outside consultants? Why? How would you specify the requirements? What personnel problems currently facing your organisation would you not remit to outside consultants? Why not?

In deciding whether or not outside consultants should be used for a specific assignment we suggest the following approach.

Describe the problem

What is the problem about which you might seek external advice? This may not be obvious, as worrying away at an issue can show that the real matter needing to be addressed is not what is immediately apparent. If, for example, the marketing manager leaves abruptly – as they often seem to do – the immediate problem will present itself as: 'We must find a replacement.' So you begin to think of ringing up the executive search consultant you used when you needed someone for the Middle East in a hurry. Working at finding a correct description of the problem could suggest that the presenting cause is easy to deal with because young X has been waiting for just such an opportunity for months and all the signals suggest that X would be ideal. The 'real' problem may turn out to be what caused the marketing manager to leave, or whether there is a string of other 'young Xs' waiting in the wings. It could require attention to succession planning reward strategy, management development, organisation structure or many more alternative possibilities.

Formulate an approach

The next step is to rough out an approach to the problem, with the emphasis here on 'rough'. If you knew the answer you would not need any further advice; if you have no idea of the answer you cannot brief a consultant (but you might give him a blank cheque!). What is needed is a clear but not inflexible strategy so that you can go through the remaining stages of making up your mind without putting the consultant, and yourself, in the wrong framework. If you decide that the problem behind the departure of the marketing manager is a combination of succession planning and remuneration policy, the approach you would formulate would be based on ideas about how those two issues could be tackled, without an absolute commitment to a single method or technique.

Work out how you could do it in-house

The '5 W-H' method, could be used at this stage, as you decide how it could be tackled by using your own existing resources, how much it would cost, how long it would take and what the repercussions would be, such as stopping work on something else.

Whether one is specifying a brief for an outside consultant or coming to terms oneself with a problem that has been presented, there is a need for some device to describe the problem as a preliminary to formulating an approach to solving it. Priestley and his colleagues (1978, p. 28) suggest a simple '5 W-H' method – What? Who? Where? When? Why? and How? A typical problem could be approached thus:

> *What is the problem?* Communications in the office are poor.
> *Who is involved?* Everyone, but most problems are at the level of first-line supervision.
> *Where is it worst?* In Accounts and in the Print Room.
> *When is it worst?* At the end of the week and at the end of the month.
> *Why does it happen?* Because of an erratic flow of work between the two departments, which is worst at those times.
> *How could it be tackled?* By getting the first-line supervisors to tackle it, smooth out the flow of work, helping them to appreciate the effect of their work flows on the other departments, etc.

This is a very simple problem with a minimal number of questions serving to do no more than illustrate the method. Each question would probably have dozens of supplementaries in order to fill out the details of a complex problem.

The main value of the consultant at this stage is the ability to raise questions that those close to the matter have not thought of. This is not because consultants are cleverer, but because they have a different pattern of experience and take for granted different things from those who are looking at the presenting problem every day.

Find out how it could be done by consultants

Provided you have done the first two steps satisfactorily, it should be possible to brief one or more outside suppliers of expertise, so that they can bid for the business. If the problem is not correctly described, there may be bids for the wrong things, and if the approach is not accurately formulated, the consultant will be obliged to carry out a preliminary study, at your expense, to formulate an approach for you. When this happens you are beginning to lose control of the operation. Even if consultants are not as rapacious and asinine as Bertie Ramsbottom suggests, they too have a business to run and will not welcome failure through an assignment being misconceived, so they will guard against the risk. The main questions to ask of the consultants are again how would it be done, how much would it cost and how long would it take.

Decide between the alternatives

A set of alternatives from which to choose gives you the opportunity to compare relative costs, times and likely outputs, as well as implications. In making the final decision the most important point to remember is that the responsibility is inescapably yours. If the consultant can produce the 'best' outcome, have you the resources to implement it? Can you wait? If you can save £10,000 by relying on your own staff and time, will you produce an outcome that adequately meets the needs of your rough-cut approach? The eventual outcome is all that matters.

The extent to which the success or failure of consultancy initiatives rests with the internal management can be demonstrated by a comparison of the impact of the same scheme 'installed' by the same team in two different companies, one directly after the other. We are unable even to hint at the identity of either, nor to describe what the initiative was, but follow-up research gave some interesting commentary on the degree of effectiveness by recording the percentage of employees who answered 'yes' in a questionnaire about the initiatives.

Question	Company A	Company B
1. Do you understand the new scheme?	87%	44%
2. Have you had targets set?	77%	29%
3. Have you had management feedback?	87%	41%
4. Have you had the training?	53%	24%
5. Do you understand the pay plan?	44%	38%

There can be all sorts of explanation for the variable response, but there is at least a very strong indication indeed that the internal management of the initiative had a great bearing on the apparently different level of effectiveness. There is a great irony in the fact that both companies are outstandingly successful in their respective fields, by almost every conceivable criterion.

Typical views about using outside consultants

A. Favourable views

1. The personnel manager knows what to do, but proposals are more likely to be implemented if endorsed by outside experts.
2. The outsider can often clarify the personnel manager's understanding of an issue.
3. Specialist expertise is sometimes needed.
4. The personnel manager has insufficient time to deal with a particular matter on which a consultant could work full-time.
5. The consultant is independent.

6. Using consultants can be cheaper than employing your own full-time, permanent specialists.

B. Less favourable views

1. The personnel function should contain all the necessary expertise.
2. In-house personnel specialists know what is best for the company.
3. Other members of the organisation are prejudiced against the use of outside advisers.
4. Using consultants can jeopardise the position of the personnel specialists and reduce their influence.

Summary propositions

10.1 Patterns of employment are changing in order to give the employer greater flexibility in staffing the organisation and to give the employee greater autonomy.

10.2 Significant reductions in working hours have usually come in times of relative prosperity.

10.3 The use of shift working is increasing.

10.4 The use of part-time working (particularly by women) has increased considerably in recent years.

10.5 The use of flexible working hours is now well established. The logical development of this principle – annual hours – is gaining increased application.

10.6 Distance working is developing slowly and presents particular problems in selection, job specification, communication and control, pay and performance.

10.7 Contracts of employment exist only for employees and can be permanent, temporary or fixed-term.

10.8 The use of outside consultants for personnel activities is rising.

10.9 In deciding between outside and in-house resources, the stages are to describe the problem, formulate an approach, work out how to do it in-house, find out how it could be done by consultants, and then decide between alternatives.

References

Atkinson, J. (1982) *Shiftworking*, IMS Report no. 45, London: Institute of Manpower Studies.

Bienefeld, M. A. (1972) *Working Hours in British Industry: An economic history*, London: Weidenfeld & Nicolson.

British Institute of Management (1985) *Managing New Patterns of Work*, London: British Institute of Management Foundation.

Caulkin, S. (1997) 'The great consultancy cop-out', *Management Today*, February, pp. 32–8.

Central Statistical Office (1994) *Social Trends 24*, London: HMSO, 1994.

Central Statistical Office (1997) *Social Trends 27*, London: HMSO, 1997.

Clutterbuck, D. (1985) *New Patterns of Work*, Aldershot: Gower.

Curtis, S. (1996) *Differences in Conditions of Employment between Temporary and Permanent Shopfloor Workers in Three Manufacturing Companies*, unpublished MSc. Dissertation, UMIST.

Falconer, H. (1990) 'Children at work', *Personnel Today*, April, p. 14.

Geary, J. F. (1992) 'Employment flexibility and human resource management: the case of three electronics plants', *Work, Employment and Society*, Vol. 4, No. 2, pp. 157–88.

Huws, U. (1996) *Teleworking: An Overview of the Research*, London: HMSO.

IDS (1983) *Flexible Working Hours*, IDS Study 301, London: Incomes Data Services Ltd.

IDS (1985) *Improving Productivity*, IDS Study 331, London: Incomes Data Services Ltd.

IDS (1996a) *Teleworking*, IDS Study 616, London: Incomes Data Services Ltd.

IDS (1996b) *Brief 579*, December, London: Incomes Data Services Ltd.

Lee, R. A. (1983) 'Hours of work – who controls and how?', *Industrial Relations Journal*, Vol. 14, No. 4.

Office des Publications Officielles des Communautés Européennes (1993) *Labour Force Survey*, Luxembourg.

Priestley, P., McGuire, J., Flegg, D., Hemsley, V. and Welham, D. (1978) *Social Skills and Personal Problem Solving*, London: Tavistock.

Rothwell, S. (1987) 'How to manage from a distance', *Personnel Management*, September, pp. 22–6.

Torrington, D. P. and Mackay, L. E. (1986) 'Will consultants take over the personnel function?', *Personnel Management*, February, pp. 34–7.

Wedderburn, A. (1975) 'Waking up to shiftwork', *Personnel Management*, Vol. 7, No. 2.

Windle, R. (1985) *The Bottom Line*, London: Century-Hutchinson.

Wood, D. (1985) 'The uses and abuses of personnel consultants', *Personnel Management*, October, pp. 40–7.

General discussion topics

1. What are the advantages and disadvantages of part-time working for the employer and for the employee? In what ways does the age and domestic situation of the employee alter the answer?
2. The chapter indicates some of the problems in employing consultants. How can these be overcome?
3. What is the future for teleworking?

CHAPTER 11

Recruitment

There is always a need for replacement employees and those with unfamiliar skills that business growth makes necessary. Recruitment is also an area in which there are important social and legal implications, but perhaps most important is the significant part played in the lives of individual men and women by their personal experience of recruitment and the failure to be recruited. Virtually everyone reading these pages will know how significant those experiences have been in their own lives.

WINDOW ON PRACTICE

On graduating from university, Howard was employed as a management trainee by a large bank and was soon assigned to taking part in 'milk round' interviews of prospective graduate recruits, which he found interesting and a boost to his ego. After two years in the bank a programme of reorganisation led to Howard being out of a job. It was seven months before he was employed again and he had undergone many disappointments and frustrations. His new post was again in recruitment and he wrote himself a

short homily on a postcard which he kept propped up on his desk. It said:

> When you turn someone down, remember:
>
> First, what the experience of rejection can do to a person.
> Second, that the rejected person may be a customer.
> Third, you may want to recruit that person later.

In this chapter we shall consider various aspects of an employer's recruitment strategy; determining the vacancy, the range of recruitment methods available, recruitment advertising, and several features of recruitment method, including employee documentation and shortlisting.

Determining the vacancy

Is there a vacancy? Is it to be filled by a newly recruited employee? These are the first questions to be answered in recruitment. Potential vacancies occur either through someone leaving or as a result of expansion. When a person leaves, there is no more than a *prima facie* case for filling the vacancy thus caused. There may be other ways of filling the gap. Vacancies caused by expansion may be real or imagined. The desperately pressing need of an executive for an assistant may be a plea more for recognition than for assistance. The creation of a new post to deal with a specialist activity may be more appropriately handled by contracting that activity out to a supplier. Recruiting a new employee may be the most obvious tactic when a vacancy occurs, but it is not necessarily the most appropriate. Listed below are some of the options.

▶ **Reorganise the work**: Jobs may be rearranged so that the total amount of work to be done in a section is done by the remaining employees without replacement of the leaver. One clue to the likelihood of this being the right move lies in the reasons for leaving. If the person has left because there was not enough to do, or because the other employees formed a tight-knit group that was difficult to break into, then there may be grounds for considering this strategy. It can also work between departments, with people redundant in one area being redeployed elsewhere.

▶ **Use overtime**: Extra output can be achieved by using overtime, although there is always the possibility that the work to be done is simply expanded to fill the greater amount of time available for its completion. Few personnel managers like the extensive use of overtime, and it lacks logic at a time of high unemployment, but it may be the best way of dealing with a short-term problem where, for instance, one employee leaves a month before another is due back from maternity leave.

▶ **Mechanise the work**: There are all sorts of ways in which the work of a departing member of staff can be mechanised, though it is seldom feasible to mechanise, automate or robotise on the basis of a single, casual vacancy. However, the non-replacement of a departing member of staff is often used to justify the expense of introducing new equipment.

▶ **Stagger the hours**: As we saw in Chapter 10, there can be staffing economies in introducing shifts, staggering hours or trying flexible working hours. It is again rarely practicable to take these steps when there is a single vacancy, although sometimes staggering hours can work in that sort of situation.

▶ **Make the job part-time**: Replacing full-time jobs with part-time jobs has become widespread and has the attraction of making marginal reductions more possible at the same time as providing the possibility of marginally increasing the amount of staff time available in the future by redefining the job as full-time. It also provides potential flexibility by making it possible to turn one full-time job into two part-time posts located in two separate places.

▶ **Subcontract the work**: By this means the employer avoids ongoing costs and obligations of employing people by transferring those obligations to another employer. It is simpler to do this when the work can be easily moved elsewhere, like some features of computer programming, than when the work has to be done on your own premises, with the comparisons of terms and conditions that inevitably take place. Also, the advantages of avoiding employment costs and obligations have to be offset against the disadvantages of less direct control and probably higher overall costs in the medium term.

▶ **Use an agency**: A similar strategy is to use an agency to provide temporary personnel, who again do not come onto the company payroll.

If your decision is that you are going to recruit, there are four questions to determine the vacancy:

1. What does the job consist of?
2. In what way is it to be different from the job done by the previous incumbent?
3. What are the aspects of the job that specify the type of candidate?
4. What are the key aspects of the job that the ideal candidate wants to know before deciding to apply?

The conventional personnel approach to these questions is to produce job descriptions and personnel specifications (see Table 11.1). Methods of doing this are well established. Good accounts are in Ungerson (1983) and Pearn and Kandola (1988).

We have found, however, that less than half of personnel departments use job analysis and its products for recruitment and selection, usually because they wish to avoid the close definition and inflexibility that careful specification often implies. Our set of four questions is offered as an alternative.

Table 11.1 Job description for senior sales assistant

Job title: Senior Sales Assistant

Context:

The job is in one of the thirteen high-technology shops owned by 'Computext'
Location: Leeds
Supervised by, and reports directly to, the Shop Manager
Responsible for one direct subordinate: Sales Assistant

Job summary:

To assist and advise customers in the selection of computer hardware and software, and to arrange delivery and finance where appropriate.
Objective is to sell as much as possible, and for customer and potential customers to see 'Computext' staff as helpful and efficient.

Job content:

Most frequent duties in order of importance

1. Advise customers about hardware and software
2. Demonstrate the equipment and software
3. Organise delivery of equipment by liaising with distribution department
4. Answer all after-sales queries from customers
5. Contact each customer two weeks after delivery to see if they need help

Table 11.1 Continued

6. Advise customers about the variety of payment methods
7. Develop and keep up to date a computerised stock control system

Occasional duties in order of importance

1. Arrange for faulty equipment to be replaced
2. Monitor performance of junior sales assistant as defined in job description
3. Advise and guide, train and assess junior sales assistant where necessary

Working conditions:

Pleasant, 'business-like' environment in new purpose-built shop premises in the city centre. There are two other members of staff and regular contact is also required with the Delivery Department and Head Office. Salary is £12,000 pa plus a twice yearly bonus, depending on sales. Five weeks' holiday per year plus statutory holidays. A six-day week is worked.

Other information:

There is the eventual possibility of promotion to shop manager in another location depending on performance and opportunities.

Performance standards:

There are two critically important areas:

1. Sales volume. Minimum sales to the value of £400,000 over each six-month accounting period.
2. Relations with customers:

   ▶ Customers' queries answered immediately
   ▶ Customers always given a demonstration when they request one
   ▶ Delivery times arranged to meet both customer and delivery department's needs
   ▶ Complaints investigated immediately
   ▶ Customers assured that problem will be resolved as soon as possible
   ▶ Customers never blamed
   ▶ Problems that cannot be dealt with referred immediately to Manager.

Methods of recruitment

Once an employer has decided that external recruitment is necessary, a cost-effective and appropriate method of recruitment must be selected. One survey (Curnow, 1989) investigated the methods used by the 1,000+ personnel professionals questioned (see Table 11.2).

The recruitment methods compared

The various methods of recruitment all have benefits and drawbacks, and the choice of a method has to be made in relation to the particular vacancy and the type of labour market in which the job falls. A general review of advantages and drawbacks is given in Table 11.3.

Table 11.2 Usage of various methods of recruitment by 1,000+ personnel professionals questioned

Advertisements in regional press	87%
Advertisements in specialist press	80%
Advertisements in national press	78%
Job centres	71%
Employment agencies	62%
Recruitment consultants	61%
Executive search consultants	36%
Career conventions	35%
Open days	32%
Recruitment fairs	32%
University 'milk rounds'	21%
Radio advertising	17%
Other forms of recruitment	6%

Source: Curnow (1989)

Table 11.3 Advantages and drawbacks of different methods of recruitment

Job Centres

Advantages:
(a) Applicants can be selected from nationwide sources with convenient, local availability of computer-based data.
(b) Socially responsible and secure.
(c) Can produce applicants very quickly.

Drawback:
(a) Registers are mainly of the unemployed rather than of the employed seeking a change.

Commercial employment agencies and recruitment consultancies

Advantages:
(a) Established as the normal method for filling certain vacancies, e.g. secretaries in London.
(b) Little administrative chore for the employer.

Drawbacks:
(a) Can produce staff who are likely to stay only a short time.
(b) Widely distrusted by employers (Knollys 1983, p. 234).

Management selection consultants

Advantages:
(a) Opportunity to elicit applicants anonymously.
(b) Opportunity to use expertise of consultant in an area where employer will not be regularly in the market.

Drawbacks:
(a) Internal applicants may feel, or be, excluded.
(b) Cost.

Executive search consultants ('headhunters')

Advantages:
(a) Known individuals can be approached directly.
(b) Useful if employer has no previous experience in specialist field.
(c) Recruiting from, or for, an overseas location.

Table 11.3 Continued

Drawbacks: (a)   Cost.
              (b)   Potential candidates outside the headhunter's network are
                     excluded.
              (c)   The recruit may remain on the consultant's list and be hunted
                     again.

Visiting universities (the 'milk round')
Advantage: (a)   The main source of new graduates from universities.

Schools and the Careers Service
Advantages: (a)   Can produce a regular annual flow of interested enquirers.
              (b)   Very appropriate for the recruitment of school-leavers, who
                     seldom look further than the immediate locality for their first
                     employment.
Drawback: (a)   Schools and the advisers are more interested in occupations than
                     organisations.

ACTIVITY BOX 11.2

We have seen the significance of informal methods of recruitment whereby new employees come as a result of hearing about a vacancy from friends, or putting their names down for consideration when a vacancy occurs. Employees starting employment in this way present the employer with certain advantages as they come knowing that they were not wooed by the employer: the initiative was theirs. Also they will probably have some contacts in the company already that will help them to settle and cope with the induction crisis.

What are the drawbacks of this type of arrangement?

Recruitment advertising

Apart from using recruitment consultants, most employers will deal with an advertising agency to help with drafting the advertisements and placing them in suitable media. The basic service such an agency will provide is considerable:

> only one copy of the text need be supplied no matter how many publications are to be used; the agency will book space; prepare the layout and typography; read and correct proofs; verify that the right advertisement has appeared in the right publications at the right time; and only one cheque has to be raised to settle the agency's monthly account.   (Plumbley 1985, p. 55)

These basic technical services are of great value to the personnel manager and are 'free' in that the agency derives its income from the commission paid by the journals on the value of the advertising space sold. The personnel manager placing, say, £50,000 of business annually with an agency will appreciate that the agency's income from that will be between £5,000 and £7,500, and will expect a good standard of service. The important questions relate to the experience of the agency in dealing with recruitment, as compared with other types of advertising, the quality of the advice they can offer about media choice, and the quality of response that their advertisements produce.

Well-known agencies can provide another benefit to the employer wishing to advertise anonymously, as the advertisement can appear under the agency's masthead. This can be more productive than using a box number in those few situations where it is prudent to conceal the company's identity in the early stages. Table 11.4 shows advantages and drawbacks of various methods of job advertising.

Table 11.4 The advantages and drawbacks of various methods of job advertising

Internal advertisement

Advantages:
(a) Maximum information to all employees, who might then act as recruiters.
(b) Opportunity for all internal pretenders to apply.
(c) If an internal candidate is appointed, there is a shorter induction period.
(d) Speed.
(e) Cost.

Drawbacks:
(a) Limit to number of applicants.
(b) Internal candidates not matched against those from outside.
(c) May be unlawful if indirect discrimination. (See Chapter 20.)

Vacancy lists outside premises

Advantage:
(a) Economical way of advertising, particularly if premises are near a busy thoroughfare.

Drawbacks:
(a) Vacancy list likely to be seen by few people.
(b) Usually possible to put only barest information, like the job title, or even just 'Vacancies'.

Advertising in the national press

Advantages:
(a) Advertisement reaches large numbers.
(b) Some national newspapers are the accepted medium for search by those seeking particular posts.

Drawbacks:
(a) Cost.
(b) Much of the cost 'wasted' in reaching inappropriate people.

Advertising in the local press

Advantages:
(a) Recruitment advertisements more likely to be read by those seeking local employment.
(b) Little 'wasted' circulation.

Drawback:
(a) Local newspapers appear not to be used by professional and technical people seeking vacancies.

Advertising in the technical press

Advantage:
(a) Reaches a specific population with minimum waste.

Drawbacks:
(a) Relatively infrequent publication may require advertising copy six weeks before appearance of advertisement.
(b) Inappropriate when a non-specialist is needed, or where the specialism has a choice of professional publications.

Advertising media

Choosing the appropriate medium for your advertisement will be a subject for advice from your advertising agency, but remembering the basis of their income you may want to take an independent view as well. The best source of information on what to choose will be previous experience. If 3 column cm of classified advertising in your local weekly free-sheet have always produced an adequate number of prospective sales representatives before, why change? Many posts, however, do not recur often enough to provide such background data. Also, the labour market is changing constantly and last year's experience may be this year's irrelevance.

The key pieces of information are circulation and readership, as these tell you both how wide the readership is and how much of that will be wasted. Table 11.5 shows the circulation and percentage share of the main daily and Sunday newspapers over two decades, indicating a decline in the sale of quality dailies over that period. To this must be added the information about who constitutes the readership. The National Readership Survey, which is commissioned annually by the media owners, gives figures based on occupations, showing, for instance, that 61,000 accountants read the *Daily Telegraph* and 73,000 graduate engineers read the *Daily Express*, suggesting that you advertise for accountants in one paper and for engineers in the other. The more general classification that is used by media sellers is a peculiar mystique of social classification.

The 'Recruitment Report' section of *Personnel Management* reports monthly on the distribution of recruitment advertising in quality newspapers (Table 11.6), but the main source of detailed information about the readership of newspapers and journals is British Rate and Data (BRAD), which includes advertising rates, dates by which advertisements have to be received, and occasional additional information by the publisher, for example:

Table 11.5 Circulation of market shares of national newspapers

| | Readership (percentages) | | | |
| | Males | | Females | |
	1971	1995	1971	1995
Sun	26	26	15	19
Daily Mirror	38	16	29	13
Daily Mail	13	11	10	10
Daily Express	28	7	20	6
Daily Telegraph	10	6	7	5
Daily Star	—	6	—	3
The Times	3	4	2	3
Guardian	3	3	2	2
Independent	—	2	—	1
Financial Times	3	2	1	1

Source: *Social Trends 27*, 1997, p. 218.

Table 11.6 Percentage share of recruitment advertising in quality newspapers, April 1994

Newspaper	Percentage share
Guardian	42.8
Daily Telegraph	12.4
The Times	10.8
Financial Times	9.6
Independent	7.0
Sunday Times	12.7
Independent on Sunday	2.9
Observer	1.7

Source: *Personnel Management*, June, 1994, p. 79.

> *Accountancy Age*, Britain's only weekly newspaper for accountants, is received by over 72,000 qualified accountants in industry, commerce, public practice, the City and both national and local government. It has the highest circulation and the highest readership among qualified accountants of any publication in the UK.   (BRAD 1984, p. 237)

Drafting the advertisement

The decision on what to include in a recruitment advertisement is important because of the high cost of space and the need to attract attention; both factors will encourage the use of the fewest number of words. The agency placing it will be able to advise on this, as they will on the way the advertisement should be worded, but the following is a short checklist of items that must be included.

Name and brief details of employing organisation

The recruiter seeking anonymity will usually eschew press advertising in favour of some other medium. The advertisement that conceals the identity of the advertiser will be suspected by readers, not least for fear that they might be applying to their present organisation. If the advertisement conceals the name but gives clues to the identity of the organisation ('our expanding high-precision engineering company in the pleasant suburbs of ——') then there is the danger that the reader will guess . . . wrongly.

The brief details will fill in some of the uncertainty about what exactly the organisation is and does. The better known the employer, the less important the details.

Job and duties

The potential applicant will want to know what the job is. The title will give some idea, including a subjective assessment of its status, but rarely will this be sufficient. Particularly for knowledge workers some detail of duties will be sought.

Potential candidates are increasingly interested in the training and development that will be available. If space permits, this should also be included.

Key points of the personnel specification

If you really believe that the only candidates who will be considered are those with a specific qualification, then this may be included in the advertisement. Not only do you preclude other applicants who would be wasting your time and theirs, you also bring the vacancy into sharper focus for those you are seeking. But do you want to limit your search to that extent? If, for instance, you ask for 'full, clean driving licence', do you really wish to exclude all those who have ever had any sort of endorsement, or only those who have current endorsements? Do you really mean a **clean** driving licence or a valid licence? Other typical key points are further qualifications and experience, as long as these can be expressed clearly. 'Highly qualified' and 'considerable experience' are valueless in an advertisement.

Salary

Many employers are coy about declaring the salary that will accompany the advertised post. Sometimes this is reasonable as the salary scales are well known and inflexible, as in much public sector employment. Elsewhere the coyness is due either to the fact that the employer has a general secrecy policy about salaries and does not want to publicise the salary of a position to be filled for fear of dissatisfying holders of other posts, or does not know what to offer and is waiting to see 'what the mail brings'. Table 11.7 lists the phrases about salary used in a single issue of one quality paper. These include some of the common jargon terms: '*c.*' is an abbreviation of the Latin *circa*, meaning 'about', 'k' means 1,000, as in kilometre, 'neg' is short for negotiable, and 'OTE' stands for on-target earnings.

The other common feature of phrases about salary is to include words that are meaningless. The advertisements containing the phrases shown in Table 11.7

Table 11.7 Phrases from a quality newspaper about salary

1. c. £60,000 + bonus + car + benefits
2. from c. £35k
3. £30,000–£40,000 + substantial bonus + car
4. You will already be on a basic annual salary of not less than £40,000
5. Six-figure remuneration + profit share + benefits
6. c. £60,000 package
7. Attractive package
8. Substantial package
9. £50,000 OTE, plus car and substantial benefits
10. £ excellent + benefits
11. £ Neg.
12. c. £60k package + banking benefits

include 'attractive', 'competitive', 'excellent', 'exceptional', 'significant' and 'substantial' as explanations of the income level. It is very difficult indeed to argue that these terms mean anything that would cause an applicant to apply for one job rather than another.

ACTIVITY BOX 11.3

Table 11.7 contains phrases about the value in pay terms of twelve different jobs. Try putting them in rank order of actual cash value to the recipient. Then ask a friend to do the same thing and compare your lists.

What to do

Finally, the advertisement tells potential applicants what to do. This will vary according to the nature of the post. It is conventional for manual employees to call at the personnel department, while managerial employees will be more disposed to write. Applicants who obey the instruction 'write with full details to . . .' will be understandably discouraged if the response to their letter is an application form to be completed, giving roughly the same information in a different way. Application forms are now generally accepted, but applicants not only feel it is unnecessary to be asked for the same information twice, they also develop reservations about the administrative efficiency of the organisation that they had been thinking of joining.

Advertising control

The personnel manager needs to monitor the effectiveness of advertising and all other methods of recruitment, first to ensure value for money, and second, to ensure that the pool of applicants produced by the various methods is suitable. Jenkins (1983, p. 259) provides a useful example of monitoring the effectiveness of advertising for management trainees in retailing.

Table 11.8 reveals a number of interesting points, the first being that employment decisions are mainly taken by applicants rather than by employers. Of the 370 originally expressing interest, over half eliminated themselves by not returning the application form. Of the twenty-three to whom jobs were offered over a third did not take up the offer. An important part of the whole employment process is making sure that inappropriate people eliminate themselves from consideration, and they can only do this when given sufficient information. Table 11.8 also provides information on approximately what number of initial applications are needed to produce a specific number of accepting candidates and what it costs to fill the vacancies by this means. We would suggest this type of simple, clear recording of developments is the most useful way of building up a stock of control data from which to develop a recruitment advertising strategy.

Table 11.8 Monitoring the effectiveness of advertising for management trainees in retailing

Medium	National press
Size of advertisement	60 column cm
Initial response	370
Booklet and application form sent out to	321
Application form returned from	127
Selection board attended by	95
Job offered to	23
Jobs accepted by	19
Employment actually started by	15
Total cost	£1,440
Cost per starter	£96

Source: Jenkins 1983, p. 259.

Employment documentation

Table 11.8 shows the importance of one type of documentation – the booklet sent out to applicants – as a means of focusing the minds of recruits on whether the job will suit them or not. We must also remember the significance of informal recruitment and the need to have information available to the casual enquirer, as well as documents for reference, like the works rules or details of the pension scheme. We shall review some of the key documents.

The job description

As we saw in Chapter 10, the job description is a basic element in providing information to applicants so that they can confirm or withdraw their application.

The advertisement

A copy of the advertisement will not only be needed for internal purposes and for the advertising agent, it can also form the basic information to the job centre and to casual enquirers.

The 'glossy'

Larger organisations tend to produce recruitment literature for general use or to target specific potential employees, like graduates. These publications are usually described as 'glossies', indicating some suspicion about their contents.

A study by Cooksey examining student attitudes towards recruitment brochures found that 'the company brochure was the single most important influence on students' decisions to apply to a particular company' (Cooksey 1988, p. 75). However, the influencing factors lie not in the glossy presentation but in the *content* of the brochure: information about the company, training, promotion prospects, etc.

ACTIVITY BOX 11.4

Recruiters are interested in the job to be done, so that they concentrate on how the vacancy fits into the overall structure of the organisation and on the type of person to be sought. Applicants are interested in the work to be done, as they want to know what they will be doing and what the work will offer to them. Think of your own job and list both types of feature.

The job to be done
1. ....
2. ....
3. ....
4. ....
5. ....

The work that is offered
1. ....
2. ....
3. ....
4. ....
5. ....

How does your listing of features in the second list alter the wording of advertisements and other employment documentation?

Correspondence

It is essential to have some method of tracking recruitment, either manually or by computer, so that an immediate and helpful response can be given to applicants enquiring about the stage their application has reached.

It is also necessary to ensure that all applicants are informed about the outcome of their application. This will reduce the number of enquiries that have to be handled, but it is also an important aspect of public relations, as the organisation dealing with job applicants may also be dealing with prospective customers. Many people have the experience of applying for a post and then not hearing anything at all. Particularly when the application is unsolicited, personnel managers may feel that there is no obligation to reply, but this could be bad business as well as disconcerting for the applicant. Standard letters ('I regret to inform you that there were many applications and yours was not successful . . .') are better than nothing, but letters containing actual information ('out of the seventy-two applications, we included yours in our first shortlist of fifteen, but not in our final shortlist of eight') are better. Best of all are the letters that make practical suggestions, such as applying again in six months' time, asking if the applicant would like to be considered for another post elsewhere in the organisation, or pointing out the difficulty of applying for a post that calls for greater experience or qualifications than the applicant at that stage is able to present.

Miscellaneous information

Among the items of peripheral value in the employment process are works rules, general terms and conditions of employment, publicity material about products, the annual report, house magazines, etc.

Recruitment monitoring and evaluation

How effective is the recruiting you undertake? It is an expensive, time-consuming process with legal pitfalls, so you need some process to monitor the effectiveness of the process. One method is that illustrated in Table 11.8. Wright and Storey (1994, p. 209) suggest four numbers to collect:

1. Number of initial enquiries received which resulted in completed application forms.
2. Number of candidates at various stages in the recruitment and selection process, especially those shortlisted.
3. Number of candidates recruited.
4. Number of candidates retained in organisation after six months.

There needs, however, to be more than this in order to get to the more intangible questions, such as 'Did the best candidate not even apply?'

The most important source of information about the quality of the recruitment process is the people involved in it. Do telephonists and receptionists know how to handle the tentative employment enquiry? What did they hear from applicants in the original enquiries that showed the nature of their reaction to the advertisement? Is it made simple for enquirers to check key points by telephone or personal visit? Is there an unnecessary emphasis on written applications before anything at all can be done? Useful information can also be obtained from both successful and unsuccessful applicants. Those who have been successful will obviously believe that recruitment was well done, while the unsuccessful may have good reason to believe that it was flawed. However, those who are unsuccessful sometimes ask for feedback on the reasons. If a recruiter is able to do that, it is also a simple development to ask the applicant for comment on the recruitment process.

Shortlisting

Shortlisting of candidates can be difficult in some instances because of small numbers of applicants and in other instances because of extremely large numbers of applicants. This can occasionally be attributed to inadequate specification of the criteria. For example:

> One advertisement that was placed in 1983, seeking management trainers and offering a salary in excess of £20,000, asked only for applicants to be of graduate level with some managerial or consulting experience. It appeared in the national press and gave very little additional information. Needless to say, it produced a huge response, as a large number of people, attracted by the salary, would meet the rather vague criteria. (Lewis 1985, p. 123)

There are, however, many instances when a job is attractive and widely understood as being similar to many others (like headteacher, sales representative or management trainee) where an inconspicuous advertisement can produce large numbers of applicants. The conventional method of handling these is to compare key points on the application form with the personnel specification, but large numbers sometimes induce a further stage of arbitrary pre-selection on the basis of some additional, whimsical criterion. Methods we have heard about include ruling out:

Applicants over 45.
Married women.
Unmarried women.
Unmarried men.
Handwritten applications.
Typewritten applications.
Applicants who have been unemployed.
Applicants with poor handwriting.

No doubt there are other arbitrary criteria being adopted by managers appalled at making sense of 100 or so application forms and assorted curricula vitae. Apart from those that are unlawful, these criteria are grossly unfair to applicants if not mentioned in the advertisement, and are a thoroughly unsatisfactory way of recruiting the most appropriate person. In addition, an increasing number of employers who fail to apply fair and objective selection and promotion procedures can expect to be given a tough time in the courts (Aikin 1988).

Ostell uses the term *screening* to describe the early stages of shortlisting:

the purpose of screening can be described as eliminating failure . . . The predictor used most frequently . . . is the application form, but references, scores on psychological tests and a preliminary interview might also be used. It is often possible to screen out the majority of applicants simply by checking whether they fulfil the basic age and educational/technical requirements for a job . . .   (Ostell 1996, p. 94)

Care with the later stages of shortlisting improves the prospects of being fair to all candidates and lessens the likelihood of calling inappropriate people for interview. Where selection is to be made by a panel, it also provides panel members with practice at working together and can clarify differences in attitude and expectation between them. Recently, however, the emphasis has changed from screening. It is now a question of deciding who should be included rather than who should be eliminated. This is not a semantic quibble, but an important change in looking for the positive aspects rather than the negative. The following outline procedure has been developed for use in that most difficult of situations – selection by a heterogeneous panel with a long list of applicants:

Stage 1 Panel members agree essential criteria for those to be placed on the shortlist.

Stage 2 Using those criteria, selectors individually produce personal lists of, say, ten candidates. An operating principle throughout is to concentrate on who can be included rather than who can be excluded, so that the process is positive, looking for strengths rather than shortcomings.

Stage 3 Selectors reveal their lists and find their consensus. If stages 1 and 2 have been done properly the degree of consensus should be quite high and probably sufficient to constitute a shortlist for interview. If it is still not clear, they continue to:

Stage 4 Discuss those candidates preferred by some but not all in order to clarify and reduce the areas of disagreement. A possible tactic is to classify candidates as 'strong', 'possible' or 'maverick'.

Stage 5 Selectors produce a final shortlist by discussion, guarding against including compromise candidates: not strong, but offensive to no one.

Summary propositions

11.1 Alternatives to filling a vacancy include reorganising the work; using overtime; mechanising the work; staggering the hours; making the job part-time; subcontracting the work; using an employment agency.

11.2 Recent trends indicate a greater use by employers of recruitment agencies and executive consultants, open days, recruitment fairs, etc. Relocation constraints have also prompted a move towards the use of regional as opposed to national recruitment advertising.

11.3 Advertising agencies and specialist publications provide a wealth of information to ensure that advertisements reach the appropriate readership.

11.4 Recruiters need to think not only of the job that has to be done, but also of the work that is offered.

11.5 Increasing the amount of information provided to potential applicants reduces the number of inappropriate applications.

11.6 The most important feature of candidate decision-making in recruitment is finding an answer to the question, 'how much will I get paid?' Advertisements are frequently misleading on this.

11.7 Care with shortlisting increases the chances of being fair to all applicants and lessens the likelihood of calling inappropriate people for interview.

References

Aikin, O. (1988) 'Subjective criteria in selection', *Personnel Management*, September, p. 59.

British Rate and Data (1984) Vol. 31, No. 12, London: BRAD.

Cooksey, L. (1988) 'Recruitment brochures – are students getting the message?', *Personnel Management*, p. 75.

Curnow, B. (1989) 'Recruit, retrain, retain: personnel management and the three R's', *Personnel Management*, November, pp. 40–7.

Jenkins, J. F. (1983) 'Management trainees in retailing', in B. Ungerson (ed.), *Recruitment Handbook*, 3rd edn, Aldershot: Gower.

Knollys, J. G. (1983) 'Sales staff', in B. Ungerson (ed.), *Recruitment Handbook*, 3rd edn, Aldershot: Gower.

Lewis, C. (1985) *Employee Selection*, London: Hutchinson.

Office of National Statistics (1997) *Social Trends 27*, London: HMSO.

Ostell, A. (1996) 'Recruiting and selecting people', in C. Molander (ed.), *Human Resources at Work*, Bromley, Kent: Chartwell-Bratt.

Pearn, M. and Kandola, R. (1988) *Job Analysis: A practical guide for managers*, London: IPM.

Plumbley, P. R. (1985) *Recruitment and Selection*, 4th edn, London: IPM.

Ungerson, B. (1983) *How to Write a Job Description*, London: IPM.

Wright, M. and Storey, J. (1994) 'Recruitment', in I. Beardwell and L. Holden (eds.), *Human Resource Management*, London: Pitman.

General discussion topics

1. What are the advantages and disadvantages of graduate recruitment fairs?
2. In June 1997 a review by IPD of the recruitment advertising industry included the following observation:

   > the quality press continues to grow while the mid-market and popular press is becoming increasingly irrelevant in recruitment terms.

   Why do you think this is?
3. Can you improve on the suggestions for shortlisting that the chapter contains?

CHAPTER 12

Selection methods and decisions

While the search for the perfect method of selection continues, in its absence personnel and line managers continue to use a variety of imperfect methods to aid the task of predicting which applicant will be most successful in meeting the demands of the job. Selection is increasingly important as more attention is paid to the costs of poor selection, and as reduced job mobility means that selection errors are likely to stay with the organisation for longer.

Legislation promoting equality of opportunity has underlined the importance of using well-validated selection procedures, and there is increasing emphasis on ensuring that the selection process discriminates fairly, and not unfairly, between applicants.

In this chapter we first consider the role of personnel management in selection, and selection as a two-way process. Next we look at selection criteria and choosing appropriate selection methods. Various selection methods are then considered, including application forms, testing, group selection and assessment centres, references, use of consultants and some less traditional methods, such as graphology. We conclude by looking at selection decision-making, the validation of selection procedures, and selection and the law. Interviews, the most popular selection method, are covered in depth in Chapter 14.

The role of personnel management in selection

Personnel managers still have a key role in the selection process, although in many organisations this is increasingly less direct as indicated in Chapter 9. From an emphasis on direct involvement in shortlisting, interviewing and control of administrative procedures, the nature of involvement is shifting towards provision of specialist advice, guidance and training, and evaluation of selection effectiveness.

Personnel managers are able to draw on their expertise to recommend the most effective selection methods for each particular job or group of jobs. They are also in a position to encourage the development and use of personnel specifications as an aid to selection. A member of the personnel department will normally be the organisation's expert on test use and have the BPS certificate of competence. In an organisation where tests are particularly appropriate selection methods, they will advise managers on the most suitable tests to use, although test administration may be devolved to department level. In a more general sense personnel managers can act as an advice centre on selection methods for line managers, and they are usually involved in the formal and informal training in selection skills, particularly interviewing skills. Increasingly 'how to do it' packs are produced by the personnel department so that line managers have specialist information about selection activities at their fingertips. Personnel departments still play a co-ordinating role in selection activities in many organisations.

In our recent research we found that personnel managers remained heavily involved in selection interviewing, particularly for managers, with over three-quarters (77 per cent) of establishments reporting this. Lower levels of involvement were identified in selection and vacancy decision-making (less than one-third of establishments identifying personnel involvement for any employee group in these areas). In all cases the personnel function was involved with managerial and non-manual employment to a greater extent than manual employment.

Selection as a two-way process

The various stages of the selection process provide information for decisions by both the employer and potential employee. This is not, however, a traditional view as employment decisions have long been regarded as a management prerogative and are still widely regarded in this way. This view is likely to persist for various reasons:

1. It is attractive to managers because it underlines their authority, and they frequently feel that the ability to choose their subordinates is a key to their own effectiveness.
2. It is supported by much academic research. Psychologists have studied individual differences, intelligence and motivation extensively and have produced a number of prescriptions for those managing selection procedures on how to make sound judgements about candidates.
3. Candidates are convinced of their helplessness in selection, which they see as being absolutely controlled by the recruiting organisation.

Despite these features of the situation, we continue to advocate a more reciprocal approach to employment decision-making which is increasingly being accepted (Lewis 1985; Wanous 1992), in the belief that managers will be more effective in staffing their organisations if they can bring about some shift of stance in that direction. We must be concerned not only with the job to be done, but also with the work that is offered.

Throughout the selection process applicants choose between organisations by evaluating the developing relationship between themselves and the prospect. This takes place in the correspondence from potential employers; in their experience of the selection methods used by the employer; and in the information they gain on interview. Applicants will decide not to pursue some applications. Either they will have accepted another offer, or they will find something in their correspondence with the organisation that discourages them and they withdraw. Jenkins (1983) gives a specific example of how applicants drop out, which we refer to in more detail in Chapter 11. After newspaper advertising 321 booklets and application forms were sent out to 321 applicants: 127 were returned, so 60 per cent withdrew at that point. Dropping out later was only slightly less in percentage terms. Posts were offered to 23 candidates and accepted by 19 of whom only 15 started. Thirty-five per cent dropped out.

This type of example illustrates that the managers in the organisation do not have total control over who is employed and that there are two parties to the bargain. Figures of the type that Jenkins provides can be viewed with pride or alarm. It might be that 194 applicants received the information booklet and were immediately able to make a wise decision that they were not suited to the organisation and that time would be wasted by continuing. On the other hand, it might be that potentially admirable recruits were lost because of the way in which information was presented, lack of information, or the interpretation that was put on the 'flavour' of the correspondence.

Herriot (1985) gives a good example of the criteria that graduates use to select potential employers. The frame of reference for the applicant is so different from that of the manager in the organisation that the difference is frequently forgotten. It would not be unrealistic to suggest that the majority of applicants have a mental picture of their letter of application being received through the letterbox of the company and immediately being closely scrutinised and discussed by powerful figures. The fact that the application is one element in a varied routine for the recipient is incomprehensible to some and unacceptable to many. The thought that one person's dream is another's routine is something the applicant cannot cope with.

If they have posted an application with high enthusiasm about the fresh prospects that the new job would bring, they are in no mood for delay and they may quickly start convincing themselves that they are not interested, because their initial euphoria has not been sustained. They are also likely to react unfavourably to the mechanical response that appears to have been produced on a photocopier that was due for the scrapheap. Again there is a marked dissonance between the paramount importance of the application to the applicant and its apparent unimportance to the organisation. Some of the points that seem to be useful about correspondence are:

1. Reply, meaningfully, fast. The printed postcard of acknowledgement is not a reply, neither is the personal letter which says nothing more than that the application has been received.
2. Conduct correspondence in terms of what the applicants want to know. How long will they have to wait for an answer? If you ask them in for interview, how long will it take, what will it involve, do you defray expenses, can they park their car, how do they find you, etc.?

Selection criteria and the person specification

Unless the criteria against which applicants will be measured are made explicit, it is impossible to make credible selection decisions. It will be difficult to select the most appropriate selection procedure and approach, and it will be difficult to validate the selection process. Selection criteria are normally presented in the form of a person specification representing the ideal candidate. There is a wide range of formats for this purpose: the two most widely known are Alec Rodger's Seven Point plan and John Munro Fraser's Five-fold framework. Both are shown in Table 12.1.

Table 12.1 Two well-used human attribute classification systems: Rodger's seven point plan and Fraser's five-fold grading

Rodger's seven point plan	Fraser's five-fold grading
Physical make-up	Impact on others
Attainments	Qualifications or acquired knowledge
General intelligence	Innate abilities
Special aptitudes	Motivation
Interests	Adjustment or emotional balance
Disposition	
Circumstances	

Lewis (1985) suggests that selection criteria can be understood in terms of three aspects: organisational criteria, departmental or functional criteria, and individual job criteria.

Organisational criteria

The organisational criteria are those attributes that an organisation considers valuable in its employees and that affect judgements about a candidate's potential to be successful within an organisation. For example, the organisation may be expanding and innovating and require employees who are particularly flexible and adaptable. These organisational criteria are rarely made explicit and they are often used at an intuitive level. They are made less subjective if a group of selectors join together to share their ideas of what characteristics are required if an individual is to be successful in the organisation.

Functional/departmental criteria

Between the generality of the organisational criteria and the preciseness of job criteria there are departmental criteria, such as the definition of appropriate interpersonal skills for all members of the personnel department.

Individual job criteria

Individual job criteria contained in job descriptions and person specifications are derived from the process of job analysis. It is these criteria, derived from the tasks to be completed, that are most often used in the selection process. A sample person specification drawn up on this basis can be found in Table 12.2.

Although it is reasonably easy to specify the factors that should influence the personnel specification, the process by which the specification is formed is more difficult to describe. Robertson and Smith (1989) identify a lack of research in this area. Van Zwanenberg and Wilkinson (1993) offer a dual perspective. They describe 'job first – person later' and 'person-first – job later' approaches. The first starts with analysing the task to be done, presenting this in the form of a job description and from this deriving the personal qualities and attributes or competencies that are

Table 12.2 Person specification for the job of senior sales assistant using Rodger's seven point plan

Physical make-up
Essential: Tidy, and dressed in a business-like manner.

Attainment
Preferred: GCSE Maths grade A;
Essential: Maths grade D–E
Preferred: Attendance at a programming course, in or out of school; or demonstrate some self-taught knowledge of programming
Essential: Good keyboard skills

General intelligence
Essential: Above-average and quick to grasp the meaning of problems

Special aptitudes
Essential: Ability to relate to people – to be outgoing and form relationships quickly

Interests
Essential: Interested in both computer hardware and software

Disposition
Essential: Patience

Circumstances
Essential: Circumstances that enable attendance at work every Saturday

necessary to do the task. The difficulty here is in the translation process and the constant change of job demands and tasks. The alternative approach suggested by van Zwanenberg and Wilkinson starts with identifying which individuals are successful in a certain job and then describing their characteristics. The authors note that the difficulty here is choosing which attributes are key and need to be specified. Wilkinson and van Zwanenberg (1994) also report on the development of a computer-based expert system which can be used to guide line managers through the development of a person specification for managerial jobs.

In addition to, or sometimes instead of, a person specification, many organisations are increasingly developing a competency profile as a means of setting the criteria against which to select. Competencies have been defined as an underlying characteristic of a person which results in effective or superior performance; they include personal skills, knowledge, motives, traits, self-image and social role (see Boyatzis 1982). The advantage of competencies is that they can be used in an integrated way for selection, development, appraisal and reward activities; and also that behavioural indicators can be derived against which assessment can take place. For a more in depth discussion of the nature and role of competencies, see Chapter 22.

Choosing selection methods

It is unusual for one selection method to be used alone. A combination of two or more methods is generally used, and the choice of these is dependent upon a number of factors:

1. **Selection criteria for the post to be filled**: for example, group selection methods and assessment centre activities would only be useful for certain types of job, such as managerial and supervisory.
2. **Acceptability and appropriateness of the methods**: for the candidates involved, or likely to be involved, in the selection. The use, for example, of intelligence tests may be seen as insulting to applicants already occupying senior posts.
3. **Abilities of the staff involved in the selection process**: this applies particularly in the use of tests and assessment centres. Only those staff who are appropriately qualified by academic qualification and/or attendance on a recognised course may administer psychological tests.
4. **Administrative ease**: for administrative purposes it may be much simpler, say, to arrange one or two individual interviews for a prospective candidate rather than organise a panel consisting of four members, all needing to make themselves available at the same time.
5. **Time factors**: sometimes a position needs to be filled very quickly, and time may be saved by organising individual interviews rather than group selection methods, which would mean waiting for a day when all candidates are available.
6. **Accuracy**: accuracy in selection generally increases in relation to the number of appropriate selection methods used.
7. **Cost**: the use of tests may cost a lot to set up but once the initial outlay has been made they are reasonably cheap to administer. Assessment centres would involve an even greater outlay and continue to be fairly expensive to administer. Interviews, on the other hand, cost only a moderate amount to set up in terms of interviewer training and are fairly cheap to administer. For the costlier methods great care needs to be taken in deciding whether the improvement in selection decision-making would justify such costs.

Selection methods

Interviewing continues to be the most popular method of selection and we devote Chapter 14 exclusively to the selection interview. In our recent research we found that the use of testing was continuing to grow. Tests were used most heavily for management employees (62 per cent of establishments), and less for non-manual and manual employees (39 per cent of establishments). They were mostly used as a guide to selection rather than a vital indication of suitability. Assessment centres were used most heavily for managers as might be expected (24 per cent of establishments), while the use of biodata for all categories of employee was less, but still notable (12 per cent of establishments). In addition to these methods we cover the use of application forms, self-assessment, telephone screening, work sampling and references in this chapter.

Application forms

Growing use is being made of the application form as a basis for employment decisions. For a long time it was not really that at all – it was a personal details form, which was intended to act as the nucleus of the personnel record for the

individual when they began work. It asked for some information that was difficult to supply, like national insurance number, and some that seemed irrelevant,
like the identity of the family doctor and next of kin. It was largely disregarded in
the employment process, which was based on an informal and unstructured
'chat'. As reservations grew about the validity of interviews for employment purposes, the more productive use of the application form was one of the avenues
explored for improving the quality of decisions.

Forms were considered to act as a useful preliminary to employment interviews and decisions, either to present more information that was relevant to such
deliberations, or to arrange such information in a standard way rather than the
inevitably idiosyncratic display found in letters of application. This made sorting
of applications and shortlisting easier and enabled interviewers to use the form as
the basis for the interview itself, with each piece of information on the form being
taken and developed in the interview.

More recently the application form has been extended by some organisations
to take a more significant part in the employment process. One form of extension
is to ask for very much more, and more detailed, information from the candidate.

Another extension of application form usage has been in weighting, or biodata. Biodata have been defined by Anderson and Shackleton (1990) as 'historical and verifiable pieces of information about an individual in a selection context
usually reported on application forms'. This method is an attempt to relate the
characteristics of applicants to characteristics of successful job holders. The
method is to take a large population of job holders and categorise them as good,
average or poor performers, usually on the evaluation of a supervisor. Common
characteristics are sought out among the good and poor performers. The degree
of correlation is then translated into a weighting for evaluating that characteristic when it appears on the application form, or the additional biodata form. The
obvious drawbacks of this procedure are first, the time that is involved and the
size of sample needed, so that it is only feasible where there are many job holders in a particular type of position. Second, it smacks of witchcraft to the applicants who might find it difficult to believe that success in a position correlates
with being, *inter alia*, the first born in one's family. However, Robertson and
Makin (1986) report that biodata were being used by 8 per cent of major British
companies at the time of their survey.

WINDOW ON PRACTICE

Marks & Spencer is one of the largest recruiters of graduates in the country and each year receives huge numbers of applications. Working with biodata analysis, the application forms are first screened in a purely mechanical way, with points being scored for certain criteria, before ini- tial shortlists are drawn up. In this way the com- pany avoids the need to spend expensive execu- tive time in scrutinising all the application forms. This is a very workable strategy when you have a very large number of applicants.

Generally, application forms are used as a straightforward way of giving a
standardised synopsis of the applicant's history. This helps applicants present their
case by providing them with a predetermined structure, it speeds the sorting and
shortlisting of applications and it guides the interviewers as well as providing the

starting-point for personnel records. In application form design the following points are worth checking:

1. Handwriting is usually larger than typescript. Do the boxes on the form provide enough room for the applicant to complete their information?
2. Forms that take too long to complete run the risk of being completed perfunctorily, or not being completed at all. Is the time the form takes to complete appropriate to the information needs of the employment decision?
3. Some questions are illegal, some are offensive, others are unnecessary. Does the form call only for information that is appropriate to employment decision-making?
4. Allan (1990) suggests that in the age of word processors there is no excuse for failing to produce separate application forms for each vacancy advertised, or for not personalising forms and making them more user-friendly. One way of increasing user-friendliness is to use introductory paragraphs explaining why the information in each section is being sought.

An example of an application form that could be used for unskilled and semi-skilled jobs is given in Figure 12.1.

ACTIVITY BOX 12.1

Design an application form for senior manage-ment posts maximising critical information, but asking only for information that is strictly relevant.

Self-assessment

There is increasing interest in providing more information to applicants concerning the job. This may involve a video, an informal discussion with job holders, or further information sent with the application form. This is often termed as giving the prospective candidate a 'realistic job preview', enabling them to assess their own suitability to a much greater extent. Another way of achieving this is by asking the candidates to do some form of pre-work. This may involve asking them questions regarding their previous work experiences which would relate to the job for which they are applying.

Telephone screening

Telephone screening can be used instead of an application form if speed is particularly important, as interviews with appropriate candidates can be arranged immediately. This method works best where a checklist of critical questions has been prepared so that each candidate is being asked for standardised information. There are, however, problems with this method. Because the organisational response to prospective employees is immediate, the decision can be haphazard unless pre-set standards are agreed in advance. The difficulty with setting standards in advance is that these may turn out to be inappropriate in either selecting too many or too few candidates to interview. The standards can, of course, be

BETA BROTHERS: JOB APPLICATION

JOB APPLIED FOR _____

PERSONAL DETAILS
Surname _____ Forenames _____
Address _____
_____ Tel no _____
Date of birth _____
_____

JOB DETAILS
Present/last job _____
Employer _____
Date started _____ Date finished _____
Immediately previous job _____
Employer _____
Date started _____ Date finished _____
Immediately previous job _____
Employer _____
Date started _____ Date finished _____
_____

EDUCATION AND TRAINING
Highest educational qualification _____
Training/apprenticeship _____
_____
_____
_____

IS THERE ANYTHING YOU'D LIKE TO ADD? Please write overleaf
_____

WHERE DID YOU HEAR OF THIS JOB? _____
_____

SIGNED _____ Date _____
_____

When you have completed this form, please return it to:
Mrs J. Rank, Personnel Officer, Beta Brothers, Toolmakers, 71 Western Estate,
Greater Manchester.

We will let you know of the progress of your application within the next 14 days.
If you do not hear from us please telephone 432–1256

Figure 12.1 A sample application form for skilled, semi-skilled and unskilled jobs

changed as enquiries are coming in, but the best candidate, who may have called early, might not be invited to interview if the standards were initially too high. Also, since organisational response has to be immediate there is no time for reflection and little opportunity to be flexible.

Other, more recent approaches to telephone interviews often form part of a structured selection procedure.

One large employer requests CVs from applicants, and, on the basis of these, invites a selected number to take part in a telephone interview. A date and time are given and an idea of the questions that will be asked so that the candidate can prepare. The interview takes about 15–20 minutes, and time is allowed for the candidate to ask questions of the interviewer as well. Candidates are also told in advance of the telephone interview that if they are successful at this stage they will be invited to a one-day assessment centre on a specified date. After the telephone interview candidates are notified in writing whether or not they will move on to the assessment centre stage of the selection procedure.

ACTIVITY BOX 12.2

What are the advantages of using telephone interviews of the type described in the box? For what types of job would you use this approach to selection?

Testing

The use of tests in employment procedures is surrounded by strong feelings for and against, and a lively debate on the value of personality tests is found in Fletcher and others (1990). Those in favour of testing in general point to the unreliability of the interview as a predictor of performance and the greater potential accuracy and objectivity of test data. Tests can be seen as giving credibility to selection decisions. Those against them either dislike the objectivity that testing implies or have difficulty in incorporating test evidence into the rest of the evidence that is collected. Questions have been raised as to the relevance of the tests to the job applied for and the possibility of unfair discrimination and bias. Also, some candidates feel that they can improve their prospects by a good interview performance and that the degree to which they are in control of their own destiny is being reduced by a dispassionate routine.

The use of tests for employment selection is, however, increasing (see, for example Fletcher 1993). Shackleton and Newell (1991) report results from their survey. They found that the use of personality tests had increased to 37 per cent compared with Robertson and Makin's (1986), undertaken five years earlier, which found a 12 per cent use. At the same time the use of cognitive tests had increased from 9.3 per cent to 41.1 per cent. Newell and Shackleton (1994) report that testing is more likely to be used for management and graduate jobs than for administrative, secretarial or manual jobs, as shown in Table 12.3.

Tests are chosen on the basis that test scores relate, or correlate, to subsequent job performance, so that a high test score would predict high job performance and a low test score would predict low job performance.

Critical features of test use

Validity

There is a number of different types of validity that can be applied to psychological tests. Personnel managers are most concerned with predictive validity, which is the extent to which the test can predict subsequent job performance.

Table 12.3 The use of psychological tests for selection purposes by job grade (Newell and Shakleton 1994, p. 18). Used with permission of the *Human Resource Management Journal*.

Job grade	Recruitment selection	
	n	%
Administrative	12	40
Secretarial	11	37
Manual	6	20
Graduates	27	90
Junior management	21	70
Middle management	24	80
Senior management	21	70

Predictive validity is measured by relating the test scores to measures of future performance, such as error rate, production rate, appraisal scores, absence rate, or whatever criteria are important to the organisation. If test scores relate highly to future performance, then the test is a good predictor.

Reliability

The reliability of a test is the degree to which the test measures consistently whatever it does measure. If a test is highly reliable, then it is possible to put greater weight on the scores that individuals receive on the test. However, a highly reliable test is of no value in the employment situation unless it also has a high validity.

Use and interpretation

Tests need to be used and interpreted by trained or qualified testers. Test results, especially personality tests, require very careful interpretation as some aspects of personality will be measured that are irrelevant to the job. Wills (1990) reports concerns that tests are carried out by unqualified testers. The British Psychological Society has now introduced a certificate of competence for occupational testing at level A and is developing a level B certificate. Both the BPS and the IPM have produced codes of practice for occupational test use. It is recommended that tests are not used in a judgemental, final way, but to stimulate discussion with the candidate based on the test results. Research by Newell and Shackleton (1994) suggests, unfortunately, that tests are not used as the basis for discussion. Feedback to those tested is also identified as a key issue, yet again Newell and Shackleton found that this does not always take place.

Context of tests

Test scores need to be evaluated in the context of other information about individuals. Selection decisions need to be made up of a number of different pieces of information. Test results cannot be seen as having a simple relationship with job performance, as, for example, there are many relevant aspects of an individual which a test cannot measure.

Problems with using tests

A number of problems can be incurred when using tests.

1. In the last section we commented that a test score that was highly related to performance criteria has good validity. The relationship between test scores and performance criteria is usually expressed as a correlation coefficient (r). If $r = 1$ then test scores and performance would be perfectly related; if $r = 0$ there is no relationship whatsoever. Correlation coefficients of $r = 0.4$ are comparatively good in the testing world and this level of relationship between test scores and performance is generally seen as acceptable. Tests are, therefore, not outstanding predictors of future performance. Robertson and Smith (1989) carried out a meta-analysis of research on the validity of test results. They found that correlations for cognitive tests were between 0.25 and 0.45, and that those for personality tests were between 0.15 and 0.10.

2. Validation procedures are very time-consuming, but are essential to the effective use of tests.

3. The criteria that are used to define good job performance in developing the test are often inadequate. They are subjective and may account to some extent for the mediocre correlations of test results and job performance.

4. Tests are job-specific. If the job for which the test is used changes, then the test can no longer be assumed to relate to job performance in the same way. Also, personality tests only measure how individuals see themselves at a certain point in time and cannot therefore be reliably re-used at a later time point.

5. Tests may not be fair as there may be a social, sexual or racial bias in the questions and scoring system. People from some cultures may, for example, be unused to 'working against the clock'. Wood and Barron (1992) provide some further examples of how tests may discriminate in an unlawful or unhelpful way.

WINDOW ON PRACTICE

Wood and Barron (1992) describe how in 1991 some guards at Paddington Station took British Rail to an industrial tribunal. These guards maintained that the selection processes that British Rail used for train drivers discriminated unfairly against ethnic minorities. As part of the settlement British Rail promised to improve the situation. One action was to run workshops on test-taking. They found that the ethnic minority guards were not used to a test-taking culture and so they produced an open learning pack which gave them helpful hints on taking tests and gave them material to practise with. As a result five of the seven guards passed the selection test which enabled them to train as train drivers.

ACTIVITY BOX 12.3

In what ways could you measure job performance for the following?

▶ A mobile telephone engineer
▶ A clerk
▶ A supervisor

Types of test for occupational use

Aptitude tests

People differ in their performance of tasks, and tests of aptitude measure an individual's potential to develop in either specific or general terms. This is in contrast to attainment tests, which measure the skills an individual has already acquired. The words aptitude and ability are often used interchangeably, as, for example, by Ghiselli (1966). However, some authors see them as slightly different things. Lewis (1985) defines ability as being a combination of aptitude and attainment. For the purposes of this chapter we shall use aptitude and ability interchangeably, and as something quite separate from attainment. When considering the results from aptitude tests it is important to remember that a simple relationship does not exist between a high level of aptitude and a high level of job performance, as other factors, such as motivation, also contribute to job performance.

Aptitude tests can be grouped into two categories. Those measuring general mental ability or general intelligence, and those measuring specific abilities or aptitudes.

General intelligence tests

Intelligence tests, sometimes called mental ability tests, are designed to give an indication of overall mental capacity. A variety of questions are included in such tests, including, vocabulary, analogies, similarities, opposites, arithmetic, number extension and general information. As Plumbley (1985) indicates, it has been shown that ability to score highly on such tests correlates with the capacity to retain new knowledge, to pass examinations and to succeed at work. However the intelligence test used would still need to be carefully validated in terms of the job for which the candidate was applying. Examples of general intelligence tests are the AH4 (Heim, in Sweetland *et al.* 1983), and the Wechsler Adult Intelligence Scale Revised (Wechsler, in Sweetland *et al.* 1983).

Special aptitude tests

These are tests that measure specific abilities or aptitudes, such as spatial abilities, perceptual abilities, verbal ability, numerical ability, motor ability (manual dexterity), and so on. There is some debate over the way that general intelligence and special abilities are related. In the United Kingdom the design of ability or aptitude tests has been much influenced by Vernon's (1961) model of the structure of abilities. Vernon suggested a hierarchical model of abilities with general intelligence at the top and abilities becoming more specific and finely divided lower down in the hierarchy. Here an individual's potential ability to perform a task is the result of a combination of the specific appropriate ability and general intelligence. In the United States abilities are generally seen as more distinct (Thurstone 1938), and less emphasis is put on general intelligence as a contributing factor. The development of tests of specific aptitudes is obviously influenced by the model of intelligence and ability that is used. Tests of special abilities are those such as the Bennett Mechanical Comprehension Test (Bennett, in Sweetland *et al.* 1983).

Trainability tests

These are used to measure a potential employee's ability to be trained, usually for craft-type work. The test consists of the applicants doing a practical task that they have not done before, after having been shown or 'trained' how to do it. The test measures how well they respond to the 'training' and how their performance on the task improves. Because it is performance at a task that is being measured, these tests are sometimes confused with attainment tests; however, they are more concerned with potential ability to do the task and response to training.

Attainment tests

Whereas aptitude tests measure an individual's potential, attainment or achievement tests measure skills that have already been acquired. There is much less resistance to such tests of skills. Few candidates for a typing post would refuse to take a typing test before interview. The candidates are sufficiently confident of their skills to welcome the opportunity to display them and be approved. Furthermore, they know what they are doing and will know whether they have done well or badly. They are in control, while they feel that the tester is in control of intelligence and personality tests as the candidates do not understand the evaluation rationale. These tests are often devised by the employer.

Personality tests

Swinburne (1985) commented that there are very many articles on training and management development which continue to emphasise the importance of personality for competence in management jobs (Harrison 1979; Hollis 1984; Willis 1984) and yet there is a dearth of papers on the use of personality questionnaires for selection, guidance or development. Swinburne argues that the lack of papers may well reflect the state of the art, in that although the need for personality assessment is high, few questionnaires lend themselves easily to occupational use. An additional reason is that there is even more resistance to tests of personality than to tests of aptitude, partly because of the reluctance to see personality as in any way measurable. In spite of this there has been a marked increase in personality test use over the last ten years and Fletcher (1993) reports that the largest increase in new tests being produced is in the area of personality.

Theories of human personality vary as much as theories of human intelligence. The psychiatrist Karl Jung was content to divide personalities into extroverts and introverts; subsequently Eysenck (1963) regarded the factors of neuroticism and extroversion as being sufficient. The most extensive work has been done by Cattell (1965), who has identified sixteen factors. Amongst them he identified: reserved/outgoing; affected by feelings/emotionally stable; submissive/dominant; tough-minded/sensitive; group dependent/self-sufficient and trusting/suspicious.

It is dangerous to assume that there is a standard profile of 'the ideal employee'. Miller (1975) quotes the example of two establishments in the same organisation using the Cattell inventory to produce a profile of systems analysts. Though the work of each group was similar, the factors most associated with success in the two locations were different.

Another problem with the use of personality tests is that they rely on an individual's willingness to be honest, as the socially acceptable answer or the one best in terms of the job are often easy to pick out (Lewis 1985). There is a further problem that some traits measured by the test will not be relevant in terms of performance on the job.

Some examples of personality tests in common use are Cattell's 16PF (Cattell *et al.* 1962) and the OPQ (Saville and Holdsworth Ltd 1984). For further information on the new fourth version of the 16PF, see Lord (1994).

Interest tests

Interest tests suffer from the same problems as personality tests, without the literature to support their theoretical usefulness. They may perhaps be useful when selecting school leavers for a range of possible jobs, but otherwise their occupational use is not usually recommended.

Interviewing

Interviewing is the most common method of selection, and both one-to-one and panel interviews are explored in Chapter 14.

Group selection methods and assessment centres

Group methods

The use of group tasks to select candidates is not new, dating back to the Second World War, but such measures have gained greater attention through their use in assessment centres. Plumbley (1985) describes the purpose of group selection methods as being to provide evidence about the candidate's ability to:

1. Get on with others.
2. Influence others and the way they do this.
3. Express themselves verbally.
4. Think clearly and logically.
5. Argue from past experience and apply themselves to a new problem.
6. Identify the type of role they play in group situations.

These features are difficult on the whole to identify using other selection methods and one of the particular advantages of group selection methods is that they provide the selector with examples of behaviour on which to select. When future job performance is being considered it is behaviour in the job that is critical, and so selection using group methods can provide direct information on which to select rather than indirect verbal information or test results. The increasing use of competencies and behavioural indicators, as a way to specifiy selection criteria, ties in well with the use of group methods.

Plumbley (1985) identifies three main types of group task that can be used, each of which would be observed by the selectors:

1. **Leaderless groups**: A group of about 6–8 individuals are given a topic of general interest to discuss.
2. **Command or executive exercises**: The members of the group are allocated roles in an extensive brief based on a real-life situation. Each member outlines his or her solution on the basis of their role and defends it to the rest of the group.

3. **Group problem-solving**: The group is leaderless and has to organise itself in order to solve, within time-limits, a problem that is relevant to the job to be filled.

Business games and case studies may also be used. There are further details about these techniques as they are used in the training situation in Chapter 23. Participants are observed during the group activities, and the observers note the quality and quantity of social and intellectual skills of each individual.

Group selection methods are most suitable for management and sometimes supervisory posts. One of the difficulties with group selection methods is that it can be difficult to assess an individual's contribution, and some individuals may be unwilling to take part.

ACTIVITY BOX 12.4

To what extent does an individual's behaviour on these group selection tasks accurately reflect behaviour on the job? Why?

Assessment centres

Assessment centres could be described as multiple method group selection (Lewis 1985). The group selection techniques outlined above form a major element of assessment centre selection, and are used in conjunction with other work simulation exercises such as in-basket tasks (described in more detail in Chapter 24), psychological tests and a variety of interviews. Assessment centres are used to assess, in depth, a group of broadly similar applicants. At the end of the procedure the judges have to come to agreement on a cumulative rating for each individual, related to job requirements, taking into account all the selection activities. The procedure as a whole can then be validated against job performance rather than each separate activity. The predictive validities from such procedures are not very consistent, but there is a high 'face validity' – there is a feeling that this is a fairer way of selecting people. The chief disadvantages of these selection methods are that they are a costly and time-consuming procedure, the time commitment being extended by the need to give some feedback to candidates who have been through such a long procedure which involves psychological assessment. Fletcher (1986) gives some guidelines on how this feedback can be organised. Time commitment is also high in the development of such activities. Smith and Tarpey (1987) describe how inter-rater reliability can vary in the assessment of in-tray exercises. Reliability was much improved by the quality of assessor training, greater clarity in marking instructions, more time allowed for marking, and a structured approach to marking. All these activities are very time-consuming. Survey evidence suggests that the use of assessment centres is increasing (Iles 1992), and Mabey (1989) reported that 37 per cent of the UK organisations he surveyed used group exercises, in-basket exercises and role-play exercises. A helpful text relating competency profiles and assessment centre activities is Woodruffe (1992).

Work sampling

Work sampling of potential candidates for permanent jobs can take place by assessing candidates' work in temporary posts or on government training schemes in the same organisation. For some jobs, such as photographers and artists, a sample of work in the form of a portfolio is expected to be presented at the time of interview.

References

One way of informing the judgement of managers who have to make employment offers to selected individuals is the use of references. Previous employers or others with appropriate credentials are cited by candidates and then requested by prospective employers to provide information. There are two types: the factual check and the character reference.

The factual check

This is fairly straightforward as it is no more than a confirmation of facts that the candidate has presented. It will normally follow the employment interview and decision to offer a post. It does no more than confirm that the facts are accurate. The knowledge that such a check will be made – or may be made – will help focus the mind of candidates so that they resist the temptation to embroider their story.

The character reference

This is a very different matter. Here the prospective employer asks for an opinion about the candidate before the interview so that the information gained can be used in the decision-making phases. The logic of this strategy is impeccable: who knows the working performance of the candidate better than the previous employer? The wisdom of the strategy is less sound, as it depends on the writers of references being excellent judges of working performance, faultless communicators and – most difficult of all – disinterested. The potential inaccuracies of decisions influenced by character references begin when the candidate decides who to cite. They will have some freedom of choice and will clearly choose someone from whom they expect favourable comment, perhaps massaging the critical faculties with such comments as: 'I think references are going to be very important for this job.' 'You will do your best for me, won't you?'

Cowan and Cowan (1989) ask whether references are worth the paper they are written on, and conclude that they are mostly misused. Two key questions should be: 'Would you re-employ this person?' and 'Do you know of any reason that we should not employ them?'

Other methods

A number of other less conventional methods such as physiognomy, phrenology, body language, palmistry, graphology and astrology have been suggested as possible selection methods. While these are fascinating to read about there is little evidence to suggest that they could be used effectively. Fowler (1990), however, comments on their greater use in the EU and pressures, therefore, for greater use in the United Kingdom. Further research (Fowler 1991) suggests that the extent of use of graphology is much higher in the UK than reported figures indicate. There is some reluctance on the part of organisations to admit that they are using graphology for selection purposes. For more information on graphology, see Lynch and Wilson (1985), and for graphology and other methods, see Mackenzie Davey (1982) and Mackenzie Davey and Harris (1982).

WINDOW ON PRACTICE

It is interesting to contrast different approaches to selection in different countries. Bulois and Shackleton (1996) note that interviews are the cornerstone of selection activity in both Britain and France, but that they are consciously used in different ways. In Britain they argue that interviews are increasingly structured and criterion-referenced, whereas in France the approach tends to be deliberately unstructured and informal. They note that in France the premiss is that 'the more at ease the candidates are, the higher quality of their answer', whereas in Britain they characterise the premiss as 'the more information you get about an individual, the better you know him/her and the more valid and reliable your judgement is' (p. 129). Tixier (1996) in a survey covering the EU (but excluding France), Switzerland, Sweden and Austria, found that structured interviews were favoured in the UK, Scandinavia, Germany and Austria. This contrasted with Italy, Portugal, Luxembourg and Switzerland where unstructured styles were preferred.

Bulois and Shackleton identify selectors in Britain as more aware of the limitations of interviews and that they attempt to reduce the subjectivity by also carrying out assessment centres and psychological tests; whereas in France these methods were identified as unnatural, tedious and frustrating. Interviews are much more likely to be supplemented by handwriting analysis in France, which together with interviews were identified as valuable, flexible and cheap sources of information. Shackleton and Newell (1991) report that handwriting analysis was used in 77 per cent of the organisations that they surveyed in France compared with 2.6 per cent of the organisations they surveyed in the UK.

Both culture and employment legislation clearly have an influence over the selection methods adopted in any country and over the way in which they are used.

Using consultants

Consultants are increasingly involved in the recruitment and selection process and will in some cases directly apply a variety of the selection methods outlined above, although it is very rare that they would make the final selection decision.

The problem with using consultants is that organisations may have difficulty in communicating their exact requirements to the consultants and that some criteria – for example, ability to fit into the organisation and be successful in it – are best judged directly by a member of the organisation rather than by an intermediary.

Final selection decision-making

The selection decision involves measuring each candidate against the selection criteria defined in the person specification, and not against each other. A useful tool to achieve this is the matrix in Figure 12.2. This is a good method of ensuring that every candidate is assessed against each selection and in each box in the matrix the key details can be completed. The box can be used whether a single selection method was used or multiple methods. If multiple methods were used

Selection criteria	*Candidate 1*	*Candidate 2*	*Candidate 3*	*Candidate 4*
Criterion a				
Criterion b				
Criterion c				
Criterion d				
Criterion e				
General comments				

Figure 12.2 A selection decision-making matrix

and contradictory information is found against any criteria, this can be noted in the decision-making process.

When more than one selector is involved there is some debate about how to gather and use the information and judgement of each selector. One way is for each selector to assess the information collected separately, and then meet to discuss assessments. When this approach is used, be prepared for very different assessments – especially if the interview was the only selection method used. Much heated and time-consuming debate can be generated, but the most useful aspect of this process is sharing the information in everyone's matrix to understand how judgements have been formed. This approach is also helpful in training interviewers.

An alternative approach is to fill in only one matrix with all selectors contributing. This may be quicker, but the drawback is that the quietest member may be the one who has all the critical pieces of information. There is a risk that all the information may not be contributed to the debate in progress. Iles (1992), referring to assessment centre decisions, suggests that the debate itself may not add to the quality of the decision, and that taking the results from each selector and combining them is just as effective.

Validation of selection procedures

We have already mentioned how test scores may be validated against eventual job performance for each individual in order to discover whether the test score is a good predictor of success in the job. In this way we can decide whether the test should be used as part of the selection procedure. The same idea can be applied to the use of other individual or combined selection methods.

The critical information that is important for determining validity is the selection criteria used, the selection processes used, an evaluation of the individual at the time of selection and current performance of the individual.

Unfortunately we are never in a position to witness the performance of rejected candidates and compare this with those we have employed. However, if a group of individuals are selected at the same time – for example, graduate trainees – it will be unlikely that they were all rated equally highly in spite of the fact that they were all considered employable. It is useful for validation purposes if a record is made of the scores that each achieved in each part of the selection process. Test results are easy to quantify, and for interview results a simple grading system can be devised.

Current performance includes measures derived from the job description, together with additional performance measures:

1. **Measures from the job description**: Quantitative measures such as volume of sales, accuracy, number of complaints, and so on may be used, or qualitative measures like relations with customers and quality of reports produced.
2. **Other measures**: These may include appraisal results, problems identified, absence data and, of course, termination.

Current performance is often assessed in an intuitive, subjective way, and while this may sometimes be useful it is no substitute for objective assessment.

Selection ratings for each individual can be compared with eventual performance over a variety of time-periods. Large discrepancies between selection and performance ratings point to further investigation of the selection criteria and methods used. The comparison of selection rating and performance rating can also be used to compare the appropriateness of different selection criteria, and the usefulness of different selection methods.

Selection, the law and equality of opportunity

The law puts pressure on employers to select employees in a non-discriminating way in terms of sex, race and disability. There is also some less effective pressure on employers not to discriminate in terms of age. These issues are dealt with in more detail in Chapter 19.

Summary propositions

12.1 Selection is a two-way process. The potential employer and the potential employee both make selection decisions.
12.2 A combination of selection methods is usually chosen, based upon the job, appropriateness, acceptability, time, administrative ease, cost, accuracy, and the abilities of the selection staff. Different countries often have a different view on which methods are most appropriate.
12.3 The application form as a selection method is frequently underused or misused.
12.4 Testing gives the appearance of accuracy, but correlations with job performance are not particularly high and they are therefore not necessarily effective predictors. Test use is, however, increasing.
12.5 Assessment centres have the advantage of providing a full range of selection methods, and are increasingly used. They have been found to be more valid than other approaches to selection.

12.6 Selection methods should be validated. A simple system is better than no
system at all.

References

Allan, J. (1990) 'How to recruit the best people', *Management Accounting*, February.

Anderson, N. and Shackleton, V. (1990) 'Staff selection decision making into
the 1990s', *Management Decision*, Vol. 28, No. 1.

Bartram, D. (1991) 'Addressing the abuse of psychological tests', *Personnel
Management*, April.

Boyatzis, R. (1982) *The Competent Manager*, Chichester: John Wiley.

Bulois, N. and Shackleton, V. (1996) 'A qualitative study of recruitment and
selection in France and Britain: the attitudes of recruiters in multinationals',
in I. Beardwell (chair), *Contemporary Developments in Human Resource
Management*, Paris: Editions ESKA, pp. 125–35.

Cattell, R. B. (1965) *The Scientific Analysis of Personality*, Harmondsworth: Penguin
Books.

Cattell, R. B., Eber, H. W. and Tatsuoka, M. M. (1962) *Handbook for the Sixteen
Personality Factor Questionnaire (16PF)*, London: NFER Publishing.

Cowan, N. and Cowan, R. (1989) 'Are references worth the paper they're
written on?', *Personnel Management*, December.

Eysenck, H. J. and S. B. G. (1963) *The Eysenck Personality Inventory*, London:
University of London Press.

Fletcher, C. (1986) 'Should the test score be kept a secret?', *Personnel
Management*, April.

Fletcher, C. (1993) 'Testing times for the world of psychometrics', *Personnel
Management*, December, pp. 46–93.

Fletcher, C. *et al.* (1990) 'Personality tests: the great debate', *Personnel
Management*, September.

Fowler, A. (1990) 'The writing on the wall', *Local Government Chronicle*,
26 January, pp. 20–8.

Fowler, A. (1991) 'An even-handed approach to graphology', *Personnel
Management*, March.

Ghiselli, E. E. (1966) *The Validity of Occupational Aptitude Tests*, Chichester: John
Wiley.

Harrison, R. G. (1979) 'New personnel practice: life goals, planning and
interpersonal skills development: a programme for middle managers in the
British Civil Service', *Personnel Review*, Vol. 8, No. 1.

Herriot, P. (1985) 'Give and take in graduate selection', *Personnel Management*,
May.

Hollis, W. P. (1984) 'Developing managers for social change', *Journal of
Management Development*, Vol. 3, No. 1.

Iles, P. (1992) 'Centres of excellence? Assessment and development centres,
managerial competence and human resource strategies', *British Journal of
Management*, Vol. 3, pp. 79–90.

Jenkins, J. F. (1983) 'Management trainees in retailing', in B. Ungerson (ed.),
Recruitment Handbook, 3rd edn, Aldershot: Gower.

Lewis, C. (1985) *Employee Selection*, London: Hutchinson.

Lord, W. (1994) 'The evolution of a revolution', *Personnel Management*, February,
pp. 65–6.

Lynch, B. and Wilson, R. (1985) 'Graphology – towards a hand-picked workforce', *Personnel Management*, March.

Mabey, B. (1989) 'The majority of large companies use occupational tests', *Guidance and Assessment Review*, Vol. 5, No. 3, pp. 1–4.

Mackenzie Davey, D. (1982) 'Arts and crafts of the selection process', *Personnel Management*, August.

Mackenzie Davey, D. and Harris, M. (1982), *Judging People*, Maidenhead: McGraw-Hill.

Miller, K. M. (1975) 'Personality assessment', in B. Ungerson (ed.), *Recruitment Handbook*, 2nd edn, Aldershot: Gower.

Newell, S. and Shackleton, V. (1994) 'The use (and abuse) of psychometric tests in British industry and commerce', *Human Resource Management Journal*, Vol. 4, No. 1.

Plumbley, P. R. (1985) *Recruitment and Selection*, 4th edn, London: Institute of Personnel Management.

Robertson, I. T. and Makin, P. J. (1986) 'Management selection in Britain: a survey and critique', *Journal of Occupational Psychology*, Vol. 59, pp. 45–57.

Robertson, I. and Smith, M. (eds.) (1989) *Personnel Selection Methods: Advances in selection and assessment*, Chichester: John Wiley.

Saville and Holdsworth Ltd (1984) *Manual of the Occupational Personality Questionnaire*, London.

Shackleton, V. and Newell, S. (1991) 'Management selection: a comparative survey of methods used in top British and French companies', *Journal of Occupational Psychology*, Vol. 64, pp. 23–36.

Smith, D. and Tarpey, T. (1987) 'In-tray exercises and assessment centres: the issue of reliability', *Personnel Review*, Vol. 16, No. 3, pp. 24–8.

Sweetland, R. C., Keyser, D. J. and O'Connor, W. A. (1983) *Tests*, Kansas City: Test Corporation of America.

Swinburne, P. (1985) 'A comparison of the OPQ and 16PF in relation to their occupational application', *Personnel Review*, Vol. 14, No. 4.

Thurstone, L. L. (1938) 'Primary mental abilities', *Psychometric Monographs*, No. 1, Chicago: University of Chicago Press.

Tixier, M. (1996) 'Employers' recruitment tools across Europe', *Employee Relations*, Vol. 18, No. 6, pp. 67–78.

van Zwanenberg, N. and Wilkinson, L. J. (1993) 'The person specification – a problem masquerading as a solution?', *Personnel Review*, Vol. 22, No. 7, pp. 54–65.

Vernon, P. (1961) *The Structure of Human Abilities*, 2nd edn, London: Methuen.

Wanous, J. P. (1992) *Organisational Entry: Recruitment, Selection, Orientation and socialisation of newcomers*, Reading, Mass: Addison-Wesley.

Wilkinson, L. J. and van Zwanenberg, N. (1994) 'Development of a person specification system for managerial jobs', *Personnel Review*, Vol. 23, No. 1, pp. 25–36.

Willis, Q. (1984) 'Managerial research and management development', *Journal of Management Development*, Vol. 3, No. 1.

Wills, J. (1990) 'Cracking the nut', *Local Government Chronicle*, 26 January, pp. 22–3.

Wood, R. and Barron, H. (1992) 'Psychological testing free from prejudice', *Personnel Management*, December.

Woodruffe, C. (1992) *Assessment Centres*, London: IPD.

General discussion topics

1. It could be argued that the selection process identifies candidates who are competent in that process rather than candidates who are most competent to perform the job on offer. Discuss this in relation to all forms of selection.
2. 'It is unethical and bad for business to make candidates undergo a selection assessment centre without providing detailed feedback and support.' Discuss.

CHAPTER 13

Ending the employment contract

Having set up the contract of employment, the personnel specialist monitors the performance of that contract to ensure that both parties are satisfied. Eventually, the contract has to be terminated, either because the mutual satisfaction no longer holds or because the contract has come to its natural conclusion: retirement, the end of a fixed-term contract or a range of other reasons such as emigration, career change or following a spouse to a different part of the country. In this chapter we look mainly at dismissal, with some comment on resignation, retirement and notice.

Dismissal

Although there has been a long-standing employee right to claim wrongful dismissal by an employer, the legal framework of current practice mainly stems from the Industrial Relations Act 1971, which first established the right of employees to claim unfair dismissal, with recourse to industrial tribunals, via ACAS conciliation, in search of a remedy.

Since 1979 the number of applications to industrial tribunals has been between 25,000 and 75,000 each year. Table 13.1 is based on figures published by ACAS and demonstrates how the number of tribunal applications has varied in recent years.

Table 13.1 clearly shows the substantial rise in the number of tribunal cases, but with a declining proportion reaching tribunal: 34 per cent in 1983, 17 per cent in 1989 and rising again to 27 per cent more recently. There are always more appli-

Table 13.1 Unfair dismissal claims over a twelve-year period

	1983	1989	1993
Cases received for conciliation	37,123	48,817	91,568
Settled by ACAS	15,591	27,749	32,798
Withdrawn	9,171	8,927	28,463
To tribunal	12,575	8,528	24,991

Source: ACAS (1985, p. 84; 1990, p. 59; 1994 p. 76).

cations during economic recessions in the wake of company collapses and staff reductions. The rise is thus mostly accounted for by claims relating to redundancy. Not all of the increase, however, arises from cases of unfair dismissal. The number of applications to tribunals relating to workplace discrimination have also increased in this period, as have claims brought under the Wages Act 1986. It is also interesting to note how the number of cases going to tribunal dropped in the mid-1980s when the qualifying period in unfair dismissal claims was raised from 1 to 2 years.

Despite the increased numbers, the proportion of actual dismissals which result in a tribunal decision in favour of the ex-employee is very small. A survey for the Department of Employment in 1983–84 showed that only 6 per cent of employers were deterred from taking dismissal action because of fears of an application to tribunal, but 65 per cent reported that they now took greater care in deciding whether or not to dismiss (Evans *et al.* 1985, p. 34).

Unfair dismissal

Every employee who has been with an employer for two years of uninterrupted service has the right not to be unfairly dismissed, the fairness being determined by the provisions of the Employment Protection (Consolidation) Act 1978, with subsequent amendments in the various Employment Acts of the 1980s and the Trade Union and Employment Rights Act 1993. The main structure of unfair dismissal legislation has, however, remained unaltered since it was first introduced in the Industrial Relations Act 1971. In some areas of employment the legal provisions have made little difference, as the existing personnel policies of the employer have provided a similar or better degree of protection. The protection of the employee is due to a specific set of rules and precedents, which have developed in that particular place of work and which are particularly relevant to it.

Obtaining a legal remedy from the tribunal involves a dependence on interpretation of the law and the situation by outsiders, and this may not necessarily be in the best interests of either participant. The tribunal members are concerned with fairness for employment as a whole; not within one industrial concentration. Furthermore, of course, the tribunal cannot intervene to prevent a dismissal from occurring; it can only act after the event. The power to reinstate an employee is rarely used and the compensation ordered by tribunals seldom reaches the maximum figures permitted under the Acts.

This does not mean that the law can safely be ignored by employers, as the level of complaints to tribunals remains low only as long as practice is ahead of legislation. Even a 'cheap' unfair dismissal could be costly in terms of the unfairness stigma which will influence employee relations generally, can have a damaging public relations effect and could jeopardise the career of the manager to blame. Thus the law determines management practice.

ACTIVITY BOX 13.1

Consider the working activities of some of your colleagues (and perhaps your own working activities). What examples are there of behaviour that you feel justify dismissal? Make a list of your ideas and check them when you have finished this chapter and see how many might be classified as unfair dismissals by a tribunal.

Determining fairness

The novel legal concept of fairness relating to dismissal is determined in two stages: potentially fair and actually fair.

A dismissal is potentially fair if there is a fair ground for it. Such grounds are:

Lack of capability or qualifications: If an employee lacks the skill, aptitude or physical health to carry out the job, then there is a potentially fair ground for dismissal.

Misconduct: This category covers the range of behaviours that we examined in considering the grievance and discipline processes: disobedience, absence, insubordination and criminal acts. It can also include taking industrial action.

Redundancy: Where an employee's job ceases to exist, it is potentially fair to dismiss the employee for redundancy.

Statutory bar: When employees cannot continue to discharge their duties without breaking the law, they can be fairly dismissed. Most cases of this kind follow disqualification of drivers following convictions for speeding, drunk or dangerous driving. Other common cases involve foreign nationals whose work permits have been terminated.

Some other substantial reason: This most intangible category is introduced in order to cater for genuinely fair dismissals that were so diverse that they could not realistically be listed. Examples have been security of commercial information (where an employee's husband set up a rival company) or employee refusal to accept altered working conditions.

Having decided whether or not fair grounds existed, the tribunal then proceeds to consider whether the dismissal is fair in the circumstances. Here there are two questions: Was the decision a reasonable one in the circumstances? And was the dismissal carried out in line with the procedure? The second is the easier question to answer as procedural actions are straightforward, and the dismissal should be procedurally fair if the procedure has been carefully followed without any short-cuts.

WINDOW ON PRACTICE

A charge nurse in a hospital attacked a hospital official, punched him and broke his glasses. He was dismissed for misconduct. Later he was convicted of assault and causing damage. A tribunal found his dismissal to be unfair because he was not given a chance to state his case and because his right of appeal was not pointed out (*Amar-Ojok* v. *Surrey AHA* (1975)).

The importance of procedure was reaffirmed by the House of Lords in the case of *Polkey* v. *AE Dayton Services* (1987). This particular case concerned the fairness of a redundancy when the employer had failed to consult the employee and had also failed to give proper notice. In giving judgment Lord Mackay ruled that the fact that consultation would have made no difference to the final outcome did not render the dismissal fair.

In determining reasonableness, according to Hepple (1992), there has been a shift in emphasis on the part of the courts since 1971. In his view tribunals have adapted their previous practice of balancing the interests of employer and employee and making judgments based on 'equity and the substantial merits of the case'. Tribunals now judge reasonableness firmly from the perspective of 'progressive management' determining that the employer has acted reasonably if the dismissal is within the range of reasonable responses open to employers in such circumstances.

In this book we have separated the consideration of discipline from the consideration of dismissal in order to concentrate on the practical aspects of discipline (putting things right) rather than the negative aspects (getting rid of the problem). The two cannot, however, be separated in practice and the question of discipline needs to be reviewed in the light of the material in Chapter 29.

The question about decisions that are reasonable in the circumstances is a more nebulous one and the most reliable guide is a common-sense approach to deciding what is fair. It would, for instance, be unreasonable to dismiss someone as incapable if the employee had been denied necessary training; just as it would be unreasonable to dismiss a long-service employee for incapacity on the grounds of sickness unless future incapacity had been carefully and thoroughly determined.

WINDOW ON PRACTICE

A Mr Litster was employed by a company on the condition that he obtained an HGV licence. When he took the test he failed, but he was not dismissed. Instead he was given a job as a fitter. *Later* he was given notice and the tribunal held that the dismissal was unfair, as the lack of the licence had not prevented him from being satisfactorily employed. A prompt dismissal would presumably have been judged as fair (*Litster* v. *Thom & Sons Ltd* (1975)).

Lack of capability or qualifications

The first aspect of capability relates to skill or aptitude. Although employers have the right and opportunity to test an applicant's suitability for a particular post before that individual is engaged, or before promotion, the law recognises that mistakes may be made so that dismissal can be an appropriate remedy for the error, if the unsuitability is gross and beyond redemption. Normally there should be warning and the opportunity to improve before the dismissal is implemented, but there are exceptions if the unsuitability of the employee is based on an attitude that the employee expresses as a considered view and not in the heat of the moment. Another exception is where the employee's conduct is of such a nature that continued employment is not in the interests of the business, no matter what the reasons for it might be.

WINDOW ON PRACTICE

An employee of a shop-fitting company tended to irritate the customers, lacking 'the aptitude and mental quality to be co-operative with, and helpful to, important clients'. His employer dismissed him and the tribunal accepted the fairness of the ground but not the procedural fairness of the decision. On appeal the tribunal judgment was overturned as specific warnings of the procedure type would not have altered the employee's performance. He had known for some time that he was at risk because of his difficulty in getting on with the customers and was not able to change his attitude (*Dunning* v. *Jacomb* (1973)).

Where an employee is going through a period of probation at the time of termination, the following are appropriate check questions:

1. Has the employer shown that reasonable steps were taken to maintain the appraisal of the probationer through the period of probation?
2. Was there guidance by advice or warning when it would have been useful or fair to provide it?
3. Did an appropriate person make an honest effort to determine whether the probationer came up to the required standard, after reviewing the appraisals made by supervisors and other facts recorded about the probationer?

The employer will always need to demonstrate the employee's unsuitability to the satisfaction of the tribunal by producing evidence of that unsuitability. This evidence must not be undermined by, for instance, giving the employee a glowing testimonial at the time of dismissal.

Lack of skill or aptitude is a fair ground when the lack can be demonstrated and where the employer has not contributed to it by, for instance, ignoring it for a long period. Normally there must be the chance to state a case and/or improve before the dismissal will be procedurally fair. Redeployment to a more suitable job is also an option employers are expected to consider before taking the decision to dismiss.

The second aspect of capability is qualifications; the degree, diploma or other paper qualification needed to qualify the individual to do the work for which employed. The simple cases are those of misrepresentation, where an employee claims qualifications he or she does not have. More difficult are the situations where the employee cannot acquire the necessary qualifications.

WINDOW ON PRACTICE

Dr Al-Tikriti was a senior registrar employed by the South Western Regional Health Authority. The practice of the authority was to allow registrars three attempts at passing the examination of the Royal College of Pathologists. Dr Al-Tikriti failed on the third attempt and was subsequently dismissed. He claimed that the dismissal was unfair on the grounds that he had had insufficient training to pass the exams. The tribunal, having heard evidence from the Royal College, decided that the training had been adequate and found the dismissal to have been fair (*Al-Tikriti* v. *South Western RHA* (1986)).

The third aspect of employee capability is health. It is potentially fair to dismiss someone on the grounds of ill-health which renders the employee incapable of discharging the contract of employment. Even the most distressing dismissal can be legally admissible, providing that it is not too hasty and providing that there is consideration of alternative employment. Employers are expected, however, to take account of any medical advice available to them before dismissing someone on grounds of ill-health. Companies with occupational health services are well placed to obtain detailed medical reports to help in such judgments but the decision to terminate someone's employment is ultimately for the manager to take and if necessary, to justify at a tribunal. Medical evidence will be sought and has to be carefully considered but dismissal remains an employer's decision, not a medical decision.

Normally, absences through sickness have to be frequent or prolonged, although absence which seriously interferes with the running of a business may be judged fair even if it is neither frequent nor prolonged, but in all cases the employee must be consulted before being dismissed.

Drawing on the judgment of the EAT in the case of *Egg Stores* v. *Leibovici* in 1977, Selwyn lists nine questions that have to be asked to determine the potential fairness of dismissing someone after long-term sickness:

> (a) how long has the employment lasted (b) how long had it been expected the employment would continue (c) what is the nature of the job (d) what was the nature, effect and length of the illness (e) what is the need of the employer for the work to be done, and to engage a replacement to do it (f) if the employer takes no action, will he incur obligations in respect of redundancy payments or compensation for unfair dismissal (g) are wages continuing to be paid (h) why has the employer dismissed (or failed to do so) and (i) in all the circumstances, could a reasonable employer have been expected to wait any longer? (Selwyn 1985, p. 241)

This case was of frustration of contract, and there is always an emphasis in all tribunal hearings that the decision should be based on the facts of the particular situation of the dismissal that is being considered, rather than on specific precedents. For this reason the nine questions are no more than useful guidelines for managers to consider: they do not constitute 'the law' on the matter.

A different situation is where an employee is frequently absent for short spells, as here the employee can be warned about the likely outcome of the absences being repeated:

> The employee . . . can be confronted with his record, told that it must improve, and be given a period of time in which its improvement can be monitored. Indeed, the employer should not overlook the powerful medicinal effect of a final warning, and a failure to give one may mean that the employee is unaware that the situation is causing the employer great concern. The effect of such a warning might be to stimulate the employee into seeking proper medical advice in case there is an underlying cause of the continuous minor ailments, it may deter the employee from taking time off when not truly warranted, and it may even lead the employee to look for other work where such absences could be tolerated. (Selwyn 1985, p. 244)

In the intriguing case of *International Sports Ltd* v. *Thomson* (1980), the employer dismissed an employee who had been frequently absent with a series of minor ailments ranging from althrugia of one knee, anxiety and nerves to bronchitis, cystitis, dizzy spells, dyspepsia and flatulence. All of these were covered by medical notes. (While pondering the medical note for flatulence, you will be interested to know that althrugia is water on the knee.) The employer issued a series of warnings and the company dismissed the employee after consulting its medical adviser, who saw no reason to examine the employee as the illnesses had no connecting medical theme and were not chronic. The EAT held that this dismissal was fair.

Misconduct

The range of behaviours that can be described as 'misconduct' is so great that we need to consider different broad categories, the first being disobedience. It is implicit in the contract of employment that the employee will obey lawful instructions; but this does not mean blind, unquestioning obedience in all circumstances: the instruction has to be 'reasonable' and the employee's disobedience 'unreasonable' before the dismissal can be fair. The tribunal would seek to establish exactly what the employee was engaged to do and whether the instruction was consistent with the terms of employment.

WINDOW ON PRACTICE

Two long-serving ambulance men were rostered for duty between 9.00 and 5.00 in May 1991. They were, however, kept unusually busy in the morning and by 2.00 had not been able to take their usual lunch-break. At 2.10 they were called out again but chose not to respond on the grounds that they were excessively tired and strained because they had worked for over five hours without a break. They returned to the ambulance station and signed off sick. They were then suspended from duty and subsequently dismissed. The tribunal rejected the ambulance men's argument that they had a legitimate need for food and drink after a long spell on duty and found in favour of the employer (*Wallburton and Stokes* v. *Somerset Health Authority* (1991)).

In the case of *Payne* v. *Spook Erection* (1984) an employee was asked to rank subordinates each week on a merit table, even though he had very little contact with some of the men whose merit he was assessing. The scheme was used as a basis for both promotion and possible dismissal. Mr Payne refused to operate this system as he averred that his assessments could often amount to no more than guesswork. Because of his disobedience he was dismissed, but this dismissal was found unfair by the EAT:

> In our judgment, a scheme bearing these characteristics can only be described as obviously and intolerably unfair. . . . To hold that an employer has the right to require the implementation of a scheme such as this would be to strike at the principles of the Employment Protection legislation and the codes of practice of recent years.   (*Payne* v. *Spook Erection* (1984))

Although it is generally fair to dismiss the employee for absence, including lateness, the degree of the absence will be an issue. Lateness will seldom be seen to justify dismissal, unless it is persistent and after warning. Absence may be appropriate for dismissal if the nature of the work makes absence unsupportable by the employer. It will normally be expected that the employer will take account of an employee's previous record before taking extreme action.

The third area of misconduct is insubordination or rudeness:

> words or conduct showing contempt for one's employers – deserved or otherwise, and as distinct from disagreement or criticism – may make it impossible for the employer to exercise the authority which the law regards as his or to assume that the job in hand will be properly done.

> (Whincup 1976, p. 85)

It is important that the insubordination should be calculated, rather than a single moment of hysteria. The willingness of the employee to apologise can also be important.

WINDOW ON PRACTICE

A woman employee with five years of satisfactory service called her manager a 'stupid punk' in a heated moment and in front of other employees. Later she refused to apologise. The tribunal held that the dismissal was unfair as it was based on a single episode in a substantial period of service. The compensation for the employee was, however, reduced to £20 because she would not apologise. (*Rosenthal* v. *Butler* (1972)).

Rudeness to customers is more likely to result in dismissal that a tribunal will find fair. Sleeping with the boss's wife seems likely to produce legal punishment as well as a cuckold's outrage.

WINDOW ON PRACTICE

A Mr Whitlow was asked by a senior manager in his company to carry out some work at the manager's house. In addition to carrying out the work, Mr Whitlow started an affair with the manager's wife. This went beyond the instructions that the manager had given him. It was held that his subsequent dismissal was fair because he had not fulfilled the basic duty of behaving in good faith toward the employer (*Whitlow* v. *Alkanet Construction* (1987)).

Another area of misconduct is criminal action. Tribunals are not courts for criminal proceedings, so that they will not try a case of theft or dishonesty; they will merely decide whether or not dismissal was a reasonable action by the employer in the circumstances. If an employee is found guilty by court proceedings, this does not automatically justify fair dismissal, it must still be procedurally fair and reasonable, so that theft off-duty is not necessarily grounds for dismissal, unless it indicates the possibility of a further offence being committed that would be grounds for dismissal. Employees with responsibility for cash might well be dismissed if they commit an offence of dishonesty while off duty.

On the other hand, evidence that would not be sufficient to bring a prosecution may be sufficient to sustain a fair dismissal. Clocking-in offences will normally merit dismissal. Convictions for other offences like drug handling or indecency will only justify dismissal if the nature of the offence will have some bearing on the work done by the employee. For someone like an apprentice instructor it might justify summary dismissal, but in other types of employment it would be unfair, just as it would be unfair to dismiss an employee for a driving offence when there was no need for driving in the course of normal duties and there were other means of transport for getting to work.

Examples include that of a college lecturer who was convicted of gross indecency in a public lavatory with another man. His subsequent dismissal by the college was held to be fair as he was responsible for a foundation course for students in their mid-teens (*Gardiner* v. *Newport CBC* (1977)). In the case of *Moore* v. *C&A Modes* (1981) a store supervisor with over twenty years' service, was found shoplifting in another store. Although this was a criminal act away from the place of work, the tribunal held that her subsequent dismissal by C&A Modes was fair, because the criminal act was directly relevant to her employment, even though the action had taken place elsewhere:

> The employer must satisfy the three-fold test laid down in British Home Stores v. Burchell. First, the employer must show that he genuinely believes the employee to be guilty of the misconduct in question; second, he must have reasonable grounds upon which to establish that belief; third, he must have carried out such investigation into the matter as was reasonable in all the circumstances.
> (Selwyn 1985, p. 187)

Redundancy

Dismissal for redundancy is protected by compensation for unfair redundancy, compensation for genuine redundancy and the right to consultation before the redundancy takes place:

> An employee who is dismissed shall be taken to be dismissed by reason of redundancy if the dismissal is attributable wholly or mainly to:
> (a) the fact that his employer has ceased, or intends to cease, to carry on the business for the purposes of which the employee was employed by him, or has ceased, or intends to cease, to carry on that business in the place where the employee was so employed, or
> (b) the fact that the requirements of that business for employees to carry out work of a particular kind, or for employees to carry out work of a particular kind in the place where he was so employed, have ceased or are expected to cease or diminish.
> (Employment Protection (Consolidation) Act 1978, s. 81)

Apart from certain specialised groups of employee, anyone who has been continuously employed for two years or more is guaranteed a compensation payment from an employer, if dismissed for redundancy. The compensation is assessed on a sliding scale relating to length of service, age and rate of pay per week. If the employer wishes to escape the obligation to compensate, then it is necessary to show that the reason for dismissal was something other than redundancy.

Although the legal rights relating to redundancy have not altered for over a quarter of a century, there are still problems of interpretation.

WINDOW ON PRACTICE

Mr Johnson was employed as a roofer. When his employer's need for roofing work declined he was made redundant. He claimed that he was not redundant because his contract had been varied so that he could be required to carry out multi-trade duties. The Employment Appeals Tribunal held that his contract was as a roofer, and the fact that he could be required to assist with other work did not alter the fact that he was redundant under the terms of his contract of employment (*Johnson* v. *Peabody Trust* (1996)).

The employer has to consult with the individual employee before dismissal takes place, but there is also a separate legal obligation to consult with recognised trade unions and the Department of Employment. If ten or more employees are to be made redundant, and if those employees are in unions that are recognised by the employer, then the employer must give written notice of intention to the unions concerned and the Department of Employment at least 30 days before the first dismissal. If it is proposed to make more than 100 employees redundant within a three-month period, then 90 days' advance notice must be given. Having done this, the employer has a legal duty to consult with the union representing the employees on the redundancies: he is not obliged to negotiate with them, merely to explain, listen to comments and reply with reasons. Employees also have the right to reasonable time off with pay during their redundancy notice so that they can seek other work.

One of the most difficult aspects of redundancy for the employer is the selection of who should go. The tradition is that people should leave on the basis of a long-standing convention known as last-in-first-out, or LIFO, as this provides a rough-and-ready justice with which it is difficult to argue. Our researches show, however, that an increasing number of employers are using other criteria, including skill, competence and attendance record. Less than two-thirds of employers have agreements on redundancy, yet these are the most satisfactory means of smoothing the problems that enforced redundancy causes.

Increasingly, employers are trying to avoid enforced redundancy by a range of strategies, such as not replacing people who leave, early retirement and voluntary redundancy.

Part-time employees can be vulnerable as they can be made redundant if their jobs are made full-time and they are not able to comply with the revised terms.

The large scale of redundancies in recent years has produced a variety of managerial initiatives to mitigate the effects. One of the most constructive has been a redundancy counselling service. Sometimes this is administered by the personnel department through its welfare officers, but many organisations use external services. Giles Burrows (1985) lists fifteen firms providing redundancy advisory services, and there have been a number of 'outplacement' courses arranged for redundant executives to enable them to set up in business on their own account. Burrows cites evidence from a study by Gibbs and Cross (1985) and concludes:

> a fraction of one per cent of the total market is reached by the nine prominent redundancy counselling organizations that were surveyed. Information gained from 21 large companies which attempted some form of resettlement assistance indicates that only 51 managers out of 7,604 made redundant were sponsored at redundancy counselling organizations.
>
> (Burrows 1985, p. 320)

Some other substantial reason

As the law of unfair dismissal has evolved since 1978 the most controversial area has been the category of potentially fair dismissals known as 'some other substantial reason'. Many commentators see this as a catch-all or dustbin category which enables emoployers to dismiss virtually anyone provided a satisfactory business case can be made. All manner of cases have been successfully defended under this heading including the following: dismissals resulting from personality clashes, pressure to dismiss from subordinates or customers, disclosure of damaging information, the dismissal of a man whose wife worked for a rival firm, and the dismissal of a landlord's wife following her husband's dismissal on grounds of capability.

The majority of cases brought under this heading, however, result from business reorganisations where there is no redundancy. These often occur when the employer seeks to alter terms and conditions of employment and cannot secure the employee's agreement. Such circumstances can result in the dismissal of the employee together with an offer of re-employment on new contractual terms. Such dismissals are judged fair provided a sound business reason exists to justify the changes envisaged. It will usually be necessary to consult prior to the reorganisation but the tribunal will not base its judgment on whether the employee acted reasonably in refusing new terms and conditions. The test laid down in *Hollister* v. *The National Farmer's Union* (1979) [ICR 542] by the Court of Appeal merely requires the employer to demonstrate that the change would bring clear organisational advantage. According to the barrister John Bowers:

> A review of the re-organization case law shows that the EAT and Court of Appeal appear to accept as wholly valid employers' claims that to compete effectively in a free market they must be allowed latitude to trim and make efficient their workforce and work methods without being hampered by laws protecting their workers.
>
> (Bowers 1990)

Automatic decisions

There are some circumstances in which the tribunal is not required to go through the process of first establishing a fair reason for the dismissal before going on to assess the employer's reasonableness. In these cases the tribunal is required to find the dismissal fair or unfair without regard to the reasonableness of the employer's actions.

Automatically unfair dismissals

The following are grounds for automatically unfair dismissal:

1. Dismissals on grounds of pregnancy.
2. Dismissals on grounds of trade union membership or potential membership.
3. Dismissals on grounds of actual or proposed trade union activity undertaken at 'an appropriate time'.
4. Dismissals resulting from an individual's refusal to join a trade union.
5. Dismissals resulting directly from a transfer in the organisation's ownership.
6. When no reason for the dismissal is given.
7. Where the employee has been unfairly selected for redundancy.
8. Dismissal as a result of a past criminal conviction which is spent under the terms of the Rehabilitation of Offenders Act.

The legislation on dismissal for trade union reasons was substantially revised in the Employment Act 1988 and the Trade Union and Labour Relations (Consolidation) Act 1992.

Prior to 1988 it was sometimes deemed fair to dismiss an employee who did not wish to join a trade union where a 'closed shop' arrangement was in operation. Parliament has also waived the two year qualifying period in cases of this kind so any employee can now bring a case of unfair dismissal if they believe their contract to have been terminated as a result of trade union membership or lack of trade union membership. Trade union activity is judged 'appropriate' if it occurs outside normal working hours or during working hours with the employer's consent.

There is now a similar waiving of the qualifying period in cases of dismissal on grounds of pregnancy. New regulations concerning maternity rights came into force in October 1994 tightening up the law in this area which apply to all female employees, part-time and full-time, whatever their length of service. Before October 1994 employers could fairly dismiss a pregnant employee if she was incapable of performing her duties on account of the pregnancy or if continued employment would result in a contravention of health and safety law. Women now have the right to medical suspension on full pay in these circumstances and will be automatically successful at a tribunal if dismissed.

Since the introduction in 1981 of Transfer of Undertakings regulations it has also been automatically unfair to dismiss an employee when a business changes hands or when a public corporation is privatised unless it can be shown that the dismissal was for economic, technical or organisation reasons. It is thus not lawful for a new owner of a business to dismiss the existing manager simply to bring someone else in with whom the new owner is familiar. The same rules apply to hospitals that change to NHS Trusts and to local authority services that are transferred following competitive tendering.

There are also a few situations in which a dismissal will be found automatically to be fair. These fall into two categories:

1. Dismissal of employees who are on strike or taking part in some other industrial action.
2. Dismissals for the purpose of safeguarding national security.

Dismissals resulting from industrial action can only be fair if all employees are treated equally. It is not fair only to dismiss some of the strikers.

Constructive dismissal

When the behaviour of the management causes the employee to resign, the ex-employee may still be able to claim dismissal on the grounds that the behaviour of the employer constituted a repudiation of the contract, leaving the employee with no alternative but to resign. The employee may then be able to claim that the dismissal was unfair. It is not sufficient for the employer simply to be awkward or whimsical; the employer's conduct must amount to a significant breach, going to the root of the contract, such as physical assault, demotion, reduction in pay, change in location of work or significant change in duties. The breach must, however, be significant, so that a slight lateness in paying wages would not necessarily involve a breach, neither would a temporary change in place of work:

> If an employer, under the stresses of the requirements of his business, directs an employee to transfer to other suitable work on a purely temporary basis and at no diminution in wages, that may, in the ordinary case, not constitute a breach of contract.   (*Millbrook Furnishing Ltd* v. *McIntosh* (1981))

Some of the more interesting constructive dismissal cases concern claims that implied terms of contract have been breached.

In 1990, a hotel employee resigned after she had been severely reprimanded by a manager in front of other employees. She claimed that she had had no option to resign because she had been made to feel humiliated and degraded. A tribunal and the EAT accepted the woman's claim of constructive dismissal on the grounds that the manager's actions had breached the implied contractual term of 'trust and confidence' (*Hilton International Hotels* v. *Protopapa* (1990)).

There is no scope for an employer to assume an employee has resigned because of having apparently repudiated the employment contract by not turning up. The breach does not exist until the repudiation is accepted by the employer in dismissing the employee. Unless dismissed, the employee still has a binding contract of employment:

> If a worker walks out of his job or commits any other breach of contract, repudiatory or otherwise, but at any time claims that he is entitled to resume work, then his contract of employment is only determined if the employer expressly or impliedly asserts and accepts the repudiation on the part of the worker.
> (*LTE* v. *Clarke* (1981))

In all matters of dismissal, the personnel specialist should follow scrupulously the suggestions regarding disciplinary and grievance handling set out in Chapter 29. Procedural fairness is a significant test in deciding whether a dismissal was actually fair and not just potentially fair; and the consistent, thorough use of procedure and interviewing can frequently make a dismissal unnecessary as all the other possibilities of restoring satisfaction between the parties are explored first.

The extent to which employers find themselves in difficulty because of not following procedure can be considerable. Jill Earnshaw (1997) carried out research for the DTI on the part played by procedural defects in unfair dismissal claims. In 40 per cent of the cases reviewed the finding went in favour of the ex-employee. The typical failings were:

- no chance given to the applicants to give an explanation;
- dismissal without any prior disciplinary hearing;
- no procedure in cases involving senior staff;
- the procedure used did not comply with the respondent's own rules;
- unwillingness to have a procedure because of disliking formality; and
- no chance for the applicant to rectify their shortcomings.

Wrongful dismissal

In addition to the body of legislation defining unfair dismissal there is a long-standing common law right to damages for an employee who has been dismissed wrongfully. Cases of wrongful dismissal are taken to the county court rather than industrial tribunals and are concerned solely with alleged breaches of contract. Employees can thus only bring cases of wrongful dismissal against his or her employer when they believe their dismissal to have been unlawful according to the terms of their contract of employment. Wrongful dismissal can, therefore, be used when the employer has not given proper notice or if the dismissal is in breach of any clause or agreement incorporated into the contract. This remains a form of remedy that is used by very few people, but it could be useful to employees who have not sufficient length of service to claim unfair dismissal, so the employer who has learned that it is possible to dismiss people unfairly if they do not have two years' service needs to remember that this does not permit wrongful dismissal. There may also be cases where a very highly paid employee might get higher damages in an ordinary court than the maximum that the tribunal can award.

Compensation for dismissal

Having considered the various ways in which the employee might have some legal redress against an employer when the employment contract is terminated, we now consider the remedies. If an employee believes the dismissal to be unfair, the employee should complain to an industrial tribunal. The office of the tribunal will refer the matter first to ACAS in the hope that an amicable solution between the parties can be reached. As was indicated at the beginning of this chapter, a number of issues are settled in this way. Either the discontented employee realises that there is no case, or the employer makes an arrangement in view of the likely tribunal finding. If an agreement is not reached, the case will be heard by an industrial tribunal and, if either party is not satisfied with the finding, they can appeal to the Employment Appeal Tribunal.

The tribunal can make two types of award: either they can order that the ex-employee be re-employed or they can award some financial compensation from the ex-employer for the loss that the employee has suffered. The Employment Protection (Consolidation) Act makes re-employment the main remedy, although this was not previously available under earlier legislation. They will not order re-employment unless the dismissed employee wants it and they can choose between reinstatement or re-engagement. In reinstatement the old job is given back to the employee under the same terms and conditions, plus any increments, etc., to which the individual would have become entitled had the dismissal not occurred, plus any arrears of payment that would have been received. The situation is just as it would have been, including all rights deriving from length of service, if the dismissal had not taken place. The alternative of re-engagement will be that the employee is employed afresh in a job comparable to the last one, but without continuity of employment. The decision as to which of the two to order will depend on assessment of the practicability of the alternatives, the wishes of the unfairly dismissed employee and the natural justice of the award taking account of the ex-employee's behaviour.

In practice, however, reinstatement and re-engagement occur in less than 5 per cent of successful unfair dismissal cases. The vast majority of applicants come to tribunal seeking financial compensation. Many applicants want their jobs back at the time they make their claim but want cash compensation instead by the time the hearing takes place. Research by Evans, Goodman and Hargreaves (1985, p. 47) showed that 78 per cent of the respondent firms which they investigated would never re-employ a dismissed employee, and only 1 per cent actually had re-employed a dismissed employee.

Tribunals calculate the level of award under a series of headings. First is the basic award which is based on the employee's age and length of service. It is calculated in the same way as statutory redundancy payments;

- half a week's pay for every year of service below the age of 22;
- one week's pay for every year of service between the ages of 22 and 41;
- one and a half weeks' pay for every year of service over the age of 41.

The basic award is limited, however, because tribunals can only take into account a maximum of twenty years' service when calculating the figure to be awarded. A maximum weekly salary figure is also imposed by the Treasury which was £210 in 1997. The maximum basic award that can be ordered is therefore £6,300. In many cases, of course, where the employee has only a few years' service the figure will be far lower.

In addition a tribunal can also order compensation under the following headings:

Compensatory awards: These take account of loss of earnings, pension rights, future earnings loss etc. The maximum level in 1997 was £11,300.

Additional awards: These are used in cases of sex and race discrimination and also when an employer fails to comply with order of reinstatement or re-engagement. In the former case the maximum award is 52 weeks' pay, in the latter 26 weeks' pay.

Special awards: These are made when unfair dismissal relates to trade union activity or membership. They can also be used when the dismissal was for health and safety reasons.

A tribunal can reduce the total level of compensation if it judges the individual concerned to have contributed to his or her own dismissal. For example, a dismissal on grounds of poor work performance may be found unfair because no procedure was followed and consequently no warnings given. This does not automatically entitle the ex-employee concerned to compensation based on the above formulae. If the tribunal judges them to have been 60 per cent responsible for their own dismissal the compensation will be reduced by 60 per cent. Reductions are also made if an ex-employee is judged not to have taken reasonable steps to mitigate his or her loss.

ACTIVITY BOX 13.2

In what circumstances do you think a dismissed employee might welcome reinstatement or re-engagement, and in what circumstances might the employer welcome it?

Written statement of reasons

The Employment Protection (Consolidation) Act gives employees the right to obtain from their employer a written statement of the reasons for their dismissal, if they are dismissed after at least twenty-six weeks' service. If asked, the employer must provide the statement within fourteen days. If it is not provided, the employee can complain to an Industrial Tribunal that the statement has been refused and the tribunal will award the employee two weeks' pay if they find the complaint justified. The employee can also complain, and receive the same award, if the employer's reasons are untrue or inadequate – provided, again, that the tribunal agrees.

Such an award is in addition to anything the tribunal may decide about the unfairness of the dismissal, if the employee complains about that. The main purpose of this provision is to enable the employee to test whether there is a reasonable case for an unfair dismissal complaint or not. Although the statement is admissible as evidence in tribunal proceedings, the tribunal will not necessarily be considered to what the statement contains. If the tribunal members were to decide that the reasons for dismissal were other than stated, then the management's case would be jeopardised.

Resignation

In any organisation there will be a stream of people leaving to move on to other things, even though tightness of the labour market has recently reduced many streams to a trickle. Even the most serious of these losses actually provides an opportunity, as a new person will come in or there will be some reshuffling among the existing stock of employees, so that individuals will find fresh scope, and new ideas and energies will be deployed. What is important for effective human resource management is to find out and analyse reasons for leaving, as this will provide information that can be used to iron out problems.

Most people simply move on, but some move on because the 'push' factors are stronger than the 'pulls'. By interviewing everyone who leaves, the personnel manager can collect the range of reasons for people resigning in order to see what the pattern is in the decisions. The difficulty is that at that time the employee has not only decided to go, but also has another job to go to, so that the reasons that first caused the employee to look around may have been forgotten in the enthusiasm about the attractions of the new job. Also, the new job must be presented as better, otherwise the leaver looks foolish. With these reservations, the personnel manager can see what features of organisational practice are unsettling people.

An important legal point about resignation is that an employer cannot avoid the possibility of an unfair dismissal by offering the employee the choice between resigning or being dismissed. Resignation under duress is likely to be construed as dismissal. This is not the same as giving an employee the choice between performing the contract and resigning. The employee who resigns in that situation is making a personal choice to resign rather than discharge those duties the employer is legally entitled to expect.

Retirement

The final mode of contract termination is retirement, and this has the advantage for the employer that there is usually plenty of notice, so that succession arrangements can be planned smoothly. It is now rare for people to retire abruptly after working at high pressure to the very end. Some sort of phased withdrawal is much preferred, so that the retiree adjusts gradually to the new state of being out of regular employment and with a lower level of income, while the employing organisation is able to prepare a successor to take office.

Table 13.2 Changes in the labour force, by gender and age, between 1971 and 1996

		Ages 25–54	Ages 55 and over
Males	1971	9,400,000	3,200,000
	1996	11,200,000	2,000,000
Females	1971	5,500,000	1,700,000
	1996	9,100,000	1,300,000

Source: *Social Trends*, 1997, p. 74

Another advantage of this arrangement is that there may be 'a life after death' with the retiree continuing to work part-time after retirement, or coming back to help out at peak periods or at holiday times. Many organisations go to great lengths to keep in touch with their retired personnel, often arranging Christmas parties, excursions and other events with people returning year after year.

Early retirement has become a widespread method of slimming payrolls and making opportunities both for some people to retire early and for others to take their place. The nature of the pension arrangements are critical to early retirement strategies, as early retirees are ideally voluntary and the majority of people will accept, or volunteer for, early retirement if the financial terms are acceptable. It is not, of course, possible to draw state retirement pension until the official retirement ages of 65 for men and 60 (moving towards 65) for women, but many people will accept an occupational pension and a lump sum in their fifties if they see the possibility of a new lease of life to pursue other interests or to start their own business. Since 1971 the number of men between 25 and 54 in the labour force has risen by nearly 20 per cent. In the same period the number over 55 who are still working has dropped by 37.5 per cent. For women the decline over the same period has been a more modest 23.5 per cent (see Table 13.2).

Notice

An employee qualifies for notice of dismissal on completion of four weeks of employment with an employer. At that time the employee is entitled to receive one week's notice. This remains constant until the employee has completed two years' service, after which it increases to two weeks' notice, thereafter increasing on the basis of one week's notice per additional year of service up to a maximum of twelve weeks for twelve years' unbroken service with that employer. These are minimum statutory periods. If the employer includes longer periods of notice in the contract, which is quite common with senior employees, then they are bound by the longer period.

The employee is required to give one week's notice after completing four weeks' service and this period does not increase as a statutory obligation. If an employee accepts a contract in which the period of notice to be given is longer, then that is binding, but the employer may have problems of enforcement if an employee is not willing to continue in employment for the longer period.

Neither party can withdraw notice unilaterally. The withdrawal will be effective only if the other party agrees. Therefore, if an employer gives notice to an employee and wishes later to withdraw it, this can be done only if the employee agrees to the contract of employment remaining in existence. Equally, employees cannot change thieir minds about resigning unless the employer agrees.

Notice exists when a date has been specified. The statement 'We're going to wind up the business, so you will have to find another job' is not notice: it is a warning of intention.

Personnel managers and the law

Personnel managers should not be overconcerned with the legalism of the tribunal system, as this is a danger that the legal system itself is regularly trying to avoid. The following is an extract from a recent EAT judgment:

> Industrial tribunals are not required, and should not be invited, to subject the authorities to the same analysis as a court of law searching in a plethora of precedent for binding or persuasive authority. The objective of Parliament when it first framed the right not to be unfairly dismissed and set up a system of industrial tribunals (with a majority of lay members) to administer it, was to banish legalism and in particular to ensure that, wherever possible, parties conducting their own case would be able to face the tribunal with the same ease and confidence as those professionally represented. A preoccupation with guideline authority puts that objective in jeopardy.   (IRLR (1984), p. 131)

The existence of an expanding body of labour legislation greatly enhances the role and authority of the personnel specialist within organisations. The law relating to employment is steadily becoming more complex and is thus inevitably outside the competence of most line managers. Legal developments can thus only increase the need for personnel specialists trained to pilot organisations through these ever more hazardous waters.

Summary propositions

13.1 Of the many dismissals that take place in a year, a minority are reported to tribunal and a small minority are found in favour of the ex-employee.

13.2 The grounds on which an employee can be dismissed without the likelihood of an unfair dismissal claim are lack of capability, misconduct, redundancy, statutory bar or some other substantial reason.

13.3 If an employee is dismissed on one of the above grounds, the dismissal must still be procedurally fair: following the agreed procedure and being fair in the circumstances.

13.4 An employee who resigns as a result of unreasonable behaviour by the employer could still be able to claim unfair dismissal: constructive dismissal.

13.5 Personnel managers will not wish to discourage employees from resigning, but they will need to monitor reasons for leaving.

13.6 When employees retire from an organisation, a phased withdrawal rather than abrupt termination is likely to be a better arrangement for both employer and employee.

13.7 When contemplating the potential fairness of a dismissal, personnel managers should concentrate on the statute and the facts of the situation rather than examining tribunal precedent.

References

ACAS (1985) *Annual Report 1984*, London: Advisory, Conciliation and
   Arbitration Service.
ACAS (1990), *Annual Report 1989*, London: Advisory, Conciliation and
   Arbitration Service.
ACAS (1994), *Annual Report 1993*, London: Advisory, Conciliation and
   Arbitration Service.
Bowers, J. (1990) *Bowers on Employment Law*, London: Blackstone.
Burrows, G. (1985) *Redundancy Counselling for Managers*, London: Institute of
   Personnel Management.
Earnshaw, J. M. (1997) 'Tribunals and tribulations', *People Management*, May,
   pp. 34–6.
Evans, S., Goodman, J. and Hargreaves, L. (1985) *Unfair Dismissal Law and
   Employment Practice in the 1980s*, DoE Research Paper No. 53, London:
   Department of Employment.
Gibbs, A. and Cross, M. (1985) *A Study of Managerial Resettlement*, London:
   Manpower Services Commission.
Hepple, B. A. (1992) 'The fall and rise of unfair dismissal', in W. McCarthy
   (ed.), *Legal Interventions in Industrial Relations*, Oxford: Blackwell.
London Transport Executive v. *Clarke* (1981) ICR 355, IRLR 166.
Millbrook Furnishing Industries Ltd v. *McIntosh* (1981) IRLR 309.
Payne v. *Spook Erection Ltd* (1984) IRLR (221).
Selwyn, N. (1985) *Law of Employment*, 5th edn, London: Butterworth.
Whincup, M. (1976) *Modern Employment Law*, London: Heinemann.

General discussion topics

1. If you were dismissed in circumstances that you regarded as legally unfair, would you prefer to seek satisfaction through ACAS conciliation or through a tribunal hearing? Why?
2. In some countries a dismissal cannot be made until *after* a tribunal hearing, so that its 'fairness' is decided before it takes effect. What do you see as the benefits and drawbacks of that system?
3. What changes would you make in the criteria for dismissal on the grounds of misconduct?

CHAPTER 14

Interactive skill:
selection interviewing

We now discuss one of the most familiar and forbidding encounters of organisational life – the selection interview. Most people have had at least one experience of being interviewed as a preliminary to employment and few reflect with pleasure on the experience. Personnel specialists have a critical role in selection interviewing, carrying out many of the interviews and encouraging good interviewing practice in others by example, support and training.

In this chapter we review the varieties of selection interview and the criticism that has been made of it, in spite of its importance as a selection tool. Interview strategy and the number of interviews and interviewers are then considered, followed by sections on preparation and conduct of the interview.

Varieties of interview

There is a wide variety of practice in selection interviewing. At one extreme we read of men seeking work in the docks of Victorian London and generally being treated as if they were in a cattle market. Men had to queue up in a series of gangways, similar to those used today to corral cattle at market, and had to vie with each other for the attention of the foreman hiring labourers for the day. Some of the older men apparently used to dye their hair in a pathetic attempt to catch the foreman's eye as being younger and fitter than they were in reality. In sharp contrast is the attitude of Sherlock Holmes to a prospective employer:

> I can only say, madam, that I shall be happy to devote the same care to your case as I did to that of your friend. As to reward, my profession is its reward; but you are at liberty to defray whatever expenses I may be put to, at the time which suits you best. (Conan Doyle 1966)

There is a neat spectrum of employee participation in the employment process which correlates with social class and type of work. While the London docks situation of the 1890s is not found today, there are working situations where the degree of discussion between the parties is limited to perfunctory exchanges about trade union membership, hours of work and rates of pay: labourers on building sites and extras on film sets being two examples. As interviews move up the organisational hierarchy there is growing equilibrium with the interviewer becoming more courteous and responsive to questions from the applicant, who will probably be described as a 'candidate' or someone who 'might be interested in the position'. For the most senior positions it is unlikely that people will be invited to respond to vacancies advertised in the press. Individuals will be approached, either directly or through consultants, and there will be an elaborate pavane in which each party seeks to persuade the other to declare an interest first.

Another indication of the variety of employment practice is in the titles used. The humblest of applicants seek 'jobs' or 'vacancies', while the more ambitious are looking for 'places', 'posts', 'positions', 'openings' or 'opportunities'. The really high-flyers seem to need somewhere to sit down, as they are offered 'seats on the board', 'professorial chairs' or 'places on the front bench'.

The purpose of the selection interview

An interview is a controlled conversation with a purpose. There are more exchanges in a shorter period related to a specific purpose than in an ordinary conversation. In the selection interview the purposes are:

1. To collect information in order to predict how well the applicants would perform in the job for which they have applied, by measuring them against predetermined criteria.
2. To provide the candidate with full details of the job and organisation to facilitate their decision-making.
3. To conduct the interview in such a manner that candidates feel that they have been given a fair hearing.

Criticism of the selection interview

The selection interview has been extensively criticised as being unreliable, invalid and subjective, although this is directed towards the decisions made and ignores the importance of the interview as a ritual in the employment process.

The most perceptive criticism is by Webster (1964), summarising extensive research. The main conclusions were:

1. Interviewers decided to accept or reject a candidate within the first three or four minutes of the interview and then spent the remainder of the interview time seeking evidence to confirm that their first impression was right.
2. Interviews seldom altered the tentative opinion formed by the interviewer seeing the application form and the appearance of the candidate.
3. Interviewers place more weight on evidence that is unfavourable than on evidence that is favourable.
4. When interviewers have made up their minds very early in the interview, their behaviour betrays their decision to the candidate.

However much this criticism is justified, it does not solve the problem, it only identifies it. Lopez points to the fact that all the complaints and denunciations boil down to the argument that it is the interviewer and not the interview that is at the heart of the problem (Lopez 1975, p. 5).

Anderson and Shackleton summarise the latest research conclusions:

> Utilized properly, depending upon its exact purpose, the interview emerges as a valid and reliable tool in candidate assessment. Moreover, its flexibility to act as a medium for mutual preview or as a final-stage forum for negotiation between the parties, renders the interview more useful in selection than narrowly focused definitions of validity and reliability can convey.   (Anderson and Shackleton 1993, p. 68)

A key skill for personnel and other managers is how to handle this most crucial of encounters. It will not disappear from employment, as we shall see in the next section, and the interview provides a number of important advantages which cannot be provided by any other means.

The importance of the selection interview

The selection interview cannot be bettered as a means of exchanging information and meeting the human and ritual aspects of the employment process.

Exchanging information

The interview is a flexible and speedy means of exchanging information, over a broad range of topics. The employer has the opportunity to sell the company and explain job details in depth. Applicants have the chance to ask questions about the job and the company in order to collect the information they require for their own selection decision. The interview is also the logical culmination of the employment process, as information from a variety of sources – such as application forms, tests and references – can be discussed together.

Human and ritual aspects

In an interview some assessment can be made of matters that cannot be approached any other way, like the potential compatibility of two people who will have to work together. Both parties need to meet each other before the contract begins to 'tune in' to each other and begin the process of induction. The interview is valuable in that way to both potential employee and potential employer. As Lopez suggests, it gives interviewees the feeling that they matter as another person is devoting time to them and they are not being considered by a computer. Also, giving applicants a chance to ask questions underlines their decision-making role, making them feel less helpless in the hands of the all-powerful interviewer. Selection interviewing has powerful ritual elements, as the applicant is seeking either to enter, or to rise within, a social system. This requires the display of deferential behaviours:

> upward mobility involves the presentation of proper performances and . . . efforts to move upward . . . are expressed in terms of sacrifices made for the maintenance of front.   (Goffman 1974, p. 45)

At the same time those who are already inside and above display their superiority and security, even unconsciously, in contrast with the behaviour of someone so obviously anxious to share the same privileged position.

Reason tells us that this is inappropriate at the end of the twentieth century as it produces an unreasonable degree of dependency in the applicant; and the books are full of advice to interviewers not to brandish their social superiority, but to put applicants at their ease and to reduce the status differentials. This, however, acknowledges their superiority as they are the ones who take the initiative; applicants are not expected to help the interviewer relax and feel less apprehensive. Also the reality of the situation is usually that of applicant anxious to get in and selector choosing among several. Status differentials cannot simply be set aside. The selection interview is at least partly an initiation rite, not as elaborate as entry to commissioned rank in the armed forces, nor as whimsical as finding one's way into the Brownie ring, but still a process of going through hoops and being found worthy in a process where other people make all the rules.

ACTIVITY BOX 14.1

For a selection interview in which you recently participated, either as selector or as applicant, consider the following:

1. What were the ritual features?
2. Were any useful ritual features missing?
3. Could ritual have been, in any way, *helpfully* reduced?

No matter what other means of making employment decisions there may be, the interview is crucial, and when worries are expressed about its reliability, this is not a reason for doing away with it: it is a reason for conducting it properly.

Interview strategy

The approach to selection interviewing varies considerably from the amiable chat in a bar to the highly organised, multi-person panel.

Frank and friendly strategy

By far the most common is the approach which Hackett (1978) described as frank and friendly. Here the interviewer is concerned to establish and maintain the rapport. This is done partly in the belief that if interviewees do not feel threatened, and are relaxed, they will be more forthcoming in the information that they offer. It is the most straightforward strategy for both interviewer and interviewee and has the potential advantage that the interviewees will leave with a favourable impression of the company.

Problem-solving strategy

A variation of the frank and friendly strategy is the problem-solving approach. It is the method of presenting the candidate with a hypothetical problem and evaluating his or her answer, like the king in the fairy tale who offered the hand of the princess in marriage to the first suitor who could answer three riddles.

These are sometimes called situational interviews. The questions asked are derived from the job description and candidates are required to imagine themselves as the job holder and describe what they would do in a variety of hypothetical situations. This method is most applicable to testing elementary knowledge, like the colour coding of wires in electric cables or maximum dosages of specified drugs. It is less effective to test understanding and ability.

WINDOW ON PRACTICE

The following intriguing poser was put to a candidate for the position of security officer at a large department store:

    If you were alone in the building and decided to inspect the roof, what would you do if the only door out on to the roof banged itself shut behind you and the building caught fire?

The retired police superintendent to whom that question was posed asked, very earnestly and politely, for six pieces of additional information, like the location of telephones, time of day, height of building, fire escapes. The replies became progressively more uncertain and the interviewer hastily shifted the ground of the interview to something else.

There is no guarantee that the candidate would actually behave in the way suggested. The quick thinker will score at the expense of the person who can take action more effectively than they can answer riddles.

Behavioural event strategy

Similar to the problem-solving strategy is the behavioural event method. The focus is on the candidate's past behaviour and performance, which is a more reliable way of predicting future performance than asking interviewees what they would do in a certain situation. Examples of questions used in this type of interview are given by Jenks and Zevnik (1989). Candidates are requested to describe the background to a situation and explain what they did and why; what their options were; how they decided what to do; and the anticipated and real results of their action. The success of this method is critically dependent on in-depth job analysis, and preferably competency analysis, in order to frame the best questions.

Stress strategy

In the stress approach the interviewer becomes aggressive, disparages the candidates, puts them on the defensive or disconcerts them by strange behaviour. The Office of Strategic Services in the United States used this method in the Second World War to select men for espionage work, and subsequently the idea was used by some business organisations on the premise that executive life was stressful, so a simulation of the stress would determine whether or not the candidate could cope.

The advantage of the method is that it may demonstrate a necessary strength or a disqualifying weakness that would not be apparent through other methods. The disadvantages are that evaluating the behaviour under stress is problematic, and those who are not selected will think badly of the employer.

The likely value of stress interviewing is so limited that it is hardly worth mentioning, except that it has such spurious appeal to many managers, who are attracted by the idea of injecting at least some stress into the interview 'to see what they are made of', 'to put them on their mettle' or some similar jingoism.

Most candidates feel that the procedures are stressful enough, without adding to them. In addition, Sidney and Brown comment:

> There is seldom any reason for assuming that the stress of dealing with a hostile . . . potential . . . employer . . . resembles the kind of stress the applicant would be asked to face if he were appointed. The [stress] interview yields possible evidence on only one aspect of personality . . . and perforce omits much else that should be relevant.   (Sidney and Brown 1961, pp. 164–5)

Number of interviews and interviewers

There are two broad traditions governing the number of interviewers. One tradition says that effective, frank discussion can only take place on a one-to-one basis, so candidates meet one interviewer, or several interviewers, one at a time. The other tradition is that fair play must be demonstrated and nepotism prevented so the interview must be carried out, and the decision made, by a panel of interviewers. Within this dichotomy there are various options.

The individual interview

This method gives the greatest chance of establishing rapport, developing mutual trust and the most efficient deployment of time in the face-to-face encounter, as each participant has to compete with only one other speaker. It is usually also the most satisfactory method for the candidate, who has to tune in only to one other person instead of needing constantly to adjust their antennae to different interlocutors. They can more readily ask questions, as it is difficult to ask a panel of six people to explain the workings of the pension scheme, and it is the least formal.

The disadvantages lie in the dependence the organisation places on the judgement of one of its representatives – although this can be mitigated by a series of individual interviews – and the ritual element is largely missing. Candidates may not feel they have been 'done' properly. Our recent research indicates that a sole interview with the line manager is very popular in the selection of blue-collar staff, being used in over one-third of cases. It is much less popular for white-collar and management staff.

Sequential interviews

This is a series of individual interviews. The series most often consists of just two interviews for blue- and white-collar staff, but more than two for managerial staff. The most frequent combination is an interview with the line manager and an interview with a representative of the personnel department. For managerial posts this will be extended to interviews with other departmental managers, top managers and significant prospective colleagues. Sequential interviews are useful as they can give the employer a broader picture of the candidate and they also allow the applicant to have contact with a greater number of potential colleagues. However, the advantages of sequential interviews need to be based on effective organisation and interviews all on the same day. Lopez (1975) argues that it is important that all interviewers meet beforehand to agree on the requirements of the post and to decide how each will contribute to the overall theme. Immediately following the interviews a further meeting needs to take place so that the candidates can be jointly evaluated. One disadvantage of the method is the organisation and time that it takes from both the employer's and the candidate's point of view. It requires considerable commitment from the candidate who may have to keep repeating similar information and whose performance may deteriorate throughout the interviews due to fatigue.

Panel interviews

This method has the specious appeal of sharing judgement and may appear to be a way of saving time in interviewing as all panel members are operating at once. It is also possible to legitimise a quick decision – always popular with candidates – and there can be no doubt about the ritual requirements being satisfied. Muir (1988) also argues that panel interviews are less influenced by personal bias, ensure the candidate is more acceptable to the whole organisation, and allow the candidate to get a better feel for the whole organisation.

The drawbacks lie in the tribunal nature of the panel. They are not having a conversation with the candidates; they are sitting in judgment upon them and assessing the evidence they are able to present in response to their requests. There is little prospect of building rapport and developing discussion, and there is likely to be as much interplay between members of the panel as there is between the panel and the candidate. Alec Rodger makes the observation:

> The usefulness of the board interview may depend a good deal on the competence of the chairman, and on the good sense of board members.
>
> A promising board interview can easily be ruined by a member who does not appreciate the line of questioning being pursued by one of his fellow-members and who interrupts with irrelevancies.   (Rodger 1975 p. 17)

Panel interviews tend to over-rigidity and give ironic point to the phrase 'it is only a formality'. Ritualistically they are superb, but as a useful preliminary to employment they are questionable.

However, the benefits of the panel interview can be gained, and the disadvantages minimised, if the interviewers are well trained and the interview well organised, thoroughly planned and is part of a structured interviewing process, as, for example, described by Campion *et al.* (1988).

ACTIVITY BOX 14.2

In your organisation how many interviews and interviewers are used? How effective is this approach and why? In what ways could the approach be improved?

The selection interview sequence

Preparation

We assume that the preliminaries of job analysis, recruitment and shortlisting are complete and the interview is now to take place. The first step in preparation is for the interviewers to brief themselves. They will collect and study a job description or similar details of the post to be filled, a personnel specification or statement of required competencies and the application forms or curricula vitae of the candidates.

If there are several people to be interviewed the interview timetable needs greater planning than it usually receives. The time required for each interview can be determined beforehand only approximately. A rigid timetable will weigh heavily on both parties, who will feel frustrated if the interview is closed arbitrarily at a predetermined time and uncomfortable if an interview that has 'finished' is drawn out to complete its allotted span. However, the disadvantages of keeping people waiting are considerable and under-rated.

WINDOW ON PRACTICE

Barbara Trevithick applied for a post as personnel officer at a hospital and was invited for interview at 2.00 p.m. On arrival she was ushered into a small, windowless room where four other people were waiting. At 2.20 a secretary came in and asked Mr Brown to come with her. At 3.00 Mr Jones was called for. At 3.45 the remaining three candidates went out in search of the secretary to ask what the remaining timetable for the day was to be. The secretary replied that she did not know but the panel members had just gone to the canteen for a cup of coffee. By now Barbara had figured out that her surname was the last in alphabetical order. Miss Mellhuish was called for interview at 4.10 and Miss Roberts left because her last train home to Scotland was due in 20 minutes. Barbara Trevithick went in for interview at 4.45 to find that two members of the panel 'had had to leave', so she was interviewed by the two surviving members: a personnel officer and a nursing officer. At the close of the interview she asked when the decision would be made and was told that the two interviewers would have to consult with their two absent colleagues in the morning. Three weeks later Barbara rang to ask the outcome, as she had not received a letter, to be told that Mr Brown had been appointed and 'I'm surprised they didn't tell you, as it was offered to him that afternoon, after the coffee break.'

The experience of Barbara Trevithick reflects the thinking of some selectors that candidates are supplicants waiting on interviewers' pleasure, they have no competing calls on their time and a short period of waiting demonstrates who is in charge. There are flaws in this reasoning. At least some candidates will have competing calls on their time, as they will have taken time off without pay to attend. Some may have other interviews to go to. An open-ended waiting period can be worrying, enervating and a poor preliminary to an interview. If the dentist keeps you waiting you may get distressed, but when the waiting is over you are simply a passive participant and the dentist does not have the success of the operation jeopardised. The interview candidate has, in a real sense, to perform when the period of waiting is over and the success of the interaction could well be jeopardised.

The most satisfactory timetable is the one that guarantees a break after all but the most voluble candidates. If candidates are asked to attend at hourly intervals, for example, this would be consistent with interviews lasting between 40 and 60 minutes. This would mean that each interview began at the scheduled time and that the interviewers had the opportunity to review and update their notes in the intervals.

Reception

Candidates arrive on the premises of their prospective employer on the lookout for every scrap of evidence they can obtain about the organisation – what it looks like, what the people look like, and what people say. Candidates will make judgements as quickly as interviewers, and we have already seen that at least one study (Webster 1964) found interviewers making their decisions within a few minutes and then using the rest of the time to confirm it. A candidate is likely to meet at least one and possibly two people before meeting the interviewer. First will be the commissionaire or receptionist. There is frequently also an emissary from the personnel department to shepherd them from the gate to the waiting-room. Both are valuable sources of information, and interviewers may wish to prime such people so that they can see their role in the employment process and can be cheerful, informative and helpful.

The candidate will most want to meet the interviewer, the unknown but powerful figure on whom so much depends. Interviewers easily forget that they know much more about the candidates than the candidates know about them, because the candidates have provided a personal profile in the application form.

Interviewers do not reciprocate. To bridge this gap it can be very useful for interviewers to introduce themselves to the candidate in the waiting-room, so that contact is made quickly, unexpectedly and on neutral territory. This makes the opening of the interview itself rather easier.

Candidates wait to be interviewed. Although there are snags about extended, open-ended waiting periods, some time is inevitable and necessary to enable candidates to compose themselves. It is a useful time to deal with travelling expenses and provide some relevant background reading about the employing organisation.

The appropriate setting for an interview has to be right for the ritual and right from the point of view of enabling a full and frank exchange of information. It is difficult to combine the two. Many of the interview horror stories relate to the setting in which it took place. A candidate for a post as Deputy Clerk of Works was interviewed on a stage while the panel of seventeen sat in the front row of the stalls, and a candidate for a Headteacher post came in to meet the interview panel and actually moved the chair on which he was to sit. He only moved it two or three inches because the sun was in his eyes, but there was an audible frisson and sharp intake of breath from the members of the panel.

Remaining with our model of the individual interviewer, here are some simple suggestions about the setting.

1. The room should be suitable for a private conversation.
2. If the interview takes place across a desk, as is common, the interviewer may wish to reduce the extent to which the desk acts as a barrier, emphasising the distance between the parties and therefore inhibiting free flow of communication.
3. All visitors and telephone calls should be avoided, as they do not simply interrupt: they intrude and impede the likelihood of frankness.
4. It should be clear to the candidates where they are to sit.

Interview structure

There are several important reasons why the employment interview should be structured:

1. The candidate expects the proceedings to be decided and controlled by the interviewer and will anticipate a structure within which to operate.

2. It helps the interviewer to make sure that they cover all relevant areas and avoid irrelevant ones.
3. It looks professional. Structure can be used to guide the interview and make it make sense.
4. It assists the interviewer in using the time available in the most effective way.
5. It can be used as a memory aid when making notes directly after the interview.
6. It can make it easier to compare candidates.

The selection interview

There are several different ways to structure the interview. We recommend the form set out in Table 14.1. This divides activities and objectives into three interview stages: opening, middle and closing. While there are few, if any, alternative satisfactory ways for conducting the beginning and the end of the interview, the middle can be approached from a number of different angles, depending on the circumstances.

The interviewer needs to work systematically through the structure that has been planned, but the structure does not have to be adhered to rigidly. As Sidney and Brown (1961) suggest, interviewers should abandon their own route wherever the candidate chooses one that seems more promising.

The opening of the interview is the time for mutual preliminary assessment and tuning in to each other. A useful feature of this phase is for the interviewer to sketch out the plan or procedure for the interview and how it fits in with the total employment decision process. It is also likely that the application form will provide an easy, non-controversial topic for these opening behaviours.

Table 14.1 Interview structure: a recommended pattern

Stage	Objectives	Activities
Opening	To put the candidate at ease, develop rapport and set the scene	Greet candidate by name Introduce yourself Explain interview purpose Outline how purpose will be achieved Obtain candidate assent to outline
Middle	To collect and provide information	Asking questions within a structure that makes sense to the candidate, such as biographical, areas of the application form, or competencies identified for the job Listening Answering questions
Closing	To close the interview and confirm future action	Summarise interview Check candidate has no more questions Indicate what happens next and when

One objective is for the two parties to exchange words so that they can adjust their receiving mechanism in order to be mutually intelligible. It also provides an opportunity for both to feel comfortable in the presence of the other. Interviewers able to achieve these two objectives may then succeed in developing a relationship in which candidates trust the interviewer's ability and motives so that they will speak openly and fully.

The interviewer's effectiveness will greatly depend on being skilled with rapport. Bayne regards a prerequisite as being a 'calm-alert' state of consciousness that can be sustained throughout the interview:

> At times the good interviewer is sharp and in focus, specific and rational; at other times intuitive, picking up nuances and rationalizations; at others stepping back to see the whole interaction, fitting things together and taking note of the amount of time left and the areas to cover . . . the interviewer's calmness helps the candidate to relax and his or her clear perception allows productive silences and the easy asking of questions. The state also counteracts habituation to interviews, when the interviewer is calm but bored. And it allows intuitive processes as well as the usual thinking, evaluating ones.
>
> (Bayne 1977)

For the middle of the interview the biographical approach is the most straightforward. It works on the basis that candidates at the time of the interview are the product of everything in their lives that has gone before. To understand the candidate the interviewer must understand the past and will talk to the candidate about the episodes of his or her earlier life – education, previous employment, etc.

The advantage of this is that the objectives are clear to both interviewer and interviewee, there is no deviousness or 'magic'. Furthermore, the development can be logical and so aid the candidate's recall of events. Candidates who reply to enquiries about their choice of 'A' level subjects will be subconsciously triggering their recollection of contemporaneous events, like the university course they took, which are likely to come next in the interview. The biographical approach is the simplest for the inexperienced interviewer to use as discussion can develop from the information provided by the candidate on the application form.

One American author has produced an interview structure, which suggests the interviewer begins with questions about the employment history of the candidate and then goes through their educational record, early home background and present social adjustment (Fear 1958). This has the advantage that it begins with what the candidate is best able to handle and later moves to those areas that are not so easy to recall.

Some authorities counsel a more detailed approach by prescribing a checklist of questions to be asked. A form designed by Dodd (1970) includes a series of boxes at every stage in which the interviewer is asked to tick 'acceptable or unacceptable'. This highly structured method does, of course, turn the interview into an interrogation rather than a conversation, making it very difficult to unearth opinions and attitudes, as well as closing certain avenues of enquiry that might appear as the interview proceeds. Furthermore, it inhibits the candidate from initiating their own topics for discussion.

Some version of sequential categories, like employment, education and training, seems the most generally useful, but it will need the addition of at least two other categories: the work offered and the organisational context in which it is to be done. The middle of the interview can be structured by systematically working through items of the job description as Green (1983) describes, or the person specification. Increasingly, where competencies have been identified for the job, these are used as the basis of the structure.

In the preparatory stage of briefing the interviewer will also prepare notes on two elements to incorporate in their plan: key issues and check-points.

Key issues will be the main two or three issues that stand out from the application form for clarification or elaboration. This might be the nature of the responsibilities carried in a particular earlier post, the content of a training course, the reaction to a period of employment in a significant industry, or whatever else strikes the interviewer as being productive of useful additional evidence.

Check-points are matters of detail that require further information: grades in an examination, dates of an appointment, rates of pay, and so forth.

In closing the interview the explanation of the next step needs especial attention. The result of the interview is of great importance to the candidates and they will await the outcome with anxiety. Even if they do not want the position they will probably hope to have it offered. This may strengthen their hand in dealings with another prospective employer – or their present employer – and will certainly be a boost to their morale. The great merit of convention in the public sector is that the chosen candidate is told before the contenders disperse: the great demerit is that they are asked to say yes or no to the offer at once.

In the private sector it is unusual for an employment offer to be made at the time of the interview, so there is a delay during which the candidates will chafe. Their frustration will be greater if the delay is longer than expected and they may start to tell themselves that they are not going to receive an offer, in which case they will also start convincing themselves that they did not want the job either! It is important for the interviewer to say as precisely as possible when the offer will be made, but ensuring that the candidates hear earlier rather than later than they expect, if there is to be any deviation.

The interviewer will need to call into play at least five key aspects of method.

1. Some data can be collected by simple observation of the candidate. Notes can be made about dress, appearance, voice, height and weight, if these are going to be relevant, and the interviewer can also gauge the candidate's mood and the appropriate response to it by the non-verbal cues that are provided.

2. The remainder of the evidence will come from listening to what is said, so the interviewer has to be very attentive throughout; not only listening to the answers to questions, but also listening for changes in inflection and pace, nuances and overtones that provide clues on what to pursue further. The amount of time that the two spend talking is important, as an imbalance in one direction or the other will mean that either the candidate or the interviewer is not having enough opportunity to hear information. Inclining the body towards the other person is a signal of attentiveness, so we need to remember our *posture*, which should be inclined forward and facing the other squarely with an open posture: folded arms can be inhibiting.

   Eye contact is crucial to good listening, but is a subtle art:

   > Effective eye contact expresses interest and a desire to listen. It involves focusing one's eyes softly on the speaker and occasionally shifting the gaze . . . to a gesturing hand, for example, and then back to the face and then to eye contact once again.   (Bolton 1987, p. 36)

The distinction between 'focusing one's eyes softly' and staring is vital, though difficult to describe, and competence in eye contact is never easy to establish. It is one of the most intimate ways of relating to a person and many managers fear that the relationship may become too close. Even if you are happy with it, you may find that the other person is uncomfortable with you looking through the 'window' of their eyes.

We have to avoid distracting the other person by physical behaviour that is unrelated to what is being said; fiddling with a pen, playing with car keys, scrutinising your fingernails, wringing your hands, brushing specks of dust off your sleeves are a few typical behaviours that indicate inattention. Skilled listeners not only supress these, they also develop minor gestures and posture variants that are directly responsive to what the other person is saying.

Being silent and deliberately leaving verbal lulls in face-to-face situations provide the opportunity for the other person to say more – perhaps more than was initially intended. Silence still has to be attentive and the longer the silence, the harder it is to be attentive.

WINDOW ON PRACTICE

Reflection

The effectiveness of listening can be aided by reflection, the listener picks up and restates the content of what has just been said. It indicates that you are attending to what the other person is saying, have understood it and you are providing the opportunity for any misunderstanding to be pointed out. The standard method is *paraphrasing*, by which the listener states the essence of what has been said. This is done concisely and gives the speaker a chance to review what has been said.

An example of how this would be done is in the following exchange:

Respondent: 'Seniority does not count for as much as it should in my present company.'
Reflection: 'You feel there is not enough acknowledgement of loyalty and long service?'

Alternative reactions would have a different effect, for example:

'You sound like someone who has been passed over for promotion', or
'Oh, I don't know about that.'

Both push the respondent on the defensive, expecting a justification of what has been said. Another alternative:

'Well, I think seniority is sometimes overemphasised'

stifles the opinion before it has been fully expressed. The diffident candidate will not develop the feeling further, so the matter cannot be resolved. There is also the danger that any one of these evaluative reactions could evoke a comeback from the respondent which complies with the view suggested by the interviewer. This is the same problem as that of the leading question.

3. In order to have something to hear, the interviewer will have to direct the candidate. This, of course, is done by questioning, encouraging and enabling the candidate to talk, so that the interviewer can learn. The art of doing this depends on the personality and style of the interviewer who will develop a personal technique through a sensitive awareness of what is taking place in the interviews. Edgar Anstey has described this as the highest stage of interviewing skill:

> Once rapport has been established, the actual questions matter less and less. The candidate senses what one is getting at, without worrying about the form of words, becomes increasingly at ease and responds more spontaneously. This is the ideal . . .   (Anstey 1977)

It is helpful to distinguish between different types of question in selection interviewing. Closed questions are used when we want precise, factual information. We close the question to control the answer ('Is it Clarke with an e, or without?'). These are useful at the point in the interview where you want clear, straightforward data.

Open-ended questions are quite different as they avoid terse replies, inviting candidates to express their opinions and to explain things in their own words and emphasis. The question does little more than introduce a topic to talk about ('What does your present job entail?'). The main purpose is to obtain the type of deeper information that the closed question misses, as the shape of the answer is not predetermined by the questioner. You are informed not simply by the content of the answers, but by what is selected and emphasised.

Probes are forms of questioning to obtain information that the respondent is trying to conceal. When this happens the questioner has to make an important, and perhaps difficult decision: do you respect the candidate's unwillingness and let the matter rest, or do you persist with the enquiry. Reluctance is quite common in selection interviews where there may be an aspect of the recent employment history that the candidate wishes to gloss over. The most common sequence for the probe takes the following form. (a) Direct questions, replacing the more comfortable open-ended approach ('What were you doing in the first six months of 1988?'). Careful phrasing may avoid a defensive reply, but those skilled at avoiding unwelcome enquiry may still deflect the question, leading to (b) Supplementaries, which reiterate the first question with different phrasing ('Yes, I understand about that period, it's the first part of 1988 that I'm trying to get clear: after you came back from Belgium and before you started with Amalgamated Widgets'). Eventually this should produce the information. (c) Closing. If the information has been wrenched out like a bad tooth and the interviewer looks horrified or sits in stunned silence, then the candidate will feel put down beyond redemption. The interviewer needs to make the divulged secret less awful than the candidate had feared, so that the interview can proceed with reasonable confidence ('Yes, well you must be glad to have that behind you').

Some common lines of questioning should be avoided because they can produce an effect that is different from what is intended. Leading questions ('Would you agree with me that . . .?') will not necessarily produce an answer which is informative, but an answer in line with the lead that has been given. Multiple questions give the candidate too many inputs at one time ('Could you tell me something of what you did at university – not just the degree, but the social and sporting side as well – and why you chose to backpack you way round the world? You didn't travel on your own, did you?'). This is sometimes found in interviewers who are trying very hard to efface themselves and let the respondent get on with the talking. However helpful the interviewer intends to be, the effect is that the candidate will usually forget the later parts of the question, feel disconcerted and ask, 'What was the last part of the question?' By this time the interviewer has also forgotten, so they are both embarrassed.

Taboo questions are those that infringe the reasonable personal privacy of the candidate. There is a proper place for the probe, but some questions have to be avoided in selection interviews, as they could be interpreted as discriminatory. It is at least potentially discriminatory, for instance, to ask women how many children they have and what their husbands do for a living. Questions about religion or place of birth are also to be avoided. Also some questions may do no more than satisfy the idle curiosity of the questioner. If there is no point in asking them, they should not be put.

4. The best place to make notes is on the application form. In this way they can be joined to information that the candidate has already provided and the peculiar shorthand that people use when making notes during conversations can be deciphered by reference to the form and the data that the note is embellishing. It also means that the review of evidence after the interview has as much information as possible available on one piece of paper. An alternative is to record notes on the interview plan where the structure is based on job specification, person specification or competencies. Interviewers are strangely inhibited about note-taking, feeling that it in some way impairs the smoothness of the interaction. This apprehension seems ill-founded as candidates are looking for a serious, businesslike discussion, no matter how informal, and note-taking offers no barrier providing that it is done carefully in the form of jottings during the discussion, rather than pointedly writing down particular comments by the candidate which make the interviewer seem like a police officer taking a statement.

5. Data exchange marks a change of gear in the interview. Rapport is necessarily rather rambling and aimless, but data exchange is purposeful and the interviewer needs to control both the direction and the pace of the exchanges. The candidate will be responsive throughout to the interviewer's control, and the better the rapport the more responsive they will be. Skilled interviewers close out areas of discussion and open fresh ones. They head off irrelevant reminiscences and probe where matters have been glossed over. They can never abandon control. Even when the time has come for the candidates to raise all their queries they will do this at the behest of the interviewer and will look to him or her constantly for a renewal of the mandate to enquire by using conversational prefixes like 'Can I ask you another question?' 'If it's not taking up your time, perhaps I could ask . . .?', 'I seem to be asking a lot of questions, but there was just one thing . . .'

6. Closing the interview can be as skilful as opening it. Most of the suggestions so far have been to encourage a response, but it is easy to nod and smile your way into a situation of such cosy relaxation that the respondent talks on and on . . . and on. A surprising number of interviewers have great difficulty closing. Braking slows the rate of talking by the candidate. You will seldom need to go beyond the first two or three, but five are described in case of you having to deal with a really tough case. (a) One or two closed questions to clarify specific points may stem

the tide. (b) The facial expression changes with the brow furrowed to indicate mild disagreement, lack of understanding or professional anxiety. The reassuring nods stop and the generally encouraging, supportive behaviours of reward are withdrawn. (c) Abstraction is when the eyes glaze over, showing that they belong to a person whose attention has now shifted away from the respondent and towards lunch. (d) To look at one's watch during a conversation is a very strong signal indeed, as it clearly indicates that time is running out. Other, milder ways of looking away are: looking for your glasses, looking at your notes or looking at the aircraft making a noise outside the window. A rather brutal variant is to allow your attention to be caught by something the respondent is wearing – a lapel badge, a tie, a ring or piece of jewellery, maybe. Putting on your glasses to see it more clearly is really rather going too far! (e) If all else fails, you simply have to interrupt.

Closing requires the interview to end smoothly. Future action is either clarified or confirmed. Also, candidates take a collection of attitudes away with them, and these can be influenced by the way the interview is closed. There is a simple procedure. (a) First signal, verbal plus papers. The interviewer uses a phrase to indicate that the interview is nearing its end ('Well now, I think we have covered the ground, don't you? There isn't anything more I want to ask you. Is there anything further you want from me?'). In this way you signal the impending close at the same time as obtaining the candidate's confirmation. There is additional emphasis provided by some paper play. A small collection of notes can be gathered together and stacked neatly, or a notebook can be closed. (b) Second signal, the interviewer confirms what will happen next ('There are still one or two people to see, but we will write to you no later than the end of the week'). (c) The final signal is to stand up: the decisive act to make the close. By standing up the interviewer forces the candidate to stand as well and there remains only the odds and ends of handshakes and parting smiles.

Summary propositions

14.1 Despite criticisms and shortcomings, the selection interview remains a central feature of the recruitment and selection process.

14.2 Typical interview strategies are frank and friendly, problem-solving, behavioural event and stress.

14.3 Aspects of interview preparation are timetabling, reception and deciding the right setting.

14.4 Features of the interview itself are the opening for preliminary mutual assessment; data-gathering, involving a logical sequence, key issues and check points; and the closure, which prepares candidates for the next step in the process.

14.5. Key aspects of method are observation, effective listening, eye contact and questioning.

14.6 The main types of questions are closed, open-ended, probes and reflection. Questions to avoid are multiples or taboo questions.

References

Anderson, N. and Shackleton, V. (1993) *Successful Selection Interviewing*, Oxford: Blackwell.

Anstey, E. (1977) quoted in R. Bayne, 'Can selection interviewing be improved?', The British Psychology Society Annual Occupational Psychology Conference, Sheffield.

Bayne, R. (1977) 'Can selection interviewing be improved?' Paper presented to The British Psychological Society Annual Occupational Psychology Conference, Sheffield.

Bolton, R. (1987) *People Skills*, Sydney: Simon & Schuster.

Campion, M. A., Pursell, E. D. and Brown, B. K. (1988) 'Structured interviewing: Raising the psychometric properties of the employment interview', *Personnel Psychology*, Vol. 41, pp. 25–43.

Conan Doyle, A. (1966) *The Adventures of Sherlock Holmes*, London: John Murray.

Dodd, J. H. B. (1970) 'Personnel selection – interviewing', *Applied Ergonomics*, September.

Fear, R. A. (1958) *The Evaluation Interview*, Maidenhead: McGraw-Hill.

Fletcher, J. (1973) *The Interview at Work*, London: Duckworth.

Goffman, E. (1974) *The Presentation of Self in Everyday Life*, London: Penguin Books.

Green, J. (1983) 'Structured sequence interviewing', *Personnel Executive*, April.

Hackett, P. (1978) *Interview Skills Training: Role Play Exercises*, London: Institute of Personnel Management.

Jenks, J. M. and Zevnik, L. P. (1989) 'ABCs of job interviewing', *Harvard Business Review*, July–August.

Lewis, C. (1986) *Employee Selection*, London: Hutchinson.

Lopez, F. M. (1975) *Personnel Interviewing*, 2nd edn, Maidenhead: McGraw-Hill.

Muir, J. (1988) 'Recruitment and selection', *Management Services*, November.

Plumbley, P. (1985) *Recruitment and Selection*, 4th edn, London: IPM.

Rodger, A. (1975), 'Interviewing techniques', in B. Ungerson, (ed.), *Recruitment Handbook*, 2nd edn, Aldershot: Gower.

Sidney, E. and Brown, M. (1961) *The Skills of Interviewing*, London: Tavistock.

Webster, E. C. (1964) *Decision Making in the Employment Interview*, Industrial Relations Centre, McGill University, Canada.

Practical exercise in selection interviewing

For this exercise you need a co-operative, interested relative, or a *very* close friend, who would welcome interview practice.

1. Follow the sequence suggested to give your partner practice in being interviewed for a job, and giving yourself practice in interviewing and note-taking.

2. After the interview, discuss your mutual feelings about the process around questions such as:

Selector   Did you ever feel you were being misled? When? Why?
Did you feel the interview got out of your control? When? Why?
How could you have avoided the problem?
How was your note-taking?
What, if anything, made you bored or cross?
What did you find most difficult?
How comprehensive is the data you have collected?

Candidate   Were you put at your ease?
Were you at any time inhibited by the selector?
Did you ever mislead the selector? When? How?
Did the selector ever fail to follow up important points? When? Which?
Were you in any way disconcerted by the note-taking?
Has the selector got a comprehensive set of data about you, so that you could feel any decision made about you would be soundly based?
What did you think of the interview experience?

3. Now swap roles.

Part III
Case study problem

You are the Human Resources Manager for a large insurance company with 2,000 employees based in a large city in the north of England and your company has just taken over another insurance company in the south of England which currently employs 1,100 staff. Both firms have a long history and to some extent cover the same insurance markets, although the company in the south of England covers two fairly large specialist areas which are not covered in the north. This was one of the reasons for the takeover, as such specialist staff require a long training and need to acquire high levels of expertise. There are 300 staff in the south who are dedicated to these specialist insurance services.

The takeover did not go smoothly as there was resistance from the southern company, and now it is complete there is considerable uneasiness. Only three years ago the southern company was party to a merger with another local firm and as a result 20 per cent of staff were made redundant. There had been promises of a bright future after these difficult times.

For financial and pragmatic reasons it has been decided that the southern office will close almost immediately and all staff will be located in newly built offices 15 miles out of the northern city. Many of the southern staff are alarmed at the idea of moving and equally alarmed that they may not be invited to move due to another round of redundancies. This especially applies to those who are over 50. The northern staff are divided in their views about the move out of the city centre. Those on the western side of the city where the new offices are located are generally delighted to be able to work near to home in an exclusive part of the county. Staff who live on the other side of the city are concerned – some are not happy to travel long distances each day, and for a variety of reasons do not want to move to the other side of the city. Some would like to move, but find that the difference in house prices is too great. Many are disappointed that they will no longer work in the city centre, which is something they had valued. Redundancy is not a possibility which was seriously considered by the northern staff.

In terms of staffing demand it has been estimated that a total staffing of 2,400 is required for the next three-year period with hopes of some increase after this period based on growth.

The required profile is broadly:

A. senior and middle management: 35
B. professional/junior management: 1700 (to include 300 specialist staff)
C. clerical administrative 600
D. manual/ancillary 65

Current staffing

	Northern	Southern	Total
A.	30	20	50
B.	1400	700	2100

(there are no specialist professional staff in the north and 300 in the south)

	Northern	Southern	Total
C.	540	370	910
D.	30	10	40

The reduction in the number of professional/junior management staff required reflects a general reduction of all types of professional staff due to the economies of scale and more sophisticated IT use. The only professional staff group to increase in size is the IT group.

The reduction in clerical/administrative staff is due largely to the use of more sophisticated IT systems.

The increase in the number of manual/ancillary staff is due to the move to a much larger site with substantial grounds, including a range of on-site facilities due to a non-city centre location.

You are informed that staffing levels and the move should be complete in six months' time and that, as HR Manager, you are to have a high profile role. You have initially been asked for a recommended strategy and plan to achieve the target resourcing figures with the least possible disruption and damage to morale.

Required

1. What information would you gather before putting your proposal together?
2. What issues would you address in the proposal?
3. What options are there for achieving the target, what impact might each have, and which would you recommend and why?

Examination questions

Undergraduate introductory

1. Where does the calculation of labour turnover fit with the human resource planning process as a whole?
2. Outline the advantages and disadvantages of (a) panel interviews, and (b) serial interviews. In which circumstances would you recommend each approach?

Undergraduate finals

3. Compare and contrast work samples with situational interviews as methods of selecting operators.
4. Describe and explain the development of a one-day assessment centre for graduate selection.

Masters

5. Outline the major factors which influence the use of part-time work in Britain, and discuss the implications of part-time work for part-time workers.
6. Under what conditions may annualised hours systems provide employers with the 'flexibility they require'?

Professional

7. Wanous (1992) in his book on organisational entry talks about the idea of 'realistic recruitment'. Design a recruitment and selection process with this in mind for a sales team manager in the software business. Explain how your choice of recruitment and selection activities would achieve this objective.
8. Your organisation is about to embark on a major recruitment campaign, for the first time in a number of years. Twelve of the first line managers will be involved in the recruitment interviewing. Their interviewing skills are weak, either because they have not been involved in the interview process before, or for a long time.

   As the Training Officer, you have been asked to provide the training for the first line managers. Outline the course that you propose, giving objectives, content, methods and timing.

Performance

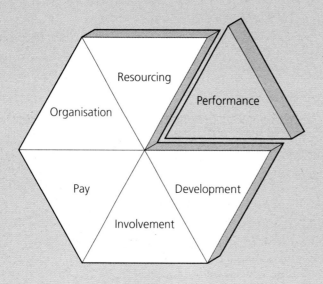

It is no good having all the right people all in the right place, but not delivering the goods. It was suggested in the book's opening chapter that there is a general move away from the contract *of* employment towards a contract *for* performance. We all have to perform effectively.

A large part of achieving effective performance is getting the organisational processes right, but within the organisational framework there are the teams, groups and individuals who do the work. Performance management is a reasonably new idea that has been developed to co-ordinate several features – targets, training, appraisal and payment – to deliver effectiveness. Within that sequence is the hardest type of meeting most managers ever have to handle: the appraisal interview. Also included here is the management of diversity, an approach which starts from the premise that the people working for the business have a very wide range of capacities and that management has to make the most of everyone, moving beyond the idea that some may be only able to make a limited contribution because of their gender, race or disability.

CHAPTER 15

Strategic aspects of performance

In our opening chapter we described the shift in emphasis away from the contract of employment towards the contract for performance. Even before the development of Taylor's Scientific Management methods a century ago, getting the most out of the workforce has always been a predominant management preoccupation, and the management literature is full of studies on the topic. Psychologists have studied motivation and leadership, ergonomists have dismantled and reconstructed every aspect of the physical environment in which people work, industrial relations specialists have pondered power relationships and reward, while sociologists discussed the design of organisations and their social structure, and operations experts have looked for ways to engineer process improvements.

In this chapter we review some major influences on our current thinking about performance. From this we explore in more detail some commonly acknowledged performance variables and then briefly review a range of current strategic performance initiatives. The following three chapters look in more detail at organisational, individual and team performance.

A change in perspective: from employment to performance

The traditional human resource management approach to enhancing individual performance has centred on the assessment of past performance and the allocation of reward (Walker 1992). The secret was seen to lie in the interplay between individual skill or capacity and motivation. There has also been a pattern of thinking which set reward as separate from performance: rewards were provided in exchange for performance. This has been powerfully influenced by the industrial relations history, as trade unions have developed the process of collective bargaining and negotiation.

The prime purpose of trade unions has always been to improve the terms and working conditions of their members. This applies in every country of the world where unions are active. There may be other objectives as well, such as bringing about political and social change in the surrounding society, but the prime purpose remains what Hugh Clegg described as:

> The most universally recognised objective of collective industrial action is the maintenance and improvement of the position of those concerned in the pay and conditions of work.   (Clegg 1970, p. 28)

With that objective, the union has only one thing to / improvements in terms and conditions, that is some op ment in productivity or performance. With the steadily unions in most industrial countries through the bulk of was inevitable that performance improvement was some only to management. Performance therefore became stereotyped no intrinsic interest to the person doing the work.

The influence of trade unions has altered and collective bargaining do dominate the management agenda as much as it used to. This is the most signi icant feature in the general change in attitudes about what we go to work for. Managements are gradually waking up to this fact and realising that there is now scope for integration in a way that was previously unrealistic. Not only is it possible to say, 'Performance is rewarded', one can now begin to say, 'Performance *is* a reward.' The long-standing motivational ideas of job enlargement, job enrichment, and so forth, become more cogent when those at work are able to look for the satisfaction of their needs not only in the job, but their performance in it.

WINDOW ON PRACTICE

Mavis has worked in a retail store for eighteen years and has recently attended a training course in customer care.

I always regarded the customer as some sort of enemy; we all did. In our coffee breaks we chatted away about the customer from hell, who was never satisfied, or who always put you down. Also I used to feel that I had to grin and·bear it in trying to be nice to these enemies in order to earn commission.

Since the course I feel much more in control and have more self-respect. I really feel that most customers will respond positively if I approach them in the right way. It is my performance that largely affects how they behave. I actually enjoy what I am doing most of the time (and I never thought I'd say that!), because I can see myself doing a bit of good as well as selling more than I used to.

Although it may seem like playing with words, this subtle shift of emphasis is fundamental to understanding the strategic approach to performance.

Influences on our understanding of performance

The Japanese influence

The success of Japanese companies and the decline of the Western organisations has encouraged an exploration and adoption of Japanese management ideas and practices in order to improve performance. Thurley (1982) described the objectives of personnel policies in Japan as performance, motivation, flexibility and mobility. Delbridge and Turnbull (1992) described type 'J' organisations (based on Japanese thinking) as characterised by commitment, effort and company loyalty. A key theme in Japanese thinking appears to be people development and continuous improvement, or 'kaizen'.

Much of this thinking and the specific management techniques used in Japan, such as JIT (just in time), have been adopted into UK organisations, often in an uncritical way and without due regard for the cultural differences between the two nations. It is only where the initiatives are developed *and modified* for their location that they appear to succeed.

The American 'excellence' literature

Peters and Waterman (1982) identified eight characteristics which they found to be associated with excellent companies – all American. These companies were chosen as excellent on the basis of their innovativeness and on a set of financial indicators, compared on an industry-wide basis. The characteristics they identified were:

- a bias for action – rather than an emphasis on bureaucracy or analysis,
- close to the customer – concern for customer wishes,
- autonomy and entrepreneurship – the company is split into small operational units where innovation and initiative are encouraged,
- productivity through people – employees are seen as the key resource, and the value of the employees' contribution is reinforced,
- hands-on, value-driven – strong corporate culture promoted from the top,
- stick to the knitting – pursuing the core business rather than becoming conglomerates,
- simple form, lean staff – simple organisation structure and small HQ staffing,
- simultaneous loose–tight properties – company values strongly emphasised, but within these considerable freedom and errors tolerated.

Peters and Waterman identified a shift from the importance of strategy and structural factors to style, systems, staff and skills (from the hard 's's to the soft 's's). In a follow-on book Peters and Austin (1985) identify four key factors related to excellence as concern for customers, innovation, attention to people and leadership.

Guest (1992) analyses why this excellence literature has had such an impact and identifies a range of methodological and analytical problems associated with the research, which question its validity. For example, he points out that no comparison was made with companies not considered to be excellent. We do not, therefore, know whether these principles were applied to a greater extent in excellent organisations. Hitt and Ireland (1987) go so far as to say that 'the data call into question whether these excellent principles are related to performance'. In addition, a number of the companies quoted have experienced severe problems since the research was carried out, and there remains the problem of the extent to which we can apply the results to UK organisations.

Whatever the reservations, the influence of the text on strategic thinking about performance remains profound. Even by using the term 'excellence' there is a change of emphasis away from the dead-pan, objective terms like profitability, effectiveness, value-added and competitive advantage towards an idea that may trigger a feeling of enthusiasm and achievement. 'Try your best' becomes 'Go for it'.

HRM and the strategy literature

The HRM strategy literature gives an indication of the personnel function's contribution to organisational performance. As we noted in Chapter 2, Guest identifies strategic integration, flexibility, commitment and quality as key factors influencing performance outcomes. Sparrow and Pettigrew (1988) have identi-fied HR policies which influence employee values and attitudes. Legge (1989), though, has pointed to some of the inherent contradictions in HRM, for example between commitment and flexibility; between individualism and teamwork and between a strong culture and adaptability. These contradictions can also be seen in some of the performance variables and strategic performance initiatives discussed below.

Some of the performance variables commonly identified

From the preceding influences it can be seen that a range of variables are emer-ging which are recognised as having a positive impact on performance. We shall explore some of the well documented examples in more detail.

Commitment

Commitment has been identified by some writers as resulting in higher perfor-mance. Commitment has been described as:

- ▶ **Attitudinal commitment** – that is loyalty and support for the organisation, strength of identification with the organisation (Porter 1985), a belief in its values and goals and a readiness to put in effort for the organisation.
- ▶ **Behavioural commitment** – actually remaining with the company and continuing to pursue its objectives.

Walton (1985) notes that commitment **is thought** to result in better quality, lower turnover, a greater capacity for innovation and more flexible employees. In turn these are seen to enhance the ability of the organisation to achieve compet-itive advantage. Iles, Mabey and Robertson (1990) add that some of the outcomes of commitment have been identified as the industrial relations climate, absence levels, turnover levels and individual performance.

Morris, Lydka and O'Creery (1992/3) argue that there is not a lot of **evidence** to link high commitment and high levels of organisational performance. Some authors have argued that high commitment could indeed reduce organisational performance. Cooper and Hartley (1990) suggest the commitment might decrease flexibility and inhibit creative problem-solving. If commitment reduces staff turnover, this may result in fewer new ideas coming into the organisation. Staff who would like to leave the organisation but who are committed to it in other ways, for example through high pay and benefits, may stay, but may not produce high levels of performance.

As well as the debate on the value of commitment to organisational perfor-mance, there is also the debate on the extent to which commitment can be managed, and how it can be managed. Guest (1992) suggests that commitment is affected by:

personal characteristics,
experiences in job role,
work experiences,
structural factors, and
personnel policies.

Morris, Lydka and O'Creery (1992/3) also identify that personnel policies have an effect on commitment. In particular they found career prospects as the most important factor in their research on graduates.

Empowerment

Keenoy (1990) argues that HRM releases untapped reserves of labour resourcefulness by facilitating employee responsibility, commitment and involvement. The organisation, it is viewed, will benefit from unleashing these reserves. Alongside this notion of 'exploiting' employee resourcefulness is the idea that this will be used in line with the needs and objectives of the organisation. It is therefore based on trust and an assumption that employees' values will be in line with those of the organisation.

The way that empowerment is facilitated is seen as realising both these expectations. Not only is it essential for appropriate training and resources to be provided for employees, but responsibility for decision-making is pushed down the hierarchy so that those who do the task make the decisions about the task. In this way employees will have a high level of ownership of what they do and bureaucratic control is not necessary as employees will manage themselves. Connock (1992) identifies empowerment as involving greater individual accountability for results with enhanced authority for work teams. He sees strategy as key, and within this, confined only by broad job accountabilities, managers and individuals have freedom to act. Connock also identifies the encouragement of innovation and continuous self-improvement as critical.

More critically, Sewell and Wilkinson (1992), in their study of total quality management (which they identify as very similar to the tenets of HRM), found that empowerment and trust may be the rhetoric, but that management power and control were the reality.

Leadership

Leadership, rather than management, has been identified as one of the keys to a high performance organisation. 'Charismatic leadership' and 'transformational leadership' give some indication of the virtues that great leadership is seen to offer. It is seen as the power to inspire and motivate, the ability to imbue employees with the desire to change the organisation and to be the best. Leaders create the vision and the strategy and present it and themselves in such a way that employees feel enthusiastic and excited by it. This, of course, is expecting a great deal of the leader, and there is always uncertainty about how many people actually possess these qualities.

Atwater, Penn and Rucker (1991) carried out some research to try to define which particular traits were present in charismatic leaders. By comparing uncharismatic and charismatic leaders they found that charismatic leaders were different in terms of being dynamic, inspiring, outgoing, sociable, insightful and enterprising.

There is a good deal of research demonstrating the value of leadership in terms of organisational performance. Leaders clearly do act as role models in the organisation. Some of the strategy literature, though, does suggest that different types of leaders fit with different types of situation, as we discussed in Chapter 9.

There is also a debate over whether leadership can be learned or whether it is innate. Peters and Waterman see it as something that can be learned, but straightforward observation of everyday events makes one question how much it can be learned and how much depends on innate personal qualities or capacities developed when young.

Culture

Leadership is a hardy perennial in the management literature, and culture is rapidly getting to match it. When in search of an answer, try culture! Meek (1992) suggests that there is a link between culture and organisational effectiveness, and that there is an assumption that the culture will unite all employees behind the stated goals of the business. Some companies have used this link to try to change the culture in an effort to improve organisational performance; we hear of businesses encouraging a 'performance culture' or a 'learning culture'. This, however, is making one very great assumption – that culture can be managed. Kilmann *et al.* (1985) support this view of culture as a variable that can be controlled. Peters and Waterman write of strong organisational cultures as being associated with excellence, and again suggest that it is possible to make a culture strong.

However, there is a strong lobby arguing that culture is an independent variable which cannot be manipulated (see, for example, Meek 1992). He argues that the culture of an organisation is not in the hands of management and therefore it is not a matter of handing down a culture to passive employees. He also suggests, however, that culture is not necessarily static and that management, as opposed to other groups, do have control over some things that will affect the culture, such as the logo and the mission statement. This argument can be extended to include systems and processes in the business, so some managements attempt to induce culture change through the introduction of a system, such as a performance management system, or through quality leadership, as at Ford (McKinlay and Starkey 1988). The impact of such systems, though, on the culture is neither straightforward nor immediate, especially remembering the likelihood of various sub-cultures within the same organisational framework, as we saw in Chapter 5.

Schein (1992) also makes the point that strong cultures are not necessarily associated with a more effective organisation, and indicates that the relationship is far more complex. He draws out some contradictions; that a strong culture may stand against flexibility and adaptability, for instance. He does maintain, though, that culture awareness is important in facilitating strategic decisions.

Flexibility

We have discussed flexibility at some length in Chapters 2 and 9. It remains here to highlight the link between flexibility and performance. Functional flexibility is particularly important where employees with a wide job remit and a wide range of skills can reduce waiting time (such as maintenance activities on breakdown), give employees a greater sense of doing a whole job and greater responsibility. All these factors have potential to improve performance.

Learning

Garratt (1990) provides the neat aphorism that for a business to survive the extent of learning has to be greater than or equal to the extent of change which it faces. De Gaus (1988) comments that learning is 'an almost priceless competitive advantage'. There is little doubt that both organisational and individual learning are associated with organisational performance. However, achieving this learning in practice is very difficult indeed. Some attention has always been given to individual learning, even if only in the form of rhetoric. Increasingly, attention is being paid to enabling the whole organisation to learn on a continuous basis and therefore become more effective.

Major performance initiatives

The variables reviewed above form the basis for many of the popular performance initiatives which companies have adopted. There are many small initiatives every day which help to improve performance, but we are concentrating here on major strategic initiatives, 'big ideas', as described by Connock (1992). Mueller and Purcell reach the heart of the issue when they say,

> It is the integration of change initiatives with other aspects of organisational life which is the key to success. It is very rare for a single initiative, however well designed to generate significant or lasting benefit.
>
> (Mueller and Purcell 1992, p. 28)

Moving to a performance culture is an all-or-nothing change in the way the business is run. This brings us to the concern that many initiatives in the same organisation will give conflicting messages to employees, particularly when they are introduced by different parts of the business. There may, for example, be contradictions between the messages of TQM and those of the learning organisation type of approach. We will explore these further in Chapter 16.

Table 15.1 lists some of the major performance initiatives. They are divided according to their primary focus, organisational, individual or team. Some of them partly cover the same ground, and it would be surprising to find them in the same business at the same time.

ACTIVITY BOX 15.1

(a) Identify the main performance initiatives in your organisation.

(h) What/who is the source of each initiative?

(c) In what ways do they mutually support each other, and in what ways do they conflict?

Table 15.1 Some major performance initiatives

Organisational focus	Learning organisation
	Investors in people
	Total quality management (TQM)
	Performance culture
	Lean production
	Just in Time (JIT)
	Standards BS5750
	ISO9000
	Customer care/orientation
Individual focus	Performance management
	Performance-related pay
	Self-development
Team focus	High performance teams
	Cross-functional teams
	Self-regulating teams

Things that go wrong

The level of satisfaction with performance initiatives is typically low (Jacobs 1993; Antonioni 1994), so we close this chapter with a summary of the problems most often reported.

The process/people balance

Schemes rarely strike the right balance between a people emphasis and a process emphasis. Concentrating on being brilliant at talking to the people, getting them going and talking them down gently if they don't quite make it will not suffice if there is not a clear, disciplined process that brings in the essential features of consistency and defining sensible goals. Getting the goals and measures right is a waste of time if there is not the necessary input to changing attitudes, developing skills and winning consent.

Looking at results rather than behaviours

Splendid, hard-working people doing the wrong thing is a recipe for disaster. The focus must be on what is achieved: results are what count. Doing things in the right way is no substitute for doing the rights things.

> The premise of a performance management type of appraisal is good but still misses the point. The approach is behavioural; it focuses on the person rather than on the performance. These programmes typically include an appraisal of such traits and behaviours as adaptability, decision-making, initiative, ability to communicate and personal development. Concentrating on such personal behaviour can lead to clashes of personality as the employee and the supervisor battle to determine whose behaviour will

> prevail . . . In a job results management system the focus shifts from the employee's behaviour to the results of the employee's behaviour.
>
> (Plachy and Plachy 1993, p. 31)

Management losing interest

A constant axiom with any initiative is the need for endorsement from senior management. With a performance initiative it has to go a great deal further. First, senior managers have to accept that it is something in which they have to participate continuously and thoroughly. They cannot introduce it, say how important it is and then go off to find other games to play:

> studies have shown that in organisations that utilise performance management, 90 per cent of senior managers have not received performance reviews in the last two years. Clearly the problem here is that PM is not used, modelled and visibly supported at the top of the organisation. Sooner or later people at lower levels catch on and no longer feel compelled to take the time to make PM work. (Sparrow and Hiltrop 1994, p. 565)

The second aspect is indicated in that quotation. Performance initiatives will not work unless people at all levels either believe in them or are prepared to give them a try with the hope that they will be convinced by the practice.

The team/individual balance

Individuals can rarely perform entirely on their own merits; they are part of a department or team of people whose activities interact in innumerable ways. Trevor Macdonald may read the television news with a clarity and sureness that is outstanding, but it would be of little value if the lights did not work or the script contained errors. Most working people, no matter how eminent, are not solo performers to that extent. Somehow the performance initiative has to stimulate both individual and team performance, working together within the envelope of organisational objectives.

> Historically the individual has been the basis of performance management strategies. However, this may be problematic in that performance variation tends to be falsely attributed to individuals, and the enhancement of individual performance does not necessarily coincide with the enhancement of the greater unit or work system. (Waldman 1994, p. 41)

ACTIVITY BOX 15.2

Think of situations in your own experience outside working life, where there has been a potential clash between individual performance and team performance. Examples might be:

(a) the opening batsman more concerned with his batting average than with the team winning the match;

(b) the person playing the lead in the amateur operatic society's production of

The Merry Widow who ignores the chorus; or

(c) the local councillor more concerned with doing what is needed to earn an MBE than with supporting the collective view of the council.

How was the potential clash avoided, or not? How could it have been managed more effectively to harmonise individual and team performance?

Leaving out the development part

A key feature of managing performance is developing people so that they *can* perform. This is the feature that is most often not delivered. In a 'box' earlier in this chapter was the story of two companies running performance management. It was the lack of follow-up on development needs that was the least satisfactory aspect of the system in both companies.

Getting it right

Here are four suggestions for running a successful performance initiative:

1. Develop and promulgate a clear vision for the business as a framework for individual/team goals and targets.
2. In consultation, develop and agree individual goals and targets with three characteristics, (a) what to do to achieve the target, (b) how to satisfy the customer rather than pleasing the boss, (c) are precise, difficult and challenging, but attainable, *with feedback*.
3. Don't begin until you are sure of (a) unwavering commitment from the top, (b) an approach that is driven by the line and bought into and owned by middle and first-line managers, (c) a system that is run, monitored and up-dated by personnel/HR specialists, (d) an agreement that every development commitment or pay commitment is honoured, or a swift, full explanation of why not.
4. Train all participants.

Summary propositions

15.1 Central to understanding management interest in performance is understanding the subtle change in attitudes: not only is performance rewarded, performance is also a reward.

15.2 In the UK our views of performance improvement have been influenced by the USA excellence literature, the Japanese experience and the HRM strategy literature.

15.3 Some commonly identified performance variables have been identified as commitment, empowerment, leadership, culture, flexibility and learning.

15.4 There is an argument that by changing these variables changes can be brought about in the performance of the business.

15.5 Things that typically go wrong with performance initiatives are getting the people/process balance wrong, looking at behaviours rather than at results, management losing interest, and getting the team/individual balance wrong.

15.6 Factors likely to produce success relate to a clear, understood vision, effective target-setting, full management commitment, training and honouring commitments.

References

Antonioni, D. (1994) 'Improve the performance management process before discontinuing performance appraisals', *Compensation and Benefits Review*, Vol. 26, No. 2, pp. 29–37.

Atwater, L., Penn, R. and Rucker, A. (1991) 'Personnel qualities of charismatic leaders', *Leadership and Organisation Development Journal*, Vol. 12, No. 2, pp. 7–10.

Clegg, H. A. (1970) *The System of Industrial Relations in Great Britain*, Oxford: Blackwell.

Connock, S. (1992) 'The importance of big ideas to HR managers', *Personnel Managers*, June.

Cooper, J. and Hartley, J. (1990) 'Reconsidering the case for organisational commitment', *Human Resource Management Journal*.

de Gaus, A. (1988) 'Planning as learning', *Harvard Business Review*, March–April, pp. 70–4.

Delbridge, R. and Turnbull, P. (1992) 'Human resource maximisation: The management of labour under just-in-time manufacturing systems', in P. Blyton and P. Turnbull (eds.), *Reassessing Human Resource Management*, Beverly Hills: Sage.

Garratt, B. (1990) *The Learning Organisation*, Hemel Hempstead: Director Books.

Guest, D. (1992) 'Right enough to be dangerously wrong; an analysis of the "In search of excellence" phenomenon', in G. Salaman *et al.* (eds.), *Human Resource Strategies*, London: Sage.

Hitt, M. and Ireland, D. (1987) 'Peters and Waterman revisited; the unending quest for excellence', *Academy of Management Executive*, Vol. 1, No. 2, pp. 91–8.

Iles, P., Mabey, C. and Robertson, I. (1990) 'Human resource management practices and employee commitment. Possibilities, pitfalls and paradoxes', *British Journal of Management*, Vol. 1, pp. 147–57.

Jacobs, H. (1993) 'The ratings game', *Small Business Reports*, Vol. 18, No. 10, pp. 21–2.

Keenoy, T. (1990) 'HRM: a case of the wolf in sheep's clothing', *Personnel Review*, Vol. 19, No. 2, pp. 3–9.

Kilmann, R. H. *et al.* (1985) *Gaining Control of the Corporate Culture*, Wokingham: Jossey-Bass.

Legge, K. (1989) 'Human resource management – a critical analysis', in J. Storey (ed.), *New Perspectives in Human Resource Management*, London: Routledge.

McKinlay, A. and Starkey, K. (1988) 'Competitive strategies and organisational change', *Organisational Studies*, Vol. 9, No. 4, pp. 555–71.

Meek, L. (1992) 'Organisational culture: origins and weaknesses', in G. Salaman *et al.* (eds.), *Human Resource Strategies*, London: Sage.

Morris T., Lydka, H. and O'Creevy, M. F. (1992/3) 'A longitudinal analysis of employee commitment and human resource policies', *Human Resource Management Journal*, Vol. 3, pp. 21–38.

Mueller, F. and Purcell, J. (1992) 'The drive for higher productivity', *Personnel Management*, Vol. 24, No. 5, pp. 28–33.

Peters, T. and Austin, N. (1985) *A Passion for Excellence*, New York: Harper and Row.

Peters, T. and Waterman, R. (1982) *In Search of Excellence*, New York: Harper and Row.

Plachy, R. and Plachy, S. (1993) 'Focus on results, not behaviour', *Personnel Journal*, Vol. 72, No. 3, pp. 28–33.

Porter, M. (1985) *Competitive Advantage*, New York: Free Press.

Schein, E. H. (1992) 'Coming to a new awareness of organisational culture', in G. Salaman *et al.* (eds.), *Human Resource Strategies*, London: Sage.

Sewell, G. and Wilkinson, B. (1992) 'Empowerment or emasculation? Shopfloor surveillance in a total quality organisation', in P. Blyton and P. Turnbull (eds.), *Reassessing Human Resource Management*, Beverly Hills: Sage.

Sparrow, P. and Hiltrop, J.-M. (1994) *European Human Resource Management in Transition*, London: Prentice Hall.

Sparrow, P. and Pettigrew, A. (1988) 'Contrasting HRM responses in the changing world of computing', *Personnel Management*, Vol. 2.

Thurley, K. (1982) 'The Japanese model: practical reservations and surprising opportunities', *Personnel Management*, February.

Waldman, D. (1994) 'Designing performance management systems for total quality implementation', *Journal of Organisational Change Management*, Vol. 7, No. 2, pp. 31–44.

Walker, K. W. (1992) *Human Resource Strategy*, New York: McGraw-Hill.

Walton, R. E. (1985) 'From control to commitment in the workplace', *Harvard Business Review* (March/April), pp. 77–84.

General discussion topics

1. To what extent can the American excellence literature be applied in a UK setting?
2. Can commitment, empowerment and job flexibility be pursued together? If yes, how can this be achieved? If no, why not – what are the alternatives?

CHAPTER 16

Organisational performance

There was a time when performance was seen primarily in terms of individual motivation and individual performance. Increasingly the focus has shifted to emphasise performance of the organisation as a whole. This change of emphasis is drawn starkly by Deming (1986) when he asserts that performance variations are the result not of individual differences, but of the systems that are implemented and controlled by managers – factors that are outside the control of the individual. While we do not fully agree with Deming's views on individual performance, we recognise that he highlights a critical perspective on the importance of the systems, processes and culture for ultimate organisational performance.

The focus of this chapter is on the whole organisation and its performance, although it is inevitable that within this individual performance and team performance issues will play a part. We shall review total quality management and learning organisations as major recent initiatives seen to affect directly organisational performance. The word 'initiative' may appear to some protagonists as inappropriate, as both these approaches may be seen as long-term and permanent changes in the philosophy of the organisation and the way that it is managed. It is unfortunate that the way that these approaches have been applied does not always (often) live up to such ideals.

The third approach we shall briefly review is that of organisation development – a perspective which has enjoyed a checkered past in terms of its perceived value. In spite of this it has not gone away and remains a valuable method and toolkit available to those organisations which are prepared to spend time to understand and apply it. Unlike total quality management and learning organisations it lacks instant impact and management appeal, and has yet to be packaged in a user friendly way.

Total quality management

There have been several quality initiatives in one form or another in recent years – perhaps the most common has been quality circles. Total quality management differs from past approaches in that these without exception were partial, piecemeal initiatives, inevitably bolted on to existing structures and systems. Total quality management, on the other hand, is intended as a holistic approach affecting every aspect of the organisation with a view to building quality into everything that is done – it is the philosophy of the way the organisation is managed. Dale and Cooper note, for example, that:

> TQM is a much broader concept than the initiatives which have gone before, encompassing not only product, service and process quality improvements but those relating to costs and productivity, and people involvement and development.   (Dale and Cooper 1992, p. 11)

Wilkinson *et al.* (1992) provide a helpful comparison of quality circles with TQM, as shown in Table 16.1.

TQM is seen by most commentators to apply to all in the organisation, not just to a selected few who work in production, and concentrated on how different parts of the organisation interact. The emphasis is on problem and defect **prevention**, rather than on fault **detection** as with quality control, with quality no longer belonging to the Quality Department, but to everyone. Quality becomes an integral part of management at all levels. TQM requires that measures of quality have been established and that when new ideas for quality improvement have been found, this best practice is then shared across the organisation to become the new expected minimum standard.

The central focus of TQM is on identifying and meeting customer needs. Customers are identified both externally, as in the eventual purchaser or user of the product or service, and internally, as in organisation departments and members who are supplied with product/material/information/services, and so on, provided by other members or departments. Total quality is not something that can be 'achieved', but is a focus for continual improvement, as in the Japanese term 'kaizen' which is well described in an article by Walker (1993). Honeycutt (1993) highlights the importance of organisational culture and environment when he says:

> The theory of continuous process improvement refers to substantive, systemic change. The challenge is to create an environment for substantive, systemic change.

Dale and Cooper (1992) state that many organisations claim TQM is their primary business strategy in influencing competitive performance, and the number of organisations claiming to have adopted TQM processes is increasing (Pike and Barnes 1994). A US study found that those organisations adopting TQM experienced overall better performance in terms of employee relations, productivity, customer satisfaction, market share and improved production. They also found that none had experienced these benefits immediately (Mendelowitz 1991). TQM is a long-term strategy for improvement, not a short-term fix.

Table 16.1 The difference between quality circles and TQM (Wilkinson *et al.* 1992)

Ideal types	Quality circles	TQM
Choice	Voluntary	Compulsory
Structure	Bolt-on	Integrated quality system
Direction	Bottom-up	Top-down
Scope	Within departments/units	Company-wide
Aims	Employee relations improvements	Quality improvements

Used with the permission of *Human Resource Management Journal.*

So TQM is popular in the extreme, but what changes are exactly being implemented? Does TQM mean the same thing in one organisation as another? It would not be surprising that organisations approached TQM in slightly different ways according to their needs. Harari (1993) notes an Ernst and Young study, which revealed that no fewer than 945 different tools were used for quality management in different organisations.

Honeycutt (1993) views TQM as an umbrella for several business concepts, but more fundamentally there are two quite different perspectives on TQM:

1. The 'hard' statistical approaches, which emphasise measurements of production, proportion of products that do not conform to specification, reasons for this, and resultant changes that are required to prevent future similar problems. This perspective depends heavily on two techniques. The first is SQC – statistical quality control – which is used to tally product defects, trace the source, make corrections, and make a record of what happens next. The second is SPC – statistical process control – which is used to analyse deviations in the production process during manufacturing.
2. The 'soft' people-based approaches, which emphasise worker empowerment, team work, devolved responsibility, open communications, involvement, participation, skill development and generating commitment to the quality objectives of the organisation.

These are pure forms and most organisations will implement some combination of these approaches. Historically, the statistical approach came first and there is a large degree of movement towards the people-based approaches. Lee and Lazarus (1993) identify a change in TQM from a technical and product focus to an 'analysis of all the processes which relate a company to its customers, suppliers and employees'. They argue what is new about TQM is the emphasis on customers, the training and empowerment of employees, top management support and commitment.

Many of the reported problems with TQM have been identified as people problems and indicate a neglect of the people issues. An IPM survey in the UK (reported in Marchington *et al.* 1993) identified that the public sector placed more emphasis on people aspects in their implementation of quality improvement.

The criteria for the 1994 Baldridge National Quality Awards in the United States include both aspects of TQM, with such aspects as quality leadership, quality information and analysis, strategic quality planning, human resource development and management, management of process quality, quality and operational results and customer focus and satisfaction.

What's involved in total quality management?

Dale and Cooper identify seven key elements of total quality management and we use their framework for this section:

Commitment and leadership of the Chief Executive

There is general agreement that commitment from the top of the organisation is essential. Senior managers need to define the quality objectives of the organisation to provide direction and clarity, and to communicate these continually within the organisation. The Chief Executive and top team also act as role models by talking about, asking about and reinforcing quality standards.

Culture change

A culture of not passing on faults to either internal or external customers is clearly important, together with a belief that all tasks can be continually improved. Critically, a culture of viewing mistakes as learning opportunities needs to be developed, and this is often where messages can become confused. Some of the quality literature refers to 'right first time' and 'zero defects' (see Crosby 1979) and this is sometimes passed on or perceived as mistakes not being allowable. If mistakes are not allowable, they are not owned up to (unless this is unavoidable), and if they are not owned up to, others cannot learn from them and the source of problems cannot be tackled.

Planning and organisation

This involves designing quality into the product and identifying fault proof features (to prevent faults in assembly); planning and communicating systems and procedures to be followed to ensure quality; designing work structures to support quality improvement (for example, task teams or cross-departmental teams) ensuring the necessary resources are made available for quality improvements; identifying how quality will be measured and monitored.

Education and training

This will be important in the areas of understanding a new approach to the management and philosophy of the organisation; operating within new structures; new criteria and performance standards; learning new skills in a team environment; learning new priorities and new tasks. In team structures team leaders will need particular help in running quality meetings and problem-solving, and in adopting a different management style. Management development generally is a key area, but one that is often overlooked. Jeffery (1992) describes how a TQM environment changes managers' tasks from control to setting direction, and from decision-making to giving guidance, information and support.

Involvement

Involving employees in the process of quality improvement is key, whether this be through suggestion schemes, team based quality meetings, or involvement in cross-function project teams looking at quality issues.

Recognition

Senior management need to recognise, celebrate and reward quality improvements. This may be in the form of publicity in company newsletters or local press, company awards and prizes, or simple praise for a job well done. It is also important that other personnel systems, for example, the appraisal system, support quality achievements.

Measurement

Level of quality according to agreed measures, costs of quality, and quality improvement targets are all important here. One of the tools used is benchmarking where an organisation or a department within it compares itself on a range of indicators to direct competitors or other organisations in the same sector. On a department basis benchmarking may use comparisons with the 'best' organisations irrespective of sector. Information on these indicators is then used as benchmarks or improvement targets for the organisation so that they can match or exceed the performance of other organisations. Simple indicators for the personnel function might include costs per new recruit or days training per head per year.

ACTIVITY BOX 16.1

In comparing your personnel department against others:

(a) Which other personnel departments would you choose to compare yourselves with and why?

(b) What quality measures or indicators would you use for the comparison and why?

OR

Think of any organisation in which you are involved in any capacity:

(a) Which other organisations would you compare this organisation with and why?

(b) What quality measures or indicators would you use for the comparison and why?

WINDOW ON PRACTICE

Mohrman *et al.* (1995) identify thirteen practices which they regard as commonly included in the practices of companies which regard themselves as operating TQM. The practices, in three groups, are as follows:

Core practices
- quality improvement teams
- quality councils
- cross-functional planning
- process re-engineering
- work simplification
- customer satisfaction monitoring
- direct employee exposure to customers

Production-oriented practices
- self-inspection
- statistical control method used by front line employees
- just-in-time deliveries
- work cells or manufacturing units

Other
- cost of quality monitoring
- collaboration with suppliers in quality efforts.

Mohrman *et al.* surveyed the 1992 Fortune 1000 listing in the United States which comprises the largest 500 manufacturers and the largest 500 service organisations. They found that 73 per cent of the organisations who responded to the survey had a quality initiative in place which covered an average of 50 per cent of employees in the organisation. The two most frequently used practices from the thirteen listed above were customer satisfaction monitoring and quality improvement teams, with 56 per cent and 59 per cent of organisations, respectively, covering 50 per cent or over of their employees in these practices. Self-inspection, collaboration with suppliers and exposure to customers are slightly less frequently used, but still within the 35–40 per cent range. The least used practice was that of work cell organisation.

What happens in practice?

In an ideal world organisations implementing TQM would follow the above steps on a continuous basis and quality improvements would ensue. This may have been the experience of some excellent organisations, but research increasingly suggests that it is not as simple as this for most. The IPM survey referred to above identifies four out of five organisations experiencing people problems in implementing quality initiatives. These problems centred on commitment to the aims of quality initiatives. Dale and Cooper identified middle managers as a block to implementation. This is sometimes because these managers see TQM as representing a greater workload for them without any immediate payoff, or alternatively due to fear of delegating responsibility and being left with no job or no power. Wilkinson *et al.* (1992) found that rather than TQM uniting middle managers behind a common cause, it actually became a source of competition. Wilkinson *et al.* (1994), reporting on an Institute of Management study, found that managers felt TQM placed a greater emphasis on teamwork, made greater demands on their time, and made management jobs more demanding in terms of both technical and people skills needed. Many managers acknowledged that it placed them under greater scrutiny from senior managers, and also that there was greater pressure from those employees below them. These same managers reported the need for further training in a variety of areas relevant to TQM, especially in the area of TQM tools and techniques (54 per cent) followed by TQM philosophy (33 per cent) and project management skills (32 per cent).

Schein (1991) also identifies the most commonly cited failure of TQM as the failure of upper and middle management to commit themselves to it. Managers often lack the passion and enthusiasm that TQM requires, and top management all too often delegate their involvement. Miller and Cargemi (1993) remind us that quality needs to be an obsession with everyone in the organisation. This requires a common understanding and a common language at all levels of the organisation. Prest (1995), in a case study of one organisation, found that senior managers were satisfied with the way that TQM was being developed within the organisation, yet first-line employees had a very different understanding of what TQM was about, the implications it had for them and the rationale for implementing it. Despite a considerable amount of training a common understanding and language had not developed and senior managers were unaware of this. Many employees were also frustrated because they were unable, for a variety of reasons, to put their new learning into practice. Employee interpretations must be critical to success, but perhaps the lack of consensus in the above study was at least partly due to the TQM programme being less than one year old, and it is recognised that TQM is not a quick fix, needing several years to become fully established (see, for example, Hill and Wilkinson 1995).

A further difficulty for managers is in wrestling with the concepts of TQM – if true, TQM requires an environment where mistakes are seen as learning opportunities. How do managers reconcile this with 'zero defect' and 'right first time' and avoid using mistakes as punishment opportunities? Political barriers are clearly another force to reckon with, for example the impact of the unions. While Mohrman *et al.* (1995) found that the unions had not been a problem in a US context, one interpretation of their data is that the unions influence the way that TQM is implemented (Hill and Wilkinson 1995).

Wilkinson *et al.* (1992) from their research identified some further issues related to difficulties in sustaining TQM:

> ‣ that TQM has been adopted as a bolt-on extra rather than a fundamental change in management approach and has not been fully integrated into the organisation.

- Where devolution had only superficially taken place within a centralised framework then employees felt their hands were tied in terms of implementing changes through TQM.
- The employee relations aspects of TQM are rarely considered – is it possible for staff to feel and display commitment after only a short training course?
- There are some contradictions in TQM as while involvement and participation are encouraged, management control is often not relinquished, and is often strengthened through the process.

There is now much literature on the failure of TQM in organisations, and the complexity of this approach to improving organisational performance is now being exposed. Many efforts at developing TQM in the British context are partial rather than total. Of the three cases described by Marchington *et al.* (1993) two of the organisations were about to re-launch TQM.

WINDOW ON PRACTICE

In a Japanese-owned organisation in the UK all employees were seen as having common status in an environment of a flattened hierarchy and responsibility being pushed down to team level. The company sought to encourage an atmosphere of trust with open communications and participation. Electronic components were assembled in teams and standard times had been identified for each activity. The teams had approximately 40–45 employees with a team leader and, within production limits the leaders had considerable discretion in the way that staff were deployed. Team members were encouraged to develop new skills and were rewarded for this, and they were encouraged to seek innovations to improve quality and productivity. The team as a whole had to cover for the absence of any team member, and electronic recording meant that the quality levels for the whole team and each individual were identified each day. All information regarding team performance in terms of absence, quality performance, conformity to standard times and production targets was displayed so that it was visible to all members. Individuals who had made mistakes were often called to the front of the line to rectify their error. The monitoring system was extended so that error rate information was placed over the head of each team member for all to see. The effect of this was to set one team member against another as the poor performance of one member affected the performance of the team as a whole.

In this example the rhetoric was to delegate day to day responsibility to the team in order to empower them and increase ownership of the task and commitment, but in reality management retained control.

(Adapted from Sewell and Wilkinson 1992.)

TQM and the personnel function

The central importance of people to TQM is an invitation to the personnel department to be involved. The bad news is that Storey (1992) reports that in some organisations TQM was implemented with very little involvement of the personnel function. In the IPM survey it was reported that around three-quarters of organisations had involved their human resource function in some way, although in many cases this was limited to operational issues such as training. What possible areas of opportunity does TQM provide?

Business strategy

Ideally the personnel function would be involved in the development of the TQM strategy itself. We have already indicated a general lack of involvement here. Before putting this down to a lack of credibility of the personnel function it is worth considering the historical development of TQM. Where TQM is seen from a 'hard' perspective the concentration is on technical quality of the product and process. Is it reasonable, then, to expect a high level of personnel involvement in strategy development? This especially applies in those organisations where TQM has just been applied to the technical/manufacturing function. What is more worrying is those organisations with a soft perspective on TQM. It is here that personnel involvement is key; however, there is no research which tells us of personnel involvement specifically in relation to the organisation's approach to TQM.

Human resource strategy

A critical area, but one that is often emphasised, is the matching of human resource strategy to TQM. For TQM to be effective it is essential that personnel strategies reinforce the quality message rather than pulling in another direction. For example, in the appraisal system, are the appraisal criteria in line with quality criteria? In terms of reward, does the organisation reward quality or something else, and does the process of reward (individual- or group-based/skill- or job-based) line up with the demands and expectations of TQM?

TQM implementation

We noted previously how the personnel function was involved more heavily in this area. Training course design and delivery, coaching managers, facilitating quality meetings are all key here; so are communications about quality and quality improvements.

TQM within the personnel function

Applying quality criteria within the personnel function is not only an essential part of TQM, but also enables the function to act as a role model for the rest of the organisation and understand first hand problems and issues. It gives the function the credibility to carry out implementation activities described above.

ACTIVITY BOX 16.2

How would you define the internal customers of the personnel function?

What would be the most appropriate way to explore customer needs and expectations for each group?

Review

The personnel function is well placed to identify some the effects and issues of the implementation of TQM. Attitude and opinion surveys are clearly one popular way. Working closely with departments as a consultant is another, and in this way richer information can be gathered giving a more in-depth understanding of issues and problems.

Learning organisations

Pedler, Boydell and Burgoyne (1989) have identified current interest in the idea of the learning organisation as a response to poor organisational performance. They describe the history of training and development in organisations in terms of critical problems and solutions. From the problem of skills shortage, leading to systematic skills training, to the problem of poor application of training, leading to an emphasis on self-development, to the problem of poor organisational performance leading to learning organisations. They define the characteristics of poor organisational performance as:

> sluggishness, an excess of bureaucracy and over-control, of organisations as straitjackets frustrating the self-development efforts of individual members and failing to capitalise upon their potential.

Becoming a learning organisation is seen by some as a way of keeping ahead of the competitors and gaining competitive advantage. We have already noted the idea that in times of constant change, learning needs to be greater than, or at least equal to, the rate of change in order for the organisation to survive (see Chapter 15, page 292).

In 1987 Pedler, Boydell and Burgoyne carried out a project entitled 'Developing the Learning Company' and interviewed staff in organisations which were pursuing learning company strategies. They asked why these strategies had been adopted, and found such reasons as the need to improve quality; the wish to become more people-oriented in relation to both staff and customers; the need to encourage 'active experimentation' and generally to cope with competitive pressures in order to survive. In Chapter 2 we also noted Pedler, Boydell and Burgoyne's (1989) definition of a learning organisation – which they identify as a 'dream' rather than a definition of current practice – was:

> an organisation which facilitates the learning of all its members and continually transforms itself.

Swieringa and Wierdsma (1992) offer an alternative definition of organisational learning:

> by the term organisational learning we mean the changing of organisational behaviour. The changing of organisational behaviour is a collective learning process.

The question is, what does this mean in practice? Beard (1993) notes that there is some confusion over this. The confusion, though, lies more in the practices adopted by organisations under the banner of a learning organisation, rather than in the fundamental ideas. Academics and theorists may place different emphases on different aspects of a learning organisation, but these are mutually supportive rather than conflicting. There is a common thread of a holistic approach and that organisational learning is greater than the sum of individual learning in the organisation. Different organisations, though, appear to have been inspired by some aspects of this approach, and having adopted these, they therefore see themselves as learning organisations. In essence they have taken some steps towards their goal, and have certainly improved the level of learning going on in the organisation, but have taken a partial rather than a holistic approach. In the next section we consider the nature of organisational learning before going on to describe a wide range of characteristics of learning organisations.

The nature of organisational learning

Although some pragmatic definitions of learning organisations centre on more and more individual learning, learning support and self-development, organisational learning is more than just the sum of individual learning in the organisation. It is only when an individual's learning has an impact on and interrelates with others that organisation members learn together and gradually begin to change the way things are done.

WINDOW ON PRACTICE

The difference between individual and organisational learning

Brian learns from the last research project team he ran that it would be much more effective if a member of the marketing department were fully involved at an early stage. Therefore he includes a marketing specialist from the outset on the next project team and finds that this reduces the time needed for the project team and results in less hassle towards the end of the project. Brian and the organisation have gained from this learning, but if *only* Brian learns this lesson the learning will be lost when he leaves the organisation. If, however, Brian discusses the idea with colleagues, or if there is heated debate at the beginning of the project team due to resistance to marketing specialists being included, and/or if there is some appraisal at the end of the project, there is some chance that others may learn from being involved in this experience. Others may feel that marketing specialists should be involved from the outset, may request that this happens, may apply it to other teams, and the new practice may become the way that the organisation operates. In this second scenario, if Brian leaves the organisation, he may take his learning with him, but the organisation also retains the learning as it has become embedded in the way that the organisation operates.

In this way mutual behaviour change is achieved which increases the collective competence, rather than just individual competence. Argyris and Schon (1978) see such learning as a change in the 'theory in use' (that is, the understanding, whether conscious or unconscious, that determines what we actually *do*) rather than merely a change in the 'espoused' theory (what we *say* we do). In other words the often unspoken rules of the organisation have changed. The question of how individual learning feeds into organisational learning and transformation, and how this is greater than the sum of individual learning, is only beginning to be addressed. Viewing the organisation as a process rather than an entity may offer some help here. Another perspective is that of viewing the organisation as a living organism. Pedler *et al.* (1991) make a useful start with their company energy flow model, shown in Figure 16.1.

Argyris and Schon (1978) describe different levels, or loops, of organisational learning, which have been developed by others. These levels are:

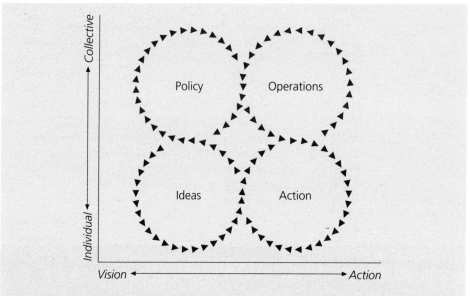

Figure 16.1 The energy flow model, from Pedlar *et al.* (1991). Used with permission of McGraw-Hill Book Company, Europe

Level 1: Single loop learning: Learning about *how* we can do better, thus improving what we are currently doing. This is seen as learning at the operational level, or at the level of rules

Level 2: Double loop learning: A more fundamental level, which is concerned with *why* questions in relation to what we are doing, rather than being concerned with doing the same things better, questioning whether we should be doing different things. This level is described as developing knowledge and understanding due to insights, and can result in strategic changes and renewal.

Level 3: Triple loop learning: This level of learning is the hardest of all to achieve as it is focused on the purpose or principles of the organisation, challenging whether these are appropriate, and is sometimes described as learning at the level of will or being.

All these levels of organisational learning are connected, as shown in Figure 16.2.

What are the characteristics of learning organisations?

There are many different approaches to describing the characteristics of a learning organisation, and we shall briefly consider three of these. First, Pedler, Burgoyne and Boydell (1991), who identify eleven characteristics of a learning organisation, which over time they have grouped into five general themes. Figure 16.3 shows both the characteristics and themes. We briefly summarise and discuss each of these dimensions next.

A learning approach to strategy

Strategy formation, implementation, evaluation and improvement are deliberately structured as learning experiences. Explicit feedback loops are built into the

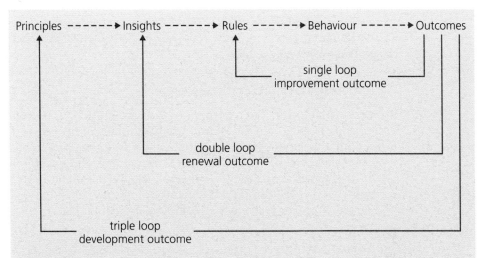

Figure 16.2 Three levels of organisational learning. Adapted from Swieringa and Wierdsma (1992)

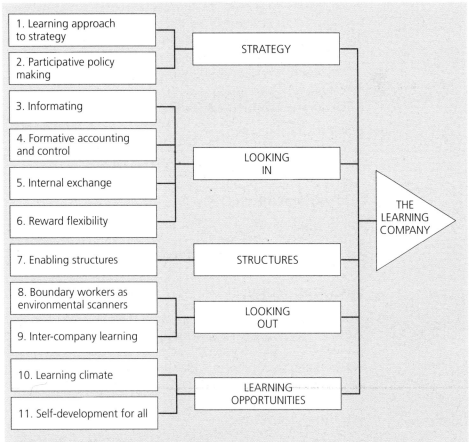

Figure 16.3 Blueprint of a learning company. From Pedlar *et al*. (1991). Used with permission of McGraw-Hill Book Company, Europe

process so that there can be continuous improvement in the light of experience. This approach is very close to Mintzberg's ideas of strategy formation (see, for example, Mintzberg 1987).

Participative policy-making

Policy-making is shared with all in the organisation, and even further, suppliers, customers and the total community have some involvement. The aim of the policy is to 'delight customers', and the differences of opinion and values which are revealed in the participative process are seen as productive tensions. A closeness to the principles of total quality management can be seen here. Nonaka and Johansson (1985) note how extensive internal consultations are carried out in Japanese organisations before taking major decisions.

Informating

Technology is used to empower and inform employees, and is made widely available. They note that such information should be used to understand what is going on in the company, and so stimulate learning, rather than used to reward, punish or control. Some clear difficulties here with the practical example we described on page 304, of information use in a total quality environment. Easterby-Smith (1989) makes the point that good news such as sales achieved, is often reported, rather than the information which would be of more value – why some orders were lost. He also notes the importance of systems that are future-oriented rather than past-oriented.

Formative accounting and control

Pedler *et al.* see this as a particular application of informating where accounting, budgeting and reporting systems are designed to assist learning. They also identify a purpose here of delighting the internal customer.

Internal exchange

This involves the general idea of all internal units seeing themselves as customers and suppliers of each other, but causing them to operate in a collaborative rather than a competitive way. This is, of course, also a key theme in TQM.

Reward flexibility

While noting that money is not seen as the sole reward, in Pedler *et al.*'s view the question of why some receive more money than others is a debate to be brought out into the open. They recommend that alternatives are discussed and tried out, but recognise that this is the most difficult of the eleven characteristics to put into practice.

Enabling structures

This means that roles should be loosely structured in line with the needs of internal customers and suppliers, and in a way that allows for personal growth and experimentation. Internal boundaries can be flexible. Easterby-Smith (1989) reports on some research with managers from different organisations. They were asked whether they had learned and developed through their past work experiences, and the results indicated that managers in different organisations would differ greatly in the extent to which they had done this. One of the key characteristics which distinguished organisations where individuals had learned and those where they had not was the use of project groups and transient structures, and individual encouragement to try new ways of working. These structures help to break down barriers between units, provide mechanisms for spreading new ideas and encourage the idea of change.

Boundary workers as environmental scanners

This relates to the need to collect data from outside the organisation, and it is seen as part of the role of all workers who have contact with suppliers, customers and neighbours of the organisation.

Inter-company learning

This entails joining with customers and suppliers in training experiences, research and development and job exchanges. Pedler *et al.* also note the possibility of learning with competitors. They also suggest that benchmarking can be used to learn from other companies.

Learning climate

Here the primary task is the encouragement of experimentation and learning from experience. To achieve this current ideas, attitudes and actions need to be questioned and new ideas tried out. Mistakes are allowed because not all new ideas will work. The importance of continuous improvement is underlined – that it is always possible to do it better. The involvement of customers, suppliers and neighbours in experimentation is suggested. A learning climate suggests that feedback from others is continually requested, is made available and is acted upon.

WINDOW ON PRACTICE

One of the authors invited a business speaker to address a course group on the subject of management development. The speaker duly arrived and delivered a summary of his organisation's management development strategy, including its efforts to become a learning organisation. Over coffee, following the lecture, the speaker requested feedback from the whole class group so that he could use this to improve his performance on the next occasion. He explained that in everything that the personnel function did they would ask for feedback and incorporate this into future activities. Asking for feedback had become a habit and was not only expected internally, but from external customers too.

Self-development opportunities for all

That means that resources and facilities for self-development are available to employees at all levels in the organisation, and that coaching, mentoring, peer support, counselling, feedback, and so on are available to support individuals in their learning.

Peter Senge (1990) takes a slightly different perspective. In his book about the art and practice of a learning organisation he identified five vital dimensions in building organisations which can learn, which he refers to as disciplines:

1. **Systems thinking**: This is an understanding of the interrelatedness between things, seeing the whole rather than just a part, and concentrating on processes. In terms of organisational actions it suggests that connections need to be constantly made and a consideration of the implications that every action has elsewhere in the organisation.
2. **Personal mastery**: This underlines the need for continuous development and individual self-development.
3. **Mental models**: This is about the need to expose the 'theories in use' in the organisation. These can block change and the adoption of new ideas, and can only be confronted, challenged and changed if they are brought to the surface rather than remaining unconscious.
4. **Shared visions**: This is expressing the need for a common purpose or vision which can inspire members of the organisation and break down barriers and mistrust. Senge argues that such a vision plus an accurate view of the present state results in a creative tension which is helpful for learning and change.
5. **Team learning**: Teams are seen as important in that they are microcosms of the organisation, and the place where different views and perspectives come together, which Senge sees as a productive process.

Senge acknowledges that he presents a very positive vision of what organisations can do, and recognises that without the appropriate leadership this will not happen. He goes on to identify three critical leadership roles: designer, teacher, steward. As designer the leader needs to engage employees at all levels in designing the vision, core purpose and values of the organisation: design processes for strategic thinking and effective learning processes. As teacher the leader needs to help all organisation members gain more insight into the organisational reality, to coach, guide and facilitate, and help others bring their theories into use. As steward the leader needs to demonstrate a sense of personal commitment to the organisation's mission and take responsibility for the impact of leadership on others.

Bob Garratt (1990) concentrates on the role that the directors of an organisation have in encouraging a learning organisation and in overcoming learning blocks. He suggests:

▶ the top team concentrate on strategy and policy and hold back from day-to-day operational issues;
▶ thinking time for the top team to relate changes in the external environment to the internal working of the organisation;

) creation of a top team, involving the development and deployment of the strengths of each member;

) the delegation of problem-solving to staff close to the operation;

) acceptance that learning occurs at all levels of the organisation, and that directors need to create a climate where this learning freely flows.

Clearly, a learning organisation is not something which can be developed overnight and has to be viewed as a long-term strategy.

Easterby-Smith makes some key points about encouraging experimentation in organisations in relation to flexible structures, information, people and reward. We have discussed flexibility and information in some detail. In respect of people he argues that organisations will seek to select those who are similar to current organisation members. The problem here is that in reinforcing homogeneity and reducing diversity, the production of innovative and creative ideas is restrained. He sees diversity as a positive stimulant (which we discuss further in Chapter 19) and concludes that organisations should therefore select some employees who would not normally fit their criteria, and especially those who would be likely to experiment and be able to tolerate ambiguity. In relation to the reward system he notes the need to reinforce rather than punish risk-taking and innovation.

A word of caution

Hawkins (1994) notes the evangelistic fervour with which learning organisations and total quality management are recommended to the uninitiated. His concern with the commercialisation of these ideas is that they thereby become superficial. He argues that an assumption may be made that all learning is good whatever is being learnt, whereas the value of learning is where it is taking us. Learning, then, is the means rather than the end in itself. Learning to be more efficient at what is being done does not necessarily make one more effective – it depends on the appropriateness of the activity itself. Nor does the literature cover adequately the barriers to becoming a learning organisation – for example, the role of politics within the organisation. If learning requires sharing of information, and information is power, then how can individuals be encouraged to let go of the power they have? In particular, both Senge and Garratt have high expectations of the leaders of organisations. To what extent are these expectations realistic, and how might they be achieved? The literature of learning organisations has a clear unitarist perspective – the question of whether employees desire to be involved in or united by a vision of the organisation needs to be addressed. For a useful critique of the assumptions behind learning organisations, see Coopey (1995). In addition, the full complexity of the ideas implicit in the words 'learning organisation' requires more explanation.

Organisational development

It is difficult to justify writing a chapter about organisational performance without mentioning organisational development (OD), which has been, and remains, a key approach to developing performance in some organisations. OD has been described by French and Bell (1984) as an approach to organisational improvement using behavioural science techniques. Hawkins (1994) sees the learning organisation as an umbrella for OD activities, while recognising there is value in the slightly different perspectives of each. Other writers have argued that the learning organisation is enabling individuals to do collectively what OD sets out to do, but that they are doing it by themselves without external help.

Typically, OD has involved an internal or external consultant/facilitator using behavioural science principles in working on organisational problem-solving. Currently, OD practitioners may be particularly involved in the introduction of change, whether it be technical, cultural or organisational. OD's method of operation centres not only on objectives and aims, but on interpersonal behaviour, attitudes and values in the organisation. There is usually an emphasis on openness between colleagues, improved conflict resolution methods, more effective team management and the collaborative diagnosis and solution of problems. OD does not necessarily include formalised training and development, although it is most likely that this will be incorporated.

Any training strategy typically centres on groups of managers, or directly on organisational processes with the assistance of the change agent or consultant, who helps the participants to perceive, face up to and resolve the behavioural problems experienced. OD is a 'macro' approach to development, as contrasted with individual training and development, which is primarily a 'micro' approach.

Specific issues that OD practitioners may be involved with include:

◗ developing processes for bringing about and implementing change;
◗ assessing organisational effectiveness and developing improvement plans;
◗ organisation structure and design;
◗ bringing about cultural change;
◗ designing effective communication processes;
◗ building effective work-groups and multidisciplinary teams;
◗ managing the implementation and organisational implications of new technology;
◗ effective work practices, such as clarification of roles and responsibilities in complex situations, work-group objective setting;
◗ stimulating innovation and creativity;
◗ problem-solving and effective decision-making processes;
◗ managing interpersonal and inter-group conflict.

(Adapted from Purves 1989.)

Van Eynde and Bledsoe (1990) found in their research that OD practitioners were now more likely to be working with client managers on more task-focused issues directly related to organisational effectiveness, and less on improvement of interpersonal relationships, than they were fifteen years ago. Team dynamics, for example, would now be dealt with inside the framework of helping a team to resolve a critical issue. Increasingly, OD consultants are involved in helping organisations to envisage the future. The researchers also found that there are increasing opportunities for OD practitioners to work with the highest levels in the organisation on changes that impact on the whole organisation.

It is through these types of intervention, and from their experiences of the processes used, that managers develop further and are more able successfully to work through similar issues in the future.

Summary propositions

16.1 There is an increasing emphasis on organisational performance and the factors that affect it.

16.2 Systems, structures, processes, resources and culture will all have an impact on organisational performance, as well as on individual motivation and ability.

16.3 Total quality management and learning organisations are two important philosophies for improving organisational performance.

16.4 Both of these approaches require a long-term perspective and are more complex than the way in which they are often presented.

16.5 Total quality management has a statistical, 'hard' strand and a people-centred 'soft' strand. Difficulties experienced in adopting TQM have mainly focused on people issues.

References

Argyris, C. and Schon, D. A. (1978) *Organisational Learning*, Reading, MA: Addison-Wesley.

Beard, D. (1993) 'Learning to change organisations', *Personnel Management*, January.

Blyton, P. and Turnbull, P. (1992) *Reassessing Human Resource Management*, London: Sage.

Coopey, J. (1995) 'The learning organisation, power, politics and ideology', *Management Learning*, Vol. 26, No. 2, pp. 193–213.

Crosby, P. B. (1979) *Quality is Free*, Maidenhead: McGraw-Hill.

Dale, B. and Cooper, C. (1992) *Total Quality and Human Resources: An executive guide*, Oxford: Blackwell.

Deming, W. E. (1986) *Out of the Crisis*, Cambridge, Mass: MIT Institute for Advanced Engineering Study.

Easterby-Smith, M. (1989) 'Creating a learning organisation', *Personnel Review*.

French, W. L. and Bell, C. H. (1984) *Organisation Development: Behavioural science intervention for organisational improvement*, 4th edn, Hemel Hempstead: Prentice Hall.

Garratt, B. (1990) *Creating a Learning Organisation*, Hemel Hempstead: Director Books.

Harari, O. (1993) 'Ten reasons why TQM doesn't work', *Management Review*, Vol. 82, No. 1, January.

Hawkins, P. (1994) 'Organisational learning; Taking stock and facing the challenge', *Management Learning*, Vol. 25, No. 1.

Hill, S. and Wilkinson, A. (1995) 'In search of TQM', *Employee Relations*, Vol. 17, No. 3.

Honeycutt, A. (1993) 'Total quality management at RTW', *Journal of Management Development*, Vol. 12, No. 5.

Jeffery, J. R. (1992) 'Making quality managers: redefining management's role', *Quality*, Vol. 31, No. 5, May.

Marchington, M., Dale, B. and Wilkinson, A. (1993) 'Who is really taking the lead on quality?', *Personnel Management*, April.

Mendelowitz, A. I. (1991) *Management Practices – US companies improve performance through quality efforts,* United States General Account Office (GAO/NSIAD-91-190).

Miller, R. L. and Cargemi, J. P. (1993) 'Why total quality management fails: perspective of top management', *Journal of Management Development,* Vol. 12, No. 7.

Mintzberg, H. (1987) 'Crafting strategy', *Harvard Business Review,* July/August pp. 66–75.

Mohrman, S. A., Tenkas, R. V., Lawler, E. E. III and Ledford, G. E. (1995) 'Total quality management – practice and outcomes in the largest US firms', *Employee Relations,* Vol. 17, No. 3.

Nonaka, I. and Johansson, J. (1985) 'Japanese management: what about the "hard skills"?', *Academy of Management Review,* Vol. 10, No. 2, pp. 181–91.

Pedler, M., Boydell, T. and Burgoyne, J. (1989) 'Towards the learning company', *Management Education and Development,* Vol. 20, Pt 1.

Pedler, M., Burgoyne, J. and Boydell, T. (1991) *The Learning Company,* Maidenhead: McGraw-Hill.

Pike, J. and Barnes, R. (1994) *TQM in Action,* London: Chapman and Hall.

Prest, A. (1995) 'Perspectives of Total Quality Management', unpublished MA thesis.

Purves, S. (1989) 'Organisation and process consultancy', unpublished paper.

Schein, L. (1991) 'Communicating quality in the service sector', in B. H. Peters and J. L. Peters (eds.), *Maintaining Total Quality Advantage,* New York: The Conference Board, pp. 40–2.

Senge, P. (1990) *The Fifth Discipline: The art and practice of the learning organisation,* London: Century Business, Random House.

Sewell, G. and Wilkinson, B. (1992) 'Empowerment or emasculation? Shopfloor surveillance in a total quality organisation', in P. Blyton and P. Turnbull (eds.), *Reassessing Human Resource Management,* London: Sage.

Storey, J. (1992) *Developments in the Management of Human Resources,* Oxford: Blackwell.

Swieringa, J. and Wierdsma, A. (1992) *Becoming a Learning Organisation,* Wokingham: Addison-Wesley.

van Eynde, D. F. and Bledsoe, J. A. (1990) 'The changing practice of organisation development', *Leadership and Organisation Development Journal,* Vol. 11, No. 2, pp. 25–33.

Walker, V. (1993) 'Kaizen – the art of continual improvement', *Personnel Management,* August.

Wilkinson, A., Marchington, M., Goodman, J. and Ackers, P. (1992) 'Total quality management and employee involvement', *Human Resource Management Journal,* Vol. 2, No. 4, 1–20.

Wilkinson, A., Redman, T. and Snape, E. (1994) 'Quality management and the manager: a research note on findings from an Institute of Management study', *Employee Relations,* Vol. 16, No. 1, pp. 62–70.

General discussion topics

1. Is quality management a threat to or an opportunity for the personnel function?
2. 'Learning organisations are dreams which can never come true.' Discuss why you agree or disagree with this statement.

CHAPTER 17

Managing individual performance

The treatment of individual performance in organisations has traditionally centred on the assessment of performance and the allocation of reward. Walker (1992) notes that this is partly due to these processes being institutionalised through the use of specific systems and procedures. Performance was typically seen as the result of the interaction between individual ability and motivation.

Increasingly, organisations are recognising that planning and enabling performance have a critical effect on individual performance. So, for example, clarity of performance goals and standards, appropriate resources, guidance and support from the individual's manager all become central.

In this chapter we start with the fundamental steps for managing individual performance, review approaches to the assessment of performance, and then explore how performance management systems attempt to integrate both enabling and assessing individual performance.

The performance cycle

The performance cycle identifies three key aspects of effective performance, as shown in Figure 17.1. These aspects can be used as stepping-stones in managing employee performance.

Planning performance

This step recognises the importance of a shared view of expected performance between manager and employee. The shared view can be expressed in a variety of ways, such as a traditional job description, key accountabilities, performance standards, specific objectives or targets, and essential competencies.

In most cases a combination of approaches is necessary. There is a very clear trend to use specific objectives with a timescale for completion in addition to the generic tasks, with no beginning and no end, which tend to appear on traditional job descriptions. Such objectives give individuals a much clearer idea of performance expectations and enable them to focus on the priorities when they have to make choices about what they do. There is a long history of research demonstrating how clarity of goals improves employee performance.

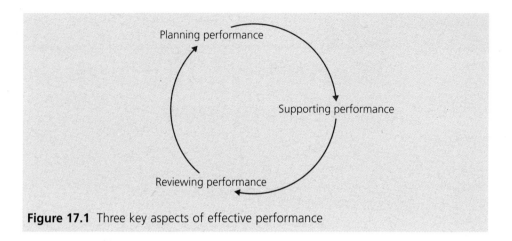

Figure 17.1 Three key aspects of effective performance

The critical point about a *shared* view of performance suggests that handing out a job description or list of objectives to the employee is not adequate. Performance expectations need to be understood and, where possible, involve a contribution from the employee. For example, although key accountabilities may be fixed by the manager, they will need to be discussed. Specific objectives allow for and benefit from a greater degree of employee input as they will have a valid view of barriers to overcome, the effort involved and feasibility. Expressing objectives as a 'what' statement rather than a 'how' statement gives employees the power to decide the appropriate approach once they begin to work on the issue. Incorporating employee input and using 'what' statements are likely to generate a higher degree of employee ownership and commitment.

Planning the training, development and resources necessary for employees to achieve their objectives is imperative. Without this support it is unlikely that even the most determined employees will achieve the performance required.

Supporting performance

While the employee is working to achieve the performance agreed, the manager retains a key enabling role. Organising the resources and off-job training is clearly essential. So too is being accessible. There may well be unforeseen barriers to the agreed performance which it falls within the manager's remit to address, and sometimes the situation will demand that the expected performance needs to be revised. The employee may want to sound out possible courses of action on the manager before proceeding, or may require further information. Sharing 'inside' information which will affect the employee's performance is often a key need, although it is also something which managers find difficult, especially with sensitive information. Managers can identify information sources and other people who may be helpful.

Ongoing coaching during the task is especially important. Managers can guide employees through discussion and by giving constructive feedback. They are in a position to provide practical job experiences to develop the critical skills and competencies which the employee needs, and can provide job-related opportunities for practice. Managers can identify potential role models to employees, and help to explain how high achievers perform so well.

Although it is the employee's responsibility to achieve the performance agreed, the manager has a continuous role in providing support and guidance, and in oiling the organisational wheels.

ACTIVITY BOX 17.1

Do managers actively support employee performance in your organisation?

If they do, by what means do they do this and how effective is it?

If they do not, why not, and what is the impact of this?

OR

Think of any organisation in which you have had some involvement:

▶ How has individual performance been supported?
▶ How effective was/is this?
▶ How would you improve the way in which performance was/is supported?

Ongoing review

Ongoing review is an important activity for employees to carry out in order to plan their work and priorities and also to highlight to the manager well in advance if the agreed performance will not be delivered by the agreed dates. Joint employee/manager review is essential so that information is shared. For example, a manager needs to be kept up to date on employee progress, while the employee needs to be kept up to date on organisational changes which have an impact on the agreed objectives. Both need to share perceptions of how the other is doing in their role, and what they could do that would be more helpful.

These reviews are normally informal in nature, although a few notes may be taken of progress made and actions agreed. They need not be part of any formal system and therefore can take place when the job or the individuals involved demand, and not according to a pre-set schedule. The purpose of the review is to facilitate future employee performance, and provide an opportunity for the manager to confirm that the employee is 'on the right track', or redirect him or her if necessary. They thus provide a forum for employee reward in terms of recognition of progress. A 'well done' or an objective signed off as completed can enhance the motivation to perform well in the future.

Using the performance cycle

The performance cycle describes effective day-to-day management of performance. As such it was often used as the reason why no formal appraisal system was in place – 'because performance is appraised informally on a continuous basis'. In reality performance was usually managed on a *dis*continuous basis, with very little action unless there was a performance problem which needed sorting out! Even then the problem was often avoided until it had become so severe that someone would begin to talk of disciplinary procedures.

The performance cycle, as we have described above, is intended to be viewed as a positive management tool to enhance employee performance and to support whatever formal appraisal or performance management system is in place.

Appraisal systems

Appraisal systems formalise the review part of the performance cycle. They are typically designed on a central basis, usually by the personnel function and require that each line manager appraise the performance of their staff on an annual, six-monthly or even quarterly basis. Elaborate forms are often designed to be completed as a formal record of the process.

Appraisal has traditionally been seen as most applicable to those in management and supervisory positions, but increasingly clerical and secretarial staff are being included in the process. Manual staff, particularly those who are skilled or have technical duties, are also subject to appraisal, although to a lesser extent than the other groups. Long (1986) notes that over the past decade there has been a substantial increase in performance reviews for non-managerial staff. Some organisations have a flexible approach whereby individuals in certain grades – for example, secretarial and clerical – can elect whether or not to be included in the appraisal system. Other organisations allow those over a certain age to opt out of the system if they so wish.

Why have an appraisal system?

The different purposes of appraisal systems frequently conflict. Appraisal can be used to improve current performance, provide feedback, increase motivation, identify training needs, identify potential, let individuals know what is expected of them, focus on career development, award salary increases and solve job problems. It can be used to set out job objectives, provide information for human resource planning and career succession, assess the effectiveness of the selection process, and as a reward or punishment in itself. Fletcher and Williams (1985) have suggested two conflicting roles of judge and helper, which the appraiser may be called upon to play, depending on the purpose of the appraisal process. If a single appraisal system was intended to improve current performance and to act as the basis for salary awards, the appraiser would be called on to play both judge and helper at the same time. This makes it difficult for the appraiser to be impartial. It is also difficult for the appraisee, who may wish to discuss job-related problems, but is very cautious about what she says because of not wanting to jeopardise a possible pay rise. Randell et al. (1984) suggest that the uses of appraisal can be divided into three broad categories, and that an appraisal system should attempt to satisfy only one of these. The categories they suggest are reward reviews, potential reviews and performance reviews. This implies that personnel managers need to think more carefully about the primary purpose of their appraisal system, and make sure that procedures, training and individual expectations of the system do not conflict.

Given that there is a choice about the way the appraisal system will be used, Randell et al. believe that the greatest advantages will be gained by the use of performance reviews. Such reviews include appraisal of past performance, meeting objectives, identification of training needs, problems preventing better performance, and so on. This poses a great problem, particularly for the private sector, but increasingly in the public sector, where there is a predilection to link pay directly to performance. Do these organisations settle just for reward reviews and forgo the advantages of performance reviews? Do they have two different appraisal systems – one for reward and one for performance at two distinctly different times of the year? Do they forget about linking performance and pay? These are key questions in relation to performance management systems, and are discussed later in this chapter.

ACTIVITY BOX 17.2

▶ What are the key purposes of performance appraisal in your organisation, or any organisation with which you are familiar?

▶ What conflicts does this create?
▶ How might these conflicts be resolved?

Torrington and Weightman (1989) suggest that, from the individual's point of view, appraisal may be seen as a time when they can gain feedback on their performance, reassurance, praise, encouragement, help in performing better and guidance on future career possibilities. For many, however, the process is seen as irrelevant to their needs and unhelpful – although this is often a reflection on the way that the process operates. Long (1986) found that there was a decreased emphasis on potential assessment and related career planning activity.

Who contributes to the appraisal process?

Individuals are appraised by a variety of people, including their immediate supervisor, their superior's superior, a member of the personnel department, themselves, their peers or their subordinates. Sometimes, assessment centres are used to carry out the appraisal.

Immediate manager

Most appraisals are carried out by the employee's immediate manager. The advantage of this is that the immediate supervisor usually has the most intimate knowledge of the tasks that an individual has been carrying out and how well they have been done. The annual appraisal is also the logical conclusion of on-going management of performance that should have been taking place throughout the year between the supervisor and the appraisee. Appraisal by the immediate manager is sometimes called appraisal by 'father'. Even when appraisal information is collected from a range of other sources, it is the immediate manager who collates and uses this information with the individual.

Manager's manager

The level of authority above the immediate manager can be involved in the appraisal process in one of two ways. First, they may be called upon to counter-sign the manager's appraisal of the employee in order to give a 'seal of approval' to indicate that the process has been fairly and properly carried out. Second, the manager's manager may directly carry out the appraisal. This is known as the 'grandfather' approach to appraisal. This is more likely to happen when the appraisal process is particularly concerned with making comparisons between individuals and identifying potential for promotion. It helps to overcome the problem that managers will all appraise by different standards, and minimises the possibility that appraisees will be penalised due to the fact that their manager has very high standards and is a 'hard marker'. Grandfather appraisal is often used to demonstrate fair play.

Member of the personnel department

Much less frequently an employee will be appraised by a member of the personnel department. This happens when there is no obvious ongoing immediate manager, for example, in a matrix organisation. Stewart and Stewart (1977) show how this can work in practice by the example of an accountancy and consultancy partnership where work teams are organised according to the particular project in hand. At the end of each project the team manager completes a summary of the performance of each member of the team. This is then forwarded to the 'development manager' in the personnel department. At the end of the appraisal year the development manager collates all the reports on a given employee and produces a composite performance appraisal which is then discussed with the individual. This type of appraisal can be tricky to organise and much depends on the skills of the co-ordinator in the personnel department.

Self-appraisal

Fletcher (1993b) argues that there is little doubt that people are capable of rating themselves, but the question is, are they willing to do this? and further, will individuals rate themselves fairly? Is it realistic to expect individuals to rate themselves as middle of the range if their salary depends on the appraisal result? Meyer (1980) reports that when employees were asked to compare themselves with others they tended to overrate themselves; however, when individuals prepared self-appraisals for appraisal interviews they were more modest. Fletcher notes that one of the most fruitful ways for individuals to rate themselves is by rating different aspects of their performance relative to other aspects, rather than relative to the performances of other people. He comments that by approaching self-appraisal in this way, individuals are more discriminating.

Self-appraisal is relatively new and not widely used. However, individuals do carry out an element of self-appraisal in some of the more traditional appraisal schemes. Some organisations encourage individuals to prepare for the appraisal interview by filling out some form of appraisal on themselves. The differences between the individual's own appraisal and the manager's appraisal can then be a useful starting point for the appraisal interview. The difference between this and self-appraisal is that it is still the superior's appraisal that officially counts, although in the light of the subordinate's comments they might amend some of the ratings that they have given. In many schemes appraisees are asked to sign the completed appraisal form to show that they agree with its conclusions. In the event of disagreement a space is provided for details of controversial items. At the other end of the scale there are 'closed' schemes which not only eschew any form of contribution from the appraisees, but also prevent the appraisees from knowing the ratings that they have been given by their appraiser.

Taylor, Lehman and Forde (1989) recommend a particularly constructive form of self-appraisal, where individuals do this as a mid-point evaluation and concentrate on development, improvement and enrichment strategies. Managers support this process and aid development by coaching. The formal appraisal by the manager does not take place until six months later.

Appraisal by peers

Latham and Wexley (1981) suggest that peer ratings are both acceptably reliable and valid and have the advantage that peers have a more comprehensive view of the appraisee's job performance. They note the problem, though, that peers may be unwilling to appraise each other, as this can be seen as 'grassing' on each other. It is perhaps for this reason that peer appraisal is not often used, despite its claimed advantages. When peer rating is used, an individual is rated by a group of peers and the results are averaged. In a time of increasing emphasis on teamwork there is a danger that peer assessment can be dysfunctional and disrupt team harmony (see Williams 1989).

Appraisal by subordinates

Appraisal information from subordinates, sometimes referred to as upward appraisal or reverse appraisal, is another less usual approach, although it is certainly increasing. Latham and Wexley (1981) identify circumstances where it can be valuable and give an example of an organisation where individuals were rated by both superiors and subordinates, and where any large discrepancies in ratings were seen as areas for follow-up investigation. It is more limited in its value than peer appraisal as subordinates are only acquainted with certain aspects of their manager's work. However, it can be especially useful in providing information on management style and people management skills, which are increasingly seen as critical. Redman and Snape (1992) argue that asking for this type of information from subordinates facilitates empowerment. Recent examples of this include the Post Office (Cockburn 1993) and W. H. Smith (Fletcher 1993a). Further research by Redman and Snape (1992) revealed that only 13 per cent of their sample of 280 respondents were subject to a formal system of upward appraisal. In general their respondents (whether subject to such as system or not) found upward appraisal less acceptable than the conventional approach, and those who did receive it were reluctant to share upward appraisal data with others.

Customer appraisal

An increasingly useful source of appraisal information is from internal and external customers. This information can be collected directly by the direct manager from internal customers – for example, the training manager may collect information from a department on the support given to them by their specified training officer. Collecting information from external customers is a bit more tricky, but can be done in a positive manner, framed in terms of improving customer services, and designed to be not too time-consuming.

Assessment centres

Assessment centres can be used in the appraisal of potential supervisors and managers. The advantage of assessment centres for this purpose is that ratings of

Almost all organisation members will have contact with a variety of internal customers. Identify your internal customers, or those of another member of staff, and design a short questionnaire to collect feedback that would be important in an appraisal situation.

What difficulties might you encounter in collecting and using this information?

NB: You can use any organisation with which you are familiar, and any role played by yourself or another person whose role you know about.

potential can be assessed on the basis of factors other than current performance. It is well accepted that high performance in a current job does not mean that an individual will be a high performer if promoted to a higher level. It is also increasingly recognised that a moderate performer at one level may perform much better at a higher level. Assessment centres use tests, group exercises and interviews to appraise potential.

Contributor balance and 360 degree appraisal

Although most appraisal systems focus on appraisal by the direct manager Fisher (1994) identifies two distinct emphases – hierarchical appraisal (by the management system) and peer appraisal (which he found in some educational institutions and private professional practice firms). Where there is more than one

WINDOW ON PRACTICE

Jacob and Flood (1995) report on how 360 degree feedback was used as part of a senior management development programme in a French agrochemicals company – Rhône-Poulenc. This approach was felt to be more accurate than an assessment centre because it collected data directly from on-the-job performance rather than from a substitute environment. The questionnaire was designed around a strategically developed competency framework – bosses, peers and subordinates took part in the process as well as the manager themselves. The identity of all contributors was anonymous, except for the immediate boss. The questionnaire took around 20 minutes to complete and was administered prior to the development programme, and at a later date after the programme. As part of the process, individual managers had to present what they had learned about themselves to others in a team setting. Despite this, Jacob and Flood state that 'most

participants have suggested that they have never experienced such powerful and apparently insightful feedback about their performance'.

In the United States, where 360 degree feedback appears to have originated, Edwards and Ewen provide an example of how this process was used to improve customer satisfaction. At Chemetals when sales staff complete a client call they leave the client with a computer disk containing an assessment questionnaire. The client is asked to complete this and mail it on to another party for analysis. Analyses at July 1993, December 1993 and July 1994 demonstrate improvements on a number of aspects of customer satisfaction, particularly in communication and responsiveness. The authors maintain that there was no training, or other initiatives, in the intervening period, and whilst they cannot exclude some influence from other factors, it appears that the 360 degree feedback was a major cause of the improved job performance.

contribution to the assessment, the extent to which the different contributors are integrated varies considerably. Fletcher (1993a) comments that upward appraisal is only likely to be used as an occasional and additional activity rather than an integral part of the appraisal process. Different contributions may be integrated on an informal basis by the direct manager in order to collect a range of perspectives and thus enhance the appraisal discussion. Where a range of contributions are more formally integrated this process is usually termed multi-rater appraisal, or 360 degree feedback. This uses a quantitative approach with a range of raters (usually self, managers, peers, customers and subordinates) completing a questionnaire on behaviour and actions of the appraisee. A good guide to the practicalities of designing and implementing a system is Edwards and Ewen (1996). They suggest that the barriers to implementation concern culture, inertia, cost, lack of research and the technology available for analysis. Ward (1995) explains how Tesco have used such a system, and suggests that such behaviours as leadership and communication can be assessed in this way. He argues that it is useful for an individual's summative ratings to be compared with functional, industry or company norms as well as against their self-assessment ratings. He also notes the importance of support with feedback and interpretation, a resultant action plan and possibly counselling.

What is appraised?

Appraisal systems can measure a variety of things. They are sometimes designed to measure personality, sometimes behaviour or performance, and sometimes achievement of goals. These areas may be measured either quantitively or qualitatively. Qualitative appraisal often involves the writing of an unstructured narrative on the general performance of the appraisee. Alternatively, some guidance may be given as to the areas on which the appraiser should comment. The problem with qualitative appraisals is that they may leave important areas unappraised, and that they are not suitable for comparison purposes. Coates (1994) argues that what is actually measured in performance appraisal is the extent to which the individual conforms to the organisation.

When they are measured quantitively some form of scale is used, often comprising five categories of measurement from 'excellent', or 'always exceeds requirements' at one end to 'inadequate' at the other, with the mid-point being seen as acceptable. Scales are, however, not always constructed according to this plan. Sometimes on a five-point scale there will be four degrees of acceptable behaviour and only one that is unacceptable. Sometimes an even-numbered (usually six-point) scale is used to prevent the central tendency. There is a tendency for raters to settle on the mid-point of the scale, either through lack of knowledge of the appraisee, lack of ability to discriminate, lack of confidence or desire not to be too hard on appraisees. Rating other people is not an easy task, but it can be structured so that it is made as objective as possible. If peformance appraisal is related to pay, then some form of final scale is normally used. A typical approach is for there to be forced distributions on this scale – so, for example, only a specified proportion of staff fall into the highest, middle and lowest categories.

Avoidance of personality measures

Much traditional appraisal was based on measures of personality traits that were felt to be important to the job. These included traits such as resourcefulness, enthusiasm, drive, application and other traits such as intelligence. One difficulty with these is that everyone defines them differently, and the traits that are used are not always mutually exclusive. Raters, therefore, are often unsure of what they are rating. Ill-defined scales like these are more susceptible to bias and prejudice. Another problem is that since the same scales are often used for many different jobs, traits that are irrelevant to an appraisee's job may still be measured. One helpful approach is to concentrate on the job rather than the person. In an attempt to do this some organisations call their annual appraisal activity the 'job appraisal review'. The requirements of the job and the way that it is performed are considered, and the interview concentrates on problems in job performance which are recognised as not always being the 'fault' of the person performing the job. Difficulties in performance may be due to departmental structure or the equipment being used, rather than the ability or motivation of the employee. Other approaches concentrate on linking ratings to behaviour and performance on the job.

Behaviourally anchored rating scales

One way of linking ratings with behaviour at work is to use behaviourally anchored rating scales (BARS). These can be produced in a large organisation by asking a sample group of raters independently to suggest examples of behaviour for each point on the scale in order to collect a wide variety of behavioural examples. These examples are then collated and returned to the sample raters without any indication of the scale point for which they were suggested. Sample raters allocate a scale point to each example, and those examples, which are consistently located at the same point on the scale, are selected to be used as behavioural examples for that point on the scale. Future raters then have some guidance as to the type of behaviour that would be expected at each point. BARS can be used in conjunction with personality scales, but are most helpful when using scales that relate more clearly to work behaviour. Table 17.1 shows an example of a BARS in relation to 'relations with clients' – for the sake of clarity just one behavioural example is given at each point on the scale, whereas in a fully developed scale there may be several at each point. Another advantage of the development of BARS is that appraisers have been involved in the process and this can increase their commitment to the outcome.

Behavioural observation scales

Behavioural observation scales (BOS) provide an alternative way of linking behaviour and ratings. Fletcher and Williams (1985) comment that these scales are developed by lengthy procedures, and are similar in some ways to BARS. They indicate a number of dimensions of performance with behavioural statements for each. Individuals are appraised as to the extent to which they display each of the characteristics. Figure 17.2 gives an example.

Table 17.1 An example of a behaviourally anchored rating scale: relations with clients

Behavioural example	Points of the rating scale
Often makes telephone calls on behalf of the client to find the correct office for him/her to go to even though this is not part of the job	A
Will often spend an hour with a client in order to get to the root of a very complex problem	B
Usually remains calm when dealing with an irate client	C
If the answer to the client's problem is not immediately to hand s/he often tells them s/he has not got the information	D
Sometimes ignores clients waiting at the reception desk for up to 10 minutes even when s/he is not busy with other work	E
Regularly keeps clients waiting for 10 minutes or more and responds to their questions with comments such as 'I can't be expected to know that' and 'You're not in the right place for that'	F

Meeting objectives

Another method of making appraisal more objective is to use the process to set job objectives over the coming year and, a year later, to measure the extent to which these objectives have been met. The extent to which the appraisee is

Leadership/staff supervision

1 Provides help, training and guidance so that employees can improve their performance

   Almost never   5   4   3   2   1   Almost always

2 Explains to staff exactly what is expected of them – staff know their job responsibilities

   Almost never   5   4   3   2   1   Almost always

3 Gets involved in subordinates' work only to check it

   Almost never   5   4   3   2   1   Almost always

4 Consults staff for their ideas on ways of making their jobs better

   Almost never   5   4   3   2   1   Almost always

5 Praises staff for things they do well

   Almost never   5   4   3   2   1   Almost always

6 Passes important information to subordinates

   Almost never   5   4   3   2   1   Almost always

The number of behavioural statements to be rated for any one dimension will be determined through the job analysis used to identify the key dimensions of performance and behavioural statements.

Figure 17.2 An example of a behavioural observation scale (Fletcher and Williams 1985, p. 45). Used with permission of Stanley Thornes Publishers

involved in setting these objectives varies considerably. If, as Stewart and Stewart (1977) suggest, these objectives are part of an organisational management by objectives scheme, then the individual may be given them, with limited negotiation available. Alternatively, if they are not part of a larger scheme there is a lot of scope for the individual to participate in the setting of such objectives. One of the biggest problems with appraisal on the basis of meeting objectives is that factors beyond the employee's control may make the objectives more difficult than anticipated, or even impossible. Another problem is that objectives will change over a period and so the original list is not so relevant a year later. Kane and Freeman (1986, p. 7) also highlight such difficulties as pressures to set 'easy' objectives, lack of comparability between the objectives of different individuals, unclear specification of measures and an emphasis on short-term, at the expense of long-term, accomplishments. They also discuss the 'fudge factor', where middle managers are pressured from the top to set challenging and stretching objectives for their people, and are pressured from below to set objectives that are not difficult to achieve. In order to please all, the middle manager fudges the issue rather than working it through. If suitable provision can be made for these contingencies and difficulties, appraisal by objectives can be effective and motivating.

Performance against job description

Some systems require the manager to appraise performance against each task specified in the job description or against each key accountability. The appraisal in this case may be in the form of narrative statements and/or a performance rating.

Performance against job competencies

When a competency profile has been identified for a particular job, it is then possible to use this in the appraisal of performance. Many appraisal systems combine competency assessment with assessment against objectives or job accountabilities.

Surveillance of actual performance

Performance appraisal need not only be centred on opinions and reactions reported back by an appraisal interview, as there are increasing opportunities for collecting primary data via various forms of electronic surveillance system. There are increasing examples of how activity rates of computer operators can be recorded and analysed, and how the calls made by telephone sales staff can be overheard and analysed. Sewell and Wilkinson (1992) describe a Japanese electronics plant where the final electronic test on a piece of equipment can indicate not only faults but the individual operator responsible for them. On another level some companies test the performance of their sales staff by sending in assessors acting in the role of customer (Newton and Findlay 1996).

Development of appraisal criteria

Stewart and Stewart (1977) suggest a variety of methods by which appraisal criteria can be identified. These include the use of the critical incident technique to identify particularly difficult problems at work, content analysis of working documents and performance questionnaires whereby managers and potential appraisers identify (anonymously) what characterises the most effective job holder and the least effective job holder (see Stewart and Stewart 1977, pp. 37–59). We previously made the point that one of the advantages of BARS was that appraisers are involved in formulating the way that appraisal scales are used. There are, similarly, advantages in involving appraisers in the identification of appraisal criteria, as well as the advantages from an information point of view. There can also be advantages in involving potential appraisees in criteria identification (Silverman and Wexley 1984).

The key question is whether the appraisal criteria are appropriate for the job in question – there are all too many examples of appraisal criteria being chosen and used based on flimsy evidence of appropriateness to the job. Appraising criteria that have little relevance to the job being done is clearly of no value whatsoever.

Effectiveness of appraisal systems

The effectiveness of appraisal systems hinges on the extent to which performance criteria are appropriate for the jobs for which they are used, and that the system itself is appropriate to the needs and culture of the organisation (see, for example, George 1986). Ownership of the system is also important – if it was designed and imposed by the Personnel Function there may be little ownership of the system by line managers. Similarly, if paperwork has to be returned to the Personnel Function the system may well be seen as a form-filling exercise for someone else's benefit and with no practical value to performance within the job. Fletcher (1993a) makes the interesting comment that all systems have a shelf-life – maybe changes are required to the system to renew interest and energy. In any case, as Fletcher also notes, organisations have changed so much, and continue to do so, that it is inevitable that the nature of the appraisal process will change too (see Fletcher 1993b). There is an increasing body of critical literature addressing the role and theory of appraisal. These debates centre on the underlying reasons for appraisal (see, for example, Townley 1989; and Barlow 1989) and the social construction of appraisal (see, for example, Grint 1993). This literature throws some light on the use and effectiveness of performance appraisal in organisations.

Performance management systems

Performance management systems are increasingly seen as the way to manage employee performance rather than relying on appraisal alone. Bevan and Thompson (1992), for example, found that 20 per cent of the organisations they surveyed had introduced a performance management system. Such systems offer the advantage of being tied closely into the objectives of the organisation, and therefore the resulting performance is more likely to meet organisational needs. The systems also represent a more holistic view of performance. Performance appraisal is almost always a key part of the system, but is integrated with ensuring that employee effort is directed towards organisational priorities, that appropriate training and development is carried out to enable employee effort to be successful, and that successful performance is rewarded and reinforced. Given that there is such an emphasis on a link into the organisation's objectives it is somewhat disappointing that Bevan and Thompson found no correlation between the existence of a performance management system and organisational performance in the private sector.

As with appraisal systems, some performance management systems will be development-driven and some will be reward-driven. A good example of a development-driven system, which does include an element of reward, is Sheard (1992) reporting on performance management at Zeneca Pharmaceuticals.

There are many different definitions of performance management and some have identified it as 'management by objectives' under another name. There are, however, some key differences here. Management by objectives was primarily an off-the-peg system which organisations bought in, and generally involved objectives being imposed on managers from above. Performance management tends to be tailor-made and produced in-house (that's why there are so many different versions), and there is an emphasis on mutual objective setting and on ongoing performance support and review.

Figure 17.3 shows a typical system, including both development and reward aspects, the main stages of which are:

1. A written and agreed job description, reviewed regularly. Objectives for the work-group which have been cascaded down from the organisation's strategic objectives. Bevan and Thompson found that performance management organisations were more likely to have an organisational mission statement and to communicate this to employees.

2. Individual objectives derived from the above, which are jointly devised by appraiser and appraisee. These objectives are results- rather than task-oriented, are tightly defined and include measures to be assessed. The objectives are designed to stretch the individual, and offer potential development as well as meeting business needs. Many organisations use the 'SMART' acronym for describing individual objectives or targets:

   specific
   measurable
   appropriate
   relevant
   timed

   This is clearly easier for some parts of the organisation than others. There is often a tendency for those in technical jobs, for example, computer

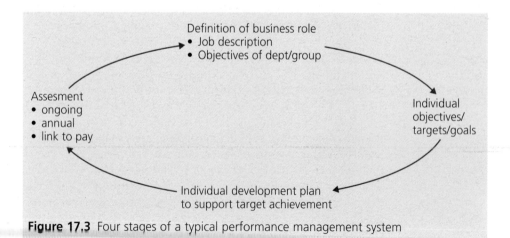

Figure 17.3 Four stages of a typical performance management system

systems development, to identify purely technical targets – reflecting heavy task emphasis – they see in their jobs. Moving staff to a different view of how their personal objectives contribute to team and organisational objectives is an important part of the performance management process. An objective for a team leader in systems development could be:

> To complete development interviews with all team members by end-July 1998.   (written March 1998)

Clearly, the timescale for each objective will need to reflect the content of the objective and not timescales set into the performance management system. As objectives are met, managers and their staff need to have a brief review meeting to look at progress in all objectives and decide what other objectives should be added. Five or six ongoing objectives are generally sufficient for one individual to work on at any time.

3. A development plan devised by manager and individual detailing development goals and activities designed to enable the individual to meet the objectives. The emphasis here is on managerial support and coaching, very much as described in the performance support phase of managing individual performance (see pages 317–18). Those organisations with a development-driven performance management system may well have development objectives alongside performance objectives to ensure that this part of the system is given proper attention.

4. Assessment of objectives. Ongoing formal reviews on a regular basis designed to motivate the appraisee and concentrate on developmental issues. Also, an annual assessment which affects pay received depending on performance in achievement of objectives. Most systems include this link with pay, but Fletcher and Williams (1992b) point to some difficulties experienced. Some organisations (both public and private) found that the merit element of pay was too small to motivate staff, and indeed was sometimes found to be insulting. Although performance management organisations were more likely to have merit or performance-related pay (Bevan and Thompson), some organisations have regretted its inclusion.

WINDOW ON PRACTICE

A large insurance company introduced a performance management system, but two years later the system had to be relaunched. The main problem was that the middle managers felt less than keen to agree objectives with their staff because their managers had not done so with them. They had received only very brief training in performance management, and although the system was designed to be reward-driven the organisation had experienced difficult times during the recession and there had been no additional money available to reward achievement of objectives.

Implementation of performance management

Performance management needs to be line-driven rather than personnel-driven (see, for example, Fletcher 1993b), and therefore mechanisms need to be found to make this happen. The incorporation of line managers alongside personnel managers in a working party to develop the system is clearly important. This not only ensures that the needs of the line are taken into account in the system design, but also demonstrates that the system is line-lead. Training in the introduction and use of the system is also ideally line-lead, and Fletcher and Williams (1992b) give us an excellent example of an organisation where line managers were trained as 'performance management coaches' who were involved in departmental training and support for the new system.

WINDOW ON PRACTICE

The scheme was introduced by training a series of nominated line manager coaches from each department. They had then to take the message back to their colleagues and train them, tailoring the material to their department (Personnel Training providing the back-up documentation). These were serving line managers who had to give up their time to do the job. Many of them were high-flyers, and they have been important opinion leaders and influencers – though they themselves had to be convinced first. Their bosses could refuse to nominate high quality staff for this role if they wished, but they would subsequently be answerable to the Chief Executive. This approach was taken because it fits with the philosophy of performance management (i.e. high line management participation), and because it was probably the only way to train all the departmental managers in the timescale envisaged) (Fletcher and Williams 1992b, p. 133).

Bevan and Thompson found incomplete take-up of performance management, with some aspects being adopted and not others. They noted that there was a general lack of integration of activities. This is rather unfortunate as one of the key advantages of Performance Management is the capacity for integration of activities concerned with the management of individual performance.

Summary propositions

17.1 Effective management of individual performance rests on managing the performance cycle – ongoing performance planning, support and review.

17.2 Appraisal is most often carried out by the immediate manager, but is enhanced by information from other parties.

17.3 There is a conflict in many appraisal systems in the role of the manager – as judge and as helper.

17.4 Performance management systems incorporate appraisal activity, but include other aspects such as a link to organisational objectives and a more holistic view of performance.

17.5 So far performance management has generally been adopted in a piecemeal way with a lack of integration between performance activities – there are, however, some good examples of carefully thought through and implemented systems.

References

Barlow, G. (1989) 'Deficiencies and the perpetuation of power: latent functions in management appraisal', *Journal of Management Studies*, Vol. 26, No. 5, pp. 499–518.

Bevan, S. and Thompson, M. (1992) 'An overview of policy and practice', in *Personnel Management in the UK: and anaylsis of the issues*, London: IPM.

Coates, G. (1994) 'Performance appraisal as icon: Oscar winning performance or dressing to impress?' *International Journal of Human Resource Management*, No. 1, February.

Cockburn, B. (1993) 'How I see the personnel function', *Personnel Management*, November.

Edwards, M. R. and Ewen, A. J. (1996) *360 Degree Feedback*, New York: Amacom, American Management Association.

Fisher, C. M. (1994) 'The differences between appraisal schemes: variation and acceptability – Part 1', *Personnel Review*, Vol. 23, No. 8, pp. 33–48.

Fletcher, C. (1993a) *Appraisal: Routes to improved performance*, London: IPM.

Fletcher, C. (1993b) 'Appraisal: an idea whose time has gone?', *Personnel Management*, September.

Fletcher, C. and Williams, R. (1985) *Performance Appraisal and Career Development*, London: Hutchinson.

Fletcher, C. and Williams, R. (1992a) 'The route to performance management', *Personnel Management*, October.

Fletcher, C. and Williams, R. (1992b) *Performance Management in the UK: Organisational experience*, London: IPM.

George, J. (1986) 'Appraisal in the public sector: dispensing with the big stick', *Personnel Management*, May.

Grint, K. (1993) 'What's wrong with performance appraisals? – a critique and a suggestion', *Human Resource Management Journal*, Vol. 3, No. 3, pp. 61–77.

Herriot, P. (1989) *Assessment and Selection in Organisations*, Chichester: John Wiley.

Jacob, R. and Flood, M. (1995) 'A bumper crop of insights', *People Management*, 9 February.

Kane, J. S. and Freeman, K. A. (1986) 'MBO and Performance Appraisal: a mixture that's not a solution, Part 1', *Personnel*, December, pp. 26, 28, 30–6.

Latham, G. P. and Wexley, K. N. (1981) *Increasing Productivity through Performance Appraisal*, Wokingham: Addison-Wesley.

Long, P. (1986) *Performance Appraisal Revisited*, London: IPM.

Maier, N. R. F. (1958) *The Appraisal Interview: Objectives, methods and skills*, New York: John Wiley.

Meyer, H. H. (1980) 'Self-appraisal of job performance', *Personnel Psychology*, Vol. 33, pp. 291–5.

Newton, T. and Findlay, P. (1996) 'Playing God? – the performance of appraisal', *Human Resource Management Journal*, Vol. 6, No. 3, pp. 42–58,

Randell, G., Packard, P. and Slater, I. (1984) *Staff Appraisal*, London: IPM.

Redman, T. and Mathews, B. P. (1995) 'Do Corporate Turkeys Vote for Christmas? – managers' attitudes towards upward appraisal', *Personnel Review*, Vol. 24, No. 7, pp. 13–23.

Redman, T. and Snape, E. (1992) 'Upward and onward: can staff appraise their managers?', *Personnel Review*, Vol. 21, pp. 32–46.

Sewell, G. and Wilkinson, B. (1992) 'Someone to watch over me: surveillance, discipline and the just-in-time process', *Sociology*, Vol. 26, pp. 271–89.

Sheard, A. (1992) 'Learning to improve performance', *Personnel Management*, September.

Silverman, S. B. and Wexley, K. N. (1984) 'Reaction of employees to performance appraisal interviews as a function of their participation in rating scale development', *Personnel Psychology*, Vol. 37.

Stewart, V. and Stewart, A. (1977) *Practical Performance Appraisal*, Aldershot: Gower.

Taylor, G. S., Lehman, C. M. and Forde, C. M. (1989) 'How employee self-appraisals can help', *Supervisory Management*, August, pp. 33–41.

Torrington, D. P. and Weightman, I. (1989) *The Appraisal Interview*, Manchester: UMIST.

Townley, B. (1989) 'Selection and appraisal: reconstituting social relations', in J. Storey (ed.), *New Perspectives on Human Resource Management*, London: Routledge.

Walker, J. W. (1992) *Human Resource Strategy*, Maidenhead: McGraw-Hill.

Ward, P. (1995) 'A 360 degree turn for the better', *People Management*, 9 February.

Williams, R. (1989) 'Alternative raters and methods', in P. Herriot, *Assessment and Selection in Organisations*, Chichester: John Wiley.

General discussion topics

1. In what ways is the concept of performance management different from the way in which management has been traditionally practised? What are the advantages and disadvantages for employees and employers?

2. 360 degree appraisal may have many advantages, but there is the argument that it can never really work because of the built-in biases, such as marking a boss well because you're due for a pay rise; marking yourself low then you can be happily surprised by others' evaluations; marking peers down to make oneself look better.

   Discuss as many built-in biases as you can think of, and think how they might be tackled and whether substantive improvements could be made.

CHAPTER 18

Team performance

The appointments pages of *Personnel Management* in 1994 were littered with advertisements looking for 'an effective team player' to 'join an established HR team', where one of the 'key organisational issues is team working' so that they can 'add value to the European HR team', 'enhance the skills of the management team', and 'facilitate effective team development'. In *People Management* in 1997 the trend continues, with, perhaps a little more focus, as organisations are seeking 'proactive', 'natural', 'enthusiastic', 'genuine' and 'effective' team players, who 'enjoy' or 'have a preference for' working in a team environment, and who are 'committed' to team working.

Few would argue that the 1990s is the age of the team and teamwork. Teamwork is used as a way of empowering employees and facilitating the development of their full potential in order to enhance organisational performance. A heavy emphasis on teamwork usually corresponds with flatter organisations which have diminished status differentials. Teamwork, of course, is not a new idea, and the autonomous working groups of the 1960s and 1970s are clear forerunners. The similarities are increasing responsibility, authority and a sense of achievement among group members. The protagonists of autonomous working groups were also intent on improving the quality of working life of employees by providing a wider range of tasks to work on (job enrichment) and a social environment in which to carry them out. The emphasis in the 1990s is quite different – performance is the unvarying aim. Higher performance is expected due to increased flexibility and communication within teams, increased ownership of the task and commitment to team goals. Some of the most famous autonomous working groups at Volvo in Sweden have now been disbanded because their production levels were too low compared with other forms of production. The teams of the 1990s are designed to outperform other production methods. They are also seen as critical in the development of a learning organisation (see, for example, Senge 1990).

So, what is a team? How does it differ from all the other groups in organisations? A team can be described as more than the sum of the individual members. In other words, a team demands collaborative, not competitive, effort, where each member takes responsibility for the performance of the team rather than just their own individual performance. The team comes first, the individual comes second, and everything the individual member does is geared to the fulfilment of the team's goals rather than their individual agenda. If you think of a football team, a surgical team or an orchestra, it is easier to see how each member is assigned a specific role depending on their skills and how individuals use their skills for the benefit of the team performance rather than selectively using them for personal achievement. In a football game, for example, a player making a run towards the goal would pass to another player in a better position to score rather than risking trying to score themselves for the sake of personal glory. We argue that such teamwork is critical to the success of delayered organisations, and we discuss this issue in Chapter 5, page 98, in the context of Drucker's (1988) metaphor of the symphony orchestra.

Moxon (1993) defines a team as having a common purpose; agreed norms and values which regulate behaviour; members with interdependent functions and a recognition of team identity. Katzenbach and Smith (1993) have also described the differences that they see between teams and work-groups, and identify teams as having shared leadership roles, mutual accountability and a specific team purpose, amongst other attributes. In organisations this dedication only happens when individuals are fully committed to the team's goals. This commitment derives from an involvement in defining how the goals will be met and having the power to make decisions within teams rather than being dependent on the agreement of external management. These are particularly characteristics of self-managing teams – perhaps the most topical of teams at present.

WINDOW ON PRACTICE

Mueller (1992) compares and contrasts German and Japanese approaches to flexible teamwork in the European automobile industry. The German approach, influenced by a long-term system of apprenticeships, relies on the heavy use of qualified and skilled production workers in their production teams. Mueller argues that the usefulness of skilled workers depends on the number of skilled tasks required to be done, and found that in the German situation a large number of skilled tasks were carried out including quality checks, machine supervision and checking, minor maintenance and machine adjustments. However they found substantial differences between the jobs of team members, depending on whether they were skilled or not. For unskilled employees jobs are limited and routine, compared with the job enrichment for skilled workers. Those unskilled with limited roles were often demotivated. The skilled workers were highly valued and some plants were considering reconstituting teams with 100 per cent of skilled workers. Mueller argues that there may be potential problems with the heavy use of skilled workers, as they may be top craftsmen but not necessarily good teamworkers. He also suggests that the current system might create

demarcations and distinctions within the production team which are alien to the new employee relations. Even for skilled workers he identifies demotivation as a problem when not enough is demanded of them, for example electricians.

Mueller compares this with the Japanese approach at Honda where qualifications are seen as less important and on-the-job learning is seen as vital. The emphasis here on attitude, teamworking and openness to change, which can be justified in relation to the accelerating pace of change and a need for a fast response to customers. There was a complete absence of job descriptions, and everyone in the team was paid the same rate. Although team leaders sometimes received a higher rate they also operated as team members as well as leaders. Everyone was considered to be skilled because on-the-job training is continuous (and in the hands of the line manager, not the training department).

The essential elements of good teamwork were seen to be single status, good communication, participation, togetherness, self-development, fairness, competitive working conditions and flexibility. Production teams were given much more autonomy.

Organisational teams differ, though, in terms of their temporary or permanent nature, the interchangeability of individual members and tasks and the breadth of tasks or functions held within the team:

Time span: Some teams are set up to solve a specific problem, and when this has been solved the team disbands. Other teams may be longer-term project-based, and may disband when the project is complete. Some teams will be relatively permanent fixtures, such as production teams, where the task is ongoing.

Interchangeability: Teams differ in the range of specific skills that are required and the expectation of all members learning all skills. In some production teams interchangeability of skills is key, and all members will have the potential and will be expected to learn all skills eventually. In other types of teams, for example, cross-functional teams (surgical teams, product development teams) each member is expected to bring their specialist skills to use for the benefit of the team, and they are not expected to be able to learn all the skills of each other member.

Task and functional range: Many production teams will often be designed to cover a whole task and within this there will be a wide range of activities. This clearly differs from the traditional line form of production where the tasks are broken down and segmented. Other teams will span a range of functions – for example, cross-functional teams involving, say, research, development, marketing and production staff.

Figure 18.1 shows how different types of teams can be represented on a framework representing interchangeability and task/functional spread.

In this chapter we shall look at the characteristics of four broad types of teams: production/service teams; cross-functional management teams; problem-solving

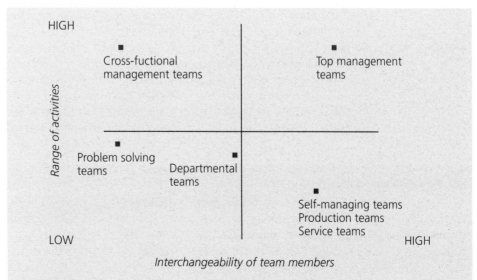

Figure 18.1 Different types of team. High range of activities indicates activities over a broad range of functions; low range of activities indicates activities within a function and within a single task

teams; and departmental teams. We then look at what factors affect teams' performance and what can be done to improve team effectiveness.

Broad team types

Production and service teams

It is these teams which are often referred to as **self-managing teams**, **self-managing work teams**, or **self-directed teams**. They are typically given the authority to submit a team budget, order resources as necessary within budget, organise training required, select new team members, plan production to meet predefined goals, schedule holidays and absence cover, and deploy staff within the team. There is a clear emphasis on taking on managerial tasks that would previously have been done by a member of the managerial hierarchy. These managerial tasks are delegated to the lowest possible organisational level in the belief that these tasks will be carried out in a responsible manner for the benefit of the team and the organisation. The payoff from this self-management has been shown in some research as 30 per cent increase in productivity (Hoerr 1989). These teams are growing in popularity in such areas as car production and the production of electrical and electronic equipment. Teams will be based around a complete task so that they perform a whole chunk of the production process and in this way have something clear to manage. For example, the team will normally include people with maintenance skills, specific technical skills and different types of assembly skills so that they are self-sufficient and not dependent on waiting for support from other parts of the organisation. The ultimate aim is usually for all members to have all the skills needed within the team. Self-managing teams may also be found in the service arena as well as the manufacturing one.

WINDOW ON PRACTICE

The British company Whitbread have established a small, up-market chain of restaurants called 'Thank God it's Friday', which is abbreviated to 'Friday's' or TGIF. The marketing is directed towards the relatively young and affluent and a part of this strategy has been to avoid the traditional hierarchy of the good-food restaurant – Maître d'Hôtel, Chef de Rang, Commis Waiter and so forth – by empowering the person with whom the customer deals directly: the Waiter. This person can take decisions on such things as complementary drinks without reference to anyone else. There is no manager, but each restaurant has a team leader known as The Coach.

In some teams a leader is appointed from the outset, but in others a leader is left to emerge. Whatever process is used, the leader is the same level of employee as other members and is as fully involved in the task of the team. They are therefore not part of the traditional managerial hierarchy, and yet they will need to take on managerial tasks such as planning, organising, supporting individuals, presenting information and representing the team to the rest of the organisation. The way that the leader carries out these activities and involves others in them will clearly have an impact on the effectiveness of the team. In some teams the leadership may vary according to the nature of task, resting with whoever has the most appropriate skills to offer.

The nature of self-management also has an impact on the role of managers outside the team. Traditionally these managers would carry out the tasks described above and would monitor and control the performance of the team. If these tasks are no longer appropriate, what is the role of the manager – is there a role at all? It will come as no surprise that the formation of self-managed teams is seen as a threat to some managers. However, Casey (1993) comments that 'self-managed teams do not deny the role of manager, they redefine it'. He also notes that the management of the team is a balance between responsibility within the team and management without, rather than an all-or-nothing situation. He suggests a move towards 90 per cent within the team in a self-management situation rather than nearer 30 per cent in a traditional management situation.

Where there are self-managed teams the role of the traditional manager outside the team changes to adviser and coach, as they have now delegated most of their responsibilities for directly managing the team. These managers become a resource to be called on when needed in order to enable the team to solve their own problems. Salem, Lazarus and Cullen (1992) comment that:

> The SMT approach requires a conscious effort on the part of the management to encourage and reinforce both the individual members and the team as a whole. Management's tools are stimulating questions designed to motivate the individual to examine himself or herself in relation to the attainment of the group's objectives.

Oliva (1992) draws a helpful framework for understanding the respective managerial roles of traditional managers and teams in a team environment, shown in Figure 18.2.

We referred to the High Performance Teams at Digital in Chapter 2 (Buchanan 1992) and you may wish to turn back to this example on page 41. Another example is Milliken, which won the Baldridge US National Quality Award in 1989. In this organisation employees are called 'associates' and the teams schedule their own work, create team objectives, enrol themselves for training and are empowered to stop production for quality or safety reasons.

The self-managing team concept has much to offer in terms of increasing employee ownership and control and thereby releasing their commitment, creativity and potential. There are, of course, potential problems with this approach too. Salem, Lazarus and Cullen (1992) identify the difficulty of returning to traditional systems once employees have experienced greater autonomy; resistance from other parts of the organisation; and peer pressure and its consequences. We would also add resistance from team members too. Let us look at some of these in more detail.

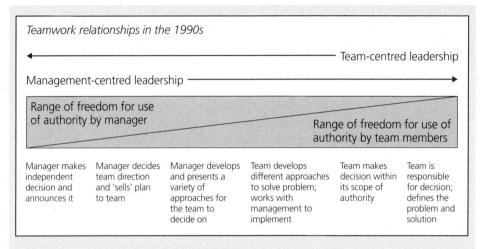

Figure 18.2 Teamwork relationships in the 1990s (Oliva 1992, p. 76). Reproduced with permission of Idea Group Publishing

Resistance from other parts of the organisation

As self-managing teams have clear knock-on effects for other parts of the organisation these other parts will react. If traditional managers do not give direction and control over to the team an immediate conflict is set up as to who makes the decisions around here; if they fail to support and coach, the team may feel abandoned and insecure. In general, the climate of the organisation needs to be supportive in terms of the value placed on individual autonomy and learning. There are situations also where the rhetoric of the organisation is about delegating responsibility to the team, but where management fail to give up ownership of the task (see the example adapted from Sewell and Wilkinson in Chapter 16, page 304).

Resistance within the team

Individuals who have spent many years being told what to do may need some time to take this responsibility for themselves. It is clear that operating self-managed teams will be easier on a greenfield site. However, for locations which want to make the transition, the importance of team selection of newcomers and of selecting skills relevant to a team environment as well as essential technical skills will be key. Salem, Lazarus and Cullen (1992) note that the most often cited individual characteristics for a team environment are 'interpersonal skills, self-motivation, ability to cope with peer pressure, level of technical/administrative experience, communication skills and the ability to cope with stress'. Other characteristics which have been noted elsewhere include the ability to deal with ambiguous situations and cope with conflict in a constructive way.

Peer pressure

The byproducts of peer pressure have been identified as lower absence levels, due to an awareness that colleagues have to cover for them; and a higher production rate so as not to let colleagues down. However, intense peer pressure can lead to stress and destroy many of the perceived benefits of team involvement from the employees' perspective. Some of the destructive aspects of peer pressure can also be seen in the Sewell and Wilkinson example in Chapter 16. Banner, Kulisch and Peery (1992) also note issues about the limits of peer involvement when they ask whether team members should exercise discipline over one another, and whether they should be responsible for the performance appraisal process.

Cross-functional management teams

Cross-functional management teams are very different from the teams described above, and members are more likely to retain other roles in the organisation. Typically they will see themselves as members of their function, whether it be marketing, research, sales, development and members of a specific project team as well. Very often the project team will surround the development of a particular product from creation to sales – for example, a new computer package, a drug, a piece of electrical equipment. Members may be allocated to the team by their home function for all or part of their time.

The thinking behind a cross-functional team is that each member brings with them the expertise in their own function and the dedication to the team task around a certain product or project. By bringing individuals together as a team the project gains through the commitment of team members to a task which they feel that they own. Bringing these individuals together enables the development of a common language and the overcoming of departmental boundaries. For a further discussion of the matrix form of organisation in which cross-functional teams are a key feature, see Chapter 5.

Meyer (1994) expresses the importance of measures of performance for cross-functional teams, and sees process measures as key rather than just measures of achievements. His argument is that process measures help the team to gauge their progress, and identify and rectify problems. It follows from this that the performance measures used need to be designed by the team and not imposed on them from senior management, as the team will know best what measures will help them to do their job. Inevitably these measures will need to be designed against a strategic context set by higher management. Meyer describes a good example of the problems that can result if managers try and control the performance measurement process rather than empowering team members.

WINDOW ON PRACTICE

At one Ford manufacturing plant multifunctional teams were used to improve product quality. Team members were trained to collect and analyse data so that they could solve their own quality problems.

Quality engineers had also been appointed in order to assist the teams. The Divisional management then asked the engineers for a Divisional Quality report, and in order to complete this the engineers asked the teams for the data that they had collected, and they summarised these.

As time went on the teams began to wait for the engineers to collect and analyse their raw data before they made any decisions regarding quality. They even began to wait for directions from the engineers before taking action. Problems that the teams had previously solved were now being solved with the help of the engineers, who began to ask for more engineers to support this process.

The intention had been to empower the teams, but the teams did not act as though they were empowered as management had still remained in control by asking for the quality reports from the engineers.

(Adapted from Meyer 1994.)

The process of agreeing their own performance measures will also enable the team to identify different assumptions and perceptions that each team member holds, and generate discussion on the exact goals of the team. All this is helpful in bringing the team together, generating a common language and ensuring that everyone is pulling in the same direction.

One special form of cross-functional management team is the top management team of the organisation – the Directors. Clearly, this team is different in that it is permanent and not project-based, but the need to work as a team rather than a collection of individuals is key. Katzenbach and Smith (1993) note that it is more difficult to get this group to work together as a team as they are more likely to be individualists. Directors often still see themselves as representatives of their function rather than members of a team, and thus will be more likely to defend their position and attempt to influence each other rather than pulling together. Garratt (1990) asks three key questions to top teams to assess whether they are truly direction-giving teams. He asks about regular processes, outside formal meetings, to discuss what's going on in the organisation and what possibilities exist; to what extent the team involve themselves in unstructured visioning before grappling with the nitty-gritty of plans and budgets; and to what extent they assess individual contributions and the skills and resources owned within the team. Garratt explains that he usually gets little evidence of any of these activities taking place.

Functional teams

Functional teams, as the name implies, are made up of individuals within a function. For example, the training section of the personnel department may well be referred to as the training team – different groups of nurses on a specific ward are sometimes divided into, say, the 'red' team and the 'blue' team. Sales staff for a particular product or region may refer to themselves as the 'games software sales team' or the 'north west sales team'. Some of the rationale behind this is to give the customer, internal or external, an identified set of individuals to liaise with. Given that these will be a smaller set than those in the whole department it will enable a much closer knowledge of the particular customer in question and a better understanding of customer needs. The extent to which these are really teams as opposed to groups of individuals will vary enormously.

ACTIVITY BOX 18.2

Think of some functional teams that you either belong to, have belonged to, or have had some contact with.

To what extent, and why, is each truly a team, or just a group of individuals with the title 'team'? Use the ideas and Figure 18.1 of this chapter to help you with this assessment.

Problem-solving teams

These teams may be within-function or cross-functional. Within-function teams may typically be in the form of quality circles where employees voluntarily come together to tackle production and quality issues affecting their work

Unfortunately, many of these teams have had little clout and recommended changes and improvements have not been possible to implement, owing to the retention of management control. Other within-function teams may consist of specially selected individuals who will be involved in the implementation of a major development within the function or department. For example, the implementation of performance management may be supported by specific coaches in each department who carry out related training, offer counselling and advice and who tailor organisation policy so that it meets department needs. These coaches may become the departmental performance management team.

Cross-functional teams may be brought together to solve an identified and specific organisational problem, and will remain together for a short period until that problem has been solved. They differ from cross-functional management teams as their role is not to manage anything, but rather to collect and analyse data and perspectives and develop an understanding of the nature of the problem. From this they will make recommendations on how to solve the problem which are then passed on to higher management. Usually their remit ends here, and there is little or no involvement in implementation. Team members will retain their normal work role at the same time as being a team member.

ACTIVITY BOX 18.3

If you have belonged to, or observed, a problem-solving team:

(a) What were the barriers to team formation?

(b) In what ways did team members support the team?

(c) In what ways did team members concentrate on themselves as individuals?

Team effectiveness

For a team to be effective they need a clear and agreed vision, objectives and set of rules by which they will work together. They will need to feel able to be open and honest with each other and be prepared to confront difficulties and differences. It is also important for members to be able to tolerate conflict and be able to use this in a collaborative way in the achievement of the team's objectives. Some researchers have commented upon the size of the team and suggest it should be small enough, say no more than 20, for communications to be feasible. Others have suggested that proximity is important in maintaining communications and team spirit. Next we explore the key issues of selection, training/development, assessment and reward in relation to team effectiveness.

Selecting team members

The effectiveness of any team depends to a large extent on the appropriateness of the team members. For self-managing teams there is a strong lobby for newcomers to be appointed by the team themselves, and indeed some would argue that unless this happens the team is not truly self-managing (see, for example, Banner *et al.* 1992). Other case studies suggest that team members, whether selected by the team or by others, are chosen very carefully in the likeness of the

team and with the 'right attitudes'. For all teamwork Katzenbach and Smith
(1993) identify three critical selection criteria: technical or functional expertise,
problem-solving and decision making skills and interpersonal skills.

Another approach to selection of team members is by understanding the team
roles that they are best able to play, so that the team is endowed with a full range
of the roles that it will need to be effective. Meredith Belbin (1993a), through
extensive research and the evolution of his original ideas, has identified nine
team roles which are important to a team and which individuals may have as
strengths or weaknesses. The absence of some or many of these roles can cause
problems in team effectiveness. Too many individuals playing the same type of
role can cause undue friction in the team and again damage effectiveness. The
key is achieving a balance. These team roles are as follows:

Co-ordinator: This person will have a clear view of the team objectives and
will be skilled at inviting the contribution of team members in achieving
these, rather than just pushing his or her own view. The co-ordinator (or
chairperson) is self-disciplined and applies this discipline to the team. They
are confident and mature, and will summarise the view of the group and
will be prepared to take a decision on the basis of this.

Shaper: The shaper is full of drive to make things happen and get things
going. In doing this they are quite happy to push their own views forward,
don't mind being challenged and are always ready to challenge others. The
shaper looks for the pattern in discussions and tries to pull things together
into something feasible which the team can then get to work on.

Plant: This member is the one who is most likely to come out with original
ideas and challenge the traditional way of thinking about things.
Sometimes they become so imaginative and creative that the team cannot
see the relevance of what they're saying, however without the plant to
scatter the seeds of new ideas the team will often find it difficult to make
any headway. The plant's strength is in major new insights and changes in
direction and not in contributing to the detail of what needs to be done.

Resource investigator: The resource investigator is the group member
with the strongest contacts and networks, and is excellent at bringing in
information and support from the outside. This member can be very
enthusiastic in pursuit of the team's goals, but cannot always sustain this
enthusiasm.

Implementer: The individual who is a company worker is well organised and
effective at turning big ideas into manageable tasks and plans that can be
achieved. They are both logical and disciplined in their approach. They are
hardworking and methodical but may have some difficulty in being flexible.

Team worker: The team worker is the one who is most aware of the others
in the team, their needs and their concerns. They are sensitive and
supportive of other people's efforts, and try to promote harmony and
reduce conflict. Team workers are particularly important when the team
is experiencing a stressful or difficult period.

Completer: As the title suggests, the completer is the one who drives the
deadlines and makes sure they are achieved. The completer usually
communicates a sense of urgency which galvanises other team members
into action. They are conscientious and effective at checking the details,
which is a vital contribution, but sometimes get 'bogged down' in them.

Monitor evaluator: The monitor evaluator is good at seeing all the options. They have a strategic perspective and can judge situations accurately. The monitor evaluator can be overcritical and not usually good at inspiring and encouraging others.

Specialist: This person provides specialist skills and knowledge and has a dedicated and single-minded approach. They can adopt a very narrow perspective and sometimes fail to see the whole picture.

ACTIVITY BOX 18.4

Think of a team situation in which you have been involved, either in a work or social/family setting:

(a) Which roles were present and which were absent?

(b) What was the effect of this balance?

An individual's potential team roles can be interpreted from some of the psychometric tests used in the normal selection procedure (for example, Cattell's 16PF). They can also be assessed in a different way. Belbin designed a specific questionnaire to identify the individual's perceived current team role strengths (that is, the roles they have developed and are actually playing). This is particularly helpful for development within the current team, but may be less useful for selection purposes. Although helpful, current team role strengths may not be automatically transferred into another team situation.

The psychometric properties of the Belbin Team Roles Self-perception Inventory (BTRSPI) have been assessed by Furnham *et al.* (1993) whose work has cast doubt on the ability of the BTRSPI to be a reliable measure of team role preference. Further research by Fisher *et al.* (1996) confirms these doubts and also questions the extent to which team role preferences identified by the BTRSPI correlate with those identified by the 16PF. Fisher notes that although they found both tests to be imperfect, the evidence available supports the 16PF rather than the BTRSPI. Belbin (1993b) maintains that the BRTSPI was never intended to be a formal psychometric test, and Fisher *et al.* conclude that, despite questions over its reliability, and since the Belbin *model* itself has intuitive appeal and some empirical support, it would be a pity to disregard it. They recommend further research.

Team leader and manager training

Both team leaders and senior managers begin to play new roles in team situations. Team leaders suddenly find themselves with a host of new responsibilities for the support of team members and the planning and organising of team activities – responsibilities for which they have little experience and often no training. Similarly managers will need some training support in moving from a directive, controlling role to a coaching and counselling role. Training needs to encompass not only new skills but an opportunity to discuss the changing philosophy of the organisation and encourage attitude change.

Team member training

Whether or not the team has an appointed leader all team members will need some training support in working in a different environment with different rules about what they should be doing and shouldn't be doing. Being more involved and taking on more responsibility, and sometimes leading activities will require some initial training support. Further training in new technical skills can often be handled within the team once at least one member has the knowledge required and has gained some training skills themselves.

Team development

Teams can be developed in many different ways, and perhaps one of the most critical early on is development through the task itself. For example, teams can develop by jointly describing the core purpose of the team, visualising the future position that they are aiming to achieve, developing the rules and procedures they will use, performance measures, and so on. If the team are given some support to do this, perhaps a facilitator from the personnel function or externally, they can not only develop vital guidelines but also understand a way of working things out together, a process, which they can use by themselves in the future.

Teams can also develop by looking at the way they have been working together since they came together. One way of doing this is by completing a team roles questionnaire to identify the strengths and weaknesses of each member. This will help to promote a better understanding of why things happen as they do, and also pave the way for some changes. On this basis some individuals can develop their potential in team roles which they are not presently using, but for which they have some preference, and in this way a better balance may be struck making the team more effective. Another process is to review what the team are good at and bad at, what different individuals can do to enable others to carry out their tasks more effectively, and what improvements can be made in the way that the team organises itself. Simple suggestions can be surprisingly effective such as 'It would really help me if you gave me a list of telephone numbers where I can leave a message for you when I need to get hold of you urgently' (cross-functional team) and 'I don't understand why we need to lay the figures out in this way and it really gets my back up – will someone take some time out to explain it to me?' Irwin, Plovnick and Fry (1974) identified four major problem areas in relation to group effectiveness – goals, roles, processes and relationships – and these four can be used to provide a framework for team development activities.

Other less direct methods of development involve working through simulated exercises as a team – for example, building a tower out of pieces of paper – and learning from this how the team operate and what they could do to operate better. Outdoor training is also used to good effect in team situations, where the team tackle new, and perhaps dangerous, activities in the outdoors. Typically, some activities involve learning to trust and to depend on each other in a real and risky situation, and the learning from this and the trust developed, can then be transferred back into the work situation.

The approach taken to team building needs to be appropriate to the stage of development of the team. Tuckman (1965) identified four stages of team development – forming, storming, norming and performing. Forming centres on team members working out what they are supposed to be doing, and trying to feel part of it. At this stage they are quite likely to be wary of each other and hide their feelings. Storming is the stage where members are prepared to express strongly held views, where there is conflict and competition, and where some push for power while others withdraw. The norming stage is characterised by a desire to begin to organise themselves. Members actually begin to listen to each other, become more open and see problems as belonging to the whole group. Performing is where a sense of group loyalty has developed and where all contribute in an atmosphere of openness and trust.

Two very useful and practical texts for managers and facilitators on team building are Woodcock (1979) and Moxon (1993).

Recognition and reward

Like individuals, teams need some form of recognition and reward for their efforts. Recognition may be in the form of articles in company newsletters or local papers about team successes, inscribing the team name on the product, or monetary rewards. A sense of team identity is often encouraged by the use of team T-shirts, coffee mugs and other usable items. It is most important that other reward systems in the organisation, say based on individual contribution, do not cut across the reinforcement for team performance. In addition for those teams where the longer-term objective is for all members to acquire the whole range of skills than a payment system, which pays for skills gained rather than job done, will be important.

Are teams always the right answer?

Team-based work seems set to increase on the premise that it will improve organisational commitment and performance. The three gritty issues which will need to be tackled are that not all employees will feel comfortable or perform their best in a team-based situation; that teamwork is not always the best approach; and that not all teams are effective teams. Critics of a team environment suggest that it can have a downward levelling effect, that it stunts creativity and is generally limiting (Stott and Walker 1995). The difficulty of generating the essential openness, trust and commitment is also a potential difficulty. Whatever the advantages of participation and consensus, it has been shown that this approach, in Japan, for example, makes decision-making a long drawn out process.

Implications for the personnel function

Team-based working gives rise to a number of implications for the personnel function:

- There will need to be increasing emphasis on training the trainers so that teams can do as much of their own training as possible.
- Training in selection techniques will need to be made available if teams are to select members without ongoing assistance from the personnel function.
- The personnel function will probably find it useful to produce guidance manuals for teams which give a framework for those personnel activities which will be carried out within the team, and which back up any training given.
- There will an increased demand, especially early on, for facilitation skills – a member of the personnel function will need to work with teams in reviewing their effectiveness and working out ways to improve.

❱ There will also probably be an increased demand for personnel consultancy skills and on-line advice.

❱ Members of the personnel function may well find they spend more time coaching senior managers in changing their role from directing to coaching.

❱ The personnel function may well become involved in efforts to change the culture of the organisation so that it is supportive of teamwork. The personnel function may be involved in supporting the changes in senior managers' roles and in helping them view problems as learning opportunities.

Summary propositions

18.1 Team-based working has been increasing due to a belief that this empowers employees, encourages them to use their full potential and results in better performance.

18.2 Three key variables in different types of teams are timespan of the team, interchangeability of team members and range of activities and functions involved.

18.3 There are four broad team types – production/service teams; cross-functional management teams; departmental teams and problem-solving teams.

18.4 Team effectiveness is dependent on the team having agreed goals and methods of working, and a climate where team members can be open and honest and use conflict in a constructive way.

18.5 Selection of team members is key and it is important to have a well-balanced team in terms of the team roles described by Belbin.

18.6 Increasing team-based work has an impact on the personnel role – including increased consultancy and facilitation, coaching of managers, training team trainers and producing team guides.

References

Banner, D. K., Kulisch, W. A. and Peery, N. S. (1992) 'Self-managing work teams (SMWT) and the human resource function', *Management Decision*, Vol. 30, No. 3, pp. 40–5.

Belbin, M. (1993a) *Team Roles at Work*, London: Butterworth Heinemann.

Belbin, R. M. (1993b) 'A reply to the Belbin team role self-report inventory by Furnham, Steele and Pendleton', *Journal of Occupational and Organisational Psychology*, Vol. 66, pp. 259–60.

Buchanan, D. (1992) 'High performance: new boundaries of acceptability in worker control', in G. Salaman *et al.* (eds.), *Human Resources Strategies*, London: Sage.

Casey, D. (1993) *Managing Learning in Organisations*, Milton Keynes: Open University Press, p. 60.

Drucker, P. F. (1988) 'The coming of the new organization', *Harvard Business Review*, Vol. 66, No. 1, January–February.

Fisher, S. G., Marcrosson, W. D. K. and Sharp, G. (1996) 'Further evidence concerning the Belbin Team role self-perception inventory', *Personnel Review*, Vol. 25, No. 2, pp. 61–7.

Furnham, A., Steele, H. and Pendleton, D. (1993) 'A psychometric assessment of the Belbin team role self-perception Inventory', *Journal of Occupational and Organisational Psychology*, pp. 245–57.

Garratt, B. (1990) *Creating a Learning Organisation*, Hemel Hempstead: Director Books.

Hoerr, J. (1989) 'The pay-off from teamwork', *Business Week*, July, pp. 56–62.

Katzenbach, J. R. and Smith, D. K. (1993) 'The discipline of teams', *Harvard Business Review*, March/April.

Meyer, C. (1994) 'How the right measures help teams excel', *Harvard Business Review*, May/June, pp. 95–103.

Moxon, P. (1993) *Building a Better Team*, Aldershot: Gower in association with ITD.

Mueller, F. (1992) 'Designing flexible teamwork: comparing German and Japanese approaches', *Employee Relations*, Vol. 14, No. 1, pp. 5–16.

Oliva, L. M. (1992) *Partners not Competitors*, London: Idea Group Publishing.

Salem, M., Lazarus, H. and Cullen, J., (1992) 'Developing self-managing teams: structure and performance', *Journal of Management Development*, Vol. 11, No. 3, pp. 24–32.

Senge, P. (1990) *The Fifth Discipline: The art and practice of the learning organisation*, London: Century Business, Random House.

Stott, K. and Walker, A. (1995) *Teams, Teamwork and Teambuilding*, Hemel Hempstead: Prentice Hall.

Tuckman, B. W. (1965) 'Development Sequences in Small Groups', *Psychological Bulletin*, Vol. 63, pp. 384–99.

Woodcock, M. (1979) *Team Development Manual*, Aldershot: Gower.

General discussion topics

1. In an organisation which is moving into teamwork the supervisor's role will change from direct supervision to team facilitation and development. What problems are these supervisors likely to experience in their change of role, and what forms of training and development would help them?
2. The need to work as a team depends on the kinds of work that are carried out. Discuss.

CHAPTER 19

Managing diversity

We discriminate between people in many aspects of our life and work. The selection process in particular directly discriminates between people in order to offer the reward of a job to one but not the others. Certain forms of discrimination are acceptable but others are not, and have been made unlawful. Facts rather than prejudice, and relevant facts rather than irrelevant facts, are important criteria in determining what type of discrimination is acceptable. Legislation, voluntary codes of practice and equality initiatives have resulted in some progress towards equality of treatment for minority groups, but there remains inescapable evidence of continuing discrimination. More recent approaches of the business case for equal opportunities, the economics of equal opportunities, the valuing and managing of diversity in organisations, and the mainstreaming of equal opportunities are a response to the insufficient progress made so far. These offer some useful perspectives and practices, although the underlying concepts also raise some issues and concerns.

We begin this chapter with a discussion of the differences between the more traditional approach to equal opportunities and the management of diversity approach, and then recap the relevant legislation and codes of practice in relation to gender, race, disability and age. Following this we consider the current position for each of these groups before moving on to considering the management of diversity in more depth.

Equal opportunities and managing diversity

There are always certain groups in any society that are discriminated against unfavourably due to the prejudices and preconceptions of the people with whom they have to deal. These preconceptions are sometimes verbalised, but often not, and the people holding these preconceptions may well be unaware of the way that they see and judge things and people.

However, verbalised or not, these preconceived ideas influence the actions of the people who hold them, and the way they deal with others. The effects of this can be seen in the employment arena, as this is inextricably linked with discrimination in the rest of society. Disadvantaged groups, who have already been identified, are women, people from other racial backgrounds, disabled people and older people, and in the UK there is legislation protecting the employment rights of the first three of these four groups.

There has been a continuing debate concerning the action that should be taken to alleviate the disadvantages that these groups suffer. One school supports legislative action, while the other argues that this will not be effective and that the only way to change fundamentally is to alter the attitudes and preconceptions that are held about these groups. The initial emphasis on legislative action was adopted in the hope that this would eventually affect attitudes. However, there have been some efforts to change attitudes directly in addition to this, for example the International Year for the Disabled in 1981 and Opportunity 2000 which has encouraged employers to commit themselves publicly to the goals of increasing the quantity and quality of women's participation in the workforce, and set relevant organisational goals together with an improvement programme (see, for example, EOR, No. 41 1992). A third, more extreme, and often less supported approach comes from those who advocate legislation to promote positive or reverse discrimination in order to compensate for a history of discrimination against specified groups and as a way of redressing the balance more immediately. The arguments for and against such an approach are fully discussed by Singer (1993). In the UK legislation provides for positive action for disadvantaged groups (that is, special support and encouragement), but not positive discrimination (that is, discriminating in their favour, sometimes called reverse discrimination).

Although the labels 'equal opportunities' and 'management of diversity' are used inconsistently, and to complicate this there are different perspectives on the meaning of managing diversity, we shall draw out the key differences which typify each of these approaches. Equal opportunities approaches have sought to influence behaviour through legislation so that discrimination is prevented. It has been characterised by a moral and ethical stance promoting the rights of *all* members of society. Management of diversity approaches, on the other hand, stress the economic and the business case for equal treatment, offering benefits and advantages for the employer if they invest in ensuring that everyone in the organisation is valued and given the opportunity to develop their potential and make a maximum contribution. The practical arguments supporting the equalisation of employment opportunity are highlighted. A company that discriminates directly or indirectly against older or disabled people, women or ethnic minorities will be curtailing the potential of available talent, and employers are not well known for their complaints about the surplus of talent. The financial benefits of retaining staff who might otherwise leave due to lack of career development or due to the desire to combine a career with family are stressed, as is the image of the organisation as a 'good' employer and hence its attractiveness to all members of society as its customers. In addition, the value of different employee perspectives and different types of contribution is seen as providing added value to the organisation. Mahon (1989) demonstrates how an equal opportunities policy at Wellcome has shifted from good employment practice to sound business sense, and from personnel policies to business issues. In line with the difference between the moral argument and the business argument defined above, Equal Opportunities is often characterised as a responsibility of the Personnel Department, whereas the management of diversity is seen as a responsibility of all managers.

Equal opportunities approaches stress disadvantaged groups, and the need, for example, to set targets for those groups to ensure their representation in the workplace reflects their representation in wider society – in occupations where groups are underrepresented, such as the small numbers of ethnic minorities who are employed as firefighters and police officers, or the small numbers of women in senior management roles. These targets were not enforced by legislation, as in the United States, but organisations have been encouraged to commit themselves voluntarily to improvement goals, and to support this by putting in place measures to support disadvantaged groups such as special training courses and flexible employment policies. Recent research suggests that this approach alienated large sections of the workforce (those not identified as disadvantaged groups) who felt that there was no benefit for themselves, and indeed that their opportunities were damaged. Others felt that equal opportunities initiatives had resulted in the lowering of entry standards, as in the London Fire and Civil Defence Authority (EOR, 1996). In contrast, the management of diversity concentrates on individuals rather than groups, and includes the improvement of opportunities for *all* individuals and not just those in minority groups. Hence managing diversity involves everyone and benefits everyone, which is an attractive message to employers and employees alike. The focus becomes changing the culture so that all are valued for their diversity and different contributions, and the approach is more integrated as special and separate groups are not singled out (as, for example, in the legislation). Kandola and Fullerton express it this way:

> Managing diversity is about the realisation of the potential of all employees . . . certain group based equal opportunities policies need to be seriously questioned, in particular positive action and targets. (1994, p. 47)

Although managing diversity offers an integrated approach which can help organisations locate equality issues in their mainstream activities, concerns centre on how the attractive idea of business advantage and benefits for all may divert attention from disadvantaged groups and result in no change to the status quo (see, for example, Ouseley 1996). Table 19.1 summarises the key differences between equal opportunities and managing diversity, and in Table 19.2 Ford (1996) contrasts the approaches in the United Kingdom with those in the United States.

Table 19.1 Major differences between 'equal opportunities' approaches and 'management of diversity' approaches

Aspect	Equal opportunities	Managing diversity
Purpose	Reduce discrimination	Utilise employee potential to maximum advantage
Case argued	Moral and ethical	Business case – improve profitability
Whose responsibility	Personnel department	All managers
Focuses on	Groups	Individuals
Perspective	Dealing with different needs of different groups	Integrated
Benefits for employees	Opportunities improved for disadvantaged groups, primarily through setting targets	Opportunities improved for all employees
Focus on management activity	Recruitment	Managing
Remedies	Changing systems and practices	Changing the culture

Table 19.2 A comparison of UK and US approaches to equality

UK	US
Legislation founded upon equal treatment, initially for race and sex (1974)	Legislation founded upon civil rights, initially for racial equality (1960s)
Codes of practice issued in 1984, promoting good employment practice	Federal contract compliance – statistical returns and targets for workforce profiles
Focus on fairness and equity at the point of selection	Focus on parity in representation of women and minority groups in recruitment
Positive action through training and advertising to offer a more diverse pool of talent from which to select. Selection decisions based on sex or race made illegal	Positive selection of women and people from minority groups when candidates of equal calibre, if targets not fulfilled, when race or sex could be taken into account
Focus on the individual in the legislation	Legislation allows group actions
Equality of treatment	Equality of outcomes

Source: Ford (1996). Reproduced with permission of the author.

A review of the legislation

This section includes legislation, voluntary codes of practice and national initiatives.

Women

The chief legislation relating to the equality of women in employment are:

- The Equal Pay Act 1970.
- The Sex Discrimination Act 1975.
- The Employment Protection (Consolidation) Act 1978.
- The Social Security Act 1989.
- The Trade Union and Employment Rights Act 1993.

The Equal Pay Act 1970

This was the first of the legislation promoting equality at work between men and women. The Act was passed in 1970, came into full force on 29 December 1975, and was amended by the 1983 Equal Pay (Amendment) Regulations Statutory Instrument 1983, No. 1794 and the 1983 Industrial Tribunals (Rules and Procedures) (Equal Value Amendment) Regulations, which came into effect from January 1984. A very good guide, particularly to the amendments, is Gill and Ungerson (1984).

The Act specifies circumstances where a woman's pay should be equal to that of a man. These are:

1. Where the woman can show that she is doing like work to a man – for example, a woman assembly worker sitting next to a male assembly worker, assembling similar items would clearly be entitled to equal pay.

2. Where a woman can show that she is carrying out work rated as equivalent to that of a man, for example, under a job evaluation scheme. In this case the woman may be in a clerical post, but if the organisation has an overall job evaluation scheme and her job is given the same points as a different job done by a man, then she can claim pay equal to the man.
3. Since 1984, where a woman can show that her work is of equal value to that of a man's. Equal value is defined in terms of the demands made by the job, and includes skill, effort and decision-making. To claim under this rule there need be no job evaluation scheme as demonstrated in the case when a cook at Camel Laird claimed that her work was of equal value to painters and joiners (see Wainwright 1985). The cook was awarded equal pay.

Selection of a comparator

There is a number of limitations on the job holder which the woman may select as a comparator. The comparator needs to be of a different sex, but employed by the same employer and at an establishment covered by the same terms and conditions.

Enforcement of the Act

A woman may claim on an individual basis to a tribunal. Appeal is possible to an Employment Appeal Tribunal, then the Court of Appeal, and finally the House of Lords. Should the job be declared equal the individual applicant may then receive equal pay, which can be backdated to a maximum of two years before the date at which she applied to the tribunal.

Genuine material factors

An employer, however, may admit that a woman's job is equal to a man's in one of the three ways defined above, but that the pay is different and should remain different 'genuinely due to a material factor which is not the difference of sex' ((S1 (3) Amended) Equal Pay Act). A genuinely material factor (GMF) applies in a slightly different way to like work and work rated as equivalent under a job evaluation scheme, from work of equal value cases. In the first the employer may cite a difference of personal factors such as length of service, superior skill or qualifications, higher productivity or red circling. In relation to equal value cases skill shortages and market forces would come into play.

The Sex Discrimination Act 1975

This Act came into force at the same time as the Equal Pay Act: December 1975. The Sex Discrimination Act promotes the equal treatment of women and men in employment and other areas. Equal treatment in employment centres on such activities as selection, the availability of opportunities for training and progression, the provision of benefits and facilities, and dismissal. The Equal Opportunities Commission was established by the Sex Discrimination Act, and its duties are primarily to:

1. eliminate discrimination on the grounds of sex or married status;
2. generally promote equal opportunities between men and women;
3. monitor the implementation of the Sex Discrimination Act and the Equal Pay Act.

The Sex Discrimination Act makes discrimination against women or men, or discrimination on the grounds of marital status, unlawful in the employment sphere. The meaning of both direct and indirect discrimination is clarified in the Act.

Ways of discriminating

1. Direct sex discrimination occurs when a person is treated less favourably due to their sex than a person of the opposite sex would be in similar circumstances. For example, advertising for a man to do a job which could equally well be done by a woman.
2. Direct marriage discrimination occurs when a married person is treated less favourably, due to their married status, than a single person of the same sex would be treated in similar circumstances. This would apply if a married woman was denied promotion because she was married, and it was considered she might leave to follow her husband's job or start a family. The Act makes no mention of discrimination against employees on the basis of their unmarried status, and this is not unlawful.
3. Indirect sex discrimination occurs when a requirement or condition is applied equally to men and women. However, the condition has the effect that in practice it disadvantages a significantly larger proportion of one sex than the other, because they find it harder to fulfil, and it cannot be justified on any grounds other than sex. Indirect sex discrimination has been demonstrated by the age limit of twenty-eight years maximum, for entry into the executive officer grade of the civil service. In the case of *Price* v. *The Civil Service Commission* it was successfully argued that this was considerably disadvantageous to women as they were often raising a family at this time, and that therefore the age limit constituted indirect discrimination (IPM 1978; EOC Sex Discrimination Decisions no. 9).
4. Indirect marriage discrimination occurs when an employer places a requirement or condition on both married and unmarried people, but the practical effect of this is that a significantly smaller proportion of married people can comply compared with single people of the same sex, and there is no other justification for the condition than their marital status. An employer who offered promotion on the basis that the employee was prepared to be away from home for considerable spells of time, when in reality this was never or rarely required, would be indirectly discriminating on the grounds of married status. If the spells away from home were needed in practice then the employer would not be acting unlawfully.
5. Victimisation occurs when an employer treats an employee of either sex less favourably than other employees would be treated on the grounds that they have been involved in, or intend to be involved in (or is suspected of either of these), proceedings against the employer under the Sex Discrimination Act or the Equal Pay Act.

Unlawful discrimination

In the employment sphere it is unlawful to discriminate on the basis of sex or married status in relation to potential and present employees:

1. **Potential employees**: It is unlawful to discriminate in recruitment arrangements, for example, in advertising and interviewing; and in the terms and conditions of a job offer, for example, in whether a permanent or temporary position is offered. It is also unlawful to discriminate in the

adoption of selection criteria, in selection methods and in other selection matters, for example in refusing or deliberately omitting to offer employment because of a person's sex.

2. **Present employees**: It is unlawful to discriminate in the provision of opportunities for promotion, transfer or training; in the provision of facilities or services such as study leave or company cars; and in unfavourable treatment, like dismissal.

Exceptions to the Sex Discrimination Act
There are some exemptions from the Act: for example, employers are allowed to discriminate due to a genuine occupational qualification (GOQ) for the job – for example, in modelling, acting or jobs such as toilet attendant.

The Act does not allow positive discrimination, but does allow positive action. For example, if a job has been done solely or mainly by members of one sex over the past year, then employers can provide special training purely for members of the other sex. They are also allowed to specifically encourage applications from this group, but not to favour them in any way in the selection procedure.

Enforcement of the Sex Discrimination Act
There are two aspects to enforcement:

1. The EOC is the only body that can take action about instructions or pressure to discriminate, about discriminatory practices or advertisements, or persistent discrimination.
2. In all other cases any individuals who feel they have suffered as a result of discrimination may make a claim to a Tribunal as described under the Equal Pay Act.

Further details about enforcement may be found in Guidelines for Equal Opportunities Employers (EOC 1986).

Practical implications of the Sex Discrimination and Equal Pay Acts.
The legislation has several implications for personnel management:

Advertisements, notes and circulars: Advertisements must not discriminate on the basis of sex or marital status. This means that job titles should either be sexless, as in 'cashier', 'machinist' or 'salesperson', or indicate an acceptability of either sex, as in 'waiter/waitress' or 'manager/manageress'. If a job title is used indicating one sex, such as 'chairman', this must be accompanied by a statement that both men and women are invited to apply. To save any misunderstandings, it may be wise to use this statement in all advertisements. Illustrations used in advertisements and in recruitment literature should depict both men and women.

Other recruitment procedures: Personnel managers also need to consider the implications of other recruitment procedures. For example, in admitting school-children into the organisation for a careers visit, care should be taken that the boys are not shown only round the parts of the factory where the traditional male jobs are to be found, while the girls are only shown around the canteen and the offices. Similarly, if local schools are visited, then both boys' and girls' schools should be included.

Selection procedures: Equal opportunities legislation reinforces the need for job analysis and the production of job descriptions and person specifications. In particular, the person specification should be carefully considered to ensure that the person requirements are not unnecessarily restrictive and indirectly discriminate between men and women, making it easier for one group to comply. Care should also be taken that any selection tests have been well validated in that they have been demonstrated to predict performance in the job, and that they have been developed using data from both sexes.

The interview: Although interviewers may not be able to banish their prejudices and stereotypes, an awareness of these may at least allow some compensation. Other methods, such as interviewing in a structured and consistent way, can also be used to help limit the effects of preconceptions. Care should also be taken to avoid questions that may indicate an intention to discriminate, even where discrimination is not intended, for example, questioning a woman about her husband and domestic arrangements (although these questions would not in themselves constitute discrimination if the equivalent questions were also put to male interviewees and the information collected used in exactly the same way). Similarly, questions about dependants are fair if asked of both sexes. In fact, discriminating against someone on the grounds of their dependants is not unfair **so long as men and women are treated equally in this respect**. It would, however, be reasonable to assume that an individual applying for a job will have made or will make suitable arrangements for the care of dependants. We recommend that questions about domestic situations and responsibilities should not be asked. Finally, it is always wise to keep notes of an interview and the reason for rejection in the event of a claim for unfair discrimination.

Review of pay strategy, systems and wage rates: In order to ensure equal pay according to the legislation, pay strategy, systems and wage rates need to be regularly reviewed and monitored to ensure that they do not discriminate against women. This includes periodic reviews of the job evaluation system if one is used.

The Employment Protection (Consolidation) Act 1978

The 1980 Employment Act provided the right to paid time off during working hours for ante-natal care. In effect this was done by adding a new section to the Employment Protection (Consolidation) Act 1978. Other rights in addition to those gained under the Employment Protection Act 1975 include the right not to be unfairly dismissed due to pregnancy or a reason connected with pregnancy; the right to six weeks' maternity pay; and the right to return to work after the birth of a child. These rights have since been extended.

The Social Security Act 1989

From 1 January 1993 it was unlawful for occupational benefit schemes (including health insurance and pensions) to discriminate directly or indirectly on grounds of sex. Areas such as survivors' benefits, optional pensions and pensionable age are, however, not covered by the Act. Other provisions related to pregnancy and maternity. In-depth explanations of the provisions may be found in Industrial Relations Review and Report (1989, no. 384).

Trade Union and Employment Rights Act 1993

This Act makes further improvements to women's employment rights, especially in relation to maternity. The main provisions which affect equal opportunities are to:

- ◗ make dismissal for any reason connected with pregnancy unlawful;
- ◗ remove the service qualification for bringing an unfair dismissal claim on the grounds of pregnancy;
- ◗ allows new provision for suspension from work on pregnancy grounds due to health and safety reasons;
- ◗ regardless of service provides for a minimum of 14 weeks' maternity leave, and specifies that during this period all other terms and conditions except for actual remuneration must be maintained.

In addition, the Act allows measures restricting the publicity of sexual harassment cases, new rules for settling sex and race discrimination cases out of court and new rights to challenge collected agreements on the grounds that they are discriminatory. The pregnancy and maternity sections of the Act substitute new sections for many provisions in the Employment Protection (Consolidation) Act.

Equal opportunity policies

Equal opportunities policies are not required by law but are recommended, and the Equal Opportunities Commission produces a model policy for those employers who wish to adapt this for use in their own organisation. A summary of the EOC's model policy is found in Table 19.3, and the IPD strongly recommend the use of such policies.

Table 19.3 Summary of EOC's model 'Equal Opportunity Policy'. Summarised from EOC (1985) *A Model Equal Opportunity Policy*

1. **Introduction**: Desirability of the policy and that it is required to be strictly adhered to.

2. **Definitions**: Direct and indirect discrimination defined.

3. **General statement of policy**: A commitment to equal treatment and the belief that this is also in the interests of the organisation. Staff in the organisation should be made aware of the policy and key personnel trained in the policy.

4. **Possible preconceptions:** Examples of preconceptions that may be erroneously held about individuals due to their sex or marital status.

5. **Recruitment and promotion**: Care to be taken that recruitment information has an equal chance of reaching both sexes and does not indicate a preference for one group of applicants. Care that job requirements are justifiable and that interviews conducted on an objective basis. An intention not to discriminate in promotion.

6. **Training**: An intention not to discriminate with some further details.

7. **Terms and conditions of service and facilities**: An intention not to discriminate.

8. **Monitoring**: Nomination of a person responsible for monitoring the effectiveness of the policy and with overall responsibility for implementation. An intention to review the policy and procedures. Intention to rectify any areas where employees/applicants are found not to be receiving equal treatment.

9. **Grievances and victimisation**: An intention to deal effectively with grievances and a note of the victimisation clauses in the Act.

Racial and ethnic origin

There has been legislation since 1968 making it unlawful for employers to discriminate directly on the grounds of race, colour, nationality or ethnic origin. The Race Relations Act 1976 replaces the 1968 Act, and extends it by, for example, making indirect discrimination illegal, using a similar approach to the Sex Discrimination Act. The 1976 Act also set up the Commission for Racial Equality with similar powers to the Equal Opportunities Commission.

The Race Relations Act 1976

The Act identifies ways in which racial minority groups may be discriminated against, and makes these illegal:

1. Direct discrimination occurs if an employer treats an employee, or prospective employee, less favourably than they treat, or would treat other employees, on the grounds of his race. Racial grounds have been defined as colour, race or nationality or ethnic or national origin. Less favourable treatment may occur, for example, in selection for recruitment, promotion, shiftwork, overtime, and so on. Discrimination may also occur in the work environment, for example, in the use of separate canteens.
2. Indirect discrimination is defined in the same way as for the Sex Discrimination Act. An example here would be requiring a good standard of written English for a manual labourer's job, but to insist that workers on a building site should wear steel helmets would not be discriminatory against Sikhs – the condition is capable of being justified irrespective of the race of the person concerned (see *Singh* v. *Lyons Maid*) (Selwyn 1978, p. 87).
3. Victimisation provisions give individuals the right of complaint to an industrial tribunal, as with the Sex Discrimination Act, if they feel they have been victimised in their employment because they have been connected with bringing proceedings under the Act.

   Some exceptions to the Race Relations Act are specified, and in these areas discrimination in recruitment, training, promotion or transfers on the grounds of 'genuine occupational qualification' is acceptable. These are:

1. **Entertainment:** If it is necessary to have a person of a particular racial group to achieve an authentic presentation.
2. **Artistic or photographic modelling**: If it is necessary to use a person from a particular racial group to provide authenticity for a work of art, visual image or sequence.
3. **Specialised restaurants**: If it is necessary to have a person from a particular racial group to sustain the special setting of an establishment where food or drink is served to the public, like a Chinese restaurant.
4. **Community social workers**: If a person provides personal services to members of a particular racial group and the services can best be provided by someone of the same racial group.

However, these do not permit discriminatory treatment in the terms and conditions of employment.

Enforcement of the Race Relations Act

The pattern of enforcement is similar to that for the Sex Discrimination Act. Individuals who feel they have been discriminated against can complain to a tribunal, and the Commission for Racial Equality can also bring complaints to a tribunal where there may be direct discriminatory practices, but no particular casualty, or in cases of discriminatory advertisements.

Practical implications of legislation promoting racial equality

The implications for the personnel manager run along the same lines as for the Sex Discrimination Act, in particular:

Advertisements
Advertisements should be carefully worded so that there is no indication that people of some racial backgrounds are preferred to others. A statement to this effect, as with the Sex Discrimination Act, may well be the best policy. Illustrations should show a mix of different races. Personnel managers also need to be careful where they place advertisements. An internally placed advertisement in an organisation employing only white people may constitute indirect discrimination against those racial groups who will have less chance to hear about the job from their friends.

Selection procedures
The use of a job description and specification are again very helpful here, and care should be taken not to draw up a specification that is unjustifiably demanding. When considering individuals from different racial groups against this specification it is important to distinguish between attainment and potential. People from disadvantaged groups often have a poor record of attainment by employers' standards, but their potential to do the job may at the same time be very good. Also, as a general rule, application forms require a level of English in excess of job requirements and so selection on that basis may constitute unfair discrimination against those whose mother tongue is not English and yet who may be suitable employees (Runnymede Trust and BPS 1980).

Selection tests
The use of selection tests should be carefully monitored. Many tests discriminate against people from minority backgrounds due to assumptions made when the tests were designed and due to the fact they may have been standardised on, for example, all-white groups of individuals. Also, people from different racial backgrounds may be at a disadvantage because the ethos of testing is more alien to their culture (IPM 1978).

Personnel managers will overcome these difficulties if they scrutinise very carefully, for example, a test that rejects 70 per cent of black applicants but only 30 per cent of white applicants. They must be able to show that this cut-off point is justifiable and that the test is valid in terms of job performance. It is also worthwhile considering whether there are equally valid selection criteria that can be used which have a less adverse impact on disadvantaged groups. If tests are used, personnel managers should try to ensure that these are 'culture-fair' (although it has been argued that this is impossible (Runnymede Trust and BPS 1980, p. 23)); that adequate pre-test orientation is given, for example, about the purpose of testing; that pre-test practice is given; and perhaps produce a self-help pamphlet.

Interviewing

One of the common problems with interviewing is the tendency of interviewers to select in their own image (Runnymede Trust and BPS 1980). This work against minority groups and also reinforces the current structure of the workforce. Interviewers need to be aware of this problem as well as the others mentioned under the Sex Discrimination Act. Interviewers also need consciously to remember that the way individuals present themselves is partly dependent on their culture and background. Things that are acceptable, or even expected, in one culture may not be acceptable in another.

Disabled people

Disabled Persons (Employment) Act 1944 and 1958

These Acts, together with some additional regulations that came into force in 1980, have been the main legislative provisions until recently. They provided for:

1. assessment of disabled people;
2. rehabilitation of disabled people;
3. retraining of disabled people;
4. a register of people with disabilities;
5. a quota scheme in respect of registered disabled people where employers of over twenty staff were required to employ sufficient disabled people to comprise at least 3 per cent;
6. reserved employment for disabled people – the jobs of car park attendant and lift attendant were reserved for disabled people only;
7. sheltered employment, for example, Remploy.

This legislation has for some time been considered as inadequate protection for disabled people. Walker comments: 'These reforms are no substitute for the establishment of clear rights to employment protection along the lines of other European countries such as West Germany' (Walker 1986, p. 45). Government statistics for 1993 (EOR, 1994 No. 56) show that only 18.9 per cent of employers fulfilled their quota obligations. There has been much discussion over the future of the quota scheme, and the Equal Opportunities Review (1994, No. 56) reports that since the scheme began, only ten firms have been prosecuted, with employers being persuaded to act responsibly rather than invoking the law.

The Disability Discrimination Act 1995

This Act came into force on 2 December 1996, at which time the requirements of the quota scheme ended, and provides greater protection for disabled people than any of the previous legislation. In terms of employment rights there are two major provisions of the Act – first, that it becomes unlawful to discriminate against current or prospective employees with a disability, because of their disability; and second, that employers must make reasonable changes to the workplace and to the employment arrangements so that a disabled person is not substantially disadvantaged. Reasonable changes include amongst other things, changes to premises and/or equipment, additional training, changes to working hours and changes to the nature of supervision.

For the purposes of the Act disability is defined as:

> A physical or mental impairment which has a substantial and long term
> effect on a person's ability to carry out normal day to day activities. People
> who have a disability and people who have had a disability, but no longer
> have one are covered by the act.   (HMSO Leaflet DL70, 1996, p. 3)

Further clarification of the definition of disability is found in HMSO Leaflet DL60
(1996).

In terms of employment less favourable treatment is unlawful in areas such as
recruitment, selection, retention, promotion, transfers, training and development, and the dismissal process. The Act covers employees, whether temporary
or permanent, and potential employees, although some jobs are excluded which
are the members of the armed forces, police officers, direct firefighters in the fire
brigade, MOD firefighters, and prison officers and prison custody officers.
Responsibility for compliance with the Act rests not only with the direct
employer. Thus an employer who offers work to contract staff through an agency
(the direct employer) is still liable for the treatment of those staff and is required
to take reasonable steps to prevent unlawful discrimination.

Less favourable treatment is allowed if this is for a substantial and relevant
reason related to the circumstances of the individual case. An example of this
might be a typist who is required to type at a certain speed due to valid job
demands. If a person with arthritis in their hands, who could only type at a much
lower speed, applied for this job, they could lawfully be rejected on the grounds
of their disability as long as the potential employer had explored whether any
adjustment in the working conditions/equipment could be made to overcome the
mismatch. It would not be lawful, however, to refuse promotion to a disabled
person on the grounds that wheelchair access was not currently possible to the
new workstation, if a straightforward rearrangement of the furniture would facilitate access. Similarly, a disabled employee with higher level of absence could not
lawfully be dismissed on these grounds if this level was only slightly higher than
that accepted from other employees. Further information on unlawful and lawful discrimination can be found in the HMSO Leaflet DL70 (1996) and in the IDS
Employment Law Supplement No. 78 (1996).

The Act gives guidance when reasonable changes by the employer are necessary and identifies the factors which influence these changes. The changes apply
to physical features such as access to the premises, fixtures, fittings, furniture,
equipment and materials. Examples of such changes include widening doorways
to facilitate wheelchair access, changing taps to make them easier to turn, altering
lighting for people with restricted vision, and allocating specific parking places.
Changes also apply to arrangements which cover how and where recruitment is
carried out, working terms and conditions, and how contractual agreement,
transfers, training and other benefits are provided. For example, employers might
need to allow absences in working hours for rehabilitation, assessment or treatment, allocate duties to another employee, provide additional training, alter
instructions in reference manuals, modify procedures for testing or assessment or
provide a reader or interpreter. However, employers do not have to make changes
if the disabled person experiences only a minor disadvantage; if they do not know
that the person has a disability (and it is reasonable that they do not know); and
if the change required to overcome the disadvantage is not reasonable. A number of factors will be taken into consideration in determining whether changes
are reasonable. These are: to what extent an alteration will improve the situation
for the disabled employee or applicant; how easy it is to make the changes; the

cost of the changes in terms of money and disruption; the employer's resources, and financial or other help that may be available.

The Act sets up two new independent statutory bodies, the National Disability Council (for England, Wales and Scotland) and the Northern Ireland Disability Council, to advise the government about disability issues and the implementation of the Act. These bodies draft the Code of Practice relevant to disabled people.

ACTIVITY BOX 19.1

Consider your own organisation, or one with which you are familiar:

(a) What changes need to be made in order to comply with the Disability Discrimination Act?

(b) What changes have been made?

(c) What changes are still outstanding?

(d) What is the impact of the changes so far?

Local placement, assessment and counselling teams and the major organisations development unit

The Manpower Services Commission Employment Division (1984) produced a Code of Good Practice on the Employment of Disabled People (1984), which was updated in 1993 by Employment Services. At Job Centres there are specialist Disablement Employment Advisers who specifically assist disabled people in their search for employment and training. They also liaise with employers regarding the employment of disabled people. These employment advisers are now part of the local Placement, Assessment and Counselling Teams (PACTs) which replace the old Disablement Resettlement Officers, the Employment Rehabilitation Service and the Disablement Advisory Service. The are seventy PACTs throughout the country. In 1987 the Major Organisations Development Unit (MODU) was set up as part of the disablement branch of Employment Services. Members of MODU provide a consultancy service to large national companies to help them recruit, develop and retain disabled employees.

Policy on the employment of disabled people

All employers with 250 or more staff, on average, are obliged to include, in the Directors' Report, a statement of their policy on the employment of disabled people. The Code of Good Practice recommends that this policy should include items about: communication and consultation in the drawing up of the policy; objectives of the policy; the role of managers, employees and their representatives; the advice and help that are planned to be used; good practices and the areas where these are particularly important; and how it is planned to monitor and assess the policy.

The disability symbol

This was introduced in 1990 and relaunched in June 1993. The scheme permits an employer to use the disability tick symbol in advertisements if they demonstrate their pursuit of five minimum commitments to disabled people. These commitments are:

- guaranteed job interviews for all disabled applicants who meet the minimum criteria for the job;
- consultation with current disabled employees;
- retention of disabled workers;
- efforts to raise disability awareness;
- production of an annual review of the commitments and the achievements that have been made.

Examples of employers who have achieved this standard are found in The Equal Opportunities Review No. 43 (1992) and No. 56 (1994).

Access to work scheme

This scheme provides help, which may be worth thousands of pounds, to provide essential equipment and facilities to enable a disabled worker to be appointed to a job.

Older workers

Older workers are the least protected of all the groups we have looked at in this chapter, and in this country there is no specific legislation relating to them. The main protection for the older employee is against redundancy, for which they will be financially compensated, but there is no protection for them in seeking fresh employment, training or promotion. The problems of unemployment in the 1980s and 1990s have tended to militate against the employment prospects of those who are older, because the working population appears to be too large for our total employment requirements. People have been put under pressure to retire early in many circumstances and find it very difficult to continue working after normal retirement age.

In the United States and New Zealand legislation has been introduced to prevent discrimination in employment on the grounds of age. There are only weak signs of this spreading to the United Kingdom, but we need to consider not only whether citizens' rights are being impaired because of the lack of such legislation, but also – as with other types of anti-discrimination legislation – whether the effectiveness of organisations is being impaired by people suggesting to older employees that they are becoming less effective and that they may be standing in the way of the legitimate career aspirations of others.

Warr reports that 86 per cent of personnel managers responding to his survey were keen to see legislation or at least a voluntary code developed by the Government to protect older workers from discrimination. There have been a number of failed attempts via Private Member's Bills to institute legislation, for example David Winnick's Bill to make age limits in advertising illegal fell at its first reading in February 1996. However the Labour Government have pledged to act in terms of legislation.

Progress on equality to date

Women

If **participation** in the labour force is an indication of decreasing discrimination then recent figures are encouraging. From 1971 to 1991 the number of women has increased by 34 per cent to 12.2 million, compared with a decrease in male participation of 0.5 per cent to 15.6 million over the same period (Skills and Enterprise Network 1996). Although much of this increase has been due to the replacement of full-time jobs with part-time jobs. Indeed Hakim (1993) puts forward the strong argument, based on an alternative analysis of the census and employment data, that the increasing participation of women in employment between the 1950s and the late 1980s is a myth, although a real increase does appear to have taken place since the late 1980s. Her analysis shows that: 'the much trumpeted rise in women's employment in Britain consisted entirely of the substitution of part-time for full-time jobs from 1951 to the late 1980's' (p. 102). Hakim concludes from the research that only an increase in full-time employment is likely to have a wider impact on women's opportunities at work and elsewhere.

Some of the more obvious signs of discrimination, such as in recruitment advertising, may have disappeared, and there is some evidence to suggest that women are beginning to enter some previously male-dominated occupations, for example, women have now been ordained as priests in the Church of England but not without deep and continuing debate. Similarly men are beginning to enter some previously female-only occupations, such as midwifery. However, there remains a high degree of subtle (for example, access to training and support for development and promotion) and not so subtle discrimination (for example continued **gender segregation** in terms of both type and level of work undertaken (EOC 1994)). There are still few women in higher levels of management and not many male secretaries. An NEDCO report states that only 4 per cent of senior and middle management, 1–2 per cent of senior executives, 1.8 per cent of executive directors and 5.1 per cent of non-executive directors are women (EOR 1993, No 47). Most women remain in clerical, catering, caring, cleaning and selling occupations, often characterised by part-time work, and in a mainly narrow range of industrial sectors. Dickens and Colling (1990) explain how continued job segregation in respect of both role and hours/arrangements is one of the influencing factors which results in discriminatory agreements between employers and unions. The majority of women still work part-time (often from choice), and part-time workers are often described as part of the secondary labour market with pay, conditions and employment rights being vastly inferior to full-time permanent workers. These differences are very gradually being equalised; for example, although women have equal access to pensions schemes under the Sex Discrimination Act, and many other inequalities in schemes are now illegal under the Social Security Act 1989, McGoldrick's (1984) comments are still appropriate. She notes that pensions schemes still work to women's disadvantage as they are normally organised and administered on the basis of traditional male employment patterns – such as rewarding long, continuous service and based on full-time rather than part-time employment. Currently precedents set in the European Parliament are the major influence on improving the status of part-time workers.

In addition, women need different forms of organisational support particularly in terms of flexibility, to enable them successfully to combine a career with parenthood. Such forms of support include career-breaks, flexible working hours, annual hours, job sharing and part-time work, childcare facilities and support. Liff (1989) also suggests that non-linear career paths are important and the restructuring of jobs. Progress in these areas is patchy. Field and Paddison (1989) comment that women in the United Kingdom spend less time out of paid employment than women in any other EU country, and that 90 per cent of women are returning to work after having children. However, there is less nursery provision for the under-fives in the United Kingdom than the rest of Europe (Anon. 1988). Anecdotal evidence suggests that childcare provision is a difficult need to meet as needs vary so considerably, that it is almost impossible for the employer to win. Some companies have surveyed present and/or potential women employees to help identify some of their support needs, as did Mothercare (Arkin 1990).

Pay differentials between men and women have changed very little except for a hike of women's pay upwards when the 1970 law came into force. Women's pay as a percentage of men's pay was 77 per cent in 1990, increased from 63 per cent prior to the Equal Pay Act. However, if overtime earnings are taken into account, the percentage reduces to 68 per cent (Gregory 1992). The gender gap in pay is the greatest in the European Union (European Commission 1994). Dickens and Colling also highlight the problem of job evaluation schemes which perpetuate old values and hence discourage rather than encourage equality of pay, and they are also subject to managerial manipulation (McColgon 1994). In addition, the TUC (1995) amongst others, report that part-timers (mostly women) shoulder the burden of low pay.

While some progress has been made towards equal pay, these factors still remain as barriers to be overcome. The abolition of the Wages Councils has not helped in this respect, but it is predicted that the minimum wage to be introduced by the Labour Government will benefit in particular women and ethhic minorities (EOR 1997).

Ten years on from the amendment regulations to the Equal Pay Act there is widespread concern about their ineffectiveness due to complexity of both the substantive and procedural law (Gregory 1992). The Equal Opportunities Review (No. 52 1993) notes that there are fourteen stages to the equal value procedure and that it has been widely criticised by the judiciary for its complexity and obscurity, with severe delays and average claims taking over two and a half years. Jarman (1994) identifies four current proposals which would improve the chances of equal value claims being made and achieved:

1. Collective remedies rather than solely individual remedies could be applied – at present equal value cases which are successful do not trigger adjustments for other women who are in the same position.
2. The provision of legal aid for equal value cases. The EOC claim that the cost of pursuing an equal value case is approximately £6,500 and in cases where there is an appeal, costs frequently exceed £50,000 (EOR, No. 52, 1993). Clearly most individuals will have difficulty in funding a claim, and cannot proceed unless their case is financed by the EOC.
3. Independent experts involved in these cases should be full time, be recruited in a different manner and given adequate training. This redresses the concern that evaluation procedures are less than scientific and many systems have a built in gender bias.
4. Eliminating the material factors clause (with some exceptions) as this clause provides entry for the 'market forces' rationale.

The use of equal opportunities policies has grown only slowly, in spite of the EOC's model Equal Opportunity Policy and the IPM's support for such policies. Our research in 1984 indicated that such policies are only produced by 60 per cent of organisations, and that on the whole they are not seen as very useful. Indeed, a large number of organisations saw their policy as irrelevant. However in 1994, using a similar sample, we found that 89 per cent of organisations had equal opportunities policies with gender being covered in 96 per cent of these.

Liff and Cameron (1997) argue that, so far, conventional equality measures have made a limited impact on women's position in the workforce.

Racial and ethnic groups

In spite of the legislation evidence of discrimination continues to exist. The Equal Opportunities Review in 1994 reports that:

> unemployment rates for ethnic minority groups were about double those of the white population, even when age, sex and level of qualification were taken into account.   (p. 25)

In 1996 this **comparative level of unemployment** has barely changed (HMSO 1996), although there are differences between the different ethnic groups. Over the ten years since 1985 the relationship between ethnic minority and white rates of unemployment has changed. The gap between whites and Indians has closed from 7 to 4 percentage points, but for black, Pakistani and Bangladeshi groups it has widened, even when taking age and qualifications into account (HMSO 1996). This is in spite of the fact that many ethnic groups achieve better qualifications at school than their white peers (OFSTED 1996; *Independent* 1996). In addition, there is continued **segregation in the labour market**, with about 29 per cent of ethnic minority male employees being employed in the hotel, catering and repairs and distribution sectors, compared with 17 per cent for men who are white. Similar percentages were found for manufacturing industry, but for construction the reverse is true, with 11 per cent of white men, but only 4 per cent of racial minorities being employed here. In terms of **pay**, non-white workers are also comparatively disadvantaged, for example, on the basis on the Autumn 1994 Labour Force Survey, the Department for Education and Employment (1995) report that black workers are paid, on average, almost 10 per cent less than white workers.

Evidence of discrimination in the recruitment process is also well documented. Noon's (1993) research involved sending speculative letters to 100 employers randomly selected from the top 1,000 employers. Two letters, identical in their request for information on the company's graduate training scheme and the qualifications of the sender, were sent to each company. The only difference was the name – John Evans and Sanjay Patel, identifying them as belonging to different ethnic groups. Although there was no statistical difference in reply rate to each individual, there was a statistical difference in the quality of reply as measures by the helpfulness in terms of information and encouragement given. Evans received the more helpful replies. Those organisations with an equal opportunities policy were less likely to discriminate in the types of reply sent to each person, but where different treatment was given this was always in favour of Evans. Brown and Gay (1986), using actors in their research in Manchester, London and Birmingham, found discrimination against ethnic minority candidates took place in one third of organisations that had advertised vacancies in the press.

In 1984 a code of practice was issued by the Commission for Racial Equality. However research in 1991 (CRE 1992) showed an almost 'universal disregard' for the code in the hotel sector, a sector of heavy employment for minority racial groups.

The number of successful cases brought before tribunals each year is insignificant compared with the scale of racial discrimination in the workplace, which research studies have revealed (Runnymede Trust 1979). There were only forty-seven successful racial discrimination cases at industrial tribunals in 1990–91 (CRE 1992). Jenkins (1986) notes some severe problems with the way that indirect discrimination is framed in the law – that it was ambiguous and placed a burden of proof to show that the discrimination was not justifiable. It is still possible to use selection criteria which demand specific individual job experiences, and also to select on the basis of 'who will fit in' due to business necessity. There are many others concerns about the current UK legislation and the authors of *Measure for Measure* note:

> The majority [of employers] make no specific efforts that advance equal opportunities practice. A significant minority have issued an equal opportunities policy statement, and pro-active organisations have developed codes of practice, monitoring and positive action programmes. All these practical means of combating racial discrimination in the workplace are optional rather than required.
>
> (DoE 1992)

In addition, there is little help from Europe. Contrary to the position of employment concerning fair treatment for women, the UK generally has better legal protection for racial minority groups, and the EU has been remarkably reticent about agreeing and issuing directives to improve this position. Harmonisation in this case would mean a drop in minimum protection rather than an improvement!

In response to the current position, the CRE have made some far-reaching recommendations in their second review (1991, reported in 1992) of the Race Relations Act. These recommendations include:

▶ A new definition of indirect discrimination.
▶ Ethnic monitoring should be legally binding as in the Fair Employment Act 1989, which requires religious monitoring in Northern Ireland.
▶ Employers should have a legal requirement to identify equality targets (not quotas).
▶ The Act should apply in more areas of employment than it presently does.
▶ The CRE should be enabled to take on an inspectoral role, to make spot-checks on employers' practices, rather than just an investigatory role to research a problem area already identified.
▶ Legal aid for all racial discrimination cases.
▶ A special tribunal division should be set up to deal with discrimination cases in order to build up expertise.
▶ Tribunal remedies, for example compensation, can apply to more than the individual bringing the case if appropriate others register their involvement.
▶ Tribunals should be able to impose non-discrimination notices, where appropriate, to apply to a situation from which an individual has successfully proved discrimination.
▶ The Tribunal should have power to impose special training on an organisation where discrimination has been proved, and/or to impose actions to encourage specific racial groups (these are permitted, but voluntary, at present).

Disabled people

Fourteen per cent of the general population have a disability (Employer's Forum on Disability 1995). Walker (1986) notes that disabled people have always experienced higher levels of unemployment than the workforce as a whole, and once unemployed have greater difficulty in returning to work and therefore often remain unemployed for longer periods. The Labour Force Survey in 1992 found that 25 per cent of registered disabled men and 18 per cent of registered disabled women were unemployed compared with 12 per cent and 8 per cent respectively of their able-bodied counterparts. Their choice of job is often restricted, and where they do find work it is likely to be in low-paid, less attractive jobs. The HMSO (1989) reported that disabled employees earned, on average, 20 per cent less than non-disabled employees. Prescott-Clarke (1990) notes that disabled people are under-represented in professional and managerial jobs. Periods of high general unemployment exacerbate these problems.

Employers traditionally have had a wide range of concerns regarding the employment of disabled people, including worries about general standards of attendance and health, safety at work, eligibility for pension schemes and possible requirements for alterations to premises and equipment. Legislation prior to the Disability Discrimination Act 1995 did nothing to address these issues and the quota scheme and protected employment scheme were renowned for their ineffectiveness. Research over the next few years will indicate the effects of recent legislation.

Older people

In a survey of 4,000 job advertisements by the Equal Opportunities Review (1994), around one-third specified age qualifications, which is slightly more than their survey four years previously. There is some evidence that the private and public sectors act differently in this respect. For example Itzin and Phillipson (1993), in their qualitative and quantitative study of local authorities, note some improvements in terms of fewer upper age limits being applied, and Worsley (1996) reporting on research by the Carnegie Third Age Programme found that the voluntary and public sector organisations they studied did not specify age limits. However Itzin and Phillipson did find that the wording of some advertisements deters older workers from applying. Words like 'innovative', 'dynamic' and 'forward-thinking' suggest a younger applicant. They also identified discrimination at both the shortlisting and interview stage, with line managers having negative perceptions of older workers – seeing them as less able to cope with change, training or technology and less interested in their careers.

From January 1996 onwards *People Management* refused to accept job advertisements which specified numerical age limits, and MacLachlan, Grant and Smith declared that they were:

> unwilling to play any part in prolonging misguided attitudes and patterns of behaviour among a minority of employers and agencies based on faulty assumptions and outdated recruitment practice.
>
> (MacLachlan *et al.* 1996, p. 22)

In December 1996 MacLachlan *et al.* reported that this policy caused no damage to advertising revenue and from January 1997 they extended the ban to include the use of the words 'young' and 'old'.

Table 19.4 The frequency and coverage of equal opportunities policies in our research sample from 1994

	Percentage answering 'yes'
Do you have an equal opportunities policy?	89
Which groups does this policy cover?	Percentage of those answering 'yes' above
Age	64
Disability	90
Gender	96
Race/ethnic origin	99
Religion	85
Sexual orientation	71

Itzin and Phillipson (1993) also found that although three-quarters of the 221 employers which responded to their questionnaire had an equal opportunities policy, only one-third of the 221 included age in this. In our research in 1994/95 we found that 64 per cent of employers who had an equal opportunities policy covered age within this. This was lower than for all other equal opportunities criteria which we asked about, as shown in Table 19.4.

Respondents to a survey of IPM members (Warr) did identify some ways in which younger employees were preferred, but also a number of ways in which older workers were preferred. Workers over 40 were seen to be more loyal and conscientious, to have better interpersonal skills and to be more efficient in the job. The Equal Opportunities Review (1992), when reviewing the research about older workers, concluded that experience in the job counteracts any age-related factors lowering productivity; that older workers are generally more satisfied with their jobs and have fewer accidents and a better absence record; and that in any case there is considerable variation within individuals.

Managing and valuing diversity

The emphasis so far in this chapter has been on separate groups who are discriminated against in employment, and we have concentrated on the meeting of legal obligations. This is an important starting point, but obviously a limited perspective, and a conceptual model of the relationship between quality of opportunity and managing and valuing diversity has been developed by LaFasto (1993), shown in Figure 19.1.

The words managing diversity have been used to represent an integrated and more fundamental perspective. Ellis and Sonnenfield describe managing diversity as:

the challenge of meeting the needs of a culturally diverse workforce and of sensitising workers and managers to differences associated with gender, race, age and nationality in an attempt to maximise the potential productivity of all employees (Ellis and Sonnenfield 1994, p. 82)

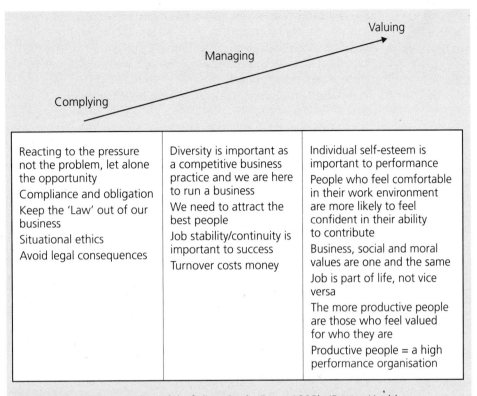

Figure 19.1 Conceptual model of diversity (LaFasto 1992). 'Baxter Healthcare Corporation', in B. W. Jackson, F. LaFasto, H. G. Schultz and D. Kelly, 'Diversity', in *Human Resource Management* 31 (1 and 2) p. 28. Reprinted with permission of John Wiley and Sons, Inc. Copyright © 1992 John Wiley and Sons, Inc.

This raises three issues: (1) the exclusion of disabled people from the definition – which sheds light on the US perspective; (2) the emphasis on awareness of differences associated with different groups – a theme which is interpreted differently in some approaches to managing diversity; and (3) the concept of culture as being at the root of managing diversity.

Groups or individuals?

Miller (1996) highlights two different approaches to the management of diversity. The first is where individual differences are identified and celebrated, and where prejudices are exposed and challenged via training. The second, more orthodox approach is where the organisation seeks to develop the capacity of all. This debate between group and individual identity is a fundamental issue as Liff explains:

> Can people's achievements be explained by their individual talents or are they better explained as an outcome of their gender, ethnicity, class and age? Can anything meaningful be said about the collective experience of all women or are any generalisations undermined by other cross-cutting ideas.
>
> (Liff 1997, p. 11)

The most common approach to the management of diversity is based on individual contribution, rather than group identity, although Liff (1997) identifies different approaches with different emphases. The **individualism** approach is based on dissolving differences. In other words, differences are not seen as being distributed systematically according to membership of a social group, but rather as random differences. Groups are not highlighted, but all should be treated fairly and encouraged to develop their potential. The advantage of this approach is that it is inclusive and involves all members of the organisation. An alternative emphasis in the management of diversity is that of **valuing differences** based on the membership of different social groups. Following this approach would mean recognising and highlighting differences, and being prepared to give special training to groups who may be disadvantaged and lack self-confidence, so that all in the organisation feel comfortable. Two further emphases are **accommodating** and **utilising** differences, which she argues are most similar to equal opportunity approaches where specific initiatives are available to aid identified groups, but also where these are also genuinely open for all other members of the organisation. In these approaches talent is recognised and used in spite of social differences, and this is done, for example, by recognising different patterns of qualifications and different roles in and out of paid work. Liff's conclusion is that group differences cannot be ignored, because it is these very differences which hold people back.

The culture question

The roots of discrimination go very deep, and in relation to women, Simmons (1989) talks about challenging a system of institutional discrimination and anti-female conditioning in the prevailing culture. Culture is important in two ways in managing diversity – first, in respect of the whole range of approaches to managing diversity, organisational culture is a determinant of the way that organisations treat individuals from different groups. Equal opportunity approaches tended to concentrate on behaviour and, to a small extent, attitudes, whereas management of diversity approaches recognise a need to go beneath this. So changing the culture to one which treats individuals as individuals and supports them in developing their potential is critical, although the difficulties of culture change make this a very difficult task.

Second, depending on the approach to the management of diversity the culture of different groups within the organisation comes into play. Recognising that men and women present different cultures at work, as well as different ethnic groups, and that this diversity needs to be managed, is key to promoting a positive environment of equal opportunity, which goes beyond merely fulfilling the demands of the statutory codes. Masreliez-Steen (1989) explains how men and women have different perceptions, interpretations of reality, languages and ways of solving problems, which, if properly used, can be a benefit to the whole organisation, as they are complementary. She described women as having a collectivist culture where they form groups, avoid the spotlight, see rank as unimportant and have few but close contacts. Alternatively, men are described as having an individualistic culture, where they form teams, 'develop a profile', enjoy competition and have many superficial contacts. The result is that men and women behave in different ways, often fail to understand each other and experience 'culture clash'. However, the difference is about how things are done and not what is achieved.

The fact that women have a different culture with different strengths and weaknesses means that women need managing and developing in a different way. They need different forms of support and coaching. Women more often need help to understand the need for making wider contacts and how to make them. In order to manage such diversity, key management competencies for the future would be: concern with image, process awareness, interpersonal awareness/sensitivity, developing subordinates and gaining commitment.

A similar argument applies to different ethnic groups, and it is generally from this perspective that managing diversity approaches in the US have developed. Jackson *et al.* (1993) propose a series of stages and levels that organisations go through in becoming a multicultural organisation:

Level 1, stage 1: The exclusionary organisation

This organisation maintains the power of dominant groups in the organisation, and excludes others.

Level 1, stage 2: The club

The club still excludes people but in a less explicit way. Some members of minority groups are allowed to join as long as they conform to pre-defined norms.

Level 2, stage 3: The compliance organisation

This organisation recognises that there are other perspectives, but doesn't want to do anything to rock the boat. It may actively recruit minority groups at the bottom of the organisation and make some token appointments.

Level 2, stage 4: The affirmative action organisation

This organisation is committed to eliminating discrimination and encourages employees to examine their attitudes and think differently. There is strong support for the development of new employees from minority groups.

Level 3, stage 5: The redefining organisation

The redefining organisation is not satisfied with being anti-racist and so examines all it does and its culture to see the impact of these on its diverse multicultural workforce. It develops and implements policies to distribute power among all groups.

Level 3, stage 6: The multicultural organisation

This organisation reflects the contribution and interests of all its diverse members in everything it does and espouses. All members are full participants of the organisation and there is recognition of a broader social responsibility – to educate others outside the organisation and to have an impact on external oppression.

ACTIVITY BOX 19.2

Think of five organisations that you know or have read about and plot where they are on each of the two frameworks we have reviewed. Explain the evidence and examples you have used in order to support where you have located them in the frameworks.

A process for managing diversity

Ross and Schneider (1992) advocate a strategic approach to managing diversity based on their conception of the difference between seeking equal opportunity and managing diversity, which is that diversity approaches are:

- ◗ internally driven, not externally imposed;
- ◗ focused on individuals rather than groups;
- ◗ focused on the total culture of the organisation rather than just the systems used;
- ◗ the responsibility of all in the organisation and not just the personnel function.

Their process involves the following steps:

1. Diagnosis of the current situation in terms of statistics, policy and culture, and looking at both issues and causes.
2. Setting aims which involve the business case for equal opportunities, identifying the critical role of commitment from the top of the organisation, and a vision of what the organisation would look like if it successfully managed diversity.
3. Spreading the ownership. This is a critical stage in which awareness needs to be raised, via a process of encouraging people to question their attitudes and preconceptions. Awareness needs to be raised in all employees at all levels, especially managers, and it needs to be clear that diversity is not something owned by the personnel function.
4. Policy development comes after awareness-raising as it enables a contribution to be made from all in the organisation – new systems need to be changed via involvement and not through imposition on the unwilling.
5. Managing the transition needs to involve a range of training initiatives. Positive action programmes, specifically designed for minority groups, may be used to help them understand the culture of the organisation and acquire essential skills; policy implementation programmes, particularly focusing on selection, appraisal, development and coaching; further awareness training and training to identify cultural diversity and manage different cultures and across different cultures.
6. Managing the programme to sustain momentum. This involves a champion, not necessarily from the personnel function, but someone who continues in his or her previous organisation role in addition. Also the continued involvement of senior managers is important, together with trade unions. Harnessing initiatives that come up through departments and organising support networks for disadvantaged groups are key at this stage. Ross and Schneider also recommend measuring achievements in terms of business benefit – better relationships with customers, improvements in productivity and profitability, for example – which need to be communicated to all employees.

Ellis and Sonnenfield (1994) make the point that training for diversity needs to be far more than a one-day event. They recommend a series of workshops which allow time for individuals to think, check their assumptions and reassess between training sessions. Key issues that need tackling in arranging training are

WINDOW ON PRACTICE

Ethnic minorities in the police service

Current employment of ethnic minorities in the police force is not representative of their presence in the labour market. In England and Wales only 1.7 per cent of the police force are from ethnic minority groups compared with 5.2 per cent of the population who are economically active. Percentages for Scotland are 0.2 per cent and 1 per cent respectively. In addition in England and Wales only 10 per cent of ethnic minorities are in the ranks above constable compared with 23 per cent for all other police staff.

In 1995 Her Majesty's Inspectorate of Constabulary (HMIC) stressed the business case for improving the current position:

> All organisations need to exploit the talents and abilities of all their members. This cannot be done without a culture which welcomes, uses and manages diversity in the workplace. . . . A workforce which reflects the society it serves provides an unrivalled source of accurate, unbiased management information and helps make policing the community more responsive and appropriate.

The Equal Opportunities Review (No. 68, 1996) reports on steps being taken by some forces to overcome the barriers to recruitment and retention of ethnic minorities – which come within the areas of recruitment, promotion and culture.

Recruitment
Evidence suggested that the PIR (Police Initial Recruitment) test was found to be adversely affecting ethnic minority groups, in addition, it was found that ethnic minority groups were deterred from applying – for Asian groups it was viewed as a less suitable career than law or accountancy, and for Afro-Caribbean groups those who joined the police were seen as traitors.

To tackle these issues advertising campaigns were designed which went beyond equal opportunity statements to address specific barriers and attitudes. In addition, familiarisation courses were provided on the premiss that ethnic minorities were less likely already to know someone who had joined the force. Strathclyde and other forces run pre-selection access courses which provide support and training for passing the PIR test. The Met have Positive Action Teams which provide guidance for ethnic minority applicants in how to prepare for the selection procedure. Other forces support outreach work where there is police involvement with community relations officers, community leaders, and careers staff.

Promotion
The HMIC identified problems in the appraisal process in terms of poor training for appraisers, no routine auditing of performance appraisal and a lack of in-depth monitoring to check for bias. The lack of ethnic minorities in CID and specialist positions was noted. Although this may be partly explained by length of service, this was not a sufficient explanation. Some forces have now set up formal mentoring programmes, assertiveness courses and special support networks.

Culture
A prevalence of racial harassment was identified and many forces now have formal policies relating to harassment. In Leicester a confidential survey found that 26 per cent of ethnic minority staff experienced harassment over the previous two years. In West Yorkshire on promotion to sergeant one of the skills tested is concerned with equal opportunities on the premiss that officers need to be able to confront and manage complaints of unacceptable behaviour. They say that this is 'sending a powerful and public message on the Force position'. Once appointed, sergeants undergo training with a significant input on equal opportunities, discrimination law, harassment and community and race relations.

(Based on EOR No. 73, 1997, – 'Ethnic Minorities in the Police Service'.)

ensuring that the facilitator has the appropriate skills; carefully considering participant mix; deciding whether the training should be voluntary or mandatory; being prepared to cope with any backlash for previously advantaged groups who now feel threatened; and being prepared for the fact that the training may reinforce stereotypes. They argue that training has enormous potential benefits, but that there are risks involved.

Organisations have a long way to go before getting to the stage of really valuing diversity, and in order for them to continue to strive it is important to reinforce the business advantages. Thompson and DiTomaso (reported by Ellis and Sonnenfield 1994) put it very well:

> Multicultural management perspective fosters more innovative and creative decision making, satisfying work environments, and better products because all people who have a contribution to make are encouraged to be involved in a meaningful way. . . . More information, more points of view, more ideas and reservations are better than fewer.

ACTIVITY BOX 19.3

The Police Service example illustrates some aspects of a management of diversity approach (as well as some aspects of an equal opportunities approach).

Explain what steps you would recommend to extend the management of diversity approach that has begun.

Equal opportunities or managing diversity?

The first question to be addressed is whether equal opportunities and managing diversity are completely different things; the second is, if so, whether one approach is preferable to the other. For the sake of clarity, in the early part of this chapter we characterised a distinct approach to managing diversity which suggests that it is different from equal opportunities. Miller identifies a parallel move from the collective to the individual in the changing emphasis in personnel management as opposed to HRM. However, as we have seen, managing diversity covers a range of approaches and emphases, some closer to equal opportunities, some very different. In reality, there remains the question of the extent to which approaches have really changed in organisations. Redefining equal opportunities in the language of the enterprise culture (Miller 1996) may just be a way of making it more palatable in today's climate, and Liff (1996) suggests that retitling may be used to revitalise the equal oportunities agenda.

Putting the question of the extent of change on one side, much of the management of diversity literature is written in such a way that it suggests a superior approach to equal opportunities, and one that is not compatible (see Kandola *et al.* 1996). However, significant disadvantages of the approach have been identified. Managing diversity can be seen as introspective as it deals with people already in the organisation, rather than getting people into the organisation – managing rather than expanding diversity (Donaldson 1993). As such Thomas (1990) suggests that it is not possible to *manage* diversity until you actually have it. Young (1990) argues that if differences are not recognised (as in the individualist approach), then the norms and standards of the dominant group are not questioned. Others however argue that a greater recognition of perceived differences will continue to provide a rationale for disadvantageous treatment.

There is much support for equal opportunities and managing diversity to be viewed as mutually supportive and a necessary interaction for progress (see Ford 1996), although Newman and Williams (1995) argue that we are some way from a model which can incorporate difference and diversity in its individualised and collective sense. To see equal opportunities and management of diversity as *alternatives* threatens to sever the link between organisational strategy and the realities of internal and external labour market disadvantage.

ACTIVITY BOX 19.4

Prepare a strategy for managing diversity which would be appropriate for your organisation, or one with which you are familiar.

Summary propositions

19.1 The essence of much personnel work is to discriminate between individuals. The essence of equal opportunity is to avoid unfair discrimination.

19.2 Equal opportunities highlights the moral argument for equal treatment, whereas managing diversity highlights the business case.

19.3 Unfair discrimination often results from people being treated on the basis of limited and prejudiced understanding of the groups to which they belong rather than on the basis of an assessment of them as individuals.

19.4 Legislation can have only a limited effect in reducing the level of unfair discrimination.

19.5 Actual changes in practice relating to equalising opportunity are taking place very slowly.

19.6 Equal opportunities approaches and the management of diversity are best viewed, not as alternatives, but as complimentary approaches which need to be interrelated.

References

Anon. (1988) 'Childcare provision 1 – employers head for the nursery', *Industrial Relations Review and Report*, October, No. 425, pp. 2–7.

Anon. (1989) 'Social Security Act 1989, guidance note', *Industrial Relations Review and Report, Legal Information Bulletin*, No. 384, pp. 2–8.

Arkin, A. (1990) 'Mothercare makes a play for women returners', *Personnel Management Plus*, July, pp. 20–1.

Brown, C. and Gay, P. (1986) *Racial Discrimination 17 years after the Act*, London: PSI.

Carr, J. (1980) 'Comments on monitoring', *Record Keeping and Monitoring in Education and Employment*, London: Runnymede Trust.

Clark, A. (1984) in D. Gill and B. Ungerson, *The Challenge of Equal Value*, London: Institute of Personnel Management.

Cockburn, S. (1991) *In the Way of Women*, Basingstoke: Macmillan.

Commission for Racial Equality (1992) *Second Review of the Race Relations Act 1976*, London: CRE.

Dickens, L. and Colling, T. (1990) 'Why equality won't appear on the bargaining agenda', *Personnel Management*, April, pp. 48–53.

Donaldson, L. (1993) 'The recession: a barrier to equal opportunities?', *Equal Opportunities Review*, No. 50, July/August.

Ellis, C. and Sonnenfield, J. A. (1994) 'Diverse approaches to managing diversity', *Human Resource Management*, Spring, Vol. 33, No.1, pp. 79–109.

Employers' Forum on Disability (1995) *Action File*, Employers' Forum on Disability, London.

Employment Service (undated) *The Disabled Persons (Employment) Acts 1944 and 1958: Employers' obligations*, Employment Service.

Equal Opportunities Commission (1985) *A Model Equal Opportunities Policy*, London: Equal Opportunities Commission.

Equal Opportunities Commission (1985) *Sex Discrimination Decisions No. 9. Women and family responsibilities, Price v. Civil Service Commission*, EOC Information Leaflet, London: Equal Opportunities Commission.

Equal Opportunities Commission (1986) *Guidelines for Equal Opportunities Employers*, London: HMSO.

Equal Opportunities Commission (1994) *The Inequality Gap*, Manchester: Equal Opportunities Commission.

Equal Opportunities Review (1992) 'Opportunity 2000', *Equal Opportunities Review*, No. 41, pp. 20–6.

Equal Opportunities Review (1992) 'Positive action on disability', *Equal Opportunities Review*, No. 43, May/June.

Equal Opportunities Review (1993) 'Formulating an equal opportunities policy', *Equal Opportunities Review*, No. 47, Jan./Feb.

Equal Opportunities Review (1993) 'Trade Union and Employment Rights Act and equal opportunities: the EOR Guide, *Equal Opportunities Review*, No. 5, July/August.

Equal Opportunities Review (1993) 'Age discrimination – no change', Equal Opportunities Review, No. 48.

Equal Opportunities Review (1993) 'EOC looks to Europe for action over UK equal pay laws', *Equal Opportunities Review*, Nov./Dec., No. 56, pp. 20–4.

Equal Opportunities Review (1994) *Equal Opportunities Review*, No. 54.

Equal Opportunities Review (1994) 'Positive about disabled people: the disability symbol', *Equal Opportunities Review*, No. 56 July/August.

Equal Opportunities Review (1994) 'Statistics: ethnic minorities in the labour market', *Equal Opportunities Review*, No. 56.

Equal Opportunities Review (1996) 'Ethnic minorities in the police service', *Equal Opportunities Review*, No. 68, July/August.

Equal Opportunities Review (1997) 'Minimum wage benefits women and ethnic minorities', *Equal Opportunities Review*, No. 73, May/June.

Field, S. and Paddison, L. (1989) 'Designing a career break system', *Industrial and Commercial Training*, Jan./Feb., pp. 22–5.

Ford, V. (1996) 'Partnership is the secret of success', *People Management*, 8 February, pp. 34–6.

Gill, D. and Ungerson, B. (1984) *The Challenge of Equal Value*, London: IPM.

Gregory, J. (1992) 'Equal pay and work of equal value: the strengths and weaknesses of the legislation', *Work Employment and Society*, Vol. 6, No. 3, September, pp. 461–73.

Hakim, C. (1993) 'The myth of rising female employment', *Work Employment and Society*, Vol 7, No. 1, March, pp. 121–33.

Harbour, T. (1980) 'Monitoring: the mass experience' in *Record Keeping and Monitoring in Education and Employment*, Proceedings of a one-day seminar, London: Runnymede Trust.

Home Office (1985) *Sex Discrimination: A guide to the Sex Discrimination Act 1975*, London: HMSO.

HMSO (1989) *Disabled Adults: Services, transport and employment*, London: HMSO.

HMSO (1996) *The Disability Discrimination Act: Definition of disability*, Leaflet DL60, London: HMSO.

HMSO (1996) *The Disability Discrimination Act: Employment*, Leaflet DL 70, London: HMSO.

Incomes Data Services (1983) *Maternity Rights*, Handbook Series No. 26, London: IDS.

Incomes Data Services (1996) *Employment Law Supplement*, No. 78, London: IDS.

Institute of Personnel Management (1978) *Towards Fairer Selection: A code for non-discrimination*, IPM Joint Standing Committee on Discrimination, London: IPM.

Itzin, C. and Phillipson, C. (1993) *Age Barriers at Work: Maximising the potential of mature and older people*, London: Metropolitan Authorities Recruitment Agency.

Jackson, B. W., LaFasto, F. Schultz, H. G. and Kelly, D. (1993) 'Diversity', *Human Resource Management*, Vol. 31, Nos 1 and 2, Spring/Summer, pp. 21–34.

Jarman, J. (1994) 'Which way forward? Assessing the current proposals to amend the British Equal Pay Act', *Work Employment and Society*, Vol. 8, No. 2, pp. 243–254, June.

Jenkins, R. (1986) *Racism and Recruitment*, Cambridge: Cambridge University Press.

Kandola, P. and Fullerton, J. (1994) *Managing the Mosaic*, London: IPD.

Kandola, R., Fullerton, J. and Mulroney, C. (1996) *1996 Pearn Kandola Survey of Diversity Practice Summary Report*, Oxford.

LaFasto, F. (1993) 'Baxter Healthcare Organisation', in B. W. Jackson *et al.*, *Human Resource Management*, Vol. 31, Nos 1–2 (Spring/Summer).

Lawrence, E. (ed.) (1986) *CSO Annual Abstract of Statistics*, No. 122, London: HMSO.

Liff, S. (1989) 'Assessing equal opportunities policies', *Personnel Review*, Vol. 18, No. 1, pp. 27–34.

Liff, S. (1996) 'Managing diversity: new opportunities for women?', *Warwick Papers in Industrial Relations No. 57*, Coventry: IRU, Warwick University.

Liff, S. (1997) 'Two routes to managing diversity: individual differences or social group characteristics?', *Employee Relations*, Vol. 19, No. 1, pp. 11–26.

Liff, S. and Cameron, I. (1997) 'Changing equality cultures to move beyond "women's problems"', *Gender, Work and Organisation*, Vol. 4, No. 1, January, pp. 35–46.

MacLachlan, R. (1996) 'Conquering ageism, *People Management*, 19 December, pp. 25–7.

MacLachlan, R., Grant, B. and Smith, P. (1996) 'Standing up to be counted', *People Management*, 11 January p. 22.

Mahon, T. (1989), 'When line managers welcome equal opportunities', *Personnel Management*, October, pp. 76–9.

Manpower Services Commission Employment Division (1984), *The Disabled Persons Register*, Sheffield: Central Office of Information and Manpower Services Commission.

Manpower Services Commission (1985) *Working Group Report on Suggestions for Improving the Quota Scheme's Effectiveness*, Sheffield: Manpower Services Commission.

Martin, J. and Roberts, C. (1980) *Women and Employment: A lifetime perspective*, Report of the 1980 DE/OPCS Women and Employment Survey, London: HMSO.

Masreliez-Steen, G. (1989) *Male and Female Management*, Sweden: Kontura Group.

McColgan, A. (1994) 'Pay equity – just wages for women', London: Institute of Employment Rights.

McGoldrick, A. (1984) *Equal Treatment in Occupational Pension Schemes*, Research Report, London: Equal Opportunities Commission.

Miller, D. (1996) Equality management – towards a materialist approach', *Gender, Work and Organisation*, Vol. 3, No. 4, pp. 202–14.

Newman, J. and Williams, F. (1995) 'Diversity and change, gender, welfare and organisational relations', in C. Itzin and J. Newman, *Gender, Culture and Organisational Change*, London: Routledge.

Noon, M. (1993) 'Racial discrimination in speculative application: evidence from the UK's top 100 firms', *Human Resource Management Journal*, Vol. 3.

Ousley, H. (1996) quoted in S. Overell, 'Ouseley in assault on diversity', *People Management*, 2 May, pp. 7–8.

O'Sullivan, A. (1989) 'Women in senior management', *MBA Review*, Vol. 1, Pt 2, pp. 5–7.

Prescott-Clarke, P. (1990) *Employment and Handicap*, London: Social and Community Planning Research.

Ross, R. and Schneider, R. (1992) *From Equality to Diversity – a business case for equal opportunities*, London: Pitman.

Runnymede Trust (1979) *A Review of the Race Relations Act*, London.

Runnymede Trust and BPS (1980) *Discriminating Fairly: A guide to fair selection*, Report by the Joint Working Party on Employment Assessment and Racial Discrimination, London.

Select Committee on the Anti-discrimination Bill (House of Lords) (1972–73), *Second Special Report from the Select Committee*, London: HMSO.

Selwyn, N. M. (1978) *Law of Employment*, London: Butterworth.

Simmons, M. (1989) 'Making equal opportunities training effective', *Journal of European Industrial Training*, Vol. 13, No. 8, pp. 19–24.

Singer, M. (1993) *Diversity-based Hiring*, Aldershot: Avebury.

Skills and Enterprise Network (1996) *Meeting the National Skills Shortage*, Nottingham: Skills and Enterprise Network.

Sly, F. (1996) 'Ethnic minority participation in the labour market: trends from the Labour Force Survey 1984–1995', *Labour Market Trends*, Vol. 104, No. 6, June.

Sly, F. (1996) 'Women in the labour market: results from the Spring Labour Force Survey', *Labour Market Trends*, Vol. 104, No. 3, March.

Smith, D. J. (1974) *Racial Disadvantage in Employment* (PEP Study of Racial Disadvantage), Vol. XL, Broadsheet 544, The Social Science Institute.

Terbourg, J. R. (1977) 'Women in management: a research review', *Journal of Applied Psychology*, Vol. 62, pp. 647–64.

Thomas, R. R. (1990) 'From Affirmative Action to affirming diversity', *Harvard Business Review*, March/April.

Trades Union Congress (1995) *Arguments for a Minimum Wage*, London: TUC.

Wainwright, D. (1985) 'Equal value in action', *Personnel Management*, January.

Walker, A. (1986) 'Disabled workers and technology: quota fails to quote', *Manpower Policy and Practice*, Spring.

Women of Europe Supplements (1989) *Women of Europe Supplements*, No. 30.

Worsley, R. (1996) 'Only prejudices are old and tired', *People Management*, 1 January, pp. 18–23.

Young, I. M. (1990) *Justice and the Politics of Difference*, Princeton, NJ: Princeton University Press.

General discussion topics

1. Discuss Liff's (1997) question:

   Can people's achievements be explained by their individual talents or are they better explained as an outcome of their gender, ethnicity, class and age? Can anything meaningful be said about the collective experience of all women or are any generalisations undermined by other cross-cutting ideas. (p. 11)

2. Which is preferable – the UK approach or the US approach to equal opportunities? What are the implications of each for all members of the organisation?

Interactive skill:
the appraisal interview

Appraising performance is not a precise measurement but a subjective judgement. It has a long history of being damned for its ineffectiveness at the same time as being anxiously sought by people wanting to know how they are doing. It is difficult to do, it is frequently done badly with quite serious results, but on the rare occasions when it is done well it can be invaluable for the business, and literally life-transforming for the appraisee. It is probably the most demanding and skilful activity for any manager to undertake:

> W. Edwards Deming has contended that performance appraisal is the number one American management problem. He says it takes the average employee (manager or non-manager) six months to recover from it. I think Dr Deming is about right, though I'd add the setting of objectives and job descriptions to the list of personnel control devices that are downright dangerous – as currently constituted.   (Peters 1989, p. 495)

This comment echoes a similar opinion expressed by Douglas McGregor thirty years earlier in the classic management text *The Human Side of Enterprise*.

With reactions like this, it makes the appraisal interview sound even more suspect than the selection interview, as we saw in Chapter 14. Its use is becoming more widespread, but if it is so difficult to get right, why does it survive? Why persist with something that Tom Peters regards as downright dangerous?

One might just as well ask why marriage survives despite its extensive failure and the innumerable personal tragedies it produces. Why do teachers grade students' work? Why do we all seek advice? Why do audiences applaud? Why do wives and husbands seek the views of their spouses on the prospective purchase of a new suit/dress/shirt/hat? The reason is simple: we all seek approval and confirmation that we are doing the right thing, and most of us yearn to advise or direct what other people should do.

At work these basic human drives are classified into activities including objective-setting, counselling, coaching or feedback on performance. They all have in common the feature of one person meeting face to face with another for a discussion focused on the performance of only one of them.

There are many appraisal schemes being designed and implemented in all areas of employment. Once installed, schemes are frequently modified or abandoned, and there is widespread management frustration about their operation. Despite the problems, the potential advantages of appraisal are so great that organisations

WINDOW ON PRACTICE

In one recent set of examination scripts for the Institute of Personnel Management the following comments were found:

> Our scheme has been abandoned because of a lot of paperwork to be completed by the manager and the time-consuming nature of the preparation by both appraiser and appraisee. Assessment dragged on from week to week without any tangible outcome, there was no follow-up and few people understood the process. The interview was spent with managers talking generalities and appraisees having nothing

to say. (from a large engineering company)

> We have had approximately one new scheme per year over the last six years. These have ranged from a blank piece of paper to multi-form exercises, complete with tick boxes and a sentence of near death if they were not complete by a specified date. (from an international motor manufacturer)

> Our scheme is not objective and has become a meaningless ritual. It is not a system of annual appraisal; it is an annual handicap. (from a public corporation)

continue to introduce them and appraisal can produce stunning results. Here is another extract from the same set of examination answers referred to above:

> I have had annual appraisal for three years. Each time it has been a searching discussion of my objectives and my results. Each interview has set me new challenges and opened up fresh opportunities. Appraisal has given me a sense of achievement and purpose that I had never previously experienced in my working life.   (from an insurance company).

Contrasted approaches to appraisal

There are two contrasted motivations that drive the appraisal interview: the motivation of management control and the motivation of self-development. These produce appraisal systems that show a mixture of both motivations, with the control approach still being the most common, especially when there is a link with performance-related pay, but the alternative development emphasis is gaining in popularity. Describing them as polar opposites helps to illustrate the key elements.

1. **The management control approach** starts with an expression of opinion by someone 'up there', representing the view of controlling, responsible authority in saying:

   > We must stimulate effective performance and develop potential, set targets to be achieved, reward above-average achievement and ensure that promotion is based on sound criteria.

   Despite the specious appeal of this most reasonable aspiration, that type of initiative is almost always resisted by people acting collectively, either by representation through union machinery or through passive resistance and grudging participation. This is because people whose performance will be appraised construe the message in a way that is not usually intended by the controlling authorities, like this:

They will put pressure on poor performers so that they improve or leave. They will also make sure that people do what they're told and we will all be vulnerable to individual managerial whim and prejudice, losing a bit more control over our individual destinies.

It is the most natural human reaction to be apprehensive about judgements that will be made about you by other people, however good their intentions.

This approach is likely to engender:

(a) Conflictual behaviour and attitudes within the organisation, including resistance by managers to the amount of administrative work involved in the process.
(b) Negotiated modifications to schemes. These are 'concessions' made to ease the apprehension of people who feel vulnerable. These frequently make the schemes ineffective.
(c) Tight bureaucratic controls to ensure consistency and fairness of reported judgements.
(d) Bland, safe statements in the appraisal process.
(e) Little impact on actual performance, except on that of a minority of self-assured high achievers at one extreme and disenchanted idlers at the other.
(f) Reduced openness, trust and initiative.

This approach works best when there are clear and specific targets for people to reach, within an organisational culture that emphasises competition. There are considerable problems, like who sets the standards and who makes the judgements? How are the judgements, by different appraisers of different appraisees, made consistent? Despite its drawbacks, this approach is still potentially useful as a system of keeping records and providing a framework for career development that is an improvement on references and panel interviews. It is most appropriate in bureaucratic organisations. The emphasis is on form-filling.

2. **The development approach** starts with the question in the mind of the individual job holder:

> I am not sure whether I am doing a good job or not. I would like to find ways of doing the job better, if I can, and I would like to clarify and improve my career prospects.

This question is addressed by job holders *to themselves*. Not: 'Am I doing what you want?', but, 'Where can I find someone to talk through with me my progress, my hopes, my fears? Who can help me come to terms with my limitations and understand my mistakes? Where can I find someone with the experience and wisdom to discuss my performance with me so that I can shape it, building on my strengths to improve the fit between what I can contribute and what the organisation needs from me?'

Those in positions of authority tend to put a slightly different construction on this approach, which is something like:

> This leads to people doing what they want to do rather than what they should be doing. There is no co-ordination, no comparison and no satisfactory management control.

This approach to appraisal:

(a) develops co-operative behaviour between appraisers and appraisees and encourages people to exercise self-discipline, accepting autonomous responsibility,
(b) confronts issues, seeking to resolve problems,
(c) does not work well with bureaucratic control,
(d) produces searching analysis directly affecting performance,
(e) requires high trust, engenders loyalty and stimulates initiative.

This approach works best with people who are professionally self-assured, so that they can generate constructive criticism in discussion with a peer; or in protégé/mentor situations, where there is high mutual respect. The emphasis is on *interviewing*, rather than on form-filling. Despite the benefits of this approach, there are two problems: first is the lack of the *systematic* reporting that is needed for attempts at management control of, and information about, the process; second is the problem of everyone finding a paragon in whom they can trust.

ACTIVITY BOX 20.1

To what extent can the benefits of both approaches be created in a single scheme?

Who should conduct the appraisal interview?

Appraisal . . . requires a strong communications effort and a supportive skill-based training programme for appraisers and appraisees . . . complex systems requiring managers to complete large volumes of paperwork soon fall into disrepute. Care must be taken that simple user-friendly and useful systems remain so. However, the appraisal process should not be reduced to the mere ticking of meaningless boxes. (Snape *et al.* 1994, p. 66)

Despite the problems the potential advantages of performance appraisal are so great that attempts are made to make it work. Appraisal is, however, valueless unless the general experience of it is satisfactory. Appraisees have to find some value in the appraisal process itself and see tangible outcomes in follow-up. Appraisers have to find the appraisal process not too arduous and have to see constructive responses from appraisees. When general experience of appraisal is satisfactory, it becomes an integral part of managing the organisation and modifies the management process.

Who does the appraisal?

Individuals are appraised by a variety of people, including their immediate superior, their superior's superior, a member of the personnel department, themselves, their peers or their subordinates. Sometimes, assessment centres are used to carry out the appraisal. You may find it helpful to refer back to Chapter 17 to remind yourself in more detail about these options.

There are, however, many problems for those carrying out the appraisal. For example:

Prejudice – the appraiser may actually be prejudiced against the appraisee, or be anxious not to be prejudiced; either could distort the appraiser's judgement.

Insufficient knowledge of the appraisee – appraisers often carry out appraisals because of their position in the hierarchy rather than because they have a good understanding of what the appraisee is doing.

The 'halo effect' – the general likeability (or the opposite) of an appraisee can influence the assessment of the work that the appraisee is doing.

The problem of context – difficulty of distinguishing the work of appraisees from the context in which they work, especially when there is an element of comparison with other appraisees.

ACTIVITY BOX 20.2

Think of jobs where it is difficult to disentangle the performance of the individual from the context of the work. How would you focus on the individual's performance in these situations?

Problems for both the appraiser and the appraisee include:

The paperwork – documentation soon gets very cumbersome in the attempts made by scheme designers to ensure consistent reporting.

The formality – although appraisers are likely to try to avoid stiff formality, both participants in the interview realise that the encounter is relatively formal, with much hanging on it.

Among the other common problems, that often cause appraisal schemes to fail are:

Outcomes are ignored – follow-up action agreed in the interview for management to take fails to take place.

Everyone is 'just above average' – most appraisees are looking for reassurance that all is well, and the easiest way for appraisers to deal with this is by a statement or inference that the appraiser is doing at least as well as most others, and better than a good many. It is much harder to deal with the situation of facing someone with the opinion that they are average – who wants to be average?

Appraising the wrong features – sometimes behaviours other than the real work are evaluated such as time-keeping, looking busy and being pleasant, because they are easier to see.

The appraisal interview

The different styles of appraisal interview were succinctly described forty years ago by the American psychologist Norman Maier (1958). His three-fold classification remains the most widely adopted means of identifying the way to tackle the interview. The *problem-solving* style has been summarised as:

> The appraiser starts the interview by encouraging the employee to identify and discuss problem areas and then consider solutions. The employee therefore plays an active part in analysing problems and suggesting solutions, and the evaluation of performance emerges from the discussion at the appraisal interview, instead of being imposed by the appraiser upon the employee.   (Anderson 1993, p. 102)

This is certainly the most effective style, consistent with the development approach to appraisal set out at the opening of this chapter, providing that both the appraiser and appraisee have the skill and ability to handle this mode. It is the basis on which this chapter is written, but it is not the only way. Maier's alternatives were first *tell and sell*, where the appraiser acts as judge, using the interview to tell the appraisee the result of the appraisal and how to improve. This 'ski instructor' approach can be appropriate when the appraisees have little experience and have not developed enough self-confidence to analyse their own performance. *Tell and listen* still casts the appraiser in the role of judge, passing on the outcome of an appraisal that has already been completed and listening to reactions. These could sometimes change the assessment, as well as enabling the two people to have a reasonably frank exchange.

A number of recent articles suggest *a contingency approach* to the personal interaction in the appraisal interview. George suggests that effective appraisal depends on the style of appraisal not conflicting with the culture of the organisation. He suggests that the degree of openness that is required is 'unlikely to materialize without an atmosphere of mutual trust and respect – something which is conspicuously lacking in many employing organizations' (George 1986, p. 32).

George also comments on the links between the appraisal system and other personnel and organisational systems:

> An investment in a system must involve statements about certain desired organizational characteristics and about the treatment of people in an organization. It is very mistaken, therefore, to regard appraisal as merely a technique or a discrete process with an easily definable boundary. (*ibid.*, p. 33)

Appraisal therefore needs to reflect the wider values of the organisation if it is to be properly integrated and survive in an effective form.

Other aspects of the contingency approach to appraisal include the appraiser's style in relation to their normal management style and in relation to the needs and personality of the appraisee. Pryor (1985) argues that appraisers should aim to achieve consistency between their normal day-to-day management style and the style that they adopt in appraisal interviews. George talks of the few really open relationships that individuals have at work and how in the appraisal situation we may be expecting interactions of a nature and quality which are not evident in most relationships. Pryor offers a reappraisal of Maier's three styles, particularly the usefulness of tell and sell and tell and listen. He suggests that they can be effectively adapted to the needs of appraisees with little experience who require less participation in the appraisal interview.

It is tempting to identify Maier's problem-solving approach as 'the best', because it appears to be the most civilised and searching, but not all appraisal situations call for this style, not all appraisees are ready for it and not all appraisers normally behave in this way.

The appraisal interview sequence

Certain aspects of the appraisal interview are the same as those of the selection interview discussed in Chapter 14. There is the inescapable fact that the appraiser determines the framework of the encounter, there is a need to open in a way that develops mutual confidence as far as possible, and there is the use of closed and open-ended questions, reflection and summarising. It is also a difficult meeting for the two parties to handle:

> The appraisal interview is a major problem for both appraisers and appraisees. The appraiser has to have a degree of confidence and personal authority that few managers have in their relationship with all those who they have to appraise. The most contentious aspect of many appraisal schemes is the lack of choice that appraisees have in deciding who the appraiser should be. Interview respondents regularly cite the interview as something that they dread. (Torrington 1994, p. 149)

For the appraisee there are concerns about career progress, job security, the ongoing working relationship with the appraiser, and the basic anxieties relating to self-esteem and dealing with criticism.

The fundamental difference between selection and appraisal that every appraiser has to remember is that the objective is to reach an understanding that will have some impact on the future performance of the appraisee: it is not simply to formulate a judgement by collecting information, as in the selection situation. A medical metaphor may help. A surgeon carrying out hip replacements will select patients for surgery on the basis of enquiring about their symptoms and careful consideration of the evidence. The surgeon asks the questions, makes the decision and implements that decision. A physician examining a patient who is overweight and short of breath may rapidly make the decision that the patient needs to lose weight and take more exercise. It is however not the physician but the patient who has to implement that decision. The physician can help with diet sheets, regular check-ups and terrifying advice; the real challenge is how to get the patient to respond.

The easy part of appraisal is sorting out the facts. The tricky bit is actually bringing about a change in performance. The interview – like the discussion in the physician's consulting rooms – is crucial in bringing about a change of attitude, fresh understanding and commitment to action.

Preparation

Brief the appraisee on the form of the interview, possibly asking for a self-appraisal form to be completed in advance. To some extent this is establishing rapport, with the same objectives, and makes the opening of the eventual interview easier.

Asking for the self-appraisal form to be completed will only be appropriate if the scheme requires this. As we have seen, self-appraisal gives the appraisee some initiative, ensures that the discussion will be about matters which the appraisee can handle and on 'real stuff'.

The appraiser has to review all the available evidence on the appraisee's performance, including reports, records or other material regarding the period under review. Most important will be the previous appraisal and its outcomes.

Most of the points made in Chapter 14 about preparing for the selection interview apply to appraisal as well, especially the setting. Several research studies (e.g. Anderson and Barnett 1987) have shown the extremely positive response of appraisees who felt that the appraiser had taken time and trouble to ensure that the setting and supportive nature of the discussion was considerate of the appraisee's needs.

Interview structure

A recommended structure for a performance appraisal interview is shown in Figure 20.1. Alternative frameworks can be found in Anderson (1993, pp. 112–13) and Dainow (1988).

Rapport is unusual because it attempts to smoothe the interaction between two people who probably have an easy social relationship, but now find themselves ill at ease with each other. This is not the sort of conversation they are used to having together, so they have to find new ground-rules. The pre-interview appraisee briefing is an important step towards this, but the opening of the interview itself still needs care. The mood needs to be light, but not trivial, as the appraisee has to be encouraged towards candour rather than gamesmanship.

ACTIVITY BOX 20.3

What do you think of the following openings to appraisal interviews heard recently:

(a) 'Well, here we are again. I'm sure you don't like this business any more than I do, so let's get on with it.'

(b) 'Now, there's nothing to worry about. It's quite painless and could be useful. So just relax and let me put a few questions to you.'

(c) 'I wonder if I will end up conning you more than you will succeed in conning me.'

(d) 'Right. Let battle commence!'

1. Purpose and rapport	Agree purpose with appraisee Agree structure for meeting Check that pre-work is done
2. Factual review	Review of known facts about performance in previous period. Appraiser reinforcement.
3. Appraisee views	Appraisee asked to comment on performance over the last year. What has gone well and what has gone less well; what could be improved; what they liked; what they disliked; possible new objectives.
4. Appraiser views	Appraiser adds own perspective, asks questions and disagrees, as appropriate, with what appraisee has said.
5. Problem-solving	Discussion of any differences and how they can be resolved.
6. Objective-setting	Agreeing what action should be taken, and by whom.

Figure 20.1 Structure for a performance appraisal interview

Factual review is reviewing aspects of the previous year's work that are unproblematic. Begin by reviewing the main facts about the performance, without expressing opinions about them but merely summarising them as a mutual reminder. This will include the outcome of the previous appraisal. This will help to key in any later discussion by confirming such matters as how long the appraisee has been in the job, any personnel changes in the period, turnover figures, training undertaken, and so forth.

The appraiser will still be doing most – but not all – of the talking, and can isolate those aspects of performance that have been disclosed which are clearly satisfactory, mention them and comment favourably. This will develop rapport and provide the basic reassurance that the appraisee needs in order to avoid being defensive. The favourable aspects of performance will to some extent be *discovered* by the factual review process. It is important that 'the facts speak for themselves' rather than appraiser judgement being offered. Not, for instance:

> Well, I think you are getting on very well. I'm very pleased with how things are going generally.

That sort of comment made at this stage would have the appraisee waiting for 'but . . .', as the defences have not yet been dismantled. A different approach might be:

> Those figures look very good indeed. How do they compare with . . .? That's X per cent up on the quarter and Y% on the year . . . That's one of the best results in the group. You must be pleased with that . . . How on earth did you do it?

This has the advantage of the evidence being there before the eyes of both parties, with the appraiser pointing out and emphasising, and it is specific rather than general, precise rather than vague. This type of approach invariably raises the question from appraisers about what to do in a situation of poor performance. Appraising stars is easy; what about the duds? The answer is that all appraisees have some aspects of their performance on which favourable comment can be made, and the appraisal process actually identifies strengths that might have been previously obscured by the general impression of someone who is not very good. You may discover something on which to build, having previously thought the case was hopeless. If there is not some feature of the performance that can be isolated in this way, then the appraiser probably has a management or disciplinary problem that should have been tackled earlier.

The appraiser then asks for the *appraisee's views* on things that are not as good as they might be in the performance, areas of possible improvement and how these might be addressed. These will only be offered by the appraisee if there has been effective positive reinforcement in the previous stages of the interview. People can only acknowledge shortcomings about performance when they are reasonably sure of their ground. Now the appraisee is examining areas of dissatisfaction by the process of discussing them with the appraiser, with whom it is worth having the discussion, because of the appraiser's expertise, information and helicopter view. There are three likely results of debating these matters:

- some will be talked out as baseless;
- some will be shown to be less worrying than they seemed when viewed only from the single perspective of the appraiser, and ways of dealing with them become apparent;
- some will be confirmed as matters needing attention.

This stage in the interview is fraught with difficulties for the manager, and is one of the reasons why an alternative style is sometimes preferred:

> some employees prefer to be told rather than invited to participate . . . the manager receives extra pay and status for making decisions, so why should the manager expect them to do his or her job as well?
>
> (Wright and Taylor 1984, p. 110)

These, however, are problems to be recognised and overcome: they are not reasons for not bothering to try.

Appraiser views can now be used in adding to the list of areas for improvement. In many instances there will be no additions to make, but usually there are improvement needs that the appraisee cannot, or will not, see. If they are put at this point in the interview, there is the best chance that they will be understood, accepted and acted upon. It is not possible to guarantee success. Demoralised collapse or bitter resentment is always a possibility, but this is the time to try, as the appraisee has developed a basis of reassurance and has come to terms with some shortcomings that he or she had already recognised.

The appraiser has to judge whether any further issues can be raised and if so, how many. None of us can cope with confronting all our shortcomings, all at the same time, and the appraiser's underlying management responsibility is that the appraisee is not made less competent by the appraisal interview. There is also a fundamental moral responsibility not to use a position of organisational power to damage the self-esteem and adjustment of another human being.

Problem-solving is the process of talking out the areas for improvement that have been identified, so that the appraisee can cope with them. Underlying causes are uncovered through further discussion. Gradually huge problems come into clearer and less forbidding perspective, perhaps through being analysed and broken up into different components. Possibilities for action, by both appraiser and appraisee, become clear.

These central stages of the interview – factual exchange, appraisee views, appraiser views and problem-solving – need to move in that sequence. Some may be brief, but none should be omitted and the sequence should not alter.

The final stage of the encounter is to agree what is to be done: objective-setting. Actions need to be agreed and nailed down, so that they actually take place. One of the biggest causes of appraisal failure is with action not being taken, so the objectives set must not only be mutually acceptable, they must also be deliverable. It is likely that some action will be needed form the appraiser as well as some from the appraisee.

Making appraisal work

There are many reports of organisations installing an appraisal system only to find that they have to change it or completely abandon it after only a short time. Other organisations battle on with their systems, but recognise that they are ineffective or inadequate or disliked. What can be done to encourage the system to work as effectively as possible?

Effectiveness will be greater if all involved are clear about what the system is for. The personnel manager and senior managers need to work out what they want the appraisal system to achieve and how it fits in with the other personnel activities that feed into it and are fed by it, such as career planning, training and human resource planning. Those who have to operate the system also have to appreciate its objectives, otherwise they are just filling in forms to satisfy the irksome personnel people, as we saw at the opening of this chapter. Finally, those whose performance is to be appraised will answer questions and contribute ideas with much greater constructive candour if they understand and believe in the purposes of the scheme.

It is vital that the system is visibly owned by senior and line management in the organisation, and that it is not something that is done for the personnel department. This may mean, for example, that appraisal forms are kept and used within the department and only selected types of data are fed through to the personnel function or other departments. Ideally, the form itself should be a working document used by appraiser and appraisee throughout the year.

The more 'open' the appraisal system is, that is the more feedback that the appraisee is given about his or her appraisal ratings, the more likely the appraisee is to accept rather than reject the process. Similarly, the greater the extent to which appraisees participate in the system, the greater the chance of gaining their commitment, subject to the reservation already made: not all appraisees are ready and willing to participate, and not all organisational cultures support participative processes.

The involvement of both appraisers and appraisees in the identification of appraisal criteria has already been noted. Stewart and Stewart (1977) suggest that these criteria must be:

1. Genuinely related to success or failure in the job.
2. Amenable to objective, rather than subjective judgement, and helpful if they are:
   (a) Easy for the appraiser to administer.
   (b) Appear fair and relevant to the appraisee.
   (c) Strike a fair balance between catering for the requirements of the present job while at the same time being applicable to the wider organisation.

Appraisers need training in how to appraise and how to conduct appraisal interviews. Appraisees will also need some training if they have any significant involvement in the process. In our recent research we found that just over a third of the organisations that had appraisal systems trained all interviewers in appraisal interviewing. A further 18 per cent said that all interviewers had some training in interpersonal skills and that appraisal was included in this. Almost a quarter provided appraisal interviewing training for those who felt that they needed it. However, over 20 per cent provided no training at all. An excellent performance appraisal system is of no use at all if managers do not know how to use the system to best effect. Sims (1988) quotes an ineffective system which was sophisticated and well designed, but which line managers did not have the skills to use.

The appraisal system needs to be administered so that it causes as few problems as possible for both parties. Form-filling should be kept to a minimum, and the time allocated for this activity should be sufficient for it to be done properly, but not so much that the task is seen as unimportant and low priority.

Appraisal systems need to be supported by follow-up action. Work plans that are agreed by appraiser and appraisee need to be monitored to ensure that they actually take place, or that they are modified in accordance with changed circumstances or priorities. Training needs should be identified and plans made to meet those needs. Other development plans may involve the personnel department in arranging temporary transfers or moves to another department when a vacancy arises. In order to do this, it is vital that appraisal forms are not just filed and forgotten.

Summary propositions

20.1 Performance appraisal has a poor track-record, but it has considerable potential, when done well.

20.2 Among the problems of appraisal are prejudice, insufficient knowledge by the appraiser of the appraisee, the halo effect, the problem of context, the paperwork, the ignoring of outcomes, appraising the wrong features and the tendency for everyone to be just above average.

20.3 Three approaches to the appraisal interview are problem-solving, tell and sell and tell and listen.

20.4 Features of the interview itself are the opening for preliminary mutual assessment; factual review; appraisee views on performance; appraiser views, to add perspective; problem-solving and objective-setting.

20.5 Appraisers must follow up on interviews, making sure that all agreed action (especially that by the management) takes place.

20.6 Training in appraisal is essential for appraisers and for appraisees.

References

Anderson, G. C. (1993) *Managing Performance Appraisal Systems*, Oxford: Blackwell.

Anderson, G. C. and Barnett, J. G. (1987) 'The characteristics of effective appraisal interviews', *Personnel Review*, Vol. 16, No. 4.

Dainow, S. (1988) 'Goal-oriented appraisal', *Training Officer*, January, pp. 6–8.

Fletcher, C. (1984) 'What's new in performance appraisal?', *Personnel Management*, February.

George, J. (1986) 'Appraisal in the public sector: dispensing with the big stick', *Personnel Management*, May.

Latham, G. P. and Wexley, K. N. (1981) *Increasing Productivity through Performance Appraisal*, Wokingham: Addison-Wesley.

Maier, N. R. F. (1958) *The Appraisal Interview: Objectives, methods and skills*, New York: John Wiley.

Meyer, H. H. (1980) 'Self-appraisal of job performance', *Personnel Psychology*, Vol. 33, pp. 291–5.

Peters, T. (1989) *Thriving on Chaos*, London: Pan Books.

Pryor, R. (1985) 'A fresh approach to performance appraisal', *Personnel Management*, June.

Sims, R. R. (1988) 'Training supervisors in employee performance appraisals', *European Journal of Industrial Training*, Vol. 12, No. 8, pp. 26–31.

Snape E., Redman, T. and Bamber, G. (1994), *Managing Managers*, Oxford: Blackwell.

Stewart, V. and Stewart, A. (1977) *Practical Performance Appraisal*, Aldershot: Gower.

Taylor, G. S., Lehman, C. M. and Forde, C. M. (1989) 'How employee self-appraisals can help', *Supervisory Management*, August, pp. 33–41.

Torrington, D. P. (1994) 'Sweets to the sweet: performance-related pay in Britain', *International Journal of Employment Studies*, Vol. 1, No. 2, pp. 149–64.

Wright, P. L. and Taylor, D. S. (1984) *Improving Leadership Performance*, Hemel Hempstead: Prentice Hall International.

Practical exercises in appraisal interviewing

Again you need a very good friend to work with, but it is best if it is someone with a job that they can talk through, so that there are real issues of concern that provide real value to them from the discussion. You take it in turns to interview each other. The aim is to talk real stuff about your respective jobs. One of you is A, the other is B.

First exercise

1. Preparation by A:
   Write down the response to the following questions on separate cards or pieces of paper:
   (a) An activity you perform in your job that is very important (this should begin with a verb, e.g. 'carrying out appraisal interviews', not a role or responsibility).
   (b) An activity you do frequently – not necessarily important, but one which occupies a good deal of time.
   (c) An activity, though important, unlikely to appear in your diary.
   (d) What is the most important activity not so far listed?

2. Interview/discussion led by B on above topics:
   (i) How are (a) and (b) similar, and how are they different?
   (ii) What makes them easier, or harder, to do than (c)?
   (iii) Which is it more important in your job to do well, (b) or (c)?
   (iv) On what criteria did you select (d)?
   (v) Which gives you most satisfaction, (a), (b), (c) or (d)?

   Now change roles.

Second exercise

Having begun the process of examining what you do with a colleague, you now move on to a similar exercise in which you have a different type of structure. It is a mini-appraisal in which you interview each other about work done in the first week of the month.

1. A interviews B for information about A's week. (15 minutes)
2. B interviews A for information about B's week. (15 minutes)
3. A and B prepare for feedback and discussion. (15 minutes)
4. B conducts appraisal interview with A about the week. (30+ minutes)
5. A conducts appraisal interview with B about the week. (30+ minutes)
6. A and B discuss with each other what they liked and disliked about the process.

Points to remember:

▶ The first interview is for information gathering.

▶ The second interview is for feedback. This should include opportunities for positive reinforcement. Only criticise with care.

▶ A final discussion could consider the question: 'How useful did you find it to discuss an aspect of your work with someone who was well-informed, but not your "boss"? Would it have been more or less useful having that discussion with your boss?'

Part IV Case study problem

Bakersfield (new) University is in a process of change in order to promote more effective service delivery to their customers within tight budget constraints. Teaching staff have increasingly taken on higher teaching hours as the staff : student ratio has increased from 1:18 to 1:26 over the past eight years. The decrease in staff numbers has been managed through the non-replacement of leavers and a limited level of early retirement. In addition to increased teaching loads staff have been exhorted to engage themselves in research to a much greater extent and to complete PhDs. The staff have increasingly felt under pressure, but have on the whole been dedicated workers. Those staff who were most seriously disillusioned by the changes taking place were generally those opting for early retirement, although this process also meant that much expertise was suddenly lost to many departments.

The pressure of work seems set to increase and the goodwill and relatively high performance of staff are increasingly at risk. In the current circumstances Departments have found it difficult to recognise the good work of staff by promotion, which had been the traditional approach. Many Department Heads have tried to deal with this by holding out the hope of future promotion and by recognition of a good job done. Some Department Heads were more effective in this than others.

The University as a whole has decided to put two major schemes into place in relation to staff performance. First, a staff appraisal scheme, and second, an individual performance-related pay scheme. Standard forms were produced for all Departments to use and guidelines produced relating to the purpose and frequency of appraisal. All Departments conformed in terms of carrying out the appraisals, but there were great differences in how this was handled in different Departments. Those Heads who had experience of successful systems elsewhere, or who were enthusiastic about this change, carried out the appraisals in a more thorough and committed way, and did try to integrate them into the running of the department and link them to Department goals. Other Heads failed to do this, and some were positively against the system as they saw it as impinging on academic freedom, and in any case had never seen themselves as true managers. The reaction of staff was mixed, often depending on their past employment experiences and length of time employed by the University.

There were similarly disparate reactions to the individual performance pay scheme. Department Heads were each allocated a small pot of money to distribute as they saw fit between their staff. There were only two months between the announcement of the availability of this money and the date for distribution. Some Department Heads announced its availability and others never mentioned it. Some made allocations based on performance appraisal results and others made a separate judgement – perhaps allocating money only to someone who was highly valued and who had threatened to leave, but who was not necessarily the best performer. Others shared the money, in different amounts, between the top three high performers, and one other shared the money out equally between all staff in the Department. Most Heads of Department allocated the money without any consultation, indeed the Heads never got together to talk about the new system and how to handle it. A small number of Heads quickly formed a Senior Staff panel to judge the allocation and one Head devised a peer assessment panel.

Staff reactions were mixed. Some were pleased that at last there was potential monetary recognition for the extra effort they had put in. But those who only found out about the system after the money had been allocated to others were angry. Some of the staff who had received the money were so embarrassed about it that they kept it secret. Union representatives complained about the 'shady' process in many departments. Only three Heads announced the criteria which had been used to allocate the money. There were complaints about the timescale – but this was improved by the immediate announcement in the University's newsletter of a similar pot of money being made available for the following year. Many objected on principle, though, to the idea of individual performance pay and felt that it undermined the teamwork that was necessary for the Department to run effectively. A number argued that if there was to be such pay next year, it should relate directly to the performance appraisal results, and hence became more concerned that these were carried out more thoughtfully.

Staff morale was damaged by these events and the University, which is aware that it mishandled these issues, is anxious to improve matters as quickly as possible.

Required

1. What were the main problems with the approach adopted by the University Authorities?
2. What options does the University have for next year? What are the advantages and disadvantages of each?
3. Which option would you recommend, and how would you implement it?

Examination questions

Undergraduate introductory

1. 'Equal opportunities legislation is an unnecessary interference for business.' Discuss.
2. Outline the major implications of the Disability Discrimination Act 1995. Why was the Act seen as necessary?

Undergraduate finals

3. What practical steps would you take if you were the personnel manager in an organisation wishing to introduce a learning organisation?
4. Present arguments for and against linking pay to an assessment of individual performance. Having done this, explain whether or not you would like to be paid in this way, and why.

Masters

5. Discuss the reasons for the relative failure of women to move into the ranks of senior management in both private and public sector organisations.
6. Why is performance appraisal a process that frequently disappoints both appraisers and appraisees? How can these problems be overcome?

Professional

7. Given the models of best practice and the problems that have emerged in training for equal opportunities in the areas of both race and gender, suggest how these might influence equal opportunities training relating to the Disability Discrimination Act 1995.
8. As a personnel consultant how would you evaluate client/customer satisfaction with your performance and why is it important to do so?

PART **V**
Development

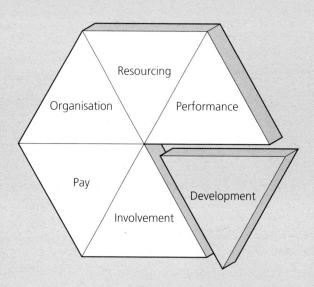

Having set up appropriate methods of organisation and systems to ensure performance, we now have to consider in more detail the ways in which people acquire skill and knowledge in order to develop their capacity to perform effectively.

One feature of development is the national framework within which vocational skills can be acquired. Here the individual employer relies on the provision of the education system and the specifications of professional and other bodies, which specify the appropriate areas of competence for vocational competence. This is then developed further within the business, especially in management development, where the skills and knowledge needed tend to be much more organisationally specific and the methods of development are geared to the ongoing processes of the business.

Individually we are all interested in our own careers. It is now unlikely that anyone will spend more than a few years with a single employer, especially at the start of their working life, so career development is something that we take on as our responsibility rather than the responsibility of our employer.

Central to all development is the teaching interaction, whether it be the instructor developing the capacity of someone else to acquire a practical skill, like driving a car or using a keyboard, or the mentor developing a protégé's self-confidence and effectiveness in social situations.

Strategic aspects of development

S

First Monday of the month again – Board meeting. This was the opportunity I'd been waiting for – with some trepidation. My function had produced firm proposals on a new training and development strategy which I was to present to the Board. Development for all was the theme, with key competencies being identified at each level of the organisation and everyone being entitled to six days off-job training per year, plus coaching on the job to meet individual development goals. A real step in the right direction at last. All I had to do was to get the Board's backing and we'd be off.

I began to present the scheme, complete with user-friendly overheads, information packs for employees and a manager guidance and support package. My colleagues listened intently, for about 5 minutes, then all hell broke loose.

'So what's going to happen to production when they're all off swanning around training – we're understaffed anyway? – that was Gary, the Production Manager.

Brian from Marketing chipped in next: 'They'll be poached as soon as they're trained if word gets out about this – we'll be doing it for nothing.'

But worst of all was Karen, the MD: 'Why are you proposing this anyway? Granted we desperately need some skills training for those new machines and to encourage flexibility – but we didn't ask for all this. How will it improve business performance? What are we going to get out of all the money this is going to cost us?'

I had hoped more of Karen. She was usually very supportive when I came up with training proposals to solve business problems – well crises would be a better word – we did what I suggested and it usually worked.

This time my words fell on stony ground – no one was interested.

Where do we go from here??????

(extract from the diary of Len Hodge, Personnel Director)

Before you read on. . .

 ▶ What went wrong in the Board meeting?

 ▶ Why do you think that the Directors reacted as they did?
 ▶ What could Len have done differently to improve his chances of success?
 ▶ Where does Len go from here?

Employee development has traditionally been seen as a cost rather than an investment in the UK, although this is certainly changing in some organisations. Comparatively speaking UK organisations give little support to training and development compared with our European partners (see, for example, Handy 1988; and Constable and McCormick 1987), and our national training framework is voluntarist, with the government's role limited to *encouraging* training rather than intervening, as in many other countries.

It is widely agreed that it is difficult to provide evidence of a causal link between employee development and organisational performance. Harrison (1993) argues that this is partly because the terms 'employee development' and 'business success' are poorly defined.

Employee development is necessarily an act of faith. It is so difficult to tie down performance improvements to the development itself (aside from other influences) and to understand the nature of the causal link. For example, is performance better because of increased or different employee development, because the reward package has improved, or because we have a clearer set of organisational and individual objectives? If there is a link with employee development initiatives, is it that employees have better skills, or are better motivated, or they have been selected from a more able group of candidates attracted to the organisation as it offers a high level of development?

Miller (1991), writing specifically of management development, points to a lack of fit between business strategy and development activity. Pettigrew and others (1988) did find, though, that development issues get a higher priority when they are linked to organisational needs and take a more strategic approach. Miller (1991) makes the point that although at the organisational level it is difficult to identify quantitatively the direct impact of strategic investment in development, this is well supported by anecdotal evidence and easily demonstrated at the macro-level.

Harrison (1993) notes a number of triggers for employee development activity which include:

- organisational strategy,
- external labour market shortages,
- changes in internal labour market needs,
- changes in internal systems and values, and last but not least,
- government initiatives and external support.

It is in this context that we consider employee development strategy. In the following chapters we look in more detail at government support for National Vocational Qualifications (NVQs) and the competence movement more generally (including the Management Charter Initiative competencies). In this chapter we shall concentrate on internal changes, especially organisation strategy, and to a lesser extent external labour market conditions.

Organisational strategy and employee development strategy

McClelland's research (1994) is one of many to show that organisations generally do not consider development issues to be part of their competitive strategy formulation, although he found that those that do identified it to be of value in gaining as well as maintaining competitive advantage.

Those organisations that do consider employee development at a strategic level usually see it as a key to *implementing* business strategy. This necessitates an emphasis on identifying development needs from an organisational perspective rather than, but not at the complete expense of, individually identified development needs.

WINDOW ON PRACTICE

One large organisation had a well-established training function and on an annual basis they sat down to plan the year ahead. They would plan how many of what types of course depending on the demand in the previous year and the availability of appropriate staff. New courses would be introduced where a need had been identified and were piloted. Course evaluation data (collected mainly from participants, but sometimes from their managers) were used to inform course demand and course structure and content.

Individuals were booked on training courses following discussion with their manager regarding their individual needs. There were often problems resulting from long waiting lists and individuals being nominated for courses for which they were not eligible (defined by the nature of their job) – it appeared that individuals sometimes nominated themselves and the manager rubber-stamped this.

Some years later, after efforts on the part of general management and training and development management to employ a more strategic approach to the business, the picture was very different. Performance management had been introduced as the cornerstone of people management resulting from a multi-functional, high-level working party. A course was devised and delivered in chunks of one and two days and this was delivered to *all* staff, with slightly differing versions for managers and non-managers. The course was an integrating mechanism for all people management activities and most importantly it promoted a cohesive *style and philosophy* of people management that the organisation felt was critical in the achievement of its business objectives. Not only was senior general management involved in the initial stages of the course, but key line managers were involved in delivering the subsequent modules.

Miller has demonstrated how management development can be aligned with the strategic positioning of the firm. He has produced a matrix demonstrating how development content and processes can reflect stable growth, unstable growth, unstable decline and competitive positions, as shown in Table 21.1. He offers the model as suggestive, only, of the 'possibilities in designing strategically-oriented management development programmes'.

Not only is it critical for individuals to be developed to meet currently identified strategic needs, but also for needs in the future. There has been an upsurge of interest in 'anticipatory learning' where future needs are predicated and development takes place in advance. The *Journal of Management Education and Development* (1994) devoted an entire issue to anticipatory learning, which included some ideas on how it might be identified and achieved. Buckley and Kemp (1987) suggest that anticipatory learning is most important at corporate level, and that a strategic approach at business unit or functional level may be shorter-term and more immediately relevant.

What can be said with confidence is that the future will be different from the present and that the skills and competencies needed will therefore be different. Of paramount importance therefore is the ability to learn. Watkins (1987) suggests that development for strategic *capability*, rather than just targeting devel-

Table 21.1 Linking management development to strategic situations (Miller 1991, p. 47). Reproduced with permission of the author

| | Environment condition | | | |
	Stable	Unstable growth	Unstable decline	Competitive
Content	Environment scanning skills	Environment scanning skills	Stakeholder relations	Competitive strategy development
	Understanding sources of stability (e.g. geographically isolated product market, state of technology)	Industry analysis skills	Executive retention skills	Competitor analysis
		Sales, marketing	Understanding competitor environment	Marketing/cost control (dependent on competitive strategy)
		Financial control		
		Creative thinking	Negotiating skills	
	Defence strategies	Team building	Diversification skills (technology, human resources)	Industry analysis (dependent on competitive strategy)
	Industrial relations skills (but depends on source of stability)	Organisation structure skills		
		Forecasting techniques		
Process	Slow pace but 'eventful'	Fast-moving	Medium pace	High-pressure
	Modest emphasis individual development	High pressure	Co-operative environment	Competitive
		Intense		
		Team-oriented	Reactive	
	Non-competitive but 'aggressive'	Proactive		
	Reactive			

opment on achieving business objectives, needs to reinforce an entrepreneurial and innovative culture in which learning is part of everyday work. He identifies the importance of acting successfully in novel and unpredictable circumstances and that employees acquire a 'habit of learning, the skills and learning and the desire to learn'.

Mabey and Iles (1993) note that a strategic approach to development differs from a tactical one in that a consistent approach to assessment and development is identified with a common skills language and skills criteria attached to overall business objectives. They also note the importance of a decreasing emphasis on subjective assessment. To this end many organisations have introduced a series of

ACTIVITY BOX 21.2

How can future development needs, say five years out, be anticipated?

Brainstorm future needs for your own organisation, or the university/college which you attend with a group of colleagues/students.

Table 21.2 A strategic approach to employee development

Issues to consider

▶ What are the key competencies that the organisation needs at each level to meet its objectives now and in the future?

▶ How are we going to assess current levels of these competencies?

▶ To what extent (as determined by the organisation's strategy and the external labour market) should these be developed internally?

▶ Which approaches to, and methods of, development will be most effective in helping us to build up the required competencies?

▶ Who is most appropriately involved in these processes?

▶ What investment will be required to achieve the employee development strategy – including finance, time, etc., and who will hold the budgets?

▶ How are we going to ensure that our employee development strategy is reinforced by and reinforces other HR strategies?

▶ How will we evaluate the effectiveness of the strategy?

development centres, similar to assessment centres (discussed in Chapter 12), but with a clear outcome of individual development plans for each participant related to their current levels of competence and potential career moves, and key competencies required by the organisation.

In Table 21.2 we offer a list of questions that are raised if an organisation wishes to adopt a strategic approach to employee development.

Influence of the external labour market

The external availability of individuals with the skills and competencies required by the organisation will also have an impact on employee development strategy. If skills and individuals are plentiful, the organisation has the choice of whether, and to what extent it wishes, to develop staff internally. If skills or individuals are in short supply, then internal development invariably becomes a priority. Predicting demographic and social changes is critical in identifying the extent of internal development required and also who will be available to be developed. In-depth analysis in these areas may challenge traditionally held assumptions about who will be developed, how they will be developed and to what extent they will be developed. For example, the predicted shortage of younger age groups in the labour market, coupled with a shortage of specific skills, may result in a strategy to develop older rather than younger recruits. This poses potential problems about the need to develop, quickly aligned with developing older workers some of whom may learn more slowly. What is the best form of development programme for employees with a very varied base of skills and experiences? Another critical issue is that of redeployment of potentially redundant staff and their development to provide shortage skills.

Prediction of skills availability is critical, as for some jobs the training required will take years rather than months. Realising in January that the skills required in August by the organisation will not be available in the labour market is too late if the development needed takes three years!

The external labour market clearly has a big impact on employee development strategy, but it is important in this respect and in relation to organisational strategy that there is a high level of integration between employee development strategy and other aspects of human resource strategy.

Integration with other human resource strategy

Where there is a choice between recruiting required skills or developing them internally, given a strategic approach, the decision will reflect on the positioning of the organisation and its strategy. In Chapter 9 we looked at this balance in some depth and you may find it helpful to re-read pages 176–9. A further issue is that of ensuring a consistency between the skills criteria used for recruitment and development.

From a slightly different perspective the organisation's development strategy, either explicit or implicit, is often underestimated in terms of its impact on recruitment and retention. There is increasing evidence to show that employees and potential employees are more interested in development opportunities, especially structured ones, rather than improvements in financial rewards. Development activity can drive motivation and commitment, and can be used in a strategic way to contribute towards these. For these ends, publishing and marketing the strategy is key, as well as ensuring that the rhetoric is backed up by action. There is also the tricky question of access to and eligibility for development – if it is offered only very selectively, it can have the reverse of the intended impact.

However, not all employees see the need for, or value of, development and this, in particular, means that the organisation's reward systems need to be supportive of the development strategy. If we want employees to learn new skills and become multi-skilled, it is skills development we need to reward rather than the job that is currently done. If we wish employees to gain vocational qualifications, we need to reflect this in our recruitment criteria and reward systems. Harrison (1993) notes that these links are not very strong in most organisations.

Other forms of reward – for example, promotions and career moves – also need to reflect the development strategy. For example, in terms of providing appropriate (e.g. matrix) career pathways if the strategy is to encourage a multi-functional, creative perspective in the development of future general management. Not only do the pathways have to be available, they also have to be used, and this means encouraging current managers to use them for their staff. In Chapter 24 we explore such career issues in more depth.

Finally, an organisation needs to reinforce the skills and competencies that it wishes to develop by appraising those skills and competencies rather than something else. Developmentally based appraisal systems can clearly be of particular value here.

Training and development roles

Salaman and Mabey (1995) identify a range of stakeholders in strategic training and development, each of which will have different interests in, influence over and ownership of training and development activities and outcomes. They identify senior managers as the *sponsors* of training and development, who will be influenced by professional, personal and political agendas; and business planners as the *clients* who are concerned about customers, competitors and shareholders. Thirdly, they identify line *managers* who are responsible for performance, coaching and resources; and fourthly, *participants* who are influenced by their career aspirations and other non-work parts of their lives. HRM staff are identified as *facilitators* who are concerned with best practice, budgets credibility and other HR strategy. Lastly, training specialists are identified as *providers*, who are influenced by external networks, professional expertise and educational perspectives. The agendas of each of these groups will overlap on some issues and conflict on others.

Most organisational examples suggest that the formation of training and development strategy is not something that should be 'owned' by the personnel and training function. The strategy needs to be owned and worked on by the whole organisation, with the personnel/training function acting in the roles of specialist/expert and co-ordinator. The function may also play a key role in translating that strategy into action steps. The actions themselves may be carried out by line management, the personnel/training function or outside consultants.

Involvement from line management in the delivery of the training and development strategy can have a range of advantages. Top management have a key role in introducing and promoting strategic developments to staff – for example, the creation of an organisation-wide competency identification programme; the creation of system of development centres or introduction of a development-based organisational performance management system. Only in this way can employees see and believe that there is a commitment from the top. At other levels line managers can be trained as trainers, assessors and advisers in delivering the strategy. This is not only a mechanism for getting them involved, but also for tailoring the strategy to meet the real and different needs of different functions and departments.

Consultants may, of course, be used at any stage. They may add to the strategy development process, but there is always the worry that their contribution comes down to an offering of their ready-packaged solution, with a bit of tailoring here and there, rather than something which really meets the needs of the organisation. It is useful to have an outside perspective, but there is an art in defining the role of that outside contribution.

In terms of delivery, consultants may make a valuable contribution where a large number of courses have to be run over a short period. The disadvantages are that they can never really understand all the organisational issues, and that they may be seen as someone from outside imposing a new process on the organisation.

Approaches to development

The approaches to and methods of development chosen need to be the most effective in achieving the skills and competencies required by the organisation. They will also need to be appropriate to the culture of the organisation. Schein (1961) produced an argument based on development as a process of influence and attitude change and showed how different approaches to development would meet differing organisation needs. For example, although there is great agreement on the value and importance of on-the-job coaching, this may not be the most appropriate method of development if the organisation wishes to encourage innovation, creativity and a holistic organisation perspective. Coaching would be a mechanism of continuing the traditions of the past, whereas cross-functional moves, job rotations, secondments and periods spent in another organisation would be more likely to produce new insights and an organisational perspective.

Another question is the organisation's approach to national initiatives such as National Vocational Qualifications and competencies identified by the Management Charter Initiative. Both of these reflect the general move from education to job-related training and both aim to develop specific competencies to a pre-defined standard. The work-based nature of these initiatives means that organisations adopting and encouraging them are landed with a heavy time commitment, particularly in the assessment process. A further issue is the extent to which the employer decides to tailor the standards specifically to meet their own needs. Similarly, a commitment to Investors in People requires significant time and effort, particularly in relation to the processes involved in development. The initial targets set for the number of employers seeking and achieving the Investors in People recognised status are proving to have been very ambitious.

Raskas and Hambrick (1994) show in the context of multi-functional development how business strategy, culture, skills required and individual characteristics need to be considered when deciding the exact approach to be adopted. A contingency approach to employee development strategy is therefore essential – there are no pre-packaged solutions.

Evaluation of training and development

One of the most nebulous and unsatisfactory aspects of the training job is evaluating its effectiveness, yet it is becoming more necessary to demonstrate value for money. Evaluation is straightforward when the output of the training is clear to see, like reducing the number of dispatch errors in a warehouse or increasing someone's typing speed. It is more difficult to evaluate the success of a management training course or a programme of social skills development, but the fact that it is difficult is not enough to prevent it being done.

A familiar method of evaluation is the post-course questionnaire, which course members complete on the final day by answering vague questions that amount to little more than 'good, very good or outstanding'. The drawbacks with these are, first, that there is a powerful halo effect, as the course will have been, at the very least, a welcome break from routine and there will probably have been some attractive fringe benefits like staying in a comfortable hotel and enjoying rich food. Second, the questionnaire tends to evaluate the course and not the learning, so that the person attending the course is assessing the quality of the tutors and the visual aids, instead of being directed to examine what has been learnt. Easterby-Smith and Tanton surveyed evaluation of training in fifteen organisations and concluded:

> All but one of the 15 organizations conducted some form of evaluation on a regular basis, and invariably this consisted of an end-of-course questionnaire. . . . The impression gained from training managers was that this was regarded largely as part of the ritual of course closure; they

> commented that completed questionnaires were normally filed away – the data thus produced was rarely used in decisions about training . . . if a negative comment is voiced by one individual, that criticism is often seen to reflect poorly on the individual rather than on the course.
>
> (Easterby-Smith and Tanton 1985, p. 25)

The authors then advocate the simple strategy of asking participants and their bosses to complete short questionnaires at the beginning of the course to focus their minds on what they hope to get from it. At the end of the course there is a further questionnaire focusing on learning and what could be applied back on the job. Later, they complete further questionnaires to review the effects of the course on the subsequent working performance. This overcomes the problem of the learning remaining a detached experience inducing nostalgic reflection but no action, but it also encourages the course participant to concentrate on what he or she is learning and not assessing objectively the quality of the service.

Hamblin (1974), in a well-quoted work, identified five levels of evaluation: (1) evaluating the training, as in the post-course questionnaire above; (2) evaluating the learning, in terms of how the trainee now behaves; (3) evaluating changes in job performance; (4) evaluating changes in organisation performance; and (5) evaluating changes in the wider contribution that the organisation now makes. Bramley (1996) suggests that performance effectiveness can be measured at individual, team and organisational levels, and that changes in behaviour, knowledge, skills and attitudes need to be considered. He makes the worthwhile point – as do others – that the criteria for evaluation need to be built into development activities from the very beginning, and not tagged on at the end. Bramley is a useful source of practical approaches to evaluation, as are Bee and Bee (1994).

Taking the broader issue of evaluating training in general rather than the experience of trainees, researchers at Warwick University concluded:

> Evaluation is notoriously difficult, but our research indicates that those firms which have the most positive attitudes (and carry out the most training) typically employ 'soft' criteria relating to broad human resource goals (recruitment and retention, career management etc.), and tend to be sceptical about 'hard' cost-benefit evaluation, related to bottom-line outcomes.   (Pettigrew, Sparrow and Hendry 1988, p. 31)

The amount of money available for training and development and the way in which costs are allocated and analysed within the business will have a significant impact on what development strategies are feasible, and supportable.

> The Manpower Services Commission survey calculated that with a total training expenditure of £2 billion per year, this works out at £200 per employee and represents only 0.15% of the average firm's turnover. This lack of investment is not only foolhardy but considerably below that of others: in fact only one seventh of the American figure and one fourteenth of the best in West Germany.   (Open University 1986, p. 5)

Two years later the Manpower Services Commission had become the Training Commission and had conducted a further survey (reported in Sloman 1989). This reached the conclusion that in 1986/87 British employers spent £14.4 billion on the provision of training for their workforce, which worked out at £800 per employee. Despite the wildly differing conclusions about how much is actually spent, they at least demonstrate that we do not spend as much on training as other countries, but not widespread agreement on who should pay more.

An analysis by the Industrial Society (1985) shows how companies in different areas distribute their training budget and what proportion it is of turnover. In answer to a questionnaire with 134 usable responses, 64.6 per cent of responding organisations said that they spent less than 0.5 per cent of their annual turnover on training their employees, including all twelve of the public service respondents. Only seven respondents spent more than 1.5 per cent. The items comprising the training budget were staff education schemes, equipment costs, training centres and consultants. The survey does not reveal whether salary costs for training staff are included, but 77 per cent of firms include trainees' expenses and only 35 per cent include trainees' salaries.

WINDOW ON PRACTICE

In a further analysis of the Price Waterhouse Cranfield survey, Holden and Livian (1992) compared some strategic aspects of training across ten European countries.*

Training as a recruitment strategy
All ten countries identified training as being used in recruitment strategy. In eight (not including Germany and Sweden) training for new recruits was seen as the most popular method (from a list of 11) of attracting recruits.

Knowledge of investment in training
Although all organisations had increased expenditure on training over the previous year, many were unclear about the actual money spent as a proportion of wages. However this varied by country. The three highest – Sweden (44 per cent of organisations did not know), Denmark (42 per cent of organisations did not know) and the UK (38 per cent of organisations did not know) – compare markedly with the lowest, France, where only 2 per cent of organisations did not know.

This no doubt reflects the French taxation system, where a tax is levied if the organisation does *not* spend 1.2 per cent of the paybill on training.

Actual investment in training
In only Sweden and France do more than a quarter of the organisations surveyed spend above 4 per cent of the paybill on training. With the exception of France, the majority of organisations in each of the other countries spent less than 2 per cent of their paybill on training.

Time spent on training
Only some 10 per cent of organisations provided over ten days' training per year – the exception to this being Spain, where 29 per cent of organisations provided this level of training. In all countries the amount of time for managerial training was greater than for other groups of employees

*The countries surveyed were Switzerland, Denmark, Germany, Spain, Finland, Italy, Norway, Netherlands, Sweden and the UK.

Summary propositions

21.1 The personnel/training function does not own employee development strategy – it must be owned by the organisation as a whole.

21.2 Employee development strategy needs to focus on the organisation strategy and objectives and involves identifying the skills and competencies required to achieve this, now and in the future.

21.3 Employee development strategy will also be influenced by the external labour market, government initiatives and competitor activity.

21.4 It is important that employee development strategy is reinforced by, and reinforces, other HR strategy.

21.5 The methods of employee development chosen need to be aligned not only with the competencies and skills to be developed, but also strategic position of the organisation, its culture and the individuals involved.

References

Bee, F. and Bee, R. (1994) *Training Needs Analysis and Evaluation*, London: IPM.

Bramley, P. (1996) *Evaluating Training*, London: IPD.

Buckley, J. and Kemp, N. (1987) 'The strategic role of management development', *Management Education and Development*, Vol. 18, Pt 3, pp. 157–74.

Constable, R. and McCormick, R. J. (1987) *The Making of British Managers*, London: BIM.

Easterby-Smith, M. and Tanton, M. (1985) 'Turning course evaluation from an ends to a means', *Personnel Management*, April.

Hamblin, A. C. (1974) *Evaluation and Control of Training*, Maidenhead: McGraw-Hill.

Handy, C. (1988) *Making Managers*, London: Pitman.

Harrison, R. (1993) *Human Resource Management: Issues and strategies*, Wokingham: Addison-Wesley.

Holden, L. and Livian, Y. (1992) 'Does strategic training policy exist? Some evidence from ten European countries', *Personnel Review*, Vol. 21, No. 1, pp. 12–23.

Industrial Society (1985) *Survey of Training Costs*, London: The Industrial Society.

Journal of Management Education and Development (1994) 'Anticipatory learning: learning for the twenty-first century', Vol. 12, No. 6.

Mabey, C. and Iles, P. (1993) 'Development practices: succession planning and new manager development', *Human Resource Management Journal*, Vol. 3, No. 4.

McClelland, S. (1994) 'Gaining competitive advantage through strategic management development', *Journal of Management Development*, Vol. 13, No. 5, pp. 4–13.

Miller, P. (1991) 'A strategic look at management development', *Personnel Management*, August.

Open University (1986) *Managing People*: 2, Milton Keynes: The Open University.

Pettigrew, A. M., Sparrow, P. and Hendry, C. (1988) 'The forces that trigger training', *Personnel Management*, Vol. 20, No. 12, pp. 28–32.

Raskas, D. F. and Hambrick, D. C. (1992) 'Multi-functional management development: a framework for evaluating the options', *Organisational Dynamics*, Vol. 21, Autumn.

Salaman, G. and Mabey, C. (1995) *Strategic Human Resource Management*, Oxford: Blackwell Business.

Schein, E. (1961) 'Management development as a process of influence', *Sloan Management Review*, Vol. 2, No. 2, May.

Sloman, M. (1989) 'On-the-job training: a costly poor relation', *Personnel Management*, Vol. 21, No. 2, February.

Watkins, J. (1987) 'Management development policy in a fast-changing environment: the case of a public sector service organisation', *Management Education and Development*, Vol. 18, Pt 3, pp. 181–93.

General discussion topics

1. Both the UK as a whole and organisations themselves would benefit if the government adopted an interventionist approach to training.

   ▶ Do you agree or disagree? Why?
   ▶ How might this intervention be shaped?

2. What opportunities are there for development strategy and reward strategy to be mutually supportive?
   Think of examples (real or potential) where reward strategies undermine development strategies.

CHAPTER 22

Competence, competencies and NVQs

There has always been a tension in education and training between what the trainee knows and what the trainee can do after the training is complete. Knowledge has an ancient history of being highly desirable and jealously guarded: look at the trouble the serpent got Eve into in the Garden of Eden. Our literature and our folklore are full of the value of knowledge, including its best-known aphorism by Francis Bacon four hundred years ago, that knowledge itself is power. This connection to power and influence is why access to knowledge is often surrounded by elaborate ritual requirements to ensure that possession of the knowledge remains valuable and rare.

In every country of the world education has been developed, with all its mystique and influence, to communicate knowledge and to develop understanding. In developing countries it is usually the first priority of economic growth. For all people the search for better understanding is a human quality that is self-perpetuating once the appetite has first been stimulated.

WINDOW ON PRACTICE

Many people love studying, but in some places it seems to have become a public nuisance. In a shopping mall on Orchard Road in Singapore a café proprietor concerned about the popularity of the establishment with students has a large notice: 'NO STUDYING IN THE CAFE.'

The search for knowledge also develops a prestige for certain types of knowledge and for the institutions that trade in that knowledge. In Britain and France the areas with the greatest prestige have been those that are closest to the arts and pondering the human condition: English, history, classical civilisation and language, philosophy and theology, followed by those allied to elite professions, like medicine and the law. Science took longer to achieve a similar prestige and it is still physics and chemistry that are valued ahead of engineering. Knowledge rather than practical skills carries status, and the educational institutions with the highest prestige are those universities with the strongest representation in these areas.

This preference for knowledge has carried through into the labour market. We still pay more to people who manipulate words than to those who manipulate materials. Reading the news on television pays much more than making the world's most advanced aircraft or electronic equipment. Writing computer programs for arcade games pays much more than making the equipment on which the games run. It has become very difficult to recruit able students to study physics at university, and it is a bitter frustration for their teachers that many of them will move, on graduation, to merchant banking or accountancy.

Elsewhere it is different. The inevitable comparison is with Germany and Japan, countries where the practical skills of engineering, for instance, carry much greater prestige. This comparison has increasingly led policy-makers and those in education to seek ways to shift the emphasis in education away from esoteric knowledge towards practical, vocational skills. This has proved remarkably difficult, as education is a large vested interest in any advanced society and change is resisted, however inevitable it may be. In the last half-century there have been the moves to set up technical schools in the late 1940s, which failed almost completely. We have had technological universities, many of which became universities much like any other. We had degrees in technology that were designated as BSc*, to show that they weren't real degrees at all. We had the industrial training boards in the 1960s, rapidly followed by polytechnics in the 1970s, but the training boards were abolished and the polytechnics developed degrees in social sciences more rapidly than in vocational science and engineering.

By the early 1980s government policy achieved an unprecedented degree of centralised control on schooling through the national curriculum and on higher education through controlling student numbers and having differential fee regimes. Central to this control has been a heightened emphasis on practical vocational skills: what the student is able to do that is vocationally useful when the training is complete. The end-result should be that the student is competent to do something that is useful. Furthermore, the education and training agenda has been placed under greater employer influence than previously. It is difficult to see that this has produced the desired results.

ACTIVITY BOX 22.1

Think of your own schooling. Single out three things you learned at school that have subsequently been useful to you in your working life.

Then single out the three topics or subjects which you found most interesting to study. What changes would you make if you could have your time over again?

Competencies

The vehicle for this attempted revolution has been an array of National Vocational Qualifications (NVQs), which are based on assessed competencies, so let us now see what competencies are. The basic idea of competency-based training is that it should be criterion-related, directed at developing the ability of trainees to perform specific tasks directly related to the job they are in or for which they are preparing, expressed in terms of performance outcomes and specific indicators. It is a reaction against the confetti-scattering approach to training as being a good thing in its own right, concerned with the general education of people dealing with general matters.

The key piece of research on competencies is by Richard Boyatsis, who carried out a large-scale intensive study of 2,000 managers, holding 41 different jobs in

12 organisations. He defines a competency as: 'an underlying characteristic of a person which results in effective and/or superior performance in a job' (Boyatsis 1982, p. 21).

It may be a trait, which is a characteristic or quality that a person has, like efficacy, which is the trait of believing you are in control of your future and fate. When you encounter a problem, you then take an initiative to resolve the problem, rather than wait for someone else to do it.

It may be a motive, which is a drive or thought related to a particular goal, like achievement, which is a need to improve and compete against a standard of excellence.

It may be a skill, which is the ability to demonstrate a sequence of behaviour that is functionally related to attaining a performance goal. Being able to tune and diagnose faults in a car engine is a skill, because it requires the ability to identify a sequence of actions, which will accomplish a specific objective. It also involves being able to identify potential obstacles and sources of help in overcoming them. The skill can be applied to a range of different situations. The ability to change the sparking plugs is an ability only to perform that action.

It may be a person's self-image, which is the understanding we have of ourselves and an assessment of where we stand in the context of values held by others in our environment. For example: 'I am creative and innovative. I am expressive and I care about others.' In a job requiring routine work and self-discipline, that might modify to: 'I am creative and innovative. I am too expressive. I care about others and lack a degree of self-discipline.'

It may be a person's social role, which is a perception of the social norms and behaviours that are acceptable and the behaviours that the person then adopts in order to fit in. It may be a body of knowledge.

If these are the elements of competency, some of them can be developed, some can be modified and some can be measured, but not all.

Boyatsis makes a further distinction of the threshold competency, which is: 'A person's generic knowledge, motive, trait, self-image, social role, or skill which is essential to performing a job, but is not causally related to superior job performance', like being able to speak the native tongue of one's subordinates. Table 22.1 summarises these.

Table 22.1 The seven threshold competencies identified by Richard Boyatsis

Threshold competencies

Use of unilateral power: Using forms of influence to obtain compliance.

Accurate self-assessment: Having a realistic or grounded view of oneself, seeing personal strengths and weaknesses and knowing one's limitations.

Positive regard: Having a basic belief in others; that people are good; being optimistic and causing others to feel valued.

Spontaneity: Being able to express oneself freely or easily, sometimes making quick or snap decisions.

Logical thought: Placing events in causal sequence; being orderly and systematic.

Specialised knowledge: Having usable facts, theories, frameworks or models.

Developing others: Helping others to do their jobs, adopting the role of coach and using feedback skills in facilitating self-development of others.

Competencies are required for superior performance and are grouped in clusters, shown in Table 22.2. The goal and action management cluster relates to the requirement to make things happen towards a goal or consistent with a plan. The leadership cluster relates to activating people by communicating goals, plans and rationale and stimulating interest and involvement. The human resource management cluster relates to managing the co-ordination of groups of people working together towards the organisation's goals. The focus on other clusters relates to maturity and taking a balanced view of events and people. The directing subordinates cluster relates to providing subordinates with information on performance, interpreting what the information means to the subordinates, and placing positive or negative values on the interpretation.

Table 22.2 The five clusters of management competencies by Richard Boyatsis (1982)

Management competency clusters

The goal and action management cluster:

Concern with impact: Being concerned with symbols of power to have impact on others, concerned about status and reputation.

Diagnostic use of concepts: Identifying and recognising patterns from an assortment of information, by bringing a concept to the situation and attempting to interpret events through that concept.

Efficiency orientation: Being concerned to do something better.

Proactivity: Being a disposition towards taking action to achieve something.

The leadership cluster:

Conceptualisation: Developing a concept that describes a pattern or structure perceived in a set of facts: the concept emerges from the information.

Self-confidence: Having decisiveness or presence; knowing what you are doing and feeling you are doing it well.

Use of oral presentations: Making effective verbal presentations in situations ranging from one-to-one to several hundred people (plus threshold competency of logical thought).

The human resource management cluster:

Use of socialised power: Using forms of influence to build alliances, networks, coalitions and teams.

Managing group process: Stimulating others to work effectively in group settings (plus threshold competencies of accurate self-assessment and positive regard).

The focus on other clusters:

Perceptual objectivity: Being able to be relatively objective, avoiding bias or prejudice.

Self control: Being able to inhibit personal needs or desires in service of organisational needs.

Stamina and adaptability: Being able to sustain long hours of work and have the flexibility and orientation to adapt to changes in life and the organisational environment.

The directing subordinates cluster:

Threshold competencies of developing others, spontaneity and use of unilateral power.

The Boyatsis framework is set out at some length because of its influence. It is the basis of the work carried out by many consultants in the training field. It has, however, suffered criticism. Academics were sceptical about the methods of investigation, and practitioners found the framework too complex to translate into action. Boyatzis may be slipping into history, but his work remains an invaluable point of reference because of the way it demonstrates the scale and complexity of the management job. Subsequently, definitions of competency and lists of competencies have come thick and fast from the training and development specialists. There is no need for us to add to those, but we can offer some clarification. First of all, competency is not the same as competence. Competence is the general ability to do something to an acceptable level (a competent witness, a competent answer, a competent driver) and is in contrast to incompetent, which is a pretty drastic condemnation. Competency is not as modern and trendy as many of its advocates believe. It appears in Shakespeare's *Merchant of Venice* and is a word that has long been available as an alternative to competence. What is new is its use in training in a quite specific way to describe a range of things one has to be able to do in order to achieve competence:

> A competency is a set of behaviour patterns that the incumbent needs to bring to a position in order to perform its tasks and functions with competence.
>
> (Woodruffe 1992)

Competencies in the United Kingdom

In the United Kingdom, competencies have been developed in line with other aspects of change in education, like experiential learning, problem-based learning, the national curriculum and GCSE, attempts to develop the ability of learners to do rather than to know, as well as introducing greater flexibility into the learning process, so that career aspirants are not restrained by elitist exclusiveness of either educational institutions or professional associations. This is partly due to a long-standing disappointment about British industrial performance, easily attributable to poor management (Constable and McCormick 1987). There is therefore a political momentum behind the competency movement over and above considerations of education and training. It has been heavily promoted by the Training and Enterprise Directorate of the Department for Education and Employment.

The principles of competencies leading to national vocational qualifications are:

1. **Open access**. There should be no artificial barriers to training, like it being available only to people who are members of a professional body, such as the Institute of Personnel and Development or the Law Society, or those in a particular age group.
2. There is a focus on what people can **do**, rather than on the process of learning. Masters' students in a university typically cannot graduate in less than twelve months. With competency-based qualifications, you graduate when you can demonstrate competency, however long or short a period it takes you to achieve the standard.
3. **National** vocational qualifications, which are the same wherever the training takes place, so that the control is in the hands of the awarding body rather than the training body, and there is only one strand of

qualification for each vocational area: no multiplication of rival qualifications. The overall control is with the National Council for Vocational Qualifications (NCVQ).

4. The feature of performance **standards** as the basis of assessment; not essays or written-up case studies, but practical demonstrations in working situations, or replicas, of an ability to do the job at a specified standard. Although training schemes are littered with euphoria about excellence, the competency basis has only one standard. The only degree of differentiation between trainees is the length of time taken to complete the qualification.

5. **Flexibility and modularisation**. People must be able to transfer their learning more or less at will between 'providers', so that they are not tied to a single institution and without needless regulations about attendance. Woolwich Building Society runs a scheme with one of the London universities whereby employees can obtain a BA in Business Studies without ever visiting the university itself.

6. **Accreditation of prior experience and learning**. You can accredit prior learning, no matter how you acquired it. If you have been able to acquire a competency by straightforward experience or practice at home, and if you can reach the performance standard, you can receive the credit for it. If prior experience enables you to demonstrate competency, you can receive credit for that as well.

7. The approach to training is the establishment of a **learning contract** between the provider and the trainee, whereby the initiative lies with the trainee to specify the assistance and facilities that are needed and the provider agrees to provide them. The idea of this is that the learner is active in committing to the learning process.

8. Flexibility in assessment is partly achieved by the **portfolio** principle, as you accumulate evidence of your competence from your regular, day-to-day working and submit it for assessment as appropriate.

9. **Continuous development**. Initial qualification is not enough. Updating and competence extension will be needed and failure to do this will lead to loss of qualification.

10. The standards to be achieved are determined by designated **lead bodies**, which are large committees of practitioners, or professional bodies, so that vocational standards are decided by those in charge of the workplace instead of by those in charge of the classroom. One of these is **MCI**, the Management Charter Initiative, which has set standards for management at the administrative and middle level and have recently published standards for the strategic level. These are intended to equate to Certificate, Diploma and MBA. Figure 22.1 lists the middle level standards.

11. **Assessment**. Written examinations are not regarded as being always the most appropriate means of assessing competence. Assessment of whether or not the learner has attained the appropriate standard must be by a **qualified assessor**, who becomes qualified by demonstrating competence according to two units of the scheme produced by the Training and Development Lead Body. Assessment may be partly by portfolio (see 8 above), but has to be **work-based**. Originally it was to be in the work place, but that proved impracticable to implement.

12. **General National Vocational Qualifications** are school- or college-based and take the place of BTec and similar qualifications.

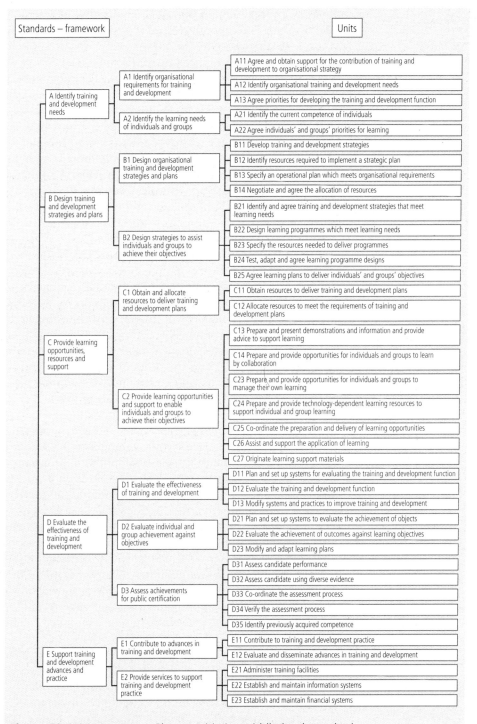

Figure 22.1 Management Charter Initiative middle-level standards

The general intention is that NVQs should run alongside traditional academic qualifications at undergraduate level.

NVQs have had a rough ride since the concept was first introduced, coming under some heavy criticism and not being extensively taken up. The most common reservations about NVQs are:

1. **Assessment**. The emphasis has been shifted away from learning towards assessment. The assessment process is itself somewhat laborious. Research by the Institute of Manpower Studies (1994) found that the most common problem about introducing NVQs was finding the time to organise the assessments. The study found that 5 per cent of employers were using NVQs and half of them reported this difficulty.
2. **Bureaucracy**. NVQs have developed an entire vocabulary to bring the concept into action, and this causes difficulties. One of the key terms is 'range indicators' and at a recent meeting of fifty personnel practitioners, no one could produce a definition that the rest of the group could accept. Also the assessment process specifies a number of different standards of performance that have to be demonstrated and assessed. Each of these has to be described succinctly and the performance measured.
3. **The generality of the standards**. Those employers who take up NVQs are likely to modify them for their own use. In a three-year research project at UMIST over twenty employer schemes for MCI have been examined, and each one is tailored to the needs of the particular business. This is for two reasons: (a) the national standards are seen as being too general, and (b) employers are concerned to train for their own needs rather than for national needs of skilled human resources. This begins to undermine the concept of a *national* qualification.
4. **The quality of the standards**. It is very difficult to ensure a satisfactory quality of assessment, where so much depends on a large number of individual assessors. The initial emphatic opposition to written examination has modified, especially as NVQs are contemplated for some of the well-established professions, such as medicine and the law.
5. **The training agenda**. Within a large vested interest like British higher education, there is obviously some resistance to the idea that educators are not competent to set the training agenda.

> There seems to be a drift towards a training agenda in management education, such that students are technically equipped to take up a task but intellectually incapable of addressing the ideas that have shaped the creation of that task.
> (Berry 1990)

One quite damning piece of research has been produced by Peter Robinson of the London School of Economics. He demonstrates that the actual take-up of NVQs is very low and has not been associated with an increase in the training available to individuals.

> Between 1991 and 1995 the only net growth in the number of all vocational qualifications awarded was at level 1 and especially level 2. There was no growth at all in the number of awards at level 3, and a slight fall in the number of awards at levels 4 and 5.
> (Robinson 1996, p. 4)

Awards of traditional vocational qualifications outstrip NVQs by a wide margin, especially at higher levels. Between 1992 and 1995:

NVQs awarded		*Traditional VQs awarded*
375,355		1,598,350
	Percentages at different levels	
26.0%	1	32.6%
63.5%	2	29.4%
8.5%	3	27.8%
1.9%	4/5	10.2%

NVQs are heavily concentrated in clerical, personal service, sales and those service sectors which are sheltered from international competition. They are under-represented in higher managerial, professional and technical occupations, in crafts, and in the internationally exposed areas of manufacturing, business and financial services.

Those who have championed the concept of employers setting the agenda are equally concerned that employers risk losing the control they have achieved.

> if we do not move towards a market system, and the Government continues to fund and intervene heavily in the development and design process, NVQs could soon be a dead duck and vocational qualifications would, once again, be knowledge-based and controlled mainly by educationalists. The opportunity for a system which matches employers' needs and individuals' aspirations to the greater benefit of UK plc would have been lost.   (Marshall 1994)

The failure of NVQs to take off has stimulated a high-level review of the whole process by senior civil servants, and it seems highly likely that there will be a fundamental change. The report was commissioned by the previous Secretary of State for Education, and it remains to be seen what the eventual policy will be, but there is a widespread belief that NVQ principles will be significantly undermined, particularly by moves to accommodate traditional vocational qualifications:

> New thinking has kindled alarm among supporters of NVQs that the system set up 10 years ago . . . is about to be fatally undermined . . . it is probable that the new framework will include hundreds of non-NVQ traditional vocational qualifications.   (Packard 1997, p. 11).

A useful review of NVQ problems and the NCVQ approach to their resolution is provided by McKiddie (1994). An excellent practical guide to the approach is in Fletcher (1991). Opposition from the academic world continues (for example, Smithers 1994), although some universities now provide programmes leading to NVQs.

Other competence-based approaches

Although there has been much controversy about NVQs, they are not the only form of competence-based training that is being provided. Boam and Sparrow (1992) describe a number of different schemes. Although competence-based training has become the received wisdom on approaches to management training, all the lists we have seen have been difficult to use in practice, mainly due to an understandable attempt to be precise or over-inclusive.

Torrington, Waite and Weightman (1992) developed a composite model to describe the work of personnel specialists working in the health service. We are therefore presenting a crude model here as a framework which could be applied to other groups of jobs. It is crude because the boundaries must be blurred: ambiguity is essential if we are to make sense.

Our analysis starts from this point, by considering not whether a person is able to do a job, but what skills are required in order to be able to do a job: not 'this is how recruitment is done', but 'these are the skills you personally need, now, in order to do recruitment excellently'. This is the approach of competence analysis, distinguishing between the competent performance of a job and the competencies required in order to perform a job excellently.

The basis of this model is an analysis of the jobs that need doing by personnel and HR managers. The following list encompasses the main areas of expertise that a large NHS personnel department could need to have. The composite is based on eight facets of the personnel operational role:

1. The personnel manager as SELECTOR
2. The personnel manager as PAYMASTER
3. The personnel manager as NEGOTIATOR
4. The personnel manager as PERFORMANCE MONITOR
5. The personnel manager as WELFARE WORKER
6. The personnel manager as HUMAN RESOURCE PLANNER
7. The personnel manager as TRAINER
8. The personnel manager as COMMUNICATOR

Every mainstream personnel management job consists of one or more of these roles. Selector and Trainer are those most commonly found to comprise a complete job. Some combination of two or three is usual. All the roles are highly interdependent. Each of these eight is then broken down into a set of *professional competencies*. An illustration is the professional competencies required in one of the eight roles, shown in Table 22.3.

Table 22.3 shows that there are some areas of overlap, so that job analysis is a technique that is used in other areas as well as selection. Each of the eight areas has a similar list.

There is also a list of generic competencies which are more general competencies used in at least two, and sometimes more, of the professional roles. These are: *managing oneself, working in the organisation, getting things done* and *working with people*.

The idea of the job composite model, therefore, is that each individual's job will be a composite of activities drawn from the professional list and from the shorter list of generic competencies. Job-specific individual training needs can then be derived by using our self-assessment questionnaire (Table 22.4), developed from these two lists of competencies.

There have been many criticisms of the type of analysis we are putting forward here, not least of which is the belief that a competence-based approach cannot take into account individual differences.

> Users of competency-based assessment should be aware that it provides one relatively partial view of performance. Its strong emphasis on the need for scientific rigour tends to lead to a rather narrow perspective which, on its own, is barely capable of reflecting the rich and often paradoxical nature of human behaviour.
>
> (Jacobs 1989, p. 36)

Table 22.3 Professional competencies in one (selector) of the personnel manager roles

The personnel manager as selector

Vacancy identification The ability to determine whether a vacancy exists and whether it needs to be filled by recruitment or by other means such as overtime or flexibility.

Job analysis The ability to examine a job or role, to identify the component parts and the circumstances in which it is performed, and to understand the variety of uses to which a job analysis can be put, e.g. as a guide to recruitment, training needs analysis, job evaluation, appraisal, and allowing individuals to see where their jobs fit in to the whole organisation. Knowledge of the process and limitations of job analysis methods.

Recruitment advertising The ability to draft succinct, attractive and effective job advertisements. Knowledge of merits and demerits of using an advertising agency and/or recruitment agency. Selection of appropriate media.

Selection process The awareness of different selection procedures and the ability to choose appropriate methods. Knowledge of benefits and problems of psychometric tests. Able to ensure that jobs are not filled 'at any price'.

Selection decision-making The ability to assess the strengths and weaknesses of a candidate on the basis of information provided, selection test data and interview assessment. The ability to identify those candidates who will fulfil the requirements of the job and the business as a whole.

Letters of offer The ability to have all communications with prospective employees (brochures, etc.) and those joining the organisation (joining instructions, etc.) conveying and, to some extent, promulgating the corporate culture.

Contracts of employment The ability to draft a contract of employment, reflecting both the job and organisation requirements and the needs of the individual employee, within a framework of legal requirements.

Induction/socialisation The ability to make the employee aware of facilities or benefits available and to assist in the development of training programme/on-the-job mentor/assignment.

Table 22.4 Personnel competencies, self-assessment questionnaire

Name _____ Date _____

Current post _____

Using the job composite model of personnel competencies, complete the following checklist by assessing your present expertise in each of the identified competencies as either A, B, C, D or E, indicating:

A   Little or no expertise;
B   Some expertise, but a need for further development or updating now;
C   Expert;
D   Considerable expertise, but some further development or updating necessary soon;
E   Not relevant to the present post.

Table 22.4 Continued

Professional competencies

1. The PM as selector
.... Vacancy identification
...... Job analysis
...... Recruitment advertising
...... Selection process
...... Psychometric testing
...... Selection decision-making
...... Letters of offer
...... Contracts of employment
.... Employee records
.... Induction/socialisation

2. The PM as paymaster
.... Job evaluation
.... Pay determination
.... Employee benefits
.... Performance-related pay
.... Salary administration
.... Salary structures
.... Pensions and sick pay
.... Taxation and National Insurance

3. The PM as negotiator
.... Consultation
.... Employee involvement
.... Negotiating bodies
.... Trade union recognition
.... Agreements and procedures
.... Grievance and discipline
.... Redundancy and dismissal
.... Industrial tribunals

4. The PM as performance monitor
.:..... Appraisal/assessment
.... Attendance management
.... Management of poor performance

5. The PM as welfare officer
.... Health and safety
.... Counselling services
.... Occupational health
.... Health and safety legislation

6. The PM as human resource planner
...... Supply and demand forecasting
.... Modelling and extrapolation
.... Manpower utilisation
.... Planning

.... Statistical method
.... Computer analysis

7. The PM as trainer
.... Identification of training needs
.... Design of training
.... Delivery of training
.... Evaluation of training

8. The PM as communicator
.... Bulletins
.... Community relations
.... Team briefing
.... In-house magazine

Generic competencies

9. Managing oneself
.... Personal organisation
.... Time management
.... Interpersonal communication
.... Assertiveness
...... Problem-solving and decision making
.... Report writing
.... Reading
...... Presentations
.... Managing stress

10. Working in the organisation
.... Networking
.... Working in groups
...... Power and authority
.... Influencing
.... Negotiating

11. Getting things done
.... Setting objectives
.... Goal planning and target setting
.... Managing external consultants
.... Using statistics
.... Information technology literacy
.... Keyboard skills

12. Working with people
.... Interviewing
.... Listening
...... Counselling
.... Conducting and participating in
        meetings
.... Team-building

One way around this problem is to construct competence analysis in terms of self-assessment, enabling staff at all levels, and varying from tyro to past master to assess their own training needs.

Our research has demonstrated the need for this approach caused by the wide differences in practice between parts of the organisation, which make it quite inappropriate to have an 'ideal' model of, for example, a personnel department. These are some of the main differences we found between Health Service Districts:

▶ The different levels of funding received.
▶ The different skills and experience of the people.
▶ The differing hierarchical position of personnel, including the relationship to the general manager.
▶ The differing relationships with Region.
▶ Differing perceptions of the personnel role held by personnel directors, their staff and their colleagues.
▶ The differing nature of the districts themselves: size, labour markets, medical specialisms, and so forth.

Below we give some hypothetical examples of the sort of competencies, both professional and generic, that particular job holders might conclude were necessary for them to do their work. These lists might be arrived at by the job holder alone or in consultation with their boss and/or colleagues.

A pay strategy post

Appropriate professional competencies:

1 Job analysis
1 Job evaluation
2 Pay determination
2 Employee benefits
2 Performance-related pay
2 Salary administration
2 Salary structures
2 Pensions/sick pay
2 Taxation and National Insurance
3 Consultation
3 Employee involvement
3 Negotiating bodies
3 Agreement and procedures
6 Planning
6 Computer analysis

Appropriate generic competencies:

9 Personal organisation
9 Interpersonal communication
9 Problem-solving and decision-making
9 Report-writing
9 Making presentations
10 Networking
10 Influencing
11 Statistics
11 Information technology literacy

11 Setting up systems and procedures
12 Conducting and participating in meetings

Most of the other competencies listed would probably be scored E (no current or foreseeable need for competence in this area). Of the competencies listed which are needed, some no doubt will have been scored A or B, suggesting some difficulty. These then need prioritising.

A recruitment officer post

Appropriate professional competencies:

1 Vacancy identification
1 Job analysis
1 Recruitment advertising
1 Selection process
1 Selection decision-making
1 Letters of offer
1 Contracts of employment
1 Induction/socialisation
3 Agreements and procedures
6 Supply and demand forecasting

Appropriate generic competencies:

9 Managing oneself
9 Time management
9 Interpersonal communication
12 Interviewing

ACTIVITY BOX 22.2

How many of the generic competencies listed in Table 22.4 are common to most jobs?

Summary propositions

22.1 There is a tension between education and training that has existed for a long time, with education carrying more status than training. Education leading to the acquisition of an ability to manipulate words and concepts usually leads to higher rewards than training in skills to manipulate materials.
22.2 The most recent attempt to strengthen vocational training has been the development of competence-based (or competency-based) qualifications, which are directed at developing the ability of trainees to perform specific tasks directly related to the work they are doing or which they are preparing to do.
22.3 The main vehicle for competency learning is the array of National Vocational Qualifications (NVQs).
22.4 In the ten years since they were initially proposed, NVQs have been continually criticised, mainly because of queries about assessment, bureaucracy, generality and the quality of the standards.

22.5 NVQs have also been resisted by two powerful vested interests: higher education and professional bodies, neither of which wishes to lose control of the training agenda.

22.6 An alternative competency-based approach is the job-composite model, based on the different roles that a job holder has to fulfil.

References

Berry, A. J. (1990) 'Masters or subjects?', *British Academy of Management Newsletter*, No. 5, February.

Boam, R. and Sparrow, P. (1992) *Designing and Achieving Competency*, Maidenhead: McGraw-Hill.

Boyatsis, R. E. (1982) *The Competent Manager*, New York: John Wiley.

Constable, J. and McCormick, R. (1987) *The Making of British Managers*, Corby: British Institute of Management.

Fletcher, S. (1991) *NVQs, Standards and Competence*, London: Kogan Page.

Institute of Manpower Studies (1994) *National and Scottish Vocational Qualifications: Early indications of employers' take-up and use*, Poole, Dorset: BEBC.

Jacobs, R. (1989) 'Getting the measure of management competency', *Personnel Management*, Vol. 21, No. 6, pp. 32–7.

Marshall, V. (1994) 'Employers beware: don't lose control of your NVQs', *Personnel Management*, Vol. 26, No. 3, pp. 30–3.

McKiddie, T. (1994) 'Personnel NVQs: preparing for take-off' *Personnel Management*, Vol. 26, No. 2, pp. 30–3.

Packard, J. (1997) 'Overhaul sparks fear for basic NVQ tenets', *People Management*, Vol. 3, No. 6, p. 11.

Robinson, P. (1996) *Rhetoric and Reality: Britain's new vocational qualifications*, London School of Economics, Centre for Economic Performance.

Smithers, A. (1994) 'Whither competences?' *Times Higher Education Supplement*, 22 April.

Torrington, D. P., Waite, D. and Weightman, J. B. (1992) 'A continuous development approach to training health service professionals', in *Journal of European Industrial Training*, Vol. 16, No. 3, pp. 3–12.

Woodruffe, C. (1992) 'What is meant by competency?' in R. Boam and P. Sparrow, *Designing and Achieving Competency*, Maidenhead: McGraw-Hill.

General discussion topics

1. The Boyatsis approach to competence-based management training has been criticised as being too complicated. Do you agree?

2. In 1996 a review of NVQs included the following comment:

   A widely-held view was that NVQs/SVQs worked best when they were focused on the workplace and that they were less suitable for those preparing to enter employment . . . for unemployed people or those in employment seeking new job opportunities, there was difficulty in accessing workplace assessment.

   How could that difficulty be overcome?

3. What are the differences between skill, competence and competency?

CHAPTER 23

Management development

If we want to develop managers so that they are effective contributors to the organisation, we need to have a clear view of what an effective contribution would look like. The use of personal competencies, as described in Chapter 22, can be helpful in describing the way that an effective manager behaves, but the truth is that there can be no universal prescription of an effective manager. Effectiveness will vary with organisational context, and on whose perspective we are adopting. What makes an effective manager is a complex of personality, innate skills, developed skills, experiences and learning.

In this chapter we do not attempt prescription. What we do is consider the growth and identity of management development, review some differing perspectives on its nature and goals, and in particular concentrate on the processes that contribute towards management development.

The growth of management development

There is a strong myth-making tradition attached to the development of effective management as those senior in organisations have sought to preserve their elite status. Initially, there was no question of acquiring skill; entry to a management position came as part of the right of ownership, the favour of the owner or the natural entitlement of those in a particular social position. As the size of organisations and the number of managers began to increase, there was a move to professionalisation to justify managerial status, with the development of professional or quasi-professional bodies, controlling entry by examination and election. This, together with organisational complexity, produced specialisation and the longest-running feature of management development: management training courses. Run by educational establishments, professional bodies, employers or consultants, there is a wide range of courses which seek to communicate some distilled wisdom relating to the management task. Although the training course is well established, it was joined during the 1960s by a fresh idea – that of developing individuals. Instead of managers being fed information in a course, their managerial capacity and potential would be developed by a wide variety of experiences, through which they would acquire greater understanding, awareness, sensitivity, self-confidence and those other aspects of effectiveness that were regarded as most important, but that could not be inculcated. This change of emphasis was accompanied by a growing use of employee appraisal to determine individual development needs, rather than leaving trainers to produce universal programmes. There was also some move towards putting the control of the development programme in the hands of the individual being developed, instead of the experts. In reporting on one such experiment Graves concludes: 'managers are better able to develop their own skills if given development opportunities rather than training . . . training should be based on managerial needs as perceived by the managers rather than development needs perceived by the trainers' (Graves 1976, p. 15). Furthermore, such development may well take place on the job in the everyday ebb and flow of events rather than in the specially contrived circumstances beloved by trainers. In this way the learning is not only relevant to the job being done, it may also alter the manager's approach to his work as he or she becomes more questioning of events and more analytical of processes: 'The remarkable and persuasive reason for saying that nonetheless managers can become more effective as learners lies in the dedication to doing things, being active, that is the hallmark of so many of them' (Mumford 1981, p. 380). Mumford continues by suggesting that the art of encouraging learning is 'to ask them to undertake activities associated with learning which build on existing managerial processes and rewards' (*ibid.*).

The focus in management development has moved on to emphasise activities such as coaching, action learning, natural learning and self-development. In line with this increased emphasis on learning in the job, there has also been an upsurge of interest in mentoring, which, like many of the best management development ideas, describes a process that is long familiar to experienced managers, but is substantially unrecognised and underused (Mumford 1985). This process is largely uncontrolled at present, although there is a clear increase in formal mentoring schemes. An understanding of mentoring and of the contributions of peers gives critical insight into the role of work relationships in the development of managers.

Interest in mentoring has also highlighted a particular problem for the development of women managers – that of finding a role model. It appears that, for the few women who are mentors or protégés, the nature of the relationship is different from that of men. This brings us to the thorny problem of whether the training and development needs of women managers are different from those of men, and whether there should be separate development programmes especially for women.

The identity of management development

We can see from the above that management training contributes to management development but is not synonymous with it, as managers also learn and develop in many other ways. Management training and management development can be differentiated in four important ways:

1. Management development is a broader concept and is more concerned with developing the whole person rather than emphasising the learning of narrowly defined skills.
2. Management development emphasises the contribution of formal and informal work experiences.

3. The concept of management development places a greater responsibility on managers to develop themselves than is placed on most employees to train themselves.

4. Although in training generally there always needs to be a concern with the future, this is especially emphasised in management development. Managers are developed as much for jobs that they will be doing as for the jobs that they are doing. Both the organisation and the managers benefit from this approach. Management development is a vital aspect of career management, and from the organisation's point of view both are methods of satisfying human resource needs while allowing individuals to achieve their career goals.

ACTIVITY BOX 23.1

▶ How can individual managers identify their own development needs?

▶ How can they be proactive in meeting these needs?

What do managers do?

> The question 'what do managers do?' has an air of naiveté, insolence and even redundancy about it. Yet it is a question which is begged by many management-related issues. . . . The vast and growing industry of management education, training and development presumably rests upon a set of ideas about what managers do and, hence, what managers are being educated, trained and developed for.
>
> (Hales 1986, p. 88)

There has been much theorising and uncertainty about the nature of managerial work. Managerial work has been studied from a variety of perspectives, including what managers do, how they distribute their time, with whom they interact, informal aspects of their work and themes that pervade management work (Hales 1986).

Among the mass of theorising has been the research of Rosemary Stewart (1976) in analysing work in terms of the relationships involved, and also some common recurrent management activities which are liaison, maintenance of work processes, innovation and setting the boundaries of the job. Mintzberg (1973) suggests that managerial work comprises various combinations of ten distinct roles in three general categories: decision-making, interpersonal and information-processing. Earlier, Scholefield (1968) had produced the suggestion that managers should do three things: operate the firm, make innovations and stabilise the organisation. Other management researchers (for example, Torrington and Weightman 1982) have concentrated on the nature of the skills involved in management work, and have investigated how managers' time is allocated between the technical, administrative and managerial aspects of their jobs. Leavitt (1978) suggests four key ideas about the nature of the managing process. First, managing always includes some influencing and implementing activities, as managers have to get other people to do things. Second, managing also includes a lot of problem-solving, with managers not only having to work against tight deadlines, but also work on a dozen problems at the same time.

Third, managers have to be problem-finders, and need to take an active rather than an entirely passive stance.

A final aspect of managing, as suggested by Leavitt (1978), is that it takes place in an organisation and that managers operate in a position that is peculiarly dependent, while seeming to be independent.

One of the central themes of managerial work is that, to a large extent, managers define the work that they will do. This is undoubtedly one of the factors which makes managerial work so hard to characterise. Hales comments that: 'Managerial jobs seem, in general, to be sufficiently loosely defined to be highly negotiable and susceptible to choice of both style and content' (Hales 1986, p. 101). And Fletcher carries this point further: 'Management is neither art nor science nor skill. At base there is nothing to do. A manager is hired for what he knows other firms do, what he can find to do, and what he can be told to do' (Fletcher 1973, p. 136).

Hales (1986) comments that this opportunity for choice and negotiation, together with variation and contingency, pressure and conflict, and lack of opportunity for reflection are central themes in managerial work. In the same vein Mumford (1987) characterises the *reality* of management as very different from the logical rational and organising processes that it may superficially appear to be about. He suggests that management is an interactive activity with multi-programmed tasks being carried out at a hectic pace and dependent on the use of informal networks. In addition, he argues that a manager's work is more often constrained than innovative and unplanned rather than proactive. It is clearly useful to have an understanding of management activities, but the *realist* school has been criticised for abstracting activities from the institutional arrangements in which and through which they act (Willmott 1987) and for separating activity from their purpose, and in particular, their relationship with the survival of the organisation (Carroll and Gillen 1987). Watson (1994) reflects the context of management well when he describes managers as 'organising: pulling things together and along in a general direction to bring about long term organisational survival'. A further issue is that in the final event management is a political activity.

All these ideas clearly have a bearing on the objectives of management development. However, a useful counterblast to all this theorising is the iconoclasm of Alistair Mant (1977), whose scepticism is so perceptive and persuasive that one is left with the feeling that he might just be right when he argues that we tend to undervalue a large number of jobs that are of true social and economic importance, such as salesman and housewife, while ascribing enormous significance to the job of manager, which seems non-existent in some of the world's more successful industrial societies.

The goals of management development

Undoubtedly, those people who design management development programmes and experiences aim to encourage the development of effective managers. One of the greatest difficulties is that although there is a lot of research about what managers do, much less is written about the relationship between this and their effectiveness. Hales (1986) comments that some of the more celebrated writings on effective management are singularly reticent about specifying what effective managers are effective at. We have already noted that the use of competency description can be helpful here, but some of the most helpful comments have been made by Pedler *et al.* (1991) who identify eleven necessary qualities of effective managers. These include command of basic facts, relevant professional knowledge, continuing sensitivity to events, problem-solving and decision-making skills, social skills, emotional resilience, proactivity, creativity, mental agility, balanced learning habits and skills and self-knowledge. A glance back at Mumford's characterisation of the reality of management will show some immediate contradictions. We can only conclude that there is much uncertainty about what managers do, and it is not surprising therefore that the goals of management development are often uncertain and frequently spurious. The goals of the organisers of development may differ markedly from those undergoing the process. Among the generalisations we can make are that management development has traditionally been an elitist process, although this may be changing with greater development for all; emphasis will be on skills at doing, rather than knowledge about; and dominant will be the capacity of the individual manager to be socially adroit and to evaluate information as a preliminary to making choices between alternatives.

Lees (1992) identifies ten purposes (explicit and implicit) of management development. Apart from the most popular rationale, that of performance improvement, he identified others which were indirectly related to performance, such as socialisation, where the aim is to reduce conflict by developing a common perspective and a common language. Other rationales, more distant from performance, were the political reinforcement of those shaping the organisation's vision; compensation, a type of welfare substitute in order to make work more bearable; and ceremonial, which represented passages in the status of managers. Research into a management development programme for hospital ward sisters, in which one of the authors was involved, revealed that for many of these sisters the management development programme served most noticeably as a rite of passage from a nursing to a management role (Holman and Hall 1996).

Following on from the last section we would suggest that it would be fruitful, among other things, to develop managers who can structure their own jobs and manage themselves and their careers. Much of the management development that takes place does so without any externally imposed goals – it takes place in the context of the job and is guided to a greater or lesser extent by managers themselves. The capacity of managers to develop others is increasingly seen as fundamental. The process of managerial development at work has been identified as incurring emotional costs (Snell 1988) and this may influence the goals themselves.

We move on to review some aspects of organising development experiences, including informal and formal training input. We discuss the nature of management learning, and based on this, how learning techniques and support can be used together with job experiences to contribute to their development as managers.

Approaches to management development

Education and training courses

A training course will usually be a key feature in a formal programme of development, and these may be standard offerings by various specialist bodies or in-house courses developed for their own specialist needs. Increasingly, these options are being combined so that there is the possibility of an externally provided course tailored to suit an organisation's particular needs.

First are the pre-experience courses: full-time education leading to academic qualification with a management sciences or business studies label and undertaken by young people as a preliminary to a career. These have been developing in the United Kingdom since the middle 1960s and have proved very popular with students at universities and polytechnics. They are often described as 'vocational' and intended to be a practical preparation for a management-type occupation on completion. They can never, however, be vocational in the same sense as degrees in areas such as medicine or architecture, because there is relatively little practical element in the course. The sandwich courses that incorporate periods of work in the 'real' world may help to bring the feet of students nearer to the ground, but they cannot give any meaningful experience in, and practice at, managerial work. The courses provide an education, normally based on a study of the academic disciplines of economics, mathematics, psychology and sociology and incorporating some work in the more specialised disciplines like industrial relations and organisational behaviour, as well as an introduction to the practical areas like accounting, marketing, personnel and production. The student should emerge with a balanced understanding of the workings of an industrial society and an industrial economy, and they will have some useful blocks of information which may well be at the frontiers of knowledge in management thought. The student should also have developed the more traditional qualities of maturity and the ability to analyse and debate that university education purports to nurture: they will not be trained to be a manager.

Second are the post-experience courses: full-time education usually leading to a diploma or master's degree with a management or business label and undertaken during a career. Although such courses were being run in this country early in the twentieth century, the great boom came after the establishment of the London and Manchester Business Schools and other management centres in the 1960s. The main difference is not only that students are older, but that they study on the basis of experience they have had and with the knowledge of the work to which they will return. Members of a course at a business school may be seconded or supported on a part-time basis by their employer at a time when they have already held a management post. The material of the course may not be very different from that of the pre-experience course, but the student's perception will be very different and their application of any new insights or skills will be more immediate.

Neither pre-experience nor post-experience courses of the type described here will feature strongly the skills element mentioned above.

The third category can be generally described as consultancy courses. Varying from a half-day to several weeks in length, they are run by consultants or professional bodies for all comers. They have the advantage that they bring together people from varying occupational backgrounds and are not, therefore, as introspective as in-house courses and are popular for topical issues. They are, however, often relatively expensive and superficial, despite their value as sources of industrial folklore, by which we mean the swapping of experiences among course members.

The most valuable courses of this type are those that concentrate on specific areas or knowledge, like developing interviewing or disciplinary skills, or being introduced to a new national initiative. This short-course approach is probably the only way for managers to come to terms with some new development, such as a change in legislation, because they need not only to find an interpretation of the development, they also need to share views and reactions with fellow managers to ensure that their own feelings are not idiosyncratic or perverse.

A fourth category is in-house courses which are often similar in nature to the consultancy courses. Such in-house courses are often run with the benefit of some external expertise, but this is not always the case. In-house courses can be particularly useful if the training needs to relate to specific organisational procedures and structures, or if it is geared to encouraging managers to work more effectively together in the organisational environment. The drawbacks of in-house courses are that they suffer from a lack of breadth of both content and input from managers, and there is no possibility of learning from people in other organisations.

Lastly, and on the fringe of education and training courses, are outdoor-type (sometimes known as outward-bound) courses. Outdoor courses attempt to develop such skills as leadership, getting results through people, self-confidence in handling people, and increasing self-awareness through a variety of experiences, including outdoor physical challenges. One course brochure states:

> A range of intellectual, emotional and physical challenges is presented which involves working in a variety of environments; in group syndicate rooms, outdoor project areas, creative workshops, on rivers and lakes and in the hills and mountains.
>
> (Brathay 1986)

Courses like these continue to be increasingly used, and their differential value is assumed to hinge on their separation from the political, organisational, environment. A natural, challenging and different environment is assumed to encourage individuals to forsake political strategising, act as their raw selves and be more open to new ideas. Burleston and Grint (1996), based on ethnographic research into outdoor programmes, found that whilst most participants did gain from the experience, the idea of providing a de-politicised environment is a naive hope rather than a reality.

The nature of learning

There has been a significant amount of work done which helps us understand how managers, and others, learn from their experiences. Kolb *et al.* (1984) argue that it is useful to combine the characteristics of learning, which is usually regarded as passive, with those of problem-solving, which is usually regarded as active. From this combination Kolb *et al.* developed a four-stage learning cycle, which was further developed by Honey and Mumford (1989).

The four stages, based on both influences, are shown in Figure 23.1.

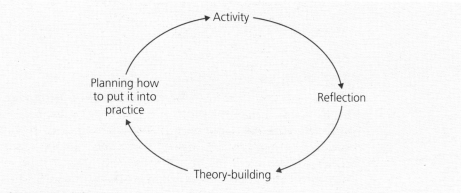

Figure 23.1 The learning cycle

WINDOW ON PRACTICE

Gwen is a management trainer in a large organ-isation running a number of in-house manage-ment courses. She has just moved into this position from her role as section leader in the research department; the move was seen as a career development activity in order to strengthen her managerial skills.

Gwen is working with her manager to learn from her experiences. Here is an extract from her learning diary based on the learning cycle:

Activity – I've had a go at running three sessions on my own now, doing the input and handling the questions.

Reflection – I find the input much easier than handling questions. When I'm asked a question and answer it I have the feeling the they're not

convinced by my reply and I feel awkward that we seem to finish the session hanging in mid-air. I would like to be able to encourage more open discussion.

Theory building – If I give an answer to a ques-tion it closes off debate by the fact that I have 'pronounced' what is 'right'. If I want them to discuss I have to avoid giving my views at first.

Planning practice – When I am asked a question rather than answering it I will say to the group: 'What does anyone think about that?' or 'What do you think? (to the individual who asked) or 'What are the possibilities here?' I will keep encouraging them to respond to each other and reinforce where necessary, or help them change tack by asking another question.

Each of these four stages of the learning cycle is critical to effective learning, but few people are strong at each stage and it is helpful to understand where our strengths and weaknesses lie. Honey and Mumford designed a questionnaire to achieve this which identified individuals' learning styles as 'activist', 'reflector', 'theorist' and 'pragmatist', and explain that:

Activists learn best from 'having a go', and trying something out without necessarily preparing. They would be enthusiastic about role play exercises and keen to take risks in the real environment.

Reflectors are much better at listening and observing. They are effective at reflecting on their own and others' experiences and good at analysing what happened and why.

Theorists' strengths are in building a concept or a theory on the basis of their analysis. They are good at integrating different pieces of information, and building models of the way things operate. They may choose to start their learning by reading around a topic.

Pragmatists are keen to *use* whatever they learn and will always work out how they can apply it in a real situation. They will plan how to put it into practice. They will value information/ideas they are given only if they can see how to relate them to practical tasks they need to do.

An understanding of the way that managers learn from experience is paral-leled by a change in emphasis in management development from formal training course offering to learning through the job itself, with appropriate support. The remainder of approaches to management development rely heavily on learning from experience.

Understanding our strengths and weaknesses enables us to choose learning activities which suit our style, and also gives us the opportunity to decide to strengthen a particularly weak learning stage of our learning cycle. Whilst Honey and Mumford adopt this dual approach, Kolb firmly maintains that learners *must* become deeply competent at all stages of the cycle. There has been considerable attention to the issue of matching and mismatching styles with development activities: see, for example, Hayes and Allinson (1996), who also consider the matching and mismatching of trainer learning style with learner learning style.

ACTIVITY BOX 23.2

Identify a management skills area which you need to develop. (You may find it particularly helpful to choose an interpersonal area, for example, assertiveness, influencing others, presentation, being more sociable, contributing to meetings, helping others.)

Keep a learning diary over the next few weeks logging anything that is relevant to your development area. Use the framework which Gwen used on page 436.

At the end of the period review what you have learned in your development area and also what you have learned about the learning cycle.

Action learning

The iconoclasm of Mant (1977), referred to earlier in this chapter, is mild compared with that of Revans (see, for example, Revans 1972, 1974), one of the great original thinkers to study management. As a professor of management he became more and more disenchanted with the world of management education that he saw developing around him. Among the many aphorisms attributed to him was: 'If I teach my son to read, how do I know he will not read rubbish; if I teach him to write, how do I know that he will not write yet another book on management education?' Despairing of the way in which the London and Manchester Business Schools were established, Revans resigned his chair in Manchester and moved to Belgium to start his first action learning project. This was based on his conviction that managers do not need education, but the ability to solve problems. His method has been basically to organise exchanges, so that a manager experienced in one organisation is planted in another to solve a particular set of problems that is proving baffling. He or she brings a difference of experience, a freshness of approach, and is not dependent on new, temporary, organisational peers for career growth. They work on the problem for a period of months, having many sessions of discussion and debate with a group of other individuals similarly planted in unfamiliar organisations with a knotty problem to solve. The learning stems from the immediate problem that is presented, and from all the others that emerge, one by one, in the steps towards a solution. This presents a need that the student has to satisfy and all the learning is in terms of what they discover they need to know, rather than what someone else feels is necessary. It is an idea of startling simplicity. Its relative unpopularity in academic circles is easy to understand, but in management circles there has been some diffidence because the action learning approach nearly always stirs something up, and not all organisations have the nerve to risk the soul-searching and upheaval that are caused.

Coaching

Coaching is an informal approach to management development based on a close relationship between the developing manager and one other person, usually their immediate manager, who is experienced in management. The manager as coach helps trainees to develop by giving them the opportunity to perform an increasing range of management tasks, and by helping them to learn from their experiences. They work to improve the trainee's performance by asking searching questions, discussion, exhortation, encouragement, understanding counselling, and providing information and feedback. It is vital that the coach is someone who has experienced those things which the trainee is now learning. Henry Boettinger, that most elegant of writers on management, makes the point:

> Only someone who can actually perform in an art is qualified to teach it. There is no question that constructive criticism from an informed bystander is helpful; actors, for instance, can learn a great deal about human motivation from psychiatrists. Nevertheless, this kind of procedure is different from the one an actor goes through to show another how to express human feelings.
>
> (Boettinger 1975)

The coach, as the immediate manager of the learner, is also in an excellent position to provide the appropriate learning opportunities in terms of new/challenging tasks, membership of working parties and committees, secondments, deputising and so on. Mumford (1994) has written an excellent guide to the ways that managers can help other managers to learn.

Mentoring

> As a training and development tool, it [mentoring] is not a new concept. For centuries wise men have offered counsel to the young. In ancient Greece, Odysseus entrusted the education of his son Telemachus to a trusted counsellor and friend. This trusted and wise friend, Mentor, reputedly became the counsellor, guide, tutor, coach, sponsor and mentor for his protégé, Telemachus.
>
> (Hunt and Michael 1983)

Mentoring is seen as offering a wide range of advantages for the development of the protégé, coaching as described above being just one of the benefits of the relationship. The mentor would occasionally be the individual's immediate manager, but more often it is a more senior manager in the same or a different function. Kram (1983) identifies two broad functions of mentoring: first, career functions, which are those aspects of the relationship that primarily enhance career advancement; and second, psychosocial functions, which are those aspects of the relationship that primarily enhance a sense of competence, clarity of identity and effectiveness in the managerial role. Figure 23.2 shows these functions in more detail and compares them with the functions of peer relationships, which we discuss in the following section. There is a much greater stress in the mentoring relationship than in the coaching relationship, on career success, and individuals selected for mentoring, because, among other things, they are good performers, from the right social background and know the potential mentors socially (Kanter 1977). There are advantages in the relationship for mentors as well as protégés. These include reflected glory from a successful protégé, the development of supporters throughout the organisation, and the facilitation of their own promotion by adequate training of a replacement (Hunt and Michael 1983).

Managers are also seen as responsible for developing talent, and mentorship may be encouraged or formalised as, for example, in the Bell Laboratories and some departments of the US Government (Stumpf and London 1981). The difficulties of establishing a formal programme include the potential mismatch of

Mentoring relationships

Career-enhancing functions
▶ sponsorship
▶ coaching
▶ exposure and visibility
▶ protection
▶ challenging work assignments

Psychosocial functions
▶ acceptance and confirmation
▶ counselling
▶ role modelling
▶ friendship

Special attribute
▶ complementarity

Peer relationships

Career-enhancing functions
▶ information sharing
▶ career strategising
▶ job-related feedback

Psychosocial functions
▶ confirmation
▶ emotional support
▶ personal feedback
▶ friendship

Special attribute
▶ mutuality

Figure 23.2 Development functions – comparison of mentoring and peer relationships (Kram and Isabella 1985). Reproduced with permission of the American Academy of Management

individuals, unreal expectations on both sides, and the time and effort involved. Gibb and Megginson (1993) surveyed a number of formal mentoring schemes and describe that such UK schemes offer a slightly different perspective from the US approach. They argue from the literature and from their research that the mentoring relationship is multi-faceted, and that in the UK in particular there is greater emphasis than in the US on learning support, often based around the restructuring of our qualification system. In these situations the protégés were more likely to have specific learning goals. An example might be mentoring in support of achieving MCI competencies or other competency-based qualifications. In the formal schemes surveyed, just under half the protégés were working on a learning contract (see page 442 for further details).

Four mentoring roles were identified by Gibb and Megginson from the literature: helping to improve performance, helping career development, acting as a counsellor and sharing knowledge. Burke and McKeen (1989) offer a thoughtful discussion of the advantages and disadvantages of formal programmes.

Peer relationships

Although mentor–protégé relationships have been shown to be related to high levels of career success, not all developing managers have access to such a relationship. Supportive peer relationships at work are potentially more available to the individual and offer a number of benefits for the development of both individuals. The benefits that are available depend on the nature of the peer relationship, and Kram and Isabella (1985) have identified three groups of peer relationships which are differentiated by their primary development functions and which can be expressed on a continuum from 'information peer' through 'collegial peer' to 'special peer'. Table 23.1 shows the developmental functions and the characteristics of each type of relationship. Most of us benefit from one or a number of peer relationships at work but often we do not readily appreciate

Table 23.1 Peer relationships and the characteristics of each type.

	Information peer	Collegial peer	Special peer
Primary functions	Information-sharing	Career strategising Job-related feedback Friendship	Confirmation Emotional support Personal feedback Friendship
Level of commitment	Demands little, but offers many benefits	Information-sharing joined by increasing level of self-disclosure and trust	Equivalent of best friend
Intensity of relationship	Social, but limited in sharing of personal experience	Allows for greater self-expression	Strong sense of bonding
Issues worked on	Increases individual's eyes and ears to organisation (work only)	Limited support for exploration of family and work issues	Wide range of support and work issues
Needs satisfied	Source of information regarding career opportunities	Provides direct honest feedback	Offers chance to express one's personal and professional dilemmas, vulnerabilities and individuality

Source: Adapted from Kram and Isabella (1985, pp. 199–20). Reproduced with permission of the American Academy of Management.

their contribution towards our development. Peer relationships most often develop on an informal basis and provide mutual support. Some organisations, however, formally appoint an existing employee to provide such support to a new member of staff through their first 12–18 months in the organisation. These relationships may, of course, continue beyond the initial period. The name for the appointed employee will vary from organisation to organisation, and sometimes the word 'coach' or 'mentor' is used – which can be confusing! Cromer (1989) discusses the advantages of peer relationships organised on a formal basis and references the skills and qualities sought in peer providers, which include accessibility, empathy, organisational experience and proven task skills.

ACTIVITY BOX 23.3

Consider each significant peer relationship that you have at work. Where does each fit on the continuum of relationships shown in Table 23.1, and what contributions does it make towards your development?

If you are in full-time education consider the contribution that each of your relationships (whether univerisity, home, work) has to your development.

Natural learning

Natural managerial learning is learning that takes place on-the-job and results from managers' everyday experience of the tasks that they undertake. Natural learning is even more difficult to investigate than either coaching, mentoring or peer relationships, and yet the way that managers learn from everyday experiences, and their level of awareness of this, is very important for their development. Burgoyne and Hodgson (1983) collected information from managers by having them 'think aloud' while doing their work. They identified three levels of learning. The first level is when the manager took in some factual information that had an immediate relevance but did not have any long-term effect on his view of the world in general. At the next level the manager learnt something that was transferable from the present situation to another – they had changed their conception about a particular aspect of their view of the world in general, this aspect being situation-specific. For example, managers use incidents to add to their personal stock of 'case law' and from this select models when dealing with future situations. In some cases managers specifically set aside time for reflective learning so that they can derive critical insights and new approaches for use in the future. Some managers also learnt through deliberate problem-solving: Burgoyne and Hodgson describe a manager who was unhappy with the way that he used his time, and who tried a new approach, was unsatisfied and so tried another, liked it and kept it. Level three learning was similar to level two, but not as situation-specific. Perhaps one of the most valuable insights from this research is that some learning occurred as a direct result of the research process, due to managers verbalising what was happening or had happened, and thus becoming more conscious of the processes taking place. Mumford comments: 'In my view the focus should be on what managers do and how they can be helped to learn from what they do' (Mumford 1985, p. 30).

Self-development

To some extent self-development may be seen as a conscious effort to gain the most from natural learning in a job. The emphasis in self-development is that each individual is responsible for, and can plan, their own development, although they may need to seek help when working on some issues. Self-development involves individuals in analysing their strengths, weaknesses and the way that they learn, primarily by means of questionnaires and feedback from others. This analysis may initially begin on a self-development course, or with the help of a facilitator, but would then be continued by the individual back on the job. From this analysis individuals, perhaps with some help at first, plan their development goals and the way that they will achieve these, primarily through development opportunities within the job. When individuals consciously work on self-development they use the learning cycle in a more conscious way than described in natural learning above. They are also in a better position to seek appropriate opportunities and help, in their learning, from their manager.

Many of the activities included in self-development would be based on observation, collecting further feedback about the way they operate, experimenting with different approaches, and in particular reviewing what has happened, why and what they have learned. A manager's guide to self-development has been published by Pedler, Burgoyne and Boydell (1991), which provides some structured analyses and activities for managers to work through.

Honey and Mumford (1989) have also produced a *Manual of Learning Opportunities* which is helpful in this respect.

A logical extension of self-development within the job is the development of career planning where individuals can work through a guidebook which helps them identify their career goals, the ways they learn, and their development needs, liaising with their supervisor to check assumptions, share information and receive help. This process has been described by Burgoyne and Germain (1984) in relation to research staff at Esso, and we shall return to this aspect of development in Chapter 24.

Self-development groups

Self-development or management learning groups are another way in which managers can support their development. Pedler (1986) describes how self-development groups originated from his work on individual self-development and provides an insight into how groups operate and develop.

Typically, a group of managers is involved in a series of meetings where they would jointly discuss their personal development, organisational issues and/or individual work problems. Groups may begin operating with a leader who is a process expert, not a content expert, and who therefore acts as a facilitator rather than, but not to the complete exclusion of, a source of information. The group itself is the primary source of information and as their process skills develop they may operate without outside help. The content and timings of the meetings can be very flexible, although clearly if they are to operate well, they will require a significant level of energy and commitment. Blennerhasset (1988) gives an example of using such groups prior to further development of information technology and demonstrates changes in individual attitudes and behaviour and beneficial effects for the organisation.

Self-development groups can be devised in a variety of contexts. They can be part of a formal educational course, for example the Diploma in Management Studies, where a group of managers from different organisations come together to support their development; they constitute the whole of a self-development 'course'; or they can be an informal group within an organisation. However the group originates, it is important that the group understands what every member hopes to get out of the group, the role of the facilitator (if there is one), the processes and rules that the group will operate by and how they agree to interact. Martin (1988) identifies some of the problems and issues in running self-development groups, particularly the nature of the facilitator role.

Learning contracts

There is increasing use of management learning contracts – sometimes used within more formalised self-development groups; on other management courses; as part of a mentoring or coaching relationship; or in working towards a competency-based qualification. These contracts are a formal commitment by the learner to work towards a specified learning goal, with an identification of how the goal might be achieved. Boak (1991) has produced a very helpful guide to the use of such contracts and suggests that they should include:

⟩ an overall development goal,
⟩ specific objectives in terms of skills and knowledge,
⟩ activities to be undertaken,
⟩ resources required,
⟩ method of assessment of learning.

The value that individual managers gain from learning contracts is dependent on their choice to participate, their identification of the relevant goal and the importance and value they ascribe to achieving it. Only with commitment will a learning contract be effective, because ultimately it is down to the individual learner manager to make it happen.

WINDOW ON PRACTICE

David wanted to improve his influencing skills and has sent the following draft learning contract to his manager for discussion:

Goal
To improve my influencing skills with both peers and more senior managers.

Specific objectives
To prepare for influencing situations.
To try to understand better the perspective of the other.
To identify the interpersonal skills required – probably active listening, reflecting, summarising, stating my needs, collaboration (but maybe more).
To be able to identify that I have had more influence in decisions made.

Activities
Watch a recommended video on influencing skills.
Re-read my notes from the interpersonal skills course I attended.

Watch how others in my department go about influencing.
Ask other people (supportive ones) how they go about it.
Identify possible influencing situations in advance, and plan for what I want and what might happen.
Reflect back on what happened, and work out how to do better next time.
Ask for feedback.

Resources
Video.
Notes.
The support of others.

Assessment
I could ask for feedback from colleagues and my manager.
My own assessment may be helpful.
Make a log over time of decisions made and my originally preferred outcome.

Appraisal, performance management and MbO

Although different in their emphasis these approaches have been grouped together as they provide some similarities in terms of management development. They can all provide some performance targets and feedback on the extent to which they have been achieved. Some developmentally-based performance management systems include specific development goals as well as performance goals, aiming for integration between the two, with an emphasis on coaching as the key development mechanism.

We have identified the main approaches to management development and have focused on learning from the work itself with support. Management development is, however, no solution to incorrect selection. Many organisations have produced competency profiles of what makes an effective manager in their context, and not all of these are easily developable – for example, creativity and being socially at ease. Sisson (1994) suggests that some of the desirable indicators for managers in the future are being an active analyst, willing to take risks, strong personal goals and wide vision. As we noted in Chapter 5, Kanter (1989) believes that the organisation of the future will require seven particular qualities from managers – the ability to operate without relying on hierarchy; competing in a way that enhances rather than undercuts co-operation; a high standard of ethics; humility to learn new things; a process focus; to be multi-faceted and ambidextrous and to gain satisfaction from results rather than contribution. Again, some of these are not so easy to develop from a very low base level. We suggest that those qualities which are harder to develop should be key criteria in the selection process.

WINDOW ON PRACTICE

Increasing attention has been given to the need to develop international managers, although specific development needs will depend on the definition of 'international managers' which is used (Storey 1992). Various lists have been produced of the key competencies, for example Zeneca (Carr 1994) identify conceptual thinking; strategic thinking; cultural adaptability; flexibility; concern for standards and impact; strategic influencing; results orientation and development orientation. The most important competencies (picked by over a quarter of respondents) identified in an Ashridge study (Barnham and Oates 1991) were identified as strategic awareness; adaptability to new situations; sensitivity to different culture; ability to work in international teams; language skills, understanding international marketing, relationship skills, international negotiating skills and self reliance – in that order.

The picture is further complicated by different cultural conceptions of management in different countries – for example, the differential emphasis on leadership/people skills, rational/analysis skills and technical/engineering skills. Lawrence (1992) contrasts different values and their impact on management development in Britain, France and Germany.

Summary propositions

23.1 The emphasis on formal development programmes is declining in favour of greater interest in approaches to on-the-job development, such as mentoring, peer relationships and self-development.

23.2 Management development is different from management training as it is broader and geared more towards the future. It places a greater responsibility on managers to develop themselves.

23.3 There is great uncertainty about what managers do, and to some extent managers define their own jobs. It would be fruitful to help them to develop the skills to do this.

23.4 It is critical to help managers to learn from their own experiences. It is also critical for managers to develop skills in helping others to develop.

23.5 Management development is no substitute for poor management selection.

References 445

References

Barnham and Oates (1991) in J. Storey (ed.) (1992) 'Making European Managers: an overview', *Human Resource Management Journal*, Vol. 3, No. 1.

Blennerhasset, E. (1988) 'Research report: Management learning groups – a lesson in action', *Journal of European Industrial Training*, Vol. 12, No. 8, pp. 5–12.

Boak, G. (1991) *Developing Managerial Competencies. The management learning contract approach*, London: Pitman.

Boettinger, H. M. (1975) 'Is management really an art?', *Harvard Business Review*, January–February.

Brathay (1986) *Brathay Leadership and Development Training*, Ambleside, Cumbria: Brathay.

Burgoyne, J. G. and Germain, C. (1984) 'Self-development and career planning: an exercise in mutual benefit', *Personnel Management*, April.

Burgoyne, J. G. and Hodgson, V. E. (1983) 'Natural learning and managerial Action: a phenomenological study in the field setting', *Journal of Management Studies*, Vol. 20, No. 3.

Burke, R. J. and McKeen, C. A. (1989), 'Developing formal mentoring programs in organizations', *Business Quarterly*, Vol. 53, Pt 3, pp. 76–9.

Burleston, L. and Grint, K. (1996) 'The deracination of politics: outdoor management development', *Management Learning*, Vol. 27, No. 2, pp. 187–202.

Carr, R. (1994) 'The development of a global human resource management approach in ZENECA Pharmaceuticals', in D. Torrington (ed.), *International Human Resource Management*, Hemel Hempstead: Prentice Hall.

Carroll, S. J. and Gillen, D. J. (1987) 'Are the classical management functions useful in describing work?', *Academy of Management Review*, Vol. 12, No. 1, pp. 38–51.

Cromer, D. R. (1989) 'Peers as providers', *Personnel Administrator*, Vol. 34, Pt. 5, pp. 84–6.

Fletcher, C. (1973) 'The end of management', in J. Child (ed.), *Man and Organisations*, London: George Allen & Unwin.

Gibb, S. and Megginson, D. (1993) 'Inside corporate mentoring schemes – a new agenda of concerns', *Personnel Review*, Vol. 22, No. 1, pp. 40–54.

Graves, D. (1976) 'The managers and management development', *Personnel Review*, Autumn.

Hales, C. P. (1986) 'What do managers do? A critical review of the evidence', *Journal of Management Studies*, Vol. 53, No. 1.

Hayes, J. and Allinson, C. W. (1996) 'The implications of learning styles for training and development: a discussion of the matching hypothesis', *British Journal of Management*, Vol. 7, pp. 63–73.

Holman, D. and Hall, L. (1996) 'Competence in management development: rites and wrongs', *British Journal of Management*, Vol. 7, pp. 191–202.

Honey, P. and Mumford, A. (1989) *A Manual of Learning Opportunities*, Maidenhead: Peter Honey.

Hunt, D. M. and Michael, C. (1983) 'Mentorship: a career training and development tool', *Academy of Management Review*, Vol. 8, No. 3.

Kanter, R. M. (1977) *Men and Women of the Corporation*, New York: Basic Books.

Klatt, L. A., Murdick, R. G. and Schuster, F. E. (1985) *Human Resource Management*, Columbus, Ohio: Charles E. Merrill.

Kolb, D. A., Rubin, I. M. and McIntyre, J. M. (1984) *Organization Psychology*, 4th edn, Englewood Cliffs, NJ: Prentice Hall.

Kram, K. E. (1983) 'Phases of the mentor relationship', *Academy of Management Journal*, Vol. 26, No. 4.

Kram, K. E. and Isabella, L. A. (1985) 'Mentoring alternatives: the role of peer relationships in career development', *Academy of Management Journal*, Vol. 28, No. 1.

Lawrence, P. (1992) 'Management development in Europe: a study in cultural contrast', *Human Resource Management Journal*, Vol. 3, No. 1, pp. 11–23.

Leavitt, H. J. (1978) *Management Psychology*, 4th edn, Chicago: University of Chicago Press.

Lees, S. (1992) 'Ten faces of management development', *Management Education and Development*, Vol. 23, Pt 2, pp. 89–105.

Mant, A. (1977) *The Rise and Fall of the British Manager*, Basingstoke: Macmillan.

Martin, P. (1988) 'Self-development groups in the context of a structured management development programme', *Management Education and Development*, Vol. 19, Pt 4, pp. 281–97.

Mintzberg, H. (1973) *The Nature of Managerial Work*, London: Harper & Row.

Mumford, A. (1981) 'What did you learn today?', *Personnel Management*, August.

Mumford, A. (1985) 'What's new in management development?', *Personnel Management*, May.

Mumford, A. (1987) 'Using reality in management development', *Management Education and Development*, Vol. 18, Pt 3.

Mumford, A. (1994) *How Managers Develop Managers*, Aldershot: Gower.

Pedler, M. (1986) 'Developing within the organisation – experiences of management self-development groups', *Management Education and Development*, Vol. 17, Pt 1, Spring, pp. 5–21.

Pedler, M., Burgoyne, J. and Boydell, T. (1991), *A Manager's Guide to Self-development*, 3rd edn, London: McGraw-Hill.

Revans, R. W. (1972) 'Action learning – a management development programme', *Personnel Review*, Autumn.

Revans, R. W. (1974) 'Action learning projects', in B. Taylor and G. L. Lippitt (eds.), *Management Development and Training Handbook*, Maidenhead: McGraw-Hill.

Scholefield, J. (1968) 'The effectiveness of senior executives', *Journal of Management Studies*, May.

Sisson, K. (1994) *Personnel Management – A comprehensive guide to theory and practice*, 2nd edn, Oxford: Blackwell.

Snell, R. S. (1988) 'The emotional cost of managerial learning at work', *Management Education and Development*, Vol. 19, Pt 4, pp. 322–40.

Stewart, A. and Stewart, V. (1976) *Tomorrow's Men Today*, London: Institute of Personnel Management.

Stewart, R. (1976) *Contrasts in Management*, Maidenhead: McGraw-Hill.

Storey, J. (1992) 'Making European managers: an overview', *Human Resource Management Journal*, Vol. 3, No. 1, pp. 1–10.

Stumpf, S. A. and London, M. (1981) 'Management promotions: individual and organizational factors influencing the decision process', *Academy of Management Review*.

Torrington, D. and Weightman, I. (1982) 'Technical atrophy in middle management', *Journal of General Management*, Vol. 7, No. 4.

Watson, T. J. (1994) *In Search of Management: culture, chaos and control in managerial work*, London: Routledge.

Willmott, H. (1987) 'Studying managerial work: a critique and a proposal', *Journal of Management Studies*, Vol. 24, pp. 249–70.

General discussion topics

1. If learning is an individual process, why is so much training done in groups? What are the implications of moving towards more individualised learning?
2. Discuss the view that the role of the trainer/facilitator is critically important in the effectiveness of a training programme.

CHAPTER 24

Career development

WINDOW ON PRACTICE

June had applied for four promotions over the last two years. She knew she was ready to move on, but had been turned down on each occasion. There was no feedback from her manager about her applications, but she was beginning to think that her career had come to a dead end.

Larry, with a PhD in chemistry, was appointed to a junior research role four years ago, and he was promoted to a senior post two years ago. He saw his role as limited and he felt he was wasting his talents. There was no logical promotion route from where he was, unless he wanted to move into management which he didn't. Larry saw his only option as moving out of the organisation.

Brenda performed really well in a senior production role. She could see only two potential promotions in the function and these were not likely to become available within the next five years. She wanted to move into marketing which would provide a fresh challenge and broaden her perspective. Her manager kept blocking her efforts to move, continued to express her value to the production function, and told her to be patient.

Phil was trapped. He was at the top of the unqualified scientist career ladder and the company had indicated that this was as far as he would go. He didn't think studying for a degree would improve his chances much either. He was well paid and tempted to stay put, although he felt bored and frustrated and had ceased to perform to the best of his ability.

Sarah felt as if she didn't count. She loved her job in the sales support team and was good at what she did. She did however want more, but not too much more. The next logical move was to apply for a position as a representative and her manager had indicated she stood a fair chance of success. This was no good to her at present as she did not feel able to combine the travelling with her family responsibilities. What she would have liked was some challenging expansion of her current role. Her requests were ignored – her manager had defined her as 'not a career woman'.

Some of the problems outlined in these five examples include lack of feedback on career development possibilities; lack of a technical promotion ladder to run in parallel with a management promotion ladder; avoidance of cross-functional moves; the desire to hold on to good people rather than encouraging their development elsewhere; lack of support for those individuals who are not seen as having the potential to move to a more senior position; lack of development opportunities within current job and the writing off of those people who do not conform to standard career development patterns. These problems typify a lack of attention to career development in the organisation. We suggest that organisations ignore career development at their peril, even for those organisations who feel that they can no longer offer long term careers, as we discuss later on.

In this chapter we shall look at the changing context of career development and then offer some definitions of career development, and consider why it is important both to the individual and the organisation. Following this we shall review some of the concepts behind career development and the impact of current employment and social characteristics on careers. We then explore what we can do to manage our own careers and what organisations can do to support this process and reap the benefits of it.

The context of career development

Careers are changing. It is now much more likely that individuals will progress in a variety of organisations rather than remaining with one for the whole of their working lives. It is also more likely that they will make one or more career transitions, that is, changing to a different career area in the same or a different organisation, during their working lives. The opportunities for upward promotion in organisations is decreasing as organisations are delayered and activities are contracted out, and yet this remains the most desirable career move for many employees. Organisations continue to work on making lateral moves and career development through job expansion a more realistic and attractive alternative. Constant organisation change and reshaping makes career planning over the longer term an exercise in fortune-telling, and in any case there is clear evidence that individuals do not plan their careers to any great extent. Yet as the old psychological contract, in which the organisation promised a long-term career in return for loyalty and commitment, is less widely relevant, individuals are expected to take charge of their own careers. The psychological contract between employer and employee needs to be renegotiated (see, for example, Herriot and Pemberton 1996). Male careers are becoming increasingly similar to the traditional fragmented pattern of women's careers (Goffee and Nicholson 1994), and there is evidence that many are generally keener to develop careers which take account of personal and family needs, including children's education, partner's career and quality of life. Career development is no longer a stand-alone issue and needs to be viewed in the context of the life and development of the whole person and not just the person as employee.

Definitions and importance of career development

A career can be defined as the pattern or sequence of work roles of an individual. Traditionally, the word would be applied only to those occupying managerial and professional roles, but increasingly it is seen as appropriate for everyone in relation to their work roles. Also traditionally, the word career has been used to imply upward movement and advancement in work roles whereas we now recognise other moves as legitimate expressions of career development, including development and extension within the job itself.

We view career development as something experienced by the individual (sometimes referred to as the *internal* career), and therefore not necessarily bounded by one organisation. This also means that the responsibility for managing a career is with the individual, although the organisation may play a key role in facilitating and supporting this.

The primary purpose of career development, then, is to meet the needs of the individual at work, although clearly it makes sense to meet organisation needs at the same time where this is possible. Career success is seen through the eyes of the individual, and can be defined as individual satisfaction with career through meeting personal career goals, whilst at the same time making a contribution to the organisation. In this respect our perspective differs from, say, Stamp (1989), who in her article on career development gives the needs of the individual and the organisation equal weight. Although in this chapter we prioritise the needs of the individual, in Chapter 4 we prioritise the needs of the organisation when we review replacement and succession planning.

Given the priority we have given to the individual in career development, it is also worth noting the general benefits that this can provide for the organisation as it:

- makes the organisation attractive to potential recruits,
- enhances the image of the organisation, by demonstrating a recognition of employee needs,
- is likely to encourage employee commitment and reduce staff turnover,
- is likely to encourage motivation and job performance as employees can see some possible movement and progress in their work, and perhaps most importantly,
- exploits the full potential of the workforce.

Before we look at how individuals can manage their career development and how organisations can support this, we need to review some of the concepts underlying the notion of career, as an understanding of these is important for both the individual and the organisation in selecting the most appropriate career activities.

Understanding careers

Career development stages

Many authors have attempted to map out the ideal stages of a successful career. These are compatible with the life stages outlined by such writers as Levinson *et al.* (1978). More specifically, Schein offers nine stages of the career life-cycle and these are shown in Table 24.1. Other authors, such as Super (1980) and Hall and Nougaim (1968), have suggested five. In this section we use the five stages outlined by Greenhaus and Callanan (1994).

Stage 1: occupational choice: preparation for work

Greenhaus and Callanan suggest that this stage may last until around age 25, or may reappear for those who wish to change career later in life. It involves the development of an occupational self-image. The key theme is a matching process

Table 24.1 Schein's stages of the career development cycle

0–21	Growth, fantasy, exploration
16–25	Entry into the world of work
16–25	Basic training
17–30	Full membership in early career
25 plus	Full membership in mid-career
35–45	Mid-career crisis
40 plus	Late career
40 plus	Decline and disengagement
	Retirement

Source: Schein (1978, pp. 40–6).

between the strengths/weaknesses, values and desired life-style of the individual and the requirements and benefits of a range of occupations. One of the difficulties that can arise at this stage is a lack of individual self-awareness. There are countless tests available to help identify individual interests, but these can only complete part of the picture. Perhaps more effective are structured exercises, which help people look at themselves from a range of perspectives. Other problems involve individuals limiting their choice due to social, cultural, gender or racial characteristics. We often use role models to identify potential occupations. On some occasions these extend the range of options we consider, but this process may also close them down. Another difficulty at this stage is gaining authentic information about careers which are different from the ones pursued by family and friends.

Stage 2: organisational entry

There is some overlap between stage 1 and stage 2 which occurs, typically, between the ages of 18 and 25, involves the individual in both finding a job which corresponds with their occupational self-image, and in starting to do that job. Problems here centre on the accuracy of information that the organisation provides, so that when the individual begins work expectations and the reality are very different. Recruiters understandably 'sell' their organisations and the job to potential recruits, emphasising the best parts and neglecting the downside. Applicants often neglect to test out their assumptions by asking for the specific information they really need. In addition, schools, colleges and universities have, until recently, only prepared students for the technical demands of work, ignoring other skills that they will need, such as communication skills, influencing skills and dealing with organisational politics. To aid organisational entry, Wanous (1992) has suggested the idea of realistic recruitment whereby organisations present a more balanced view of what to expect from the organisation and the job. Candidates are then in a better position to choose for themselves, and if they choose to join, they have a more accurate picture of what to expect. There is evidence to suggest that pointing out the negative as well as the positive aspects of a job does not deter applicants from accepting an offer. Once someone has joined the organisation, appropriate induction programmes and a mentoring scheme can facilitate an understanding of what the job and organisation are really like.

Stage 3: early career – establishment and achievement

The age band for early career is suggested by Greenhaus and Callanan as between
25 and 40 years.

The establishment stage involves the process of fitting into the organisation and
understanding how things are done around here. The new recruit not only needs
to learn the specific tasks of the job, but also how the organisation works and what
things are rewarded and punished. Individuals seek to be recognised as belonging
and need some form of approval from the organisation. Thorough induction programmes are important, but more especially it is important to provide the new
recruit with a 'real' job and early challenges rather than a roving commission from
department to department with no real purpose (as often found on trainee
schemes). Feedback and support from the immediate manager are also key.

The achievement part of this stage is concerned with demonstrating competence and gaining greater responsibility and authority. It is at this stage where
access to opportunities for career development becomes key.   Development
within the job and opportunities for promotion and broadening moves are all
aided if the organisation has a structured approach to career development involving career ladders, pathways or matrices. Feedback remains important, as do
opportunities and support for further career exploration and planning.

Stage 4: mid-career

Greenhaus and Callanan suggest that this stage usually falls between the ages of
40 to 55, and may involve further growth and advancement or the maintenance
of a steady state. In either case it is generally accompanied by some form of re-
evaluation of career and life direction. A few will experience decline at this stage.
For those individuals who continue to advance, organisational support as described
above remains important. For others a different type of support may be required as
some people whose career has reached a plateau will experience feelings of failure.
Motivation and job performance may decrease. Greenhaus and Callanan suggest
that organisational support in these cases needs to involve the use of lateral
career paths, job expansion, developing these individuals as mentors of others,
further training to keep up to date and the use of a flexible reward system.

Stage 5: late career

The organisation's task in this stage, from 50 onwards, is to encourage people to
continue performing well. Despite the stereotypes that abound defining older
workers as slower and less able to learn, Mayo (1991) argues that if organisations

believe these employees will do well and treat them as such, then they will perform well. Greenhaus and Callanan point out that the availability of flexible work patterns, clear performance standards, continued training and the avoidance of discrimination are helpful at this stage, combined with preparation for retirement.

The profile of a traditional/ideal career and some alternatives are shown in Figure 24.1.

Career anchors

Based on a longitudinal study of 44 male Sloan graduates completed in 1973, 10–12 years after graduation, Schein identified a set of five 'career anchors' and proposed that these explained the pattern of career decisions that each individual had taken. Schein (1978) described career anchors as much broader than motivation, and inclusive of the following:

▶ self-perceived talents and abilities,
▶ self-perceived motives and needs,
▶ self-perceived attitudes and values.

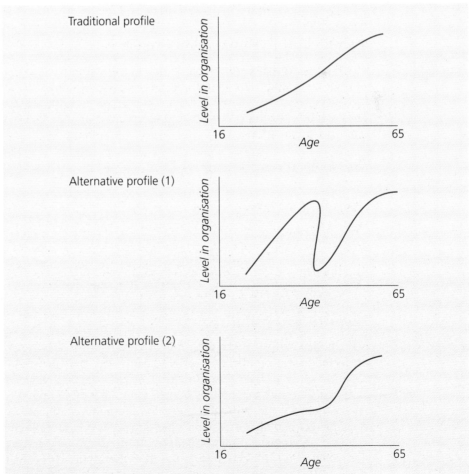

Figure 24.1 Traditional ideal and alternative career profiles

Our perception of ourselves in these areas comes from direct experiences of work – from successes, from self-diagnosis and feedback. The conclusions that the individual comes to through work experiences both drive and constrain future career development. Schein sees career anchors as a holistic representation of the person, which takes into account the interaction between the factors identified above. Career anchors can be used to identify a source of stability in the person which has determined past choices and will probably determine future ones.

The most problematic aspect of career anchors is the accuracy of the individual's self-perceptions, and the question of what happens in mid-career to those who feel their attitudes and values are changing. Schein acknowledges that career anchors are learned rather than reflecting latent abilities. The identification and assessment of one's own career anchors can be very helpful to those who do not feel comfortable with the career path they are following.

Career anchors are the sort of things that people are very reluctant to abandon. Not only do we all need to identify and understand what our anchors are in order to make sure we are doing the right thing, we also need to appreciate that there are things that we shall continue to need even if we make a career change.

Schein originally identified five career anchors and later supplemented them with another four. Schein suggests that people may have more than one career which is important to them. The original five are:

Technical/functional competence

Those who have this as their career anchor are interested in the technical content of their work and their feelings of competence in doing this. They tend not to be interested in management itself, as they prefer to exercise their technical skills. They would, however, be prepared to accept managerial responsibilities in their own functional area.

Managerial competence

For those with this career anchor, the exercising of managerial responsibility is an end in itself, and technical/functional jobs just a way of getting there. These individuals are most likely to end up in general managerial jobs and possess three key competences. The first is analytical competence to solve problems with incomplete information in areas of uncertainty. The second is the interpersonal competence to influence and control; and the third is emotional resilience, and the ability to be stimulated by crises rather than be paralysed by them.

Security and stability

It is characteristic of those with this career anchor to be prepared to do what the organisation wants of them in order to maintain job security and the present future benefits which go with this. They will conform to the organisation's requirements and trust that they will be well looked after. Most will therefore remain with one organisation for life, although there are alternative patterns such as remaining in the same geographical area whilst moving between different employers, and making separate financial provision for the future. Because they have not sought career success in terms of hierarchical promotion those with this career anchor often feel a sense of failure, and find it hard to accept their own criteria for career success. This group are more likely to integrate career with home life.

Creativity

Individuals with creativity as a career anchor feel the need to build something new. They are driven by wanting to extend themselves, get involved in new ventures and projects and could be described as entrepreneurial. Should their new ventures turn into thriving businesses they may become bored by the need to manage it and are more likely to hand this aspect over to others.

Autonomy and independence

The desire to be free of organisational constraints in the exercise of their technical/functional competence is what drives those with this career anchor. These people tend to find organisational life restrictive and intrusive into their personal lives and prefer to set their own pace and work style. They will usually work alone or in a small firm. Consultants, writers and lecturers are typical of the roles that this group occupy.

The four additional anchors which Schein proposed are:

Basic identity

Those with this career anchor are driven by the need to achieve and sustain an occupational identity. Typically these people are in lower-level jobs where their role is represented visually perhaps with badges or uniforms. In this way their role is defined externally, and some may seek for example to be associated with a prestigious employer.

Service to others

The driving force here is the need to help others, often through the exercise of interpersonal competence or other skills. The need is not to exercise such competence as an end in itself, but for the purpose of helping others; typical examples here would be teachers and doctors.

Power, influence and control

This career anchor can be separate from the managerial anchor or may be a pronounced part of it. Those driven by this career anchor may pursue political careers, teaching, medicine, or the church as these areas may give them the opportunity to exercise influence and control over others.

Variety

Those who seek variety may do so for different reasons. This career anchor may be relevant for those who have a wide range of talents, who value flexibility or who get bored very easily.

Derr (1986) proposed an alternative set of career types with the emphasis on the development of this aspect of self-identity as an ongoing process. Derr's five types are shown in Table 24.2.

Table 24.2 Derr's career orientations (1986)

Getting high	Excited by the actual content of the work done
Getting ahead	Motivated by advancement in their chosen field and will want to climb the organisation's career ladder
Getting secure	Seeking a solid position in the organisation
Getting free	Seeking an autonomous working environment to create and structure one's own work
Getting balanced	Values career but attaches greater importance to family and other non-work interests

Complicating issues and organisational implications

Much of the original work done on describing career stages and career anchors was carried out by analysing the experiences of those who were both male and white, so the analyses are clearly inadequate for our contemporary world of work. The development by Schein of his original set of career anchors is an indication of how understanding is being reshaped, but we still lack satisfactory explanations of career development that can embrace the full variety of ethnic backgrounds, gender and occupational variety.

There is considerable evidence that racial minorities and women limit their career choices, both consciously and unconsciously, for reasons not to do with their basic abilities and career motives. Social class identity may have the same impact. Employers need at least to be aware of such forces and ideally would explore such constraints with their employees to encourage individual potential to be exploited to the full.

The acceptance of such idealised career development stages as described above leaves little room for family and other interference in career development, and until recently there has been no place in career development and even in the thinking about careers for those who do not conform to the career stages outlined. There are hopeful signs of increasing recognition that career and life choices need to be explored in unison. There has also been little recognition of the commercial environment and the impact that this has on career development stages for many individuals. We look at four major influences below: parenting; partner's career; lifestyle values, and the demise of the old psychological contract.

Parenting

Parenting is a powerful influence, particularly, but *not only*, on women's careers. This may create the desire to take a few years out from employment; putting a halt on advancement aspirations while children are young; or taking a different career path which combines more effectively with child-raising. Pringle and Gold (1989) note that the interruption of a woman's career pathway is often identified as one of the reasons for the lower status and salary they receive in management positions. Such people are often classified as not interested in their career development. The following quote from a female chartered accountant, reported by Lewis and Cooper (1989), is telling:

> If you are trying to get back into the profession at the age of 40, there isn't much chance. This is the problem, the child rearing years are the same years

when you have to build your career. For a woman who drops out for a period of, say five to ten years, it would be difficult to get back. You would be out of touch anyway.

A more positive reaction would be to view their career development curve as having a different, but equally legitimate shape.

WINDOW ON PRACTICE

Jennifer is a thoroughly professional lecturer who appears to enjoy her job immensely. When asked about her career ambitions she described her present job as taking time out of her career plan. Prior to lecturing she was committed to her role as Personnel Adviser in a large company and had ambitions to be Personnel Director. On the birth of her children she knew that she could not effectively combine her Personnel Adviser role and childrearing to her satisfaction. Hence her decision to take a different career path for ten years with the objective of returning to industry when her children were older.

Paul was a lecturer in the same department, and was intent upon an academic career. Soon after he joined he agreed with his partner to take sole responsibility for the children. Over the next eleven years Paul did little research and publication but concentrated very effectively on his teaching role. When his children left home he devoted all his energy to his career, taking on much more responsibility and applying for promotion. He had delayed the start of the 'achievement' phase of his career and consequently pursued it more intensely and desired that his employer would support his continued promotion at a later stage in his life.

Partner's career

Career choices are increasingly likely to be taken in combination with the career choice of a partner rather than in isolation, although the burden of adapting one's own career choices to fit in with those of a partner still falls on women. Traditional patterns of job-seeking activity for dual-career couples would be for the man to choose a job first and the woman to follow. Lewis and Cooper (1989) identify a range of alternatives, including direct reversal of the traditional pattern. More egalitarian strategies are that:

- each partner seeks opportunities independently and the best joint option is chosen,
- both partners seek to be employed by the same organisation on a joint basis,
- both partners share the same job,
- each partner selects the best opportunity for them and geographical distance is dealt with by one partner living away from home during the working week.

As alternative strategies become more common, career decisions become more complex and organisations need to work harder at understanding and working with the influences at play. Geographical mobility generally becomes more difficult, and Evans (1986) notes that resistance to this is increasing.

Changing lifestyle values

As we move towards the end of the 1990s there is increasing evidence that, for some, the value of work is changing. While the 1980s were characterised by the idea that 'lunch is for wimps', there has been a shift, perhaps encouraged by increasing work intensification and pressure, towards valuing a slower and gentler pace, which allows more room for personal interests, environment and family. 'Downshifting' has been described as swapping a life of total commitment to work and possible high rewards, for less demanding, or part-time, work or self-employment – or a combination of the three. Guides on how to downshift are increasingly appearing (for example, Ghazi and Jones 1997), which help individuals evaluate the best option for themselves, recognising both the sacrifices and the benefits. To some extent this movement, may be the rationalisation of lack of traditional career opportunities and the need to develop a portfolio career, but the protagonists make a pretty convincing case of downshifting from choice.

Demise of the old psychological contract

Many organisations can no longer offer a traditional career, or can only offer this to a selected few. Enforced redundancies, short-term contracts, availability of part-time rather than full-time work, all break the idealised image of career. This, however, does not mean the abandonment of the concept of career, and the idea of a new psychological contract is developing. The foundation of this is that employees offer high productivity and total commitment while with their employer, and in return the employer offers enhanced *employability* rather than long-term employment. The offer of employability centres on giving employees the opportunity to develop skills that are in demand, and allows them the opportunities to practise these and keep up to date. This support is intended to equip the employee with the skills and experiences they need to obtain another appropriate job when they are no longer needed by their present employer.

Individual career management

If we identify a career as the property of the individual, then clearly the responsibility for managing this rests on the individual, who should identify career goals, adopt strategies to support them and devise plans to achieve the goal.

In reality, however, there is a considerable amount of research indicating that many people fail to plan. Pringle and Gould (1989), for example, found a lack of career planning in their sample of fifty 'achieving' men and women managers. Only around a quarter of people had plans for the future and many identified luck, opportunity or being in the right place at the right time as the reason they had achieved promotions. Harlan and Weiss (1982) found both men and women drifting into positions created through coincidences.

Of course, we don't know how well these people would have done had they planned – they may have done even better. Whether this is the case or not, we would argue that planning is an essential ingredient of individual career management even if only to provide a framework for decisions about the opportunities that arise through identification of priorities. We would also argue that the more an individual attempts to manage their career, the more likely it is that opportunities will arise and the more likely we are to be able to do something constructive with them.

Mayo suggests that in defining a career goal it is too difficult for a person to try to specify the ultimate goal of their career. He suggests that career aiming points are more appropriate if based on a 10–15-year timespan, maybe shorter for younger people. This lines up well with Greenhaus and Callanan, who provide a strong case for career goals to be identified in the context of the career stage which the individual has reached at the time. They also argue that career management needs to be an ongoing process, and suggest a career management model, appropriate to any stage in the career development cycle, an adapted version of which we show in Figure 24.2.

A career goal will be specific to the individual – for example, to become an internal senior organisational consultant by the age of 35. The range of strategies that an individual may adopt in pursuit of their goal can be described in terms of more general groups. The list below describes the type of strategies, identified from a review of the literature by Gould and Penley (1984).

▶ **Creating opportunities**. This involves building the appropriate skills and experiences that are needed for a career in the organisation. Developing those skills which are seen as critical to the individual's supervisor and department are most useful, as is exercising leadership in an area where none exists at present.

▶ **Extended work involvement**. This necessitates working long hours, both at the workplace and at home, and may also involve a preoccupation with work issues at all times.

▶ **Self-nomination/self-presentation**. The individual who pursues this strategy will communicate the desire for increased responsibility to their managers. They will also make known their successes, and build an image of themselves as someone who achieves things.

▶ **Seeking career guidance**. This involves seeking out a more experienced person, either within the organisation or without, and looking for guidance or sponsorship. The use of mentor relationships would come into this category.

▶ **Networking**. Networking involves the development of contact both inside and outside the organisation in order to gain information and support.

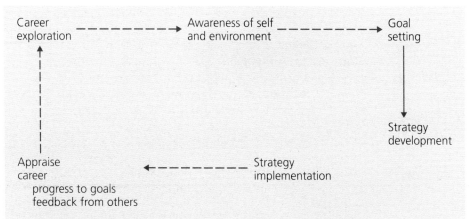

Figure 24.2 Career management model. Adapted from *Career Management*, 2nd edition, by Jeffrey Greenhaus and Gerald Callanan. Copyright © 1993/4 by Harcourt Brace and Company

▶ **Interpersonal attraction**. This strategy involves building the relationship with one's immediate manager on the basis that they will have an impact on career progression. One form of this is 'opinion conformity'; that is, sharing the key opinions of the individual's manager, perhaps with minor deviations. Another is expressed as 'other enhancement', which may involve sharing personal information with one's manager and becoming interested in similar pursuits.

Gould and Penley interviewed 414 clerical, professional and managerial employees of a municipal bureaucracy to establish which strategies they used to relate this to salary progression as one indicator of career progression. They found the following:

▶ Managers used these strategies more than non-managers.
▶ Non-plateaued managers used them more than plateaued managers.
▶ Salary progression was related to the use of extended work involvement, creating opportunities, and for non-managers only 'other enhancement'.
▶ Men were more likely to use extended work involvement than were women.
▶ For managers the use of networking and self-nomination/self-presentation were best related to salary progression.

These results obviously need to be interpreted in the context of the employing organisation – different career strategies will be most effective in different contexts. The findings are still illuminating and there are some clear pointers here to the disadvantages that women experience with career progression – for example, the greater limitations on extended work involvement and the difficulty of breaking into male networks:

women in management often find it difficult to break into the male-dominated 'old boy network' and therefore are denied the contacts, opportunities and policy information it provides.

(Davidson and Cooper 1992, p. 129)

The career strategies explored above are clearly most appropriate in the early and mid-career stages, and other strategies will best fit other stages.

ACTIVITY BOX 24.2

What general types of career strategy would be appropriate for:

▶ organisational entry?

▶ late career?

Compare your views with people you know who are in each of these career stages.

While the strategies above were derived from careers within an organisational context, similar strategies could be appropriate for employees forced to look more widely in developing their careers. Waterman *et al.* (1994), in an article on the career resilient workforce, suggest that individuals need to:

▶ Make themselves knowledgeable about relevant market trends.
▶ Understand the skills and knowledge needed in their area and anticipate future needs.

▶ Be aware of their own strengths and weaknesses.
▶ Have a plan for increasing their performance and employability.
▶ Respond quickly to changing business needs.
▶ Move on from their current employer when a win/win relationship is no longer possible.

Organisational support for career development

Although career management is primarily the individual's responsibility, there is a great deal that organisations can do to support this. Organisations can help individuals with:

▶ Career exploration – providing tools and help for self-diagnosis and supplying organisational information.
▶ Career goal-setting – providing a clear view of the career opportunities available in the business, making a wider range of opportunities available to meet different career priorities.
▶ Career strategies and action planning – providing information and support; what works in this organisation; what's realistic.
▶ Career feedback – providing an honest appraisal of current performance and career potential.

The ways that organisations can make this contribution is through the following activities:

Career pathways and grids

A career path is a sequence of job roles or positions, related via work content or abilities required, through which an individual can move. Publicised pathways are helpful to an individual in identifying a realistic career goal within the organisation. Traditional pathways were normally presented as a vertical career ladder. The emphasis was on upward promotion within a function, often formally or informally using age limits and formal qualifications for entry to certain points of the ladder. Joining the pathway at other than the normal entry point was very difficult. These pathways tended to limit career opportunities as much as they provided helpful information. The emphasis on upward movement had the result that career progress for the majority was halted early on in their careers. The specifications of age and qualification meant that the pathways were restricted to those who had an 'ideal' career development profile (for example, it excluded those who had taken career breaks, or who had lots of relevant experience but no formal qualifications). Lack of flexibility in these pathways tended to stifle cross-functional moves and emphasised progression via management rather than equally through development of technical expertise. An example of a traditional career pathway is shown in Figure 24.3.

There is now increasing use of alternative approaches, which are often designed in the form of a grid, with options at each point, so that lateral, diagonal and even downwards moves can be made, as well as the traditional upwards ones. In addition, these grids may be linked into grids for other parts of the business, and therefore facilitate cross-functional moves. Ideally, positions are described in

Figure 24.3 Traditional career pathway

behavioural terms, identifying the skills, knowledge and attitudes required for a position rather than the qualifications needed or age range anticipated. An example of a career grid is shown in Figure 24.4.

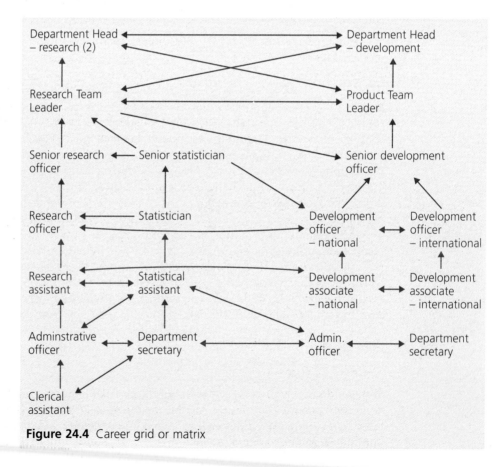

Figure 24.4 Career grid or matrix

Not only do career pathways and grids need to be carefully communicated to employees, they also need to reflect reality, and not just present an ideal picture of desirable career development. Managers who will be appointing staff need to be fully apprised of the philosophy of career development and the types of move that the organisation wishes to encourage. It is important that the organisation reinforces lateral moves by developing a payment system that rewards the development of skills and not just organisation level.

Managerial support

Managerial support is critical, not only in terms of appointing staff, but also in supporting the career development of their current staff. Direct feedback on current performance and career potential is vital, especially in the form of strengths and weaknesses, and what improvement would be critical. The immediate manager is in a good position to refer the individual to other managers and introduce them into a network which will support their career moves. In addition the manager is in the ideal position to provide job challenges and experiences within the current job which will equip the incumbent with the skills needed for the desired career move. Walker notes that:

> The manager can provide valuable input in terms of honest feedback relative to the individual's capabilities, information about the organisation's needs and future direction, and ideas and suggestions for training and use of company resources.
> (Walker 1992, p. 208)

Unfortunately, as Evans (1986) notes, managers often do not see these responsibilites as part of their job and see them as belonging to the personnel department. Managers often feel constrained by their lack of knowledge about other parts of the organisation, and often withdraw from giving accurate feedback about career potential, particularly when they know that what they have to say is not what the individual wishes to hear. Managers are also sometimes tempted, in their own interests, to hold on to good employees rather than encouraging them to develop elsewhere.

ACTIVITY BOX 24.3

As a member of the personnel function pursuing an organisational philosophy of flexible career moves and continuous career development, how would you:

  ▶ encourage managers to adopt this philosophy?

  ▶ prepare them for the skills they will need to use?

What other career development support could immediate managers give in addition to the suggestions made above?

Career counselling

Occasionally immediate managers will be involved in career counselling in terms of drawing out the strengths, weaknesses, values and interests of their staff. In many cases, however, those who seek such counselling would prefer to speak in confidence to someone independent of their work situation. In these circumstances a member of the personnel department may act as counsellor. In more complex cases, or those involving senior members of staff, professionals external to the organisation may be sought. This is also more likely to be the case if the career counselling is offered as part of an outplacement programme resulting from a redundancy.

Career workshops

These workshops are usually, but not always, conducted off-site, and offered as a confidential programme to help individuals assess their strengths and weaknesses, values and interests, identify career opportunities, set personal career goals, and begin to develop a strategy and action plan. Career goals will not necessarily be restricted to the current employing organisation – and one objective of the workshop is often to broaden career perspectives. Workshops may last 2–3 days, and normally involve individual paper-and-pencil exercises, group discussions, one-to-one discussions and private conferences with tutors. For some people these can be quite traumatic events as they involve whole-life exploration, and often buried issues are confronted which have been avoided in the hurly-burly of day-to-day life. The most difficult part for many individuals is keeping the momentum going after the event by continuing the action planning and self-assessment of progress.

Self-help workbooks

As an alternative to a workshop there is a variety of self-help guides and workbooks which can assist you to work through career issues by presenting a structure and framework. Organisations such as 'Lifeskills' provide a range of workbooks appropriate for different stages of career development.

Another excellent example is the work of Burgoyne and Germain (1982) at Esso Chemicals. The two driving forces here were the need to spend more effective career planning time with employees and the anticipated needs of the organisation in the year 2000.

A guide was produced that staff could work through at their own speed using friends and colleagues to check out their responses and assessments. The guide was designed to help them integrate career planning and self-development, and covered the following areas:

- your skills and job,
- your life and work,
- the world in which you live and work,
- exploring career options,
- what can you learn to help you in the future?
- how do you solve problems?
- what should you be planning to learn?
- how best do you learn?
- how do you keep up to date?
- opportunities and resources for learning,
- planning your self-development.

It is critical that in completing the guide individuals also had a series of meetings with their immediate manager to test out their assessments and assumptions and share information.

Career centres

Career centres can be used as a focal point for the provision of organisational and external career information. The centre may include a library on career choices and exploration, information on organisational career ladders and grids, current opportunities to apply for, self-help workbooks and computer packages.

Assessment and development centres

Assessment centres for internal staff have traditionally taken the form of pass/fail assessment for a selected group of high-potential managers at a specific level. They were focused on organisational rather than individual needs. Recently changes to some of these centres have moved the focus to the individual, and there has been less limitation in who is allowed to attend. The emphasis in these centres, usually termed 'development centres', is to assess the individual's strengths and weaknesses and provide feedback and development plans so that each individual can make the most of his or her own potential. The outcome is less pass/fail but more action plans for personal and career development.

It is a sad reflection that in our recent research, career-related activities did not appear to have a high profile, as shown in Table 24.3.

Whatever career activities are in place in the organisation it is important to ensure that:

▶ There is a clear and agreed careers philosophy communicated to all in the organisation.
▶ Managers are supported in their career development responsibilities.

Table 24.3 Career activities in our recent research sample

Answers to the question: Does your company provide any of the following in order to assist people in their development? Please circle as many as appropriate for the various categories of employee.

	Manual	Non-manual	Managerial
Formal mentoring scheme	2%	15%	24%
Self-development plans	14%	30%	46%
Structured cross-functional moves	3%	16%	22%
Formal career pathways (vertical moves only)	3%	12%	14%
Formal career pathways (vertical and horizontal moves)	2%	17%	19%
Career counselling	7%	23%	27%
Career workshops	1%	4%	6%
Self-help workbooks	3%	6%	6%
Internal assessment centres	2%	9%	16%
None	30%	32%	31%

- Career opportunities are communicated to staff.
- There is an appropriate balance between open and closed internal recruitment.
- The reasons for the balance are explained.
- Knowledge, skills and attitude development are rewarded as well as achievement of a higher organisational level.
- Attention is given to career development within the current job.

Although the range of activities above focus on careers within an organisation, most are still appropriate for employers providing development leading to employability rather than long-term employment. Waterman *et al.* (1994) stress that employers need to move to an adult/adult relationship with their employees from a parent/child one, be prepared to share critical organisational information; and let go of the old notion of loyalty, thus accepting that good employees will leave. Hiltrop (1996) provides a good range of suggestions for managing the changing psychological contract.

ACTIVITY BOX 24.4

- What are the advantages and disadvantages of open and closed internal recruitment?
- In which circumstances might it be appropriate to give a greater emphasis to closed recruitment?
- In which circumstances might it be appropriate to give a greater emphasis to open recruitment?

Perhaps the most outstanding challenge is to come to terms with the fact that careers have changed due to a changing organisation structure and competitive demands; individuals in our current labour market have a greater say in their career and how it relates to their whole life; and that alternative career profiles are equally legitimate.

Summary propositions

24.1 Careers are owned by individuals and the primary responsibility for managing them falls to the individual; organisations have a role in supporting and encouraging this.

24.2 It is important for individuals and organisations to understand the dynamics of careers and the changing psychological contract in order that they may manage or support them more effectively.

24.3 Career development can be described in stages for example – occupational choice, organisational entry, early career, mid-career, late career. These stages may follow a traditional pattern but there are equally legitimate alternative forms, and increasingly so.

24.4 Career anchors represent the self-perceived talents, values and needs of individuals. They help to explain past career choice and have a bearing on future choices. Individual people usually have a combination of anchors.

24.5 Individuals can most effectively manage their careers on a continuous basis. Career management involves identifying a career goal, career strategies and a career action plan, together with collecting feedback and monitoring their progress.

24.6 Organisations can support and encourage individual career management by providing flexible and realistic career grids, honest feedback, opportunities for individual career exploration and planning.

References

Burgoyne, J. and Germain, C. (1982) 'Self-development and career planning: an exercise in mutual benefit', *Personnel Management*, April, pp. 21–3.

Davidson, M. J. and Cooper, C. (1992) *Shattering the Glass Ceiling*, London: Paul Chapman.

Derr, C. B. (1986) *Managing the New Careerists: The diverse career success orientations of today's workers*, Wokingham: Jossey-Bass.

Evans, P. (1986) 'New directions in career management', *Personnel Management*, December, pp. 26–9.

Ghazi, P. and Jones, J. (1997) *Getting a Life: a downshifter's guide*, London: Hodder and Stoughton.

Goffee, R. and Nicholson, N. (1994) 'Career development in male and female managers – convergence or collapse?', in M. J. Davidson and R. J. Burke (eds.), *Women in Management: Current Research Issues*, London: Paul Chapman Publishers.

Gould, S. and Penley, L. (1984) 'Career strategies and salary progression: a study of their relationships in a municipal bureaucracy', *Organisational Behaviour and Human Performance*, Vol. 34, pp. 244–65.

Greenhaus, J. H. and Callanan, G. A. (1994) *Career Management*, London: Dryden Press.

Hall, D. T. and Nougaim, K. (1968) 'An examination of Maslow's need hierarchy in an organisational setting', *Organisational Behaviour and Human Performance*, Vol. 13, pp. 12–35.

Harlan, A. and Weiss, C. L. (1982) 'Sex differences in factors affecting managerial career advancement', in P. A. Wallace (ed.), *Women in the Workforce*, London: Auburn House, ch. 4.

Herriot, P. and Pemberton, C. (1996) 'Contracting careers', *Human Relations*, Vol. 49, No. 6, pp. 757–90.

Hiltrop, J.-M. (1996) 'Managing the changing psychological contract', *Employee Relations*, Vol. 18, No. 4, pp. 36–49.

Levinson, D. J., Darrow, C. N., Klein, E. B., Levinson, M. H. and McKee, B. (1978) *The Seasons of a Man's Life*, New York: Knopf.

Lewis, S. and Cooper, C. L. (1989) *Career Couples*, London: Unwin Hyman.

Mayo, A. (1991) *Managing Careers: strategies for organisations*, London: IPM.

Pringle, J. K. and Gold, U. O'C. (1989) 'How useful is career planning for today's managers?', *Journal of Management Development*, Vol. 8, No. 3, pp. 21–6.

Schein, E. (1978) *Career Dynamics: Matching individual and organisation needs*, Reading, MA: Addison-Wesley.

Stamp, G. (1989) 'The individual, the organisation and the path to mutual appreciation', *Personnel Management*, July, pp. 28–31.

Super, D. E. (1980) 'A life span, life space approach to career development', *Journal of Vocational Behaviour*, Vol. 16, pp. 282–98.

Walker, J. W. (1992) *Human Resource Strategy*, Maidenhead: McGraw-Hill.

Wanous, J. P. (1992) *Recruitment, Selection, Orientation and Socialisation of Newcomers*, Wokingham: Addison-Wesley.

Waterman, R. H., Waterman, J. A. and Collard, B. A. (1994) 'Toward a career-resilient workforce', *Harvard Business Review*, July–August.

General discussion topics

1. What is the career management challenge for the 1990s? What appropriate strategies and actions might there be for employers and employees?
2. 'No matter how much we encourage individuals to plan their careers, at the end of the day it comes down to opportunity and chance.'
   Do you think that this comment is a fair reflection of the way that individuals manage their careers?

CHAPTER 25

Interactive skill: teaching

Within the personnel function, and in all other management roles, there is always a need to enable people to learn. There are all manner of ways in which this can be done, especially with the development of technical aids, but this chapter concentrates on the face-to-face learning situation: teaching. We use that simple, traditional term despite its connotations of narrowness. Many people visualise teaching as a process in which someone who knows instructs someone who does not. But enabling people to learn goes beyond simple instruction. Learners frequently have to discover for themselves, as this is the only way in which they will understand, and they frequently can only learn by their interaction with other people in a group, as it is the group process alone that can help them develop their social skills.

Teaching a person to do something is different from teaching someone to understand something, and understanding something intellectually is different from understanding and changing how you interact with other people. In this chapter we are going to consider two different approaches to teaching: learning in groups and job instruction, with the most detail about the last, which remains essential despite the increasing emphasis quite rightly placed on other types of learning:

> Notwithstanding the amazing developments that have taken place in recent years with alternative modes of delivery, there is still a great demand for classroom-based, tutor delivered training. People do, however, demand and expect training to be lively and stimulating. They will not put up with dull and irrelevant training . . .
> (Truelove 1992, p. 172)

Approaches to learning

Different types of learning require fundamentally different methods and approaches by the teacher. One recent, popular classification is to distinguish between memorising, understanding and doing (MUD). This was the result of research by Downs and Perry (1987). Their work was based on identifying blockages to learning, especially by adults, and was widely promoted in the late 1980s by, among others, the Manpower Services Commission. A more detailed classification was shown in the CRAMP taxonomy (ITRU 1976), developed after a study of the work of the Belbins (Belbin and Belbin 1972) and following an earlier analysis by Bloom (1956). This system divides all learning into five basic types.

1. **Comprehension** is where the learning involves knowing how, why and when certain things happen, so that learning has only taken place when the learner understands: not simply when the learner has memorised. Examples would be having enough understanding of how German grammar works to be able to get the words of a sentence in the right order, or knowing enough of the law of employment to decide whether or not someone has been dismissed unfairly.

2. **Reflex learning** is involved when skilled movements or perceptual capacities have to be acquired, involving practice as well as knowing what to do. Speed is usually important and the trainee needs constant repetition to develop the appropriate synchronisation and co-ordination. Many of the obvious examples lie outside the interests of most personnel managers, like juggling, gymnastics or icing a cake, but there are many examples in most organisations, such as driving a fork-lift truck, spot welding, fault-finding and typing. One of the most widespread in management circles is the use of a keyboard. It is interesting how the status of the keyboard has altered. On promotion to supervisory, administrative or managerial positions, ex-secretaries have regarded it as essential that they should never use a keyboard again for fear that they would revert to being seen as 'merely a secretary'. Now the use of a keyboard is an essential managerial adjunct to making the most of information technology (Hall and Torrington 1989).

3. **Attitude development** is enabling people to develop the capacity to alter their attitudes and improve their social skills. Much of the customer care training currently being conducted has this as its basis. The theory is that dealing with customers requires people to be confident of their own ability to deal with others, shedding some of their feelings of insecurity and discovering how they are able to elicit a positive response. This can partly be achieved by the process of 'scripting', whereby staff have a set formula to follow. We are all familiar with making a telephone call which brings a response along the lines of, 'Good morning. Bloggs, Blenkinsop, Huggins and Scratchit. Mandy speaking. How may I help you?' Attitude development aims to enable people to develop positive attitudes about themselves and their relationships with others, so that they can cope effectively with other people.

4. **Memory training** is obviously concerned with trainees remembering how to handle a variety of given situations. Pharmacists learn by rote a series of maximum dosages, for example, and an office messenger will need to remember that all invoices go to Mr Brown and all cheques to Mrs Smith. Police officers remember the registration numbers of cars better than most of us, and we all need to remember telephone numbers and PIN numbers. This is distinguished from comprehension because understanding is not necessary, only recall, and it is worth referring back to the example above of understanding German grammar. Learning grammatical rules by rote does not enable one to use that knowledge, because understanding is also required. Learning your PIN number does not require any understanding at all.

5. **Procedural learning** is similar to memory except that the drill to be followed does not have to be memorised, but located and understood. An example is the procedure to be followed in shutting down a plant at Christmas, or dealing with a safety drill.

Most forms of training involve more than one type' of learning, so that the apprentice vehicle mechanic will need to understand how the car works as well as practising the skill of tuning an engine, and the driver needs to practise the skill of coordinating hands, feet and eyes in driving as well as knowing the procedure to follow if the car breaks down. Broadly speaking, however, comprehension-type learning is best approached by a method that teaches the whole subject as an entity rather than splitting it up into pieces and taking one at a time. Here the lecture or training manual is typically used. Attitude change is now often handled by group discussion, but reflex learning is best handled by part methods, which break the task down into sections, each of which can be studied and practised separately before putting together a complete performance, just as a tennis player will practise the serve, the smash, the forehand, the backhand and other individual strokes before playing a match in which all are used. Memory and procedural learning may take place either by whole or by part methods, although memorisation is usually best done by parts.

ACTIVITY BOX 25.1

(a) Think of things that you have learned in the recent past and identify whether the learning was comprehension, reflex, attitude development, memorisation or procedural.
(b) How would you classify learning for the following?

- Swimming
- Calorie-counting in a diet
- Parenting
- Safe lifting
- Selection interviewing
- Learning Russian
- Running a business
- Preparing for retirement

Types of learner

Learners differ according to their prior knowledge, the quality and nature of their previous education and their age. CRAMP (comprehension, reflex learning, attitude development, memory training, procedural learning) was developed on the basis of research among adults and most of the teaching carried out under the aegis of personnel management is with adults, so we need some understanding of how learners differ. An excellent analysis has been produced by Robert Quinn (1988) based on earlier work by Dreyfus *et al.* (1986). It also appears in Quinn's work on management skills (Quinn *et al.* 1990). He believes that mastery of an activity involves a learning process that takes place over an extended period of time and the capacity to learn evolves at the same time. The inference of this is that our approach to organising facilities for others to learn will be influenced by how far their learning capacity has developed. There are five stages:

1. **The Novice** learns facts and rules without criticism or discussion, accepting that there are ways of doing things that others have devised, and that's that.

2. **The Advanced Beginner** goes a little further by being able to incorporate the lessons of experience, so that understanding begins to expand and embellish the basic facts and rules. As you begin to experience working in an organisation, aspects of cultural norms become apparent that are just as important as the basic rules. You find out the subtleties of the dress code and working relationships and extend competence by trying out very slight departures from the rigidity of the rules.

3. **Competency** represents a further development of confidence and a reduced reliance on absolute rules by recognising a wider variety of cues from the working context. There is a greater degree of learning by trial and error, experimenting with new behaviours. It is not abandoning the rules, but being able to use them more imaginatively and with an interpretation that suits one's own personal strengths and inclinations.

4. **Proficiency** is where the learner transcends analysis and begins to use intuition:

   > Calculation and rational analysis seem to disappear. The unconscious, fluid, and effortless performance begins to emerge, and no one plan is held sacred. You learn to unconsciously 'read' the evolving situation. You notice cues and respond to new cues as the importance of the old ones recede. (Quinn *et al.* 1990, p. 315)

5. **Expert** is the term used to describe those rare people who produce a masterly performance simply by doing what comes naturally, because all the learning has fused together to develop a capacity based on having in their heads 'multi-dimensional maps of the territory' that are unknown to other people; they are thus able to meet effortlessly the contradictions of organisational life.

This is a neat and helpful model, although it could also be used as an excuse for sloppy thinking and an inability to see that there has been a sea-change that undermines the expert's certainties. Personnel students have ground into them the risks of snap judgements in selection interviewing ('I can tell as soon as they come through the door') and there will always be a temptation for established managers to take short cuts on the basis of their assumed expertise without realising that the rules have been changed, so that they are playing the wrong game.

WINDOW ON PRACTICE

David teaches a teacher-training course which has a mixture of students. Most are recent graduates with little working experience but well-developed study skills. A minority are a little older, usually mothers with growing children, who have experience, but whose study skills are rusty. He finds that the mature students tend to dominate discussion at the beginning of the course, as they constantly relate everything to their own experience and circumstances, while the recent graduates feel at a loss and put down. After a few weeks the younger students become more assertive in discussion as they gain confidence from their developing understanding, and the mature students are less dominant because they are beginning to question some of the taken-for-granted certainty of their earlier opinions. Mutual respect gradually develops and both groups learn from each other. David classifies the recent graduates as novices rapidly becoming advanced beginners and the mature students as competents who have to revert to novices in order to move on to proficiency.

Leading group discussion

Members of a discussion group both compete and co-operate. They will co-operate in the shared task of seeking understanding and developing answers, but they will also compete in wanting to appear shrewd, fluent and perceptive, especially if there are inequalities of status in the group. They will be even more anxious not to appear foolish. Members of the group will look to the teacher for structure at the beginning: a strong indication of how to get started and assistance in developing the social interaction of the group process. As discussion unfolds the teacher will become less obviously necessary to the group, but will still need to control the exchanges to ensure their effectiveness. This later control is the hardest part, as the voluble need to be reigned in frequently and the diffident encouraged.

Small informal groups are being used more extensively in business life, especially since the introduction of team briefing, quality circles and similar attempts at employee involvement. This is an important aspect to the background of using group methods in teaching. Working in groups becomes more familiar, so learning in groups becomes more the accepted norm. The increasing use of groups generally is based on the belief that some tasks are better undertaken by groups than by individuals. Blau and Scott (1963) offer three reasons for this view:

1. The sifting of suggestions in social interaction serves as an error-correction mechanism.
2. The social support furnished in interaction facilitates thinking.
3. The competition among members for respect mobilises their energies for contributing to the task.

For the teacher that analysis provides the value of using groups for learning: clarification, thinking and motivation. One must, however, avoid the risk of thinking that group-working is the *only* effective means of teaching, especially when one considers the time that is involved. Not only do groups move at the speed of the lowest learner, there is also the problem that each group member may have a problem that others do not share, so much time may be spent by the group laboriously reaching only a modest level of learning development.

WINDOW ON PRACTICE

The Higher Education Funding Council for England has undertaken the assessment of teaching assessment throughout the universities it supports. A part of this process is assessing the effectiveness of individual teaching sessions. Here is an extract from one of these assessments:

The student group was a mixture of those in their late teens who had recently left school and a number of married women 'returners' who were preparing to re-enter the labour market. There was an easy relationship between the teacher and the students, so that discussion of the case study began without delay and everyone took some part. There was, however, increasing diversity and generality in the discussion that often dwelt on personal opinions of the group members on matters that had no relevance to the case study. When the session closed after 50 minutes one was left with the impression that all students had enjoyed a conversation but it was difficult to believe that much learning had taken place.

Group leadership and group roles

In all informal groups the position of the leader is crucial, and in teaching situations the leadership role is clearer than in most, as the teacher is the acknowledged expert in the group, although many teachers may feel no more than competent or proficient! The size of the group will influence group effectiveness, according to the task. The larger the group the greater the problems of coordination. Most experienced teachers feel that groups relying mainly on discussion as the means of learning begin to lose their effectiveness if there are more than twelve or fifteen members, and that numbers should be lower when the material is particularly abstruse. It is interesting to compare with other group learning situations. A class in school will seldom be so small, but the student learning depends on a higher level of individual student activity, such as reading a passage in the book, working out an equation, translating a poem, or carrying out an experiment. Apprentice classes are able to work with larger numbers, again because so much of the learning is practical work by the individual student. Hare (1962) argues that there should always be an odd number of group members so that a single group member could be in a minority without the same pressure to conform with the majority that would exist in a smaller group, and there are enough people for members to shift roles easily. Where the group task is not wholly one of social interaction, then the size could increase.

The membership of the group will be either more or less homogeneous, or it will be mixed. Most personnel managers organising teaching will be working with homogeneous groups in the sense that they will have a number of points in common, such as membership of the company, or all being recently recruited, or all needing to understand the new computing system. Typically the teacher will probably increase the homogeneity by, for instance, grouping all the supervisors in one group, all the engineers in another and all the marketing staff in a third. Similarity of interests and background aids co-operation and understanding.

Mixed group composition is better when the differences of perspective or interest are the core of the training task, because they are differences that have to be overcome, or where a diversity of opinion and expertise is needed to achieve understanding.

Every group leader needs to be able to assess the members of the group and work out how to mobilise their diverse competences and contributions to best effect. Here is a list of types of people and their distinctive contributions to group discussion. It is modelled on the work of Meredith Belbin which was described fully in Chapter 18.

1. **The Shaper** influences discussion by developing thoughtful argument and following through particular topics that have been raised, always wanting to make sense of things and get them into shape.
2. **The Ideas Person** contributes novel suggestions and is likely to provide possibilities of breaking out of stalemate situations, or distracting everyone with a fresh idea just at the point where most people are about to succeed in mastering something else.
3. **The Radical** believes that the group's task cannot begin until something else has been done first – and the 'something else' is always beyond the group's control. Groups discussing employee relations issues are vulnerable to discussion that rapidly settles down to bemoaning capitalist society, the failure of the labour movement or male repression of women.

4. **The Steady Eddy** is always cautious and aware of problems. This anxiety not to rock the boat can help a group to calm down when the radicals and the ideas people get going, but a group comprised entirely of Steady Eddies would achieve little. They can be useful for knowing what next week's topic is and for explaining that the right books are not in the library.

5. **The Team Worker** keeps the group going by joking when discussion gets too tense and always finding points on which to agree with other people. They are more useful than Steady Eddies, but it gets a bit boring when everyone agrees with everything.

6. **The Monitor** likes to review progress and summarise what has been said. In most teaching situations this is the main role of the leader, but a leader who is a natural ideas person will value a monitor to keep track of what is happening.

7. **The Shrinking Violet** has difficulty in getting into the discussion and is intensely concerned not to sound foolish, requiring careful assistance – but not condescension – from the leader. They have to be assisted because they worry everyone else as well as themselves. The silent figure who never speaks can soon become identified as someone who thinks deeply and has probably spotted flaws in the argument that no one else can see.

8. **The Completer** likes to push things along, get things done and formulate conclusions. The trouble is that this may be done too soon and may deflect the group from facing up to tricky issues.

ACTIVITY BOX 25.2

Rewrite the above list in the ranked order that most accurately describes your behaviour in group learning situations. Could you alter that ranking by changing your mode of participation? Do you want to? Why?

At the next meeting you attend, classify each participant in one only of the eight categories. Does the meeting need different people?

The group work sequence

Preparation

Do all members of the group know each other? With a close-knit team, like a senior management group, introductions will obviously not be needed, but there may be a new member of the group, there may be members whose presence puzzles others (or themselves), and sometimes the group will be made up of relative strangers. The group leader has four basic strategies available for making sure that people know each other:

1. **Assume introductions are not needed**: The leader does not make any introductions, assuming them to be unnecessary.

2. **Introduce individuals**: Leader makes introductions 'from the chair', of those who are new to those who are established and vice versa, for example: 'I think we mostly know each other, but Chris is with us for the first time, as last week he was on assignment in Italy. Chris, on your right is Roger, from customer service, Sheila, from Distribution and Jan, who . . .'

3. **Ask people to introduce themselves**: 'Perhaps we could just go round the group, saying who we are and what our role is. I'm Simon Rowntree, from Central Personnel. I've been seconded for three months to act as trainer on all these sessions. On my right is . . .?'

4. **Ask people to introduce others**: The Leader asks pairs in the group to interview each other for 5 minutes and then introduce the person they have interviewed to everyone else. This method is particularly useful for a group of strangers, as it initiates discussion and eliminates the self-consciousness felt by many in saying 'I am . . .'

The Leader sets the scene by reminding everyone of why they have assembled and summarising what it is they have to do. At this stage members of the group will welcome clear guidance and a suggested structure for the meeting, but the Leader will need their consent by signing off with a comment like:

'Is that all right?'
'Is there anything I've missed, do you think?'

The Leader now opens the discussion by introducing the topic – or the first of several topics – for the group to develop. There are various ways of doing this:

Setting out background information

Adding to the initial introductory comments by providing more general information in a way that will focus the thinking of group members.

Providing factual data

Giving group members specific details about the initial topic and inviting their analysis.

Offering an opinion

Leading the group towards a conclusion by declaring your own beliefs first is a strong but risky opening. If you are articulating a view that most people will support, then the group will make quick progress, but you may prevent people developing true understanding. In your inescapable role as expert, you may not be challenged. If there is likely to be dissent, then proceedings will be slowed down, as members of the group have first to grapple with the task of disagreeing with the Leader, and then they have to sound out support for their own views.

Asking a question

Directing everyone's thinking by posing a question that opens up the topic. It is wise to move from the general to the particular, by setting up the initial discussion around the broader aspects of the question which can later be brought into much sharper focus.

Although the teacher will be less dominant as the discussion gets underway, there is still a need for control and direction, using the following methods:

Bringing people in

Without direction some group members will never speak and others will scarcely stop, but productive discussion will result from a blend of contributions from Shapers, Steady Eddies, Completers, and so on. The teacher will not only bring people in in a general way ('What do you think, Frank?') but will also shape the discussion by bringing people in for specific comment ('How does John's idea fit in with what you were saying earlier, Helen?').

Shutting people up

Curbing the voluble is difficult and can make everyone feel awkward if it is not well done, yet the discussion will not work if it is dominated by one or two people. Equally, the teacher will fail if the voluble person is expressing a point of view for which there is broad support, so that the understanding is not moving on. Techniques for the teacher to use in shutting people up are:

- put one or two closed questions to a person in the middle of a diatribe,
- give them a job to do ('Could you just jot down for us the main points of that, so that we can come back to it later?'),
- orient them towards listening ('Can you see any problems with what Sheila has suggested?').

There is little need to sustain discussion on matters where everyone is agreed. Agreeing with each other is useful for social cohesion, but the Leader needs regularly to direct discussion back to points of disagreement and misunderstanding. It helps to bring in someone who has previously been neutral or silent on the matter and who may therefore have a different perspective.

Periodically the discussion will need to be summarised and a new direction introduced. Members of the group need to confirm the summary. This is usually a job for the teacher, but there may be a Monitor in the group to take it on.

Occasionally someone in the group will make a contribution that others do not understand, so the teacher will seek clarification, ensuring that the responsibility for the confusion is *not* on the person making the statement. 'Could you just go over that again, Fred' is better than 'I think what Fred is trying to say is . . .'

The session must close and not simply run out of time. It is superficially pleasing when everyone is still keenly discussing when time is up, but it does leave things up in the air. The teacher needs to pick out from the discussion one or two workable hypotheses or points of general consensus and put them to the meeting for acceptance. Group members will look to the teacher for that type of closure so that they have confirmation that their time has been well spent: only the teacher can really see the wood for the trees. The best discussions finish on time!

Job instruction

The first step in learning a skill is for the learner to understand the task and what needs to be done to produce a satisfactory performance. This provides the initial framework for, and explanation of, the actions that are to be developed later, although more information will be added to the framework as the training proceeds. The job of the teacher at this point is to decide how much understanding is needed to set up the training routine, especially if part methods are to be used for the later practice. Trainees are usually keen to get started with 'hands-on' experience, so long and detailed preliminaries are best avoided.

The second step is to practise the performance, so the instructor has to decide how to divide the task up into separate units or subroutines to aid learning. Typists begin their training by learning subroutines for each hand before combining them into routines for both hands together, but pianists spend very short periods of practice with one hand only. The reason for this seems to be that typists use their two hands in ways that are relatively independent of each other with the left always typing 'a' and the right always typing 'p', so that co-ordination of the hands is needed only to sequence the actions. In playing the piano there is a more complex integration of the actions performed by the two hands so that separate practice can impair rather than enhance later performance. A further aspect of learning to type is to practise short letter sequences that occur frequently, such as 'and', 'or', 'the', 'ing' and 'ion'. These can then be incorporated into the steadily increasing speed of the typist. A feature of this type of development is the extent to which the actions become automatic and reliable. The amateur typist will often transpose letters or hit the wrong key, writing 'trasnpose' instead of 'transpose' or 'hte' instead of 'the'. The skilled typist will rarely do this because the effect of the repeated drills during training will have made the subroutines not only automatic but also correct.

The third element is feedback, so that learners can compare their own performance with the required standard and see the progress they are making. The characteristics of good feedback are immediacy and accuracy. If the feedback comes immediately after the action, the trainee has the best chance of associating error with the part of the performance that caused it, whereas delayed feedback will demonstrate what was wrong, but the memory of what happened will have faded. If you are being taught to drive a car, one of the early lessons is changing gear. If you think you understand what the instructor tells you, you need to try it out straightaway, so that you have first the feedback of your own performance in seeing if you execute the manoeuvre effectively and then the feedback from the instructor, who screams in anguish before telling you what you did wrong. If you are learning photography you do not have that element of immediate feedback, so that you have to recall everything that took place in taking the photograph when you eventually receive the prints.

The second characteristic of feedback is that it should be as accurate as possible in the information it provides on the result and the performance. The driving instructor may say, 'That's fine', or may say, 'That was better than last time because you found the gear you were looking for, but you are still snatching. Try again and remember to ease it in.' The second comment provides a general indication of making progress, it provides an assessment of the performance and specific comment that should improve the next attempt.

The job instruction sequence

Preparation

The instructor will have two sets of objectives: organisational and behavioural. Organisational objectives specify the contribution to the organisation that will be made by the learner at the end of training. It will be general but necessary. If a company trains its own word processor operators and secretaries, for instance, it might be that the organisational objectives will be to teach people to word process and to transcribe from handwritten copy or dictating machine, but not to take shorthand. These are different from educational objectives, which focus on the trainee or student rather than on organisational needs, so that tutors in secretarial colleges are more likely to organise training round what will be useful in a number of occupational openings. The instructor will need to work out organisational objectives which may or may not include broader educational features.

Behavioural objectives are specifically what the learner should be able to do when the training, or training phase, is complete. Organisational objectives for trainee word processor operators may be simply to ensure a constant supply of people able to type accurately and at reasonable speed. In behavioural terms that would be made more specific by setting standards for numbers of words to be typed to a predetermined level of accuracy per minute.

ACTIVITY BOX 25.3

Think of a training experience involving learning how to *do* something that you are contemplating for yourself or for someone else in your organisation. Note down organisational objectives and behavioural objectives for the training.

Next the instructor will decide what learning methods are to be used. We have already seen that the main elements of job instruction are understanding, practice and feedback, so the instructor decides how much initial explanation is needed, and how many other explanations will be necessary at different stages of the training, together with the form that is appropriate. Words alone may be enough, but audio-visual illustration and demonstration will probably be needed as well. There are rapid developments in computer-based training and interactive video that can provide frequent explanations and feedback on trainee performance (Rushby 1987).

The two questions about practice are to decide on the subroutines and any necessary simulation, like the working of a flight simulator in pilot training. Most feedback is by the instructor talking to the learner, but it may be necessary to devise ways of providing greater accuracy or speed to the feedback by methods like television recording or photography. The most common method of job instruction is the *progressive part* method. This had its most comprehensive explanation by Douglas Seymour (1966). The task to be undertaken by the learner is broken down into a series of subroutines. The learner then practises routine 1, routine 2 and then 1+2.

The next step is to practise routine 3, 2+3 and 1+2+3, so that competence is built up progressively by practising a subroutine and then attaching it to the full task, which is constantly being practised with an increasing number of the different components included. The components are only practised separately for short periods before being assimilated, so there is no risk of fragmentary performance.

This only works if the job can be subdivided into components. Where this is not possible, simplification offers an alternative. In this method the task to be performed is kept as a whole, but reduced to its simplest form. Skilled performance is then reached by gradually increasing the complexity of the exercises. In cookery the learner begins with simple recipes and gradually develops a wider repertoire.

There are some specialised methods of memory training which can be listed here, as well as ways of training for perceptual skill. Both types of ability appear to be increasing in importance in organisational life.

The most familiar way of memorising is the *mnemonic* or *jingle*, wherein a simple formula provides the clue to a more comprehensive set of data. Laser is much easier to remember than light amplification by stimulated emission of radiation and most people employed in schools will remember how the Great Education Reform Bill of 1988 was reduced to the shorthand of GERBIL in staff room discussions. If the initial letters are not easily memorable, the mnemonic is replaced by the jingle. The denseness of ROYGBIV has led generations of school children to remember that Richard Of York Gave Battle In Vain as a way of recalling the sequence of red, orange, yellow, green, blue, indigo and violet in the spectrum. Arthur Spits in Claude's Milk is a rather less familiar way of remembering that there are five types of arthropod: Arthropods, Spiders, Insects, Crustaceans and Myriapods. One does have to be sure, however, both that the mnemonic or jingle will itself be remembered and that it will subsequently be possible to remember what is to be recalled.

ACTIVITY BOX 25.4

What do the following sets of letters mean: DERV, DFE, DSS, RADAR, TINA LEA, UNESCO, UNPROFOR ?

Apart from the obvious, why should anyone remember the phrase, 'Most Engineers Prefer Blondes'?

For some tasks the use of *rules* reduces the volume of material to be memorised. There are many fault-finding rules, for instance, where the repairer is taught to use a systematic series of rules. The stranded motorist who telephones the vehicle rescue service for assistance will probably be asked a first question, 'Have you run out of petrol?' The answer 'Yes' identifies the fault, while 'No' leads to the second question, 'Is there any spark?' so that the engineer who comes to help already has some areas of fault eliminated.

Deduction is a method that puts information into categories so that if something does not fit into one category the learner then uses deduction to conclude that it must belong in another. At the beginning of this chapter was the example of the office messenger remembering that invoices go to Mr Brown and cheques to Mrs Smith. If there was also a Ms Robinson, who received all sales enquiries, complaints, unsolicited sales promotion material, tax returns, questionnaires, applications for employment, and so on, the messenger would not need to remember what did go to Ms Robinson, but what did not: invoices to Mr Brown, cheques to Mrs Smith and everything else to Ms Robinson. Some interesting examples of using deduction in training are to be found in Belbin and Downs (1966).

For memorisation of information the *cumulative part* method is slightly, but significantly, different from the progressive part method already described in that the learner constantly practises the whole task, with each practice session adding an extra component. This is distinct from progressive part in which components are practised separately before being built into the whole. This can be especially useful if the more difficult material is covered first, as it will then get much more rehearsal than that coming later.

A method for the development of perceptual skills is *discrimination*, which requires the learner to distinguish between items that appear similar to the untrained eye or ear. In a rough-and-ready way it is the procedure followed by the birdwatcher or the connoisseur of wine. First the trainee compares two items which are clearly dissimilar and identifies the points of difference. Then other pairs are produced to be compared, with the differences gradually becoming less obvious. Discrimination can be aided by *cueing*, which helps the learner to identify particular features in the early attempts at discrimination by providing arrows or coloured sections. Some people start learning to type with the keys coloured according to whether they should be struck with the left or right hand, or even according to the particular finger which is appropriate. Gradually the cues are phased out as the learner acquires the competence to identify without them.

Magnification is a way of developing the capacity to distinguish small faults in a process or even small components in machinery. Material for examination is magnified at the beginning of training and then reduced back to normal as competence is acquired. Inspectors of tufted carpet start their training by being shown samples of poor tufting that have been produced using much larger material than normal. Later they examine normal material under a magnifying glass and eventually they are able to examine the normal product. A helpful discussion of magnification method can be found in Holding (1965).

The various training methods to be used are put together in a training programme. This sets out not only what the instructor is going to do, but also the progress the trainee is expected to make. Of critical importance here is pacing; how much material has to be taken in before practice begins, how long there is to practise before being able to proceed to a new part, and how frequently progress is checked by the teacher. Individual trainees will each have their own rate at which they can proceed and will need differing levels of initial explanation and demonstration before practice can start. Training programmes require sufficient flexibility to accommodate the varying capacities that learners bring to their training.

A useful feature of the training programme is providing scope for learners to be involved in determining their own rate of progress and some self-discovery, to avoid spoon-feeding. At the outset trainees are so conscious of their dependency that all measures that build up confidence, independence and autonomy are welcome.

The instruction

When instructor and trainee meet for the first time there is a mutual appraisal. The process is basically 'getting to know you', but the exchanges are important, as the two people have to work together and the learner will be uncertain in an unfamiliar situation, and absolutely dependent upon the instructor. Some instructors and some training programmes appear deliberately to emphasise the inferiority of the learner as a prerequisite of the training process; Hollywood frequently produces films about the training of marines or other members of the American military that show the trainees being systematically humiliated by instructors who could have given lessons to Attila the Hun. Individual instructors in less melodramatic situations sometimes like to assert their superiority, but it is essential that the learners feel confident in the instructor as someone skilled in the task that is to be learned and enthusiastic about teaching it to others. They will also be looking for reassurance about their own chances of success by seeking information about previous trainees.

The explanation of procedure will follow as soon as the meeting phase has lasted long enough. Here is the first feature of pacing that was mentioned as part of preparation. There has to be enough time for meeting to do its work, but long, drawn-out introductions can lead to impatience and wanting to get started.

The procedure is the programme, with the associated details of timing, rate of progress, training methods and the general overview of what is to happen. The most important point to the trainee is obviously the end. When does one 'graduate'? What happens then? Can it be quicker? Do many people fail? What happens to them? The instructor is, of course, more interested in the beginning of the programme rather than the end, but it is only with a clear grasp of the end that the trainee can concentrate on the beginning. Clarifying the goal reinforces the commitment to learning.

With long-running training programmes where an array of skills has to be mastered, the point of graduation may be too distant to provide an effective goal so that the tutor establishes intermediate goals: 'By Friday you will be able to . . .'. This phase benefits from illustration: a timetable, a chart of the average learning curve, samples of work by previous trainees – all make more tangible the prospect of success and more complete the mental picture of the operating framework that the learner is putting together. It is also helpful to avoid the explanation becoming mechanical, like the tourist guide at a stately home. If the instructor has explained the procedure so often that it has become automatic, it is no longer the vivid stimulus to learning that is so necessary. It is a time for as much interchange as possible, with questions, reiteration, further explanation, clarification and confirmation.

WINDOW ON PRACTICE

Repetition does not necessarily make material automatic. Acker Bilk played 'Stranger on a Shore' thousands of times, and many excellent teachers re-use exactly the same material repeatedly. The Scottish playwright James Barrie studied medicine in his youth and took with him to university a set of verbatim anatomy notes that had been compiled by his father thirty years earlier.

His father said the lectures were so interesting that it would be better if he did not have to make notes. As Barrie attended the lectures, he was astonished to find that little had changed. At one point the lecturer took hold of a gas bracket and related an anecdote. On looking at his father's notes he saw, 'At this point Professor X took hold of a gas bracket and told this story . . .'

The task that the trainee has to perform first is demonstrated and explained. The purpose is not to display the teacher's advanced skills, but to provide a basis for the learner's first, tentative (and possibly incorrect) attempts. The demonstration is thus done without any flourishes, and as slowly as possible, because the teacher is not only demonstrating skill but also using skill to convince the trainees that they can do the job. Accompanying the demonstration, an explanation gives reasons for the different actions being used and describing what is being done so that the learners can watch analytically. Their attention is drawn to features they might overlook, the sequence of actions is recounted and key points are mentioned.

The task must be presented to the learner in its simplest possible form, with a straightforward, unfussy, accurate demonstration accompanied by an explanation

which emphasises correct sequence, reasons why, features that might be overlooked in the demonstration and the key points that lead to success. Where possible,
the tutor should not mention what not to do. Incorrect aspects of performance
can be dealt with later; at this stage the direction should be on what to do.

The presentation is followed, and perhaps interrupted, by questions from the
learners on what they did not follow or cannot remember. The success of this will
depend on the skill of the instructor in going through the opening stages of the
encounter. Many trainees are reluctant to question because they feel that the
question reveals their ignorance, which will be judged as stupidity. The experienced instructor can stimulate the questioning and confirming by the trainees by
putting questions to them. This is effective only when done well, as there is the
obvious risk of inhibiting people by confronting them with their lack of understanding. The most unfortunate type of questions are those which cross-examine:

'Now, tell me the three main functions of this apparatus.'
'Can anyone remember which switch we press first?'

Little better are the vague requests for assent:

'Do you understand?'
'Am I making myself clear?'
'Is that all right, everybody?'

These are leading questions. They will be some use as there will be nods and
grunts from the trainees to provide response, but it is most unlikely that people
will do more than offer the easy, regular 'yes'. The job of the teacher is to help
learners build the picture in their own minds without the feeling that they are
being tested. This will only come with good rapport. After the presentation the
trainees have their first attempt at the task.

They expect to do badly and need confidence from the tutor, who has to steer
a difficult path between too much or too little intervention. Too much and the
trainees do not 'feel their feet' and acquire the confidence that comes from sensing the strength and purpose of your own first faltering steps. Too little intervention means that trainees learn about their lack of competence, which is reinforced
by a performance that falls short of what the presentation had suggested as being
possible. This shows the importance again of presentation, which has to be
pitched at the level that will make initial performance feasible, without building
up expectations that cannot be realised.

Among the considerations for teachers are the varying potential of individual
trainees and the ritual elements of training. Some trainees will be able to make
initial progress much more rapidly than others, so that pegging all to the same
rate of advance will inhibit both. The ritual features depend on the acknowledgement by the trainee of the absolute, albeit temporary, superiority of the tutor.
It has already been pointed out that there is a reluctance to question during presentation; there are also intermittent displays of deference to the teacher. This
enables learners to perform badly during practice without losing face. However,
deference to a superior figure is normally offered on the assumption that the
novice is being helped towards the advanced level of skill that the superior
posesses. If early practice of a taught skill produces abject performances by the
learners, then they either lose confidence or resent the instructor for highlighting
their inadequacy.

Learning theory tells us the importance of the law of effect, which practice makes possible, but it also tells us that there is likely to be a point at which the learner makes a sudden leap forward – the point at which the penny drops and there is a shared excitement. In the words of Professor Higgins about Eliza: 'I think she's got it. By Jove, she's got it.' Practice leads up to the point where the learning spurts forward and it then provides the reinforcement of that learning by continued rehearsal and confirmation.

The most effective reinforcement for learners is realising that they can perform, like the child who at last finds it possible to remain upright and mobile on a bicycle. Learners cannot usually rely on their own interpretation of success: they will need constant assessment by the teacher. Many of the textbooks on teaching and learning emphasise the value of praise, a little of which apparently goes a long way, for example:

> When they are learning people need to know where they stand, they need to know how they are progressing. The knowledge of their progress spurs them on to greater achievements. In this respect praise is always far more helpful than criticism.
>
> (Winfield 1979)

Effective reinforcement enables trainees to understand both the result and the actions or behaviour which produced the result, so the tutor needs to identify the particular ways in which progress is being made and explain their merit, as well as explaining what caused the progress to happen. When trainees are approaching full competence, with the associated self-confidence, then they are able to cope with more direct criticism.

Summary propositions

25.1 A useful classification of types of learning is CRAMP: comprehension, reflex learning, attitude development, memory training, procedural learning.

25.2 Selecting the right approach to learning is helped by identifying the learner as being in one of these categories: novice, advanced beginner, competent, proficient or expert.

25.3 Where learning takes place through group discussion, the type of contribution from individual members can be classifed as follows: shaper, ideas person, radical, steady Eddy, team worker, monitor, shrinking violet and completer.

25.4 Preparing for group work involves deciding about introductions: either assume introductions not needed or, introduce individuals or, ask people to introduce themselves or, ask people to introduce others.

25.5 There are four basic methods of starting group discussion: giving background, providing facts, offering an opinion or asking a question.

25.6 During group discussion the main jobs for the leader are: bringing people in, shutting people up, focusing on points of disagreement and misunderstanding, summarising and changing direction.

25.7 Alternative methods in job instruction are: progressive part, simplification, mnemonics or jingles, rules, deduction, cumulative part, discrimination and magnification.

References

Belbin, E. and Belbin, R. M. (1972) *Problems in Adult Retraining*, London: Heinemann.

Belbin, E. and Downs, S. (1966) 'Teaching and paired associates', *Journal of Occupational Psychology*, Vol. 40, pp. 67–74.

Blau, P. M. and Scott, W. R. (1963) 'Processes of communication in formal organisations', in M. Argyle (ed.), *Social Encounters*, Harmondsworth: Penguin Books.

Bloom, B. S. (1956) *Taxonomy of Educational Objectives: The cognitive domain*, London: Longman.

Downs, S. and Perry, P. (1987) *Helping Adults to Become Better Learners*, Sheffield: Manpower Services Commission.

Dreyfus, H. L., Dreyfus, S. E. and Athanasion, T. (1986) *Mind over Machine: The power of human intuition and expertise in the era of the computer*, New York: Free Press.

Hall, L. A. and Torrington, D. P. (1989) 'How personnel managers come to terms with the computer', *Personnel Review*, Vol. 8, No. 6.

Hare, A. P. (1962) 'Small groups', *American Behavioral Scientist* (May/June).

Harrison, R. (1988) *Training and Development*, London: Institute of Personnel Management.

Holding, D. H. (1965) *Principles of Training: Research in applied learning*, Oxford: Pergamon.

ITRU (Industrial Training Research Unit) (1976) *Choose an Effective Style: A self-instructional approach to the teaching of skills*, Cambridge: ITRU Publications.

Quinn, R. E. (1988) *Beyond Rational Management: Mastering the paradoxes and competing demands of high performance*, San Francisco: Jossey Bass.

Quinn, R. E., Faerman, S. R., Thompson, M. P. and McGrath, M. R. (1990) *Becoming a Master Manager*, New York: John Wiley.

Rushby, N. (ed.) (1987) *Technology-based learning: selected readings*, London: Kogan Page.

Seymour, W. D. (1966) Industrial Skills, London: Pitman.

Truelove, S. (1992) *Handbook of Training and Development*, Oxford: Blackwell.

Winfield, I. (1979) *Learning to Teach Practical Skills*, London: Kogan Page.

Practical exercises in teaching

First exercise

Devise a training programme that will teach someone to complete a straight-forward task, taking care to go through all the steps of preparation that have been mentioned in this chapter. Then teach someone to complete the task.

Some of the tasks you could consider are:

- folding a table napkin,
- laying out a tray to serve someone a full English breakfast in bed,
- doing a conjuring trick,
- teaching the rudiments of sign language,
- making a cake,
- packing a collection of tinned food in a box,
- laying out a tray, as above, but for someone who is left-handed.

Second exercise

The next time you attend a meeting or take part in any sort of group discussion, try to work out which members of the group adopt the different roles described on pages 474–5 of this chapter. Then ask yourself these questions:

1. Why did those people adopt those roles? Was it an aspect of their personality, or because of the particular topic that was being discussed, or some other reason?
2. To what extent did people take up a role because of the role adopted by someone else?
3. How much competition was there and how much co-operation, as described in the chapter?
4. Who were the most effective group members in terms of enabling the group to reach agreement or develop understanding? Why were they effective?

Third exercise

At a different meeting, identify which of the following impediments to constructive discussion and understanding or action were present:

- some people talking too much and others making no contribution,
- poor agenda or no agenda,
- poor chairing.

After the meeting try to work out what caused the problems, but think it through fully. For instance, did the people who talked too much do so because they thought it was expected of them, because they always talk too much, because they did not understand what was happening, or for some other reason?

How could these problems have been overcome? Would you have been able to deal with them?

Fourth exercise

The next time you are involved in leading a discussion (after you have done the second exercise) try using the behaviours described on pages 476–7. Later, ask yourself these questions:

1. Which of them worked and which failed? What was the reason for the success and failure?
2. What did you make of the way other people reacted to you and to your tactics? Did they welcome your approach and respond to it, or did they try to ignore you? Why was this?
3. What have you learned from this exercise? What will you do differently next time?

(Do not wait for a formal meeting to try this. A chat with two or three of your friends in a pub could be very appropriate if it turns into a discussion or even an argument rather than just small talk.)

Part V Case study problem

Micropower is a rapidly growing computer software firm, specialising in tailor-made solutions for business. Increasingly training for other businesses in their own and other software packages has occupied the time of the consultants. This it sees as a profitable route for the future and such training is now actively sold to clients. Consultants both sell and carry out the training. As an interim measure, to cope with increasing demand, the firm is now recruiting some specialist trainers, but the selling of the training is considered to be an integral part of the consultant's role.

Micropower have just issued a mission statement which accentuates 'the supply of and support for sophisticated computer solutions', based on a real understanding of business needs. The firm considers that it needs to be flexible in achieving this and has decided that multi-skilling is the way forward.

All consultants need to sell solutions and training at all levels, and be excellent analysts, designers and trainers. Some 200 consultants are now employed; most have a degree in IT and most joined the firm initially driven to specialise in the technical aspects of software development and spent some years almost entirely office-based before moving into a customer-contact role. A smaller proportion were keen to concentrate on systems analysis, and were involved in customer contact from the start.

In addition there are 300 software designers and programmers who are primarily office-based and rarely have any customer contact. It is from this group that new consultants are appointed. Programmers are promoted to two levels of designer and the top level of designer may then, if their performance level is high enough, be promoted to consultant. There is some discontent amongst designers that promotion means having to move into a customer-contact role, and there are a growing number who seek more challenge, higher pay and status, but who wish to avoid customer contact. Another repercussion of the promotion framework is that around a quarter of the current consultants are not happy in their role. They are consultants because they valued promotion more than doing work that they enjoyed. Some have found the intense customer contact very stressful, feel they lack the appropriate skills, are not particularly comfortable with their training role and are unhappy about the increasing need to 'sell'.

Required

1. What immediate steps could Micropower take to help the consultants, particularly those who feel very unhappy, perform well and feel more comfortable in their new roles?

2. In the longer term how can Micropower reconcile its declared aim of multi-skilling with a career structure which meets both organisational and employee needs?

3. What other aspects of human resource strategy would support and integrate with the development strategy of multi-skilling?

4. Micropower wish to develop a competency profile for the consultant role. How would you recommend that they progress this, and how might the profile be used in the widest possible manner in the organisation?

Part V Examination questions

Undergraduate introductory

1. Outline the nature and purpose of National Vocational Qualifications. What has been their impact so far?
2. Discuss the advantages and disadvantages of on-job training and development compared with off-job training and development. In which circumstances might each be more appropriate?

Undergraduate finals

3. Identify the factors which determine 'skill need' in an organisation. Discuss how managers ensure that workers develop the skills and knowledge necessary for their roles within organisations.
4. What practical steps would you take if you were the personnel manager in an organisation wanting to introduce training for people to enable them to manage their own careers more effectively?

Masters

5. What is a career, how is it changing and how should it be managed?
6. Choose one of the following: (a) career planning workshops; (b) mentoring; (c) succession planning. Define it and briefly describe the forms it can take in an organisation. Discuss the criteria on which its success can be evaluated and consider whether some criteria are (i) more appropriate, and (ii) more easily measured, than others.

Professional

7. Explain to a line manager the value of coaching as a way of developing a subordinate.
8. 'Employment development should be handed over to line managers.' Summarise your views on this statement.

PART **VI**
Involvement

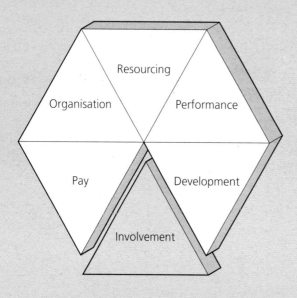

All jobs have the potential to be alienating, making the job holder indifferent or hostile both to the job and to the management who are seen as responsible for obliging the employee to continue doing the job.

Involvement is largely concerned with preventing or alleviating that type of alienation. Because the issues are often collective, concerning a number of people in a similar situation, many involvement procedures incorporate the recognition of trade unions and ways of making that recognition productive for both parties. Working safely in a healthy environment is included here as there is a legal obligation to involve employee representatives in monitoring management arrangements for safe working. Safe working is ultimately a matter of employees working safely because they understand and follow the practices that are provided for their personal safety.

Whether unions are recognised or not, there are always points of disagreement between managers and the managed and here we have two rather 'heavy' words: grievance and discipline. Few managers like to participate in these processes, but they are very interesting and provide the opportunity of major change and improvement for the manager who handles them well.

CHAPTER 26

Strategic aspects of involvement

S

When we surveyed the activities and priorities of personnel specialists in the early 1980s, there was no doubt about the pre-eminence of employee relations as being the activity on which they spent most of their time and as being most central to the personnel function (Mackay and Torrington 1986, pp. 149, 161). Only in recruitment and selection did they feel that they had a slightly greater degree of discretion and scope in decision-making (pp. 146–8). Furthermore it was a time of increasing management assertiveness in this area (p. 79) (see Table 26.1).

In our more recent research we asked a question about union influence at the respondent's place of work in the previous three years. The answers showed a very small increase and roughly the same number of replies for decrease and no change. Nearly a quarter said the question did not apply as they had no union presence (see Table 26.2).

This sort of information certainly indicates a continuation of the general trend that was apparent ten years before. During the early stages of the work by the Personnel Standards Lead Body in developing the occupational map at the beginning of the 1990s, one group of consultants decided that employee relations was not a part of personnel work at all! It certainly has lost the pre-eminent position it held through most of the post-war period, with training and development, performance management, team building and other activities taking greater attention.

The agenda has also changed. The focus is no longer on collective bargaining and procedural agreements, but on holistic approaches to the relationship with the workforce, such as employee involvement, total quality management and team briefing. No longer is there an attempt to control affairs by getting a firm agreement to a set of arrangements that will not be changed by either side, but rather there is an attempt to reach a much less settled relationship, within which

Table 26.1 Replies in interviews on employee relations with senior personnel specialists

Is there a more 'bullish' approach being taken to employee relations in this organisation?	%	No.
Yes, more bullish	61.0	25
No, it was always bullish	10.0	4
No, not more bullish	29.0	12

Table 26.2 Replies to the question: 'Has the influence of unions at your workplace changed in the last three years?'

The influence of unions at your workplace in the last three years	%	No.
Increased	3.3	7
Decreased	35.0	75
Stayed the same	34.1	73
Not applicable	22.4	48

(Eleven respondents [5.1 per cent] did not reply.)

working practices change constantly and the employment relationship is less formalised. To some commentators the agenda is human resource management, not as a term to describe the varied activities of personnel specialists, but as a description of the current management approach to industrial relations. The arena has become both bigger and smaller, as the focus has shifted away from national-level determination of terms and conditions towards arrangements determined within the enterprise, at the same time as the European context of labour law and the social contract have expanded the general context.

The two main trends have been more local determination and more emphasis on commitment:

> two core themes appear to underscore many of the new developments. One is to internalise the personnel function as far as possible within the enterprise, thereby loosening employee relations from wider labour market institutions and influences. . . . The other is to establish gemeinshaft arrangements inside the enterprise in an effort to increase corporate identity and loyalty amongst employees. (Teague 1991, p. 4)

By the late 1990s we find employee relations alive and well as a management activity, although not as salient as industrial relations were in the 1970s, and the overriding characteristic of employee relations is employee involvement. The change of government in 1997 is unlikely to bring in a major change of emphasis. It is likely that trade unions will come in from the cold to some extent at the national level, especially in being increasingly consulted by government, but it is difficult to see any real change in employee relations within businesses.

The development of employee involvement

The whole concept of employee involvement has its roots in broader concepts such as industrial democracy and workers' control, which themselves have an ancient lineage. Over 2,000 years ago there was a series of so-called 'Servile Wars' in Rome, where slaves rose up against their overseers. The last of these was led by a Thracian shepherd, Spartacus, who assembled an army of 90,000 rebellious slaves before eventual defeat. His example was remembered in modern times when a movement was started in Berlin at the beginning of the twentieth century called the Spartacists. This was led by Rosa Luxemburg, who has become an icon of the labour movement.

The inspiration for industrial democracy was the Marxist analysis of how the proletariat is exploited by the capitalists and the middle class, with the inevitable result that the proletariat will eventually overthrow the capitalist system and establish a system of workers' control. This idea received considerable impetus from the inequities of the factory system that followed the industrial revolution, alluded to in our opening chapter.

This was the time when 'industry' came to mean the large-scale manufacture of goods as well as meaning habitual diligence. The size of employing organisations began to grow, industrial cities mushroomed, there was large-scale migration from the country to the city, expanding population, division of labour, ghastly working conditions and the emergence of the new social class, the bourgeoisie. Perhaps of greatest importance, there was a degree of speed of change in people's lives that was unprecedented.

The degree of exploitation of the urban proletariat was so extreme, in such a novel form, that its members attempted collective organisation to resist it. The early trade unions were ineffective and seldom lasted, but by 1880 the British trade union movement had established itself and taken on a form that has not been much altered since. Not only were the methods of industrial action set, so too were the subtle class distinctions between the craft and general unions. It was an essentially British invention and the basic intractability of British trade unions today, as they find it so difficult to adapt policies and practices appropriate to the times, can be seen as a problem of a movement that began when employee representation was being thought up for the first time. At the same time that trade unions were becoming established as part of the social order, the revolutionary philosophy of Karl Marx was being propounded. Asserting that social change results from a class struggle for control of the means of production, Marx predicted the eventual, inevitable victory of the proletariat despite the contemporary subjection of the worker whose labour is bought and sold as a commodity under capitalism, with the economic and human interests of employees being sacrificed. He also argued that the conflict in the social relations of industry is a result of the inherent exploitation.

Marxism has not had the same effect on the British labour movement as has been seen in other countries of Europe, where it is common to have some unions that are communist and some that are Catholic, but it has had an undoubted influence on thinking about industrial relations, mainly because it provides an explanation of the phenomenon and an integrating conceptual framework.

While Marxists argue that change in industrial relations will only be peripheral and unimportant until the complete social revolution has taken place, a more generally accepted view was proposed by Sidney and Beatrice Webb in the late nineteenth century. They concentrated on the industrial order rather than the more general social order and saw trade unions as organisations to further the interests of their members within the system of industrial government, mainly by influencing the wage-work bargain. Any political action was seen as a means towards the end of reforming the way industry is governed rather than transforming the whole society of which industry is a part. This can be described as the mainstream of industrial relations thinking, which reached its apogee in the 1960s in the work of Flanders, Clegg and the recommendations of the Donovan Commission (1968).

Through the first half of the twentieth century trade unions, employers' associations and the various institutions of collective bargaining developed steadily.

The General Strike of 1926 was a trauma from which two main lessons were learned. The union movement learned that a general strike would bring no miracles of social change in a British context and those who had so implacably opposed it, particularly in the employer ranks, learned that 'beating' the strike did not cause the trade unions to wither and die, even though they suffered considerable losses in membership, funds and morale.

The next major development came in the middle 1960s, but in 1958 there was a new academic explanation of industrial relations. Dunlop set out his idea of industrial relations as a system with different types of relations at the varying levels of plant, enterprise, industry or nation in any political or economic setting. He attempted to put forward a comprehensive model that would aid subsequent research. Initially the reaction was mainly of interested disagreement, but recent years have seen more detailed and constructive attempts to move forward from his position.

By the time Dunlop produced his book, most British managers were resigned to a rather defeatist attitude towards the organisation of employment where trade unions were recognised. Bit by bit more was conceded to the unions, who had effected a vice-like grip on production around which nothing could be altered. Restrictive or protective practices were deeply entrenched. This coincided with bad news in the product market. Exports were slipping and the economic growth of other countries was outstripping that of Britain. Productivity bargaining became fashionable as managements sought initiatives with trade unions that had previously seemed impracticable. A Royal Commission was set up to make proposals for change regarding trade unions and employers' associations. It was chaired by Lord Donovan and the report is always known as the Donovan Report. Its actual title was 'The Royal Commission on Trades Unions and Employers' Associations' and that was interesting, as it was set up to look at the collective entities rather that the processes in which they were engaged. The report of the Commission reflected a significant change in thinking. The trouble lay not with trade unions, nor with employers, but with the processes for their interactions. Collective bargaining itself needed reform. National agreements were frequently inadequate as a framework for employment relations in a factory as their formality and precision was shadowed by a series of informal, imprecise arrangements that governed what actually happened on the floor of factories.

ACTIVITY BOX 26.1

The Donovan analysis drew a distinction between the formal system of industrial relations, which was a series of agreements and procedures agreed and organised at the level of a complete industry, and the informal system, which was the actual behaviour of managers, shop stewards and employees.

To what extent has the usefulness of that distinction altered in the period since 1968, and what has caused the change?

It was these informal understandings that needed attention in order to improve the disorder of the workplace. They should be reviewed and a greater degree of formality introduced so that everyone knew more reliably where they stood. No dramatic legislative intervention; no fundamental restructuring in the direction of industrial democracy; and no question of the government taking over. The Royal Commission commented favourably on the productivity agreements that were being concluded, seeing in these deals many of the features which it saw as being necessary at plant level: managers and shop stewards taking responsibility for their own affairs within a loose framework of national agreements, and gradually bringing about the changes in employment and working relationships that were so urgent.

Productivity bargaining received another boost from a new body, the National Board for Prices and Incomes. For the first time there was a statutory prices and incomes policy, which sought to control income growth by statute rather than exhortation and example. One of the agents of this policy was an investigative Prices and Incomes Board. This was soon to become politically unacceptable, but for a few years it produced a series of excellent reports on a variety of investigations into employment matters and advocated the extension of productivity bargaining as a means of achieving economic growth as well as improved industrial relations. Although it was to disappear so soon, it helped to develop the idea of plant-level agreement, which was the productivity bargaining inheritance and brought about that major, and apparently, long-term shift of emphasis towards local agreement on the features of the employment contract. This has now become the norm throughout the private sector of employment, with the business – or even the division of the business – being the arena in which matters of employment practice are resolved. Moves in this direction in the public sector are being made, but more cautiously.

The proposals of the Donovan Commission were not universally accepted. A few weeks before it was published another document was produced called *Fair Deal at Work* (1968). This was a statement of policy by the Conservative Party; then in opposition. The proposals were radically different in tenor and were not widely discussed or analysed because the Royal Commission report followed so soon afterwards. The importance of *Fair Deal at Work* was seen in 1970, when a change of government brought in draft legislation based on the earlier policy statement. This became the Industrial Relations Act of 1971, one of the most controversial pieces of legislation in the post-war period. There was a fundamental difference between it and the Royal Commission view. Instead of seeking the reform of collective bargaining and more effective management, *Fair Deal at Work* and the Industrial Relations Act set out to contain collective bargaining and to control trade unions. The resistance of unions was fierce and the reaction of managements generally apathetic or hostile. Within four years the Act was repealed. There were other legacies of the Act that it is not appropriate to discuss here, but one rather intangible effect was a further strengthening of the 'establishment' position of unions. The General Strike of 1926 may have demonstrated that unions would not wither on the vine, but the Industrial Relations Act brought a form of official acceptance that had previously been missing. For a Conservative government to introduce legislation conferring the legal right to belong to a union and various other union rights was a significant step, even if the unions did not want most of the rights they were given.

The twentieth-century British view of industrial democracy was based on the idea that employers were powerful, the state was powerful and it was therefore important that trade unions should be powerful, so that the three stakeholders in industrial relations should be in some form of power balance. This was articulated by Clegg (1960). During the 1970s there was a lively debate about industrial democracy and various forms of employee participation in the management decision-making processes of business. This was driven by the relatively strong position held by trade union leaders in the various industries and the need of a Labour government to gain their support at a time of a slender majority in the House of Commons. The most thorough-going idea was for the introduction of industrial democracy, which was by then conceived as the participation of employees being developed via representative democracy at the boardroom level to influence, or to make, the major strategic decisions of the organisation.

The main focus of the debate was the Committee of Inquiry on Industrial Democracy, chaired by Lord Bullock. Their majority proposal was that boards of companies should be reconstituted to give equal representation to shareholder and employee representatives, with a smaller number of independents holding the balance.

ACTIVITY BOX 26.2

In addition to the main report of the Bullock Committee (1977), there was a minority report from some members who were 'completely opposed to the introduction into existing Boards of representives of special interests. This might provoke confrontation or extend the scope of collective bargaining into top-level management decision-making.'

Is there any counter-argument to that criticism that you would make in the light of subsequent events?

The proposals were met with varying degrees of horror in management circles and less than rapture among trade unions. The eventual government reaction to the ideas was contained in a White Paper over twelve months later, which declared that there would not be a standard form of participation, like that proposed by the Committee of Inquiry, imposed by law. Increased participation would result mainly from exhortation, although companies employing 5,000 people or more would be legally obliged to discuss with employees all major proposals affecting the workforce and those employing 2,000 or more would be required to concede a legal right to employee representation a few years later.

The 1979 change of government led to these proposals being shelved, but interest continued among both managers and trade unionists. Dowling *et al.* surveyed the attitudes of executives in twenty-five large private companies and the regional officers of fourteen trade unions. Both groups were opposed to worker directors and were relieved that the likelihood of such legislation had receded:

> Managers tended to favour forms of 'participation' which emphasized communication and consultation, whereas the trade union officials favoured extensions to the range of issues subject to collective bargaining or joint regulation.
> (Dowling *et al.* 1981, p. 190)

In 1984 Hanson and Rathkey published the results of a survey of shopfloor opinion they carried out in four companies that would have been affected by the Bullock proposals to try to establish a shopfloor view of the industrial democracy idea. One of their most conclusive findings was that employees were very little interested in making decisions without management involvement. Also twice as many people wanted involvement only in matters concerning their own work and conditions as those who wanted involvement in both that and issues concerning the management of the company as a whole.

The managerial interest was usually in some form of sharing control in order to regain control and they were clearly committed to the idea that managers are the people to make decisions, although employees may be consulted and have things explained to them in order to obtain their commitment to management objectives. Difficult trading conditions had also increased managerial willingness to disclose information about company affairs. An amendment to the Employment Act 1982, introduced by the House of Lords, is a requirement for companies with more than 250 employees to include in their annual report a statement of action taken to introduce or develop arrangements for employee participation. Specifically: systematically providing employees with information on matters which concern them; consulting with employees or their representatives on management decisions likely to affect employees' interests; encouraging employee involvement through means such as shareholding; providing information on financial and economic matters affecting the business.

Management interest was centred on the idea of employee involvement as a way of meeting the demands of the 1982 Act, although ACAS were not initially impressed:

> The pressing need is for employees to be further involved in consultative and decision-making processes in the organizations in which they work, if their talents and energies are to be released and their willing commitment secured to the measures necessary for economic recovery. ACAS officials report that progress in this area has been slow and there remains much to be done.   (ACAS 1985, p. 16)

Another view of participation was that it should develop first at the place of work itself, with autonomous working groups taking over their own supervision, and with managers giving much more attention to the design of jobs and finding ways in which individual employees can participate more in the day-by-day decisions that affect their work. The argument supporting this is that board-level decisions are of little interest or immediacy to employees and that their participation will be apathetic or incompetent, while what they really care about is what they themselves do from day to day, as implied by the Hanson and Rathkey survey.

Another type of initiative is harmonisation of terms and conditions between different categories of employee. A third of the respondents in our earlier research had made some moves in this direction (Mackay and Torrington 1986). Changes were mainly in holidays, hours and method of payment. These general moves have continued, but at a slower pace, and running alongside them has been the core/periphery approach to the workforce. As we have shown elsewhere, temporary and part-time employees frequently 'enjoy' poorer terms and conditions than their full-time counterparts.

In more recent years the impetus for employee involvement has tended to come from two sources. First, despite its inapplicability in the UK, the inclusion of statements on participation in the European Union Social Chapter has influenced practice here. The second driver has been the need to find communication mechanisms to replace those inherent in collective bargaining as negotiation with trade unions has become less significant.

The most popular current methods of involvement appear to be team briefing and total quality management, although the Investors in People initiative is promising. Our recent research showed that 61 per cent of respondents used team briefing and 79 per cent had used team briefing. Nine per cent had achieved Investors in People status, while another 44 per cent were working towards it.

ACTIVITY BOX 26.3

To what extent do you regard the harmonisation of terms and conditions of employment
between different categories of employee as
genuine employee involvement?

A further form of involvement that has grown in coverage recently is the company council, often designed in such a way as to meet the requirements of the
European Works Councils directive. We shall consider each of these shortly, but
this review of how employee involvement has developed can be wound up by
considering the idea that involvement progresses in cycles or waves. This was
scouted by Ramsay (1991) and developed in the seminal work of Marchington and
his colleagues (1992, 1993). While Ramsay saw a pattern that amounted to rein-
venting the wheel, the Marchington analysis sees that each wave of development
is different from its predecessors, even though there may be similarities in their
stimuli. Like so many aspects of management practice, there are fashions, so that
joint consultation was in vogue at one time, team briefing became the popular
notion of the early 1980s, followed by employee share ownership, total quality
management, and so forth. This is similar to the analysis put forward in our opening chapter, that personnel management is constantly picking up new ideas and
orientations. They rarely disappear, but the emphasis is constantly changing.

Any initiative in employee involvement carries a further question about which
employees are to be involved. There have frequently been comments about senior
management attempts to involve shop floor employees having the effect of ignoring
those not working on the shop floor. More recently there has been the issue of
full-time and part-time employees and whether their rights are similar.

An example of this was in the spring of 1994, when one nationally known
engineering company introduced a small number of temporary employees. They
were on contracts of six or thirteen weeks and represented less than 5 per cent of
the total shopfloor workforce. Concerned about security of employment, union
representatives only agreed to the initiative providing that the level of payment was
formally pegged at 10 per cent less than the full-time rate and with significant
benefits, such as sickness payment and holiday entitlement being withheld.

Team briefing

Teamwork has been one of the key ingredients of the new industrial
relations and human resource management movements. *Fortune* business
magazine in the United States heralded it as 'possibly the productivity
breakthrough of the 1990s'.   (Storey and Sisson 1993, p. 91)

That is a bold claim and it covers aspects of work organisation that are rather broader
than team briefing. Teamworking is a direct descendant of the concept of autonomous
working groups, which had their highest profile in the Volvo plant at Kalmar, and a
rather vague movement of the 1960s, called Quality of Working Life (QWL). At Volvo
there were the twin aims of improving the quality of working life and enhancing productivity. The QWL was directed mainly at making life more tolerable, as the title
implies, and it is difficult to see what impact it had. More recently teamworking
has become more comprehensive in its approach and its objectives. It is very fully
explained in the work of Buchanan (1993; Buchanan and McCalman 1989).

The timeliness of this approach was linked to the shop steward tradition, as well as to the production and market imperatives which were its main drives. The shop steward had been the main focus of representation and loyalty in the collective bargaining framework of industrial relations. As the collective bargaining influence waned, there was a vacuum that needed to be filled. Managements seized on the opportunity to maintain and develop group cohesion around work activities that were aligned directly with organisational requirements. Teamworking aims to focus work activity among small, face-to-face groups of about a dozen members, who are mutually supportive and who operate with minimal supervision.

Within the teamworking framework and ethos, team briefing is an initiative that attempts to do a number of different things simultaneously. It provides authoritative information at regular intervals, so that people know what is going on, the information is geared to achievement of production targets and other features of organisational objectives, it is delivered face to face to provide scope for questions and clarification, and it emphasises the role of supervisors and line managers as the source of information:

> They are often used to cascade information or managerial messages throughout the organisation. The teams are usually based round a common production or service area, rather than an occupation, and usually comprise between four and fifteen people. The leader of the team is usually the manager or supervisor of the section and should be trained in the principles and skills of how to brief. The meetings last for no more than 30 minutes, and time should be left for questions from employees. Meetings should be held at least monthly or on a regular pre-arranged basis.   (Holden 1997, p. 624)

With goodwill and managerial discipline, team briefing can be a valuable contributor to employee involvement, as it deals in that precious commodity, information. Traditionally, there has perhaps been a managerial view that people doing the work are not interested in anything other than the immediate and short term and that the manager's status partly rests on knowing what others don't know. For this reason all the managers and supervisors in the communications chain have to be committed to making it a success, as well as having the training that Holden refers to above. Team briefing gets easier once it is established as a regular event. The first briefing will probably go very well and the second will be even better. It is important that management enthusiasm and commitment do not flag just as the employees are getting used to the process.

During the early 1980s there was a boost to the team briefing process because so many managements had so much bad news to convey. When you are losing money and profitability, there is a great incentive to explain to the workforce exactly how grim the situation is, so that they do not look for big pay rises. Team briefing as a means to maintain the team ethos continues, but the main method of team working has changed to the quality initiative.

Total quality management

Total quality management – universally abridged to TQM – can be regarded as one of the biggest developments in management over the latter part of the twentieth century. Although a bold and sweeping statement, it has survived and flourished for a sustained period, it has achieved a British Standard definition and has attained the magical 'senior management support' which all personnel managers seem to regard as essential. What may be even more significant is that it has crossed international boundaries, especially the crucial boundary between East and West, as the basic concept was invented by an American, taken to Japan because of American indifference and re-exported when it was so successful:

> many of the products the Japanese now sell successfully were invented in America and manufactured according to standards set by an American. Here, in his own country, he is largely unknown – almost a prophet without honor. Yet in Japan, he is a national celebrity.
>
> (Stoner, Freeman and Gilbert 1995, p. 7)

The prophet without honour at home was the late W. Edwards Deming, who went to Japan as a struggling engineer in 1950 to propose a management approach to achieving quality production. Thirty years later it was picked up by the Americans and is now established throughout the world as a fundamental approach to management which can apply in any culture.

Initially TQM was an engineering approach, concerned with measurement and with procedures being managerially imposed in organisations, lacking the voluntary nature of the earlier quality circles (Sewell and Wilkinson 1992). In Britain TQM is gradually being seen as needing an extra dimension, developing from its engineering basis to give more attention to social factors, such as commitment, self-control and trust. Guest (1992) is one of several analysts who has identified a logical link between the needs of HRM and the opportunity of TQM.

Total quality management can only appear in a chapter on employee involvement if it goes beyond the type of managerially determined electronic surveillance described by Graham Sewell and Barry Wilkinson above. The recent path-breaking work by Adrian Wilkinson and his colleagues (1991, 1992, 1994) suggests that TQM in Britain is taking that course.

Investors in People

The Government commits a considerable proportion of its annual expenditure to vocational training. Opposition parties, employer bodies and trade unions claim that the commitment should be even greater. All interests share a concern that British training has not succeeded in developing the skilled and committed workforce that is needed in the current economic context of intense international competition.

Among a range of national initiatives is Investors in People (IIP), which aims to develop employer commitment to developing their staff in line with business objectives. This is widely regarded as an initiative of considerable potential, as it should achieve the twin objectives of skill and commitment at the same time as improving business effectiveness. Very few companies have achieved the required standard and there was little sign that the national objectives would be reached until the Spring of 1994, when IIP was relaunched. By the Autumn the level of commitment to the IIP concept had increased, although only 350 companies had achieved the standard.

It may be that more skilful marketing and clearer explanation are what is required to make IIP successful. We believe that is only a small part of what is needed. What will convince employers and employees is a convincing analysis and explanation of the tangible benefits that IIP is producing in the businesses where the standard has been achieved. The unanswered questions include:

1. **Process benefits**: How has IIP changed attitudes of training expenditure away from cost and towards investment? How is the return on training measured? Does IIP help to justify training expenditure? Does it provide a focus for existing initiatives?
2. **Business benefits**: What have been the benefits to the business from the IIP award? How have these benefits been measured? How do they split between the tangible and the intangible? Are they real or assumed?
3. **Employees**: What have been employee attitudes toward IIP? How has their commitment been won? How have anxieties about employment insecurity been allayed (if it has)? What do employees see as the personal benefits to them?
4. **The personnel function**: How has the personnel function featured in IIP, as instigator and creative leader, as administrative support, as bystander, or as something else? Is the personnel function the key to success in IIP?

IIP offers an excellent prospect of real progress in finding a way to create more effectively competitive business through developing the skills and commitment of those who work in the businesses. It may be just one more wave in employee involvement, but it is an initiative that is proving popular among managers of all sorts and its developing take-up suggests it will now flourish.

European Works Councils

In September 1996 the European Union's Works Council Directive came into effect. While not applicable in the UK, many companies based here are nevertheless obliged to set up councils by virtue of the fact that they employ substantial numbers of staff in other EU countries. Furthermore, many UK subsidiaries of larger European firms have had to comply and introduce company councils along the lines demanded by the new law. However, there is nothing new about the idea of setting up a company council. According to a survey by IRS (1995, pp. 9–16), three-quarters of their sample had established such arrangements *before* 1990.

The methods used to elect representatives, the frequency with which councils meet, and the range and scope of discussions will all vary from organisation to organisation – as will the extent to which the council has a role in determining policy and practice. (For detailed information on these matters, see IDS Study 1994, 1996; IRS 1995; and Carley 1995; all of which include case studies showing how different organisations have approached the setting-up and running of councils.) However, most of the recent initiatives have complied with only the minimum requirements as set out in the EU Directive. These are:

- Councils must have between 3 and 30 members.
- These individuals must be elected to the council by the workforce.
- Regular council meetings are to be held annually at which management are obliged to give reports concerning progress, prospects, the financial situation and plans relating to sales, production, employment, investment and/or the corporate structure.

▶ Special meetings are to be held in 'exceptional' circumstances when, for example, large-scale redundancies or plant relocations are being contemplated.

▶ Councils have the right to be informed and consulted about 'any measure liable to have a considerable effect on employees' interests'.

▶ Only matters that are 'community scale' need be discussed. There is no legal requirement to cover affairs affecting employees in only one EU country.

European Works Councils are not therefore instruments of industrial democracy and there is no right to co-determination with management over areas of employment policy, as has long been the approach in Germany.

While it is too early to tell what effects EWCs are going to have, it is difficult to avoid viewing them as falling somewhat between two stools, with the result that they are in danger of being seen as costly irrelevances. They have too few teeth and meet too rarely to have any real impact on decision-making or to play a significant role in communication, yet they remain frustratingly rule-bound and costly to organise.

Strategy and employee involvement

The position adopted on employee involvement by a management is one of the most profound of all strategic issues, with ethical, social and political dimensions, as well as affecting all aspects of human resource management.

Many managers look for what one might call the bottom-line argument. Does employee involvement 'work'? Does it enhance employee commitment and effectiveness? There is a simplistic answer to that sort of question which runs that it must 'work' because it makes sense: people will support that which they have helped to create. Without involvement there will be no commitment and motivation, both of which are much lauded as necessary features of corporate culture. There are, however, limitations to the validity of that argument.

The channel of involvement is through the work that people do, yet the work that some people do lacks sufficient job content for involvement to offer any scope for the degree of personal commitment that involvement requires. There is a constant cry that there is a shortage of skilled people, yet many jobs call for little skill. If one is engaged in routine, mind-numbing tasks, offers of involvement are difficult to understand and respond to. In jobs of this nature the best prospect for the people doing the work is to find some degree of mental and emotional detachment from it, rather than involvement.

WINDOW ON PRACTICE

Mary, a programmer, is married to John, a brick-layer. They take it in turns to work full-time while the other looks after the domestic duties and picks up casual work. They each aim to work full-time for 4–5 months a year and to spend 2–3 months travelling round Europe in their motor caravan with their two small children. They both find it reasonably easy to obtain the short spells of working that they need, as they are both highly skilled and efficient. To them employee involvement is an irrelevance and they seek clearly defined tasks with specific objectives.

Some people find the implications of involvement stressful, as they feel under pressure to display acceptable behaviours, like enthusiasm and withholding criticism, which they regard as artificial and unnecessary.

The decline of the organisation as an entity also reduced the scope for involvement. If the employer distances the employees by some form of casualisation, the message is clear: 'You are not a part of the business. We are keeping you at arm's length. There are insiders and outsiders; you are an outsider, not a stakeholder.'

A different type of justification for employee involvement is that it is a straightforward legal and moral obligation of any employer to treat employees decently and with respect. That includes providing information, explanation of management decisions, training and career opportunities, opportunities to complain and to suggest improvements. If that is the management motivation towards involvement, then it is providing opportunity rather than making demands that go beyond the bounds of the employment contract, so there is as much scope to opt out of involvement as there is to opt in.

The management strategy on involvement will therefore stem from the values and personal priorities of the management team as well as the type of business that is being managed. It is difficult to devise involvement strategies that are equally appropriate for all members of the business. The opportunities for involvement of senior managers are infinitely greater than those of security guards, because their jobs are so much more varied and individualised. The need for employee involvement in, say, a theatre company is much stronger than in running a pub with part-time bar staff.

Summary propositions

26.1 A collective approach to employee relations and employee involvement does not now have the emphasis it had in the period before 1980.

26.2 Employee involvement practices have evolved from a specifically British view of industrial democracy as a means of balancing the relative power of employers, trade unions and the state, which was propounded by Hugh Clegg in the 1960s.

26.3 It is possible to identify waves in employee involvement approaches, with different ideas being adopted as others recede in popularity.

26.4 The current popular ideas are team briefing, total quality management, investors in people and European Works Councils. All these are firmly managerial, with the power balance ideas of industrial democracy largely missing.

26.5 The approach a business adopts to employee involvement will depend on the personal views and priorities of the management team, as well as the nature of the business itself.

References

ACAS (1985) *Annual Report, 1984*, London: HMSO.

Buchanan, D. (1993) 'Principles and practice of work design', in K. Sisson (ed.), *Personnel Management*, 2nd edn, Oxford: Blackwell.

Buchanan, D. and McCalman, J. (1989) *High Performance Work Systems*, London: Routledge.

Lord Bullock (1977) *Report of the Committee of Enquiry on Industrial Democracy*, London, HMSO.

Carley, M. (1995) 'Talking shops or serious forums?' *People Management*, July.

Clegg, H. A. (1960) *A New Approach to Industrial Democracy*, Oxford: Blackwell.

Conservative Political Centre (1968) *Fair Deal at Work*.

Dowling, M., Goodman, J., Gotting, D. and Hyman, J. (1981), 'Employee participation: survey evidence from the north west', *Employment Gazette*, April.

Dunlop, J. T. (1958) *Industrial Relations Systems*, London: Harper and Row.

Guest, D. (1992) 'Human resource management in the U.K.', in B. Towers (ed.), *Handbook of Human Resource Management*, Oxford: Blackwell.

Hanson, C. and Rathkey, P. (1984) 'Industrial democracy: a post-Bullock shopfloor view', *British Journal of Industrial Relations*, Vol. 22, No. 2, pp. 154–68.

Holden, L. (1997) 'Employee involvement', in I. Beardwell and L. Holden (eds.), *Human Resource Management*, 2nd edn, London: Pitman.

IDS Study (1994) *Company Councils*, September, Incomes Data Services. London.

IDS Study (1996) *European Works Councils*, April, Incomes Data Services. London.

IRS (1995) 'Employee representation arrangements 2: company councils', *Employment Trends*, 590.

Mackay, L. E. and Torrington, D. P. (1986) *The Changing Nature of the Personnel Function*, London: IPM.

Marchington, M. P., Goodman, J. F. B., Wilkinson, A. J. and Ackers, P. (1992) *New Developments in Employee Involvement*, Employment Department Research Series No. 2, London: HMSO.

Marchington, M. P., Wilkinson, A. J. and Ackers, P. (1993) 'Waving or Drowning in Participation?'; *Personnel Management*, March, pp. 46–50.

Ramsay, H. (1991), 'Re-inventing the Wheel? A Review of the Development and Performance of Employee Involvement', *Human Resource Management Journal*, Vol. 1, No. 4, pp. 1–22.

Royal Commission on Trade Unions and Employers' Associations (1968) *Report*, London: HMSO. (The Donovan Commission).

Sewell, G. and Wilkinson, B. (1992) 'Empowerment or Emasculation? Shopfloor Surveillance in a Total Quality Organisation', in P. Blyton and P. Turnbull (eds.), *Reassessing Human Resource Management*, London: Sage.

Stoner, J. A. F., Freeman, R. E. and Gilbert, D. R. (1995) *Management*, 6th edn, Englewood Cliffs, NJ: Prentice Hall International.

Storey, J. and Sisson, K. (1993) *Managing Human Resources and Industrial Relations*, Milton Keynes: Open University Press.

Teague, P. (1991) 'Human Resource Management, Labour Market Institutions and European Integration', *Human Resource Management Journal*, Vol. 2, No. 1.

Wilkinson, A. J. (1994) 'Managing Human Resources for Quality' in B. G. Dale (ed.), *Managing Quality*, 2nd edn, London: Prentice Hall International.

Wilkinson, A. J., Allen, P. and Snape, E. (1991) 'TQM and the Management of Labour', *Employee Relations*, Vol. 13, No. 1, pp. 24–31.

Wilkinson, A. J., Marchington, M. P., Goodman, J. F. B. and Ackers, P. (1992) 'Total Quality Management and Employee Involvement', *Human Resource Management Journal*, Vol. 2, No. 4, pp. 1–20.

General discussion topics

1. Why should employees be involved, and what should they be involved in?
2. To what extent would you regard the history of employee involvement in Britain as a history of failure?
3. Is TQM an aspect of human resource management or a much narrower approach to effectiveness, with an over-reliance on statistical measures?

CHAPTER 27

Trade union recognition and consultation

Trade union recognition remains widespread in Britain, despite the steep decline in trade union membership levels over the past two decades. In 1979, according to Government figures, a total of 13.3 million workers were members of 453 separate trade unions. By 1995 there were only 8.3 million in 238 unions (*Labour Market Trends* 1997). While a number of reasons have been put forward to explain this trend, a major cause is the expansion of industries which have not tradition-ally recognised trade unions, combined with a comparative decline in the more heavily unionised sectors. The current situation is thus very varied, with union membership holding up in public sector organisations, larger manufacturing con-cerns and in the transport and distribution sectors, and far lower levels in other private sector companies. This pattern is reflected in the number of organisations which formally recognise trade unions for bargaining purposes. Here, too, the extent of the decline has varied from sector to sector. The Workplace Industrial Relations Survey (Millward *et al.* 1992) provides comprehensive information about all aspects of industrial relations, and Table 27.1 shows the trends between 1980 and 1990. Overall, just under half of all employees in the UK are covered by a collective agreement of one kind or another.

The extent to which the decline in trade union influence is terminal is a matter of debate, with some seeing unions as no longer relevant to an advanced society; others believe that unionism has moved to a more marginal position in employee relations; while some sense the prospect of a resurrection, based on support from the European Commission, the Labour Party and a new style of leadership within the TUC itself:

Table 27.1 Changes in the proportion (%) of establishments recognising trade unions between 1980 and 1990

	Manufacturing		Services		Public Sector	
	1980	*1990*	*1980*	*1990*	*1980*	*1990*
Manual workers	65	44	33	31	76	78
Non-manual workers	27	23	28	26	91	84
All employees	65	44	41	36	94	87

Source: Millward *et al.* 1992

> There are signs the tide is turning in favour of the unions. Mind-blowing militants still wave red flags, but they are nobodies going nowhere. The rise of middle class unemployment, the hopelessness of many young people without jobs, the entrenchment of union reform and the resentment created by boardroom greed all favour the restoration of responsible trade unionism.
>
> (Jones 1994, p. 45)

It remains to be seen whether this resurrection will actually take place, but we can be sure that some personnel managers are in establishments where unions are not recognised and where recognition is unlikely, some are in establishments where they are working towards recognition, and many others are in a situation where unions are recognised to some degree for at least part of the workforce. A fourth group will have experienced, or may yet experience, situations in which unions have had recognition withdrawn. In most cases, therefore, the issue of the extent and type of union recognition remains an issue of some significance in the day-to-day management of the personnel function. Perhaps the situation is best described by Marchington:

> Diversity is more noticeable than similarity, uneven developments are more typical than common trends, and changes take place in different directions in different workplaces.   (Marchington 1995, p. 82)

There is no standard pattern and certainly no grand design. It is probably true to say that trade unions remain unfashionable, despite the election of a Labour Government in 1997, but the general attitude towards them is rarely now as hostile and suspicious as it was throughout the 1980s.

Defining recognition

Recognition, in the context of employee relations, is defined fairly narrowly in law. As a legal concept, the term has become increasingly important in recent years with the extension of consultation rights to recognised trade unions on a variety of workplace issues such as collective redundancy, transfer of undertakings, health and safety and occupational pensions. Section 178 of the 1992 Trade Union and Labour Relations (Consolidation) Act retains the established legal definition of recognition as being a situation in which, via either a formal written agreement or custom and practice, employers engage in collective bargaining with union representatives about all or some the following matters:

1. Terms and conditions of employment, or the physical conditions in which any workers are required to work.
2. Engagement or non-engagement, or termination or suspension of employment or the duties of employment of one or more workers.
3. Allocation of work or the duties of employment as between workers or groups of workers.
4. Matters of discipline.
5. The membership or non-membership of a trade union on the part of a worker.
6. Facilities for officials of trade unions.
7. The machinery for negotiation or consultation and other procedures, relating to any of the foregoing matters, including the recognition by

employers or employers' associations of the right of a trade union to represent workers in any such negotiation or consultation or in the carrying out of such procedures.

The decision to recognise or to withdraw recognition from a trade union thus has implications far beyond the terms of the agreement itself. Once recognised, the union gains a whole raft of defined legal rights to exercise on behalf of its members. Aside from the consultation rights identified above, these include the right to receive collective bargaining information and the right for stewards to have reasonable time off work for industrial relations, trade union and public duties. Furthermore, the Transfer Regulations of 1981 require that union recognition continues and collective agreements remain in force after the transfer of an undertaking to new ownership, providing that the transferred undertaking retains 'an identity distinct from the remainder of the transferee's undertaking'.

At the time of writing, there is no legal requirement on the part of employers to recognise trade unions – although such a right was at one time available to union organisers under the Employment Protection Act 1975. Since the repeal of these provisions in 1980 there has been no statutory right for a trade union to be recognised for any purpose, even in situations where the vast majority of the workforce are union members. However, it now seems likely that the law is to change again, following the election of a new Government committed to removing the employer's right to refuse recognition in situations where over 50 per cent of employees in a particular undertaking vote for recognition in a secret ballot.

Collective consent

Management always needs the collective consent of its employees: it also needs a mandate to manage. In many situations this is at least partly delivered by trade union recognition. The recent changes in union membership, employment legislation, high unemployment and economic recession have provided academic analysts with the challenge of describing how employee relations strategies have changed. We still lack a full explanation, but one of the best-known approaches has been the attempt of Purcell and Sisson (1983) to categorise management styles in industrial relations. These are summarised in Table 27.2 and the key distinguishing feature is of a collective view of the workforce. From a personnel management perspective this is a useful way of separating out this category of personnel work from the rest as being those aspects in which one is dealing with categories and collectives of people, rather than with individuals.

This is a useful set of categories, although some organisations do not fit easily into any one of them. Most large, long-established companies will be in one of the last three; most public sector organisations will be in category 4; and many of the newer businesses will be in some version of category 2.

ACTIVITY BOX 27.1

Which of the five categories Table 27.2 most closely fits your establishment? Does the category vary for different groups of employees?

Table 27.2 Categories of management styles in employee relations

Style	Characteristics
1. Traditional	Fire-fighting approach. Employee relations not important until there is trouble. Low pay. Hostile to trade unions. Authoritarian. Typical in small, owner-managed businesses.
2. Paternalist	Unions regarded as unnecessary because of employer's enlightenment. High pay. Concentration on encouraging employee identification with business objectives.
3. Consultative	Union participation encouraged through recognition. Problem-solving, informal approach to employee relations. Emphasis on two-way communications.
4. Constitutional	Similar to consultative, but emphasis on formal agreements to regulate relationship between two powerful protagonists.
5. Opportunistic	Large company devolving responsibility for employee relations to subsidiaries, with no common approach but emphasis on unit profitability.

Source: Purcell and Sisson (1983, pp. 112–18).

Taking a strictly managerial view of trade unions and their recognition, the interest is the degree to which recognition will deliver collective consent to a general framework of rules and guidelines within which management and employees operate. Collective consent implies the acceptance of a situation, while agreement has the more positive connotation of commitment following some degree of initiative in bringing the situation into existence.

We are not, therefore, necessarily describing active employee participation in managerial decision-making. The range is wider, to include the variety of circumstances in which employees consent collectively to managerial authority, so long as they find it acceptable.

In order to couch the discussion in terms that can embrace a variety of styles, we set out seven categories of consent, in which there is a steadily increasing degree of collective employee involvement. We begin with a category in which there is straightforward and unquestioning acceptance of management authority, and then move through various stages of increasing participation in decision-making and the necessary changes in management style as the power balance alters and the significance of bargaining develops and extends to more and more areas of organisational life.

1. **Normative**: We use this term in the sense of Etzioni (1961), who described 'normative' organisations as being those in which the involvement of individuals was attributable to a strong sense of moral obligation. Any challenge to authority would imply a refutation of the shared norms and was therefore unthinkable. Many of the exercises in corporate culture are construed by some as strategies to develop this type of consent, with strong emphasis on commitment and the suppression of views opposed to managerial orthodoxy.

2. **Disorganised**: In organisations that are not normative there may be collective consent simply because there is no collective focus for a

challenge, so disorganised consent is where there may be discontent but consent is maintained through lack of employee organisation to articulate and endorse the dissatisfaction. A Victorian sweatshop would come into this category.

3. **Organised**: When employees organise it is nearly always in trade unions and the first collective activities are usually in dealing with general grievances. It is very unlikely that there will be any degree of involvement in the management decision-making processes. Employees simply consent to obey instructions as long as grievances are dealt with.

4. **Consultative**: Consultation is a stage of development beyond initial trade union recognition, even though some employers consult with employees before – often as a means of deferring – trade union recognition. This is the first incursion into the management process as employees are asked for an opinion about management proposals before decisions are made, even though the right to decide remains with the management.

5. **Negotiated**: Negotiation implies that both parties have the power to commit and the power to withhold agreement, so that a decision can only be reached by some form of mutual accommodation. No longer is the management retaining all decision-making to itself; it is seeking some sort of bargain with employee representatives, recognising that only such reciprocity can produce what is needed.

6. **Participative**: When employee representatives reach the stage of participating in the general management of the business in which they are employed, there is a fundamental change in the control of that business, even though this may initially be theoretical rather than actual. Employee representatives take part in making the decisions on major strategic issues like expenditure on research, the opening of new plants and the introduction of new products. In arrangements for participative consent there is a balance between the decision-makers representing the interests of capital and those representing the interests of labour, though the balance is not necessarily even.

7. **Controlling**: If the employees acquire control of the organisation, as in a workers' co-operative, then the consent is a controlling type. This may sound bizarre, but there will still be a management apparatus within the organisation to which employee collective consent will be given or from which it will be withheld.

All of the above categories require some management initiative to sustain collective consent. In categories (1) and (2) it may be exhortation to ensure that commitment is kept up, or information supplied to defer organisation. In each subsequent category there is an increasing bargaining emphasis which becomes progressively more complex.

The implication is that there is a hierarchy of consent categories, through which organisations steadily progress. Although this has frequently been true in the past, it is by no means necessary. Some may begin at (6) or (7): there is no inflexible law of evolution and change can move in the opposite direction as well. Some of the recent instances of partial or complete de-recognition of trade unions could be characterised as examples of regression back down the hierarchy.

ACTIVITY BOX 27.2

At the end of Chapter 26 four current approaches to employee involvement were set out: team briefing, total quality manage- ment, Investors in People and European Works Councils. Where would you place each of those in these seven categories of consent?

Trade union recognition and bargaining units

When a trade union has recruited a number of members in an organisation, it will seek recognition from the employer in order to represent those members. The step of recognition is seldom easy but is very important as it marks a highly significant movement away from unilateral decision-making by the management. We can examine some of the questions to be considered.

Why should a union be recognised at all?

If the employees want that type of representation, they will not readily co-operate with the employer who refuses. In extreme cases this can generate sufficient antagonism to cause industrial action in support of recognition. In such situations the employer may be forced to grant partial recognition or even concede the demand for full negotiating rights over a whole range of issues. In many countries employers are compelled to recognise trade unions where there is such a desire on the part of the workforce. The desirability of collective bargaining is stressed in the EU Social Chapter and is accepted as being within the scope of state regulation across much of the continent. How far and in what way similar recognition rights will be introduced in the UK has yet to be confirmed, but it seems likely that in some circumstances employers who are not minded to agree recognition agreements will be compelled to do so where there is a clear demand from their employees.

However, there are also positive reasons for considering recognising trade unions, relating to the benefits that can flow as a result: there are employee rep- resentatives with whom to discuss, consult and negotiate so that communication and working relationships can be improved:

> There are a number of reasons why employers should choose to work with, rather than against, unions at the workplace. Firstly, management may regard trade union representatives as an essential part of the communication process in larger workplaces. Rather than being forced to establish a system for dealing with all employees, or setting up a non-union representative forum, trade unions are seen as a channel which allows for the effective resolution of issues concerned with pay bargaining or grievance handling. It is also the case that reaching agreement with union representatives, in contrast to imposing decisions, can provide decisions with a legitimacy which otherwise would be lacking. It can also lead to better decisions as well.　　　　　(Marchington and Wilkinson 1996, p. 237)

There is also a variety of arguments that can be put against choosing to recog- nise a trade union and resisting doing so. Employers are often apprehensive about the degree of rigidity in employment practice that union aims for security of employment appear to imply, and therefore consider to what extent collective consent can be achieved by other means, providing that the management work hard at both securing and maintaining that consent.

A survey undertaken by IRS (1995a, pp. 3–9) asked company representatives to outline the advantages and disadvantages of trade union recognition. The benefits suggested included the stable structure such a relationship gives to the management of employees, the promotion of smooth industrial relations and its role in providing a mechanism for upward communication from the staff. A further perceived advantage was its cost-effectiveness as a communication tool when compared to more individualised approaches. The drawbacks principally related to a perception that unions tend to resist change and take a long time to get things done. The result is a reduction in the ability of managers to respond quickly and flexibly to market pressures and opportunities.

When should a union be recognised?

A union should be recognised only when it has sufficient support from the employees, but there is no simple way of determining what is sufficient. In the late 1970s, when the Advisory, Conciliation and Arbitration Service was responsible for making recommendations on recognition claims, there were a number of occasions where recognition was advocated in situations where less than 40 per cent of the workforce were union members. In so doing they took into account the degree of union organisation and efficiency, the number of representatives, the size of constituency and the degree of opposition to recognition from non-union employees. There may thus be situations in which recognition has advantages to offer even when there is no clear majority of employees who have joined the union or unions concerned. A frequent encouragement for the management of a business to recognise a union relatively quickly is where there is the possibility of competing claims, with some employees seeking to get another union established because they do not like the first.

WINDOW ON PRACTICE

An interesting footnote to British industrial relations is the elimination of trade unions at the Government Communications Headquarters at Cheltenham. GCHQ produces a signal intelligence to support the security, defence, foreign and economic policies of the British government. Like most public sector bodies, there has been a strong tradition of union representation among the several thousand staff who are employed. In the early 1980s the Government became concerned about the possible risk to security of this type of representation in a body where such sensitive data were handled. There was a particular apprehension about the possibility of industrial action impeding urgent defence initiatives. In January 1984 union members were offered £1,000 each to 'buy out' their membership. All but a small number accepted the offer, but the action was regarded as a serious attack on union rights and there were a series of legal moves, including an appeal to the European Court of Human Rights, to have the ban declared invalid. In October 1988 fourteen of the employees who had not resigned their union membership were dismissed. The incoming 1997 Government was pledged to restore negotiating rights, and fulfilled the pledge within two weeks of taking office, although maintaining a ban against industrial action. In July those who had been dismissed returned to work.

For whom should a union be recognised?

A union should be recognised for that group of employees who have a sufficient commonality of interests, terms and conditions for one union to be able to represent them and the management be able to respond. This group of employees are sometimes described as those making up a bargaining unit; the boundaries of the units need careful consideration by the management to determine what is most appropriate and what consequent response to recognition claims they will make. Traditionally a number of boundaries have generally been acknowledged, with manual employees being represented by different unions from white-collar employees, and skilled employees being represented by a different union from the semi-skilled and unskilled as well as from those possessing different skills.

These traditional boundaries have increasingly become blurred. The Trade Union Reform and Employment Rights Act 1993 provides employees with a statutory right to join the union of their choice, regardless of what might be convenient for the local management, so that the famous Bridlington agreement on dealing with disputes between unions about membership is effectively redundant. The trend towards 'single status' arrangements and the bringing together of previously separate negotiating procedures round a 'single table' has further removed hard-and-fast demarcations of this kind. Furthermore, the increasing tendency for unions to merge to form 'super-unions' representing all types of employees has removed many of the old distinctions between white- and blue-collar unions. That said, it is clear from the 1995 IRS survey (IRS 1995a, pp. 3–9) that a good number of companies still treat these groups differently in terms of the scope of collective bargaining engaged in on their behalf. In most cases this involves granting full recognition to manual grades but only partial recognition to their white-collar counterparts.

A common type of new recognition arrangement is where an employer agrees recognition terms with one union only. These are popularly known as 'single-union' agreements, but they are more far-reaching in their departure from traditional arrangements than simply focusing on a single union. They are typically on greenfield sites and in businesses of technological sophistication. Their essential novelty is the closeness and extent of the working relationship between management and union. Union officials find that they have less freedom of action on some matters than their members expect, but also find they are involved in the full range of human resource management questions, not simply the familiar terrain of collective bargaining. The agreements are also frequently accompanied by 'no strike' clauses, which supposedly remove the need for industrial action by providing for independent arbitration in situations where management and union fail to reach agreement. Single-status arrangements also often feature in single-union deals. Such agreements, by definition, therefore involve negotiating on the basis of one set of terms and conditions for all employees.

For what should a union be recognised?

A union can seek recognition on anything that might be covered in a contract of employment, but the employer may agree to recognition only for a limited range of topics. The irreducible minimum is assistance by a union representative for members with grievances, but the extent to which matters beyond that are recognised as being a subject of bargaining depends on which consent category the business is in. It also depends on the possible existence of other agreements that could take some matters out of the scope of local recognition. A feature of some new-style agreements is an acceptance that certain matters are potentially subject to negotiation with the recognised union (e.g. pay and redundancy), while in other areas the union has the right only to be consulted.

Although there is not now a legal right to recognition, different statutes provide rights for independent trade unions that have been recognised. These are:

1. The right for both union and officials and members to time off work for trade union reasons.
2. The right to consultation on redundancies.
3. The right to have information disclosed to them for the purposes of collective bargaining.
4. Rights to be consulted ahead of redundancies.
5. Various rights in connection with the transfer of undertakings to new ownership.
6. The right to both consultation and information on matters of health and safety.
7. Rights to information on occupational pensions.

Management organisation for recognition

The 'category of consent' for a business will influence its style of management and the structure of its management organisation, with the most important change coming when an organisation moves from the second to the third category mentioned earlier in this chapter (see under Collective Consent). That is the point at which there is some guarantee of commitment by management to procedure and the acknowledgement that a limited range of management decisions could be successfully challenged by the employees, causing those decisions to be altered.

As personnel managers have become more dominant in the management handling of employee relations issues, the traditional pattern of personnel and line management has altered. There is still, however, a notional distinction between the personnel and line roles. The Commission on Industrial Relations has made this comment:

1. The line manager is necessarily responsible for industrial relations within his particular area of operations. He needs freedom to manage his plant, department or section effectively within agreed policies and with access to specialist advice.
2. The personnel manager should help by supplying expert knowledge and skill and by monitoring the consistent execution of industrial relations policies and programmes throughout the company. He needs the backing of top management and must establish the authority which comes from giving sound advice.
(CIR 1973, p. 26)

The same publication indicates (*ibid.*, p. 13) that the simple distinction between advisory and executive roles is more useful as an instrument of analysis than as a means of describing current practice, which varies so much. Some employers give full executive authority to industrial relations specialists. Parker, Hawes and Lumb illustrate the variation with two quotations from company policy statements:

> Management responsibility for the conduct of industrial relations is . . .
> delegated by the accountable line manager to his senior industrial relations
> executive who will make industrial relations decisions or review such
> decisions and ensure their consistency with established policy, practices and
> procedure . . .
>
> The management of employees is the responsibility of line management; the
> role of personnel specialists is to advise and assist line management in the
> exercise of that responsibility and to provide requisite supporting services.
>
> (Parker *et al.* 1971, p. 23)

Although the use of the exclusive male gender is now dated, the fundamental
nature of the responsibility split seems to remain. What has changed is the nature
of the advice offered. It used to be thoughtful, genuinely intended to be helpful and
was sometimes welcome, but its basis was simply general experience and good
intentions. The recipient could use or ignore it at will, depending on the common-
sense assessment of its value. Legislation has caused the need for advice of the type
offered by a professional. This is thoughtful, intended to be helpful, but may not be
welcome. It will be based on an informed examination of statute and precedent, and
will include a full appreciation of the strategic implications of whatever is being considered. No personnel manager can now regard the general company strategy as
something of concern only for other members of the management team. Although
this is such an obvious point, it needs reiteration as a number of those applying for
courses in personnel management retain a view that personnel is much more even-
handed and some commentators castigate personnel managers for adopting a managerial approach. One recent commentary criticised personnel managers for
abandoning their social and religious principles, adopting a managerial rather than
independent professional stance, ignoring the pluralistic nature of work organisations and consolidating an exploitative relationship between people at work (Hart
1993). Today's personnel manager is inescapably and necessarily a representative of
management interests. In union recognition issues in particular, there is no point in
having a personnel manager involved who does not adopt that perspective.

The personnel manager therefore carries a quite different type of authority. It
may also be that people see the need not only for advice, but also for representation by someone who knows the esoteric rules of procedure and behaviour in a
highly stylised form of discussion.

As well as advice, the employer needs to see that all employment matters are
administered in a way that is consistent with the legislative framework, and part of
that requirement is that managerial actions should be consistent with each other.

In many management decisions in relation to employees the correctness lies
not only in the intrinsic quality of the decision but also in the consistency of management handling of similar matters previously and in other parts of the business.
In employment law consistency is an important feature of justice, and it can be
achieved in a company, either by having inflexible rules or by having a single
source of control on decisions made.

The need for specialist advice based on a sound knowledge of the law and the
need for an associated control over a wide range of management decisions have
changed the range of options open to the employer in deploying personnel
experts. The personnel officer may be charged with the task of deciding action on
all employment matters and then implementing those decisions. Alternatively,
the officer may monitor tentative decisions by others, which are agreed or vetoed
before they are confirmed and implemented by those who formulated them.

Management strategy for union recognition

There is a sequence of steps in the strategy of a management for union recognition.

Management attitudes

However dominant personnel specialists may be on employee relations matters, the other members of management do not simply leave them to get on with trade union recognition while they pursue their other and more interesting preoccupations. The step of recognition, or the extension of recognition, and all that follows can affect other policy matters such as the introduction of new products, investment in new plant, the manning of equipment and the opening or closure of establishments.

Equally, policy decisions to do with marketing, manufacturing, financing or new technology are likely to have employment repercussions. Union recognition or extension of recognition represents the introduction of change which can have major implications in all parts of the life of the business. For this reason it is important that collective management attitudes towards recognition should have as wide a degree of consensus as possible. Then policy on recognition and its consequences can be fully integrated with other aspects of policy.

The previous three sentences represent a homily that has been repeated for years, and managers are frequently sceptical about such bland exhortations to do something which they know to be extremely difficult. Some of the problems lie in the specialised nature of the issue. The very existence of trade unions is resented by some and the alleged behaviour of trade unionists has been given as the reason for the fall of governments, let alone managerial ineffectiveness. The reasons justifying trade union recognition in general, and on some contentious matters in particular, are not readily appreciated, and when understood may still be disputed. Another difficulty is the need for a positive rather than grudging approach to recognition. If the management recognise a trade union only because they feel there is no alternative, then they will derive scant benefit from the arrangement. As with other aspects of change in organisations it can be an initiative towards improvement and development, or it can be a defensive reaction to something distasteful and unwanted. It is also typical for the new convert to trade union recognition to be disappointed with the outcome. The conventional illustration of this attitude is where management have been persuaded that rank-and-file employees will make a contribution to better management decisions if they are involved through their union being recognised. A few months later there are bitter, disillusioned remarks about the unwillingness of the employees to discuss anything other than trivial matters like the colour of their overalls.

These and other problems about the integration of policy and a management consensus on recognition can probably only be resolved by full and lengthy discussion by members of management to find and then agree on a collective view.

Preparing to recognise

Does a management respond or initiate on recognition? Does it wait for a claim and then treat it on its merits, or does it invite a claim? The answer to these questions will come from a consideration of timing. It has already been suggested that care has to be taken with a recognition claim that the time is ripe, not too soon or too late. There is always a danger that recognition will be harder if deferred. The findings of the Commission on Industrial Relations undertaken in 1973 found several situations like this which remain relevant for personnel managers in the 1990s:

> the success of the company's products in the markets of the world meant that management had to concentrate, to the virtual exclusion of all else, on increasing output . . . The problems arising from the needs and aspirations of a large number of people had been largely shelved under the presence of the more immediate need to meet production targets. (CIR 1973, p. 12)

Another argument in favour of a recognition initiative by the management is that most of the areas of employment where recognition has not yet been granted are white-collar; one of the traditional reasons for white-collar employees not joining unions is their feeling that the management do not approve. They may tend to identify with the management and do not want to do things that are disliked.

Preparing to recognise requires a decision on whether to wait or to initiate. It also requires decisions on strategy about which union would be most 'appropriate', what the boundaries of the bargaining units could be and on what matters recognition would be contemplated.

Organisation, communication and responsibility

How are the management to organise themselves to make recognition work? This process will involve a re-examination of the decision-making processes so that the additional input of employee consent can be incorporated with the other variables to be evaluated. It does not mean that managers have to get permission from their employees before they do anything – even though this is how union recognition is often caricatured. The decision-making processes have to be examined and the boundaries of managerial roles redrawn. Any recognition step involves moving one or more items off the list that are customarily a subject for unilateral decision and onto the list of those for joint regulation. When that happens it will involve not only a different approach but also a different process of discussion and validation within the management ranks.

The contract for recognition

Ideally, there will be some written statement to which both parties assent; this will include the basic factual information about which union is a party to the agreement, what the bargaining unit is and what the subjects of recognition are. It may include much more, as it is an opportunity to declare aspects of the policy of the business – either the policy of the management or the policy of management and employee representatives combined. This can pave the way for openness between the parties, awareness of what is happening and consistency in management.

WINDOW ON PRACTICE

Collective agreements between employers and unions form the basis of many employment relationships. Although they are rarely legally binding in themselves, their terms are often incorporated into individual contracts of employment, either expressly or by implication or, more rarely, through agency. Such agreements also give detail to the employment structure beyond individual employee–employer relationships by covering essentially collective matters such as the provision of negotiating machinery for management and trade unions. (IDS 1997, p. 123)

Such a statement will also have the advantage of focusing the attention of policy-makers on the purposes and implications of it. The drafting of the statement could well be the basis of the full and lengthy discussion suggested earlier in this chapter. The CIR give us a useful summary of the benefits of a written statement of policy:

> Firstly, the processes involved in producing the document will themselves have been valuable in focusing minds on the purpose of the policy. They clarify intentions and eliminate uncertainties which may exist when reliance is placed on custom and practice or when policy is a matter of surmise. Secondly, a written document provides an objective reference point in the communication of policy to managers, employees and their representatives. Thirdly, by making clear the starting point of policy it provides a basis for change. A written policy need not be inflexible but should be reviewed and adapted as circumstances require. By being written it should, in fact, be easier to change than policies which are embedded in custom and practice, tradition and precedent.   (CIR 1973, p. 6)

We have already referred to the move by some employers to sign single-union agreements when setting up new plants. These avoid, on the one hand, a long-running series of arguments with unions seeking recognition and, on the other hand, the problems of fragmented bargaining arrangements. It also shifts any rivalry between unions to the stage before recognition. Pirelli General approached five different unions in south Wales:

> In each case the company outlined in some detail its proposed personnel philosophy and policies for the new factory, and each union was asked whether it wished to be considered for single recognition on those broad terms. All five unions . . . responded positively and enthusiastically. The prize . . . was the creation of new jobs and new union recruits in an area of very high unemployment.   (Yeandle and Clark 1989, p. 37)

Derecognition

Derecognition of trade unions is often seen in published literature as being redolent of fundamentally undesirable 'macho' approaches to employee relations. While outright derecognition against the stated wishes of the workforce has been relatively rare, the TUC Labour Research Department has formally recorded a number of significant cases in recent years (see IRS 1996a, p. 4; 1996b, p. 4). The vast majority of these have related to specific grades of employees rather than the entire workforce. In other cases partial derecognition has occurred where the scope of matters covered by collective bargaining is narrowed. Such situations often accompany moves by employers to establish personal employment contracts and/or to move towards pay rises based on individual performance or contribution. The result is the retention of collective bargaining machinery, but a tendency for it to be used more and more rarely in important decision-making.

It could be argued that partial derecognition of this kind ultimately leads to full derecognition as fewer staff see any particular advantage in joining the union. Over time the union becomes so numerically weak that there is no longer a persuasive case for its continued recognition – even over the limited range of issues for which it retains bargaining rights.

In such circumstances there is a good case for accepting that the union is no longer performing a useful representative function and that employees' interests might thus be better served with the introduction of other forms of representative participation such as those outlined in the previous chapter.

Summary propositions

27.1 'Recognition' is a term defined in law and which, once secured by trade unions, confers on them a number of very significant rights.

27.2 Employee consent to the exercise of management authority may be strengthened if the management recognise a trade union to provide a focused, collective questioning of that authority and consequent co-operation.

27.3 Management need to decide what bargaining units there should be, which union should be recognised for each unit, when it should be recognised and what the scope of recognition should be.

27.4 Managements at new sites often seek a 'new-style' recognition agreement with a single union and covering a wide range of human resource matters.

27.5 The step of recognition requires re-examination of management decision-making processes and will involve the personnel manager in taking the leading role in employment matters.

27.6 A written statement of policy on recognition can provide the basis for mutually beneficial development of collective consent.

27.7 Derecognition of unions is very rare, although there are instances where the support for the union withers away to such an extent that recognition becomes either token or meaningless.

References

Commission on Industrial Relations (1973) *The Role of Management in Industrial Relations*, London: HMSO.

Etzioni, A. (1961) *A Comparative Analysis of Complex Organisations*, New York: Free Press.

Hart, T. (1993) 'Human resource management: time to exorcize the militant tendency', *Employee Relations*, Vol. 15, No. 3, pp. 29–36.

IDS (1997) *Trade Unions, Employment Law Handbook*, series 2, no. 12, London: Incomes Data Services Ltd.

IRS (1995a) 'Employee representation arrangements: the trade unions', *Employment Trends 586*, London: Industrial Relations Services.

IRS (1995b) 'Brophy and the GMB', *Employment Trends 583*, London: Industrial Relations Services.

IRS (1996a) 'News section', *Employment Trends 612*, London: Industrial Relations Services.

IRS (1996b) 'News section', *Employment Trends 616*, London: Industrial Relations Services.

Jones, M. (1994) 'The tide is now turning in favour of the unions', *The Sunday Times*, 28 August, p. 45.

Labour Market Trends (1997) 'Statistical update: membership of trade unions in 1995', February, London: Department of Education and Employment.

Marchington, M. P. (1995) 'Employee relations', in S. Tyson (ed.), *Strategic Prospects for HRM*, London: IPD.

Marchington, M. P. and Parker, P. S. (1990) *Changing Patterns of Employee Relations*, Hemel Hempstead: Harvester Wheatsheaf.

Marchington, M. P. and Wilkinson, A. J. (1996) *Core Personnel and Development*, London: IPD.

Millward, N., Stevens, M., Smart, D. and Hawes, W. (1992) *Workplace Industrial Relations Survey*, Aldershot: Dartmouth.

Parker, P. A. L., Hawes, W. R. and Lumb, A. L. (1971) *The Reform of Collective Bargaining at Plant and Company Level*, London: HMSO.

Purcell, J. and Sisson, K. (1983) 'Strategies and practice in the management of industrial relations', in G. S. Bain (ed.), *Industrial Relations in Britain*, Oxford: Blackwell.

Yeandle, D. and Clark, I. (1989), 'Growing a compatible IR set-up', *People Management*, Vol. 21, No. 7, July, pp. 36–9.

General discussion topics

1. Have trade unions outlived their usefulness?
2. How would you improve on the suggestions about management organisation for recognition outlined in the chapter?
3. Why has collective bargaining in the private sector of employment been so extensively decentralised?

CHAPTER 28

Health, safety and welfare

There is always a conflict between the needs of the employer to push for increased output and efficiency and the needs of the employee to be protected from the hazards of the workplace. In the mid-nineteenth century these tensions centred almost entirely on the long hours and heavy physical demands of the factory system. In the closing years of the twentieth century the tensions are more varied and more subtle, but concern about them remains as great, being expressed by employers, employees, trade unions, government agencies and campaign groups.

Increasingly, aspects of protection are being provided by statute, and James comments:

> As a result of the directives adopted by the European Community, UK health and safety law is undergoing its most fundamental process of change since the passing of the Health and Safety at Work Act 1974.   (James 1992)

In addition some aspects result from the initiatives of managements, employees and their representatives. No matter what the source of the initiative or the nature of the concern, the personnel manager is often the focus of whatever action has to be taken.

In this chapter we first consider definitions of health, safety and welfare, and then discuss the development and importance of this area of work and the role of personnel management. Following this we cover legislation relating to health, safety and welfare and then look at the management of health and safety matters. We conclude by discussing some more general aspects of occupational health and welfare.

Definitions of health, safety and welfare

The dictionary defines 'welfare' as 'well-being', so health and safety are strictly aspects of employee welfare, which have been separately identified as being significant areas of welfare provision for some time. Others (e.g. Beaumont 1984), have noted that welfare can be very broadly defined. Using Fox (1966) as an example, he notes that welfare has been defined to encompass not only the early concern with workers' physical working conditions (sanitation, canteens, hours of work, rest pauses, etc.), but also the 'human relations school of thought', due to the achievement of job satisfaction being seen as a way to achieve higher productivity. He also notes the importance attached to counselling by early welfare workers and the human relations school.

There are two primary areas of benefit to the individual from the provision of welfare facilities – physical benefits and emotional/psychological benefits. Physical benefits would stem primarily from measures to improve health and safety, as well as from the provision of paid holidays, reduced working hours, and such like. Emotional welfare stems chiefly from any provisions made to improve mental health, for example, counselling, improved communications, or anything involving the 'human relations' needs of people at work. These benefits are, however, highly interrelated, and most welfare activities would potentially have both physical and emotional benefits. It can also be argued that employers provide for the material and intellectual welfare of their employees, in the material provisions of sick pay and pensions, and in the intellectual benefits that come from the provision of satisfying work and appropriate training and development. However, since these aspects are covered elsewhere in this book, we shall concentrate on physical and emotional welfare in this chapter.

Many provisions are less clearly seen as welfare when, for example, they are long-standing provisions made by many employers, such as canteens and time off for doctor's appointments. Other provisions are less clearly seen as welfare when they are enshrined in the contract of employment and therefore seen as standard. Holiday entitlement would come into this group: however, the amount of holiday is far from standard. In the UK holiday entitlement generally ranges from three to six weeks a year, which compares very favourably with the two weeks to which many US employees are entitled.

The development and importance of health, safety and welfare provision and the role of personnel management

The development of health, safety and welfare provision is to a large extent interrelated with the development of personnel management itself. As mentioned in Chapter 1, one of the early influences on the development of personnel management was the growth of industrial welfare workers at the beginning of the twentieth century. Enlightened employers gradually began to improve working conditions for employees and the industrial welfare worker was often concerned in implementing these changes. Much of this work was carried out voluntarily by employers, although not necessarily from altruistic motives alone. Another influence on personnel management was that of the 'human relations school', in particular the work of Elton Mayo at the Hawthorne plant of the Western Electric Company. Here there was an employee counselling programme, which operated from 1936 to 1955. It was found that such a programme was beneficial both for the mental health of the employees and their work. Other aspects of welfare provision, particularly in respect of safety, such as limitations on the hours of work of children, were enshrined in the law from as early as the 1840s and these again have become identified with the personnel function. Our research in 1994 shows that in 41 per cent of those firms with a safety officer, this person comes within the ambit of the personnel function. In those firms without a health and safety officer the personnel department had a primary responsibility for health and safety. The activities of the personnel department in relation to health and safety are shown in Table 28.1. As health and safety legislation has become more pervasive, in particular with the Health and Safety at Work Act 1974, and the surge of regulations stemming from it (many resulting from the need to harmonise health and safety regulation throughout the EU), the personnel department has taken on the role of advising managers on the consequences of this, as with the constant updating of other employment.

However, personnel managers often find their welfare origin a source of embarrassment, feeling that it has contributed to their 'soft' image, and accordingly were not sorry when the emphasis on welfare decreased between the 1950s and the 1970s. There is considerable support for the view that the personnel function can achieve authority and status in the organisation only when its activities have moved substantially beyond the welfare function (Fox 1966). More recently:

> the personnel function seeks to be, and often is, a full member of the
> management team, aiming to participate and contribute to the success
> and survival of the organization. . . . It is the credibility of personnel
> management in the eyes of other managers that matters, not their credibility
> in the eyes of the workforce.   (Mackay 1986, p. 3)

Watson (1977) has also noted the need for personnel to distance itself from its welfare image in order to facilitate full acceptance as part of the management team.

During the 1970s, however, there was some attempt to rediscover welfare (Kenny 1975). In the 1980s this renewed interest was maintained; the personnel function still had a role to play in welfare provision. The issues have changed from the early days. There has been a change in emphasis from purely physical to both physical and emotional welfare. In aspects of occupational health related to stress and personal problems, the involvement of line managers (Slaikeu and Frank 1986) and separate occupational counselling services have been advocated. There has also been more attention to health promotion as well as accident prevention. Whatever role personnel managers may play in health, safety and welfare, our research indicates that they do not rate this area of their work very highly in terms of the time that they devote to it and the importance they accord it among their other activities. Health, safety and welfare was ranked tenth out of fourteen for time spent and twelfth out of fourteen for importance to the business, which are similar results to those of ten years ago.

The importance of health, safety and welfare from the employees' point of view is clear – their lives and futures are at risk. Health and safety has been given increasing emphasis by the trade unions, especially from the late 1960s. Eva and Oswald (1981), in their book on the trade union approach to health and safety, identify a number of health and safety concerns of the unions in the early 1970s, which include the rising number of accidents; new technologies creating new hazards and new diseases; and new diseases caused by working conditions being detected. Since that time some improvements have been made:

> For the third successive year the rate of fatal accidents fell in 1992–3 to 1.3
> per 100,000 employees, generally less than a quarter of the rate 30 years
> ago. The rate of major injuries fell to 81 per 100,000.
>   (Anon, reporting on the 1992–3 Health and Safety Commission
>   annual report)

Table 28.1 Activities of the personnel department in relation to health and safety activities

Activity	Role of Personnel Department			
	Undertakes wholly	Undertakes in part	Does not undertake	Total*
Formulating policy statement on safety	25	40	34	99
Formulating safety regulations	20	29	51	100
Formulating safe systems of work	12	40	48	100
Formulating accident reporting procedures	30	38	32	100
Recording industrial accidents and notifiable diseases	35	32	33	100
Formulating accident investigation procedures	27	29	44	100
Advising management of health and safety legislation	32	35	33	100
Designing, providing, recording health and safety training	29	39	32	100
Compiling, analysing health and safety statistics	31	24	45	100
Designing safety publicity, leaflets	19	18	61	100
Liaising with occupational health and other bodies	35	30	36	101
Liaising with inspectorate	28	26	46	100
Monitoring health and safety policy, procedures	28	36	36	100
Advising on provision of protective clothing	18	31	51	99

*Figures are percentages of 214 potential responses indicating the role of personnel from our research sample in 1994

The Health and Safety Commission acknowledges that as well as representing genuine improvements in safety, these reflect the move away from high-risk heavy industry. The annual report also notes that 140,365 injuries cause an absence from work over three days, and that an estimated 3,000 of the deaths were due to asbestos. With such a rate of injury and death few would fail to acknowledge the continued importance of health and safety issues.

From the point of the view of the employer, there is a variety of reasons for supporting health, safety and welfare provision, apart from the ethical perspective and their legal obligations. It would be unfair to say that it does not play a part in employers' motives for improving these provisions, but there are other major influencing factors. The number of working days lost due to accidents at work was 10.5 million in the year 1981/2 (Health and Safety Executive 1985). If this figure were reduced by only a small percentage, the employer would save a considerable amount of money and trouble. One of the side-effects of employees with personal problems is that the quality of their work is often affected, as indicated by Knox and Fenley: 'One of the earliest signs of problem drinking is a detrimental change in attitude, performance and efficiency at work which can be detected by an alert supervisor many years before other serious consequences of alcoholic dependence' (Knox and Fenley 1985, p. 32). There is also a general feeling that employees whose health, safety and welfare needs are well looked after by the employer will be more productive and loyal employees, and may cause fewer industrial relations problems, as indicated by the following quotes from a personnel director: 'It's very difficult for people who have been treated well to take a militant attitude to one per cent one way or the other on a pay deal' (Mackay 1986, p. 13); and a personnel manager: 'Let's be honest. From our point of view, I far prefer to have a contented employee, because he's doing a good job and generating income for the company' (*ibid.*).

However, there is a continual conflict between health, safety and welfare considerations and other business priorities, as Beaumont *et al.* comment:

> Many safety officers interviewed suggested that, as a result of the recession, production considerations consistently tended to outweigh health and safety matters as a priority in management calculations. As one health and safety officer put it, trying to bring about improvements in health and safety now was very much an uphill battle.   (Beaumont *et al.* 1982, p. 38)

More recently Leach (1995) reported a line manager (who had previously been a safety officer): 'I think in general managers don't see [health and safety issues] as important as . . . other issues that they would deal with disciplinary on. I mean you do take short cuts, I do myself. I mean I am not practising a lot of what I used to preach, there's no doubt about it. Managers know it is a part of their job, but I don't think they personally see [health and safety offences] as an offence as such.'

Health, safety and welfare legislation

In the area of health and safety legislative intervention has existed continuously for well over a century, longer than for any other matter we consider. Prior to 1974 the principal statutes were the Factories Act 1961, the Offices, Shops and Railway Premises Act 1963 and the Fire Precautions Act 1971. These three Acts have all been brought up to date by the Health and Safety at Work Act 1974. In addition there is a host of health and safety Regulations primarily extending the Health and Safety Act to expand specific areas of the legislation, the most significant of which is the Control of Substances Hazardous to Health Regulations 1988 (COSHH). Increasingly, regulations have been based on EU directives, such as noise control and the manual handling of heavy loads, use of visual display units

(VDUs), and use of carcinogens and biological agents. Regulations are also supplemented by an increasing number of Codes of Practice which are not legally enforceable.

Health and Safety legislation is increasing at a high rate and the IPD (1997) note that 'This is now the most highly regulated area of employment and more proposals are on the table.' EU Directives are implemented via national law such as implementing further regulations under the Health and Safety at Work Act. The reason that EU Directives have increased so rapidly in this area is because the Single European Act 1987 added another article to the Treaty of Rome. This allowed Health and Safety Directives to be accepted by a qualified majority vote as a move towards harmonising EU health and safety legislation.

The Factories Act 1961

This Act applies to all factories where two or more persons are employed in manual labour by way of trade or for the purpose of gain in a range of operations. The Act sets out to ensure that minimum standards are maintained in factories on cleanliness, space for people to work in, temperature and ventilation, lighting, toilet facilities, clothing, accommodation and first-aid facilities. Many of the standards are fairly obvious, like keeping factories clear of the effluvia from drains, but some of them provide very precise levels that have to be met. Part of the enforcement machinery is the Factory Inspector, whose authority was reinforced under the Health and Safety at Work Act.

The Offices, Shops and Railway Premises Act 1963

The Offices, Shops and Railway Premises Act was introduced to extend to these buildings protection similar to that provided for factories. The legislation covers the type of premises described, and the general provisions are very similar to those of the Factories Act, dealing with cleanliness, lighting, ventilation and so on. There are differences in terms of the minimum space provision and temperature requirements.

The Fire Precautions Act 1971

The Fire Precautions Act lists designated premises for which a fire certificate is required, and this list includes premises being used as a place of work. When issuing a fire certificate a fire authority can impose requirements on the certificate holder. These may concern such things as:

- The means of escape from the building.
- Instruction and training for employees on what to do in the case of a fire.
- Limits to the number of people on the premises.

The Health and Safety at Work Act 1974

The Health and Safety at Work Act 1974 is an attempt to provide a comprehensive system of law, covering the health and safety of people at work:

> The objectives of the Act, which are very ambitious, include both raising the standards of safety and health for all persons at work, and protection of the

public, whose safety and health may be put at risk by the activities of persons at work. Because it is of general application, it brings within statutory protection many classes of persons who were previously unprotected.   (Howells and Barrett 1982, p. 1)

The Act is an enabling Act and, as Howells and Barrett (1982) comment, for this reason its provisions are of necessity wide and remain somewhat vague, except where they have been interpreted by the courts or augmented by regulations produced under the Act by the Secretary of State. By September 1985, 147 regulations had been issued under the Act (Health and Safety Executive 1986), although some of these are modifications or repeals of existing health and safety laws. The Act imposes, for the first time, criminal liability to comply with its provisions. The legislation is based largely on the recommendations of the Robens Committee (1970–72) and creates various new bodies and reinforces the authority of others as detailed below.

The Health and Safety Commission

The Health and Safety Commission was formed under the Act and has a chairman and between six and nine other members appointed by the Secretary of State to represent employers, employees and local authorities. The commission is responsible for carrying out the policy of the Act and providing advice to local authorities and others to enable them to discharge the responsibilities imposed upon them by the Act. It issues codes of practice and regulations, as well as having the power to make investigations and inquiries.

The Health and Safety Executive

The Commission, together with the Secretary of State, appoints three people to form the Health and Safety Executive whose duty it is to make adequate provision for the enforcement of the Health and Safety at Work Act, and to undertake the daily administration of affairs. There can also be other enforcement bodies as well as the Executive, for example local authorities.

The Factory Inspectorate

Factory inspectors had been employed for some time prior to the 1974 Act, and we have previously mentioned them regarding the enforcement of the 1961 Factories Act. As the enforcing authority of the Health and Safety at Work Act, the Executive is given the power to appoint inspectors. The role of the Inspectorate was strengthened by the 1974 Act as they were given the power to issue improvement and prohibition notices to appropriate employers. In general, inspectors have the right to enter employers' premises; carry out examinations/investigations; take measurements, photographs and recordings; take equipment and materials and examine books and documents. Initially, the number of inspectors was increased, from 681 in 1973 to 986 in 1980. However, by 1985 the number had fallen to 823. See Davis (1979) for further coverage of this aspect.

The Employment Medical Advisory Service

The Employment Medical Advisory Service was set up in 1972 to provide general advice to the government on industrial medicine matters and a corps of employment medical advisers to carry out medical examinations of employees whose health may have been endangered by their work. Responsibility for this service is now delegated by the Secretary of State to the Health and Safety Commission.

Enforcement of the Health and Safety at Work Act

Employer health and safety policy

Every employer is required to prepare a written statement of their general policy on health and safety, and the organisation and arrangements for carrying out that policy which are in force at the time. All employees must be advised of what the policy is. It is perhaps inevitable that many employers have regarded this as a statutory chore and have gone through the motions of articulating a policy in terms of the bare minimum that is possible, rather than thinking out a policy statement that will have genuine impact on safe working. The report of the Inspectorate for 1976 is very critical of companies where this happens, especially where the policy is a hollow statement without action to implement the declared intentions. Other specific criticisms were the lack of information in policy statements about particular hazards and how they could be dealt with, and a failure to stress management responsibility for safety as strongly as those of safety representatives (Health and Safety Commission 1978).

Booth (1985) makes similar criticisms based on research carried under the auspices of the Printing and Publishing Industry Training Board. He comments that of the 121 policy documents investigated, most expressed a clear commitment to health and safety, but few contained appropriate details of the necessary arrangements for implementing the policy.

Another requirement of the Act is updating: 'it is the duty of every employer to prepare, and as often as may be appropriate revise, a written statement of general policy with respect to the health and safety at work of his employees' (Health and Safety at Work Act 1974, s. 2(3)). If a safety policy is produced as something then to be filed away and forgotten, there is little chance that arrangements for coping with new hazards or changed working conditions will be made. The need for safety policy statements to be specific to the circumstances makes it difficult to offer models, but a useful starting point is provided by Armstrong:

> The general policy statement should be a declaration of the intention of the employer to safeguard the health and safety of his employees. It should emphasize four fundamental points: first, that the safety of employees and the public is of paramount importance; second, that safety will take precedence over expediency; third, that every effort will be made to involve all managers, supervisors and employees in the development and implementation of health and safety procedures; and fourth, that health and safety legislation will be complied with in the spirit as well as the letter of the law.
> (Armstrong 1977, p. 337)

Devise a health and safety policy for your organisation. Include information about:

1. General policy on health and safety.
2. Specific hazards and how they are to be dealt with.
3. Management responsibility for safety.

4. How the policy is to be implemented.

OR

Obtain the Health and Safety Policy from any organisation and assess the policy in the light of Armstrong's quotes and our four points identified in the first part of this activity box.

Managerial responsibility

The management of the organisation carry the prime responsibility for implementing the policy they have laid down; they also have a responsibility under the Act for operating the plant and equipment in the premises safely and meeting all the Act's requirements whether these are specified in the policy statement or not. In the case of negligence, proceedings can be taken against an individual, responsible manager as well as against the employing organisation. The appointment of a safety officer can be one way of meeting this obligation. The officer does not become automatically responsible for all managerial failures in the safety field, but does become an in-house factory inspector.

Employee responsibility

For the first time in health and safety legislation a duty is placed on employees while they are at work to take reasonable care for the safety of themselves and others, as well as their health, which appears a more difficult type of responsibility for the individual to exercise. The employee is, therefore, legally bound to comply with the safety rules and instructions that the employer promulgates. Rose (1976) reported that nine employees had been prosecuted under this section of the Act.

Employers are also fully empowered to dismiss employees who refuse to obey safety rules on the grounds of misconduct, especially if the possibility of such a dismissal is explicit in the disciplinary procedure. An employee who refused to wear safety goggles for a particular process was warned of possible dismissal because the safety committee had decreed that goggles or similar protection were necessary. His refusal was based on the fact that he had done the job previously without such protection and did not see that it was now necessary. He was dismissed and the tribunal did not allow his claim of unfair dismissal (*Mortimer* v. *V. L. Churchill* (1979)).

Safety representatives

To reinforce the employees' role in the care of their own health and safety, provision has been made for the appointment of safety representatives by trade unions. The Safety Representatives and Safety Committees Regulations 1978 set out the functions of safety representatives and provide for various types of inspection and investigation which they may carry out. Safety representatives have a legal duty of consultation with employers and are entitled to paid time off for training to enable them to carry out their function. There is also a Code of Practice for Safety Representatives recommending that they keep themselves informed, encourage co-operation with management and bring matters to their employer's attention (Davis 1979). However, in practice, things do not always work out this well, as Codrington and Henley comment:

The innovations of [HASWA] can only produce significant improvements in the construction industry's appalling safety record if there are improvements in trade union site organization, for without it safety representatives have very little real power or authority. . . . With a declining membership and increasing fragmentation of employment relationships on site, the construction unions will only have limited resources available to encourage the development of safety representatives' activities.

(Codrington and Henley 1981, p. 308)

Safety committees

Although the Act does not specifically instruct employers to set up safety committees, it comes very close:

it shall be the duty of every employer, if requested to do so by the safety representatives . . . to establish, in accordance with regulations made by the Secretary of State, a safety committee having the function of keeping under review the measures taken to ensure the health and safety at work of his employees and such other functions as may be prescribed.

(Health and Safety at Work Act 1974, s. 2(7))

The safety representatives also have to be consulted about the membership of the committee, and detailed advice on the function and conduct of safety committees is provided in the guidance note on safety representatives (Health and Safety Commission 1976).

Research by Leopold and Coyle (1981) has shown that there has been a great increase in the number of safety committees in operation since the passing of the Act, especially in companies employing fewer than 200 people and in those industries where there was previously a low level of accidents. They also found the effectiveness of such committees to be much dependent on the employment of trained safety officers. This was generally confirmed by the work of Donnelly and Barrett (1981).

Safety training

There is a general requirement in the Act for training to be given, along with information, instruction and supervision, to ensure 'the health and safety at work of his employees'. There is thus fairly wide scope to determine what is appropriate in the differing circumstances of each organisation.

We deal more fully with safety training and other methods of persuasion later in this chapter.

Codes of practice

The Commission is empowered to follow the growing practice of issuing codes of practice for people to follow in various situations. Codes have been issued covering such aspects as:

- The protection of persons against ionising radiation.
- Control of lead pollution at work.
- Time off for the training of safety representatives.
- Control of substances hazardous to health (various).

The codes are not legally enforceable, but the use or not of the codes may be interpreted in a legal case as an indication of the employer's efforts in that area of health and safety.

Improvement notices

Inspectors can serve improvement notices on individuals whom they regard as being in breach of the HASWA provisions, or earlier legislation, like the Factories Act 1961. This notice specifies the opinion of the inspector and the reasons for it, as well as requiring the individual to remedy the contravention within a stated period. Most frequently, this will be issued to a member of the management of an organisation, depending on which individual the inspector regards as being appropriate, but such a notice could also be issued to an employee who was deliberately and knowingly disobeying a safety instruction.

Prohibition notices

An alternative, or subsequent, power of the inspector is to issue a prohibition notice, where he believes that there is a risk of serious personal injury. This prohibits an operation or activity being continued until specified remedial action has been taken. In 1983, 3,805 prohibition notices were issued compared with 12,268 improvement notices (HSE 1986).

It is possible for employers to appeal against both improvement and prohibition notices. In 1978 an employer appealed successfully against a prohibition notice issued against a hand-operated guillotine that had been used – as had nine similar machines – for eighteen years without accident. Another successful appeal was against an improvement order that was issued requiring safety shoes to be provided free of charge to employees. The tribunal found that the cost of £20,000 in the first year and £10,000 a year thereafter was disproportionate to the risk involved, and that the fact of the shoes being provided free did not make it more likely that they would be worn (IDS 1978).

Control of Substances Hazardous to Health Regulations 1988

These regulations, which came into force on 1 October 1989, were made under the Health and Safety at Work Act 1974. They comprise nineteen regulations plus four approved codes of practice, and were described by Norman Fowler, Secretary of State in 1988, as the most far-reaching health and safety legislation since the Health and Safety at Work Act (Powley 1989).

The purpose of the legislation is to protect all employees who work with any substances hazardous to their health, by placing a requirement on their employer regarding the way and extent that such substances are handled, used and controlled.

The regulations apply to all workplaces, irrespective of size and nature of work – so for example, they would apply equally to a hotel as to a chemical plant, and in firms of a handful of employees as well as major PLCs. The regulations not only place a responsibility for good environmental hygiene on the employer, but on employees too. All substances are included, except for asbestos, lead, materials producing ionising radiations and substances underground, all of which have their own legislation (see e.g. Riddell 1989).

The regulations require employers to focus on five major aspects of occupation in respect of hazardous substances. These are:

1. Assessing the risk of substances used, and identifying what precautions are needed. This initial assessment of substances already in use, and those that are intended for use is a major undertaking in terms of both the number of substances used and the competency of the assessor. Cherrie and Faulkner

(1989) report that one employer in their survey used over 25,000 different substances! The assessment needs to be systematic, and key questions to ask are contained in the HSE's guide, *Introduction to COSHH*. Assessors may be internal or external consultants or specialists. Should the internal approach be adopted, the assessors require rigorous training and education as at ICI, described by Mountfield (1989).

2. Introducing appropriate measures to control or prevent the risk. These may include:
   (a) removing the substance, by changing the processes used,
   (b) substituting the substance,
   (c) controlling the substance where this is practical, for example, by totally or partially enclosing the process, or by increasing ventilation or instituting safer systems of work and handling procedures.
   These measures would be designed to undercut Maximum Exposure Limits (MEL) and meet Occupational Exposure Standards (OES). (For a fuller explanation of MEL and OES, see Powley 1989.)

3. Ensure that control measures are used – that procedures are observed and that equipment involved is regularly maintained. Where necessary, exposure of the substance to employees should be monitored. This would particularly apply where there could be serious health measures were they to fail or be suboptimal. Records of monitoring should be made and retained.

4. Health surveillance. Where there is a known adverse effect of a particular substance, regular surveillance of the employees involved can identify problems at an early stage. When this is carried out, records should be kept and these should be accessible to employees.

5. Employees need to be informed and trained regarding the risks arising from their work and the precautions that they need to take.

Although the legislation has been widely publicised and produced in a clear and appropriate format, as judged, for example, by Foy (1989), there is early survey evidence of the lack of awareness, understanding and training in smaller firms from Cherrie and Faulkner (1989). The authors recommend three major initiatives to prepare this sector of employers better, which are that:

1. A major publicity campaign should be aimed specifically at small firms.
2. Small organisations need better access to professional health and safety advice.
3. The regulations must be enforced effectively.

Further regulations resulting from EU directives

The following information is based in the IPD Executive brief, *Europe: Personnel and Development* (1997).

Management of Health and Safety at Work Regulations 1992

This implements the Framework and Temporary Workers Directives. The Framework Directive is an umbrella Directive, in a similar way as the Health and Safety at Work Act is an umbrella Act. Additional rules known as 'daughter directives' covering specific areas have been issued within the framework of this directive. By July 1997 there were twelve such daughter directives.

Workplace (Health, Safety and Welfare) Regulations 1992

This implements the first daughter directive, the Workplace Directive, which sets out minimum design requirements, including provision of rest and no smoking areas.

Provision and Use of Work Equipment Regulations 1992

This implements the Work Equipment Directive (the second daughter directive), and sets of minimum standards for the safe use of machines and equipment.

Personal Protective Equipment at Work Regulations 1992

This implements the third daughter directive on Personnel Protective Equipment, and requires employers to provide appropriate protective equipment, and workers to use this correctly.

Manual Handling Operations Regulations 1992

This implements the fourth daughter directive on Heavy Loads, and requires employers to reduce the risk of injury by providing lifting equipment where appropriate and training in lifting.

Health and Safety (Display Screen Equipment) Regulations 1992

This implements the Display Screen Equipment (VDU) Directive (fifth daughter directive), and requires employers to provide free eye tests, glasses where appropriate, regular breaks, appropriate training and organisation of equipment to reduce strain.

COSHH (Amendment) Regulation 1992

This implements the Carcinogens Directive, increasing the safeguards on employees by providing for risk assessments every five years.

Biological Agents Directive

Implemented via COSHH Regulations 1994 and requiring employers to safeguard employees from biological agents at work.

Construction (Design and Management) Regulations

Requires the incorporation of health and safety considerations into such activities including a nominated person responsible for co-ordinating, implementing and monitoring measures.

Health and Safety (Safety Signs and Signals) Regulations 1996

Requires harmonisation of both visual and acoustic signs, to specific guidelines.

Protection of Pregnant Workers Directive

Implemented in 1994 via a range of UK Acts and Regulations.

Drilling Industries Directive

Implemented by Regulations in 1995 and 1996 harmonising standards of protection for workers in mineral extraction in both on- and off-shore boreholes.

Mines and Quarries (Miscellaneous Health and Safety Provisions) 1995

Introduces harmonised standards of protection for workers in surface and underground mineral extracting industries.

There is a number of draft directives under negotiation and consideration covering such areas as transport workers, chemical agents, physical agents and further amendments to the carcinogen regulations.

Directives outside the Framework Directive: The Control of Asbestos at Work (Amendment) Regulations 1992 and The Asbestos (Prohibitions) Regulations 1992

This implements the Asbestos Directive (which does not come under the framework directive) and concerns worker protection.

Other directives outside the Framework Directive involve medical stores on ships and safety in explosive atmospheres. In addition there are two areas which are not yet fully implemented in the UK:

Young workers
Setting minimum age limits and maximum working hours.

Working time
Which should have been implemented by November 1996. The UK argued that this area does not come under Health and Safety but was overruled by the European Court of Justice. New regulations are being drafted.

The management of health, safety and welfare

There is a number of ways in which managerial responsibility can be discharged to implement the policy statement and ensure compliance with legal requirements.

Making the work safe

Making the work safe is mainly in the realm of the designer and production engineer. It is also a more general management responsibility to ensure that any older equipment and machinery that is used is appropriately modified to make it safe, or removed. The provision of necessary safety wear is also a managerial responsibility – for example, making sure goggles and ear protectors are available.

Enabling employees to work safely

Whereas making the work safe is completely a management responsibility, the individual employee may contribute his or her own negligence to work unsafely in a safe situation. The task of the management is two-fold; first, the employee must know what to do; second, this knowledge must be translated into action: the employee must comply with the safe working procedures that are laid down. To meet the first part of the obligation management need to be scrupulous in communication of drills and instructions and the analysis of working situations to decide what the drills should be. That is a much bigger and more difficult activity than can be implied in a single sentence, but the second part of getting compliance is more difficult and more important. Employee failure to comply with clear drills does not absolve the employer and the management. When an explosion leaves the factory in ruins it is of little value for the factory manager to shake his head and say: 'I told them not to do it.' We examine the way to obtain compliance shortly, under the discussion about training and other methods of persuasion.

The initiative on safe working will be led by the professionals within the management team. They are the safety officer, the medical officer, the nursing staff and the safety representatives. Although there is no legal obligation to appoint a safety officer, more and more organisations are making such appointments. One reason is to provide emphasis and focus for safety matters. The appointment suggests that management mean business, but the appointment itself is not enough. It has to be fitted into the management structure with lines of reporting and accountability which will enable the safety officer to be effective and which will prevent other members of management becoming uncertain of their own responsibilities – perhaps to the point of thinking that they no longer exist. Ideally, the safety officer will operate on two fronts: making the work safe and ensuring safe working, although this may require an ability to talk constructively on engineering issues with engineers as well as being able to handle training and some industrial relations-type arguments. Gill and Martin (1976) have demonstrated that there is usually a clear dissonance between what is prescribed and what takes place, because the engineering approach produces complex and detailed manuals based on the belief that safety is a technical rather than human problem, whereas the people who do the work tend to produce different working practices based on experience:

> When we came to study the chemical plants we found an apparent paradox. On the one hand there existed a comprehensive body of written safety practices and procedures to cater for every conceivable contingency, and on the other hand actual working practice often differed considerably from the rules specifying safe working practices. Nevertheless the plants ran well and both the frequency of dangerous incidents and accidents were very low by national standards.   (Gill and Martin 1976, p. 37)

The medical officer (if one is appointed) will almost certainly be the only medically qualified person and can therefore introduce to the thinking on health and safety discussions a perspective and a range of knowledge that is both unique and relevant. Second, the medical officer will probably carry more social status than the managers dealing with health and safety matters and he or she will be detached from the management in their eyes and his or her own. Doctors have their own ethical code, which is different from that of the managers. They are an authoritative adviser to management on making the work safe and can be an authoritative adviser to employees on working safely. They are an invaluable member of the safety committee and a potentially important feature of training programmes.

Occupational nurses also deal directly with working safely and often play a part in safety training, as well as symbolising care in the face of hazard.

WINDOW ON PRACTICE

Health and Safety and the use of contractors

As large firms increasingly contract out their operations the Health and Safety Commission is paying greater attention to this area, and Frank Davis, the Chair of the Commission warned: 'No firm – whatever the industrial sector – can afford to be complacent about the activities of contractors' (Royal Society for Prevention of Accidents Congress, May 1996)

Lucas Industries (who subcontract a range of activities, some high-risk), as part of a major reorganisation, reviewed their health, safety and environment systems in order to improve their performance. They concluded that current systems were reactive, not auditable or integrated with other systems, lacked clear ownership, were too dependent on internal specialists, and did not address concerns about high risk activities.

Their new approach seeks to rectify these problems. They developed a questionnaire for contractors to complete, relating to health and safety issues and they assessed this against what they could reasonably expect from a contractor of that size in that business. This enabled Lucas to take the initiative by assessing the risk and then discussing this assessment with the contractor. Where necessary, contractors were given encouragement and help to improve. Only those contractors who were already operating at the appropriate level or who would improve to this level, would be on the Lucas Register of Contractors. Contractors were invited to attend a half-day awareness raising workshop based on the questionnaire topics and focused on risk assessment. A newly designed Contractors Registration Form was implemented to be completed jointly by the contractor and Lucas. This covers such issues as the task, materials, substances and equipment used, services needed, work environment and conditions and site hazards. Via this form the contractors and Lucas agree and record controls and precautions and safe systems of work. Where possible these forms are displayed where the work is carried out in order to make the risk assessment visible.

Further progress may involve training the contractor's workforce, more guidance to contractors, and a monitoring and auditing review mechanism.

Safety training and other methods of persuasion

Safety training has three major purposes: (1) employees should be told about and understand the nature of the hazards at the place of work; (2) employees need to be made aware of the safety rules and procedures; and (3) they need to be persuaded to comply with them. The first of these is the most important, because employees sometimes tend to modify the rules to suit their own convenience. Trainers cannot, of course, condone the short-cut without implying a general flexibility in the rules, but they need to be aware of how employees will probably respond. In some areas the use of short-cuts by skilled employees does not always mean they are working less safely, as Gill and Martin (1976) have demonstrated, but there are many areas where compliance with the rules is critical, for example, the wearing of safety goggles.

Persuading employees to keep to the safety rules is difficult and there often appears to be a general resistance on the part of the employees. A study by Pirani and Reynolds (1976) throws some light on this, as they used the repertory grid technique to obtain from both managers and employees a construct of the safety conscious employee:

> The management sample saw this 'ideal' safety-conscious operative as a half-witted, slow but reliable person who gave little trouble. They saw him as a worker who could be left safely alone but prone to making trivial complaints. He certainly was not depicted as a worker to be respected. The major construct to emerge from the operatives' data alone was that the ideal safety conscious man was rather a 'cissy' and somewhat unsociable. It is important to note, however, that individual operatives did not see him in these terms but felt that this was how the rest of the operatives would view him – a feeling substantiated by a large sample of operatives.
>
> (Pirani and Reynolds 1976, p. 26)

Safety training needs to be carried out in three settings: at induction, on the job and in refresher courses. A variety of different training techniques can be employed, including lectures, discussions, films, role-playing and slides. These methods are sometimes supplemented by poster or other safety awareness campaigns and communications, and disciplinary action for breaches in the safety rules. Management example in sticking to the safety rules no matter what the tempo of production can also set a good example. A four-stage systematic approach to health and safety training is described by Culliford (1987).

Research by Pirani and Reynolds (1976) indicated that the response to a variety of methods of safety persuasion – poster campaigns, film shows, fear techniques, discussion groups, role-playing and disciplinary action – was very good in the short term (over two weeks) but after four months the initial improvement had virtually disappeared for all methods except role-playing. From this it can be concluded that: first, a management initiative on safety will produce gratifying results in the obeying of rules, but a fresh initiative will be needed at regular and frequent intervals to keep it effective; and second, the technique of role-playing appears to produce results that are longer-lasting.

ACTIVITY BOX 28.2

If you work in an organisation, analyse the health and safety roles of the Personnel Department, Line Manager, Senior Management, Safety Officer and Safety Representative. Consider:

- similarities and differences
- gaps and overlaps
- purposes and pressures
- reinforcements and contradictions

of and between each group.

OR

Analyse any employment experiences which you have had in terms of the training, support and encouragement you have received in relation to health and safety issues. In particular comments on:

- the variety of health and safety roles in relation to you as a worker
- the impact of this
- the health and safety concerns expressed by others and identified by yourself
- the impact of this

Also important is external training for managers, supervisors and safety representatives. Following the 1974 Act, a substantial provision for health and safety training and education was introduced in colleges of further education, but by 1985 there was a decline in the take-up of places (Booth 1985).

Job descriptions and the role of the supervisor

Attention can be drawn to the safety aspects of work by inserting a reference to safe working practices in job descriptions. In particular, the supervisor's role in ensuring safe working practices should be made as specific as possible in the supervisor's job description.

Risk assessment

Risk assessment is one of the newer approaches to health and safety which concentrates on accident prediction, as opposed to the more traditional prevention of recurrence after the event (Booth 1985). This approach reflects current concerns that expenditure on health and safety matters should be cost effective, and the Royal Society paper (1983) on the subject discusses risk decision-making based on cost–benefit models.

Occupational health and welfare

Occupational health and welfare is a broad area, which includes both physical and emotional well-being. The medical officer, occupational health nurse and welfare officer all have a contribution to make here. In a broader sense so do the dentist, chiropodist and other professionals when they are employed by the organisation. The provision of these broader welfare facilities is often found in large organisations located away from centres of population, especially in industrial plants, where the necessity of at least an occupational health nurse can be clearly seen.

In terms of physical care the sorts of facility that can be provided are:

1. Emergency treatment, beyond immediate first-aid, of injuries sustained at work.
2. Medical, dental and other facilities, which employees can use and which can be more easily fitted into the working day than making appointments with outside professionals.
3. Immediate advice on medical and related matters, especially those connected with work.
4. Monitoring of accidents and illnesses to identify hazards and danger points, and formulating ideas to combat these in conjunction with the safety officer.
5. On-site medicals for those joining the organisation.
6. Regular medicals for employees.
7. Input into health and safety training courses.
8. Regular screening services. For example, cervical cancer screening at British Shipbuilders, Leyland Vehicles and United Biscuits.
   (*Personnel Management* 1986)

In terms of emotional welfare (although this cannot necessarily be clearly separated from physical welfare) Slaikeu and Frank (1986) make a convincing case for provision by the employer:

> Research shows that marital, family, financial or legal crises are workers' most prevalent problems. Poor resolution of such crises can lead to long-term psychiatric damage resulting in depression, alcoholism, physical illness and even death. Untreated and unresolved crises affect worker productivity and contribute to labour turnover; the annual cost to US business of alcoholism alone is put at five billion. The 'hard' costs of ill and unhappy employees (absence, recruitment, and training expenses) are high enough. Still greater are inefficient and inadequate job performance, discredit to the company and diminished morale engendered among co-workers. The bottom line?
>
> Estimated cost for 'emotional problems' in US business and industry is $17 billion a year. (*Management Today*, p. 35)

This, however, only deals with the emotional problems that employees bring with them to work and the effects that these have on their work. What about problems that are caused by the work itself, and the interaction between 'home' and 'work' problems? There is not only a financial argument for the provision of health and welfare assistance here, but possibly a moral argument as well. It is very difficult, of course, to ascribe some problems to a definite cause, however Eva and Oswald (1981) argue that conditions of work, speed of work, how boring or demanding the job is, and how the job affects family and social life are all major elements in the causation of stress.

Stress at work is not a new idea, although it was originally viewed in terms of executive stress (for example, Levinson 1964), and seen only to apply to those in senior management positions. The literature on the subject of stress at work is large (for example, Cooper and Marshall 1980; Palmer 1989; Nykodym and George 1989). Stress is now also seen to apply to those in manual work (Cooper and Smith 1985). It is the response of individuals to work pressures, though, that the level of pressure determines whether they display the symptoms of stress. Different people react to the same pressures in different ways. It has been shown that the experience of stress is related to 'type A' coronary-prone behaviour. Stress is a threat to both physical and psychological well-being. Glowinkowski summarises the effects:

> While stress can be short-lived it can represent a continuous burden leading to short-term outcomes such as tension, increased heart rate, or even increased drinking or smoking. In the long term, stress is said to cause disorders such as depression, coronary heart disease, diabetes melitus and bronchial asthma. . . . Indeed, while stress may be a direct causal factor in heart disease, its effects may be indirect. Stress may increase smoking and cause overeating, which are also high risk factors in coronary artery disease
>
> (Glowinkowski 1985, pp. 1–2)

In relation to the variety of psychological and physical problems, the employer can provide a number of facilities to ease the difficulties that employees may be experiencing.

Someone to talk to/someone to advise

This could be the individual's manager, or the personnel manager, but it is often more usefully someone who is distinct from the work itself. An occupational health nurse, welfare officer or specialised counsellor are the sort of people well placed to deal with this area. There are two benefits that come from this, the first being advice and practical assistance. This would be relevant, for example, if the individual had financial problems, and the organisation was prepared to offer some temporary assistance. Alternatively, the individual could be advised of alternative sources of help, or referred, with agreement, to the appropriate agency for treatment. The second benefit to be gained is that from someone just listening to the individual's problem without judging it – in other words counselling. De Board (1983) suggests that the types of work-related problems that employees may need to be counselled on are: technical incompetence, underwork, overwork, uncertainty about the future and relationships at work. Counselling aims to provide a supportive atmosphere to help people to find their own solution to a problem.

Organisation of work

This is a preventive measure involving reorganisation of those aspects of work that are believed to be affecting the mental health of employees. This may include changes that could be grouped as 'organisational development', such as job rotation and autonomous work-groups. Eva and Oswald (1981) suggest greater control over the speed and intensity of work, an increase in the quality of work and a reduction in unsocial hours. Individually-based training and development programmes would also be relevant here. Specifically for the executive, there is growing use of the 'managerial sabbatical'. Some American companies have begun to give a year off after a certain number of years' service in order to prevent 'executive burnout'. In the UK, the John Lewis Partnership has a programme allowing six months away from work.

Positive health programmes

Positive health programmes display a variety of different approaches aimed at relieving and preventing stress and associated problems, and promoting healthy lifestyles. There is increasing activity in terms of healthy eating and no smoking campaigns and support, together with the provision of resources for physical activity. Corporate wellness programmes have been in place for a longer period in the US, where the prime motivation was the reduction of medical costs (most employers providing this as a benefit for their employees). In the UK the programmes are more often seen as an employee benefit in themselves, with the hope that this will also encourage higher productivity and reduce absence levels. However, Mills (1996) argues that although there is a weak positive relationship between healthier lifestyles and the bottom line, there is little evidence that health promotion programmes are actually working. He argues that only a small number of employees are affected by such programmes and that these are likely to be the ones who already have healthier lifestyles. Mills suggests that blue-collar employees, who have the least control over their working lives also tend to have less healthy lifestyles and are more resistant to health promotion. He suggests that all three factors are interrelated and connected in a complex manner with employee motivation. If Mills is right, this presents a challenge to organisations and suggests at the very least they should evaluate positive health programmes as well as investigating the impact of the prevailing management style.

Some approaches to corporate wellness include the use of yoga and meditation. Others, like 'autogenic training', are based on these principles, but are presented in a new guise. Autogenic training is developed through exercises in body awareness and physical relaxation which lead to passive concentration. It is argued that the ability to do this breaks through the vicious circle of excessive stress, and that as well as the many mental benefits, there are benefits to the body including relief of somatic symptoms of anxiety, and the reduction of cardiovascular risk factors (Carruthers 1982). A newer approach is 'chemofeedback', which is geared towards the connection between stress and coronary heart disease, high blood pressure and strokes. Chemofeedback (Positive Health Centre 1985) is designed as an early warning system to pick up signs of unfavourable stress. The signs are picked up from the completion of a computerised questionnaire together with a blood test. This approach is being offered as a 'stress-audit' on a company-wide basis.

Other issues currently in the health and safety arena are passive smoking, alcohol and drug abuse, the control of AIDS and the threat of violence.

ACTIVITY BOX 28.3

We are buying their [the employees'] skills and their energy and industry and commitment. Whilst they are at work we don't feel we've got responsibility to manage their social life, marriages,

religious faith or anything else . . .
(Personnel Manager)

How do you think employees see the provision of facilities at work to deal with their personal, emotional problems?

Summary propositions

28.1 Occupational welfare is the 'well-being' of people at work, encompassing occupational health and safety.

28.2 There are four aspects of welfare at work: physical, emotional, intellectual and material.

28.3 The history of personnel management is interrelated with the development of welfare. Many personnel managers find this association a disadvantage when trying to develop the authority and status of personnel management.

28.4 There was a surge in interest in health, safety and welfare in the late 1960s and early 1970s and this culminated in the Health and Safety at Work Act 1974, and its associated regulations.

28.5 By the early 1980s the interest in safety had waned, but there was increasing interest in occupational health and welfare, particularly related to stress, alcoholism and counselling.

28.6 The efforts of the EU to ensure harmonisation of health and safety has resulted in a major surge of legislation in the early 1990s.

References

Anonymous (1994) 'Record low for workplace deaths', *Employment Gazette*, January, p. 9.

Armstrong, M. (1977) *Handbook of Personnel Management Practice*, London: Kogan Page.

Beaumont, P. B. (1984) 'Personnel management and the welfare role', *Management Decision*, Vol. 22, No. 3.

Beaumont, P. B., Leopold, J. W. and Coyle, J. R. (1982) 'The safety officer: an emerging management role?', *Personnel Review*, Vol. 11, No. 2.

Booth, R. (1985) 'What's new in health and safety management?' *Personnel Management*, April.

Carruthers, M. (1982) 'Train the mind to calm itself', *General Practitioner*, 16 July.

Central Statistical Office (1985) *Social Trends*, No. 15, London: HMSO, p. 112.

Cherrie, I. and Faulkner, C. (1989) 'Will the COSHH regulations improve occupational health?', *Safety Practitioner*, February, pp 6–7.

Codrington, C. and Henley, I. S. (1981) 'The industrial relations of injury and death', *British Journal of Industrial Relations*, November.

Cooper, C. L. and Marshall, I. (1980) *White Collar and Professional Stress*, Chichester: John Wiley.

Cooper, C. L. and Smith, M. I. (eds.) (1985) *Job Stress and Blue Collar Work*, Chichester: John Wiley.

Culliford, G. (1987) 'Health and safety training', *Safety Practitioner*, July, pp. 10–14.

Davis, K. P. (1979) *Health and Safety*, Wokingham: Van Nostrand Reinhold.

de Board, R. (1983) *Counselling People at Work: an introduction for managers*, Aldershot: Gower.

Donnelly, E. and Barrett, B. (1981) 'Safety training since the Act', *Personnel Management*, June.

Eva, D. and Oswald, R. (1981) *Health and Safety at Work*, London: Pan Books.

Fox, A. (1966) 'From welfare to organization', *New Society*, 9 June.

Foy, K. (1989) 'COSHH package appraisal', *Safety Practitioner*, February, pp. 18–19.

Gill, I. and Martin, K. (1976) 'Safety management: reconciling rules with reality', *Personnel Management*, June.

Glowinkowski, S. P. (1985) 'Managerial stress: a longitudinal study', unpublished PhD thesis, UMIST, Manchester.

Health and Safety Bulletin (1997) 'Controlling contractors', *Health ahd Safety Bulletin* No. 254, February, pp. 11–14.

Health and Safety Commission (1976) *Safety Representatives and Safety Committees*, London: HMSO.

Health and Safety Commission (1978) *Health and Safety in Manufacturing and Service Industries (1976)*, London: HMSO.

Health and Safety Executive (1986) *Health and Safety Executive Statistics (1983)*, London: HMSO.

Health and Safety Executive (1988) *Introducing COSHH*, London: HMSO.

Howells, R. and Barrett, B. (1982) *The Health and Safety at Work Act: a guide for managers*, London: Institute of Personnel Management.

Incomes Data Services (1978) *IDS Brief No. 145*, London: Incomes Data Services.

Institute of Personnel and Development (1997) *Europe: personnel and development*, IPD Brief, July.

James, P. (1992) 'The health and safety agenda', *Personnel Management*, March, p. 23.

Kenny, T. (1975) 'Stating the case for welfare', *Personnel Management*, Vol. 7, No. 9.

Knox, I. and Fenley, A. (1985) 'Alcohol problems at work: some medical and legal considerations', *Personnel Review*, Vol. 14, No. 1.

Leach, J. (1995) *Devolution of Personnel Activities – the reality*, MA thesis.

Leopold, I. and Coyle, R. (1981) 'A healthy trend in safety committees', *Personnel Management*, May.

Levinson, H. (1964) *Executive Stress*, New York: Harper & Row.

Mackay, L. E. (1986) *The Workforce and the Personnel Function*, unpublished paper, Manchester: UMIST.

Mills, M. (1996) 'Body and soul', *People Management*, 2 September, pp. 36–8.

Mountfield, B. (1989) 'Preparing for COSHH at ICI', *Occupational Health Review*, June/July, pp. 6–7.

Nykodym, N. and George, K. (1989) 'Stress busting on the job', *Personnel*, July, pp. 56–9.

Palmer, S. (1989) 'Occupational stress', *The Safety and Health Practitioner*, August, pp. 16–18.

Personnel Management (1986) *Mortimer* v. *V. L. Churchill* (1979), News and notes, March.

Pirani, M. and Reynolds, J. (1976) 'Gearing up for safety', *Personnel Management*, February.

Positive Health Centre (1985) *Chemo Feedback*, London: Positive Health Centre.

Powley, D. (1989) 'Life under the COSHH', *Manufacturing Engineer*, September, pp. 24–31.

Riddell, R. (1989) 'Why COSHH will hit hard on health and safety', *Personnel Management*, September, pp. 46–9.

Rose, P. (1976) 'Surveying the new safety structure', *Personnel Management*, November.

Royal Society (1983) *Risk Assessment: a study group report*, London: The Royal Society.

Slaikeu, K. and Frank, C. (1986) 'Manning the psychological first aid post', *Management Today*, February.

Torrington, D. P., Mackay, L. E. and Hall, L. A. (1985) 'The Changing Nature of Personnel Management', *Employee Relations*, November/December.

Watson, T. J. (1977) *The Personnel Managers*, London: Routledge & Kegan Paul.

General discussion topics

1. Good health is good business. Discuss.
2. To what extent and by what processes can organisations reduce stress for employees who are members of dual career families?
3. How can organisations utilise training and development to develop a culture that is receptive to health and safety?

CHAPTER 29

Grievance and discipline

Grievance and discipline are areas of management where there is constant vacillation between the authority of the individual person and the authority of office, conferred by the system. Organisations are systems to distribute power and obedience, and the individuals who become employees of the organisation surrender a segment of their personal autonomy to become relatively weaker, making the organisation inordinately stronger. The benevolence of the organisation cannot be guaranteed, so individual employees seek to limit its power in relation to themselves.

Usually, the authority to be exercised in a business is impersonalised by the use of role in order to make it more effective. If a colleague mentions to you that you have overspent your budget, your reaction might be proud bravado unless you knew that the colleague had a role such as company accountant, internal auditor or financial director. Everyone in a business has a role – most people have several – and each role confers some authority. The canteen assistant who tells you that the steak and kidney pudding is off is more believable than the managing director conveying the same message. Quality assurance staff in factories are likely to wear white coats and send unfavourable reports in writing so as to deploy the authority of their role rather than test the authority of their own selves.

Dependence on role is not always welcome to those in managerial positions, who are fond of using phrases like 'I know how to get the best out of people', 'I understand my chaps' and 'I have a loyal staff'. This may be due in part to their perception of their role as being to persuade the reluctant and command the respect of the unwilling by the use of personal leadership qualities, and it is indisputable that some managers are more effective with some groups of staff than with others, but there is more to it than personal skill: we are predisposed to obey those who outrank us in any hierarchy.

The Milgram experiments with obedience

Obedience is the reaction expected of people by those in authority positions, who prescribe actions which otherwise may not necessarily have been carried out. Stanley Milgram (1974) conducted a series of experiments to investigate obedience to authority and highlighted the significance of obedience and the power of authority in our everyday lives.

Subjects were led to believe that a study of memory and learning was being carried out which involved giving progressively more severe electric shocks to a learner who gave incorrect answers to factual questions. If the learner gave the correct answer the reward was a further question; if the answer was incorrect there was the punishment of a mild electric shock. Each shock was more severe than the previous one. If the subject queried the procedure because it seemed bizarre or brutal, a standard response was received from the authority figure conducting the experiment, such as:

1. 'Please continue' or 'Please go on.'
2. 'The experiment requires that you continue.'
3. 'It is absolutely essential that you continue.'
4. 'You have no other choice: you must go on.'

These responses were given sequentially: (2) only after (1) had failed, (3) after (2), and so on.

The 'learner' was not actually receiving shocks, but was a member of the experimental team simulating progressively greater distress as the shocks were made stronger. Eighteen different experiments were conducted with over 1,000 subjects, with the circumstances varying between each experiment. No matter how the variables were altered the subjects showed an astonishing compliance with authority even when delivering 'shocks' of 450 volts. Up to 65 per cent of subjects continued to obey throughout the experiment in the presence of a clear authority figure and as many as 20 per cent continued to obey when the authority figure was absent.

Milgram was widely criticised for this study, largely because of questions about the ethics of requiring subjects to behave in such a distressing way, but we cannot evade the fact that he induced a high level of obedience from a large number of people who would otherwise have considered their actions to be wrong. Understandably, the reaction of Milgram to his own results was of dismay that:

> With numbing regularity good people were seen to knuckle under to the demands of authority and perform actions that were callous and severe. Men who are in everyday life responsible and decent were seduced by the trappings of authority, by the control of their perceptions, and by the uncritical acceptance of the experimenter's definition of the situation into performing harsh acts.   (1974, p. 123)

Our interest in Milgram's work is simply to demonstrate that we all have a predilection to obey instructions from authority figures, even if we do not want to. Milgram explains the phenomenon of obedience for us by an argument which he summarised thus:

> (1) organized social life provides survival benefits to the individuals who are part of it, and to the group; (2) whatever behavioural and psychological features have been necessary to produce the capacity for organized social life have been shaped by evolutionary forces; (3) from the standpoint of cybernetics, the most general need in bringing self-regulating automata into a co-ordinated hierarchy is to suppress individual direction and control in favour of control from higher level components; (4) more generally, hierarchies can function only when internal modification occurs in the elements of which they are composed; (5) functional hierarchies in social life

are characterised by each of these features, and (6) the individuals who enter into such hierarchies are, of necessity, modified in their functioning.

(*ibid.*, p. 132)

He then points out that the act of entering a hierarchical system makes people see themselves acting as agents for carrying out the wishes of another person, and this results in these people being in a different state, described as the agentic state. This is the opposite to the state of autonomy when individuals see themselves as acting on their own. Milgram then sets out the factors that lay the groundwork for obedience to authority.

1. **Family**: Parental regulation inculcates a respect for adult authority. Parental injunctions form the basis for moral imperatives as commands to children have a dual function. 'Don't tell lies' is a moral injunction carrying a further implicit instruction: 'And obey me!' It is the implicit demand for obedience that remains the only consistent element across a range of explicit instructions.

2. **Institutional setting**: Children emerge from the family into an institutional system of authority: the school. Here they learn how to function in an organisation. They are regulated by teachers, but can see that the teachers themselves are regulated by the headteacher, the school governors and central government. Throughout this period they are in a subordinate position. When, as adults, they go to work it may be found that a certain level of dissent is allowable, but the overall situation is one in which they are to do a job prescribed by someone else.

3. **Rewards**: Compliance with authority is generally rewarded, while disobedience is frequently punished. Most significantly, promotion within the hierarchy not only rewards the individual but ensures the continuity of the hierarchy.

4. **Perception of authority**: Authority is normatively supported: there is a shared expectation among people that certain institutions do, ordinarily, have a socially controlling figure. Also, the authority of the controlling figure is limited to the situation. The usher in a cinema wields authority which vanishes on leaving the premises. As authority is expected it does not have to be asserted, merely presented.

5. **Entry into the authority system**: Having perceived an authority figure, this figure must then be defined as relevant to the subject. The individual does not only take the voluntary step of deciding which authority system to join (at least in most of employment), but also defines which authority is relevant to which event. The firefighter may expect instant obedience when calling for everybody to evacuate the building, but not if asking employees to use a different accounting system.

6. **The overarching ideology**: The legitimacy of the social situation relates to a justifying ideology. Science and education formed the background to the experiments Milgram conducted and therefore provided a justification for actions carried out in their name. Most employment is in realms of activity regarded as legitimate, justified by the values and needs of society. This is vital if individuals are to provide willing obedience, as it enables them to see their behaviour as serving a desirable end.

Managers are positioned in an organisational hierarchy in such a way that others will be predisposed, as Milgram demonstrates, to follow their instructions.

Managers put in place a series of frameworks to explain how they will exact obedience: they use *discipline*. Because individual employees feel their relative weakness, they seek complementary frameworks to challenge the otherwise unfettered use of managerial disciplinary power: they may join trade unions, but they will always need channels to present their *grievances*.

WINDOW ON PRACTICE

Of all the strange creatures in science fiction, among the most durable are the Daleks of Dr Who. They moved smoothly and rapidly in pursuit of their prey, with turret-like heads that swivelled weird antennae searching for their victims. Although they were remorseless robots, they were reassuringly vulnerable, especially to one of Dr Who's friends, the Brigadier. Of particular significance in making them safe for small children to watch were their voices, strident but high-pitched and verging on hysteria. Their opening battle cry was a relentless monotone, 'Exterminate . . . exterminate . . .' but when they were baffled or outwitted, the voices rose to a paranoid screech, 'You will obey . . . you will obey.' Once you heard that you could come out from under the bedclothes, because you knew they were asserting in vain an authority they could not implement. Dr Who and his companions were not in the Daleks' hierarchical structure and would not see themselves in an agentic state, so the Daleks could not prevail.

In this chapter we are concerned uniquely with discipline and grievance within business organisations, but it is worth pointing out that managers are the focal points for the grievances of people outside the business as well, but those grievances are called complaints. You may complain *about* poor service, shoddy workmanship or rudeness from an employee, but you complain *to* a manager.

Personnel managers make one of their most significant contributions to business effectiveness by the way they facilitate and administer grievance and disciplinary issues. First, they devise and negotiate the procedural framework of organisational justice on which both discipline and grievance depend. Second, they are much involved in the interviews and problem-solving discussions that eventually produce solutions to the difficulties that have been encountered. Third, they maintain the viability of the whole process which forms an integral part of their work: they monitor to make sure that grievances are not overlooked and so that any general trend can be perceived, and they oversee the disciplinary machinery to ensure that it is not being bypassed or unfairly manipulated.

Grievance and discipline handling are one of the roles in human resource management that few other people want to take over. Ambitious line managers may want to select their own staff without personnel intervention or by using the services of consultants. They may try to brush their personnel colleagues aside and deal directly with trade union officials or organise their own management development, but grievance and discipline is too hot a potato.

Though it may seem like a thankless task that is 'pushed onto' personnel, it is now a major feature of personnel influence and authority within the organisation. The requirements of the law regarding explanation of grievance handling and the legal framework to avoid unfair dismissal combine to make this an area where personnel people must be both knowledgeable and effective. That combination provides a valuable platform for influencing other aspects of management. The personnel manager who is not skilled in grievance and discipline is seldom in a strong organisational position.

What do we mean by discipline?

Discipline is regulation of human activity to produce a controlled performance. It ranges from the guard's control of a rabble to the accomplishment of lone individuals producing spectacular performance through self-discipline in the control of their own talents and resources.

First, there is managerial discipline in which everything depends on the leader from start to finish. There is a group of people who are answerable to someone who directs what they should all do. Only through individual direction can that group of people produce a worthwhile performance, like the person leading the community singing in the pantomime or the person conducting an orchestra. Everything depends on the leader.

Second, there is team discipline, whereby the perfection of the performance derives from the mutual dependence of all, and that mutual dependence derives from a commitment by each member to the total enterprise: the failure of one would be the downfall of all. This is usually found in relatively small working groups, like a dance troupe or an autonomous working group in a factory.

Third, there is self-discipline, like that of the juggler or the skilled artisan, where a solo performer is absolutely dependent on training, expertise and self-control.

Discipline is, therefore, not only negative, producing punishment or prevention. It can also be a valuable quality for the individual who is subject to it, although the form of discipline depends not only on the individual employee but also on the task and the way it is organised. The development of self-discipline is easier in some jobs than others and many of the job redesign initiatives have been directed at providing scope for job holders to exercise self-discipline and find a degree of autonomy from managerial discipline. Figure 29.1 shows how the three forms are connected in a sequence or hierarchy, with employees finding one of

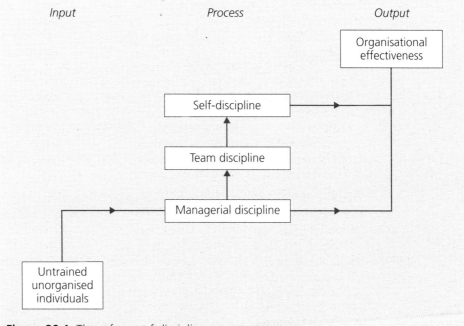

Figure 29.1 Three forms of discipline

three ways to achieve their contribution to organisational effectiveness. However, even the most accomplished solo performer has been dependent on others for training, and advice, and every team has its coach.

ACTIVITY BOX 29.1

Note three examples of managerial discipline, team discipline and self-discipline from your own experience.

Managers are not dealing with discipline only when they are rebuking late-comers or threatening to dismiss saboteurs. As well as dealing with the unruly and reluctant, they are developing the coordinated discipline of the working team, engendering that *esprit de corps* which makes the whole greater than the sum of the parts. They are training the new recruit who must not let down the rest of the team, puzzling over the reasons why A is fitting in well while B is still struggling. Managers are also providing people with the equipment to develop the self-discipline that will give them autonomy, responsibility and the capacity to maximise their powers. The independence and autonomy that self-discipline produces also produces the greatest degree of personal satisfaction – and often the largest pay packet. Furthermore the movement between the three forms represents a declining degree of managerial involvement. If you are a leader of community singing, nothing can happen without your being present and the quality of the singing depends on your performance each time. If you train jugglers, the time and effort you invest pays off a thousand times, while you sit back and watch the show.

What do we mean by grievance?

Contemporary British texts virtually ignore grievance handling, but the Americans maintain sound coverage. Mathis and Jackson (1994) have a particularly helpful review. Some years ago Pigors and Myers (1977, p. 229) provided a helpful approach to the topic by drawing a distinction between the terms dissatisfaction, complaint and grievance as follows:

> **Dissatisfaction**: Anything that disturbs an employee, whether or not the unrest is expressed in words.
> **Complaint**: A spoken or written dissatisfaction brought to the attention of the supervisor and/or shop steward.
> **Grievance**: A complaint that has been formally presented to a management representative or to a union official.

This provides us with a useful categorisation by separating out grievance as a formal, relatively drastic step, compared with commonplace grumbling. It is much more important for management to know about dissatisfaction. Although nothing is being expressed, the feeling of hurt following failure to get a pay rise or the frustration about shortage of materials can quickly influence performance.

Much dissatisfaction never turns into complaint, as something happens to make it unnecessary. Dissatisfaction evaporates with a night's sleep, after a cup of coffee with a colleague, or when the cause of the dissatisfaction is in some other way removed. The few dissatisfactions that do produce complaint are also most likely to resolve themselves at that stage. The person hearing the complaint explains things in a way that the dissatisfied employee had not previously appreciated, or takes action to get at the root of the problem.

Grievances are rare since few employees will question their superior's judgement (whatever their private opinion) and fewer still will risk being stigmatised as a troublemaker. Also, many people do not initiate grievances because they believe that nothing will be done as a result of their attempt.

Personnel managers have to encourage the proper use of procedures to discover sources of dissatisfaction. Managers in the middle may not reveal the complaints they are hearing, for fear of showing themselves in a poor light. Employees who feel insecure, for any reason, are not likely to risk going into procedure, yet the dissatisfaction lying beneath a repressed grievance can produce all manner of unsatisfactory work behaviours from apathy to arson. Individual dissatisfaction can lead to the loss of a potentially valuable employee; collective dissatisfaction can lead to industrial action.

Roethlisberger and Dickson (1939, pp. 225–69) differentiated three types of complaint, according to content. The first kind referred to tangible objects in terms that could be defined by any competent worker and could be readily tested:

▶ 'The machine is out of order.'
▶ 'This tool is too dull.'
▶ 'The stock we're getting now is not up to standard.'
▶ 'Our cement is too thin and won't make the rubber stick.'

Second were those complaints based partly on sensory experience, but primarily on the accompanying, subjective reactions:

▶ 'The work is messy.'
▶ 'It's too hot in here.'
▶ 'The job is too hard.'

These statements include terms where the meaning is biologically or socially determined and can therefore not be understood unless the background of the complainant is known; seldom can their accuracy be objectively determined. A temperature of 18 degrees centigrade may be too hot for one person but equable for another.

The third type of complaint they differentiated were those involving the hopes and fears of employees:

▶ 'The supervisor plays favourites.'
▶ 'The pay rates are too low.'
▶ 'Seniority doesn't count as much as it should.'

These complaints proved the most revealing to the investigators as they showed the importance of determining not only what employees felt, but also why they felt as they did; not only verifying the facts ('the manifest content'), but also determining the feelings behind the facts ('the latent content').

Roethlisberger and Dickson concluded, for instance, that one employee who complained of his supervisor being a bully was actually saying something rather different, especially when the reason given was the fact that the supervisor did not say 'good morning'. Later, it was revealed that the root of his dissatisfaction was his attitude to any authority figure, not simply the supervisor about whom he had complained.

Each of the types of dissatisfaction manifested in this analysis is important for the management to uncover and act upon, if action is possible. Action is likely to be prompt on complaints of the first type, as they are neutral: blame is being placed on an inanimate object and individual culpability is not an issue. Action may be taken on complaints of the second type where the required action is straightforward – such as opening a window if it is too hot – but the problem of accuracy is such that there may be a tendency to smoothe over an issue or leave it 'to sort itself out' in time. The third type of complaint is the most difficult, and action is therefore less likely to be taken. Supervisors will often take complaints to be a personal criticism of their own competence, and employees will often translate the complaint into a grievance only by attaching it to a third party like a shop steward, so that the relationship between employee and supervisor is not jeopardised.

The framework of organisational justice

Now we look at the ways of dealing with the dissatisfaction that causes grievance and discipline.

ACTIVITY BOX 29.2

Think of an example from your own experience of dissatisfaction causing inefficiency that was not remedied because there was no complaint. Why was there no complaint?

The organisation requires a framework of justice to surround the everyday employment relationship so that managers and supervisors, as well as other employees, know where they stand when dissatisfaction develops. Figure 29.2 shows a framework of organisational culture.

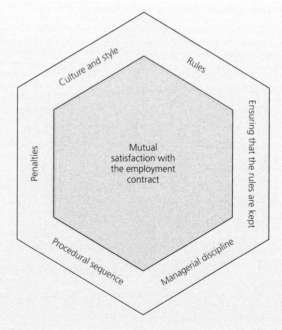

Figure 29.2 The framework of organisational justice

Awareness of culture and appropriateness of style

The culture of an organisation profoundly affects the behaviour of people within it and develops norms that are hard to alter. It is important to recognise the importance of this influence. If, for instance, everyone is in the habit of arriving ten minutes late, a 'new broom' manager will have a struggle to change the habit. Equally, if everyone is in the habit of arriving punctually, then a new recruit who often arrives late will come under strong social pressure to conform, without need for recourse to management action. Culture also affects the freedom and candour with which people discuss dissatisfactions with their managers without allowing them to fester.

The style managers adopt in handling grievances and discipline will reflect their beliefs. The manager who sees discipline as being punishment, and who regards grievances as examples of subordinates getting above themselves, will behave in a relatively autocratic way, being curt in disciplinary situations and dismissive of complaints. The manager who sees disciplinary problems as obstacles to achievement that do not necessarily imply incompetence or ill-will by the employee will seek out the cause of the problem. The problem may then be revealed as one requiring firm, punitive action by the manager, but it may alternatively be revealed as a matter requiring management remedy of a different kind. In either case the manager will be supported by the bulk of the employees. The manager who listens out for complaints and grievances, gets to the bottom of the problems and finds solutions will run little risk of rumbling discontent from people obsessed by trivial problems.

Rules

Every workplace has rules; the difficulty is to have rules that people will honour. Some rules come from statutes, like the tachograph requirement for HGV drivers, but most are tailored to meet the particular requirements of the organisation in which they apply. For example, rules about personal cleanliness are essential in a food factory but less stringent in a garage.

Rules should be clear and readily understood. The number of rules should be sufficient to cover all obvious and usual disciplinary matters. To ensure general compliance it is helpful if rules are jointly determined, but it is more common for management to formulate the rules and for employee representatives eventually to concur with them. Employees should have ready access to the rules through the employee handbook and noticeboard, and the personnel manager will always try to ensure that the rules are known as well as published.

The Department of Employment (1973) suggested that rules fall into six categories, relating to different types of employee behaviour:

1. Negligence is failure to do the job properly and is different from incompetence because of the assumption that the employee can do the job properly, but has not. The incompetent employee, unable to do the job properly, should not be subject to discipline.
2. Unreliability is failure to attend work as required, such as being late or absent.
3. Insubordination is refusal to obey an instruction, or deliberate disrespect to someone in a position of authority. It is not to be confused with the use of

bad language. Some of the most entertaining cases in industrial tribunals have involved weighty consideration of whether or not colourful language was intended to be insubordinate.

4. Interfering with the rights of others covers a range of behaviours that are deemed socially unacceptable. Fighting is clearly identifiable, but intimidation may be more difficult to establish. Less clear as a basis for rules that must be obeyed is the prohibition of practical jokes and pernicious gossip.

5. Theft is another clear-cut aspect of behaviour that is unacceptable when it is from another employee. Theft from the organisation should be supported by very explicit rules, as stealing company property is regarded by many offenders as one of the perks of the job. How often have you taken home a box of paper clips or a felt tip pen without any thought that you were stealing from the employer?

6. Safety offences are those aspects of behaviour that can cause a hazard.

WINDOW ON PRACTICE

In a recent discussion with a group of senior managers, the following were identified as legitimately taken at will by employees:

Paper clips, pencils, disposable pens, spiral pads, local telephone calls, plain paper, computer paper and disks, adhesive tape, overalls and simple uniform.

Among the more problematic were:

Redundant or shop-soiled stock. One DIY store insisted that the store manager should personally supervise the scrapping of items that were slightly damaged, to ensure that other items were not slightly damaged on purpose.

Surplus materials. One electricity supplier had some difficulty in eradicating the practice of surplus cable and pipe being regarded as a legitimate perquisite of fitters at the end of installation jobs, as they suspected their engineers were using the surplus for private work. Twelve months later the level of material requisition had declined by 14 per cent.

The Institute of Personnel Management (1979) conducted a survey of disciplinary practice in nearly 300 organisations and found that the three main reasons for disciplinary action were: poor timekeeping, unauthorised absence and poor standards of work. So the rules most frequently invoked were those relating to negligence and unreliability. Rules are not, however, just a basis for imposing penalties. Their greatest value is in providing guidelines on what people should do, and the majority will comply. The number of drivers killed on the roads has declined sharply because the great majority of drivers obey the law on wearing seat belts. The date for introducing the legislation was, however, deferred twice to ensure that it was introduced at a time when there would be general acceptance rather than widespread defiance of the law.

Ensuring that the rules are kept

Although the majority of car drivers wear seat belts, the majority of dog owners never had dog licences. It is not sufficient just to have rules; they are only effective if they are observed. How do we make sure that employees stick to the rules?

1. Information is needed so that everyone knows what the rules are and why they should be obeyed. Written particulars may suffice in an industrial tribunal hearing, but most people follow the advice and behaviour of their colleagues in determining how they will behave, so informal methods of communication are just as important as formal statements.

2. Induction is a means of making the rules coherent and reinforcing their understanding. The background can be described and the reason for the rule explained, perhaps with examples, so that the new recruit not only knows the rules but understands why they should be obeyed.

3. Placement and relocation can both avoid the risk of rules being broken, by placing a new recruit with a working team that has high standards of compliance. If there are the signs of disciplinary problems in the offing, then a quick relocation can put the problem employee in a new situation where offences are less likely.

4. Training increases the new recruit's awareness of the rules, improving self-confidence and self-discipline. For established employees there will be new working procedures or new equipment from time to time, and again training will reduce the risk of safety offences, negligence or unreliability.

5. Review of the rules periodically ensures that they are up-to-date, and also ensures that their observance is a live issue. If, for instance, there is a monthly works council meeting, it could be appropriate to have a rules review every twelve months. The simple fact that the rules are being discussed will keep up the general level of awareness of what they are.

6. Penalties make the framework of organisational justice firmer if there is an understanding of what penalties can be imposed, by whom and for what. It is not feasible or desirable to have a fixed scale, but neither is it wise for penalties to depend on individual managerial whim. This area has been partially codified by the legislation on dismissal, but the following are some typical forms of penalty:

   (a) **Rebuke**: This is the simple 'Don't do that' or 'Smoking is not allowed in here' or 'If you're late again, you will be in trouble'. This is all that is needed in most situations, as someone has forgotten one of the rules, or had not realised it was to be taken seriously, or was perhaps testing the resolution of the management. Too frequently, managers are reluctant to risk defiance and tend to wait until they have a good case for more serious action rather than deploying their own, there-and-then authority.

   (b) **Caution**: Slightly more serious and formal is the caution, which is then recorded. This is not triggering the procedure for dismissal, it is just making a note of a rule being broken and an offence being pointed out.

   (c) **Warnings**: When the management begin to issue warnings, great care is required as the development of unfair dismissal legislation with its associated code of practice has made the system of warnings an integral part of disciplinary practice which has to be followed if the employer is to succeed in defending a possible claim of unfair dismissal at tribunal. For the employer to show procedural fairness there should normally be a formal oral warning, or a written warning, specifying the nature of the offence and the likely outcome of the offence being repeated. It should also be made clear that this is the first, formal stage in the procedure. Further misconduct could then warrant a final written warning containing a statement that further repetition would lead to a penalty such as suspension or dismissal. All written warnings should be dated, signed and kept on record for a period agreed by rules known by both sides. Details must be given to the employee and to his or her representative, if desired. The means of appeal against the disciplinary action should also be pointed out.

(d) **Disciplinary transfer or demotion**: This is moving the employee to less attractive work, possibly carrying a lower salary. The seriousness of this is that it is public, as the employee's colleagues know the reason. A form of disciplinary transfer is found on assembly-lines, where there are some jobs that are more attractive and carry higher status than others. Rule-breakers may be 'pushed down the line' until their contempt is purged and they are able to move back up. Demotion is rare and seldom effective because the humiliation is so great. Those demoted usually either leave or carry on (probably because they cannot leave) with considerable resentment and having lost so much confidence that their performance remains inadequate.

(e) **Suspension**: A tactic that has the benefit of being serious and avoids the disadvantage of being long-lasting, like demotion. The employer has a contractual obligation to provide pay, but not to provide work, so it is easy to suspend someone from duty – with pay – either as a punishment or while an alleged offence is being investigated. If the contract of employment permits, it may also be possible to suspend the employee for a short period without pay.

(f) **Fines**: These are little used, because of contractual problems, but the most common is deduction from pay for lateness.

The important general comment about penalties is that they should be appropriate in the circumstances. Where someone is, for instance, persistently late or absent, suspension would be a strange penalty. Also penalties must be within the law. An employee cannot be demoted or transferred at managerial whim, and fines or unpaid suspension can only be imposed if the contract of employment allows such measures.

7. Procedural sequence is essential to the framework of organisational justice. It should be the clear, unvarying logic of procedure, and be well known and trusted. Procedure makes clear, for example, who does and who does not have the power to dismiss. The dissatisfied employee who is wondering whether or not to turn a complaint into a formal grievance, knows who will hear the grievance and where an appeal could be lodged. This security of procedure, where step B always follows step A, is needed by managers as well as by employees, as it provides them with their authority as well as limiting the scope of their actions.

8. Managerial discipline. Finally, managers must preserve general respect for the justice framework by their self-discipline in how they work within it. With very good intentions some senior managers maintain an 'open door' policy with the message: 'My door is always open . . . call in any time you feel I can help you.' This has many advantages and is often necessary, but

it has danger for matters of discipline and grievance because it encourages people to bypass middle managers. They welcome the opportunity to talk to the organ grinder rather than the monkey. There is also the danger that employees come to see the settlement of their grievances as being dependent on the personal goodwill of an individual rather than on the business logic or their human and employment rights.

Managers must also be consistent in their handling of discipline and grievance issues. Whatever the rules are, they will be generally supported only as long as they deserve such support. If they are enforced inconsistently they will soon lose any moral authority and depend only on the fear of penalties. Equally, the manager who handles grievances quickly and consistently is well on the way to enjoying the support of a committed group of employees.

The other need for managerial discipline is to test the validity of the discipline assumption. Is it a case for disciplinary action or for some other remedy? There is little purpose in suspending someone for negligence when the real problem is lack of training. Many disciplinary problems disappear under analysis, and it is sensible to carry out the analysis before making a possibly unjustified allegation of indiscipline.

Grievance procedure

The formality of the grievance procedure is often resented by managers, who believe that it introduces unnecessary rigidity into the working relationship: 'I see my people all the time. We work side by side and they can raise with me any issue they want, at any time they want . . .' The problem is that many people will not raise issues with the immediate superior that could be regarded as contentious, in just the same way that managers frequently shirk the rebuke as a form of disciplinary penalty. Formality in procedure provides a framework within which individuals can reasonably air their grievances and avoids the likelihood of managers dodging the issue when it is difficult. It avoids the risk of inconsistent *ad hoc* decisions and the employee knows at the outset that the matter will be heard and where it will be heard. The key features of grievance procedure are fairness, facilities for representation, procedural steps and promptness.

1. Fairness is needed not only to be just but also to keep the procedure viable. If employees develop the belief that the procedure is only a sham, then its value will be lost and other means will be sought to deal with grievances. Fairness is best supported by the obvious even-handedness of the ways in which grievances are handled, but it will be greatly enhanced if the appeal stage is either to a joint body or to independent arbitration – usually by ACAS – as the management is relinquishing the chance to be judge of its own cause.
2. Representation can be of help to the individual employee who lacks the confidence or experience to take on the management single handedly. A representative, such as a shop steward, has the advantage of having dealt with a range of employee problems and may be able to advise the person with the grievance whether the claim is worth pursuing. There is always

the risk that the presence of the representative produces a defensive management attitude affected by a number of other issues on which the manager and shop steward may be at loggerheads, so the managers involved in hearing the grievance have to cast the representative in the correct role for the occasion.

3. Procedural steps should be limited to three. There is no value in having more just because there are more levels in the management hierarchy. This will only lengthen the time taken to deal with matters and will soon bring the procedure into disrepute. The reason for advocating three steps is that three types of management activity are involved in settling grievances. Having said that, it is quite common for there to be more than three steps where there is a steep hierarchy, within which there may be further, more senior, people to whom the matter could be referred. The reason for more steps has nothing to do with how to process grievances but is purely a function of the organisation structure.

   The first step is the preliminary, when the grievance is lodged with the immediate superior of the person with the complaint. In the normal working week most managers will have a variety of queries from members of their departments, some of which could become grievances, depending on the manager's reaction. Mostly the manager will either satisfy the employee or the employee will decide not to pursue the matter. Sometimes, however, a person will want to take the issue further. This is the preliminary step in procedure, but it is a tangible step as the manager has the opportunity to review any decisions made causing the dissatisfaction, possibly enabling the dissatisfied employee to withdraw the grievance.

   The hearing is when the complainant has the opportunity to state the grievance to a more senior manager, who is able to take a broader view of the matter than the immediate superior and who may be able both to see the issue more dispassionately and to perceive solutions that the more limited perspective of the immediate superior obscured. It is important for the management that the hearing should finalise the matter whenever possible, so that recourse to appeal is not automatic. The hearing should not come to be seen by the employees as no more than an irritating milestone on the way to the real decision-makers. This is why procedural steps should be limited to three.

   If there is an appeal, this will usually be to a designated more senior manager, and the outcome will be either a confirmation or modification of the decision at the hearing.

4. Promptness is needed to avoid the bitterness and frustration that can come from delay. When an employee 'goes into procedure', it is like pulling the communication cord in the train. The action is not taken lightly and it is in anticipation of a swift resolution. Furthermore, the manager whose decision is being questioned will have a difficult time until the matter is resolved. The most familiar device to speed things up is to incorporate time limits between the steps, specifying that the hearing should take place no later than, say, four working days after the preliminary notice and that the appeal should be no more than five working days after the hearing. This gives time for reflection and initiative by the manager or the complainant between the stages, but does not leave time for the matter to be forgotten.

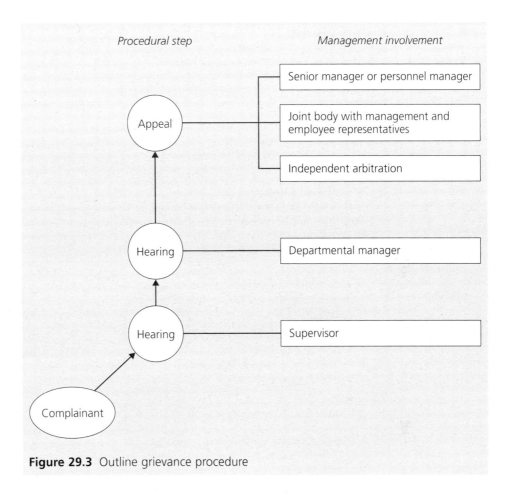

Figure 29.3 Outline grievance procedure

Where the organisation has a collective disputes procedure as well as one for individual grievances, there needs to be an explicit link between the two so that individual matters can be pursued with collective support if there is not a satisfactory outcome. An outline grievance procedure is in Figure 29.3.

Disciplinary procedure

Procedures for discipline are very similar to those for grievance and depend equally on fairness, promptness and representation. There are some additional features.

Authorisation of penalties

The law requires that managers should not normally have the power to dismiss their immediate subordinates without reference to more senior managers. Whatever tangible penalties are to be imposed, they should only be imposed by people who have that specific authority delegated to them. Usually this means that the more serious penalties can only be imposed by more senior people, but there are many organisations where such decisions are delegated to the personnel department.

Investigation

The procedure should also ensure that disciplinary action is not taken until it has been established that an offence has been committed that justifies the action. The possibility of suspension on full pay is one way of allowing time for the investigation of dubious allegations, but the stigma attached to such suspensions should not be forgotten.

Information and explanation

If there is the possibility of disciplinary action, the person to be disciplined should be told of the complaint, so that an explanation can be made, or the matter denied, before any penalties are decided. If an employee is to be penalised, then the reasons for the decision should be explained to make sure that cause and

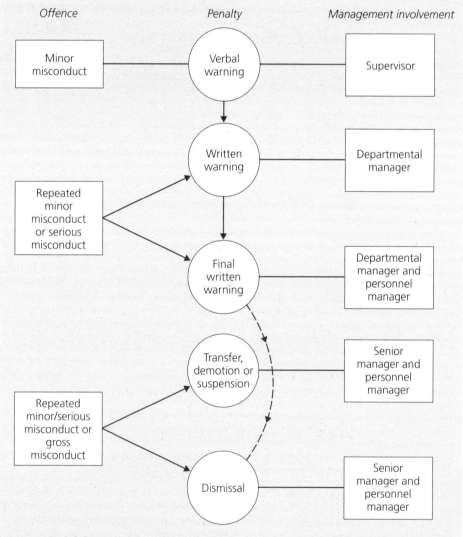

Figure 29.4 Outline disciplinary procedure

effect are appreciated. The purpose of penalties is to prevent a recurrence. An outline disciplinary procedure is in Figure 29.4.

Disputes

Procedures for the avoidance of disputes are mainly drawn up in national negotiations between employers' associations and trade unions or between single employers and unions. Disputes can arise for a wide range of reasons, but their essence is that they are collective: employees are acting in concert, and nearly always using union machinery, to persuade the management to alter a decision. Sometimes the grievance of an individual can escalate into a collective dispute if employees together feel that a matter of principle is at stake. Disciplinary penalties, especially dismissals, can also become matters for collective employee action, when the dismissal is regarded as unfair or victimisation.

There are usually more steps in a procedure for collective dispute than for individual grievances and provisions to preclude strikes, lock-outs or other forms of industrial action before procedure is exhausted.

Are grievance and discipline processes equitable?

For these processes to work they must command support, and they will only command support if they are seen as equitable, truly just and fair. At first it would seem that it is concern for the individual employee that is paramount, but the individual cannot be isolated from the rest of the workforce. Fairness should therefore be linked to the interests that all workers have in common in the business, and to the managers who must also perceive the system as equitable if they are to abide by its outcomes.

Procedures have a potential to be fair in that they are certain. The conduct of employee relations becomes less haphazard and irrational – people 'know where they stand'. The existence of a rule cannot be denied and opportunities for one party to manipulate and change a rule are reduced. Procedures also have the advantage that they can be communicated. The process of formalising a procedure that previously existed only in custom and practice clarifies the ambiguities and inconsistencies within it and compels each party to recognise the role and responsibility of the other. By providing pre-established avenues for responses to various contingencies there is the chance that the response will be less random and so more fair. The impersonal nature of procedures offers the possibility of removing hostility from the workplace, since an artificial social situation is created in which the ritual displays of aggression towards management are not seen as personal attacks on managers.

The achievement of equity may not match the potential. Procedures cannot, for instance, impart equity to situations that are basically unfair. Thus attempting to cope with an anomalous pay system through grievance procedure may be alleviating symptoms rather than treating causes. It is also impossible to overcome accepted norms of inequity in a plant, such as greater punctuality being required of manual employees than of white-collar employees.

A further feature of procedural equity is its degree of similarity to the judicial process. All adopt certain legalistic mechanisms, like the right of individuals to be represented and to hear the case against them, but some aspects of legalism, such as burdens of proof and strict adherence to precedent, may cause the application of standard remedies rather than the consideration of individual circumstances.

WINDOW ON PRACTICE

The 'red-hot stove' rule of discipline offers the touching of a red hot stove as an analogy for effective disciplinary action:

1. The burn is immediate. There is no question of cause and effect.
2. You had warning. If the stove was red-hot, you knew what would happen if you touched it.
3. The discipline is consistent. Everyone who touches the stove is burned.
4. The discipline is impersonal. People are burned not because of who they are, but because they touch the stove.

ACTIVITY BOX 29.3

Think of an attempt at disciplinary action that went wrong. Which of the features of the red-hot stove rule were missing?

Notions of fairness are not 'givens' of the situation; they are socially constructed and there will never be more than a degree of consensus on what constitutes fairness. Despite this, the procedural approach can exploit standards of certainty and consistency which are widely accepted as elements of justice. The extent to which a procedure can do this will depend on the suitability of its structure to local circumstances, the commitment of those who operate it and the way that it reconciles legalistic and bargaining elements.

Summary propositions

29.1 The authority of managers to exercise discipline in relation to others in the organisation is underpinned by a general predilection of people to obey commands from those holding higher rank in the hierarchy of which they are members.

29.2 The exercise of that discipline is limited by the procedural structures for grievance and discipline.

29.3 Grievance and discipline handling are two areas of human resource management that few other people want to take over and provide personnel managers with some of their most significant contributions to business effectiveness.

29.4 Discipline can be understood as being either managerial, team or self-discipline, and they are connected hierarchically.

29.5 Dissatisfaction, complaint and grievance is another hierarchy. Unresolved employee dissatisfaction can lead to the loss of potentially valuable employees. In extreme cases it can lead to industrial action.

29.6 Grievance and disciplinary processes both require a framework of organisational justice.

29.7 The procedural framework of disciplinary and grievance processes is one of the keys to their being equitable.

References

Department of Employment (1973) *In Working Order*, London: HMSO.

Institute of Personnel Management (1979) *Disciplinary Procedures and Practice*, London: IPM.

Mathis, R. L. and Jackson, J. H. (1994) *Human Resource Management*, 7th edn, Minneapolis/St Paul: West.

Milgram, S. (1974) *Obedience to Authority*, London: Tavistock.

Pigors, P. and Myers, C. (1977) *Personnel Administration*, 8th edn, Maidenhead: McGraw-Hill.

Roethlisberger, F. J. and Dickson, W. J, (1939) *Management and the Worker*, Cambridge, Mass.: Harvard University Press.

General discussion topics

1. Do you think Milgram's experiments would have had a different outcome if the subjects had included women as well as men?
2. What examples can individual members of the group cite of self-discipline, team discipline and managerial discipline?
3. 'The trouble with grievance procedures is that they encourage people to waste a lot of time with petty grumbles. Life at work is rarely straightforward and people should just accept the rough with the smooth.'
   What do you think of that opinion?

CHAPTER 30

Interactive skill: grievance and disciplinary interviewing

We said in Chapter 20 that the appraisal interview was the hardest aspect of management for any manager to undertake. The subject of this chapter is the least popular of all management activities: talking to people when things have gone wrong. Reading most books on management you might think that things never go wrong. The writing has such an upbeat tone that it is *entirely* positive, enthusiastic, visionary, forward-looking and all the other qualities that are so important. Sometimes, however, things really do go wrong and have to be sorted out. The sorting out involves at some point a meeting between a dissatisfied manager and an employee who is seen as the cause of that dissatisfaction, or between a dissatisfied employee and a manager representing the employing organisation that is seen as the cause of the employee's dissatisfaction. Procedures can do no more than force meetings to take place: it is the meetings themselves that provide answers.

Many contemporary views of discipline are connected with the idea of punishment, as we saw in the last chapter; a disciplinarian is one seen as an enforcer of rules, a hard taskmaster or martinet. To discipline school children is usually to punish them by keeping them in after school or chastising them. Disciplinary procedures in employment are usually drawn up to provide a pre-liminary to dismissal, so that any eventual dismissal will not be viewed as unfair by a tribunal. This background makes a problem-solving approach to discipline difficult for a manager, as there is always the sanction in the background making it unlikely that the employee will see the manager's behaviour as being authentic. There will always be a feeling – somewhere between outright conviction and lingering uncertainty – that a manager in a disciplinary interview is looking for a justification to punish rather than looking for a more constructive solution. The approach of this chapter is based on the more accurate notion of discipline implied in its derivation from the Latin *discere*, to learn and *discipulus*, learner. In disciplinary interviews the manager is attempting to modify the working behaviour of a subordinate, but it does not necessarily involve punishment.

The idea of grievance similarly has problems of definition and ethos. In the last chapter we used the convenient scale of dissatisfaction–complaint–grievance as an explanation, but that is a convenient technical classification. The general sense of the word is closer to the dictionary definitions which use phrases like 'a real or imaginary wrong causing resentment' or 'a feeling of injustice having been unfairly treated'. Notions of resentment and injustice seem too heavy for situations where the basic problem is that the maintenance crew have fallen down on the job or the central heating is not working properly. Where we have unresolved problems about our jobs – even when we are deeply worried by them – we are often reluctant to construe our feelings as 'having a grievance'. We just want to get more information, or an opportunity for training, a chance to talk to someone a bit more senior. Very few people indeed want to be seen to be grumbling. Customers are generally reluctant to grumble about the service they receive, because it is too much trouble, because no one would listen, or just because they do not want to make a fuss; yet they can simply walk away. Compared with customers, employees are much less inclined to complain, or even to point out problems, for fear of being categorised as a nuisance.

Despite the difficulties, the aim of this chapter is to formulate an approach to the interview that achieves an adjustment in attitude, with the changed attitude being confirmed by subsequent experience. Either the manager believes that the employee's subsequent working behaviour will be satisfactory, or the employee believes that his or her subsequent experience in employment will be satisfactory. The interview only succeeds when there is the confirmation.

In his profound and simple book of 1960, Douglas McGregor advocated an approach to management based on the strategy of *integration and self-control*. He regarded forms and procedures as having little value and emphasised the importance of social interaction as well as the difficulty of achieving any change in people's interactive behaviour:

> Every adult human being has an elaborate history of past experience in this field and additional learning is profoundly influenced by that history. From infancy on, his ability to achieve his goals and satisfy his needs – his 'social survival' – has been a function of his skills in influencing others. Deep emotional currents – unconscious needs such as those related to dependency and counterdependency – are involved. He has a large 'ego investment' and his knowledge and skill in this area, and the defences he has built to protect that investment are strong and psychologically complex.
>
> (McGregor 1960, p. 75)

Managers undoubtedly spend a great deal of their time in interviews of one type or another and grievance and disciplinary interviews are among the least popular parts of their managerial day; nearly as difficult as performance appraisal and potentially even less pleasant. It may be that the ability of managers to handle the grievance/discipline interview will be the most important test of their effectiveness in organising the efforts of their working group.

Just as we set grievance and discipline alongside each other in the last chapter, similarly we examine here the grievance/disciplinary encounter in the same framework, as both are trying to tackle dissatisfaction with the employment situation of a particular person, where resolution of the problem is not straightforward. If Jim sets fire to the Plant Director's office and admits to the police that he did it for a lark because he was bored, then any disciplinary interview ought not be too difficult. If Joe is not working as well as he used to, but nobody quite knows why and he refuses to say anything about it to anyone, then there is the less straightforward situation with which the approach of this chapter might help.

ACTIVITY BOX 30.1

What grievance or disciplinary incidents can you recall where the situation was not clear-cut and where an interview with a manager pro- duced a resolution to the problem that was effective, although quite different from what had been anticipated by the manager at the beginning of the interview?

The nature of grievance and disciplinary interviewing

Many grievance or discipline interviews are simple: giving information, explaining work requirements and delivering rebukes, but from time to time every manager will need to use a problem-solving approach, involving sympathy, perception, empathy and the essential further feature that some managers provide only with reluctance: time. The method will be analytical and constructive; not only for the interviews built in to the grievance and discipline procedure, but also for interviews that avoid recourse to the rigid formality of procedure. We see such interviews as one of the means towards *self-discipline* and *autonomy* of employees, reducing the need for supervision. The sequence we advocate has discipline and grievance intertwined for much of the process but diverging in the interview itself.

As we have shown in the previous chapter, a grievance may be expressed only in manifest form, requiring interviewing to understand its latent content in order that appropriate action is taken to remove the underlying dissatisfaction. Discipline problems will have underlying reasons for the unsatisfactory behaviour and these need to be discovered before solutions to the problems can be attempted.

WINDOW ON PRACTICE

There is a risk of some managers looking for problems that do not exist anywhere other than in the imagination of the manager. George was a supervisor in charge of several cleaning gangs and he prided himself on his avuncular concern for their welfare (some of the more cynical cleaners described him as 'bloody nosey').

One day, Mildred stopped at his office to say that she was going to leave at the end of the month, because she had decided to give up work. Mildred had been a cleaner in the company for fifteen years and was highly regarded by George. She was 59 and her husband had recently retired. Her two children were both independent, so she and her husband had decided that she would give up work in April, so that they could both get used to retirement during the summer rather than wait until her 60th birthday in November.

George decided that there was 'more to this than met the eye' and spent half an hour asking Mildred a series of questions about her health, her children, her relationship with her husband and how she spent her spare time. Mildred became more and more exasperated, eventually storming out to see her shop steward.

Sometimes people say what they mean, mean what they say and that's that: problem-solving interviewing is definitely not required.

The discipline and grievance sequence

Figure 30.1 is a model of the interviews we are going to describe.

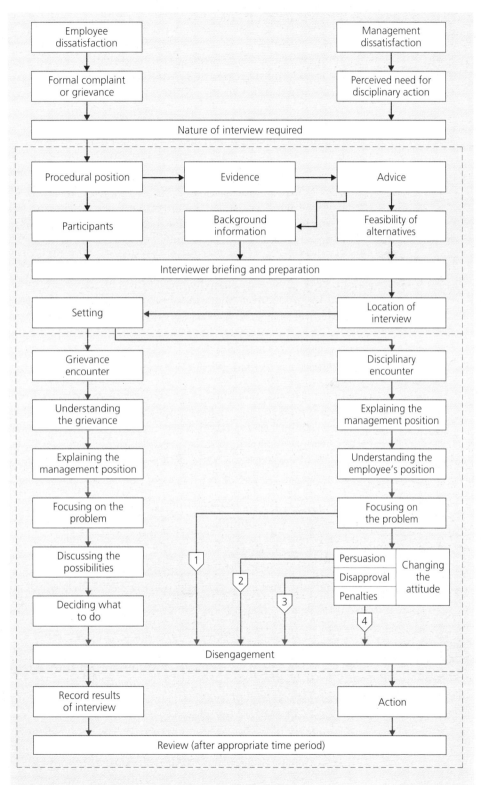

Figure 30.1 The grievance and disciplinary interviews

Preparation

The first requirement is to check the procedural position and to ensure that the impending interview is appropriate. In a grievance situation, for instance, is the employee pre-empting the procedure by taking the matter to the wrong person or to the wrong point in procedure? This is most common when the first-line supervisor is being bypassed, either because the employee or the representative feel that it would be a waste of time, or perhaps because the supervisor is unsure of the appropriate action and is conniving at the procedure being side-stepped. It is also possible that the supervisor knows what to do but is shirking the responsibility or the potential unpopularity of what has to be done. Whatever the reason for such bypassing it is usually to be avoided because of the worrying precedents that it can establish.

In disciplinary matters even more care is needed about the procedural step, as the likelihood of penalties may already have been set up by warnings, thus reducing the scope for doing anything else in the impending interview apart from imposing a further penalty. In the majority of cases we believe that interviews will precede procedure, in which case the parties to the interview are less constrained by procedural rules. In these situations the manager will be at pains to establish that the interview is informal and without procedural implications. Alternatively the interview may be in a situation where the likelihood of a move into procedure is so remote that the manager will be at pains to avoid any such reference, for fear of the complainant taking fright.

Who will be there? Here there are similar procedural considerations. In procedure there is the likelihood of employee representation, out of procedure there is less likelihood of that, even though the employee may feel anxious and threatened without it. If the manager is accompanied in the interview, the employee may feel even more insecure, and it is doubtful how much can be achieved informally unless the employee feels reasonably secure and able to speak frankly.

What are the facts that the interviewer needs to know? In grievance it will be necessary to know the subject of the grievance and how it has arisen. This type of information will have been filtered through the management hierarchy and may well have been modified in the process, so it needs to be considered carefully and any additional background information collected.

Disciplinary interviews always start at the behest of the management so the manager will again need to collect evidence and consider how it may have been interpreted by intermediaries. This will include some basic details about the interviewee, but mainly it will be information about the aspects of the working performance that are unsatisfactory and why. Too often this exists only in opinions that have been offered and prejudices that are held. This provides a poor basis for a constructive interview, so you need to ferret out details, with as much factual corroboration as possible, including a shrewd guess about the interviewee's perspective on the situation.

It is almost inevitable that the interviewee will start the interview defensively, expecting to be blamed for something and therefore ready to refute any allegations, probably deflecting blame elsewhere. The manager needs to anticipate the respondent's initial reaction and be prepared to deal with the reaction as well as with facts that have been collected. Unless the interview is at an early, informal stage, the manager also needs to know about earlier warnings, cautions or penalties that have been invoked.

For both types of interview there will be more general information required. Not just the facts of the particular grievance or disciplinary situation, but knowledge to give a general understanding of the working arrangements and relationships, will be required. Other relevant data may be on the employee's length of service, type of training, previous experience, and so forth.

Most managers approaching a grievance or disciplinary interview will benefit from advice before starting. It is particularly important for anyone who is in procedure to check the position with someone like a personnel officer before starting, as the ability to sustain any action by management will largely depend on maintaining consistency with what the management has done with other employees previously. The manager may also have certain ideas of what could be done in terms of re-training, transfer or assistance with a domestic problem. The feasibility of such actions need to be verified before broaching them with an aggrieved employee or with an employee whose work is not satisfactory.

Where is the interview to take place? However trivial this question may seem it is included for two reasons. First, because we have seen a number of interviews go sadly awry because of the parties arriving at different places; this mistake seems to happen more often with this type of encounter than with others. Second, because there may be an advantage in choosing an unusually informal situation – or an unusually formal location, according to the manager's assessment. A discussion over a pie and a pint in the local pub may be a more appropriate setting for some approaches to grievance and disciplinary problems, although they are seldom appropriate if the matter has reached procedure. Also employees frequently mistrust such settings, feeling that they are being manipulated or that the discussion 'does not count' because it is out of hours or off limits. If, however, one is trying to avoid procedural overtones, this can be a way of doing it.

Unusual formality can be appropriate in the later stages of procedure, especially in disciplinary matters, when proceedings take on a strongly judicial air. An employee is not likely to take seriously a final warning prior to probable dismissal if it is delivered over a pint in a pub. The large, impressive offices of senior managers can provide appropriate settings for the final stages of procedure.

ACTIVITY BOX 30.2

What incidents have you experienced or heard about where the location of the interview was clearly unsuitable?

The grievance interview

The first step in the grievance interview is for the manager to be clear about what the grievance is; a simple way of doing this is to state the *subject* of the grievance and get confirmation from the employee that it is correct. The importance of this lies in the probability that the manager will have a different perspective on the affair from the employee, particularly if it has got beyond the preliminary stage. A supervisor may report to a superior that Mr X has a grievance and 'will not take instructions from me', but when the interview begins Mr X may state his grievance as being that he is unwilling to work on Saturday mornings. In other situations it might be the other way round, with the supervisor reporting that Mr X will not work Saturday mornings and Mr X saying in the interview that he finds the style of his supervisor objectionable. Even where there is no such confusion, an opening statement and confirmation of the subject demonstrate that they are talking about the same thing.

Having clarified or confirmed the subject of the grievance, the manager will then invite the employee to state the case. This will enable the employee to explain why she or he is aggrieved, citing examples, providing further information and saying not just 'what' but also 'why'. Seldom will this be done well. The presentation of a case is not a particularly easy task for the inexperienced, and few aggrieved employees are experienced at making a case of this type. Furthermore there is the inhibition of questioning the wisdom of those in power and some apprehension about the outcome. After the declaration of the case the manager will need to ask questions in order to fill in the gaps that have been left by the employee and to clarify some points that were obscure in the first telling. As a general rule it seems better to have an episode of questioning after the case has been made, rather than to interrupt on each point that is difficult. Interruptions make a poorly argued case even more difficult to sustain. There may, however, be disguised pleas for assistance that provide good opportunities for questioning to clarify: 'I'm not very good with words, but do you see what I'm getting at . . .?', 'Do you see what I mean?', or 'Am I making myself clear?' Among the communication ploys that the manager will need at this stage could be the method of *reflection* that is described by Beveridge:

> a selective form of listening in which the listener picks out the emotional overtones of a statement and 'reflects' these back to the respondent without making any attempt to evaluate them. This means that the interviewer expresses neither approval or disapproval, neither sympathy nor condemnation. Because the respondent may be in an emotional state, sympathy is liable to make him feel resentful and angry. Any attempt to get the respondent to look objectively and rationally at his problem at this stage is also likely to fail; he is still too confused and upset to be able to do this and will interpret the very attempt as criticism.   (Beveridge 1968, p. 121)

After all the necessary clarification has been obtained the manager will restate the employee grievance, together with an outline of the case that has been presented, and will ask the employee to agree with the summary or to correct it. By this means the manager is confirming and demonstrating an understanding of what the grievance is about and why it has been brought. The manager is not agreeing with it or dismissing it; all that has happened is that the grievance is now understood.

This phase of the interview can be summarised in sequential terms:

Manager	Employee
1. States subject of grievance	
	2. Agrees with statement
	3. States case
4. Questions for clarification	
5. Re-states grievance	
	6. Agrees or corrects

The grievance is now understood

The next phase is to set out the management position on the grievance. This is not the action *to be taken* but the action that *has been taken* with the reasons for it, and may include an explanation of company policy, safety rules, previous grievances, supervisory problems, administrative methods and anything else which is needed to make clear why the management position has been what it has been. The manager will then invite the employee to question and comment on the management position to ensure that it is understood and the justifications for it are understood, even if they are not accepted. The objective is to ensure that the parties to the discussion see and understand each other's point of view.

The management position is now understood

Setting out the two opposed positions will have revealed a deal of common ground. The parties will agree on some things, though disagreeing on others. In the third phase of the interview the manager and employee sort through the points they have discussed and identify the points of disagreement. At least at this stage the points on which they concur can be ignored as the need now is to find the outer limits. It is very similar to the differentiation stage in negotiation.

Points of disagreement are now in focus

As a preliminary to taking action in the matter under discussion, the various possibilities can be put up for consideration. It is logical that the employee suggestions are put first. Probably this has already been done either explicitly or implicitly in the development of the case. If, however, specific suggestions are invited at this stage they may be different ones, as the aggrieved employee now understands the management position and is seeing the whole matter clearly following the focusing that has just taken place. Then the manager will put forward alternatives or modifications, and such alternatives may include – or be limited to – the suggestion that the grievance is mischievous and unfounded so that no action should be taken. Nevertheless in most cases there will be some scope for accommodation even if it is quite different from the employee's expectation. Once the alternative suggestions for action are set out, there is time for the advantages and disadvantages of both sets to be discussed.

Alternatives have now been considered

A grievance interview is one that falls short of the mutual dependence that is present in negotiation, so that the decision on action is to be taken by the manager alone; it is not a joint decision even though the manager will presumably be looking for a decision that all parties will find acceptable. In bringing a grievance the employee is challenging a management decision and that decision will now be confirmed or it will be modified, but it remains a management decision.

Before making the decision the manager may deploy a range of behaviours to ensure that the decision is correct. It may be useful to test the employee's reaction by thinking aloud, 'Well, I don't know, but it looks to me as if we shall have to disappoint you on this one . . .'. There may be an adjournment for a while to seek further advice or to give the employee time to reflect further, but there will be little opportunity for prevarication before the manager has to decide and then explain the decision to the employee. In this way the manager is not simply deciding and announcing, but supporting the decision with explanation and justification in the same way that the employee developed the case for the grievance at the beginning. There may be employee questions, who may want time to think, but eventually the management decision will have to be accepted, unless there is some further procedural step available.

Management action is now clear and understood.

The disciplinary interview

Discipline arises from management dissatisfaction rather than employee dissatisfaction with the employment contract, so the opening move is for a statement of why such dissatisfaction exists, dealing with the *facts* of the situation rather than managerial feelings of outrage about the facts. The importance of this is that the interview is being approached by the manager as a way of dealing with a problem of the working situation and not – yet – as a way of dealing with a malicious or indolent employee. If an employee has been persistently late for a week, it would be unwise for a manager to open the disciplinary interview by saying 'Your lateness this week has been deplorable' as the reason might turn out to be that the employee has a seriously ill child needing constant attendance through the night. Then the manager would be seriously embarrassed and the potential for a constructive settlement of the matter would be jeopardised. An opening factual statement of the problem, 'You have been at least twenty minutes late each day this week . . .' does not prejudge the reasons and is reasonably precise about the scale of the problem. It also circumscribes management dissatisfaction by implying that there is no other cause for dissatisfaction: if there is, it should be mentioned.

Now the manager needs to know the explanation and asks the employee to say what the reasons for the problem are. The manager may also ask for comments on the seriousness of the problem itself, which the employee may regard

WINDOW ON PRACTICE

In the booklet *I'd Like to Have a Word With You*, Tietjin describes various types of difficult interviewee, one of which is 'the professional weeper':

> This is the person who can turn on tears like turning on a tap. Some people are quite unmoved by tears, but lots of bosses find tears and emotion very hard to cope with. They are either very embarrassed or very apologetic that their words could have had such an effect. (1987, p. 26)

Another difficult interviewee is the 'counter-attacker':

who operates on the maxim that the best defence is attack. Once you have stated your reasons for the interview, he will leap straight into the discussion, relishing the opportunity to 'have it out'. The obvious danger is that you respond to his aggression, that a battle of words will ensue and that nothing else will happen. (p. 28)

Notice that Ms Tietjin leaves the gender open in the first instance and specific in the second!

as trivial, while the manager regards it as serious. If there is such dissonance it needs to be drawn out. Getting the employee reaction is usually straightforward, but the manager needs to be prepared for one of two other types of reaction. Either there may be a need to probe because the employee is reluctant to open up, or there may be angry defiance. Disciplinary situations are at least disconcerting for employees and are frequently very worrying and surrounded by feelings of hostility and mistrust, so that it is to be expected that some ill-feeling will be pent up and waiting for the opportunity to be vented.

First possible move to disengagement

If the employee sees something of the management view of the problem and if the manager understands the reasons for it, the next requirement is to seek a solution. We have to point out that a disciplinary problem is as likely to be solved by management action as it is to be solved by employee action. If the problem is lateness, one solution would be for the employee to catch an earlier bus, but another might be for the management to alter the working shift to which the employee is assigned. If the employee is disobeying orders, one solution would be to start obeying them, but another might be for the employee to be moved to a different job where orders are received from someone else. Some managers regard such thinking as unreasonable, on the grounds that the contract of employment places obligations on individual employees that they should meet despite personal inconvenience. The answer to this type of query seems to lie in the question not of how people *should* behave, but how they do. Can the contract of employment be enforced on an unwilling employee? Not if one is seeking such attitudes as enthusiasm and co-operation, or behaviour such as diligence and carefulness. The disenchanted employee can always meet the bare letter rather than the spirit of the contract, but there is some evidence of increasing strictness:

> There appears to be growing managerial concern about absence and timekeeping. . . . There has been a move towards closer monitoring of attendance and the enforcement of standards. In one firm subjected to case study analysis, absence control was high on the managerial agenda . . . workers were more aware of pressures to work harder and tightening discipline.
> (Edwards 1989, p. 320)

The most realistic view of the matter is that many disciplinary problems require some action from both parties, some require action by the employee only and a small proportion require management action only. The problem-solving session may quickly produce the possibility for further action and open up the possibility of closing the interview.

The simple, rational approach that we have outlined so far may not be enough, due to the unwillingness of employees to respond to disciplinary expectations. They may not want to be punctual or to do as they are instructed, or whatever the particular problem is. There is now a test of the power behind management authority. Three further steps can be taken, one after the other, although there will be occasions when it is necessary to move directly to the third.

Second possible move to disengagement

Persuasion

A first strategy is to demonstrate to employees that they will not achieve what they want, if their behaviour does not change:

> 'You won't keep your earnings up if your output doesn't meet the standard.'

> 'It will be difficult to get your appointment confirmed when the probationary period is over if . . .'

By such means employees may see the advantages of changing their attitude and behaviour. If they are so convinced, then there is a strong incentive for them to alter, because they believe it to be in their own interests.

Third possible move to disengagement

Disapproval

Another strategy is to suggest that the continuance of the behaviour will displease those whose goodwill the employee wishes to keep:

> 'The Management Development Panel are rather disappointed . . .'

> 'Some of the other people in the department feel that you are not pulling your weight.'

A manager using this method will need to be sure that what is said is both true and relevant. Also the manager may be seen by the employee as shirking the issue, so it may be appropriate to use a version of 'I think this is deplorable and expect you to do better.'

We asked for a restraint from judgement in the early stages of the interview, until the nature of the problem is clear. The time for judgement has now come, with the proper deployment of the rebuke or the caution.

Fourth possible move to disengagement

Penalties

When all else fails or is clearly inappropriate – as with serious offences about which there is no doubt – penalties have to be invoked. In rare circumstances there may be the possibility of a fine, but usually the first penalty will be a formal warning as a preliminary to possible dismissal. In situations that are sufficiently grave summary dismissal is both appropriate and possible within the legal framework.

Disengagement

We have indicated possible moves to disengagement at four different points in the disciplinary interview. Now we come to a stage that is common for both grievance and disciplinary encounters from the point of view of describing the process, although the nature of disengagement will obviously differ. Essentially the manager needs to think of the working situation that will follow. In a grievance situation can the employee now accept the decision made? Are there faces to be saved or reputations to be restored? What administrative action is to be taken? In closing a disciplinary interview, the manager will aim for the flavour of disengagement to be as positive as possible so that all concerned put the disciplinary problem behind them. In those cases where the outcome of the interview is to impose or confirm a dismissal, then the manager will be exclusively concerned with the fairness and accuracy with which it is done, so that the possibility of tribunal hearings is reduced, if not prevented. It can never be appropriate to close an interview of either type leaving the employee humbled and demoralised.

WINDOW ON PRACTICE

The American Eric Harvey has reduced what he calls 'positive discipline' to three simple steps:

1. Warn the employee orally.
2. Warn the employee in writing.
3. If steps 1 and 2 fail to resolve the problem, give the employee a day off, *with pay*.
(Harvey, 1987)

A similar, very positive, approach was outlined in a seminal paper by Huberman in 1967.

Summary propositions

30.1 Grievance and disciplinary interviews are central to the process of sorting things out when there is a management/employee problem, but most managers dislike such interviews intensely.

30.2 Grievance and disciplinary interviews are one of the means towards people at work achieving self-discipline and autonomy, reducing the need for supervision and reducing the need for recourse to the formality of procedure.

30.3 The steps in conducting a grievance interview are first to understand the nature of the grievance, then to explain the management position, focus on the problem, discuss possibilities and then to decide what to do.

30.4 The disciplinary interview starts the other way around, first explaining the management position, then understanding the employee's position and focusing on the problem. If that does not produce a satisfactory disposal, the manager may have to move through three more steps: persuasion, showing disapproval or invoking penalties.

References

Beveridge, W. E. (1968) *Problem-Solving Interviews*, London: Allen and Unwin.

Edwards, P. K. (1989) 'The three faces of discipline', in K. Sisson (ed.), *Personnel Management in Britain*, Oxford: Blackwell.

Harvey, E. L. (1987) 'Discipline versus punishment', *Management Review*, March, pp. 25–9.

Huberman, J. C. (1967) 'Discipline without punishment', *Harvard Business Review*, May, pp. 62–8.

McGregor, D. (1960) *The Human Side of Enterprise*, Maidenhead: McGraw-Hill.

Tietjen, T. (1987) *I'd Like a Word With You*, London: Video Arts Ltd.

Practical exercises in grievance and discipline

First exercise

Reflection is a specialised technique, which is especially appropriate for grievance and discipline. It is reflecting back something a respondent has said in order to get more comment on the same topic. It has been defined by W. S. Beveridge as:

> a selective form of listening in which the listener picks out the emotional overtones of a statement and 'reflects' these back to the respondent without any attempt to evaluate them . . . the interviewer expresses neither approval or disapproval, neither sympathy or condemnation.   (1968, p 57)

In the next few conversations you have, practise reflection and see what effect it has on the development of the exchanges with the other person. Then think further about the type of discipline and grievance situations in which reflection would be useful.

Second exercise

This exercise needs the co-operation of your spouse, other trusted relative or close friend.

1. Identify an incident that the other person experienced some time in the past, which was unpleasant or disconcerting at the time, and about which your friend feels either guilty or unfairly treated.
2. Take the respondent through the events again, using the methods suggested in this chapter, including decision-making to agree on what should have been done.
3. Change roles and repeat the process with an incident from your past.

Third exercise

In the booklet *I'd Like to Have a Word With You*, Tina Tietjen identifies ten categories of difficult respondent in disciplinary interviews. One of these is 'the professional weeper':

> This is the person who can turn on tears like turning on a tap. Some people are quite unmoved by tears, but lots of bosses find tears and emotion very hard to cope with. They are either very embarrassed or very apologetic that their words could have had such an effect.   (Tietjen 1987, p. 26)

How would you respond to the professional weeper? Can you recall a situation when you have had to cope with tears and emotion? How will you do it next time?
    Another of her categories is 'the counter-attacker' who

> operates on the maxim that the best defence is attack. Once you have stated your reasons for the interview, he will leap straight into the discussion, relishing the opportunity to 'have it out'. The obvious danger is that you will respond to his aggression, that a battle of words will ensue and nothing else will happen.

How would you respond to the counter-attacker? Do you find it difficult to avoid rising to the bait of being drawn into an argument? How will you do it next time?
    Now get your close friend to play one of these roles of professional weeper or counter-attacker, while you play the part of the manager.

Case study problem

Industrial dispute at British Airways

British Airways is an international company by any standards and, by 1990 was the world's most popular and most profitable airline. Because of its extensive network and the salient position of Heathrow as the world's busiest airport, it was relatively straightforward to become the most popular airline, but achieving high profitability was more difficult. There was over-staffing and the need for radical measures:

> The organisation had a bureaucratic style of management, damaging industrial relations and a poor reputation for customer service. . . . There was a drastic reduction in staff numbers from 60,000 to 38,000. This was achieved by a combination of voluntary severance and natural wastage.
>
> (Hopfl, 1993, p. 117)

In order to maintain market leadership the airline embarked on a famous programme of staff training to develop commitment to customer service, and the quality of service to the customer improved markedly, so that British Airways was able to maintain its premier position despite ever-increasing competition.

There were, however, mounting problems with the staff as the pressure on margins continued. In 1996 a strike by pilots was narrowly averted, but 1997 brought one stoppage and the threat of another.

On 9 July a 72-hour strike by cabin staff began. It was an official stoppage called by the Transport and General Workers Union following protracted negotiations and a ballot among its members working for the airline. According to British Airways only 142 cabin crew formally joined the strike, but 1,500 (compared with a normal daily average of 120) reported sick – a novel strategy! 834 reported for work as usual.

The management reaction was to announce that all strikers would forfeit the travel perks and promotion prospects for three years. Film was also taken of strikers on picket lines. The threats were later withdrawn and the filming was stopped. The situation was complicated by the existence of a rival union, Cabin Crew '89, which had broken away from the TGWU in 1989. This union, known as CC89, supported the management position and all their members worked normally through the stoppage.

Another interesting feature of the dispute was reported by *The Times*:

During the past few years, BA, like many companies in Britain, has appointed middle and senior managers who fear for their jobs. To get on, they believe, they must show they are tough. I have heard these 'performance managers' brusquely warning vacillating staff that if they follow their union and refuse to work, they will 'face the consequences.' This has irked the cabin crew far more than the dispute over pay and conditions. They no longer feel part of a team and believe they are being bullied.

(Elliott 1997, p. 41)

As usual, the dispute moved on to talks to find a resolution, but BA had lost many flights and its reputation was as severely dented as its financial position. The share price dropped from 763p to 583p before recovering to 635p, and there were varying reports about how many millions of pounds the dispute was costing

Required

1. Do you think it is inevitable that the pressures of international competition drive companies into a situation where unilateral managerial decision-making must prevail and there is simply no time for the consultation and compromise that is involved in union negotiation?
2. This case provides an excellent example of the problems that can arise from having two unions representing the same group of employees and competing with each other for membership. How would you try and deal with this situation *now* – not back in 1989?
3. How accurate do you regard Harvey Elliott's views to be as a general comment on current management practice?

References

Elliott, H. (1997) 'BA is Plunging towards Disaster', *The Times*, 10 July.
Hopfl, H. (1993) 'Culture and Commitment: British Airways', In *Case Studies in Organizational Behaviour and Human Resource Management*, ed. D. Gowler, K. Legge and C. Clegg, 2nd edn, London: Paul Chapman Publishing, pp. 117–25.

Part VI Examination questions

Undergraduate introductory

1. Explain the difference between these four terms:
    (a) Industrial relations,
    (b) Employee relations,
    (c) Collective bargaining,
    (d) Employee involvement.
2. What are the aims and objectives of British trade unions?

Undergraduate finals

3. What is meant by the term 'derecognition'? How extensive is derecognition in contemporary Britain, and what employment practices, if any, have employers initiated to take the place of trade unions?
4. 'Good health is good business.' Discuss.

Masters

5. How just can the framework of organisational justice ever be when managers have so much more power than employees?
6. Analyse critically the assertion that employers develop employee involvement schemes in order to empower their employees.

Professional

7. Explain the main components of a grievance procedure.
8. Explain the difference between bargaining and grievance handling.

PART **VII**
Pay

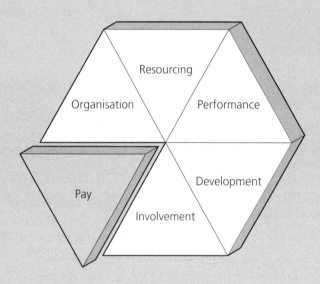

Pay

PART VII PAY

31 **Strategic aspects of payment**
32 **Job evaluation**
33 **Incentives, performance pay and fringe benefits**
34 **Pensions and sick pay**
35 **Interactive skill: negotiation**

If we were all paid the same amount for working, life would be very straightforward, but not many of us would be satisfied with the arrangement! This part of the book deals with the ways in which what we are paid differs between us. There must always be a reason to justify the difference.

It may be that one person is paid more than another because of having a higher level of skill, so the skilled artisan is paid more than the labourer, or it may be that the difference is justified by experience, so that the experienced school teacher will be paid more than the newly qualified teacher. Managers have always been interested in making arrangements for the better performer to be paid more than the average performer, and we can see lots of schemes currently that are working towards that objective. Aspects of payment do not only affect our working life; there is an effect also on our pension at the end of our working life and an effect on what happens if we are too ill to go into work.

Pay is a feature of management arrangements where fairness is always both important and problematic, so job evaluation is a means of introducing fairness into the calculations.

CHAPTER 31

Strategic aspects of payment

Pay is all sorts of different things. It is basically a transaction, as an employer pays £X in exchange for generally specified time, skills, commitment and loyalty. But pay is also a label (the £2,000-a-day libel lawyer), a status symbol (professors are paid more than senior lecturers) and a determinant of your standard of living. Pay is also likely to be a discriminator according to your sex (average earnings for women are lower than for men) and social class (average earnings for manual workers are lower than for non-manual workers), and is one of the main influences on the degree to which you value your employment. It is not just the amount you are paid, but the nature of the contract. Salaried posts in the main are for what you *are* as well as for what you do. The Government Minister in charge of the Treasury is paid to *be* Chancellor of the Exchequer, not just to prepare and deliver an annual budget.

The reason why pay is a crucial issue for managers is that managers decide what employees should be paid, so they influence all of these factors in the lives of John Brown and Mary Smith. Managers mediate between the customer and the worker as a supplier of goods and services, and we are all highly sensitive to issues like our social status. This is why trade unions were created and pay review bodies formed. This is why we have laws to control at least some aspects of the pay bargain. If you are an employee at any level someone decides what you are worth, and few things matter more to us than how we are valued.

This type of management mediation between customer and worker applies only to employees; it is different for the self-employed and sole traders. In writing this book we have one thing in common with Catherine Cookson and Jeffrey Archer: we have all recently published books. Every copy of this book that is sold puts a modest amount of money in our pockets, that is predetermined by a royalty agreement. There is no employer intervention to vary the amount. If the publisher sells a huge number, then our royalty payments rise in strict proportion. If they sell few, then our royalty payments are disappointing, but there is no argument about worth or value, because there is no mediation.

Management approaches to payment

A strange thing about payment is that managers seem to shy away from actually using the word. We hear about 'compensation', 'reward' or 'remuneration', yet the idea of compensation is making amends for something that has caused loss or injury. Do we want to suggest that work necessarily causes loss or injury? Reward suggests a special payment for a special act. Much current management thinking on pay issues is to induce more special effort by employees, but the bulk of the pay bargain for an individual is not affected by performance. Remuneration is a more straightforward word which means exactly the same as payment but has five more letters and is misspelt (as renumeration) more often than most words in the personnel manager's lexicon.

We use the general term 'payment' as this part of the book includes material about pensions and sick pay, but the current general term is certainly 'reward'. This term is used to identify the system of payment as a central, integrated feature of the approach to HRM. The traditional collective bargain was separated from the management of the people receiving the money: the concept of reward is to have some sort of multiple helix, where motivation, skill, career and performance are all intertwined to produce added value to the individual career and corporate aspects, with the pay reflecting, describing and moving with the other elements continuously.

The approach to payment adopted by employers typically takes one of three forms, the focus is either on *service*, on *skills* or on *performance*. The focus on service is characterised by open-ended agreements about continuity of employment, incremental pay scales and annual reviews. Focusing on skills produces higher rates of pay with greater or rarer skills, while a focus on performance emphasises target-setting, adapting to change and a close relationship between what the employee achieves and what the employee is paid. Over all three approaches is the need to have a system of payment that is fair. But what is fairness in payment?

Fairness and performance in payment

One basis for deciding who should be paid what is an assessment of fairness – 'a fair day's pay for a fair day's work'. The employer believes that the employee should be paid a fair amount in relation to the skill and effort that has to be exercised, and employees feel there is a reasonable level of payment that can be expected for the contribution made. When both sets of expectations can be satisfied, then we have in place a further dimension of the employment contract described in the first chapter.

The axiom of a fair day's pay for a fair day's work is not necessarily either fair or just. Karl Marx described it as a conservative motto and it undoubtedly impedes change in pay arrangements. What is seen as fair is putting something back to what it used to be: the restoration of a differential or the rectification of an anomaly. Change is almost defined as unfair because it undermines the status quo and reduces standards. By inhibiting change, the fairness principle also impedes restructuring.

Another criticism is that any differences in relative payment are related to the work undertaken, yet that is intrinsically no more logical than the quite different concept of 'from each according to their ability: to each according to their needs'.

Despite these criticisms of the fairness principle, it remains the most useful basis for any discussion of payment because it is the notion used by both employers and employees in considering the acceptability of payment arrangements, actual or proposed, although the other principle of supply and demand is always present.

> Supply and demand have long been held to be at the heart of the wage
> determination process, at least in the opinion of economists. The supply of
> manpower should be equated with the organization demand if performance
> is to be underpinned.   (Smith 1983, p. 26)

Supply and demand remain only a partial explanation of pay determination, even
in the more sophisticated formulae of marginal productivity theory or wages fund
theory. Whatever limited validity these economists' explanations may have in
explaining national labour market behaviour, the mutual assessment of what is fair
remains the most useful starting point for the personnel manager assessing what is
to be done within the organisation and for individual employees deciding the
acceptability of their level of payment. A group of employees strongly persuaded
that they are underpaid will not change their minds if it is explained to them that:

> wages had to be paid out of a fund from the accummulated revenues
> deriving from past production, and the size of fund, and therefore wages,
> were determined by the ratio of supply to amounts of revenue set aside for
> labour.   (*ibid.*, p. 29)

The other basis for deciding relative payment is performance, with above-
average performance producing above-average pay and above-average increases
in pay. This has certainly been very popular since the late 1980s for payment
arrangements related to management posts, and a development of the earlier
notion of management by objectives:

> The trend towards performance, rather than merit, assessment is a trend
> towards rewarding output rather than input. It stems from the concept of
> performance management – a much wider development than just a change
> in payment practices.   (Fowler 1988)

Neither fairness nor performance is an easy principle to implement. Judgements
of fairness are typically supported by pay systems based on incremental scales and
job evaluation, yet the most widespread reason for industrial action has always
been dissatisfaction with relative pay. Performance-related payment arrangements are only relatively easy to run when everyone is doing better. The difficulty
of below-average pay for below-average performers is indicated by the fact that
schemes typically deliver enhanced pay even when performance by objective
criteria like company profitability declines.

Employee objectives for the contract for payment

Those who are paid and those who administer payment schemes have objectives
for the payment contract which differ according to whether one is the recipient
or the administrator of the payments. The contract for payment will be satisfactory in so far as it meets the objectives of the parties. Therefore we consider the
range of objectives, starting with employees.

First objective: purchasing power

The absolute level of weekly or monthly earnings determines the standard of living of the recipient, and will therefore be the most important consideration for
most employees. How much can I buy? Employees are rarely satisfied about their

purchasing power, and the annual pay adjustment will do little more than reduce dissatisfaction. The two main reasons for this are inflation and rising expectations.

Second objective: felt-fair

We have already discussed the notion of fairness in payment. Here we have the term 'felt-fair', which was devised by Elliott Jaques (1962), who averred that every employee had a strong feeling about the level of payment that was fair for the job. Here we move away from the absolute level of earnings to the first of a series of aspects of relative income. In most cases this will be a very rough, personalised evaluation of what is seen as appropriate.

The employee who feels underpaid is likely to demonstrate the conventional symptoms of withdrawal from the job: looking for another, carelessness, disgruntlement, lateness, absence, and the like. Perhaps the worst manifestation of this is among those who feel the unfairness but who cannot take a clean step of moving elsewhere. They then not only feel dissatisfied with their pay level, they also feel another unfairness too: being trapped in a situation they resent. Those who feel they are overpaid (as some do) may simply feel dishonest, or may seek to justify their existence in some way, like trying to look busy. That is not necessarily productive.

Third objective: rights

A different aspect of relative income is that concerned with the rights of the employee to a particular share of the company's profits or the nation's wealth. The employee is here thinking about whether the division of earnings is providing fair shares of the Gross National Product. 'To each according to their needs' is overlaid on 'a fair day's pay . . .' This is a strong feature of most trade union arguments and part of the general preoccupation with the rights of the individual. Mainly this is the longstanding debate about who should enjoy the fruits of labour.

Fourth objective: relativities

'How much do I (or we) get relative to . . . group X?' This is a version of the 'felt-fair' argument. It is not the question of whether the employee believes the remuneration to be reasonable in relation to the job done, but in relation to the jobs other people do.

There are many potential comparators, and the basis of comparison can alter. The Pay Board (1974) pointed out three. First is the definition of pay. Is it basic rates or is it earnings? Over how long is the pay compared? Many groups have a level of payment that varies from one time of the year to another. Second is the method of measuring the changes: absolute amount of money or percentage. £5 is 10 per cent of £50 but 5 per cent of £100. Third is the choice of pay dates. Here we can see a change since the Pay Board report, as not all groups receive annual adjustments to their pay, nor at the same time.

Fifth objective: recognition

Most people have an objective for their payment arrangements of their personal contribution being recognised. This is partly seeking reassurance, but is also a way in which people can mould their behaviour and their career thinking to produce progress and satisfaction. It is doubtful if financial recognition has a significant and sustained impact on performance, but providing a range of other forms of recognition while the pay packet is transmitting a different message is certainly counter-productive.

Sixth objective: composition

How is the pay package made up? The growing complexity and sophistication of payment arrangements raises all sorts of questions about pay composition. Is £200 pay for 60 hours' work better than £140 for 40 hours' work? The arithmetical answer that the rate per hour for the 40-hour arrangement is marginally better than for 60 hours is only part of the answer. The other aspects will relate to the individuals, their circumstances and the conventions of their working group and reference groups. Another question about composition might be: Is £140 per week plus a pension better than £160 per week without? Such questions do not produce universally applicable answers because they can be quantified to such a limited extent, but some kernels of conventional wisdom can be suggested as generalisations:

1. Younger employees are more interested in high direct earnings at the expense of indirect benefits, like pensions, which will be of more interest to older employees.
2. Incentive or performance-related payment arrangements are likely to interest employees who either see a reliable prospect of enhancing earnings through the ability to control their own activities, or who see the incentive scheme as an opportunity to wrest control of their personal activities (which provide little intrinsic satisfaction) away from management by regulating their earnings.
3. Married women are seldom interested in payment arrangements that depend on overtime: married men frequently are.
4. Overtime is used by many employees to produce an acceptable level of purchasing power particularly among the lower-paid.
5. Pensions and sickness payment arrangements beyond statutory minima are a *sine qua non* of white-collar employment, and are of growing importance in manual employment.

Employer objectives for the contract for payment

In looking at the other side of the picture, we consider the range of objectives in the thinking of employers, or those representing an employer interest *vis-à-vis* the employee.

First objective: prestige

There is a comfortable and understandable conviction among managers that it is 'a good thing' to be a good payer. This seems partly to be simple pride at doing better than others, but also there is sometimes a feeling that such a policy eliminates a variable from the contractual relationship. In conversation with one of the authors a chief executive expressed it this way:

I want to find out the highest rates of pay, job-for-job, within a fifty-mile radius of my office. Then I will make sure that all my people are paid 20 per cent over that. Then I know where I am with them as I have taken money out of the equation. If they want to quit they can't hide the real reason by saying they're going elsewhere for more cash: they can't get it. Furthermore, if I do have to fill a job I know that we won't lose a good guy because of the money not being right.

Whether high pay rates succeed in getting someone the reputation of being a good employer is difficult to see. What seems much more likely is that the low-paying employer will have the reputation of being a poor employer.

Second objective: competition

More rational is the objective of paying rates that are sufficiently competitive to sustain the employment of the right numbers of appropriately qualified and experienced employees to staff the organisation. A distinction is drawn here between competition thinking and prestige thinking, as the former is more designed to get a good fit on one of the employment contract dimensions rather than simply overwhelm it. It permits consideration of questions such as: how selective do we need to be for this range of jobs? and: how can we avoid over-paying people and inhibiting them from moving on? Every employer has this sort of objective, even if only in relation to a few key posts in the organisation.

Third objective: control

There may be ways of organising the pay packet that will facilitate control of operations and potentially save money. The conventional approach to this for many years was the use of piecework or similar incentives, but this became diffi-cult due to the unwillingness of most employees to see their payment fluctuate wildly at the employer's behest. Theoretically, overtime is a method of employer control of output through making available or withholding additional payment prospects. In practice, however, employees use overtime for control more exten-sively than employers. Gradually, other ways in which employers could control their payroll costs are being eliminated or made more difficult by legislation. Redundancy, short-term lay-off and unfair dismissal are all now more expensive, and it is increasingly unreasonable, unlawful and impracticable to regard women as a reservoir of inexpensive, temporary labour.

Fourth objective: motivation and performance

Employers also seek to use the payment contract to motivate employees and thus to improve their work performance. The subject of incentive payment systems is discussed in detail in Chapter 33 but some features of payment and its influence on performance are worth mentioning here.

Prior to the 1980s incentive payment systems were primarily used as part of the payment package for manual workers and sales staff. The design of such schemes is simple, with a built-in bias towards rewarding the volume of products manufactured or sold. Wherever the quality of output is a matter of significance such approaches are, therefore, inappropriate. Two extreme ex-amples indicate the weakness of this approach. Someone engaged in manufacture

The case of the AIDS counsellor

The difficulty of determining a fair and satisfactory rate of pay for particular individuals is illustrated in the following example of a nurse employed by a large NHS hospital as a counsellor for haemophilia patients who have contracted AIDS through blood transfusion.

The nurse concerned was employed on a senior sister's grade but was required to work in the community, undertaking counselling duties with patients and their families. The nature of the job, however, meant that she was required to work very irregular and unpredictable hours and could not delegate duties to anyone else or share the burden of cases with others. In 1994 she requested a regrading with the full support of her managers who perceived her to be a uniquely good performer. No performance-related scheme had, however, been developed.

Regrading the nurse was not straightforward. The first stumbling block came when her duties were assessed according to grading criteria negotiated by the relevant NHS Whitley Council.

Although several attempts were made to try to make the job fit the criteria for the higher grade, the task proved impossible. Authorising a regrading on these grounds would have set a precedent leading to large numbers of regrading claims.

The next approach taken was to analyse the nurse's job using the hospital's computerised job evaluation system. This route also failed because the results of the analysis suggested that the job was already graded too highly. To regrade in spite of this would render the decision indefensible were an equal value claim to be brought by a male nurse employed at the same grade.

Finally an attempt was made to justify the proposed regrading by discovering at what level other hospitals paid nurses undertaking similar roles. It was found, however, that other AIDS counsellors were paid on the same or lower grades.

It thus proved impossible to pay the nurse concerned a rate which she and her managers regarded as 'fair' because no decision to regrade could be objectively justified.

of diamond-tipped drilling bits would serve the employer poorly if payment were linked to output. If it were possible to devise a payment system that contained an incentive element based on high quality of workmanship or on low scrap value that might be more effective. If school-teachers were paid a 'quantity bonus' it would presumably be based either on the number of children in the class or on some indicator like the number of examination passes. The first would encourage teachers to take classes as large as possible, with probably adverse results in the quality of teaching. The second might increase the proportion of children succeeding in examinations, but would isolate those who could not produce impressive examination performance.

In recent years a great deal of attention has been paid to the development of incentive payment systems which go beyond rewarding the quantity of output to take account of job performance as a whole. In particular there has been a marked increase in the use of performance-related pay (PRP) for management and professional staff, especially for senior managers; organisations have sought either to re-establish or to introduce for the first time schemes which reinforce the messages required to produce improved performance and increased productivity.

Private sector employers in particular now increasingly believe that they are not providing an appropriate or competitive package for their directors and senior executives unless there is some element of risk money to add on to the basic salary and reward the achievement of company growth, profitability and success. At the same time, companies have been re-examining the use of bonus schemes for more junior employees in order to increase motivation and to reward them for their contribution. The use of PRP is also growing in the public sector following active promotion of its benefits by Government Ministers.

Fifth objective: cost

Just as employees are interested in purchasing power, the absolute value of their earnings, so employers are interested in the absolute cost of payment, and its bearing on the profitability or cost-effectiveness of their organisation. The importance of this varies with the type of organisation and the relative cost of employees, so that in the refining of petroleum employment costs are modest, in teaching or nursing they are substantial. The employer interest in this objective is long-term as well as short-term. Not only do employees expect their incomes to be maintained and carry on rising, rather than fluctuating with company profitability, but the indirect costs of employing people can also be substantial.

The elements of payment

The payment of an individual will be made up of one or more elements from those shown in Figure 31.1. Fixed elements are those that make up the regular weekly or monthly payment to the individual, and which do not vary other than in exceptional circumstances. Variable elements can be varied either by the employee or the employer.

Bonus	Profit allocation		Variable elements • Irregular • Variable amount • Usually discretionary
	Discretionary sum		
Incentive	Group calculation basis		
	Individual calculation basis		
Overtime payment			
Premia	Occasional		
	Contractual		
Benefits	Fringe benefits		Fixed elements • Regular • Rarely variable • Usually contractual
	Payments in kind	Other	
		Accommodation	
		Car	
	Benefit schemes	Other	
		Pension	
		Sick pay	
Plussage	'Fudge' payments		
	Special additions		
Basic rate of payment			Basic

Figure 31.1 The potential elements of payment

Basic

The irreducible minimum rate of pay is the basic. In most cases this is the standard rate also, not having any additions made to it. In other cases it is a basis on which earnings are built by the addition of one or more of the other elements in payment. One group of employees – women operatives in footwear – have little more than half of their earnings in basic, while primary and secondary schoolteachers have virtually all their pay in this form.

Plussage

Sometimes the basic has an addition to recognise an aspect of working conditions or employee capability. Payments for educational qualifications and for supervisory responsibilities are quite common. There is also an infinite range of what are sometimes called 'fudge' payments, whereby there is an addition to the basic as a start-up allowance, mask money, dirt money, and so forth.

ACTIVITY BOX 31.1

If your employer offered you a 'remuneration package', which could be made up from any of the items in Figure 31.1 provided that the total cost was no more than £X, what proportion of each item would you choose and why? Does your answer suggest ideas for further development of salary policies?

Benefits

Extras to the working conditions that have a cash value are categorised as benefits and can be of great variety. Some have already been mentioned; others include luncheon vouchers, subsidised meals, discount purchase schemes and the range of welfare provisions like free chiropody and cheap hairdressing.

Premia

Where employees work at inconvenient times, like shifts or permanent nights, they receive a premium payment as compensation for the inconvenience. This is for inconvenient rather than additional hours of work. Sometimes this is built into the basic rate or is a regular feature of the contract of employment so that the payment is unvarying. In other situations shift working is occasional and short-lived, making the premium a variable element of payment.

Overtime

It is customary for employees working more hours than are normal for the working week to be paid for those hours at an enhanced rate, usually between 10 and 50 per cent more that the normal rate according to how many hours are involved. Seldom can this element be regarded as fixed. No matter how regularly overtime is worked, there is always the opportunity for the employer to withhold the provision of overtime or for the employee to decline the extra hours.

Incentive

Incentive is here described as an element of payment linked to the working performance of an individual or working group, as a result of prior arrangement.

This includes most of the payment-by-results schemes that have been produced by work study, as well as commission payments to salespeople, skills-based pay schemes and performance-related pay schemes based on the achievement of agreed objectives. The distinguishing feature is that the employee knows what has to be done to earn the payment, though he or she may feel very dependent on other people, or on external circumstances, to receive it.

Bonus

A different type of variable payment is the gratuitous payment by the employer that is not directly earned by the employee: a bonus. The essential difference between this and an incentive is that the employee has no entitlement to the payment as a result of a contract of employment and cannot be assured of receiving it in return for a specific performance. The most common example of this is the Christmas bonus.

We include profit-sharing under this general heading although the share owner-ship confers a clear entitlement. The point is that the level of the benefit cannot be directly linked to the performance of the individual but to the performance of the business. In some cases the two may be synonymous, with one dominant individual determining the success of the business, but there are very few instances like this, even in the most feverish imaginings of tycoons. Share-ownership or profit-sharing on an agreed basis can greatly increase the interest of the employees in how the business is run and can increase their commitment to its success, but the performance of the individual is not directly rewarded in the same way as in incentive schemes.

The difference between wages and salaries

Since the 1970s the traditional divide in the respective treatment of 'waged' and 'salaried' employees for payment administration purposes has declined. It is clear, however, that there remain a number of differences in emphasis that affect not only the payer of the wages or the salary, but also the attitude of the recipient. This tends both to emphasise and reflect the tendency to identify core and peripheral workforces as we saw in our discussion of labour markets.

Some of the most obvious differences between wages and salaries are shown in Figure 31.2.

Salaries	Wages
Annual rate	Hourly rate
Paid monthly	Paid weekly
Paid by bank transfer	Paid in cash
Performance-related pay	Incentive schemes
Occupational pensions	No fringe benefits
Liberal expenses paid	No expenses paid
Company cars	No cars

Figure 31.2 Ways in which wage-earning and salary-earning differ

There are also less tangible differences which reflect the attitudes of the recipients of wages and salaries as perceived by organisation decision-makers. For example, the nature of incentive payments has traditionally been different. Wage-earners are paid tightly measured incentives based on individual or team production levels, whereas salaried staff are rewarded for their performance over a longer timescale with pre-defined incremental scales up which they may progress.

The last difference to mention is probably the most important, as it is a part of all the others. Those receiving salaries are likely to identify with the management interest in the organisation. This was suggested by the studies by Batstone and his colleagues (1977), and Bain (1972) has pointed out that management encouragement is one of the features that needs to be present before white-collar unions expand. Salaried employees are most likely to see themselves doing a piece of the job of management, which has had to be split up because it – and the organisation – have grown too big for top management to handle alone, but unquestionably it is a part of management. Wage-earners see themselves as doing the work that the management would never do and which is independent of management apart from the labour-hiring contract.

ACTIVITY BOX 31.2

Some employers who have moved wage-earners to salaried status have been surprised that the employees do not assume the same attitudes to work as those who are already salaried. Why do you think this is?

Recent survey evidence (IRS 1989; IDS 1992) indicates that in many of the above areas the traditional divide between the way wage-earners and salaried staff are treated has greatly declined. Single-status arrangements are increasingly becoming the norm, especially in respect of access to occupational pensions and in the frequency and in the method of payment. Where a status divide persists it is commonly in the means used to determine basic pay levels and in the design of grading structures. In these organisations manual workers and the lower graded service staff are now likely to be paid monthly directly into a bank account while the level of their pay continues to be determined through annual negotiations with their representatives. By contrast, individuals in occupations traditionally identified as 'salaried' are more likely to benefit from annual incremental progression or pay rises achieved through promotion up a recognised career ladder. A more detailed analysis of trends in this field can be found in Price and Price (1994).

Incremental salary structures

A typical organisation will have a salary structure of groups, ladders and steps.

Groups

The first element of the structure is the broad groupings of salaries, each group being administered according to the same set of rules. The questions in making decisions about this are to do with the logical grouping of job holders, according to their common interests, performance criteria, qualifications and, perhaps, bargaining arrangements and trade union membership. The British Institute of Management study (1973) used a framework of four groups:

1. **Senior and middle management**: Directors, heads of major functions and their immediate subordinates.
2. **Junior management**: Responsible to the above and including supervisory staff.
3. **Technical and specialist**: Personnel with technical or professional skills and/or qualifications (excluding those working in a managerial capacity), e.g. work study officer, technician, draughtsman/woman.
4. **Clerical**: All clerical occupations including secretarial staff (British Institute of Management 1973).

The broad salary ranges are then set against each group, to encompass either the maximum and minimum of the various people who will then be in the group or – in the rare circumstance of starting from scratch – the ideal maximum and minimum levels.

As the grouping has been done on the basis of job similarity, the attaching of maximum and minimum salaries can show up peculiarities, with one or two jobs far below a logical minimum and others above a logical maximum. This requires the limits for the group to be put at the 'proper' level, with the exceptions either being identified as exceptions and the incumbents being paid a protected rate or being moved into a more appropriate group.

Salary groups will not stack neatly one on top of another in a salary hierarchy. There will be considerable overlap, recognising that there is an element of salary growth as a result of experience as well as status and responsibility. A typical set of groups could be as illustrated in Figure 31.3.

There are various alternatives to this now rather dated type of arrangement, such as separating senior and middle management; incorporating technical and specialist personnel into appropriate management groups according to seniority; including manual employees as a salaried group. Another alternative is not to have groups at all, but simply a single system of ladders and steps, so that all employees have their payment arrangements administered according to one set of criteria. The argument against such a system is that it applies a common set of assumptions that may be inappropriate for certain groups. In general management, for instance, it will probably be an assumption that all members of the group will be interested in promotion and job change; this will be encouraged by the salary arrangements, which will encourage job holders to look for opportunities to move around. In contrast, the research chemist will be expected to stick at one type of job for a longer period, and movement into other fields of the company's affairs, like personnel or marketing, will often be discouraged. For this reason it will be more appropriate for the research chemist to be in a salary group with a relatively small number of ladders, each having a large number of steps; while a general management colleague will be more logically set in a context of more ladders, each with fewer steps. It should be noted, however, that employers operating a system of separate occupational pay spines must be able to defend their system against possible equal value claims (see Chapter 32).

Another way of dealing with specialists is to take them out of the corporate salary structure altogether and pay them according to salaries prescribed by an acknowledged outside body. This is done most frequently for nurses working in industry, who are often paid according to scales published by the Royal College

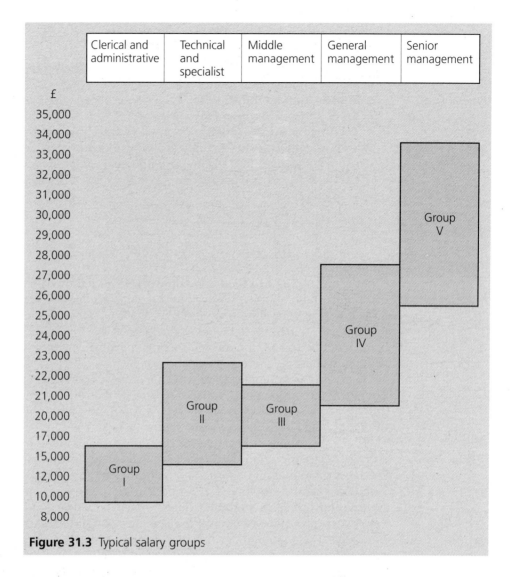

Figure 31.3 Typical salary groups

of Nursing. A device like this can solve the problem of one or two specialised employees whose general rank or standing in the organisation is not consistent with the necessary level of payment.

The grouping stage in salary administration has thus identified a number of employees whose remuneration will be organised along similar lines.

Ladders and steps

Because employees are assumed to be career-oriented, salary arrangements are based on that assumption, so each salary group has several ladders within it and each ladder has a number of steps (often referred to as 'scales' and 'points'). As with groups there is considerable overlap, the top rung of one ladder being much higher than the bottom rung of the next. Taking the typical general management group that was mentioned above, we could envisage four ladders, as shown in

Figure 31.4. The size of the differential between steps varies from £200 to £600 according to the level of the salary and the overlapping could be used in a number of ways according to the differing requirements. Steps 6 and 7 on each ladder would probably be only for those who had reached their particular ceiling and were unlikely to be promoted further, while steps 4 and 5 could be for those who are on their way up and have made sufficient progress up one ladder to contemplate seeking a position with a salary taken from the next higher ladder.

The figures attached to the ladders in this example are round, in the belief that salaries are most meaningful to recipients when they are in round figures. However, ladders are sometimes developed with steps having a more precise arithmetical relationship to their relative position, so that each step represents the same percentage increase. Equally, some ladders have the same cash amount attached to each step.

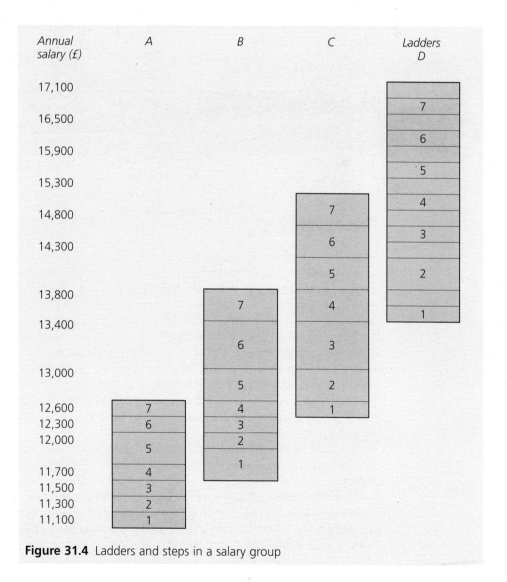

Figure 31.4 Ladders and steps in a salary group

Some commentators place importance on the relationship of the maximum to the minimum of a ladder, described as the span, and the relationship between the bottom rung of adjacent ladders, referred to as the differential. Bowey (1972) suggests that the most logical arrangement is a 50 per cent span and a 20 per cent differential. There is no inscrutable logic behind those precise figures, so that 49 per cent and 21 per cent would not be 'wrong', but they have a similar value to the use of round figures referred to in the last paragraph. There is a neatness and symmetry about the method, which can commend itself to salary recipients.

The self-financing increment principle

It is generally believed that fixed incremental payment schemes are self-regulating, so that introducing incremental payment schemes does not mean that within a few years everyone is at the maximum. The assumption is that just as some move up, others retire or resign and are replaced by new recruits at the bottom of the ladder. This will clearly not be the case when staff turnover is low.

ACTIVITY BOX 31.3

If incremental scales cease to be self-financing through lack of labour market movement, what advantage is there to the employer in keeping them?

Pay comparisons

Salary structures have to have an internal logic that makes sense to at least the majority of the salary recipients, but they also have to be consistent with what is being paid elsewhere, as was considered in the chapter on labour markets. There are a number of ways in which comparisons can be made. The most reliable is to use salary surveys, which are carried out by consultants. The method is to obtain information from a number of employers and then arrange the anonymous information into a range of categories for comparison, such as size of company by turnover and number of employees. More difficult is to define the jobs for which salaries are being compared, both in terms of the job specialisation and the degree of responsibility and accountability of the post holder. Incomes Data Services and Industrial Relations Services publish regular reviews of what the surveys are saying.

Salary clubs are informal collections of employers who meet periodically to share information about relative rates of pay for categories of staff they all employ.

A service found especially valuable by its users is the pay comparison information provided by the Hay-MSL management consultancy, where the regular pay reports are based on jobs evaluated by the Hay-MSL system, so there is an unusual degree of reliability in the like-for-like comparisons.

Salary decisions

Who decides where in the salary structure the individual fits? The answer to that question at one extreme is 'job evaluation and fixed increments' and at the other extreme it is the capricious whim of another individual. The first means that decisions are not made about individuals but about systems, and the individual salary emerges from the inexorable process of increments. The second means that decisions on salaries are made without constraint and, perhaps, without logic. Between these two extremes we can list the sequence of decisions that are involved in a typical annual salary review:

1. How much the salary budget for the next year will be.

    Decision made by the senior decision-making individual or coalition after submissions of evidence from personnel, finance and other specialists, including an interpretation of labour market indicators and trade union negotiations, if any.

2. How the additional budget provision is to be divided between general increases (cost-of-living) and individual increases (performance or 'merit').

    This decision is probably made at the same time as the first, but evidence and advice from personnel is given more weight than any other. Possibly a wholly personnel decision.

3. How performance or 'merit' increases are decided.

    Recommendation from individual's superior, according to clear-cut rules, vetted by personnel to ensure consistency of approach by all superiors and that no previous undertakings are overlooked.

4. How individuals hear the news.

    Face-to-face by line superior, written confirmation from personnel.

A strategic approach to payment administration

Since the late 1980s a number of authorities have expressed the view that the way payment is managed is undergoing a fundamental change. This view has been most eloquently expressed by Armstrong and Murlis in successive editions of their book *Reward Management* where they describe the way they perceive the role of the salary administrator to have changed since the early 1980s:

> Salary administration was very much seen as a back-room function in which numerate specialists worked out details of policies that came from elsewhere – from government, from head office or from general management. There was little obvious link between what happened on the remuneration front and over all business strategy, let alone an organization's human resource strategy – if it had one. There was certainly little line management involvement in, or ownership of, the pay practice that emerged.
>
> (Armstrong and Murlis 1994, p. 16)

They go on to describe how they perceive practice to have changed. In particular they stress the significance of reward strategies which have led to the replacement of traditional grading structures with less bureaucratic means of determining an individual's pay. As a result it is possible to reward individual contribution to organisational success through payments related to profit, performance or skills acquisition to a far greater extent than was previously the case.

WINDOW ON PRACTICE

Attitudes towards payment arrangements vary radically between different countries. In a survey in Singapore 1,500 respondents were asked to pick three of the following five factors which they believed would have a significant impact on wage determination: wages in the same industry, wages in a different industry, union representation, government influence and productivity. The proportion of respondents identifying the five factors as significant were:

Productivity	33.5%
Government	29.1%
Wages in the same industry	27.1%
Unions	18.3%
Wages in a different industry	14.8%

The same survey demonstrated that the main cause for differences between individual perspectives was the quality and quantity of information they received from their employer (Torrington and Tan Chwee Huat 1994).

While there has, unquestionably, been a greater interest in incentive payments during the past 10–15 years, it is unclear whether this represents a shift in employer practice of the degree described above. Criticism of this view has been expressed by Smith (1993) who questions the extent to which the various developments in incentive pay have in fact derived from a new-found strategic approach to pay. Rather, he believes, they amount to 'no more than a collection of expedient manoeuvres to deal with the boom conditions of the late 1980s'. According to this view, the continued growth in profit-related pay owes more to Government encouragement than to a serious attempt on the part of employers to use pay strategically as a means of improving productivity. The argument that developments in incentive pay are born of short-term considerations on the part of employers is further backed up by evidence of declining labour productivity during the late 1980s and early 1990s.

Summary propositions

31.1 For both parties to the employment contract the main consideration is that the payment arrangement should be 'fair'.

31.2 Employee and employer have different frames of reference that determine their respective views of fairness.

31.3 The main elements of payment are basic rate, plussage, benefits, premia, overtime, incentive and bonus.

31.4 Despite moves towards harmonisation, there remain major differences between wages and salaries.

31.5 The traditional divide between the 'salaried' and 'wage-earning' employee is of increasingly little importance.

31.6 A typical salary structure has groups, ladders and steps which interconnect to describe and encourage career progression.

31.7 The idea that incremental salary systems keep the total cost of salaries stable around the mid-point of scales is seldom correct when there is little staff turnover.

References

Armstrong, M. and Murlis, H. (1994) *Reward Management: A handbook of salary administration*, London: Kogan Page.

Bain, G. S. (1972) *White Collar Unions: A review*, London: IPM.

Batstone, E., Boraston, I. and Frenkel, S. (1977) *Shop Stewards in Action*, Oxford: Blackwell.

Boddy, D. (1977) 'Salary payment and salary costs', *British Journal of Industrial Relations*, March.

Bowey, A. (1972) *Salary Structures for Management Careers*, London: IPM.

British Institute of Management (1973) *Salary Administration. Survey report no. 16*, London: British Institute of Management.

Casey, B., Lakey, J. and White, M. (1992) *Payment Systems: A look at current practice*, Employment Department Research Series No 5, London: Policy Studies Institute.

Fowler, A. (1988) 'New directions in performance pay', *Personnel Management*, November, Vol. 20, No. 11.

Incomes Data Services (1992) *Integrated Pay*, Study no 509, London: IDS.

Industrial Relations Services (1989) 'Harmonisation: a single status surge?', *IRS Employment Trends*, 501, London: IRS.

Jaques, E. (1962) 'Objective measures for pay differentials', *Harvard Business Review*, January/February, pp. 133–7.

Lupton, T. and Bowey, A. M. (1974) *Wages and Salaries*, Harmondsworth: Penguin Books.

National Board for Prices and Incomes Report no. 132 (1969) *Salary Structures*, Cmnd 4187, London: HMSO.

Office of Manpower Economics (1973) *Incremental Payment Schemes*, London: HMSO.

Pay Board (1974) *Relativities*, London: HMSO.

Price, L. and Price, R. (1994) 'Change and continuity in the status divide', in K. Sisson (ed.) *Personnel Management: A comprehensive guide to theory and practice in Britain*, Oxford: Blackwell.

Roberts, C. (ed.) (1985) *Harmonization Whys and Wherefores*, London: IPM.

Smith, I. (1983) *The Management of Remuneration: Paying for effectiveness*, London: IPM.

Smith, I. (1993) 'Reward management: A retrospective assessment', *Employee Relations*, Vol. 15.

Torrington, D. P. and Tan Chwee Huat (1994) *Human Resource Management for South East Asia*, Singapore: Simon & Schuster.

General discussion topics

1. Can payment ever be fair?
2. The chapter lists employer and employee objectives in payment. What changes would you make in that list?
3. The chapter distinguished between wages and salaries. To what extent do you regard that distinction as obsolete?

CHAPTER 32

Job evaluation

One of the main tasks of payment administration is setting the differential gaps. It is necessary always to juggle the three factors of performance, market rate and equity. It is rarely possible or wise to pay people only according to their performance or contribution, and linking payment only to developments in the labour market can make working relationships very difficult. There is always the vexed question of how much more than Y and how much less than Z should X receive? The relative contribution of each individual of the three is difficult to measure, so some acceptable assessment of each job is made. The difficult problem of assessing performance is overlaid with the even more difficult problem of making comparisons.

The standard way of tackling this problem is using a form of job evaluation. In 1993 a major survey was undertaken by Industrial Relations Services (IRS), which examined the use of job evaluation in 164 organisations employing a total of 700,000 people. They found that 75 per cent of the sample used job evaluation in determining the pay of some employees compared with 65 per cent in a similar survey undertaken in 1990. More recent evidence confirms this broad trend, with a majority of those responding to separate surveys undertaken by the IPD, *Personnel Today*, the Hay Consultancy and the CBI all indicating that their use of job evaluation was increasing (IDS 1996, pp. 4–6). Few organisations abandon it once introduced. It is clear from these surveys as well as that carried out by Spencer (1990a) that the chief reason for the introduction of job evaluation is to achieve fairness in pay policy or to increase employees' sense of fairness. It is also commonly used as a tool in organisation restructuring and in harmonising the terms and conditions enjoyed by different groups of employees.

Another important reason for the increased use of job evaluation is the need to comply with the Equal Pay Act, as modified in 1984, which places as central in assessing equal pay claims the question of whether or not a job evaluation scheme is in use. It is significant that the trend towards the introduction of job evaluation in all the major retailing groups in the early 1990s followed threats of legal action to secure equal pay between check-out operators and other groups. Recent judgments in the European Court of Justice have further focused attention on the role of job evaluation in equal value cases.

In this chapter we consider first the background to the problems of getting relative payment right and then the job evaluation methods which are used. Finally, we consider the equal pay aspects.

Relativities and differentials

There are four different types of pay relationship that personnel managers need to understand, as dissatisfaction with relative pay can come from any of these sources.

Differentials

Differentials is the term used to describe pay differences within a single group of people whose jobs are sufficiently similar in content for comparisons to be logical. This will either be by unilateral management decision, by following agreed procedures probably involving members of the group whose jobs are being compared, or by agreement between one set of negotiators representing management interests and one representing employee interests – the simple model of the bargaining relationship. If the management negotiates with one bargaining agent on behalf of, say, manual employees who are skilled, semi-skilled and unskilled, then any disagreement about different levels of pay between the different categories of employee are for those two parties to resolve. The resolution is normally within their competence, unless the negotiators are so unresponsive to the feelings of their members that one category of employees withdraws its support and seeks separate representation.

Internal relativities

A more difficult type of pay relationship to control is that of internal relativity. Here the employer is constant, but the employees are represented by different agents as a result of being in different bargaining units. The most common internal relativity problem is between manual and non-manual employees, where one union or group of unions represents the manual employees and another represents the non-manuals, although bargaining may be much more fragmented in some companies – the problem of multi-unionism. Although more difficult to control than differentials, there is at least one common factor, the employer.

External relativities

Employees do not, however, restrict themselves to making comparisons between their own pay and that of others within their company, even though this may be the most cogent comparison. They will compare themselves with those in other companies, industries and services. Occasionally there will be a common element in the union, which negotiates better terms with one employer than another for groups of employees who see themselves as being similar.

WINDOW ON PRACTICE

External relativities can sometimes make a nonsense not only of differentials, but of performance-related pay as well. In one international bank some employees working in highly skilled areas are paid on a basis of salary plus a performance-related element that can be ten times the salary. There is such anxiety about the possibility of staff being enticed away by a competing bank that the additional amount is paid in anticipation of the performance rather than as a result of it.

More often the comparison is with completely different groups of employees. The long-running industrial dispute involving ambulance crews at the end of 1989 centred on the question of external relativity between them and members of the police and fire services.

The difficulty is shown most sharply in public sector pay bargaining, where there are large numbers of employees doing apparently similar work with pay scales that are broadly the same in all parts of the country. Every recipient of the pay is likely to make comparisons with friends and neighbours who are better off, or who seem to be better off. Public sector employees are extensively unionised and union research departments prepare detailed analyses of comparative pay rates, again picking those comparators that produce comparisons most favourable to their own cause. Any pay claim always has some comparator, as this is what gives it credibility.

A potential problem of external relativity is in the employment of peripheral employees by contractors of consultants, who may be working alongside permanent staff enjoying less attractive (or apparently less attractive) terms and conditions.

External identification

In one specialised category the employee identifies with an external employee grouping for purposes of determining the appropriate pay level. These people are usually taken out of intra-organisational bargaining. The obvious examples are company doctors and nurses, where the appropriate rates of pay are determined by bodies external to the company which proceeds to pay on that basis, unless there is some wish to pay above that rate. Other examples would be such professional groups as solicitors, surveyors and architects, and there will be many others where the number of employees will be so small, as well as specialised, that some external reference is the most appropriate way of determining the rate. The company employing one or two chemists or actuaries or other specialists would probably accept scales of pay published by the appropriate professional body rather than try to produce a pay structure that accommodated a range of specialists all identifying with an external professional grouping.

ACTIVITY BOX 32.1

Taking your own job, score from 0 to 5 the relative importance to you of the four types of pay relationship described in the 'Relativities and Differentials' section of this chapter. 0 = no importance, 5 = very important. Now do the same exercise with three or four other jobs and job holders that you know, such as members of your own family. How do you explain any differences?

Limitations on management action

If managers can accept and understand the range of limitations upon their actions in connection with pay comparisons, they can begin to develop a strategy to deal with them. There are five major constraints upon management action.

The product market

The influence of the product market varies according to how important labour costs are in deciding product cost, and in how important product cost is to the customer. In a labour-intensive and low-technology industry like catering, there will usually be such pressure on labour costs that the pay administrator has little freedom to manipulate pay relationships. In an area like magazine printing, the need of the publisher to get the product on time is so great that labour costs, however high, may be of relatively little concern. In this situation the pay negotiators have much more freedom to deal at least with differentials.

In their analysis of the footwear industry, Goodman and his colleagues (1977) found that a major reason why the industry was characterised by peace rather than conflict was the need for employer collaboration on labour matters because of the intensive competition in the product market.

The labour market

We have suggested that external relativity is the most intractable type of pay relationship for personnel specialists because it is so completely beyond their control. It may not be beyond their understanding, and understanding could offer the opportunity at least to pre-empt some problems so as to deal with them before or when they arise rather than being taken by surprise. Accountants and craft-workers, for instance, come very close in our categorisation to those who identify with an external employee grouping, as their assessment of their pay level will be greatly influenced by the 'going rate' in the trade or the district. A similar situation exists with jobs that are clearly understood and where skills are readily transferable, particularly if the employee is to work with a standard piece of equipment. Driving heavy goods vehicles is an obvious example, as the vehicles are common from one employer to another, the roads are the same, and only the loads vary. Other examples are secretaries, switchboard operators and computer operators. Jobs that are less sensitive to the labour market are those that are organisationally specific, like most semi-skilled work in manufacturing, general clerical work and nearly all middle-management positions.

Collective bargaining

Perhaps the most obvious constraint for management is the operation of collective bargaining. Employees do not join trade unions in order to comply with managerial wishes, but to question them, and the differential structure that fits in with management requirement will not necessarily fit in with employee expectations.

Although the influence of trade unions on pay determination has lessened, the extension of collective bargaining to white-collar and managerial groups has reduced the scope for unilateral decisions about differential structures. One of the influences of collective bargaining is in the use of internal relativities as the basis for negotiations. The members of a low-pay group will narrow the gap between themselves and those in a high-pay group; whereupon the higher-paid will seek to widen the gap again by 'restoring the differential'. Before long there will follow more arguments from the lower-paid that the gap has widened – and should be narrowed.

Academics have long argued about the effect of trade unions and collective bargaining on the relative level of wages. The evidence is contradictory with one study seeming to indicate that the now illegal closed shop was associated with relatively high wages (Blanchflower *et al.* 1990) and another showing that skilled non-union workers are just as likely as their unionised counterparts to benefit from high wage levels (Stewart 1990).

Technology

Technology has an effect on most things, and pay is no exception. As technology changes so there will arise the need for new skills in the business and people who are recruited possessing those skills will tend to import a pay level with them. The external identification principle may justify special treatment for one or two such employees, but once the numbers begin to increase, then they must be assimilated into the pay structure, almost certainly upsetting it in the process.

Internal labour market

Just as there is a labour market of which the company is a part, so there is a labour market within the organisation which also needs to be managed so as to ensure effective performance. According to Doeringer and Piore (1971) there are two kinds of internal labour market: the enterprise and the craft. The enterprise market is so-called because the individual enterprise defines the boundaries of the market itself. Such will be the situation of manual workers engaged in production processes, for whom the predominant pattern of employment is one in which jobs are formally or informally ranked, with those jobs of the highest pay or prestige usually being filled by promotion from within and those at the bottom of the hierarchy usually being filled only from outside the enterprise. It is, therefore, those at the bottom that are most sensitive to the external labour market. Doeringer and Piore point out that there is a close parallel with managerial jobs, the main ports of entry being from management trainees or supervisors, and the number of appointments from outside gradually reducing as jobs become more senior. This *modus operandi* is one of the main causes of the problems that redundant executives face.

Recent American research has stressed the importance of this kind of internal labour market in determining relativities. An interesting metaphor used is that of the sports tournament in which an organisation's pay structure is likened to the prize distribution in a knock-out competition such as is found, for example at the Wimbledon Tennis Championships. Here the prize money is highest for the winner, somewhat lower for the runner up, lower again for the semi-final losers and so on down the rounds. The aim, from the point of view of the tournament organisers, is to attract the best players to compete in the first round, then subsequently to give players in later rounds an incentive to play at their peak. According to Lazear (1995, pp. 26–33), the level of base pay for each level in an organisation's hierarchy should be set according to similar principles. The level of pay for any particular job is thus set at a level which maximises performance lower down the hierarchy among employees competing for promotion. The actual performance of the individual receiving the pay is less important.

The second type of internal labour market identified by Doeringer and Piore is the craft, where barriers to entry are relatively high – typically involving the completion of an apprenticeship or qualification. However, once established, seniority and hierarchy become unimportant as jobs and duties are shared among the individuals concerned. Such arrangements are usually determined by custom and practice, but are difficult to break down because of the vested interests of those who have successfully completed their period of apprenticeship.

Internal labour markets often have a far more profound effect on individual employee attitudes towards pay than comparisons with the external labour market:

> It seems to us at least arguable that most people are little interested in whether other people are better off, or whether they have become better off than others, provided they themselves are treated fairly in relation to most of those with whom they work. No grand design here.   (IDS 1977, p. 17)

Why this should be the case is open to question. It might simply be because people are ignorant of what similarly qualified counterparts in other organisations are being paid. Alternatively, it might arise from the belief that, whatever is paid elsewhere, there is a need for fairness within the organisation in terms of the distribution of hard-earned rewards.

Management policy decisons and pay relationships

Although there are limitations to managerial freedom of action on pay relationships, there is still a need for managerial initiative in policies to influence differentials and relativities. These are mostly to do with employee groupings or deciding on job families.

The job family is a collection of jobs which have sufficient common features for them to be considered together when differential gaps are being set. What are the management decisions to be made?

Why not one big (happy) family?

The first question is whether there should be sub-groupings within the organisation at all, or whether all employees should be paid in accordance with one overall salary structure. Internal relativities disappear; there is only a differential structure. This arrangement has many attractions, as it emphasises the integration of all employees and may encourage them to identify with the organisation as a whole, it is administratively simple and can stimulate competition for personal advancement. It also allows more flexibility in the pay that is arranged for any individual. Interest in the development of single pay structures has increased in recent years for a number of reasons. It has accompanied a more general interest among employers in taking a company-wide approach to a whole range of personnel initiatives. New technologies often demand a more flexible workforce, leading to a blurring of the organisational distinction between groups of workers. Harmonisation of the terms and conditions of employment follows, so that all employees work the same number of hours, are given the same training opportunities and enjoy the same entitlement to occupational pensions, sick pay and annual leave. Such practices have also been conspicuously imported into British subsidiaries of Japanese and American companies, which typically have longer experience of single-status employment practices.

Interest has also arisen following recent judgments in which courts have awarded equal pay to employees who have sought to compare their jobs with those of other individuals in wholly different job families. As a result, employers who continue to operate different mechanisms for determining the pay of different groups of employees have had difficulty in defending their practices when faced with equal value claims.

A number of pay structuring schemes built on the principle of a single pay spine have been developed. Both Paterson (1972) and Jaques (1961) used a single-factor scheme of job evaluation to determine the differentials. Paterson's decision-band method evaluated all jobs in terms of the decisions taken by the employee while Jaques's single factor is the timespan of the discretion that the employee is expected to exercise. Other organisations have developed single pay spines using the computer-assisted multi-factor job evaluation schemes which are now available. Useful case histories of the introduction of such schemes have been produced by ACAS (1983) and IDS (1992).

In practice, however, it is very difficult to develop a single pay structure which is acceptable to all parties. The 1993 IRS survey into job evaluation practices found that while over half the organisations in their sample used job evaluation for all their employees, only a quarter had a single scheme which applied to the whole workforce. The more diverse the skills, values and union affiliation of the employees, the more difficult is such a single job family. The problems are well illustrated in the National Health Service where there is a diversity of skills that can probably not be matched in any other area of occupational life. While several NHS Trusts have sought to develop single pay structures, to date very few have managed to implement their schemes because they are unable to overcome the difficulty of encompassing doctors, nurses, paramedical cadres, ancillary staff, administrators and technicians in a single scheme. The factors used to compare job with job always tend to favour one grouping at the expense of another; one job at the expense of another. The wider the diversity of jobs that are brought within the purview of a single scheme, the wider will be the potential dissatisfaction, with the result that the payment arrangement is one that at best is tolerated because it is the least offensive rather than being accepted as satisfactory.

The limitations of the single-factor evaluation scheme have been pungently criticised by Alan Fox (1972) on the grounds that it discriminates in favour of those in posts that are traditionally better paid anyway and therefore inhibits change of pay differentials towards a more broadly acceptable structure. Other difficulties about a single, integrated system of payment are those of responding to the external labour market and the impact of collective bargaining. If the only variables to control were within the business, it would be easier to sustain than in a situation where sectional interests are actively seeking to alter the structure specifically in their favour.

It is also invariably the case that any move towards a single pay structure is costly. Whichever job evaluation scheme is used to develop the new pay spine there will always be winners and losers among existing employees, as some will now be more highly ranked than others. While those who have hitherto been underpaid can be given pay increases it is not possible to reduce the salaries of those who are overpaid without breaching the contract of employment. This problem is associated with all job evaluation exercises, but is especially acute where moves towards a single pay spine are being made.

It is difficult to predict how many organisations will ultimately manage to overcome these problems and develop single pay structures. Spencer (1990a) reports that 35 per cent of new job evaluation schemes cover all the employees in the organisation. IRS (1993), however, found that over the previous five years more employers in their sample had moved away from the single-scheme approach than had adopted it.

ACTIVITY BOX 32.2

In what type of situations do you think a single, integrated job evaluated pay structure would be appropriate? Where would such a pay structure be inappropriate? What are the most likely management problems in each case?

Bargaining units

In our chapter on trade union recognition there was mention of the need to decide the boundaries of bargaining units. A job family and a bargaining unit will normally coincide, as the matter principally being discussed – pay – is common to both concepts. However, job families are created to deal with differential gaps rather than internal relativities even though they influence the internal relativity structure, and it is quite feasible to have bargaining units with more than one job family within them. A company might, for instance, negotiate with a trade union to determine a single salary scale for clerical, computer and administrative staff and then evaluate jobs in two separate families in the bargaining unit to determine the place within the scale for the different jobs. This procedure would be justified by the argument that the skills and requirements of computing staff are specialised, so that differentials are appropriately decided only by comparison with other computing jobs, while the relative position of computing staff is settled by collective bargaining.

In taking this course of action, however, a company would be in danger of losing an equal pay case brought by a female clerical officer claiming that her work was of equal value to that of a male computer operator. This has been the position since October 1993 when the European Court ruled in the case of *Enderby* v. *Frenchay Health Authority* that employers could not rely for defence on the operation of separate bargaining arrangements for different groups of staff.

The family structure

Another decision to be made is whether there will be any degree of overlap on the pay scales that relate to each family. There is no right answer to this question, although some overlap is usual, as suggested in the last chapter. No overlap at all (a rare arrangement) emphasises the hierarchy, encouraging employees to put their feet on the salary ladder and climb, but the clarity of internal relativities may increase the dissatisfaction of those on the lower rungs and put pressure on the pay system to accommodate the occasional anomaly, especially if climbing is not well supported. Overlapping grades blur the edges of relativities and can reduce dissatisfaction at the bottom, but introduce dissatisfaction higher up.

Another reason why pay scales for different job families usually overlap is to accommodate scales of different length. A family with a flat hierarchy will tend to have a small number of scales with many steps, while the steep hierarchy will tend to have more scales, but each with fewer steps. One of the main drawbacks of overlapping scales is the problem of migration, where an employee regards the job as technical at one time and makes a case for it to be reclassified as administrative at another time, because there is no further scope for progress in the first classification. Another aspect of migration is the more substantive case of employees seeking transfer to other jobs as a result of changes in the relative pay scales, which reduce rigidity in the internal labour market.

It is usual for executive pay to be discussed and administered differently from the pay of other employees. This is largely because traditional theoretical formulations of economists have no place for executives, who are neither wage-earners in the normal sense nor owners, yet they are both earners and acting on behalf of the owner(s). A further reason for regarding executives as a special case is the result of a number of investigations that have demonstrated a relationship between executive pay and organisational features such as sales turnover and number of employees. An admirable summary is to be found in Husband (1976) of work by analysts who argue that there is a typical relationship between the number of earners and the number of salaries at different levels.

In recent years the moves towards performance-related pay have been much greater for executives than for other categories of employee and they are rarely included in job evaluation.

Job evaluation methods

Job evaluation is the most common method used to compare the relative values of different jobs in order to provide the basis for a rational pay structure. Among the many definitions is this one from ACAS:

> Job evaluation is concerned with assessing the relative demands of different jobs within an organization. Its usual purpose is to provide a basis for relating differences in rates of pay to different in-job requirements. It is therefore a tool which can be used to help in the determination of a pay structure.
> (ACAS 1984)

It is a well-established technique, having been developed in all its most common forms by the 1920s. In recent years it has received a series of boosts. First, various types of incomes policy between 1965 and 1974 either encouraged the introduction of job evaluation or specifically permitted expenditure above the prevailing norm by companies wishing to introduce it. More recently the use of job evaluation is the hinge of most equal pay cases. Despite its popularity it is often misunderstood, so the following points have to be made:

1. Job evaluation is concerned with the job and not the performance of the individual job holder. Individual merit is not assessed.
2. The technique is systematic rather than scientific. It depends on the judgement of people with experience, requiring them to decide in a planned and systematic way, but it does not produce results that are infallible.
3. Job evaluation does not eliminate collective bargaining. It determines the differential gaps between incomes; it does not determine pay level.

4. Only a structure of pay rates is produced. Other elements of earnings, such as premia and incentives, are not determined by the method.

There are many methods of job evaluation in use and they are summarised in Smith (1983, pp. 68–106) and in Armstrong and Murlis (1994, pp. 99–110). Where a non-analytical or 'whole job' scheme is used a panel of assessors examines each job as a whole, in terms of its difficulty or value to the business, to determine which should be ranked more highly than others. No attempt is made to break each job down into its constituent parts. By contrast, an analytical scheme requires each element or factor of the job to be assessed. Since 1988 it has been the practice of courts only to accept the results of analytical schemes in equal pay cases.

We have already seen the problems connected with those analytical schemes which are built around an analysis of single factors, like those of Jaques and Paterson. The reliability of the outcome can be improved using multi-factor schemes but they have the disadvantage of being harder to understand and appear to depend on mechanical decision-making rather than on human judgement. This may produce 'better' decisions, which are less acceptable.

The most widely used analytical schemes are based on points-rating systems, under which each job is examined in terms of factors such as skill, effort and responsibility. Each factor is given a weighting indicating its value relative to the others and for each factor there are varying degrees. A score is then given depending on how demanding the job is in terms of each factor, with the overall points-value determining the relative worth of each job. Traditionally the analysis has been carried out by a panel of managers and workforce representatives who examine each job description in turn and compare it, factor by factor, with degree definitions. In recent years there has been increased interest in computer-assisted job evaluation systems which award scores to each job on the basis of information gathered from job analysis questionnaires. These developments are described by Murlis and Pritchard (1991) and by Spencer (1990b).

The best-known set of factors, weightings and degrees is that devised for the National Electrical Manufacturers Association of the United States, but the International Labour Organisation has produced a list of the factors used most frequently:

Accountability	Mental fatigue
Accuracy	Physical demands
Analysis and judgement	Physical skills
Complexity	Planning and co-ordination
Contact and diplomacy	Problem-solving
Creativity	Resources control
Decision-making	Responsibility for cash/materials/
Dexterity	confidential information/equipment or process/
Education	records and reports
Effect of errors	Social skills
Effort	Supervision given/received
Initiative	Task completion
Judgement	Training and experience
Know-how	Work conditions
Knowledge and skills	Work pressure
Mental effort	

The points values eventually derived for each job can be plotted on a graph or simply listed from the highest to the lowest to indicate the ranking. Then – and only then – are points ratings matched with cash amounts, as decisions are made on which points ranges equate with various pay levels.

It is virtually inevitable that some jobs will be found to be paid incorrectly after job evaluation has been completed. If the evaluation says that the pay rate should be higher then the rate duly rises, either immediately or step by step, to the new level. The only problem is finding the money, and introducing job evaluation always costs money. More difficult is the situation where evaluation shows the employee to be overpaid. It is not feasible to reduce the pay of the job holder without breaching the contract of employment. There have been two approaches. The first, which was never widespread and appears almost to have disappeared, is buying out. The overpaid employee is offered a large lump sum in considera- tion of the fact of henceforth being paid at the new, lower rate. The second and more general device used is that of the personal rate or red circling. An example could be where the rate for the job would be circled in red on the salary admin- istrator's records to show that the employee should continue at the present level while remaining in that post, but a successor would be paid at the lower job- evaluated rate.

The most widely used proprietary scheme is the Hay Guide Chart-Profile Method. IRS (1993) surveyed the use of job evaluation in 120 organisations and found that 77 employed the Hay method for some or all the jobs covered. It is used particularly widely in the evaluation of management jobs. The method is based on an assessment of four factors; know-how, problem-solving, account- ability and working conditions. Jobs are assessed by using each of three guide charts, one for each factor. A profile is then developed for the job showing the relationship between the factors, a ranking is eventually produced and the rates of the jobs considered in order to produce a new pay structure. At this stage comes one of the greatest advantages of this system. The proprietors have available a vast amount of comparative pay data on different undertakings using their sys- tem, so their clients cannot only compare rates of pay within their organisation (differentials and internal relativities); they can also examine their external rela- tivities. The method of operating this system and several other consultants' methods is described by Armstrong and Murlis (1994, pp. 508–31).

Employee participation in job evaluation

The degree of participation by non-managerial employees in job evaluation varies from one business to another. In some cases the entire operation is conducted from start to finish without any employee participation at all. Some degree of par- ticipation is more common. Apart from negotiating on pay levels and bargaining units, the main opportunities for employee contribution are as follows.

Job families

Employees collectively need to consent to the family structure and they can prob- ably add to the deliberations of managers about what that structure should be, as they will be well aware of the sensitive points of comparison.

Job descriptions

Traditionally job descriptions have been crucial to the evaluation and it is common for job holders to prepare their own, using a pro-forma outline, or for supervisors to prepare them for jobs for which they are responsible. Spencer (1990b) reports 88 per cent of his respondents answering that job descriptions were prepared by involving job holders and 94 per cent involved supervisors. Superficially, this is an attractive method, as there is direct involvement of the employee, who cannot claim to have been misrepresented. Also, it delegates the task of writing job descriptions, enabling it to be completed more quickly. The drawback is similar to that of character references in selection. Some employees write good descriptions and some write bad ones: some overstate while others understate. Inconsistency in job descriptions makes consistency in evaluation difficult.

An alternative is for job descriptions to be compiled by job analysts after questioning employees and their supervisors, who subsequently initial the job description which the analyst produces, attesting to its accuracy.

Panel evaluation

The awarding of points is usually done by a panel of people who represent between them the interests and expertise of management and employee. This is not only being 'democratic', it is acknowledging the need for the experience and perspective of job holders as well as managers in arriving at shrewd judgements of relative worth. Naturally, panel memberships alter so that employees are not asked to evaluate their own jobs. Although there is an understandable general tendency for employee representatives to push ratings up, and for management representatives to try to push them down, this usually smooths out because both parties are deriving differential rankings and not pay levels. The only potential conflict of interest will be if employee representatives and managers have divergent objectives on the shape of the eventual pay structure, with big or small differential gaps.

Job analysis questionnaires

Proprietary, computer-assisted job evaluation methods involve trained analysts putting a series of detailed questions to job holders from a multiple-choice questionnaire. The results are then fed into a computer which generates a score for each job. There is therefore no need for a panel to reach decisions based on written job descriptions. While there is clearly direct employee involvement in providing answers to the Job Analysis Questionnaire, the absence of a panel including workforce representatives can reduce the level of employee influence on the outcome of the exercise. This is particularly the case with those proprietary schemes which are customised to meet the needs of the purchasing organisation.

Equal value

The Equal Pay Act 1970 established that a woman could bring a case to an industrial tribunal claiming entitlement to equal pay with a man working at the same establishment if the claimant and her chosen comparator were engaged in 'like work' or work rated as equivalent under an employer's job evaluation study. A man can equally bring a case comparing his pay to that of a female colleague but this has very rarely occurred in practice. An amendment to the Act, which came into effect in 1984, broadened the definition of 'equal value' so that it became possible for a case to be brought if the claimant believes that her work is equal to that of her comparator in terms of the demands made upon them. This amendment followed a European Court ruling which judged the existing Equal Pay Act to fall short of the standard established by the EEC Equal Pay Directive. Since then other European Court rulings have further extended the scope of equal value law.

Like work

When presented with a claim for equal pay an industral tribunal will first seek to establish whether the claimant is engaged in 'like work' with the more highly paid man she has named as her comparator. The work does not have to be identical to justify equal pay under this heading, but must either be the same or of a broadly similar nature. In practice this means that the difference in pay can only be justified if there is 'a difference of practical importance' in the work done or if there is 'a genuine material factor' which justifies the higher rate of pay enjoyed by the male comparator.

An example of a difference of practical importance might be the level of responsibility of the man's job when compared to that of the claimant. An employer might, for example, be justified in paying a man more than his female colleague working on a comparable production line if the articles being manufactured by the man were of substantially greater value. Similarly a discriminatory payment could be justified if a man worked under less supervision than a woman engaged in otherwise like work. A common example would be a man working without supervision on night shifts.

Where there is no practical difference of this kind a discriminatory payment can only be justified where there is a 'genuine material factor other than sex' which can explain the difference in pay levels.

Work rated as equivalent

Cases brought under this section of the Act relate to jobs which are different in nature but have been rated as equivalent under the employer's job evaluation study. The existence of such a study can also provide the basis of an employer's defence in equal value claims.

A definition of a job evaluation scheme is included in the Act:

> A woman is to be regarded as employed on work rated as equivalent with that of any man if her job and his have been given an equal value, in terms of the demand made on a worker under various headings (for instance, effort, skill, decision), on a study undertaken with a view to evaluating in these terms the jobs done by all or any of the employees in an undertaking.
>
> (Equal Pay Act, s. 1.5)

Recent case law has further narrowed the definition of acceptable job evaluation schemes. In the case of *Bromley* v. *H&J Quick* (1988) the Court of Appeal ruled that the identification of benchmark jobs and paired comparisons was 'insufficiently analytical' as this did not involve evaluation under headings as required by the Act. The widely used method of job evaluation whereby only a sample of benchmark jobs are analysed cannot, therefore, be relied upon as a basis for an employer's defence. The jobs of the applicants and their chosen comparators must each have been evaluated analytically. In addition, a tribunal will look at the means by which scores derived from a job evaluation scheme are used to determine the rate of pay and will take account of a job evaluation study which has been completed but not implemented.

To be acceptable to a tribunal the job evaluation scheme in use must also be free of sex bias. Employers should ensure, therefore, that the factor weightings do not indirectly discriminate by over-emphasising job requirements associated with typical male jobs, like physical effort, at the expense of those associated with jobs predominantly undertaken by women such as manual dexterity or attention to detail.

Work of equal value

A woman who is not engaged in like work, work of a broadly similar nature, or work rated as equivalent is still entitled to bring an equal pay claim if she believes her work to be of equal value. In these cases the claimant names as her chosen comparator a man employed by the same undertaking who may be engaged in work of a wholly different nature. If the tribunal decides that there are grounds to believe that the work is of equal value, it will then appoint an independent expert, nominated by ACAS, to carry out a job evaluation study. The report of the independent expert will then be used by the tribunal as a basis of the decision on whether or not to make an award of equal pay to the claimant. A woman may bring an equal value claim in this way even if she has male colleagues engaged in like work and paid at the same rate as her.

A number of significant equal value cases have been brought to tribunals in recent years. In *Hayward* v. *Cammell Laird* (1984) a cook was awarded pay equal to that of men employed as joiners and laggers, but only after an appeal to the House of Lords three years after making the initial complaint. In 1990 the shop-workers' union USDAW dropped an equal value case against Sainsbury's when the employer agreed to carry out a job evaluation exercise. The union had claimed that predominantly female check-out operators were engaged in work of equal value to that of predominantly male warehousemen. This led to an 11 per cent rise in Sainsbury's retail wage bill and to a series of similar USDAW settlements with other major retailers during 1990 and 1991.

The Danfoss case

A significant recent development arose in a case brought to the European Court in 1989 with the title Handels-OG *Kontorfunktionaererenes Forbund i Danmark* v. *Dansk Arbejdsgiverforening* (acting for Danfoss), usually referred to as the Danfoss Case. The European Court's judgment greatly extended the basis on which equal value claims can be brought to challenge pay structures by accepting a case built on the assertion that *on average* in the same employment group men were paid more than women. It went on to rule that where this was the case it was for the employer to show that the pay scheme in operation was free from gender bias.

Genuine material factor defences

If it is established, to the satisfaction of an industrial tribunal, that the claimant is engaged in like work, work rated as equivalent, or work of equal value, the employer must show that the difference in the respective rates of pay is not due to sex discrimination but to a 'genuine material factor not of sex'.

There are many defences which potentially fall into this category. Among the most significant is the practice of red-circling whereby an individual's rate of pay is protected for a period following redeployment or a new job evaluation exercise. In most cases, provided it can be clearly shown that the red circle was awarded for reasons other than the individual's sex, this will be an acceptable material factor defence. Less reliable defences are those based on arguments concerning labour market conditions. A common example would be the situation in which a man is offered a job on a higher rate than an equally well-qualified woman, who is already in a similar post, on the grounds that he asked for a higher salary as his condition for accepting the job.

In 1993 the European Court has ruled in the case of *Enderby* v. *Frenchay Health Authority* that a difference in the collective bargaining arrangements under which the pay rates for jobs of equal value are determined is not a sufficient objective justification.

Broadbanding

A good case can be made against the introduction and continuation of rigid job evaluation schemes, in spite of the legal reasons for maintaining such systems. A number of writers have argued that job evaluation is bureaucratic in character and inflexible in effect. In making internal equity the main determinant of pay rates within an organisation, job evaluation prevents managers from offering higher or lower salaries to new employees and thus hinders effective competition in labour markets. It is also argued that it encourages individuals to focus on getting promoted rather than on improving performance in their current jobs. This may lead them to play damaging political games in a bid to weaken the position of colleagues or even to undermine their own supervisors. Inflexibility also occurs when individuals refuse to undertake duties or types of work associated with higher grades. Job evaluation encourages this kind of thinking by decreeing that higher pay should be associated with the carrying out of specific job tasks.

Attention has recently been given to the introduction of 'broadbanding' as a way of retaining the positive features of job evaluation while reducing the less desirable effects described above (see IDS 1996; and IPD 1997). Essentially this involves retaining some form of grading system while greatly reducing the numbers of grades or salary bands. The process typically results in the replacement of a structure with ten or twelve distinct grades with one consisting of only three or four. Pay variation within grades is then based on individual performance, skill or external market value rather than on the nature and size of the job. The great advantage of such approaches is their ability to reduce hierarchical thinking. Differences in pay levels still exist between colleagues but they are no longer seen as being due solely to the fact that one employee is graded more highly than another. This can reduce feelings of inequity provided the new criteria are reasonably open and objective. As a reult, teamwork is encouraged as is a focus on improving individual performance in order to secure higher pay.

In theory, therefore, broadbanded structures increase the extent to which managers have discretion over the setting of internal differentials, introduce more flexibility and permit organisations to reward performance or skills acquisition as well as job size. Their attraction is that they achieve this while retaining a skeleton grading system which gives order to the structure and helps justify differentials. Time will tell how acceptable such approaches are to the courts when it comes to judging equal value claims.

Summary propositions

32.1 The personnel manager needs to understand four types of pay comparison: differentials, internal relativities, external relativities and external identification.

32.2 Management freedom of action in deciding relative pay rates is constrained by the product market, the labour market, collective bargaining, technology and the internal labour market.

32.3 Management policy decisions about organising pay relationships relate mainly to job families, bargaining units, the structure of job families and deciding whether or not executives are a special case.

32.4 Job evaluation schemes are either based on whole job comparisons (non-analytical) or on an assessment of the value of each factor which makes up the job (analytical). The most widely used proprietary scheme is Hay Guide Chart profile method.

32.5 Employees participate in the job evaluation process at any or all of the following stages: job families, job descriptions, evaluation.

32.6 Under the amended Equal Pay Act, women may claim equal pay with that of a man if the work is the same, is broadly similar, has been rated as equal in a job evaluation scheme, or is of equal value in terms of the demands made an them.

32.7 There has been a great deal of interest recently in the introduction of broadbanding. This involves reducing the number of grades to allow managers more flexibility in setting pay levels for individual employees.

References

ACAS (1983) *Integrated Job Evaluation at Continental Can*, London: Advisory Conciliation and Arbitration Services. (This was earlier produced as no. 291 of Industrial Relations Review and Report, March 1983.)

ACAS (1984) *Job Evaluation*, London: Advisory, Conciliation and Arbitration Services.

Armstrong, M. and Murlis, H. (1994) *Reward Management*, London: Kogan Page.

Blanchflower, D., Oswald, A. and Garret, M. (1990) 'Insider power in wage determination', *Economica*, Vol. 57, No. 2, pp. 143–70.

Doeringer, P. B. and Piore, M. J. (1971) *Internal Labor Markets and Manpower Analysis*, Lexington, Mass: Heath.

Enderby v. *Frenchay Health Authority* [1991] IRLR 44.

Equal Opportunities Commission (1982) *Job Evaluation Schemes Free of Sex Bias*, Manchester: Equal Opportunities Commission.

Fowler, A. (1992) 'How to choose a job evaluation system', *Personnel Management Plus*, October.

Fox, A. (1972) 'Time span of discretion theory: an appraisal', in T. Lupton (ed.), *Payment Systems*, Harmondsworth: Penguin Books.

Ghobadian, A. (1990) 'Job evaluation: trade union and staff association representative's perspectives', *Employee Relations*, Vol. 12. No. 1.

Gill, D. and Ungerson, B. (1984) *Equal Pay: The challenge of equal value*, London: IPM.

Goodman, J. F. B., Armstrong, E. G. A., Wagner, A. and Davies, J. E. (1977) *Rule-Making and Industrial Peace*, Beckenham: Croom Helm.

Hayward v. *Cammell Laird Shipbuilders Ltd* [1984] TLR 52.

Husband, T. M. (1976) *Work Analysis and Pay Structure*, Maidenhead: McGraw-Hill.

IDS Focus (1977) *The Pay Merry-go-round*, London: Incomes Data Services Ltd.

IDS Study (1985) *Blue Collar Job Evaluation*, London: Incomes Data Services Ltd.

IDS Study (1992) *Integrated Pay Structures*, London, Incomes Data Services Ltd.

IDS Focus (1996) *Job Evaluation*, London, Incomes Data Services Ltd.

International Labour Organisation (1986), *Job Evaluation*, Geneva: ILO.

IPD (1997) *The IPD Guide to Broadbanding*, London: Institute of Personnel and Development.

IRS (1993) 'Job evaluation in the 1990s', *Industrial Relations Review and Reports*, October.

IRS (1994) 'Developments in job evaluation: shifting the emphasis', *Industrial Relations Review and Reports*, January.

Jaques, E. (1961) *Equitable Payment*, London: Heinemann.

Lazear, E. P. (1995) *Personnel Economics*, London: MIT Press.

Lowry, P. (1983) 'Equal pay for work of equal value: how the new regulations will work', *Personnel Management*, September.

Lupton, T. and Bowey, A. M. (1974) *Wages and Salaries*, Harmondsworth: Penguin Books.

Metcalf, D. (1977) 'Unions, incomes policy and relative wages in Britain', *British Journal of Industrial Relations*, July, pp. 157–75.

Murlis, H. and Pritchard, D. (1991) 'The computerised way to evaluate jobs', *Personnel Management*, April.

Oakes v. *Lester Beasley and Co.* [1976] IRLR 172.

Paterson, T. T. (1972) *Job Evaluation*, London: Business Books. (This method has now been adopted and developed by the consultants Arthur Young as their own proprietary method.)

Roberts, K., Clark, S. C., Cook, F. G. and Semeonoff, E. (1975) 'Unfair or unfounded pay differentials and incomes policy', *Personnel Management*, August, pp. 29–37.

Rubenstein, M. (1994) *Discrimination: a guide to the relevant case law on race and sex discrimination and equal pay*, London: Industrial Relations Services.

Smith, I. (1983) *The Management of Remuneration*, London: IPM.

Spencer, S. (1990a) 'Devolving job evaluation', *Personnel Management*, September.

Spencer, S. (1990b) 'Job evaluation; a modern day genie for management information?', *Employment Gazette*, May.

Stewart, M. (1990) 'Union wage differentials: product market influences and the division of rents', *Economic Journal*, Vol. 100, No. 4, pp. 1122–37.

Wainwright, D. (1985) 'Equal value in action: the lessons from Laird's', *Personnel Management*, January.

General discussion topics

1. 'Job evaluation does not produce equitable payment: it merely produces a ramshackle method of justifying the status quo.' Do you agree with this statement?
2. The chapter describes four types of pay relationship, two internal and two external. Which do you regard as (a) the most important, and (b) the most difficult for management to control?
3. Why not one big (happy) family?

CHAPTER 33

Incentives, performance pay and fringe benefits

Incentive payments remain one of the ideas that fascinate managers as they search for the magic formula. Somewhere there is a method of linking payment to performance so effectively that their movements will coincide, enabling the manager to leave the workers on automatic pilot, as it were, while attending to more important matters such as strategic planning or going to lunch. This conviction has sustained a continuing search for this elusive formula, which has been hunted with all the fervour of those trying to find the Holy Grail or the crock of gold at the end of the rainbow.

Performance-related pay is the topical version of this idea, with a significant change of emphasis. Incentives are to stimulate performance, while performance pay is to reward it; incentives are for the rank and file, while performance payments were introduced for the managerial elite (although their application has extended). Incentive thinking is preoccupied with the problem of control and avoiding costs getting out of hand, because 'they' will take the management to the cleaners if they are given half a chance. Performance pay thinking is dominated by the need to reward the deserving so that they too can share in the prosperity of the business at the same time as creating it.

Incentives: the traditional approach

Incentives and performance pay are part of a complex arrangement to express and to maintain the working relationship between the employer and the employee. They demonstrate not just what the management is trying to achieve, but also what the managers believe about the relationship. Elaborate incentive systems frequently represent a working relationship in which manager and worker are far apart with considerable mutual mistrust and little common interest. Elaborate systems of fringe benefit often represent a situation in which management is attempting to emphasise the degree of common interest, although they do not always succeed in overcoming mistrust. Schemes of performance pay typically carry the implicit view that those who may receive the payments are loyal, keen and hard-working: the possibility of the scheme being manipulated to achieve levels of payment which are not justified is never mentioned.

Around a third of male manual employees and over 15 per cent of non-manual males receive incentive payments of the traditional type, making up between 15 and 25 per cent of the total pay package. The proportion of female employees receiving incentive payments is lower, although the proportion of earnings that are accounted for by incentives is often higher. The reasons why they persist include some of the reasons why they have lost favour, such as the way in which managements frequently avoid a problem by buying a way past it through juggling with the incentive arrangement. If there were not an incentive pay scheme in existence it could not be used for that sort of short-circuiting operation. Other reasons are their use to overcome resistance to change, the attractiveness sometimes to employees who feel they are gaining an element of control over their own workplace, the possible help from a supervisory point of view and probably more important than any of these – a deep-seated conviction in the minds of many managers that incentive schemes ought to work as they seem basically sensible.

WINDOW ON PRACTICE

Many job descriptions for supervisory positions include reference to responsibility for ensuring that the appropriate health and safety at work regulations are adhered to. Few supervisors, however, left to themselves would see this aspect of their work as a priority. In one organisation known to the authors it was decided to try to raise the profile of health and safety issues by including objectives in this field into managers'

annual performance targets. It, therefore, became clear that the level of performance-related payments in the following year would, in part, be determined by the extent to which the health and safety objectives had been met.

The result was the swift establishment of departmental health and safety committees and schemes whereby staff could bring safety hazards to the attention of supervisors.

Payment by results schemes

Historically, the most widely used incentive schemes have been those which reward employees according to the number of items or units of work they produce or the time they take to produce them. This approach is associated with F. W. Taylor and the phase in the development of personnel management described in Chapter 1 under the heading 'The Humane Bureaucrat'. Little attention has been paid to the operation of piecework schemes in recent years and there is clear evidence to show that they are in decline, both in terms of the proportion of total pay which is determined according to payment by results (PBR) principles and in terms of the number of employees paid in this way. The results of a survey carried out by the IPM and NEDO in 1991, however, showed that PBR was still widely used, in some shape or form, by employers of manual workers. One in five of the organisations surveyed operated individual PBR schemes for manual grades and 23 per cent used group PBR, including over half the public sector organisations.

Individual time saving

It is rare for a scheme to be based on the purest form of piecework, a payment of X pence per piece produced, as this provides no security against external influences which depress output such as machine failure or delays in the delivery of raw materials. The most common type of scheme in use, therefore, is one where the incentive is paid for time saved in performing a specified operation. A standard time is derived for a work sequence and the employee receives an additional payment for the time saved in completing a number of such operations. If it is not possible to work due to shortage of materials or some other reason, the time involved is not counted when the sums are done at the end of the day.

Standard times are derived by the twin techniques of method study and work measurement which are the skills of the work study engineer. By study of the operation, the work study engineer decides what is the most efficient way to carry it out and then times an operator actually doing the job over a period, so as to measure the 'standard time'. Work-measured schemes of this kind have, however, been subject to a great deal of criticism and are only effective where people are employed on short-cycle manual operations with the volume of output varying between individuals depending on their skill or application.

The main difficulty, from the employee's point of view, is the fluctuation in earnings that occurs as a consequence of a varying level of demand for the product. If the fluctuations are considerable then the employees will be encouraged to try to stabilise them, either by pressing for the guaranteed element to be increased, or by storing output in the good times to prevent the worst effects of the bad, or by social control of high-performing individuals to share out the benefits of the scheme as equally as possible.

Measured daywork

To some people the idea of measured daywork provides the answer to the shortcomings of individual incentive schemes. Instead of employees receiving a variable payment in accordance with the output achieved, they are paid a fixed sum as long as they maintain a predetermined and agreed level of working. Employees thus have far less discretion over the amount of effort they expend. Theoretically, this deals with the key problem of other schemes by providing for both stable earnings and stable output instead of 'as much as you can, if you can'.

The advantage of measured daywork over time-saving schemes, from the management point of view, is the greater level of management control that is exercised. The principal disadvantage is the tendency for the agreed level of working to become a readily achievable norm which can only be increased after negotiation with workforce representatives.

Group incentives

Sometimes the principles of individual time-saving are applied to group rather than individual output to improve group performance and to promote the development of team working. Cannell and Long (1991) provide evidence to suggest that private sector organisations are increasingly replacing individual PBR schemes with group-based arrangements. Where jobs are interdependent, group incentives can be appropriate, but it may also put great pressure on the group members, aggravating any interpersonal animosity that exists and increasing the likelihood of stoppages for industrial action. Group schemes can also severely reduce the level of management control by allowing the production group to determine output according to the financial needs of individual group members.

Plant-wide schemes

A variant on the group incentive is the plant-wide bonus scheme, under which all employees in a plant or other organisation share in a pool bonus that is linked to the level of output, the value added by the employees collectively or some similar formula. The attraction of these methods lies in the fact that the benefit to the management of the organisation is 'real' because the measurement is made at the end of the system, compared with the measurements most usually made at different points within the system, whereby wages and labour costs can go up while output and profitability both come down. Theoretically, employees are also more likely to identify with the organisation as a whole, they will co-operate more readily with the management and each other, and there is even an element of workers' control.

The difficulties are that there is no tangible link between individual effort and individual reward, so that those who are working effectively can have their efforts nullified by others working less effectively or by misfortunes elsewhere.

ACTIVITY BOX 33.1

Where manual employees are employed on some form of payment by results, the New Earnings Survey shows that the percentage of average earnings made up by incentive payments is under 20 per cent for men and over 30 per cent for women. How would you explain this difference?

Commission

The payment of commission on sales is a widespread practice about which surprisingly little is known as these schemes have not come under the same close scrutiny that has been put on incentive schemes for manual employees. They suffer from most of the same drawbacks as manual incentives, except that they are linked to business won rather than to output achieved.

Tips

The practice of tipping is generally criticised as being undesirable for those receiving tips – it requires them to be deferential and obsequious – and for those giving them – because it is an unwarranted additional charge for a service they have already paid for. It is also often described as an employer device to avoid the need to pay realistic wages. Despite the criticism the practice persists, although it is of varying significance in different countries of the world.

The attraction of tipping is the feeling by employees that they can personally influence the level of their remuneration by the quality of service they give, and the feeling by the tipper of providing personal recognition for service received. This does not answer the criticism that tipping is usually for reasons of convention rather than direct acknowledgement of special service. From the employer's point of view the tipping convention can help ensure application to customers' wishes by employees, but can present problems in coping with known 'bad tippers'.

Disadvantages of PBR schemes

The whole concept of payment by results was set up to cope with a stable and predictable situation, within the boundaries of the workplace. External demands from customers were irritations for others – like sales representatives – to worry about. The factory was the arena, the juxtaposed parties were the management on the one hand and the people doing the work on the other, and the deal was output in exchange for cash. The dramatic changes of the 1980s and 1990s, which have swept away stability, dismantled the organisational boundary and enthroned the customer as arbiter of almost everything have also made PBR almost obsolete.

According to the New Earnings Survey the proportion of manual workers receiving PBR payments has been in steady decline since 1983. This trend can be explained, in part, by changing technologies and working practices. A payment system that puts the greatest emphasis on the number of items produced or on the time taken to produce them is inappropriate in industries where product quality is of greater significance than product quantity. Similarly a manufacturing company operating a just-in-time system will rely too heavily on overall plant performance to benefit from a payment scheme that primarily rewards individual effort.

In addition to the problem of fluctuating earnings, described above, there are a number of further inherent disadvantages which explain the decline of PBR-based remuneration arrangements.

Operational inefficiencies

For incentives to work to the mutual satisfaction of both parties, there has to be a smooth operational flow, with materials, job cards, equipment and storage space all readily available exactly when they are needed, and an insatiable demand for the output. Seldom can these conditions be guaranteed and when they do exist they seldom last without snags. Raw materials run out, job cards are not available, tools are faulty, the stores are full, customer demand is fluctuating or there is trouble with the computer. As soon as this sort of thing happens the incentive-paid worker has an incentive either to fiddle the scheme or negotiate its alteration for protection against operational vagaries.

Quality of work

The stimulus to increase volume of output can adversely affect the quality of output, as there is an incentive to do things as quickly as possible. If the payment scheme is organised so that only output meeting quality standards is paid for, there may still be the tendency to produce expensive scrap. Operatives filling jars with marmalade may break the jars if they work too hurriedly. This means that the jar is lost and the marmalade as well, for fear of glass splinters.

Renewed emphasis on quality and customer satisfaction mean that employers increasingly need to reward individuals with the most highly developed skills or those who are most readily adaptable to the operation of new methods and technologies. PBR, with its emphasis on the quantity of items produced or sold, may be judged inappropriate for organisations competing in markets in which the quality of production is of greater significance than previously.

The quality of working life

There is also a danger that PBR schemes may demotivate the workforce and so impair the quality of working life for individual employees. In our industrial consciousness payment by results is associated with the worst aspects of rationalised work: routine, tight control, hyper-specialisation and mechanistics. The worker is characterised as an adjunct to the machine, or as an alternative to a machine. Although this may not necessarily be so, it is usually so, and generally expected. Payment in this way reinforces the mechanical element in the control of working relationships by failing to reward employee initiative, skills acquisition or flexibility. There is also evidence to suggest that achieving high levels of productivity by requiring individuals to undertake the same repetitive tasks again and again during the working day increases stress levels and can make some employees susceptible to repetitive strain injuries.

The selective nature of the incentive

Seldom do incentive arrangements cover all employees. Typically, groups of employees are working on a payment basis which permits their earnings to be geared to their output, while their performance depends on the before or after processes of employees not so rewarded, such as craftsmen making tools and fixtures, labourers bringing materials in and out, fork-truck drivers, storekeepers and so forth. This type of problem is illustrated most vividly by Angela Bowey's study of a garment factory, where employees 'on piecework' were set against those who were not, by the selective nature of the payment arrangement (Lupton and Bowey 1975, pp. 76–8).

The conventional way round the problem is to pay the 'others' a bonus linked to the incentive earned by those receiving it. The reasoning for this is that those who expect to earn more (like the craftsmen) have a favourable differential guaranteed as well as an interest in high levels of output, while that same interest in sustaining output is generated in the other employees (like the labourers and the storekeepers) without whom the incentive-earners cannot maintain their output levels. The drawbacks are obvious. The labour costs are increased by making additional payments to employees on a non-discriminating basis, so that the storekeeper who is a hindrance to output will still derive benefit from the efforts of others, and the employees whose efforts are directly rewarded by incentives feel that the fruits of their labour are being shared by those whose labours are not so directly controlled.

Obscurity of payment arrangements

Because of these difficulties, incentive schemes are constantly modified or refined in an attempt to circumvent fiddling or to get a fresh stimulus to output, or in response to employee demands for some other type of change. This leads to a situation in which the employees find it hard to understand what behaviour by them leads to particular results in payment terms. This same obscurity is often found in the latest fashion in performance-related pay. In a recent unpublished study comparing performance management in two blue-chip companies, less than half the people in management posts claimed to understand how the payments were calculated. Many of those actually misunderstood their schemes!

Performance-related pay

While the 1980s and 1990s have seen a decline in the use of PBR schemes, such as those described above, there has been considerable growth in the coverage of incentive schemes which reward individual contribution to the business on the basis of performance and overall contribution rather than simply on effort and output. Performance-related pay (PRP), unlike traditional PBR incentives, looks beyond straightforward measures of output and provides a means whereby individual effectiveness, flexibility and work quality can also be rewarded. It has its roots in schemes set up to motivate managers and executives but has increasingly spread downwards through organisations to cover non-manual grades and nowadays some manual grades as well.

In 1991 a survey looking at incentive schemes in 360 organisations was carried out jointly by the IPM and NEDO (Cannell and Wood 1992). The questionnaire responses indicated that 68 per cent of private sector organisations and 43 per cent of public sector organisations had introduced PRP for some or all their non-manual employees. Twenty-eight per cent of private sector employers used PRP to determine the final pay levels of all employees. The extent of the recent growth in the use of PRP was shown by the fact that 40 per cent of the schemes for non-manual employees had been introduced between 1981 and 1991. Of further interest was the finding that once introduced PRP was hardly ever withdrawn, although modifications to original scheme designs were common.

Our own survey data showed that relating pay to performance is a widespread current practice for those in managerial roles, although less common for others. Furthermore the figures show this approach to payment as being significantly more common than payment by results, skill-based pay, competence pay, profit-related pay or profit-sharing. Next most common was some form of bonus payment. The precise nature of these schemes varied considerably, so that many of those for manual employees would fit a textbook definition of payment by results, though that was not the term used by the respondents. Most of those for non-manual and managerial staff were like the Christmas bonus, others were linked to individual or group performance without the nature of the linkage being clearly spelled out. Table 33.1, therefore, shows that gearing payment to

Table 33.1 Percentage of employees in 215 organisations paid on various bases

Which of the following payment arrangements do you use for the different categories of employee?	Manual (%)	Non-manual (%)	Managerial (%)
Performance-related	12.9	32.4	52.4
Profit-related	6.7	12.4	14.8
Profit-sharing	4.8	9.1	9.5
Bonus scheme	24.8	28.6	38.6
Skill-based	10.0	4.8	4.3
Competence-based	3.3	2.3	4.9
Payment by results	2.4	3.3	8.6

performance is the dominant feature of current reward systems. In contrast linking reward to skill or competence is little used.

It is safe to say that relating pay to performance represents the current orthodoxy, despite some major problems.

The attractions of PRP

The growth in performance-related pay undoubtedly owes as much to the appearance of fairness as to its supposed incentive effects. In seeking to reward individuals for their personal contribution to business success the principles that underlie PRP make it attractive to employers and employees alike. Unlike payment systems which reward everyone on a particular grade equally whatever their contribution, or schemes which only reward the quantity of output, PRP appears to accord with widely supported concepts of distributive justice. Marsden and Richardson (1991) surveyed the attitudes of over 2,000 members of the Inland Revenue after the introduction of a system of relating pay to performance. It was one of the earliest such schemes in the British Civil Service, was deeply unpopular and was scrapped after its first year. Despite these huge drawbacks over half of all the respondents described relating pay to performance as being fair in principle.

In theory the incentive effect derives from the underlying principle of fairness. Individual employees are encouraged to make a greater contribution because they know they will be financially rewarded for doing so. Performance-related pay, when it works well, also ensures that individual work objectives match overall business goals. This occurs by clearly reflecting the employer's priorities and values in the criteria on which the award of performance related payments are based.

Furthermore, PRP provides a means whereby individuals can be motivated in an organisational environment with flatter hierarchies and, in consequence, fewer promotion opportunities. It also suits the needs of organisations in an era of relatively low inflation in which annual salary increases are no longer automatic but have to be earned.

Forms of PRP

The most widely used form of PRP is that which relates annual incremental progression to individual performance. An excellent level of performance will thus be rewarded the following year by a substantial increase in the individual's base salary. Conversely, an employee who has been assessed as having performed poorly will only be rewarded with a rise to cover cost of living increases or will receive no pay rise at all. The problem with this form of PRP is its tendency to cause the organisation's pay bill to rise unless there is a high level of staff turnover. An alternative approach is to pay one-off bonuses to reward individual or team performance; sums which are not consolidated into base pay rates.

The schemes also vary considerably in terms of the proportion of pay which is performance-related. The question of how much, in percentage terms, a good performer should be rewarded in comparison with a poor one will inevitably depend on the organisation's product market and the culture it wishes to develop. Armstrong and Murlis offer the following advice:

As a rule of thumb, those whose performance is outstanding may deserve and expect rewards of at least 10% and more in their earlier period in a job. People whose level of performance and rate of development is well above the average may merit increases of 8–10%, while those who are progressing well at the expected rate towards the fully competent level may warrant an increase of between 5% and 7%. Increases of between 3% and 5% may be justified for those who are still developing steadily. Performance-related increases of less than 3% are hardly worth giving.

(Armstrong and Murlis 1994, p. 216)

Assessing performance

It is feasible to base performance-related pay rises on managerial assessments of each individual's 'whole job' performance. Each supervisor can be asked to assess his or her subordinates' individual contribution over the year on the basis of a set of performance criteria such as time-keeping, attendance, effort, initiative and customer care. Such a system, however, while relatively straightforward to operate, is open to charges of unfairness and subjectivity with the awards being judged to be arbitrary.

A more effective method is to link pay to the achievement of pre-set performance targets. Here each individual agrees performance objectives with their manager at the beginning of the year and is rewarded twelve months later according to the extent to which those objectives have been achieved.

In our own survey we found varying practice. Respondents were asked to report the nature of performance review, as shown in Table 33.2. These data need cautious interpretation, as respondents may well feel that the first category is so obviously 'politically correct' that they will register their response there even if the actual practice is not quite as rigorous as their reply indicates. Even with this cautionary note, we still get a picture of clear emphasis on formal, regular, objective-setting performance review.

Table 33.2 Practice in reviewing the performance of employees in 215 organisations

How, if at all, is performance reviewed in your organisation for the various categories of employee?	Manual (%)	Non-manual (%)	Managerial (%)
A formal system of regular appraisals with reviews of past performance, setting of objectives and formal reviews of performance against these	38.9	66.8	77.3
Informal but regular reviews involving a chat about past performance and agreed action for the future	15.3	15.1	11.1
Informal, *ad hoc* reviews, undertaken especially when there is a performance problem	25.7	10.7	4.3
Not reviewed	20.1	7.3	7.2

A relatively new approach to setting objectives has been devised by Kaplan and Norton (1996), of Harvard. It is known as the 'balanced scorecard' method, in which objective measurements are put in place to answer four questions:

1. How should we appear to our shareholders? (The financial perspective)
2. How should we appear to our customers? (The customer perspective)
3. What business processes must we excel at? (The internal perspective)
4. How will we sustain our ability to change and improve? (The learning and growth perspective)

Drawbacks of PRP

The long history of incentive schemes, and particularly of trade union involvement in their development, has been to make them collective and impersonal. The idea of performance pay is usually to make it individual and personal, so that some do better than others – or some do worse than others. Therein lies the problem. If the performance pay arrangement is to be effective, it must have an apparent impact on individual performance, but selective individual reward can be divisive and lead to overall ineffectiveness unless everyone perceives the rules to be fair.

The least successful PRP schemes, therefore, are those which cover employees whose performance is most difficult to measure effectively. In the early 1990s there were moves by the government to promote PRP for nurses, doctors and teachers, and they were widely criticised for this reason. Journalists employed by the BBC went as far as to take industrial action in the summer of 1994 over

WINDOW ON PRACTICE

Peter and Patrick are sales consultants for a financial services company and both had business targets for a six-month period. Peter met his target comfortably and received the predetermined bonus of £6,000 for reaching on-target earnings. Patrick failed to reach his target because his sales manager boss left the company and poached two of Patrick's prime customers just before they signed agreements with Patrick, whose bonus was therefore £2,000 instead of £6,250.

Joanne was a sales consultant for the same company as Peter and Patrick. Before the sales manager left, he made over to her several promising clients with whom he had done considerable preparatory work and who were not willing to be 'poached' by his new employer. All of these signed agreements and one of them decided to increase the value of the deal ten-fold without any reference to Joanne until after that decision was made, and without knowing that she was now the appropriate contact. Her bonus for the period was £23,400.

Henry is a production manager in a light engineering company with performance pay related to a formula combining output with value-added. Bonus payments were made monthly in anticipation of what they should be. One of Henry's initiatives was to increase the gearing of the payment by results scheme in the factory. Through peculiarities of company accounting his bonus payments were 'justified' according to the formula, but later it was calculated that the production costs had risen by an amount that cancelled out the value-added benefits. Also 30 per cent of the year's output had to be recalled due to a design fault.

Peter had his bonus made up to £6,250. Joanne had her bonus reduced to £8,000, but took legal advice and had the cut restored, whereupon Peter and Patrick both threatened to resign until mollified by *ex-gratia* payments of £2,000 each. Peter resigned three months later. Henry was dismissed.

proposals to relate their pay to performance. All these groups fear that the diffi-culties associated with measuring their performance will lead to subjective and possibly unfair judgements being made by their assessors.

It is also very difficult to measure performance in many management jobs which, by their very nature, require great flexibility on the part of job holders. The problem here is that as soon as performance objectives and indicators have been agreed, the goalposts change, rendering the agreed performance criteria out of date long before the end of the year. As a result the pay award that is finally made does not adequately reflect the individual's actual performance.

When PRP does not work it can easily serve to demotivate employees and can act divisively to damage relationships within a team thus defeating its original purpose. There can be no doubt that organisations have to take great care in its introduction if they are to make it work successfully as an incentive.

The effect of PRP on the paybill

> Individualized pay seems tailor-made for a period of competitive expansion. . . .
> By all accounts this has had a considerable initial effect on company
> performance. But at the same time it produced a tremendous inflationary
> spiral. The systems introduced have generally been highly geared, with a high
> pay threshold as a carrot to attract employees and secure acceptance of the
> new arrangements. Awards for below standard performance have often been
> higher than the general run of increases in other industries.   (IDS 1988, p. 5)

When schemes are individualised, it is always difficult to keep pay rises down for the poorer performer. Few managers have the stomach for passing on the bad news and then hoping to get a satisfactory working performance out of the person who has not had a pay rise. It is also difficult to keep pay rises under control for the average and better performers. Eight per cent in year 1 may be such a highly appreciated reward that it will help maintain a high performance in year 2. A movement then to 10 per cent may have a similar effect, but 10 per cent repeated in year 3 would have less impact and become 'consolidated' as the expected norm. The alternative is the 'tremendous inflationary spiral' described by IDS.

If a business is struggling, it cannot afford unfettered performance pay. Sometimes, there is a management justification for performance payments being made only to those in key management posts on the grounds that only they can initiate significant change and improvement in overall business performance. Furthermore, the payments made to this small number of individuals amount to a small proportion of the organisation's total expenditure. The payments are still likely to be inflationary, as the hankering after equity by others in the organisation will put strong pressure on pay levels at every point.

WINDOW ON PRACTICE

Sophie is a secretary with a financial services business in the City of London, and was thrilled to get the job three years ago as it paid £16,000 a year, which was much more than she had been paid in her previous job at an estate agent. She was even more pleased when she received a bonus in her first year of 10 per cent. Her salary is now £22,000 and she has just had an annual bonus of 40 per cent.

Twenty years ago, inflation was sometimes attributed to consolidation, as progressively the proportion of pay that was basic as opposed to payment by results was increased, the rewards for the performance gradually being consolidated in the pay that people received regardless of the performance. Currently, this can be seen happening in a very public way in the published accounts of private companies, which include directors' emoluments. There have been several instances of company chairmen having a significant proportion of their income linked to company performance, yet the other directors decide to reward the chairman with a special payment as compensation for the fact that the success of the business has faltered.

The more exuberant schemes are gradually being replaced by arrangements that are better controlled, but the problems remain and it seems as if performance pay still suffers many of the weaknesses that were found in incentive payment schemes during the 1920s and 1930s.

There have been numerous case studies published in recent years examining the introduction of PRP in both the public and private sectors. The most thorough treatment of the problems which have arisen is found in Cannell and Wood (1992) and in Marsden and Richardson (1991). A shorter review is in Torrington (1995).

Skill-based pay

A further kind of incentive payment scheme is one which seeks to reward employees for the skills or competencies which they acquire. It is well established in the United States and, according to an IPM survey undertaken in 1991, is becoming more common among British employers. It is particularly prevalent as a means of rewarding technical staff, but there is no reason why the principle should not be extended to any group of employees for whom the acquisition of additional skills might benefit the organisation.

There are several potential benefits for an employer introducing a skill-based pay scheme. Its most obvious effect is to encourage multi-skilling and flexibility enabling the organisation to respond more effectively and speedily to the needs of customers. A multi-skilled workforce may also be slimmer and less expensive. In addition it is argued that, in rewarding skills acquisition, a company will attract and retain staff more effectively than its competitors in the labour market. The operation of a skill-based reward system is proof that the sponsoring employer is genuinely committed to employee development.

Most skill-based payment systems reward employees with additional increments to their base pay once they have completed defined skill modules. A number of such schemes are described in detail in a study published by Incomes Data Services (1992a). Typical is the scheme operated by Venture Pressings Ltd where staff are employed on four basic grades, each divided into ten increments. Employees progress up the scale by acquiring specific skills and demonstrating proficiency in them to the satisfaction of internal assessors. New starters are also assessed and begin their employment on the incremental point most appropriate to the level of skills they can demonstrate.

In many industries it is now possible to link payment for skills acquisition directly to the attainment of National Vocational Qualifications (NVQs) for which both the setting of standards and the assessment of individual competence are carried out externally.

A skill-based pay system will only be cost-effective if it results in productivity increases which are sufficient to cover the considerable costs associated with its introduction and maintenance. A business can invest a great deal of resources both in training its workforce to attain new skills, and in rewarding them once those skills have been acquired, only to find that the cost of the scheme outweighs the benefit gained in terms of increased flexibility and efficiency. Furthermore, in assisting employees to become more highly qualified and in many cases to gain NVQs, an employer may actually find it harder to retain its staff in relatively competitive labour markets. Employers seeking to introduce skill-based systems of payment therefore need to consider the implications very carefully and must ensure that they only reward the acquisition of those skills which will clearly contribute to increased productivity.

Profit-sharing and profit-related pay

There are a number of different ways in which companies are able to link remuneration directly to profit levels. In recent years the Government has sought to encourage the incidence of such schemes and has actively promoted their establishment with advantageous tax arrangements. Underlying their support is the belief that linking pay to profits increases the employee's commitment to his or her company by deepening the level of mutual interest. As a result, it is argued that such schemes act as an incentive encouraging employees to work harder and with greater flexibility in pursuit of higher levels of take-home pay.

Profit-sharing

The traditional and most common profit-sharing arrangement is simply to pay employees a cash bonus, calculated as a proportion of annual profits, on which the employee incurs both a PAYE and a national insurance liability.

An alternative is the Approved Deferred Share Trust (ADST), which was established under the Finance Act 1978. In this arrangement the company allocates the proportion of profit not in cash to employees, but to a trust fund which purchases company shares on behalf of the employees. The shares are then allocated to eligible employees on some agreed formula. The employee shareholder pays tax only when the shares are sold, and there is no additional national insurance contribution by employee or employer. ADST schemes seldom allow shares to be sold in the first two years after purchase and if they are sold in the following two years the employee pays tax on one of two values – either the price paid originally or the final selling price. If the shares are sold during the fourth year of ownership the tax obligation reduces to three-quarters of what it would have been the year earlier. After five years of ownership there is no tax obligation at all. Share dividends are received and taxed in the normal way. A variant of this arrangement was made possible by the Finance Act 1980 under which Save As You Earn Schemes can be established, enabling employees, if they wish, to purchase company shares through monthly deductions from salary.

The incidence of profit-sharing has increased in recent years and was operated in some shape or form by 55 per cent of the companies participating in the survey undertaken by the IPM and NEDO in 1991 (Cannell and Wood 1992). In the same year the Inland Revenue estimated that 1.3 million employees received shares or share options, but many more will have benefited from profit-sharing by opting to take cash payments instead of shares.

The level of bonus that employees can expect to receive as a result of profit-sharing schemes varies considerably. According to an Incomes Data Services survey of thirty-two companies carried out in 1993, the average level of bonus received by employees covered by profit-sharing schemes was £200–£300. Before the recession, however, awards worth over £500 were commonly paid.

Profit-related pay

In a profit-sharing scheme a bonus, either in the form of cash or shares, is paid to employees depending on the level of the company's annual profits. A profit-related pay scheme differs in that it automatically links a portion of an employee's basic pay to profit levels. Tax relief is available up to the point at which the profit-related part of the salary is the lower of either 20 per cent of an employee's total pay, or £4,000. This allows anyone earning between £8,000 and £20,000 an equivalent gross salary increase of around 7 per cent provided the company reaches its stated profit targets.

Tax relief on profit-related pay was first introduced in 1987 but failed to attract many companies. A large proportion of those which did participate were simply converting existing profit-sharing arrangements so as to take advantage of the tax relief. Between December 1991 and December 1993, however, the number of schemes rose from 2,000 to over 6,400. By December 1996 3.7 million employees were covered in 14,000 schemes. The acceleration in the number of applications followed the Government's decision to increase the amount of tax relief available and to publish a set of model rules to assist employers in setting up schemes. Interest has undoubtedly also been increased as a result of the recession, with employers taking advantage of Inland Revenue rules to give pay increases at no cost to the company.

In December 1996 it was announced that tax relief on these schemes would be phased out, finally ending on 1 January 2000. The Chancellor of the Exchequer contended that the principle of linking pay to profitability had been established, and it was no longer appropriate that a minority of employees should enjoy £1.5 billion in tax relief when that had to be made up by the other 22 million taxpayers. It remains to be seen whether or not his prediction about the continuation of schemes is justified.

> In a survey published in April, consultants Arthur Andersen described the phase-out of tax relief on PRP as 'a time bomb waiting to happen'. It estimates that a typical business will experience an extra 3.5 per cent increase in their payroll costs, if forced to top up employees' pay. In extreme cases, it says the costs could be as much as 8.4 per cent.   (IDS 1997a, p.1)

Disadvantages of profit-related schemes

The obvious disadvantage of the schemes described above from the employee's point of view is the risk that pay levels may decline if the company fails to meet its expected profit levels. If no profit is made it cannot be shared. Companies are not permitted to make guarantees about meeting payments and will have their schemes revoked by the Inland Revenue if they do so. In any event it is likely that pay levels will vary from year to year.

For these reasons it is questionable to assert that profit-related schemes do in fact act as incentives. Unlike performance-related pay awards they do not relate specifically to the actions of the individual employee. Annual profit levels are clearly influenced by a whole range of factors which are both internal and external to the company. An employee may well develop a community of interest with the company management, shareholders and with other employees but it is unlikely to seriously affect the nature of his or her work. It is also the case that both poor and good performers are rewarded equally in profit-related schemes. The incentive effect will therefore be very slight in most cases and will be restricted to a general increase in employee commitment.

ACTIVITY BOX 33.2

Given the disadvantages of profit-related schemes, what are the relative advantages to the employer of ADST and profit-related pay schemes?

Fringe benefits

Features of payment other than wages or salary have grown in importance steadily since the 1960s, and the United Kingdom has a level of provision that is not found in other western countries. This is especially marked in the executive, management and professional area. Gill (1989) quotes the exceptional case of a retired company chairman who was made a consultant with a package that included £92 a day for lunch, four centre court tickets for Wimbledon every year, and four tickets for each opera season at Covent Garden. A less unusual example is: 'A banker's £35,000 salary typically brings with it a bonus averaging about £9,000 a year, a car and petrol, free health insurance, life insurance cover of £100,000, an interest-free loan of £6,000 and a £60,000 mortgage at 5 per cent interest.'

This type of development has been mainly due to taxation advantages, either to the employer or the employee, although there is a further refinement, known as the cafeteria approach, whereby the employee can choose between alternatives in putting together a personalised pay and benefits package. This idea has been current for some time without being widely adopted:

> While some UK employers do offer an element of choice over individual elements of the benefits package, very few have adopted a more structured approach where individual choice is seen as a benefit in its own right. Some companies have toyed with the idea of flexible compensation but have not, up to now, regarded the potential advantages as sufficient to outweigh the complexity involved. (Woodley 1990, p. 42)

Over recent years we have all begun to reflect on our payment arrangements in a more calculated way than before with the introduction, for instance, of the option to change from an employer's pension arrangements to a private pension plan, to make additional voluntary contributions, various possibilities of share ownership, and so forth. Perhaps the cafeteria approach to benefits is an idea whose time has at last come.

Despite their great attraction, fringe benefits can exacerbate status problems, with the have-nots bitterly resenting the privilege of the haves.

Other benefits

Employers provide a wide range of other benefits, from free hairdressing in company time to loans to buy season tickets. One of these is the London allowance. According to IDS (1997b) the typical inner London allowance was £3,000–£3,500 a year with some companies paying higher salary-related allowances and one in five employers paying less than £2,000.

WINDOW ON PRACTICE

The 1996 Labour Force Survey calculated the problems of travelling to work in London when compared with elsewhere in the country. The travel to work time for the country as a whole is 24 minutes. For central London it is 55 minutes, for the rest of inner London 41 minutes and 29 minutes for outer London. Another difference was in the method of travel. In central London 16 per cent travel to work by car and 68 per cent by train. In outer London and the rest of the country 70 per cent travel by car.

Some employers also have a lower 'ROSELAND' (rest of south-east England) payment. There is an increasing practice, particularly among retailers, of fitting the allowance to a particular location instead of to a general geographical area. This enables them to target allowances as needed on a store-by-store basis according to prevailing labour market condition.

Incentives, fringe benefits and personnel management

The very costly aspects of remuneration discussed in this chapter are seldom managed in a positive way with a sense of purpose about why they are provided and what they are to achieve. Usually, an extra is provided because it is a good bargain. Membership of the local health club can be obtained at half price by the employer, so it seems like too good an opportunity to miss. Many benefits are provided simply because it is the accepted practice, like the company car. Incentive schemes are set up in the belief that they should work, but without any evidence that the method actually proposed will work in that situation. The various schemes are seldom co-ordinated, with different executives responsible for different features. Sometimes the responsibility of the personnel manager is total, sometimes it is nil, yet all these features affect the basic activity of personnel work: matching the expectations of employer with the expectations of employee. Furthermore they form an increasing proportion of employment costs.

Incentives and fringe benefits need to be firmly incorporated within payment policy with the personnel manager reviewing everything that is provided and proposed. What is it? What is it for? Does it achieve its purpose? Is that purpose worth achieving? Does it fit within the overall payment policy? Who administers the feature being considered? Is that the appropriate person? How much does each feature cost? How much trouble does it cause? What benefit does it confer?

Unless incentive and fringe benefit provisions are positively managed, they can become an expensive and ineffective element in the employment relationship.

Summary propositions

33.1 Incentives cannot be understood in isolation from the whole of the working relationship between employer and employee. Incentive arrangements demonstrate what managers believe about that relationship.
33.2 Typical problems with incentive schemes include having to cope with operational inefficiencies, fluctuation in earnings, the effect of incentives on the quality of work produced and on the quality of working life for the producers, as well as the selective nature of incentives and the frequent obscurity of the incentive arrangement itself.
33.3 Performance-related payments tend to be inflationary and present operational problems when overall organisational effectiveness declines.
33.4 Methods of payment by results include individual time-saving, group incentives, measured daywork, plant-wide schemes, productivity schemes, commission and tipping.
33.5 Fringe benefits are not intended to have a direct motivational effect, but are tax-efficient ways of providing additions to the remuneration package and some degree of choice within it. They are more common and diverse for management employees than for others and can cause considerable problems of relative status.
33.6 Fringe benefits include cars, mileage allowance, profit-sharing and many other small perquisites.
33.7 Fringe benefits are an area where personnel managers feel they have little discretion and influence.
33.8 Unless incentive payments and fringe benefits are managed positively, this increasingly costly aspect of the remuneration package can become an expensive and ineffective element in the employment relationship.

References

Armstrong, M. and Murlis, H. (1994) *Reward Management: A handbook of remuneration strategy and practice*, London: Kogan Page.
Cannell, M. and Long, P. (1991) 'What's changed about incentive pay?', *Personnel Management*, October.
Cannell, M. and Wood, S. (1992) *Incentive Pay: Impact and evolution*, London: IPM.
Gill, L. (1989) 'Fitting the perk to the person', *The Times*, 31 October.
Incomes Data Services (1988) 'Performance pay', *IDS Focus 49*, London: Incomes Data Services.
Incomes Data Services (1992a) 'Skill-based pay', *IDS Study 500*, London: Incomes Data Services.
Incomes Data Services (1992b) 'Profit-related pay', *IDS Study 520*, London: Incomes Data Services.
Incomes Data Services (1992c) 'Sharing profits', *IDS Focus 64*, London: Incomes Data Services.

Incomes Data Services (1993) 'Performance appraisal for manual workers', *IDS Study 543*, London: Incomes Data Services.

Incomes Data Services (1994) 'Bonus schemes', *IDS Study 547*, London: Incomes Data Services.

Incomes Data Services (1997a) *IDS Report 738*, London: Incomes Data Services.

Incomes Data Services (1997b) 'London allowances', *IDS Study 627*, London: Incomes Data Services.

Kaplan, R. S. and Norton, D. P. (1996) *The Balanced Scorecard: Translating Strategy into Action*, Newhaven, CT: Harvard Business School Press.

Lewis, P. (1991) 'Performance-related pay: pretexts and pitfalls', *Employee Relations*, Vol. 13, No. 1.

Lupton, T. and Bowey, A. M. (1975) *Wages and Salaries*, Harmondsworth: Penguin Books.

Marsden, D. and Richardson, R. (1991), *Motivation and Performance Related Pay in the Public Sector: a case study of the Inland Revenue*, London School of Economics.

Torrington, D. P. (1995) 'Pay for performance or skill?' *Finance and Administration*, July–October, pp. 60–2.

Woodley, C. (1990) 'The cafeteria route to compensation', *Personnel Management*, May, pp. 42–5.

General discussion topics

1. What are the relative advantages of (a) a system of straight salary that is the same each month, and (b) a system of salary with an individual performance-related addition so that the total payment each month varies?
2. In what circumstances might it be appropriate to base individual payment on team performance?
3. What do you think about Peter, Patrick, Joanne and Henry?

CHAPTER 34

Pensions and sick pay

The provision of pensions and sick pay has been viewed as the mark of a 'good' employer, and yet employees have not until recently seen these as benefits which attracted their interest. There is now, however, an increasing public awareness of pensions matters, stimulated by governmental actions and legislation, the media and the pensions industry. The potential for fraud in occupational pension schemes has been highlighted by the alarming evidence discovered after Robert Maxwell's death, and some serious problems with personal pension schemes have also come to light. Sick pay too has attracted greater attention since statutory sick pay was introduced in 1986, and especially since the SSP scheme was revised in 1991, 1994 and 1995, each time placing a greater financial burden for sick pay directly on the employer.

This chapter is organised into two principal sections. In the first we look at the reasons for increased awareness about pensions provision, various categories of pension schemes, pensions information and the role of the personnel department. In the second we discuss the role of the personnel department in state and occupational sick pay, and then look at sick pay and absence monitoring and control.

Increased awareness about pensions provision

Pensions are increasingly seen as 'deferred pay' rather than a reward for a lifetime of employment (IDS 1982), and as such are attracting more attention from employees and trade unions, and are seen as more negotiable than in the past. As the state pension scheme is changed and changed again, and its future form becomes more uncertain, greater attention is being paid to company schemes. Concern over the future of the State Earnings Related Pension Scheme has directed attention to other schemes, including both occupational and personal schemes. The nature of work has changed dramatically since the first company pension schemes emerged. There has been a move from lifetime employment with one employer towards greater job mobility for all groups of employees. Sometimes this movement is deliberate, for example, the young executive who joins a new company to further her career; sometimes it is involuntary, as in the case of redundancy. This has prompted an interest in the way that company pension schemes provide for those employees who have had more than one, frequently many, employers. The increasing likelihood of fairly lengthy unemployment between one job and the next, together with increasing attention to the role of women who characteristically have broken records of employment due to family commitments, have highlighted the assumptions on which most company pension schemes are based. The plight of those who, having been made redundant at 50 are never to find work again, has made people more aware of the potential role of pensions schemes.

Our expectations in general have risen, with ideas of early retirement from choice, 'while you're still young enough to enjoy it', and increasing expectations that retirement should not necessarily be a time for 'tightening your belt', but a time to reap the rewards from one's work and to do things that there was never time for before. Retirement is now seen more as a beginning than an end, and consequently the pensions that support this new beginning are seen as more important at an earlier age than before. In addition to this, as information is more generally available, employees expect more information about their pension schemes and about the benefits to which they will eventually become entitled.

ACTIVITY BOX 34.1

Robert Noble-Warren (1986) talks about 'life-time planning' as a series of 'rest and recuper-ation' periods throughout life as well as the planning of financial provision. Lifetime plan-ning has to start with a statement of your life's objectives.

What are your life's objectives and what work, rest and financial plans can you make to achieve these?

Types of pension scheme

There are four levels of pension schemes: state schemes, company pension schemes, industry pension schemes and individual schemes.

State schemes

The state runs two schemes: a basic scheme and SERPS (State Earnings Related Pension Scheme). Every employee is obliged to contribute a standard amount to the basic scheme which currently provides an old age pension on reaching the age of 65 for men and 60 for women. By 2020 the pensionable age for both men and women will be 65 and in the ten years prior to this date there will be a gradual phasing in of the new pensionable age for women.

For those employees who earn over a certain amount (known as the lower earnings limit) a percentage of salary earned between this limit and a higher salary level (known as the upper earnings limit) is also payable. Both these pay-ments are deducted from wages as part of the national insurance contribution. The individual who has paid into SERPS as well as the basic scheme will receive a higher pension from the state on retirement in proportion to the additional amount that they have contributed. The employer also makes a contribution into the state pension scheme in a way similar to the individual employee. The state pension scheme is organised on a pay-as-you-go basis. This means that there is no state pension fund as such, and the money that is paid to today's pensioners comes from today's taxes and national insurance contributions. The money that will be paid to today's contributors, when they become pensioners, will come not from the investment of their and their employers' contributions, but from the contributions of the workforce and their employers in the future. This approach to pension provision is causing great concern as the number of pensioners is increasing rapidly. Hopegood (1994) notes that at present there are 3.3 people of working age to every pensioner, a figure which reduces to 2.7 by 2030. There has been much criticism of the state pension scheme (see, for example, Butler and Pirie 1983), and the last Conservative Government at one time put forward proposals for the abolition of SERPS. The Social Security Act 1986 brought in a phased reduction of benefits under SERPS from April 1988. Implications of this and other aspects of the Act are discussed in Amy (1986).

Company schemes

There is a number of advantages to companies in setting up pensions schemes. Nash (1989) gives a good description of these, which include pensions as part of the mechanism to recruit and retain good people, the generation of goodwill and loyalty, the improvement of industrial relations, and a mechanism for managing early retirement and redundancy. In addition to these the provision of such a scheme enhances the employer's image, which can have pay-offs in many areas.

Company schemes vary considerably, and we shall consider their specific arrangements in more depth in the section on 'Varieties of Company Pension Schemes'. They are normally funded by contributions from the employee (say, 6 per cent of salary) and a similar contribution from the employer. Sometimes large companies and public sector organisations offer non-contributory pensions, in which case the employee pays nothing. In general, company schemes provide an additional retirement pension on top of the basic state pension, and sometimes on top of SERPS. Most often, however, the company will avoid employee and employer payments into SERPS by means of 'contracting out'. A company can contract out of SERPS only if its pension scheme meets certain requirements. The Occupational Pensions Board (OPB) will decide whether contracting out will be allowed, and if so they will issue a contracting out certificate. The rules on contracting out were changed in April 1997 (IRS 1997) and these require employers to pass a new test relating to overall scheme quality, the 'reference test scheme', rather than the old test, which was based on being able to pay 'guaranteed minimum pension'. It is argued that the new scheme is expected to produce pensions which are equal to or better than SERPS. Contracting out increased by 80 per cent between 1986/7 and 1992/3 and has reached 15.5 million employees (DSS, undated).

Company schemes generally provide better and wider-ranging benefits than the state schemes and they provide some flexibility. They are most often found in large organisations and the public sector, but some smaller organisations also run such schemes. Garlick (1986) reports that over eleven million employees are members of company pension schemes, but Hayward (1989) records that there are still around ten million employees who are solely dependent on state provision. Men and women have equal access to company schemes, and the Social Security Act 1989 brought further changes which enforced equal treatment of men and women in the schemes. The Pensions Act 1995 consolidates two equality measures. First, the incorporation of previous European Court of Justice cases (for example the Barber judgment). This overrides the rules of schemes to incorporate equality in the access to schemes and in the treatment of scheme members. In particular benefits must be equal for members from 1990. Second, the equalisation of state pension ages, mentioned earlier, is consolidated in the

Act. In spite of these changes in legislation men and women will continue to fare differently in terms of pensions benefits due to the patterns of women's employment being different than male patterns on which pensions schemes are typically based (see, for example, Ginn and Arber 1996). There is a tendency for a higher proportion of managerial workers than other groups to be in pensions schemes. Blue-collar workers are least likely to be in schemes. Part-time employees are sometimes excluded, as are those on temporary contracts, although this very much depends on the employer.

Company schemes rarely pay their pensioners in the pay-as-you-go manner operated by the state, but create a pension fund, which is managed separately from the business. The advantage of this is that should the company go broke, the pension fund cannot be seized to pay debtors because it is not part of the company. The money in the pension fund is invested and held in trust for the employees of the company at the time of their retirement. Very large organisations will self-administer their pension fund, and appoint an investment manager or a fund manager. The manager will plan how to invest the money in the fund to get the best return and to ensure that the money that is needed to pay pensions and other benefits will be available when required. An actuary can provide mortality tables and other statistical information in order to assist planning. Smaller organisations may appoint an insurance company or a bank to administer their pension funds, and so use their expertise. Pension funds can be invested in a variety of different ways, and Garlick comments that: 'They often deploy assets greater than the market capitalization of the companies that sponsor them and have come to dominate investment on the stock market' (Garlick 1986, p. 7).

The fund may also be used to purchase property and lend mortgages to others. Government and local government stock with specified redemption dates are also useful forms of investment as they may be selected to provide cash when claims are expected. Toulson argues that the investments made by the pension fund should meet the following criteria: 'Wise investment includes at least three criteria. Investments must be safe; they must be profitable; they must also be capable of being realized when cash is required to pay benefits' (Toulson 1982, p. 8). Booth (1986), however, notes that an increasing number of funds are investing in venture capital projects, which is basically investment in new businesses. This long-term investment is much more risky, and Booth does suggest that only a small proportion of overall funds should be invested in this manner. The structure of some pension schemes and the success of the investments have meant large surpluses of money building up in the scheme. This has enabled both employer and employee to take a contributions holiday, as at Lucas Industries who have taken a two-year contribution holiday (quoted in Garlick 1986).

Another advantage of setting up a pension fund, apart from the protection of the money, is that if the scheme is approved by the Superannuation Funds Office (SFO) of the Inland Revenue, various tax advantages can be claimed. Both employer and employee can claim tax relief on the contributions that they make to the scheme, and there are also tax advantages for the pensions benefits that are paid out.

In spite of all the advantages of company pension schemes Hearn (1992) gives of range of examples where companies have been guilty of pension fraud. The best-known example of this is the fraud discovered on the death of Robert Maxwell where the company pension funds had been used for other purposes. The Maxwell scandal led to the formation of the Pension Review Committee, headed by Professor Goode. This committee reported back in Autumn 1993 and after a period of consultation further pensions legislation is expected. Recommendations include the replacement of the Occupational Pensions Board by a Pensions Regulator with greater powers, including, for example, the power to carry out spot-checks and investigations. Further details of recommendations can be found in Allen (1994). The Pensions Act 1995 was an outcome of the Goode Report.

The major provisions of the 1995 Act are:

1. The statutory right for pension scheme members to select a proportion of pension trustees, who would normally be employees of the company. These trustees will have a right to paid time off work for their trustee duties, and appropriate training. They will be protected from dismissal for performing their trustee duties. The limits of authority of pension trustees are defined (see for example IRS 1995).
2. Pension schemes are required to have a formal procedure for resolving disputes.
3. Minimum funding levels of pensions are defined.
4. A new requirement for schemes to increase pension in payment earned after a certain date, up to a limit of 5 per cent per year.
5. Advisers to the scheme are required to 'blow the whistle' if they are concerned about malpractice.
6. Compensation for pension fund deficits is provided for in cases of employer's insolvency where there has been misappropriation of pension fund assets.
7. Provision for the courts in divorce proceedings to earmark pension benefits for divorced spouses of pension scheme members.
8. The equality clauses relating to equal access and treatment and retirement ages, discussed above.
9. The setting of a new watchdog – the Occupational Pensions Regulatory Authority (OPRA) – which has wider-ranging powers than the old Occupational Pensions Board. (The key duties of OPRA are shown in the Window on Practice below.)
10. The setting up of a Pensions Compensation Board, distinct from OPRA, which will be able to make payments to pension schemes which are wound up due to the insolvency of the employer, and where there are insufficient funds to meet pension commitments because of fraud or a similar offence.

For a fuller discussion see IRS (1995).

WINDOW ON PRACTICE

The key duties of OPRA are to:

1. Investigate reports of serious breaches of duties of trustees, employers and advisers connected with pension schemes.
2. Penalise trustees (both individuals and organisations) for wrongdoing.
3. Dismiss trustees for breach of duty and appoint substitutions.
4. Maintain a register of disqualified trustees.
5. Initiate criminal proceeding against individuals who misappropriate pension fund assets.
6. Authorise older pension schemes to be wound up, or substitute alternative arrangements where this is in the members' interests.

Industry-wide schemes

Sometimes employers and employees will contribute to an 'industry-wide' pension scheme, as an alternative to a company scheme. The reasoning behind these schemes is described very well by Incomes Data Services when they say:

> These schemes are particularly useful in industries where there is a large number of small companies, and employees tend to be mobile within the confines of the industry. The companies would not be large enough to run their own schemes, and the employees would not welcome being tied to a company pension scheme
> (IDS 1982, p. 13)

The operation of such schemes is very similar to company schemes except that a number of different companies contribute to the same scheme.

Personal pensions

Increasing attention is being paid to the possibility of personal pensions. Self-employed people have always needed to be concerned with making their own provisions for retirement, as they are excluded from joining SERPS. More general attention has been focused on this area due to increasing job mobility and the perceived greater portability of personal pensions. A personal pension is arranged, usually through an insurance company, and the individual pays regular amounts into their own 'pension fund' in the same way that they would with a company fund. The employer may or may not also make a contribution to the fund. At present there are very few employers who take part in this arrangement, but in July 1984 the Government issued a consultative document on personal pensions (DHSS 1984), suggesting that all employees should have the right to make their own pension arrangements, and from 1988 these recommendations have become operational. There has been a very mixed reaction to the proposals. The Institute of Directors, for example, has been in favour. Moody comments on less favourable responses when he says:

> The concerns seem to be about whether occupational schemes will be damaged, whether there will be administrative chaos, whether individuals will be misled by plausible salesmen and finish up with inadequate pensions, whether personal pensions will prove to be an irrelevance for pension scheme members or even whether they could result in the erosion of the state earnings-related scheme.
> (Moody 1984, p. 34)

The IPM working party, in response to the Government's consultative document, suggested that a better solution would be to allow members of company pension schemes to make additional pension provision via personal schemes (quoted in Moody 1984).

Over half a million people have taken out personal pensions since 1988, most transferring when they moved from their current employer, whilst some have opted out of their employer's scheme. There has been considerable concern recently that the pensions advice given to those taking out personal pensions has been inadequate. Of special concern are those who have opted out of well-regarded schemes such as the mineworkers, nurses and teachers. Marsh *et al.* (1994) note that some have clearly lost out by their actions, and compensation is being claimed in many cases. The Securities and Investments Board investigation in

1994 recommended that some 350,000 (this figure has now increased to 600,000) investors who had either transferred or opted out of their occupational pension scheme in favour of a personal pension must have their cases reviewed in respect of mis-selling. Insurance companies and others selling pensions have been asked to review these cases with the priority being where the investor is retired or has died. Redress is required to compensate for the financial loss suffered due to unsatisfactory advice. Where possible, individuals are to be reinstated into their old occupational pension scheme, and if this is feasible the company scheme will need to calculate the amount required for reinstatement, which if reasonable (according to SIB guidelines), will be paid by the seller of the personal pension. However, few of these cases had been resolved by 1997, and in June of this year the Government called in the large insurance companies to put pressure on them to resolve all cases by 1998. Each was required to submit plans to demonstrate how the target would be achieved. By July the Government named two insurance companies who had so far evaded the issue and failed to make any genuine attempt to identify how they could meet the target date.

Varieties of company pension scheme

We have already looked at the ways that money is paid into the pension fund, and we shall now look at the way that money is paid out in the form of a pension. There is a variety of schemes which each pay out money to pensioners on a different basis. The most common type of scheme is that based on the final salary of the employee, but there are three other forms of well-known scheme. These are a flat rate scheme, an average salary scheme and a money purchase scheme. Table 34.1 shows all these schemes and other forms of pension that are available.

Table 34.1 Pensions provision

Provider	Type of scheme	Additional benefits
State provision	Basic pension Earnings-related pension SERPS	No facility for additional benefits on top of SERPS
Company provision	Flat rate scheme Average salary scheme Money purchase scheme Final salary scheme	Sometimes additional benefits provided by 'top-hat' scheme or additional voluntary contributions
Industry-wide provision	Flat rate scheme Average salary scheme Money purchase scheme Final salary scheme	Sometimes additional benefits provided by 'top-hat' scheme or additional voluntary contributions
Personal provision	Employee-funded money purchase scheme Employee and employer funded money purchase scheme	Sometimes additional benefits provided by further investment in the scheme

Flat rate schemes

Flat rate schemes take into account the length of service of the employee, but not the wage or salary that they were earning prior to retirement. A fixed rate of money is payable each year on retirement which is determined purely by the employee's length of service.

Average salary schemes

Average salary schemes take into account both length of service and the salary that the employee has earned in each of those years. The critical figure is the average of all the yearly salaries that the employee has earned. They are usually worked out at one-fiftieth of each annual salary the employee has earned. If there was little inflation and the employee had only made a short trip up the promotion ladder, the average salary would be close to the final salary of the employee. In this case a pension that equated to a proportion of the average salary may be quite acceptable. In a case of high inflation and an employee who had started at the bottom and worked her way up to the top, 'a pension that equated to a proportion of her average salary would be less than acceptable. Some companies will now re-evaluate in line with inflation the contributions made into such a scheme, but many do not, and re-evaluation takes no account of career progression. See Figure 34.1 for an example of an average salary scheme.

Final salary schemes

A final salary scheme, as the name suggests, takes into account the employees' final salary as well as the length of time that they have contributed to the

```
25-year period
Final salary (for 4 years)        = £12,000
Salary (for 10 years)             = £10,000
Salary (for 11 years)             = £ 6,000
   4 years' contribution at £12,000 =          1/50 of £12,000 x  4 = £   950
10 years' contribution at £10,000 =           1/50 of £10,000 x 10 = £2,000
11 years' contribution at £  6,000 =          1/50 of £  6,000 x 11 = £1,320
                                              Pension per annum of   £3,070


40-year period
Final 25 years as above                                          = £3,070
Salary (for 8 years)              = £4,000
Salary (for 7 years)              = £2,000
8 years' contribution at £4,000 =             1/50 of £4,000 x 8  = £  640
7 years' contribution at £2,000 =             1/50 of £2,000 x 7  = £  280
                                              Penion per annum of    £3,990
```

Figure 34.1 Average salary schemes: over a 25-year and a 40-year period

pension fund. For each year of contribution employees earn the right to receive a specified proportion of their final salary as a pension. The better schemes offer one-sixtieth. This means that for each year of contribution to the fund the employee is entitled to receive one-sixtieth of their final salary in the form of a pension. Some worked examples are shown in Figure 34.2. The other commonly used fraction is one-eightieth. Employees in schemes that are based on one-sixtieth would, after forty years of contribution, be able to receive two-thirds of their final salary as a pension, and this is the maximum that is allowable (Toulson 1982). Employees in schemes that are based on one-eightieth would receive half their final salary as a pension after forty years of contributions.

Money purchase schemes

Money purchase schemes are organised in a totally different way from the schemes above, and there are no promises about what the final level of pension will be. Employees and employers contribute to these schemes in much the same way as to the other types of these schemes that is, a certain percentage of current salary. The pension benefits from the scheme are entirely dependent on the money that has been contributed and the way that it has been invested. If investments have been very profitable and there has been little inflation, then the final pension may turn out to be adequate. Money purchase schemes result in a lump sum available at retirement and this is used to buy a pension. However, in times of very high inflation this type of scheme has severe drawbacks, and this accounted for their decline in popularity in the 1970s. Money purchase schemes are, however, seen as more flexible and more easily transferable, and there has been a revival of interest in such schemes (IDS 1982) as the most suitable basis for personal, portable pensions. The Social Security Act 1986 simplified the requirements for opting out of SERPS, which facilitated the use of money purchase and other personal schemes.

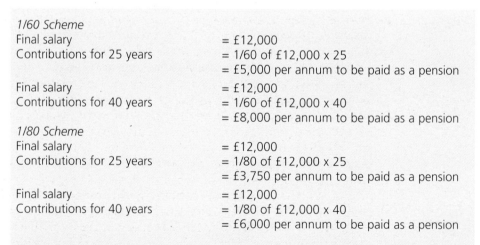

1/60 Scheme
Final salary	= £12,000
Contributions for 25 years	= 1/60 of £12,000 x 25
	= £5,000 per annum to be paid as a pension
Final salary	= £12,000
Contributions for 40 years	= 1/60 of £12,000 x 40
	= £8,000 per annum to be paid as a pension

1/80 Scheme
Final salary	= £12,000
Contributions for 25 years	= 1/80 of £12,000 x 25
	= £3,750 per annum to be paid as a pension
Final salary	= £12,000
Contributions for 40 years	= 1/80 of £12,000 x 40
	= £6,000 per annum to be paid as a pension

Figure 34.2 Final salary schemes: examples of various contribution periods with a 1/60 and a 1/80 scheme

In addition to the pension scheme, which forms the major investment for retirement purposes, there are two other types of contribution which may be made for this purpose.

Top-hat schemes

Noble-Warren (1986) notes that top-hat schemes were originally used to top up an individual's pension entitlements with a new employer to ensure that they matched what the individual would have received with the old employer. Top-hat schemes are operated like money purchase schemes, and are particularly flexible because they may be funded by a single or occasional payment, and there is no commitment to pay a certain amount each month while in employment.

Additional voluntary contributions

Additional voluntary contributions are a different way of improving retirement benefits. Incomes Data Services points out that although this may well be an efficient form of saving, there are a number of disadvantages:

> ▶ There is normally no employer's contribution.
> ▶ Once a person starts contributing, he [sic] is not usually allowed to stop unless he [sic] leaves the company.
> ▶ He [sic] cannot normally get the money back until retirement age. (IDS 1982, pp. 15–66).

Company pension schemes and the problem of early leavers

We mentioned at the beginning of this chapter that pensions were traditionally seen as a reward for a lifetime's employment, and the way that pensions are structured reflects this. Early leavers may have one or more of three options in making their pension arrangements when they begin work for a new employer. One option can be claiming back the contributions that the individual has made into the pension scheme, and sometimes interest may be paid on these. Deductions are also made in accordance with tax laws, and of course, the employer's contribution is lost. Another alternative may be opting for a preserved pension. With a final salary scheme, if there were no inflation, and if the individual progressed very little up the career ladder, a preserved pension from an old employer plus a pension from the recent employer would equate well with the pension they would have received had they been with the new employer for the whole period. However, if these conditions are not met, which in recent times they have not been, individuals who have had more than one employer lose out on the pension stakes. In some cases it is possible to transfer pension contributions to another scheme, and a transferred pension is often financially the best option. However, transfer value is not necessarily the same as original value, due to the way schemes use different sets of actuarial assumptions.

The disadvantages of leaving one employer's pension scheme and joining a new one have been one of the driving forces behind the recent interest in personal, portable pensions.

Pensions information and the role of the personnel department

Employees expect more information about their pensions, both in general terms and about their specific circumstances. The personnel department has become increasingly involved in pensions, which until recently have been mainly the province of the finance department or the secretariat. This involvement partly stems from increasing use of the computer, and the development of integrated, or at least linked systems, covering personnel, pensions and payroll. It also stems from greater trade union and employee interest in, and awareness of, pensions, and the potential of pensions to become another area for negotiation. As information becomes ever increasingly available, employees expect to know more about the benefits to which they will become entitled at retirement. The computer is ideal to provide up-to-date statements of contributions and entitlements, and many employers now send these to employees on an annual basis. Pensions modelling also enables employees to be given information about the pension consequences of selecting certain leaving dates. Pensions is increasingly becoming an area where choices have to be made and personnel managers can be in a good position to provide information and advice. The importance of pensions information, and a user-friendly approach to presenting it, is described by Hunt (1988).

Some employers provide an annual report of the pension fund for employees, but many do not. Garlick notes that accountants suggest that there should be four essential components in this annual report:

1. The general activity, history and development of the scheme contained in a trustees' report.
2. The value and transactions of the fund covered by audited accounts.
3. The actuary's report showing the progress of a scheme towards meeting its potential liabilities and obligations to members.
4. A separate report setting out the investment policy of the fund and its performance relative to its stated policy.

(Garlick 1986, p. 10)

Pension schemes need to be reviewed frequently to ascertain what benefits they are providing for the company in the light of changing circumstances. Personnel managers can draw on their specialist knowledge of labour markets, the changing nature of employment and the characteristics of the company's manpower to help assess the appropriateness of the pension scheme. Moody (1984a) suggests that a pensions checklist could be used, such as that in Table 34.2. Although written in 1984 this checklist still represents good practice. You

Table 34.2 Pensions checklist

▶ Are pensions related to final salary?

▶ If so, is the fraction used both adequate and competitive?

▶ Do portions of a year count for benefit?

▶ Is entry to the scheme monthly, quarterly or must people wait until the scheme anniversary?

▶ Does the scheme provide immediate cover for lump-sum death benefits on joining service (if otherwise eligible)?

Table 34.2 Continued

▶ Is the lump-sum death benefit payable under discretionary trust thereby avoiding delay or capital transfer tax?

▶ Can part-time staff join the scheme? If so, is membership compulsory and how are benefits calculated when members change from full- to part-time status, or vice versa?

▶ Can life cover continue for a period after leaving service for people made redundant?

▶ Does the scheme provide for the maximum cash permitted in lieu of pension on retirement?

▶ Does the scheme give fair value for money to people leaving service before retirement?

▶ Do the rules contain the requisite transfer in and out provisions?

▶ Are the definitive deed and rules available or, as is often the case, are they still in draft form?

▶ Is there a simplified and readable explanatory booklet describing the scheme?

▶ Are members given any form of annual report from the trustees and regular statements of their benefits?

▶ Are members in any way involved in the running of the pension scheme?

▶ Is the personnel department closely involved in pensions policy and the running of the scheme?

▶ Is the scheme used positively as an aid to recruitment and are leavers fully aware of what they may be losing?

▶ Is there a pre-retirement training scheme?

▶ Is there any form of post-retirement escalation on pensions in course of payment or pro-retirement escalation for people who have left service?

▶ Does the scheme contain the flexibility to cope with early retirement problems?

▶ Are there provisions for pensions to be augmented at the discretion of the trustees?

▶ Do the rules permit members to make additional voluntary contributions (which attract full tax relief) to augment their benefits in whatever way they choose?

Source: Moody (1984). Reproduced with the permission of IPD Publications.

will note that the item 'Are members in any way involved in the running of the pension scheme?' now has statutory footing in respect of the appointment of trustees, usually employees, elected by members.

Sick pay and the role of the personnel department

As with pensions schemes, the provision of sick pay is seen as the mark of a good employer. Sick pay is an important issue due to the need for control and administration of absence. Recent figures (Industrial Society 1996) suggest that sickness absence represents 3.9 per cent of working time, although there are large differences between sector and job type. The personnel manager and the personnel department have a variety of roles to play in relation to sick pay, particularly since the introduction of statutory sick pay in 1983 when state sick pay in addition to occupational sick pay have been administered by the employer.

Advice

The personnel manager is the most appropriate person to advise employees about SSP and the occupational scheme (if there is one) and how these schemes apply in individual circumstances. In particular, managers may need to advise staff who are nearing the end of their sick pay entitlement as to the remainder of their benefit and what special arrangements may be made in their case.

Home visits

Personnel managers, or welfare officers, may visit employees at home, who have been away sick for a considerable period. Such visits are partly intended just to keep in touch with the employee and their progress, but also for the advisory purposes outlined above, and for planning purposes. For example, it might be appropriate to discuss with the employee the possibility of early retirement when sick pay runs out. These visits are sometimes organised on a more regular basis, say every month, and may be included as part of the sick pay procedure. In these circumstances they are intended partly as a deterrent to those claiming sick pay under false pretences. Because of this, trade union officials are generally unenthusiastic about home visits.

Dismissal and transfer

The personnel manager will be involved in the dismissal of those employees who are unlikely to be able to return. Dismissal would be on the grounds of incapability. This is a serious step for the personnel manager to consider, and Incomes Data Services suggest the following aspects are worthy of consideration:

- The nature, length and effect of the illness or disability on the employee's past and likely future service to the company.
- The importance of the job and the possibilities of temporary replacement.
- Whether it is against the employee's, the organisation's or even the public's interest to go on employing the individual.

In many circumstances the personnel manager will be able to investigate a much happier option, that of finding suitable alternative work in the organisation to which the employee may be transferred when sufficiently fit.

Sick pay and absence policy and procedures

Personnel managers are well placed to contribute to or instigate the development of occupational sick pay policy and of the procedures used to administer both occupational sick pay and SSP. Personnel managers, too, have a part to play in such procedures, apart from the obvious administrative role, for example they may be involved in interviewing employees with a high level of absence prior to the initiation of disciplinary procedures, in cases where there is a lack of evidence of genuine sickness.

Administrative procedures

The personnel manager will be the organisation's expert on SSP, and will normally be responsible for its administration, collating information from line managers and feeding relevant information into the payroll section, unless this is done electronically. There are several specialised computer packages available to assist personnel departments with this administrative responsibility, and the introduction of SSP spurred many departments into purchasing a computer. Absence and sick pay recording is particularly important as the DSS may ask to inspect records going back for up to three years. Where possible the records kept for the DSS should be combined with any additional absence and sick pay information so that there is only one sick pay record for each individual, thus avoiding the problems of duplication.

Monitoring of sick pay and absence

The monitoring and analysis of absence and sick pay is an important aspect of personnel work. Based on this information the personnel manager will be able to assist line managers by providing guidelines along which to take action regarding such matters as suspected abuse of the sick pay system.

Disciplinary procedures

The personnel manager will be involved at some stage in disciplinary matters resulting from the abuse of the sick pay scheme, depending on the requirements of the organisation's disciplinary procedure.

State and statutory sick pay

State or statutory sick pay was first administered by employers in April 1983 as a result of the Housing Benefits Act 1982. Since then the administration of the scheme has been amended by the Health and Social Security Act 1984 and the Social Security Act 1985. The changes came into force in April 1986. Under the SSP scheme the employer payed the employee, when sick, an amount equivalent to that which they would in the past have received from the DSS. The employer reclaimed the money that has been paid out from national insurance contributions which would normally have been forwarded to the government. Although low, state sickness benefit does take into account the needs of the person involved, so that a married person with two children would receive more pay than a single person. Since SSP was first administered by employers the scheme has changed more than once. The most recent changes in April 1994 result in the employer taking the full financial responsibility for SSP for the first four weeks of absence, after which they can claim back 100 per cent of sick pay paid from the state (see for example IDS 1994). Most employees are entitled to state sickness benefit; however, there are some exceptions which include employees who fall sick outside the EU, employees who are sick during an industrial dispute, employees over pensionable age and employees whose earnings are below the earnings limit. SSP is built around the concepts of qualifying days, waiting days, certification, linked periods, transfer to the DSS and record periods.

Qualifying days

Qualifying days are those days on which the employee would normally have worked, except for the fact that he or she was sick. For many Monday to Friday employees this is very straightforward. However, it is more complex to administer for those on some form of rotating week or shift system. Sick pay is only payable for qualifying days.

Waiting days

Three waiting days have to pass before the employee is entitled to receive sick pay. These three days must be qualifying days, and on the fourth qualifying day the employee is entitled to sickness benefit, should he or she still be away from work due to sickness.

Certification

A doctor's certificate for sickness is required after seven days of sick absence. Prior to this the employee provides self-certification. This involves notifying the employer of absence due to sickness by the first day on which benefit is due – that is, immediately following the three waiting days.

Linked periods

The three waiting days do not always apply. If the employee has had a period of incapacity from work (PIW) within the previous eight weeks, then the two periods are linked and treated as just one period for SSP purposes, and so the three waiting days do not have to pass again.

Transfer to the DSS

The employer does not have to administer SSP for every employee indefinitely. Where the employee has been absent due to sickness for a continuous or linked period of twenty-eight weeks the responsibility for payment passes from the employer to the DSS. A continuous period of twenty-eight weeks' sickness is clearly identifiable. It is not so clear when linked periods are involved. An employee who was sick for five days, back at work for four weeks, sick for one day, at work for seven weeks and then sick for two days would have a linked period of incapacity of eight days. Alternatively, an employee who was sick for four days, back at work for ten weeks and then sick for five days would have a period of incapacity this time of five days.

Record periods

The DSS requires employers to keep SSP records for three years so that these can be inspected. Gill and Chadwick (1986) point out that the new linking and transfer rules mean that, in theory, an employer could be paying SSP to an individual for almost ten years before twenty-eight weeks' linked PIW came to an end. The DSS, however, do not require records for the whole of a linked PIW if this is greater than three years.

In 1995 further modifications were made to the SSP procedures (see for example IRS 1995). In particular the previous two levels of SSP payable were reduced to one (the higher) level, resulting in extra costs for employers. In addition a refund scheme for employers is now available which applies if SSP made exceed a certain proportion of national insurance contributions.

Occupational sick pay

Occupational sick pay (OSP) is administered in a variety of different ways and the employee's pay while sick can vary between statutory benefit (as above) and full normal pay. Most schemes are individual to the employer and are administered according to different rules from state sick pay. However, with the introduction of SSP, Chadwick argues: 'However, as I hope I have illustrated, two different schemes, OSP and SSP, with totally differing sets of rules and regulations, can only cause confusion for your employees and, perhaps, additional employee relations problems' (Chadwick 1983, p. 29).

The introduction of SSP was an ideal opportunity for employers to review their sick pay arrangements, tighten up procedures and reconsider benefits. A number of employers, however, take the view that occupational sick pay will be abused and either fail to introduce a system or are very cautious about improving it. Employers are understandably concerned about the effects of high absence levels, which increase costs due to temporary cover, overtime or overmanning, and due to delayed or lost production. Additional problems are created by the need for reorganisation when employees are absent. However, some authors argue that this problem is exaggerated or has only a temporary effect: 'A common myth, often elevated into a "fact" by certain employers during negotiations, is that the introduction of, or improvement to an occupational sick-pay scheme will result in increased absenteeism' (Cunningham 1981, p. 55). Incomes Data Services have a slightly different view: 'Any increase in benefit or a reduction of waiting days is normally matched by a marked rise in absenteeism from the date of implementation, but this tends to fall back towards previous levels after a number of months' (IDS 1979, p. 12).

Some industries are better than others in the provision of sick pay, for example shipbuilding, leather and textiles, clothing and footwear are less well provided for than insurance, banking, gas, electricity, water, mining and public administration (DHSS 1977). Similarly, some grades of employee fare better than others. Higher-paid workers are more likely to be in a scheme (DHSS 1977), and, in particular, white-collar and management staff are still better provided for than most manual workers, with a number of employers running two separate sick pay schemes.

ACTIVITY BOX 34.2

▶ How would you argue in favour of harmonisation of sick pay provision?

▶ What objections may be raised against such a scheme and how would you deal with these?

Occupational sick pay schemes vary according to waiting days, period of service required, amount of benefit available, length of benefit entitlement, the funding of the scheme and administrative procedures.

Waiting days

Many occupational sick pay schemes have no waiting days at all, and the employee is paid from the first day of sickness. This is one area where there is a clear difference between manual and non-manual schemes, and Incomes Data Services comment: 'The manual unions, in particular, see the use of waiting days as the most obvious difference between staff and manual sick-pay schemes' (IDS 1979, p. 57). Many manual schemes still have three waiting days in line with the SSP regulations.

Period of service required

Some employers provide sick pay for sickness absence from the first day of employment. Others require a qualifying period to be served. For some this is a nominal period of four weeks, but the period may be three or six months, or a year or more. There is a major difference here from SSP, which is available immediately after employment has begun.

Amount of benefit

Some employers offer a flat rate benefit which is paid in addition to the money provided via SSP. Others, however, link benefits to level of pay. The problem with flat rate schemes is that they quickly become out of date and need to be renegotiated from time to time. The best schemes offer normal pay for a specified period (minus the amount received via SSP). This is very straightforward for those staff who receive a basic salary with no other additions. It is more difficult to define for those whose pay is supplemented by shift allowances or productivity bonuses. Some employers will pay basic pay only with no additions, others may pay basic plus some or all additions, or give an average of the pay that has been earned over the weeks prior to sickness.

The amount of benefit may not be the same throughout the whole period of sickness. Sometimes an employer will pay a period on full pay, and then a period on half-pay, or some other combination.

Length of entitlement

The length of entitlement to sick pay varies considerably and is often dependent on the employee's length of service, so that entitlement to sick pay gradually increases in line with total length of service. Entitlement can vary between a few weeks and a year or more. Very often smaller entitlements will be expressed in terms of the number of weeks payable within any one year. However, unused entitlement can often be carried forward from one year to the next. Public sector employees are often well-off in respect of length of benefit and many employers provide six months' full pay followed by six months' half-pay after three years of service.

Funding of schemes

Most employers run non-contributory sick pay schemes. However, a few do require contributions from their employees. The majority of sick pay schemes are based on the individual employer, but there are some industry-wide schemes. Some employers provide sick pay schemes via insurance companies by paying premiums so that employees claim their sick pay from the insurance company. There is a number of disadvantages with these schemes, including the loss of future entitlement to some state benefits.

Administrative procedures

Each employer will develop administrative procedures which suit their own particular sick pay scheme. However, a number of general points have to be considered when designing procedures, as shown in Figure 34.3.

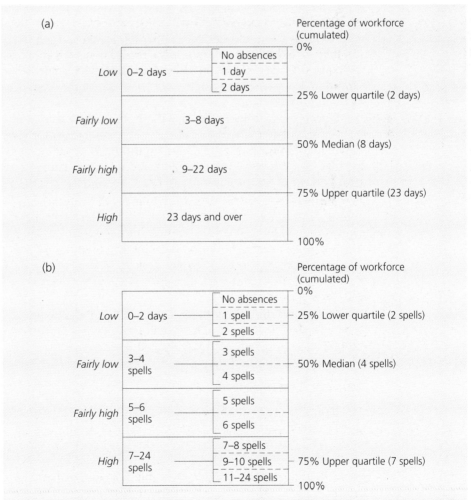

Figure 34.3 An example of the analysis of absence: (a) classification of employees by number of days lost; (b) classification of employees by number of absence spells (Behrend 1978, p. 13).

Absence and sick pay monitoring and control

The personnel department has a distinct role to play in the monitoring and control of absence levels and sick pay. In addition to the practical problems, high absence is bad for morale and suggests an employer unconcerned about the employees' behaviour. Control begins with formulating administrative procedures, as outlined in Table 34.3.

Procedures, however, are useless unless they are recognised and adhered to. It is, therefore, essential that employees know what is expected of them when they are sick – that they know whom to inform, when they need to do this and what information they need to give. If there is an employee handbook, the rules of the sick pay scheme and absence procedures should be included, and this information should be emphasised by line managers. Employees need to be aware of sick pay policy, and what is regarded as acceptable and unacceptable behaviour in relation to the scheme. They need to know how the disciplinary procedure will be implemented with regard to abuse of the sick pay scheme, and the type of information that management will use in order to decide when to invoke the procedure. Sick pay should not, however, be presented in a completely negative way, and the reasons why the organisation provides sick pay and the benefits available should be clearly presented to encourage the employee to take a responsible attitude towards the scheme, so that the use of disciplinary procedures is a rare rather than a frequent event.

Managers also need to be very clear about their role in absence and sick pay procedures, in particular regarding the transfer of information and the interviewing of absentees on their return or after a certain level of absence has been reached. Some form of periodic check needs to be made to ensure that these features are working properly and not being buried under the heavy demands of the production schedule.

Table 34.3 Formulating administrative procedures

- How, to whom and when should employees notify they are sick?
- When is a doctor's certificate required, to whom should it go?
- Any arrangements for return to work interviews?
- How is absence information to be transferred from the line manager to personnel, and from personnel to payroll?
- What should happen if employees are sick whilst on holiday or on a bank holiday?
- What sickness and absence records are to be kept and who will keep them, in what form?
- How are poor attenders to be identified, and what investigations should be made and action taken?
- What methods should be used to keep in touch with long-term sick employees?
- What arrangements are there to transfer older long-term sick employees on to a retirement pension?
- How do the OSP procedures integrate with the SSP procedures?

A further aspect of control is the monitoring of sick absence and other absence. Information for this monitoring can be used in the development of control procedures. For example, lists may be produced of those employees claiming most sick pay entitlement and managers may be asked to interview these employees in order to provide further information and explanation. Monitoring of sick absence is entirely dependent on the keeping of complete and reliable records. Useful analyses of this information can be produced by comparing different individuals; groups, such as age groups or skill level groups; departments; times of year; or comparing absence over a few years to identify trends. Comparison with the absence levels of other employers may also be illuminating. It is helpful to look at total amount of absence, number of spells of absence and length of each spell of absence. An excellent guide to the monitoring of absence is by Behrend (1978). An example of the type of analysis that Behrend has used with the help of computers is illustrated in Figure 34.3.

The computer has also been used quite extensively in absence analysis, and one example of this is by Fell (1983).

Another important factor in absence control is to consider whether sick pay policy and procedures encourage longer spells of absence than necessary due to the use of waiting periods and the backdated payment for waiting periods if they are part of a longer period of absence.

ACTIVITY BOX 34.3

Suggest an absence monitoring and control system for your organisation, or any with which you are familiar, describing the role of the line manager and the personnel department.

Summary propositions

34.1 The personnel department is becoming increasingly involved in the area of pensions.

34.2 Both the personnel manager and the line manager have a key role to play in absence control.

34.3 Pensions are still seen as the mark of a good employer, and are increasingly seen as deferred pay rather than a reward for long service.

34.4 Many employers feel a moral obligation to provide for employees when they are sick. There are also practical advantages such as a healthier workforce, being seen as a caring employer and being more able to attract new employees.

34.5 Pensions have traditionally been an area where employees have been allowed little choice. The opportunities for choice are gradually increasing, as is legislation to promote good practice

34.6 Some pension schemes have difficulty in coping with inflation and career progression, and most schemes fail to provide adequately for early leavers.

34.7 Absence control is important, as high absence levels cost money, lower morale and suggests an employer's lack of interest in their employees.

References

Allen, S. (1994) 'Sea-change for the pensions industry', *Personnel Management*, March.

Amy, R. (1986) 'Pensions after 1988: sizing up the options', *Personnel Management*, December.

Behrend, H. (1978) *How to Monitor Absence from Work: From head-count to computer*, London: IPM.

Booth, G. (1986) 'Choosing an investment manager', in Institute of Directors, *The Directors' Guide to Pensions*, London: The Director Publications Ltd.

Brown, T. (1987) 'Pensions: a fund of crucial decisions', *Personnel Management*, August.

Butler, G. and Pirie, M. (1983) *The Future of Pensions*, London: Adam Smith Institute.

Central Statistical Office (1985) *Social Trends*, No. 15, London: HMSO.

Chadwick, K. (1983) 'A prescription for statutory sick pay and the supplementary benefits', *Personnel Management*, March.

Cunningham, M. (1981) *Non-wage Benefits*, London: Pluto Press.

DHSS (1977) *Report on a Survey of Occupational Sick Pay Schemes*, London: HMSO.

DHSS (1984) *Portable Pensions: a consultative document*, London: HMSO.

DSS (undated) *Pension Scheme Contributions from 1986/7 to 1992/3*, London: HMSO.

Fell, A. (1983) 'Putting a price on lost time', *Personnel Management*, April.

Garlick, R. (1986) 'The case for company pensions', in Institute of Directors, *The Directors' Guide to Company Pensions*, London: The Director Publications Ltd.

Gill, D. and Chadwick, K. (1986) 'The new prescription for SSP', *Personnel Management*, April.

Ginn, J. and Arber, S. (1996) 'Patterns of employment, gender and pensions: the effect of work history on older women's non-state pensions', *Work Employment and Society*, Vol. 10, No. 3, pp. 469–90.

Hayward, S. (1989) 'Coping with pensions changes', *Director*, December.

Hearn, A. (1992) 'All change on the pensions front?', *Personnel Management*, October.

Hopegood, J. (1994) 'Money-go-round: Solving the age-old SERPS puzzle – government uncertainty may make it sensible for most people to opt out of earnings related pension schemes', *Daily Telegraph*, 19 March.

Hunt, P. (1988) 'Must pensions always be a turn-off?', *Personnel Management*, November.

Incomes Data Services (1979) *IDS Guide to Sick Pay and Absence*, London: Incomes Data Services.

Incomes Data Services (1982) *Pensions for Early-leavers*, IDS Study, No. 274, London: Incomes Data Services.

Incomes Data Services (1994) *Absence and Sick Pay Policies*, IDS Study, No. 556, June, London: Incomes Data Services.

Industrial Relations Services (1995) 'New state incapacity benefit: impact on employees and employers', *Employment Trends*, No. 584, May, pp. 4–10.

Industrial Relations Services (1995) 'Pensions Act heralds a new era of activity', *Employment Trends*, No. 597, December, pp. 5–9.

Industrial Relations Services (1997) 'Shake-up for contracted out pension schemes', *Employment Trends*, No. 625, February, pp. 2–3.

Industrial Society (1996) *Maximising Attendance: Managing best Practice*, London: Industrial Society.

Marsh, P., Smith, A., Cohen, N., Rich, M., Peston, R., Rudd, R. and Jack, A. (1994) 'The personal pensions time bomb: thousands pay dearly for company agents' poor advice', *Financial Times*, 28 February.

McGoldrick, A. (1984) *Equal Treatment in Occupational Pension Schemes*, Research Report, Manchester: Equal Opportunities Commission.

Moody, C. (1984a) 'Pensions and other forms of non-cash remuneration', in D. Guest, and T. Kenny (eds.), *A Textbook of Techniques and Strategies in Personnel Management*, London: IPM.

Moody, C. (1984b) 'The perils of portable pensions', *Personnel Management*, December.

Nash, T. (1989) 'Know your own pension', *Director*, January.

Noble-Warren, R. (1986) 'Lifetime planning', in Institute of Directors, *The Directors' Guide to Pensions*, London: The Director Publications Ltd.

Toulson, N. (1982) *Modern Pensions*, Cambridge: Woodhead-Faulkner.

Taylor, S. and Earnshaw, J. (1994) 'The provision of occupational pensions in the 1990s: an exploration of employer objectives', *Employee Relations*, Vol. 17, No. 2, pp. 38–53.

General discussion topics

1. Some organisations are said to have an 'absence culture' while others are said to have an 'attendance culture'. How do these terms differ, and how might an organisation move from an absence to an attendance culture?

2. What do you consider to be employer perspectives for providing occupational pensions, both historically and in the current climate?

   Compare your views with Taylor and Earnshaw's (1995) research: 'The provision of occupational pensions in the 1990's: an exploration of employer objectives', *Employee Relations*, Vol. 17, No. 2, pp. 38–53.

CHAPTER 35

Interactive skill: negotiation

Negotiation is a longstanding art, which has developed into a major mode of decision-making in all aspects of social, political and business life, even though there is always a feeling that it is no more than a substitute for direct, decisive action. Henry Kissinger was US Secretary of State when protracted negotiations eventually brought to an end the war in Vietnam. He commented:

> A lasting peace could come about only if neither side sought to achieve everything that it had wanted; indeed, that stability depended on the relative satisfaction, and therefore the relative dissatisfaction, of all the parties concerned.
>
> (Kissinger 1973)

In employment we have acquired the institutions of collective bargaining as a means of regulating some parts of the employment relationship between employer and organised employees. To some this is the cornerstone of industrial democracy and the effective running of a business, but to others it is seen as impairing efficiency, inhibiting change and producing the lowest, rather than the highest, common factor of co-operation between management and employees.

Is negotiation rightly viewed as an activity that is only second best to unilateral decision-making? If the outcome is no more than compromise, the choice seems to be between negotiation and capitulation. Some would argue that capitulation by one side would be a better outcome for both than a compromise that ignores the difficulties and dissatisfies both. There is, however, an alternative to splitting the difference in negotiation and that is where the differences in view and objective of the parties are accommodated to such an extent that the outcome for both is better than could have been achieved by the unilateral executive action of either.

Any negotiation is brought about by the existence of some goals that are common to both parties and some goals that conflict. Between employer and employees the desire to keep the business in operation is one of the goals they usually have in common, but there may be many that conflict, and the two parties negotiate a settlement because the attempt by one to force a solution on the other would either fail because of the other's strength or would not be as satisfactory a settlement without the approval of the other party. Both parties acknowledge that they will move from their opening position and that sacrifices in one area may produce compensating benefits in another. Many years ago G. C. Homans expressed the situation thus:

> The more the items at stake can be divided into goods valued more by one party than they cost to the other and goods valued more by the other party than they cost to the first, the greater the chances of a successful outcome.
>
> (Homans 1961, p. 62)

Traditionally, work on negotiation in relation to employment has always been based on the assumption that it is dealing with the collective aspects of the relationship: the management or the employers being pitched against the unions or the workers. We have always written this chapter in that way, but this time we add material on the negotiation of the individual bargain between the management and an individual person or consultancy selling services. Another recent change has been the growing interest of language specialists in the various processes of negotiation (for instance, Mulholland 1991).

The nature of conflict in the employment relationship

The approach to collective negotiations depends on the view that conflict of interests is inevitable between employer and employee because there is an authority relationship in which the aims of the two parties will at least sometimes conflict. A further assumption is that such conflict does not necessarily damage that relationship.

This has led a number of commentators to discuss negotiation in terms of equally matched protagonists. The power of the two parties may not actually be equal, but they are both willing to behave as if it were. The negotiation situation thus has the appearance of power equalisation, which can be real or illusory, due to the search for a solution to a problem. When both sides set out to reach an agreement that is satisfactory to themselves and acceptable to the other, then their power is equalised by that desire. Where the concern for acceptance by the other is lacking, there comes the use of power play of the forcing type described later in this chapter:

> negotiators seek to increase common interest and expand cooperation in order to broaden the area of agreement to cover the item under dispute. On the other hand, each seeks to maximize his own interest and prevail in conflict, in order to make the agreement more valuable to himself. No matter what angle analysis takes, it cannot eliminate the basic tension between cooperation and conflict that provides the dynamic of negotiation.
>
> (Zartman 1976, p. 41)

The relative power of the parties is likely to fluctuate from one situation to the next; this is recognised by the ritual and face-saving elements of negotiation, where a power imbalance is not fully used, both to make agreement possible and in the knowledge that the power imbalance may be reversed on the next issue to be resolved.

The classic work of Ann Douglas (1962) produced a formulation of the negotiating encounter that has been little modified by those coming after her. Walton (1969) has written a most helpful book, too little known in the United Kingdom, about the application of this thinking to the interpersonal relationships between equals in the management hierarchy. However, this needs further thought if it is to be applied to the negotiations that take place between representatives of management and representatives of employees about terms and conditions of employment. Cooper and Bartlett point out the difficulty:

> If equality is available to all . . . conflicting groups can meet. All they need to shed are their misperceptions and their prejudices. Any differences are psychological rather than economic. The truth of the matter is, of course, that . . . there are glaring inequalities of wealth and power. Each society contains its own contradictions which arise from the distribution of money, of status and control. So conflict resolution is not just a matter of clearing away mistrust and misunderstanding, replacing them with communication. It is also concerned with political matters such as the re-allocation of power.
>
> (Cooper and Bartlett 1976, p. 167)

Sources of conflict in the collective employment relationship

Many texts on organisational behaviour include sections on reducing conflict and management talk is full of the need for teamworking, corporate culture and collaboration, so why do we find one area of working life where conflict is readily accepted, even emphasised?

Although the processes of civilisation tend to constrain it there is a natural impulse to behave aggressively to some degree at some time. It has a number of outlets, for example, watching football, wrestling or boxing. Another outlet for aggression is in negotiations within the employing organisation, which is a splendid arena for the expression of aggressiveness and bravura without actually incurring the physical risks that would be involved in violent combat. Dr Johnson summed up the attractions of vigorous disagreement when he said, 'I dogmatise and am contradicted, and in this conflict of opinions I find delight.'

Divergence of interests

Probably the main source of industrial relations conflict is divergence of interests between those who are classified as managers and those who are seen as non-managers. One group is seeking principally such things as efficiency, economy, productivity and the obedience of others to their own authority. The members of the other group are interested in these things, but are more interested in features like high pay, freedom of action, independence from supervision, scope for the individual and leisure. To some extent these invariably conflict.

Potential benefits of such conflict

It is widely believed that conflict of the type described here – and described frequently and more luridly in the press – is counterproductive, and that all should make strenuous efforts to eliminate it. There are, however, some advantages.

Clearing the air

Many people feel that a conflict situation is improved by getting bad feelings 'off their chests' and bringing the matter into the open. Sometimes combatants feel closer as a result.

Introducing new rules

Employment is governed by a number of rules – formal rules that define unfair dismissal and the rate of pay for various jobs, as well as informal rules like modes of address. Management/union conflict is usually about a disagreement over the rules and the bargain that is struck produces a new rule: a new rate of pay, a new employment practice or whatever. It may be the only way of achieving that particular change, and it is a very authoritative source of rulemaking because of the participation in its creation.

Modifying the goals

The goals that management set can be modified as a result of conflict with others. Ways in which their goals will be unpopular or difficult to implement may be seen for the first time and modifications made early instead of too late. A greater range and diversity of views are brought to bear on a particular matter so that the capacity for innovation is enhanced.

Clash of values

More fundamental is the possible clash of values, usually about how people should behave. These may be variations of allegiance to the positions of different political parties on questions like 'What is production for?', or differences of social class attitude to what constitutes courtesy. Most frequently the clash is about the issue of managerial prerogative. Managers are likely to believe and proclaim that management is their inalienable right, so that those who question the way their work is done are ignorant or impertinent. Non-managers may regard management as a job that should be done properly by people who are responsive to questioning and criticism.

Competitiveness

One of the most likely sources is the urge to compete for a share of limited resources. Much of the drive behind differential pay claims is that of competing with other groups at a similar level, but there may also be competition for finance, materials, security, survival, power, recognition or status.

Organisational tradition

If the tradition of an organisation is to be conflict-prone, then it may retain that mode obdurately, while other organisations in which conflict has not been a prominent feature may continue without it. It is axiomatic that certain industries in the United Kingdom are much more likely to display the manifestations of extreme conflict in industrial relations than others. Indicators like the number of working days lost through strikes show a pattern of distribution which varies little between different industries year by year. The nature of the conflict can range between the extremes of pettiness, secrecy, fear and insecurity on the one hand, to vigorous, open and productive debate on the other, with many organisations exhibiting neither.

Understanding of respective positions

Combatants will come to a better understanding of their position on the issue being debated because of their need to articulate it, set it forth, develop supporting arguments and then defend those arguments against criticism. This enables them to see more clearly what they want, why they want it and how justifiable it is. In challenging the position of the other party, they will come to a clearer understanding of where they stand, and why.

Potential drawbacks of such conflict

These advantages may not be sufficient to balance the potential drawbacks.

Waste of time and energy

Conflict and the ensuing negotiations take a great deal of time and energy. Conflict can become attritive when over-personalised, and individuals become obsessed with the conflict itself rather than what it is about. Negotiation takes a lot longer than simple management decree.

Emotional stress for participants

People vary in the type of organisational stress to which they are prone. The need to be involved in negotiation is a source of stress which some people find very taxing, while others find it stimulating.

Organisational stress

Accommodating conflict often causes some inefficiency through the paraphernalia that can accompany it: striking, working to rule, working without enthusiasm, withdrawing co-operation or the simple delay caused by protracted negotiation.

Risks

Engaging in negotiation may be necessary as the only way to cope with a conflictual situation, but there is the risk of stirring up a hornets' nest. When conflict is brought to the surface it may be resolved or accommodated, or if the situation is handled badly it may get worse.

Worsening communications

The quality and amount of communication is impaired. Those involved are concerned more to confirm their own viewpoint than to convey understanding, and there are perceptual distortions like stereotyping and cognitive dissonance. The attitudes behind the communications may also become inappropriate as there are greater feelings of hostility and attempts to score off others.

Bargaining strategies

A reading of Schmidt and Tannenbaum (1960) and Lawrence and Lorsch (1972) helps us to identify various strategies that are adopted to cope with conflict and some of the likely effects.

Avoidance

To some extent conflict can be 'handled' by ignoring it. For a time this will prevent it surfacing so that it remains latent rather than manifest: the danger being that it is harder to deal with when it eventually does erupt. Opposing views cannot be heard unless there is apparatus for their expression. The management of an organisation can fail to provide such apparatus by, for instance, not having personnel specialists, not recognising trade unions and not recognising employee representatives. If the management organise the establishment as if conflict of opinion did not exist, any such difference will be less apparent and its expression stifled. This is a strategy that is becoming harder and harder to sustain due to the developing legal support for employee representation.

Smoothing

A familiar strategy is to seek the resolution of conflict by honeyed words in exhortation or discussion where the emphasis is on the value of teamwork, the assurance that 'we all agree really' and an overt, honest attempt to get past the divergence of opinion, which is regarded as a temporary and unfortunate aberration. This is often an accurate diagnosis of the situation and represents an approach that would have broad employee support in a particular employment context, but there is always the risk that the smoothing ignores the real problem, like giving a massage to someone who has suffered a heart attack.

Forcing

The opposite to smoothing is to attack expressions of dissent and deal with conflict by stamping it out. This is not easy and has innumerable, unfortunate precedents in both the political and industrial arenas.

Compromise

Where divergence of views is acknowledged and confronted, one possibility is to split the difference. If employees claim a pay increase of £10 and the management say they can afford nothing, a settlement of £5 saves the face of both parties but satisfies neither. However common this strategy may be – and sometimes there is no alternative – it has this major drawback: that both parties fail to win.

Confrontation

The fifth strategy is to confront the issue on which the parties differ. This involves accepting that there is a conflict of opinions or interests, exploring the scale and nature of the conflict and then working towards an accommodation of the differences which will provide a greater degree of satisfaction of the objectives of both parties than can be achieved by simple compromise. We suggest that this is the most productive strategy in many cases and offers the opportunity of both parties winning.

It is this fifth strategy which we consider in the remainder of this chapter.

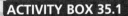

ACTIVITY BOX 35.1

Consider an industrial dispute or disagreement which you have recently witnessed or read about.

1. Was the management strategy one of avoidance, smoothing, forcing, compromise or confrontation?
2. Was this an inappropriate strategy?
3. If the answer to the last question was 'yes', why was an inappropriate strategy used?

Bargaining tactics

In preparing for negotiation there are a number of things which bargainers must set in their minds before they begin.

Resolution or accommodation

Conflict can be resolved so that the original feelings of antagonism or opposition vanish, at least over the issues that have brought the conflict to a head. The schoolboy story of how two boys 'put on the gloves in the gym' after a long feud and thereafter shook hands and became firm friends is a theoretical example of a conflict resolved. This type of outcome has a romantic appeal and will frequently be sought in industrial relations issues because so many people feel acutely uncomfortable when involved in relationships of overt antagonism.

Alternatively, the conflict may be accommodated, so that the differences of view persist, but some *modus vivendi*, some form of living with the situation, is discovered. In view of the inevitability of the conflict that is endemic in the employment relationship, accommodation may be a more common prospect than resolution, but it is an interesting question for a negotiator to ponder when approaching the bargaining table: which is it – resolution or accommodation?

Tension level

Most negotiators feel that they have no chance to determine the timing of encounters. This is partly due to reluctance; managers in particular tend to resort to negotiation only when necessary, and the necessity is usually a crisis. A more proactive (instead of reactive) approach is to initiate encounters, to some extent at least trying to push them towards favourable timings.

A feature of timing is the tension level. Too much, and the negotiators get the jitters, unable to see things straight and indulging in excessive interpersonal vituperation: too little tension, and there is no real will to reach a settlement. Ideal timing is to get a point when both sides have a balanced desire to reach a settlement.

Power balance

Effective negotiation is rarely limited to the sheer exploitation of power advantage. The best settlement is one in which both sides can recognise their own and mutual advantages (Fowler 1990, pp. 11–16). The background to any negotiation includes the relative power of the disputants. Power parity is the most conducive to success:

> Perceptions of power inequality undermine trust, inhibit dialogue, and decrease the likelihood of a constructive outcome from an attempted confrontation. Inequality tends to undermine trust on both ends of the imbalanced relationship, directly affecting both the person with the perceived power inferiority and the one with perceived superiority.
>
> (Walton 1969, p. 98)

The greater the power differential, the more negative the attitudes.

Synchronising

The approaches and reciprocations of the two parties need a degree of synchronising to ensure that an approach is made at a time when the other party is ready to deal with it. Management interpretation of managerial prerogative often causes managers to move quickly in the search of a solution, virtually pre-empting negotiation. When what they see as a positive overture is not reciprocated, then they are likely to feel frustrated, discouraged and cross; making themselves in turn unready for overtures from the other side.

Openness

Conflict handling is more effective if the participants can be open with each other about the facts of the situation and their feelings about it. The Americans place great emphasis on this, and we must appreciate that openness is more culturally acceptable in the United States than in the United Kingdom, but we note their concern that negotiators should own up to feelings of resentment and anger, rather than masking their feelings behind role assumptions of self-importance.

WINDOW ON PRACTICE

John Dunlop is known as one of the great theorists of industrial relations and the processes in collective bargaining. David Farnham summarises the ten points of his framework for analysing the negotiating process:

1. It takes agreement within each negotiating group to reach a settlement between them.
2. Initial proposals are typically large, compared with eventual settlements.
3. Both sides need to make concessions in order to move towards an agreement.
4. A deadline is an essential feature of most negotiating.
5. The end-stages of negotiating are particularly delicate, with private discussions often being used to close the gap between the parties.
6. Negotiating is influenced by whether it involves the final, intermediate or first stages of the conflict resolution process.
7. Negotiating and overt conflict may take place simultaneously, with the conflict serving as a tool for getting agreement.
8. Getting agreement does not flourish in public.
9. Negotiated settlements need procedures to administer or interpret the final agreement.
10. Personalities and their interactions can affect negotiating outcomes.

(Farnham 1993, p. 337.)

The negotiation sequence

Having reviewed the background to bargaining and negotiation, we now consider the various stages of the negotiating encounter in which aspects of ritual are especially important, making perhaps for formality and awkwardness rather than relaxed informality. However, the ritual steps are not time-wasting prevarication, but an inescapable feature of the process.

Preparation

In Figure 35.1 there is a summary of the various stages in the negotiating process itself.

Agenda

The meeting needs an agenda or at least some form of agreement about what is to be discussed. In some quarters a naive conviction persists that there is some benefit in concealing the topic from the other party until the encounter begins,

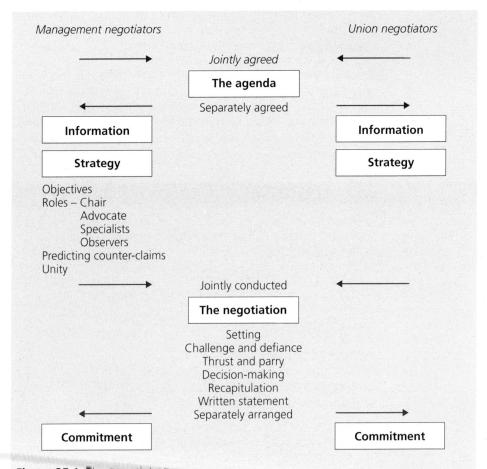

Figure 35.1 The negotiating process

presumably because there is something to be gained from surprise. In fact, this only achieves a deferment of discussion until members of the other party have had a chance to consider their position. The nature of the agenda can have an effect on both the conduct and outcome of the negotiations. It affects the conduct of the encounter by revealing and defining the matters that each side wants to deal with. It is unlikely that other matters will be added to the agenda, particularly if negotiations take place regularly between the parties, so that the negotiators can begin to see, before the meeting, what areas the discussions will cover.

The agenda will influence the outcome of negotiations as a result of the sequence of items on it as the possibilities of accommodation between the two positions emerge in the discussions. If, for instance, all the items of the employees' claim come first and all the management's points come later, the possibilities do not turn into probabilities until the discussions are well advanced. An agenda that juxtaposes management and employee 'points' in a logical fashion can enable the shape of a settlement to develop in the minds of the negotiators earlier, even though there would be no commitment until all the pieces of the jigsaw were available. Many negotiations take place without an agenda at all, sometimes because there is a crisis, sometimes because neither party is sufficiently well organised to prepare one. Morley and Stephenson (1977, pp. 74–8) review a number of studies to draw the conclusion that agreement between negotiators is facilitated when there is the opportunity for them to experience 'orientation' – considering on what to stand firm and on what to contemplate yielding – or where there is an understanding of the issues involved. An agenda is a prerequisite of orientation.

Information

Both parties will need facts to support their argument in negotiation. Some information will be provided to employee representatives for the purposes of collective bargaining and both sets of negotiators have to collect what they need, analyse it so that they understand it, and confirm that the interpretation is shared by each member of their team.

Strategy

The main feature of preparation is the determination of strategy by each set of negotiators. Probably the most helpful work on negotiation strategy has been done by Fowler (1990), with his careful analysis of bargaining conventions and possibilities. In this chapter we limit our considerations to four aspects of strategy.

Objectives

What do the negotiators seek to achieve? Here one would ask them to produce clear and helpful objectives. When the question has been put to management negotiators entering either real or contrived negotiations in recent years the following have been some of the statements of objectives:

> 'Get the best deal we possibly can.'
> 'Maintain factory discipline at all costs.'
> 'Remain dignified at all times.'
> 'Look for an opening and exploit it to the full.'

Apart from their general feebleness, all these declarations have a common, negative quality. The initiative is with the other party and the only management strategy is to resist for as long as possible and to concede as little as possible. If this is the best management negotiators can contrive, then their prospects are indeed bleak. They are bound to lose; the only unresolved question is how much. They cannot gain anything because they do not appear to want anything.

More positive objectives are those that envisage improvements, which could flow from a changing of the employment rules – changes in efficiency, working practices, manning levels, shiftwork patterns, administrative procedures, flexibility, cost control, and so forth. Unless both parties to the negotiations want something out of the meeting there is little scope for anything but attrition.

Roles

Who will do what in the negotiations? A popular fallacy is that negotiation is best conducted by 'everyone chipping in when they have something to say' and 'playing it by ear'. This is the style for a brainstorming, problem-solving group discussion, and negotiation is quite different. Problem-solving implies common interests; negotiation implies conflicting interests between groups who are opposed in debate. Negotiators need a specific role, that they stay in. The roles are:

1. **Chair**: In the majority of cases the management provides this function, and one of the management team will chair the discussion and control the meeting.
2. **Advocate**: Each party requires one person who will be the principal advocate to articulate the case and to examine the opposing case. This provides focus to the discussion and control of the argument. Although it is common for the roles of chairman and advocate to be combined in one person for status reasons, this can put a great strain on the individual, who is bowling and keeping wicket at the same time.
3. **Specialists**: The third role is that of specialist. One person who fully understands the details of the management proposal or arrangement that is being questioned, another to provide expert comment on any legal points, and so forth. The important emphasis is on what the specialist does *not* do. One would not expect this particular negotiator to become involved in the general debate, as this is confusing and moves control from the advocate. The specialist's role is to provide advice when required, rather like the civil servants who regularly pass notes to Ministers appearing before House of Commons Committees. Negotiating does not benefit from free-for-all, unstructured discussion.
4. **Observers**: There is no need for all those attending to speak in order to justify their presence. There is an important part to be played by those who do no more than observe the discussions. They get less emotionally involved in the interplay and point-scoring, and are able to evaluate the situation as it develops. When there are adjournments the observers often initiate the discussions within their team as strategy is redefined and further tactics considered.

Predicting counter-claims

No strategy survives intact the first encounter with the opposition, but its chances are improved if the negotiators have tried to predict what they will hear from the opposition. In this way they will be prepared not only to advance their own arguments, but also to respond to arguments put to them.

Unity

Because negotiations are the confrontation of different sets of interests, each team works out a united position before negotiations begin and expresses that unity in negotiation. If the position is to be modified, then they will agree the modification. This is another aspect of the vital difference between this activity and problem-solving. It is the differences between the parties that have to be handled; differences within the parties are simply a nuisance.

The negotiation

Setting

The number of people representing each side will influence the conduct of negotiations. The larger the number the greater the degree of formality that is needed to manage the meeting; this is an argument in favour of negotiations between very small teams. On the other hand, meetings between two or three people in 'smoke-filled rooms' give rise to allegations of manipulation and are difficult for members of trade unions to countenance in view of their dependence on democratic support. Another problem is that different phases of negotiation call for different arrangements. Relatively large numbers can be an advantage at the beginning, but are often a hindrance in the later stages:

> it is not uncommon for the trade union side to field a sizeable team – a union official, perhaps, supported by a shop stewards' committee. It is unwise for a single manager to attempt to negotiate alone with such a team. Negotiation demands a high level of concentration and quick thinking and it is difficult for one person to maintain full attention to everything that is said, and to detect every nuance in the discussion. This does not mean that the management team must equal the trade union team in size. Indeed, to go beyond a fairly small number runs the risk of poor coordination between team members and the possibility that differing views will emerge within the team as negotiations proceed.
> (Fowler 1990, p. 35)

When asked to suggest an appropriate number, most experienced negotiators opt for three or four on each side.

The nature of the seating arrangements needs to reflect the nature of the meeting, and that means that the sides face each other, with the boundaries between the two being clear. The importance of the physical arrangements were demonstrated by the Paris Peace Talks, which were intended to bring an end to the Vietnam War. The start of talks was delayed for some weeks due to the delegations not being able to agree about the shape of the table.

Challenge and defiance

The somewhat melodramatic term 'challenge and defiance' is used to describe the opening stage of the negotiations, for the deliberate reason that there is a deal of theatricality about the various processes.

Negotiators begin by making it clear that they are representing the interests of people whose will and desire transcends that of the representatives themselves.

They also emphasise the strength of their case and its righteousness as well as the impossibility of any movement from the position they are declaring. The theatricality lies in the realisation by both sides that there will be movement from the relative positions that they are busy declaring to be immovable. The displays of strength are necessary for the negotiators to convince themselves that they are right and to convince the opposition.

The substantive element of this phase is to clarify what the differences are. By the time it draws to a close the negotiators should be quite clear on the matters that divide them, where and how. This, of course, is an important part of the process: differentiation precedes integration.

It is important for the participants to keep the level of interpersonal animosity down. This is a part of the emphasis on their representative role that has already been mentioned. Different behaviours are needed later that depend on an open, trusting relationship between the negotiators, so this must not be impaired by personal acrimony at the opening. It is similar to the ritual whereby a lawyer may refer to a legal adversary as 'my learned friend'.

Thrust and parry

After the differences have been explored, there is an almost instinctive move to a second, integrative stage of the encounter. Here negotiators are looking for possibilities of movement and mutual accommodation:

> Douglas distinguishes between the public role-playing activities of the first stage and the 'psychological' (individual) activities of the second stage as being concerned, respectively, with inter-party and interpersonal exchange. Behaviourally the inter-party exchange is characterized by official statements of position, ostensibly committing the party or parties to some future action congruent with that position. The interpersonal exchange, on the other hand, is characterized by unofficial behaviours which do not so commit the parties in question.   (Morley and Stephenson 1970, p. 19)

Thus the statements made by negotiators are of a much more tentative nature than earlier, as they sound out possibilities, float ideas, ask questions, make suggestions and generally change style towards a problem-solving mode. This has to be done without any commitment of the party that is being represented, so the thrusts are couched in very non-committal terms, specifically exonerating the party from any responsibility. Gradually, the opportunities for mutual accommodation can be perceived in the background of the discussion. We can now incorporate the idea of target points and resistance points advanced by Walton and McKersie (1965).

The target point of a negotiating team is the declared objective – what they would really like to achieve. It will be spelled out in challenge and defiance. The resistance point is where they would rather break off negotiations than settle. This point is never declared and is usually not known either. Although negotiators frequently begin negotiations with a feeling of 'not a penny more than . . . ', the point at which they would actually resist is seldom the same as that at which they think they would resist. Normally the resistance points for both parties slide constantly back and forth during negotiations.

Decision-making

Through thrust and parry all the variations of integration will have been considered and explored, even though negotiators will have veered away from making firm commitments. The third phase of their encounter is when they reach an agreement, and it is interesting to pause here with the comment that agreement is inevitable in all but a small minority of situations, because the bargainers need each other and they have no one else with whom to negotiate. The employees want to continue working for the organisation. Even if they take strike action, they will eventually return to work. The management need the employees to work for them. Employees collectively cannot choose a different management with whom to negotiate and managers can seldom choose a replacement workforce with whom to bargain. They have to reach agreement, no matter how long it takes.

After an adjournment the management will make an offer. The decision about what to offer is the most difficult and important task in the whole process, because the offer can affect the resistance point of the other party. The way in which the other's resistance point will be affected cannot be predetermined. A very low offer could move the other's resistance point further away or bring it nearer; we cannot be sure until the negotiations actually take place.

The offer may be revised, but eventually an offer will be accepted and the negotiations – not the full process – are over.

Negotiations on the contract for collective consent are thus significantly different from those other types of bargaining in which people engage. The negotiations to purchase a second-hand car or a house may seem at first sight to be similar, but in both those situations either party can opt out at any stage and cease to deal any further. The possibility of losing the other is always present, just as is the possibility of negotiating with a different 'opponent'. For this reason the political analogies are more helpful. A peace treaty has to be agreed between the nations that have been at war, and no one else.

Recapitulation

Once a bargain has been struck the tension of negotiation is released and the natural inclination of the negotiators is to break up and spread the news of the agreement that has been reached. It is suggested that they should resist this temptation and first recapitulate all the points on which they have agreed and, if necessary, make arrangements on any minor matters still outstanding that everyone had forgotten.

In the wake of a settlement there is usually a number of such minor matters. If they are dealt with there and then they should be dealt with speedily because of the overriding feeling for agreement that has been established. If discussion of them is deferred because they are difficult, then agreement may be hard to reach later as the issues stand on their own, instead of in the context of a larger settlement.

Written statement

If it is possible to produce a brief written statement before the meeting is ended, both parties to the negotiations will be greatly helped. The emphasis here is on producing a brief written statement before the meeting ends, not as soon as possible afterwards. This will help all the negotiators to take away the same interpretation of what they have done and make them less dependent on recollection. In most circumstances it can also be used to advise non-participants: retyped as a memorandum to supervisors, put up on notice-boards, read out at union meetings, and so on. This will reduce the distortion that can stem from rumour. Until the agreement is in writing it rests on an understanding, and understanding can easily change.

Commitment of the parties

So far agreement has been reached between negotiators only, and it is of no value unless the parties represented by those negotiators accept it and make it work. This requires acceptance at two levels: first in words and then in deeds.

Employee representatives have to report back to their membership and persuade them to accept the agreement. To some extent management representatives may have to do the same thing, but they customarily carry more personal authority to make decisions than do employee representatives.

Although this is a difficult and uncertain process, it is no more important than the final level of acceptance, which is where people make the agreement work. Benefits to the employees are likely to be of the type that are simple to administer – like an increase in the rates of pay – but benefits to the business, like changes in working practices and the variation of demarcation boundaries, are much more difficult. They may quickly be glossed over and forgotten unless the changes are painstakingly secured after the terms have been agreed.

WINDOW ON PRACTICE

Lemuel Boulware, Vice-President for Employee Relations in the General Electric Company of the United States, tried to side-step the ritual dance described above by developing a strategy which he called 'truth in bargaining'. The essence was that his first offer was also his last. He claimed that in conventional bargaining everyone knew that the first offer would be improved, so it was artificially low. He intended to be direct and truthful, making one offer that would not be varied so as to save time and speculation about the final outcome.

This policy had short-run success, but trade unions objected to Boulwarism on the grounds that it eliminated the constructive interchange of normal bargaining and diminished the importance of union representatives in negotiation. Eventually they challenged the policy successfully in the US courts on the grounds that it was not bargaining in good faith.

ACTIVITY BOX 35.2

1. What was Lemuel Boulware's mistake?
2. Why is the process (as well as the result) of negotiating important to both management representatives and employee representatives?
3. Is the process of negotiation important to the members of management and to the employees who are represented, but not participating in the negotiations; or are they only interested in the result?
4. In view of the assertive, take-it-or-leave-it approach of some managements during the 1980s, is Boulware just a historical footnote, or is there still a lesson to be learned from his experience?

Negotiating with individuals

The majority of people at work are employed at the rate for the job, even though there may be some marginal variations in individual circumstances. There is, however, a small number of people who genuinely negotiate an individual arrangement. Sometimes they are employees, more often they are free-lance providers of specialist services. To some extent we considered this aspect of employing people in Chapter 10 but we need a further comment here.

Although there are not the same elaborate rituals that surround the collective bargain, there is still a fundamental conflict of interest in that the two parties are not 'on the same side', but there is also the key difference in that the parties can walk away from each other. They are not (yet) bound to each other by a contract of employment; the employer can readily decide to contract with a different supplier and the supplier of services will not be wholly dependent on a single employer. Also the employer is keen that the supplier should produce a *performance*, not simply honouring the agreement with poor grace, but performing at a high level.

Some individuals get great satisfaction from the idea of negotiating their own deal. It gives them a clear sense of their own value and a feeling of autonomy, being in control of their own destiny. It was earlier suggested that collective negotiations are at least partly a way of people dealing with their aggressive tendencies. In individual situations it is slightly different in that the gaming element is stronger and everyone becomes their own entrepreneur.

The negotiating process is broadly the same in that the first stage is to muster up all the information you need. Exactly what do you want done? What is the standard to which it has to be completed? What are your time scales? What latitude do you have? When you sit down to negotiate, there is again the general searching stage of defining the negotiating range, clarifying what you want and hearing what the supplier wants and needs. You have the useful advantage that the prospective supplier has to tender, knowing that there are, or may be, others tendering for the same work, so the supplier has to pitch the tender at a level attractive enough to interest you not only in the price but also in the quality of service being offered.

Those employing services have to know what they can and cannot do. William Oncken (1984) has coined the term 'freedom scale' to describe the degree of discretion you want to enjoy. His scale is:

Level 5   Act on your own, routine reporting only.
Level 4   Act, but advise at once.
Level 3   Recommend, then take resulting action.
Level 2   Ask what to do.
Level 1   Wait until told.

Although Level 5 sounds very status-full and macho, you may prefer in some negotiations to have less freedom, so that you cannot be expected to commit yourself without time for thought. Remember the representation element that was so central to collective negotiation.

WINDOW ON PRACTICE

Roger Fisher and William Ury (1986) suggest four basic rules to govern any negotiation:

1. Separate the people from the problem. Don't focus on the clash of personalities or bruised egos, but on the problem that needs resolution.
2. Focus on interests, not positions. If you get locked in to a particular position, you may not achieve the real objective of your negotiation. Always be looking for alternative possibilities.
3. Make the pie bigger. Generate other possibilities beyond what your 'opponent' is asking for by thinking of options that are low cost to you and high benefit to them.
4. Insist on using objective criteria. Prevent the negotiation becoming a contest of wills by looking for objective standards or criteria that can be used by both parties to test the reasonableness of any position that is adopted.

Summary propositions

35.1 The practice of negotiation is based on a need to resolve or accommodate matters on which there is a conflict of interest about the appropriate rate for the job between those who employ and those who are employed.

35.2 In collective issues negotiation can clear the air, introduce new rules, modify an unworkable management position or produce better understanding of respective positions.

35.3 Among the problems of negotiation are the waste of time, the stress and the risks.

35.4 The most common bargaining strategies are avoidance, smoothing, forcing, compromise or confrontation.

35.5 Aspects of preparation are setting the agenda, collecting information, deciding a strategy, agreeing objectives and roles.

35.6 The stages in collective negotiation are challenge and defiance, thrust and parry, decision-making, recapitulation, agreeing a written statement and ensuring the commitment of the parties.

35.7 In individual negotiations a negotiator will want to get agreement to an appropriate position of the 'freedom scale'.

References

Cooper, B. M. and Bartlett, A. F. (1976) *Industrial Relations: A study in conflict*, London: Heinemann.

Douglas, A. (1962) *Industrial Peacemaking*, New York: Columbia University Press.

Dunlop, J. T. (1984) *Dispute Resolution*, London: Auburn.

Farnham, D. (1993) *Employee Relations*, London: IPM.

Fisher, R. and Ury, W. (1986) *Getting to Yes: Negotiating agreement without giving in*, New York: Penguin.

Fowler, A. (1990) *Negotiation Skills and Strategies*, London: IPM.

Homans, G. C. (1961) *Social Behaviour: Its elementary forms*, London: Routledge & Kegan Paul.

Kissinger, H. (1973) *New York Times*, 25 January.

Lawrence, P. R. and Lorsch, J. W. (1972) *Managing Group and Intergroup Relations*, Homewood, Ill.: Dorsey.

Morley, I. and Stephenson, G. M. (1970) 'Strength of case, communication systems and the outcomes of simulated negotiations', *Industrial Relations Journal*, Summer.

Morley, I. and Stephenson, G. M. (1977) *The Social Psychology of Bargaining*, London: George Allen & Unwin.

Mulholland, J. (1991) *The Language of Negotiation*, London: Routledge.

Oncken, W. (1984) *Managing Management Time: who's got the monkey?*, Englewood Cliffs, NJ: Prentice Hall.

Schmidt, W. and Tannenbaum, R. (1960), 'Management of differences', *Harvard Business Review*, November/December, pp. 107–15.

Walton, R. E. (1969) *Interpersonal Peacemaking: Confrontations and third party consultation*, Reading, Mass.: Addison-Wesley.

Walton, R. E. and McKersie, R. B. (1965) *Towards a Behavioural Theory of Labour Negotiations*, London: McGraw-Hill.

Zartman, I. W. (1976) *The 50% Solution*, New York: Anchor Press/Doubleday.

Practical exercises in negotiation

First exercise

You again need your close friend to help you. It is probably better not to do this exercise with a spouse: either it will be hopelessly unreal, or the negotiating behaviours will be such as to subject the relationship to needless strain.

Identify a valuable possession that you might be willing to sell for a suitable price – house, car, stereo system – and that your friend might be willing to buy from you. A realistic, albeit hypothetical, willingness on both sides is a necessary feature of selecting the possession to be 'sold'. Plan your approach for negotiating the sale, including objectives, target points and resistance points. Ask your friend to carry out similar preparation as a prospective buyer.

Conduct the negotiations, attempting to avoid simple haggling about the price. When you reach potential agreement or failure to agree, discuss your feelings about the experience.

Second exercise

The above exercise was relatively easy as there was only one person on each side, either party could abandon the negotiations and negotiate with someone else, and the issue in dispute was the simple question of price. Also the negotiators were representing only themselves. This next exercise gets a little nearer the real thing by involving more people and more issues, but is inevitably a more artificial situation.

You need three friends, A again to negotiate with you, B to be represented by you and C to be represented by your adversary. Although each of you is playing a role, try to avoid play-acting as far as possible. Dissuade A, for instance, from being deliberately bloody minded and speaking with a Liverpool accent in order to play the part of a caricature shop steward.

You all need to read document I. Your adversary represents the TGWU members in the plant. Now:

1. B consults with your friend C to determine three matters they would like on the agenda for a meeting with you.
2. You have similar consultations with friend B.
3. You agree an agenda for negotiations with friend A.
4. You and B finalise your objectives; A and C finalise theirs.
5. You and A conduct negotiations, while B and C observe silently and unobtrusively.*
6. You and A reach agreement, or failure to agree, and then discuss the process with B and C.

* It is important that the observers influence the progress of negotiations as little as possible. Chuckles, sharp intakes of breath and solemn shakes of the head can quickly wreck the learning experience. As far as possible observers should be out of view of the negotiators in this exercise.

Document I

You are being moved to be general manager of a subsidiary manufacturing plant that has had three different general managers in the last eight months. You have been told of the following major problems:

1. There is a rising rate of staff turnover on the shop floor. To maintain the complement of 420 people on production, 230 new recruits have been engaged in the last six months. In the previous six months 163 were recruited. The local level of unemployment has remained unaltered at 9 per cent.
2. Demand for the product fluctuates with a lead-time for delivery of 4–6 weeks after orders are placed. You can see no possibility of smoothing this fluctuation. The present method of coping is to rely on overtime when demand is high and turning a blind eye to 'sickness' absence when things are slack. You have been told that the men like the overtime and the young married women like the 'sickness' absence, so it is quite a convenient arrangement.
3. Twenty-seven maintenance craftsmen and associated skilled personnel are all members of Union X. The remaining shop floor employees are represented by Union Y, although only 40–50 per cent are members. There have been seven stoppages in recent months due to breakdowns in negotiations about incentive payments. Union Z has begun recruiting members among white collar staff, who have objected to plans for harmonisation of terms and conditions between themselves and the shop floor personnel.

Case study problem

Salary versus benefits in financial services

We saw in this part the way in which there is a balance to be struck between the level of salary and the benefits that are associated with that salary. The case problem at the close of Part VI was an example, as employees were concerned that a salary increase of more than 20 per cent would not be as satisfactory as the previous situation, where their benefits – including greatly reduced air fare – were much greater. The problem is always in finding the right balance.

You have just been appointed to review the salary and benefits package in a financial services company, where the benefits package includes mortgages and loans at preferential rates, a non-contributory pension scheme and profit sharing. There is some feeling in the company that the value of these benefits has shrunk in recent years as the preferential terms have become less attractive. You have been asked to consider ways in which the benefits arrangements can be made more flexible, so that employees have a degree of choice between the benefits they enjoy, but you are concerned that the increase in costs of administration may be too high to justify such a move.

Research by the consultants Towers Perrin (1996) covered responses from 250 UK companies and showed that half the respondents were now allowing employee choice between different benefits, compared with only one in ten five years previously. The only significant benefit where individual choice has been reduced is in car benefits.

You carry out a questionnaire survey among staff members which provides you with the following data:

1. Would you be willing to exchange part of your salary for improvements in your benefits package? Yes: 28%. No. 72%
2. What do you feel about the present combination of salary and benefits: (a) about right as it is? (b) improving benefits more important than improving salaries? (c) improving salaries more important than improving benefits? (a) 42%. (b) 9%. (c) 49%.
3. In reply to a question about the relative value of different types of benefit, the following was the rank order:
   (a) Non-contributory pension
   (b) Profit-sharing

     (c) Preferential mortgage rates
     (d) Flexible holiday arrangements
     (e) Free life insurance
     (f) Private health care insurance
     (g) Fees refunded for approved training schemes
     (h) Sports club membership
     (i) Extended maternity leave/paternity leave
     (j) Luncheon vouchers.

Required

1. Why do you think there is such strong preference for improving salary rather than benefits?
2. What are the benefits (and disadvantages) to the employer in increasing the range of choice for individuals between a range of benefits?
3. Do you agree with the rank order of the ten benefits shown above? What changes would you make to produce your own personal list?

Reference

Towers Perrin (1996) *The Benefits Package of the Future*, London: Towers Perrin.

Part VII Examination questions

Undergraduate introductory

1. Explain the difference in the objectives of employer and employee when considering the payment arrangements of the employee.
2. What are the differences between wages and salaries?

Undergraduate finals

3. 'Job evaluation is redundant: it is only the Equal Pay Act that keeps it going.' Discuss.
4. How effective are payment systems in improving effort levels and performance?

Masters

5. If you are managing a system of payment with the objective that those being paid should regard the system as being fair, would you relate the payment to the demands of the job or to the relative performance of individuals doing the job?
6. 'Individual performance pay is only one ingredient of a performance management system and a relatively insignificant one at that.' Do you agree or disagree with this statement? Explain your reasons?

Professional

7. What are the advantages and disadvantages of broad-banded pay structures?
8. What should be the main benefits of an employee benefits policy?

PART VIII
Ethics

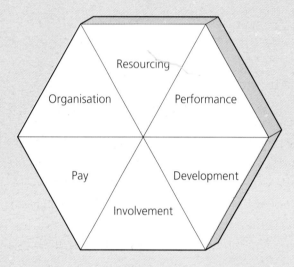

Personnel management began as an expression of employer concern for the welfare of workers. Throughout the twentieth century that pre-occupation with employee welfare has continued, even though it has been modified by a greater emphasis on employee rights. There has also developed a much greater concern about the ethical implications of management action in relation to the surrounding society in which the business is set.

This concluding chapter reviews those developments and the present situation. Experience of employment is frequently harsh, despite the general improvement in living conditions. Insecurity is commonplace and may be a contributory factor in some of the contemporary social problems of racial tensions, alienation and crime. Personnel managers remain at the heart of management concern with these issues.

Personnel, ethics and human resource management

Personnel management has always had an ethical dimension, as it began as the practical application of nonconformist paternalism which was the driving force of the Industrial Revolution. The odd thing is that practitioners have for so long been trying to bury this aspect, while academic commentators have grumbled that personnel practitioners fail to deliver on it. Thirty years ago it was possible to write a chapter in a book on personnel management with the title 'The Social Role of Personnel' (Torrington 1968, pp. 147–60) and generate a series of reviews that all vehemently disagreed with the implicit proposition that there actually *was* a social role for the personnel manager in the business.

Since then there has been a resurgence (although that might be too strong a term to describe the phenomenon) of interest in ethics, but now it is not a vain attempt of the nice personnel people to act as the conscience of the company. Instead, it is a much more general management interest. Kenneth Blanchard is an American academic and consultant of considerable reputation, including being the author of the best-selling *The One-Minute Manager*. He teamed up with Norman Vincent Peale, who had written in 1952 *The Power of Positive Thinking*, which had sold no fewer than twenty million copies. Together they produced a slim, popular book about ethics in management which they described as follows:

> ethical behaviour is related to self-esteem. We both believe that people who feel good about themselves have what it takes to withstand outside pressure and to do what is right rather than do what is merely expedient, popular or lucrative. We believe that a strong code of morality in any business is the first step toward its success. We believe that ethical managers are winning managers. (Blanchard and Peale 1988, p. 7)

It is interesting that the idea is 'sold' as a means to an end rather than as an end in itself, and it sounds almost as 'expedient, popular or lucrative' as the alternative that they are disparaging. We will return to the general management interest in business ethics later in the chapter, but we can get Blanchard and Peale in clearer perspective if we consider some definitions.

Any dictionary will indicate that ethics can be both singular and plural. In the singular it relates to *the moral value of human conduct and the principles that ought to govern that conduct*. The plural form describes *a social, religious or civil code of behaviour considered to be correct, especially that of a particular group or profession*. In the business context we can therefore understand ethics as a part of the culture of the individual business corporation that sets norms of behaviour by which people in the business will abide because they have some moral authority as well being convenient. It is also a set of guidelines followed by people in a particular group or profession because it makes practical sense in enabling them to do their jobs. Barristers will not represent two different clients if there is likely to be a conflict of interest between the clients. Doctors will generally refrain from sexual relationships with their patients. In both cases there are sound practical reasons, quite apart from any moral dimension.

Business ethics and social responsibility

The early management concern with ethics was as was discussed in the opening chapter, with comments about some of the Victorian philanthropists, like Lord Leverhulme. An American contemporary was Andrew Carnegie, who was born in Scotland but made a considerable fortune after emigrating to the United States and devoted the last years of his life to giving most of it away. In 1900 he wrote a book called *The Gospel of Wealth*, which set out a statement of corporate social responsibility that was quite as paternalist as his British counterparts. He believed that corporate social responsibility had two principles, charity and stewardship. The more fortunate in society had an obligation to aid the less fortunate (charity) and those with wealth should see themselves as owning that wealth in trust for the rest of society by using it for purposes which were socially legitimate (stewardship).

Carnegie was very influential, largely because he dispensed charity on such a massive scale, but the paternalism gradually drew more and more criticism and the involvement in social responsibility waned. It was more or less destroyed altogether by Milton Friedman, who argued that those in business were not qualified to decide on the relative urgency of social needs. He contended that managers who devoted corporate resources to pursue personal interpretations of social need might be misguided in their selection and would unfairly 'tax' their shareholders, employees and customers:

> There is one and only one social responsibility of business: to use its
> resources and energy in activities designed to increase its profits as long as it
> stays within the rules of the game, engaging in open and free competition,
> without deception and fraud.   (Friedman 1963, p. 163)

The 1980s saw the return of interest in business ethics. Like many developments it was rooted in the United States, but has been echoed at various volume levels in other countries. To many people it remains an incongruous concept:

> Many persons educated in the humanities (with their aristocratic traditions)
> and the social sciences (with their quantifying, collectivist traditions) are
> uncritically anti-capitalist. They think of business as vulgar, philistine, and
> morally suspect. . . . Three accusations come up.
> (a) In pursuit of profits, won't businesses act immorally whenever
>   necessary?
> (b) Aren't executive salaries out of line? Isn't dramatic inequality wrong?
> (c) Isn't it wrong to subject workers and middle managers in their mature
>   years to so much inequity? Isn't it wrong to let people go abruptly and
>   without a parachute?   (Novak 1996, pp. 7–8)

That was an American perspective, but would be echoed by many people in Europe. There is also the more general feeling that any commercially-driven activity has dominant motivations that are inevitably opposed to social considerations. Another version of the same view, echoing Friedman, is that those in management positions should *not* make moral judgements as they have no authority to do so. Instead they should respond to public opinion as expressed by customers' purchasing decisions, demonstrations by pressure groups or by government legislation.

WINDOW ON PRACTICE

One relatively recent form of control on management decision-making is *whistle-blowing*, which describes the practice of an employee metaphorically blowing a whistle to attract attention from the outside to some ethical malpractice within the business. Originally this was lone individuals taking great risks with their employment, but the method has now altered through the establishment of a charity *Public Concern at Work*, which gives free legal advice to potential whistle-blowers. Its Director claims that most issues are now settled within the business:

> 90% of clients who follow our advice report a successful outcome. This has much to do with our policy that, if raised responsibly within the organisation, concerns about malpractice will be addressed properly by those in charge.   (Dehn 1997)

An alternative point of view sees business practice as a product of its past:

> Wealth or values creation is in essence a moral act. The individual entrepreneurs who first organised production systematically were steeped in largely Nonconformist religious convictions that blocked most customary routes to advancement in British society of the eighteenth and early nineteenth centuries [who] . . . shared a belief that their works on this earth would justify them, that the Kingdom of Heaven was to be built by them, here and now.   (Hampden-Turner and Trompenaars 1993, p. 3)

These authors then argue that the moral values that drive wealth creation are rooted in the national and organisational cultures of the wealth-creating corporations, although that is frequently forgotten because of the prominence given to the 'value-empty' discipline of economics, of which Milton Friedman was the supreme example:

> The qualities of work performed by these corporations depend as much on the durable values of their work cultures as they once depended on the values of their founders. In our survey of 15,000 executives we found that culture of origin is the most important determinant of values. In any culture, a deep structure of beliefs is the invisible hand that regulates economic activity.   (*ibid.*, p. 4)

The further simple logic supporting the need for ethical guidelines is that actions in business are the result of decisions by human beings, and human beings tend to seek justification for their actions beyond the rule of value for money. Frequently this takes the form of grotesque rationalisation. The various Mafia families apparently have a very strong code of conduct, based on strong family cohesion and a convenient interpretation of the Roman Catholic faith. This

'justification' enables them to peddle drugs, launder money, run large-scale pros-
titution and extortion, to say nothing of killing people, without a sense of guilt.

Fortunately the great majority of people do not resort to such extreme behaviour, but will still look to justify to themselves actions they take that can have
unpleasant consequences for other people. The person who is totally rational in
decision-making is a rare creature in business life.

Sometimes the moral justification comes from a value system that is independent
of the business itself and where individual opinion can be sharply divided. Some
doctors and nurses are happy to work in abortion clinics, while others refuse, as
some people are passionately committed to the woman's right to choose and others
are equally passionately pro-life. Some people are enraged about the destruction
of green land to build motorways, while others are enthusiastic. Other actions
and decisions are more generally supported by the external value system. Few
would disagree that people at work should be honest and that claims about a
product or service should be accurate. Most would also agree with the general
proposition of equal opportunity for all, although there may be sharp disagreement
about what exactly that means in practice.

Some standards of ethics derive from voluntary agreement by members of a
particular industry, like editors of national newspapers, or statutory 'watchdogs'
like those monitoring the activities of privatised public utilities. The problems of
pensions and similar financial services being mis-sold in the 1980s has produced
the Personal Investment Authority with quite swingeing powers intended to prevent a repetition of that sort of problem. Then there are the ethical standards that
are generated within a particular business. The Royal Dutch/Shell Group of
Companies rely largely for their international effectiveness on the values shared
by all their companies and employees. No new joint venture will be developed
unless the partner company accepts them.

> The business principles are a set of beliefs which say what the Shell group
> stands for and covers in general terms its responsibilities to its principal
> stakeholders, its shareholders, employees, customers and society. They are
> concerned with economic principles, business integrity, political activities,
> the environment, the community and availability of information.
>
> (Haddock and South 1994, p. 226)

These principles were first set out in 1976 and were not imposed from the top,
but were a codification of already accepted behaviour. The principles are revised
from time to time and one of the challenging tasks for the central HR function
was to introduce a code of practice relating to drugs and alcohol, which took
considerable discussion and consultation before agreement could be reached.

Individuals encounter moral dilemmas frequently in their working lives and
are likely to find them very difficult. In carrying out research a few years ago about
performance appraisal practice in a large building society, it was possible to see the
rise in sickness absence at the time of the annual appraisal discussion, and this was
most marked among apprais*ers*: those who had to pass on bad news. We saw in
Chapter 29 that few managers wish to take over responsibility for grievance and
discipline from personnel people, and making the decision to dismiss someone for
almost any reason other than gross misconduct is a most unpopular management
task because it seems that the interests of the business are being considered at the
expense of the interests of individual employees. At times like this managers are
very anxious to find some justifying framework for their actions.

ACTIVITY BOX 36.1

Eric was deaf, mute and suffered from cerebral palsy. He had been unemployable all his adult life, but in his late twenties he started to follow round the local authority refuse collectors emptying dustbins. As the lorry reached the end of a street, Eric would go ahead of it and drag dustbins out from behind the houses to the front. His handicap made it a very slow and painful process, but it was something he could do and he worked until he dropped with exhaustion. This completely unofficial arrangement was accepted by the refuse collectors as they were able to complete their rounds more quickly and they were on an incentive payment arrangement and Eric's participation enabled them to complete their rounds in slightly less time. At the end of the week they had a collection and gave Eric a few pounds. This transformed his life, as he had a purpose and had some mates.

1. Do you feel that Eric was being exploited by the refuse collectors?

Local authority officials heard about what Eric was doing and said it had to stop.

2. Why do you think they made this decision? Do you agree with it?

A personnel manager in the neighbourhood heard about Eric and arranged for him to be taught to operate a sewing machine. He was then employed in the personnel manager's factory to maintain and repair all the overalls: a straightforward job carried out skilfully and conscientiously.

3. Do you feel that Eric was being exploited by the personnel manager?
4. As Eric was able to draw invalidity benefit, do you feel that the job should have been offered first to someone who was able-bodied?

In the following three years studies demonstrated twice that the overalls could be repaired more cheaply by subcontracting the work to another company, but that decision was not taken. Eric carried on as an employee.

5. Why do you think they did not make that decision? Do you agree with it?

By the early 1990s one-third of leading British companies had a written code of ethics, which was nearly double the number in 1987 (Sasseen 1993, p. 31). The key issue with ethical codes is the extent to which they are supported by the people to whom they apply. They are not rules that can be enforced by penalties for non-compliance. It is necessary that they are understood, appreciated and willingly honoured by the great majority of those who are affected. There will then be considerable social pressure on the few who do not wish to comply. Imposing ethics is very tricky. While researching equal opportunity some years ago, an interesting situation was found in an American computer company with a rapidly growing British subsidiary. The company had a high-profile commitment to 'positive action to seek out and employ members of disadvantaged groups'. This was reinforced in the annual appraisal system for managers, who had to indicate what they had done in the last twelve months to implement a 'programme of employment and development for minorities'. The company annual report made a claim that this initiative was advancing at all international locations. In Britain, however, it was found that:

> Without exception, all managers to whom we spoke ignored that part of their appraisal. . . . They put a line through the offending clause and wrote 'not applicable in the UK' . . . despite the corporate objective of 'citizenship', applicable in the UK, requiring recruitment officers to seek out the

disadvantaged in the community. . . . Suggestions by the researchers that such an active recruitment policy was an obligation on the part of management. . . . invoked the reaction, 'we're not a welfare organisation'.

(Torrington, Hitner and Knights 1982, p. 23)

Personnel managers, welfare and ethics

Academics have always criticised personnel managers, who have been held accountable for management failures in the employment field and have been derided as powerless because of their apparent inability to carry out simple tasks like introducing genuine equality of opportunity and humanising the workplace. Thirty years ago Flanders criticised them, and their managerial colleagues, for getting the balance wrong between who did what in management:

> Confusion over the role of personnel management can produce a compromise that gets the worst of all worlds. In major areas of industrial relations policy – such as employment, negotiations, communications and training – line management may shed all the details of administration, while retaining ultimate authority and an illusion of responsibility.

(Flanders 1964, p. 254)

As interest in HRM intensified during the 1980s, other inadequacies were reported. Daniel (1986) found that personnel specialists were normally excluded from decisions about reorganisation resulting from new technology; Purcell and Gray (1986) reported personnel departments being run down; Guest (1989) said that personnel managers lacked a necessary strategic view; and Armstrong (1989) claimed that the future of the personnel profession was doomed without a better understanding of accountancy. The undercurrent of all these critiques was that, because of their shortcomings, personnel people were not bringing about necessary social change in the workplace. These are simply examples of the continuing, conventional wisdom that personnel specialists are ineffectual.

WINDOW ON PRACTICE

One of the most telling caricatures of the personnel manager comes not from academia but from a Tyneside shopfloor:

> Joe, an old labourer, is trudging through the shipyard carrying a heavy load on his shoulders. It is a filthy, wet day and the sole of his shoe is flapping open. The personnel manager, passing at the time, stops him, saying 'Hey Joe, you can't go round with your shoe in that state on a wet day like this' and reaching into his back pocket takes out a bundle of bank notes. Joe beams in anticipation. 'Here' says the personnel manager, slipping the elastic band off the bundle of notes, 'put this round your shoe, it will help keep the wet out'.

(Murray 1972, p. 279)

Quite the most vigorous recent denunciation of personnel people for not putting the world to rights has been from Tim Hart (1993) with his onslaught on HRM and the spineless acceptance of its corrosive influences by personnel people. He had three points of criticism:

1. HRM is amoral and anti-social because it has moved away from the principles of the famous social philanthropists who realised that the standard economic paradigm of labour utility needed to be tempered with social and religious values. HRM ignores the pluralistic nature of work organisations and personnel managers have abandoned their welfare origins.
2. Personnel managers, aided and abetted by the Institute of Personnel Management, have lost their claim to independent professional standing, as HRM is a managerial rather than professional approach, producing a purely reactive response to situations.
3. HRM is ecologically destructive because it consolidates an exploitative relationship between people at work which is then reproduced in our approach to relationships in the wider society and with our environment.

Other management specialists do not receive these criticisms, either because their activities are more limited in their social implications or because their academic commentators are more interested in the technical rather than social aspects of what they are doing.

Personnel people have long held a strong interest in ethics, although it was usually caricatured as welfare. Some of the academic critics argue that personnel managers should remain aloof from the management hurly burly so that 'professional values will be paramount and prevail over other interests' (Hart 1993, p. 30). The problem with that simplistic argument is that personnel managers do not have a separate professional existence from the management of which they are a part. Personnel management is a management activity or it is nothing.

The company doctor and the company legal adviser are bound by codes of professional ethics different from those of managers, but they are employed for their specialist, technical expertise and they are members of long-established, powerful professional groupings with their own normal places of work. When they leave their surgeries or their courtrooms to align themselves with managers in companies, they are in a specialised role. They can maintain a non-managerial, professional detachment, giving advice that is highly regarded, even when it is highly unpopular. Furthermore they advise; they do not decide. For instance, any dismissal on the grounds of ill health is a management decision and not a medical decision, no matter how explicit and uncompromising the medical advice may be.

Personnel specialists do not have separate places and conventions of work which they leave in order to advise managements. They are employed in no other capacity than to participate closely in the *management* process of the business. They do not even have the limited degree of independence that company accountants have, as their activities are not subject to external audit, and it is ludicrous to expect of them a full-fledged independent, professional stance.

The change in general management orientation during the 1980s towards the idea of the leaner and fitter, flexible organisations, downsizing, delayering, outplacement and all the other ideas that eventually lead to fewer people in jobs and fewer still with any sort of employment security have usually been implemented by personnel people. Personnel managers cannot behave like Banquo's ghost and be silently disapproving. What they can do is to argue vigorously in favour of what they see as the best combination of efficiency and justice, but they can only argue vigorously if they are present when decisions are made. If they are not generally 'on side', they don't get to the decision-making and they probably don't keep their jobs. They are either a part of management, valued by their colleagues, despite their funny ideas, or they are powerless. There are no ivory towers for personnel managers to occupy, and no more employment security for them than for any other member of the business, so the voice of a personnel manager crying in the wilderness is one that no one wants to hear, let alone pay a salary to and provide a company car for.

In the different era of the 1970s Legge (1978) propounded her formulation of the conformist and deviant innovator as alternative strategies for the personnel manager to pursue. The conventions of employment security then, especially of managers, were such that personnel specialists could perhaps pursue a deviant path with impunity. Now it is more difficult:

> The 'deviant innovator' bolt hole based on a plea to consider the merits of social values and to ponder the value of an independent 'professional stance' appeared to be offering a less secure refuge.   (Storey 1992, p. 275)

They can still do it, if they are valued by their managerial colleagues for the wholeness of their contribution, and if they accept the fact that they will often lose the argument: they cannot do it by masquerading as an unrepresentative shop steward. They have no monopoly of either wisdom or righteousness, and other members of the management team are just as likely as they are to be concerned about social values. What is impressive is the strength of feeling on these issues that is found in so many personnel managers and the courage with which many advocate their policies.

Personnel managers have not abandoned their interest in welfare; they have moved away from an approach to welfare that was trivial, anachronistic and paternalist. In the personnel manager's vocabulary the term 'welfare' is code for middle-class do-gooders placing flowers in the works canteen. Personnel managers increasingly shun the traditional approach to welfare not for its softness, but because it is ineffectual. It steers clear of the work that people are doing and concentrates on the surroundings in which the work is carried out. It does not satisfy personnel managers in their obsession with getting progress in the employment of people, and it certainly does not do enough to satisfy the people who are employed. In many undertakings personnel specialists are taking their management colleagues along with them in an enthusiastic and convinced attempt to give jobs more meaning and to humanise the workplace. Their reasoning is that the business can only maintain its competitive edge if the people who work there are committed to its success, and that commitment is volitional: you need hearts and minds as well as hands and muscle. Investment in training and the dismantling of elaborate, alienating organisation structures do more for employee well-being than paternalistic welfare programmes ever did.

In 1994 the Institute of Personnel Management merged with the Institute of Training and Development to create the Institute of Personnel and Development, a professional body with 80,000 members and thus the largest single organisation of its type in the world. One of its key objectives is the establishment, monitoring and promotion of standards and ethics for its profession. Its first declared aim is:

> to advance continuously the management and development of people to the benefit of individuals, employers and the community at large.

(IPD 1996b, p. 2)

The third part of its mission statement is:

> to uphold the highest ideals in the management and development of people.
> *(ibid.)*

That provides a clear view of a social role. In passing it is worth noting that the mission statement of the antecedent body, the IPM wording was:

> The mission of the Institute of Personnel Management is to be the professional body for all those responsible for the optimum use of human resources to the mutual benefit of the enterprise, each person and the community at large.   (IPM 1993)

It sounds as if people may be taking the place of human resources after all!

ACTIVITY BOX 36.2

What are the essential differences between the 1993 and the 1996 statements and what, if any, are their implications for the work that personnel specialists do?

IPD provides a network of people working in the field, a headquarters staff who commission research and publish journals, as well as codes of professional conduct. There are very few sanctions, but there is a constituency and a reference group. All of this is largely sustained by the qualifying process; at any one time one-third of IPD members are students. The professional education scheme of the Institute is largely conducted through the institutions of higher education and is therefore in touch with research and forward thinking on social as well as managerial issues. IPD involvement with higher education, including those with the strongest research orientation, is probably greater than for any other specialist management body.

WINDOW ON PRACTICE

The IPD Code

The IPD Code of Professional Conduct (1996b) identifies seven areas in which its members must respect standards of conduct:

Accuracy. They must maintain high standards of accuracy in the information and advice they provide to employers and employees.

Confidentiality. They must respect the employer's legitimate needs for confidentiality and ensure that all personnel information (including information about current, past and prospective employees) remains private.

Counselling. With the relevant skills, they must be prepared to act as counsellors to individual employees, pensioners and dependants or to refer them, where appropriate, to other professionals or helping agencies.

Developing others. They must encourage self-development and seek to achieve the fullest possible development of employees in the service of present or future organisation needs.

Equal opportunities. They must promote fair, non-discriminatory employment practices.

Fair dealing. They must maintain fair and reasonable standards in their treatment of individuals.

Self-development. They must seek continuously to improve their performance and update their skills and knowledge.

If IPD were ever to lose its influence among personnel specialists then the practice of personnel management would be no more than the exercise of competence – amoral and anti-social.

Ethics across national boundaries

The international dimension of the social responsibility question has still to be developed. During the last half of 1992 several powerful western countries suffered serious economic problems because of speculation against their currencies and much of this was at the hands of major banks. Logging operations in South America are ravaging the rain forests, which are essential to life continuing on the planet. Error, or neglect, in the management of manufacturing processes can produce a tragedy like that of Bhopal in India, Chernobyl in Ukraine or the various discharges of crude oil that have occurred all over the world. We have already referred to the concern about values in Shell, yet this business suffered serious difficulties about its plans for the disposal of the Brent Spar oil rig. Since the first formal warning by the American Surgeon General about the risks of smoking, tobacco consumption has been falling in western countries, so the tobacco companies have increased their marketing in less developed countries.

Ethical standards vary. The Recruit affair was a major Japanese scandal involving allegations of corruption among the country's most senior politicians. In the aftermath there was much American criticism of Japanese business practices and a flurry of righteous indignation in western newspapers about the need to use 'slush funds' in various countries to obtain business. Becker and Fritzsche (1987) carried out a study of different ethical perceptions between American, French and German executives. Thirty-nine per cent of the Americans said that paying money for business favours was unethical. Only 12 per cent of the French and none of the Germans agreed. In the United States Japanese companies have been accused of avoiding the employment of ethnic minority groups by the careful location of their factories (Cole and Deskins 1988, pp. 17–19). On the other hand, Japanese standards on employee health and safety are as high as anywhere in the world (Wokutch 1990). In Southeast Asia the contrast in prosperity between countries like Malaysia and Singapore on the one hand and Indonesia and the Philippines on the other means that there are ethical questions about the employment of illegal immigrants that are superficially similar to those of Cubans and Mexicans in the United States, but which do not occur in other parts of the world (Torrington and Tan Chwee Huat 1993, Chapter 3). There are very low wages and long working hours in China, and in Europe, Britain initially refused to accept the social chapter of the Maastricht Treaty harmonising employment conditions across the European Union.

The disparate nature of ethical standards between countries will be one of the key issues to be addressed by personnel managers operating in the international arena in the future. There will gradually be a growing together of national practice on working hours, but it will take a lot longer for rates of pay to harmonise. One can visualise common standards on health and safety developing much more quickly than equality of opportunity between the sexes and across ethnic divisions.

There seem to be games being played between governments and multinational companies:

> Corporations in the international arena . . . have no real desire to seek international rules and regulations . . . that would erode the differential competitive advantage which accrues as a consequence of astute locational decisions. Indeed the strategies are centred on endless negotiations, or the ability to play off the offer from one nation against that of another. . . . Examples of this strategy can be found in the recent negotiations over CFC restrictions, ozone depletion and the preservation of the Amazon rain forest.
> (McGowan and Mahon 1992, p. 172)

Some current and developing ethical dilemmas

We conclude this chapter by suggesting some of the less obvious ethical dilemmas for those in management positions. Issues like the environment and equalising opportunity are extensively discussed, but there are others that receive less attention.

Life in the business

What sort of quality does working life have and what sort of quality will it have in the future? Twenty years ago there was a team of experts employed at Government expense in a Quality of Working Life Unit. Their task was to suggest ways in which that quality could be improved, mainly through job redesign initiatives. Since then the general belief is that quality of working life has declined, partly through overwork and partly through fear of losing employment.

> Few people go off to work these days with a song in their hearts . . . many people dread each day because they have to work in places where they feel abused and powerless. What is happening to us? Why are talented, productive people being thwarted and sabotaged? Why do we treat each other so badly? Why are tyrannical bosses tolerated? Does the bottom line really justify the hurt and frustration we experience?
> (Wright and Smye 1996, p. 3)

Schor (1992) carried out research in the United States from which she claimed that the average American was working 164 more hours a year in the 1990s than in the 1970s.

As we saw at the beginning of this book, we now lack the comfortable feelings of security that the employing organisation used to provide. Whether people are less secure in their jobs than twenty years ago is difficult to establish, but there is no doubt that they *feel* less secure. Furthermore, the delayering and downsizing to become leaner and fitter has mainly affected people in middle-range posts, who used to be the most secure and who valued their security most highly.

As the gradual shift in organisation from entity to process continues we shall have to find ways that make work less stressful and more satisfying, despite the absence of certain of its traditionally most attractive features: security and community.

Information technology and the workplace

We have plenty of predictions of what the computer and the microprocessor can do and what will then logically happen: manufacturing will progressively be taken over by robots, rapid transfer and manipulation of data, the paperless office, people working from home instead of coming into a centre, and so forth: the golden age of the post-industrial society and the information super highway. The ethical dilemma is to wonder what will be done to make up what the computer will take from us: the conviviality and communal feeling of organisational life.

Managers have long had the opportunity to spend more of their time, and make more of their decisions, by rational planning and operational research methods than in fact they do. The strange thing is that there continues to be a preference among managers in general and personnel managers in particular to spend their time talking with people and to make their decisions as a result of discussion and shrewd judgement. Will managers now begin to eschew face-to-face discussion in favour of face-to-terminal decision-making, or will they continue to confer and keep busy while others feed to them an ever-increasing flow of processed information requiring interpretation, evaluation and further discussion? Research findings suggest that managers work the way they do at least partly because they like it that way.

> The manager actually seems to prefer brevity and interruption in his work. Superficiality is an occupational hazard of the manager's job. Very current information (gossip, hearsay, speculation) is favoured; routine reports are not. The manager clearly favours the . . . verbal media, spending most of his time in verbal contact.   (Mintzberg 1973, pp. 51–2)

The date and male gender of that quotation may be significant. Most of the studies of managerial work have been of men and of men and women working in a male-dominated culture. It may be that the increasing proportion of managerial jobs done by women will alter the stereotype. The women authors of *Corporate Abuse* are quite clear about the need to care for souls:

> Studies of work flow suggest there is five times more opportunity to experience joy in the workplace on a daily basis than in the home environment if it is a workplace that is in tune with the needs of the soul. . . . Once we have a community of fully nurtured souls, the possibility of creativity is limitless. Everyone in the workforce will be tapped into his or her own power source as well as being part of a larger community of effort and partnership.   (Wright and Smye 1996, pp. 248–9)

This rings strangely in management ears, but maybe this is the way to re-discover the sense of community that employing organisations used to provide.

How great will the influence of the computer on human resource management work actually become? How will we make up for what the computer takes away? If there is a general tendency for people to work at home, taking their terminal with them, how popular will that turn out to be? It is over a century since the household ceased to be the central productive unit and the men, and later the women, began to spend a large part of their waking hours at a different social centre: the factory, shop or office – the organisational entity. To be housebound has become a blight. We can see how it used to be:

> In 1810 the common productive unit in New England was still the rural household. Processing and preserving of food, candlemaking, soap-making, spinning, weaving, shoemaking, quilting, rug-making, the keeping of small animals and gardens, all took place on domestic premises.
>
> Although money income might be obtained by the household through the sale of produce, and additional money be earned through occasional

wages to its members, the United States household was overwhelmingly self-sufficient. . . . Women were as active in the creation of domestic self-sufficiency as were men.

(Illich 1981, pp. 111–12)

Since that time we have dismantled, or allowed to wither, all the social mechanisms that supported that self-sufficiency, and developed instead the social institution of the workplace as the arena for many of our human needs, like affiliation, interaction, team working and competition. It really seems most unlikely that the move away from working in the household will be reversed. In every country of the world roads and railways are jammed with people at the beginning of the day going to work or returning, despite the tendency for the organisational entity to decline.

The world wide web may not turn everyone into a homeworker, but it is still having a significant impact. There is the slightly isolating nature of the work that computerisation produces. The individual employee is not one of many in a crowded workshop, but one of a few scattered around a mass of busy machines. The clerical employee spends more time gazing at a computer terminal and less talking to colleagues. What employee behaviour will this engender and what attitudes will be associated with that behaviour?

WINDOW ON PRACTICE

Susan is not a high-flier, but an extremely competent and conscientious secretary who is happy to work part-time so as to maintain an active family role. She explains what she has progressively 'lost':

> When I started I worked for one boss. He was a bit of a pain at times, but I got very involved, partly because he was so disorganised. He relied on me and I could follow all the ups and downs of his office politics. There was good camaraderie with other secretaries, who really ran the place. Not at all PC, but interesting and worthwhile. Nowadays there is more concentration on just doing the basic job of setting out letters and endless hours staring at that bloody screen. I feel more and more isolated.

As more people become able to use the computer, especially for word processing, there will be a net loss of jobs. This has been seen in its most dramatic form in the publishing of newspapers, where typesetting has been eliminated through journalists typing their copy directly at a computer terminal.

The central ethical dilemma seems to be that we are allowing information technology gradually to take away the social institution of the organisation on which we have become so dependent. How will this scenario unfold?

ACTIVITY BOX 36.2

What difference has the computer made to your working life so far? What further effect do you expect it to have in the next five years? How readily would you be (or are you) a homeworker?

Employment

If employing organisations are not to provide the security of a job for life, how will people find employment, both as a way of earning their livelihood and as a means of finding their place in society? There has been much brave talk of people managing their own careers and concentrating on ensuring their continuing employability. Charles Handy enunciated his concept of portfolio living, whereby people put together a portfolio of different activities so that they could control their own lives without becoming dependent on a single employer. This is fine for the able, well-educated and independently-minded, but human society has not evolved to the point where that description fits everyone; it probably fits only a minority.

There have always been large proportions of any society who were dependent. The golden age of Ancient Greece was based on slavery, as was the earlier Pharoanic period in Egypt. The lord of the manor had his tenants, mass production required masses of people and the world has always required large numbers for their armies. Not only were there dependent people, but society depended on them. We are now moving into this strange new world where there seems to be no place for that large proportion of the population.

It is unrealistic to expect every middle-aged redundant unskilled operative or every school-leaver without GCSEs to develop their own flexible employability. They need someone or something to provide them with the opportunity to work. Current economic wisdom is that jobs can only come through the activity of the market. This is one of the common political debating points: where are the jobs going to come from? Surely, however, it is one of the salient questions for human resource management. If personnel managers have social responsibility, how will *they* improve job prospects in the economy?

There is a logical inconsistency in the per capita hours of work apparently increasing at the same time as so many people are not able to work.

Self-improvement

For a long time we have lived with inflation that was, in many ways, the engine of growth. Not only did we spend in order to avoid higher prices next month, but we always felt we were making progress when our take-home pay kept going up. Rationally we know that we were not necessarily doing better at all, but it vaguely *felt* as if we were. Recently the level of inflation has been so firmly controlled that we no longer have that spurious feeling of making progress, as cost-of-living adjustments either do not exist or seem so small.

Without the mirage of progress provided by inflation, people need to have a more genuine sense of being able to do better. We have already considered the advantages and drawbacks of relating pay to performance, which is the main way in which it has been possible recently to see an improvement in one's material circumstances, but this really pays off only for a minority.

Delayering has taken out another yardstick of progress, as the scope for promotion is much reduced. This may reduce costs and may replace the phoney improvement of promotion by the possibility of real improvement through finding new opportunities, but we should remember that the business that is 'lean and mean' feels very mean indeed to the people who are inside it.

A nice challenge for personnel managers is to develop novel aspects of corporate culture that will recognise achievement and give a sense of progress for all those who seek it, without generating envy:

> Conspicuous privilege, ostentation, and other forms of behaviour, even when not necessarily wrong, typically provoke envy. Unusually large salaries or bonuses, even if justified by competition in a free and open market, may offer demagogues fertile ground on which to scatter the seeds of envy. It is wise to take precautions against these eventualities.   (Novak 1996, p. 144)

Personal management

No, the sub-heading is not an example of the naive student's mistake in spelling 'personnel' wrong. It is a suggestion that one ethical challenge in human resource management is to ensure that the processes of management are seen to be carried out by people who can be seen, talked to, argued with and persuaded.

While it is clearly important for managers to avoid an over-preoccupation with procedural trivia, which reinforces the status quo and inhibits change, management is not all about strategy and human resource management has only a modest strategic element. It is the operational or technical aspects of personnel management that require the skill and confer the status. Is there anything harder for a manager to do well than carry out a successful appraisal interview? Are there many more important jobs to be done than *explaining* strategy, or making the absolutely right appointment of someone to a key role? This is operational management for personnel specialists, yet so often we find that the personnel manager has retreated to the strategy bunker to think great thoughts and discuss the shape of the world with like-minded people consuming endless cups of coffee, while the appraisal and the selection and the communication is left to 'the line'.

There used to be a management approach knows as MBWA, or management by walking about. This exhorted managers to get out of their offices and walk about to see what was going on and to be available. We have already referred in this chapter to the apparent preference among managers to spend their time in face-to-face discussion rather than in solitary activities. The trouble is that more and more of their contacts are with other managers rather than with people in the front line.

We suggest that it is important to maintain the work of personnel specialists as largely 'a contact sport', dealing face to face with people in all sorts of jobs in all parts of the business, so that, although the business employs you, there is an agent of that employing business with whom you can reason and debate.

Future personnel managers will need a shrewd strategic sense and a set of operational managerial skills of the type that we have described in these pages. They will also need an ethical sense, able to set management action in its context, understanding the implications (as IPM put it) 'for the enterprise, each person and the community at large'. Many aspects of management work can be developed into a science: successful personnel management is an art.

Summary propositions

36.1 In the business context, ethics are part of the corporate culture that sets norms of behaviour by which people in the business will abide because they have some moral authority as well as being convenient.

36.2 Ethical standards vary been different national cultures, making international standards difficult.

36.3 Ethical codes are only valid if they are appreciated and willingly implemented by the great majority of those to whom they apply.

36.4 Personnel management has always had a strong ethical dimension, although personnel managers and the practice of human resource management are regularly criticised for failure in social responsibility.

36.5 The Institute of Personnel and Development has a code for its members setting standards of conduct in accuracy, confidentiality, counselling, developing others, equal opportunities, fair dealing and self-development.

36.6 Among current and developing ethical dilemmas are the quality of life in the business, information technology in the work place, employment, self-improvement and personal management.

References

Armstrong, P. (1989) 'Limits and possibilities for HRM in an age of management accountancy', in J. Storey, (ed.), *New Perspectives on Human Resource Management*, London: Routledge.

Becker, H. and Fritzsche, D. J. (1987) 'A comparison of the ethical behavior of American, French and German managers', in *Columbia Journal of World Business*, Winter, pp. 87–95.

Blanchard, K. and Peale, N. V. (1988) *The Power of Ethical Management*, London: Heinemann.

Cole, R. E. and Deskins, D. R. (1988) 'Racial factors in site location and employment patterns of Japanese auto firms in America', in *California Management Review*, Fall, p. 11.

Daniel, W. W. (1986) 'Four years of change for personnel', *Personnel Management*, Vol. 18, No. 12, December, pp. 40–5.

Dehn, G. (1997) 'Blow the whistle, save a life', *The Times*, 8 April.

Flanders. A. (1964) *The Fawley Productivity Agreements*, London: Faber and Faber, p. 254.

Friedman, M. (1963) *Capitalism and Freedom*, Chicago: University of Chicago Press.

Guest, D. (1989) 'Personnel and HRM: can you tell the difference?', *Personnel Management*, January, Vol. 21, No. 1, pp. 48–51.

Haddock, C. and South, B. (1994) 'How Shell's organisation and HR practices help it to be both global and local', in D. P. Torrington (ed.), *International Human Resource Management*, Hemel Hempstead: Prentice Hall International.

Hampden-Turner, C. and Trompenaars, F. (1993) *The Seven Cultures of Capitalism*, New York: Doubleday.

Hart, T. J. (1993) 'Human resource management; time to exorcize the militant tendency', *Employee Relations*, Vol. 15, No. 3, pp. 29–36.

Illich, I. (1981) *Shadow Work*, London: Marion Boyars.

Institute of Personnel Management (1993) *Annual Report*, London: IPM.

Institute of Personnel and Development (1996a) *IPD Professional Standards*, London: IPD.

Institute of Personnel and Development (1996b) *Code of Professional Conduct*, London: IPD.

Legge, K. (1978) *Power, Innovation and Problem-solving in Personnel Management*, Maidenhead: McGraw-Hill.

McGowan, R. A. and Mahon, J. F. (1992) 'Multiple games, multiple levels: gamesmanship and strategic corporate responses to environmental issues', *Business and the Contemporary World*, Vol. 14, No. 4, pp. 162–77.

Mintzberg, H. (1973) *The Nature of Managerial Work*, London: Harper & Row.

Murray, J. (1972) 'The role of the shop steward in industry', in D. P. Torrington (ed.), *Handbook of Industrial Relations*, Gower: Epping, Essex.

Novak, M. (1996) *Business as a Calling: work and the examined life*, New York: Free Press.

Purcell, J. and Gray, A. (1986) 'Corporate personnel departments and the management of industrial relations', *Journal of Management Studies*, Vol. 23, No. 2, pp. 205–23.

Sasseen, J. (1993) 'Companies clean up', *International Management*, October.

Schor, J. B. (1992) *The Overworked American*, New York: Basic Books.

Storey, J. (1992) *Developments in the Management of Human Resources*, Oxford: Blackwell.

Torrington, D. P. (1968) *Successful Personnel Management*, London: Staples Press.

Torrington, D. P., Hitner, T. J. and Knights, D. (1982) *Management and the Multi-Racial Workforce*, Aldershot: Gower.

Torrington, D. P. and Tan Chwee Huat (1993) *Human Resource Management for South East Asia*, Singapore: Simon & Schuster.

Wokutch, R. E. (1990) 'Corporate social responsibility, Japanese style', *Academy of Management Executive*, May, pp. 56–72.

Wright, L. and Smye, M. (1996) *Corporate Abuse*, New York: Macmillan.

General discussion topics

1. The chapter opens by explaining that personnel managers have been busy trying to deny their ethical/welfare role. Why do you think this is?
2. To what extent do you regard Tim Hart's criticisms as valid?
3. What examples can members of the group produce that would put them in the position of feeling that the demands of their job were in conflict with what they regarded as being right? How would they deal with this and how do the Milgram experiments on obedience explain – or fail to explain – their actions?

Index

Ben Elton's television credits include *The Young Ones*, *Blackadder* and *The Thin Blue Line*. He has written three hit West End plays, a film and two musicals, *The Beautiful Game*, with Andrew Lloyd Webber and *We Will Rock You*, with Queen. He is also the author of a string of major bestselling novels, including *Popcorn*, which won the Crime Writers' Association's Golden Dagger Award, *Blast from the Past* and *Inconceivable*.

Ben lives in London with his wife Sophie and their three children.

KT-161-871

Critical acclaim for *Dead Famous*:

'One of Ben Elton's many triumphs with *Dead Famous* is that he is superbly persuasive about the stage of the story: the characterisation is a joy, the jokes are great, the structuring is very clever and the thriller parts are ingenious and full of suspense. And not only that – the satire (of Big Brother, of the television industry, of the arrogant ignorance and rabid inarticulacy of yoof culture) is scathing, intelligent and cherishable.

As House Arrest's twerpy contestants would put it, wicked. Double wicked. Big up to Ben Elton and respect, big time. Top, top book'
Mail on Sunday

'Brilliant . . . Ben has captured the verbal paucity of this world perfectly . . . devastatingly accurate in its portrayal . . . read Elton's book'
Janet Street-Porter, *Independent on Sunday*

'As spirited and entertaining a performance as ever from Elton'
Observer

'Elton has produced a book with pace and wit, real tension, a dark background theme, and a big on-screen climax'
Independent

'Wry, fast and fiendishly clever'
The Times

DEAD FAMOUS

Ben Elton

BLACK SWAN

DEAD FAMOUS
A BLACK SWAN BOOK : 0 552 14902 0

Originally published in Great Britain by Bantam Press,
a division of Transworld Publishers

PRINTING HISTORY
Bantam Press edition published 2001
Black Swan edition published 2002

1 3 5 7 9 10 8 6 4 2

Set in 10/11pt Melior by
Falcon Oast Graphic Art Ltd.

Black Swan Books are published by Transworld Publishers,
61–63 Uxbridge Road, London W5 5SA,
a division of The Random House Group Ltd,
in Australia by Random House Australia (Pty) Ltd,
20 Alfred Street, Milsons Point, Sydney, NSW 2061, Australia,
in New Zealand by Random House New Zealand Ltd,
18 Poland Road, Glenfield, Auckland 10, New Zealand
and in South Africa by Random House (Pty) Ltd,
Endulini, 5a Jubilee Road, Parktown 2193, South Africa.

Printed and bound in Great Britain by
Clays Ltd, St Ives plc.

With thanks to:

in the UK:
Andrew, Anna, Caroline, Claire, Craig, Darren, Mel,
Nichola, Nick, Sada and Tom
and
Amma, Brian, Dean, Elizabeth, Bubble, Helen, Josh,
Narinder, Penny, Paul and Stuart;

and in Australia:
Andy, Anita, Ben, Blair, Christina, Gordon, Jemma,
Johnnie, Lisa, Peter, Rachel, Sara-Marie, Sharna and Todd,

without whom this novel would not have been written.

David. Real job: actor. Star sign: Aries.

Jazz. Real job: trainee chef. Star sign: Leo (cusp of Cancer).

Kelly. Real job: sales consultant. Star sign: Libra.

Sally. Real job: female bouncer. Star sign: Aries.

Garry. Real job: van driver. Star sign: Cancer.

Moon. Real job: circus trapeze artiste and occasional lap dancer. Star sign: Capricorn.

Hamish. Real job: junior doctor. Star sign: Leo.

Woggle. Real job: anarchist. Star sign: claims to be all twelve.

Layla. Real job: fashion designer and retail supervisor. Star sign: Scorpio.

Dervla. Real job: trauma therapist. Star sign: Taurus.

The murder took place on day twenty-seven in the house.

Nomination

DAY TWENTY-NINE. 9.15 a.m.

'Television presenter, television presenter, television presenter, television presenter, train driver.'

Sergeant Hooper looked up. 'Train driver?'

'I'm sorry, my mistake. Television presenter.'

Chief Inspector Coleridge dumped the thick file of suspect profiles onto his desk and turned his attention once more to the big video screen that had been erected in the corner of the incident room. For the previous two hours he had been watching tapes at random.

Garry lounged on the green couch. The pause button was down and Garry's image was frozen. Had the tape been running, the picture would have been much the same, for Garry was in his customary position, legs spread wide, muscles flexed, left hand idly fondling his testicles.

A blurred blue eagle hovered above his right ankle. Coleridge hated that eagle. Just what the hell did this pointless lump of arrogance and ignorance think he had in common with an eagle? He pressed play and Garry spoke.

'Your basic English Premier League team consists of ten idiots and one big gorilla hanging about up at the front, usually a black geezer.'

Coleridge struggled to care. Already his mind was drifting. How much rubbish could these people talk?

13

Everybody talked rubbish, of course, but with most people it just disappeared into the ether; with this lot it was there for ever. What was more, it was evidence. He *had* to listen to it.

'. . . What the ten idiots have to do is keep kicking the ball up to the gorilla in the hope that he'll be unmarked and get a lucky shot in.'

The world had heard these sparkling observations before: they had been chosen for broadcast, the people at Peeping Tom Productions having been thrilled with them. The words 'black' and 'gorilla' in the same sentence would make a *terrific* reality TV moment.

' "Bold, provocative and controversial",' Coleridge muttered under his breath.

He was quoting from a newspaper article he had found inside the box of the video tape he was watching. All of the *House Arrest* tapes had arrived with the appropriate press clippings attached. The Peeping Tom media office were nothing if not thorough. When you asked for their archive, you got it.

The article Coleridge had read was a profile of Geraldine Hennessy, the celebrated producer behind *House Arrest.*

'We're not BBC TV,' Geraldine, known to the press as Geraldine the Gaoler, was quoted as saying. 'We're B*P*C TV: Bold, Provocative, Controversial, and allowing the world a window into Garry's casual, unconscious racism is just that.'

Coleridge sighed. Provocative? Controversial? What sort of ambitions were those for a grown-up woman? He turned his attention to the man sitting opposite Garry, the one on the orange couch: flashy Jason, known as Jazz, so cool, so hip, such strutting self-confidence, always grinning, except when he was sneering, which he was doing now.

'That's it, mate,' Garry continued, 'no skill, no finesse, no planning. The entire national game based

14

on the strategy of the lucky break.' Once more he rearranged his genitals, the shape of which could clearly be made out beneath the lime-green satin of his sports shorts. The camera moved in closer. Peeping Tom clearly liked genitals; presumably they were BPC.

'Don't get me wrong about saying the big bloke's black, Jazz,' Garry added. 'Fact is, most League strikers are these days.'

Jazz fixed Garry with a gaze he clearly believed was both enigmatic and intimidating. Jazz's body was even better than Garry's and he too kept his muscles in a pretty continuous state of tension. They seemed almost to ripple up and down his arms as he idly fondled the thick gold chain that hung round his neck and lay heavy on his beautiful honed chest. 'Gorilla.'

'What?'

'You didn't say "bloke", you said "gorilla".'

'Did I? Well, what I mean is gorillas are big and strong, ain't they? Like your lot.'

Over by the kitchen units Layla, the blonde hippie supermodel in her own mind, tossed her fabulous beaded braids in disgust. Inspector Coleridge knew that Layla had tossed her lovely hair in disgust, because the video edit he was watching had cut abruptly to her. There was no way that Peeping Tom was going to miss that snooty little middle-class sneer. Coleridge was quickly coming to realize that Peeping Tom's editorial position was firmly anti intellectual pretension.

'We consider ourselves to be the People's Peeping Tom,' Geraldine was quoted as saying in the article. Clearly she also considered Layla to be a stuck-up, humourless, middle-class bitch, for that was how the edit was portraying her.

Coleridge cursed the screen. He had been watching Jazz, he wanted to watch Jazz, but one of the principal handicaps of his investigation was that he could only watch whoever Peeping Tom had wanted to be watched at the time, and Inspector Coleridge had a very different agenda from that of Peeping Tom. Peeping Tom had been trying to make what they called 'great telly'. Coleridge was trying to catch a murderer.

Now the camera was back with Garry and his testicles.

Coleridge did not *think* that Garry was the murderer. He knew Garry, he had banged up twenty Garrys every Saturday night during his long years in uniform. Garry's type were all the same, so loud, so smug, so cocky. Coleridge thought back to how Garry had looked two nights before, in the aftermath of a murder, when they had faced each other over a police tape recorder. Garry hadn't looked so cocky then, he had looked scared.

But Coleridge *knew* Garry. Garrys got in fights, but they didn't murder people, unless they were very unlucky, or drunk and at the wheel of a car. Coleridge most certainly did not like this strutting, pumped-up, tattooed, cockney geezer, but he did not think that he was *evil*. He did not think that he was the sort of person to sneak up on a fellow human being, plunge a kitchen knife into their neck, pull it out again and then *bury it deep into their skull*.

Coleridge did not *think* that Garry would do something like that. But, then again, Coleridge had been wrong before, lots of times.

The nation didn't think that Garry was the murderer either. He was one of their favourites. Gazzer the Geezer had been amongst the early tabloid tips to win the game before it had turned into a real-life whodunit, and he rarely topped the poll when the media considered the identity of the killer.

Coleridge smiled to himself, a sad, rather superior smile. The only sort of smile he seemed able to muster these days. The nation did not really *know* Gazzer.

They thought they did, but they didn't. They had been given only his best bits, his chirpy one-liners, his unnerving ability to spot what he thought to be a snob or a clever dick, the relentless and gleeful way he wound up the snooty, self-important Layla. And the bold chunky penis end that had once been glimpsed peeping out from beneath his running shorts. An image that had immediately found its way onto T-shirts sold at Camden Lock market.

'Cyclops! In your bed!' Garry had shouted as if addressing a dog, before relocating the offending member. 'Sorry, girls, it's just I don't wear no pants, see. They make my love furniture sweaty.'

That was all the nation saw of Garry, just bite-sized chunks of honest, no-nonsense, common-sense geezer, and on the whole they liked him for it.

On the screen, Garry, like the video editor who had created the tape that Coleridge was watching, had noted Layla's doubtful response to his homily on racial characteristics and, sensing the reaction of a snob and a clever dick, had decided to press his point.

'It's true!' he protested, laughing at Layla's discomfort. 'I know you ain't supposed to say it, but bollocks to fucking political correctness. I'm paying Jazz a compliment. Blacks are faster and stronger and that's a proven fact. Look at boxing, look at the Olympics. Fuck me, the white blokes ought to get a medal for having the guts to compete at all! It's even worse with the birds. You seen them black birds run? Half a dozen bleeding ebony amazons charge past the finishing tape in a pack and then about ten minutes later a couple of bony-arsed gingers from Glasgow turn up.'

Bold stuff: bold, provocative and controversial.

'Yes, but that's because . . .' Layla stuttered, knowing she must refute these appalling sentiments.

'Because fucking what?'

'Well . . . because black people have to turn to sport

17

on account of the fact that other opportunities in society are closed off to them. That's why they're disproportionately over-represented in physical activities.'

Now Jazz chipped in, but not to support Layla. 'So what you're saying, right, is that in fact a load of white geezers could actually beat us blacks at running and boxing and stuff like that if only they weren't so busy becoming doctors and prime ministers? Is that it, Layles?'

'No!'

'You're the fucking racist, girl, that is disgusting!'

Layla looked as if she was going to cry. Garry and Jazz laughed together. No wonder the nation preferred them to her. A large section of the viewing public saw Gazzer and Jazz as their representatives in the house. Jovial, no bullshit, down-to-earth blokes. Top lads, diamond geezers. But how would the nation feel, Coleridge wondered, if it had to suffer them twenty-four hours a day? Suffer them as the other inmates did? Day after day, week after week, with their unabashed arrogance bouncing off the walls and ceiling. How irritating would that be? How much might someone secretly hate them? Enough to attack either of them in some way? Enough to force one or both of them on to the defensive? Enough to provoke them to murder?

But people didn't murder each other because they found each other irritating, did they? Yes. As a matter of fact, in Coleridge's experience, they did. Irritation was the commonest motive of all. Sad, petty, human disputes blown up suddenly and unintentionally into lethal proportions. How many times had Coleridge sat opposite some distraught family member as they struggled to come to terms with what they'd done because of *irritation*?

'I couldn't stand him any more. I just snapped.'

'She drove me to it.'

Most murders took place in a domestic situation between people who knew each other. Well, you couldn't get a much more domestic situation than *House Arrest*, and by the time of the murder the inmates knew each other very well, or at least knew the bits of each other that were on show, which is all anybody ever knows about anyone. These people did virtually nothing but talk to and about each other every waking moment of the day and night.

Perhaps one of them really had simply become irritating enough to get themselves killed?

But they were *all* irritating. Or at least they were to Coleridge. Every single one of them, with their toned tummies and their bare buttocks, their biceps and their triceps, their tattoos and their nipple rings, their mutual interest in star signs, their *endless* hugging and touching, and above all their complete lack of genuine intellectual curiosity about one single thing on this planet that was not directly connected with themselves.

Inspector Coleridge would happily have killed them all.

'Your problem is you're a snob, sir,' said Sergeant Hooper, who had been watching Coleridge watch the video and had followed his train of thought as surely as if Coleridge had had a glass head. 'Why the hell would anybody want to be a train driver these days anyway? There *aren't* any train drivers as a matter of fact, just some bloke that pushes the start button and goes on strike every now and then. It's hardly a noble calling, is it? I'd much rather be a TV presenter. Frankly, I'd rather be a TV presenter than a copper.'

'Get on with your work, Hooper,' said Coleridge.

Coleridge knew that they all laughed at him. They laughed at him because they thought he was old fashioned. Old fashioned because he was interested in things other than astrology and celebrity. Was he the last man on earth interested in anything other than astrology and celebrity? Things like books and trains? He was only fifty-four years old, for heaven's sake, but as far as most of his officers were concerned he might as well have been two hundred. To them Coleridge was just so *weird*. He was a member of the Folio Society, a lay minister, he never failed to visit a war memorial on Armistice Day, and he grew plants from seeds rather than buying them ready-made from a garden centre.

The fact that it had fallen to Coleridge to watch the *entire* available footage of *House Arrest*, to sit and watch a group of pointless twenty-somethings living in a house together and subjected to constant video surveillance, was a cruel joke indeed. It was safe to say that under normal circumstances there was no other show in the history of television that Coleridge would have been less inclined to watch than *House Arrest*.

Coleridge gripped the handle of the proper china mug he insisted on using despite the fact that it required washing up. 'When I want your opinion, Hooper, on train drivers or any other subject for that matter, I shall ask for it.'

'And I will always be happy to oblige, sir.'

Coleridge knew that the sergeant was right. Who could blame today's youth for its lack of sober ambition? In the days when little boys wanted to grow up to be train drivers they had wanted to grow up to be the master of a vast machine. A fabulous spitting, steaming, snarling, living beast, a monster in metal that required skill and daring to handle, care and understanding to maintain. Nowadays, of course, technology was so complex that nobody knew how anything worked at all except Bill Gates and Stephen Hawking. The human race was out of the loop, to employ a phrase he often heard Hooper using. No wonder all young people wanted was to be on television. What else was there to do? He stared wearily at the huge piles of video tapes and computer disks that seemed to fill most of the room.

'Well, let's go back to the beginning, shall we? Attack this thing in order.' He picked up a tape marked 'First broadcast edit' and put it into the machine.

One house. Ten contestants. Thirty cameras. Forty microphones. One survivor.

The words punched themselves onto the screen like fists slamming into a face.

Frantic, angry rock music accompanied the post-punk graphics and the grainy images supporting them.

A spinning hot-head camera.

A barbed wire fence.

A snarling guard dog.

A girl with her back to the camera removing her bra.

A close-up of a mouth, screaming and contorted with rage.

More big guitar noise. More jagged graphics.

Nobody watching could be in the slightest doubt that this was telly from the hip and for the hip. The message was clear: boring people should seek their entertainment elsewhere, but if you happened to be young, bigged up and mad for it, this was the show for you.

Nine weeks. No excuses. No escape.

House Arrest.

A final blast of swooping, feedback-laden guitar and the credits were over. For one last moment the Peeping Tom house was empty and all was calm. A big, bright friendly space, with a wide tiled living area, pleasant communal bedrooms, stainless steel washrooms and showers and a swimming pool in the garden.

The front door opened and ten young people spilled through it, spreading out into the large open plan living area. Ten people who, the pre-publicity had assured the nation, had never met before in their lives.

21

They whooped, they shrieked, they hugged, they said 'Wicked!' over and over again. Some went into the bedrooms and jumped up and down on the beds, others did chin-ups on the doorframes, one or two stood back a little and watched, but everybody seemed to be of the opinion that the adventure of a lifetime had just begun and they simply could not be starting off on it with a more wicked crew.

Having clearly established the fact that the viewing public were in the company of a party crowd, the camera began to introduce the housemates individually. The first to be picked out was an impossibly handsome young man with soft puppy eyes, boyish features and long shoulder-length hair. He wore a big black coat and carried a guitar. A graphic stamped itself across the man's face, letters made out of bricks, like prison walls.

David. Real job: actor. Star sign: Aries.

'Pause, please, constable.'

The image froze and the assembled officers studied the handsome face on the screen, a face disfigured by the angry graphic stamped across it.

'Real job: actor,' Coleridge said. 'When did he last work?'

Trisha, a young detective constable who had just finished pinning up the last of the seven suspect photographs, turned her attention to David's file. 'Panto, Prince Charming. Two Christmases ago.'

'Two years ago? Then it's hardly a real job, is it?'

'That's what Gazzer says later on in the show, sir,' Hooper chipped in. 'David gets quite arsey about it.'

'Arsey?'

'Annoyed.'

'Thank you, sergeant. It will speed matters up considerably in this incident room if we all speak the same language. Is there any evidence that this boy *can* actually act?'

'Oh yes, sir,' said Trisha. 'He had a very good start. RADA graduate and quite a lot of work at first, but recently it just hasn't been happening for him.'

Coleridge studied David's face frozen on the screen. 'Bit of a come-down, this, eh? I can't imagine that appearing on *House Arrest* was what he had in mind when he left drama college.'

'No, it does look a bit desperate, doesn't it?'

Coleridge looked once more at David. The face was flickering and jumping about because the police VCR was old and clapped out and did not like pausing. David's mouth was slightly open in a grin and the effect made him look like he was gnawing at the air.

'What does he live off while he's doing his real job of not acting?'

'Well, I wondered about that, sir,' said Hooper, 'and I have to admit it's a bit obscure. He doesn't sign on, but he seems to do pretty well for himself – nice flat, good clothes and all that. He told Peeping Tom that his parents helped him out.'

'Look into it, will you? If he's in debt or steals or sells drugs and one of the other people in the house had found out ... Well, there might be something, the ghost of a motive . . .' But Coleridge did not sound convinced.

'The telly people would have heard it, wouldn't they, sir? I mean, if another inmate had found something out about him? Don't they hear everything?' Trisha asked. 'Not *absolutely* everything,' Hooper, who was a reality TV buff, replied. 'They *see* everything, but they don't *hear* everything – most but not all. Sometimes, when the inmates whisper, it's hard to make out what they're saying, and every now and then they leave their microphones off and have to be told to put them back on. And they sometimes tap them when they speak. The contestants in the first series worked that one out. Remember Wicked Willy? The bloke who

23

got chucked off for trying to manipulate the votes? That was his little trick.'

'Well, that would be worth watching out for, wouldn't it?' Trisha said. 'Microphone tapping – very conspiratorial.'

'Unfortunately most of the bits where you can't hear weren't stored on disk because they were useless for broadcast.'

'Oh, well,' said Coleridge. 'As my mother used to say, life wasn't meant to be easy. Next one, please. Move on.'

'Check it out, guys! A swimming pool!'

Jazz had opened the patio doors and spun round to announce his discovery. The graphic punched bricks into his handsome young face:

Jazz. Real job: trainee chef. Star sign: Leo (cusp of Cancer).

'This is better than Ibiza!' He performed a little acid-style dance on the edge of the pool while doing a convincing vocal impression of a drum and bass track. 'Duh! Boom! Chh chh boom! Chh chh boom! Chhh chhh BOOM!

Now a girl came running out to join Jazz. A pretty girl with a happy laughing face and a small jewel stud through one nostril.

Kelly. Real job: sales consultant. Star sign: Libra.

'Wicked!' shouted Kelly.

'Chh chh boom!' Jazz replied.

Kelly began to jump up and down, clapping her hands together with excitement. 'Wicked! Unreal! *Amped up!*' She shouted, and, kicking off her baggy hipsters, she jumped into the pool.

'Sales consultant?' Coleridge enquired. 'What does that mean?'

'Shop girl,' said Hooper. 'Miss Selfridge.'

Coleridge stared at Kelly's flickering image on the screen. 'Did you see those trousers she was wearing? They showed half her bottom.'

'I've got a pair exactly the same,' Trisha remarked.

'Well, frankly, Patricia, I'm surprised. You could see her knickers poking out of the top.'

'That's the point, sir.'

'It is?'

'Yes, sir, no sense paying for a CK G-string if people can't see it, is there?'

Coleridge did not ask what CK stood for. He wasn't falling into obvious traps like that. 'What sense of her own worth does that girl have if she chooses to *boast* about her underwear?'

Coleridge wondered if he was the only person in the world who felt so completely culturally disenfranchised. Or were there others like him? Living secret lives, skulking in the shadows, scared to open their mouths for fear of exposure. People who no longer understood the *adverts*, let alone the programmes.

On the TV screen Kelly burst back out of the water, and as she did so one of her breasts popped momentarily over the top of her sodden vest. By the time she surfaced for a second time she had got it covered up. 'Oh my God!' shouted Kelly. 'I'm wearing my microphone. Peeping Tom'll kill me.'

'She was wrong about that,' Hooper remarked. 'Kelly's famous boob. I remember it well. Definitely worth the cost of a mike. They used it in the trailers, all hazy in slow-motion, very cheeky, very nice. It was in the papers, too – "It's *House A-BREAST*!" Most amusing, I thought.'

'*Could* we get on, please?' Coleridge snapped testily.

Hooper bit his lip. He pressed play and a young woman with tattoos and a Mohican haircut strutted out of the house to look at the swimming pool.

25

Sally. Real job: female bouncer. Star sign: Aries.

'They should say "Real job: token lesbian",' said Trisha. 'She's the gay one. They have to have a gay or a dyke, I think it's part of the Broadcasting Standards Commission guidelines.'

Coleridge wanted to object to the word 'dyke' but he wondered whether perhaps it had become the officially accepted term without his noticing. Language changed so quickly these days. 'Do you think those tattoos mean anything?' he asked instead.

'Yeah, they mean keep clear 'cos I'm one scary hard bitch,' Hooper replied.

'I think they're Maori,' Trisha said. 'They certainly look Maori.'

Sally's arms were entirely covered in tattoos; there was not a single square inch of flesh left showing from her wrists to her shoulders. Great thick stripes of blue-black snaked and coiled across her skin.

'You know she's the number-one Internet choice for having done it,' Hooper noted, adding, 'She'd be strong enough. Look at the muscles on it.'

'That knife was very sharp,' Coleridge snapped. 'Any one of the people in that house would have been strong enough to pierce a skull with it if they felt strongly enough about the skull they were piercing. And would you kindly keep comments about the Internet to yourself? The fact that there are millions of bored idiots out there with nothing better to do than tap rubbish down telephone lines has absolutely nothing to do with this investigation.'

Silence reigned briefly in the incident room. Coleridge was so unabashed in the way he treated them all like schoolchildren; it was difficult to know how to react.

'This bouncer business,' Coleridge said, returning to the subject of Sally. 'Known to us?'

'Soho nick have talked to her occasionally,' said

Tricia, leafing through Sally's file. 'She's cracked a few heads, but only in self-defence.'

'Her mother must be very proud.'

'She also got into a bit of a fight at last year's Gay Pride march. Took on a couple of yobs who were jeering.'

'Why do these people feel the need to define themselves by their preferences in bed?'

'Well, if they didn't talk about it, sir, you wouldn't know, would you?'

'But why do I *need* to know?'

'Because otherwise you would presume they were straight.'

'If by that you mean heterosexual, I would not presume any such thing, constable. I would not think about it at all.'

But Trisha knew that Coleridge was deceiving himself. Trisha was quite certain that Coleridge presumed *she* was a heterosexual. It simply would not occur to him to think otherwise. How she longed to shock him to his foundations and prove her point by announcing that she was as entirely and absolutely a lesbian as the tattooed girl on the screen. *Actually, sir, all my lovers are women and what I particularly enjoy is when they bang me with a strap-on dildo.*

He would be *astonished*. He thought she was such a *nice* girl.

But Trisha didn't say anything. She kept quiet. That was why she secretly admired women like Sally, irritating and graceless though they might be. *They* did not keep quiet. They made people like Coleridge think.

'Let's move on,' said Coleridge.

'Nice knockers, girl!' Sally shouted at Kelly, who was just emerging from the pool.

Garry, all muscles and shaved head, was the next to emerge from the house. On seeing Kelly, soaking wet

27

with her skimpy singlet clinging to her fit young body, he dropped to his knees in mock worship. 'Thank you, God!' he shouted to the skies. 'Something for the lads! *We like that!*'

Garry. Real job: van driver. Star sign: Cancer.

'Or the girls!' Sally shouted back. 'You never know, she might play for my team.'

'You a dyke, then?' Garry enquired, turning to her with interest.

'Derr!' said Sally, pointing to the front of her vest on which were written the words 'I eat pussy'.

'Oh, is that what it means? I thought it meant you'd just been to a Chinese restaurant!' Garry laughed hugely at his joke, which was to provoke a minor scandal when it was broadcast later that evening, being considered highly bold, provocative and controversial.

Inside the house a bald woman in a leopardskin-print mini-skirt was exploring the living area. 'Check it out, guys! There's a welcome basket! Wicked!'

Moon. Real job: circus trapeze artiste and occasional lap-dancer. Star sign: Capricorn.

'Fags, chocolate, champagne! Wicked!'

'Get stuck in!' shouted Garry from the patio doors.

The others quickly assembled around the basket and the four bottles of Sainsbury's own-brand champagne were immediately opened. They all collapsed onto the orange, green and purple couches on which they would lounge for so much of the long days to come.

'Right, since we're chilling out and kicking back, I might as well tell you now,' Moon shouted in her exaggerated Mancunian accent, 'because at the end of the day you're all going to find out anyways. First of all, I'm going to win this fookin' game, all fookin' right? So the rest of you bastards can just forget it! All right?' This exhibition of bravado was received with friendly cheers.

'Second, I've done lap-dancing, right? I took money

off sad blokes for letting them see me bits, I'm not proud of it, but at the end of the day I was fookin' good at it, right?'

This provoked more cheers and shouts of 'Good on you!'

'And third, I've had a boob job, right? I was dead unhappy with my self-image before, and my new tits have really empowered me as a person in my own right, right? Which at the end of the day is what it's all about, in't it? Quite frankly, at the end of the day, I feel that these are the boobs I was supposed to have.'

'Gi's a look, then, darling, and I'll tell you if you're right!' Gazzer shouted.

'Easy, tiger!' Moon shrieked, revelling in the attention. 'Take it easy. We've got nine fookin' weeks in here, don't want to peak too soon. Oh God, though, what have I said? I feel terrible. Me mum never knew 'bout me being a stripper, she thinks I'm dead proper, me. So-rry, Mum!'

'I've got nothing against a bit of cosmetic surgery,' Jazz reflected. 'I've never regretted my knob reduction, at least now it don't poke out the bottom of me trousers!'

The housemates laughed and shrieked and said 'Wicked!' but there were some who laughed more than others. A quiet-looking girl with raven-dark hair and green eyes only smiled. Sitting beside her was a rather straight-looking young man dressed in smart but casual Timberland.

Hamish. Real job: junior doctor. Star sign: Leo.

'He doesn't look happy,' Coleridge observed, staring at Hamish's handsome face, which was caught in a rather sullen expression.

'He's thinking about winning,' said Hooper. 'He went in with a strategy. Keep your head down, don't get noticed, that's his little motto. "Only the noticed get

29

nominated." He went into the confession box every night and said that. It's a very complex game,' Hooper continued. 'They have to play their fellow housemates one way and the public another. Be unobtrusive enough not to get nominated but interesting enough not to get evicted if they do get nominated. I think that's why people find the programme so fascinating. It's a genuine psychological study. Like a human zoo.'

'Is it?' Coleridge snapped caustically. 'In that case I wonder why the producers never seem to miss a single opportunity to broadcast sex talk or to display breasts.'

'Well, breasts are fascinating too, aren't they, sir? People like looking at them. I know I do. Besides which, when people go to the *real* zoo, what do they like looking at most? Monkeys' bums and rumpo, that's what.'

'Don't be ridiculous.'

'I'm not being ridiculous at all, sir. If you had the choice of watching two elephants either having their tea or having it off, which would you choose? People are interested in sex. You might as well face it.'

'I think we're straying from the point.'

'Do you, sir?' said Trisha, who was looking at Hamish's face on the screen. 'I don't. This house was riddled with sexual tension and that's got to be relevant, hasn't it? For instance, just look who Hamish is staring at.'

'It's impossible to say.'

'You'll see in the wide shot, it's coming up next.' Trisha touched the play button on the ancient VCR and, sure enough, the picture cut to a wide shot of the laughing, slightly drunken group lolling about on the couches.

'He's looking at Kelly now, sir, and then he starts staring at Layla. He's checking them out. The psychologist on the show says that during the first hours in the

30

house the group will be thinking principally about who they're attracted to.'

'Now that *is* a surprise, constable! And there was me imagining that they were thinking about the value of their immortal souls and the definition of God.' Coleridge regretted his outburst. He did not approve of sarcasm and he liked Trisha and valued her as an officer. He knew that she did not speculate idly. 'I'm sorry. I'm afraid I'm still having some difficulty getting over my exasperation with these people.'

'That's all right, sir. They certainly are a bunch of pains. But I do think it's important that we find out who fancies whom. I mean, in this unique murder environment jealousy has to be a fairly likely motive.'

'Who do you think fancies Woggle, then?' Hooper asked, laughing at the figure who had just appeared on the screen.

Woggle. Real job: anarchist. Star sign: claims to be all twelve.

'I mean, let's face it,' Hooper continued. 'If you were looking for a potential murder victim out of this lot, it would have to be Woggle, wouldn't it? I mean, that bloke is just asking for it.'

'Any white bloke with dreadlocks is asking for it in my opinion,' Trisha remarked, adding, 'Woggle was Geraldine the Gaoler's private little project, sir.'

'What do you mean by that, constable?'

Trisha was referring to one of the confidential internal policy briefings that she had secured from the Peeping Tom offices on the day of the murder. 'He was the only inmate of the house that Peeping Tom actually *approached*, rather than the other way round. In Geraldine Hennessy's opinion he was, and I quote, "guaranteed good telly. A natural irritant, like the grain of sand in the oyster shell around which a pearl will grow".'

'Very poetic,' Coleridge remarked. 'I must say, it's a

stretch of the imagination to think of Mr Woggle as a pearl, but it takes all sorts, I suppose.'

'She saw him on the lunchtime news on the day of the annual May Day riots, sir.'

'Ah. So he was arrested? Now that is interesting.'

'He wasn't arrested, sir, he was being interviewed by the BBC. It was Woggle's claim to fame.'

'I saw that interview you did 'bout anarchy and all that malarkey,' Moon was saying to Woggle, sensing a kindred alternative spirit. 'You were fookin' magic, babe. Double wicked.'

'Thank you, sweet lady,' Woggle replied.

'But what was the story with the medieval jester's hat? Was it, like, making a point or what?'

'It was indeed making a point, O bald woman. When the so-called wise men have run out of answers it is time to talk to the fools.'

'So they talked to you, then,' said Jazz drily.

'Correctomundo, soul brother.' Woggle flashed what he believed was a smile of devilish subtlety but which, owing to his beard and the state of his teeth, looked like a few broken Polo mints buried in a hair-filled bathroom plug-hole.

'I couldn't get to work that day,' Kelly complained. 'They closed Oxford Street. How's stopping people doing their shopping going to help anybody?'

Woggle did his best to explain, but his politics were not overburdened with detail or analysis. He seemed to recognize something he called 'the system', and he disapproved of this system in its entirety. 'That's it, really,' he said.

'So what *is* the system, then?' Kelly asked.

'Well, it's all that capitalist, global, police, money, hamburger, American, fox-hunting, animal-testing, fascist-groove-thing, isn't it?' Woggle explained in his dull, nasal monotone.

'Oh, right. I see.' Kelly sounded unconvinced.

'What we need is macrobiotic organic communities interacting with their environments in an atmosphere of mutual respect,' Woggle added.

'What the *fahk* are you talking about?' Garry enquired.

'Basically it would be nice if things were nicer.'

Once more Inspector Coleridge pressed pause. 'I presume Woggle's antagonism to "the system" does not prevent him from living off it?'

'No, sir, that's right,' Trish replied. 'The one system he truly does understand is the social security system.'

'So the state can keep him fed and watered while he seeks to overthrow it? Very convenient, I must say.'

'Yes, sir, he thinks so too,' said Hooper. 'Later on he has a huge row with the rest of them about it because they refuse to celebrate the irony of the fact that the state is funding him, its most bitter enemy.'

'Presumably because they, like the rest of us, have to fund the state.'

'That's basically their point, yes.'

'Well, I'm delighted to discover that these people and I have at least one opinion in common. This Woggle, any history of fraudulent claims? False addresses? Double-drops, financial skulduggery, that sort of thing? Anything that might make him vulnerable to discovery?'

'No, sir, on that score he's completely clean.'

There was a brief pause and then, almost uniquely, all three of them laughed. If there was one thing that Woggle wasn't, it was clean.

'Shit, man,' Jazz observed, aghast. 'Haven't you ever heard of soap?'

Woggle had taken up what was to become his habitual position, crouching on the floor in the room's only

33

corner, his bearded chin resting on bony knees which he hugged close to his chest, his great horned dirty toe-nails poking out from his sandals.

Woggle was dirty in a way that only a person who has just emerged from digging a tunnel can be dirty. He had come straight to join the *House Arrest* team from his previous home, a 200-metre tunnel under the site of the proposed fifth terminal at Heathrow Airport. Woggle had suggested to Geraldine the Gaoler that perhaps he should take a shower before joining the team, but Geraldine, ever watchful for the elements that could be said to make up 'good telly', assured him that he was fine as he was. 'Just be yourself,' she had said.

'Who's that?' Woggle had replied. 'For I am the sum of all my past lives and those I have yet to live.'

Woggle stank. Digging tunnels is hard physical work and every drop of sweat that he had sweated remained in the fabric of his filthy garments, a motley collection of old bits of combat gear and denim. If Woggle had worn a leather jacket (which, being an animal liberationist, of course he would never do) he would have looked like one of those disgusting old-style hell's angels who never washed their Levi's no matter how often they urinated on them.

'Guy, you are rank!' Jazz continued. 'You are high! Here, man, have a blow on my deodorant before we all get killed of asphyxiation and suffocate to death here!'

Woggle demurred. 'I consider all cosmetics to be humanoid affectations, yet one more example of our sad species' inability to accept its place as simply another animal on the planet.'

'Are you on drugs or what?'

'People think that they are superior to animals, and preening and scenting themselves is evidence of that,' Woggle droned with the moral self-assurance of a Buddha, 'but look at a cat's silky coat or a robin's joyful wings. Did any haughty supermodel ever look that good?'

34

'Too fucking right she did, guy,' said Jazz, who personally used two separate deodorants and anointed his skin daily with scented oils. 'I ain't never gone to sleep dreaming about shagging no cat, but Naomi and Kate are welcome any time.'

Layla spoke up from the kitchen area where she was preparing herbal tea. 'I have some cruelty-free organic cleansing lotions, Woggle, if you'd like to borrow them.'

Layla. Real job: fashion designer and retail supervisor. Star sign: Scorpio.

'They won't be cruelty-free after the plastic bottles end up in a landfill and a seagull gets its beak stuck in one,' Woggle replied.

'Don't be fooled by that fashion designer thing, sir,' said Hooper. 'She's another shop girl. It comes out later in the second week. Layla cannot believe it when Garry points out that she and Kelly do basically the same job. Layla thinks she's about a million miles above Kelly. There was quite a row.'

'Garry likes annoying them all, doesn't he?'

'Oh yes, anything for a reaction, that's Garry.'

'And this young lady Layla takes herself very seriously?'

'She does that, all right. Some of the biggest clashes in the first week are between her and David the actor, over who's the most sensitive.'

'They both reckon themselves poets,' Trisha chipped in.

'Yes, I can see that there's a lot of concealed anger there,' Coleridge remarked thoughtfully. 'A lot of failed ambition for both of them. It could be relevant.'

'Not for Layla, sir, surely? She got chucked out before the murder happened.'

'I am aware of that, sergeant, but seeing as how we don't know anything at all it behoves us to investigate everything.'

Hooper hated the fact that he worked under a man who used words like 'behoves'.

'This girl Layla's resentment and feelings of inadequacy could have found some resonance in the group. She may have been the catalyst for somebody else's self-doubt. Who knows, sometimes with murder it's entirely the wrong person that gets killed.'

'Eh?' said Hooper.

'Well, think about it,' Coleridge explained. 'Suppose a man is being taunted by his girlfriend about his powers in bed. Finally he storms out into the dark night and on his way home a stranger steps on his heel. The man spins round and kills the stranger, whereas really he wanted to kill his girlfriend.'

'Well, yes, sir, I can see that happening with a random act of anger, but the murder happened long after Layla left . . .'

'All right. Suppose you have a group of friends, and A has a dark, dark secret which B discovers. B then begins to spread the secret about and this gets back to A, but when A confronts B, B convincingly claims that the blabbermouth is in fact C. A then kills C, who actually knew nothing about it. *The wrong person gets killed.* In my experience there are usually a lot more people involved in a murder than the culprit and the victim.'

'So we keep Layla in the frame?'

'Well, not as an actual murder suspect, obviously. But before she left that house it is entirely possible that she sowed the seed that led to murder. Let's move on.'

Trisha pressed play and the camera panned across from Woggle to settle on the tenth and final housemate.

Dervla. Real job: trauma therapist. Star sign: Taurus.

She was the most beautiful, everybody agreed that, and the most mysterious. Quiet and extremely calm, it was never easy to work out what was going on behind those smiling green Irish eyes. Eyes that always seemed to be laughing at a different joke from the rest of the group. By the time of the murder Dervla had been the bookies' number-two favourite to win the game, and she would have been number one had Geraldine Hennessy not occasionally and jealously edited against her, making her look stuck-up when in fact she was merely abstracted.

'So what's a trauma therapist when it's at home, then?' Garry asked. He and Dervla were stretched out beside the pool in the pleasant aftermath of the morning's champagne.

'Well, I suppose my job is to understand how people react to stress, so that I can help them to deal with it.' Dervla replied in her gentle Dublin brogue. 'That's why I wanted to come on this show. I mean, the whole experience is really just a series of small traumas, isn't it? I think it'll be very interesting to be close to the people experiencing those traumas and also to experience them myself.'

'So it's got nothing to do with winning half a million big ones, then?'

Dervla was far too clever to deny the charge completely. She knew that the nation would almost certainly be scrutinizing her reply that very evening.

'Well, that would be nice, of course. But I'm sure I'll be evicted long before that. No, basically I'm here to learn. About myself and about stress.'

Coleridge was so exasperated that he had to make himself another mug of tea. Here was this beautiful, intelligent woman, to whom he was embarrassed to discover he found himself rather attracted, with eyes like emeralds and a voice like milk and honey, and yet she was talking utter and complete *rubbish*.

'Stress! *Stress!*' Coleridge said, in what for him was almost a shout. 'Not much more than two generations ago the entire population of this country stood in the shadow of imminent brutal occupation by a crowd of murdering Nazis! A generation before that we lost a *million* boys in the trenches. *A million innocent lads.* Now we have "therapists" studying the "trauma" of getting thrown off a television game show. Sometimes I despair, I really do, you know. I despair.'

'Yes, but, sir,' Trisha said, 'in the war and stuff people had something to stand up for, something to believe in. These days there isn't anything for us to believe in very much. Does that make our anxieties and pain any less relevant?'

'Yes, it does!' Coleridge stopped himself before he could say any more. Even he could occasionally tell when he was sounding like a bigoted, reactionary old idiot. He took a deep breath and returned to the subject of the young woman on the screen.

'So, this Dervla girl went into the house with the purely cerebral intention of observing case studies in stress?'

'Yes,' said Trisha, referring to her file on Dervla, 'she felt that the nomination process with its necessary winners and losers offered a perfect chance to study people's reactions to isolation and rejection.'

'Very laudable I must say.'

'And she also added that "she hopes one day to be a television presenter".'

'Now why does that not surprise me?' Coleridge sipped his tea and studied the screen. 'One house, ten contestants,' he said almost to himself. 'One victim.'

DAY THIRTY. 7.00 a.m.

It was now three days since the murder, and Coleridge felt as if his investigation had scarcely begun. No forensic evidence of any value had emerged from the search of the house, the suspect interviews had revealed nothing but apparent shock and confusion, the observers at Peeping Tom could not suggest even a hint of a motive, and Coleridge and his excellent team had been reduced to sitting about in front of a television making wild guesses.

Coleridge closed his eyes and breathed slowly. Focus, he had to focus, forget the storm that was raging around him and *focus*.

He tried to free his mind, rid it of all thoughts and preconceptions, make of it a blank page upon which some invisible hand might write an answer. *The murderer is . . .* But no answer came.

It just didn't seem credible that there had even *been* a murderer, and yet there had most definitely been a murder.

How could it be possible to get away with murder in an entirely sealed environment, every inch of which was covered by television cameras and microphones?

Eight people had been watching the screens in the monitoring bunker. Another had been even closer, standing behind the two-way mirrors in the camera runs that surrounded the house. Six others had been present in the room left by the killer to pursue his victim. They were still there when he or she returned shortly thereafter, having committed the murder. An estimated *47,000* more had been watching via the live Internet link, which Peeping Tom provided for its more obsessive viewers.

All these people saw the murder happen and yet somehow the killer had outwitted them all.

Coleridge felt fear rising in his stomach. Fear that his long and moderately distinguished career was about to end in a spectacular failure. A world-famous failure, for this was now the most notorious case on the planet. Everybody had a theory – every pub, office, and school, every noodle bar in downtown Tokyo, every

Turkish bath in Istanbul. Hour by hour Coleridge's office was bombarded with thousands of emails explaining who the killer was and why he or she had done it. Criminologists and Crackers were popping up all over the place – on the news, in the papers, on-line and in every language. The bookies were taking bets, the spiritualists were chatting to the victim and the Internet was about to collapse under the weight of traffic of webheads exchanging theories.

Indeed, the only person who seemed to have absolutely no idea whatsoever of the killer's identity was Inspector Stanley Spencer Coleridge, the police officer in charge of the investigation.

He walked through the house, trying to gain some sense of its secrets. Asking it to give him some clue. Not the real house, of course. The police forensics team had completed their business there in a day and had then been obliged to return it to its owners. This was a replica house that Peeping Tom Productions had been happy to lend to the police. The plasterboard and glue version that the producers had used during the months of camera rehearsal, during which they had ensured that every single angle was covered and that there truly was no place to hide. This replica house had no roof or plumbing and did not include the garden, but internally its colours and dimensions were precise. It gave Coleridge the *feel*.

He cursed himself. Standing in the imitation space, he felt that he had become like one of the actual housemates: he had no useful thoughts in his head whatsoever, only *feelings*.

'Feelings,' Coleridge thought. 'The *modus operandi* of an entire generation. You don't have to think anything, or even to believe anything. You only have to *feel*.'

Like the real house, the replica house, which stood on an empty sound stage at Shepperton Film Studios, consisted of two bedrooms, a shower room, a bathroom in which laundry could be done in a big steel trough, a toilet, an open-plan living, kitchen and dining area, a store room, and the room known as the confession box, where the inmates went to speak to Peeping Tom.

Three dark corridors ran along the edges of the house that did not open out on to the garden, and it was along these corridors that the manned cameras travelled, spying on the inmates through the huge two-way mirrors that took up most of the walls. These cameras, combined with the remote-controlled 'hot-head' ones situated inside the house, ensured that there was not a single square centimetre of space in which a person might avoid being observed. The only room that was not covered by the manual camera runs was the toilet. Even Peeping Tom's obsessive voyeurism had drawn a line at having cameramen standing 18 inches from the inmates while they evacuated their bowels. The duty editors had to watch, however, as the toilet contained a hot-head, which missed absolutely nothing. They had to listen, too, as the cubicle was also wired for sound.

Coleridge was reminded of the catchphrase that had adorned so many roadside posters in the run-up to broadcast. 'THERE IS NO ESCAPE' they had read. For one of the inmates that statement had proved horribly prophetic.

The house and garden complex was surrounded by a moat and twin lines of razorwire fencing patrolled by security guards. The monitoring bunker in which the production team worked was situated 50 yards beyond the fence and was connected to the camera runs via a tunnel under the moat. It was along this tunnel that Geraldine and the horrified Peeping Tom night crew had run on that dreadful night after they had witnessed a murder on their television monitors.

The murder.

41

It was eating Coleridge up.

For the umpteenth time he walked across the replica of the floor that the victim had crossed, to be followed moments later by the killer. Then he went and stood in the camera run, looking in on the room, just as the operator had done on the fatal night. He re-entered the living space and opened a drawer in the kitchen unit, the top one, the one the killer had opened. There were no knives in the drawer Coleridge opened; it was only a rehearsal space.

Coleridge spent almost three hours wandering around the strange, depressing replica, but it told him nothing more about what had happened during the few, brief moments of dreadful violence than he already knew. He asked himself how he would have carried out the murder had he been the killer. The answer was, in exactly the same way as the killer. It was the *only* way it could have been done with any chance of getting away with it. The killer had seen his or her one opportunity to kill with anonymity and had seized it.

Well, that was *something*, Coleridge told himself. The speed with which the killer had grasped his or her chance surely proved that he had been waiting and watching. He or she had *wanted to kill*.

What could possibly have happened to engender such hatred? Without any evidence to the contrary, Coleridge had to presume that these people had all been complete strangers to each other less than a month before. He and his team had been studying the background of all the housemates but had so far found not one shred of a suggestion that any of them had known each other prior to entering the house.

So why would a stranger plan to kill a stranger?

Because they were strangers no more. Something must have happened or been said in those three weeks that had made murder inevitable. But what? There had certainly been some dreadful goings-on in the house, but nothing had been observed that looked remotely like a motive for the crime.

It could not be ruled out that two of the inmates had not been strangers. That some ancient enmity had been unwittingly introduced into the house? That some bleak and terrible coincidence in the selection process had led to murder?

Whatever the answer, Coleridge knew that he wouldn't find it there in that gloomy old hangar at Shepperton. It was inside the real house, it was inside the *people* inside the real house.

Wearily, he returned to his car, to which Hooper had retreated half an hour earlier, and together they began their drive back to Sussex, where the real Peeping Tom house was located, a journey of about twenty miles which if they were lucky would only take them the rest of the morning.

DAY THIRTY. 9.15 p.m.

While Coleridge and Hooper nosed their way along the M25, Trisha was interviewing Bob Fogarty, the editor-in-chief of *House Arrest*. After Geri the Gaoler, Fogarty was the most senior figure in the Peeping Tom hierarchy. Trisha wanted to know more about how the people she had been watching came to be presented in the way they were.

'*House Arrest* is basically fiction,' said Fogarty, handing her a styrofoam cup of watery froth and nearly missing her hand in the darkness of the monitoring bunker. 'Like all TV and film. It's built in the edit.'

'You manipulate the housemates' images?'

'Well, obviously. We're not scientists, we make television programmes. People are basically dull. We have to make them interesting, turn them into heroes and villains.'

43

'I thought you were supposed to be observers, that the whole thing was an experiment in social interaction?'

'Look, constable,' Fogarty explained patiently, 'in order to create a nightly half-hour of broadcasting we have at our disposal the accumulated images of thirty television cameras running for twenty-four hours. That's seven hundred and twenty hours of footage to make one *half-hour* of television. We couldn't avoid making subjective decisions even if we wanted to. The thing that amazes us is that the nation *believes* what we show them. They actually accept that what they are watching is real.'

'I don't suppose they think about it much. I mean, why should they?'

'That's true enough. As long as it's good telly they don't care, which is why as far as possible we try to shoot the script.'

'Shoot the script?'

'It's a term they use in news and features.'

'And it means?'

'Well, say you're making a short insert for the news, investigating heroin addiction on housing estates. If you simply went out to some urban hellhole with a camera and started nosing around, you could be looking for the story you want till Christmas. So you *script* your investigation before you leave your office. You say . . . all right, we need a couple of kids to say they can get smack at school, we need a girl to say she'd whore for a hit, we need a youth worker to say it's the government's fault . . . You write the whole thing. Then you send out a researcher to round up a few show-offs and basically tell them what to say.'

'But how could you do that on *House Arrest*? I mean, you can't tell the housemates what to say, can you?'

'No, but you can be pretty sure of the story you want to tell and then look for the shots that support it. It's the only way to avoid getting into a complete mess. Look at this, for instance . . . This is Kelly's first trip to the confession box on the afternoon of day one.'

DAY ONE. 4.15 p.m.

'It's brilliant, wicked, outrageous. I feel just totally bigged-up and out there,' Kelly gushed breathlessly from the main monitor. She had come to the confession box to talk about how thrilling and exciting it all was.

'I mean, today has just been the wickedest day ever because I really, really love all these people and I just know we're all going to get along just brilliantly. I expect there'll be tension and I'll end up hating all of them for, like, just a moment at some point. But you could say that about any mates, couldn't you? Basically I *love* these guys. They're my posse. My crew.'

Deep in the darkness of the editing suite Geraldine glared at Fogarty. 'And that's what you want her to say, is it?'

Bob cowered behind his styrofoam cup. 'Well, it's what she did say, Geraldine.'

Geraldine's eyes flashed, her nostrils flared and she bared her colossal overbite. It was as if the Alien had just burst out of John Hurt's stomach.

'You stupid cunt! You stupid lazy cunt! I could get a monkey to broadcast what she actually said! I could get a work-experience school-leaver pain-in-the-arse spotty fucking waste-of-space teenager to broadcast what she *actually* said! What I pay you to do is to *look* at what she *actually* said and *find* what we *want her to say*, you *cunt*!'

Fogarty threw a commiserating glance at the younger, more impressionable members of staff.

'Who is Kelly, Bob?' Geraldine continued, throwing an arm towards the frozen image of the pretty young brunette on the screen. 'Who is that girl?'

Fogarty stared at the television. A sweet smile beamed back at him, an open, honest, naïve countenance. 'Well . . .'

'She's our bitch, Bob, she's our manipulator. She's one of our designated hate figures! Remember the audition interviews? All that pert ambition? All that artless knicker-flashing. All that *girl power bollocks*. Remember what I said, Bob?'

Fogarty did remember, but Geraldine told him anyway.

'I said, "Right, you arrogant little slapper, we'll see how far you get towards presenting your own pop, style and fashion show once the whole nation has decided you're a back-biting, knob-teasing fucking *dog*," didn't I?'

'Yes, Geraldine, but on the evidence of today she's turned out to be really quite nice. I mean, she's a bit of an airhead, and vain, certainly, but she's not really a bitch. I think we'll find it quite hard to make her look that nasty.'

'She'll *look* however we want her to look and *be* whatever we want her to be,' Geraldine sneered.

DAY THIRTY. 9.20 a.m.

'Does Geraldine normally talk to you like that?' Trisha asked.

'She talks to everybody like that.'

'So you get used to it, then?'

'It's not something you get used to, constable. I have an MSc in computing and media. I am *not* a stupid cunt.'

Trisha nodded. She had heard of Geraldine

46

Hennessy before her *House Arrest* fame. Most people had. Geraldine was a celebrity in her own right. A famously bold, provocative and controversial broadcaster, Trisha ventured.

'Rubbish!' said Bob Fogarty. 'She's a TV whore masquerading as an innovator and getting away with it because she knows a few popstars and wears Vivienne Westwood. What she does is steal tacky, dumbed-down tabloid telly ideas, usually from Europe or Japan, smear them with a bit of hip, clubby, druggy style, and flog them to the middle class as post-modern irony.'

'So you don't like her, then?'

'I loathe her, constable. People like Geraldine Hennessy have ruined television. She's a cultural vandal. She's a nasty, stupid, dangerous bitch.'

In the gloom Trisha could see that Fogarty's cup was shaking in his hand. She was taken aback. 'Calm down, Mr Fogarty,' she said.

'I am calm.'

'Good.'

Then Fogarty played Kelly's confession as it had been broadcast.

'I'll end up hating all of them.'

Seven words were all she said.

DAY ONE. 4.30 p.m.

Kelly left the confession box and went back into the living area of the house. Layla gave her a sympathetic little smile and stroked her arm as she walked by. Kelly turned back, smiled and then they had a little hug together.

'Love you,' said Layla.

'Love you big time,' Kelly replied.

'You stay strong, OK?' said Layla.

47

Kelly assured Layla that she would certainly attempt to stay strong.

Kelly was so pleased that Layla was hugging her. Earlier in the day they had had a small tiff over Layla's insistence on including walnut oil on the first group shopping list. Layla pointed out that since she ate mainly salad, dressings were very important to her and that walnut oil was an essential ingredient.

'Also it lubricates my chakras,' she'd said.

Kelly had suggested to Layla that with their limited food budget, walnut oil was surely rather an expensive luxury item.

'Well, I think that's an entirely subjective observation, babes,' Layla replied, relishing her own eloquence, 'and quite frankly depends on how much you value your chakras.'

David then weighed in, supporting Layla. He pointed out that as far as he was concerned the bacon that Kelly had suggested they order, because she cooked a wicked brekkie, was hardly an essential item . . . 'except perhaps to the pig that donated it', David observed piously from the unimpregnable fortress of his lotus position. 'Personally I would far rather order walnut oil than corpse.'

All the other boys leapt in and supported Kelly, but David and Layla's effortless occupation of the moral high ground had made Kelly feel rotten and for a minute she had thought she would cry. Instead she went into the confession box and told Peeping Tom how much she loved everybody.

Now she had re-emerged and Layla had rewarded her with a hug.

Kelly was wearing only a T-shirt and a tiny pair of shorts and Layla was dressed with similar minimalism in a little silk sarong and matching bikini top. Their tight little tummies touched and their breasts pushed against each other.

Across the room the hot-head camera clamped to the ceiling whizzed and whirred and zoomed towards them with unseemly haste.

DAY THIRTY. 9.45 a.m.

'You know that even though the weather was warm and sunny Geraldine insisted that the central heating be on at all times, don't you?' Fogarty said.

Trisha was astonished. 'You made it hot in order to get people to take their clothes off?'

'Of course we did. What do you think? Peeping Tom wanted bodies! Not baggy jumpers! Twenty-four degrees Centigrade is the optimum good telly temperature, warm but not sweaty. Geraldine always says that if she could make it twenty-five degrees in the room and minus five in the vicinity of the girls' nipples she'd have the perfect temperature.'

Trisha looked at Fogarty thoughtfully. He certainly was going out of his way to make his employer look bad. Why was that? she wondered.

'Anyway,' the man concluded, 'Miss High and Mighty, oh so brilliant, Machiavellian genius Geraldine Hennessy got it totally wrong with Kelly, although she has never admitted it. She thought that just because *she* didn't like Kelly nobody else would, but the public did like her and apart from Woggle she was the most popular one on the show. We had to change tack and from day two we edited in Kelly's favour.'

'So sometimes the subject does lead the programme?'

'Well, with a little help from me, I must admit. I gave Kelly plenty of cute angles. I was buggered if I was going to do Geraldine's dirty work.'

49

DAY THIRTY-ONE. 8.30 a.m.

After reading Trisha's report of her interview with Fogarty, Coleridge called a meeting of all his officers.

'Currently,' he said firmly, 'I am of a mind that we are pursuing the wrong seven suspects *and* the wrong victim.'

This comment, like so many that Coleridge made, was met with blank stares. He could almost hear the whoosh as it swept over their heads.

'How's that, then, boss?' said Hooper.

'Boss?'

'Inspector.'

'Thank you, sergeant.'

'How's that, then, inspector?' Hooper persevered wearily. 'How is it that we're pursuing the wrong suspects and the wrong victim?'

'Because we are looking at these people in the way that the producers and editors of Peeping Tom Productions want us to look at them, not as they *are*.' Coleridge paused for a moment, his attention drawn to an officer at the back of the room who was chewing gum, a *female* officer. He longed to tell her to find a scrap of paper and dispose of it, but he knew that the days when an inspector could treat his constables in that manner had long gone. He would not be at all surprised if there was a court in Brussels that could be cajoled into maintaining that the freedom to chew gum was a human right. He confined his reaction to a withering stare, which caused the girl's jaw to stop moving for all of three seconds.

'We must therefore be extremely cautious in our views, for apart from a brief interview with each of the surviving housemates after the murder, we know these people only through the deceiving eye of the television camera, that false friend, so convincing, so plausible, so *real* and yet, as we have already seen, so fickle and so false. We must therefore begin at the beginning with all of them and presume nothing. Nothing at all.'

50

And so the grim task of reviewing the *House Arrest* tape archive continued.

'*It's day three under* House Arrest *and Layla has gone to the refrigerator to get some cheese.*' This was the voice of Andy, *House Arrest's* narrator. '*Layla's vegan cheese is an important part of her diet, being her principal source of protein.*'

'You see how television pulls the wool over our eyes!' Coleridge exclaimed in exasperation. 'If we weren't concentrating, we might actually have formed the impression that something of interest had occurred! This man's talent for imbuing the most gut-wrenchingly boring observations with an air of significance normally reserved for matters of life and death is awe-inspiring.'

'I think it's the Scottish accent,' said Hooper. 'It sounds more sincere.'

'The man could have covered the Cuban Missile Crisis without altering his manner at all . . . It's midnight in the Oval Office and President Kennedy has yet to hear from Secretary Khrushchev.'

'Who was Khrushchev?' Hooper asked.

'Oh, for God's sake! He was General Secretary of the Soviet Union!'

'Never heard of it, sir. Is it affiliated to the TUC?'

Coleridge hoped that Hooper was joking but decided not to ask. Instead he pressed play again.

'*Layla has just discovered that some of her cheese has gone missing,*' said Andy.

'He says it as if she's just discovered penicillin,' Coleridge moaned.

DAY THREE. 3.25 p.m.

Layla slammed the fridge door angrily. 'Hey right, I mean, yeah, I mean, come on, OK? Who's been eating my cheese?'

51

'Oh yeah, right. That was me,' said David. 'Isn't that cool?' David always spoke to people in the sort of soft, faintly superior tone of a man who knows the meaning of life but thinks that it's probably above everybody else's head. Normally he talked to people from behind because he tended to be massaging their shoulders, but when he addressed them directly he liked to stare right into their eyes, fancying his own eyes to be hypnotic, limpid pools into which people would instinctively wish to dive.

'I mean, I thought it would be cool to have a little of your cheese,' he said.

'Oh, yeah,' Layla replied. 'Half of it, actually . . . But that's totally cool. I mean totally, except you will replace it, right?'

'Sure, yeah, absolutely, whatever,' said David, as if he was above such matters as worrying about whose cheese was whose.

'*Later*,' said Andy the narrator, '*in the girls' room, Layla confides in Dervla about how she feels about the incident involving the cheese.*'

Layla and Dervla lay on their beds.

'It's not about the cheese,' Layla whispered. 'It's so *not* about the cheese. It's just, you know, it was my cheese.'

DAY THIRTY-ONE. 8.40 a.m.

'I'm honestly not sure if I can continue with this investigation,' said Coleridge.

DAY THIRTY-ONE. 2.00 p.m.

'Actually it was Layla's cheese that gave Geraldine her first crisis.'

Trisha had returned to the monitoring bunker to speak once more with Bob Fogarty. She and Coleridge had agreed that Fogarty was the person who knew most about the housemates and also about the workings of Peeping Tom. 'Why was there a crisis over the cheese?' she asked Fogarty.

'Well, because the duty editor resigned and took both his assistants with him. I had to come in myself and cover. Don't you call that a crisis? I call it a crisis.'

'Why did he resign?'

'Because unlike me he still had some vestige of professional pride,' Fogarty reflected bitterly, dropping a square of milk chocolate into his cup of watery foam, something Trisha had never seen anyone do before. 'As a highly trained, grown-up adult, he simply could not continue to go home to his wife and children each evening and explain that he'd spent his entire working day minutely documenting a quarrel between two complete idiots about a piece of cheese.'

'And so he resigned?'

'Yes. He sent Geraldine an email saying that *House Arrest* was a disgrace to the British television industry, which, incidentally, it is.'

'And what did Geraldine do?'

'What do you think she did? She leaned out of her window and shouted, "Good riddance, you pompous cunt!" at him as he got into his car.'

'She didn't mind, then?'

'Well, it was very inconvenient certainly, particularly for me, but we soon got a replacement. People want to come to us. We make "cutting-edge television", you see.' Fogarty's voice was bitter with sarcasm. 'We're at the sharp end of the industry, we're hip, challenging and innovative. This is, of course, an industry where they thought it was challenging and innovative when the newsreaders started perching on the fronts of their desks instead of sitting behind them . . . Damn!'

Fogarty fished about in his cup with a teaspoon, searching for the square of chocolate. Trisha concluded that he had been intending only to soften the outside rather than melt it completely. People develop strange habits when they spend their working lives in dark rooms.

'God, I was jealous of that bloke who left,' Fogarty continued. 'I came into television to edit cup finals and Grand Nationals! Drama and comedy and science and music. What do I end up doing? I sit in the dark and stare at ten deluded fools sitting on couches. *All day*.'

Trisha was discovering one of the great secrets of *House Arrest*. The people who worked on it *loathed* the people they were charged with watching.

'It's all just so boring! *No one* is interesting enough to be looked at the way we look at these people, and particularly not the sort of person who would *wish* to be looked at. It's catch twenty-two, you see. Anyone who would *want* to be in that damn stupid house is by definition not an interesting enough person to be there.' Fogarty stared at his bank of television monitors. A long, sad, hollow silence ensued.

'It's the *hugging* I hate most, you know,' he said finally, 'and the *stroking* . . . And above all the endless *wittering on*.'

'You should meet my boss,' said Trisha. 'You two would really hit it off.'

Fogarty fell silent once more before resuming his theme.

'If that lot in the house had any idea of the contempt in which we hold them from our side of the mirrors, the cruel nicknames we give them . . . 'Nose-picker', 'Sad slap', 'the Farter' . . . If they knew the damning assessments we make as we chop up their comments to suit our needs, the complete lack of respect we have for any of their motives . . . well, they'd probably wish they'd *all* got murdered.'

Coleridge and his team were becoming increasingly frustrated with Woggle. The problem was that he kept getting in the way of the other housemates. The people at Peeping Tom had thought him such good telly that large chunks of what footage remained from the early days of the show concerned his exploits and the other housemates' ever more frustrated reactions to them.

'If it had been Woggle that was murdered we could have made a circumstantial case against any of them,' Coleridge complained. 'I'm sick of the sight of him myself and I didn't have to live with the man.'

'You can't blame the producers for pushing him,' Hooper said. 'I mean, for a while there the country was obsessed. "Wogglemania", they called it.'

Coleridge remembered. Even he had been aware of the name popping up on the front pages of the tabloids and on page three or four of the broadsheets. At the time he had not had the faintest idea who they were talking about. He had thought it was probably a footballer or perhaps a celebrity violinist.

Hooper ejected the video tape that they had just finished and put it on the small 'watched' pile, then took another tape from the colossal 'have not yet watched' pile and put it into the VCR.

'You do know that the "have not yet watched" pile is just a satellite of a much bigger one, don't you, sir? Which we have in the cells.'

'Yes, I did know that, sergeant.'

Hooper pressed play and once more the sombre Scottish brogue of Andy the narrator drifted across the incident room.

'*It's day four in the house and Layla and Dervla have suggested that a rota be organized in order to more fairly allocate the domestic chores.*'

Coleridge sank a little further into his chair. He knew

55

that he couldn't allow himself another mug of tea for almost fifty minutes. One an hour, fourteen pint mugs a working day, that was his limit.

DAY FOUR. 2.10 p.m.

'I want to have a house meeting,' said Layla. 'So would it be cool if everybody just chilled? So we can all just have a natter maybe?'

Across the room Moon's bald head poked out from the book she was reading, a book entitled *You Are Gaia: Fourteen Steps to Becoming the Centre of Your Own Universe.*

'It's dead spiritual, this book,' Moon said. 'It's about self-growth and development and personal empowerment, which at the end of the day I'm really into, if you know what I mean, right?'

'Yeah, Moon, wicked. Look, um, have you seen the state of the toilet?'

'What about it?'

'Well, it's not very cool, right? And Dervla and I . . .'

'I'm not fookin' cleaning it,' said Moon. 'I've been here four days and I ain't even done a poo yet. I'm totally fookin' bunged up, me, because I'm not getting my colonic irrigation, and also I reckon the electrical fields from all the cameras are fookin' about with me yin and me yang.'

'Layla's not asking you to clean the toilet, Moon,' said Dervla gently. 'We just think it would be good to organize some of the jobs that have to be done around the house, that's all.'

'Oh. Right. Whatever. I'm chilled either way. But at the end of the day I'm just not scrubbing out other people's shite when I haven't even done one. I mean, that would be *too* fookin' ironic, that would.'

'Well, I don't mind doing heavy work, like lifting

and shifting,' said Gazzer the Geezer, pausing in the push-ups that he had been doing pretty continuously since arriving in the house, 'but I ain't cleaning the bog, on account of the fact that I don't mind a dirty bog anyway. Gives ya something to aim at when you're having a slash, don't it?'

The look of horror on Layla's delicate face filled the screen for nearly ten seconds.

'Well, never mind the toilet, Garry. What about the washing-up?' Dervla enquired. 'Or do you not mind eating off mouldy plates either?'

David, beautiful in his big shirt, did not even open his eyes when he spoke. 'Perhaps for the first week or so we should just do our own chores. I'm detoxing at the moment and am only eating boiled rice, which I imagine will be rather easier to clean off plates than whatever bowel-rotting garbage Garry, Jazz and Kelly choose to gorge themselves on.'

'Suits me,' said Gazzer. 'I always clean my plate with a bit of bread anyway.'

'Yes, Garry,' said Layla, 'and I'm not being heavy or anything, but perhaps you should remember that the bread is for *everyone*. I mean, I hope you think that's a chilled thing to say? I'm not trying to diss you or anything.'

Gazzer simply smirked and returned to his push-ups.

'Wouldn't doing our washing-up individually be a bit silly, David?' said Kelly.

'And why would that be, Kelly?' David opened his eyes and fixed Kelly with a soft, gentle, tolerant smile that was about as soft, gentle and tolerant as a rattle-snake.

'Well, because . . . Because . . .'

'Please don't get me wrong. I feel it's really important that you feel *able* to say to me that I'm stupid, but why?'

'I didn't mean . . . I mean, I didn't think . . .' Kelly said no more.

David closed his eyes once more and returned to the beauty of his inner thoughts.

Hamish, the junior doctor, the man who did not wish to be noticed, made one of his rare contributions to the conversation.

'I don't like house rotas,' he said. 'I had five years of communal living when I was a student. I know your sort, Layla. Next you'll be fining me an egg for not replacing the bogroll when I finish it.'

'Oh, so it's *you* that does that, is it?' said Dervla.

'I was giving an example,' said Hamish hastily.

'I'll tell you what's worse than a bogroll finisher,' Jazz shouted, leaping into the conversation with eager enthusiasm: 'a draper! The sort of bastard who finishes the roll, all except for a *single sheet*, which he then proceeds to *drape* over the empty tube!'

Jazz may have been a trainee chef, but that was just a job, not a vocation. It was not what he wanted to do with his life at all. Jazz wanted to be a comedian. *That* was why he had come into the house. He saw it as a platform for a career in comedy. He knew that he could make his friends laugh and dreamt of one day making a rich and glamorous living out of this ability. Not a stand-up, though; what he wanted to be was a *wit*. A raconteur, a clever bastard. He wanted to be on the panel of a hip game show and trade inspired insults with the other guys. He wanted to be a talking head on super-cool TV theme nights, cracking top put-downs about ex-celebrities. He wanted to host *an award ceremony*. That was Jazz's ambition, to be one of that élite band of good old boys who made their living out of just saying *brilliant* things *right off the cuff*. He wanted to be hip and funny and wear smart suits and be part of the *Zeitgeist* and just take the *piss* out of everything.

58

First, however, Jazz needed to get noticed. He needed people to see what a cracking good bloke and dead funny geezer he was. Since entering the house he had been looking for opportunities to work his ideas for material into the conversation. The mention of empty toilet rolls had been a gift.

'The draper is a toilet Nazi!' Jazz cried. 'He doesn't have to replace the roll, no, 'cos it ain't *finished* yet, is it? He's left just enough for the next bloke's fingers to go straight through and right up his arse!'

Jazz's outburst was met with a surprised silence, not least perhaps because he had chosen to deliver most of it directly into one of the remote cameras that hung from the ceiling.

'You don't even know if they'll broadcast it, Jazz,' said Dervla.

'Gotta keep trying, babes,' Jazz replied. 'Billy Connolly used to gig to *seagulls* when he was a Glasgow docker.'

'Look! Please!' Layla protested. 'Can we *please* just chill! We are trying to organize a rota.'

'Why don't we just take it easy and see what happens?' said Hamish. 'Things will get done, they always do.'

'Yes, Hamish, they will get done by people like me and Layla,' said Dervla, the soft poetry of her voice becoming just a little less soft and poetic, 'after which people like you will say, "See, look, I told you things would get done," but the point will be that *you* didn't do them.'

'Whatever,' Hamish replied, returning to his book. 'Make a rota if you want. I'm in.'

DAY THIRTY-ONE. 3.10 p.m.

'You see, sir,' said Hooper, pressing pause once more, 'Hamish backs off, he doesn't want to be noticed. Only the noticed get nominated.'

59

Coleridge was confused. 'Didn't Hamish go to the confession box and say that his ambition was to have sex before he left the house?'

'That's him – the doctor.'

'Well, wouldn't saying something like that get him noticed?'

Hooper sighed. 'That's different, sir, the confession box is for the *public*. Hamish needs to be a bit saucy in there so that if he does get nominated for eviction by the *housemates*, the public won't want to evict him because he says he's going to have sex on television.'

'But surely that would be an excellent reason *for* evicting him,' Coleridge protested.

'Not to most people, sir.'

DAY FOUR. 2.20 p.m.

The shrugs of the rest of the group indicated that Layla and Dervla had won the day, and since the inmates of the house were allowed neither pencil nor paper Jazz, drawing on his training as a chef, suggested that they make the rota grid out of spaghetti.

'Spag sticks to walls,' he said. 'That's how you check it's done. You chuck it at the wall and if it sticks it's done.'

'Well, that's fahkin' stupid, Jazz,' said Gazzer. 'I mean, then you'd have to scrape your dinner off the wall, wouldn't you?'

'You don't throw all of it, you arsehole, just a strand or two.'

'Oh, right.'

'*Jazz lightly boils some spaghetti*,' said Andy the narrator, '*and makes a rota grid on the wall.*'

'Bitching,' said Jazz, admiring his handiwork. 'Now each of us can be represented by grains of boiled rice. The starch will make them stick.'

'Wicked!' shouted Moon. 'We can each personalize our grains, like them weird fookers in India or wherever who do rice sculptures. I saw it on Discovery, they do all this incredible tiny detail and the really, really philosophical thing about it is, it's too fookin' small to see.'

'Well, that's just fahkin' stupid, isn't it?' Gazzer opined.

'It's not! It's a fookin' philosophical point, ain't it? Like if a tree falls in a forest but nobody hears it. Did it make a noise or whatever. These blokes don't do it for you or me. They decorate grains of rice for God.'

'You've lost me.'

'That's because at the end of the day you're dead thick, you are, Garry. You think you're not, but you are.'

They all began to discuss how they could individualize their grains of rice, and it was at this point that Woggle spoke up from his corner. 'People, I have yet to speak, and I think that this domestic fascism is totally divisive. The only appropriate and equitable method of hygiene control is to allow work patterns to develop via osmosis.'

They all looked at Woggle.

'Listen, guy, I have to tell you,' said Jazz. 'The only thing developing via osmosis on you is mould.'

Layla tried to be reasonable. 'Surely, Woggle, you're not saying that any type of group organization is fascism?'

'Yes, I am.'

There was a pause while the nine people who were trapped in a small house with this creature from the black latrine took in the significance of his answer. They were going to have to live with a man who considered organizing the washing-up tantamount to invading Poland.

61

Woggle took the opportunity of their stunned silence to press his advantage. 'All structures are self-corrupting.'

'What *are* you talking about, guy?' said Jazz. 'Because I have to tell you, man, you are sounding like a right twat.'

'Centrally planned and rigidly imposed labour initiatives rarely produce either efficient results or a relaxed and contented workforce. Look at the Soviet Union, look at the London Underground.'

'Woggle,' Layla was now sounding slightly shrill, 'there are ten of us here and all I'm saying is that in order that the house stays nice it would be a good idea to rotate the housework.'

'What you are saying, sweet lady,' Woggle replied in his irritating nasal tone, 'is that a person can only be trusted to act responsibly if he or she is ordered to do so.'

'I am *so* going to hate you,' said Jazz, speaking for the group.

'In the greater scheme of things,' Woggle said, 'within the positive and the negative energy of creation, hate is merely the other half of love, for every season has its time. Therefore in terms of the universe as a whole, actually, you love me.'

'I fucking don't,' said Jazz.

'Yes, you do,' said Woggle.

'I fucking *don't*!' said Jazz.

'You do,' said Woggle.

Woggle never gave up.

DAY FIVE. 9.00 a.m.

Dervla pushed the bar of soap up under her T-shirt and washed her armpits. She was just beginning to get used to showering in her underwear; it had felt very uncomfortable on the first morning and rather silly, like being on a school trip and insisting on undressing under the covers. The alternative, however, meant exposing her naked body full frontal to the viewing millions, and Dervla had absolutely no intention of doing that. She had watched enough reality TV to know what the producers liked most and took great care as she lathered under her arms. It would be extremely easy to inadvertently pull up her vest and expose her breasts and she knew that behind the two-way mirrors in the shower cubicle wall a live cameraman was watching, waiting for her to do just that. One flash would be all that was required and her tits would be hanging around somewhere on the Internet till the end of time.

Having showered, Dervla went to brush her teeth, and it was while doing this that she noticed the letters on the mirror. For a moment she thought that they had been left in the condensation by the previous occupant of the shower room, but when more appeared she realized with a thrill that they were being written from the other side of the mirror.

Although Dervla had been incarcerated for only four days, already she had begun to feel as if she and her fellow inmates were the only people left on earth. That their little sealed bubble was all that was left in the world. It was quite a shock to be reminded that it wasn't. That outside, beyond the mirror, just inches away but in another world, someone was trying to talk to her.

'*Shhhhh!*'

That was the first word that had appeared. Written as Dervla watched, letter by letter appearing through the steam and condensation, right near the bottom of the mirror, just above the basin taps.

'*Don't stare,*' came next, and Dervla realized that she was standing bug-eyed, still holding her toothbrush in her mouth, looking at the letters. Quickly she re-adjusted her gaze, looking at her own reflection as toothbrushers are wont to do.

After a moment she allowed her eyes to flick down again.

'*I like you*,' said the words. '*I can help you. Bye now.*'

There was a pause and then the anonymous communicator's final letters. '*XXX.*'

Dervla finished brushing her teeth quickly, wrapped a towel around her, took off her wet knickers and vest, dressed as fast as she could and went outside to sit in the vegetable garden. She needed to think. She could not decide whether she was angry or excited about this un-sought-for development. On balance she reckoned that she was both. Angry because this man (she felt certain it was a man) had clearly singled her out for his special attention. He had been watching her and now he wanted to use the power he had over her to intrude on her space. That gave her rather an uncomfortable feeling. What were his motives? Was he attracted to her? Was he perving on her? What other reason could he have for risking his job in such a manner? On the other hand, perhaps he was doing it for a laugh? Perhaps he was just a wild and crazy guy who fancied the crack of manipulating Peeping Tom? Dervla was well aware of how much the media preferred scandals and skulduggery in the house to honest relationships. It was always the bad boys and girls who got the publicity. If this mysterious letter-writer managed to open up a dialogue with her, the story would certainly be worth more than a cameraman's wage.

That was a thought. Perhaps he was already in the pay of a newspaper? The press were always trying to drop leaflets and parachutists and hang-glider pilots into the house; it must have occurred to them to try to bribe a cameraman. Now another thought occurred to her: perhaps this person was no friend at all, but an *agent provocateur*! Seeking to tempt her into breaking the rules! Was this entrapment? A sting? Were Peeping Tom or the newspapers trying to catch her out? If so, then were they trying the same trick on the others?

Dervla imagined her exposure as a cheat, the earnest tones of the voiceover man revealing her shame. Revelling in it. '*We decided to test each of the inmates by offering them an illegal channel of communication with the outside world. Dervla was the only housemate to take the bait, the only willing cheat . . .*'

That would be it, expulsion in disgrace, for ever more to be labelled 'Devious Dervla,' 'Dastardly Dervla' . . . *Dirty Dervla.*

Her mind swam. She forced herself to focus her thoughts.

It simply couldn't be Peeping Tom doing this. Entrapment was immoral – she wasn't at all sure if it wasn't an actual crime. If a respectable production company did that, then nobody would ever trust them again. No, it couldn't be Peeping Tom.

What if it was the media? Well, so what? So far she had done nothing wrong and she would be careful to keep it that way. Besides, any paper that had bribed a cameraman could not publish anything about it without revealing their source, and they would certainly wait a while to do that. Dervla reckoned that at the very least she had time to sit back and see how the situation developed. And if it really was a friend, somebody who had taken a shine to her and wanted her to win . . . Who could tell? Perhaps it might give her the edge. It would certainly be nice to get a bit of outside information . . . And she hadn't actually *asked* for any help, so it wasn't really immoral. Not to look in the mirror, surely?

DAY THIRTY-TWO. 9.20 p.m.

One wall of the incident room had become known as 'the Map'. On it Trisha had affixed photographs of the ten housemates, which she had then connected by a great mass of criss-crossing lines of tape stuck to the plaster with Blu-Tack. On the strips of tape Trisha and her colleagues had written short descriptive sentences such as 'attracted to', 'loathes', 'had row about cheese', and 'spends too long in the toilet'.

Hooper had attempted to recreate Trisha's map on his computer, using his photo scanner and untold gigabytes of three-dimensional graphic-arts software programming. Sadly the project defeated him and a little bomb kept appearing and telling him to restart the computer. Soon Hooper was forced to slink back to the drawing pins and Blu-Tack along with everybody else.

Now Coleridge was standing in front of the map solemnly contemplating the ten housemates and the ever-growing web of interconnecting relationships. 'Somewhere,' he said, 'somewhere in this dense mass of human intercourse must lie our motive, our catalyst for a murder.' He spoke as if he were addressing a room full of people, but in fact only Hooper and Trisha were there, everybody else having long since gone home. They had decided that the evening's subjects for discussion would be Layla the beautiful 'hippie' and David the dedicated actor.

On one of the tapes that connected their two photographs Trisha had written: 'Friends for first day or two. Turned sour.'

'So what was this early friendship based on?' Coleridge asked. 'It can't have been much if it went sour so quickly.'

'Well, they have a lot in common,' Trisha replied. 'They're both vegans and obsessed with diets and

66

dieting, which seems to have formed a bond between them. On the very first evening they had a long and rather exclusive conversation about food-combining and stomach acids. I've lined up the tape.'

Sure enough, when Trisha pressed play there on the screen were David and Layla, set slightly apart from the rest of the group, having the most terrific meeting of minds.

'That is *so* right,' said Layla.

'Isn't it?' David agreed.

'But it's amazing how many people still think that dairy is healthy.'

'Which it *so* isn't.'

'Did you know that eggs killed more people in the last century than Hitler?'

'Yes, I think I did know that, *and* wheat.'

'Ugh, wheat! Don't get me started on *wheat*!'

Now the sombre tones of Andy the narrator intruded briefly. '*David and Layla have discovered that they have a lot in common: they both miss their cats dreadfully.*'

'Pandora is the most beautiful and intelligent creature I have ever met,' David explained, 'and sadly I include human beings in that statement.'

'I *so* know what you mean,' Layla replied.

Trisha stopped the tape. 'Fogarty the editor told me they got very excited about David and Layla that night. They thought that they might even troll off to the nookie hut and have it off there and then, but all that happened was a shoulder massage.'

'But they were definitely friends?' Coleridge asked.

'I think it's more that they hated everybody else. Looking at the tapes, it's pretty obvious that they thought themselves a cut above the others. On the first day or two the cameras often caught them exchanging wry, superior little glances. Peeping Tom broadcast them, too. The public hated it. David and

67

Layla were the absolute least popular people in the house.'

'But of course they didn't know this.'

'Well, there's no way they could have done. They were sealed off. In fact, watching them you get the impression that they think people will love them as much as they love themselves. Particularly him.'

'Yes, David certainly is a cocky one,' Coleridge mused. 'Arrogant almost beyond belief, in fact, in his quiet, passive-aggressive sort of way.'

Hooper was surprised to hear Coleridge using a term as current and overused as passive-aggressive, but there was no doubt that the phrase summed up David exactly.

They looked at David on the screen and stared into his soft, puppy-dog eyes. All three were thinking the same thing.

'It would certainly take a very confident person to believe that they could get away with what our murderer got away with,' said Coleridge. 'No one with the slightest self-doubt would ever have attempted it.' He returned to the theme of friendship. 'So familiarity quickly took its toll on David and Layla's closeness. Like many a friendship too eagerly begun, it had no staying power.'

'That's right,' said Trisha. 'It started going wrong with the cheese and went downhill from there.'

'They were too alike, I reckon,' said Hooper. 'They got in each other's way. They wanted the same role in the house, to be the beautiful and sensitive one. It all fell irrevocably to pieces over Layla's poem.'

DAY FIVE. 9.00 p.m.

The row began with the best intentions. David had suggested, in an attempt to engineer a *rapprochement*

68

between himself and Layla (and hence avoid her nominating him), that since he was trained and practised in the art of recitation perhaps he should learn one of Layla's poems and recite it for her. Layla had been touched and flattered and because there were no papers or pens allowed in the house David had set to learning the poem orally directly from the author.

'Lactation,' said Layla.

'That's very, very beautiful,' said David.

'It's the title,' Layla explained.

'I understand,' said David, nodding gently, as if the fact that 'Lactation' was the title required a heightened level of perception to come to terms with.

'Shall we take it two lines at a time?' Layla asked.

By way of an answer David closed his eyes and put his hands together at the fingertips, his lips gently touching his index fingers.

Layla began. ' "Woman. Womb-an. Fat, full, belly, rich with girl child. Vagina, two-way street to miracles." '

David breathed deeply and repeated the first two lines of Layla's poem. It was clear from his manner that he thought Layla would be amazed and thrilled to have her words lent wings by such a richly liquid and subtle voice.

If she was, she hid it well. 'Actually, that first line is meant to be very upbeat, joyful,' Layla said. 'You're being too sombre. I always say it with a huge smile, particularly the words "girl child". I mean, think about it, David, doesn't the thought of a strong, spiritual woman's belly engorged with a beautiful girl child just make you want to smile?'

David was clearly aghast. 'Are you giving me *direction*, Layla?' he asked.

'No, I just want you to know how to say it, that's all.'

'The whole point about getting an *actor* to work on a piece of writing, *Layla*, is in order to get another artist's interpretation of it. An actor will find things in a poem that the author did not even know were there.'

'But I don't want the things that aren't there, I want the things that are.'

David seemed to snap. 'Then you'd better recite it yourself,' he said, jumping angrily to his feet. 'Because quite frankly it stinks. Apart from the repulsive imagery of fat, engorged female stomachs, from, I might add, a woman with less flesh on her than a Chupa Chups stick, I am a *professional* actor and I simply will not take direction from an *amateur* poet! Particularly after I have paid her the *enormous* compliment of actually taking an interest in her pisspoor work!' And with that David headed outside for a dip in the hot spa.

DAY THIRTY-TWO. 10.15 p.m.

'Very short fuse, Master David,' Coleridge observed thoughtfully. 'Short enough for murder, do you think?'

Rewinding slightly and freezing on David's furious face, it did seem possible.

'He certainly looks like he wants to murder her,' said Hooper. 'But of course it wasn't Layla that ended up getting killed, was it?'

'As we have discussed endlessly, sergeant. If the motive were obvious our killer would be awaiting trial right now. All we can hope to find is the seed from which a murder will grow.'

Hooper informed Coleridge as briskly as he dared that he was aware of this.

DAY FIVE. 9.15 p.m

After David had left the room, Layla did indeed take his advice and recite the poem herself, grinning like a baboon with a banana wedged sideways in its mouth throughout.

Jazz, Kelly, Dervla and Moon listened respectfully, and when it was over, they all said that they thought it was very, very good.

Woggle opined from his corner that poetry was merely an effort to formalize language and as such indicated a totalitarian mindset. 'Words are anarchists. Let them run free,' he said. But the others ignored him, something that they had learned to do as much as possible, while counting the minutes to nomination day.

'That was the business, that poem, Layles. It was dead wicked, that, so fair play to yez,' Moon said in her Mancunian accent, which seemed to be getting thicker by the day.

'Did you notice my red lipstick?' Layla gushed.

They all had.

'Some anthropologists believe that women paint their lips red in order to make their mouths reminiscent of their vaginas.'

'Steady on, girl,' said Gazzer from over by the kettle. 'Just had my dinner.'

'They say that women do it to make themselves more attractive to men, but I do it as a celebration.'

'Of what?' Jazz asked innocently.

'Of my vagina.'

'Oh, right.'

'Any time you want someone to help you celebrate it, Layles,' said Garry.

'Sherrup, Garry,' said Moon. 'It's not about fookin' blokes, it's about bein' a strong and spiritual woman, in't it, Layles?'

'Yes, it is, Moon, that's exactly what it's about.'

Kelly was still a bit confused. 'Well, I don't get what these anthropologists are on about. Why would any girl want to have a face like a fanny?'

Layla had to think about this for a moment. She had never been asked before. People she knew just tended to nod wisely and ask if there was any more guacamole.

'I don't think they mean *exactly* like one. It's just an impression of genitalia in order to steer the male towards procreation.'

'Oh, right, I see,' said Kelly.

'It's why female monkeys turn their bottoms pink. If they didn't they would have died out as a species long ago. Trust the woman to find a way.'

Everybody nodded thoughtfully.

'Did you know that monkeys have star signs?' said Moon. 'Yeah. This mystic went to London Zoo and did horoscopes for all the advanced primates, and do you know what? She got them all bang on, their personalities and everything. It were fookin' weird.'

DAY SEVEN. 8.00 a.m.

For the previous day or two Dervla had made a point of always being the first up in the morning so that she might have the shower room to herself. On this occasion, however, she found Moon had beaten her to it, not because Moon had suddenly transformed herself into an early riser, but because she was only just on her way to bed.

'I've been sat up all night reading that Red Dragon book Sally brought in. You know, the first one with Hannibal Lecter in it. Fookin' amazing, I were fookin' terrified. I reckon that's the scariest kind of murder that, when there's no fookin' reason for it except that the bloke's fookin' mad for topping people, you know, a serial psycho.'

Dervla waited while Moon brushed her teeth and staggered off to bed.

'Wake me if I'm missing out on any food,' Moon said as she left the bathroom.

Now Dervla was alone, standing before the basin mirror in her underwear. She sensed movement behind the mirror. The housemates were occasionally aware of the people behind the mirrors: there were tiny noises and at night sometimes, when the lights in the bedrooms were off, shapes could vaguely be made out through the mirrors. Dervla knew that her friend had come to meet her.

'Mirror, mirror on the wall,' she said, as if having a private joke with herself, 'who'll be the winner of us all?' She pretended to laugh and put some toothpaste on her brush. None of the editors watching could have imagined that she was talking to anyone.

Soon the writing appeared, just as it did every morning. Ugly ungainly letters. The messenger was clearly having to write backwards and perhaps, Dervla thought, at arm's length.

'*Woggle number one with public,*' said the message.

She nearly blew it. She nearly blurted Woggle's name out loud she was so surprised to discover that he was in the lead. Fortunately she stayed cool, allowing her eyes to flick downwards only momentarily.

Her anonymous informant completed his message. '*Kelly 2. You 3,*' it said, and then, '*Good Luck XXX.*'

Dervla finished brushing her teeth and washed her face. So she was running third. Not bad out of ten. It was certainly a surprise that Woggle was so popular, but when she thought about it she supposed he must have a lot of novelty value. It would soon wear off.

Kelly was much more of a threat.

She was a lovely girl. Dervla liked her. Clearly the public did too. Never mind, Dervla thought to herself, there were eight weeks to go yet. A lot could happen in eight weeks and surely Kelly couldn't stay so happy and so sunny for ever.

Before leaving the bathroom Dervla wiped the words off the mirror and blew a little kiss at her reflection. She thought that her friend the cameraman might appreciate a small friendly gesture.

DAY THIRTY-TWO. 11.35 p.m.

Coleridge tiptoed from the kitchen into the living room with his second can of beer. Upstairs his wife was asleep. She had been asleep when he'd arrived home and would still be asleep when he left the house again at six the following morning. She had left Coleridge a note pointing out that although they lived in the same house she had not actually set eyes on him for three days.

Coleridge searched out a Biro and scribbled, 'I haven't changed,' beneath his wife's message.

The note would still be there the next night, only by then Mrs Coleridge would have added 'more's the pity'.

She didn't mean it, she liked him really, but, as she often remarked, it's easy to think fondly of somebody you never see.

Coleridge had brought home with him the Peeping Tom press pack relating to week one in the house. On the front was attached a photocopied memo written on Peeping Tom notepaper. It was headed 'Round-up of housemates' public/press profiles at day eight.' The writer had been admirably succinct.

Woggle is the nation's pet. Mega-popular.

David is the bastard. Hated.

Kelly has phwoar factor. Popular.

Dervla is an enigmatic beauty. Popular.

Layla is highly shaggable but a pain. Disliked.

Moon is a pain and not even very shaggable. Disliked.

74

Gazzer and Jazz liked. (Not by feminists and intel-
lectuals.)

Sally, not registered much. When has, disliked.
(Note: gay community think S. an unhelpful stereo-
type. Would have preferred a fluffy poof or lipstick lez.)

Hamish not registered.

Coleridge leafed through the clippings. Most of them
confirmed the Peeping Tom memo. There was, however, some discussion about the fact that *House Arrest
Three* was defying expectations and performing much
better than had been predicted.

'The saggy soufflé rises!' one headline said, referring
to its prediction of the previous week that soufflés do
not rise twice, let alone three times. This was news to
Coleridge, who had not realized that when the third
series of *House Arrest* had been announced there had
been much speculation that the reality show bubble
had already burst. Coleridge had presumed that this
sort of show was a guaranteed success, but he was
wrong. The press clippings revealed that many shows
conceived in the heady days when it seemed that any
show with a loud and irritating member of the public
in it was a guaranteed winner had failed to live up to
their promise. And at the start of week one the new
series of *House Arrest* was confidently expected to be
a big failure. But it had defied all the grim expectations, and after seven shows had been broadcast it
was already doing as well as its two predecessors.
Nobody was more surprised about this than Geraldine
herself, something that she freely admitted when she
appeared on *The Clinic*, a hip late-night chat show, in
order to promote week two.

Coleridge slipped the video into his home VCR and
instantly found himself struggling to reduce the volume as the screaming, blaring frenzy of the opening
credits filled his living room and no doubt shot straight
upstairs to where his wife was trying to sleep.

*

'Big up to yez,' said the hip late-night girl, welcoming
Geraldine on to the programme. 'Cracking first week in
the house. We like that.'

'Top telly that woman!' said the hip late-night guy.
'Respect. Fair play to yez.'

'Go, Woggle, yeah!' said the girl. 'We *so* like Woggle.'

'He da *man*!' said the guy. 'Who da man?'

'*He* da man,' said the girl. 'Woggle, he da man!'

There was much cheering at this. The public loved
Woggle.

'Amazing,' said Geraldine when the cheering had
died down. 'I mean, I thought he would be interesting
and stir things up a bit, but I never realized he'd strike
such a chord with the viewers.'

'Yeah, well, he's like a sort of pet, isn't he?' said the
girl. 'Like Dennis the Menace, or Animal from the
Muppets or whatever.'

'I mean, you wouldn't want to live with him yourself, but it's top fun watching other people do it, big
time!'

'Woggle, he da man!'

'Da *top* man. Respect! But the whole show is totally
wicked,' the guy added quickly, 'so fair play to all of
the posse in the house!'

'Respect!'

'Kelly's my girl! Ooojah ooojah!'

'You would fancy Kelly!' said the girl, punching
her partner in the ribs. 'Dervla's easily the most
beautiful.'

'Dervla's beautiful, that is true, and she melts my ice
cream big time, so fair play to her for that, but Kelly,
well, Kelly has . . . something special.'

'Big knockers?'

'What can I tell you? It's a boy thing.'

The boys in the audience let it be known that they
agreed with this sentiment.

'And don't we so *hate* David?' said the girl. 'We *so* do hate him.'

'We *so* do not, not hate him,' added the guy.

There was much booing at the mention of David's name, and the show's producer dropped in a shot taken directly from the live Internet link to the house. David was sitting crosslegged on the floor playing his guitar, clearly thinking himself rather beautiful. There was more booing and laughter at this.

'Sad *or what*?' shrieked the hip girl.

Sipping his beer and watching all of this, three and a half weeks after it had been recorded, Coleridge was struck by how astonishingly brutal it was. The man on the screen had absolutely no idea that he was being jeered and ridiculed. It was as if the country had turned into one vast school playground with the public as bully.

'All right, that's enough of that,' said the guy, clearly having an attack of conscience. 'I'm sure his mum likes him.'

'Yeah. Big up to David's mum! But can you *please* tell him to cut that *hair*?'

'And to stop playing that *guitar*!'

The interview passed on to the unexpected success of the third series so far.

'So you defied the snooties and the sneerers, and the show's a huuuuugge hit,' said the guy, 'which is quite a relief, Geri, am I right? Tell me I'm right.'

'You are so right,' said Geraldine, 'and if I wasn't a bird I'd say my balls were on the line with this one. I've sunk every penny I have into it. My savings and all of my severance pay from when I left the BBC. I'm the sole director of Peeping Tom Productions, mate, so if it fails I haven't got anybody to blame but me.'

'Gutsy lady!' the girl enthused. 'We like that! Respect!'

'Too right I'm a gutsy lady, girl,' said Geraldine. 'I gave up a cushy job as controller of BBC1 to do the *House Arrest* thing, and everybody expected this third series to fall on its arse.'

'Yeah, Geri, you really went out on a limb leaving the Beeb,' the hip late-night guy said. 'I know your name has often been mentioned as a possible future Director General.'

'Yes, I think they wanted to offer it to me,' she said, 'but stuff that, I'm a programme maker, I ain't spending my day kissing politicians like Billy here's arse. I ain't grown up yet.'

The camera pulled out to reveal Billy Jones, who was the other guest on *The Clinic*, and who was smiling indulgently. Billy was the Minister for Culture and had agreed to appear on *The Clinic* as part of the government's strategy to reach out to youth.

'I regret greatly that I shan't be having my arse kissed by a lady so charming as you, Geraldine,' Billy Jones said, and got a laugh.

'So, Billy,' said the girl, turning to him with a serious expression on her face. 'How do you rate *House Arrest*, then? Top telly or pile of poo?'

'Oh, *House Arrest* is *so* top telly,' said the Minister of Culture. 'No *way* is it a pile of poo.'

'And what about people who say that telly is dumbed down? That we need more, I don't know, history programmes and classic drama-type stuff?'

'Well, certainly there is a place for history-type stuff and all that classic drama malarkey, but at the end of the day politicians, teachers and social workers need to be *listening* to young people, because I don't think, right, that history and stuff is really very relevant to what young people are interested in today.'

'Big up to that,' said the hip late-night guy. 'We like that!'

'Because at the end of the day,' Billy continued, 'what politicians and teachers and stuff need to do is connect with what kids are really into, like the Internet. We think that the Internet and the web are terribly important, and of course these wicked experiments in reality TV like *House Arrest*.'

By the time the show was ending and the final band was being introduced, Coleridge had fallen asleep. He woke up to the vision of a sweating American skinhead wearing only board shorts and 90 per cent tattoo coverage shouting 'I'm just a shitty piece of human garbage,' at the screen.

He decided it was time to go to bed. Geraldine had had a lucky escape with her show, that was clear. By rights, it seems, it should have been a flop.

David, on the other hand, had not been so lucky. He was the fall guy, the national joke, and Geraldine had made him so. If David had known this, Coleridge reflected, he might have been tempted to take some kind of revenge on Peeping Tom, but of course he could not have known, could he?

DAY THIRTY-THREE. 10.15 a.m.

The picture of Woggle on the map on the incident room wall was almost completely obscured by the numerous tapes that terminated on it. Trisha had just completed the pattern by running a ribbon to him from Dervla, with the words 'pubic hair row' written on it.

Dervla had seemed so determined to be quiet and serene, so like the muse in an advert for Irish beer. But you couldn't maintain that if you followed Woggle into the bathroom.

DAY EIGHT. 9.30 a.m.

'*It's day eight in the house,*' said Andy the narrator, '*and Dervla has just had a shower.*'

'Woggle!' she shouted, emerging from the shower room, clutching a bar of soap.

'Yes, sweet lady.'

'Can you *please* remove your pubic hairs from the soap after you have finished showering?'

It was their own fault, of course. Woggle would have been quite happy not to shower at all, but the group had made a personal appeal to him to wash thoroughly at least once a day.

'That way in a month or two you might be clean,' Jazz had observed.

Now they were paying the price for their finickiness. Woggle's matted pubic mullet had never seen such regular action, and the unaccustomed pressure was causing it to moult liberally.

Dervla waved the hairy bar of soap in his face. She had thought hard before confronting Woggle. Quite apart from the fact that she did not like scenes, she also knew from her secret informant that Woggle was a very popular person outside the house. Would having a row with him alienate her from the public? she wondered. On the other hand, perhaps it would do the public good to get some idea of what she and the other housemates were having to deal with. In the end, Dervla could not help herself: she just *had* to say something. Woggle tended to do his cursory ablutions in the middle of the night, and, being first up, it was always Dervla who encountered his residue.

'Each morning I have to gouge a small toupee off the soap, and the next morning there it is again, looking like a member of the Grateful Dead!'

'Confront your fear of the natural world, O she-woman. My knob hair can do you no harm. Unlike cars of which you have admitted you own one.' In one single bound Woggle had got from his lack of social grace to her responsibility for the destruction of the entire planet. He was always doing that.

'It's got nothing to do with fucking cars!' Dervla was shocked to hear herself shout. She had not raised her voice in years. Hers was a calm, reflective spirit, that was her thing, and yet here she was shouting.

'Yes, it has, O Celtic lady, for your priorities are weirding me out, man, messing with my head zone. Cars are evil dragons that are eating our world! Whereas my hair is entirely benign, non-volatile dead-cell matter.'

'It is benign non-volatile dead-cell matter that grew out of your *scrotum*!' Dervla shouted. 'And it makes me want to puke! Sweet Virgin Mary Mother of Jesus Christ, where does it all come from! We could have stuffed a mattress by now! Are you using some kind of snake oil ointment down there?'

Unbeknown to Dervla, Woggle was actually a little hurt by her attack. Nobody ever credited Woggle with having feelings because he seemed so entirely oblivious to everybody else's. But Woggle actually liked Dervla, and he fancied her, too. He had even been to the confession box to confess his admiration.

'There is definitely a connection between us,' he said. 'I'm fairly certain that at some point in another life she was a great Princess of the Sacred Runes and that I was her Wizard.'

Confronted now by this attack from one he clearly rated so highly, Woggle attempted to assume an air of dignified distance. 'I remain unrepentant of my bollock hair,' he muttered. 'It has as much right to a place in this house as does every other item of human effluvia, such as, for instance, the pus from Moon's septic nipple ring, which I respect.'

It was a clever ploy. Moon had insisted that the

whole group look at her septic nipple the night before and had won herself no friends in the process.

'Hey! Leave my fookin' nipple out of it, Woggle!' Moon shouted now from where she sprawled on the purple couch. 'I've told you. How was I to know that dirty bastard in Brighton was using shite metal 'stead of gold, which he said it was. He said it were fookin' gold, didn't he? The bastard. Besides, I'm using Savlon on my nipple and I don't leave what comes out of it all over the fookin' soap.'

'Yes, don't try and change the subject,' Dervla insisted. 'Moon's doing what she can about her nipple infection and you should clean the soap after you use it. And not just the soap: clean out the plughole too. It looks like a St Bernard dog died there and rotted.'

'I shall clean up my hair,' Woggle said with what he assumed was an air of ancient and mighty dignity.

'Good,' said Dervla.

'*If*,' Woggle continued, 'you promise to renounce your car.'

DAY THIRTY-THREE. 2.30 p.m.

Every time the 'not yet watched' pile of tapes began to look a little smaller and less intimidating, somebody brought up more from the cells. They seemed to go on for ever.

'*It's day eight, and Jazz and Kelly are chatting in the garden.*'

DAY EIGHT. 3.00 p.m.

'What's the worst job you've ever had?' said Jazz.

He and Kelly were sitting by the pool revelling in the sunshine and the fact that they must look absolutely terrific on camera in their tiny swimming costumes.

'No doubt about that,' Kelly replied. 'Being a film extra. I hated it.'

'Why's that, then?' asked Jazz. 'It don't sound too bad to me.'

'Well, I think it's all right if you're not interested in being an actor. Then you just take the money and eat the lunch and try and spot a star, but it's really rough if you actually want to get into the profession properly like I do. Then being an extra makes you feel like you're just never going to get anywhere.'

'So you want to be an actress, then?'

'Oh God, I'd love it. That would be sooooo cool! Except you don't say actress any more, you know. They're all just actors nowadays, even the women, because of feminism. Like Emma Thompson or Judi Dench or Pamela Anderson or whatever. They're not actresses, they're actors.'

'Is that right? Sounds a bit weird to me.'

'Well, I think so too, actually. I mean, they're women, aren't they? But we've all got to get used to it, otherwise it's offensive, apparently. I'm not sure, but I *think* it goes back to a time when apparently all actresses were prostitutes, and I suppose Judi Dench doesn't want anyone thinking that she's a prostitute. Well, you wouldn't, would you?'

'No, not if you're a classy bird like her, certainly not,' Jazz conceded. 'So that's what you want to be then – a lady actor?'

'Absolutely, that's why I'm in here. I'm hoping I'll get noticed. I went in the confession box the other day and did a speech I'd learnt off *The Bill* about a girl doing cold turkey in the cells.'

'Fahkin' hell, girl, well pushy.'

'Yeah, I rolled around on the floor and cried and everything. Don't know if they'll show it, though. I'd do anything to get to be an actress. That's why I did the extra work. I thought I might learn something and even make a few contacts, but I hated it.'

David was swimming in the pool. Elegantly completing a series of gentle, desperately mannered laps in a perfectly unhurried breaststroke. A breaststroke which announced to the world that not only did David swim absolutely beautifully but that he had absolutely beautiful thoughts while he was doing it.

He had been listening to what Kelly was saying. 'I don't believe that anyone who would take extra work can truly want to be an actor, Kelly. I advise you to find a more realistic dream.'

'You what?' said Kelly.

'Fuck off, David,' said Jazz. 'Kelly can dream what she likes.'

'And I can offer her advice if I wish. Kelly's a big girl. She doesn't need you to protect her, Jason.'

'Jazz.'

'I keep forgetting.'

'Come on, then, David,' said Kelly. 'What do you mean, a more realistic dream?'

David hoisted himself up out of the water, quite clearly conscious as he did so of the splendid, glistening, dripping curves and tone of his muscular arms. He paused halfway out of the pool, arms stretched taut, taking his weight, shoulders rippling and strong, firm, shadowy clefts at his collar bone. His legs dangled in the pool and the hard, wavy plane of his stomach pressed against the terracotta edge. 'I meant exactly what I said.'

David emerged from the pool completely, in one single, graceful, uncluttered movement. 'Acting is the most demanding vocation imaginable. Harder, I think, perhaps, than any other.'

'Bomb-disposal expert?' said Jazz, but David ignored him.

'You have to believe in yourself utterly, and consider

84

your dream to be not a dream but a duty. If you're prepared at the very beginning to accept second best, then I suggest it is inevitable that you will never achieve your end. I personally would wash dishes, clean cars, wait on tables, rather than accept any job in the profession other than one I considered worthy of my dream. John Hurt resolved at the outset of his career to accept only leading roles, you know. I'm told he suffered thirteen years of unemployment as a result. But, ah, what triumph was to follow.'

'Well, what about all the actors who aren't John Hurt?' Jazz asked. 'The ones who suffered thirteen years of unemployment and then suffered another thirteen years of unemployment and then died of alcohol poisoning. What if that's what happened to you?'

'If that were my fate,' said David, 'then at least I would know that I had never compromised and that although my talent was not recognized I had never betrayed it. I would far rather be Van Gogh, tormented in life and dying unrecognized, than some comfortable portrait painter who prostitutes his talent for lack of faith in it. Winning is all. Consolation prizes are not worth having. I truly, truly believe that, Jason. I know you think me a pompous arrogant bastard . . .'

'Yes,' said Jazz.

'And perhaps I am. But I mean what I say. You have to have everything or nothing, and so you will never be an actor, Kelly, and I say that as a friend who has your best interests at heart. Do yourself a favour. Find another dream.'

DAY THIRTY-THREE. 2.35 p.m.

Hooper pressed stop. 'David knows what he's doing, he just doesn't know it isn't working.'

'You what?' asked Trisha.

'Well, he's not stupid. He must know he's coming across as arrogant and mean. I think it's his strategy. It's not always the nice people who stay the course in these shows. Sometimes it's the bastards. I reckon David wants to get noticed, noticed as someone great-looking, arrogant and uncompromising. In other words, a leading man, a star. I don't think that man cares what he does or what people think of him. He just wants to be a star.'

DAY EIGHT. 11.20 p.m.

The girls were lying on their beds drinking hot chocolate. The talk quickly turned to Woggle, as it had done on many previous evenings.

'He's a nutter,' Moon said. 'He should be in a loony bin. He's mad, he is.'

'He is strange,' said Kelly. 'I just worry that he might do himself some harm or something. We had a kid like him at our school, except he had a Mohican instead of dreadlocks. Always sitting on his own and swaying, he was, just like Woggle, and he ended up writing on his arms with a knife, there was blood everywhere, the school nurse fainted, it was gross.'

Then Sally spoke. After Woggle, Sally was the most isolated of the group, and had so far come to prominence only once, when she had insisted on raising her Rainbow Lesbian and Gay Alliance flag in the back garden. It had not been a major incident, however, because despite Sally's very best efforts nobody had objected.

Moon's comments about loony bins had touched a nerve.

'Woggle's not mad!' Sally snapped. 'He's just filthy and horrible and politically unfocused. That's all. He's not mad.'

'Well, he is a bit mad, Sally,' Kelly said. 'Did you see him trying to save that ant from the water that splashed out of the pool? I mean, how mad is that?'

The venom of Sally's reply took everybody aback. 'Listen, Kelly, you know absolutely nothing about it, all right?' she hissed. 'Nothing! People like you are so prejudiced and ignorant about mental illness. It's pathetic! Absolutely pathetic and also disableist!'

'I only said he was a bit mad, Sally.'

'I know what you said, and I find it totally offensive. Just because a person has mental health issues doesn't make them a disgusting anti-social pariah.'

'Yes, but he *is* disgusting, Sally,' Kelly protested. 'I mean, I feel sorry for him and everything, but . . .'

'And that's the point I'm making, you stupid ignorant cow! He's disgusting, he's not mad. The two are not the same thing. Everybody's so fucking prejudiced. Fucking grow up, why don't you?'

Kelly looked like she had been slapped in the face. Sally's anger had risen up so quickly that her fists were clenched and it almost seemed that she would lash out.

In the monitoring bunker they twiddled desperately at their controls to get the hot-head remotes to swivel and focus on the relevant faces. Geraldine ordered both operators in the camera runs to push their dollies round to the girls' bedroom immediately. That rarest of all events in reality television seemed to be developing: a moment of genuine, spontaneous drama.

'Hey, steady on, Sally,' said Dervla. 'Kelly's entitled to her opinion.'

'Not if it's oppressive of minorities, she isn't.'

'I haven't got an opinion,' wailed Kelly, tears springing up in her eyes. 'Honestly.'

'You do, you just don't recognize your own bigotry!'

Sally snapped. 'Everybody hates and stigmatizes the mentally ill and blames them for society's problems. They're denied treatment, ignored by the system and then when once in a blue moon something happens, like some poor schizo who never should have been returned to the community gets stuck inside their own dark box and sticks a knife in someone's head or whatever, suddenly every mild depressive in the country is a murderer and it's just ignorant fucking bollocks!'

Sally was getting more and more upset. The other girls had not seen this side of her before. The knuckles on her clenched fists had turned white; there were angry tears in her eyes.

Kelly appeared horrified to have been the cause of all this hurt, but also astonished at how emotional Sally had so quickly become. 'I'm sorry, Sally, all right?' Kelly said. 'If I've said something stupid I'm sorry. I didn't mean to, but really there's no need to cry about it.'

'I'm not fucking crying!' Sally shouted.

Moon had been lying on her bed listening to the conversation with a look of tolerant bemusement on her face. Now she raised herself up and joined in. 'Sally's right, but she's also wrong,' she said with a patronizing air of authority. 'Woggle ain't genuinely mad, he's just a twat with body odour, but on the other hand I wouldn't be too certain about how nice and cosy the average loony is, Sally . . .'

Sally tried to interrupt angrily but Moon continued.

'Or "people with mental health issues" as you choose to put it. I've seen nutters, real nutters, dangerous fookin' bastard nutters, and let me tell you, darling, society's right to be scared of them, I know I fookin' was.'

'That is just ignorant shit,' said Sally. 'What would you know about it? How would you know anything about the mentally ill?'

'Well, what would you know about it yourself, Sally?' said Dervla thoughtfully. Her face had a slightly troubled look about it.

But before Sally could answer Dervla's question, Moon pressed on. 'I know plenty about it, Sally!' she barked, seeming suddenly to be as upset as the other girl, 'and I'll tell you why: because I spent two years, did you hear me, love? Two fookin' years in a mental hospital. Have you got that? A hospital for the insane, a loony bin and that is why, Sally, I fookin' hate nutters.'

For a moment the room fell silent. The other girls were simply astonished at this sudden and unexpected bombshell.

'You never did,' said Kelly. 'You're having a laugh.'

But it appeared that Moon was not having a laugh.

'So don't tell me about people with mental health issues, Sally! I lived with them, I slept in their rooms, ate at their tables, walked the same corridors, stared at the same shitty walls for two years. So don't give me any of that *One Flew Over the Cuckoo's Nest* crap! Like *they*'re the bloody sane ones – the fookin' heroes.'

Sally clearly wanted to reply, but could find no words in the face of Moon's onslaught, which continued unabated: 'Oh yeah, I'm sure there's plenty of nice ones about the place, plenty of nice sweet little manic-depressives who don't hurt anybody but their mums and dads and themselves ... but I'm talking about *nutters*. The ones that scream and tear at themselves in the night. All night! The ones that lash out when you pass them on the ward, trick you with their cunning, grab you, touch you, fookin' try and *eat you*.'

The other four young women sat on their beds and stared at Moon. Sally's passion had come as a surprise, but this was something more, much, much more. This was shocking. Moon had been so cheerful, so funny right from the first day, and now this.

89

'But why? Why were you there, Moon?' Dervla's voice was calm. Sweet and reassuring, like a doctor's or a priest's, but those who knew her would have heard the anxiety in it. They would have known that she was scared. 'Were you ill?'

'No, I wasn't ill,' said Moon bitterly. 'But my fookin' uncle was ill. My uncle is a sad sick ill bastard.' She stopped, and seemed to be considering whether to go on.

Layla asked if she wanted a hand to hold. Moon ignored her.

'He abused me, right? Not the full business, never rape, but plenty enough. A year it went on until one day I told my ma, that cow. I can say it now because she's dead. I never thought she'd believe her brother and not me, but he was a powerful man in the local community, I suppose, a doctor. And he had friends, counsellors, other doctors and the like, and between them they managed to make it all look my fault. I was a nasty lying little slut and a dangerous fantasist to boot. Maybe it woulda' been different if me dad had been around, but God knows where he is. God knows *who* he is.'

'They managed to get you committed?' Dervla asked, astonished.

'Yeah, you wouldn't have thought it could happen, would you? To a young teenage girl, in our day and age, but it did, and I got put away for trying to tell the world that I'd been touched up by my uncle.'

There was silence in the room. For the first time since they had all entered the house, nobody had anything to say.

The silence was echoed in the monitoring bunker, where Bob Fogarty, Pru, his assistant editor, various production managers and all their PAs were stunned.

'That is incredible,' said Fogarty.

'Yes, it is, isn't it?' said the voice of Geraldine Hennessy. 'An incredible load of bollocks.'

They turned round in surprise. Nobody had noticed Geraldine enter the bunker, but in fact she had been watching for some time. She had come on from dinner with her current boyfriend in tow, a beautiful nineteen-year-old dancer whom she had met backstage at the Virgin summer pop festival.

'I never thought Moon would be the one to go for the lying trick, I really didn't. I must say I'm impressed.'

'She's lying?' the various editors and PAs asked in astonishment.

'Of course she's lying, you stupid bunch of cunts. Do you really think I'd put an abused kid out of a loony hospital into my happy little game show? Bollocks! Woggle's as mad as I go. That bald bitch's mum and dad are alive and well and living in Rusholme. He's a tobacconist, she works in a dry cleaner's.'

There was great relief in the bunker at this and also excitement. It seemed that perhaps the game inside the house might turn out to be more interesting than they had feared.

'Look at her smirking to herself 'cos it's dark and the others can't see,' Geraldine said, pointing at one of the remote camera feeds. 'She knows *we* can see, though, oh yes! She's having a laugh, isn't she? She knows the public loves a stirrer. You get much more famous being naughty than nice. Get me a coffee, will you, Darren? Use the machine in my office, not the shite this lot drink.'

The impossibly beautiful nineteen-year-old boy grumpily stirred his perfect body and went off to do as he was bidden.

'Lucky you did your research, Geraldine,' Fogarty remarked. 'If you didn't know Moon was lying I imagine we'd all be pretty nervous now.'

'I'd have known anyway,' Geraldine replied

pompously. 'Those idiot proles in there might manage to manipulate each other, possibly even the public, but not me, mate.'

'You think you would have guessed she was lying even if you didn't know?'

'Of course I would. That woman's never been near a mental hospital in her life. She's watched too many films, that's all. People don't scream and shriek in those places. If they do they get sedated pretty fucking sharpish, let me tell you, and the only grabbing and touching that goes on is by the nurses. Mental hospitals are *quiet* at night. All you can hear is weeping, shuffling and wanking.'

For a moment Geraldine had a faraway look in her eye. To her assembled staff she seemed almost human. The next moment she was herself again. 'Right, package all that stuff up. I'm not using it now, I'm concentrating on Woggle. Besides, I'm not having some bald cunt like Moon influencing the public this early on. I influence the public, not the bloody inmates. Keep it, though. Could be useful later.'

'What, you mean put it in out of sequence?' Fogarty was taken aback.

'Maybe,' replied Geraldine. 'Who'd notice the difference?'

'But . . . but the time codes on the video . . . They'd be out of sequence. We couldn't adjust them.'

'Of course you can, you silly arse. They're just numbers on a screen, you can change them. Just go into the Apple menu and dig out the control panel.'

'I know *how* to do it, Geraldine,' Bob Fogarty replied coldly. 'I meant we couldn't do it morally, professionally.'

'Our moral and professional duty is to provide good telly to the public, who pay our wages. We are not fucking anthropologists, we are entertainers, mate. Turns. We work on the end of the pier along with the illusionists, the mystics, the magicians, the hypnotists and all the other cheating shysters who make up this great business we call show. Now stick the whole thing in a separate file and hide it somewhere.'

The team said no more, working on in silence, hoping that if Geraldine did want to do something as outrageous as broadcasting house events out of sequence it would not be them whom she instructed to do it. Back on the screens the attention of the editing team was drawn by a flurry of bras and knickers. The girls were getting ready for bed.

'Nipple-watch!' shouted Geraldine. 'Jump to it.'

They all had their styles. Sally got into bed in her T-shirt and knickers. Kelly allowed the occasional flash as she whipped off her shirt and dived into bed. Moon was happy to wander about in front of the infra-red cameras entirely naked. Layla and Dervla were the most coy: both put on long nighties before removing their underwear. When Geraldine saw this on the first night she had made a mental note to catch both of these prudes out at some point, in the showers, probably, or perhaps the pool, and put their nipples out in the Sunday night special compilation. She wasn't having hoity-toity little scrubbers like them holding back on the flesh. What did they think they were on telly for?

The atmosphere in the bedroom was sombre. On previous nights the girls had laughed and giggled as they got into their beds, but on this occasion there was silence. Moon's revelations had rocked them all. Not just because it had been such a sad and shocking tale, but also because her distress would so obviously appeal to the public's sympathy and give her the edge when eviction time came. It was very strange to have to remember all the time that every conversation was a conversation between rivals who were competing against each other for the affection of the public.

Then Moon spoke. 'Oh, by the way, girls,' she said. 'All that stuff I just told you. That were rubbish, by the way. Sorry.'

There was another moment's silence.

'*What!*' Layla, who rarely shouted, was furious.

'Don't worry about it, love,' Moon said in a calm, matter-of-fact voice. 'I were 'aving a laugh. Take me mind off me septic nipple.'

'You said you'd been *abused*!'

'Well, everybody says they've been abused these days, don't they?' Moon replied. 'Blimey, if you look at the posters them charities put out, apparently every fookin' kid in the country's getting touched up on a more or less continual basis.'

'What's your game, Moon?' said Dervla with barely controlled fury.

'Told you. Just thought I'd have a laugh,' Moon said. 'Plus, I thought our Sally was getting a bit too serious, hopping into Kelly a bit strong about fookin' loonies, that's all.'

'You rotten bitch,' said Layla.

'You cow,' said Kelly.

'That was a pretty low trick, Moon,' said Dervla. 'I don't think sexual abuse is a very funny subject.'

'Well, it passed the time, didn't it?' Moon said. ''Night.'

There was another long pause. Finally Kelly broke the silence. 'So were you telling the truth about your breast implants, then?' she asked.

'Oh, yeah, couldn't do without me kajungas, could I? I reckon they help me with me balance when I'm on the trapeze.'

As peace once more descended upon the room, Dervla thought she heard Sally sob.

DAY THIRTY-THREE. 5.10 p.m.

It had been six days since the murder, and Sergeant
Hooper and his team continued with the huge task of
trawling through the vast archive of unseen Peeping
Tom footage. Searching diligently for any hint of an
incident that might have turned somebody's mind to
murder. It was gruelling work even for Hooper, who
was a big *House Arrest* fan, fitting their audience profile and advertiser expectations perfectly. Hooper was
the opposite of Coleridge, a very modern copper, a hip,
mad-for-it, bigged-up, twenty-first-century boy with
baggy trousers, trainers, an earstud and a titanium
Apple Mac Powerbook. Hooper and his mates never
missed any of the various reality TV shows, but even
he was being ground down by the task he now faced.
Fortunately not *all* seven hundred and twenty hours a
day of camera activity were available to the police, the
vast bulk of it having been discarded on a daily basis
by the Peeping Tom editors. But there were still hundreds of hours left, and watching it was like watching
paint dry. Worse, at least paint *did* eventually dry. This
lot seemed to stay wet for ever.

Hamish picking his nose again . . . Jazz scratching
his bum.

The girls doing their yoga, *again*.

Garry doing more press-ups.

Garry doing chin-ups on the doorframes.

Garry running on the spot . . .

Hooper was beginning to despise the people in the
house, and he did not want to. Quite apart from the fact
that he did not think it would help him in his detection work, in a way these were his people. They had
similar interests and ambitions, a similar honest conviction that they had a right to be happy. Hooper did
not want to start thinking like Coleridge. What *was* that
man like? Always *banging on* about the housemates

having no sense of 'duty' or 'service' or 'community'. As if wanting to have it large made you an enemy of society.

Nonetheless, they were seriously beginning to wear him down. It was just that they never *did* anything, and, more irritatingly, they never *thought* anything. That most defining of all human characteristics, the capacity for abstract thought, was pressed solely into the service of . . . of . . . Nothing.

Hooper cursed inwardly. He was even beginning to *think* like Coleridge.

And of clues to a murder there were none.

Until Trisha spotted something.

Not much, but something.

'Have a look at this, sergeant,' she said. 'Arsey little moment between Kelly the slapper and David the ponce.'

'Arsey, constable? Slapper? Ponce?' Hooper replied, in Coleridge's schoolmasterly tone, and they both smiled grimly at the thought of the linguistic strictures under which they were obliged to work.

It was only a minor incident, just a whisper of a possibility, but then the police had long since given up any hope of happening upon the obvious.

'We are looking for a catalyst,' Hooper explained to the assembled officers. 'In chemistry, sometimes the tiniest element, if added to other compounds, can cause the most explosive results. That's what we're looking for: a tiny psychological catalyst.'

It had sounded good when Coleridge had said it to Hooper, and it sounded even better when Hooper showed off with it to his constables. Coleridge might have the lines, but Hooper felt that he knew how to deliver them.

The potential catalyst that Trisha had found was tiny indeed. It had not even been interesting enough for Peeping Tom to broadcast it, but Trisha found it interesting, and so did Hooper.

Kelly, Jazz and David were in the hot tub together. As usual, David was talking.

'It's interesting what you said yesterday about wanting to be an actress, Kelly. Because actually everybody in here is acting. You know that, don't you? This house is a stage and all the men and women merely players.'

'Not true,' Jazz replied, with his customary abundance of self-confidence. 'I'm being my true self, guy. What you see is what you get, because everything I got is too good to hide.'

'Oh, what nonsense. Nobody is ever truly themself.'

'And how do you know that, Mr Clever Arse Mind Games?'

'Because we don't completely know ourselves.'

'That's rubbish, that is.'

'Well, admit it, Jason.'

'Jazz.'

'Whatever. Haven't you ever surprised yourself, spotted some new and different personal angle that you've never seen before?'

'Well, I once squatted over a mirror. That was a bit of a shock, I can tell you,' said Jazz, and Kelly laughed loudly, a big, brash, irritating laugh.

Irritating to David, anyway.

'I was staring straight up my arse, man,' Jazz continued, grinning broadly, 'and even I was having trouble loving it!'

David was suddenly angry. He took himself very seriously and liked others to do the same.

'I can assure you, Jason, that we are all actors in life, presenting ourselves as we wish others to see us. That is why those of us who actually *are* actors, like myself, understand our world and the people in it more fully than ordinary folk do. We know the tricks, we read the

97

signs. We recognize that we live in a world full of performers. Some of us are subtle, some are hams, but every one of us is *acting*. Seeing through your performance, *Jazz*, is my bread and butter.'

Jazz didn't reply for a moment. 'That's bollocks,' he said finally, which was sadly well below his usual natural wit.

David smiled.

Then Kelly leaned forward and whispered something in David's ear. It was hard to catch, but there was no doubt about what she said. What Kelly said to David was: 'I *know* you.'

Then she leaned back against the side of the tub and looked straight into David's eyes.

David returned her stare, his superior smirk undaunted. He seemed unruffled.

He was about to be ruffled. Very.

For Kelly leaned forward once more and whispered something else into David's ear.

DAY THIRTY-THREE. 5.30 p.m.

This time neither Sergeant Hooper nor Trisha could quite catch what Kelly said. None of the officers working in the room could work it out at all.

It sounded something like 'Far corgi in heaven.'

'That can't be right, surely,' said Hooper.

'It would seem unlikely,' Trisha agreed.

Whatever it was that Kelly whispered, David had understood it and had not liked it.

There on the screen his expression clearly changed, subtly – he was too good an actor for his face to give much away – but his expression changed. Suddenly the smug, superior smile had disappeared.

He looked scared.

Hooper showed Coleridge the tape the following morning.

'Whatever "Far corgi in heaven" means, sir, and that is certainly not quite what she said, it indicates to me that Kelly knew David before they entered the house.'

'It's possible,' conceded the inspector.

'I reckon probable, sir,' said Hooper, running the tape once more. 'When she says "I know you" I thought at first she meant she knew him psychologically, because that's what David was talking about.'

'Of course.'

'But then she says the other stuff, the corgi bit, and that's clearly something that only David understands, some secret or experience from the outside world that they share.'

'No doubt about that, sergeant,' Coleridge agreed, 'but it doesn't necessarily mean they'd met. Kelly may have recognized something in David that enabled her to work something out about him.'

'I don't count Kelly as the brightest apple in the barrel, sir. Working things out is not really her thing. I think they'd met.'

'Well, if they had then that is certainly a most significant discovery. Our whole catalyst theory is based on the presumption that they were all strangers. If two of them knew each other then that changes the dynamics across the whole group.'

For the first time the two detectives felt they might have a shred of a lead.

'So how do you read it, then, sergeant? Do you think that whatever Kelly recognized in David she recognized from the start?'

'Not unless she was as good an actress as she'd like to be. That first day was an absolute blank for her, I reckon. She just ran around shrieking, jumping in the pool and falling out of her top. Can't say I noticed a single reflective moment. No, I think that whatever it was that made the penny drop for Kelly happened later. At some point David gave himself away, and Kelly spotted something about him that she recognized.'

'In that case I imagine it would have occurred not too long before she revealed her knowledge to David.'

'For sure. Kelly does not strike me as the sort of girl to keep a juicy thing like that to herself. She couldn't wait to slap our Dave in the face with it, particularly after the way he put her down the previous day about her acting ambitions.'

'Well, if that's correct, then whatever she saw she must have seen between the conversation around the pool and the conversation in the hot tub. What were they doing on the evening of day eight?'

'Tattoos!' said Hooper. 'They were comparing tattoos! I've seen the tape.'

'Well, let's take another look at it.'

By the time Hooper had reloaded the video tape, Trisha had joined them, and together they sat down to study the faces of Kelly and David as the group discussed tattoos.

Supper was over and with the exception of Woggle the housemates were all sitting about on the couches. They had just completed a small task set by Peeping Tom in which each housemate was loaned a pencil and paper and had to write down their predictions of who they thought would be left in the house at the end of week seven. They were also encouraged to jot down any other thoughts they might have about how things would pan out. All the pieces of paper were then put in a big brown envelope marked 'Predictions', which was solemnly sealed and placed at the back of the kitchen unit.

It was after that that the conversation turned to

tattoos. They all had something to exhibit except Dervla and Jazz.

'I'm too black,' Jazz said, 'besides which my skin is too beautiful to be improved.'

'I don't have an explanation as to why I don't have any tattoos,' said Dervla. 'Except to say that it is extraordinary to me that these days when people talk about their tattoos it's the people who *don't* have them who have the explaining to do. Maybe that's why I don't want one.'

'Good for you,' said Coleridge, sipping from his china mug.

Hooper and Trisha said nothing. Hooper had the Everton football club badge tattooed on his shoulder and Trisha had a butterfly on her left buttock.

On the screen Garry was explaining that the eagle on his ankle stood for strength, honour and truth.

'What does the clenched fist on your shoulder stand for? Wanker?' Jazz enquired.

'No, it bleeding well doesn't,' Garry replied. 'Even though I am Olympic class in that particular sport.'

The girls groaned.

'My clenched fist also stands for strength, honour and truth. What's more, I'm going to get another one done across me back. I'm going to get "strength, honour and truth" written out in gothic script. It's my motto.'

The group indicated that they had rather gathered this.

Then Moon showed the floral arrangement that ran up her spine. 'The flowers are symbols of peace and inner strength. They're spiritual blooms, and I think Egyptian princesses used to get buried with them in a bouquet, although I might have got that wrong. It might be fookin' Norse women, but either way they're all dead significant and spiritual.'

Kelly showed the phoenix that was flying up from between her buttocks. Sally demonstrated the female warrior fighting a dragon that surrounded her belly button, and Layla showed the tiny butterfly on one of her buttocks.

'I've got one just like that,' said Trisha, outraged. 'The bloke who did it told me it was a unique one-off.'

Coleridge nearly choked on his tea. It had never even *occurred* to him that one of his officers, one of his *lady* officers, was tattooed. Particularly Patricia, whom he had thought such a steady girl.

Layla then proudly spread her legs and showed off the other butterfly she had, which was fluttering about right at the top of her perfectly lovely, smooth, groomed inner thigh.

'I keep it there,' Layla said, 'to remind my lovers of the importance and the beauty of delicacy and light-ness of touch.'

Coleridge groaned and looked away from the screen.

'Got one of those, Trish?' said Hooper.

'No *way*, not there. It's bad enough having a bikini wax without some hell's angel getting up you with his ink needle.'

'Be quiet, both of you!' barked Coleridge.

Now Layla was showing the little Eastern symbol on her shoulderblade. 'It's Tibetan,' she explained. 'A Buddhist symbol indicating a tranquil inner light.'

Everyone agreed that this was particularly lovely.

Except David.

'Tibetan?' he asked, a hint of indulgent surprise in his voice.

'Yes, Tibetan,' said Layla defensively.

'Oh . . . OK, right. Whatever.'

Layla wanted to kill him. 'What do you mean "Whatever"? It's fucking Tibetan!'

'Steady, Layla,' grinned Jazz. 'Hang on to your tran-quil inner light.'

'Look, Layla,' said David gently. 'It's very beautiful and it can and should mean whatever you want it to mean. It doesn't matter whether it's Tibetan or Thai, which is what it actually is: it's *your* tattoo, and it means whatever you want it to.'

Who would have thought that Layla's fabulous calm could have been shattered so easily. Her face was red with embarrassment and anger. 'It's Tibetan, you bastard,' she repeated. 'I know it's Tibetan.'

David gave an annoying little smile and shrug as if to say 'You're wrong, but it's beneath me to argue.'

'It is Tibetan! It means tranquil inner fucking light!' Layla shouted, and stormed off to get herself a soothing cup of herbal tea.

'I heard about this bloke, a gay bloke,' Garry said, 'who had this Chinese proverb put up his arm which meant "gentle seeker after truth". Anyway, one day he pulls this poofter Chinkie at a noodle bar in Soho, and his new boyfriend says, "Actually it means you are a stupid, gullible, round-eyed cunt." '

Garry, Jazz, Sally and Kelly laughed hugely at this. Hamish and Moon smiled. Layla, standing over by the kettle, bit her lip, red-faced with fury, and David closed his eyes for a moment as if gathering strength from his own stillness.

Then Hamish showed the Celtic Cross on his forearm, and finally it was David's turn. He had been waiting for it.

'I have only one tattoo,' he explained, as if this in itself was evidence of his exquisite taste and heightened perception. 'And it is very, very beautiful.'

With that David lifted the leg of his baggy silk trousers and revealed, inscribed upon his left ankle, wound three times around his leg, the first four lines of the 'to be or not to be' soliloquy from *Hamlet*.

'No butterflies, no Tibetan shopping lists, no fiery dragons. Simply the most perceptive investigation of the essential absurdity of man's existence ever committed to paper.'

'Or in this case skin,' Jazz pointed out, but David ignored him.

'Existentialism three hundred years before existentialism was invented. Humanism in a brutal and barbaric world. A tiny light that has illuminated every century since.'

'Yeah, all right, but why have it written on your leg?' asked Jazz, speaking for the nation.

'Because it saved my life,' said David with clear-eyed, unblinking sincerity. 'When I was in my dark time and saw no possibility of living in this world I fully intended to end my own life. Believe me, I had entirely resolved upon suicide.'

'Except you didn't do it, did you?' Garry said. 'Funny, that.'

'No, I didn't. Instead through one long night I read *Hamlet* three times from cover to cover.'

'Fuck me. I'd *rather* fucking kill myself,' Garry said, but David pressed on regardless.

'That sad prince also contemplated the terrible act of self-murder just as I was doing, but he rose above it, rose above it and achieved a grand and private nobility.'

'Is that why you didn't do it yourself, then, David?' asked Moon, obviously trying to be supportive of David's confessional. 'Because nothing that you were feeling could ever be as bad as *Hamlet*.'

'We did it at school,' said Garry. 'Believe me, nothing is as bad as *Hamlet*.'

'Oh, fookin' shurrup, Garry,' said Moon. 'David knows what I mean, don't you, David?'

'Yes, I do, Moon, and the answer is yes and no. Without doubt the sombre princeling's torment taught me much. But in fact I resolved against suicide because I realized reading that play that I did not wish to leave a world that could contain something as beautiful as

104

Shakespeare's verse, or indeed a flower, or a sunrise or the smell of fresh-baked bread.'

'Now you've lost me,' said Moon. 'What's fookin' bread got to do with it?'

'I believe, Moon, that once a person recognizes beauty they become alive to the possibility of beauty in all things. And so I decided to keep the words which the young Prince of Denmark spoke at his time of deepest sadness about me always. Just to remind me that the world is beautiful and to despair of it is an insult to God.'

Jazz wanted to tell David that he was a pretentious prat, but he didn't. There was something about David, something so handsome and compelling, something so utterly blatant about his colossal conceit that Jazz could not help but be a little bit moved.

None of them were sure about David. The obvious sincerity of David's self love was quite compelling. A love as true as the love David had for himself could not be simply dismissed, it was almost noble. They stared, unable to decide what to think about David.

Except Kelly.

The incident hadn't been noticed in the monitoring box on the night it happened because the editors were concentrating on the wide-angle shot, and Kelly's back had been to the camera, but the police had all the available video coverage of the scene: for once they got a little lucky. One of the live cameramen had been taking a reverse angle, and the disk had not been wiped. It was a three-shot of Kelly, Moon and Hamish on the orange couch.

Kelly was smiling, a big broad wicked smile. Hardly the reaction she would normally have had to David's tale of suicidal angst, no matter how absurdly pompous it might have sounded.

'She'd seen that tattoo before,' said Hooper.

'Yes, I rather think she had,' Coleridge agreed.

DAY THIRTY-FOUR. 10.00 a.m.

While various junior officers went off to run the phrase 'Far corgi in heaven' around the Internet and through various voice decoders, Coleridge and his inner team put David to one side for a moment and returned to the subject of Woggle.

'It seems to me that, for all that the public knew, there really *was* only one housemate in week two,' Coleridge said, glancing through the digest of the broadcast edits that Trisha and her team had prepared for him. 'Woggle, Woggle, Woggle and once more Woggle.'

'Yes, sir,' Trisha replied. 'Briefly he became a sort of mini national phenomenon. Half the country were talking about him and the other half were asking who was this Woggle bloke that everybody was talking about. Don't you remember it?'

'*Very* vaguely, constable.'

'The more revolting he got and the more he denied that he was revolting the more people loved him. It was a sort of craze.'

'I'll never forget when they showed him picking the fleas out of his dreadlocks,' remarked another constable. 'We were in the pub and it was on the telly; everybody just sort of gasped. It was soooo gross.'

'Gross if you were watching it. Pretty unbearable if you were living with it,' said Trisha. 'Those fleas nearly brought the whole thing to a halt there and then. Shame they didn't, really, then nobody would have got killed.'

'And we wouldn't have to watch this torturous drivel,' said Coleridge. 'Didn't those sadists at Peeping Tom offer them any flea powder?'

'Yes, they did, but Woggle refused to use it. He said that his fleas were living creatures, and while he

106

didn't much like the itching he had no intention of murdering them.'

'Good lord,' Coleridge observed. 'An abstract opinion! A moral point of view. I'd given up all hope.'

'Well, it wasn't abstract to the housemates, sir. And Woggle's flea debate gripped the nation.'

DAY TEN. 3.00 p.m.

Woggle was sitting in his corner ringed by the other housemates.

'My fleas are forcing you to address your double standards,' Woggle protested. 'Would you hunt a fox?'

'Yes, I fucking would,' said Garry, but the others had had to admit that they would not, David, Layla and Moon even to having been vaguely active in the most recent anti-hunting campaigns.

'Fox-hunting is an abomination,' David said with his usual air of quiet superiority.

'Yet you would hunt my fleas,' Woggle said. 'Explain to me the difference between a fox and a flea.'

Clearly nobody really knew where to start.

'Well . . .' said Kelly, slightly nervously, 'foxes are cute and fleas aren't.'

'Oh, don't be so silly, Kelly,' David snapped.

'She is not being silly,' said Woggle. 'She has articulated a universal truth, for it is the shame of humankind that we judge the value of a life in aesthetic terms. That which we find beautiful we nurture, that which we find ugly we destroy. Oh, cursed are we, the human virus that infects this perfect planet.'

David had clearly had enough of this. He wasn't having the moral high ground pulled from under him. 'Foxes do very little harm. Hunting them is a sport, not a necessity, that is what makes it despicable and

107

utterly unacceptable to decent modern people living in twenty-first-century New Britain.'

'Fox-hunters say foxes do lots of harm. They say that foxes are vermin,' Woggle replied.

'I deny their claims.'

'Where'd you live, then, Dave?' asked Gazzer, who was always interested in a wind-up. 'On a farm?'

'I live in Battersea,' David replied angrily. 'But that's not the . . .'

Gazzer and Jazz laughed at David's discomfort, which made David furious. He loathed the way people pretended that you had to live in the country to understand anything about foxes.

'This is a serious debate,' he snapped. 'It is not about cheap point-scoring.'

Woggle agreed with him and pressed his advantage. 'The difference between foxes and my fleas, comrade, is that my fleas irritate you and foxes don't. But the fascist farmers and the Nazi hunters claim that foxes irritate them. They *claim* that foxes eat the chickens and terrorize the hedgerows.'

'I absolutely refute their claims,' David insisted, 'but the point is anyway—'

'The *point* is, O Adolf of the insect kingdom, the point is, *Herr Hitler*, that, whether foxes are rural terrorists or not, *I* would not kill them just as I would not kill my fleas, bite me though they will. This is because I am a morally developed individual, whilst *you*, on the other hand, are a vicious murdering bastard hypocrite scumbag member of the Gestapo who should be letterbombed.' Woggle's thin nasal voice had become firm; he obviously meant what he was saying. He actually leapt to his feet.

'Your concern for animal welfare,' Woggle shouted, the flesh around his bushy eyebrows suddenly glowing red, 'goes *exactly* as far as the point where your *own* interests are threatened, and no further. You are just like the tens of millions of vile scum in this country who would ban fox-hunting and seal-clubbing but happily gorge themselves on factory-bred fried chicken and mutated beefburgers! If you would hunt my fleas I suggest you do so with due self-knowledge. I suggest you wear a red coat, O *Genghis Khan*, and blow a bright horn. I suggest that you smear the blood of my dead fleas on the faces of your young after the kill and have a party to celebrate with stirrup cup served in beakers carved from the hooves of slaughtered stags! For you are no better than Lord Blood Sport of Bastardshire, David! You, who profess to care so much, are in fact the self-appointed Master of the Peeping Tom flea hunt!'

*

The curious thing was that when Woggle's flea rant was broadcast at the end of the first week of *House Arrest*, most people watching managed to find common ground with what he said. The anti-fox-hunters, of course, welcomed their most prominent ever national spokesman, while the country sports people hailed a man who forced urban animal activists to confront the selective nature of their agendas.

Woggle was like the Bible: everybody claimed he proved their point. And people just loved him. Suddenly it was as if Woggle was the nation's pet dog, dirty, smelly and intrusive, but somehow rather lovable.

If the nine other inmates of the house had had any idea of the extent of Woggle's popularity outside the house they would not have done what they did. But sealed off as they were from the outside world, they never dreamt that this flea-ridden crusty who could not sit down without leaving a stain was becoming a hero.

It wasn't fair, of course. Geraldine knew that it wasn't fair, but not surprisingly she didn't care.

Geraldine knew that nobody could have lived with Woggle and put up with it. The fact was that the other nine inmates had been incredibly tolerant; most people would probably have killed Woggle already. But, like life, television is not fair and Geraldine, having unwittingly created a national craze, was happy to edit towards it.

She therefore chose not to broadcast the patient and fairly considerate efforts that the housemates made to persuade Woggle to wash his clothes, clear up after himself and above all to deal with his fleas. She did not show how Kelly brought him blankets in the night and Dervla ensured that his dietary requirements were included on the house shopping lists. She showed only moments of the lengthy discussions that Garry, Jazz and Woggle had about football, a passion they all shared. No, Geraldine cut straight to the day when Garry, Jazz, David and Hamish leapt on Woggle as he lay in the garden and forcibly stripped him, burnt his clothes and covered his writhing, protesting form with flea powder.

DAY ELEVEN. 7.30 p.m.

The incident occurred on the second Thursday under *House Arrest*, the day of the first nominations.

The Peeping Tom rules were pretty much the same as all the similar shows that had gone before it. Each week, each of the housemates was asked to secretly nominate two people for eviction. The two most nominated people were then subjected to a public telephone vote to decide who should be thrown out of the house.

In order to allow people a chance to get to know each other there had been no voting in the first week and therefore day eleven was the first nomination day. The nominating took place in the afternoon, and in the evening the public got to see who had nominated whom, before the cameras cut live to the house to show the housemates being told who would be up for eviction on the following Sunday. Once this live moment of broadcasting was over, and everyone's face had been studied for traces of relief, glee, spite, etc., the rest of the evening's show returned to the usual round-up of the day's activities in the house.

The first thing that the public saw on that eleventh night of *House Arrest* was the nominations. All but one of the housemates voted for Woggle. The strange thing was that the housemate who did not vote for Woggle was not Woggle, because even Woggle voted for Woggle, which was a first for any reality TV show.

'I am voting for myself to be evicted from this house,' Woggle droned into the confession box camera, 'because I absolutely and entirely reject this highly divisive and gladiatorial system which is based on the inherently hierarchical principle that society must produce winners and losers, a principle aimed at the inevitable consequence of the emergence of a single oligarch, which is, let us be quite clear about this, nothing less than fascism. I therefore offer myself up as a sacrifice in protest against the transparently cynical deployment of a spurious democratic process in order to undermine genuine democracy. My other vote is for Jason, because his deodorants block my sinuses.'

After this astonishing display, which could only endear Woggle further to his adoring public, the other nominations seemed rather dull by comparison.

David voted for Woggle and also Layla, because he thought Layla was an irritating and pretentious pseud.

Kelly voted for Woggle and also Layla, because she thought that Layla looked down on her.

Jazz voted for Woggle and also Sally, because he found Sally's pious attitude to being a lesbian irritating.

Hamish voted for Woggle and also David, because he thought he'd have a better chance with the women with David out of the way.

Layla voted for Woggle and also David, because she thought David was an irritating and pretentious pseud.

Garry voted for Woggle and also Layla, because he thought she was a snob.

Moon voted for Woggle and also Garry, because she thought he was a fookin' sexist twat.

Sally voted for Woggle and also Moon, because of what Moon had said about the mentally ill.

Dervla voted for David and for Layla, because she was sick of their bickering. Dervla would have voted for Woggle. She certainly wanted Woggle out of the house – she was no more immune to him than anybody else was. But unlike the rest of the housemates, Dervla knew how popular Woggle was with the public. The mirror had told her.

It was a constant theme of the messages.

Woggle stood at number one, Kelly at number two and Dervla was stubbornly placed third.

'*Be nice to Woggle. People love him*,' the message-writer had said on the morning after Dervla had confronted Woggle over the hair on the soap. Since that time, Dervla had been careful to follow the advice.

When the nominations were announced on live television Woggle was acting very strangely. He was sitting in his usual corner but he had covered himself in a blanket and was swaying softly beneath it. He was humming to himself, almost keening. The other nine housemates sat on the couches.

'This is Chloe,' the announcement said. Chloe was the 'face' of *House Arrest*, the girl who worked the studio chats. 'The two housemates nominated for eviction this week are . . . in alphabetical order . . . Layla and Woggle.'

Everybody tried not to show it, but the relief was

palpable. Only four more days and Woggle would be gone. Even Layla was not unduly worried. Although hurt that she had been the other nominee, she knew that she would live to fight another day, because, like most of the others, she simply could not imagine the public not voting Woggle out. Surely they must find him as revolting as the housemates did.

Dervla, of course, knew better.

DAY THIRTY-FOUR. 4.15 p.m.

'The public did find Woggle revolting,' Bob Fogarty said, fishing a semi-melted square of chocolate out of his foaming plastic cup, 'but they just loved him for it, and by the time episode eleven was over, he'd become a national hero. It was so deceitful and unfair, I felt ashamed. I complained to that bitch Geraldine, but she said it came with the job and that cunts like me had forfeited our right to have principles.'

Once more Trisha had gone to the editing bunker in an effort to try to bridge the gap between what the public had seen and what had actually happened. It seemed just possible to her that the clue to solving the murder might lie in understanding how this trick was worked.

After all, everybody had *seen* the murder.

Fogarty sucked noisily on his chocolate. Trisha watched his mouth with growing distaste.

'That cow knew very well that she had been wickedly skewing public sympathy away from the main group and towards Woggle right from the start.'

'So when the attack on him came, shown in the context Geraldine had made you create, it looked absolutely damning?'

'It certainly did, and the nation went potty, as I'm sure you know. I told Geraldine that we were giving

113

Woggle too much of the running. I mean, quite apart from the fact that we were seriously demonizing nine relatively innocent people, we were also turning the show into a one-trick pony, which in my *humble* opinion was not good telly at all in the long term. Geraldine knew that, of course, but the footage was just irresistible. It made the other boys look like absolute *bastards*. Awful. Like something out of *Lord of the Flies*.'

DAY ELEVEN. 1.45 p.m.

The housemates had been called into the confession box to make their nominations in alphabetical order, therefore Woggle had gone in last.

'What's he doing in there?' Jazz said, after a minute or two had passed.

'I hope he's died and rotted,' David replied.

'He wouldn't have to die to rot, he's rotting already,' said Gazzer.

'We'll be doing him a favour,' Jazz concluded. 'Saving him from himself.'

To Jazz, the worst thing on earth would be to be filthy. He lived to preen.

When Woggle finally emerged from the little room, the boys were lying in wait.

'Afternoon, fellow humanoids,' said Woggle, wandering out into the garden. 'Happy summer solstice.'

Without a word, they jumped him. Hamish and Jazz held him down while Garry and David pulled off his ancient combat trousers.

'What's going on?' he shouted, but the boys were too intent on their mission to reply.

Woggle's skinny legs kicked about, glaring white in the bright sunlight. He was wearing filthy old Y-fronts with a hole in them where one of his balls had worn the cloth away. As he struggled with his attackers both balls fell through this hole. It didn't look funny, it looked sad and pathetic.

'No, no! What're you doing!' Woggle yelled, but still the boys ignored him. They had drunk the last of the house cider and were feeling righteous. This had to be done. Woggle had it coming to him. You could not just give people fleas and then expect them to do nothing about it.

'Get them pants off him, they'll be infested too!' Jazz shouted.

'I ain't touching them,' Garry replied.

'Nor me,' said Hamish.

'Fuck this,' said Jazz and, letting go of Woggle for a moment, he ran to the chicken coup and grabbed the gloves they used to clean out the birds. When he returned, Woggle had managed to twist himself round so that when Jazz pulled his underpants off him his bony white arse was on view to the cameras.

Next they pulled off his shirt, ripping the buttons as they did so, and finally they wrenched Woggle's filthy string vest up over his head. Now Woggle was naked. A struggling, shrieking, pale, bony little creature with a great mop of dreadlocks and his beard flying and flapping in the summer sun.

'This is assault! I am being defiled! Get off me!' he shouted.

'I'm being assaulted and defiled by your fleas!' Hamish cried, speaking for them all. 'My fucking armpits are bleeding.'

There was a barbecue at the back of the house and the boys had already cranked it up in preparation for the attack. Jazz threw Woggle's clothes and his sandals onto the fire. There was a strange fizzing sound. 'Fuck me!' he cried. 'I can hear the fleas popping!'

'Not popping, screaming!' Woggle shouted.

'Let's shave his head!' shouted David. 'He's bound to have lice.'

'No,' said Jazz firmly. 'You can't mess with a man's barnet, even Woggle's.'

'Fascists!' shouted Woggle, but his voice degenerated to a cough as Garry and Hamish began dousing him in flea powder. For a few moments they were all engulfed in a great cloud, and when they had finished Woggle was a luminous ghostly white from head to toe. Even his hair and beard were white as snow.

They left Woggle prostrate and naked in the middle of the lawn. As he turned briefly towards one of the garden cameras, flesh-coloured lines began to streak his death-white face as the tears sprang from his eyes.

DAY THIRTY-FOUR. 5.00 p.m.

'That was the image Geraldine made me close the show with,' Fogarty told Trisha. 'We didn't show any of this . . .' He tapped an assortment of the buttons on his editing console and there appeared on the bank of screens the coverage from inside the house recorded immediately following the attack.

The housemates were taking no pleasure from the incident. There was no whooping, no hollering. They were all genuinely sorry for Woggle. Dervla was already making him some herbal tea (which he accepted in silence), and Kelly was planning a tofu and molasses comfort cake. The mood was subdued but resolved. As one, they felt that the men had acted in order to counter a pressing social issue which threatened the wellbeing of the group.

In the editing suite Fogarty retreated to the little kitchenette area to get more of his chocolate from the fridge. Trisha wondered why he kept it cold when he was going to put it in his coffee.

116

'It's sad, isn't it?' Fogarty remarked. 'They actually deluded themselves that the nation would applaud their ability to police their own community.'

On the screens the self-justification continued.

'We could have gone on strike and asked for him to be ejected,' Hamish was saying, 'but what would we have looked like? A bunch of kids who couldn't handle their own problems.'

'Yes,' said Layla. 'The whole point of being here is to discover whether we can work together. If we had just gone running to Peeping Tom with our first group problem we'd basically have failed the test.'

Fogarty shook his head in disbelief. 'Incredible. That girl Layla is bright enough, and yet she actually believed all that bullshit about *House Arrest* being a genuine experiment in social engineering. It's a TV programme, for God's sake! How could she not realize that the single and only point of the whole bloody exercise is to attract advertisers?'

'Well, it certainly did that, didn't it?' said Trisha.

'Oh yes, our ratings shot up and with it Peeping Tom's revenue.' Fogarty turned his attention back to the screens. 'Watch this,' he said. 'There's more that we didn't broadcast.'

On the screens Woggle came in from the garden.

He refused Kelly's offer of cake without a word.

He also turned his back on the various offers of clothing and water.

Layla suggested that she read him one or two of her healing poems. 'Or else we could hold hands and hum together.'

Woggle did not even look at her. Instead he took up a blanket to cover his nakedness and retreated silently to his corner.

'This is it, coming up now,' said Fogarty. 'Dervla's confession.'

Sure enough, there was Dervla slipping into the confession box.

'Of course I understand the boys' frustration,' she said. 'We are after all suffering quite considerably here. But I did want to say that I feel enormous sorrow over Woggle's distress and wished that a better way could have been found to deal with his health issues. Deep down I think he is beautiful.'

Fogarty stopped the tape. 'Now I believed then and I believe now that Dervla is a lovely, lovely girl and that she was really upset about Woggle. But do you know what that shitty little cynic Geraldine made of it?'

'What?'

'She reckoned that Dervla had worked out that Woggle would be popular on the outside and was trying to curry favour with the public by supporting him.'

'Wow, you'd have to be pretty perceptive.'

'And pretty calculating, which I don't think she is.'

'On the other hand, she *was* the only person who didn't nominate him.'

'You're worse than Geraldine! She said exactly that! Said that if she didn't know better she'd think that Dervla had inside information.'

'But that's impossible, isn't it?'

'It certainly is. Let me tell you that if anyone was cheating I'd know. I see *everything*.'

'But if she *did* have a secret advantage, and one of the others found out about it . . .' Trisha stared into Dervla's deep-green eyes, trying to read the thoughts that Dervla had been thinking in the confession box. Before death had changed everything.

DAY THIRTY-FOUR. 8.00 p.m.

Trisha returned to the station without eating. Having watched Fogarty sucking chocolate for an hour, she

118

had lost her appetite, which she regretted now because it looked like it was going to be another long night.

'Let's get through Woggle this evening, shall we?' Coleridge suggested. I don't think I could face coming back to him tomorrow. What happened after the flea powder attack?'

'The public weren't happy, sir,' said Hooper. 'Within hours of show eleven going out there was a crowd outside the Peeping Tom compound calling for Garry, Hamish, David and Jazz to be arrested for assault. Geraldine Hennessy had to play music into the house to drown out the chants.'

Trisha put the tape Fogarty had given her into the VCR. 'People weren't happy inside the house either. Look at Woggle. He's devastated.'

'The rest of them don't look too good either.'

'They feel guilty about it.'

It was clear from the subdued conversation and unhappy faces that everybody was feeling very uncomfortable.

They took refuge in cleaning, frenzied cleaning. With Woggle, the carrier and principal breeding ground, de-flead, it was possible to begin cleansing the rest of the house, which the nine of them did with a vengeance. Every mattress and sheet was taken outside, washed, dried, powdered, then washed again. Every garment of clothing, every cushion and cloth. Everybody showered and applied more powder. They got through ten containers of it, all of which had had to come out of their weekly shopping budget. Not only had Woggle's fleas half eaten them alive, but they had also cost them the equivalent of eight precious bottles of wine or thirty cans of lager.

Throughout the whole of this day-long cleaning process Woggle remained beneath his blanket in his corner, swaying slowly and singing to himself. A traumatized troll, as one newspaper was to put it.

At the end of the day came the first eviction.

'They broadcast two episodes on eviction nights,' Hooper explained to Coleridge, 'which is very thoughtful, because it gives the nation just enough time to pop out for a beer and curry between the shows.'

'Don't talk about food,' said Trisha. 'I haven't eaten all day.'

'You can have half of my evening Mars Bar if you wish,' Coleridge suggested, but without enthusiasm.

'No, thank you, sir,' said Trisha. 'I'm a bit off chocolate at the moment.'

Coleridge struggled hard not to show his mighty relief.

'Anyway,' said Hooper, doggedly persevering with the matter at hand. 'The first broadcast on a Sunday is a live broadcast of the announcement of the person who's going to be evicted, and the second is live coverage of the departure.'

'Marvellous,' said Coleridge. 'An opportunity to spend an entire evening watching someone you don't know being asked to leave a house you've never been to by a group of people you've never met and whom you will never hear of again. It's difficult to imagine a more riveting scenario.'

'You have to be into it, sir, that's all. If you get into it it's brilliant.'

'Of course it is, Hooper. I wonder if when the ancient Greeks laid the foundation stones of western civilization they ever dreamt such brilliance possible?'

'Like I say, if you're not into it you won't get it.'

'From Homer to *House Arrest* in only twenty-five hundred years, a record to be proud of, don't you think?'

'Sir!' said Hooper. 'We're doing fourteen-hour days minimum to get through this! You have absolutely no right to extend them by constantly going off on one!'

There was an embarrassed silence, which lasted for

the time it took for Coleridge to unwrap his Mars Bar. Hooper's face was red. He was tired, angry and annoyed. Coleridge, who had had no idea he was being so irritating, was slightly sad.

'Well,' he said finally. 'Let's get on.'

DAY FOURTEEN. 7.30 p.m.

'People under House Arrest, this is Chloe. Can you hear me? The first person to leave the house will be,' Chloe left a suitably dramatic pause, '. . . Layla.'

Layla looked like she had been hit in the face with a cricket bat, but nevertheless managed to enact the time-honoured ritual required from people in such situations.

'Yes!' she squeaked, punching the air as if she was pleased. 'Now I can get back to my cat!'

'Layla, you have two hours to pack and say your goodbyes,' Chloe shouted, 'when we will be back live for *House Arrest*'s first eviction! See you then!'

Layla was stunned.

They were all stunned.

Even Woggle beneath his blanket was stunned. He had presumed like everyone else in the house (except Dervla) that his presence there had been evenly reported and, although he considered his conduct to be exemplary, he had not expected public sympathy. Years of sneers and contempt from almost everybody he met for almost everything he said and did had led Woggle to presume that the viewing public's attitude to him would be the same as that of the four fascists who had stripped him in the garden and attacked him without *any* provocation.

But the public's attitude wasn't the same at all, they loved their little goblin, the traumatized troll. He was their pet, and although Woggle could have no idea of

121

the dizzy heights to which his popularity had risen, he was astonished and thrilled enough simply to have avoided eviction.

He poked his head out of his blanket briefly. 'Fuck you,' he said to the assembled inmates and then submerged himself once more beneath his cover.

Then Layla howled with anguish. She actually *howled*. The injustice of it all was clearly nearly unbearable. The tears streamed down her face as she rocked back and forth on the purple couch in an agony of self-pity. She could obviously not believe that the public had chosen Woggle over her! *Woggle!*

Layla went to the confession box to vent her spleen.

'You bastards!' she stormed. 'It's fucking obvious what you've done! Somehow you've made him the victim, haven't you? You've been having a laugh and we're the joke, aren't we? *I'm* the joke! You know what Woggle's like! What we've had to put up with! He doesn't clean up, he doesn't help out, he stinks like the rotting corpse of a dead dog's arse! *Everyone* wanted him out, but you haven't shown all that, have you? No! You can't have done or he'd be going, not me!'

DAY THIRTY-FOUR. 8.40 p.m.

'If she'd shown a bit more spirit like that before, she wouldn't have been nominated,' said Hooper, who had enjoyed watching Coleridge wincing at some of Layla's choice of phrases.

'But she's wrong about the eviction,' said Trisha. 'Certainly, Peeping Tom skewed the coverage in Woggle's favour, but everyone could still see what a slob he was. Layla would have been voted out whatever. The mistake the people who go on these shows make is to imagine that anybody actually *cares* about

122

them. As far as we're concerned, they're just acts on the telly, to be laughed at.'

On screen Layla was beginning to break down. 'I think some of my flea bites will leave scars, you bastards! The ones around my bottom have gone septic!'

'Ugh!' said Trisha.

'Too much information!' Hooper protested.

'If I do get ill I shall sue you,' Layla fulminated. 'I swear I will! I'm going now, but one more thing: I know you won't broadcast this, Geraldine Hennessy, but I think you're a complete and utter shit and I will hate you for ever!'

'*Hate you for ever*,' Coleridge repeated. 'That's a long time, and it was only three weeks ago. I doubt she'd have got over it yet.'

On the screen Layla went into the girls' bedroom to get her bag. Kelly joined her. 'I'm really, really sorry, Layla,' Kelly said. 'It must feel rotten.'

'No, no, it's fine really . . .'

But then Layla broke down again, falling into Kelly's arms and sobbing.

'*Kelly is comforting Layla, but what Layla doesn't know is that Kelly nominated her for eviction*,' said the voice of Andy the narrator.

'They just *love* pointing it out when that happens,' Hooper remarked. 'It's the best bit of the show.'

'You have to be strong, right?' Kelly said, holding Layla close. 'Be a strong woman, which is what you are.'

'That's right, I am, I'm a strong, spiritual woman.'

'Go, girl. Love you.'

'Love you, Kelly,' said Layla. 'You're a mate.'

Then Layla went back into the living area and hugged everybody else, including, even, extremely briefly, Woggle.

Her hug with David lasted nearly a minute.

'The evictees always do that,' said Hooper. 'Have a great big hug. Pretending they're all big mates really.'

123

'I think while they're doing it they mean it,' Coleridge said. 'Young people live on the surface and for the moment. That's just how it is these days.'

'You are so right, sir,' put in Trisha. 'I'm twenty-five and I've never held a considered opinion or experienced a genuine emotion in my life.'

For a moment Coleridge was about to insist to Trisha that he was sure this was not the case, but then he realized she was being sarcastic.

'Layla, you have thirty seconds to leave the Peeping Tom house,' said Chloe's voice on the television.

DAY FOURTEEN. 9.30 p.m.

As she stepped out of the house Layla was bathed in almost impossibly bright light, which turned her and the house behind her bleach white. A huge bald security man in a padded bomber-jacket stepped forward and took her arm. He led her onto the platform of a firework-bedecked cherry picker which lifted her up and over the moat while the crowd cheered. Peeping Tom took great pride in its house exits; they turned them into what appeared to be huge parties. They bussed in crowds, let off fireworks and criss-crossed the air with search lights. As Layla was lifted high over the shrieking throng a rock band played live from the back of a lorry.

Then came the short limousine journey to the specially constructed studio and the live interview with Chloe, the beautiful, big-bosomed, ladette-style 'face' of Peeping Tom. Chloe was no mere pretty face, however, like the girls who presented the more mainstream shows. No, Chloe was a pretty face with a tattoo of a serpent on her tummy and another of a little devil on her shoulder, which was of course much, much more real.

Chloe met Layla at the door of the limo. She looked rock-chick stunning in black leather trousers and a black leather bra, while Layla looked hippie-chick stunning in a tie-dye silk sarong and cropped silk singlet. The women hugged and kissed as if they were long-lost sisters instead of complete strangers, one of whom was paid to talk to the other.

The crowd went berserk. Literally berserk. They whooped, they hollered, they screamed, they waved their home-made placards. There was absolutely no provocation for this madness beyond the presence of television cameras and the well-established convention that this was how up-for-it young people were supposed to behave in the presence of television cameras.

Finally the whooping died down, or at least died down enough for Chloe to make herself heard. It would continue, ebbing and flowing in volume, throughout the interview, but Chloe used her window of opportunity to express her own feelings of exuberance.

'Whooo!' she shouted. 'All right! Unreal! Wicked! Whooo!'

The audience concurred with these sentiments entirely and returned to their own whooping refreshed.

Chloe threw a proudly muscular arm around Layla. 'Do we love this chick or what? Is she not one strong, special lady?'

Further whoops and hollers indicated that the audience did indeed love Layla very much.

'We are soooooo proud of you, girl, you're brilliant.'

Once more the proceedings became mired in shouting and screaming. Chloe fought to make herself heard, or perhaps merely to make it clear that she was the most excited and up for it of them all.

'So how are you feeling, girl?' Chloe whooped.

The atmosphere was infectious. Layla smiled broadly. 'Wicked!' she said.

'All right!'

'Yeah, really amped up.'

'Go, girl!'

'But also quite spiritual.'

'I *so* know what you mean.'

'Yeah, like I've grown.'

'And you so have, girl. Respect to that!' Chloe turned to the mob and shouted, 'Do we love this ace lady or what!?'

And the mob whooped and hollered with renewed energy.

'So were you really, really shocked to be nominated?'

'Well, you know, all life is a season and seasons change. I really, really believe that.'

'That is so true.'

'You have to be positive in your own head space, the mind is a garden, it needs constant weeding.'

'Fantastic, and what about Jazz's cooking. Was that wicked or what?'

'Totally wicked.'

And so, with the in-depth psychological grilling over, Chloe turned to the big screen and showed Layla who had nominated her.

First came David. There he sat, on nomination day, looking beautiful and sincere as he addressed the confession box camera.

'And the second person I'm nominating is Layla, because although I think she's a very strong spiritual woman, she doesn't give a lot to the group as a whole.'

The nation watched Layla watching the screen. Her manic grin did not forsake her. 'David's great,' she said. 'I really love him totally, but you know when two strong, spiritual, loving, caring, strong people meet, sometimes their head spaces don't always connect, but that's OK, I really love him and I know he loves me.'

'And of course you nominated him,' said Chloe.

'Yeah, isn't that weird! It just shows what a connection we actually had.'

Dervla was a surprise. 'After David, I nominate Layla,' Dervla said, looking excruciatingly sincere, thoughtful and beautiful. 'She's a lovely, lovely girl, a very gentle, caring and beautiful spirit, but I feel that in the end her loveliness would be able to blossom more beautifully outside of the house.'

Which everybody, even Layla, knew translated as 'She's a pain in the arse.'

Then came Garry. 'Layles is a very, very tasty bird, and also I reckon she means well, but basically she's a bit snooty for my liking, you know what I mean? Reckons herself and all that.'

Layla smiled bravely at this, a smile which was meant to say, 'Yes, people often mistake my spirituality for conceit.'

And then finally there was Kelly. 'This is really, really difficult, but at the end of the day I have to choose someone, and I'm choosing Layla because I think she reckons she's better than me, and maybe she is, but it's still a bit hurtful.'

Chloe leant forward and squeezed Layla's hand, thereby offering comfort and showing off her lovely bosom simultaneously.

'You OK, girl?' said Chloe. 'Strong?'

'Yeah, strong.'

'You stay strong, girl,' Chloe insisted.

Layla rose to the challenge. 'I think David and Gazzer are brilliant,' she said, 'and Dervla and Kelly are great, really, really, strong ladies. The truth is that they all have to choose someone and sometimes my strength and my spirituality get misunderstood by people. But at the end of the day, right, I love those guys, they're my posse.'

'Big up to that! Respect!' Chloe shouted, and then abruptly got up and walked off into the crowd, leaving Layla sitting alone.

'So, one gone, only eight more rejects and we'll have

a winner!' Chloe shouted into the camera that was tracking backwards in front of her. 'Who's out next? Stinky man? Booby woman? David and his most irritating guitar-playing? Jazz with the top bod? Gazz who speaks for ENGERLAND!? Angry Sal? Dull Hamish? Bald lady? Or Dervla, our oh-so-sensitive little Irish Colleen. You are the executioners! You can crush their little dreams! YOU decide! The phone lines will be open after the next nominations! Respect! Love on ya.'

DAY THIRTY-FOUR. 10.20 p.m.

The three police officers watched as Layla disappeared behind the baying crowd, heading straight for obscurity.

'I think we should definitely talk to her,' Coleridge said. 'There's a lot of anger there and we need to know more about it.'

'Besides which,' observed Hooper, 'she knows them all better than we ever will. Perhaps she has a theory.'

'Everybody's got a theory,' Coleridge replied ruefully, 'except us.'

On the screens the remaining housemates still looked shell-shocked.

'Well, O hunters and killers,' Woggle said through a broken-toothed smile, 'the people sided with life over death and light over darkness. It appears that the revolution beginneth.'

David got to his feet.

'You're right there, Woggle. I'm going to have a word with Peeping Tom.'

DAY FOURTEEN. 10.45 p.m.

'I'm fookin' coming with yez,' said Moon.

David and Moon stormed into the confession box

128

together, where David made it clear that he had drawn the same conclusion that Layla had done earlier in the evening.

'You've betrayed us, Peeping Tom,' he said. 'You know we did our best with Woggle. But we saw the banners out there and the people all shouting for him. They think we're shits.'

'It's not a question of betrayal,' Peeping Tom replied, Peeping Tom being Geraldine, of course, who was frantically scribbling down her replies and handing them to her 'voice', a quiet, gentle, soothing lady named Sam, who normally did voiceovers for washing-up liquid commercials.

'The public have simply seen something in Woggle that they find attractive,' the soothing voice continued.

'They find him attractive because that's how you must have made him look!' David snarled. 'I'm a professional, I'm in the business, I know your tricks. Well, let me tell you I've had enough! I didn't come in here to be manipulated and made a fool of. I want out. You can get me a taxi because I'm leaving,' he said.

'Me fookin' too!' added Moon. 'And I reckon the rest'll go too, and then all you'll be left with is the plague pit with Woggle in it. It's fookin' obvious you're taking the piss.'

DAY THIRTY-FOUR. 10.25 p.m.

Hooper pressed pause. 'This is very interesting, sir. None of this stuff was ever broadcast. I had absolutely no idea that the inmates were so sussed out to what was going down.'

'Sussed out to what was going down?'

'It means . . .'

'I know what it means, sergeant. I'm not an imbecile.

129

I was just wondering if you'd given any thought at all to how ugly it sounds?'

'No, sir, actually I hadn't. Would you like me to hand in my warrant card for using inelegant sentences in the course of an investigation?'

DAY FOURTEEN. 10.46 p.m.

'Walking out would be very foolish. You would be sacrificing the chance of winning the half-million-pound prize,' Peeping Tom said, and Sam put every ounce of her ability to soothe into each syllable.

'I don't care,' David said. 'Like I said, I know this business. We're just a bunch of stooges to Woggle's funny man. I came in here to get the chance to show the world who I am, but you've turned it into a freak show, an endurance test, and I don't want to play any more.'

'Me fookin' neither,' said Moon.

There was another pause while Peeping Tom considered a reply. 'Give us two days,' the soothing voice said finally. 'He'll be out.'

'Two days?' David replied. 'Don't lie to me. There isn't another eviction for a week.'

'Give us two days,' Peeping Tom repeated.

DAY THIRTY-FOUR. 10.30 p.m.

'That's amazing,' said Trisha. 'Geraldine Hennessy must have known about Woggle all along. It's obvious she had it ready up her sleeve.'

'The sly bitch!' Hooper agreed. 'She said she got sent those clippings anonymously.'

'Kindly explain what you're talking about and please don't refer to our witnesses as bitches.'

'None of what we've just seen was broadcast, sir. We've only seen it because we impounded the tapes.'

'I'm amazed it wasn't wiped,' Hooper added.

'That'll be Fogarty. He *hates* Geraldine Hennessy.'

'What are you talking about?' Coleridge demanded once more.

'You must be the only person in the country who doesn't know, sir. Woggle was wanted by the police. But it only emerged on day fifteen. It's obvious now that Geraldine Hennessy knew all along; that's why she was able to promise to get him out.'

DAY FIFTEEN. 9.00 p.m.

'I simply cannot believe that they have just made the whole thing up about Woggle,' Layla told the assembled press on the morning after her departure. She had spent all of the preceding night looking at tapes of the show and press cuttings collected for her by her family. It had been a grim business. She discovered that what coverage there had been of her had made her look like a snooty, self-obsessed airhead. Much of that impression had been given in the first handful of shows, for increasingly during the second week Woggle appeared to be the only issue of any real interest in the house.

'It was so *not* all about Woggle,' Layla protested. 'There were nine other people in that house – interesting, strong, spiritual, beautiful people. It has fallen to me to speak up for all of us. We have spent our time under House Arrest interacting, talking, loving, hugging, being irritated and inspired by each other. Woggle, on the other hand, spent his time in the house being a dirty and unreasonable slob and spreading disease, and it is *so* not all about him.'

But as far as the public were concerned it *was*, and

131

that morning even more so, because that was the morning that Geraldine put her Woggle policy into drastic reverse.

The sensational news became public about halfway through Layla's press conference, and as it swept through the room Layla saw the interest in her and anything she might have to say diminish very rapidly to zero.

Geraldine had had to act, and act quickly. Woggle had been a colossal success, but he was now in danger of being an even more colossal failure. If the other inmates walked out now, as they were perfectly entitled to do, Peeping Tom would be left in default of seven more weeks of nightly television that it was contracted to deliver to the network. Peeping Tom would be bankrupted. Which was why Geraldine sent the old press clippings of the photo of Woggle kicking the girl to the police.

The incident had happened four years previously, and Woggle had looked quite different. He had been a little chunkier and had a pink Mohican haircut, but if you looked closely at the large nose and the bushy eyebrows and the spider's web tattooed on the man in the picture's neck, there was no doubting that it was Woggle. Actually Geraldine had been surprised that the papers had not dug it up themselves, but since Woggle had never been caught or identified it would have taken a good memory for faces to recall four years previously, when the photo had been splashed across all the front pages with the headline 'WHO ARE THE ANIMALS?'

It had been a hunt-saboteur operation that got out of hand. Woggle and a number of fellow sabs had invaded a kennels in Lincolnshire with the intention of freeing the dogs. The master of hounds and a number of stable hands had confronted them and an ugly row had developed. The sabs struck first, trying to force their way past the master, and when he refused to yield they had knocked him to the ground with an iron bar. A general fight then broke out, and Woggle had waded in with his boots and a bicycle chain. This was a side of Woggle of which the people in the house and indeed his fans the viewing population had no idea. There was much about Woggle of which the house-mates disapproved (everything, in fact) but it would never have occurred to them that a propensity for violence was one of his faults.

But, on occasion, it was. Although as Woggle and his old animal-liberationist colleagues sometimes pointed out, 'We're only ever violent to humans.' Like most zealots, Woggle had his dark, intolerant side, and while he valued the wellbeing of dumb creatures and even insects most highly, he was singularly unconcerned about his fellow man. Therefore when he had found himself confronted by a stable hand wielding a rake, he waded in and whacked her. The fact that she was only fifteen and weighed less than he did did not concern him. Chivalry was not an issue when it came to defending foxes. As far as Woggle was concerned, if you were a fox-murderer, or an associate of fox-murderers, you had sacrificed your right to any consideration. It did not matter if you were small and blonde and cute, you were fair game and deserved what you got. And this girl was small, blonde and cute, which was why, when the newspapers were choosing between the horrific images of violence taken by the master's wife from the upstairs window of her farmhouse, there had been no contest. It was an image that briefly shocked a nation: the jolly blonde ponytailed cutie in gumboots and a Barbour jacket spread out on the ancient cobbles of the stable yard with blood in her hair, while the ugly, crusty, pierced, punk thug lashed out at her with his great steel-capped boots. It had been a public relations disaster for the sabs, compounded by the fact that the fifteen-year-old in question was a dog-mad, fox-loving member of the RSPCA who regularly petitioned the local hunt to switch to the drag method.

Woggle had brought the press clipping to show Geraldine on the last night before he and the others were scheduled to go into the house. He had been delighted to have been chosen and had not told Peeping Tom about his past until this point, in case it counted against him. He was very much looking forward to going under House Arrest, not least because it guaranteed him full board and a dry roof, which was quite a tempting prospect after months spent in a tunnel. Now, however, he was worried that the subsequent notoriety might cause him to be identified as the man in the picture and possibly get him arrested.

'So why are you showing me all this now, Woggle?' Geraldine had asked.

'I don't know. I thought maybe if you knew about it then if anybody says anything you could say that you'd checked it out and it wasn't me but some other bloke with a spider tattoo.'

Woggle, like all the other house inmates, had been so taken in by Peeping Tom's protestations about the contestants' welfare being their first concern that he actually thought that Geraldine would be prepared to lie to the press and the police on his behalf. In fact her only concern on being confronted with Woggle's confession had been whether she could possibly get away with letting a person who was wanted for assault into a highly pressurized and confined social environment.

In the end she had decided to risk it. It had only been a scuffle at an animal-rights protest, and Woggle looked like such a peaceful old hippie. Besides which, there were only hours left before the game started, and Woggle was potentially such very good telly that she simply could not face the idea of giving him up.

'We can always deny any knowledge of it if the cunt goes mad and bops someone for eating a ham sandwich,' Geraldine said to Bob Fogarty. 'I mean, the cops and the press never caught him at the time, so why should we have recognized him now?'

So Geraldine had hidden the old clippings in a drawer and thought no more about them. Until day fifteen, when she found Peeping Tom in a situation where, having made a hero out of Woggle, she needed, as she said at the emergency planning meeting held in the small hours of the morning, 'to get the cunt out sharpish'.

It did not take long for the photograph of Woggle kicking the teenage girl to find its way back to Peeping Tom Productions. Geraldine had sent it to the police at 9.15 a.m. with an accompanying letter explaining that she had received it at the office that morning from an anonymous source.

By 9.30 one of the press ringers at Scotland Yard had alerted the papers and by 9.45 they and the police had been beating a path to Peeping Tom's door. Inside the house, knowing nothing of these developments, the mood was very sombre.

Woggle had spent the night under his blanket in his usual corner. The others had been drinking out in the garden until the chill had forced them in at around four. They all felt very sorry for themselves, Woggle because he had been assaulted and defiled, the others because their lovely exciting adventure was being ruined by Woggle.

When it came, relief for the eight and disaster for the one struck like a thunderclap.

DAY FIFTEEN. 10.00 a.m.

'This is Chloe,' the tannoy announced. 'Woggle, would you please gather up your things. You are to leave the house in ten minutes.'

Garry, Kelly and Jazz cheered, the others, ever mindful of the game that they were playing, masked their inner delight beneath thoughtful, sensitive faces.

Woggle popped his head out from under his blanket. 'You can't chuck me out, I haven't been voted,' he said. 'I know my rights and I'm not fucking going.'

'Woggle, this is Chloe. We are not chucking you out. The police wish to interview you. Get your things.'

There was stunned silence.

'Fucking hell, Woggle, what you done?' Garry asked.

'Nothing, bollocks, I'm not going. They'll have to come and get me.'

And so they did, and that evening, in one of the television coups of the year, the nation watched as three uniformed police officers entered the Peeping Tom house and arrested Woggle for assault. Most of the other inmates were too stunned to react, but in what was without doubt a brilliant effort at audience manipulation Dervla suddenly cast herself in the roll of feisty, quick-thinking friend of the oppressed. She leapt up from the couch and gave Woggle the name of her solicitor.

'Insist on being allowed to look up the number in the book,' she said, allowing her Irish accent to ring out more strongly than usual, perhaps thinking it a fitting brogue in which to conduct a civil liberties protest. 'If you call directory inquiries they'll say you've used up your phone call. I know their tricks.'

David was not going to be upstaged. He stepped boldly in between the policemen and Woggle, who was still sitting on the floor.

'Be aware, officers, that I have committed all of your

faces and your numbers to memory. I am an actor and am trained in the art of mental retention. If anything happens to Mr Woggle you shall answer to me.'

It sounded great, and it would have sounded even better if the leading copper had not brought David down to earth by pointing out that since the arrest was being recorded by six separate video cameras he did not think that there would ever be a problem identifying the arresting officers. Then the policeman turned to Woggle.

'Get up, please, sir.'

'No. I ain't moving. I am the Peeping Tom One. Free the Peeping Tom One!'

'You can't arrest him for having fleas,' said Dervla.

'Why not?' Garry interjected. 'Should have done it weeks ago.'

Kelly stepped forward and put some apples and biscuits in Woggle's lap. 'In case they don't feed you.'

'Oh, for God's sake, Kelly,' David sneered. 'Like you give a toss.'

'He's a human being,' Kelly protested.

'That's debatable,' said Jazz, who was over at the kitchen area putting the kettle on and trying to look cool and unconcerned. 'I'm young, gifted and black,' his hip, easy stance was saying. 'Coppers come through my door every day.' In fact Jazz had never been arrested in his life, but the pose looked great and his standing with the public rocketed.

'We are bearing witness to this arrest,' Dervla said firmly.

'Yes, we are,' Moon added, rather weakly.

Hamish clearly decided that he couldn't compete and, following his plan that only the noticed get nominated, he got up and went into the boys' bedroom for a lie-down.

'Sir,' the lead policeman said, 'we do not know your name beyond the fact that you are known as Woggle.

137

However, we have strong photographic evidence to suggest that you are the person wanted by Lincolnshire Police in connection with the serious assault of one Lucy Brannigan, a girl of fifteen at the time of the attack.'

The other inmates stopped in their tracks, stunned.

'What? Sexual assault?' Garry asked.

'Come along, sir,' said the policeman.

'I can't believe it, Woggle,' said Jazz. 'I knew you were a dirty disgusting little toe-rag, but I never thought you were a nonce.'

Everybody drew back from the little figure squatting in the corner. Dervla disengaged herself and disappeared into the girls' bedroom.

Woggle wasn't having this. 'She was a fox-murderer!' he shouted. 'An animal-torturer! It was a fair fight and I kicked her in the head. She bloody deserved it, the fascist! If you live by the sword you die by the sword.'

And as if to prove this point the policemen picked Woggle up and carried him away. As they took him, struggling, through the door the blanket fell away to reveal Woggle's skinny body, still naked and covered in white flea powder.

He looked pathetic. It was the final indignity.

DAY THIRTY-FOUR. 11.50 p.m.

On the drive home Coleridge attempted to banish Woggle from his mind by listening to Radio 4. The thing about Radio 4 for Coleridge was that no matter what they were talking about he always got caught up in it. He had often found himself sitting in his car outside his house waiting to hear the end of some discussion about crop rotation in West Africa, or some other subject he had never heard of and would never think of again. Even the shipping forecasts made good listening, conjuring up as they did strange emotions and race memories of dark rocky coastlines, furious typhoons and the long lonely watches of the night.

The subject being discussed that night as Coleridge drove home was an economic slump in rural Ireland. The shift of money and young people to the cities, coupled with cuts in European agricultural grants, had left some villages in desperate financial straits. Negative loans and mortgages were forcing many households to the edge of despair. Coleridge's ears pricked up at the mention of one of the villages worst affected, Ballymagoon. Where had he heard that name recently? he wondered.

It wasn't until he was opening his second can of beer (and thinking about having a bit of ham with it) that Coleridge remembered. He had read the name on a suspect profile. Ballymagoon was the village in which Dervla was born.

DAY THIRTY-FIVE. 9.30 a.m.

'*It's day fifteen in the house, and after supper, in order to take their minds off Woggle's arrest, Peeping Tom sets the housemates a topic for discussion,*' Andy the narrator intoned portentously. '*The topic tonight is their deepest feelings.*'

Coleridge stirred his second mug of tea of the working day. Those he had at home did not count.

Trisha bustled in, pulling off her coat.

'You've arrived just in time, Patricia,' said Coleridge. 'Our suspects are about to discuss that most significant and sublime of all subject matters: themselves.'

'Suspects *and* victim, sir.'

It was early, and Trisha was not in the mood for Coleridge's superior tone, besides which, she felt that some respect at least was due to the dead. Coleridge merely smiled wearily.

On the screen Garry had taken the floor. 'I'm not going to mess you about,' he said. 'I've not always been a very nice person.'

'You still ain't,' Jazz chipped in, but nobody laughed. Instead they all hung on to the intense, caring expressions that they had had assumed when Garry had begun.

Coleridge pressed pause. 'You see how none of them share Jazz's joke? This is confession time. It's serious stuff. A matter of faith. Garry is worshipping at the altar of his own significance, and Jazz is laughing in church.'

'Sir, if we have to stop every time any of these people annoy you we'll never get through even this tape.'

'I can't help it, Patricia. They've ground me down.' But Coleridge knew he was being stupid and resolved to make an effort.

Garry began his story. 'Like I said, I was a bit of a geezer, you know what I mean? Little bit o' this, little bit o' that, dodgy stuff, done some rotten things that I don't mind admitting I'm not proud of, but at the end of the day, right, I done 'em and that's me and I can't change that. Truth is, I wanted it large and I wasn't too fussed about who I had a go at to get it. You know what I'm saying?'

There were murmurs of sympathy but not very enthusiastic ones.

'I think the truth of the matter was, right,' Garry continued, 'I didn't love myself.'

Now they all nodded earnestly. This they understood. Garry's other influences – the fighting, the boozing, the dodgy dealing – might have been different from their own, but when it came to that central subject of not quite loving oneself enough, they understood exactly what he meant.

'I know exactly what you fookin' mean,' Moon said.

'I don't think I was letting myself in,' Garry continued.

Coleridge's resolve to keep quiet had lasted less than a minute. 'Oh, for heaven's sake! Why do they all talk as if they're in therapy! Even *Garry*. Just *listen* to him! "I wasn't letting myself in." What on earth does *that* mean? He's a *yobbo*, for heaven's sake! Not a sociology graduate! Where do they *learn* all these ridiculous empty phrases?'

'Oprah, sir.'

'Who?'

Trisha could not tell whether Coleridge was joking. She let it go.

Back in the house, oblivious to how much they would one day annoy a senior police officer, the confessional continued.

'I just know *exactly* what you mean, I really do,' Moon was saying, 'and I think it's really dead strong of you that you can say it.'

Nourished by the support, Garry pressed on. Loving himself by pretending to hate himself. 'Anyway, I was getting into a lot of coke at the time, you know, quite a big habit, doing five hundred notes a week, bosh, straight up my hooter. Yes, please. Thank you very much. We like that. Blowing a grand was nothing to me. Nothing. I'm not proud of it, right, but that was me, right? I was having it large and what I wanted I fahking had, you know what I'm saying? I was a bad boy. I ain't proud of it.'

Coleridge thought about remarking that for a man who professed so much not to be proud of his behaviour, Gazzer was doing a pretty good job of showing the world just how proud of it he was. He decided against it, though. He could see that Patricia was getting sick of him.

On screen the rest of the group nodded earnestly at

Gazzer while clearly itching for the moment when they could take the floor themselves.

'But you know what saved me? You know what really worked me out?' Suddenly Garry was choking up. There were tears welling up in his eyes and his voice was cracking.

'Don't go on if you don't want to, mate,' said David, his voice awash with concentrated sincerity and sympathy. 'Take a break. Come back to it. Give yourself space. Now, when I—'

'No, no,' said Garry quickly. He wasn't losing hold of the conch that easily, not now he was on a roll. 'I'm all right, mate, thanks, but it helps to talk about it.'

David sank back onto the couch.

Garry took up the thread of his story. 'I'll tell you what changed me. My little lad, that's who, little Ricky. My kid. He means everything to me, everything. I'd fahkin' die for him, I would, I really would.'

There was much sincere and committed nodding at this. The body language of the group was highly supportive. Their eyes, on the other hand, told a different story. As the shot cut from one listener to another the message was clear: it said, 'I am bored out of my brains, I do not care about you and your little lad, and I wish you'd just *shut up and let me speak.*'

''Cos, like, I have Ricky most weekends, right, and he's just brilliant, I mean he's just so amazing, I'm so proud of him and like everything he says is just brilliant, right? You know what I mean? I'm not being funny or nothing, he's my little kiddie and he's like the best thing that ever happened to me.' Garry's voice was choking with emotion but he persevered.

'And one weekend I'd had it large the night before, you know what I'm saying? Did the lot, right, booze, coke, spliff, I ain't proud of it, and I was feeling well rough, and Ricky's mum brings him round and she says, "It's your day with him," and I'm thinking,

142

"Fahkin' hell! Oh no! This is all I need with a head like a sack full of broken glass." So I says, "I'll have him tomorrow," but she says, "You'll have him today," and she's gone, right? So I'm thinking, "Fahk, I'll take him round me mum's." But then, little Ricky says, "Don't you want to play with me, then, Daddy?" And you know what? He cured my hangover, there and then, just with his little smile and by saying that. So I stuck *Spot the Dog* on while I got myself together and then we went to the café for breakfast and after that we went down the park and had loads of ice cream and stuff. It was just brilliant, I mean really amazing, because I'm so proud of him and there's so much that I can learn from him, right? And at the end of the day, I know I have to treasure every moment with him and cherish him, because he's the most precious thing I've got.'

Gazzer wiped tears from his eyes. He had surprised himself. He didn't cry much in the usual run of things, but getting all that stuff about Ricky out had been brilliant. He felt genuinely moved.

The group paused for a nod. They were obviously anxious to leap straight in with stories of their own, but they held back, awarding Garry a moment of reflection and respect. None of them wanted to be portrayed on the television as taking somebody else's emotions lightly. Particularly when a little kiddie was involved.

It was into this pious pause that Kelly unwittingly slung her bucket of cold water. 'So what are you doing in here, then, Garry?' she asked.

'What?'

Kelly did not look as if she was trying to be horrid, but it certainly came across that way.

'I mean, if you have such a great time with him, and learn so much, what are you doing in here? You might be in here for nearly two and a half months. How old is he?'

'Nearly four.'

143

Garry was trying to work out what was going on. Was this woman *criticizing* his heartfelt confessional? Surely that was against the rules?

'Well, I think you're mad, then,' Kelly continued. 'I mean, at that age he'll be changing every day. You're going to miss it.'

'Yeah, I know that, Kelly, that's fahking obvious. I might even miss his birthday and I'm gonna be dead choked up—'

'So what are you doing in here, then?' Kelly repeated.

'Well, because . . . Because . . .'

Now Coleridge could contain his frustration no longer. He almost shouted at the screen, which was very unlike him. 'Well, come on, lad! Be honest, why don't you, for once in your life? Surely it's obvious! Because you have a *right* to be in that damned stupid house. You have a *right* to do *exactly* as you please. To lead an entirely selfish and irresponsible life while wallowing in the mawkish sentimentality of fatherhood when you feel like it! Come on, lad! Be a man! Answer the girl.'

'Sir,' said Trisha. '*Shut up.*' She stopped, shocked at her audacity.

'I'm sorry, sir, I . . .'

'I did not hear anything, constable,' said Coleridge quietly, resolving once more to try to contain himself.

On the screen Garry was still lost for words.

'Don't get me wrong,' Kelly continued. 'I'm not knocking you for having a kid or nothing like that. My sister's got two by different blokes and they're brilliant. I just think, you know, if you do have a kid, shouldn't you be out there trying to look after it? Instead of sitting in here. That's all. I mean, only seeing as how you love him so much.'

Garry, normally so quick with a clever line and a put-down, was at a loss. 'Well, as it happens, Kelly,' he said finally, 'I'm doing this for him.'

'How's that work, then?' said Kelly.
'To make him proud of me.'
'Oh, I see.'

On the following evening's edition of *House Arrest* Dr Ranulf Aziz, the show's resident TV psychologist, gave his opinion for the benefit of the viewers.

'See Garry's body language now, his shoulders hunched, his jaw set, this is a classic quasi-confrontational stance, with overtones of semi-concealed malice and undertones of mental violence. We see it mirrored in the animal kingdom when a great beast is denied access to the best portion of the kill. Garry's arms are firmly folded, just as a lion or a tiger might shift its weight to its rear haunches, demonstrating current passivity but a willingness to attack violently and with extreme rage.'

Chloe, the sparkly, spunky, batty, booby *House Arrest* babe, put on her intelligent face. 'So you're saying Gazzer's a bit naffed off?'

'That is indeed what I'm saying, Chloe. Gazzer is a bit naffed off big-time.'

Gazzer was more than naffed off. He was speechless with rage, his heart and soul were a boiling, bubbling pit of hurt and anger.

He covered it well, in that he only looked furious. 'Yeah, well, whatever,' he said.

'I didn't mean to say anything, Gazz,' Kelly replied. 'You know, I'm just saying, that's all.'

'Yeah, right, whatever,' Garry said again. 'Who wants a cup of tea, then?' He turned away from the group but there was no escape from the cameras, and a hot-head followed him to where the kettle was. There were tears in Garry's eyes and he was biting his lip so hard that a thin line of blood could be seen emerging.

How dare she? It was incredible. It wasn't his fault

that him and the mother didn't get on any more. What was he supposed to do, camp outside their house twenty-four hours a day? He had to have a life, didn't he?

He *did* love his kid. She had no right. No right at all.

DAY SEVENTEEN. 10.00 a.m.

Layla had been back at work for only an hour when she left again.

Back at work? It was incredible. Terrible. Devastating.

During all the time she had been in the house, and indeed ever since she had received the thrilling news that she had been selected to join the *House Arrest* team, Layla had hardly dared to think of what she would be doing three days after leaving. Of course, she had allowed herself to dream a little and in her wildest fantasies had imagined herself juggling offers to model gorgeous clothes and to present exciting television programmes about beauty products and alternative culture. In her worst moments of fear and doubt she had feared being lampooned in the tabloids and having to go on radio chat shows to defend her dippy-hippie ways. What she never *ever* imagined, however, was that she would be going back to work.

The brutal fact was that nobody was interested in her. The story of Woggle's rise and spectacular fall had been *the* Peeping Tom story of the first fortnight, and now even that was becoming old news. The show had moved on. Layla had been useful to the press only in so much as she could talk about Woggle, and now that this one small nugget of notoriety had disappeared, she was just the beautiful but vain hippie one who got chucked out first.

The one who wrote shit poetry. The one who was

obviously entirely and completely absorbed in her own beauty and wonderfulness.

That was how Peeping Tom had presented her, when they presented her at all. As a snooty, stupid cow whose one redeeming feature was that she was highly shaggable. However, since the Woggle story had placed matters of the heart firmly on the Peeping Tom back-burner, even that tainted card had been totally underplayed.

Added to all of this was the fact that Layla's final act in the house had been to go into the confession box and to tell the world that she had clusters of septic flea bites around her anus. This had been the sole snippet of Layla's last rant that Geraldine had chosen to broad-cast, and it considerably dampened her immediate sexual allure on the outside.

Layla had gone into the house with a chance of star-dom and she had emerged just two weeks later as a desperate wannabe who had turned into a sad loser. Even her friends were looking at her differently.

'Couldn't you have stopped the others from being quite so mean to Woggle?' the more radical of them said. 'I mean, in a way he was right. What *is* the differ-ence between a fox and a flea?'

'I think you should have let David read your poem for you when he offered,' her mother said. 'I'm afraid that refusing did look rather precious, dear.'

Layla felt that her life was ruined, and for what? Nothing. She was despised and, more pressingly, she was broke. Peeping Tom did not pay its contestants (except the winner). They were given a small stipend to maintain their rent or mortgages while they were in the house, but that was it. Ex-contestants were expected to fend for themselves, but the only offers of paid employment that Layla had received since leaving the house were to pose nude for men's magazines. In the end, with weekly shopping to be done and bills to be paid, she had no choice but to ask for her old job back, which had been as a shop girl in a designer clothes shop.

'What do you want to come back for?' the manager said, astonished at Layla's enquiry. 'You're famous, you've been on telly, you must be rolling in it.'

Nobody believed that Layla, who had been on telly every night for a fortnight, could possibly need a job in a shop.

But she did, and they were happy to take her back, thrilled to have a famous person working for them. Thrilled, that was, until they found themselves with a shop full of idiots with nothing better to do than snigger from behind the dress racks at somebody who had been on the television.

'I voted for you to leave,' said one mean-looking teenager. 'I rang twice.'

'I saw one of your nipples in the shower,' said another.

'Do you reckon Kelly's going to shag Hamish, then?'

They all called her Layla, or, worse still, Layles. They knew her name, they knew *her*, or at least they thought they did.

A middle-aged man brought her a small bottle of walnut oil, which for a moment Layla thought was nice, but then he asked her to go out with him and she realized that people thought that the sort of girl who went on *House Arrest* (and got chucked straight off) was the sort of girl who would shag you for half the ingredients of a salad dressing.

At shortly after ten a photographer from the local newspaper arrived. 'Must be the quickest "Where are they now?" feature in the history of showbiz,' he said, snapping away without asking.

The shop manager had called the paper. 'I thought you'd be pleased, Layles. I mean, after all, you must have done it for the publicity.'

148

Layla put down the jumper she had been trying to fold for some time, took £9.50 from the till, which was pay for one hour's work, and went home. Once there she picked up the phone and asked Directory Inquiries for the phone number of *Men Only* magazine.

They were delighted to get her call. 'What we wondered was would you do an erotic shoot with this beautiful girl who had her kitchen done up on *Changing Rooms*? We thought we could call it Celeblezzy, you know, just as a joke, like.'

Layla put down the phone. She was *so* angry. Angry with Peeping Tom Productions, of course, but particularly angry with the people who had nominated her for eviction. She tortured herself by watching the tape over and over again. There they were sitting in the box, so smug, so self-important. They had sealed her fate, they had doomed her to being the first out.

David. Dervla. Garry and *Kelly*.

Kelly was the real humiliation, that little ladette slapper had had the gall to nominate *her*.

Dervla she hated also. Those weasel words from the confession box burned into her soul. 'She's a lovely, lovely girl, a very gentle, caring and beautiful spirit, but I feel that in the end her loveliness would be able to blossom more beautifully outside of the house.' What a stuck-up, hypocritical Irish cow. The truth was she had wanted Layla out because she hadn't wanted someone better looking and more intelligent than her grabbing the sensitive male vote.

Dervla and Kelly. For some reason it was the women that hurt the most. Probably because Layla felt that she was so much better at *being* a woman than they were. They should have supported her, they should have made her their champion against pseuds like David and yobbos like Garry and Jazz. Their rejection of her was, she felt, almost *sexist*.

Dervla and Kelly. Those were the two she really

hated. But particularly Kelly. That same Kelly who had nominated her and then hugged her and kissed her when she was voted out, and said she loved her. Kelly, who had pretended to be upset, who had so compounded her humiliation for all the world to see.

DAY SEVENTEEN. 8.00 p.m.

It had been two days since Woggle's exit, and the *House Arrest* experience had returned to the basic formula of whining, back-biting and wondering who fancied whom.

'*It's day seventeen in the house,*' said Andy the narrator. '*After lunch, a meal of pasta and vegetable sauce, which Sally cooks, the group talk about first love.*'

'Well, it's gotta be Chelsea FC, hasn't it?' said Gazzer. 'You never forget the first time you see the Blues.'

'Because they're so shite,' Jazz opined.

'Even when they're shite they're beautiful.'

'We're talking about proper love, Gazzer,' said Moon. 'Not fookin' football.'

'So am I, gel. Let's face it, the love a bloke has for his team transcends all others. Think about it. I fancy loads of birds, *all* blokes fancy loads of birds, 'cept poofs, and they fancy loads of blokes. Gay or straight, men like to put it about a bit, full stop. But when it comes to football, you only ever support one team, don't you? You're *faithful*, Moon, it's true love.'

Watching from the depths of the monitoring bunker, Geraldine Hennessy could see that without Woggle life in the house was beginning to look dull. She needed to do something quickly to pep things up. Her solution was to give the housemates more to drink.

'What is the number-one interest people have in

watching these programmes?' she asked her production team at their morning meeting the next day. There was silence. Geraldine's minions all learned quickly that most of her questions were rhetorical.

'To see if any of the inmates shag, am I right? Of course I'm right. When you get down to it, that's what it's all about. But basically it *never* fucking happens, does it? Nobody ever actually does it! We all keep up the pretence that it's *going* to happen, us and the newspapers and the bleeding Broadcasting Standards Commission, we all *pretend* that it's all so bleeding titillating when it patently isn't. But nobody ever actually does the business. And why is that, I ask myself?'

She was indeed asking herself, for her cowed minions remained silent.

'Because nobody is ever *pissed* enough, that's why! Which, in a nutshell, is the problem with reality TV! Not enough booze! Oh, we can give them hot spas and massage rooms and nookie huts and all that bollocks, but in the long run no one is going to do the nasty, insert the portion, prise open the clam, heat up the sausage or cleave the bearded monster with the one-eyed lovesnake unless they are completely arseholed!'

Everybody shuffled their papers and looked embarrassed. They all knew that they were involved in a fairly tawdry exercise, but they fervently wished that Geraldine would not revel in it quite so much.

Then Geraldine announced that she was changing the rules. She was going to separate the food and alcohol budgets in order to remove the usual constraint of having to sacrifice a meal for a drink.

There were protests, of course, once it was announced, from the watchdogs and the bishops. Geraldine took the moral high ground, her usual defence for descending into the gutter. 'We believe that people should be treated as adults,' she sniffed. 'If you set up a valid experiment such as ours and then police it from the outside as if it was some fifth-form trip, you learn nothing about the people involved. Our intention is to facilitate and encourage genuine social interaction.'

Nobody was fooled, of course. The tabloids put it most succinctly with their leader comment: 'It's *House A'pissed*! Lets get 'em drunk and watch 'em shag.'

Of course even Geraldine had to draw a line somewhere. These people were locked in a house with no TV, no writing equipment, no sense of time and almost nothing to do except a few foolish tasks, for weeks on end. Given the chance, most people would start drinking the moment they got up in the morning and carry on until collapsing into unconsciousness at night. Peeping Tom could not allow that. There were, after all, strict broadcasting standards to observe. Therefore, Peeping Tom banned daytime drinking and also rationed it during weekday evenings. At weekends, however, it was party time, and the housemates could have as much to drink as they liked.

'And my rule in life has always been,' Geraldine told a press conference, 'that the weekend starts on Thursday.'

That afternoon, the Thursday following the drama of Layla's eviction and Woggle's arrest, found the store room where Peeping Tom left the house supplies filled with booze.

Under normal circumstances Thursday should have meant another round of eviction nominations, but because of Woggle's unexpected departure it was announced that the evictions for that week would be cancelled and that things would be picked up as normal on the following Thursday. If ever there was an excuse for a party, this surely had to be it.

DAY THIRTY-SIX. 1.00 p.m.

Coleridge had spent another fruitless morning out at Shepperton Studios wandering around the replica Peeping Tom house, foraging in his imagination for some stroke of insight that might lead on to a theory.

Something was forming in his mind, the beginnings of an idea, but it was just a theory. There was nothing much so far to back it up. Still, better to be chewing on something rather than nothing, even if it did prove to be a red herring in the end. He returned to the station to find a faxed letter from the Irish Garda waiting for him. It was in response to an inquiry he had made to them about Ballymagoon, the village which Coleridge had heard mentioned on the radio and which was at the centre of an economic slump in rural Ireland. Dervla's home village.

Suspect family still resident in village, the letter read. *Both parents and two younger sisters continue to live at family home. Family do not appear to have escaped effects of slump. Considerable financial hardship, car sold, negative equity on house and farm, mounting debts. Recent request for loans denied.*

Well, thought Coleridge, if ever a girl had a pressing reason for wanting to win half a million pounds it was Dervla. On the other hand, he knew from many years of experience that when it came to money most people did not need a pressing reason to covet half a million pounds.

Nonetheless, her parents *were* in danger of losing their farm. And volunteering to be on *House Arrest was* quite a strange choice for a girl like Dervla to make. Of all of the housemates, she was undoubtedly the most ... Coleridge struggled for the word ... 'beautiful' sprang into his mind, but he fought it out again. Finally he settled upon 'different.' Dervla was the most different.

There was no doubt about it that, as motives went, money was always a good one. Coupled with imminent family shame it was terrific . . . Except killing one housemate was scarcely going to guarantee her victory. It was only week four, there were seven other competitors, and it seemed unlikely that she had been planning to kill them all.

She could not even have known that she was a popular housemate. None of them knew anything about what the world was thinking.

Something to save for later was about all Coleridge could construe from his fax from the Irish police. He put it in the Dervla file and asked a constable to add a 'motive' note to her photograph on the wall map. Then he joined Trisha and Hooper at their habitual position in front of the video screen.

They were looking at day eighteen.

'Look at all that booze. Must be over a hundred quid's worth,' said Trisha.

'It was the only way to get things going,' Hooper replied. 'Geraldine Hennessy said as much to the press at the time.'

'Surely these people must have realized that they were being manipulated?' Coleridge observed. 'Getting them drunk is such a transparent ploy.'

'*Of course* they realized it, sir, but you have to try and understand that they're not like you. *They don't mind.* And frankly if I was stuck in a sealed house with David and his guitar for weeks on end and somebody stuck five crates of booze on the table, I'd get stuck in myself.'

'But have they no sense of personal privacy? Dignity?'

Hooper could disguise his exasperation no longer. 'Well, sir, being as how they've all volunteered to be on the programme and they've been wandering around in their knickers ever since, I would say that the answer to that would probably have to be no.'

154

'Don't take that tone with me, sergeant.'

'What tone, sir?'

'You know damn well what tone.'

'I do not know what tone.'

'Well, don't take it anyway.'

On the screen, while the other housemates began their evening's drinking, Moon got up and made her way to the confession box. 'I just wanted to say . . . that I've been thinking about the trick I played on Sally and the girls the other night, you know, when I said all that stuff about being abused and institutionalized . . .'

Moon then went into a lengthy ramble about herself and what a mad-for-it gangster she was, a straight-talker who just said what she felt like and at the end of the day people would have to take her as they found her. Finally, she got to the apology.

'What I'm saying is, I don't want people to think it was cruel and the like, especially 'cos I could hear her sobbing afterwards and all that, and I expect the public could too. Even though if you ask me it was a bit of an over-reaction . . . but what I'm saying is, if Sally's been abused or whatever and has got, you know, mental health stuff going on or whatever, then fair play to her, right, because at the end of the day I wouldn't like it myself if I thought someone was taking the piss out of me for being a nutter, particularly if I actually was a nutter, like Sally seems to be, although I'm not saying she is, if you know what I'm saying? So that's all I'm saying, right. If you know what I'm saying.'

All of this was news to Coleridge. Geraldine had never broadcast the original discussion that had taken place in the girls' bedroom; nor had she broadcast Moon's apology in the confession box.

'Sally has "mental health" stuff going on?' Coleridge asked.

'It seems so,' said Trish, ejecting the Moon confession tape.

'I talked to Fogarty the editor, and he told me that Sally pretty much said as much one night when the girls were chatting. They never broadcast it but Geri the Gaoler kept the tape for possible future use. That's why we didn't see it in our first trawl, it was still hidden on the edit suite hard disk. Fogarty sent it over. This is it.'

And so Coleridge, Hooper and Trish listened in on the conversation that had taken place in the girls' room on the eighth night when Moon had lied about her past and Sally had shown herself so sensitive about the subject of mental health. For all three of them watching, one phrase stood out above all the others. Something that Sally had said as she sat there in the dark, her voice shaking with emotion.

'. . . when once in a blue moon something happens, like some poor schizo who never should have been returned to the community gets stuck inside their own dark box and sticks a knife in someone's head or whatever, suddenly every mild depressive in the country is a murderer.'

Trisha had marked down the time code of the comment and now they rewound the tape and listened to it again.

'*Sticks a knife in someone's head.*'

'Sticks a *knife* in someone's head.'

With the knowledge of hindsight, it was certainly an unfortunate choice of words.

'Coincidence, do you think?' Coleridge said.

'Probably. I mean, if Sally was the murderer, how would she have known nearly four weeks beforehand how she was going to do it? We've already established that the murder was an improvisation.'

'We haven't established anything of the sort, constable,' Coleridge snapped. 'We have *supposed* such a thing because it seems difficult to see how it could have been planned. However, *if* someone in the house

156

had an attraction for knives, *if* one of them was mentally predisposed towards stabbing, then we might *suppose* that this would make the murder method less a matter of chance and more one of inevitability.'

There was silence in the incident room for a moment before Coleridge added, 'And Sally is a very, very strong woman.'

'So Sally's the killer, then?' Trisha said with a hint of exasperation. 'That's an awfully big supposition to make from one little comment.'

'I am not supposing anything, constable. I'm ruminating.'

Ruminating? Did he speak like that for a joke? Who ruminated? People thought, they considered, they might even occasionally ponder, but nobody had *ruminated* for fifty years.

'Sally chose to use a phrase that exactly describes the murder. She said "stick a knife in someone's head". We have to consider the implications of that.'

'Well, how about considering this, sir . . .' Trisha fought down the feeling she had in her stomach that she might be being defensive on Sally's behalf out of some absurd sisterly and sexual solidarity. She truly believed that she would as happily convict a lesbian as any other person . . . On the other hand she did rather resent the fact that people were so eager to suspect Sally.

'She's very strong,' they kept saying. 'Very *very* strong.'

It wasn't Sally's fault that she was strong and muscular. Trisha herself would have loved to have been that strong. Although perhaps not quite as muscular.

'Go on, Patricia,' said Coleridge.

'Well, I was just wondering whether perhaps Moon *wanted* us to be reminded of what Sally had said. Perhaps she said all that stuff in the confession box because she wanted us to ruminate along the lines that you are ruminating along, sir.'

Coleridge raised a thoughtful eyebrow. 'That is also a possibility,' he conceded, 'and one upon which we must certainly ru— which we must certainly bear in mind.'

They turned their attention back to the screen.

DAY EIGHTEEN. 8.15 p.m.

Moon walked out of the confession box, having made her little speech about Sally, and announced her intention of getting immediately 'shitfaced'.

'I'm going to go large,' she said, pulling the ring on a can of Special Brew. 'I'm mad for it. I'm going to get shitfaced and rat-arsed!'

'Funny that, isn't it?' Jazz said. 'How we choose to describe having a good night.'

'You what?' said Moon.

'Funny way of describing a party, Moon,' he said.

'You what, Jazz?'

Jazz, ever watchful for opportunities whereby he could work on his patter and continue what he saw as his ongoing public audition for a career in comedy, had spotted what he thought was a fruitful opening. 'Well, the English language is the most extensive in the world, but that's the best you can do to describe having a good time. Tonight I'm going to have such a good time that it will be as if my face was covered in shit! My mood will resemble that of a rat's arse! What's all that about, then?'

'Eh?' said Moon.

Dervla tried to be supportive. 'Very amusing, Jazz,' she said, opening a bottle of wine. 'I'd laugh but I'm not yet sufficiently shitfaced.' And she smiled, hugging herself as if she had a special secret.

'*Kelly 1. Dervla 2.*' The secret hand had written in the condensation. '*Hang in there, Gorgeous. XXX.*'

The recipient of this little love note grinned broadly through the toothpaste foam.

So now she had risen to second place in the affections of the public. Not bad at all after only two and a half weeks. Only Kelly was ahead of her and Dervla felt far better equipped to stay the course than she believed Kelly was. After all, it was going to be a long, long game for those who survived, and Dervla was confident in her reserves of inner strength. Kelly, she felt, was not so well equipped for the struggle. She was too open, too sweet, too vulnerable, not so mentally attuned to stay the distance. Dervla felt that all she had to do was hang on. If she could just survive the process, she would win the game.

That was all she had to do.

Survive.

Jazz broke in on Dervla's reverie. 'So're you going to get shitfaced too, then, Dervo?' he said, throwing a friendly arm around her. 'Can I join you?'

'I'd be delighted, kind sir,' she replied.

Jazz's smooth, beautiful, scented face smelt sweet close to hers, his arm was strong.

'I never heard you swear before, Dervs,' he laughed. 'You're loosening up, my darling.'

'Ah, to be sure, even us nuns like to let our wimples down occasionally.'

Jazz had been working up a little idea and, encouraged by Dervla's friendly attitude, he decided to give it a trial run. 'You know what?' he said. 'You give so much away about yourself when you brush your teeth.'

Dervla almost leapt away from him. In fact, she jumped so suddenly that she caused them both to spill their drinks. Everybody turned in surprise.

'What the *fuck* do you know about me brushing my teeth?' she snapped angrily. It was rare that anybody heard Dervla say 'fuck'.

'Here, steady on, girl,' said Garry. 'Mind the language. I ain't as rough as you, you know.'

Dervla appeared shattered. She tried to collect herself. 'I mean, what do you mean, Jazz? What about me brushing my teeth?'

Jazz struggled for words, confused by her defensive reaction. 'Well, not just you, Dervs,' he said. 'I mean anybody, what I'm saying is people's toothbrushes give a lot away about them.'

'Oh, anybody,' Dervla said. 'So it's not like you've been watching me brush my teeth or anything?'

Now it was Jazz's turn to react. 'What you saying, girl? That I'm some sort of tooth pervert? I never seen none of you brushing your teeth, right? On account of the fact that when I ablute, girl, I ablute alone, it's a personal thing, OK? Because my body is a temple and I go there to worship.'

They all laughed and Dervla apologized. The moment passed, and Jazz pressed on with his comic material.

'What I'm saying, right, is that I ain't never seen none of you brush your teeth. But I bet I know who everybody's brush belongs to.'

This caused a moment of semi-drunken attention. From everyone, that is, except Hamish and Kelly. Kelly was already too far gone to take much interest in the conversation, and Hamish was too busy taking an interest in Kelly. Hamish had come into the house with the intention of having sex on television and in Kelly he was scenting a possible opportunity. He had put his hand on Kelly's knee and she was giggling.

Meanwhile, Jazz expanded on his theme. 'Like there was a time,' he continued, 'when a toothbrush was a functional item, they was all the same, man, there was different colours, but that was it. Now your toothbrush is a *fashion statement*, man! We are talking a *designer* commodity here!'

'Stop waffling and get on with it,' said David. 'Whose brush is whose?'

'Just setting the scene, guy, just setting the scene.'

'Whose brush is whose?

'Well, Gazzer's has gotta be the one like mine. It's hip, it's flash, it's well hard and it's the business! It's got shock absorbers, man! It's got a big soft round aero-dynamically palm-friendly handle, rear suspension and a detachable head. It's got a spring-loaded crumple zone at the front, it looks like a ray gun, and it's in Chelsea's away colours. Am I right, Gazz?'

'Fuck me, you're Sherlock fucking Holmes, Jazz.'

'Yes, I am, guy, because it is el-e-fucking-mentary. Now, Dervo, you got the one with the age-fading stripe, that's what I reckon.'

Dervla attempted to maintain a poker face. 'Why's that, Jazz?'

' 'Cos you are one fastidious lady, OK? You are sweet and clean and you don't want no dirty old worn-out thing stuck in your mouth.'

'Shame!' shouted Gazzer, at which Dervla blushed.

'Shut up, Gazz,' Jazz admonished. 'Dervo is a fucking lady, so don't you go making no off-colour comments implying no blow jobs, all right? Anyway, the point is, am I right, girl? When you was in the chemist and you was buying a brush for your perfect pearly toothypegs, did you choose a basic bristle or did you choose the one what tells you when it's time to buy a new one?'

Dervla blushed again. 'All right, I did, you swine!' Dervla laughed, perhaps a little too loudly.

'All right then, Jason.' David still insisted on refer-ring to Jazz by his full name. 'Which one's mine?'

'Easy, man, piece of piss. You're the blue one, the

one without nothing on it at all, no spring-loaded bit in the middle, no go-faster stripe, just a plain basic brush.'

'Well, as it happens, you're right,' said David, slightly resentfully. 'I must say that I'm rather flattered that you understood that I was the sort of person who was unlikely to fall for all that marketing rubbish. I want a brush that gets the job done and shuts up about it. A toothbrush is a toothbrush, not a pair of trainers or a sports car.'

'But you're wrong, guy,' said Jazz. 'I didn't pick you for being no down-to-earth geezer, no way. I got you right because you're a bigger wanker than any of us.' Jazz was laughing, but David wasn't.

'Oh, and how is that, then?' he asked, attempting to maintain his rapidly evaporating air of superiority.

'Because you chose the *classic*, man! That's what they call that sort of brush these days. You ain't got no bog-standard brush in your toothmug, David, no way, guy, what you got's a Wisdom *classic*. And they're not easy to find these days either, not every chemist stocks them, and you got to search your way through all the pink spongy ones and the transparent bendy ones to find them. Because you see, David, it's the flash gimmicky brushes that are the *norm* these days. *They're* the bog-standard brushes, the ones ordinary people buy. What you got is the designer item, the retro classic, which you have to seek out, like you obviously did. Just like you must have looked high and low to get that retro-looking pair of old-style trainers you got on, and they're called "classics" too. Made just for that bit of the market that reckons it's got *style* and *class* and would never be a part of a *trend*, oh no, not them, they favour *classic* styles, or to put it another way, David, they're wankers.'

It was a good performance and everybody laughed loudly. David obviously felt he had better laugh along too, but he did not do a very convincing job of it. In fact he looked furious. Livid. And also astonished. Jazz had caught him out. David had obviously never expected any intellectual threat from Jazz's direction and yet this loudmouthed, conceited *trainee chef* had made him look a fool. What was more, it would probably be broadcast on national television.

In the back of his mind David kept a little book into which he would put the names of people with whom he intended to get even. Jazz had just reserved himself an entire page.

DAY EIGHTEEN. 10.00 p.m.

Kelly announced that it was time to go to bed. She had had a terrific night, she said, but now the room was really beginning to spin. As she got up she fell back down again, straight into Hamish's lap.

'Sorry,' said Kelly.

'Fine by me,' Hamish replied. 'You should do it more often.'

Kelly giggled and put her arms round Hamish's neck. 'I think I fell on something hard,' she said, laughing drunkenly. 'Give us a kiss.'

Hamish did not require any further encouragement and so they kissed. Kelly started with puckered lips but Hamish went in mouth open and for a moment or two Kelly responded, her jaw working against his.

In the monitoring bunker they cheered. This was the first proper kiss of *House Arrest Three*. They knew Geraldine would be thrilled.

'If he puts his hand up her top we win the magnum,' said Pru, Bob Fogarty's assistant, who was the duty editor that night.

Peeping Tom Productions had indeed promised a

magnum of vintage Dom Pérignon to the crew who were lucky enough to record the first grope.

Back in the house, sitting on the green couch, Moon was not impressed. 'Fookin' hell, Kelly, if you're not careful you'll suck his fookin' head off. What do his tonsils taste like?'

But Kelly was enjoying herself. She was drunk and feeling naughty, and Hamish was a lovely-looking boy.

'Very nice,' she said, getting up unsteadily, 'and now I'm going to bed.'

'I'll help you,' said Hamish, leaping up to great cheers from the rest of the group.

'Thank you, kind sir,' Kelly replied, giggling.

'Don't forget, Peeping Tom is peeping,' Dervla warned.

'I don't care,' Kelly replied, and she didn't. Quite suddenly she had decided that she was not ready for bed yet. Why not sneak off with Hamish for a little while? Who knows, she might even kiss him again. Why not, it was a party, wasn't it? And so together they staggered off towards the girls' bedroom, leaving the other six housemates to further boozing.

'Don't hurry back!' shouted Jazz.

'Yeah, not until we've drunk the rest of the booze, anyway,' Garry added.

In the monitoring bunker they were keeping their fingers crossed. This was certainly the most sexually promising development so far. Breathlessly, the editors, assistant editors and PAs watched as the drunken couple staggered from camera to camera, spinning across through each screen in turn.

Halfway to the bedroom they altered course. It was Kelly's idea. She grabbed Hamish's shirt and steered him out through the big sliding doors and out into the warm night. Together they staggered towards the pool and for a moment the watchers wondered whether they might luck out with a bit of skinny dipping.

'Camera four, under the pool, double quick!' Pru barked into her intercom, and down in the camera runs around the house a black draped dalek-like shape began to glide along the corridor, down the ramp and into the spying position under the pool's glass bottom.

But although the drunken couple teetered on the edge, kissing deep and laughing loud, they did not fall in.

'Oh my God! I think they're making for Copulation Cabin!' Pru could scarcely contain her excitement. 'Somebody ring Geraldine.'

Copulation Cabin was a wooden hut that had been placed beyond the swimming pool and filled with cushions and draped lamps. It looked like somebody had attempted to create an Arabian love tent in a garden shed, which was exactly what had happened. Peeping Tom had put it there in the transparent hope that if they supplied a place where people could get away from the prying eyes of the other housemates they might have sex. It was hoped that the existence of no fewer than *five* cameras covering this tiny space would not dampen the ardour.

Kelly led Hamish into the cabin and they collapsed together in a laughing boozy heap on the cushions.

Hamish had fancied Kelly from the start, and for him the cameras were a turn-on. Quite apart from the terrific thrill of the idea of bedding Kelly while millions of jealous men looked on, he felt that it would be a wonderful starting point towards presenting his own quasi-medical sex show on the television, which in his fantasies was called *Dr Nookie Talks*.

The kissing was becoming more intense: long, passionate, drunken kisses. Showy, chewy, gurgling kisses. Kisses that were in fact more about exhibitionism than passion, because if there was one thing that both Kelly and Hamish knew for sure, even in their drunken state, it was that this moment would make the cut of the following night's show and also that it would be in the papers the following morning.

What a wildly exciting thought that was! That simply by clamping their mouths together they were making themselves into stars!

Hamish boldly chanced a hand, spurred on by genuine lust and pure vainglorious exhibitionism. Gently he slipped it under the hem of the baggy vest that Kelly was wearing. It had been clear to him all evening and to the four million viewers who would later be watching on television that Kelly was not wearing a bra.

'Uh-oh, that's second base,' Kelly breathed, and removed his hand.

In the bunker they were on the edge of their seats.

'Did he touch a tit? Did we win the magnum?'

'I don't think so, she stopped him.'

'Cow! Let him have a squeeze, girl, go on. Think of England!'

'I think he might have touched it, I really do.'

'We'll have to wait for the replay.'

'Plenty of time yet, anyway. Look at them.'

In Copulation Cabin Hamish's disappointment over the failed grope was already forgotten. Kelly seemed to be turning hot again.

'I've got an idea,' she said. 'Let's sleep here tonight, eh? Then we can be really famous: Hamish and Kelly sleep together in poolside love nest! Ha ha!' Then she pulled off her jeans.

'Yes!' they cried in the monitoring bunker, punching the air with their fists as Kelly's gorgeous bottom, clad (if 'clad' could be considered the word) in a tiny G-string, was revealed.

'Oh, yes!' they shouted once more, their fingers positively quivering over their editing controls.

'Come on,' Kelly breathed, 'get your kecks off, you ain't sleeping in my love nest in dirty stinky boy trousers.'

Hamish did not need asking twice and immediately began pulling down his immaculate chinos. As he struggled to get them off over his shoes, which he had neglected to remove, the full erection struggling within his underpants was plain for all to see.

'Naughty,' said Kelly. 'Did you make that for me?' And with that she pulled the rugs up and over them.

'Damn,' they said in the bunker. 'We never should have given them anything to cover themselves with.'

In the darkness under the blankets Kelly put her hand over her microphone and whispered. 'That'll give 'em something to think about, eh?'

Kelly had reached her limit. Quickly, Hamish tried to push her on. 'Why don't we *really* give them something to think about, Kelly?'

'What sort of girl do you think I am?' Kelly giggled. She was already drifting off to sleep. 'I'm tired.' She whispered it so quietly that even Hamish had trouble hearing her. And her hand was over her microphone.

Nobody would have heard it but him.

The booze and the soft cushions were taking their toll. Kelly was losing consciousness. Inwardly Hamish cursed. Hamish kissed her. He kissed her again, whispering in her ear, trying to revive a mood, which had never really been the mood he thought it was anyway.

'No,' Kelly murmured. 'Don't be silly. Too tired, too drunk, too comfy.'

Or at least that's what it sounded like. She was so far away by this time that she wasn't speaking clearly.

Hamish held Kelly close. Her arms were still around him, exactly where she had placed them before she had fallen asleep. His body was pressing up against her, his whole bursting, desperate body. He slipped his hand back under Kelly's shirt, the hand that she had only recently removed. This time she did not remove it. She was asleep. Hamish held her breast.

In the bunker there were no celebrations. The crew did not realize that they had won their magnum. They could not see. They did not know.

'What are they doing under there?' Pru asked.

'Not very much, I'm afraid,' said the PA. 'Too bloody pissed. I know the feeling.'

*

Under the blankets Hamish gave Kelly's breast a little squeeze. Gently and then more boldly he allowed his fingertips to play with the glorious, sexy little nipple ring. He pulled at it a little. Kelly did not even stir.

Hamish was a doctor and he knew that Kelly was not asleep. She was unconscious. Hamish's head was swimming in the darkness.

The darkness! Hamish suddenly realized how dark it was. They were completely concealed. It was black as coal beneath the thick, heavy, musky blankets.

Slowly, being careful not to move the blanket that covered them, Hamish began to edge his hand down Kelly's body. Down across her ribs, which rose and fell so deeply, and so regularly, across her smooth, flat tummy, until finally slipping it beneath the tiny triangle of her G-string.

Hamish was blind with excitement. The prospect of touching such forbidden fruit had completely intoxicated his already drunken mind. Now Kelly let out a deep snore.

In the bunker they heard Kelly's snore and, noting that the blanket beneath which Hamish and Kelly lay was scarcely moving, they concluded ruefully that the excitement of the night was over.

But the excitement wasn't over: it was reaching fever pitch. Hamish had his hand between Kelly's legs now, he was touching her, discovering her, discovering to his surprise that Kelly had a little secret . . . her labia was pierced. This she had not revealed to the group; her nipple rings she had mentioned often, but this most private piece of jewellery she had kept to herself. Until now.

As Hamish gently explored, a phrase suddenly appeared in his fuddled consciousness, a phrase which he remembered from his class on forensic medicine. The phrase was *digital penetration*.

That's what he was doing now. That was what it would be called if anybody ever knew.

Suddenly Hamish became aware of the appalling risk that he was running. He was committing a *serious crime*. This crazy drunken improvisation, this *sex prank*, was assault. He could go to prison.

Hamish began to remove his hand, but reluctantly, very reluctantly. And as he did so, for a moment he pulled aside the thin, damp gusset of Kelly's G-string and in that moment, in that one blinding moment of lust, he seriously considered taking his straining, aching erection from inside his own underpants and with it entering Kelly's unconscious body.

The thought lasted only for a moment. Drunk as he was, the terrible, life-changing risks that he had already run were clear to him. In fact it was the momentary contemplation of this even greater abuse that truly brought home to Hamish the gravity of what he had already done.

Digital penetration. That was serious enough, for God's sake, leave it. Leave it. Quickly, gently, with the practised and steady hand of a doctor, Hamish rearranged Kelly's gusset in an impression of how he had found it, pushing the warm wet string into the crease of her vagina and then threading it up between her buttocks.

All the while he was deadly careful to avoid moving the heavy blankets and rugs that covered them. It was imperative that the people whom he knew were watching thought that he, like Kelly, had been asleep.

Having removed his hand, Hamish began to pretend to snore a little, not too much, just the occasional little noise to accompany Kelly's deep, drunken slumber.

Reaching down to feel himself, Hamish realized that his pants were wet. Unwittingly he must have ejaculated or at least leaked considerably during his excitement. Had he stained the cushions? Or, worse still, her knickers? If he had, could he pass it off as an embarrassing accident? Tense with fear, he felt about to discover if any evidence of his shame had escaped. It seemed not. He had been lucky.

Kelly was unconscious and he had left no sign.

The blankets were thick and they had scarcely moved.

He was safe. He truly believed that he was safe. But the risk. The *risk* he had run! It made him cold to even think of it.

Now Hamish let his body twitch a little, as if he had been sleeping and had startled himself awake. Kelly did not stir as he pulled back the rug, scratching his head, rubbing his eyes and looking around as if to say 'Where am I?'

Then he feigned a smile and winked at the camera. 'Nearly, eh?' he whispered up at the little red pin light. 'I can't believe it, and it was me that fell asleep first. For God's sake, don't show this on the telly. My mates will never ever let me live it down.'

With that he got up from the cushions, put his trousers back on, gently rearranged the rug over Kelly's unconscious form and returned to the party.

He was greeted with a chorus of leery cheers.

'Sorry to disappoint you people,' said Hamish, 'but we both nodded off. I think I went first, if you can believe that.' Hamish desperately hoped that they could.

Then he retreated to his bed and to a very troubled night, as over and over again he asked himself if there was any way that Peeping Tom could have known the terrible thing he had done.

Digital penetration.

Silently in the darkness he thanked God for stopping him before he had done something even worse.

DAY NINETEEN. 7.00 a.m.

Kelly groaned once and she was awake. 'What the f . . . ?' Then she remembered. She was in Copulation Cabin. The Shag Shack, Bonkham Towers, Haveitoff House. Even before the show had started, when Peeping Tom had announced this refinement to the house structure, the press had had about fifty names for it. And now she was in it, in front of the nation. What *must* she look like?

'Don't worry,' she said to the camera that hung directly overhead. 'Nothing happened.'

She reached out from under the rug for her jeans, grinning sheepishly. Like Hamish before her, she felt obliged to address the camera.

'Was I *arseholed* last night . . . ? Still you have it to do, eh?'

Kelly's shapely legs emerged now and she donned her jeans with considerable elegance considering her hangover. 'Bet Hamish feels rotten too.'

171

She smiled once more at the camera, but beneath the smile lay unease. Why did she feel so dirty? Why did she feel such a sad old slapper? Just the hangover, surely? After all, she knew that nothing had happened. *Had* anything happened? Had she let Hamish get further than he should have done?

Definitely not. She was sure about it. She remembered everything clearly, she had snogged him and then she had crashed out. Going exactly as far as she had intended to go.

So why this feeling? Why this unease?

There was something, something about herself that she could not quite define, except that she wondered ... *Had* anything happened? How could it have? She remembered it all, she always remembered, that was one of her characteristics as a drinker, she *always remembered what she did. What she didn't do.*

And she remembered it now. She had kissed him, and crashed out. And yet ... She had this feeling that she'd been ...

Abused? Was that it? Did she feel abused? Surely not. Never.

It was an illusion. It had to be. The Peeping Tom house was the safest place on earth. There were cameras watching *all the time*. Nobody would take such a risk under those circumstances. Least of all Hamish. He was a good bloke. And a doctor.

Someone else? Later? No. It was absolute madness. Even as she sat there thinking, she knew that there were five cameras watching her. Five all-seeing chaperons there to look after her. She smiled up at them once more. 'Yeah, lucky nothing happened, eh? You're my protectors, aren't you, Peeping Tom? My dad don't have to worry, does he? Nothing's going to happen while you're watching.'

*

In the monitoring bunker Geraldine, who had arrived breathlessly in the small hours to be confronted with the night's disappointments, was livid.

'That's not the *idea*, you *stupid* cow!' she shouted at Kelly's face on the monitors. 'That's not the fucking idea at all!'

Kelly emerged from the hut and dived straight into the pool. She did not even take off her jeans. It was a spontaneous action, a sudden need to be *clean*. And another £500 microphone gone.

Behind the glass doors the house slept. Jazz, Moon and Sally had not even bothered to rise from the couch.

Even Hamish had finally fallen asleep, but his dreams were troubled and studded with guilt. And when he awoke it was worse. Did she know? Did anybody know? What had the camera seen? Nothing. If they had, then Peeping Tom would have intervened, otherwise they would have been compounding a felony. Surely, no. Hamish felt certain that from the outside nothing would have seemed amiss or, if it had, then nothing had been said. Discovery could only come from within. Did Kelly remember? How could she? She had been asleep. She had *definitely* been asleep.

DAY NINETEEN. 8.00 a.m.

Kelly did not go to bed. Having changed out of her wet clothes, she made herself a cup of tea and sat down on the green couch, trying to put from her mind the suspicions with which she had awoken.

It was here that Dervla found her an hour later as she made her way to the shower room. Dervla, like the rest of them, had been up late, but she did not want to sleep in, she never slept in, she always wanted to get to the shower room first. She wanted to look in the mirror.

173

'Good morning, Kelly,' Dervla said. 'Things got a bit close with Hamish there for a bit, didn't they?'

'What do you mean? We were only having a laugh.'

Kelly's defensive tone made Dervla smile. Perhaps something had gone on, after all.

'Well, you were both pretty drunk, weren't you? And he was drooling over you all evening, tongue fair hanging out, so it was. If the poor fella hadn't have nodded off first I think you'd have had to beat him off with a stick.'

'Nodded off first. Is that what he said happened?'

'That's what he said . . . Are you all right, Kelly?'

'Yes! Yes, absolutely fine,' Kelly replied, about twenty times too eagerly, and lapsed into silence.

Dervla headed for the shower room, left Kelly to it. She could hear the camera moving about beyond the glass.

'Morning, Mr Cameraman,' she said as she soaped herself beneath her T-shirt. 'I hope you feel better than I do.' She slid a slippery, sudsy hand inside her knickers.

Beyond the glass the camera's electric motor gave a little hum as it pulled focus. Dervla might have heard it had the shower not been running.

The message was already being written as Dervla approached the basin to brush her teeth. The writer's tone had changed.

'*K is your enemy,*' it said. '*Fucking slut is still ahead. She cockteases the boys to avoid nomination.*' And then the unseen finger underlined the first four words . . .

'*K is your enemy.*'

DAY THIRTY-SIX. 11.50 p.m.

Sergeant Hooper was thinking about ringing for a cab. He had had a long and fruitless day on the murder inquiry followed by a pretty monumental amount of beer and curry and it was time to pull the pin.

It had been a decent night out with the lads, but it was about to go boring on him. It wasn't that he particularly objected to pornography, although he was not a big consumer of it himself, it was just that he had never seen the point of watching it with your mates. As far as he was concerned, the purpose of porn was to stimulate sex, either sex with yourself or sex with a partner. That was what it was for. To be masturbated over or to be watched with a girlfriend as a way of expanding the horizons of your own nocturnal activities. What he was not into doing was sitting bleary-eyed on a friend's couch holding a kebab in one hand, a can of Stella in the other and drooling over it with a bunch of pissed-up off-duty coppers.

'You lot are sad,' he said. 'I'm going to finish me beer and leave you to it. Don't stain the sofa now.'

'You don't understand, Hoops,' said Thorpe, a detective constable from Vice. 'This isn't about sex, it's about quality. We're critics. Porn is an art form and we are aficionados. Do you know that at the blue movie Oscars in Cannes they have an award for best come shot?'

'I find that very hard to swallow,' said Hooper, unwittingly earning himself about five minutes of hysterical drunken laughter.

'Pornography is a legitimate film genre,' insisted Blair. 'Every bit as important as, for instance, the adventure movie or the romantic comedy.'

'Like I said, Blair, you're sad,' Hooper replied. 'Why can't you just be honest? You watch this stuff because it gives you a hard-on. Well, fair play to you, mate, I can understand that, I just don't see why you need company.'

'You're wrong, Hoop, you just don't understand at all. This is a social thing. We discuss the movies, the acting, the groaning, the relative success of a golden shower, whether the dick you see being slipped actually belongs to the bloke you see slipping it. What we have here is a critics' forum. You seem to be under the impression that all porn movies are the same.'

'Aren't they?'

'No more than horror movies are all the same, or westerns. Is *Butch Cassidy* the same as *A Fistful of Dollars*? Of course it isn't. Is *The Exorcist* the same as a Hammer Horror? I don't think so. Well, it's the same with porn. For instance, this one I'm putting on now. This is from the tacky end of the market, real hard-core humping. A proper down-and-dirty porn nasty.'

'Thanks for the warning, mate,' said Hooper, draining his beer. 'I think I'll give it a miss. I'll find a cab on the street.'

'You're mad. You're missing out on a classic of its type, a cultural icon. The *Fuck Orgy* series is a milestone of its genre.'

Hooper was already heading for the door when the little bell rang in his head. 'What series?' he said, turning back.

'*Fuck Orgy*. Legendary no-holds-barred, in-your-face porn. No stupid plot, no lengthy preamble, it does exactly what it says on the tin. *Fuck Orgy* is the name and fuck orgy is most definitely the game. This is number three, an early one, really only for the connoisseurs. The series hadn't found its feet yet. The recognized triumph of the collection is *Fuck Orgy Nine*, which won no less than—'

'Is there a *Fuck Orgy Eleven*?' Hooper enquired urgently.

'There certainly is. They've made fifteen so far. I can get you them all if you like . . . What are you looking so pleased with yourself about?'

Hooper was indeed smiling. He believed that he had

176

found out what Kelly had whispered to David in the hot tub. The thing that had made him look so concerned.

DAY THIRTY-EIGHT. 9.00 a.m.

As he removed his coat and hat in the cloakroom Chief Inspector Coleridge was surprised to hear cheering and shouting coming from the incident room. He walked in to see a group of his officers, both male and female, clustered round a video monitor from which strange moans and groans were emanating.

'She will *never* get that in her mouth!' a constable was saying.

'It can't be real!' shrieked one of the girls. 'It must be digitally enhanced.'

Now Coleridge realized what sort of video they were watching, and was about to begin the process of disciplining the lot of them when Hooper pressed the freeze-frame button and turned to his boss.

'Ah, sir,' he said. 'Sorry about the noise, but we're all a bit pleased with ourselves this morning. I think we know where Kelly had met David before.'

On the screen a young woman was frozen in the act of performing oral sex on a man who appeared to have been crossed with a donkey. The woman was most definitely not Kelly.

'That's not Kelly,' said Coleridge testily, 'and I don't see David either. What's your point?'

'Look behind the main lady, sir. Look at the two girls reaching round to feel her knock— breasts, the one on the right, she's partially obscured by the man's dick— penis, but it's Kelly all right.'

'Good heavens,' said Coleridge. 'So it is.'

'She said that she'd been a movie extra, sir. Now we know what sort of movie she was an extra in. No wonder she didn't rate it very highly. This film is Kelly's 'Far Corgi In Heaven', by the way.'

'Curious title.'

'Not when you know that what she actually said was *Fuck Orgy Eleven*.'

'Oh, I see. Well, I never . . . And the owner of that . . . um, appendage . . . Is that David?'

'No, sir, that's just one of the numerous disassociated penises that the movie features. This is David.' And Hooper fast-forwarded a little to reveal the entrance of the star of the film: an outrageous bisexual figure in a long purple wig and high-camp make-up, pink lips, glittery eye shadow and a fur and feather posing pouch, which he was in the process of removing.

'David, sir,' said Hooper, 'or Boris Pecker as he is known in the *Fuck Orgy* series. He also appears at times under the names of Olivia Newton Dong, Ivor Whopper and half of a mock Scottish gay-porn comedy double act known as Ben Doon and Phil McCavity.'

'Good heavens.'

'I talked to his agent this morning. He tried to hold out on me at first, but in the end he didn't fancy getting nicked for obstructing the police in their inquiries. Our David has a secret double life as a porn star. Apparently he's much in demand.'

'So that's how he manages to live so fat despite apparently not working.'

'Yes, sir, the high-and-mighty serious actor who would never take on extra work and believes it is better to be unemployed than prostitute your talent.'

'What a nasty little hypocrite our friend is.'

'Exactly. Remember the hard time he gave Kelly that day about getting a different dream because she'd already compromised any hope she had of being an actress?'

'I do indeed.'

'Well, look at him.'

The tape played on and David, or Boris Pecker, barely recognizable in his outrageous make-up, walked among the writhing copulating bodies. He was stark naked save for the purple fright wig and a pink bow on his penis.

'My name is Lord Shag!' he said. 'Bow before the power of my awesome schlong!' At which point all the naked extras stopped cavorting about and prostrated themselves before him.

'I'm amazed that none of the papers has picked up on this,' Coleridge remarked.

'Well, look at him, sir. All the make-up, the wig, the high-camp act. Would you have recognized him if you didn't know?'

'No, I suppose not.'

'And nor would anyone else. Unless of course they recognized some absolutely clear distinguishing feature. Watch Kelly.'

Kelly was very close to David, lying at his feet, her eyes barely two inches from his left ankle.

'To be or not to be, sir,' said Hooper smiling.

DAY THIRTY-EIGHT. 10.15 a.m.

While Hooper and Coleridge contemplated David's starring role in *Far Corgi in Heaven*, Trisha had once more made the trip out to the Peeping Tom complex in order to speak to Bob Fogarty.

'This business about Kelly and Hamish in the shag shack,' she had said to him on the phone before setting off. 'The day after it happened, Kelly went to the confession box, but we've only got the edited version of it here. Do you think you still have the original?'

'Nothing is ever actually wiped from a hard disk,' Fogarty told her, delighted to be able to talk about computers. 'Unless it's specifically recorded over, it just

179

hangs around in the digital shadows for ever. Pressing delete or putting it in the trash simply hides it. If you know how to look you can get most things back on a computer. That's how porno people get caught.'

'Well, try to dig up Kelly's confession from day nineteen for me, then. I'll bring you a bar of chocolate.'

Fogarty had found the footage Trisha wanted and now they were sitting watching it together.

'*It's seven fifteen on day nineteen,*' said Andy the narrator, '*and Kelly comes to the confession box because she is worried about the events of the previous night.*'

'Hullo, Tom.'

'Hullo, Kelly,' said Sam, the soothing voice of Peeping Tom.

'Um, I just wanted to ask you about the party last night and . . . um . . . when I went off to the um . . . the little hut with Hamish.'

'Yes, Kelly,' said Peeping Tom.

'Well, I was a bit drunk, you see . . . Well, actually I was very drunk, and what I wanted to ask was . . . Did anything happen? I mean, I know nothing did, I'm sure nothing did, and I love Hamish, he's great, but, well . . . I can't really remember and, well, I just wanted to know.'

'Why don't you ask Hamish, Kelly?'

'Well, he was drunk too and . . . Well, it's a bit embarrassing, isn't it? Saying to some boy "Did we do anything last night?" '

'Peeping Tom reminds you of the rules, Kelly, that no outside influences or information are allowed to housemates. This includes retrospective discussion of an individual's behaviour. Peeping Tom expects you to *know* what you did.'

'I do know what *I* did, I just want to know what . . .'

Kelly stopped. She sat in silence for a moment, her eyes seeming to plead with the camera.

Trisha looked hard at Kelly. What had she been about to say? Could it have been 'what *he* did'?

'Please, Peeping Tom, I'm not asking for detail, all I'm asking is whether anything happened in the hut.'

There was a pause. 'Peeping Tom will get back to you on this, Kelly.'

'What!' Kelly gasped. 'Just tell me! Surely you don't have to think about it! I mean, you were watching. *Did anything happen?*'

Kelly's voice was shaking. 'Is this a gag? Are you having a laugh? Like when someone crashes out at a party and wakes up with their head shaved and toothpaste smeared all over them? Come on, I can take a joke. Did I make a fool of myself? Did anyone make a fool of *me*?'

'I myself was not on duty last night, Kelly. We must consult with the relevant editors. You can wait in the box if you wish.'

And so Kelly sat and waited.

Trisha and Fogarty watched her waiting.

'She doesn't look very comfortable, does she?' Fogarty observed. 'She thinks that she got drunk and did the naughty, naughty. She didn't, of course. You've seen the footage. Very boring.'

Finally the voice of Peeping Tom returned. 'Peeping Tom has spoken to the editor concerned, Kelly, and we have decided that it is within order for us to assure you that you and Hamish kissed and cuddled, after which you both fell asleep under the blankets and no further movement was observed.'

Kelly looked relieved. She had just wanted to be reassured. 'Thanks, Peeping Tom,' she said. 'Please don't show this, will you? I mean, I was just being stupid and I wouldn't want to say anything about Hamish because he's great and I love him . . . You won't show it, will you?'

'Peeping Tom can make no promises, Kelly, but will bear your request in mind.'

'Thanks, Peeping Tom.'

'And of course as you've seen, we did show it,' said Fogarty, 'or at least an edited version. Geraldine *loved* it. She said it was *terrific* telly. "A sad, drunken old slapper pleading to be told she didn't make a twat of herself the night before," was how Geraldine put it. Said it happened to her all the time, that she was always bumping into blokes at parties who claimed to have shagged her rigid the previous Tuesday and who she didn't know from a bar of soap.'

'Quite a character, isn't she, your Geraldine?'

'She's a slag. That's all.'

'Strange how Kelly thought that she could say all that on camera and then ask you not to show it.'

'I know, they all do that. Amazing, really. They actually think we'd put their wishes before the prospect of a bit of good telly. They're always creeping into the box and saying, "Oh, please don't show that bit." I mean, if for one moment they stopped to think, they might ask themselves why we spent over two and a half million pounds setting up the house. I don't think it was to provide them with a nice shortcut into showbusiness, do you?'

'No, but then stopping to think isn't really what these people are about, is it? They're too busy stopping to feel.' Trisha realized that for a moment she had sounded exactly like Coleridge. She was twenty-five years old and had started to talk like a man in his fifties, going on seventies. She really would have to get out more.

'It's pathetic, really,' said Fogarty. 'They even thank us when we give them some little treat or other, usually designed to get them to take their clothes off. It's Stockholm Syndrome, you know.'

'When captives fall in love with their tormentors.'

'Exactly, and begin to rely on them, to *trust them*. I mean, how can that girl not have realized that as far as we're concerned she's a prop, an extra, to be used, abused and utterly misrepresented as we see fit?'

'I suppose it is pretty obvious, now you come to mention it. But I suppose it's not just the housemates who fall for it. The public believes in you too.'

'The public! The public, they're worse than us! At least we get paid to bully these people. The public do it for fun. They know they're watching ants getting burnt under a magnifying glass, but they don't care. They don't care what we do to them, how we prod them, as long we get a reaction.' Fogarty stared angrily at the screen upon which Kelly was still frozen. 'The people in that house think that they're in a cocoon. In fact it's a redoubt. They're surrounded by enemies.'

DAY TWENTY. 6.15 p.m.

'*It's two-fifteen,*' said Andy the narrator, '*and after a lunch of rice, chicken and vegetables cooked by Jazz, Sally asks Kelly to help her dye her hair.*'

Geraldine stared at the screen showing various camera angles of Kelly applying shampoo to Sally's mohican haircut prior to dyeing it.

'A new low,' mused Geraldine. 'I thought Layla's cheese was our nadir but I reckon watching some great lump of a bird getting her hair washed has got to plumb new and unique depths in fucking awful telly, don't you? Fuck me, in the early days of TV they used to stick a potter's wheel on between the programmes. Now the potter's wheel *is* the fucking programme.'

Fogarty gritted his teeth and continued with his tasks. 'What shot do you want, Geraldine?' he enquired. 'Kelly's hands on her head? Or a wide?'

'Put Sally up on the main monitor – the close-up of

her face, through the mirror. Run the whole sequence, right from where she bends down over the basin.'

Fogarty punched his buttons while Geraldine continued her reverie. 'Tough time for us, this. Eviction night tomorrow but no eviction. That cunt Woggle has deprived us of our weekly climax. We are in a lull. A low point, a stall. The wind is slipping out of our fucking sails, Bob. The Viagra pot is empty and our televisual dick is limp.'

Andy the narrator emerged from the voiceover recording booth to get a cup of herbal tea. 'Perhaps I could tell them what everyone had for pudding,' he suggested. 'David made a soufflé, but it didn't really rise. That's quite interesting, isn't it?'

'Get back in your box,' said Geraldine.

'But Gazzer didn't finish his, and I think David was a little bit offended.'

'I *said*, get back in your fucking box!'

Andy retreated with his camomile.

'Always trying to grab himself a few more lines, that bastard. I've told him, if he does one more beer ad voiceover he's fucking out. I'm going to get a bird to do it next time, anyway . . . Stop it there!'

Fogarty froze the image of Sally's face. Dribbles of shampoo foam ran down her temples; Kelly's fingertips could be made out at the top of the screen. Sally's hand was at her mouth, frozen in the moment of inserting a segment of tangerine into it.

'Run it on, but mute the sound,' Geraldine instructed.

They studied Sally's silent countenance for a few moments, as her jaw moved about, her lips pursed and her cheeks became slightly sucked in, then the lips parted a fraction and the tip of her tongue licked them.

'Very nice,' Geraldine observed. 'I love a bit of muted mastication, the editor's friend. Right, chop the tangerine off the front and run that sequence mute under Kelly's dialogue about finding head massage sensual.'

Fogarty gulped before replying. It reall〉
this time he had had enough. 'But . . . bu
that comment to David while they were h
chicken and vegetables that Jazz cooked. If we drop
over Sally's face it will look as if . . . as if . . .'

'Ye-es?' Geraldine enquired.

'As if she's getting a thrill out of massaging Sally's
head!'

'While Sally,' Geraldine replied, 'with her grinding
jaw and tense cheeks, sucky-sucky lips and little wet
tongue tip, is positively creaming her gusset, and *we*,
my darling, have got what can only be described as a
half-decent lezzo moment.'

The silence in the monitoring bunker spoke loudly of
the unease felt by Geraldine's employees. Geraldine
just grinned, a huge, triumphant grin, like a happy
snarl.

'We are in a ratings trough, you cunts!' she shouted.
'I'm paying your wages here!'

DAY TWENTY-TWO. 6.10 p.m.

'Such a shame there was no eviction last night,' the
young woman was saying. 'The last one was terrific,
although I was sorry to see Layla go. I mean I know she
was pretty pretentious, but I respected the integrity of
her vegetarianism.'

'Darling she was a *poseur*, a complete act, I *hated*
her,' said the man, a rather fey individual of about thirty.

Chief Inspector Coleridge had been listening to them
chat for about five minutes, and did not have the
faintest idea who or what they were talking about.
They seemed to be discussing a group of people that
they knew well, friends perhaps, and yet they
appeared to hold them in something approaching
complete contempt.

185

What do *you* think about Layla going, then?' said the man, whose name was Glyn, turning finally to Coleridge.

'I'm afraid I don't know her,' Coleridge answered. 'Is she a friend of yours?'

'My God,' said Glyn. 'You mean you don't know who Layla is? You don't watch *House Arrest*?'

'Guilty on both counts,' said Coleridge, attempting a little joke. He knew that they knew he was a policeman.

'You simply do not know what you're missing,' said Glyn.

'And long may that remain the case,' Coleridge replied.

It was an audition evening at Coleridge's local amateur dramatic society. Coleridge had been a member of the society for over twenty-five years and had attended thirty-three such evenings previous to this one, but he had never yet been offered a lead. The nearest he had got was Colonel Pickering in *My Fair Lady*, and that was only because the first choice had moved to Basingstoke and the second choice got adult chicken pox. The next production of the society was to be *Macbeth*, and Coleridge really and truly wanted to play the killer king.

Macbeth was his favourite play of all time, full of passion and murder and revenge, but one glance at Glyn's patronizing, supercilious expression told Coleridge he has as much chance of playing Macbeth as he had of presenting Britain's next entry for the Eurovision song contest. He would be lucky to score a Macduff.

'Yes, I am intending a very *young* production,' Glyn drawled. 'One that will bring *young people* back into the theatre. Have you seen Baz Luhrman's *Romeo and Juliet*?'

Coleridge had not.

'That is my inspiration. I want a contemporary, *sexy Macbeth*. Don't you agree?'

Well, of course Coleridge did not agree. Glyn's production would run for three nights at the village hall and would play principally to an audience that wanted armour and swords and big black cloaks.

'Shall I read, then?' he asked 'I've prepared a speech.'

'Heavens, no!' Glyn said. 'This isn't the audition, it's a *prelim chat*. A chance for *you* to influence *me*, give me your feedback.'

There was a long pause while Coleridge tried to think of something to say. The table that divided him from Glyn and Val was a chasm. 'So when is the actual audition?' he finally said.

'This time next week.'

'Right, well, I'll come back then, shall I?'

'Do,' said Glyn.

DAY TWENTY-THREE. 3.00 p.m.

Sally was not yet satisfied with her new bright-red mohican hair.

'I just want a tuft,' she said, 'like a shaving brush.'

'Well, just you leave it at that,' Moon said. '*I'm* the bald bird in this house. Can't have two of us, we'll look like a fookin' game of billiards.'

Sally did not reply. She rarely replied to anything Moon said, or even looked at her.

Dervla was relieved that Kelly elected to administer the haircut in the living area. It had been agony for her on the Saturday when Sally had done the dyeing in the bathroom. Dervla always rubbed out her messages, of course, and they were only condensation anyway, but seeing Sally with her face so close to the very place where they appeared had been most disconcerting. As

187

Kelly washed Sally's hair and the mirror steamed up, Dervla had been gripped with an irrational fear that a message might suddenly appear, there and then, right in front of Sally's eyes. She knew that this was unlikely, unless of course the man had decided to start writing to Sally.

'All done,' said Kelly.

'I like it,' Sally replied, having inspected the little red tuft which was all that remained of her hair. 'When I get out I'm going to have my head tattooed.'

'What will you get done, then?' Kelly asked.

'I thought perhaps my star sign. It's the ram, except obviously I'm not having a male animal on my head, so I'd have to have a ewe.'

'Well, that doesn't sound very empowering, Sally,' Dervla observed.

'Be a fucking lioness, Sal,' said Jazz. 'I mean, let's face it, them pictures they make out of the stars are just total bullshit anyway. Three bloody dots and they draw a bull round it, or a centaur. It's ridiculous. If you actually do join the dots all you get is a splodge, like an amoeba or a puddle. Born under the sign of the puddle.'

'Actually, Jazz,' said Moon, 'it's not just about the fookin' shapes, is it? It's about the personality, the characteristics of people born under certain signs.'

'It's bollocks,' Jazz insisted. 'People say . . . Oh, Virgo, dead brave, or Capricorn, really clever and introspective. Where are the star signs for all the stupid boring people, eh? I mean, the world's full of them. Don't they get to be represented celestially? Taurus – we're really dull and don't get our rounds in . . . I could tell you who was a Libra, they're very flatulent.'

'You know fook all, you do, Jazz,' said Moon. 'Do you know that?'

188

'So what's a sweatbox when it's at home?' asked Gazzer.

'It says here that it's an ancient Native American tradition,' Hamish replied.

'Native American?'

'Red Indian to you, I imagine,' said Dervla.

The housemates had been given their instructions for the weekly task, and so far Gazzer was not impressed.

'So what the fahk is it?'

'Exactly what it sounds like,' said Hamish, who was reading the instructions. 'A box in which you sweat. From what it says here it sounds pretty similar to a sauna, except a bit more friendly. It says this is a historical task because they were used by Native American fighting men.'

'And women,' Sally interjected. 'Native American fighting women.'

'Were there any?' asked Kelly. 'I thought they were just squaws.'

'That's because history is written by men,' Sally assured her. 'Women warriors have been denied their place in the chronicles of war, just like women artists and scientists never got credit for doing an amazing amount of art and science which their husbands took credit for.'

'Wow, I had no idea,' said Kelly, genuinely surprised.

'Well, think about it, Kelly. History . . . *his* story.'

'Oh, yeah.'

'Can we get back to this fahkin' sweatbox?' Gazzer protested. 'What are we supposed to do about it?'

Hamish applied himself once more to Peeping Tom's note. 'Well, we have to build one, for a start. They'll give us instructions and all the stuff we need, and when we've built it we have to use it.'

'Use it?' Dervla enquired.

'Well, apparently after these Native Americans had had a fight, or a sports day or whatever, they'd wait till it got dark and then get into a hot confined space all squeezed up tight together and sweat.'

'It sounds totally homoerotic,' said Sally. 'Most military rituals are, if you didn't know.'

DAY THIRTY-EIGHT. 4.45 p.m.

'Homoerotic, oh, for heaven's sake,' Coleridge snapped.

'Sounds reasonable to me,' Hooper replied.

'Yes, of course it does, sergeant! So easy to say, so impossible to contradict. Why is it that everybody these days insists on presuming a sexual motive for absolutely everything? Military rituals homoerotic? *Why*, for heaven's sake!'

Was Freud to blame? Coleridge rather thought that he might be, or else Jung, or perhaps some imbecile from the sixties like Andy Warhol.

'Whatever you say, sir,' said Hooper.

Coleridge let it go, as he let so much go that bothered him these days. At the end of the day, as the inmates of the house were so fond of saying, it wasn't worth it.

'I still cannot quite believe that these people actually agreed to do this task. I mean, four hours in that thing, naked.'

'Well, Dervla tried to object, didn't she?'

'Ah, yes,' Coleridge thought, Dervla objected, the one he secretly rather liked. For a moment he felt glad that she had objected. Then inwardly he cursed himself. He had absolutely no business liking any of them, or being glad about what they did or didn't do.

DAY TWENTY-FIVE. 8.00 p.m.

The sweatbox, which the housemates had been instructed to build in the boys' bedroom, was half finished. The false floor had been laid, underneath which the heating elements were to be installed; the support poles for the roof were in position and work had begun on stitching the thick plastic for the walls. The construction so far looked rather small and uninviting, with very little prospect of its looking any better when it was finished.

'I am so not sitting naked in that thing with a lot of nude boys,' Dervla said.

'For four hours, they say,' said Jazz.

'No way,' Dervla repeated.

'Why not? None of the rest of us fookin' object,' said Moon.

'What's that got to do with anything?' Dervla asked.

'Well, what's so special about you is what I'm saying? Anyway, don't you want to look sexy on the telly?'

Of course Dervla wanted to look sexy on the telly, or else she would never have applied to be on the telly in the first place, but she also understood that real allure depended on retaining a bit of mystery. She had a good body, but she knew that like all bodies it was even better when left to the imagination. Besides which, she had her misty green eyes and sparkling smile to rely on; she did not need to go flashing her knockers about the place.

Dervla went to the confession box and asked to be allowed to perform the task in her bathing suit. 'It's high cut on the thigh and a lovely pattern,' she said.

The answer when it came was broadcast to the whole house.

'This is Peeping Tom,' said a much sterner voice than usual, a voice that normally did ads for BMWs and aftershave. 'The traditional Native American

191

sweatbox experience was undertaken naked, and this is the manner in which Peeping Tom requires the task to be performed. As with any of the group tasks, all housemates must comply with the rules and if any single housemate fails to do so then the whole group will be deemed to have failed and will therefore lose a percentage of their food and drink for the following week.'

It was jaw-dropping cynical and Geraldine knew it, which was why she had no intention of allowing this outrageous instruction to be aired publicly. Clearly she was blackmailing Dervla into stripping, but the public were to be given the illusion that the housemates one and all simply could not wait to get their clothes off.

'I cannot believe they're trying to get away with this,' Dervla fumed.

Then Sally spoke up. 'Actually, Dervla, I really think that we should do this, because I am worried that we might come across as racist if it looks like we think we're too good for a legitimate ethnic custom, particularly one with such obviously homoerotic overtones.'

Sally was pleased that Peeping Tom had provided her with an opportunity to hold forth on the one area about which she felt truly passionate.

'As a lesbian woman of mixed race I know what it's like to have my customs and rituals held in fear and contempt by the majority community. Peeping Tom is offering us the opportunity to experience the bonding rituals of an oppressed indigenous group. I think we should try to learn from it.'

DAY TWENTY-SIX. 9.15 a.m.

Bob Fogarty waited until the following morning's production meeting to make his complaint. He wanted his objections to be noted publicly. It was difficult for him

192

to find his moment because Geraldine was roaring with laughter so much as she recalled Sally's unlikely take on the weekly task.

'All I'm trying to do is persuade them to feel each other up and it turns out I'm a champion of minority rights. Anyway, all ethnic and sexual bollocks aside, Dervla will have to get 'em out for the lads or nobody gets a drink next week.'

Fogarty had to stand up to get her attention. 'Geraldine, we are coercing this girl into taking her clothes off against her wishes.'

'Yes, Bob, we all know that. Why are you standing up?'

'Because I think it's morally corrupt.'

'Oh, do fuck off.'

Fogarty had finally had enough. 'Ms Hennessy, I cannot prevent you from using profanity to punctuate your sentences, but I am a grown man and a highly qualified employee and I am entitled to insist that you do not use such language towards me or those who work under me.'

'No, you're fucking not, you cunt. Now sit down or fuck off.'

Fogarty did neither. He just stood there, shaking.

'You think you can do me for constructive dismissal?' Geraldine asked. 'For swearing? Grow up, Bob. Even this cunt of a country isn't that pathetic yet. If you walk out it's a straight resignation and you get bugger-all. Now, are you staying or are you going?'

Fogarty sat down.

'Good. You may be an arsehole, but you're a talented arsehole and I don't want to lose you. And besides which,' Geraldine went on, 'Dervla is free to leave that house at any time. She could have walked out there and then, and she could walk out now. But she hasn't done, has she? And why? Because she wants to be on telly, that's why, and at the end of the day, if she has to take her clothes off to do it, then you can bet your last quid she'll allow herself to be persuaded.'

Bob stared down into his coffee. He looked like a man who needed a bar of chocoate. 'We're corrupting her,' he mumbled.

'What?' Geraldine barked.

'I said, we're corrupting her,' but this time Fogarty said it even more quietly.

'*Look!*' shouted Geraldine. 'I'm not asking the snooty stuck-up cow to show us her bits full on, am I? There are guidelines, you know. We *do* have a Broadcasting Standards Commission in this country. The polythene walls of that box are going to be translucent and the lights will be off. The idea is to make it so dark that the anonymity will persuade some of them to have it off, which I can assure you will be a lot more interesting than precious little Dervla's sacred little knockers. I want it to be literally dark as hell in that box.'

Eviction

DAY TWENTY-EIGHT. 6.00 p.m.

Coleridge pushed the record button on his audio tape-machine.

'Witness statement. Geraldine Hennessy,' he said before sliding the little microphone across the desk and setting it down in front of Geraldine.

'Bit of a reversal for you, eh, Miss Hennessy?'

'Ms.'

'I'm sorry, Ms Hennessy. Bit of a reversal, you being the one getting recorded, I mean.'

Geraldine merely smiled.

'So tell me about the night it happened.'

'You know as much as I do. The whole thing was recorded from start to finish. You've seen the tapes.'

'I want to hear it from you. From Peeping Tom herself. Let's start with the sweatbox. Why on earth did you ask them to do it?'

'It was a task,' Geraldine replied. 'Each week we set the inmates challenges to perform to keep them busy and see how they react when working together. They get to pledge a part of their weekly booze and food budgets against their chances of success. We gave them wood and tools and polythene, a couple of heating units and all the instructions, and as it happens they did a bloody good job.'

'You told them how to make it?'

'Of course we did, or how else would they have done it? If I gave you some wood and plastic and told you to construct a Native American sweatbox to seat eight, could you do it?'

'Probably not, I suppose.'

'Well, nor could this lot either. We gave them the designs and the materials and told them exactly where to put it to suit our hot-head camera. This they did and it took them three days. Then on the Saturday evening, as the sun went down, we gave them a shitload of booze and told them to get on with it.'

'Why did you let them get drunk?'

'Well, it's obvious, isn't it? To try to get them to have sex. The show had been going for three weeks and apart from a near miss with Kelly and Hamish in Bonkham Towers we'd had scarcely a hint of any nooky at all. I wanted to get them going a bit.'

'Well,' said Coleridge pointedly, 'you certainly did that.'

'It wasn't my fucking fault somebody got killed, inspector.'

'Wasn't it?'

'No, it fucking wasn't.'

Coleridge absolutely hated to hear a woman swear, but he knew he could not say anything about it.

'Look, I'm not a social worker, inspector. I make telly!' Geraldine continued. 'And I'm sorry if it offends you, but telly has to be sexy!'

She said it as if she was talking to a senile octogenarian. Coleridge was in fact only two years older than she was, but the gap between them was chasmic. She had embraced and joined each new generation as it rose up to greet her, remaining, in her own eyes at least, forever young. He, on the other hand, had been born old.

'Why did it have to be so dark?'

'I thought it would loosen up their inhibitions if

they couldn't see each other. I wanted them all completely anonymous.'

'Well, you certainly succeeded in that, Ms Hennessy, which is the principal factor inhibiting my investigation.'

'Look! I didn't know anybody was going to fuck off and murder someone, did I? Forgive me, but in my many years of making television it has never crossed my mind to arrange my work on the offchance that you coppers might want to look at it later in the light of a homicide investigation.'

It was a fair point. Coleridge shrugged and gestured Geraldine to continue.

DAY TWENTY-SEVEN. 8.00 p.m.

The sweatbox stood waiting in the boys' bedroom, but for the time being the housemates remained in the living area, trying to get drunk enough to take the plunge.

'Well, we gotta do four hours in there,' Gazzer said, 'and if we don't want to get caught all nudey when the sun comes up we'll have to get started by one at the latest.'

'I want to get it over with long before that,' said Dervla, gulping at her strong cider.

'Well, don't get too pissed, Dervo,' Jazz warned. 'I don't think the confines of a sweatbox are a very clever environment to honk up in.'

Peeping Tom had given them all the luxuries that they needed to get in an appropriately silly mood: plenty of booze, of course, also party hats, party food and sex toys.

'What are they, then?' Garry asked.

'Love balls,' Moon replied. 'You stick 'em up your twat.'

'Blimey.'

'I've got a pair at home. They're great, keep you permanently aroused, except they can be dead embarrassing. I don't wear knickers much, you see, and I were wearing me love balls to go shopping, right, and they fell out in the supermarket and went bouncing up the fookin' veggies isle. This old bloke picked 'em up for me, no fookin' idea at all. "Excuse me, dear, I think you dropped these." '

Jazz fished in the party box and brought out a sort of plastic tube. 'What's this, then?' he asked.

'Knob massager,' said Moon, who seemed to be something of an expert on the subject. 'You stick your knob in it and it whacks you off.'

'Ah well, you see, me, I'm a traditionalist,' said Jazz. 'Why get a machine to do something that is best done by hand?'

Everybody was getting quite deliberately drunk, slowly convincing themselves that they were at a party. That they were amongst friends instead of amongst rivals and competitors.

'Quite frankly,' said Moon, 'at the end of the day, ninety-five per cent of sex toys never get near a knob or a vag. People buy 'em for a laugh, to give as embarrassing birthday presents and whatever. It's like "What are we going to get Sue for her eighteenth?" "Oh, I know, let's get her a fookin' great big dildo with a swivel end. That'll be a laugh when she opens it in front of her gran." Nobody actually *uses* this shite. Quite frankly, I've got a pair of nipple clamps at home and I use them for keeping my bills together.'

Along with the sex toys, Peeping Tom had supplied a coolbox full of ice creams. The modern variety of expensive iced versions of well known chocolate bars. They all dipped in excitedly.

'I remember when there was ice creams and there was KitKats,' Jazz observed, 'and the idea of the two trespassing on each other's territory was simply not an issue, it just was *not* going to happen. Unimaginable. Kids today reckon it's the norm.'

'Mars Bars started the rot,' Dervla observed. 'I'm old enough to remember the excitement, it seemed such an incredible idea at the time, a *Mars Bar* made of ice cream. Stupid. Now they do ice cream Opal Fruits.'

'Starbursts, they're called now,' said Jazz with mock contempt. 'Get with the plot, girl. You probably still think a Snickers is a Marathon. It's fucking globalization gone mad, that is. We have to call our sweets the same as the Yanks do. There ought to be protests.'

'And what was wrong with Mivvis and Rockets anyway, I'd like to know?' Dervla added. 'We enjoyed them.'

'We are the last generation,' said Jazz solemnly, 'that will have known the joys of truly crap lollies. No kid will ever again be asked to suck the red and orange stuff out of a block of ice and be told that it's a treat.'

In the monitoring bunker Geraldine was already getting frustrated. When she had supplied them with ice cream it had been in the hope that they might eat it off each other's bodies, not talk about it.

'You're a philosopher, Jazz,' said Dervla.

'What's that, then? Irish for wanker?' asked Gazzer.

'It means,' said David, 'that there are more things in heaven and earth than you could ever dream of.'

'You don't have any idea what I dream about, Dave mate.'

'Naked women?'

'Fuck me! You're fucking clairvoyant, you are. You've got a gift.'

But Jazz was not being diverted so easily. He had struck on a subject which he knew his book on comedy would recognize as the stuff of top routines.

'It's like these days everything is pretending to be

something it's not, nothing is happy as it is. Take Smarties, not happy any more, now you have to have little mini Smarties and great big fuck-off Smarties.'

'And of course fookin' Smarties original,' Moon chipped in.

'Well, that is, of course, your Smarties Classic like with toothbrushes, *David*. Everything has to pretend it's something else, and it won't stop, you know, not now it's started. Everything we love will change, get repackaged and flogged back to us as an improvement . . . Fish-fingers. I'll bet you one day they start doing mini-fish-fingers, giant fish-fingers . . .'

'Ice cream fish-fingers,' said Dervla.

'That's coming, I swear that's coming,' Jazz replied.

Dervla was laughing now. 'It's salad dressing, but in a bar!'

'You got it, girl!'

'All your favourite breakfast cereals, in a series of bite-sized soups!'

'Yeah, all right, all right.'

Jazz was taken aback to have had the comic baton wrested from his hand so easily. He was supposed to be on the roll, not Dervla. She was a trauma therapist.

In the monitoring bunker Geraldine's impatience was growing. 'Come on!' she shouted. 'Get your kit off and get in the sweatbox, you cunts!'

Perhaps they heard her in the house, or else maybe they had got drunk enough by this time, but for whatever reason the conversation now turned to the forthcoming task.

'So how are we going to do it, then?' Sally asked. 'I'm not just getting undressed in here with all the lights on.'

'Do it in the bedroom, then,' said David. 'It's dark in there.'

'No way,' said Dervla. 'They have infrared cameras or whatever. We'd look like flipping porn stars, so we would.'

'Very nice,' Gazzer observed.

Kelly flicked a look across at David, just a look, and a little smile. If he noticed he did not return it.

'I don't give a fook, me,' said Moon pulling off her shoes.

'Well, I do,' said Sally. 'Just because the sweatbox represents a legitimate ethnic experience doesn't mean we have to do a striptease.'

'Why not?' said Moon. 'That's the only reason they're making us fookin' do it, ain't it?'

'I don't know, Moon,' said Hamish. 'They've given us sheets to cover up with if we have to go to the loo.'

'Ah, but that's just for show, a mask to hide their true agenda,' Dervla said.

'Exactly,' Moon concurred. 'Which is for us to show the lot and if possible have it off as well.'

'You can be so cynical, you,' said Hamish.

'Hamish,' Moon insisted. 'They've supplied us with fookin' chocolate-flavoured *condoms*, for God's sake.'

'I've got nothing to hide.' Garry laughed. 'If anybody wants to see my knob they only have to ask. Quite frankly, sometimes they don't even have to ask.'

'Yes, well, I do not have any desire to see your penis,' said David. 'We have to do this task or we get half-rations next week, but that's no reason for us to feel obliged to allow our bodies to be exploited.'

'Fookin' hell, David,' Moon sneered. 'You wander round the house in your little pose pouch the whole time exploiting what a great bod you've got, which I'll admit you have, but you still look a right ponce because you're obviously so fookin' pleased with it, and now you won't even get your kecks off for this week's task.'

'A man in his underwear, Moon,' David responded,

'is no more naked than a man in his swimming costume.'

Geraldine crushed her styrofoam cup in her hands. 'Oh, for fuck's *sake*, you precious bunch of *cunts*. Get your KIT OFF.'

Eventually the task had to be begun, and so they all made their way into the darkened bedroom and began to strip off with varying degrees of bravado. Dervla was easily the most cautious, keeping her undies on right up to the point of entering the sweatbox, before throwing them off in a flurry and scuttling inside.

Geraldine was fairly satisfied. 'I think we got one of her tits, didn't we?' she asked. 'Certainly her bum. We'll stick that in the trailers. The whole nation's been waiting to see a bit more of sweet pure little Dervo.'

Inside the sweatbox the darkness was absolute. Dark as the grave, as the newspapers were to remark the following morning.

And it was hot. Very, very hot.

Following the instructions given, Jazz and Gazzer had laid out a false floor made of scented pine wood, underneath which were electric heating units, which had been on all afternoon.

'Ooh, it smells dead lovely,' Moon remarked.

'Ow! This floor's burning my bum,' squealed Kelly.

'You'll get used to it,' Dervla assured her. 'Give yourself a minute to acclimatize.'

The floor was indeed hot on their bare flesh, but not unbearably so. In fact it was rather pleasant, exciting almost.

'Sweet Mother of Jesus,' Dervla's voice continued in the darkness. 'Now I know why they call it a sweatbox.' She had been inside for only a few moments, but

204

already she could feel the perspiration streaming down her skin. Her forehead and armpits were instantly dripping wet.

'Well, it's giving *me* a sweaty box, that's for sure!' Moon shrieked, and they all laughed with her. 'Oh, my God! Who's arse was that!'

'Mine!' three or four voices answered simultaneously.

They could all feel their flesh gliding across each other's but the darkness was total. Nobody knew whose bottom belonged to whom.

'Four hours,' said Hamish. 'We need another drink.'

Somehow, and with much groping about, plastic bottles containing warm Bacardi and Coke (mainly Bacardi) were handed round.

'I could get to like this,' Garry remarked, and to varying degrees he spoke for them all.

In every sense, the party was warming up.

DAY TWENTY-NINE. 8.00 p.m.

Having spent the day reviewing the footage from the very first day in the house, Coleridge and Hooper turned once more to the tape of the night of the murder. The same images that Geraldine, the Peeping Tom production team and 47,000 Internet subscribers had watched live less than forty-eight hours before. Those same strange, fuzzy, bluish-grey pictures that the nightsight cameras had transmitted from the boys' bedroom. A bedroom that seemed innocent and empty, entirely normal, save for the weird-looking plastic box in the middle of the room, a box which they knew contained eight drunk, naked people, the only evidence of whom were the strange bulges that seemed to undulate against the polythene walls from time to time. It was an eerie and depressing sight for the two policemen, knowing as they did that one of those living bulges was shortly to die.

'He could have done it inside the box,' said Hooper thoughtfully. 'Why didn't he do it in the box?'

'Or she,' Coleridge reminded Hooper, 'or she. We refer to the murderer as a he for convenience's sake but we must never ever forget that it could be a woman.'

'Yes, all right, sir, I know. But what I'm saying is that nobody would have known, if he or she had done it inside the box, if a hand had reached out in the darkness holding a small knife, which the murderer could easily have sneaked in with him. It would have been relatively simple to just slit a throat in the dark and wait until people smelt blood, or felt it. By the time anybody realized that the warm stuff flowing all over them wasn't sweat they'd all have been drenched in it. Maybe that's what he planned.'

'There was no small knife in the box when we searched it, or in the room.'

'Well, sir, if he'd suddenly decided to follow the victim to the toilet instead, he could have put it back in the kitchen drawer when he got the bigger one.'

'I don't think so, sergeant. How could he have been sure of his kill in that darkness? Whether he'd stabbed the right person and whether he'd finished the job properly? Chances are it would have been a terrible mess. He would have just cut off a nose or something, or somebody else's nose, or his own fingers.'

'Well, he had to do it some time. How would he have known that a better chance was going to emerge?'

'He didn't know, but he was waiting. If the chance hadn't come, my guess is that he would have carried on waiting.'

'For how long? Until his prey got voted out and escaped him altogether?'

'Ah, but he or she knew that the prey hadn't been nominated that week, giving at least eight days' grace.'

'All I'm saying,' the sergeant insisted, 'is that if I was desperate to kill somebody in that house, I would have reckoned a crowded, darkened sweatbox, inside which everybody was drunk, to be about the best shot I was going to get.'

'Well, the drinking is a factor, surely. I suppose he knew that people would have to start going to the lavatory at some point.'

'He couldn't be certain.'

'No, he couldn't be certain of anything. However and whenever he chose to do it, this was always going to be a risky sort of murder.'

Coleridge looked at the time code on the video. They had pressed pause at 11.38. He knew that when he pressed play the code would tick over to 11.39 and Kelly Simpson would emerge from the sweatbox to take what would be the final brief walk of her life.

Kelly Simpson, so young, so excited, so certain of her splendid fun-filled destiny, gone into that stupid, pointless house to die. In Coleridge's mind there appeared the image of how she had been on that very first day in the house, jumping into the pool with excitement, shrieking about how 'wicked' it all was. And wicked was without doubt the word, because the time was now 11.38 on Kelly's last day in the house, and in a few more minutes she would be in a pool once more. A pool of her own blood.

'The point I'm making, sir,' Hooper pressed on, 'is that if he was planning to kill her, which we have presumed he was, then he must have been considering the possibility of doing her inside the sweatbox. He could not have known for certain that she would go to the loo, or that he would be able to conceal his identity when he followed her into it.'

Coleridge stared at the screen for a long time. Difficult to believe that there were eight people in that foolish little plastic construction. 'Unless the catalyst for the murder did not occur until after they had entered the box,' he mused. 'Unless whatever it was that made the killer want Kelly dead did not occur until moments before she ran to the toilet, and in fact he ran after her in an act of spontaneous fury.'

'Or fear,' Hooper added.

'Yes, that's right. Or fear. After all, since none of these people knew each other before they entered the house . . .'

'Or so we have been told, sir.' This remark came from Trisha, who had just returned with a round of teas.

'Yes, that's right, constable, so we have been told,' said Coleridge. 'We have been working on the theory that the catalyst that provoked the murder must have taken place at some point between the housemates entering the house and their entering the box. But of course something terrible might have happened *once they were inside* the box.'

'Well, it would certainly explain why the people at Peeping Tom have no idea about a motive,' Trisha conceded, sugaring Coleridge's tea for him.

'It would indeed. And this situation was after all developing into an orgy.'

Coleridge pronounced the word 'orgy' with a hard 'g'. Hooper wondered whether he did it deliberately and rather thought he must.

'Quite a volatile environment, I should imagine. An orgy,' Coleridge continued.

'Are you suggesting a rape, sir?' said Trisha. 'That someone forced themselves upon Kelly and then killed her in order to avoid the consequences?'

'It wouldn't be the first time a rape turned into a murder.'

'But the others? We've talked to them all. They didn't notice anything. I mean, you simply could not keep a thing like that quiet.'

'Couldn't you? In that environment? Besides, consider

the possibility that they were all conspirators. That they were all covering up for the one who actually did the dirty work.'

'You mean perhaps they *all* wanted Kelly dead?'

'Perhaps,' said Coleridge. 'It would certainly explain the startling lack of evidence in any of their statements.'

'You think that perhaps she had something on them, that she knew something about them all?'

Coleridge accepted his mug of tea from Trisha without looking at her. Instead he continued to stare at the box on the screen. He was imagining something very ugly. 'Or because they'd all done something to her,' he said finally.

'Some kind of group abuse?' Hooper said. 'A gangbang?'

Coleridge wanted to tell Hooper to use some other more suitable term, but he knew that there wasn't one. For the umpteenth time he pressed play and 11.38 ticked over to 11.39. Kelly emerged from the sweatbox.

DAY TWENTY-SEVEN. 11.39 p.m.

Geraldine was thrilled. Thrilled and very excited.

When asked to describe the scene later to the police, everyone who had been in the box with her that night commented on just how happy had been her mood. Almost hysterical, one or two of them had said.

And well Geraldine might have been happy. It was clear to them all as they watched the grey, translucent plastic box almost begin to *throb* that her plan was working and that real sex truly was on the cards. They had been in the box for just half the allotted four hours, and there had clearly already been some quite specific

209

erotic activity, and it seemed certain that there would be more.

The shouts and shrieks and smart-alec comments of the first rush of embarrassed excitement had died down, and now only murmurs and whispers could be heard. The people inside the box were clearly very drunk and very disoriented after their two hours of sweating and writhing in the complete darkness of their little plastic hut.

Clearly anything might happen. And of course it did.

It was about ten minutes after Jazz's voice had been heard suggesting a touching game in which people were to attempt to identify each other in the darkness that the plastic flaps at the entrance to the sweatbox parted, and Kelly emerged.

'Aye aye,' said Geraldine. 'Piss break.'

Bob Fogarty winced and concentrated on his monitors.

On the screens Kelly straightened herself up. Her naked body was gleaming and dripping with sweat.

'Very nice,' whispered Geraldine, tense with excitement. 'Very, very, *very* nice.'

Kelly seemed to be in a hurry. She did not bother to take up one of the great long sheets that Peeping Tom had thoughtfully provided for such eventualities, but simply ran naked out of the boys' bedroom, across the living area and into the sole lavatory, which served the needs of the whole group.

'Beautiful!' Geraldine exclaimed. 'I never thought they'd use the cover-up sheets once they got amped up. Except maybe that snotty cow Dervla. Moon was right, I only put them there to make it look like I'm not a total perv, which of course I am, along with the rest of the population, I might add.'

Kelly's run had certainly been thrilling for the watchers in the monitoring bunker. The show's first moment of absolute, in-focus, full-frontal nudity.

'Minge and all,' as Geraldine delightedly put it. 'Now we won't have to keep running that same tired old shot of her tit coming out in the pool.'

'Superb image quality, too,' commented Fogarty.

'The body or the pictures?' Geraldine enquired.

'I'm a techy, I don't do aesthetics,' Fogarty replied with angry embarrassment.

He was right about the quality, though. This was no grainy-blue sneaky night-shot like the ones they occasionally caught in the bedrooms. Kelly had run right through the living area, which was permanently neon lit, and although the lights had been dimmed to avoid light intruding into the boys' bedroom when the door was open, it was still a glorious shot.

'Nice one, Larry,' Geraldine called into the microphone, addressing the one live cameraman on duty. 'Glad we decided to keep you on.'

Geraldine was referring to the fact that there had only the previous day been a debate about dispensing with night operators altogether, because so little ever actually happened in the house at night, and seeing as how the entire environment was covered by remotes anyway. Geraldine had, however, insisted on retaining at least one person in the camera runs at night for just such an eventuality as had occurred. A naked girl running right across the room needed the personal touch. The coverage from the hot-heads not only came from above but also encompassed three different arcs of vision, and would have had to be cut up accordingly. On the other hand Larry, the live cameraman, had got one long beautiful, tit-bouncing, thigh-wobbling, tummy-stretching, full-frontal shot with pubic hair in full and constant focus. A shot that would play absolutely beautifully in slow motion.

'Terrific work, out of the blue like that,' Geraldine continued, giving credit where it was due. 'Looks like

211

there's still a role for you human beings in making television. Stick with her at the toilet door, Larry, and get her again when she comes out.'

Inside the toilet, of course, there was only remote coverage, a single camera mounted high in a corner above the door. This camera was looking down now on Kelly as she sat on the seat of the lavatory, her head in her hands.

In the monitoring box there was a slightly embarrassed silence. None of the production team had ever quite got used to this bit of their job. Listening to people pee and poop. In the daytime at least there were other things going on, something else to look at and listen to, but not at night. When any of the housemates went at night it was just them and the six people watching and listening from the box. This was always a strangely intense and rather degrading experience for the editing team. They felt like the most awful perverts.

On this occasion, of course, there should have been plenty of distraction coming from inside the translucent plastic box, but suddenly the party seemed to have arrived at something of a lull. The high hilarity, grunting and giggling of the touching game had rather abruptly died down into what sounded like something approaching a drunken stupor. Murmured conversations and giggles could be made out, but nothing very clear. Nothing distracting enough to take the team's minds off the girl on the toilet.

And so they sat there, grown-up, educated, professional people, waiting to watch a young woman empty her bladder and very possibly also her bowel. They all felt very stupid.

'Get on with it then, darling,' said Geraldine. 'You can't have stage fright after three weeks. We've all heard you piss before.'

'Maybe she's having a little cry or something,' said

212

Fogarty. 'She doesn't normally hang her head like that when she pees.'

'Somebody in the sweatbox pushed her a bit too far, do you think?' Geraldine replied eagerly. 'Well, we shall no doubt hear all about it in the confession box tomorrow.'

'She's just sitting like that 'cos she's drunk,' observed Pru, the assistant editor.

'Probably.'

Together they all continued to stare at the girl on the toilet. It was, after all, their job.

'That reminds me,' said Geraldine. 'I'm busting.' She had been in the bunker for many hours, drinking coffee almost continuously. 'Bet I'm back before she's been.' Geraldine rather prided herself on the efficiency of her physical functions.

'*And* I'm going to have a shit,' she remarked over her shoulder as she left. Geraldine knew how unpleasant her staff found her and she delighted in compounding it, surprising them by going further than even their grim expectations.

'Far, far too much information,' Fogarty said ruefully after Geraldine had left the room.

They waited in silence.

'I think she is upset,' said Pru.

'Who? Geraldine? I doubt it.'

'No, Kelly. She doesn't want a pee, she's just gone in there to get away, hasn't she?'

'Possibly, I suppose.'

'Well, she's not doing a wee, is she? She's just sitting there. She just wanted to get out of that sweatbox, but she knows if she does she'll forfeit the task and Geraldine will fine the group half their budget. The only way she can get a break is by pretending to have a pee.'

Shortly after this Geraldine returned and drew the same conclusion as Pru. 'She's skiving off,' Geraldine sneered. 'She's having a bunk. She's not *having* a piss, she's *taking* the piss, and I'm not putting up with that. I'm going to give her a Peeping Tom announcement to pee or get off the potty. Where's my voice? Where's Sam? I'm going to tell that young slapper to get her lovely body back in that sweatbox or pay the price.'

'Hang on,' said Pru. 'Something's happening.'

DAY TWENTY-NINE. 8.10 p.m.

The line of numbers at the bottom of the screen of the incident room television showed that it was 11.44. Eleven forty-four and twenty-one seconds, twenty-two seconds, twenty-three seconds.

Coleridge still found it difficult to watch, even after numerous viewings. He had heard that the whole sequence was already available on the Internet and had been downloaded many tens of thousands of times. As long as he lived Coleridge did not believe he would understand how a single race of beings could include both Jesus Christ and the sort of people who would download a video of a young woman being murdered. He rather supposed that had been the Messiah's point, but that didn't make it any easier to understand or accept.

He, Hooper and Trish watched as, while Kelly sat naked and unsuspecting on the toilet, at the other end of the house, in the boys' bedroom, the plastic flaps of the sweatbox moved. There was a sort of flurry of activity as a hidden figure swiftly gathered up one of the sheets that Peeping Tom had allowed for lavatory trips, spread it out to cover the entrance and on leaving the box enveloped his or her self in it. Try as they might, and using the best image-enhancement technology available, the police had been unable to gain any information whatsoever from that blurred bluish image. For a moment a hand was visible, but it was not possible to even tell if it was male or female, or even to say whether it wore a ring.

Then, carefully, covered from head to toe in the sheet, the hunched figure made its way out of the boys' bedroom and into the glaring tube lighting of the living area. From there it went to the kitchen units, where it provided the police with another tantalizing glimpse of hand as it reached into one of the kitchen drawers and took out the largest kitchen knife available, a beautiful Sabatier. Then, as the murmuring and giggling that emanated from inside the sweatbox continued gently to waft into the microphones, the cloaked figure crossed the rest of the living room, went into the utility area and approached the toilet door.

DAY TWENTY-SEVEN. 11.44 p.m.

'Who the fuck is that, then?' said Geraldine, watching the sheeted figure emerge from the boys' bedroom.

'Don't know,' said Pru and Fogarty together.

'Someone's having a laugh,' opined Fogarty. 'Going to scare Kelly.'

Now the figure crossed to the kitchen units and picked up the knife from the kitchen drawer.

'That I do not like,' said Geraldine. 'That is not funny.'

The figure was making its way towards the toilet now.

'They're all far too pissed for this type of nonsense,' said Geraldine. 'We need to make an announcement. Tell whichever silly cunt is in that sheet to stop fucking around and put that fucking knife back in the drawer before he gets us censored by the bleeding Standards Commission. Sam's not here. You do it, Pru, quick, bang the intercom on.'

215

But there was no time.

The figure in the sheet suddenly threw open the toilet door and swept inside.

Kelly must have seen her killer's face, but she was the only person who did. Every housemate knew the location of all the cameras intimately and whoever burst into that toilet knew that the only camera covering him was the one above the door. As he entered, he raised the sheet high above his head with both hands, one of which also held the knife. Kelly must have looked up in surprise, but it was not possible to see her expression in that final moment because the sheet was billowing above and behind the killer, cutting them both off from the view of the camera.

Now, as Geraldine and her editing team watched, the sheet seemed to fall downwards onto Kelly. This, it was to transpire, was the first plunge of the knife. The one that skewered Kelly's neck.

In the monitoring box they still thought it was a wind-up. They had no reason to think anything else.

'What *is* that cunt doing?' Geraldine said, as the billowing sheet raised itself up again before plunging down once more.

DAY TWENTY-NINE. 8.30 p.m.

'I think he had been planning on making only one blow,' said Coleridge. 'After all, he couldn't afford to get any blood on him.'

'Tough call, that, if you happen to be knifing somebody.'

'Just one huge blow, straight into the brain. Instant death.'

'And no geyser of blood.'

'Exactly, but the girl must have moved her head and he hit the neck.'

216

'Fortunately for him not the jugular.'

'No, not the jugular. He got away without getting marked, just.'

'One lucky bastard.'

Coleridge was forced to agree: the killer had indeed been one lucky bastard.

'I still say it would take a man to deliver a blow like that, and a strong one,' Hooper continued.

'It doesn't. We proved that,' said Trisha with a touch of impatience. She herself had spent an unpleasant afternoon at a local butcher's shop plunging knives into pigs' skulls.

'I know that a woman *could* have done it, but at what risk?' Hooper insisted. 'If the knife had got stuck in the bone of the skull, for instance – that happened with the pigs, Trish, half the times you tried it. What's more, the force required is huge, and there's no guard on a kitchen knife. You were wearing gloves, but your hand slipped occasionally. What if hers had done? She'd have cut off her own fingers. Kelly would have grabbed the sheet. It would have been all up. The chances of a woman pulling off a blow like that are quite small.'

'Except for Sally,' Coleridge said. Big, beefy Sally. The Internet's murderer of choice.

'Why on earth would Sally murder Kelly?' said Trish, a little too quickly.

'Why would any of them?' Coleridge answered. 'The only thing we can say for sure is that any one of them *could* have done it. The killer was right-handed and so are all of the remaining housemates. However, I concede that it is more *probable* that one of the stronger ones did it. Probably a man.'

They all turned back to the screen. The figure had thrown open the door at 11.44 and twenty-nine seconds. The first blow had fallen two and a half seconds later, the next and final one two seconds after that. The killer had been inside the lavatory for considerably less than ten seconds in all.

'If it wasn't all so damned clinical,' Coleridge observed, 'I would have said that the attack was frenzied.'

The tape played on. The killer had clearly taken two sheets from the pile when he left the sweatbox, for now as he raised himself up from making the second blow he threw one over his victim. The other one continued to cover him as he left the toilet.

'And you talked to the cameraman on duty, constable?' Coleridge enquired.

'Yes, I did, sir,' Trish replied, 'at length. His name is Larry Carlisle. He saw the figure in the sheet enter the lavatory and moments later he saw the figure emerge.' Trisha gathered up her case notes and quoted from the transcript of her interview with the cameraman . . .

' "I saw the figure follow the victim into the toilet at approximately twenty to midnight. He re-emerged shortly thereafter and headed back across the living area towards the boys' bedroom. I did not cover him with my camera as I had been instructed to continue to watch the toilet for Kelly in order to obtain more good nude footage. I remained there, watching the door, until the alarm was raised. I recall thinking that she was having a long time in the loo. I had only twenty minutes to go until my shift finished and I was beginning to think I'd have to leave her for the next bloke. Anyway, about four or five minutes after the figure in the sheet emerged, they all rushed down from the monitoring bunker, and you know the rest." '

'Four or five minutes?' said Coleridge when Trisha had finished reading.

'That's what he said.'

'According to the people in the box and the time codes it was no more than two.'

'I suppose if you're just standing staring at a door it would be easy to misjudge a period of time.'

'How long did he say elapsed between Kelly emerging from the bedroom and the killer following her?'

'He said two, but gets that wrong as well, because it was around five.'

Coleridge got out the big red ledger in which he kept his notes for the case and wrote down Carlisle's name and the discrepancies the man had made in his timings. Coleridge wrote in longhand, and it always seemed to take him about a week to complete a sentence.

DAY TWENTY-EIGHT. 7.00 p.m.

Geraldine's witness statement had arrived at the point of the murder. She told the same story as all the others. 'I saw the bloke in the sheet come out of the sweatbox, cross the living area, go into the toilet and kill Kelly.'

'How long would you say Kelly had been on the toilet before the killer emerged?' Coleridge asked.

'About four or five minutes, I think.'

'Did you actually see the murder?'

'Well, not actually, obviously, the sheet was in the way. We just saw the sheet billow up and down twice and wondered what was up. Then the bloke buggered off sharpish back to the sweatbox, leaving Kelly covered in his spare sheet.'

'You saw the sheeted figure return to the sweatbox and go inside it?'

'Yes, we all did.'

'What happened then?' Coleridge asked.

'We sat and watched. Kelly was still on the bog but covered in this sheet.'

'You didn't think that was strange?'

'Well, of course we thought it was fucking strange,

219

but the whole thing's fucking strange, isn't it? We didn't know what was happening. As far as we knew there'd been a bit of malarkey with the sheets, that was all. I mean, come on, inspector, we weren't *expecting* a murder, were we? I think we sort of presumed she'd fallen asleep. They were all completely pissed. It would have been strange if things *hadn't* been strange.'

'Then what?'

'Well, we saw the puddle, didn't we?'

'How long would that have been after the figure in the sheet had left the toilet?'

'I don't know. Five minutes, max.'

'Yes, that's what the operator in the camera run said.'

'Does it matter?'

'The editor and his assistants thought it was more like two.'

'Maybe it was, I don't know, it seemed like five minutes. Time drags a bit when you're sitting staring at a bird on a bog covered in a sheet. What's it say on the video time code?'

'Two minutes and eight seconds.'

'Well, you know, then. What are you asking me for?'

'So then you saw the puddle?'

'Yeah, suddenly we could see a wet sort of dark shiny glow spreading out from around the toilet.'

'Blood?'

'Well, we know that now, don't we?'

'It must have occurred to you then.'

'Well, of course it did, but it just seemed so impossible.'

'The sheet was already sodden with it. Why didn't you see that?'

'As you know, the sheet was dark blue. The stain didn't show up on the night camera. All the sheets in the house are dark colours. Our psychologist reckons it's more conducive to people having sex on them.'

'So what then?'

220

'Well, I'm embarrassed to say, inspector, that I screamed.'

DAY TWENTY-SEVEN. 10.00 p.m.

They had been inside the sweatbox for a few minutes now, waiting for their eyes to get used to the darkness. It was useless trying to see anything, however. The blackness was complete.

'Let's play truth or dare,' Moon's voice called out of the darkness.

'Dare?' said Dervla. 'Jesus, what more of a dare could we think of than this? We've already had to strip naked, for heaven's sake.'

'I can think of a few things,' Gazzer grunted.

'Well, keep them to yourself, Gaz,' Dervla replied, managing to make her voice sound almost prim, which was some achievement considering the situation they were all in. 'Because I'm not shaggin' any of yez.'

Dervla's voice and intonation were getting closer to Dublin with every syllable she spoke. She always took refuge in the comfort and protection of the tough, highly credible accent of her childhood when she felt vulnerable. 'Jesus, me mother'd kill me, so she would.'

'All right, then,' Moon conceded. 'Let's just play truth, then. Somebody ask a question.'

Now another voice rang out of the darkness, a voice that was jarring and bitter. 'What would be the fucking point of asking you to tell the truth, Moon?' It was Sally's voice, and it struck a disturbing note. Its hard, nasty edge cut through the drunken badinage.

'Hey, Sally,' Moon replied, angry and defensive. 'I were having a fookin' laugh, all right. Get over it, why don't you?'

'What's that, then?' Garry asked. 'What's been going on with you birds?'

221

'Ask Sally,' said Moon. 'She's the one who can't take a joke.'

But Sally remained silent. And would not get over it either. She had no intention of getting over it, ever. Moon had done a despicable thing. She had hijacked the terrible suffering of the abused and the mentally disturbed to score cheap points. One day Sally intended to make Moon aware of the offence that she had caused.

'Oh, fook it, then,' Moon continued, 'and fook you, Sally.'

There was a movement in the box. Somebody was leaving.

'Who's that?' Hamish asked.

'Who's got out?' said Jazz.

Sally was already outside the box. 'I'm going for a slash,' she said.

'Well, make sure you come back,' said Jazz. 'We all have to do this or we all fail.'

'I know,' Sally assured him.

In the monitoring box they watched as Sally came out of the boys' bedroom and crossed the living area to the toilet. Sally had not bothered to take up a sheet to cover herself, but Geraldine was less than thrilled.

'Well, not bad, I suppose, but she's hardly one of the lookers,' she moaned. 'And, anyway, we've seen her bloody great kajungas hundreds of times. What we need is Kelly or Dervo to give us a full frontal.'

Geraldine stared wearily at the screen. 'And I *do* wish she'd get that bikini line done. I mean, look at it. It's just not necessary. I've known lesbians with beautifully styled fur burgers.'

Bob Fogarty reached for a comforting pound or two of chocolate.

*

While Sally was away Moon resumed her theme. 'Come on, are we having a truth game or what? Let's have a juicy question.'

And of course Garry asked the inevitable one. 'All right. We all have to say who we'd shag in the house if we had to do it or die.'

'Dervla,' said Jazz, and as he said it he realized that he had responded rather embarrassingly quickly. He was rewarded with a chorus of 'Whoos'.

'Jazz fancies Dervo. Jazz fancies Dervo,' Kelly chanted drunkenly.

'Well, I'm very flattered, Jazz,' said Dervla, 'but as I said I'm not after looking for any nookie, so I'm not.'

'But if you were, Dervs,' Garry said, pressing his point. 'Who would it be?'

'You have to answer,' said Moon. 'We all have to answer.'

'Oh, all right, then,' Dervla replied. 'Jazz, I suppose, but only because he's been a gentleman and named me.'

'Me too, I'll have him after you've finished with him,' said Moon, ''cos I reckon you're dead fookin' lush, Jazz. I can say it in here because it's dark and I'm pissed and you can't see me going red, but at the end of the day I'd bang your fookin' brains out if I had a chance, so fair play to ya 'cos I think you're brilliant.'

'Bang his brains out? That'd take all of ten seconds!' shouted Garry.

'You're just jealous, Gazzer,' Jazz shouted back, 'because it's two nil to me! Two nil! Two nil! Two nil.' Jazz had turned his score into a chant.

Sally returned from the toilet. There was much groaning and giggling as she squeezed her way in among the naked bodies.

'I'll tell you one thing, Jazz,' she said. 'Listening to you and Gazzer I'm glad I'm a lesbian.'

'Yes, you'd better watch it, Jazz,' Dervla added. 'I'm thinking about changing my vote.'

'Well, I'll have Hamish, then,' Kelly shouted. 'Because he's a doctor and you've got to respect that, haven't you?'

Actually Kelly fancied Jazz, like all the other girls except Sally, but she nominated Hamish because she wanted to be nice to him. She had been feeling guilty about the strange half-formed suspicion that she had harboured after their drunken night together and in particular about the fact that she had spoken to Peeping Tom about the matter. Not in so many words, of course, but she had gone to the confession box to ask whether anything had happened, which was a pretty clear indication of what she was thinking. That had been really bad of her. It must have looked to everyone like she was worried that Hamish had attempted to take advantage of her drunken state. Kelly knew that was a pretty major thing to imply about anybody, particularly a doctor, and particularly since she had by now definitely decided in her mind that nothing untoward had occurred in Copulation Cabin that night. Kelly wanted to make amends, and she reckoned by naming him as her preferred partner she was making clear that she harboured no further suspicions.

Hamish was thrilled. He had noted Kelly's unscheduled trip to the confession box and had been horribly disturbed by it. Now, however, he knew that he was safe. Kelly had named him as her partner of choice, and if she had been harbouring any suspicions about his character or conduct she would scarcely have done that, would she?

'Besides which,' Kelly continued, 'doctors have such sensitive hands, and a girl does love a gentle touch.'

Garry and Jazz cheered drunkenly. Hamish gulped at the hot salty air. *'Sensitive hands'*? . . . *'gentle touch'*? Was it a coincidence? Did she know? Had she been conscious all along and enjoying his . . . his explorations, his . . . *digital penetration*? It was possible surely, after all Kelly was quite a wild one. Hamish smiled broadly, a big happy smile which nobody could see. It was all going to be all right, maybe even better than all right. Maybe he might even get another chance at her.

'Cheers, Kelly!' Hamish shouted out. 'I'm deeply flattered and most certainly reciprocate the nomination.'

'And I shall join you, my son,' Garry shouted. 'No offence to the other girls, but it's got to be Kelly, ain't it? I mean just for the knockers alone.'

'Forget it, Garry,' Hamish replied. 'Personally I'm not into threesomes.'

'Listen to these two!' Kelly shrieked. 'I'm being fought over, girls. I think it's dead romantic.' Which, considering she was sitting naked in a communal sweatbox, showed how drunk Kelly had become.

'What about you, then, Sally?' Jazz asked. 'Who'd you have if you had to have someone?'

'I'd have Dervla, thank you very much,' Sally replied quietly. 'I think we'd make a lovely couple at the next Pride Festival.'

'Well, I'm delighted and flattered,' said Dervla from somewhere in the darkness. 'I think that's a terribly sweet thing to say, Sally, and if I batted for your team I should take you up on the offer without further ado.'

'All *right*!' shouted Garry. 'Can I watch?'

'So you've got two nominations then, Dervo,' said Jazz. 'Impressive score, girl. Equal to the Jazz meister.'

'Do lezzo votes count, then?' asked Garry. 'I mean, I'm not being homo whatsit or nothing, but I'd have thought they'd be in a different category, wouldn't they?'

'What absolute rubbish, Garry,' snapped Dervla, 'and you are being homo whatsit.'

'No way,' Garry defended himself. 'I'm a big supporter of lesbian love. I could watch it all day. In fact

225

I've got some excellent videos if anyone's interested, for when we all get out.'

This comment put Kelly in mind of David and her little secret bit of knowledge about him. So Garry collected porn. She wondered whether he had any of the *Fuck Orgy* series. 'Who do you nominate, then, David?' she asked.

'To have sex with, out of our little group?' David replied, his voice being heard in the pitch-black sweatbox for the first time. 'Why, who else but myself? For me sex is nothing without love and commitment, and you all know that I love no one on this earth so much as I love *moi.*'

They all laughed, as David had hoped they would. He was perfectly well aware that he must have been coming across to the public as extremely vain. He always came across as extremely vain, and the reason for this was because he *was* extremely vain. But the funny thing about David's vanity was that it was both his most irritating and his most charming feature. There was something almost endearing or at least comical about how much David loved himself, and as people got to know him they began to see the fun in it. David hoped that this would work for him in the house. All his life he had progressed from being the one people simply hated, through being the one people loved to hate, until eventually ending up being a person people hated themselves for loving. It was a complex equation, but it was pretty much how things worked socially for David, and he thought he might have a similar relationship with the public. He imagined that his little joke about sex with himself (should it be broadcast) would do much to improve his standing with the voting public. David was an acquired taste, and he believed that once the penny dropped with people that he *knew* how vain he was, they would start to like him more.

'Not bad, not bad,' said Geraldine crouching over the monitoring controls. 'At least they're talking about sex. Got some lovely stuff to broadcast there. I loved David's wanking joke. He's really coming into his own. Might put a few quid on him to make the final three. Wouldn't that be a surprise?'

'I hope they continue to speak up,' the sound editor said. 'Don't forget they aren't wearing their radio mikes. We're relying on the ones dropping from the ceiling.'

'I know that, but what could we do? You can't fit bloody battery packs onto naked people. They'd get in the way. Besides, what would you hang the mikes off?'

'All right, come on, then,' said Moon. 'Another truth question. Who's got one, then? Here, I've got one. Has anybody ever paid for sex?'

'Fahkin' hell, Moon,' Gazzer laughed. 'I've paid for it the next day all right, when I told the girlfriend I'd just knocked off her sister or her best mate or whatever.'

'No, I mean paid money for gratification. Been with a tart or summat.'

The reason Moon was asking became clear with her next comment. 'All right, then. Who's ever *been* paid for sex, because I know I fookin' 'ave.'

This revelation definitely caused a flurry of interest.

'I'm not proud of it or anything, but at the end of the day I needed the money, right. I were doing arts and social studies at Preston uni, when it was the poly, and I hadn't got the fees, and I were fooked if I was going to stand behind a bar all night making the same money I could get in twenty minutes lying on my back.'

Everyone was enjoying themselves except Sally. She hated Moon so much, her endless boasting and story-telling. So what if she'd been a prostitute? Who cared? Besides, Sally didn't believe it. She didn't believe

227

anything that Moon said any more, and she never ever would again.

'I've been in a porn movie,' Kelly said. 'Does that count as being paid for sex?'

Silent in the darkness, David tensed. Where was she going with this?

'Well, it depends if you've actually done it for the camera or not,' Garry said. 'I've got this film, it's called *LA 100* and all it is, right, you'll never believe this, but it's true. All it is is this bird shagging *a hundred* blokes in a row. Can you believe that! I couldn't till I saw it. One after the other. In you go, my son, wallop, thank you very much, lovely jubbly, we like that! Next!'

'I don't believe it,' said Dervla. 'You couldn't shag a hundred times, it would be impossible.'

'No, no, honest. It was all kosher, they had authentic adjudicators with clipboards and everything. This bird really did do the ton. And at the end of the day, fair play to her, I say.'

'Yeah, well, I never actually had sex in the movie I did,' Kelly conceded. 'I wouldn't do that. You can forget it, they're all such sleazy bastards, those porn actors. You wouldn't risk it. I was just an extra, you know, a pair of knockers in the background. I had to kiss this other girl's nipples, but that was it and we just had a laugh about it, but there was plenty of them actually at it, let me tell you, and it was disgusting: shagging and sucking and slobbering and all. The star took it both ways at the same time. I could not believe it, *both ways*, bonking and being bonked. I mean, come on.'

'Not easy rhythmically, I would imagine,' Jazz opined. 'I should think you'd need a metronome, or there could be a nasty pile-up.'

'You wouldn't know whether you was coming or going!' Garry roared, and they all roared with him.

Except David. Where is she going with this? he was

thinking, his fists clenched with tension. *Where is she going with this?*

'He was called Boris Pecker, and he just stood there poking away at these girls in front of him while he got poked at by these blokes from behind him. Unbelievable, it was.'

David was already sweating profusely, but if it were possible he actually began to sweat a little more. Was she about to reveal all? Was this common, ignorant cow going to give him away? David longed to reach out into the darkness and shut that big fat mouth up before it could say any more. He longed to gag it, to ram it shut, to silence it for good.

It was obvious to David that Kelly was directing her remarks at him, and it was a bitter blow. He had almost begun to relax about that whispered moment of recognition that they had shared together in the hot tub. It had shocked him deeply at the time, but as the days wore on and she did not mention it again he had started to imagine that perhaps he had heard her wrong, or at the very least that his secret was safe with her.

And now . . .

Now she was teasing him, no, *taunting* him, with her knowledge of his secret, the secret that could destroy his dreams for ever.

Because there was only one thing in David's life that really mattered to him and that was his acting. All he had ever wanted, all he ever would want, was to be an actor, a celebrated actor, of course, a star. At one time in his life, just after he had left RADA, it had almost seemed as if this dream might come true. He had won prizes, got some decent first jobs, and his talent was spoken of highly amongst influential casting agents. But somehow it hadn't lasted. While others in his graduation class had found their way to the National Theatre, the RSC, and even Hollywood, his flame had sputtered and dimmed.

But David still believed from the depths of his soul that he had a fighting chance. He *was* a good actor, his was surely a talent too rare to go unnoticed for ever. What was more, he was handsome, achingly handsome. All he needed was a break, and that was why he had applied to join *House Arrest*. He knew, of course, that it was a pretty desperate final gambit, but he was a pretty desperate man, a *completely* desperate man, in fact.

After *House Arrest* David would be a telly name. He simply could not believe that this would not get him *somewhere*, a nice little Shakespearean lead at the Glasgow Citizen's, or perhaps the West Yorkshire Playhouse . . . and then, if the notices were good, a short London transfer would follow . . . and then . . . then he would be back on track!

Back on track to catch up with all the bastards from his year who were doing so much better than he was. Back on track to be able to open the arts pages of the newspapers once more without having to curse every single fucking profile of some bastard ten years younger than him who had just redefined the art of playing Shakespeare in a promenade production in a garden shed on the Isle of Dogs.

But none of this would *ever* happen if people knew that David Dalgleish, actor, artist, man who took no job unworthy of his talent, was in fact none other than Boris Pecker! Olivia Newton Dong! *Ivor Biggun!*

Then he would be a laughing stock. 'Porn star' was not a label it was possible to shake off, particularly not the type of porn star that he had been, a fuck and suck man. Oh, certainly, a little bit of Polanski or Ken Russell early in one's career was fine. Without doubt one could bare one's youthful arse for a name director with impunity; it was actually considered rather classy. Even an early dabble in soft core classics was survivable, particularly if you were a girl. A daringly graphic *Lady Chatterley* rarely did any harm, nor did a corsets-off *Fanny Hill.*

But not *Fuck Orgy Eleven.*

Not *The Banging Man.*

Not . . . *Pussy Picnic.*

David wondered where Kelly was sitting. It was difficult to tell inside the hot, rank darkness. It crossed his mind that if he could reach her, he could strangle her where she sat and nobody would notice.

That would shut the bitch up.

But Kelly did not need shutting up, not immediately, anyway, because as time ticked on in the darkness of the sweatbox she made no further mention of David's secret. She had been having a laugh, teasing him. He certainly deserved a bit of winding-up. Kelly's inside knowledge did not have remotely the significance for her that it had for him. She had no idea of the emotional turmoil and hatred that she was causing, and soon the conversation moved on.

Now a series of fumbling, stumbling drinking games developed. Much booze was drunk and even more was spilt as the plastic bottles were passed about in the darkness. The alcohol hissed and steamed as it dripped between the hot wooden floorboards and onto the heating units beneath. It turned the sweatbox into a kind of sauna, using wine and spirits to create the steam instead of water.

David began to relax a little, but only a little. He believed that Kelly had been warning him, warning him to be nice to her and not to nominate her. Showing him that she held his future in her hands and that she could deploy her weapon whenever she chose. Well, if that was the case, David thought, she was playing a dangerous game. He was a proud man. He could not and would not put up with being blackmailed, particularly by a know-nothing nonentity like Kelly. But he would have to bide his time.

The drinking continued. There were songs and jokes, nice ones and dirty ones, some too dirty even for Geraldine to be able to broadcast.

And the atmosphere was slowing down. Slowing down and heating up. The heat, the booze and the housemates' utter disorientation in the darkness were beginning to take their toll. People were getting lazier and bolder, their defences were evaporating like the alcohol that was dripping onto the heaters.

'OK, then, let's see how well we *really* know each other, eh?' said Jazz in a hoarse, slurred voice. 'We're all mixed up and totally out of it, right? So everybody feel about with their left hand and when they touch someone, they have to identify them, right? But just by feel – no talking till you know.'

A mighty, boozy cheer greeted this suggestion, although, drunk as she was, Dervla was not too sure about it. However, everybody else seemed to be greeting the idea with such enthusiasm that she felt bound to go along with it. She did not want to end up on everybody's nomination list for being a killjoy and a prude.

'OK,' said Jazz. 'Everybody knows where I am 'cos I've been talking and I would like to be identified by my donga, not my voice, on account of the fact that I'm hung like a Derby winner, so I'm just going to slide around a bit, mix us all up good, right? Then let the feeling begin. Here I go, these are the last words I will say . . .'

There were drunken cheers, whoops and groans as the others felt Jazz's smooth, taut, sweating body moving about inside the tight, slippery little group of cramped and naked forms.

The observers in the monitoring bunker could scarcely contain their excitement. The translucent plastic walls of the sweatbox bulged and heaved. Even in the eerie blue light of the night cameras there were clearly discernible body parts constantly emerging and then disappearing in the shapes in the plastic. Elbows, heads, buttocks – sexy, exciting buttocks. There seemed to be a real possibility of an orgy developing.

'We should have made the plastic completely transparent,' Geraldine drooled. 'The sad cunts would have stood for it too, except Saint fucking Dervla, of course.'

'I don't agree,' Fogarty replied. 'Firstly, we couldn't have broadcast it if we'd done that. Secondly, it would have been all steamed up anyway, and thirdly, it wouldn't have been half as exciting even if we could see, because it's the anonymity that's so intoxicating. We don't know who's who and nor do they.'

'When I want your opinion, Bob, I'll ask for it.'

Inside the box the darkness was as intense as the excitement. Dervla felt Jazz slide across her. She felt his taut skin and beautiful rock-hard muscles against her own bare flesh.

'My God,' she thought. 'He doesn't know it's me he's sliding over.'

Jazz was pretending to be a snake, hissing and writhing. She could feel his muscular stomach in her lap as he giggled and wriggled across her and then . . . then she felt his penis dragging across her thighs, big and heavy, obviously already semi-hard. She could not resist it. Through the darkness she placed her hand in its path, palm upwards, deliberately letting him glide into it.

Then very gently she squeezed. It felt wonderful in that coal-black anonymity to be doing something so outrageous. She could feel herself sweating all the more as Jazz stopped his wriggling and slithering for a moment and allowed the object of her attentions to grow bigger and harder in her hand. In that moment, for Dervla, Jazz was no longer the beery-leery jack-the-lad fly-boy king of clubbing cool that she knew and was beginning to rather like, he was a Greek or a Roman God, a living, breathing version of all those wonderful works of art she saw on her summer holidays in Europe. He was a fantastical night-time love muse.

Then she heard his voice and of course it was only Jazz. 'Is that you, Kelly, you naughty, naughty slapper, you?'

'What?' said Kelly's voice from the vicinity of Jazz's feet.

'Ah,' said Jazz. 'So not Kelly, then.'

Dervla gave a tiny gasp and let go, shocked at her audacity!

She had been gripping Jazz's penis! That was terrible! Absolutely terrible. She would have to face him at breakfast in the morning! Her, the chief objector to crudity. The Lady High and Mighty. The good girl of the group. What if he knew it was her?

He did know.

Her tiny gasp had given her away. Even amongst the general grunting and giggling, Jazz had caught its tone.

'Who, then, I wonder,' he said, and then he sang a line of 'When Irish eyes are smiling.'

Dervla felt herself go crimson in the darkness. What if he told Peeping Tom? What if he went into the confession box and told the nation that she had grabbed his penis in the darkness and squeezed it until it was hard? Then her thoughts were interrupted, because Gazzer made them all roar with laughter.

'Fuck me, I'm glad Woggle ain't in here!'

Everybody shrieked. It was such a terrible, terrible, madly hilarious thought, to be stuck in a crowded sweatbox with Woggle. To have to feel him, smell him.

Dervla laughed too, and suddenly she didn't care about having touched Jazz. In fact she was proud of it. She hoped he did tell. She knew the other inmates

234

thought her a prude, and it was certain that the public thought so too. It wouldn't do her chances of winning any harm at all to add a bit of generous, good-humoured ladette behaviour to the mix. Jazz thought that she was beautiful, he had made that clear often enough, and she *was* beautiful.Why shouldn't she touch his dick? He had loved it, it had made him hard. And the truth was she had loved it too, it had felt terrific. Having that big, strong, veiny piece of male flesh in her small soft hand had turned her on like a tap. As the waves of laughter that had greeted Gazzer's observation began to recede, Dervla topped them.

'Hey, Jazz,' she called out jubilantly into the darkness. 'I just felt your willy!'

'Any time, fine lady, any time!' Jazz shouted back and again they all roared.

In the camera corridor the one operator on duty recoiled as if he had been electrocuted.

Larry Carlisle had been covering the entrance to the sweatbox viewed across the living room and through the open door of the boys' bedroom, which had been left slightly ajar. Now, as he twitched involuntarily, the lens of his camera swung wildly upwards covering, for a moment, nothing more interesting than the ceiling. Fortunately for Carlisle nobody in the monitoring bunker was watching his camera feed at that moment because a much better picture of the shadowy box was being supplied by the remote hot-heads in the bedroom itself. Quickly Carlisle regained control of his camera and returned its focus to the proper place.

But he still had to struggle to stop his hand from shaking on the controls. Carlisle could scarcely contain his bitter anger. *His girl*, the gorgeous but prudish girl behind the mirror, the girl who was so careful to never show *him* anything, had just gripped the black one's cock! It was outrageous, it was disgusting. It was a betrayal of the purity of the relationship that they had established together.

They shrieked, they laughed, they whooped. Nobody could quite believe that Dervla had been the first to get so specifically raunchy. It emboldened them all, seeming to give the whole game genuine class.

The cleverer, more manipulative people in the box realized that Dervla's sudden sexiness was a pretty clever trick in terms of the public's perception of her. There was nothing that kept up audience interest better than surprises, particularly sexual ones, and Dervla's grabbing of Jazz had certainly been that. Moon, David, Hamish and Garry all realized that Dervla had raised the stakes and they would have to lift their game accordingly.

Moon decided then and there that she would later confess to Peeping Tom that she had had intercourse inside the box and had no idea with whom it had been. She resolved to admit to this whether it had happened or not, but actually she thought it probably would happen, because now the touching and feeling began with a vengeance.

'So are we going to play this identification game or what?' shouted Jazz.

'Yes!' came the reply.

'OK, then, go for it!' Jazz shouted. 'Everybody move around and nobody talk, OK? And when you've had a really good squirm, cop a feel and guess who you've got.'

Suddenly it was all shrieks and giggles and boozy lust as they slipped about together.

Hamish was almost beside himself with excitement. This was the reason he had come into the house. Like Moon, he wanted to have sex, and then he wanted everyone to know about it. With Kelly, preferably, but frankly any female partner would do. He felt a hand stroking his back, gently teasing his sweaty spine, gently running all the way down to the cleft of his buttocks. Was this the one? Should he turn about and try to make love to whoever was touching him?

He heard a whisper in his ear. 'Sally?' It was David's voice.

'You've been in this house too long, mate,' Hamish whispered back.

'Fuck!' David barked, snatching his hand away as if Hamish was a red-hot stove.

'Shhh!' whispered Jazz from nearby.

David was annoyed. His mistake made him feel vulnerable. He wondered if Kelly had heard. All his doubts flooded back once more. Was she laughing at him in the darkness? Was she thinking to herself that Boris Pecker would not have minded at all who he found himself feeling up? Would she tell? Would she suddenly blurt it out and tell? David wanted to leave the sweatbox there and then, he wanted to run. But perhaps that in itself might provoke Kelly.

'Funny how he couldn't take a bit of sex,' she would say. 'I would have thought it would have been right up his street.'

'Up his arse, more like,' Gazzer would say after Kelly had explained, and then David would be a laughing stock, a national joke. David decided he had better stay put. He reached for one of Geraldine's artfully placed plastic bottles of warm, strong booze and drank deep.

Hamish was not going to make the mistake that David had made. It was a woman's thigh he was holding, for sure. So soft and smooth and not too firm. Kelly? he thought. Possibly, but just as easily Dervla or even Moon. Not Sally, he was delighted to conclude, and probably not small enough for Dervla, but you couldn't be sure. Whoever it belonged to it was fun to touch and squeeze. Hamish was feeling much better about himself now. Kelly's kind gesture earlier in the game had truly put his mind at rest, and now he felt safe and powerful and ready for anything.

He let his hand slip around from the outside to the inside of the thigh that he was holding. The flesh was hot and slightly clammy, it seemed almost to tug gently at his fingertips as he slid them across it. Whoever's thigh it was, and he was sure now it wasn't Dervla's, she seemed quite happy to be touched. Her opposite leg was moving, her other inner thigh gently brushing against the back of Hamish's hand. Hamish's lips brushed against a soft shoulder. He kissed it.

There were hands on Hamish now. Someone was stroking his buttocks, but he ignored it. The girl he was holding was the one he wanted.

Kelly was now very drunk. As drunk as she had been the week before, when she had passed out. She had had to get drunk in order to get into the sweatbox, and she knew that if she didn't get into the sweatbox she would lose the game. Now that she was inside and this hand was touching her she no longer really felt a part of her body, it was as if she was hovering above it and some other Kelly was being touched and caressed. It was not an unpleasant feeling, just slightly detached and uninvolved. This was how Kelly always felt about sex, possibly because she was always drunk when she did it. She liked sex, she was pretty sure of that, but somehow she always ended up wishing that she liked it more. Secretly she was sure that the missing ingredient was love, and she knew that she would have to wait for that. You couldn't plan it.

The hand was being more daring now, working its way up to the very top of her thigh. Kelly didn't *think* she minded, although she knew that she would probably stop him quite soon, whoever he was. On the other hand, why not let him play? This was what you did, wasn't it? If you were a top bird, a mad-for-it, gagging-for-it personality like she was? You didn't bottle out.

That wasn't what it was about at all, was it? You went for it, you lived it large. One thing you weren't was a killjoy.

Now the hand was brushing at Kelly's most intimate self. Now she would stop him, move the hand away. But she didn't. She had become distracted. Something in her memory was stirring.

Hamish moved his hand and touched the little metal ring hidden within the folds of Kelly's private flesh. And now he knew who it was he was touching. He was thrilled: this was who he had hoped it would be: Kelly, the one he fancied most, the one who had named him as her choice if sex were on the agenda. Well, sex was on the agenda. This was his chance.

He found her ear and whispered into it and as he whispered he gave the little ring the gentlest of flicks with his finger.

'Kelly,' he said, with a big broad smile.

And at that moment, in that very instant, they both knew.

Kelly was certain that she had not told a soul about her pierced labia, not even the girls. She had been specifically holding the information back to use as a triumphant, sexy revelation at some strategic moment later in the game, when she felt the need to shine.

But the voice in her ear knew. The voice of Hamish. *Hamish* knew because the moment he had touched that tiny wire he had whispered her name. And now Kelly saw the truth. The bastard had touched her vagina before. The half-formed suspicions that had troubled her aching head the morning that she had woken up in that horrible little sex cabin were suddenly turned to cast-iron facts.

'My God!' Kelly breathed, momentarily more surprised than angered. 'You felt me up when I was passed out. You fingered me. You knew I was pierced.' Her voice was a whisper; the shock of the revelation was still sinking in. All of the other people in the box were busy with their own affairs.

Nobody heard her. *Nobody heard.*

Like Kelly, Hamish had realized the moment that he said it, in the instant that he breathed those two give-away syllables 'Kell-y', that he had made a terrible, terrible mistake. But as yet it was still a secret. Only they knew; the others were all too busy with their own giggling, their own fumbling.

'Please,' Hamish pleaded into Kelly's ear. 'Don't tell them.'

But in the way her body recoiled from him he knew that she would. How could she not? Why *should* she not? She would tell the others, she would tell the world, and he would be finished. Of course, he would deny it, it was her word against his, but people liked Kelly, they would believe her. The minimum he could expect was national shame, and the worst . . . prosecution for sexual assault. For *digital penetration*. His career was over, that was for sure. Doctors could not afford that kind of scandal. What woman would trust him with her body now?

He almost laughed. Here they all were, pawing at each other like animals in muck, and he was in danger of being prosecuted for sexual assault! Hamish's blind black vision turned red with fury. The slag! The disgusting fucking slag! She had been happy enough to let him feel her up just then, to let him *finger* her. And yet now she would ruin him utterly for having done exactly the same thing before.

Hamish's rush of fear and fury were fully matched by what Kelly was feeling. She was outraged, disgusted. She wanted to be sick. This bastard had mauled her while she lay unconscious! Put his hand *inside her*. Had he raped her? He could have raped her. Probably not, Kelly's fevered brain was telling her. If he had raped her she would have known, for sure. But would she? Perhaps he was small, perhaps he had been very careful. She remembered the sensation with which she had woken up. That discomfort, the sudden over-whelming urge to dive into the pool. Had he *put it in her*? How would she ever know?

'Please, don't tell,' Hamish whispered once more, and suddenly his hand was at her mouth.

Now Kelly was struggling to get out of the sweatbox, pushing herself through the laughing, groping bodies that surrounded her, trying to find the exit flaps.

'She's getting out!' thought Hamish. 'What will the bitch do?'

David was also aware that it was Kelly who was rushing for the exit. Kelly, the woman who with her special knowledge of him held his fate in her hands . . . *The bitch*, the one who had been taunting him. 'What's on her mind?' he thought. 'What will the cow do?'

Kelly passed Dervla in her panting, sweating struggle to get out. Dervla knew it was Kelly, because she could hear her hurried breathing. To Dervla's mind she sounded excited, almost triumphant. What had she to be so excited about? Dervla thought about the message that she had read in the mirror that morning. '*The bitch Kelly still number one.*'

Did Kelly know that she was number one? That she was winning? Was that why she was so excited? Dervla felt a massive surge of irritation towards the silly young woman who was squirming across her. What was so special about Kelly? She wasn't particularly bright, her morals were not very impressive, her dress sense was questionable and yet there she was, seem-ingly unmovable in the lead. All the confidence that Dervla had felt before about playing a longer game than Kelly evaporated. Kelly was going to win.

She was going to grab all the fame and she was going to grab the half-million quid, too. The half-million quid, about which Dervla had privately been dreaming since the day her application had been accepted. The half-million quid that would save her family . . . her beloved mother and father, her darling little sisters, from disaster.

Dervla wondered why Kelly was running out so suddenly and so breathlessly. What was she up to?

Sally shrank back into the corner of the sweatbox in which she had been hiding since almost the moment she had entered it, pushing away any hands or limbs that intruded on her space. Sally pushed Kelly away as she passed, and as she did so Sally thought to herself, 'That girl's in a hurry to get out of the sweatbox.' And with that thought, despite the heat, Sally's blood ran cold. For a memory had come upon her and claimed her for its own. It was the memory of her mother, on the only occasion in her life when Sally had ever spoken to her, sitting behind a glass screen speaking through an intercom.

'I don't know why a person like me does the things she does,' Sally's mother's voice had crackled. 'You just get stuck in the dark box and then it happens.' Suddenly Sally believed she knew how her mother had felt. She too was stuck in the black box. The black box was real.

Gazzer was thinking the same thing that he always felt about Kelly. He kept it well hidden, but one day he intended to get even with that bitch. Inside the house or out he would pay her back for what she had implied about his little lad, his wonderful Ricky. Telling the whole nation that he was a selfish, scrounging, absent father who didn't give a fuck. That was basically what she had implied. Well, Gazzer would show her. Sooner, or later. Or sooner.

Kelly was past them all and out. She gulped down the fresher, cooler air that hit her as she emerged from the flaps of the sweatbox, and, with her bile still rising in her throat, she rushed out of the boys' room and headed for the toilet.

A few minutes later Geraldine and her editing team watching the monitoring screens saw somebody appear at the front of the sweatbox, swathe themself in a sheet and follow Kelly to the toilet, pausing only to pick up a knife.

And kill her.

DAY TWENTY-SEVEN. 11.46 p.m.

'Oh my God! Oh, please God, no!'

It was unlike Geraldine to ask assistance from anybody, least of all the Almighty, but these were, of course, very special circumstances. The puddle on the floor around Kelly had suddenly appeared and was spreading rapidly.

'Fogarty, you and Pru come with me. You too!' Geraldine barked at one of the runners. 'The rest of you stay here.'

Geraldine and her colleagues rushed out of the monitoring bunker and down the stairs into the tunnel which ran under the moat, connecting the production complex to the house. From the tunnel they were able to gain access to the camera runs and from these runs there were entrances to every room in the house.

Larry Carlisle, the duty cameraman, heard a noise behind him. Later he was to explain to the police that he had been expecting to see his relief clocking on early, and had been about to turn and tell the next man not to run and make such a clatter when Geraldine and half the editing team had rushed past.

'Through the store room!' Geraldine barked, and in a moment she and her colleagues found themselves blinking in the striplit glare of the house interior. Later they were all to recall how strange it felt, even in that moment of panic, to be there inside the house. None of them had entered the house since the inmates had taken it over and now they felt like scientists who had suddenly found themselves on a petri dish along with the bugs they had been studying.

Geraldine took a deep breath and opened the toilet door.

DAY TWENTY-EIGHT. 7.20 p.m.

'Why did you pull the sheet off?' Coleridge asked. 'You must know that it's wrong to disturb the scene of a crime.'

'It's also wrong to ignore an injured person in distress. I didn't know she was dead, did I? I didn't even know there'd been a crime, as a matter of fact. I didn't know anything. Except that there was blood everywhere, or something that looked like blood. If I really try to remember what I was thinking at the time, inspector, I honestly still think that I half hoped it was a joke, that somehow the inmates had managed to turn the tables on me for letting them down over Woggle.'

Coleridge pressed play. The cameras had recorded everything: the little group of editors standing outside the toilet, Geraldine reaching in and pulling at the sheet. Kelly being revealed still sitting on the toilet, slumped forward, her shoulders resting on her knees. A large dark pool, flowing from the wounds in her neck and skull, growing on the floor. Kelly's feet in the middle of the pool, a flesh-coloured island growing out of a lake of red.

And, worst of all, the handle of the Sabatier kitchen knife sticking directly out of the top of Kelly's head, the blade buried deep in her skull.

'It was all so weird, like a cartoon murder or something,' Geraldine said. 'I swear with that knife hilt sticking out of her head she looked like a fucking

244

Teletubby. For a quarter of a second I *still* wondered whether we were being had.'

DAY TWENTY-SEVEN. 11.47 p.m.

'Give me your mobile!' Geraldine barked at Fogarty, her voice shrill but steady.

'What . . . What?' Bob Fogarty's eyes were fixed on the horrifying crimson vision before him, the knife. The knife in the *skull*.

'Give me your mobile phone, you dozy cunt!' Geraldine snatched Fogarty's little Nokia from the pouch at his belt.

But she could not turn it on; her hand was shaking too much. She looked up at the live hot-head that was still impassively recording the scene. 'Somebody in the edit suite call the fucking police! . . . Somebody watching on the Internet! Do something useful for once in your crap lives! Call the fucking police!'

And so it was that the world was alerted to one of the most puzzling and spectacular murders in anybody's memory or experience: by thousands of Internet users jamming the emergency services switchboards and, failing to get through, calling the press.

At the same time, at the scene of the crime, Geraldine seemed unsure what to do next.

'Is she . . . dead?' said Pru, who was peering over Fogarty's shoulder, trying to keep the bile from rising in her throat.

'Prudence,' said Geraldine, 'she's got a kitchen knife stuck through her fucking brain.'

'Yes, but we should check all the same,' stammered Pru.

'You fucking check,' said Geraldine.

But at this point Kelly saved them from further speculation about her state of health by keeling off the toilet seat and falling to the floor. She went head first, pulled forward over her knees by the weight of her own head. This resulted in her butting the floor with the handle of the knife, which buried the blade another inch or two into her head, as if it had been hit by a hammer. It made a sort of creaking sound which caused both Pru and Fogarty to be sick.

'Oh, great. Fucking brilliant,' Geraldine said. 'So let's just throw up all over the scene of the crime, shall we? The police are going to fucking love us.'

Perhaps it was the idea of what people might think of them that led Geraldine to turn once more to the watching cameras. 'You lot in the box. Switch off the Internet link. This isn't a freak show.'

But it was a freak show, of course, a freak show that had only just begun.

'What the fuck's going on?' It was Jazz, emerging from the boys' bedroom, a sheet stuck to his honed, toned and sweaty body. What with his sheet and his muscley physique, Jazz looked like Dervla's fantasy of him, a Greek God startled on Mount Olympus. He could not have looked more ridiculously out of place if he had tried.

Jazz stood on the threshold of the room staring, stunned by the bright lights and the extraordinary and unexpected presence of intruders in a house that he and his fellow inmates had had exclusive use of for weeks.

Dervla appeared behind him. She too had taken up a sheet and looked equally out of place staring at the casually dressed intruders, behind whom was the corpse. It was beginning to look as if a toga party had crashed into a road accident.

Geraldine realized that the situation was about to spiral out of control. She did not like situations that were out of control; she was a classic example of that tired old phrase, 'the control freak'. 'Jason!

246

Dervla!' she shouted. 'Both of you get back in the boys' bedroom!'

'What's happening?' Dervla said. Fortunately for them neither she nor Jazz could see into the lavatory. The gruesome sight was blocked from them by the cluster of people at its doorway.

'This is Peeping Tom!' Geraldine shouted. 'There has been an accident. All house inmates are to remain in the boys' bedroom until told otherwise. Get inside! NOW!'

Astonishingly, such was the hostage mentality that had developed amongst the housemates that Jazz and Dervla did as they were told, returning to the darkness of the boys' bedroom, where the others were emerging from the sweatbox, hot, naked and confused.

'What's going on?' David asked.

'I don't know,' Dervla replied. 'We're to stay in here.'

Then somebody in the edit suite took it upon themselves to turn on all the lights in the house. The seven inmates were caught almost literally in the headlights. They stood around the redundant sweatbox blinking at each other, naked, reaching for sheets, blankets, towels, anything to cover their red-skinned, sweaty embarrassment, memories of the previous two wild hours turning their hot red faces still redder. It was as if they were all fourteen years old and had been caught in the process of a mass snog by their parents.

'Oh my God, we look *so* stupid,' said Dervla.

Outside, Geraldine was taking charge. Later on it was generally agreed that, having got over her shock, she had acted with remarkable cool-headedness.

Having confined the seven remaining inmates to one room, she ordered everybody to retrace their steps and do everything possible to avoid further altering the scene of the crime.

'We'll stand in the camera run,' she said, 'and wait for the cops.'

DAY TWENTY-EIGHT. 6.00 a.m.

Six hours later, as Coleridge left the scene of the crime, the light was beginning to break on an unseasonably grim and drizzly morning.

'Murder weather,' he thought. All of his homicide investigations seemed to have taken place in the rain. They hadn't, of course, just as his boyhood summer holidays had not all been bathed in endless cleansing sunshine. None the less, Coleridge did have a vague theory that atmospheric pressure played a tiny role in igniting a killer's spark. Premeditated murder was, in his experience, an indoor sport.

From beyond the police barriers hundreds of flash-bulbs exploded into life. For a moment Coleridge wondered who it might be that had caused such a flurry of interest. Then he realized that the photographs were being taken of him. Trying hard not to look like a man who knew he was being photographed, Coleridge walked through the silver mist of half-hearted rain and flickering strobe light towards his car.

Hooper was waiting for him with a bundle of morning papers. 'They're all basically the same,' he said.

Coleridge glanced at the eight faces splashed across every front page, one face set apart from the others. He had just met the owners of those faces. All but Kelly, of course. He had not met her, unless one could be said to have met a corpse. Looking at that poor young woman curled up on the toilet floor, actually stuck to it with her own congealed and blackened blood, a kitchen knife sticking out of the top of her head, Coleridge knew how much he wanted to catch this killer. He could not abide savagery. He had never got used to it; it scared him and made him question his faith. After all, why would any sane God possibly want to engineer such a thing? Because he moved in mysterious ways, of course; that was the whole point. Because he

248

surpasseth all understanding. You weren't *meant* to understand. Still, in his job it was hard sometimes to find reasons to believe.

Sergeant Hooper hadn't enjoyed the scene much either, but it was not in his nature to ponder what purpose such horror might have in God's almighty plan. Instead he took refuge in silly bravado. He was thinking that later he would tell the women constables that Kelly had looked like a Teletubby with that knife coming out of the top of her head. It was the same thought that Geraldine had had. Fortunately for Hooper he never ventured such a remark within Coleridge's hearing. Had he done so he would not have lasted long on the old boy's team.

DAY TWENTY-EIGHT. 2.35 a.m.

They had received the call at one fifteen, and had arrived at the scene of the crime to take over the investigation by two thirty. By that time, probably the biggest mistake of the case had already been made.

'You let them *wash*?' Coleridge said, in what was for him nearly a shout.

'They'd been sweating in that box for over two hours, sir,' the officer who had been in charge thus far pleaded. 'I had a good look at them first and had one of my girls look at the ladies.'

'You *looked* at them?'

'Well, blood's blood, sir. I mean, it's red. I would have spotted it. There wasn't any. I assure you we had a very good look. Even under their fingernails and stuff. We've still got the sheet, of course. There's a few drops on that.'

'Yes, I'm sure there is, the blood of the victim. Sadly, though, we do not have a problem identifying the victim. She's glued to the lavatory floor! It's the killer

249

we're looking for, and you let a group of naked suspects in a knife-attack wash!'

There was no point pursuing the matter further. The damage was done. In fact, at that point in the investigation Coleridge was not particularly worried. The murder had been taped, the suspects were being held, all of the evidence was entirely contained within a single environment. Coleridge did not imagine that it would be long before the truth emerged.

'This one's got to be a bit of a no-brainer,' Hooper had remarked as they drove towards the house.

'A what?' Coleridge enquired.

'A no-brainer, sir. It means easy.'

'Then why don't you say so?'

'Well, because . . Well, because it's less colourful, sir.'

'I prefer clarity to colour in language, sergeant.'

Hooper wasn't having this. Coleridge wasn't the only one who had been woken up at one in the morning. 'What about Shakespeare, then?' Hooper reached back in his mind to his English Literature GCSE for a quote. He retrieved a sonnet:

'What about "Shall I compare you to a summer's day? Thou art more lovely and more temperate." Perhaps he should have just said, "I fancy you"?'

'Shakespeare was not a policeman embarking on a murder inquiry. He was poet employing language in celebration of a beautiful woman.'

'Actually, sir, I read that it was a bloke he was talking about.'

Coleridge did not answer. Hooper smiled to himself. He knew that one would annoy the old bastard.

And Coleridge was annoyed once more, for, once they had arrived at the house, it became very quickly clear to him that this investigation was by no means straightforward at all.

The pathologist had no light to shed on the subject.

'What you see is what you get, chief inspector,' she said. 'At eleven forty-four last night somebody stabbed this girl in the neck with a kitchen knife and immediately thereafter plunged the same knife through her skull, where it remained. The exact time of the attack was recorded on the video cameras, which makes a large part of my job rather redundant.'

'But you concur with the evidence of the cameras?'

'Certainly. I would probably have told you between eleven thirty and eleven forty, but of course I could never be as accurate as a time code. Bit of luck for you, that.'

'The girl died instantly?' Coleridge asked.

'On the second blow, yes. The first would not have killed her had she gone on to receive treatment.'

'You've watched the tape.'

'Yes, I have.'

'Do you have any observations to offer?'

'Not really, I'm afraid. I suppose I was a little surprised at the speed with which the blood puddle formed. A corpse's blood doesn't flow from a wound, you see, because the heart is no longer pumping it. It merely leaks, and an awful lot leaked in two minutes.'

'Significant?'

'Not really,' the pathologist replied. 'Interesting to me, that's all. We're all different physiologically. The girl was leaning forward, so gravity will have increased the speed of blood loss. I suppose that accounts for it.'

Coleridge looked down at the dead girl kneeling on the floor in front of the toilet. A curious position to end up in, for all the world like a Muslim at prayer. Except that she was naked. And, of course, there was the knife.

'Who would have thought the old man to have had so much blood in him,' Coleridge murmured to himself.

'Excuse me?'

'*Macbeth*,' said Coleridge. 'Duncan's death. There was also a lot of blood on that occasion.'

Coleridge had gone to bed with the *Complete Works* the night before, preparing for the amateur dramatics audition that he knew he would fail.

'Well, there normally is a lot of blood when people get stabbed,' stated the pathologist matter of factly. 'So that's your lot for the moment,' she continued. 'We might find something on the knife handle. The killer wrapped the sheet round it for grip and also, one presumes, in order to avoid leaving prints. They'd all been in a sweatbox, secreting copiously, so some cellular matter might have soaked through. Could possibly get an ID from that.'

'Nobody's touched the knife, then?' After the washing incident Coleridge was ready to believe anything.

'No, but we'll obviously have to touch it to get it out of her head. We'll almost certainly have to cut the skull as well. Grim work, I'm afraid.'

'Yes.' Coleridge leaned over the body, trying to see as far as he could into the toilet cubicle without stepping in the pool of congealed blood. He put his hands against the walls to support himself. 'Hold my waist, please, sergeant. I don't want to fall onto the poor girl.'

Hooper did as he was told and Coleridge, thus suspended, took in the scene. Kelly's naked bottom stared up at him and, beyond that, the toilet bowl.

'Very clean,' he remarked.

'What, sir?' Hooper asked, surprised.

'The lavatory bowl, it's very clean.'

'Oh, I see, I thought you meant . . .'

'Be quiet, sergeant.'

'That was Kelly.' Geraldine spoke from behind him. 'Scrubbed the toilet twice a day. She can't stand dirty bogs . . .' Her voice trailed away as she reminded herself that Kelly was past caring about anything now. 'I mean, she couldn't stand it . . . She was a very neat and tidy girl.'

Coleridge continued his investigation. 'Hmmm, not a particularly thorough girl, though, I fear. She missed a few small splashes of what I think is vomit on the seat. Thank you, you can pull me back now.'

With Hooper's help and by walking his hands backwards along the walls, Coleridge rejoined the pathologist.

'What about the sheet worn by the killer?' he asked. 'The one he took back into the boys' bedroom?'

'You might be luckier with that. I mean, all that sweating must have loosened some skin. Some of it would certainly have stuck to the sheet.'

The original officer on the scene chipped in at this point.'We think that the sheet the killer used was the same one as the black lad, Jason, put on when he emerged from the room after the event, sir.'

'Ah,' said Coleridge thoughtfully. 'So if by any chance Jason were our man, then he would have a convenient alibi for any residue of his DNA on the sheet.'

'Yes, I suppose he would.'

'It'll take a day or two at the lab,' said the pathologist. 'Shall I send it off?'

'Yes, of course. Not a lot of point in my looking at it,' Coleridge replied. 'I see that the lavatory door has a lock.'

'That's right,' said Geraldine. 'It's the only one in the house. It's electronic and they can open it from either side, in case one of them faints or decides to top themselves or whatever. We can also spring it from the control room.'

'But Kelly didn't use the lock?'

'No. None of them did.'

'Really?'

'Well, I suppose if you've got a camera staring at you while you do your thing privacy becomes sort of irrelevant. Besides, there's a light that says when the loo's occupied.'

'So the killer would not have expected to encounter a lock?'

'No, not since about the second day.'

Coleridge inspected the door and the lock mechanism for some moments.

'I only had it fitted as an afterthought,' said Geraldine. 'I thought we ought to give them at least the *impression* of privacy. If only she'd used it.'

'I'm not sure it would have helped,' said Coleridge. 'The killer was obviously very determined, and the restraining bar on this lock is only plywood. It would have taken very little force to kick it open.'

'I suppose so,' said Geraldine.

Coleridge summoned the police photographer to ensure that photographs of the door and its catch were taken, and then he and Sergeant Hooper retraced the killer's steps from the lavatory back to the boys' bedroom.

'Nothing to be got from the floor, I suppose.'

'Hardly, sir,' said Hooper. 'The same eight people have been back and forth over these tiles twenty-four seven for the last four weeks.'

'Twenty-four seven?'

Hooper gritted his teeth before replying. 'It's an expression, sir. It means twenty-four hours a day, seven days a week.'

'I see . . . Quite useful. Economic, to the point.'

'I think so, sir.'

'American, I presume?'

'Yes, sir.'

'I wonder if any item of colloquial English will ever again emanate from this country.'

'I wonder if anybody apart from you remotely cares, sir.' Hooper knew that he was safe to be as cheeky as he liked. Coleridge was no longer listening to him, nor was he really thinking about the changing nature of English slang. That was just his way of concentrating. Coleridge always turned into an even bigger bore than usual when his mind began to gnaw at a problem. Hooper knew that he was in for weeks of grim pedantry.

After another half-hour or so of searching, during which nothing of interest was discovered, Coleridge decided to leave the lab people to their work. 'Let's go and meet the suspects, shall we?'

DAY TWENTY-EIGHT. 3.40 a.m.

The housemates were being held in the Peeping Tom boardroom, situated on the upper floor of the production complex across the moat from the house. The seven tired, scared young people had been taken there after being questioned briefly at the scene and then allowed to shower and dress. Now they had all been sitting together for over an hour, and the truth of the night's terrible event had well and truly sunk in.

Kelly was dead. The girl with whom they had all lived and breathed for the previous four weeks, and with whom they had all been groping and laughing only a few hours before, was dead.

That was the *second* most shocking thing any of them had ever in their lives been forced to try to come to terms with.

The most shocking thing of all was the self-evident fact that one of them had killed her.

The penny had dropped slowly. At first there had been much weeping and hugging, expressions of astonishment, confusion, sadness and solidarity. They had felt as if they were the only seven people in the world, bonded by a glue that no outsider would ever understand. It was all so strange and confusing: the four

255

weeks of isolation and game-playing, then the mad, drunken excess of the sweatbox, the sudden onrush of raw sexual energy that had taken them all by surprise . . . and then the death of their comrade and the house suddenly *full of police*. That had almost been the strangest thing of all. To find their house, the place where nobody could enter and none could leave save by a formal and complex voting procedure, full of police officers! Of course, they had been intruded on before, when Woggle was arrested, but that had been different. The housemates had remained in the majority, in some way in control. This time they had been reduced to a huddled little ghetto in the boys' bedroom, pleading to be allowed to wash themselves.

All this common and unique experience had at first served to create a gang mentality for the seven surviving housemates . . . Jazz, Gazzer, Dervla, Moon, David, Hamish and Sally.

But as they sat together around the big table in the Peeping Tom boardroom, rapidly sobering up, that solidarity had begun to evaporate like the alcohol in their systems. To be replaced by fear, fear and suspicion. Suspicion of each other. Fear that they themselves might be suspected.

One by one Coleridge saw them, these people who were shortly to become so familiar to him. And with each brief interview the depressing truth became clearer. Either six of them genuinely knew nothing, or they were each protecting all the others, because none of them had anything to say to him that shed any light upon who had left the sweatbox in order to kill Kelly.

'To be honest, officer,' Jazz told Coleridge, 'I could not have told you what was up and what was down inside that box, let alone where the exit was. It was totally dark, man. I mean *totally*. That was the point of it. We'd been in there two hours, and we were just *so* pissed, I mean, *completely*—'

'How did you know it was two hours?' Coleridge interrupted.

'I didn't know, I heard since. Man, I would not have known if it was two hours, two minutes or two *years*. We was out to it, floating, zombied, brain-fucked to the double-max degree, and we was getting it on! I was getting it on! Do you understand? Four weeks without so much as a touch of a woman, and suddenly I was *getting it on*. Believe me, man, I wasn't thinking about where no exit was. I was happy where I was.'

This was the common theme of the majority of the interviews. Each of them had been utterly disoriented inside that box, losing all concept of space and time, and contentedly so, for they had been enjoying themselves.

'It was so fookin' hot in there, inspector,' Moon assured him, 'and dark, and we were drunk. It was like floating in space or summat.'

'Did you notice anybody leave?'

'Maybe Kelly?'

'Maybe?'

'Well, I didn't even know where the entrance was by then. At the end of the day, I don't think anybody knew fook all about anything, to be quite honest. But I did feel a girl suddenly moving, like, *amongst* us all . . . and quite quickly, which was a bit of a surprise because we were all so chilled.'

'You were chilled?' Coleridge thought he must have misheard. He wanted things to be clear for the tape.

'The witness means relaxed, sir,' Hooper interjected.

'Whatever the witness means, sergeant,' Coleridge snapped, 'she can mean it without your leading her to it. What did you mean, miss?'

'I meant relaxed.'

'Thank you. Please continue.'

'Well, I think that maybe after I felt the girl move there was like a little waft of cooler air. I think maybe

I realized that somebody was going for a piss or whatever, but quite frankly, at the end of the day, I weren't that bothered. I mean I were giving somebody – I *think* it were Gazzer – a blow-job at the time.'

Interview after interview told the same story: varying degrees of sexual activity plus the idea that someone, probably a girl, had scrambled over them shortly before the game was brought to an abrupt halt. They each remembered this moment because it had rather jarred the 'chilled' atmosphere that had developed.

'And this movement happened quite suddenly?' Coleridge asked each of them. They all agreed that it had, that there had been a sudden flurry of limbs and soft warm skin, followed by the faintest waft of cooler air. With hindsight it was clear that this must have been Kelly rushing off to the lavatory.

'Could anybody have sneaked off after her?' Coleridge asked them. Yes, was the reply, they all felt strongly that in the cramped, crowded darkness and confusion of it all, it would have been possible for a second person to follow Kelly out of the sweatbox unnoticed.

'But you yourself were unaware of it.'

'Inspector,' said Gazzer, and he might have been speaking for them all, 'I wasn't aware of anything.'

Sally's were the only recollections that differed substantially from the norm. When she appeared Coleridge had been taken aback. He had never seen a woman whose arms were completely covered in tattoos before and he knew that he would have to try not to let it prejudice his view of her.

'So you were not involved in the sexual activity?' Coleridge asked.

'No. I decided to try and use the exercise to improve my understanding of other cultures,' Sally replied. 'I found a corner of the box, ignored what the others were doing and concentrated on recreating the consciousness of a Native American fighting woman.'

Coleridge could not stop himself from reflecting that to the best of his knowledge all the Native American fighting had been done by men, but he decided to let it go. 'You didn't want to join in the, um, fun?' he asked.

'No, I'm a dyke, and all the other women who were in that box are straight, or at least they think they are. Besides, I had to concentrate on something other than them, you see. I *had to concentrate.*'

'Why?'

'I don't like dark, confined spaces. I don't like getting into black boxes.'

'Really? Is this something you have much experience of?'

'Not for real, no. But in my head I imagine it all the time.'

Coleridge noted that the cigarette Sally held in her hand was shaking. The column of smoke rising above it was jagged. Like the edge of a rough saw. 'Why do you imagine dark boxes?'

'To test myself. To see what happens to me when I go there.'

'So on being confronted by a real physical black box, you decided to use it as a test of your mental strength.'

'Yes, I did.'

'And did you pass the test?'

'I don't know. I don't remember anything about what happened in that box. It just totally weirded me out and so I went somewhere else in my head.'

And press her though he might, Coleridge could get nothing more out of Sally.

'I'm not holding out on you,' she protested, 'I swear. I liked Kelly. I'd tell you if I knew something, but I don't remember anything at all. I don't even remember *being* there.'

'Thank you, that'll be all for now,' Coleridge said.

As Sally was leaving she turned at the door. 'One thing, though. Anything Moon tells you is a lie, all right? That woman wouldn't know the truth if it stuck a knife in her head.' Then she left the room.

'Do you think she was trying to tell us Moon did it?' Hooper said.

'I have no idea,' Coleridge replied.

Both David and Hamish struck Coleridge as evasive. Their statements were much the same as Garry's, Jason's and Moon's had been, but they seemed less frank, more guarded.

'I couldn't tell you where Kelly was in the box,' said Hamish. 'I know I was feeling up one of the girls, but to be honest I couldn't tell you which.'

Something about his manner struck Coleridge as jarring. Later on, when discussing it with Hooper, the sergeant admitted that he had felt the same way. They had both interviewed enough liars to be able to spot the signs. The defensive body language, the folded arms and squared shoulders, the body pushed right back in the seat as if preparing for attack from any side. Hamish was probably lying, they thought, but whether it was a big lie or a little one they could not tell.

'You're a doctor, it says here,' Coleridge observed.

'I am,' said Hamish.

'I would have thought that a doctor might have been a little more aware. After all, there were only four women in that darkness. You'd known them all for a month. Are you seriously telling me that you were groping one of them and had no idea which?'

'I was very drunk.'

'Hmmm,' said Coleridge after a long pause. 'So much for doctors and their sensitive hands.'

Coleridge would have known that David was an actor without having to refer to Peeping Tom's notes. There was something mannered about his expressions of grief; not that this meant he wasn't sorry, but it did mean he was conscious of how he was presenting his sorrow. The pauses before he spoke were too long, the frank manly eye contact a little too frank and manly. He smoked a number of cigarettes during his interview, but since he clearly did not inhale it struck Coleridge that the cigarettes were props. He held them between his thumb and forefinger, his hand cupped around the burning end which pointed towards his palm. Not a very practical way to hold a cigarette, Coleridge thought, but it certainly gave an impression of anguish. When David wasn't looking earnestly into Coleridge's eyes, he was staring intently at his cupped cigarette.

'I loved Kelly. We were mates,' he said. 'She was such a free and open spirit. I only wish I'd known her better. But I certainly was not aware of her in the box. To be honest, Dervla would be more my type if I'd been fishing, but I'm afraid I was too drunk and disoriented to take much interest in anyone.'

It was all so vague, so confused. Coleridge inwardly cursed these scared, bewildered young people. Or he cursed six of them, at any rate. The murderer he could only grudgingly respect. Six people had been present when the murderer left the box and also when he returned and yet they had all been too damned drunk and libidinous to notice.

Only Dervla, to whom he spoke last, was clearer in her recollection. This was of course Coleridge's first experience of Dervla, but immediately he liked her. She seemed to be the steadiest of the bunch, intelligent but also giving the impression of being frank and open. He found himself wondering what madness had moved a nice, clever girl like her to get involved with an exercise as utterly fatuous as *House Arrest* in the first place. He could not understand it at all, but then Coleridge felt that he no longer understood anything very much.

Dervla alone seemed to have been relatively aware of her surroundings during those last few minutes in the sweatbox. She recalled that when the agitated girl had made her hurried exit, she herself must have been close to the flaps, for she had definitely felt the waft of cooler air. She was also quite certain that the figure she felt slide across her and exit through the flaps had most definitely been Kelly.

'I felt her breasts slide across my legs, and they were big, but not as big as Sally's,' she said, reddening at the thought of the scene that she must be conjuring up in the minds of the detectives.

'Anything else about her?' Coleridge asked.

'Yes, she was shaking with emotion,' said Dervla. 'I know that I felt a real sense of tension, almost of panic.'

'So she was upset?' Coleridge asked.

'I'm trying to remember what I thought at the time,' Dervla said. 'Yes, I think I thought she was upset.'

'But you don't know why.'

'Well, a lot of strange things were happening inside that box, inspector, things that would be embarrassing enough to recall in the morning without having to relate them to police officers.'

'Strange things?' Coleridge asked. 'Be specific, please.'

'I can't see how it's relevant.'

'This is a murder investigation, miss, and it's not your place to decide what's relevant.'

'Well, OK, then. I don't know what Kelly was doing before she bolted, but I know she'd been feeling pretty wild earlier in the evening. We all had, and still were. I myself was getting close to the point of no return with Jason, or at least I think it was Jason. I *hope* it was Jason.' She glanced down, and her eyes rested on the little revolving cogs on the cassette tape recorder. She reddened.

'Go on,' said Coleridge.

'Well, after Kelly slid across me and went off, Jazz and I . . . carried on with our um . . . canoodling.'

Coleridge caught Hooper smiling at this choice of word and glared at him. There was nothing in his opinion remotely amusing about discussing the circumstances that led up to a girl's being murdered.

'And that was it, really,' Dervla concluded. 'Shortly after that we heard all the commotion, and Jazz went out to see what was going on and who was in the house. I remember that at that point I actually felt relieved at the interruption. It gave me a chance to collect myself and realize what I was doing, just how far I'd let myself get carried away. I was happy that something had occurred to stop the party.'

Dervla stopped herself, realizing how terrible this must sound. 'Of course, I felt differently when I realized what had actually happened.'

'Of course. And you don't know anything about what might have upset Kelly?'

'No, I don't, but I suppose somebody must have pushed their luck a bit with her, if you know what I mean. I always thought that Kelly was a bit of a tease on top but what my mother would call a "nice girl" underneath. I don't think she'd have gone all the way in that box.'

'Really?'

'Yes. The other night Hamish followed her out into the nookie hut, but I don't think he got anywhere . . . Not that I'm saying anything about Hamish, you understand.'

'Were you aware of anybody following Kelly out of the box last night?'

'No, I was not.'

'You've said yourself that you were situated near the entrance. You're sure you noticed nothing?'

'As I've told you, I was occupied at the time. The whole business was rather a giddy affair.'

Later, Coleridge was to ponder Dervla's choice of words and phrases: 'canoodling', 'giddy affair', as if she was talking about an innocent flirtation at a barn dance rather than an orgy.

After Dervla had completed her interview and returned to the conference room, Coleridge and Hooper discussed her evidence for some time.

'Very mysterious that she had no sensation of the second person leaving the box,' Hooper said.

'Yes,' Coleridge replied. 'Unless . . .'

Hooper finished his sentence for him. 'Unless she was the person who left.'

One Winner

DAY TWENTY-EIGHT. 7.30 p.m.

The door closed behind David. He picked up his guitar from the orange couch and began playing a mournful song. He was the last one in. They'd all come home.

There was never any real question in their minds that they would go on with it. Even as they were driven away from the house in seven separate police cars in the early morning following the murder, they were able to get some idea of the scale of interest that would henceforth be shown in them. The corpse was hardly cold, and yet already the word was out and the whole world was rushing to their door.

By the time they left the police station, without charge, eight hours later, there were over a thousand reporters waiting for them.

A thousand reporters. On a recent trip to Britain the President of the United States had rated only two hundred and fifty.

And once Peeping Tom announced that the seven remaining contestants intended to *continue with the game*, the media and the public went berserk with excitement. For these were no longer just seven contestants in a TV game show, as Geraldine continued publicly to maintain, they were seven suspects in a murder hunt. The only seven suspects.

All day and all night it seemed as if people could

talk about nothing else. Bishops and broadcasting watchdogs deplored the decision as a collapse of moral standards. Opportunistic politicians applauded it as evidence of a more open and relaxed society that was 'at ease with its traumas'. The prime minister was invited to comment on the matter during Parliamentary Question Time, and earnestly promised that he would 'listen to the people', attempting, if possible, to 'feel their pain' and get back to parliament the moment he had an idea about how they felt.

Many people expressed surprise that the seven contestants were legally free to go back into the house, but of course there was nothing to stop them. Even though it was clear that one of them had murdered Kelly, the police were unable to find evidence to detain any of them. They were all free to go for the time being, free to do what they wanted, and what they wanted, it soon turned out, was to go back into the house.

Efforts were made by concerned individuals to implement the law that states that people cannot profit from media exploitation of their crimes. But what profit? The inmates of the house were not being paid for their efforts. And what crime? Six of the people had not committed one, and the identity of the person who had done it remained a complete mystery. Once he or she was detected, it would of course be possible to prevent them from appearing on television, but until then there was nothing that could be done to restrain any of them.

DAY TWENTY-EIGHT. 6.50 p.m.

'I say we fahkin' go for it.'

Garry had been the first to speak. He was a geezer and a hard one at that, and he wasn't squeamish about using a toilet in which someone had been knifed.

'I've been in a lot of bogs with blood on the floor,' he said, thinking to himself that this comment would play rather well on the telly, before he remembered that he was outside the house and for the first time in a month there were no cameras being trained on him. 'So I say fahk it, let's have it large.'

Geraldine had managed to collect all seven of the tired, confused housemates as they left the police station and wrestle them onto a waiting minibus. It had not been easy: the offers of money had burst forth with a roar the moment the station door had opened. Any one of the remaining housemates could have got a hundred thousand for an exclusive interview there and then. Fortunately, Geraldine had brought a megaphone with her and she was entirely unembarrassed about using it. 'You'll do much better if you bargain collectively,' she shouted, 'so get on the bus!'

Finally, with the help of the ten huge security men she had brought with her, she managed to get her precious charges inside the vehicle and there they sat like obedient children while the police tried to clear a path for them to depart. Outside, hundreds of cameras were clicking and whirring, microphones were being banged against the windows; the noise of the shouted questions was cacophonous.

'Who do you think did it?' 'How do you feel?' 'Did she deserve it?' 'Was it a sex thing?'

Even inside the bus Geraldine had to use her megaphone to get their attention. She knew what she required of the housemates, and she got right down to telling them.

'Listen to me!' she shouted.

The seven shell-shocked people stared back at her.

'I know you're all sorry about Kelly, but we have to be practical. Look at what's going on outside! The entire world's press have turned up, and for what? Not for Kelly, she's gone, but for *you*, that's who. So think about that for a minute.'

While the seven housemates thought about it the minibus began to edge its way through the roaring sea of journalists.

'Why did you people get into this thing in the first place?' Geraldine continued. 'Why did you write to Peeping Tom?'

They were confused: there had been so many reasons given at the start of the whole business. 'To really stretch myself as a person . . .' 'To explore different aspects of who I am . . .' 'To discover new horizons and life adventures . . .' 'To provide a goal, and to be a role model.'

They had all known the codes, the things that they were *supposed* to say. The new language of pious self-justification. All rubbish, of course, and Geraldine knew it. She knew why they had applied to be on Peeping Tom, and no amount of pretentious New Age waffle could disguise it. They had done it to *get famous* and that was why Geraldine knew that they would all go back into the house.

The bus was finally pulling away from the mob at the police station, and the motorbike photographers were beginning their pursuit, weaving in and out of the traffic, oblivious to their own safety or anybody else's, intoxicated by the hunt.

'So,' Geraldine barked, 'let's leave aside for a moment the issue of who kill . . . of how poor Kelly died, and consider the opportunity that her sad demise has opened up for you people. I am talking about fame beyond frontiers, beyond your wildest dreams. This show will be broadcast worldwide, no question about that. By the time you come out of our house your faces will be recognizable in every town, village and *home* on the planet. Think about that. If you guys split up now the story's over in a week, you'll all make a few

270

quid talking about Kelly to the papers and that'll be it. But if you stick together! If you go back into the house together! You'll be the biggest story on earth day after day after day.'

'You mean people will be watching to try to work out which one of us killed Kelly?' Dervla said.

'Well, that certainly,' Geraldine conceded. 'But the police are trying to work that out anyway, so you might as well make a profit out of it. Besides, there's so much more to this, the human angle of how you all cope with the tragedy, with each other. Believe me, this is a century-defining definition of what constitutes good telly.'

Geraldine could see that they were all still struggling with the terrifying and bewildering change in their circumstances.

Sally spoke up in a sad small voice, a voice no one had heard her use before. 'I thought that maybe it would be nice just to go home for a bit.'

'Exactly!' Geraldine exclaimed. 'That's what I'm saying.'

'No, I mean my real home.'

'Oh, I see . . . Fuck that. The house is your real home now.' Geraldine's own life was so entirely defined by her work that she simply could not understand the idea that somebody might be seriously considering putting toast and Marmite and a bit of a cry on the sofa with Mum before participating in the greatest tele-vision event in decades.

'All right, let's look at it this way,' Geraldine said, able to adopt a quieter, more conciliatory tone now that they had left the roaring crowd behind them. 'If one of you killed her, then that means six of you didn't, right? Six people who can either slink away having had your big chance ruined by a cruel psychopath, or six people who can have the guts to stand up for themselves. Don't forget that you have a *right* to pursue this journey of personal empowerment, you have a *right* to be stars.

Because, at the end of the day, you're all strong, fabulous, independent people, so I say just go for it! Crack on, because you're brilliant, you really are. And I really, really mean that.'

But still they wavered.

To go back into that house . . .

To sleep in those beds . . .

To use the toilet. The toilet where only hours before . . .

Having tried conciliation, Geraldine picked up her cosh once more and played her strongest card of all: the truth. 'All right, let's really get down to it, shall we? Yesterday you were all part of a crappy, unoriginal little cloned game show that we've all seen ten times before. You've all watched them and you all know that the people on them basically look like a bunch of arrogant self-absorbed arseholes. Do you think you looked any different? Think again. I'll show you the tapes if you like. Blimey, the public preferred *Woggle* to you lot. Stars? Fuck off. Disposable minor celebs is all you were. That's the truth. I'm levelling with you for your own good.'

'Now look here . . .' David began to protest.

'Shut up, David, this is my fucking bus and I'm fucking talking.'

David shut up.

'*Now*, however,' Geraldine continued, 'you can change all that. If you have the guts, you have the chance to be a part of the most fascinating television experiment of all time. A live whodunit! A nightly murder mystery with a *real live victim* . . .'

She realized what she'd said the moment she said it. 'Oh, all right, then, a real dead victim if you like. The point is that this will be the biggest show in history, and you are the stars of it! Kelly has given you the chance to be the thing *she* wanted most of all, to be a star! Do you hear me? Genuinely, properly famous, and to get it all you have to do is continue to play the game.'

Geraldine looked at their faces. She had won her argument. It had not taken long.

Together they quickly concocted a press release, which they issued through the bus window as they approached the house. 'We, the seven remaining housemates of *House Arrest Three*, have elected to continue with our sociological experiment as a tribute to Kelly and her dreams. We knew Kelly and know that she loved this show. It was a part of her, and she gave her life for it. We feel that for us to give up now and to jettison all that she worked for would be an insult to the memory of a beautiful strong woman and human being, whom we loved very, very much. *House Arrest* continues because it is what Kelly would have wanted. We are doing it for her. Crack on!'

'That's fookin' beautiful, that is,' Moon said.

Then Sally started to cry and in a moment they were all crying. Except Dervla. Dervla was thinking about something else.

'Just one thing,' she said, as the bus forced its way through the crowds who had gathered round the Peeping Tom compound.

'Yeah, what?' said Geraldine brusquely. Having secured their agreement, she wanted no further discussion, *particularly* from Princess fucking Dervla.

'Suppose the killer strikes again?'

Geraldine pondered this for a moment. 'Well, it's never going to happen, is it? I mean, come on, you'll all be on your guard, and we'd never do something like the sweatbox thing again. Obviously all anonymous environments and closed-in group activities are out. No more bunches of people, everything open and spread out. Really you should be sorry. I mean, imagine if it *were* possible for it to happen again. Just how fucking big would the remains of you be *then*?'

DAY TWENTY-EIGHT. 8.00 p.m.

They had been back inside for half an hour, but no one had spoken. Some lay on their beds, some sat on the couches. Nobody had yet used the toilet.

'This is Chloe,' the voice sounded through the house from the concealed speakers. 'In order to maintain the integrity of the game structure we have decided to treat Kelly's absence as an eviction from the house. Therefore there will be no further evictions this week. As a special treat, and in view of your long and tiring day, a takeaway meal for you has been placed in the store cupboard.'

Jazz went to get it. 'Chinese,' he said, returning with the bags.

It was the only word uttered in the house until long after they had finished the food.

Finally David broke the silence. 'So one of us killed Kelly?'

'So it would fookin' seem,' Moon replied.

There was silence again.

There was silence also in the monitoring bunker as the hours ticked by.

Late that night Inspector Coleridge slipped into the box and sat down beside Geraldine. He wanted to see for himself how the show was put together. When he spoke Geraldine actually jumped.

'You know that if I could have stopped you carrying on with this, I would.'

'I don't see why you would want to,' Geraldine replied. 'How many policemen get the chance to watch their suspects in the way you're doing? Normally when no charges are pressed the prey is gone, off covering its tracks and hiding its secrets. If this lot are holding onto any secrets, then they'd better keep them pretty close.'

'I would have liked to stop you on moral grounds. The whole country is watching your programme because they know that one of the people on it is a murderer.'

'Not just that, inspector, as if that wasn't good enough telly in itself,' Geraldine replied gleefully. 'They're also watching because there is always the chance that it might happen again.'

'That possibility had occurred to me.'

'And I can assure you that it's occurred to our little gang of wannabes. How good is that?'

'Murder is not a spectator sport.'

'Isn't it?' Geraldine asked. 'All right, then. If you didn't have to watch this because you're investigating it, would you still watch it? Come on, be honest, you would, wouldn't you?'

'No, I wouldn't.'

'Well, then, you're even more boring than I thought you were.'

Silence descended as they watched the housemates clearing away the debris of their meal.

'Why are they doing it, do you think?' Coleridge asked.

'Why do you think? To get famous.'

'Ah yes, of course,' said Coleridge. 'Fame.'

Fame, he thought, the holy grail of a secular age. The cruel and demanding deity that had replaced God. The one thing. The only thing, it seemed to Coleridge, that mattered any more. The great obsession, the all-encompassing national focus, which occupied 90 per cent of every newspaper and 100 per cent of every magazine. Not faith, but fame.

'Fame,' he murmured once more. 'I hope they enjoy it.'

'They won't,' Geraldine replied.

275

Coleridge sat in the larger of the two halls in the village youth centre awaiting his turn among all the other hopefuls. He was very, very tired, having been up for most of the previous two nights investigating a real live 'murder most foul'.

Now he was in the realms of fiction, but the words of the great 'Tomorrow and tomorrow and tomorrow' speech, one of his favourites, seemed to be draining from his mind.

He tried to concentrate, but people kept asking him about the Peeping Tom murder. It was understandable, of course – the whole affair was colossal news, and they all knew that Coleridge was a senior policeman. He would not have dreamt of telling them about his direct association with the crime. 'I expect my colleagues will do their best,' he said, trying to fix his mind on being a poor player about to strut and fret his hour upon the stage.

To Coleridge's great relief his picture had not been shown on any of the news broadcasts during the day, and he did not expect it to be in the morning papers either. He simply did not look enough like a 'top cop' to warrant inclusion. When the press did print a photo it was of Patricia, there being nothing they liked more than a comely 'police girl'.

Finally, it was Coleridge's turn to audition, and he was called into the smaller room in order to perform before Glyn and Val's searching gaze. He gave it everything he had, even managing the ghost of a tear when he got to 'out, brief candle'. There was nothing like the murder of a twenty-one-year-old girl to remind a person that life truly was a 'walking shadow'.

When he had finished, Coleridge felt that he had acquitted himself well.

Glyn seemed to think so too. 'That was lovely. Absolutely lovely and very moving. You clearly have great depth.'

Coleridge's hopes soared, but only for a moment.

'I always think that *Macduff* is the key role in the final act,' said Glyn. 'It's a small part, but it needs a big actor. Would you like to play it?'

Trying not to let his disappointment show, Coleridge said that he would be delighted to play Macduff.

'And since you won't have many lines to learn,' Val chipped in chirpily, 'I presume I can put you down for scenery-painting and the car pool?'

DAY TWENTY-NINE. 9.30 p.m.

Episode twenty-eight of *House Arrest* went out in an extended ninety-minute special edition on the evening following the day after the murder. It should have been episode twenty-nine that night, but there had been no show on the previous evening, partly out of respect and partly because the inmates of the house had spent all day at the police station.

All except one inmate, who was in the morgue.

The special edition show included the lead-up to the murder and the murder itself. There was a tasteful ten-second edit for the actual moment when the sheet rose and fell, a pointless precaution, since it had been aired endlessly on the news anyway. Also included in the show was the return of the housemates into the house in order to bring the chronology up to date. The whole thing was generally considered to have been very good telly indeed. Straight after the broadcast, and by way of absolving themselves from all criticism and responsibility, the network aired a live discussion programme about the morality of their having continued to broadcast the show at all. Geraldine Hennessy appeared on the discussion, along with various representatives of the great and the good.

'I fear that what we have just watched was depressingly inevitable,' said a distinguished poet and broadcaster. Distinguished, as Geraldine would point out to him afterwards in hospitality, principally for appearing on discussion programmes.

'Reality television, as it is called,' drawled the distinguished broadcaster, 'is a return to the gladiatorial arenas of ancient Rome. What we are watching is conflict, conflict between trapped and desperate antagonists who compete for the approval of the baying crowd. Like the plebeians of old, we raise and lower our thumbs to applaud the victor and condemn the vanquished. The only difference is that these days we do it via a telephone poll.'

Geraldine shifted in her seat. She hated the way supposed intellectuals leeched off popular culture while loftily condemning it.

'Personally,' the distinguished broadcaster continued, 'I am astonished that it has taken so long for murder to become a tactic in these entertainments.'

'Yes, but does that justify its being broadcast?' the shadow minister for home affairs leapt in, angry that the discussion had been underway for over two minutes and that he had yet to speak. 'I say most definitely not. We have to ask ourselves what sort of country we wish to live in.'

'And I would agree with you,' said the distinguished poet, 'but will you have the courage to deny the mob? The public must have its bread and circuses.'

Geraldine swallowed an overwhelming desire to unleash a four-letter tirade and resolved to be reasonable. That was, after all, why she had come on the show. The last thing she needed at this crucial moment in her career was to be taken off the air. 'Look,' she said. 'I don't like what has happened here any more than you do.'

'Really?' sniffed the poet.

'But the truth of the matter is if we don't put it out one of the low-rent channels will. The moment the inmates decided to carry on with the show, we didn't have a choice in the matter. If we had refused to go on, some publicist or other would have packaged the lot of them up and sold them to the highest bidder. Cable or satellite, probably. A programme like this could finally bring those carriers into the heart of the mainstream.'

'You could have refused to let them use the house,' the programme's distinguished host interrupted.

'There are any number of similar houses currently empty overseas,' Geraldine said. 'I think I saw that the original Dutch one was being sold on the Internet, cameras and all. That would have been perfect. Besides which, the simple truth of the matter is that you could put these people in a garden shed and the public would watch them.'

'Because one of them is a murderer,' said the shadow minister. 'There is blood and gore to be enjoyed here. But let us not forget, Ms Hennessy, a girl has died.'

'Nobody is forgetting that fact, Gavin, but not everybody is attempting to make political capital out of it,' said Geraldine. 'There is a genuine public interest here in what is, after all is said and done, a major public event. The audience feel, I think legitimately, that they are a *part* of this murder. In many ways they feel some responsibility for it. They have been shocked and traumatized. They are grieving and they need to *heal*. They need to remain connected to what is happening in order to begin that healing process. We cannot suddenly cut them out of the loop. Kelly was much loved, an enormously popular contestant. She truly was the people's housemate, and in many ways this is the people's murder.'

It was a brilliant, jaw-droppingly audacious gambit, and totally unexpected. Everybody knew that the real reason Geraldine and the channel wanted to continue broadcasting was money, pure and simple. The stark truth was that Kelly's murder had turned *House Arrest* from a moderately successful programme into a television colossus. Episode twenty-six of the show, the last to be shown before the murder, had achieved a 17 per cent audience share. The episode that had just been broadcast, the one that included the murder, had been watched by almost 80 per cent of the viewing public. Almost half of the *entire* population. Thirty-second advert slots in one of the three commercial breaks had sold at fifteen times their normal price.

'To prevent further broadcasts would be entirely élitist,' Geraldine continued. 'What we would be saying is that *we* know what is good for the public. We, the high and the mighty, the great and the good, will decide what the proles can be trusted to watch. That is totally unacceptable in a modern democracy. Besides which, let me remind you that this event has already been seen live on the Internet. It's already part of the culture. It is already *out there*. Do you condone the social disenfranchisement of people who do not own a computer? Are they to be denied their chance to grieve? To come to terms with Kelly's death just because they are not on-line?'

Even the distinguished poet and broadcaster was caught off balance by such a breathtaking display. He was no slouch at pressing every argument into the service of self-promotion, but he was quickly realizing that with Geraldine Hennessy he was punching in a different league.

'Our responsibility to the public,' Geraldine concluded, 'is *not* to take responsibility for the public. Our duty is to enable them to take responsibility for *themselves*. Allow *them* to make a choice. We can only do that by continuing to broadcast. *That* is the responsible and moral thing to do.'

The last thing any of the other panellists wanted was to be seen to be élitist.

'We certainly must listen to what *the people* want,' said the shadow minister. 'Already Kelly Simpson has become part of their lives. They have seen her murdered, they have a right to view her legacy.'

'As I said,' Geraldine repeated. 'They have to be given the opportunity to grieve and to heal.'

The distinguished poet made a late attempt to give the impression that it was actually he who had led the argument to the place where Geraldine had taken it. 'As I believe I implied,' he said, 'in many ways this event crosses the Rubicon in the democratization of the human experience. Reality television has already shown us that privacy is a myth, an unwanted cloak which people eagerly discard like a heavy garment on a summer's day. Death was the last truly private event, but thanks to *House Arrest* it is private no longer. In our open, meritocratic age, no human experience need be seen as "better" or more "significant" than any other, and that includes the final one. If Kelly had the right to be seen living, then surely we must grant her the right to be seen dying.'

Geraldine had won her argument as she had fully expected to.

The simple truth was that people wanted to watch, and it would have been very difficult to deny them that opportunity. And not just in Britain either. Within thirty-six hours of the murder occurring it had been broadcast in *every single country on earth*. Even the rigidly controlled Chinese state broadcaster had been unable to resist the allure of such a very, very good bit of telly.

This worldwide exposure had been the cause of considerable frustration in the Peeping Tom office, which had been caught completely offguard by the sudden surge of international interest in *House Arrest*. When the flood of requests for tapes of the murder came in they had been handled like the ordinary clip requests that arrived in the office every day from morning TV and cable chat shows.

The clips had been *given away*!

Normally Peeping Tom was glad of the publicity. The nation was getting bored with reality television, and it was essential to give the impression that, when Jazz made an omelette or Layla got annoyed about the boys' flatulence, a national event was taking place. Therefore, Peeping Tom Productions actively sought out opportunities to air their show on other programmes. So when every news and current-affairs show on earth had suddenly requested a clip, the Peeping Tom Production secretaries had simply followed procedure and handed them over for nothing. In fact, running off the huge number of tapes requested had actually *cost* Peeping Tom thousands of pounds.

No one involved would ever forget Geraldine's reaction when she realized what had happened. There simply wasn't enough foul language in the vocabulary to encompass her rage. In private, however, she had to acknowledge that it was her fault. She should have thought more quickly. She should have recognized immediately how profitable this murder was going to become.

Geraldine soon made good her mistake, and, from that point on, broadcasters who wanted to show any further footage of *House Arrest* were asked to pay a very heavy price indeed. But no matter how high Geraldine pushed that price, it was paid without a murmur.

Within a week of the murder, Geraldine, the sole owner of Peeping Tom Productions, had become a millionaire many, many times over. Although, as she was to explain in numerous interviews, this fact was of course in no way her reason for wishing to continue to broadcast. Oh no, as she had already made abundantly clear, she did that because it was her *duty*. She did that in order to give the public an opportunity to *grieve*.

Geraldine also dropped heavy but vague hints about substantial charitable donations, the details of which had of course yet to be finalized.

DAY THIRTY. 10.30 a.m.

Some commentators had predicted that such unprecedented international interest in *House Arrest* could not be sustained, but they were wrong. Night after night viewers watched while the seven housemate suspects attempted to coexist in an atmosphere of shock, grief and deep, deep suspicion of each other.

Peeping Tom had announced that, until the police made an arrest, the game would continue as if nothing had happened. Nominations would take place as usual and the inmates would be given a task to learn and perform together in order to earn their weekly shopping budget. In the week following the murder, the task they were given was to present a synchronized water ballet in the swimming pool.

Geraldine had pinched the idea from the Australian version of the show, but in this new context it could not have been more perfect. Geraldine had also been acutely aware of the problem of maintaining the high level of excitement generated by the murder episode and its aftermath, and the idea of subjecting the seven housemates to a water ballet was hailed by many critics as a stroke of genius. The sight of these tired, nervous, desperate people, one of whom was a murderer, all rehearsing classical dance moves together while wearing high-cut Speedo swimwear, ensured that viewing figures for *House Arrest* went up. The sound of Mantovani's most soothing string selections wafting through the house lent an even more sinister and surreal note to the exercises and the bickering.

'You're supposed to raise your *right* fookin' leg, Gazzer!' Moon shouted as Garry attempted to execute a movement known as the Swan.

'Well, I've done my fahkin' groin in, haven't I? I'm not a fahkin' contortionist.'

'Point your toes, girl,' Jazz admonished Sally. 'It says we'll be judged on elegance and fucking grace.'

'I'm a bouncer, Jazz, I don't do fucking grace.'

Even an innocent comment like this caused many a worried look between the housemates and much discussion on the outside. Sally had only been replying to Jazz, but to be reminded that she had more than a casual acquaintance with violence ... Well, it did make you think.

Sometimes they confronted the ever-present agenda head on.

'This fahkin' swimming suit's riding right up my bum,' said Gazzer. 'If I could get hold of the bloke whose idea this was I'd stick a fahkin' knife in his head!' It was meant to be a joke, a dark and courageous joke, but nobody laughed when it was replayed *ad nauseam* in the *House Arrest* trailers, and Gazzer briefly climbed a notch or two in the 'whodunit' polls of the popular press.

DAY THIRTY-ONE. 11.20 a.m.

Coleridge was taking a break from reviewing the Peeping Tom archive when the pathologist's report came in.

'Well, the flecks of vomit on the toilet seat were Kelly's,' he remarked.

'Yuck,' said Trisha.

'Yuck indeed,' Coleridge agreed. 'And, yucker still,

there were traces of bile in her neck and in the back of her mouth. They think she'd been gagging. There's no doubt about it: when Kelly left that sweatbox she must have been extremely upset.'

'Poor girl. What a way to spend your last few minutes, trying not to puke up all over people in a tiny plastic tent. God, she must have been drunk.'

'She was. The report says eight times over the limit.'

'That's pretty seriously arsehole— legless. No wonder she was having trouble keeping it down.'

'The report also says that her tongue was bruised.'

'Bruised . . . You mean bitten?'

'No, bruised, reminiscent of someone forcing a thumb into her mouth.'

'Ugh . . . So somebody wanted to shut her up?'

'That would seem the obvious interpretation.'

'Perhaps that's why she was gagging, because someone had their thumb in her mouth. No wonder she wanted to get out of that sweatbox in such a hurry.'

'Yes, although if someone in that box had put a hand into Kelly's mouth sufficiently hard to bruise her tongue, you'd think that *someone* would have heard her complain, wouldn't you?'

DAY THIRTY-TWO. 7.30 p.m.

As the week went on the group began to get the hang of the ballet, and footage of them performing 'The Flight of the Swan' in unison, first out of the pool and then in it, became the most expensive four-minute item of video tape in the history of television.

Besides the ballet, there was of course the simple drama of the inmates' coexistence in the house for the viewing public to pore over and enjoy. Each of the inmates was forever looking at the others, eyeing them as potential murderers . . . as actual murderers. Every glance took on a sinister significance, sly, sideways looks, long piercing stares, hastily averted gazes. When properly edited, every twitch of every facial muscle on every housemate could be made to look like either a confession or an accusation of murder.

And then there were the knives. Flush with money, Geraldine now maintained six cameramen in the camera run corridors at all times, ten at mealtimes. And the sole brief of most of these camera operators was to watch out for knives. Every time a housemate picked one up, to spread some butter, chop a carrot, carve a slice of meat, the cameras were there. Zooming in as the fingers closed around the hilt, catching the bright flash as the overhead strip-lighting bounced off the blade.

The Peeping Tom psychologist stopped trawling the footage for flirtatious body language and started searching for the murderous variety. He was soon joined by a criminologist and an ex-chief constable, and together they discussed at length which of the seven suspects looked most at ease with a knife in their hand.

DAY THIRTY-TWO. 11.00 p.m.

The evenings were the worst times for the housemates. It was then, with nothing much to do, that they had time to think about their situation. When they spoke about it to each other, which was not often, they agreed that the worst aspect of it all was the not knowing. The rules of the game had not changed – they were allowed no contact with the outside world – and since their brief bewildering day in the eye of the storm they had heard and seen absolutely nothing.

The sound of madness had been abruptly and completely turned off. It was as if a door had been slammed, which of course it had. Collectively and alone they longed for information. *What was happening?*

Even Dervla with her secret source of information was in the dark. She had wondered whether her message-writer would stop after the murder, but he hadn't.

'They all think you're beautiful, and so do I.'

'You look tired. Don't worry. I love you.'

One day Dervla risked mentioning the murder, pretending that she was talking to herself in the mirror. 'Oh, God,' she said to her reflection. 'Who could have done this thing?'

The mirror did not tell her much. *'Police don't know,'* it said. *'Police are fools.'*

DAY THIRTY-THREE. 9.00 a.m.

The forensic technician brought the report on the sheet that had shrouded the killer to Coleridge personally.

'Glad of the opportunity of a break from the lab,' he said. 'We don't get out much and it's not often that anything involving celebrities comes our way. I don't suppose there's any way you could blag me a trip behind the scenes, is there? Just next time you're going. I'd love to see how they do it.'

'No, there isn't,' Coleridge replied shortly. 'Please tell me about the sheet.'

'Absolute mess. Tons of conflicting DNA. Dead skin, bit of saliva, other stuff. You know sheets.'

Coleridge nodded and the technician continued.

'I think they must have been sharing this one, or else they all slept together, because there's strong evidence of four different male individuals on it, one of whom is particularly well represented. There are also traces of a fifth man. I presume that the prominent DNA represents the four boys left in the house and the fifth is

Woggle. Let's face it, he'd leave a pretty strong trail, wouldn't he? Of course, I can't be sure without samples from them all to compare it with.'

'All of them? On that one sheet?'

'So it would seem.'

DAY THIRTY-THREE. 11.00 a.m.

'*It's eleven o'clock on day thirty-three*,' said Andy the narrator, '*and the housemates have been summoned to the confession box in order to give a sample of their DNA. The police request is voluntary but none of the housemates refuse*.'

'Charming,' Dervla observed drily. 'Today's task is to attempt to eliminate yourself from a murder investigation.'

Gazzer seemed disappointed. 'I thought I was going to have to have one off the wrist and give 'em a splash of bollock champagne,' he said, 'but they only wanted a scrape of skin.'

DAY THIRTY-FOUR. 8.00 p.m.

Layla stumbled away from the church, her eyes half blinded with tears. The priest had asked her what had made her feel the need of a faith that she had rejected when she was fifteen.

'Father, I have a death on my conscience.'

'What death? Who has died?'

'A girl, a beautiful girl, an innocent I despised. I hated her, Father. And now she's dead and I ought to be released. But it's worse, she's everywhere, and they're calling her a saint.'

'I don't understand. Who was this girl? Who's calling her a saint?'

288

'Everyone. Just because she's dead they print her picture and say she was a lovely girl and innocent and that she wouldn't hurt a fly. Well, she hurt me, Father! She hurt me! And now she's dead and she should be gone, but she isn't! She's still here. She's still everywhere, a star!'

The priest looked hard at Layla through the grille. He had never watched *House Arrest*, but he did occasionally see a newspaper.

'Hang on a minute,' he said. 'I know you, don't I? You're . . .'

Layla ran. Even in church she could not escape the shame of her poisonous notoriety as a nonentity. There was no sanctuary from her anti-fame. The fact that she was a failure, the first person to be thrown out of that house. And Kelly had nominated her and then *kissed her* in front of millions. The whole nation had seen Layla accept Kelly's sympathy. And now Kelly was dead and Layla did not feel any better at all.

DAY THIRTY-FIVE. 7.30 p.m.

It was the first eviction night following the murder.

An executive editorial decision had been taken that Chloe should remain upbeat and positive about events. This was, after all, the house style.

'We all *so* miss Kelly big time, because she was such a *top lady* and a sweet young life cruelly snuffed out, which just should *not* have happened, right? Kelly was a laugh, she was a gas, she was bigged up, amped up, loads of fun and just *lovely*. And no way did she deserve such a pants thing to happen to her, not that anybody does. Ooooooh, Kelly, we *miss you*! We all just want to give you a *big hug*! But the show goes on and as the other inmates have made it clear, this whole gig right now is a tribute to Kelly's gorgeous memory.

So you just amp it up in heaven, Kezzer babe, 'cos this one's for you. All right! Let's give it up large for another week *in the house*!'

This announcement was of course followed by the now famous credits. *One house. Ten contestants. Thirty cameras. Forty microphones. One survivor.* A sentence which now carried with it a highly provocative double meaning, but which, it was felt, it would be even more provocative to change. Either way, it was difficult to imagine better telly than this.

'House, can you hear me? This is the voice of Chloe.'

'Yes, we can hear you,' said the seven people assembled on the couches, and for a moment everything seemed back to normal. It was almost possible to imagine that nobody had died.

'The fourth person to leave the Peeping Tom house will be . . .'

A huge dramatic pause.

'David! David, it's time to go!'

'Yes!' said David, punching the air in triumph, following the necessary practice of appearing absolutely delighted to be going.

'David, pack your bags. You have one and a half hours to say your goodbyes, when we will be back live to see you leave the house!'

The nominees for that week had been David and Sally.

Everyone had nominated Sally, because she had become so depressed, and a majority had voted for David, because he was a pain in the arse.

By coincidence, the two people whom the inmates had nominated for eviction were also the nation's two biggest suspects for the murder. Outside the house the eviction vote had turned into a national referendum on who had murdered Kelly. David won by a shade, and when the results were announced it was for a moment almost as if the crime had been solved.

'It's David!' the press wires hummed. 'As we have suspected all along.'

'Yes! It's David!' they shouted on the radio and on the live TV news links. Some even added, 'We are expecting an arrest shortly,' as if while in the house David had been enjoying some kind of sanctuary from the law but now that the people had spoken he could expect no further reprieve.

Inside the house the 90 minutes of allotted departure time ticked by slowly. It did not take David long to pack, and there was only so much group hugging and swearing of undying loyalty that you could do to somebody whom you heartily disliked and whom you suspected might be a murderer. Under normal circumstances the correct etiquette at evictions would be for everybody to put up a hysterical pretence that, despite everything, they adored the person departing and were desperately sorry to see them go. But on this particular night, the tiniest whiff of real reality could not be prevented from intruding.

Not on the outside, though. Outside the house the rules of TV still applied.

David stepped out to the throbbing beat of 'Eye Of The Tiger' and into the white light of a thousand flash cameras. The crowd was enormous. David had been terrified moments before, but now he found himself uplifted by the noise of the crowd. For this one moment at least he was the star he so desperately wanted to be. The eyes of the entire world were upon him and to his credit he pulled off those few seconds with great aplomb. His beautiful shoulder-length hair was lent life by a light breeze, his big black coat billowed romantically. He gave a sardonic smile, threw wide his arms and gave a deep bow.

The crowd, who appreciated a bit of theatre, rewarded David with a redoubled cheer.

Then, smiling broadly, David swept a hand through

his beautiful hair and boarded the platform of the cherry picker to be lifted up over the moat. When he arrived at the other side he bowed deep once more and kissed Chloe's hand. The crowd whooped again while simultaneously observing that David was an even bigger arsehole than they had previously thought.

Together David and Chloe took the short limousine ride to the studio. The music throbbed, the lights bobbed and weaved and the crowd shouted and waved their placards. 'WE LOVE DERVLA!' and 'JAZZ IS LUSH!'

Finally David and Chloe managed to get to the couch, where only Layla had sat before, and begin their chat.

'Wow!' shouted Chloe. 'Amped up! All right! You OK, Dave?'

'Yes, Chloe, I'm fine.'

'*Wicked!*'

'Absolutely. Wicked indeed.'

'Look, fair play to you, David,' Chloe gushed. 'Respect and all that big-time. You've been through it, and we all haven't, and it must have been an incredibly weird experience and all that, but I've got to ask you this, you know that, don't you? Of course you do, you know what I'm going to ask, I can see it in your face, you do know, don't you? What I'm going to ask? Of course you do, so let's get it over with. The big question everybody wants to know is, "Did you kill Kelly?"'

'No, absolutely not. I loved Kelly.' David gave it his best shot – the short pause before answering to focus fully and assume the appropriate look of pained sincerity, the tiny catch in the voice, but it did him no good. The crowd wanted a result; they booed, they jeered; a chant developed: 'Killer. Killer. Killer.'

David was stunned. He hadn't expected this.

'Sorry, babe. They think you did it, babe,' said Chloe.

'Sorry and all that, but at the end of the day there it is, babe.'

'But I didn't do it, I promise.'

'*All right, then,*' said Chloe, perking up. 'Let's see if anybody thinks somebody *else* did it.'

There were substantial cheers for this proposition, some without doubt coming from the same people who had only moments before condemned David. The situation, like the police investigation, was confused.

'Well, fair play to you, Dave,' said Chloe. 'There are a lot of young ladies on your side, I can see that, and can you blame them? Wicked!'

And, of course, at this the cheering redoubled.

'So come on, then, David. If you didn't do it, who do you think did?'

'Well, I don't know. I'd have to say Garry, but it's just a guess. I really don't know.'

'Well, we'll just have to wait to the end of the series to find out, won't we? said Chloe, which was an outrageous and entirely unfounded statement, but it sounded convincing enough, such is the seductive power of television.

'In the meantime,' Chloe shouted, 'let's take a look at some of Dave's finest moments *in the house*!'

DAY THIRTY-FIVE. 10 p.m.

Coleridge's team had to deal with thousands of calls from cranks. Every second ring of the phone heralded yet another clairvoyant who had seen the culprit in a dream.

Hooper kept a little tally. 'Dervla appears in most of the male clairvoyants' dreams, and Jazz in the birds'. Funny that, isn't it?'

This call was different, though. It came just as the closing credits of the *House Arrest Eviction Special*

293

were rolling on the TV in the police incident room. When Hooper picked up the phone there was something about the caller's calm and steady tone that made him decide to listen.

'I am a Catholic priest,' said the rather formal, foreign-sounding voice. 'I recently heard a confession from a very distressed young woman. I cannot of course tell you any details, but I believe you should be looking not only at the people who remain in the house, but also those who have left it.'

'Have you been speaking to Layla, sir?' Hooper replied. 'Because we have so far been unable to locate her.'

'I can't say anything more, except that I believe that you should continue trying to find her.' At that the priest clearly felt that he had already said enough, because he abruptly concluded the conversation and rang off.

DAY THIRTY-SIX. 11.00 a.m.

The results of the house DNA tests took three days to arrive, which Coleridge thought was outrageous.

As expected, the individuals represented on the sheet were the male housemates. Jazz, most prominently, Gazzer, David and Hamish equally clearly, and Woggle the least. Woggle, of course, had not been available to supply a sample, having famously skipped bail and disappeared. However, when he left the house he had accidentally left his second pair of socks behind, which despite having since been buried in the garden by the other boys, yielded copious quantities of anarchist DNA.

'So the sheet points towards Jazz, then,' said Hooper.

'Well, perhaps, but we'd expect his presence to be detected more strongly, since he wore the sheet after Geraldine and her team had arrived.'

294

'Yes, convenient, that, wasn't it?' Hooper observed drily. 'Covers his tracks very nicely, except that if one of the others had worn it too we would expect their presence to show more strongly also. After all, the killer would have been sweating like a pig when he put it on.'

'But all the other three have come up equally.'

'Exactly, sir.'

'Which is a bit weird in itself, isn't it?' said Trish. 'Sort of supports the idea that they were all in it, and they had a pact, to divide suspicion.'

'Well, anyway, at least it rules the girls out,' said Hooper.

'You think so?' Coleridge enquired.

'Well, doesn't it?'

'Only if the sheet under discussion was the one the killer used to hide under, which it *probably* is, but we can't be certain. We know that it's the sheet Jazz grabbed after the Peeping Tom people had entered the house, but can we be sure it was the one that the killer dropped onto the pile when he returned to the sweatbox?'

'Well, it was on top.'

'Yes, but the pile was fairly jumbled, and all the sheets were the same dark colour. More than one sheet may have been on top, so to speak. The tape is not entirely clear.'

'So it doesn't help us at all, then?' said Trish.

'Well, I think it could strengthen a case; it just couldn't make one. If there was further evidence against Jazz, this sheet would help, that's all.'

DAY THIRTY-SEVEN. 9.30 p.m.

For six hours the house had been completely empty, the thirty cameras and forty microphones recording

295

nothing but empty rooms and silence. Six hours of nothing, which had been diligently watched by millions of computer-owners all over the world.

It had begun at three o'clock that afternoon when the police arrived and collected all of the housemates, taking them away without explanation. Naturally this caused a sensation. The lunchtime news bulletins were filled with breathless stories of group conspiracies, and halfway round the world, down in the southern hemisphere, newspaper editors preparing their morning editions considered risking pre-emptive headlines announcing 'THEYALLDUNNIT!'

The reality made everybody look stupid, particularly the police.

'A tape measure!' said Gazzer as he and the others re-entered the house. 'A fahkin' tape measure! That's what Constable Plod's using to catch a killer!'

It had been Trisha's idea to take all of the housemates down to the Peeping Tom rehearsal house at Shepperton and ask them to walk the journey taken by the killer, thereby enabling a comparison to be made with the number of strides taken on the video. Coleridge had thought it was worth a try, but the results had been disappointing and inconclusive. A tall person might have scuttled, a short one might have stretched. The sheet made it impossible to work out clearly the nature of the killer's gait, and so the inmates were released without further comment.

Gazzer's frustration was echoed across the nation. 'The fahkin' FBI have got spy satellites and billion-dollar databases, and what have our lot got? A fahkin' tape measure!'

DAY THIRTY-EIGHT. 7.00 p.m.

Hooper had to ring David's doorbell for a long time before he could get him to answer it. While he waited on the steps of his apartment building the three or four reporters who were hanging about fired questions at him.

'Are you here to arrest him?'

'Was he in league with Sally?'

'Was it all of them that did it? Was it planned in the sweatbox?'

'Do you accept your incompetence in so far not making an arrest?'

Hooper remained silent until finally he was able to announce his credentials into David's intercom and gain admittance.

David greeted him at the lift dressed in a suit of beautiful silk pyjamas. He looked tired. He had been home for only three days but he was already heartily sick of the one thing he had gone into the house to get: fame.

'They don't want me,' he moaned when finally Hooper found himself inside the beautiful flat that David shared with his beautiful cat. 'They want the man that bitch Geraldine Hennessy created. A vain, nasty probable murderer. Vain and nasty I can handle, lots of stars are guilty of that, but probable murderer is something of a career no-no. If only that silly girl had not got herself killed. It's ruined everything for me.' He was entirely unabashed about his take on Kelly's death.

'You think I'm a right bastard, don't you?' he continued, making Hooper coffee from his beautiful shiny cappuccino machine. 'Because I don't pretend to forget my own interests and reasons for going into that house now that the girl is dead? Well, excuse me, but I do not intend to add hypocrisy to my many other faults, which seem now to have become a part of the national consciousness. She was a stranger to me, and if she hadn't been killed I might have had my chance to shine. To show people all the things I have to offer. To be the leading man. Instead it appears that I've been cast in the role of villain.'

'And are you a villain?'

'Oh, for Christ's sake, sergeant! You're worse than that silly bitch Chloe. If I had killed her do you think I'd be telling you? But, as it happens, I didn't. What possible motive could I have?'

'*Fuck Orgy Eleven.*'

David took it well. He clearly had not been expecting this, but he hardly let it show. 'Oh, so you know about that, then? Well, all right. I admit it, I'm a porn star. It's not a crime, but it's not very classy either, and by some appalling coincidence it turned out that the girl Kelly knew. Yes, of course I was hoping that she would keep quiet about it. But I can assure you, I didn't feel strongly enough about it to murder her.'

They talked for a little while longer, but David had very little to add to the statement he had made on the night of the murder. Except to expand on his reasons for suspecting Gazzer. 'He really truly hated her for what she said about his son, you know. He tried to cover it up a bit, but I know how to spot the signs. I'm an actor, you see . . .' David's voice trailed off. His handsome arrogance seemed to evaporate from him and he looked tired. Tired and sad.

Hooper got up to leave, but as he did so he asked one more question. 'If Kelly had not been killed,' he said, 'if the show had proceeded as they normally do, do you honestly believe that the sort of exposure you or anyone else could get on these things could ever lead to proper work – I mean, as a real actor or whatever?'

'Not really, no, sergeant,' David conceded. 'But, you see, I was desperate. Desperate to be a famous actor, certainly, but if I couldn't have that I was happy to settle for just being famous.'

'Well, you got your wish,' said Hooper. 'I hope you enjoy it.'

Outside the building the assembled press pack snapped and barked as he forced his way through to his car.

DAY THIRTY-NINE. 7.00 p.m.

'*It's Thursday night,*' said Andy the narrator, '*and time for the housemates to make their nominations for this week's eviction.*'

Again everybody nominated Sally.

'She's just got so strange,' Jazz said, when Peeping Tom asked him why he'd nominated her. 'I mean, she sleeps on her own out in the garden and she's so intense. It's a real strain having her around.'

The other four housemates who nominated her all had much the same reason. Moon put it most succinctly. 'I'm just sick to death of her being so fookin' moody . . .'

And then there was the little matter that they were all quite clearly scared of her.

Of course, besides these negative thoughts they all added that they loved Sally and that she was a top girl.

The other person nominated was Garry, his sick jokes having by this time begun to grate on the inmates.

'I mean, I love him, of course,' said Dervla, 'but if he does that screeching noise from *Psycho* one more time when I go to the toilet . . .'

'He's a diamond geezer,' Jazz assured the camera, 'but putting ketchup on Moon's neck while she was having a kip was totally out of order. I mean, he's brilliant, I love him, but you know what? At the end of the day I'm sick of him.'

When the nominations were announced Sally said nothing. She sat and stared into the distance for about half an hour before retreating to what had once been thought of as the nookie hut.

Garry assured everybody that he was happy to stay or go. 'At the end of the day I've got a top life out there. I've got my little lad, I'm looking forward to going to the pub. I'm happy to crack on and big it up. Long as none of you lot stick a knife in my head before I get a chance to snuggle up on that couch with Chloe.'

Later on that evening Sally returned to the living area, and when she spoke it was to nobody in particular. 'You all think I did it, don't you?' she said. 'And you know what? Maybe I did.'

In the monitoring bunker Geraldine did a little dance. 'Thank you, Sally, you gorgeous fat dyke, you! Out lines do not get any better than that. Stick it on the end, Bob, and bang to credits, then when the credits are over, play it again . . . "Maybe I did." Su-fucking-perb!'

DAY FORTY. 8.15 p.m.

Trisha had gone to see Sally's mother, a nervous, worried woman, who had been expecting her. 'I wondered how long it would take you people to get to me, and after what Sally said on the telly I knew you'd be here this morning.'

'Tell me about Sally,' Trisha said.

'Well, you obviously know that my late husband and I were not her birth parents.'

'Yes, we knew Sally was adopted.'

'Ever since the murder happened I haven't been able to sleep,' she said, staring down at her teacup. 'I know *exactly* what Sally will be thinking, I know it. She'll be worrying that people will think that it was her, because of . . . But you can't pass mental illness on, can you? Well, it isn't likely anyway. I've asked doctors, they've told me.'

'What was wrong with Sally's mother?'

300

'Paranoid schizophrenia, but I don't really know what that means. They seem to use these terms so often these days. Sally found out two years ago last Easter. I don't think adopted kids should be allowed to find out about where they came from. They never used to be. Adoption meant a completely new beginning, your new family *was* your family. These days they act as if adoptive parents are just caretakers. They're not *real*, they're not *birth*!'

'Is that what Sally said to you?' Trisha asked. 'That you weren't a real parent?'

'Well, she loved me, I know that, so she certainly never meant to hurt me. But she used to talk all the time about wanting to find her birth mother, her *blood*, as she put it. It broke my heart. I'm her real mother, aren't I? That was the deal.'

'So she found out that her mother had been a mental patient?'

'Well, I told her. I thought better coming from me than from some bloody librarian at the Public Records Office.'

'Is that why Sally was adopted? Because of her mother's mental instability?'

'You really don't know, do you? You actually don't know.' Mrs Copple was surprised.

'We don't know much at all, Mrs Copple. That's why we've come to you.'

'Oh dear. I don't want to tell you. If I do you'll suspect her, but you can't inherit what that woman had, at least it's not likely. I've talked to doctors. I've looked it up on the net.'

'Please, Mrs Copple, I'd much rather talk about this here with you now, at your home.' It was a gentle threat, heavily veiled but effective.

'Her mother was in prison. She killed someone . . . with a knife. That's why Sally was put up for adoption.'

'What about the father? Couldn't he have had her?'
'It was Sally's father who her mother killed.'

DAY FORTY-ONE. 2.15 p.m.

Trisha did everything she could to keep Sally's sad past a secret. She knew that if it came out Sally would be crucified in the press. Being aware of what leaky places police stations are, she asked to see Coleridge privately to explain her findings.

'There's no suggestion of abuse or provocation,' Trisha said. 'By all accounts Sally's father was a decent sort of man, if rather weak. Her mother was just pathologically unbalanced, and one night she just flipped.'

'Why did she get prison?' Coleridge asked. 'It seems obvious that the woman was ill.'

'Senile judge? Incompetent defence? Who knows, but the prosecution managed to get her tried as a sane defendant. Maybe it was because she was black. This was twenty years ago, remember. Anyway, she got life for murder in the first degree.'

'But appealed, of course.'

'Of course, and won, but sadly not before she'd stabbed two other inmates in Holloway with a sharpened canteen spoon. After that she went to a hospital for the criminally insane, where she still lives. Sally had been born shortly before her father was killed, and I imagine that these days they might have established some link with postnatal depression or whatever, but then they just banged her up and left her. She's thoroughly institutionalized now, apparently. Sally found out a couple of years ago and went to see her. Shook her up quite a bit.'

'Well, it would do. Does Sally have any mental problems?'

'Yes, depression and plenty of it, right back to

puberty. Been on numerous prescriptions and hospitalized once. The adoptive mother thinks it must have all been bound up with working out that she was gay, but I don't know about that, it certainly never . . .'

Trisha was about to say that it had never bothered her, that at the age of fourteen when she had finally worked out that she was a lesbian it had in fact been an enormous relief, explaining as it did the abject confusion that she had been experiencing in her relationships with both boys and girls. But she decided to leave the sentence hanging. Now was not the time.

'Whatever the reason, Sally has definitely had problems with depression, and of course ever since she found out about her mother she's been worrying that she's going the same way.'

'And what's the likelihood of that? I mean in medical terms?'

'Well, she's more likely to flip than, say, you or I, but the chances only become truly significant if both parents were sufferers. Then some doctors say it rises to nearly forty per cent.'

'What on earth were these appalling Peeping Tom people doing letting a serial depressive with a family history of mental illness into their grotesque exercise in the first place?'

'They claim that they didn't know, sir, and I believe them. Sally didn't tell them, and they would have had to dig pretty deep to find out, what with medical confidentiality and all that. It's not as if Sally's considered dangerous at all. I only found out because her mother told me.'

Coleridge leaned back in his chair and sipped at his little paper cup of water. It had been Hooper who had led the movement to get a water cooler installed in the incident room. Coleridge had resisted it fiercely, believing the whole business to be just another example of everybody these days wanting to look like Americans. However, now that the thing had been installed, he rather liked to be able to sip at clear cold water while he ruminated, and it had helped him to cut down on tea.

'So, tell me, Patricia,' he said. 'What are your thoughts? Do you think this information about Sally is significant – I mean, to our murder inquiry?'

'Well, sir, it certainly explains Sally's touchiness about mental health. But on the whole I'm tempted to say that this puts her more *out* of the frame than into it. I mean, now we know why she said what she said the night she quarrelled with Moon.'

'Yes, I'm inclined to agree with you, constable, although it must be admitted that the similarity between Sally's mother's crime and the crime committed in the house is a pretty nasty coincidence. Anyway, whatever we might think, I doubt that the press will consider Sally exonerated if they ever get hold of this.'

DAY FORTY-TWO. 7.00 a.m.

Mrs Copple was awoken by the ringing of the telephone. Almost at the same time her doorbell began to sound. By seven thirty there were forty reporters in her front garden and her life was ruined.

'SALLY'S THE ONE. JUST ASK HER MUM' was the most pithy of the headlines.

'The press always find out everything,' Coleridge said sadly when Trisha told him what had happened. 'They're much better than us. Nothing can ever be kept from them. They don't always publish, but they always know. They're prepared to pay, you see, and if you're prepared to pay for information, somebody will always be found to give it to you in the end.'

'Housemates, this is Chloe, can you hear me?'

Yes, they could hear her.

'The fifth person to leave the Peeping Tom house will be . . .'

The traditional pause . . .

'Sally!'

In that moment Sally made a little bit of TV history by becoming the first evictee from a programme of the *House Arrest* type not to shout 'Yes!' and punch the air in triumph as if delighted to be going.

Instead she said, 'So everybody out there thinks I did it too.'

'Sally,' Chloe continued, 'you have ninety minutes to say your goodbyes and pack your bags and then we'll be back to take you to your appointment with live TV!'

Sally went over to the kitchen area and made herself a cup of tea.

'I don't think you did it, Sally,' said Dervla, but Sally only smiled.

Then she went into the confession box. 'Hallo, Peeping Tom,' she said.

'Hallo, Sally,' said Sam, the soothing voice of Peeping Tom.

In the monitoring bunker Geraldine crouched close to the monitor, pen and pad in hand, ready to give Sam her lines. She knew she must play this one very carefully. Dangling before her was the prospect of some very good telly indeed. The result turned out to be even better than she had hoped.

'I expect by now the press have found out about my mum,' said Sally. 'How she's been held at Ringford Hospital for the last twenty years.'

'Horrible place,' whispered Geraldine, 'the worst loony bin of the lot.'

'Ever since Kelly died I've been wondering,' said

305

Sally. 'Could I have done it? Is there some way I could have gone into a sort of trance? Got into the sweatbox and turned into my mother? I know that my mum told me she couldn't remember a thing about when she did it, and when the police talked to me I couldn't really remember even being in the sweatbox. So perhaps I did it and can't remember that either? Was I in a box *inside* a box? My own black box? To be honest, I don't know. I don't *think* it was me. Paranoid schizophrenics don't cover their tracks, wear sheets and avoid getting even one drop of blood on themselves. I think it was too good to have been me. I don't think I could commit the perfect murder. I know my mother didn't when she killed my father . . . but it *could* have been me. I have to accept that. I just can't remember.'

'Fu-u-u-ucking hell,' Geraldine breathed. 'This is fa-a-a-a-abulous.'

'One thing I do know,' said Sally, 'is that everybody will think it was me and that I'll never escape that as long as I live. It's obvious that the police haven't got a clue. They'll probably never arrest anyone, so for the rest of my life I'll be seen as the black dyke nutter who murdered Kelly. Therefore, I've decided to make the rest of my life as short as possible.'

And with that Sally produced a kitchen knife from within the sleeve of her shirt. She had palmed it when she had made herself a cup of tea.

DAY FORTY-TWO. 9.00 p.m.

When Chloe went back on air she was able to announce yet another dramatic exit from the house. Not live as planned, because Sally had departed an hour earlier in an ambulance, her attempted suicide having been watched live on the Internet all over the world. She had managed to stab herself twice in the chest before Jazz burst into the confession box, having been alerted to do so by Peeping Tom.

Nobody yet knew whether she would survive her wounds or not.

Chloe explained all of this to the viewers, and promised a regular update throughout the show. 'I'm afraid that we cannot show you the footage of Sally's final, brilliant, heartfelt, totally honest and spiritual visit to the confession box, because apparently suicide is a crime and our legal people are worried that some authoritarian government office or other might attack us for showing you the *truth*. Right! I mean how fascist is that? Apparently you're not *grown up* enough to see what's actually *going on* in this world, which is *so* all about mind control and Brave New 1984-type stuff, which is not what Sally wanted at all!'

It was not a vintage performance, but Chloe's autocue had been hastily assembled. The message was clear enough. Any attempt to stop Peeping Tom from exploiting the anguish of a deeply disturbed young woman was an *outrageous* infringement of the civil liberties of the viewer.

Chloe was able to show the public the footage of Jazz's heroic and dramatic entrance into the confession box, when he managed to grab Sally's hand and wrest the knife from her grasp. After that she introduced a compilation of footage of Sally's brilliant weeks in the house.

Peeping Tom would of course have liked to cut live to the house to show the reactions of the other housemates to Sally's horrifying act, but sadly they couldn't, because Geraldine was currently in the house conducting a crisis negotiation with the remaining inmates. Trying to persuade them to carry on with the show.

'We can't, we just can't,' Dervla was saying. 'Not now. People will think we're absolute ghouls.'

Even as the Peeping Tom nurse had been rushing

along the corridor under the moat in order to help Sally, the other inmates had been clamouring to leave. This would be financially disastrous for Peeping Tom, of course, particularly after such a dramatic crowd-pleaser as Sally's attempted suicide. They stood to lose tens, possibly hundreds of millions of pounds.

'You're wrong, Dervla, you're wrong,' Geraldine said. 'They love you out there, they admire your courage, they respect you, and if you have the guts to see this through they'll respect you even more. Nobody thinks any of you five killed Kelly, they all think it was Sally, and it probably was. She just about confessed to it before she stabbed herself. In a way that's kind of an end to the whole murder thing, isn't it? Now all you lot have to do is sit out the rest of the game.'

'No way,' said Dervla. 'I want out.'

'Me too,' said Jazz, still shaking violently from his encounter with Sally.

The others agreed. They had had enough.

In the end Geraldine offered the inducement that she had been expecting to have to use much earlier. 'I'll tell you what I'll do. I'm doing pretty well out of all this, I won't deny it. There's no reason why you lot shouldn't profit too. How about this? The prize is currently half a million. What if we double it *and* guarantee the other four a lump too ... let's say a hundred grand for the next one out, two hundred for the one after that, three hundred for whoever comes third, and four hund ... No, half a mill for the runner-up? How about that? Not bad moolah for sitting on your arses for another few weeks, eh? If you agree now, the *minimum* all of you will make is a hundred grand.'

This offer pretty much clinched it, the prospect of being rich *and* famous being enough inducement for anyone.

'Just one extra thing,' said Dervla. 'If the police make an arrest on the outside – you know, David or whoever

308

– you have to tell us, OK? We can't be the only people in the country who don't know.'

'Fine, whatever, I promise, absolutely,' said Geraldine, thinking to herself that she would have to give that one some thought.

DAY FORTY-THREE. 9.00 a.m.

The morning after Sally's attempted suicide Coleridge was forced for the first time to allow a public statement to be issued, something which he believed to be no part of the police's responsibilities. But Sally was out of danger, and the world press wanted to know whether the police intended to arrest her.

'No,' Coleridge said, reading laboriously from prepared notes, 'there are no plans to arrest Miss Sally Copple for the murder of Miss Kelly Simpson, for the obvious reason that there is absolutely no evidence against her. Her own statements regarding a hereditary disposition towards murder and the fear that she might have done it while in a trance do not constitute grounds for an arrest. The investigation continues. Thank you and good day.'

After he had retreated into the building, Hooper and Trisha joined him.

'So what do you think, then, sir?' Hooper asked. 'I mean, I know we have no proof, but do you think Sally did it?'

'I don't,' Trisha said quickly, causing both Hooper and Coleridge to look at her curiously.

'I don't think she did it either, Patricia,' said Coleridge. 'And I don't *think* she did not do it either.'

Coleridge was of course a show-off in his small way, and he enjoyed the confused looks that this little paradox engendered. 'I *know* she did not do it,' he said. 'The killer is without doubt still in place.'

309

DAY FORTY-THREE. 4.40 p.m.

Dervla's little secret finally began to unravel when Coleridge started to view Geraldine's 'bathroom tapes', the hoarded compilation of flesh-revealing shots that she was saving for an X-rated Christmas video.

'She just seems to love brushing her teeth,' Coleridge observed.

Geraldine had retained quite a lot of footage of Dervla's dental hygiene routine, because this was the point of the day when quiet and reserved Dervla was at her most sexy and coquettish. Not just because she was either in her underwear or a wet T-shirt or a towel, having just had her shower, but also because standing at the mirror, particularly in the early weeks, she seemed so jolly and full of fun, smiling and winking at her reflection in the glass. It was almost as if she was *flirting* with herself.

'She's not like that when she does her teeth in the evening,' Coleridge remarked.

'Well, maybe she's a morning type of person,' said Hooper. 'So what? She's not the first girl to smile at her reflection.'

Coleridge flipped the switch on a second VCR machine, a rather complicated new one that he had only partly mastered. He had been able to convince the bureaucrats who administered his budget that the nature of the evidence he had at his disposal justified the hiring of a great deal of video and TV equipment. His only problem now was that it was so very complicated. Hooper could work it all, of course, and made no secret of displaying his superiority.

'What I could to for you, sir, is upload the tapes from the VCR onto digital format in my camcorder, bung it across a flywire into the new iBook they gave us, chop up the relevant bits and crunch it down via the movie-making software, export it to a Jpeg file and email it

310

straight to you. You could watch it on your mobile phone when you're stuck at traffic lights if we get you a WAP.'

Coleridge had only just learned how to use the text message service on his phone. 'I do not have my phone on when I am in my car, sergeant. And I hope that you don't either. You'll be aware, of course, that using one when driving is illegal.'

'Yes, sir, absolutely.'

They returned to the job in hand. Coleridge had lined up a moment of tape from a discussion that the group had had on day three about nominations.

'I'm at my most vulnerable to nomination in the mornings,' Dervla was saying, 'because that's when I'm going to snap at people and hurt their feelings. I'm crap at mornings, I just don't want to talk to anyone.'

Coleridge turned off his second machine and returned to the tape showing Dervla brushing her teeth.

'She may not like talking to anyone,' Coleridge observed, 'but she certainly likes talking to herself.'

On screen Dervla winked again into the mirror and said, 'Hallo, mirror, top of the morning to you.'

'Now watch her eyes,' Coleridge said, still staring intently at the scene. Sure enough, on the screen Dervla's sparkling green eyes flicked downwards and remained on what must have been the reflection of her belly button for perhaps thirty seconds.

'Maybe she's contemplating her navel, sir. It's a very cute one.'

'I'm not interested in observations of that kind, sergeant.'

Now Dervla's eyes came up again, smiling, happy eyes. 'Oh, I love these people!' she laughed.

'This tape is from day twelve, the morning after the first round of nominations,' Coleridge said. 'You'll

311

recall that nobody nominated Dervla, although, of course, she's not supposed to have any idea about that.'

Hooper wondered whether Coleridge was onto something. Everybody knew that Dervla was in the habit of laughing and talking to herself before the bathroom mirror. It had always been seen as rather an attractive, fun habit. Could there be more to it than that?

'Look, I've had some of the technical boffins make up a toothbrushing compilation,' said Coleridge.

Hooper smiled. Only Coleridge thought you needed 'boffins' to edit a video compilation. He himself made little home movies on his PowerBook all the time.

Coleridge put in his compilation tape and together they watched as time and again Dervla dropped cryptic little comments at her reflection in the mirror before brushing her teeth.

'Oh God, I wonder how they see me out there,' she said. 'Don't kid yourself, Dervla girl, they'll all love Kelly, she's a lovely girl.'

Coleridge switched off the video. 'What were Dervla's chances of winning the game at the point when Kelly was killed?'

'The running popularity poll on the Internet had her at number two,' Hooper replied, 'as did the bookies, but it was pretty irrelevant, because Kelly was number one by miles.'

'So Kelly was Dervla's principal rival in terms of public popularity?'

'Yes, but of course she couldn't have known that. Or at least she's certainly not supposed to.'

'No, of course not.'

Once more Coleridge pressed play on the video machine that held his toothbrushing compilation.

'I wonder who the public loves most?' Dervla mused archly to herself. Moments later her eyes flicked downwards.

DAY FORTY-FOUR. 12.00 p.m.

Coleridge picked up the phone. It was Hooper, calling from the Peeping Tom production office. He sounded pleased.

'I've got the duty log here, sir. You remember Larry Carlisle?'

'Yes, the operator who was working in the camera runs on the night of the murder?'

'That's the one. Well, he's been a busy boy, seems to have taken advantage of the fact that a number of people stopped working on the show out of boredom. He's done twice as many shifts as anyone else, often eight hours on, eight hours off. Loves the show, can't seem to get enough of it. And, what's more, he's covered the bathroom on almost every morning so far. If Dervla's chatting through the mirror to anyone, she's chatting to Larry Carlisle.'

'The operator who was working on the night of the murder,' Coleridge repeated.

DAY FORTY-FIVE. 7.58 a.m.

Coleridge had been in the dark hot corridor for only a few minutes and already he loathed it. He felt like a pervert, it was disgusting.

The east–west camera run of the Peeping Tom house was known as 'Soapy' to the teams who serviced it, on account of the fact that part of the run covered the mirrored shower wall and the mirrors above the basins, which often became splashed with suds and foam. The north–south run was known as 'Dry'.

Soapy and Dry had smooth, highly polished black floors, and were entirely cloaked in thick black blankets. Any light came from inside the house and shone through the long line of two-way mirrors that ran along the inside wall of the corridor. The camera operators were covered completely in black blankets and slid about silently like great coal-dark ghosts.

Coleridge had already seen Jazz walk out of the boys' bedroom and across the living space to use the toilet. That same toilet that had been Kelly's last port of call upon this earth. The only part of the house that was not visible through the two-way mirrors. Coleridge gritted his teeth as he was forced to listen to what seemed to him to be the longest urination in history. Coleridge could find no words to describe the horror and contempt he felt for the whole tawdry business. Was there ever a better example of humankind's utter lack of nobility and grace? Here, where with such care, such immense ingenuity, such untold resources, the comings and goings of a communal bathroom were recorded for posterity.

It was eight o'clock and time for a change of shift in Soapy corridor. Coleridge heard the faintest swish as a heavily padded door was opened and Larry Carlisle crept in, dressed from head to foot in black. He even wore a ski mask, which further increased the grim and chilling atmosphere of the corridor. Without a word Carlisle disappeared under the blanket that covered the camera and its dolly while the previous operator emerged from the other side and crept away.

Coleridge slunk back into the darkness, drawing his black cowled cassock close about him. Carlisle had not been informed of Coleridge's presence, and imagined himself alone in the corridor as usual.

At the other end of the house Dervla emerged from the girls' bedroom and wandered into the living area. She entered the bathroom and approached the shower, where she took off her shirt to reveal her usual shower attire of cropped vest and knickers.

Coleridge turned away, a natural instinct for him in

the circumstances. There was a lady in a state of undress and he had no business looking at her.

Carlisle also followed his natural instincts, those of a reality TV cameraman, in that he slid along the darkened corridor to get as close as he could to the flesh.

Dervla stepped into the shower and began to wash herself, her hands running all over her body with soap. Coleridge forced himself to look again. It was not that he found the sight of Dervla soaping her near-naked body unattractive; quite the opposite. Coleridge bowed to no man in his appreciation of the female form, and Dervla's in particular with its youthful, athletic grace was just his type. It was *because* he was attracted that Coleridge wanted to look away. He was a deeply Christian man; he believed in God and he knew that God would be extremely unimpressed if Coleridge started getting hot and bothered while looking at unsuspecting young women in their underwear. Particularly when he was on duty. Coleridge, that is, not God. God, in Coleridge's opinion, was always on duty.

Making absolutely certain in his own mind that his mind was on the job and nothing else, Coleridge turned back from the darkened wall and looked once more on the girl showering herself and the black-cloaked cameraman recording it.

Then he saw something that almost made him cry out. It was as much as he could do to stop himself from leaping forward and arresting the dirty little swine there and then.

Carlisle had a second camera. The man had emerged from beneath the thick black cape, having left his professional camera locked in position on its dolly, covering the young woman in the shower in a wide shot. Now he was using a small, palm-held digital camcorder, and was clearly making his own private video.

Coleridge watched in furious disgust as Carlisle

placed his little lens within millimetres of the soapy glass, clearly desperate to get as close to the unsuspecting woman as possible. Shamelessly he explored Dervla's body, zooming in on her navel, her cleavage, the faint darkened outline of her nipples showing through the material of her top. Then Carlisle crouched down to the level of Dervla's groin and began recording a long continuous close-up of her crutch area. Dervla's legs were slightly apart, the knickers thin and lacy. There was the faintest hint of soft wet hair escaping onto the uppermost part of her thighs. Water cascaded from her gusset in a sparkling stream.

When Dervla had finished showering she turned off the taps, knotted a towel across her breasts, removed her sodden undergarments from beneath it and crossed to the basin to brush her teeth.

Carlisle quickly turned off his personal camera and disappeared back under the black cape in order to push his professional camera over to cover the two-way mirror above the basin.

Beyond the mirror Dervla looked briefly at her own reflection and shook her head.

Coleridge had never been behind a two-way mirror before, and it was almost possible to believe that the girl was shaking her head not at herself but at the camera lens that hovered immediately in front of her nose. She did not speak, but she sang a snatch of an old Rod Stewart song, her voice faint beyond the glass but audible. 'I don't wanna talk about it,' she sang.

And then: 'Hey, boy, don't bother me.' After that she was silent and avoided engaging directly with her reflection.

Now Coleridge saw Carlisle's hand reach out beyond the front of his camera. He was holding something – a small white pouch which he took by a corner and shook. There was a tiny rattling sound in the deathly silence of the dark tunnel, and Coleridge realized with surprise what the pouch was: he had shaken one like it himself only a few weeks before during a hill walk in Snowdonia. It was a walker's instant heat pack, an envelope full of chemicals and iron filings designed to produce a great heat in moments of need. He watched, amazed, as Carlisle crunched the pouch in his fist to form a blunt point, and began to trace letters on the glass. Clearly the heat was intended to warm the condensation on the other side.

Carlisle wrote slowly, partly no doubt in order to give the heat time to conduct through the glass, but also, it seemed to Coleridge, because Carlisle was enjoying himself. His forefinger was gently stroking the glass, following the line traced by the heat pack, almost as if, by touching the two-way mirror, Carlisle felt he was in some way touching Dervla. Coleridge strained to see what Carlisle was writing. The letters were inscribed backwards, of course, but they were not difficult to follow.

On the other side of the glass Dervla was watching too, her eyes darting downwards as the message appeared.

'*Don't worry. People still care about you,*' emerged though the condensation.

Dervla's expression did not change. She kept her eyes fixed on the letters.

Behind the glass in the dark corridor, unaware that he was being observed by a police inspector, Carlisle stretched out his arm and wrote a few more words.

'*Nobody out here thinks you did it.*'

Three separate pairs of eyes watched as the words were slowly spelled out: '*But you're number one now. The people love you . . . and so do I.*'

Coleridge was an accomplished watcher of faces, and he knew Dervla's well from many hours of study. As he looked he saw clearly the distaste that flickered across her face.

'La de da,' she said, with a shrug of indifference, and began to brush her teeth.

Coleridge could sense Carlisle's tension as the cameraman fumbled to lock focus on his machine and get sight of Dervla through his own little camcorder. Clearly Carlisle coveted every image of his secret love, and once more he pushed his little lens as close to the glass as he dared without tapping it. First he stole himself a close-up of the dark tuft of hair in Dervla's armpit, revealed to him because her arm was raised to brush her teeth. Then he panned across a little in order to capture the faint jiggling of her breasts beneath the towel caused by the movement of her arm. Finally, with the practised timing brought by experience, he swung his sights upwards just in time to capture the unwitting girl spitting the toothpaste from between her lips. Coleridge could hear the tiny motor of the camcorder hum as Carlisle zoomed into extreme close-up on Dervla's wet, white, foaming mouth.

When she had finished, Dervla went out of the bathroom and back to the girls' bedroom. The house was silent once more. All of the inmates were in the two bedrooms on the opposite side of the house from Soapy corridor. Coleridge pressed the button on the little communicator that the Peeping Tom sound department had given him, which alerted Geraldine in the control room to the fact that he had seen enough.

A moment or two later Carlisle left his camera, having been recalled by Geraldine under some professional pretext, as she had promised to do.

Coleridge followed Carlisle out as he left the corridor. Once outside, blinking in the striplight of the communication tunnel that linked the house with the control complex, Coleridge laid his hand on Carlisle's collar in time-honoured fashion, and asked him to accompany him to the station.

DAY FORTY-FIVE. 12.00 noon

'Oh my God, I think I'm going to be sick. I really do think I'm going to be sick.'

Coleridge was showing Dervla some of the contents of the camcorder that he had taken from Larry Carlisle. Stacked up beside the VCR were seventeen similar mini-cassettes, retrieved by the police from Carlisle's home.

'You seem to have become something of an addiction for this man,' Coleridge said. 'Viewing his tape collection, it looks like he simply could not get enough of you.'

'Please don't. It's horrible, horrible.'

There was so much of it. Hours and hours of tape. Close-ups of Dervla's lips when she talked, when she ate, her eyes, her ears, her fingers, but most of all, of course, her body. Carlisle had recorded virtually every single moment that she had spent in the bathroom from day three onwards, becoming ever more practised at gaining close-ups of any intimate area that had been carelessly revealed to him.

Often in the shower the weight of the water had pulled at Dervla's sodden knickers, revealing the top of her pubic hair and, when she turned round, an inch or so of the cleft of her bottom. Carlisle had clearly lived for these moments, and he zoomed in to extreme close-up whenever the opportunity arose.

'I can't believe I've been so stupid,' Dervla said, her voice choking with disgust and embarrassment. 'Of course, I should have guessed why he was being so encouraging towards me, but I had no idea . . . I . . .'

Dervla, normally so strong, so self-assured, contemplated the creepily silent dislocated images of her own body on the screen, a body rarely viewed whole but broken up into intrusive, intimate close-ups, and she wept. The tears ran down her face as the soapy water on the screen ran down her stomach and her thighs.

'Did you get messages in the mirror every day?'

'Not every day, but most days.'

'What did they say?'

'Oh, nothing very startling. "*How are you?*" That kind of thing. "*You're doing great*".'

'So he talked about the game.'

'Well, not in any great detail. He was writing backwards in condensed steam, after all.'

'Did he ever mention Kelly?'

'No.'

It was a fool's lie.

'Actually, yes, I think he did mention her,' Dervla said quickly.

'Yes or no, Miss Nolan?'

'I just said yes, didn't I? Sometimes . . . a little . . . he mentioned them all.'

Half a lie. Was that any better? Or worse?

'I don't know why he sent me messages,' she added. 'I never asked him to.'

'He's in love with you, Miss Nolan.'

'Please don't say that.'

'He loves you, Dervla, and that is something that you are going to have to deal with, because I doubt that what he has done is going to get him any kind of prison sentence. When you come out of the house he'll be waiting for you.'

'You really think so?'

'That's my experience of obsessives. They can't just turn it off. You see, he thinks you love him back. After all, you've been flirting with him for weeks.'

'I haven't . . .' But even as she said it Dervla knew that denial was pointless. 'I . . . just sort of fell into it,' she continued. 'It was a laugh, a game. It's so *boring* in that house. The same dull stupid people that you can't even really get to like because you're in competition with them. You've no idea . . . And then there was this jokey thing going on, just for me. I had a secret friend on the outside who wished me luck and told me I was doing all right. You can't imagine how weird and insecure it is in that house, how vulnerable you feel. It was nice to have a secret friend.'

Dervla looked at the screen on which Larry Carlisle's tape was still playing. She was in the shower again, her hand inside the cups of her sodden bra, soaping her breasts, the shape of her nipples clearly visible. 'Can we turn that off, please?'

'I want you to see this next bit.'

The image on the screen flickered and changed to the girls' bedroom. It was night and all the girls appeared to be asleep.

'My God, he had a nightsight on his camcorder!' Dervla gasped.

'I'm afraid to say, my dear, that this man did not miss anything.'

On the screen Dervla was lying in bed. It had clearly been a hot night, as she was covered by only a single sheet. She was asleep, or so it seemed until her eyes opened for a moment and flickered about the room. Now the camera panned down from her face to her body. It was possible to make out Dervla's hand gently moving beneath the sheet, moving downwards to below her waist, the outline of her knuckles standing out against the cotton as her fingers moved gently beneath it. The camera returned to focus once more on Dervla's face: her eyes were closed but her mouth was open. She was sighing with pleasure.

Sitting in Coleridge's office, Dervla turned deep crimson with angry embarrassment. 'Please!' she snapped. 'This isn't fair.'

Coleridge switched off the tape. 'I wanted you to see

and to know just how little respect this man has had for you. You and he have been partners of sorts. You are partners no longer.'

Dervla felt scared. 'Surely, inspector, you can't really be thinking that there's any connection between this silly lark and . . . and . . . Kelly's death?'

Coleridge waited for a moment before replying. 'You said his messages mentioned Kelly?'

'Well, yes, they did but . . .'

'What did they say?'

'They said . . . they said that people liked her and that they liked me. They liked us both.'

'I see. And did he ever tell you who they liked more? Your ranking, so to speak.'

Dervla looked the chief inspector in the eye. 'No. Not specifically.'

'So you did not know that prior to Kelly's death you were in second place after her.'

'No, I did not.'

'Just remind me once more, Miss Nolan. How much is the prize worth for the winner of this game?'

'Well, it's gone up since, but at the time of the murder it was half a million pounds, chief inspector.'

'How are things at your parents' farm in Ballymagoon?'

'I beg your pardon?'

'I believe your parents are in danger of losing their farm and family home. I was wondering how all that was going. How they were taking it, so to speak.'

Dervla's face turned cold and hard. 'I don't know of late, inspector. I've been inside the house. But I imagine they'll survive. We're tough people in our family.'

'Thank you. That will be all, Miss Nolan,' Coleridge said. 'For the moment.'

DAY FORTY-FIVE. 1.30 p.m.

At first Geraldine had not wanted Dervla back in the house. 'Fuck her, the cheating little cow. I'll teach her for cock-teasing my cameramen and giving the show a bad name.'

Geraldine was angry and embarrassed that such a thing could have been going on under her nose without her having any idea about it. Her professional pride was deeply wounded, and she wanted to have her revenge on Dervla, of whom she was jealous anyway. Soon, however, wiser counsel prevailed. To eject Dervla would almost certainly mean admitting the reason for it, which would only compound Geraldine's embarrassment. Dervla was now the most popular and most fancied housemate, added to which was the fact that she had been removed by the police for further questioning, which massively increased her fascination.

Her photograph was all over the morning's papers, looking pale and beautiful as she was led from the house. The press had been forced to rethink their conviction that Sally was the killer, and their banner headlines read 'POLICE DETAIN DERVLA', 'DERVLA ARRESTED'. Soon she would be all over the evening news with reporters standing outside the house breathlessly announcing that the police had failed to lay charges against her. This was exactly the kind of incident that Geraldine needed to keep the whole story at the top of the nation's, and indeed the world's, agenda.

All in all, Dervla was too important to the show to let go.

'It'll mean keeping that disgusting pervert Carlisle,' Geraldine complained. 'If we sack him but leave her alone the cunt will blackmail us. At least I know I would.'

DAY TWENTY. 12.40 p.m.

William Wooster, or Woggle as he was more generally known, was released on bail of £5000, which was stood by his parents. The police had appealed against bail being granted on the grounds that Woggle, being a member of the itinerant, alternative community and a known tunneller, might easily abscond. The judge took one look at Dr and Mrs Wooster, him in tweeds, her in pearls, and decided that it would be an insult to two such obvious pillars of the community to deny them the company of their wayward son.

Woggle absconded within two hundred yards of the court.

After his brief appearance before the majesty of the law he and his parents had fought their way through the crowd of reporters who were waiting outside the courtroom, got into the waiting minicab and had driven off together. That, however, was as far as Woggle was prepared to go in this return to family life. Woggle waited for the first red traffic light and, when the cab pulled up to stop, simply got out and ran. His parents let him go. They had been through this so many times before and were just too old for the chase. They sat together in the car, contemplating the fact that the company of their son had this time cost them over £1000 a minute.

'Next time we won't do this,' said Woggle's dad.

Woggle ran for about a mile or so, dodging this way and that, fondly imagining that his dear old father was tearing after him waving his umbrella. When he finally believed himself safe, he decided to stop in a pub for a pint and a pickled egg. It was here that he was forced for the first time to come to terms with the extent of the blow that Peeping Tom had dealt him. For it was not just the police and the press who knew him now. Everybody knew him, and they did not like him, not one little bit.

A group of men surrounded him at the bar as he waited to be served. 'You're that cunt, aren't you?' said the nastiest looking of the gang.

'If you mean am I beautiful, warm, welcoming and hairy, yes, then you could say I was a cunt.'

It was a piece of bravado that Woggle had cause to regret as the man instantly decked him.

'I offer up the hand of peace,' Woggle said from the floor.

The man took it and dragged him outside by it, where the whole gang comprehensively beat Woggle up.

'Not so easy when you ain't kicking little girls, is it?' said the thugs, as if by attacking him with odds at six to one they were doing something brave. They left him lying in the proverbial pool of blood with broken teeth filling his mouth and hatred filling his soul. Hatred not for the thugs, who as an anarchist he considered merely unenlightened comrades, but for Peeping Tom Productions.

He skulked away from the pub, dressed his wounds as best he could in a nearby public toilet and then went underground. Literally. He returned to the tunnels whence he had come. There better to nurse his colossal sense of grievance. To dig it deeper into his angry heart with every stone and ounce of earth that he moved.

They had brought him low. All of them. The people on the inside of the house and the ones across the moat in the bunker.

Dig, dig, dig.

Geraldine Hennessy. That witch. He had thought that he could trust her, but he had been mad.

Dig, dig, dig.

You could not trust anyone. Not straights, not muggles, not fascist television people, and certainly not those *bastards* in the house. Particularly the ones who had pretended to be his friend. He hated them most. Not Dervla, of course, not the Celtic Queen of the Runes and Rhymes. Dervla was all right, she was a beautiful summer pixie. Woggle had seen the tapes and she had not nominated him. But the other one, the one who had made the tofu and molasses comfort cake! What a hypocritical *slag* that bitch had been! He'd eaten it, too. Late at night when she wasn't looking. Well, he'd show her.

Dig, dig, dig.

He hadn't wanted to kick that girl. She'd come at him with her dogs and now the whole country loathed him and he was facing a prison sentence. Woggle was scared of prison. He knew that the people in prisons were even straighter than the ones on the outside. They didn't like people like Woggle. Especially people like Woggle who kicked fifteen-year-old girls.

That was why he had gone back underground. To hide and to plan. Woggle decided as he scraped away at the earth that if he was going down, he was not going down alone. He would have his revenge on them all.

Dig, dig, dig.

DAY FORTY-FIVE. 3.00 p.m.

Trisha and Hooper checked the lab report for the final time, took deep breaths, and walked into Coleridge's office.

The police had had the two-way mirror glass through which Carlisle had been sending his messages to Dervla removed and sent to the forensic lab for analysis. The conclusions had come back within a few hours, and it seemed to Trisha and Hooper that they rather changed everything.

'We think this builds a pretty strong case against the cameraman, Larry Carlisle, sir.'

Coleridge looked up from the notes he had been reading.

'Look at this.' Hooper produced the summary of the evidence found by the forensic technicians. 'Carlisle wrote his messages with his instant heat pack, but he also traced them with his finger. The heat from the pack warmed the condensation on the other side.'

'I know that, sergeant. I told you.'

'Well, because Dervla wiped away the steam on her side it looked as if the messages were gone for ever. But the residue his finger left on the glass on his side remained. There are stains, sir. Stains and smears.'

'Stains and smears?'

'Semen, I'm afraid.'

'Ye gods.'

'I've spoken to Carlisle. He admits that he regularly masturbated during his duty shifts. He claims they all did.'

'Oh no, surely not!' Coleridge protested.

'Carlisle seemed to think it was hardly surprising, sir. As he said, once Geraldine cut the shifts down to one man, the operator was all alone in a darkened corridor for eight hours, covered in a big blanket. They're all men and they're staring at beautiful young women undressing and taking showers.'

Hooper almost added, 'What would you do?' but he valued his job and restrained himself.

'Carlisle says they sometimes called the corridors the peep booths,' Trisha added.

Coleridge stared out of the window for a moment. Three years. That was all he had left, then he could retire and go away for ever and listen to music and reread Dickens and tend the garden with his wife, give more time to amateur dramatics and never have to consider a world of secretly masturbating cameramen ever again. 'You're saying he wrote his messages in semen?'

'Well, there weren't puddles of it. I think it was more a case of traces of the stuff being left on his fingers.'

Trisha noticed that during this part of the conversation Coleridge addressed himself exclusively to Hooper. He absolutely did not look at her. Coleridge was a man who still believed that there were some things which were better off not discussed in mixed company. Not for the first time Trisha found herself wondering how it was that Coleridge ever came to be a police officer at all. But on the other hand, he was incorruptible, believed passionately in the rule of law and was acknowledged as a superb detective, so perhaps it was not necessary that he also live in the same century as everybody else.

'All right,' Coleridge said angrily. 'What did the lab say?'

'Well, sir, it's all pretty jumbled up and overlaid, but when dusted, four messages can be made out and some of others are partly there. They all give Dervla the current popularity score. Two of the clear ones are pre Woggle's eviction and put Dervla in third place behind him and Kelly, then with Woggle gone the two girls both move up one. Dervla knew the score from the start. Carlisle told her.'

'But she denied it when we asked her. What a foolish young woman.'

'Well, she could obviously see that her knowing her position relative to Kelly would give her a motive for murder. Half a million pounds is a lot of money, particularly if your mum and dad are broke.'

'And she *was* closest to the exit in the sweatbox,' Trisha added.

'The least that she's been guilty of is withholding evidence, and I intend to make sure that she regrets it,' said Coleridge.

'Well, of course, sir, but we think Carlisle is the issue,' said Trisha. 'Dervla was his motive. He wanted desperately to be the one who helped her to win, and he was convinced that Kelly stood in the way.'

'You think his desire for her to win could be a strong enough motive for murder?'

'Well, he's pathologically obsessed with her, sir, we know that. And you only have to look at the tapes he made to see how weird and warped that love is. Surely it's possible that this aching, gnawing proximity to the object of his affections totally unbalanced him.'

'Love is usually the principal motive in crimes of passion,' Hooper chipped in, quoting Coleridge himself, 'and this was clearly a crime of passion.'

'Do you remember what happened to Monica Seles, sir, the tennis player?' said Trisha eagerly. 'Exactly what we're suggesting happened here. A sad, besotted psycho fan of her rival Steffi Graf stabbed Seles in the insane belief that such an action would advance Graf's career, and that Graf would thank him for it.'

'Yes,' conceded Coleridge. 'I think the example is relevant.'

'But consider this, sir,' Hooper jumped in. 'Not only did Larry Carlisle have the motive, he had the *opportunity*.'

'You think so?' said Coleridge.

'Well . . . *almost* the opportunity.'

'In my experience opportunities for murder are never "almost".'

'Well, there's one bit we can't work out, sir.'

'I look forward to hearing you admit that to a defence lawyer,' Coleridge observed drily, 'but carry on.'

'Until now we've all been working on the assumption that the murderer was one of the people in the sweatbox.'

'For understandable reasons, I think.'

'Yes, sir, but consider the case against Carlisle, who was even *closer* to the victim. First of all he sees Kelly emerging from the boys' bedroom and sweeping naked across the living area towards the toilet. Carlisle captures this moment beautifully and gets complimented

329

from the monitoring box for his efforts. Now Kelly disappears into the toilet and Carlisle is instructed to cover the door in the expectation of getting more good nude material when she emerges.'

'But she doesn't emerge.'

'No, because he kills her, sir. It could so easily have been him. Put yourself in his shoes, the shoes of a besotted man, a man who from the very beginning has been risking his job, his future in the industry, his marriage – don't forget, sir, Carlisle is married with children. He's been risking *everything* for the love of Dervla—'

'A love that's mirrored by his hatred of Kelly,' Trisha chipped in. 'Look at this, sir.' She had brought a large folder into the room with her, the sort of folder that an artist or graphic designer might use to keep their portfolio of work in. Inside it were a series of photographs that the people at Forensic had taken of their work on the tunnel side of the two-way mirror.

In the first photo it was impossible to make anything out. All that could be seen was a streaky, dusted surface where a finger had clearly traced numerous letters on top of one another. Then Trisha produced a second copy of the photograph, and then a third, on which the relevant experts had struggled to make sense of the mess; here in different-coloured translucent pastel shades they had followed different sentences, sometimes getting a clear reading, sometimes making informed guesses.

'Look at that one, sir,' said Trisha, pointing to a sentence that was traced out in red. 'Not very nice, is it?'

DAY TWENTY-SIX. 8.00 a.m.

'*The bitch Kelly still number one. Don't worry my darling. I will protect you from the cocksucking whore.*'

330

Dervla reached forward to the mirror and angrily rubbed out the words. She had come to dread brushing her teeth in the morning. The messages had been getting steadily angrier and uglier, but she could say nothing about it for fear of revealing her own complicity in the communication. Of course, she no longer encouraged him, she no longer spoke to the mirror, and had wracked her brains to think of a way of telling the man on the other side to stop. The only idea that she had had was singing songs with vaguely relevant lyrics.

'I don't wanna to talk about it'. 'Return to sender.' 'Please release me, let me go.'

But the messages kept coming. Each one uglier than the last.

'*I swear to you my precious, I'd kill her for you if I could.*'

DAY FORTY-FIVE. 3.10 p.m.

' "I'd kill her for you if I could," ' Coleridge read out. 'Well, that's pretty damning, isn't it?'

'So there he is,' Hooper pressed on eagerly. 'The man who wrote that message, standing with his camera pointing at the toilet door, knowing that the object of his hatred is inside. What does he do? He locks his camera in the position he has been told to maintain, creeps back along Soapy corridor, up Dry, through the wall hatch into the boys' bedroom, picks up a sheet from outside the sweatbox, emerges from the bedroom covered in it, and the rest we know. It's Carlisle we see cross the living area to pick up the knife from the kitchen drawer, Carlisle who bursts in on Kelly, and Carlisle who murders her.'

'Well . . .' said Coleridge warily.

'I know what you're going to say, sir. I know, I know.

331

What about the bedroom? It's covered by cameras too . . .'

'It had occurred to me, yes,' Coleridge answered.

'If he'd entered the room from Dry and gone and picked up a sheet at the sweatbox we would have seen it and we didn't.'

'Yes, and not only did we not see it, but what we *did* see was a person emerge from the sweatbox and pick up the sheet.'

'Yes, sir, but only on video. No one who was in the sweatbox recalls a second person leaving it. Therefore either one, some or all of them are lying.'

'I agree.'

'*Unless* the video is lying. Carlisle is a trained camera operator. We know from his extraneous activities that his interest in the tools of television is not merely professional. Is there some way that he could have corrupted the evidence of the hot-head camera in the bedroom? The imaging of the figure emerging into the sheet is pretty unclear. Trisha and I have been wondering if he could have somehow *frozen* the picture being broadcast for a few moments—'

'After all, the image had remained unchanged for hours already,' Trisha interrupted. 'Is it possible that he somehow looped a few seconds or simply paused it for long enough to cross the room to the sweatbox?'

'After which it would all happen in real time as we saw it,' Hooper concluded.

'He would have had to pull the same trick on the way back,' said Coleridge. 'We saw the murderer return to the sweatbox, don't forget.'

'I know. There are a lot of problems with the theory,' pressed Hooper, 'but don't forget, sir, that Carlisle was very hazy about the timings of when the events happened. Do you remember that he claimed that only two minutes had passed from when Kelly went to the toilet to when the killer emerged from the bedroom, while everybody in the monitoring bunker said it was five, which was proved on the time code. And he claimed that as much as five minutes passed after the killer had re-emerged until the murder was discovered, whereas in fact it was only two. Again the people in the box and the actual time code all concurred. Those are big discrepancies, sir, but understandable ones, of course, if it was actually Carlisle who committed the murder. Anybody might imagine that two minutes was five and that five was two if they had spent those minutes killing someone with a kitchen knife.'

'Yes,' conceded Coleridge. 'I think they might. I suggest you speak to the relevant boffins in order to see how these remote cameras might be interfered with. And of course we'd better have another word with *Miss Nolan*.'

DAY FORTY-SIX. 2.30 p.m.

The sight of Dervla being escorted from the house by the police for the second time in one day caused a sensation both outside and in. Surely this must mean that she was now the number-one suspect?

Geraldine could scarcely contain her delight. 'The fucking cops are flogging our show for us,' she crowed. 'Just when everybody thought Loopy Sal' done it, they nick the virgin princess *twice*! Fuck me sideways, it's brilliant. But we have to make plans. A lot of moolah's riding on this. If they don't give us Dervla back we'll cancel this week's eviction, all right? Can't lose two of the cunts in one week, just can't afford it. A week of this show is worth more money than I can count!'

Hamish and Moon were up for eviction this week, but if Dervla went it seemed that they would get a reprieve. The nominations had been the most relaxed since the relatively calmer days of Woggle and Layla.

With Sally gone there had been a general lifting of the gloom, besides which Sally was a prime suspect for having committed the murder, so her absence had made the house feel safer.

It felt safer no longer, of course. There had been shock and fear at Dervla's second removal by the police.

'Fookin' 'ell, I thought I were all right with her,' said Moon. 'We've been sharing a fookin' bedroom! I lent her a jumper.'

'I don't believe it,' said Jazz. 'The cops are fishing, that's all.'

'Just because you fancy her don't mean she ain't a mad knife-woman, Jazz,' Garry said.

Jazz didn't reply.

DAY FORTY-SIX. 4.00 p.m.

Dervla's lip quivered. She was trying not to cry. 'I thought if I told you I knew the scores you'd suspect me.'

'You stupid stupid girl!' Coleridge barked. 'Don't you think that lying to us is probably the best way to engender our suspicion?'

Dervla did not reply. She knew that if she did she really would cry.

'Lying to the police is a criminal offence, Miss Nolan,' Coleridge continued.

'I'm sorry. I didn't think it would matter.'

'Oh, for God's sake!'

'It was only between him and me, and he was on the outside! I didn't think it would matter.' Now Dervla *was* crying.

'Right, well, you can start telling the truth now, young lady. You were, I take it, aware at all times of your standing with the public, and of Kelly's?'

'Yes, I was.'

'What would you say was Larry Carlisle's attitude towards Kelly?'

'He hated her,' Dervla replied. 'He wanted her dead. That was why I tried to stop him sending me messages. His tone changed so completely. It was vile. He called her some terrible things. But he was on the outside. He couldn't have . . .'

'Never you mind what he could and couldn't do. What we're concerned about here, my girl, is what *you* did.'

'I didn't do anything!'

Coleridge stared at Dervla. He thought of his own daughter, who was not much older than the frightened girl sitting opposite him.

'Are you going to charge me?' Dervla asked in a very small voice.

'No, I don't think there'd be much point,' said Coleridge. Dervla had not been under oath when she had given her statement and she *had* been under stress. Coleridge knew that any half-decent brief could make a convincing case that she had simply been confused when she gave her evidence. Besides, he had no wish to charge her. He knew the truth now and that was all he was interested in.

And so Dervla went back into the house.

DAY FORTY-SEVEN. 11.00 a.m.

The days dragged by in the house and the tension remained unrelenting. Every moment they expected either word of an arrest from the outside, as Geraldine had promised, or another visit from the police to take one of the remaining housemates into custody. But nothing happened.

They cooked their meals and did their little tasks,

always watching, always wondering, waiting for the next development. Occasionally a genuine conversation would bubble up out of the desultory chats and interminable silences that now characterized most of the house interaction, but these moments never lasted long.

'So who believes in God, then?' Jazz asked as they all sat round the dining table, pushing their Bolognese around their plates. Jazz had been thinking about Kelly, and about heaven and hell, and so he asked his question.

'Not me,' said Hamish, 'I believe in science.'

'Yeah,' Garry agreed, 'although religion is good for kiddies, I think. I mean, you've got to tell them something, haven't you?'

'I'm quite interested in Eastern religions,' said Moon. 'For instance, I reckon that Dalai Lama is a fookin' ace bloke, because with him it's all about peace and serenity, ain't it? And at the end of the day, fair play to him because I really really respect that.'

'What sort of science do you believe in, then, Hamish?' Dervla asked.

'The Big Bang Theory, of course, what else?' Hamish replied pompously. 'They have telescopes so powerful nowadays that they can see to the very edges of the universe, to the beginning of time. They know to within a few seconds when it all began.'

'And what was there *before* it all began, then?' asked Moon.

'Ah,' said Hamish. 'You see, everybody asks that.'

'I wonder why.'

'Yeah, Hamish,' Jazz taunted. 'What was there before?'

'There was nothing there before,' said Hamish loftily. 'Not *even* nothing. There was no space and no time.'

'Sounds like in here,' Jazz replied.

'Fook all that, Hamish, it's bollocks.'

'It's *science*, Moon. They have evidence.'

'I don't see what you're arguing about,' said Dervla. 'It seems to me that accepting the Big Bang theory or any other idea doesn't preclude the existence of God.'

'So do you believe in him, then?'

'Well, not *him*. Not an old man with a big beard sitting in a cloud chucking thunderbolts about the place. I suppose I believe in *something*, but I don't hold with any organized religion. I don't need some rigid set of rules and regulations to commune with the God of my choice. God should be there for you whether you've read his book or not.'

Coleridge and Trisha had caught this conversation on the net. The *House Arrest* webcast played constantly in the incident room now.

'I should have arrested that girl for obstruction,' he said. 'There's one young lady who could do with a few *more* rules and regulations.'

'What's she done now?' said Trisha. 'I thought you liked her.'

'For heaven's sake, Patricia, did you hear her? "The God of my choice." What kind of flabby nonsense is that?'

'I agreed with her, actually.'

'Well, then, you're as silly and as lazy as she is! You don't *choose* a god, Patricia. The Almighty is not a matter of whim! God is not required to *be there for you*! You should *be there for him*!'

'Well, that's what you think, sir, but—'

'It is also what every single philosopher and seeker after truth in every culture has believed since the dawn of time, constable! It has always been commonly supposed that faith requires some element of humility on the part of the worshipper. Some sense of awe in the smallness of oneself and the vastness of creation! But not any more! Yours is a generation that sees God as some kind of vague counsellor! There to tell you what you want to hear, when you want to hear it, and to be entirely forgotten about inbetween times! You have invented a junk faith and you ask it to justify your junk culture!'

'Do you know what, sir? I think if you'd been around four hundred years ago you'd have been a witch-burner.'

Coleridge was taken aback. 'I think that's unfair, constable, and also unkind,' he said.

The brief conversation around the dinner table had died out as perfunctorily as it had begun, and the housemates had returned to the uncomfortable contemplation of their own thoughts.

What could possibly be going on out there?

They speculated endlessly, but they did not *know*. They were cut off, at the centre of this mighty drama and yet playing no part in it. Not surprisingly, they had begun to turn detective, conjuring up endless theories in their own minds. Occasionally they took their thoughts to the confession box.

'Look, Peeping Tom,' said Jazz on one such occasion. 'This is probably really stupid. I never even thought to say anything about it till now, I just think maybe I ought to say it so you can tell the police, and then it's done, right? Because I reckon it ain't nothing anyway. It's just I was in the hot tub with Kelly and David. I think it was about the beginning of the second week and Kelly whispered something in David's ear that freaked him out. I think she said, 'I know you,' and he didn't like it at all. It did his head in big time. Then she said the weirdest thing. I don't know what, but I think she said, pardon my French, "Fuck Orgy Eleven", and he was pole-axed, man. That, he *did not* like.'

'Great,' said Hooper, who had now joined Trisha at the computer. 'Two weeks staring at those bloody tapes.

338

We wrestle one piss-poor clue out of the whole thing, and now it turns out this bastard knew about it all along anyway.'

'Well, at least he left it till now to tell us,' said Trisha, 'and gave you the satisfaction of working it out for yourself.'

'I'm thrilled.'

Hooper may not have been thrilled, but everybody else was, because it took the press, who were also monitoring the Internet, all of five minutes to find out what *Fuck Orgy Eleven* was, and of course who Boris Pecker was. The news of this juicy development hit the papers the following morning, to the delight of the legions of *House Arrest* fans. David's downfall was complete.

DAY FORTY-NINE. 10.00 a.m.

It was eviction day, but many long hours would have to pass before the excitement of the evening. As usual the Peeping Tom production team had been racking their brains trying to think of things for the housemates to do. It wasn't that interest in the show was waning, far from it. *House Arrest* remained the single most watched show on the planet. Geraldine had just brokered a worldwide distribution deal for the following week's footage of US$45 million. It was more a matter of professional pride. Peeping Tom knew that it was running a freak show, but, freak show or not, it was still a television programme and they were responsible for it. The general feeling at the production meetings was that some artistic effort was required, if only for form's sake.

The week's task had been a success. Geraldine had challenged the housemates to create sculptures of each other, and this inspired thought, with all its possibilities for psychological analysis, had provoked an incident of genuine spontaneous drama. An incident that once more confounded the sceptics who thought that *House Arrest* had run out of shocks.

The trouble started when Dervla returned from her second visit to the police station. She was tired and upset after her grilling from Coleridge. Then there had been all the gawpers and reporters outside the house, screaming at her, asking if she had killed Kelly, and if it had been a sex thing. And finally there had been the looks of doubt and suspicion on the faces of her fellow housemates when she re-entered the house. Even Jazz looked worried.

All in all, she was in no mood for jokes, so when she noticed that Garry had placed a kitchen knife in the hand of his half-finished representation of her, she flipped.

'You bastard!' Dervla screamed, white with fury. 'You utter, utter bastard.'

'It was a fahking joke, girl!' said Garry, laughing. 'Joke? Remember them? After all, you are the coppers' favourite, love!'

At which point Dervla slapped him across the face with such force that Garry toppled backwards over the orange couch.

'Fahk that!' said Garry, leaping up, tears of pain and anger in his eyes. 'Nobody slaps the Gaz, not even a bird, all right? I intend to give your arse a right proper spanking, you nasty little Paddy bitch!'

'Oi,' said Jazz, and leaped forward with the intention of intervening, but this act of chivalry turned out to be unnecessary. Dervla did not need any help, for as Garry advanced upon her, fists clenched, intent upon mayhem, she spun round upon one foot and in a single smooth movement planted the other one firmly into Garry's face.

He fell to the ground instantly, blood gushing from his nose.

'Blimey,' said Geraldine in the monitoring bunker.

Dervla had been practising kickboxing since she was eleven and was by now a master at it, but she never told anybody if she could help it. She had discovered early on that once people knew, it was all they ever wanted to talk about. People were always asking for demonstrations and asking earnest questions: 'OK, say if three, no, *four* blokes, *with* baseball bats, jumped you *from behind*, could you take them out?'

On the whole Dervla had kept her special skill private. Now, however, the world knew and frankly she didn't care. She realized that she had a score to settle, and that it had nothing to do with Garry.

Suddenly weeks of pent-up fear and rage exploded within her. Dervla knew that lurking not ten feet from her was almost certainly the message-writer, Larry Carlisle, the agent of her recent distress. Ignoring Garry, who was crumpled up on the floor howling in pain, Dervla turned to face the mirrors on the wall. 'And if you're out there, Carlisle, you disgusting little pervert, that's *exactly* what you'll get if you come within a hundred miles of me when I get out of this house. You made the police suspect me, you bastard! So you just leave me alone or I'll kick your fucking head off and pull your balls out through your neck!'

'Wow,' said Geraldine in the monitoring bunker. 'Is *he* going to have some explaining to do when he gets home.'

Thus it was that the affair of the perving cameraman unexpectedly entered the public domain, giving Peeping Tom yet another day of high drama. Carlisle was sacked, of course, but Dervla, who should by rights have also been kicked off the show for conniving with him, was allowed to stay.

'Dervla did not solicit these messages, nor did she welcome them,' said Geraldine piously, which was complete rubbish, of course, but the press did not care because nobody wanted to remove Dervla from the mix, particularly now that she had suddenly become so interesting. Particularly after Geraldine broadcast a selection of Carlisle's private footage of Dervla in the shower.

All of that excitement, however, had been some days before, and the voracious public appetite for surprises now needed feeding again. The hours until eviction would have to be filled. Geraldine decided to dig out the predictions package.

'*Peeping Tom has instructed the housemates to open the "predictions" package, which they had all been a part of preparing at the end of week one,*' said Andy the narrator. '*The package has lain untouched at the back of the kitchen cupboard since the day it was produced.*'

'Uh'd fugodden all abah did,' said Garry, who was still nursing a swollen nose. Garry had decided to accept his surprise beating at Dervla's hands in good part and let it be known both to her and in the confession box that there were no hard feelings on his side. 'At the end of the day,' he said through his bloody sinuses, 'if you get bopped you get bopped. No point crying about it. In fact, getting hit by a bird is good for me and has made me more of a feminist.'

Garry was not stupid. There was a big difference between the hundred grand that the next person out would get and the million that would go to the winner. He wanted to stay in the game while the money grew, and he guessed that sour grapes would not help his cause at all. Therefore, once the doctor had treated his nose, which had been neatly broken, he shook Dervla's hand and said, 'Fair play to you, girl,' and the nation applauded him for it.

Inside, of course, Garry was seething. To have been duffed up by a bird, a *small* bird, on live TV. It was his worst nightmare. He'd never be able to show his face down the pub again.

Watching Garry's efforts to make up with Dervla on the police computer, Hooper did not believe a word of it. 'He hates her. She's number one on our Garry's hate list,' he said.

'The place that Kelly used to occupy,' Trisha mused. 'And Kelly, of course, got killed.'

They had all forgotten about the predictions envelope, and there was eager anticipation as Jazz solemnly opened it and they all dipped in. The whole thing reminded them of a happier, more innocent time in the house.

Peeping Tom had supplied some wine and there was much laughter as all the wrong predictions made six weeks earlier were read out.

'Woggle reckoned he'd be the only one left,' said Jazz.

'Fook me, Layla picked herself to win the whole thing!' laughed Moon.

'Listen to David!' shrieked Dervla. '"I believe that by week seven I will have emerged as a healing force within the group."'

'In your dreams, Dave!' Jazz shouted.

The laughter died somewhat when they came to Kelly's prediction. Moon read it out, and it was a moment of pure pathos.

'"I think that all the others are great people. I love them all big time and I shall be made up if I am still around by week seven. My guess is I'll be out on week three or four."'

There was silence as they all realized how right Kelly had been.

'What's that one, then?' Moon asked, pointing at a piece of paper that had not yet been read out.

Hamish turned it over. It was written in the same blue pencil that Peeping Tom had provided for everybody but the handwriting was a scrawled mess, as if somebody had been writing without looking and also with their left hand. This, the police handwriting expert was later to confirm, was indeed how the message had been written.

'What does it say?' asked Moon.

Hamish read it out. '"By the time you read this Kelly will be dead."'

It took a moment for it to dawn on them just what had been said.

'Oh, my fook,' said Moon.

Somebody had known for certain that Kelly would die. Somebody had actually written out the prediction. It was too horrible to imagine.

'There's more. Shall I read it?' Hamish asked after a moment.

They all nodded silently.

'"I shall kill her on the night of the twenty-seventh day."'

'Oh my God! He knew!' Dervla gasped.

Still Hamish had not finished. There was one final prediction in the note. '"One of the final three will also die."'

'Oh, my God,' Moon gasped. 'No one's touched that envelope in six fookin' weeks. It could have been any of us wrote that.'

DAY FORTY-NINE. 12.05 a.m.

Woggle had taken to sleeping in his tunnel. He felt safe there. Safe from all the people who did not understand

344

him. Safe to dig away at his hate. Planting it deeper with every blow of his pick. Watering it with his sweat.

Occasionally at night he would emerge to get water and to steal food. But more and more he existed entirely underground. In his tunnel.

The tunnel that he had dug to take his revenge.

Dig, dig, dig.

He would show them. He would show them all.

One evening, when the time had nearly come for what he had to do, Woggle took his empty sack and crept from his tunnel once more, but this time his mission was not for food. This time he made his way to a squat in London where he had once lived, a squat occupied by anarchists even stranger and more stern in their resolve than he was. These anarchists Woggle knew had the wherewithal to make a bomb.

When Woggle crept back to his tunnel just before the morning light the sack he carried was full.

DAY FORTY-NINE. 7.30 p.m.

Hamish was evicted in the usual manner, but nobody noticed very much. Try as Chloe might to drum up some interest in his departure, all anybody wanted to talk about was the sensational news that another murder was to take place.

The whole world buzzed with the news that one of the final three would die.

'It's curious, isn't it?' Coleridge said, inspecting the ugly scrawled note that lay in Geraldine's office in a plastic evidence bag.

'It's fucking chilling, if you ask me,' said Geraldine. 'I mean, how the hell would he have known he was going to be in a position to do Kelly on day twenty-seven? I hadn't even had the idea for the sweatbox then. Besides, he might have been evicted by then. I mean, he couldn't get back into the house, could he? And what about this stuff about killing one of the last three? I mean, nobody knows who the last three will be. It's up to the public.'

'Yes,' said Coleridge. 'It is all very strange, isn't it? Do you think there'll be another murder, Ms Hennessy?'

'Well, I don't really see how there can be . . . On the other hand, he was right about Kelly, wasn't he? I mean, the predictions envelope was put in the cupboard at the end of week one. There've been cameras trained on that cupboard ever since. There is no way it could have been interfered with. Somehow the killer *knew*.'

'It would certainly seem so.'

At that point Geraldine's PA entered the office. 'Two things,' said the PA. 'First, I don't know how you did it, Geraldine, but you did. The Americans have agreed to your price of two million dollars *a minute* for the worldwide rights to the final show, the *Financial Times* are calling you a genius . . .'

'And the second thing?' asked Geraldine.

'Not such good news. Did you see Moon in the confession box? They want a million each, right now, up front, to stay in the house for another moment.'

'Where's my cheque book?' said Geraldine.

'Isn't that against the rules?' Coleridge asked.

'Chief inspector, this is a *television* show. The rules are whatever we want them to be.'

'Oh yes, I was forgetting. I suppose that's true.'

'And this show,' Geraldine crowed triumphantly, 'goes right down to the wire.'

DAY FIFTY-THREE. 6.00 p.m.

Over the next few days the police did everything they could to gain some information from the note that had

346

been found in the predictions envelope. They re-entered the house and took samples of everybody's handwriting, both right and left. They fingerprinted the kitchen cupboard. They pored for hours over the surviving footage from week one when the predictions had been written.

'Nothing. We've learnt nothing at all,' said Hooper.

'I didn't expect that we would,' Coleridge replied.

'Oh well, that's a comfort, sir,' said Hooper as testily as he dared. 'I just don't see how it could have happened.'

'And there,' said Coleridge, 'is the best clue you're going to get. For it seems to me that it *couldn't* have happened.'

Trisha had been on the phone. Now she put the receiver down with a gloomy face. 'Bad news, I'm afraid, sir. The boss wants you.'

'It is always a pleasure to see the chief constable,' Coleridge said. 'It makes me feel so much better about retiring.'

DAY FIFTY-THREE. 8.00 p.m.

The chief constable of the East Sussex Police was sick to death of the Peeping Tom murder. 'Murder is not what we here in New Sussex are all about, inspector. Here I am, trying to build a modern police service' – the chief constable did not allow the term police *force* – 'a service that is at ease with itself and comfortably achieving its goal targets in the key area of law upholdment, and *all* anybody wants to talk about is *your* failure to arrest the Peeping Tom murderer.'

'I'm sorry, sir, but these investigations take time.'

'New Sussex is a modern, thrusting, dynamic community, inspector. I do not like having our customer service profile marred by young women falling off lavatories with knives in their heads.'

'Well, I don't think any of us do, sir.'

'It's an image-tarnisher.'

'Yes, sir.'

'Quite apart, of course, from the human dimensions of the tragedy *vis-à-vis* that a customer is dead.'

'That's right.'

'And now we have this appalling new development of further threats being made. We are a modern community, a dynamic community and, I *had hoped*, a community where groups of sexually and ethnically diverse young people could take part in televised social experiments without being threatened with illegal life termination.'

'By which you mean murder, sir.'

'Yes, I do, chief inspector, if you wish to so put it, yes I do! This new threat is making us look like fools! We must be seen to be taking it very seriously indeed.'

'By all means, sir, let us *be seen* to take it seriously, but I am of the opinion that we do not need to *actually* take it seriously.'

'Good heavens, chief inspector! A murder has been announced! If the law upholdment service doesn't take it seriously then who will?'

'Everyone else, no doubt, sir, particularly the media,' said Coleridge calmly. 'But as I say, I do not think that *we* need to. I do not think that there will *be* another murder.'

'Oh yes, and what grounds do you have for this confidence?'

'I don't think that the killer *needs* a second death. One was enough, you see.'

The chief constable did not see, and he did not think much of Coleridge's enigmatic tone. 'One was too bloody many, Coleridge! Do you know that when this story broke I was about to make public my new policy document style initiative entitled *Policing The Rainbow*?'

'No, sir, I was not aware.'

'Yes, well, you weren't the only one who was not aware. *No one* was aware. The damn thing sank without trace. *Weeks* of work, ignored, absolutely ignored because of this ridiculous murder. It's not easy catching the eye of the Home Secretary these days, you know.'

DAY FIFTY-SIX. 7.30 p.m.

'Moon,' said Chloe 'you have been evicted from the house.'

'Yes!' Moon shouted, punching the air, and for once an evictee actually meant what she said. Moon had her million pounds plus the two hundred thousand Geraldine had promised for the next one out, and she was ecstatic to be free. She had no desire to be one of the last three, not now one of them was under sentence of death.

The three remaining inmates looked at each other. Gazzer, Jazz and Dervla. One more week. Another million to the winner. Half a million to the runner-up. Three hundred thousand even for the one who came third.

If all three survived, of course.

Worth the risk, certainly. Gazzer would use it to pursue a life of luxury. Jazz would start his own TV production company. Dervla would save her family from ruin ten times over. Definitely worth the risk.

Nobody spoke. They did not speak much at all any more, and they had all taken to sleeping in separate parts of the house. Even Jazz and Dervla, who had become close, could no longer trust each other. After all, it was they who had been closest to the exit on the night Kelly was killed. And now there was this new

349

threat. The whole process was nothing more than a long, grim waiting game.

Gazzer, Jazz, Dervla and the whole world, all waiting for the final day.

DAY SIXTY. 1.30 a.m.

Woggle was digging for as much as sixteen hours a day now. Not consecutively: he would dig for a few hours then sleep a while and, on waking, begin again immediately. Days did not matter to Woggle. It was hours that counted. Woggle had one hundred and fifteen of them left until the final episode of *House Arrest* began. He would have to hurry.

DAY SIXTY-TWO. 9.00 a.m.

Coleridge decided that it was time to take Hooper and Patricia into his confidence and admit to them that he knew who had killed Kelly.

He had had his suspicions from the start. Ever since he had seen the vomit on the seat of that pristine-clean toilet bowl. But it was the note that convinced him he was right, the note predicting the second murder. The murder he did not believe would happen because it did not need to.

What Coleridge lacked was proof and the more he thought about it, the more he knew that he never would have proof, because no proof existed, and therefore the killer was going to get away with the crime. Unless . . .

The plan to trap the killer came to Coleridge in the middle of the night. He had been unable to sleep and in order to avoid disturbing his wife with his shifting about and sighing he had gone downstairs to sit and think. He had poured himself a medium-sized Scotch and added the same amount again of water from the little jug shaped like a Scottish terrier. He sat down with his drink in the darkened sitting room of his house, the room he and his wife referred to as the drawing room, and considered for a moment how strange all the familiar objects in the room looked in the darkness of the middle of the night. Then his mind turned to the killer of Kelly Simpson, and how it might be that Coleridge could arrange to bring that foul and bloody individual to justice. Perhaps it was the words 'foul' and 'bloody' falling into his head that turned his thoughts from Kelly to *Macbeth* and the rehearsals that would commence a fortnight hence and thereafter take place every Tuesday and Thursday evening throughout the autumn. Coleridge would have to attend these rehearsals because Glyn had asked Coleridge if, given that he was in only the last act, he would be prepared to take on various messenger roles and attendant lords. 'Lots of nice little lines,' Glyn had said. 'Juicy little cameos.'

Oh, how Coleridge would have loved to play the bloody, guilty king, but of course it was not to be. He had never been given a lead.

Coleridge's mind strayed back in time to the first production that had stirred him as a boy: the Guinness *Macbeth*. How Coleridge had gasped when Banquo's ghost had appeared at the feast, shocking the guilty king into virtually giving the game away. They had done it quite brilliantly: Coleridge had been nearly as shocked as Macbeth was. These days, of course, the ghost would probably be on video screens or represented by a fax machine. Coleridge had already heard Glyn remark that his ghosts were going to be *virtual*, but way back then people weren't embarrassed by a bit of honest theatre. They liked to see the blood.

'Never shake your gory locks at me,' Coleridge

murmured under his breath. And it was then that it occurred to him that what was required to trap his murderer was a bit of honest theatre. Coleridge resolved that, if he could not find any genuine proof, natural justice required that he make his own. It was a desperate idea, he could see that, and there was scarcely time to put it into action. But it offered a chance, a small chance. A chance to avenge poor, silly Kelly.

The following morning Coleridge spoke to Hooper and Trisha. 'Banquo's ghost,' he said. 'He pointed a finger, all right?'

'Eh?' said Hooper.

Trisha knew who Banquo's ghost was. She had studied English literature at A-level, and had actually done three months' teacher training before deciding that if she was going to spend her life dealing with juvenile delinquents she would rather do it with full powers of arrest. 'What's Banquo's ghost got to do with anything, sir?' she asked.

But Coleridge would say no more and instead gave her a shopping list. 'Kindly go and make these purchases,' he said.

Trisha scanned the list. 'Wigs, sir?'

'Yes, of the description that I've noted. I imagine the best thing would be to look up a theatrical costume dresser in *Yellow Pages*. I doubt that the civilians in Procurements will view my requests with much favour, so for the time being I shall have to finance them myself. Can you be trusted with a blank cheque?'

DAY SIXTY-THREE. 6.30 p.m.

If Woggle's calculations were correct, he was directly under the house. He had the location right, he had the

352

time right and he had the heavy canvas bag that he had been dragging along behind him in the latter stages of his tunnelling.

Woggle knew, as he crouched in the blackness of his tunnel, that a few feet above him the three remaining housemates, whoever they were, would be preparing for the final eviction. Well, he'd give them and Peeping Tom a send-off they would not forget.

DAY SIXTY-THREE. 9.30 p.m.

And so it came to the end game.

The killer's last chance to kill, and Coleridge's last chance to catch the killer before the whole edifice of *House Arrest* was broken up and scattered. Every instinct he possessed informed Coleridge that if he did not make an arrest that evening the killer would escape him for ever.

Yet how could he make an arrest? He had no evidence. Not yet, anyway.

Coleridge was not the only one feeling frustrated. The viewing public felt the same way; the final eviction show was almost over and so far nothing much had happened. The largest television audience ever assembled were watching what was proving to be the biggest non-event in the history of broadcasting.

It was not as if Peeping Tom had not put in the effort. All the ingredients were in place for a television spectacular. There were fireworks, weaving searchlights, rock bands, three separate cherry pickers for three separate trips across the moat. The world's press was there, the baying crowds were there. Chloe the presenter's wonderful breasts were there, almost entirely on display as they struggled to burst free from the confines of her pink leather bra.

Perhaps most intriguingly of all, five out of the six

previous evictees were also there. All of the suspects had returned to the scene of the crime.

In fact the ex-housemates were obliged to come back for the final party under the terms of their contracts, but they would probably have come anyway. The lure of fame remained as strong as ever, and with the exception of Woggle, who had jumped bail, Peeping Tom had assembled them all. Even Layla had made the effort and spruced herself up, as had David, Hamish, Sally (who got a huge cheer when she entered, walking slowly but on the way to recovery), and Moon.

After the opening credit music, played live on this special occasion by the month's number-one boy band, who performed on an airship floating overhead, the cameras cut live to the last three people in the house. The sense of expectation in the audience was huge. They had been assured by the mystery killer that one of the three people that they could see on the huge screen was going to die.

But it didn't happen. The bands played, people cheered, Kelly's old school choir sang John Lennon's 'Imagine' in her honour, and one by one the final three were voted out of the house, but *nobody was killed at all*.

First came Garry. 'Yeah, all right! Fair play! Big it up! Respect!'

Then Dervla. 'I'm just glad it's over and I'm not dead.'

And finally Jazz. 'Wicked.'

Jazz had been the favourite to win ever since his dramatic intervention to save Sally's life in the confession box. Dervla's kickboxing attack on Garry had closed the gap considerably, but it could not make up for the fact that people knew she had been cheating, and so Jazz emerged a clear and popular winner. Garry was nowhere, having been losing ground all week.

And that was it. They were all out of the house, safe

354

and sound, and no matter how much the viewing public might wish it, it seemed unlikely that any of the three finalists, grinning with happy relief and holding onto their cheques, was going to leap on to one of the others and murder them.

The whole thing was rapidly coming to a close. A deeply sugary tribute to Kelly in words and music had been played, giving the impression that she had been a sort of cross between Mother Teresa and Princess Diana. Elton John had provided the music which further increased this impression. And now Chloe was doing her wind-up speech, making appropriate comments about how awesome and wicked it all was, and trying not to look too disappointed that nothing more exciting had happened.

Inspector Coleridge stood beside Geraldine in the studio. He was trying to look indulgent and relaxed, but he kept looking over his shoulder to glance at the big door at the back of the studio. He was waiting for Hooper and Patricia to appear, but so far there had been no sign of them. He knew that if they did not come in the next few moments and provide him with the proof he needed, the killer would escape.

'Well, you were right,' said Geraldine grudgingly. 'Nobody did get killed. You know, I really thought the bastard might pull it off. I suppose it was stupid, but he did do such an extraordinary job the first time round. Either way, it makes no difference to me. The show was pre-sold.' She looked at her watch. 'Fifty-three minutes so far, that's a hundred and six million dollars. Very nice, very nice indeed.'

Geraldine addressed Bob Fogarty in the control box via her intercom: 'Bob, give Bimbo Chloe a message to wind it up as slow as she dares, words of one syllable, please. When she's finished, replay the Kelly tribute and then stick on the long credits, every second is money.'

Coleridge looked at the door once more: still no sign of his colleagues. It was all about to slip away from him. He knew that somehow he must delay the end of the show. Banquo's ghost would only work on air. There had to be a feast. Macbeth's confusion would mean nothing if it happened in private.

'Hold on a minute, Ms Hennessy,' he said quietly. 'I think I can earn you a few more million dollars.'

Geraldine knew a sincere tone of voice when she heard one. 'Keep the cameras rolling!' she barked into her intercom, 'and tell my driver to wait. What's on your mind, inspector?'

'I'm going to catch the Peeping Tom killer for you.'

'Fuck me.'

Even Geraldine was surprised when Inspector Stanley Spencer Coleridge asked if it would be possible for him to be given a mike.

A hand-held microphone was quickly thrust into his hand, and then to everyone's complete surprise Coleridge stepped up onto the stage and joined Chloe. All over the world and in every language under the sun, the same question was asked: 'Who the hell is that old guy?'

'Please forgive me, Chloe . . . I'm afraid I don't know your surname,' Coleridge said, 'and I hope that the public will forgive me also if I trespass for a moment on their time.'

Chloe stared about her wildly, wondering where the security men were, seeing as a senior citizen appeared to be making a stage invasion.

'Run with it, Chloe,' the floor manager whispered at her through her earpiece. 'Geraldine says he's kosher.'

'Oh, right. Wicked,' said Chloe in an unconvinced voice.

Everybody stared at Coleridge. He had never felt such a fool, but he was desperate. There was still no sign of Hooper and Patricia. He knew that he would

356

have to stall. He looked out at the sea of expectant, slightly hostile faces. He tried not to think of the hundreds of millions more that he could not see but who he knew were watching. He fought down his fear.

'Ladies and gentlemen, my name is Chief Inspector Stanley Coleridge of the East Sussex Police, and I am here to arrest the murderer of Kelly Simpson, spinster of the parish of Stoke Newington, London Town.' He had no idea where the 'spinster' bit had come from except that he knew he must spin it out, *spin it out at all costs*. He had absolutely no idea how long he would have to stall.

Once the sensation caused by his opening remark had died down, Coleridge turned and addressed the eight ex-housemates, who had been assembled by Chloe on the podium. The eight people whose faces he had stared at for so long. The suspects.

'This has not been an easy case. Everyone in the world has had a theory, and motives there have been aplenty. A fact that has caused my officers and myself some considerable confusion over the last few weeks. But the identity of this cruel killer, that despicable individual who saw fit to plunge a knife into the skull of a beautiful, innocent young girl, has remained a mystery.'

Something rather strange was happening to Coleridge. He could feel it deep in the pit of his stomach. It was a new sensation for him, but not an unpleasant one. Could it be that he was *enjoying himself*? Perhaps not quite that. The tension was too great and the possibility of failure too immediate for enjoyment, but he certainly felt . . . exhilarated. If he had had a moment to think, he might have reflected that circumstance had granted him that thing which he most craved and which his local amateur dramatic society had so long denied him: an audience and a leading role.

'So,' said Coleridge, addressing the camera with the red light on top, presuming correctly that this was the live one. 'Who killed Kelly Simpson? Well, in view of the wealth of suspicion that has been visited upon various innocents, I think it fair to begin by clearing up who definitely did *not* kill Kelly Simpson.'

'This bloke's a natural,' Geraldine whispered to the floor manager. She was deeply impressed with this new side of Coleridge's character, and well she might have been, for every minute that he spoke was earning her an extra two million dollars.

Spin it out. Spin it out, Coleridge thought to himself, a sentiment which Geraldine would have applauded wholeheartedly.

'Sally!' Coleridge said, turning dramatically to face the eight suspects. 'You were the victim of a terrible coincidence. Your poor mother's suffering, which you had hoped would remain a private matter, has become public knowledge. You have anguished over your fears that the curse that blighted your mother's life might also have blighted yours. You've tortured yourself with the question Did I Kill Kelly? Was your true personality revealed in the darkness of that black box?'

Sally did not answer. Her eyes were far away. She was thinking of her mother sitting in the terrible little room where she had sat for most of the last twenty years.

'Let me assure you, Sally, that never for *one moment* did I imagine that the killer was you. You had not the ghost of a motive save family history, and the coincidence of that history repeating itself in so exact a manner is so unlikely as to be virtually impossible. Many families have some mental disorder in their line . . . Why, the producer of this very show could say as much, couldn't you, Ms Hennessy?'

'Eh?' said Geraldine. She was enjoying Coleridge's

performance hugely, but had not expected to be drawn into it.

'I gather from interviews my officers have held with your staff that on the two occasions when both Sally and Moon spoke about life inside mental hospitals you remarked quite clearly that it was not like that at all. You in fact explained clearly what it *was* like. I can only presume that you yourself have some experience?' Coleridge glanced once more at the studio door. No sign. *Spin it out.*

'Well, as it happens you're right.' Geraldine spoke into the boom mike, which had hastily descended above her head, the studio crew having reacted according to their instincts. 'My mum was a bit of a fruitcake herself, Sally, and my dad, as it happens, so believe me, I sympathize with the outrageous prejudice you have had to put up with.'

'A sentiment that does you great credit,' Coleridge said. 'Particularly since medical opinion informs me that when *both* a person's parents suffer serious mental instability, their offspring has a thirty-six per cent chance of inheriting their challenges.'

Geraldine did not much like having her family's linen so publicly washed, but at two million dollars a minute she felt she could put up with it.

Coleridge turned once more to the suspects. 'So, Sally, I hope that you can learn from this terrible experience that you need not fear the burden of your past. You did not kill Kelly Simpson, but you were very nearly killed yourself, as I intend to show.'

This comment was greeted with gasps from the audience, which Coleridge did his best to milk.

'Now, what about the rest of you? Did Moon kill Kelly? Well, did you, Moon? You're a wicked liar, we know that from the tapes. The public never saw you make up a history of abuse in order to score cheap points against Sally, but I did, and it occurred to me

359

that a woman who could invent such grotesque and insensitive deceits might lie about pretty much anything, even murder.'

The cameras turned on Moon.

'Extreme close up!' shouted Bob Fogarty from the control box.

Moon was sweating. 'Now just a fookin' . . .'

'Please, if we could try to moderate our language,' Coleridge chided. 'We are on live television, after all. Don't upset yourself, Moon. If there were as many murderers as there are liars in this world we should all be dead by now. You did not kill Kelly.'

'Well, I know that,' said Moon.

'Nobody has really known anything during this investigation, Moon. Heavens, even Layla has come under suspicion.'

The cameras swung to face a shocked Layla.

'What?'

'Oh yes, such was the apparent impossibility of the murder that at times it seemed possible to imagine that you had wafted in through an airvent on that grim night. After all, everybody saw Kelly nominate you in that first week and then hug and kiss you goodbye. That must have hurt a proud woman like you.'

'It did,' said Layla, 'and I'm ashamed to say that, when I heard about the murder, for a moment I was glad Kelly died. Isn't that terrible? I've sought counselling now though, which is helping a lot.'

'Good for you,' said Coleridge. 'For let us be quite clear: there is no circumstance or situation in our world today that cannot benefit from counselling. You were simply being selfish, Layla, that was all, but I'm sure that somewhere you can find somebody to tell you that you had a right to be.' Coleridge was being deeply sarcastic, but the crowd did not get it and applauded him, assuming, as did Layla, that Coleridge's comment was a love-filled Oprah moment of support.

'Layla was long gone by the time Kelly died,' Coleridge continued, 'but Garry wasn't, were you, Gazzer? So how about you? Did *you* kill Kelly? You certainly *wanted* to kill her. After the whole country saw her teach you a few home truths about the responsibilities of fatherhood there was no doubt you had a motive. Wounded pride has been a cause for murder many times in the past, but on the whole I suspect that you don't care quite enough about *anything* to take the sort of risk this killer took. But what about you, Hamish? Only you know what passed between Kelly and yourself the night you reeled drunkenly together into that little cabin. Perhaps Kelly had a story to tell, but, if she did, fortunately for you we'll never hear it. Did you wish her silenced as you sat together in that awful sweatbox? Did you reach out a hand to stop her mouth?'

Hamish did not answer, but just glared at Coleridge fiercely, biting his lip.

'Perhaps you did, but you didn't kill her. Now then, what about David?' Coleridge turned his gaze to the handsome actor, whose face was still proud and haughty despite all that he'd been through. 'You and Kelly also shared a secret. A secret you hoped to keep hidden, and with Kelly's death you thought it safe.'

'For heaven's sake, I didn't . . .'

'No, I know you didn't, David. Sadly for you, though, because of her death and the subsequent investigation, the world has discovered your secret anyway and, like her, I doubt now that you will ever achieve your dream.'

'Actually, I've had some very interesting offers,' said David defiantly.

'Still acting, David? I recommend you try facing up to the truth. In the long run life is easier.'

As David glared at him Coleridge looked once more at the door at the back of the studio. There was still no sign of Hooper and Patricia. How long could he keep on stalling? He was running out of suspects.

'Dervla Nolan, I have always had my doubts about you,' said Coleridge, turning to her and pointing his finger dramatically.

Once more the focus of the cameras shifted.

'Have you now, chief inspector?' Dervla replied, her green eyes flashing angry defiance. 'And why would that be, I wonder.'

'Because you played the game so hard. Because you have a rogue's courage and risked it all by communicating with the cameraman Larry Carlisle through the mirror. Because you were closest to the entrance of the sweatbox and could have left it without anybody else's knowing. Because you needed money desperately. Because you had been told that, with Kelly dead, you would win. Not a bad circumstantial case, Ms Nolan. I think perhaps a good prosecuting lawyer could make it stick!'

'This is just madness,' said Dervla. 'I loved Kelly, I really . . .'

'But you didn't win, did you, Dervla?' Coleridge said firmly. '*Jazz* won. In the end, good old Jazz was the winner. Everybody's friend, the comedian, the man who was *also* in the key position in the sweatbox and could have left it without being noticed! The man whose DNA was so prominent on the sheet that the murderer used. The man who so conveniently covered his tracks by putting the sheet back on after the murder. Tell me, Jazz, do you honestly think that you would have won if Kelly had not died?'

'Hey, just a minute,' Jazz protested. 'You ain't trying to say that . . .'

'Answer my question, Jason. If Kelly had survived that night, the night she brushed past you in the sweatbox and someone followed her out in order to kill her, would you have won? Would that cheque you are now holding not have had her name on it?'

'I don't know ... Maybe, but that doesn't mean I killed her.'

'No, Jazz, you're right. It doesn't mean that you killed her, and of course you didn't. *Because none of you did.*'

The sensation that this statement caused was highly gratifying. Coleridge's emotions were torn. Part of him, the main part, was in absolute torment, desperately awaiting the arrival of his colleagues. An arrival which if put off much longer would be useless anyway. But there was another part of Coleridge, and that was Coleridge the frustrated performer: this part was loving every minute of his great day.

'You are all innocent,' he repeated, 'for it is a fact that no one who shared the sweatbox with Kelly on the night she died killed her!'

'It was Woggle, wasn't it?' Dervla shouted. 'I should have guessed! He hated us all! He took revenge on the show!'

'Ah ha!' shouted Coleridge. 'Woggle the tunneller! Of course! Everybody's mistake in this investigation – *my* mistake – was to presume that the murder was committed by a person who was a housemate at the time. But what of the *ex-housemates* – not Layla, but Woggle! How simple for a committed anarchist like him, a saboteur, an expert underground tunneller, to break into the house and take his revenge on the show, and in particular on the girl who nominated him and then insulted him with a tofu and molasses comfort cake!'

The studio erupted. All around the world the press lines jammed. So Woggle had done it after all, the evil kicker of teenage girls had surpassed even his previous levels of brutality.

'Of course it wasn't Woggle!' said Coleridge impatiently. 'Good heavens, if that highly distinctive fellow had popped up through the carpet I think we would have noticed, don't you? No, let's stop looking for opportunity and start to consider *motive*. What are the common motives for murder? I suggest that hate is one. Hatred drives people to kill, and my investigations have discovered that there was one truly hate-filled relationship souring the Peeping Tom experience, and it did not fester inside the house. It was the hatred that Bob Fogarty, the senior series editor, felt for Geraldine Hennessy, the producer!'

Coleridge pointed above the heads of the audience to the darkened window situated high in the wall at the back of the studio. 'Behind that window sits the Peeping Tom editing team,' Coleridge continued, 'and they are led by a man who believes that his boss, Geraldine Hennessy, is a television whore! He said as much to one of my officers. Bob Fogarty claimed that Hennessy's work represented a new low in broadcasting, she had ruined the industry he loved and that he longed for her downfall! But! He did *not* kill Kelly.'

Coleridge could detect a tiny edge of impatience in the crowd. He knew that he could not play the trick he was playing for much longer. The spin was running out. But it no longer mattered. Coleridge was smiling, for at the back of the studio he saw the big door open and Hooper steal through it. Hooper gave Coleridge the briefest of thumbs-up signals.

Geraldine did not see the smile spreading across Coleridge's face. She was too busy smiling herself because, glancing down at her watch, she worked out that the mad policeman had been on the stage for five and a half minutes and had therefore earned her an extra eleven million dollars, and clearly the idiot had not finished yet.

The smile was about to be wiped from Geraldine's face.

'So!' said Coleridge dramatically. 'We know now who did *not* kill Kelly Simpson. Let us come to the real business at hand and establish who *did* kill her. Nothing happened in that dreadful house without first being arranged, manipulated and packaged by the producer. Nothing, ladies and gentleman, not even murder most foul. Therefore let us be quite clear about this. The murderer was ... *you*, Geraldine Hennessy!' Coleridge pointed his finger and the cameras swung around to follow its direction.

For once Geraldine found herself at the wrong end of the lens.

'You're out of your mind!' Geraldine gasped.

'Am I? Well, I think you'd know something about that, Ms Hennessy.'

Trisha entered the editing box carrying a plastic bag filled with video tapes. She went up to Bob Fogarty and whispered in his ear.

'I can't leave now,' Fogarty protested.

'I can cover it,' said his assistant, Pru, eagerly. All her life she had longed for just such a chance.

'I'm afraid I must insist, sir,' said Trisha, whispering once more into Fogarty's ear.

Fogarty rose from his seat, took up his family-sized bar of milk chocolate, and left the editing box.

Pru took over the controls. 'Camera four,' she said. 'Slow creep in on Coleridge.'

Down on the stage the object of this command was in full flow.

'Perhaps you will allow me to explain,' Coleridge said. 'First let us consider motive.' Coleridge was standing tall now, strong and commanding. This was not just because his performance muscles, which had for so long lain dormant, were flexing themselves, but also because he knew that success could only come with confidence. She had to believe that the game was up.

'Well, a motive is simple enough, it's the oldest one of the lot. Not hate, not love, but greed. Greed, pure and simple. Kelly Simpson died to make you rich, Ms Hennessy. The whole media establishment expected series three of *House Arrest* to be a failure. The Woggle affair drew attention to you, certainly, but it was Kelly's death that turned your show into the biggest television success story in history, *as you knew it would!* Can you deny it?'

'No, of course not,' Geraldine said. 'That doesn't mean I killed her.'

Geraldine was alone now on the studio floor. The happy throng of excited young audience members and studio staff had drawn back to form a large circle. Geraldine stood in the middle of this, like a lioness at bay, the focus of that vast room, three big studio cameras hovering around her, for all the world like great hunting animals of prey.

Beyond them, still standing on the stage with Chloe and the eight housemates, was Coleridge, returning Geraldine's defiant stare. 'You have been clever, Ms Hennessy, brutally, fiendishly clever. I do believe your finest hour, perhaps, was allowing the early profits from the worldwide interest that Kelly's murder produced to be given away. Oh yes, that certainly made me wonder, when your editor, Bob Fogarty, told us of your fury at the missed opportunity, a million lost? Perhaps two? And then, I thought, what a small price to avoid suspicion falling immediately upon your shoulders, as since then you have milked *hundreds of millions* of dollars from your ghoulish crime.'

'Now you be careful, chief inspector,' Geraldine said. 'You're on live television here. The whole world is watching while you make a fool of yourself.' The mention of money had put the spirit back into Geraldine. Coleridge's accusation had certainly been a shock, but she could not imagine on what grounds he was going to base it, let alone prove it. Meanwhile, the *House Arrest* drama continued and the profits kept on mounting.

'You may bluster all you wish, Ms Hennessy,' Coleridge replied, 'but I intend to prove that you are the murderer and then I intend to see you punished under the full majesty of the law. Let me say now that I knew even on the night of the crime that things were not as they appeared. Despite your impressive efforts, there was *just so much* that was wrong. Why was it that cameraman Larry Carlisle, the only person to witness the cloaked murderer follow Kelly to the lavatory, thought that the killer had emerged only two minutes after Kelly left the sweatbox, while the people watching *on video* could see very well from their machines that it had been more like five?'

'Larry Carlisle has been proved to—'

'Not a very reliable witness, I accept that, but on this occasion I suggest reliable enough. Otherwise, why was it that the blood which flowed from Kelly's wounds seemed to accumulate so very quickly? The doctor was surprised, and so was I. *Who would have thought the young girl to have so much blood in her*, to paraphrase the Bard. A great deal of blood to flow in the *two minutes* that was supposed to have passed between the murder and your arriving on the scene, Ms Hennessy, but not so much if you reckon on the *five minutes* that Carlisle thought had passed.'

'Not all blood flows at the same speed, for fuck's sake!' Geraldine barked, forgetting for a moment that she was on live television.

'Then there was the vomit,' said Coleridge. 'Kelly had been drinking heavily, and she rushed to the lavatory in a mighty hurry, didn't she? But according to what we saw, when she arrived she simply sat down. More curious still, even though the lavatory bowl had clearly been scrubbed clean, the lavatory *seat* had a few flecks of vomit on it. Vomit which has been confirmed as having emanated from Kelly. How could this be? I asked myself. Watching the tape again I can see that Kelly does not throw up, she merely sits . . . and yet *I know that she was sick*. I have vomit from her mouth, I have her vomit from the lavatory seat. Without doubt this is a girl who ran into the lavatory, knelt before it and was sick. Yet when I watch the tape, *she just sits down*.'

Up in the studio editing box, Pru was having the gig of her life. She had taken over the controls of the edit box and, working live and entirely off-script, she had first managed to ensure perfect camera coverage of the scene unfolding down in the studio, barking cool clear instructions to the shocked team of operators. And now she excelled herself by managing to dial up footage of the murder tape and drop it into the broadcast mix as Coleridge spoke. Once more viewers around the world watched the familiar footage of Kelly entering the toilet and sitting down, this time seeing it in an entirely new and mystifying context.

Down on the studio floor the thrilling confrontation continued.

'Next I come to the matter of the *sound* on the tapes that were recorded during the murder. In the earlier part of the evening much of what was said inside that grim plastic box was clearly audible, and, I might add, little of it did any of the people you see standing on this stage much credit.'

Coleridge turned to the eight ex-housemates. 'Really, you all ought to be ashamed of yourselves. You're not animals, you know.'

'It wasn't me!' Layla protested like an anxious school child. 'I'd been evicted, I wasn't there!'

Such was the authority of Coleridge's performance that, instead of telling him to mind his own business, the other seven housemates, even Gazzer, blushed and stared unhappily at their feet.

'But I'm straying from the point,' Coleridge admitted, 'which is that while Kelly remained in the sweatbox we could hear what was being said, but from the moment that Kelly entered the lavatory the sound becomes vague, a mere cacophony of murmuring. Why? Why could we no longer make out any of the voices?'

'Because they were all too pissed, of course, you stupid—' Geraldine bit her lip. She knew he had no proof. She had no need to lose her cool.

'I don't think so, Ms Hennessy. Seven people do not simultaneously begin to mumble in unison. What had happened? Why had the sound changed? Was it because the sound that I could hear on the tape of the murder was *not* the sound that was being generated in the sweatbox? Could it be that the person who made that tape did not wish for any discernible voices to be heard from the box during the murder because *she did not know who it was who was going to be killed*? Strange it would be indeed if the voice of the victim could still be heard in the sweatbox after her death. Was this the reason that the sound on the murder tape was so revealingly anonymous?'

Geraldine remained silent.

'Let us leap forward for a moment in time, to when the note predicting the second murder was discovered. Oh, what a fine sensation that made. But for me, Ms Hennessy, that note was the absolute proof I needed to convince me that the murder was *not* committed by a housemate.'

'Why, babe?'

Coleridge almost jumped. He had forgotten that Chloe was standing beside him. Throughout his speech she had been attempting, not very subtly, to remain in shot, and she now made a play to really get involved.

Chloe felt she had a right, she was the presenter of the show, after all.

'Why, Chloe? Because it was utterly ridiculous, that's why. Impossible, a transparent piece of *theatre*. None of the contestants could *possibly* have known at the end of week one when and how Kelly Simpson would die. Even if they had been planning to kill her it is quite absurd to think that they would have been able to see into the future in such detail and be assured that an opportunity would arise on the twenty-seventh day. So how did that note come to be among the predictions in the envelope? An envelope which we had seen the housemates fill and seal on day eight? Clearly someone from the outside had put that prediction note there, put it there at the *time that they killed Kelly*. That note was a little extra piece of drama that you could not resist, Ms Hennessy. You were desperate to maximize your price for footage of the final week, and yet you knew that with each passing day the murder grew colder and with each eviction the chances of the killer still being in the house lessened. Hence your absurd, ridiculous note, a note which fooled the world but which served only to convince me that there definitely would *not* be another murder.'

'Excuse me, sorry to interrupt, babe.' It was Chloe again, delighted to have another chance to get into the action. 'They've asked me from the box to ask you to tell us how she did it. I mean we've got as much time as you like, but the problem is that we're live and at some point we have to cut to an ad break, but we do all *really really* want to know.'

'Justice has its own pace, miss,' said Coleridge grandly. He was grimly aware that he had no proof. If he was to gain a conviction then he needed a confession, and only Banquo's ghost, only a set of shaking gory locks, could get him that. The time had to be right, the killer had to *sweat*.

'Fine, babe,' said Chloe. 'They say it's cool. Respect. Whatever.'

'Surely you must all have guessed how she did it anyway?' said Coleridge. 'I mean, isn't it obvious?'

The sea of blank faces in the audience was most gratifying.

'Ah, but of course, I was forgetting. You have not had the privilege as I have of visiting Shepperton Studios, a place where *an exact replica* of the house exists. A place where Geraldine Hennessy made a video recording. A recording of a murder that *was yet to happen.*' Coleridge had abandoned all pretence at quiet reserve. He was an actor now, an actor in a smash hit.

'One dark night shortly before the *House Arrest* game began, Geraldine Hennessy crept onto the set of her replica house. With a crank and a clang she turned on the studio lights and activated the remote cameras that would shortly thereafter be installed in the real house. She also pushed one manual camera into position in front of the lavatory door, where she locked it off, just as a month or so later she would instruct Larry Carlisle to do. Then Ms Hennessy stripped naked and put on a dark wig, a wig that was the colour of Kelly Simpson's hair. She then entered the replica lavatory, where she was recorded by the only camera in the room, high above and behind her. Swiftly she sat down and put her head into her hands, not a difficult deception to pull off – the foreshortening quality of an overhead camera angle would make any differences in height and figure an irrelevance, and, when looked at from almost directly above, one hunched figure on a lavatory looks much the same as another. So, a month or so before it actually happened, Kelly's final trip to the lavatory had been ... I can't say *re*constructed – I'd therefore better say *pre*constructed.'

Coleridge was having a wonderful time. Banquo's ghost was waiting in the wings, Macbeth (perhaps he should say Lady Macbeth) stood before him in all her arrogance; all he had to do now was bring her to the point where her spirit collapsed, and he truly believed he could do it. In thirty-five years of dedicated and usually successful police work, Coleridge could never have been said to have shone. But on this night, as he neared the end of his long career, he was sparkling.

'So,' he continued, 'Hennessy playing Kelly sits on the lavatory and now, across the replica living area, in the boys' bedroom, where a small sweatbox has been constructed – a sweatbox built to exactly the same specifications for construction and positioning that were later given to the housemates – a cloaked figure emerges. Your accomplice in the drama, Ms Hennessy. The figure crosses the living area, picks up a knife and bursts into the lavatory, raising his sheet behind him to block the camera's view. He then makes two plunging movements. A clever bit of deception that, Ms Hennessy: *two* blows, the first a miss hit, giving the impression that what occurred was a desperate improvisation rather than a cold and cunning decep-tion. One single death blow might have appeared just *too* pat. Then, having left a sheet over you, hunched up on the lavatory, your accomplice goes back across the little stage at Shepperton and gets back into the replica sweatbox.'

'Who? Who was the accomplice?' gasped Chloe.

'Why, Bob Fogarty, of course. It could *only* be Bob Fogarty, the man who made such a heavy-handed point of hating Ms Hennessy, a man with video-editing skills equal to your own, Ms Hennessy. Because I put it to you, Geraldine Hennessy, that the world never saw Kelly murdered! That dark event remains unrecorded. It is the tape that you and Fogarty made at Shepperton that was played that night and which has so absorbed the interest of the public ever since! Your *construction* of a murder that had yet to happen and which you and

372

he dropped into edit mix at the point at which the *real* Kelly entered the lavatory. I have taken some advice on this matter and have been told that the opening of the door would be a good point at which to switch the tapes. From that moment on, you and all the people in the monitoring bunker were watching the tape you had made and *not the actual feed from the cameras*. You yourself have boasted that computer time codes can easily be falsified, and with you and Fogarty working together it was a simple matter to switch your television monitors over to playing the tape.'

Geraldine tried to speak, but no sound came. The floor manager did what all floor managers do and brought her a plastic cup of water.

'Now that Kelly was in the lavatory, although you of course could no longer see her, you used the remote-controlled lock that you yourself had insisted on having installed and sealed the lavatory door, trapping poor Kelly and thus insuring yourself against the possibility of her completing her lavatorial functions before you could get to her. You then excused yourself from the monitoring bunker, saying that like the girl on the screen you too needed to spend a penny, and you rushed off to do your terrible deed!'

There was sensation in the studio and, of course, across the globe. Seldom can any television performer have had so attentive an audience. All over the world pans boiled dry, dinners burned and babies' cries went unheeded. There was no talk of cutting to an ad break now.

'Go on,' sneered Geraldine. 'What am I supposed to have done then?'

'You ran under the moat, along the connecting tunnel, I imagine having first grabbed for yourself a strategically placed smock. I feel certain that somewhere there is an incinerator in London that could tell a tale of a blood-stained coverall. You ran into the corridor and from there you made your way into the boys' bedroom. Once inside the house you grabbed a sheet from the top of the pile that you had instructed the housemates to place outside the sweatbox. That polythene construction in which the people you see standing here tonight were sweating with drunken lust—'

'Not me, I'd been evicted,' Layla piped up, but Coleridge swept on.

'You covered yourself with the sheet, emerged into the living area and went to get the knife, pausing briefly at the kitchen cupboard to take out the predictions envelope, tear it open and put its contents inside a new but identical envelope. It was then, of course, that you added your extra note, predicting a second murder. No one saw any of this, of course, because the editors were watching the video that you and Fogarty had made a month before, a video on which Kelly Simpson was sitting peacefully on the lavatory, and for the time being no other figures were to be seen. There was the live cameraman to consider, of course, but Larry Carlisle had been instructed to cover the lavatory door and wait for Kelly. *This* is why Carlisle claimed a much shorter time had elapsed after Kelly went to the lavatory before the killer emerged, because the figure he saw rush past him in a sheet was you, *the real killer*. Meanwhile, in the monitoring bunker, your accomplice Fogarty and the editing team were still watching a peaceful house in which a lone girl was sitting on the lavatory. You, Ms Hennessy, would be *back in the monitoring bunker* before your tape revealed a besheeted figure entering the lavatory.'

There were gasps and applause from the audience.

'Unreal,' said Chloe. 'Mental. Absolutely mental. Just totally wicked.'

Geraldine remained aloof and silent, seemingly held at bay by the three cameras pointing at her.

'But I'm getting ahead of myself,' said Coleridge. 'Poor Kelly Simpson is still alive . . . Although only for a few more moments. The door to the lavatory springs open, unlocked at the appointed time by your colleague in the bunker, you burst in on the unsuspecting girl, but you do not find her as you had hoped, sitting on the lavatory as per your impersonation on the video you had made. No, she is kneeling *in front* of the lavatory, being sick. This is no good – everything must be as it is on the tape: the girl must die sitting and, most importantly, she cannot have been sick because she is not seen being sick on your tape. You grab her, you spin her round, she no doubt thinks that someone has come to help her, but no, you've come to kill her. With admirable coolness you stab her first in the neck and then, deploying the full force of your passion, your strength and your *greed*, you bury the blade in her skull, working quickly, knowing that seconds count. You flush the toilet and clean the vomit from the bowl. You do a good job, Ms Hennessy, but not quite good enough. A few tiny flecks are left on the seat. Then, and at this point I can only gasp at your icy cool, you *clean out the dead girl's mouth*. Did you have a cloth? Toilet paper would have stuck to her teeth. Your shirt cuff, perhaps? I don't know, but crucially I do know that in doing what you did you marked the dead girl's tongue! Kelly was only seconds dead and so could still bruise, unfortunately for you, Ms Hennessy. You could not, of course, clear the vomit from the back of her mouth and her throat, but you had done your best, a best which was very nearly good enough. But time is short, Kelly is bleeding. If she bleeds too much on you, you're done for. Quickly you place the corpse in the same sitting position that you yourself took on your tape. You put a second sheet on top of the dead girl and, covering yourself once more in your own sheet, you leave the lavatory. Again, Larry Carlisle sees the besheeted figure exit the lavatory minutes before the editors do, because on their screens still *nothing has happened yet*; on their screens Kelly Simpson is still alive! I applaud you, Ms Hennessy, you designed the process so that Larry Carlisle's story concurred exactly with what was seen in the monitoring bunker. It was only the timings that you could not fix.'

Once more there were murmurs of appreciation in the studio.

'Now you run, back through the living area and into the boys' bedroom,' Coleridge said, his voice rising, 'pausing only to take the sheet you have been using to cover yourself and quickly wipe it round all of the boys' beds in order that a confusion of skin cells and other DNA matter will be present on it. Perhaps you wore gloves and a hair scarf? I don't know, since at the time I was too stupid to consider the possibility of testing for anyone other than the people who had been in the sweatbox.'

There were cries of 'No!' at this. Coleridge was the hero of the hour and the audience would not hear a word said against him, even by himself.

'You go back into the corridor,' Coleridge continued, 'you run through the tunnel, hide your coverall and arrive back in the monitoring bunker just in time to see *your identical* version of the murder take place on screen. You have created the perfect alibi: you're sitting safely and prominently with your editors when the murder takes place, so nobody could suspect you. The murder, like everything that happens on these so-called "reality" programmes, was built in the edit, it was nothing more than television "reality".' Coleridge paused momentarily for breath. He knew that shortly he must bring on his ghost.

'All that remained for you to do then, Ms Hennessy, was to switch your viewing monitors back from showing your video to the genuine reality of the live camera feed. This, I imagine, was a big test. Was Fogarty ready with his altered time codes? Had you placed the sheet on Kelly's body *exactly* as it was in your Shepperton video? If you had, then the switchover would be smooth. If you hadn't, there would be a jump of position. Once more I congratulate you, Ms Hennessy. I've watched the tape many times and even now I'm only half sure I can tell where you make the switch, and of course you never imagined that anybody would be looking for such a thing.'

'That's because there's nothing to look for. There was no switch, you *utter cunt*! I didn't kill her and you know it. You've made this up because you're too fucking thick to work out which one of those sad bastards standing beside you actually did it!'

Editors worldwide taking live sound and vision from Peeping Tom struggled to activate their bleeper machines.They all missed it; they had been too absorbed in what Coleridge was saying. Geraldine's string of obscenities went out to the world, a genuine moment of reality TV.

Coleridge did not look at Geraldine. He looked past her to the back of the studio, where once more Hooper silently gave him the thumbs-up. He knew that the time had come to introduce Banquo's ghost to the feast.

'Ah, but Ms Hennessy,' Coleridge said, 'I do not make these accusations lightly. I have proof, you see, because I have the evidence of your *other murders*.'

'What!'

'Let them shake their gory locks at you, Ms Hennessy! Let them point their bloody fingers.'

'What the *fuck* are you talking about, you silly old cunt!' said Geraldine.

A slightly bashful look flickered across Coleridge's face. 'Perhaps I have been slightly indulgent in my language. I should of course say your other murder *preconstructions*! Because you see, Ms Hennessy, it occurred to me that you could not possibly have known who it was who would leave the sweatbox in order to go to the toilet that night. It was a virtual certainty that *somebody* would, of course, and it was on that assumption that your whole murder plan was based. But you could not know *who*. I reasoned therefore that for your plan to work you would need to have recorded your scenario featuring not just poor Kelly but at the very least all of the other girls, so that when a girl, *any* of the girls, emerged and headed for the lavatory, you could activate the appropriate tape and go and kill her. That is perhaps the saddest aspect of this investigation. I have found many possible motives for killing Kelly, but not one of them is remotely relevant, because she died by *pure chance*. She was murdered simply because she was the *second* girl to go to the toilet. Ah! I hear you say. Second? Why second? Surely Sally went to the lavatory at the very beginning of the evening? Why was she not murdered? I shall tell you why: because since entering the house Sally had *dyed and cut her hair*! Sally's dark mohican had become no more than a red tuft, a fact which definitely saved her life, for had you not altered your looks, Sally, then *you*, not Kelly, would have died, and your murder would have looked like this!'

And with a nod and a wave which quite frankly he enjoyed, Coleridge gestured to the technicians in the editing box that he was ready.

Pru, who had been acting under instructions from Trisha, pressed the cue button which she had hastily marked 'Sally'. And to the astonishment of the entire world the naked figure of Sally, but Sally with her old mohican haircut, could be seen entering the toilet, or at least it easily *could* be Sally. Being a high, overhead shot, all that could really be seen were flashes of bare female limb, in this case tattooed, and of course the distinctive top of the head. The girl who could be Sally then sat on the toilet, put her head in her hands and was murdered by the same person in the sheet in exactly the same way that Kelly had been.

'Oh my God,' the real Sally murmured, suddenly aware of how close she had come to death.

Now the screen flickered and a second video was shown. This time it was the bald pate of Moon that was viewed from overhead entering the toilet. Again the sheeted figure stole across the living area, took up the knife and acted out the murder.

'Fookin' hell!' Moon shrieked. 'Are you saying that if I'd gone for a piss . . . ?'

'Indeed I am, miss,' Coleridge replied. 'Indeed I am. Interesting, isn't it, how Geraldine Hennessy selected women with such particular heads of hair, or in your case, Moon, lack of it.'

Now the distinctive raven hair of Dervla was seen entering the toilet and, of course, the story was the same.

Finally, to everybody's surprise, the beaded ringlets of Layla appeared, and once more the murder was enacted.

'Oh yes, Layla was there too,' said Coleridge, 'Layla with her blond beaded braids. For how could Geraldine Hennessy have known before the series began who it was that would be evicted?'

Again there was applause.

'All those girls were played by *you*, Ms Hennessy,' Coleridge shouted, pointing his finger at Geraldine, who was now beginning to look rather worried, 'as I have no doubt the digital enhancement of the tapes will prove!'

'I told that fucking swine Fogarty to burn those tapes!' Geraldine shrieked.

Banquo's ghost had done its work.

Geraldine knew that the game was up. Further deception was pointless. Coleridge had her tapes.

Except, of course, he didn't have them, because he had tricked her.

Fogarty had burnt the tapes, as he was currently trying to tell her, shouting at the soundproofed walls of the little viewing gallery into which Trisha had taken him, from where he had watched the whole thing on a monitor.

'I did burn the tapes! I did, you silly cow!' he shouted at the screen, tears of terror welling up in his eyes. 'He's tricked you. He made those tapes himself.'

'I made them, actually,' Trisha told Fogarty rather proudly. 'Me and Sergeant Hooper out at Shepperton this afternoon. Hell of a rush to get back . . . I hated wearing that bald wig – it really pulls at your hair when you take it off.'

Trisha had had a good day. It had meant being naked in front of Sergeant Hooper, of course, but in fact this had brought about a happy and unexpected result. Hooper had been much taken with Trisha naked and had instantly asked her to go out with him.

'Sorry, sarge. I'm gay,' she replied and so finally she said it and she had felt much better ever since.

Down on the studio floor Coleridge arrested Geraldine in front of hundreds of millions of people. Finest hours rarely get any finer.

'So what if I did kill her?' Geraldine shrieked. 'She got what she wanted, didn't she? She got her fame! That's all any of them wanted. They're desperate, all of them. They probably would have gone through with it even if they'd known what I was planning, the *pathetic cunts*! Ten to one chance of dying, nine to ten chance of worldwide fame? They'd have grabbed it! That was my only mistake! I should have got their fucking permission.'

DAY SIXTY-THREE. 10.30 p.m.

Because of Coleridge's moment of theatre, the final
eviction show overran by half an hour, and half an
hour after that, exactly one hour late, owing to his forgetting that the clocks had gone forward, Woggle blew
up the house.

'Ha ha, you witches and you warlocks, how about
that?' Woggle shouted, emerging from his escape tunnel as the last bits of brick and wood descended.
Woggle had planned for this to be the crowning
moment of the eviction show, the moment when he,
Woggle, showed his contempt for the lot of them and
upstaged all their petty egos by destroying the house at
the very apex of Peeping Tom's party. However,
because of his error, most of his hoped-for audience
were making their way to their cars when the bomb
went off.

Geraldine, the principal target of his revenge, did not
see it at all because she was in the back of a sealed
police van on her way into custody.

Coleridge saw it, though, and judged it a good effort
and, on the whole, justified. However, this did not stop
him from arresting Woggle for jumping bail.

DAY SIXTY-THREE. 11.00 p.m.

When Coleridge got home he was delighted to find that
his wife had watched it all.

'Very theatrical, dear, not like you at all.'

'I had to do something, didn't I? I had no proof. I
needed to trick her into a public confession and to do
it tonight. That was all.'

'Yes, well, you did very well. Very very well indeed,
and I'm just glad we don't have to watch any more of
that appalling programme. Oh, by the way, someone

called Glyn phoned, from the am-dram society. He said he'd been meaning to phone for ages. He was terribly complimentary about your audition, said that you had done a brilliant reading, which apparently blew him away, and that on reflection he wants you to play the lead after all.'

Coleridge felt a thrill of eager anticipation. The lead! He was to give the world his Macbeth after all. Of course Coleridge wasn't stupid. He knew that he had only got the part because he had been on television. But why not? If everybody else could play the game, why couldn't he? Fame, it seemed, *did* have its uses.

THE END

INCONCEIVABLE
Ben Elton

'EXTREMELY FUNNY, CLEVER, WELL-WRITTEN, SHARP
AND UNEXPECTEDLY MOVING . . . THIS BRILLIANT,
CHAOTIC SATIRE MERITS REREADING SEVERAL TIMES'
Nicholas Coleridge, *Mail on Sunday*

Lucy desperately wants a baby. Sam wants to write a hit
movie. The problem is that both efforts seem to be
unfruitful. And given that the average IVF cycle has about
a one in five chance of going into full production, Lucy's
chances of getting what she wants are considerably better
than Sam's.

What Sam and Lucy are about to go through is absolutely
inconceivable. The question is, can their love survive?

Inconceivable confirms Ben Elton as one of Britain's most
significant, entertaining and provocative writers.

'THIS IS ELTON AT HIS BEST – MATURE, HUMANE,
AND STILL A LAUGH A MINUTE. AT LEAST'
Daily Telegraph

'A VERY FUNNY BOOK ABOUT A SENSITIVE SUBJECT
. . . BEN ELTON THE WRITER MIGHT BE EVEN FUNNIER
THAN BEN ELTON THE COMIC'
Daily Mail

'A TENDER, BEAUTIFULLY BALANCED ROMANTIC
COMEDY'
Spectator

'MOVING AND THOROUGHLY ENTERTAINING'
Daily Express

Now filmed as *Maybe Baby*.

0 552 14698 6

BLACK SWAN

BLAST FROM THE PAST
Ben Elton

'ELTON AT HIS MOST OUTRAGEOUSLY ENTERTAINING'
Cosmopolitan

It's 2.15 a.m., you're in bed alone and the phone wakes you.

Your eyes are wide and your body tense before it has completed so much as a single ring. And as you wake, in the tiny moment between sleep and consciousness, you know already that something is wrong.

Only someone bad would ring at such an hour. Or someone good with bad news, which would probably be worse.

You lie in the darkness and wait for the answer machine to kick in. Your own voice sounds strange as it tells you that nobody is there but a message can be left.

You feel your heart beat. You listen. And then you hear the one voice in the world you least expect . . . your very own Blast from the Past.

'ONLY BEN ELTON COULD COMBINE UNCOMFORTABLE QUESTIONS ABOUT GENDER POLITICS WITH A GRIPPING, PAGE-TURNING NARRATIVE AND JOKES THAT MAKE YOU LAUGH OUT LOUD'
Tony Parsons

0 552 99833 8

BLACK SWAN